A Guide to Reviewing
Nous, les jeunes

Focusing on communication in everyday situations, *Nous, les jeunes* helps students develop proficiency in listening, speaking, reading, and writing in French. It also increases students' knowledge and appreciation of diverse cultures in French-speaking countries.

Use the list below as a convenient guide to reviewing *Nous, les jeunes.* Page references provide examples of key features.

▶ Clearly delineated sections with specific communicative functions provide a "purpose" for language learning (page 153).

▶ At the beginning of each instructional unit, **Premier Contact** acquaints students with the new topic by providing copies of authentic documents for increased comprehension and cultural awareness (page 92).

▶ Each section opens with an appealing situation rich in ideas for lively communication (page 171).

▶ In each section, **Comment le dire** summarizes the key expressions needed to achieve the communicative functions (page 391).

▶ Each section includes a cultural note—**Savez-vous que...?**—that provides interesting facts about French-speaking people to increase students' cultural awareness (page 198).

▶ **Try Your Skills** activities provide "real-life" opportunities for students to use new language skills (pages 36-44).

▶ A special **Prononciation** page in each unit helps students pronounce French as accurately as possible (page 183).

▶ Cross-referenced to the communicative functions in each unit, **Vérifions!** helps students monitor their progress (page 414).

▶ **A Lire** provides reading selections for practice and pleasure, including letters, interviews, articles, stories, and poems (page 334). **Avant de lire** offers pre-reading strategies to help students develop reading skills in French (page 86). Following each selection, activities check comprehension and relate reading to students' personal experiences (page 231).

▶ Review units allow students to reinforce their newly acquired skills and to develop increasing proficiency in new, interesting ways (pages 272-284). Two review units provide instruction in the use of the dictionary (page 284).

▶ Throughout the textbook, photographic essays depict the lifestyles of French-speaking people and enhance students' understanding of French attitudes and customs (pages 285-292).

▶ A wealth of supplements, including the *Teacher's Edition* and the *Teacher's ResourceBank*™, provides a rich variety of teaching resources for *Nous, les jeunes.*

HBJ Harcourt Brace Jovanovich
School Department

Nous, les jeunes

The French program that has everybody talking!

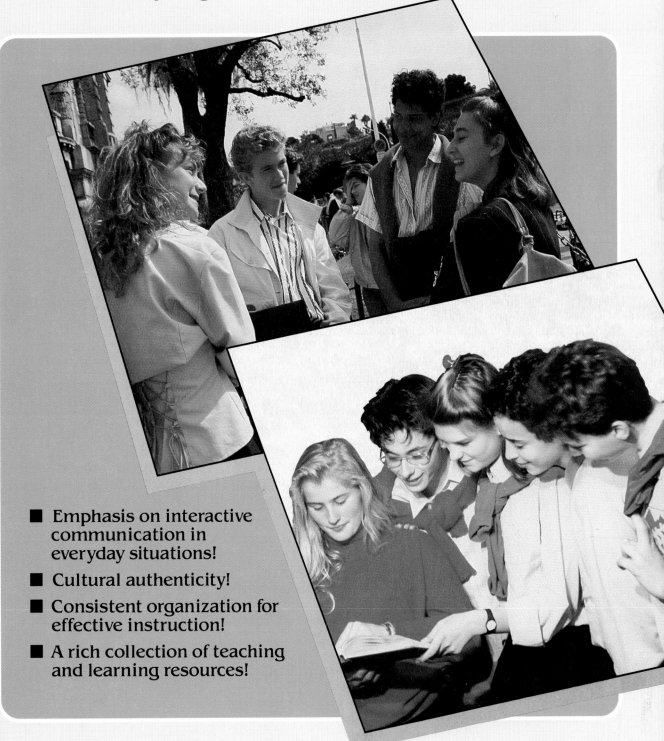

- Emphasis on interactive communication in everyday situations!
- Cultural authenticity!
- Consistent organization for effective instruction!
- A rich collection of teaching and learning resources!

Functional language for proficient communication

From asking about a friend's health to offering advice, from expressing amazement to asking for permission, **Nous, les jeunes** immerses students in the world of *real* language in *real* situations!

Learning activities that develop basic concepts

Through a variety of activities, **Nous, les jeunes** provides specific practice for basic vocabulary and grammar concepts.

Each section opens with an appealing situation rich in ideas for lively communication.

Application activities for proficient communication

Motivating activities invite students to apply what they have learned to real-life situations.

A balance of activities for learning and application helps students become proficient in listening, speaking, reading, and writing in French.

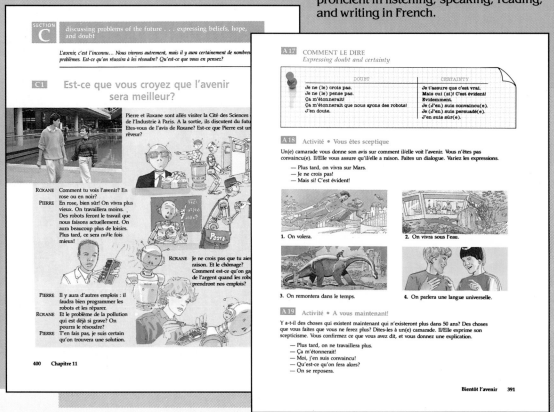

Application activities in **Try Your Skills** provide "real-life" opportunities for students to use their new language skills.

Reading selections in a variety of formats--including letters, interviews, character sketches, and articles, as well as narratives—help students develop reading skills in French. Activities, following each selection, check comprehension and relate reading to students' personal experiences.

Sample pages are reduced.
Actual sizes are 8"x10". All pages are from *Level 2*.

Cultural awareness to broaden understanding

Positive cultural attitudes

To help students understand and appreciate French-speaking people and countries, *Nous les jeunes* interweaves cultural insights and information. Teaching more than just the language, the program depicts everyday life, such as family and peer relations and social customs, in the French world.

Cultural authenticity

To immerse students in French culture, the textbook includes facsimiles of authentic documents, photos shot on location, French art, numerous cultural notes, and such special features as colorful photographic essays. To ensure authenticity, the textbook was written by native speakers of French and is based on many interviews with French students. In addition, the annotated *Teacher's Edition* and *Teacher's ResourceBank* ™ provide abundant cultural information and realia to enhance learning experiences.

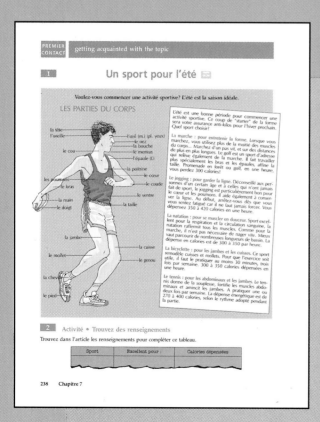

At the beginning of each unit, **Premier Contact** acquaints students with the new topic by providing copies of authentic documents for global reading comprehension and cultural awareness.

Each section includes a cultural note—**Savez-vous que...?**—that provides interesting facts about French-speaking people to increase students' cultural awareness.

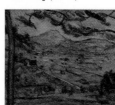

Depicting the lifestyles of French-speaking people, colorful photo essays enhance students' understanding of French attitudes and customs.

Sample pages are reduced. Actual sizes are 8"x10". All pages are from *Level 2*.

Consistent organization for effective teaching and learning

Manageable content

Designed as a one-year course, **Nous, les jeunes** promotes active learning at a comfortable pace. Instruction progresses logically without overwhelming students, introducing a manageable amount of new grammar and vocabulary to support the communicative functions.

Clear learning objectives

Consistent unit organization with clearly defined objectives ensures success in learning. As students move through each new lesson, they build self-confidence and self-motivation.

Clearly delineated sections with specific communicative functions provide a "purpose" for language learning.

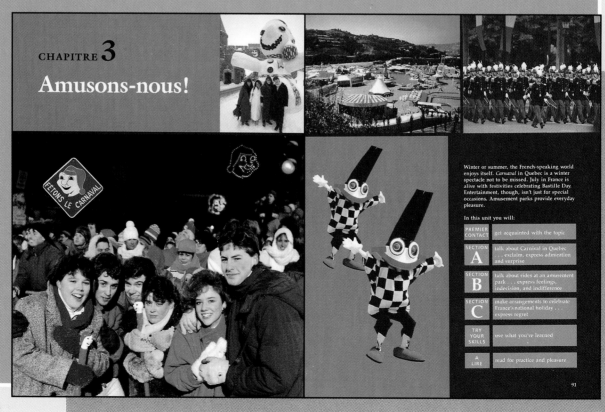

CHAPITRE **3**

Amusons-nous!

FÊTONS LE CARNAVAL

Winter or summer, the French-speaking world enjoys itself. *Carnaval* in Quebec is a winter spectacle not to be missed. July in France is alive with festivities celebrating Bastille Day. Entertainment, though, isn't just for special occasions. Amusement parks provide everyday pleasure.

In this unit you will:

PREMIER CONTACT	get acquainted with the topic
SECTION A	talk about Carnival in Quebec . . . exclaim, express admiration and surprise
SECTION B	talk about rides at an amusement park . . . express feelings, indecision, and indifference
SECTION C	make arrangements to celebrate France's national holiday . . . express regret
TRY YOUR SKILLS	use what you've learned
A LIRE	read for practice and pleasure

91

Frequent review

Periodic review helps students apply what they have learned to new and different situations. Self-checks in each unit allow students to monitor their grasp of important concepts and skills. Review units provide numerous activities that teachers may select to reinforce learning and satisfy special needs.

Cross-referenced to the communicative functions, **Vérifions!** helps students monitor their progress.

VERIFIONS!

 SECTION A

Do you know how to ask someone to lend you something?
Ask your friend to lend you 100 francs in three different ways.

Can you insist if your first request is refused?
Give two different expressions to accomplish this.

Have you learned how to refuse a request for a favor?
Refuse your friend's request, using two different expressions.

Do you know what to say as you grant a request?
Your friend has asked to borrow a few francs. What two different expressions might you use as you lend the money?

Can you express a need?
Say that you need a certain amount of money. Say that you need to buy something.

Have you learned how to use the object pronouns *me, te, nous,* and *vous*?
Restate each sentence, adding the French equivalent of the English pronoun in parentheses.
1. Elle prête quinze francs. *(me)*
2. J'attends là-bas. *(you, pl.)*
3. Il téléphone à huit heures. *(us)*
4. Nous allons aider. *(you, sing.)*

 SECTION B

Do you know how to give advice?
Ask your friend why he/she doesn't do each of the following things.
1. chercher un job
2. mettre une annonce

Have you learned to use *plus, jamais, rien,* and *que* with *ne*?
Restate each sentence, adding the French equivalent of the English given in parentheses.
1. J'ai gardé les chiens. *(never)*
2. Elle est serveuse. *(no longer)*
3. Nous avons mangé. *(nothing)*
4. Tu as huit francs. *(only)*

Can you ask people how they feel about their activities?
Ask your friend how he/she likes his/her job. Use three different expressions.

Do you know how to express pleasure and disappointment?
Tell your friend in at least two different ways how much you like your new job. Now express disappointment with your new job three different ways.

 SECTION C

Do you know how to give reasons for doing something?
Give three different reasons for having a job, using **moyen, façon,** and **occasion.**

Have you learned to use the object pronouns *me, te, nous,* and *vous* with the passé composé?
Rewrite each sentence, changing the verb to the **passé composé.** Make any necessary spelling changes in the past participle.
1. Il nous invite, Pierre et moi?
2. Paul t'offre un cadeau, Marie?
3. Nathalie! Anne! Je vous attends.
4. Tes parents te paient, Marianne?

226   Chapitre 6

Throughout the textbook, a simple color-code system helps students recognize new material, activities, and cultural information (not shown).

Sample pages are reduced. Actual sizes are 8"x10". All pages are from *Level 2.*

A wealth of teaching resources for a range of needs

Flexible resources

Nous, les jeunes provides a range of resources to satisfy a variety of teaching preferences and individual learning rates and styles.

Teacher's Edition

The easy-to-use annotated *Teacher's Edition* contains numerous convenient features:

- A scope and sequence chart for each unit
- Detailed teaching suggestions— including ideas for cooperative learning—conveniently located before each unit
- Cultural background notes for each section of every unit
- Provisions for students of different abilities
- Scripts and answers for listening comprehension exercises
- Annotated pupil's pages with answers to exercises

Sample pages are reduced.
Actual sizes are 8"x10" (*Teacher's Edition, Level 2*).

B11 **Activité • Chez les Legal**

You might assign the activity as a written check-up. Have students write out the answers to the eight questions, replacing nouns with pronouns.

SLOWER-PACED LEARNING Before doing the activity as recommended here, work with the entire class, first to identify the direct object in each sentence and then to decide which pronoun will replace it.

B12 **Activité • A votre avis**

SLOWER-PACED LEARNING Have students look at the drawings in B5, page 166, and decide which member of the Legal family does each task. They should give complete sentences in French. Then turn their sentences into questions, and have them practice answering with the correct direct-object pronoun. Finally, students may pair off to do the activity.

CHALLENGE Have students say their dialogues in this manner:

— C'est à M. Legal d'arroser le jardin?
— Oui, c'est à lui de l'arroser.

B13 **Activité • A vous maintenant!**

Begin by having students write down lists of household chores. Circulate among students as they work in pairs. Listen carefully to make sure they are using the direct-object pronouns correctly. Give help where needed.

B14 **Activité • Chacun sa tâche**

SLOWER-PACED LEARNING Before students work in pairs, have them identify an appropriate verb for each activity suggested in the note on the refrigerator: la cuisine → faire la cuisine; la voiture → laver la voiture. If students find the structure of the answer too difficult, they may simply respond to the question like this: **M. Ballard l'arrose.**

CHALLENGE After students have done the activity as directed, have them go through the tasks again, using the model below:

—C'est à qui d'arroser le jardin?
—C'est à M. Ballard de l'arroser.
—C'est à qui de faire la cuisine?
—C'est à Mme Ballard de la faire.

B15 **Activité • Et chez vous?**

If students ask why different forms of **faire** appear after **qui** in the example, explain that the true subject of **faire** here is the word before **qui.** Do not go into more detail at this time. The use of **qui** as a relative pronoun is presented in Unit 11, C14, page 406.

SLOWER-PACED LEARNING If students find the sentence structure too complex, simplify the dialogue as follows:

—Tu fais les courses chez toi?
—Oui, je les fais. (Non, je ne les fais pas.)

Chapitre 5   Teacher's Notes   T109

CHAPITRE **5**

B11–15

Teacher's Notes provide specific strategies for each part of the unit—including basic material, activities, and reading selections. Notes include special projects, variations of textbook exercises, and suggestions for accommodating different learning styles. Tabbed pages allow quick location of **Teacher's Notes.**

Challenge and **Slower-Paced Learning** activities satisfy individual learning needs.

Teacher's ResourceBank™

The *Teacher's ResourceBank*™ includes useful *Teacher's Resource Materials* —learning and teaching strategies, proficiency practice cards, games, songs, vocabulary lists with exercises, realia, components correlation charts, a glossary of grammatical terms, and a pronunciation guide. The *Teacher's ResourceBank*™ also contains a Unit Theme Posters Sampler, an Overhead Transparencies Sampler and Planning Guide, the *Student's Test Booklet*, the *Teacher's Test Guide,* and the *Unit Cassette Guide.* A three-ring binder with convenient tabbed dividers provides organized storage for these teaching resources.

Additional components for students and teachers

Exercise Workbook with Teacher's Edition

The *Exercise Workbook (Cahier d'Exercices)* provides practice in grammar and vocabulary. The accompanying *Teacher's Edition* contains answers for all activities.

Activity Workbook with Teacher's Edition

Rich in illustrations and realia, the *Activity Workbook (Cahier d'Activités)* provides entertaining and challenging activities to develop communication skills. The accompanying *Teacher's Edition* contains answers for all activities.

Testing Program

The comprehensive Testing Program—consisting of the *Student's Test Booklet, Teacher's Test Guide,* and *Test Cassettes*—assesses both achievement and proficiency in French. The perforated *Student's Test Booklet* includes section quizzes, unit tests, review tests, mid-year and final examinations, and proficiency-based tests. The *Teacher's Test Guide* includes recording scripts for the listening portions of all quizzes and tests, speaking tests for each unit, suggestions for administering and scoring tests, and an answer key. *Test Cassettes* contain the listening portions of all quizzes and tests as well as a model for administering the speaking portion of a proficiency-based test.

Teacher's Resource Materials

Teacher's Resource Materials provides a variety of copying masters, including:

■ Proficiency practice cards with situations and activities for use with each review unit to help students improve communication skills
■ Games to enrich and enliven learning
■ French songs for group singing activities
■ Vocabulary lists with exercises for reinforcement and enrichment
■ Realia—including authentic menus, transportation schedules, and forms—with teaching suggestions and cross-references to textbook units
■ Components correlation charts
■ A glossary of grammatical terms with examples
■ A pronunciation guide with suggestions for pronunciation practice
■ Answer forms for listening comprehension exercises

Unit Cassettes

Cassettes for instructional and review units include the authentic material in Premier Contact, basic material, selected activities, listening comprehension and pronunciation exercises, reading selections, and photo essays—all recorded by native speakers with pauses for student repetition and response, where appropriate. They also provide French songs.

Unit Cassette Guide

The *Unit Cassette Guide* includes an index to the *Unit Cassettes,* recording scripts for all *Unit Cassettes,* and answer forms for the listening comprehension exercises in the textbook.

Overhead Transparencies

Overhead Transparencies, with copying masters, accompany each instructional and review unit. Full-color map transparencies include overlays with geographical names. In addition, a Planning Guide contains suggestions for classroom use.

Unit Theme Posters

Colorful posters feature captivating photographs to enhance each unit in the textbook.

Nous, les jeunes
Teacher's Edition

HBJ HARCOURT BRACE JOVANOVICH, PUBLISHERS
Orlando   San Diego   Chicago   Dallas

Requests for permission to make copies of any part of the work should be mailed to: Copyrights and Permissions Department, Harcourt Brace Jovanovich, Publishers, Orlando, Florida 32887

Printed in the United States of America
ISBN 0-15-381751-8

We do not include a Teacher's Edition automatically with each shipment of a classroom set of textbooks. We prefer to send a Teacher's Edition only when it is part of a purchase order or when it is requested by the teacher or administrator concerned or by one of our representatives. A Teacher's Edition can be easily mislaid when it arrives as part of a shipment delivered to a school stockroom, and, since it contains answer materials, we would like to be sure it is sent directly to the person who will use it, or to someone concerned with the use or selection of textbooks.

If your class assignment changes and you no longer are using or examining this Teacher's Edition, you may wish to pass it on to a teacher who may have use for it.

CONTENTS

TO THE TEACHER

SCOPE AND SEQUENCE CHARTS AND TEACHER'S NOTES

TO THE TEACHER

In creating the new Harcourt Brace Jovanovich French Program, we have incorporated suggestions from foreign language teachers in all parts of the country. We are grateful to you for talking and writing to us. We feel that, based on your suggestions and on what we have observed about general trends in foreign language teaching, we have produced a program that you and your students will profit from and enjoy.

Philosophy and Goals

The primary goal of the Harcourt Brace Jovanovich French Program is to help students develop proficiency in the four basic skills: listening, speaking, reading, and writing. At the same time, it aims to increase the students' knowledge and appreciation of the diverse cultures of the countries whose language they are learning.

In order to become proficient in a foreign language, students must not only learn the vocabulary and structures of the language but also apply what they have learned. Thus, students learn and practice the material in each unit; they also have many opportunities to apply their skills. Given ample opportunity for creative expression, students are on their way to developing proficiency.

The emphasis is on communication. The approach is based on the communicative purposes of young people at this level—to invite, inform, inquire, exclaim, agree, disagree, compliment, express emotions and opinions, and so on. These communicative purposes, or functions, in turn determine the selection and the amount of vocabulary and grammar that students need to learn. The communicative functions, grammar, and vocabulary are presented in culturally authentic situations that appeal to young people. They are followed by a variety of activities that promote both learning and application of the language, ultimately leading students to function with increasing proficiency in many new situations. The question to be asked constantly in measuring students' success is "What can they do with the language they are learning, and how well?"

Description of the HBJ French Program

We have designed the materials of this program to be highly adaptable. You will be able to offer a variety of experiences in learning and using the foreign language, choosing materials that correspond to the learning needs of each student. The various parts of the program are

Components
of the
program

- Pupil's Edition
- Teacher's Edition
- Activity Workbook
- Activity Workbook, Teacher's Edition
- Exercise Workbook
- Exercise Workbook, Teacher's Edition
- Overhead Transparencies
- Unit Theme Posters
- Testing Program
    Student's Test Booklet
    Teacher's Test Guide
    Test Cassettes
- Audio Program
    Unit Cassettes
    Unit Cassette Guide
- Teacher's Resource Materials

**Organization
of the textbook**

Pupil's Edition

The student textbook is the core of the program. The book contains twelve units, grouped into three Parts. Each Part consists of a photo essay *(Aperçu culturel)*, three instructional units *(Chapitre)*, and one review unit *(Chapitre de révision)*. The book ends with a reference section. Here students will find summaries of the communicative functions, grammar, and vocabulary found in both **Nouveaux copains** and **Nous, les jeunes.** Culturally authentic photographs, art, and realia appear throughout the book.

Organization of Instructional Units

Each instructional unit starts with two pages of photographs that illustrate the theme of the unit. Also appearing on these pages are a brief introduction and an outline of the unit that lists, section by section, the performance objectives, or communicative functions, that the students should expect to achieve.

The first section of the unit, called *Premier Contact,* provides authentic materials to be read for global comprehension and cultural awareness. These materials are followed by activities that should stimulate discussion.

Communicative functions

The instructional portion of each unit is divided into three sections—Section A, Section B, and Section C. The communicative functions are repeated at the beginning of the section, followed by a brief introduction to the theme of the section. Each section includes basic material presented in the form of a dialogue, narrative, or letter; a grouping of the words or phrases necessary to the communicative function *(Comment le dire)*; grammar *(Structures de base)*; a cultural note *(Savez-vous que... ?)*; a listening comprehension exercise *(Ecoutez bien)*; and numerous activities *(Activités)*, both oral and written. The activities range from those that help students acquire new skills and knowledge through practice to those that provide opportunities for them to apply their newly acquired skills in simulated real-life situations. Personalized questions encourage students to relate the material to their own experiences. Many of the activities recommend that students work in pairs or groups.

Color coding

All headings are color-coded. Blue signifies new material, communicative functions, and grammar. Orange signals activities. Green calls attention to the cultural notes.

Application

Following Section C is another section called Try Your Skills. The activities in the section are generally open-ended. They create situations in which students can apply what they have learned, bringing together the communicative functions, grammar, and vocabulary presented in the preceding sections. The Try Your Skills section is essential to the development of proficiency.

Pronunciation

The next section, *Prononciation,* helps students isolate and practice the sounds and spelling of French. The section includes pronunciation, letter-sound correspondence, and dictation exercises.

Self-check

A one-page self-check, *Vérifions,* follows the *Prononciation* section. Here a few key questions and check-up exercises help students assess their achievement of the objectives listed in the opening pages of the unit. You may use the self-check after completing Sections A, B, and C and Try Your Skills, or you may choose to use the appropriate part of the self-check after completing the corresponding section of the unit.

On the page opposite the self-check is a list of active vocabulary words *(Vocabulaire)* and their English equivalents, grouped by section. Below the list, a word-study exercise *(Etude de Mots)* focuses attention on the vocabulary list; it gives students practice in developing word-attack skills while expanding their French vocabulary.

The unit closes with one or more short reading selections *(A Lire)* linked to the theme of the unit. The selections may be in the form of a poem, short story, article, or survey. The activities accompanying the reading selections seek to develop reading skills in the foreign language and to encourage critical thinking through open-ended questions.

The basic material, some of the activities, the listening comprehension and pronunciation exercises, and the reading selections of each unit are recorded on the Unit Cassettes.

Organization of Review Units

The three review units *(Chapitre de révision)*—Units 4, 8, and 12—are considerably shorter than the nine instructional units. A review unit presents familiar material in a different context. No new active vocabulary, grammar, or communicative functions are presented. Like the Try Your Skills section within an instructional unit, a review unit contains activities that encourage students to combine and apply the skills they acquired in the preceding instructional units. The situations presented in the review unit may differ from those the students encountered previously; using skills in new situations is crucial to developing proficiency. Finally, Units 4 and 8 end with a page entitled *Consultons le dictionnaire,* which instructs students how to use the dictionary, while Unit 12 contains a review of pronunciation. Selected material from the review units is also recorded on the Unit Cassettes.

Teacher's Edition

The Teacher's Edition is designed to be of maximum assistance to you. It includes the pages of the Pupil's Edition, fully annotated with background notes, answers to activities, teaching suggestions, and variations.

In addition, special Teacher's Notes—pages tabbed in blue—accompany each unit. For your convenience the Teacher's Notes for each unit are placed immediately before the annotated pupil pages of that unit. The Teacher's Notes address not only each section of the unit but every item within the section. The teaching suggestions are cross-referenced to the corresponding material (A1, A2, and so on) in the pupil pages.

The Teacher's Notes begin with a detailed Scope and Sequence chart for the unit that also contains suggestions for the consistent re-entry of previously learned material. Below the chart is a list of the relevant ancillary components of the program and suggested materials that you may wish to prepare or gather. The Teacher's Notes state objectives, provide cultural background, suggest motivating activities, and offer teaching suggestions for all basic material; for the functions, grammar, and culture notes; and for each activity. To help you adapt instruction to meet different learning styles, suggestions are given on how to accommodate slower-paced learning and how to provide a challenge. Also included are suggestions for using cooperative learning and TPR (Total Physical Response) techniques (see page T7) and for combining the different language skills. The scripts of the listening comprehension, pronunciation, and dictionary exercises also appear in the Teacher's Notes.

Activity Workbook

The Activity Workbook (*Cahier d'Activités*) offers additional activities, puzzles, and games that give students practice with communicative functions, vocabulary, and structure in a variety of entertaining and challenging ways. Culturally authentic photographs, art, and realia add an appealing visual dimension. All the activities are cross-referenced to those in the textbook.

The Teacher's Edition of the Activity Workbook provides you with the answers to the activities, printed in place.

Exercise Workbook

The Exercise Workbook (*Cahier d'Exercices*) contains exercises of a more structured nature, all of which are cross-referenced to the textbook. The grammar points taught in the textbook are restated in the Exercise Workbook, where they are followed by extensive practice.

The Teacher's Edition of the Exercise Workbook, like that of the Activity Workbook, contains the answers to the exercises, printed in place.

Testing Program
Student's Test Booklet

Section quizzes

Unit tests

Proficiency-based tests

The Student's Test Booklet has three parts. The first part contains quizzes based on every section of the nine instructional units in the textbook. The second part includes a unit test for each instructional unit, three review tests covering the three Parts of the textbook, a midterm test, and a final exam. Listening comprehension is an integral part of each quiz and test. The third part of the Student's Test Booklet contains two proficiency-based tests that are designed to assess students' levels of proficiency in all four language skills. You may wish to use the first test for practice during the second half of the school year and the second proficiency-based test at the end of the year. Although related to the content of the textbook, the proficiency-based tests do not measure students' mastery of specific material. Rather, they present a variety of situations in which students are expected to demonstrate their ability to function in French.

Teacher's Test Guide

Speaking tests

The Teacher's Test Guide consists of several parts. The introduction describes the testing program and offers suggestions on how you may administer and score the quizzes and tests.

Following the introduction are the recording scripts of the listening parts of the quizzes, tests, and proficiency-based tests.

The next section of the Teacher's Test Guide presents speaking tests for each unit in the textbook. Although these tests are optional, you are urged to administer them at the appropriate times. Suggestions for administering and scoring the speaking tests are given in the introduction to the Teacher's Test Guide.

The answer key to the entire testing program forms the final part of the Teacher's Test Guide.

Test Cassettes

The listening parts of the quizzes, tests, and proficiency-based tests are recorded on cassettes. Included is a recording of an examiner administering the speaking portion of a proficiency-based test to a student; it is intended to serve as a model if you are not familiar with proficiency testing.

Audio Program

Unit Cassettes

For each unit the recordings include *Premier Contact,* the new or basic material, some of the activities, the listening, pronunciation, and dictionary exercises, and the reading selections. The texts of the three photo essays are also recorded. Where appropriate, pauses are provided for student repetition or response. In the textbook, items that are recorded are designated by means of a cassette symbol ⬚ . The scripts of the recordings are provided in the Unit Cassette Guide. One of the Unit Cassettes contains several songs; the lyrics are provided in the Teacher's Resource Materials.

Unit Cassette Guide

The Unit Cassette Guide includes the reference index to the Unit Cassettes, scripts of the Unit Cassettes, and student answer forms for the listening exercises in each unit.

Overhead Transparencies

Copying masters

A set of overhead transparencies with copying-master duplicates supplements the textbook. The set includes one transparency for each section of the nine instructional units, one for each of the three review units, and three maps. Each transparency depicts a situation that is closely related to the one in the corresponding section of the unit. The transparencies are accompanied by a Planning Guide booklet that offers suggestions on how to use them effectively.

Teaching suggestions

The transparencies are a valuable teaching aid. Students may be asked to describe what they see and then to imagine themselves in the situation and converse appropriately. Used in this manner, the transparencies serve to involve students in interactive communication. You may wish to use the transparencies in your presentation of basic material. As students learn new vocabulary and communicative functions, transparencies from previous units may be reintroduced to provide additional situations for the practice of the new material. When students view a new transparency, they may be encouraged to re-enter previously learned communicative functions and vocabulary. The copying masters enable you to distribute copies of the transparencies for use in cooperative learning groups, for individual or group writing assignments, and for homework.

Unit Theme Posters

Twelve full-color posters are available. Each poster displays one or more photographs relevant to the theme of the corresponding unit in the textbook. An accompanying flyer suggests ways in which you might use the posters. Aside from creating a cultural ambiance in the classroom, they can be an effective teaching aid when you present and review a unit.

Teacher's Resource Materials

Proficiency
practice

The Teacher's Resource Materials booklet contains numerous teaching aids. One section discusses learning and teaching strategies, such as Total Physical Response (TPR), group learning, study hints, and suggestions for planning total immersion experiences. Another provides copying masters for role-playing situations to be used with each review unit. You may reproduce and distribute them to the students to stimulate extemporaneous communication, oral or written.

Vocabulary
exercises

Also included in the Teacher's Resource Materials are the vocabulary lists of the nine instructional units with the words regrouped according to their parts of speech. Supplementary vocabulary exercises complement each list. Enrichment vocabulary and useful classroom expressions complete the vocabulary section.

Realia

Games/songs

The booklet contains several pages of realia, reproductions of authentic documents, which you may reproduce for classroom use. In addition, there are suggestions for classroom games and the lyrics of favorite songs. The music has been recorded on one of the Unit Cassettes. Also included are a pronunciation guide, a glossary of grammar terms, and a listing of additional sources of instructional materials (magazines, films, software, and so on).

Using the HBJ French Program

The following procedures and techniques are suggested to meet diverse learning styles and classroom circumstances and to help students achieve communicative competence.

Developing Proficiency in the Four Skills

Listening

From the beginning, students are eager to say things in the foreign language, but they should also hear authentic language, even if they do not grasp the meaning of every word. You will wish to provide an abundance of listening activities.

Authentic
input

For this purpose, the textbook is a primary source. *Premier Contact*, the basic material, and selected activities in each unit are recorded so that students may hear authentic language spoken by a variety of native speakers. In addition, each section of every unit contains a listening exercise. When playing the recordings in class, consider that students need time to listen to the new material before you ask them to repeat it or apply it.

Listening
strategies

Listening requires active mental participation. You may want to share these listening strategies with your students: (1) they should listen for key words that tell what the situation is about; (2) they should not feel that they must understand every word; (3) they should make guesses and verify their hunches by repeated listening.

The TPR (Total Physical Response) technique is an effective means of developing proficiency in listening. TPR is a physical response to an oral stimulus. Students listen to instructions or commands and give nonverbal responses according to their comprehension of the message. These responses may include moving about the classroom, interacting silently with classmates, drawing, or arranging pictures in sequence. Some activities in the student textbook call for TPR responses. Suggestions for applying the TPR technique to other activities are given in the Teacher's Edition.

By minimizing the use of English in the classroom from the beginning, you provide more opportunity for students to hear the foreign language. You may want to make a practice of relating personal experiences and local or world happenings to the students in the foreign language. Students will pick up a great deal of this "incidental" language.

Speaking

Students want most to be able to speak the foreign language they are studying. Keep in mind that the speaking skill is the most fragile; it takes careful nurturing and encouraging, uninhibited by rigid standards. It is more important to encourage fluency first; accuracy will follow.

Each of the units in the textbook focuses on the speaking skill. The majority of the activities are designed to lead to interaction and communication among students. Managed properly, these activities will provide the optimum speaking experiences for the students. The use of various grouping techniques will facilitate this procedure (see page T14).

The development of the speaking skill follows this pattern: (1) repeating after adequate listening; (2) responding, using words and expressions of the lesson (up to this point no degree of proficiency should be expected); (3) manipulating learned material and recombining parts; (4) using what was previously learned in a new context.

When students use a previously learned expression spontaneously in a simulated situation as a natural thing to say at that time, they are truly beginning to speak the language. Students must be engaged in the application phase in order to develop proficiency beyond the novice level. Application activities are found particularly in the Try Your Skills section of each unit and in each review unit.

Reading

It is appropriate for students to read material they have been practicing, but they should also develop their reading skills using unfamiliar material. Require students to skim, scan, draw inferences, determine the main idea, and so forth. They should begin their reading by extracting the general ideas before they approach the details of a reading selection. The aim should be global comprehension in reading just as in listening.

You may help students approach reading selections through prereading strategies. Key words or expressions that might cause difficulty may be clarified, preferably in the foreign language. Students may be encouraged to examine the title and illustrations of a reading selection in search of clues to its meaning. You may elicit students' background knowledge of the subject of the reading through preliminary discussion; comprehension is definitely influenced by the prior information that students bring to a reading selection.

Also consider conducting directed reading lessons, requiring students to read selected passages silently with a purpose: to find answers to questions; to find reasons for actions and events; to find descriptions of characters. Students may be asked to write down all they recall of the content of a passage they have just read silently. In the follow-up lesson, you will wish not only to inquire about the who, what, and where of the content but also to encourage critical thinking by asking why.

The TPR technique may be used to develop reading proficiency as well as listening proficiency. In the case of reading, students are expected to respond nonverbally to directions they have read.

Critical
thinking

Writing

The development of the writing skill is analogous to that of the speaking skill. Although the first stage may consist of copying, learning to spell, filling in the blanks, and writing from dictation, this training does not constitute writing. Writing is transferring thoughts to paper. Hence, students should progress from directed writing to more creative expression. To this end, a variety of controlled and open-ended writing activities appear in the textbook. The Teacher's Notes identify other activities suitable for writing practice and suggest additional writing activities.

Writing
activities

Communicative Functions

When people communicate with each other—either orally or in writing—they use language for a specific purpose: to describe, persuade, argue, express emotions and opinions, praise, complain, agree, and so on. The term "communicative functions," or simply "functions," is used to refer to these purposes for which people communicate.

In the HBJ French Program, the objectives of each instructional unit are phrased as communicative functions. They are clearly stated on the unit opener and are repeated on the section openers so that students can readily see the purpose for learning the language. Within the sections, the communicative functions are presented in new, or basic, material in a culturally authentic situation of interest to young people.

Introduction to the Theme

Students become acquainted with the theme of the unit in the *Premier Contact* section. The material in this section does not have to be taught in sequence, nor does it have to be completed before starting Section A. *Premier Contact* includes two authentic documents, which may be advertisements, magazine or newspaper clippings, personal preference tests, brochures, or other items of realia. The activities that follow the documents check global comprehension and encourage students to relate the information in the documents to their own lives. The *Premier Contact* section should motivate the students to learn more about the topic and to learn the language they will need in order to discuss it.

The authentic documents may contain vocabulary and structures that are unfamiliar to the students. If any such unfamiliar elements seem to be interfering with comprehension, stop and act them out (or explain or translate them, as seems appropriate). The goal of the *Premier Contact* section is not to teach new vocabulary and structures but to stimulate interest in the subject; the students are supposed to be reading for global comprehension only.

New (Basic) Material

Each section of an instructional unit opens with the presentation of basic material. In some sections there may be more than one piece of new material. The basic material may take different forms; it may be a dialogue, an interview, a monologue, or a narrative. Its purpose is to introduce the expressions, grammar, and vocabulary necessary to the communicative function or functions to be learned in the section. Previously learned functions may reappear in the basic material where appropriate. Also, in any basic material there will necessarily be new functions besides those to be practiced in the section. Another purpose of the basic material is to provide cultural information, either directly or indirectly.

Before introducing any basic material, consult the list of communicative functions in the Scope and Sequence chart in the Teacher's Notes for that unit. The new material should be presented in ways that emphasize these communicative functions.

Students should approach basic material with these questions in mind: "What is the communicative purpose of the native speakers in the particular situation, and how are they using their language to accomplish it?" Students should not be required to memorize the basic material. The dialogues and narratives in the textbook are only samples of what a particular speaker of French might say in a given situation; they should not be taught as fixed and rigid sentences. The aim should be to transfer the communicative functions from the basic material to other situations. Students should use the language functions to communicate naturally and spontaneously in real situations.

To help the students, the communicative function is restated and the expressions necessary to achieve it are grouped together under the heading *Comment le dire.* As the title suggests, this is how you say it, how you accomplish the communicative purpose or function. The expressions listed are primarily those introduced in the basic material. There may also be expressions from previous units that are appropriate to the communicative function; expressions that are learned to carry out one function may also be applied to carry out others. *Comment le dire,* then, is a statement of a communicative function and the expressions to accomplish it.

After the students have read the basic material and done the related activities, direct their attention to the expressions in *Comment le dire.* You might make some statements in French and have students choose appropriate responses from the expressions listed. Or, you might have students suggest ways to use French to elicit the expressions from classmates.

The activities that follow *Comment le dire* give students opportunities to carry out the intended communicative function by applying the expressions in real-life situations.

You will find detailed suggestions on how to present basic material and *Comment le dire* in the Teacher's Notes preceding each unit. All basic material is recorded on the Unit Cassettes.

Activities

**Practice/
application**

The heading *Activité* identifies the activities in the textbook. There are two basic types of activities: (1) those that reinforce learning of the new material through practice and (2) those that require students to apply what they have learned.

The activities that follow the basic material are arranged in a planned progression from practice to application of the communicative functions, grammar, and vocabulary. Try Your Skills sections and review units contain only activities of the application type. Many application activities are designed to have the students converse in pairs or groups in order to foster communication and encourage creative expression.

The activities in the textbook may take many different forms. Those that relate to the basic material include questionnaires, sentence completions, true-or-false statements, identifications, and the sequencing of events. Personalized questions encourage students to relate the basic material to their own experiences. (Be careful to respect the privacy of individuals.) Grammar explanations are followed by practice exercises. Then, since the grammar is meant to support the communicative function(s), additional activities lead students to use the grammar in communicative situations.

Writing

Writing activities of two kinds appear throughout the textbook. Controlled exercises provide practice in writing the forms and structures of the language. Others provide opportunities for creative written expression. For further writing practice, many of the oral activities may be assigned to be written.

Listening

One or more listening comprehension activities, identified by the heading *Ecoutez bien*, appear in each instructional section of a unit. These listening activities are recorded on the Unit Cassettes, and student answer forms for them are located in both the Unit Cassette Guide and the Teacher's Resource Materials booklet. The scripts of the listening activities are reproduced in the Teacher's Notes preceding each unit in the Teacher's Edition, as well as in the Unit Cassette Guide.

**Optional
activities**

A few activities have been identified in the Teacher's Notes as optional. Usually found at the end of a section, these activities are intended to enrich vocabulary. You may choose to use them or not, as time permits.

Pronunciation

In each instructional unit, after the Try Your Skills section, you will find a *Prononciation* section. This section is designed to teach the sounds, rhythm, and flow of French. The sounds are presented first in a listening-speaking exercise that gives the students practice in saying them. Then a letter-sound correspondence exercise provides practice in reading the symbols that represent the sounds. Finally, sentences to be written from dictation afford practice in transcribing the sounds. These exercises are recorded on the Unit Cassettes; the scripts are located in the Teacher's Notes preceding each unit in the Teacher's Edition and in the Unit Cassette Guide.

Recordings

This cassette symbol ▭ signals the activities that are recorded on the Unit Cassettes. Frequently, activities have been modified to adapt them for recording. You will find that a communicative activity in the textbook may be more structured when recorded. For this reason, you will want to consult the scripts in the Unit Cassette Guide before you play the cassettes. In certain circumstances, you may wish to play the recorded version of an activity first and then have the students perform the activity as it was intended for the classroom.

Answers to all activities are indicated (in blue) in the annotated pupil pages of the Teacher's Edition.

Grammar

In each section of every unit except the review units, the main grammar points relating to the functional objectives of the unit are summarized.

Grammar may be approached inductively or deductively, depending on the nature of the item and on student learning styles. Younger students, in general, respond favorably to an inductive approach that leads them to draw conclusions about the forms they have been practicing and applying.

On the other hand, because of the relative complexity of some structures, there may be a need to explain them before the students practice and apply them. In this case, the deductive approach may be more effective. Determine for yourself which approach is more suitable.

Grammar and proficiency

Regardless of the approach, it is important to remember that in the development of proficiency, grammar is a means and not an end. Only the grammar that is relevant to the communicative function is necessary.

Vocabulary

Vocabulary and proficiency

As in the case of grammar, consider the extent to which the amount and type of vocabulary presented serves the communicative purpose at hand. The introduction of excessive or irrelevant vocabulary, however interesting, may only complicate the task. The goal is to use vocabulary to communicate. Like grammar, vocabulary is a means, not an end.

Vocabulary is presented in context and listed at the end of each unit. A word-study activity following the list helps students understand and remember the vocabulary by pointing out word families, relationships, derivations, and so on.

You may use word games, puzzles, and mnemonic aids to teach vocabulary. An effective motivational practice is to have students devise their own games, puzzles, illustrative posters, and picture dictionaries to be used by their classmates.

Culture

Cultural expression

We hope to instill cultural awareness by exposing students to different kinds of cultural expression—authentic written and spoken language, a rich collection of photographs showing a cross-section of people and places, an abundance of realia, and special culture notes. We want students to get to know what French-speaking young people are like and to develop a feel for the everyday life in the foreign culture.

Throughout this Teacher's Edition we have noted additional cultural points that may interest you and your students or that clarify situations depicted in the units. The Teacher's Notes preceding each unit provide additional background information on the unit themes. You may want to consult these pages as you prepare to introduce each unit. Include in your teaching as much of this information as you find helpful.

Photo essays

Sources for cultural awareness are present on almost every page of the textbook. They are especially concentrated, however, in the photo essays that precede the three Parts of the text. To help you in presenting the photo essays, we have included in the Teacher's Notes background information on the various topics and some details about specific photographs.

Projects

Encourage your students to personalize the French-speaking cultures as they study and practice the themes and vocabulary of the units. Suggestions for projects are given in the units and in the Teacher's Notes; assign as many projects as possible. In doing projects, students not only practice their skills, but they also share in an experience that helps them learn about the particular country's culture in a direct and personal way.

You can enhance students' cultural awareness and appreciation by utilizing community resources and, if possible, by taking school trips to regions or countries where the foreign language is spoken.

Review

Quizzes

Frequent feedback is essential to assess your students' progress toward proficiency and their need for review. The quizzes based on each section of a unit are one means of assessment. They are short and are best checked immediately during the same class period.

The textbook itself is structured to ensure adequate review. The self-check (*Vérifions*) and the Try Your Skills section at the end of each unit, as well as the three review units, provide opportunities for students to review and recombine previously presented material.

Re-entry

In addition, you will want to make a practice of systematically re-entering material from previous units. To aid you in re-entering grammatical structures, the textbook provides formal re-entry presentations called *Vous en souvenez-vous?* You will find suggestions for the re-entry of previously learned material in the Scope and Sequence chart in the Teacher's Notes preceding each instructional unit.

Testing and Evaluation

Evaluation is an ongoing process. Informal assessment should take place in the classroom on an almost daily basis, whether by observing students during their group work or by engaging individuals or groups briefly in conversation. The section quizzes and the unit tests in the Student's Test Booklet provide a formal check on progress in the areas of listening, reading, and writing. You may wish to administer a short speaking test after each unit. To save you preparation time, speaking tests are supplied in the Teacher's Test Guide.

Unlike achievement, which is the realization of the immediate objectives of a lesson, proficiency develops slowly. Therefore, assessments of proficiency should be made less frequently. Proficiency-based tests are a vital part of this program. There is one practice test and a final test. Meant to be given during the second half of the year, they require students to demonstrate their abilities in all four foreign language skills in situations beyond—but not completely unrelated to—the textbook.

Suggestions for Classroom Management

Classroom Climate

As you know, students are more enthusiastic and responsive in a friendly, nonthreatening atmosphere of mutual respect that fosters self-confidence. A tense atmosphere may inhibit the spontaneous use of the foreign language, which is so necessary to the development of proficiency.

You may wish to consider the importance of organization and keeping students on task. Ground rules for classroom procedures will help you create an effective environment for learning. These procedures should include an explanation of how English is to be used as well as the distribution of a list of classroom expressions in French that students will gradually be able to use with confidence.

Another—but not the least—consideration is the positive effect of a classroom decorated with posters, maps, pictures, realia, and students' papers and projects.

English in the Classroom

The use of the foreign language in the classroom is basic to helping students develop listening proficiency. Students should be accustomed to hearing classroom directions in the foreign language. You will find lists of classroom expressions in French in the vocabulary section of the Teacher's Resource Materials.

It is natural for students to ask for explanations and want to make comments in English. You may wish to set aside a short segment of time at the end of a class period for clarifications in English.

Classroom Strategies

Two fundamental approaches to classroom instruction can be described as teacher-centered and student-centered. Both have a place in the foreign language classroom. In either approach the student is the primary focus.

A teacher-centered approach is most effective in the learning phase. You may wish to use this approach for directed teaching activities, such as presenting new material and conducting drills and question/answer sessions. Consider using various student-centered activities, such as simulated social situations and conversations, in the application phase to develop the independence that eventually leads to proficiency beyond the novice stage.

Grouping

Grouping maximizes opportunities for interaction among students in life-like situations. It is an especially useful strategy in classes that have combined levels of students with varied learning styles and abilities.

Cooperative learning

Cooperative learning is one way in which students and teachers can achieve learning goals. In cooperative learning, small groups of students collaborate to achieve a common goal. There are four basic benefits of a cooperative learning group: (1) positive interdependence; (2) face-to-face interaction; (3) individual accountability; (4) appropriate use of interpersonal skills. Following are some suggestions for structuring cooperative learning activities.

Forming cooperative learning groups

1. Be sure the task is clear to everyone.
2. Set a time limit. Completion of the task and reporting to the class should take place during the class period.
3. Circulate among the students and assist them as needed.
4. Assign specific tasks to each group member.
5. Clarify any limitations of movement during the activity.
6. Select the group size most suited to the activity. Pairs are appropriate for many activities.
7. Assign students to groups. Heterogeneous groups are more desirable. Groups should not be permanent.
8. Evaluate the group's task when completed and discuss with the group the interaction of the members.

Many activities in the textbook lend themselves to cooperative learning.

Providing for Different Learning Styles

Different students learn best in different ways. Some learn new material most easily when they are allowed to listen to it and repeat it. Others do best when they see it in writing. Still others respond best to visual experiences—photographs, drawings, overhead transparencies. And some students need to be involved physically or emotionally with the material they are learning to respond concretely and personally. Moreover, all students need variety in the learning experience; the same student may respond differently on different days.

Slower-paced learning

Slower-paced learning requires that you present and adapt materials differently than you do when a greater challenge is called for. The Teacher's Notes that precede each unit contain numerous suggestions for teaching strategies to be used in a slower-paced learning environment and in a challenge situation.

In general, you may wish to consider strategies for slower-paced learning that involve breaking down an activity into smaller tasks and then rebuilding it gradually. Accept short answers and elicit passive, non-verbal responses more often. For students who need a greater challenge, consider expanding activities and adding new twists that require critical thinking and creativity.

Challenge

Forming heterogeneous cooperative learning groups and pairing students of different abilities can be effective means of assisting all students, both academically and socially.

Homework

Homework that reinforces and enriches class work should be an integral part of instruction. You may want to consider giving differentiated homework assignments to suit the varied needs of students instead of issuing identical assignments to all. For this purpose, the Activity Workbook and the Exercise Workbook provide numerous exercises of various types that are designed to meet different learning styles.

Homework should be collected and checked; otherwise students will not respect the practice. You may devise a system for students to check their own homework, but take care to avoid spending an entire class period checking homework. Long-term homework projects as well as short-term assignments are effective.

Use of Audio-Visual Materials

Students need to hear a variety of voices speaking French. The Unit Cassettes provide the students with a listening program so that they can practice the sounds of French, develop listening proficiency, and get practice in manipulating the language.

Students also need to see authentic representations of the foreign culture. The photographs in the textbook—in each unit and in the photo essays—can be used to motivate students before they launch into new material and also to increase cultural awareness. In addition, the unit theme posters and the transparencies related to each section of a unit depict culturally authentic situations.

You may want to use an overhead projector with a transparency instead of writing on the board to focus students' attention more directly. Where the facilities exist, students may create their own skits based on the units and record them on a videocassette for classroom viewing. Showing rented films, displaying posters, and sharing realia are other means you may consider to add a visual dimension to classroom instruction.

Planning

Pacing

It is helpful to devise a schedule of instruction for the year. Planning ahead is essential to setting the pace most appropriate for your classroom. The textbook is designed to be completed in one school year. Where needed, you can control the time spent on each unit by including or omitting optional exercises, by reading all or only one of the reading selections at the end of the unit, by doing some or all of the activities in the review unit, by insisting on total mastery of material before progressing or relying on the cumulative acquisition of the language.

Your schedule will vary according to the grade and ability level of your students and the number of interruptions in your school program. In general, an instructional unit can be taught in three weeks; in some cases an additional day may be needed for the unit test. A review unit will take one week, including the review test. Sufficient time should remain for discussing the cultural notes and photo essays, administering the midterm, final, and proficiency-based tests, and conducting optional enrichment activities.

Lesson Plans

You will probably want to prepare a daily lesson plan that incorporates various language skills. Plans may vary, but the basic lesson should include the following, to some degree, at least over a span of two days.

- A warm-up activity, usually involving review
- A quiz or test when appropriate
- The presentation of new material preceded by a motivating activity and a statement of objectives
- Developmental activities and guided practice
- Application by the students of what they have learned
- Summarizing statements, preferably elicited from the students
- Closure (review with students of what they have learned)
- Assignment, planning ahead, or previewing the next lesson
- Periodic long-range planning with the students

Unit Planning Guide

The following plan suggests how the material in Unit 3 may be distributed over fifteen days. You may wish to prepare similar lesson plans, adjusting them to suit the needs and interests of your students. For a faster pace, the activities in parentheses may be assigned as homework or omitted.

	Daily Plans	Unit Resources
Day 1	Objective: To get acquainted with the topic Unit opener: discussion Premier Contact 1 Activités 2, 3 Premier Contact 4 Activités 5, 6	Unit 3 Poster Unit 3 Cassette
Day 2	Objective: To talk about Carnival in Quebec Section A: motivating activity Basic material A1 Activités A2, (A3), A4, A5	Unit 3 Cassette Activity Workbook Exercise Workbook
Day 3	Objective: To describe Carnival in Quebec Savez-vous que... ? A6 Vous en souvenez-vous? A7 Structures de base A8 Activités A9, A10	Activity Workbook Exercise Workbook

	Daily Plans	Unit Resources

Day 4	Objectives: To talk about parades; to exclaim; to express admiration and surprise
	    Basic material A11
	    Activités A12, (A13)
	    Comment le dire A14
	    Activités A15, (A16), (A17), A18, A19
	    Assign review of Section A
		Overhead Transparency 7
		Unit 3 Cassette
		Activity Workbook
		Exercise Workbook

Day 5	Objective: To talk about rides at a fair
	    Quiz on Section A
	    Section B: motivating activity
	    Basic material B1
	    Activités B2, (B3)
		Quiz 7
		Overhead Transparency 8
		Unit 3 Cassette
		Activity Workbook
		Exercise Workbook

Day 6	Objective: To ask for agreement; to express indecision and indifference
	    Structures de base B4
	    Activité B5
	    Comment le dire B6
	    Activités B7, (B8)
	    Basic material B9
	    Activités B10, (B11), B12
		Overhead Transparency 8
		Unit 3 Cassette
		Activity Workbook
		Exercise Workbook

Day 7	Objective: To express feelings
	    Structures de base B13
	    Activités B14, (B15), (B16), B17
	    Comment le dire B18
	    Activités B19, B20
	    Savez-vous que… ? B21
	    Activité B22
	    Assign review of Section B
		Unit 3 Cassette
		Activity Workbook
		Exercise Workbook

Day 8	Objective: To talk about celebrating France's national holiday
	    Quiz on Section B
	    Section C: motivating activity
	    Basic material C1
	    Activités C2, (C3), C4, (C5)
	    Savez-vous que… ? C6
		Quiz 8
		Overhead Transparency 9
		Unit 3 Cassette
		Activity Workbook
		Exercise Workbook

Day 9	Objective: To express regret
	    Vous en souvenez-vous? C7
	    Structures de base C8
	    Activités C9, (C10), C11, C12
	    Comment le dire C13
	    Activités C14, (C15), (C16), C17
	    Assign review of Section C
		Unit 3 Cassette
		Activity Workbook
		Exercise Workbook

	Daily Plans	Unit Resources

Day 10	Objective: To use what you've learned
	    Quiz on Section C
	    Basic material Try Your Skills 1
	    Activités 2, 3
		Quiz 9
		Unit 3 Cassette
		Activity Workbook

Day 11	Objective: To use what you've learned Activités (4), 5, 6, (7)	Unit 3 Cassette Activity Workbook

Day 12	Objective: To use what you've learned
	    Activités 8, 9, (10)
	    Prononciation
		Unit 3 Cassette
		Activity Workbook

Day 13	Objective: To prepare for Unit 3 Test
	    Vérifions!
	    Vocabulaire
	    Etude de mots
		Activity Workbook
		Exercise Workbook
		Overhead Transparencies
		    7, 8, 9
		Unit 3 Poster

Day 14	Objective: To assess progress Unit 3 Test	Unit 3 Test

Day 15	Objective: To read for practice and pleasure
	    A Lire: La Marseillaise
	    Activités: Connaissez-vous votre hymne
	      national? Ecrit dirigé
	    (Choice of other reading selections)
		Unit 3 Cassette

Beyond the Classroom
In School

A vibrant foreign language program extends outside the classroom to other disciplines, the entire school, the community, and beyond.

Relating to other disciplines

By its very nature, the study of foreign languages is interdisciplinary. You may wish to consider cooperating with social studies teachers to promote global education. Since you deal with the music, art, and literature of the foreign culture, you complement the work of the art, music, and English teachers. Foreign language study raises students' level of general linguistic awareness, thereby reinforcing their work in English language arts. Learning about sports in other countries may increase the enthusiasm for sports among your students.

Foreign language classes should have an impact on the total school environment. You may have the students label areas of the building and prepare public address announcements in the foreign language. Staging assemblies, participating in school fairs, and celebrating foreign festivals schoolwide are other ways to provide students with opportunities to use their knowledge and skills outside the classroom, particularly during National Foreign Language Week in March.

Outside School

Your efforts to heighten enthusiasm for foreign language study might reach out into the community through field trips to ethnic restaurants, museums, embassies, and local areas where the foreign language is spoken. Encourage your students to present special foreign language programs in nursing homes and hospitals. If you receive radio and television programs in French, or if foreign movies are shown in your region, you will want your students to take advantage of them to improve their language skills as well as their cultural awareness.

The ultimate extension of foreign language study is a trip to or a stay in a country where the language is spoken. Working with school authorities, you may be able to arrange trips abroad for your students.

Total immersion

However, a total foreign language experience need not require travel outside the area. For a day, a weekend, or a longer period during a school vacation, the foreign culture can be recreated at the school, at a camp, or at a university to provide a total immersion experience. This activity requires detailed planning and preparation. Suggestions for planning total immersion experiences are presented in the Teacher's Resource Materials.

Whatever the nature of the endeavor to extend foreign language study beyond the classroom, you will need to develop guidelines with the students in addition to any school rules governing such activities. Adherence to an organized plan results in a more productive experience.

Career Awareness

For many students, foreign language study will form the basis of their life's work or enhance it.

Career awareness activities can be a strong motivating force to learn a foreign language. Students should be made aware of the types of professions and occupations prevailing in the foreign culture and those in their own culture that either depend on foreign language skills or are enhanced by such skills.

You may want to collaborate with guidance counselors in your school to provide up-to-date information concerning career opportunities related to foreign languages. Many schools have career fairs in which you might consider participating.

Conclusion

Many teachers have found the following guidelines practical in planning their foreign language courses. You, too, may find them useful.

- Establish a positive climate.
- Have a classroom decor that reflects the foreign culture.

- Establish a fair-but-firm policy for classroom management.
- Take student interests into consideration when planning.
- Have a written plan.
- Discuss objectives with the students.
- Provide for varied learning styles and rates.
- Avoid lecturing.
- Maximize student involvement.
- Provide positive verbal and nonverbal feedback.
- Evaluate class procedures and outcomes with the students.

The aim of proficiency-oriented instruction is not that students learn language lessons. Rather, the goal is to encourage and guide students to use what they have learned in new situations. Without this application phase in the instructional procedure, proficiency will not be achieved. Therein lies the challenge to the foreign language teacher. We wish you much success in this exciting undertaking.

Specific suggestions for teaching each unit appear in the blue-tabbed pages preceding the unit. Additional suggestions and answers to activities are provided in the annotated pupil pages.

Nous, les jeunes

HBJ
Foreign Language Programs

FRENCH

- **Nouveaux copains**
  Level 1

- **Nous, les jeunes**
  Level 2

- **Notre monde**
  Level 3

Nous, les jeunes

HBJ HARCOURT BRACE JOVANOVICH, PUBLISHERS
Orlando   San Diego   Chicago   Dallas

Printed in the United States of America
ISBN 0-15-381750-X

For permission to reprint copyrighted material, grateful acknowledgment is made to the following sources:

Bayard Presse: Adapted from "Aimeriez-vous avoir un confident?" in *Okapi* Magazine, No. 381, October 1–15, 1987. Adapted from "Grand Sondage Okapi-L'Express-Louis Harris" (Retitled: "Sondage") in *Okapi* Magazine, No. 383, November 1–15, 1987. Adapted from "A la maison, ce n'est pas encore l'égalité," "Interlocuteurs privilégiés," "Petits poucets et gros budget," "Les postes clés du budget des 15–18 ans," and "Le bas de laine des 15–20 ans" in *Juniorscopie* by Geneviève Welcomme and Claire Willerval.
Carnaval de Québec, Inc.: From the lyrics of the song "Carnaval, Mardi-Gras, Carnaval" by R. Vézina and P. Pétel, sung by Pierrette Roy.
Editions Denoël: Adapted from "Souvenirs de vacances" in *Les vacances du petit nicolas* by René Goscinny, illustrated by Jean-Jacques Sempé. © 1962 by Editions Denoël.
EF Ecole Européenne de Vacances: Adapted from "Londres Informations" in *EF,* 1987 Séjours linguistiques Février, Pâques et été.
L'Ecole des Loisirs: "L'embouteillage" from *La Ville enchantée* by Jacques Charpentreau. Published by L'Ecole des Loisirs, 1976.
l'officiel des loisirs: Advertisement for ZYGOFOLIS from cover of *l'officiel des loisirs, côte d'azur,* No. 0020, May 25–31, 1988.
Faits et Opinions/Gallup Paris: Adapted chart, "L'homme au foyer" (Retitled: "Monsieur, est-ce que vous faites... ?") from *L'Express,* March 1984.
Editions Gallimard: Adapted from "Il faut que ma mère soit heureuse" in *Piranha* Magazine, October 1986.
Mirapolis: Cover of brochure advertising "MIRAPOLIS—1ᵉʳ Grand Parc d'Attractions Français."
Warner Chappell Music France SA: Lyrics of the song "En sortant du lycée," by Michel Jourdan and Bernard Estardy. © by Warner-Chappell Music France.

PHOTO CREDITS: Cover: HBJ Photo/Stuart Cohen

All HBJ Photos by Daniel Aubry 1 (cl, b), 4 (cl), 7 (r), 54 (t, b), 56, 67, 70, 75, 91, 102, 103, 105, 110, 111, 114, 116, 118 (t, cr), 152, 153, 163 (b), 165, 171, 172, 182 (tr, bl), 188, 196, 204, 211, 215 (cl), 221, 272 (cr, bl), 273, 274, 278 (tr), 279 (c, b), 281, 294, 295, 298 (l), 299, 301 (r), 308, 309, 311 (tr, cb), 313 (tl), 316, 317, 319 (tl, br), 321, 323, (lc, tr, ct, br), 324, 367 (l), 392 (t, br), 393 (tl, bl, br), 423 (tl); Stuart Cohen 25 (cl, cr), 198, 215 (b); Robert Didsbury 29, 112, 230; Claire Dufour 2 (tl), 5, 90 (cl), 96, 98 (tr), 101, 143–150; Herman Emmet 95 (b), 118 (cl, b); Patrice Maurin 1 (tr, cr), 2 (tr, b), 4 (b), 6 (tl, tr), 8 (tl), 128, 129 (t, b), 131 (bl, br), 133, 136 (t, c, bl), 138, 140, 188 (tl), 236, 237, 240, 246, 247, 254, 255, 256, 263 (t), 285–292, 313 (tr), 381 (tr), 404; Peter Menzel 90 (t, cr, b), 94, 95 (t, c), 98 (tl, bl, br), 100, 101 (b), 127; May Polycarpe 1 (c), 2 (cr), 3, 4 (t, cr), 5 (tl, cl, tr), 6 (br), 7 (t, cl, bl), 8 (bl, tr, br), 10, 11, 14, 15, 17, 18, 22 (b), 25 (bl), 30, 31, 50, 51, 54 (c), 55, 60, 61, 156, 163 (t), 181, 182 (tl), 187, 192, 193, 200, 207, 215 (t, cr), 339, 340 (bl, ct, cb, cr, br), 342, 343, 344, 345, 347, 349, 352, 353 (t), 359, 360, 364–366, 367 (r), 369, 385, 393 (tr), 423 (bl, tr, br), 424 (br), 427, 429; Annette Stahl 392 (bl), 393 (cr); Emmanuel Rongieras d'Usseau 21, 22 (t), 25 (tl, tr, br), 182 (br); George Winkler 6 (bl), 37 (b); HBJ Studio 43, 92, 109, 277, 303, 315, 389, 403 (br), 409, 424 (tr), 431 except Herve Donnezan/Photo Researchers, Inc. 23 (t); Romilly Lockyer/The Image Bank 23 (cl); B. Roussel/The Image Bank 23 (cr); Paolo Koch/Photo Researchers, Inc. 23 (b); Mike Mazzaschi/Stock, Boston 36 (t); François Gohier/Photo Researchers, Inc. 36 (b); Travelpix/FPG 37 (t); Vance Henry/Taurus Photos 39; Weinberg-Clark/The Image Bank 41 (l); R. Semois/Belgian Tourist Office 41 (r); Thomas Marotta/FPG 59; Lehr/Sipa-Press 63 (tl); Ginies/Sipa-Press 63 (tr); Benaroch/Sipa-Press 63 (cr); Robb Kendrick/Retna Ltd. 63 (cl); Serge Arnal/Stills/Retna Ltd. 63 (bl); Camacho/Stills/Retna Ltd. 73 (t, cl, cr); Youri Lenquette/Stills/Retna Ltd. 73 (b); Frank Driggs Collection 88 (both); David Redfern/Retna Ltd. 89; Canadian Government Travel Bureau 119; Bernard Asset, Agence Vandystadt/Photo Researchers, Inc. 129 (c); Walter S. Clark/

(continued on p. 486)

Writer
Emmanuel Rongieras d'Usseau

Contributing Writers

Monique Branon
Woodside, NY

Noëlle Gidon
Université de Paris VIII
Paris, France

Barbara Kelley
Parkway Central High School
Chesterfield, MO

William F. Mackey
Université Laval
Québec, Canada

Editorial Advisors

Guy Capelle
Université de Paris VIII
Paris, France

Nunzio Cazzetta
Smithtown High School West
Smithtown, NY

Charles R. Hancock
Ohio State University
Columbus, OH

William Jassey
Norwalk Board of Education
Norwalk, CT

Ilonka Schmidt Mackey
Université Laval
Québec, Canada

Consultants and Reviewers

Melinda Jones
Diamond Bar High School
Diamond Bar, CA

Sally Sieloff Magnan
University of Wisconsin
Madison, WI

Mandel Perodin
Bridgehampton High School
Bridgehampton, NY

Vincent Sausto
Pascack Valley Regional
   High School District
Montvale, NJ

Mary Slavinski
Horace Greeley High School
Chappaqua, NY

Peter Thornley
Edgewater High School
Orlando, FL

John Thomas Wissman
Ysleta High School
El Paso, TX

Field Test Teachers

Kathy Benson
Groveport-Madison
   High School
Groveport, OH

Jean Cadet
Hudson High School
Hudson, FL

Janet Crockett
Pasadena High School
Pasadena, TX

William Green
Menlo-Atherton
   High School
Atherton, CA

ACKNOWLEDGMENTS

We wish to express our gratitude to the people pictured in this book and to the many others who assisted us in making this project possible.

In some instances, the people whose photos appear in the book have been renamed. Listed here are their real names, their role(s) in the book in parentheses, and the unit(s) in which their photos appear.

Jérôme Cohen, Alexia Nadal, Sylvain Couvain, Sandrine Peres, Cover; Jim Achache, AC 1, (Henri), Unit 11; Mme Achache (Mme Noguier), Unit 11; Sandrine Aubrit (Sandrine), Unit 7; Mme Nicole Balland (professeur), Unit 1, Unit 10; Céline Barran, AC 3; Claire Batreau, AC 1, AC 3; Emmanuelle Bédard (Anne-Sophie), AC 2; Héloïse Bédard (Héloïse), AC 2; Marie-Céline Bédard (Mme Dufour), AC 2; Olivier Bédard (Paul), AC 2; Paul-André Bédard (M. Dufour), AC 2; Jérôme Berthier (Jérôme), Unit 4; Armand Betoulle (M. Desmarest), AC 3; Dina Betoulle (Mme Desmarest), AC 3; Jean-Luc Betoulle (Jean-Luc), AC 3; Stéphane Betoulle (Stéphane), AC 3; Guillaume Blamard (Eric), Unit 2; Marc Boisvin (Julien), Unit 2; Mme Borelli (Françoise), Unit 10; Stéphane Boujenah, Unit 5; Nathalie Braquet (Emmanuelle), Unit 2; Stéphanie Busson (Hélène), Unit 5, Unit 6; Guillaume Cabrère, AC 1; Nathalie Caissotti, Unit 6, (Florence), Unit 10; Frédérick de Cenarchans (Bruno), Unit 8; Elodie Cenni (Emilie), Unit 1; Sonia Chmilewsky, Unit 2; Frank Clausse (rock group), Unit 2; Audrey Couëdel (Nicole), Unit 3, Unit 6; Tristan Couëdel (Simon), Unit 3; Antoine Coussieux (Antoine), Unit 4; Frédéric Delaître (Alexandre), Unit 1; Fabrice Denys (Fabrice), Unit 7; Adama Dione (cousin), Unit 12; Imane Dione (baby), Unit 12; Jeff Dubé (Robert), Unit 3; Vanessa DuHomme, AC 1; Hervé Elmozino (rock group), Unit 2; Sébastien Fagot, AC 1, AC 3; Dominique Fard (rock group), Unit 2; Gregory Ferrière, AC 1, (Laurent), Unit 5, Unit 6; Franck Gasparro (Philippe), Unit 1; Johan Geffray (Patrice), Unit 5, Unit 6; M. Ghioly (M. Legal), Unit 6; Lysianne Ghioly (Mme Legal), Unit 6; Pascale

Ghioly (Murielle), Unit 6; Lionel Gosse, AC 1; Christina Haddock (Lucie), Unit 3; No Hausner (Bruno's sister), Unit 8; Valérie Hot (Fabienne), Unit 12; Mariem Ka (Marianne), Unit 6; Mme Ka (grandmother), Unit 12; Matthieu de Laborde (Matthieu), Unit 7; Ivan Lecourt, AC 3; Betty Madiouma (Angèle), Unit 12; Pierre-Olivier Malmont, AC 3; Eric Mancini (Martin), Unit 1, (Philippe), Unit 2, Unit 6; M. Marchesi (M. Legal), Unit 5; Mme Marchesi (Mme Legal), Unit 5; Olivier Marchesi (Julien), Unit 5; Christophe Moracchini (Jacques), Unit 5; Sophia Nadic (Isabelle), Unit 5, (Julie), Unit 10; Prosper N'Criessan, AC 1; Sandrine Nebulat (Nicole), Unit 2, (Muriel), Unit 5, Unit 6; Maria Nicolier (Isabelle), Unit 8; Sherry Norales, AC 3; Victor Ogilvie (Corinne's father), Unit 5; Mlle Ogilvie (Corinne), Unit 3, Unit 5; Mme Partouche (Mme Gastaldi), Unit 10; Alexandra Partouche (Alexandra), Unit 5, Unit 9, Unit 10; Luc Pastur (Claude), Unit 2; Elodie Pépin (Isabelle), Unit 1; Franckie Perotte (Thomas), Unit 2; Christelle Piscina, AC 1, (Charlotte), Unit 11; Frank Pllonghini (rock group), Unit 2; Emmanuelle Riem, Unit 6; Christopher Rigaud (Marc), Unit 1, Unit 6; Benoît Roman (Xavier), Unit 5, Unit 6; Stéphane Rosario, AC 3; Olivier Sardou (Romain), Unit 2; Patrick Sardou (rock group), Unit 2; Michaella Thiercelet (Claire), Unit 1; La famille Thiercelin, Unit 5; Cyril Torres, AC 1; Stéphanie Vatinos, AC 3; Isabelle Visbeca, AC 1; Antoine Vitale (Roland), Unit 2; Sophie Weiss (Caroline), Unit 2, Unit 5; Vladimir Weiss (Damien), Unit 2, Unit 5; Laure Yvars (Laure), Unit 2; Valérie Yvars (Laure's mother), Unit 2.

Our special thanks to Marie-Lou de Burette for introducing us to many young people in France, to the Collège Alphonse Daudet and the Lycée Masséna in Nice for allowing us to photograph at the schools, and to the Betoulle family in France and the Bédard family in Quebec for opening their homes and sharing their lives with us.

CONTENTS

COMMUNICATIVE FUNCTIONS	GRAMMAR	CULTURE
Reading for global comprehension and cultural awareness		The cost of books, school supplies, and clothes for school in France
Socializing • Greeting old and new friends • Asking how others are **Expressing attitudes, opinions** • Expressing an opinion, agreeing, and disagreeing	Review of the **passé composé** with **avoir**	Back to school in France: **la rentrée** The ideal **lycée**
Socializing • Asking others how they spent the summer **Expressing feelings, emotions** • Expressing satisfaction and dissatisfaction **Expressing attitudes, opinions** • Expressing indifference	The **passé composé** with **être**	How French students spend their vacation Regions of France Vacations in France for employees and students
Socializing • Making excuses **Exchanging information** • Talking about the last school year • Making resolutions for the new school year	Review of **aller** + infinitive	Grades and report cards Teacher-parent contact: **le carnet de correspondance**
Recombining communicative functions, grammar, and vocabulary		Learning English while vacationing in Ireland Camping and canoeing in the **Ardenne**
Reading for practice and pleasure		A French boy boasts of his feats at summer camp

CHAPITRE 2
Après l'école 50

COMMUNICATIVE FUNCTIONS	GRAMMAR	CULTURE
Reading for global comprehension and cultural awareness		Local recreation center offerings
Exchanging information • Answering a negative question affirmatively • Talking about recreational activities **Socializing** • Inviting friends	The independent pronouns **moi, toi, lui, elle, nous, vous, eux, elles**	Leisure activities of French young people
Exchanging information • Choosing leisure activities **Persuading** • Offering encouragement	Review of the verb **prendre** The verbs **apprendre** and **comprendre**	Activities at the **Maison des Jeunes** Music preferences of French teenagers
Exchanging information • Talking about forming a rock group • Asking and telling how long something has been going on **Socializing** • Asking for, giving, and refusing permission	The verb **devoir** The pronoun **en**	Forming music groups
Recombining communicative functions, grammar, and vocabulary		Music, dance, and theater at the **MJC** Favorite pastimes of French young people
Reading for practice and pleasure		A French girl sings about the best time of her day Famous jazz and rock musicians

COMMUNICATIVE FUNCTIONS	GRAMMAR	CULTURE
Reading for global comprehension and cultural awareness		Activities during **Carnaval** in Quebec Celebrations of July 14, French "Independence Day"
Exchanging information • Talking about Carnival in Quebec **Expressing feelings, emotions** • Exclaiming, expressing admiration and surprise	Review of adjectives Adjectives ending in **-al** and **-if**	**Carnaval** festivities
Socializing • Talking about carnival rides • Asking for agreement **Expressing feelings, emotions** • Expressing fear, pain, hunger, thirst, discomfort **Expressing attitudes, opinions** • Expressing indecision and indifference	The verb **vivre** The formation and position of adverbs	A French amusement park
Socializing • Making arrangements **Expressing feelings, emotions** • Expressing regret	Review of questions Asking questions using **est-ce que** and inversion	Bastille Day in France
Recombining communicative functions, grammar, and vocabulary		The Bastille Day parade
Reading for practice and pleasure		Story of the **Marseillaise** Who is **Bonhomme Carnaval**? The **Carnaval** song
Reviewing communicative functions, grammar, and vocabulary		The sights of Brussels The Belgian Grand Prix The Festival of the Cats

DEUXIEME PARTIE

COMMUNICATIVE FUNCTIONS	GRAMMAR	CULTURE
Reading for global comprehension and cultural awareness		Sharing confidences with parents and friends
Socializing • Refusing invitations • Asking permission **Expressing attitudes, opinions** • Expressing obligation	The present subjunctive with **il faut que…** and **vouloir que…** The present subjunctive of **faire**	The French family Family responsibilities
Exchanging information • Talking about family responsibilities • Assigning responsibility **Expressing attitudes, opinions** • Complaining	The direct-object pronouns **le, la, les**	Chores in the French household
Expressing feelings, emotions • Sharing confidences • Asking for advice **Persuading** • Giving advice and encouragement	The verb **voir** Review of the object pronouns **le, la, les, lui, leur, y, en** with the **passé composé**	The role of family and friends in the lives of French young people
Recombining communicative functions, grammar, and vocabulary		Celebrating a birthday
Reading for practice and pleasure		Impossible love for a French boy and his girlfriend French friends discuss family restrictions A French girl's poem A family in Burkina Faso

COMMUNICATIVE FUNCTIONS	GRAMMAR	CULTURE
Reading for global comprehension and cultural awarensss		French spending and saving habits
Persuading • Asking a favor • Insisting **Socializing** • Refusing or granting a favor **Exchanging information** • Expressing a need	Review of the object pronouns **le, la, les, lui, leur** The object pronouns **me, te, nous, vous**	Allowances and bank accounts
Persuading • Giving advice **Exchanging information** • Inquiring about others' activities **Expressing feelings, emotions** • Expressing pleasure and disappointment	Review of the negative **ne... pas** Other words used with **ne: plus, jamais, rien, que**	Jobs for French teenagers
Exchanging information • Talking about the advantages of working **Expressing attitudes, emotions** • Giving reasons for doing something	Review of the object pronouns **le, la, lui, leur** with the **passé composé** The object pronouns **me, te, nous, vous** with the **passé composé**	How French teenagers spend their money
Recombining communicative functions, grammar, and vocabulary		Inquiring about a job
Reading for practice and pleasure		A French girl's invention French teenagers start their own businesses Money: a self-test

COMMUNICATIVE FUNCTIONS	GRAMMAR	CULTURE
Reading for global comprehension and cultural awareness		Health benefits of sports French breakfast habits
Exchanging information • Talking about health **Expressing feelings, emotions** • Complaining about health **Socializing** • Expressing concern	The reflexive pronouns with verbs in the present tense and in the **passé composé** The verb **se sentir**	Sleeping habits of French teenagers
Persuading • Talking about eating well • Giving and justifying advice **Expressing attitudes, opinions** • Expressing doubt, uncertainty, and dislikes	The verb **boire** The verb **suivre**	Fast food in France
Persuading • Talking about fitness • Assuring and reassuring • Encouraging **Expressing feelings, emotions** • Expressing fatigue • Pitying	The verb **courir** Review of the present subjunctive Irregular subjunctive forms: **aller, avoir,** and **être**	Health clubs in France
Recombining communicative functions, grammar, and vocabulary		Fabrice's nightmare French anti-smoking publicity
Reading for practice and pleasure		A health fanatic pens a poem A French doctor's prescription Colorful French gym classes
Reviewing communicative functions, grammar, and vocabulary		Switzerland: languages, sights, and products

COMMUNICATIVE FUNCTIONS	GRAMMAR	CULTURE
Reading for global comprehension and cultural awareness		Tours of **Lyon** The **Guignol** theater
Exchanging information • Comparing city and country **Expressing feelings, emotions** • Saying you miss something **Persuading** • Consoling someone	Making comparisons with nouns The imperfect ✓	**Lyon** and its cultural life Country life in **Bourgogne**
Socializing • Renewing old acquaintances **Exchanging information** • Talking about past experiences	Review of the **passé composé** and the imperfect ✓ The uses of the **passé composé** and the imperfect ✓ The use of **être en train de**	Transportation to and within **Lyon** Weekend activities in France
Exchanging information • Making comparisons • Reporting a series of events **Persuading** • Making suggestions	Making comparisons with adjectives and adverbs	The sights of **Lyon**
Recombining communicative functions, grammar, and vocabulary		A French girl talks about living in **Champagne, Strasbourg,** and **Bordeaux**
Reading for practice and pleasure		Parisians cope with strikes A Parisian traffic jam in verse A family moves to Paris

COMMUNICATIVE FUNCTIONS	GRAMMAR	CULTURE
Reading for global comprehension and cultural awareness		History of **Arles** The **Camargue** region
Exchanging information • Making preparations for a trip **Expressing feelings, emotions** • Expressing impatience **Socializing** • Making excuses	Review of the interrogative pronouns **qui, que, qu'est-ce que, quoi** The interrogative pronouns **qui est-ce qui, qui est-ce que, qu'est-ce qui**	School trips and government-sponsored educational projects in France The city of **Berre** and its industry
Exchanging information • Talking about sightseeing • Making comparisons **Expressing feelings, emotions** • Expressing relief and regret	Review of making comparisons with nouns, adjectives, and adverbs Making comparisons: superlatives of adjectives and adverbs The past subjunctive ✓	The sights of **Arles** **Provence** Cezanne and Van Gogh
Exchanging information • Telling about past events **Expressing attitudes, opinions** • Expressing lack of interest	The past infinitive ✓	**Arles:** the national center of photography
Recombining communicative functions, grammar, and vocabulary		Events at the photography convention in **Arles** The village of **Les Saintes-Maries-de-la-Mer**
Reading for practice and pleasure		Adventure in the **Château de Rambouillet**

	BASIC MATERIAL

COMMUNICATIVE FUNCTIONS	GRAMMAR	CULTURE
Reading for global comprehension and cultural awareness		The **minitel** The **Explora** exhibit at **la Villette**
Expressing attitudes, opinions • Predicting what the future will be like • Expressing doubt and certainty	The future tense	French technology
Expressing attitudes, opinions • Imagining your future **Expressing feelings, emotions** • Expressing intentions, goals, wishes, and dreams	The future of irregular verbs The future with **quand**	The French space program
Expressing attitudes, opinions • Discussing problems of the future • Expressing beliefs, hope, and doubt	The relative pronouns **qui** and **que**	A visit to the **Cité des Sciences et de l'Industrie**
Recombining communicative functions, grammar, and vocabulary		A French girl's responses to a survey about her future
Reading for practice and pleasure		A science lesson in a French classroom An unusual day in France
Reviewing communicative functions, grammar, and vocabulary		A Senegalese girl introduces her French friend to her country

FOR REFERENCE

MAPS

Nous, les jeunes

OBJECTIVE To read in French for cultural awareness

CULTURAL BACKGROUND *Page 1* French speakers do indeed come from all over the world, since French is one of only two languages (English is the other) spoken on all five continents. You might remind students that **Fort-de-France** is the capital of **Martinique.**

Page 2 There are more than 40 amusement parks in France, and several more are being built. They're very popular among French families for day and weekend trips. The oldest, dating back to the early 1960s, is **la Mer de Sable** near Ermenonville, about 40 kilometers north of Paris. This park has an old-American-West theme.

Watching television is a common evening pastime. The most popular shows are sports telecasts, which attract 29.6 percent of the population. The least popular are art and cultural programs, which attract only 5.4 percent of the population.

Page 3 Pets are very popular in France, and their popularity is growing. Thirty-four percent of French households now have a dog. It is estimated that the dog population of France will double by the year 2000. To satisfy the growing demand, the French are importing approximately 400,000 dogs each year, mostly from England.

Page 4 Despite the relative rigor of schooling in the **lycées,** the dropout rate is low, only four percent after the first year **(la seconde),** and even lower after the second year **(la première).** If students dropout, they do it earlier, during and after the **collège** years. In fact, fewer than half of the students in the first year of **collège (la sixième)** go on to study at a **lycée.**

Because of their heavy school workload, French teenagers do not go out during the week as often as American teenagers do, but socializing with friends on weekends is everyone's favorite activity.

Page 5 In France one must be 14 years old to work. Between the ages of 14 and 16, one is permitted to work during school vacations only.

Baby-sitting is by far the most popular job among French teenagers. The average baby-sitter earns 20 to 25 francs per hour. Other popular summer jobs besides those mentioned in the text are lawn mowing, working as an **au pair** (*mother's helper*), selling newspapers, working as a cashier or salesclerk, and making deliveries for local stores. Some teenagers work as camp counselors **(monos,** slang for **animateurs/animatrices),** but in order to get such a job, one must be 17 years old and have been certified.

Page 6 Music, theater, chess, and computer operations are popular courses at most **MJCs (Maisons des Jeunes et de la Culture).** Others are photography, art, sports, yoga, choral singing, and dance.

Page 7 Two hours a week of physical education are compulsory in French **lycées,** although many **lycées** give three hours of instruction in **EPS (Education physique et sportive).** Most of that time is devoted to track and field and to gymnastics.

Both team and individual sports are popular among French teenagers; many join teams organized by the **UNSS (Union nationale du sport scolaire).** In the **UNSS,** the most popular team sports among boys are (in descending order)

European-style handball, soccer, basketball, volleyball, and rugby. Handball is also the most popular among girls, followed by basketball and volleyball. For boys the most popular individual sports in the **UNSS** are track and field, cross-country, swimming, tennis, and cycling. Girls like rhythmic gymnastics best, followed by dance and track and field.

SUGGESTED TEACHING PROCEDURE

Play the cassette or read the text and captions aloud as students follow along in their books. Pause occasionally to ask comprehension questions: **Qu'est-ce qui indique que le lycée occupe une place très importante dans la vie des jeunes? Nommez quelques corvées domestiques des jeunes.** Students may consult their books to answer.

Have the students read the text and captions a second time, silently. Then invite them to ask their own questions about the information presented. Questions should be in French.

SLOWER-PACED LEARNING Explain any expressions students might not understand, in French if possible: **se balader—marcher.** Use simple true-or-false statements to check comprehension.

CHALLENGE Invite students to make comparisons with American culture in general and their own lives in particular. You might ask these questions:

> Est-ce que le dîner en famille est aussi important ici qu'en France?
> Est-ce que les corvées domestiques mentionnées sont typiques chez
>   nous aussi? Quelles corvées est-ce que vous faites?
> Comparez la vie scolaire d'un lycéen français à celle d'un américain.
> Qu'est-ce que vous faites avec vos copains quand vous avez du temps libre?

Suggested Activity

Have students make two lists, one of cultural differences between France and the United States, and the other of cultural similarities. After they've made their lists, divide the class into cooperative learning groups of three or four. Group members should compare their lists and discuss their findings. They may not agree; explain that this doesn't mean that one person is wrong and another right, but that people see things in different ways. After several minutes of discussion, invite one member from each group to report general conclusions to the class.

SLOWER-PACED LEARNING Brainstorm with the students a list of observations about French teenagers, based on the photo essay: **Les lycéens ne travaillent pas après l'école, Les jeunes font des corvées domestiques,** and so on. Write the sentences on the board or on a transparency, and have students copy them. Then proceed as above, having students make up two lists (differences and similarities) before breaking into small groups for discussion.

Suggested Activity

Have students scan the photo essay to find ways to express likes and preferences **(C'est sympa! C'est chouette! C'est super! On adore!)** and ways to express dislikes **(C'est pas le pied! Quelle barbe!).** List the expressions on the board or on a transparency. Ask students to say how they feel about some of the activities mentioned in the photo essay.

APERÇU CULTUREL 1

Nous, les jeunes

Nous venons de Paris, Montréal, Fort-de-France et des quatre coins du monde. Nous nous appelons Sébastien, Corinne, Grégory ou Claire. Nous sommes tous différents, et pourtant, nous sommes tous un peu les mêmes : nous sommes les jeunes d'aujourd'hui, adultes de demain. Nous aimons nos parents, nos frères et sœurs, nos copains; nous aimons rire et être ensemble, nous aimons la vie!

Vivre en famille, c'est sympa. Souvent, nous n'osons pas parler à nos parents, mais ils sont là pour nous aider à résoudre les difficultés de la vie. Nous passons beaucoup de temps ensemble, et nous partageons joies et chagrins, espoirs et regrets…

Une visite au musée, c'est toujours éducatif!

Le dîner est un moment très important de la soirée.

Qu'est-ce qu'il y a à la télé ce soir?

Toute la famille au parc d'attractions

A la maison, il y a toujours mille petites choses à faire : ranger notre chambre ou préparer le repas, par exemple. C'est vrai, les corvées domestiques, c'est pas le pied, mais nous aidons volontiers nos parents. Après tout, c'est normal de participer, vous ne trouvez pas?

Zut! Pour manger, il faut mettre la table!

Ah, faire la vaisselle... Mes pauvres mains!

Sortir le chien, c'est agréable...

mais passer l'aspirateur, quelle barbe!

Le lycée occupe une place très importante dans notre vie. Nous avons beaucoup de cours : français, maths, langues étrangères, gym, biologie, histoire-géo, informatique, physique, chimie, musique, dessin... Nos journées sont très longues, et après l'école, nous étudions à la maison. Heureusement, il y a les copains!

Quel monde dans la cour du lycée!

Salut, les copains!

Chut! On est en classe...

Les devoirs, toujours les devoirs!

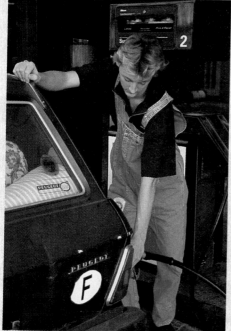

Les voitures, ça vous intéresse? Alors, travaillez dans une station-service.

L'argent de poche, c'est un problème international! Nos parents nous donnent souvent une petite somme par semaine, mais comment économiser pour acheter la stéréo de nos rêves? La solution : trouver un petit job. Malheureusement, nous n'avons pas beaucoup de temps pendant l'année scolaire. Alors, nous travaillons surtout en juillet ou en août.

Vous pouvez aussi distribuer des prospectus...

ou faire du baby-sitting, si vous aimez les enfants!

Et pourquoi pas vendre des fleurs sur le marché?

Les cours et les devoirs, c'est fatigant! Heureusement, il y a le mercredi après-midi, le week-end et les vacances... Quand nous sommes enfin libres, nous pouvons faire un tas d'activités passionnantes. Bien sûr, nos passe-temps sont très variés. Il y en a pour tous les goûts, pour les rêveurs comme pour les cérébraux!

*Un futur
Jimi Hendrix?*

Nous, on fait du théâtre dans la rue, et on adore!

Les échecs, c'est super compliqué!

Vous aussi, vous aimez l'informatique?

La gym, c'est très bon pour la santé! Mais après l'école, quels sports pratiquons-nous? Ça dépend beaucoup des saisons (été ou hiver, printemps ou automne?), et aussi d'où nous habitons (mer, montagne, ville, campagne?). Sports d'équipe ou sports individuels, sports traditionnels ou originaux, nous avons vraiment le choix!

On n'est pas les Harlem Globetrotters, mais on s'amuse!

En été, on peut faire de la natation ou de la planche à voile.

Le ski sur gazon, vous connaissez?

La danse, quel sport gracieux!

Bien sûr, les copains, c'est très important! Nous partageons nos petits secrets, nous parlons de tout et de rien. Nous aimons bien sortir ensemble, surtout le samedi soir et le dimanche, parce que pendant la semaine, nous n'avons pas le temps. Qu'est-ce que nous faisons? Ça varie beaucoup.

Pour discuter, nous allons souvent au café.

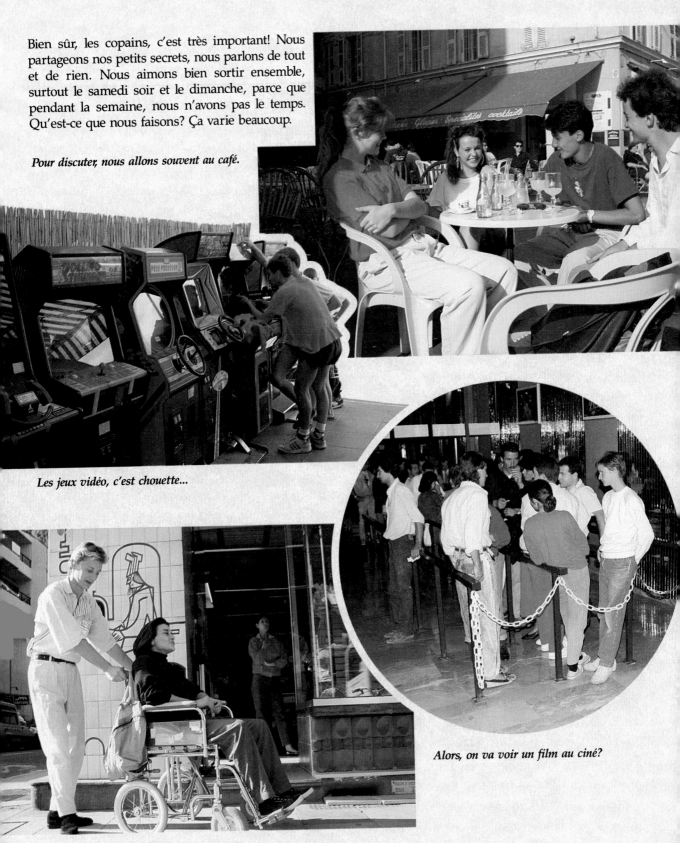

Les jeux vidéo, c'est chouette...

Alors, on va voir un film au ciné?

mais se balader entre amis, c'est super!

CHAPITRE 1

CHAPITRE 1 Nous revoilà

	BASIC MATERIAL	COMMUNICATIVE FUNCTIONS
PREMIER CONTACT	**Retour de vacances (1)** **Shopping rentrée (4)**	Reading for global comprehension and cultural awareness
SECTION A	**Nous revoilà (A1)** **Nous revoilà (suite) (A9)**	**Socializing** • Greeting old and new friends • Asking how others are **Expressing attitudes, opinions** • Expressing an opinion, agreeing, and disagreeing
SECTION B	**Où est-ce qu'ils sont allés pendant leurs vacances? (B1)**	**Socializing** • Talking about summer vacation **Expressing feelings, emotions** • Expressing satisfaction, dissatisfaction **Expressing attitudes, opinions** • Expressing indifference
SECTION C	**Les résolutions (C1)**	**Socializing** • Making excuses **Exchanging information** • Talking about the last school year • Making resolutions for the new year
TRY YOUR SKILLS	**Des cartes postales (1)**	

- **Prononciation** (the rhythm of French; dictation) **45**
- **Vérifions!** 46 - **Vocabulaire** 47

A LIRE	**Souvenirs de vacances** (A French boy boasts of his accomplishments at summer camp.)

WRITING A variety of controlled and open-ended writing activities appear in the Pupil's Edition. The Teacher's Notes identify other activities suitable for writing practice.

COOPERATIVE LEARNING Many of the activities in the Pupil's Edition lend themselves to cooperative learning. For guidelines, see page T14.

Scope and Sequence

1

GRAMMAR	CULTURE	RE-ENTRY
	The cost of books, school supplies, and clothes for school in France	
	Back to school in France: **la rentrée** The ideal **lycée**	**The passé composé** with **avoir** Greetings Getting acquainted Expressing opinions Weather expressions
The **passé composé** with **être** (B7)	How French students spend their vacation Regions of France Vacations in France for employees and students	The verb **être** Months of the year Expressing likes and dislikes
	Grades and report cards Teacher-parent contact: **le carnet de correspondance**	**Aller** + infinitive The verb **prendre**

Recombining communicative functions, grammar, and vocabulary

Reading for practice and pleasure

UNIT RESOURCES   **Cahier d'Activités, Cahier d'Exercices,** Unit 1 Cassettes, Transparencies 1–3 (also 31, 31A), Quizzes 1–3, Unit 1 Test
TEACHER-PREPARED MATERIALS   **Premier Contact**   School-supply catalogue and ads, French magazines; **Section A**   School calendar; **Section B**   Vacation souvenirs and pictures, map of England, flashcards for B7; **Try Your Skills**   Map of France

PREMIER
CONTACT

The authentic material in **Premier Contact** introduces the theme of the unit. Concentrate only on the general content of these documents. A detailed treatment of the grammar and vocabulary is not intended. Since students should be reading for global comprehension, they need not know the meaning of every word. For this reason, new words in **Premier Contact** have been omitted from the unit vocabulary list and the French-English Vocabulary at the end of the book.

OBJECTIVES   To read for global comprehension and cultural awareness; to get acquainted with the topic

1   Retour de vacances

Play the cassette. As they listen with books closed, have students write down the number of the question, and beside it, the letter of the response that applies to them. Then ask the questions, and have students read their responses from the book.

SLOWER-PACED LEARNING   Allow students to open their books and to read along silently as they listen to the cassette. Then answer questions they might have about new expressions: **carrément ennuyeuses, je me suis ennuyé(e), je me suis bien amusé(e), à l'étranger.**

2   Activité • Trouvez d'autres réponses

Prepare a transparency of the eight questions, without responses, leaving room below each question. As students think of alternate responses, add the best ones to the transparency.

3   Activité • Sondage

CHALLENGE   Work with the students to make up a more extensive questionnaire. As students suggest questions, write them on the board and have the students copy them. When the questionnaires are ready, allow students to circulate and conduct their interviews.

4   SHOPPING RENTREE

Present new vocabulary words using a school-supply catalogue or ads as visual aids. Then play the cassette as students follow along in their books. Based on the current exchange rate, have students figure what each item would cost in American dollars. Ask students how much they spend on their supplies. What do they buy? How does this differ from what French students buy?

5   Activité • Trouvez les mots

Students should write the five words along the top of a sheet of paper and then select related words from the reading to list underneath. Have students guess the English equivalents of the words they've listed.

6   Activité • Le budget de la rentrée

Have students list the things they've already bought or will need to buy for the new school year. Next to each item, have them write the approximate price in French francs. They might do this activity for homework.

CHALLENGE   Borrow some recent newspapers from the school library, and show students how to check the current exchange rate. Then bring in some recent French magazines, and invite students to comment on the prices of advertised items.

 SECTION A

OBJECTIVES   **To socialize:** greet old and new friends; ask how others are; **to express attitudes, opinions:** express an opinion, agree, and disagree

CULTURAL BACKGROUND   The school year is about the same length in France as in the United States. French students have fewer single days off, but their vacation periods are longer. **Les vacances de Noël** and **les vacances de Pâques** are generally two full weeks long. **Les vacances d'hiver** (in February) last about ten days. **Les vacances de la Toussaint** *(All Saints' Day)* at the beginning of November also last about ten days. The summer vacation **(les grandes vacances)** is a little more than two months long.

MOTIVATING ACTIVITY   Review months and days of the week. Show the school calendar for the year to students. Have them talk in French about the opening, closing, and holiday dates. Also, have them express their opinion as to whether the summer vacation is too long **(trop longues),** too short **(trop courtes),** or just right **(bien).**

 A1

Nous revoilà

Introduce new vocabulary **(bronzé, un nouveau/une nouvelle)** by greeting students and telling them about your summer vacation. Demonstrate **dragueur** and ask students if they know a boy who is one.

Play the cassette and have students follow along in their books. Have them summarize the opinion about summer vacation given by each character. Next personalize some of the expressions by doing a survey: **Qui est content de rentrer? Qui n'est pas content? Pourquoi?** Encourage the students to find lines in the dialogues that reflect their own opinions. Ask volunteers to read them aloud.

Finally, have the students role-play the dialogues, encouraging them to change the dialogues to reflect their own opinions.

SLOWER-PACED LEARNING   Stop the cassette after each dialogue and check comprehension by asking simple questions. If necessary, summarize each dialogue and play it again before going on to the next one.

CHALLENGE   Have students prepare and present to the class original dialogues based on the ones in the text.

A2   ## Activité • Vrai ou faux?

Have one student read each statement and call on classmates either to confirm or to correct. For homework, have students write out all six sentences, making any necessary corrections.

A3   ## Activité • Et vous?

Ask several students each question. Then have the students work in pairs to ask each other the questions, using **tu.** For homework, have students write out their answers in paragraph form.

A4 COMMENT LE DIRE

Using the phrases for expressing an opinion, make several strong statements: **A mon avis, la rentrée, c'est ennuyeux! Je trouve que la musique d'aujourd'hui est mauvaise!** Invite students to agree or disagree, using the expressions in their books.

SLOWER-PACED LEARNING   Have students make two columns on a sheet of paper, one labeled **D'accord** and the other **Pas d'accord.** Make several statements of agreement or disagreement, and have students place a check mark in the appropriate column. Use exaggerated body language and gestures to aid comprehension.

> —A mon avis, ce film est un navet!   —Il fait trop froid pour nager!
> —Au contraire, c'est un bon film!   —Vous avez raison! Jouons au tennis!

A5 Activité • Et vous?

Assign these statements to five students. Each one should say his or her statement. Others in the class should volunteer responses that express their own feelings. Students might also do this as a chain drill: the student who responds makes the next statement, and so forth.

CHALLENGE   Have students in the class make up their own statements and choose someone to agree or disagree with them.

A6 Activité • Exprimez votre opinion

For cooperative learning, divide the class into groups of three or four students each, and have them discuss each situation in French. One student might volunteer to express the conclusions reached by the group in each case.

CHALLENGE   Have the various groups write their own situations, which you might duplicate and distribute for class discussion the next day.

A7 Activité • Ecrivez

Have students list their classes, their teachers, and their last vacation. Beside each of these, they should write an appropriate adjective. Encourage them to use adjectives in addition to those given in the box. Next take one list; show how it can be expanded into sentences and then a paragraph. Assign this activity as homework. The next day, collect and correct.

A8 Activité • A vous maintenant!

For cooperative learning, form groups of three or four, with one student in each group selected to lead the discussion and to summarize the group's opinion(s) for the class.

CHALLENGE   Some students may wish to prepare a dialogue to present to their classmates.

A9 NOUS REVOILA (SUITE)

Review summer weather expressions in both the present and the **passé composé.** Have students say what the weather is like today and what it was yesterday. Introduce **Comment allez-vous?** and have students practice using it with you.

Have them practice using **Comment vas-tu?** with each other.

Play the cassette. Have students repeat the dialogue in pairs. Then have each pair switch roles and repeat the dialogue once more. Remind students to substitute **monsieur** for **madame** when appropriate.

A 10 Activité • Avez-vous compris?

First review the dialogues in A1 by playing the cassette for A1. Have students write the names of the characters on a sheet of paper and take notes as they listen. Then ask the questions, or have students ask each other the questions.

A 11 COMMENT LE DIRE

Ask the students these questions. Encourage not only the responses given in the box but any other acceptable replies. Then you might play various roles: tell students who you are and have them greet you. Respond in various ways.

> —Je suis un élève français. Je visite votre école. Je m'appelle Claude.
> —Bonjour, Claude. Comment vas-tu?
> —Très bien, merci. Et toi?
> —Pas mal.

For homework, have students choose an identity. In class the following day, they circulate and introduce themselves to each other according to their new identity.

A 12 Activité • A vous maintenant!

Students should have their books closed. Give the direction to a student. After the student has phrased the question, have other students respond. Repeat until most of the class has participated.

A 13 Activité • Discussion en classe

For cooperative learning, divide the class into groups of five. Have them role-play the dialogue, taking turns as the teacher.

A 14 VOUS EN SOUVENEZ-VOUS?

Review the examples given in number 1. Have students change all six forms to the negative, as described in number 2. Show how some adverbs are inserted, as in number 3: **Vous avez déjà fini le repas? Je n'ai pas encore fini. Elle a souvent parlé de vous.** Give two or three examples using the past participles of irregular verbs listed in number 4. Write them on the board and have students copy them into their notebooks.

Then ask students to work in pairs or cooperative learning groups to make up their own sentences for the rest of the verbs in number 4. Circulate; when you see a good example, ask a member of the group to write it on the board for the class to copy.

SLOWER-PACED LEARNING   On a transparency, make a list of sentence endings, such as the ones on the next page. Ask students to supply the missing parts, using the irregular past participles in number 4. Choose a good sentence completion, write it on the transparency, and have students copy it into their notebooks.

_____ le livre.	_____ la tour Eiffel.
_____ ton devoir?	_____ mon stylo.
_____ la porte.	_____ ses chaussures.

CHALLENGE   Ask students to tell about their activities from the past summer, using the following verbs: **visiter, voyager, travailler, nager, prendre, jouer, faire, passer, lire.** You might write these on the board so that students will not try to use verbs conjugated with **être.**

A 15   Activité • A-t-elle passé de bonnes vacances?

First do the activity orally, having individuals change each verb to the correct form in the **passé composé.** Next, as a self-check, have students write out the sentences.

SLOWER-PACED LEARNING   Have students give the past participle for each verb. Then have them change the verb in the sentence.

A 16   Activité • Qu'est-ce qu'ils ont fait?

Have students look at the pictures and identify the activity in each, using the present tense. Then have them describe the pictures in the **passé composé.**

SLOWER-PACED LEARNING   On the board or on a transparency, list phrases that describe the pictures: **attraper un coup de soleil, rencontrer un garçon, lire des bédés,** and so on. Have students match the phrases to the pictures and then say what happened, using the **passé composé.**

A 17   Activité • A vous maintenant!

Elicit from students how they would ask the questions. Write out several on the board as models: **Tu as lu un livre? Quel livre? Tu as voyagé? Où?** Have students pair off to do this activity. Have them switch roles to do it once more. Circulate among students; then spot-check by asking several individuals to tell their partners' answers.

A 18   Activité • Sondage

Have students circulate, asking four or five other students each question. Have volunteers report what they found out.

SLOWER-PACED LEARNING   As a listening exercise, ask questions beginning with **qui: Qui a déjà voyagé au Canada? Qui a déjà étudié l'espagnol?** Have a show of hands to see which students have done the activities mentioned.

CHALLENGE   Have students add questions of their own to the poll.

A 19   Activité • Parlez et écrivez

Have students circulate, asking four or five other students each question and taking notes on their answers. Call on a few to report, and write the results of the survey on the board.

SLOWER-PACED LEARNING   Allow students to jot down their answers to the questions before they begin to circulate.

CHALLENGE   As a homework assignment, have the students prepare a newspaper article based on the survey.

A 20 Activité • Les achats de la rentrée

SLOWER-PACED LEARNING   Start the list on the board. Have each student go up and add one item. Continue until there are no more ideas. Then have students pair off to ask each other questions, referring to the list.

CHALLENGE   This activity can be made into a game. Ask students to think of and list as many items as they can. They needn't be real purchases. Set a time limit. The student with the longest list wins.

A 21 Savez-vous que... ?

The **lycée Balzac** has hosted many American exchange students. It does have exceptionally attractive features. The swimming pool is housed in a separate building near the main entrance, which is the only gate by which students may enter, so that they can be observed by the **concierge.** There are several dining rooms: one for older students, one for younger ones, one for teachers, and a small one for the principal and his guests or fellow administrators. The top floor of the main building contains a large private apartment, with balconies and beautiful views of the Paris skyline, where the principal **(le proviseur)** lives with his family.

Play the cassette twice. Students listen with books closed the first time and with books open the second time. Go over the list of suggestions given, asking students whether they agree or disagree that these are important features of a school.

CHALLENGE   Have students make their own list of features that should be part of **un lycée cool** in the United States.

A 22 Activité • Ecoutez bien

Listen to the following conversations. Is the person who answers happy about returning to school or not? On a separate sheet of paper, number from 1 to 6. *(pause)* Be prepared to write **oui** or **non** after each number. **Ecoutez bien.**

1. —Tu as passé de bonnes vacances?
   —Merveilleuses! J'ai fait des tas de choses. J'ai très envie de repartir! *(non)*

2. —Tu as bronzé, dis donc!
   —Oui, il a fait un temps splendide. Maintenant, pour le premier jour d'école, il pleut! Quelle barbe! *(non)*

3. —J'ai pas du tout envie de recommencer l'école. Et toi?
   —Moi, oui. Je ne m'amuse pas en vacances. Je suis très contente de revoir mes amies de l'année dernière. *(oui)*

4. —Viens, on va dire bonjour à la nouvelle!
   —D'accord! C'est bien, l'école. Il y a toujours des nouvelles! *(oui)*

5. —Je suis content de te revoir!
   —Moi aussi! Alors, qu'est-ce que tu as fait pendant tes vacances? *(oui)*

6. —Alors, content de recommencer l'école?
   —Bof! C'est quand les prochaines vacances? *(non)*

Et maintenant, vérifions. *Read each dialogue again and give the correct answer.*

SECTION
B

OBJECTIVES **To socialize:** talk about summer vacation; **to express feelings, emotions:** express satisfaction and dissatisfaction; **to express attitudes, opinions:** express indifference

CULTURAL BACKGROUND French schools do not have the organized sports programs and competitive teams with which we are familiar. Therefore, vacations are the time for teenagers to be physically active: swimming, sailing, biking, hiking, and so on. They offer chances to meet other young people and expand one's horizons by traveling and immersing oneself in another culture. Some French students come to the United States by participating in **un échange culturel.** Many spend a summer in England, taking part in **un séjour linguistique.**

MOTIVATING ACTIVITY If you have any souvenirs from your summer vacation, bring them to class and tell the students a little about your own vacation. Use some of the expressions from the dialogues. Have students talk about the best or the worst summer vacation, other than the past one, they ever spent.

B1 — Où est-ce qu'ils sont allés pendant leurs vacances?

Bring in pictures to present the new vocabulary: **faire du canoë-kayak, faire de la spéléologie, une station-service, au bord de la mer, faire de la bicyclette.** Ask students **Avez-vous déjà fait du canoë-kayak? De la spéléologie? Faites-vous souvent de la bicyclette?** and so on. Explain the term **un séjour linguistique.**

   Place the pictures on the chalk ledge along with a map of England and number them. Tell students that they are going to hear what seven young French people did during vacation. As students listen to the cassette, they should write the name of the person next to the number of the appropriate vacation activity.

   After playing the cassette, assign the eight roles to different students and have them read through the dialogues. Divide the class into groups to role-play the dialogues; allow students to keep their books open.

B2 — Activité • Pourquoi?

Have students complete this activity orally or in writing. They should answer in complete sentences.

B3 — Activité • Trouvez les synonymes

Call out the underlined words **(beaucoup, contents,** and so on) and have students respond with synonyms. Then have individuals read the sentences aloud, making the necessary substitutions.

B4 — COMMENT LE DIRE

Ask students about their summer vacations, personalizing your questions: **C'était comment, vos vacances au parc de Yellowstone?** Students should choose responses from the chart.

SLOWER-PACED LEARNING If students are unsure of any words, act them out or explain them. Then have them ask you questions about your vacation, weekend, and so on. Exaggerate body language and gestures as you give the various responses. Ask each student to take a few minutes to memorize *one* response of each type; then ask questions to elicit the responses.

CHALLENGE   Model a few questions that the students can ask each other:

—Qu'est-ce que tu as fait le week-end dernier?
—J'ai vu un film.
—C'était bien?

Have students work in pairs to ask and respond to similar questions.

B5   Activité • Ça vous a plu?

Tell students to pretend they enjoyed the experience, and call on individuals to respond. Then tell students to pretend they hated the experience, and call on others to answer. Have students pair off, assigning one to be the mother (or father) and the other to be the camper. Students should then switch roles and repeat the activity.

B6   Activité • A vous maintenant!

Model the questions by asking a student **Est-ce que vous avez fait de la voile? Ça vous a plu?** Then have students carry out the activity in pairs.

SLOWER-PACED LEARNING   Brainstorm the questions with the class first. Have students write out the questions and answers before practicing them aloud.

B7   STRUCTURES DE BASE

Ask a few questions in the **passé composé** with the auxiliary verb **avoir: Qu'est-ce que vous avez fait hier soir? Qu'est-ce que vous avez fait dans le cours d'anglais la semaine dernière?** After you've talked a bit, ask what the helping verb is and have one or two students write some examples on the board, using different verbs.

Ask a student to leave the room (the student can stand outside the open door): **Debbie, voulez-vous sortir pour un moment?** After she has left, say **Debbie est sortie. Elle est sortie.** Ask **Qui est sorti?** Repeat the procedure with a boy: **Paul est sorti. Il est sorti.** Ask **Qui est sorti?** Say **Debbie et Paul sont sortis. Ils sont sortis.** Ask **Anne et Michel sont sortis?** Have the class answer: **Non, Debbie et Paul sont sortis.** Bring the students back into the classroom. Introduce the negative: **Isabelle n'est pas sortie.** Have the students practice negative sentences.

Walk to the door and say: **Je suis allé(e) à la porte.** Then, using a TPR technique (see page T7), ask a student to go to the door. Say **Pierre, allez à la porte, s'il vous plaît.** Ask **Pierre, vous êtes allé au bureau?** Elicit the response: **Non, je suis allé à la porte.** Repeat the procedure with several students, eliciting affirmative and negative sentences. Then do the same with two students, teaching **vous êtes allés** and **nous sommes allés.** Have the class practice the **nous** and **vous** forms.

In various parts of the classroom, post students holding up flashcards with the names of French cities. Have students take turns going from one "city" to another and returning to their seats. Students can then practice asking questions and responding: **Où est-ce que tu es allé(e)? Tu es allé(e) à Lyon?** After some practice, write sentences that the students generated on the board or on a transparency, pointing out the agreement of the past participles. Discuss all persons, singular and plural. Have the students copy the sentences into their notebooks.

Have students act out other verbs, and encourage them to describe the actions: **il est arrivé, je suis entré(e), elle est partie,** and so on. Have the class practice the **liaison** sounds in verbs that begin with a vowel.

For the next few days, practice the verbs by asking personalized questions: **Où êtes-vous allé(e) hier soir? A quelle heure êtes-vous parti(e) ce matin? A quelle heure êtes-vous arrivé(e) à l'école?**

SLOWER-PACED LEARNING After students have gained confidence in using these verbs orally, begin to do written work. Don't expect students to master all the past participle agreements right away.

B 8 Activité • Le dernier jour de vacances

Students should give the answers orally. Then have them write out the sentences. Have students tell what they did on the last day of their vacations.

B 9 Activité • Où est-ce qu'ils sont allés?

Have students work in pairs to reread B1 in search of the answers. Then call on individuals to tell where each French **ami(e)** went on vacation and what he or she did there. Then assign this as written homework. For more practice, have students ask each other where they went on vacation.

B 10 Activité • Le voyage de Sylvie

Divide the class into groups of three and have each group change the story, using one of the following: **Sylvie et sa sœur, Sylvie et son frère, Sylvie et moi.**

B 11 Activité • Ecrit dirigé

SLOWER-PACED LEARNING Have students write down only the verb forms. Call on individuals to read each sentence aloud, using the appropriate verb form. Then assign the entire paragraph to be written.

B 12 Activité • A vous maintenant!

Have the students report their partners' answers to the rest of the class.

B 13 Activité • Ecrivez

You might first provide students with a model by describing a real or imaginary trip you took to Paris.

SLOWER-PACED LEARNING For cooperative learning, have students work in pairs to discuss a trip to Paris and to prepare one written account of it together.

B 14 Savez-vous que… ?

Play the cassette or read the passage aloud as students follow along in their books. Ask questions in order to check comprehension. If you know of any foreign student exchange programs in the area, describe them for the students.

Have students read silently the publicity for the **séjour linguistique** in London. Tell students to imagine they are going to London, and have them tell you what they are going to do there.

B15 Activité • Ecoutez bien

Open your book to page 29. *(pause)* Copy the chart in B15 on a separate sheet of paper. *(pause)* Listen as Sylvie and Guillaume talk about their vacations. Then fill in the chart, telling where they went, how the weather was, what they did, and if they are pleased with how things went. You don't have to write complete sentences. You may want to take notes as you listen. **Ecoutez bien.**

GUILLAUME   Salut, Sylvie!
SYLVIE   Salut, Guillaume!
GUILLAUME   Alors, tu as passé de bonnes vacances?
SYLVIE   Merveilleuses! Je suis restée chez moi, à Paris. C'était génial. Je me suis beaucoup amusée!
GUILLAUME   Il a fait beau?
SYLVIE   Un temps super! Et toi, qu'est-ce que tu as fait?
GUILLAUME   Oh, moi, je suis allé au bord de la mer. C'était pas terrible. Il a plu tout le temps. J'ai fait un peu de planche à voile. Et toi, qu'est-ce que tu as fait?
SYLVIE   J'ai pas arrêté! J'ai fait du jogging, j'ai vu tous mes amis, j'ai écouté des disques... Quoi d'autre?... Ah, oui, j'ai organisé une boum et j'ai invité vingt personnes! Ah, quelles vacances!

Et maintenant, vérifions. *Read the information in the chart.*

	Où?	Temps?	Activités?	Content(e)?
Sylvie	*Paris*	*super*	*jogging, amis, disques, boum*	*oui*
Guillaume	*mer*	*pluie*	*planche à voile*	*non*

SECTION C

OBJECTIVES   To socialize: make excuses; **to exchange information:** talk about the last school year; make resolutions for the new year

CULTURAL BACKGROUND   The pressure to do well in school is strong on French students. One reason is the difficult national examination (**le baccalauréat,** or **le bac** for short) administered in parts after each of the last two years of the **lycée: la première** and **la terminale.** Since a student must pass this exam in order to enter a university and about one-third do not pass the first time, many students repeat the **terminale** and then take the **bac** again. Students may repeat the **terminale** year a third time; if by then they have not passed the **bac,** they must leave school. Most young people who fail the exam enter the working world or join the military. Everyone is free to take the **bac** again as many times as he or she may wish, but it is difficult to pass without the benefit of recent schooling.

There are educational opportunities for those who don't pass the exam. For example, students who are interested in studying law can take a two-year pre-law course without having passed the **bac.** However, a stiff exam at the end of the first year eliminates 80 percent of the students. Another option is to take the **ESEU (Examen spécial d'entrée à l'université).** This exam is open to all adults 24 years or older, or to 20-year-olds who have at least two years of work experience. Slightly more than one-half pass this exam.

MOTIVATING ACTIVITY Have students list in French the courses they are taking this year. Have them label each one as **facile** or **difficile.** Finally, have them indicate by a brief phrase what they expect to have to do in each course.

C1 Les résolutions

Tell students they are going to hear a conversation among four French young people who are making resolutions for the new school year. Present through gestures and/or pictures some of the new vocabulary: **redoubler, tomber malade, souffrir, nul/nulle, mon fort.** After the students have listened to the cassette, assign roles to be read aloud. Then ask comprehension questions beginning with **qui: Qui n'a pas travaillé l'année passée? Qui va aller au cinéma cette année?**

C2 Activité • Avez-vous compris?

SLOWER-PACED LEARNING Form cooperative learning groups of three students each. Have students help each other find the answers in the text and write them down.

C3 Activité • Qu'est-ce que vous en pensez?

Brainstorm possible ways to express opinions: **C'est vrai, Il/Elle a raison (tort), Je suis d'accord.** Write them on the board or on a transparency. Elicit some opinions for each question. Then form groups of three students each. Allow time for discussion and then call for opinions from each group.

C4 Activité • Et vous?

Have students pair off to ask each other these questions. Circulate among them, listening but not interrupting. Correct errors you overhear afterward in a general summary for the class.

C5 Activité • Ecrivez

Have a group of three or four students copy and complete this activity on a transparency while the others copy and complete it in their notebooks. Then show the transparency and correct it. Students may use it as a model to correct their own paragraphs.

SLOWER-PACED LEARNING Write this completion activity on a transparency for students to do along with you. Then have them copy it.

CHALLENGE Ask students to use these sentences as the basis of a composition to be written at home. Tell them to expand it wherever possible. Call for volunteers to read their compositions aloud before you collect and correct them.

C6 Activité • Enquête

Have students write the questions they will ask. Allow the students to circulate, conducting their survey of classmates. After a reasonable time, spot-check by calling for reports on results.

SLOWER-PACED LEARNING Ask for a show of hands as you ask these questions. Record the results on the board or on a transparency.

C7 **COMMENT LE DIRE**

Have students list courses in which they are not satisfied with their performance. Then, selecting from the excuses given here, they should write down the reasons for their unsatisfactory performance. Finally, have them make a resolution (how they can achieve better results) in each case.

C8 **Activité • Quelle est votre excuse?**

Encourage students to suggest original excuses in addition to the ones in C7.

C9 **Activité • A vous maintenant!**

SLOWER-PACED LEARNING Before having the students pair off, play the role of the parent and model possible parental comments. The class should brainstorm responses. Then have the students pair off; assign *one* subject to each pair.

CHALLENGE Have students make up their own personal report cards, listing their classes in French, but leaving blanks for grades and comments. Collect and distribute these cards at random. Each student should write grades and comments (anonymously) on the card he or she receives. Collect again and return cards to their original owners. Reactions should be in French. Encourage students to use the expressions they learned in A4 to agree and disagree with the comments.

C10 **VOUS EN SOUVENEZ-VOUS?**

Review the present-tense forms of **aller.** Give several examples of the use of **aller** with the infinitive, both affirmative and negative, with phrases that indicate future time: **Je vais étudier ce soir. Je ne vais pas aller au cinéma demain.** Ask students to write a few sentences about what they are going to do tonight or next weekend. Then have them form groups and question each other about their plans. Choose one person from each group to report.

C11 **Activité • Qu'est-ce qu'ils vont faire?**

Have students work in groups or in pairs to come up with the answers from C1 and then to suggest as many other solutions as they can. Have them share their solutions with the class.

SLOWER-PACED LEARNING Write six sentence endings on a transparency: **travailler dur, faire de la gymnastique, faire un séjour en Angleterre cet été,** and so on. Elicit completions based on C1: **Isabelle va faire un séjour en Angleterre cet été.**

C12 **Activité • On prend des résolutions**

CHALLENGE Have pairs make up situations for last year. Then allow them to read their situations aloud and to call on someone to state a change that will take place.

C13 **Activité • En dehors de l'école**

Have students pair off to ask each other what they are going to do this year, using the six suggestions, plus others they may think of. Then call on individuals to report what their partners are going to do.

C 14 Activité • Ecrivez

Circulate to assist students as they write. Ask for volunteers to write their resolutions on the board. Follow up by asking why they made a particular resolution.

C 15 Savez-vous que... ?

SLOWER-PACED LEARNING Briefly summarize, in French, the content of this paragraph. Then play the cassette as students follow along in their books. Ask students what they can glean from the comments in the **carnet** about school life in France. You might have them make up a similar page of comments and announcements to take home.

C 16 Activité • Ecoutez bien

Emilie is very busy, but Isabelle keeps trying to find a time when they can do something together. Open your book to page 35. *(pause)* Read the items in C16 to yourself. *(pause)* Listen to the conversation between the two girls, and be prepared to indicate your answers on a separate sheet of paper. Ready? **Ecoutez bien.**

ISABELLE	Qu'est-ce que tu vas faire ce soir, Emilie?
EMILIE	Eh bien, je vais étudier mon anglais. Je suis complètement nulle. Quand le prof parle, j'y comprends rien.
ISABELLE	Et demain? Tu veux venir au cinéma avec moi?
EMILIE	Impossible! J'ai des maths à faire.
ISABELLE	Jeudi, alors?
EMILIE	Non, pas jeudi. Vendredi matin, j'ai histoire. Je veux préparer la leçon.
ISABELLE	Bon! Qu'est-ce que tu fais ce week-end?
EMILIE	Ce week-end, je vais rester chez moi et travailler!
ISABELLE	Eh bien, tu es sérieuse!
EMILIE	Il faut bien! Je suis mauvaise en tout. Et je n'ai pas du tout envie de redoubler encore cette année.

Et maintenant, vérifions.

1. **b** Elle va étudier son anglais.
   c Elle va faire ses maths.
   a Elle va préparer sa leçon d'histoire.
2. **b** sortir.

3. **a** vrai
   b faux
   c faux
4. **c** mardi

OBJECTIVE To recombine communicative functions, grammar, and vocabulary

CULTURAL BACKGROUND In the summer, **Arcachon** is a bustling resort town with crowded beaches and hotels. French people love to eat the local oysters. The **Auvergne** is in the heart of the **Massif central.** It is a little off the beaten path for tourists, but those who go there appreciate its unspoiled scenery. The Pyrenees Mountains are not as popular as the Alps, but they attract their share of tourists. In the summer the region offers hikes at all levels of difficulty. Hikers can see wildlife that exists nowhere else in France: brown bears, eagles, and mountain antelopes **(ibards).**

MOTIVATING ACTIVITY   Invite students to bring in any postcards that may have been sent to their own family or friends from France, Germany, or other countries. If possible, have them say something in French about their cards.

1

Des cartes postales

Display a map of France that shows neighboring countries. Help students locate **Arcachon, l'Auvergne, les Pyrénées, l'Allemagne.** Ask what they think one might do on a vacation in each area. On the board or on a transparency, write at random the names of the people who sent the postcards and the names of the places they visited. Then play the cassette. Have students match the names and places.

2

Activité • Racontez

Do this activity in two steps. First have students put the verbs into the proper **passé composé** forms: **est allée/a fait, ont visité/sont rentrées,** and so on. Then have them find the necessary information in Skills 1 to complete each sentence. Do this as an oral activity before assigning it to be written.

3

Activité • Ecrivez

Make two wide columns on the board. Write **L'été passé** at the top of one and **L'été prochain** at the top of the other. Write a short model sentence below each heading:

L'été passé	**L'été prochain**
J'ai visité le Québec.	Je vais visiter la France.

Ask volunteers to add sentences to each column. Have students write their own two lists of sentences about past and future summer activities and then combine the information in two cohesive paragraphs. Collect, correct, and return the next day.

4

Activité • Ecrivez

Help students organize and write the response to this postcard. Read through the text of the card in French first, clarifying the meaning if necessary. Have students pick out the specific topics to address: **l'école, les profs, les copains, les résolutions.** Write these on the board or on a transparency. Then have students reread A1, B1, and C1 to decide how Emilie would answer the questions. Write at least one answer for each question on the board or on a transparency. Finally, ask students to write the date on their papers and to write Emilie's response to her friend. Collect and check, or have papers handed in the next day.

CHALLENGE   Have students write a postcard to an imaginary French friend about the opening of their school.

5

Activité • Catastrophe!

Have the entire class brainstorm possible "catastrophes" that might occur in these two situations. Then form cooperative learning groups of three or four students. Each group should choose one of the two situations. One member of each group should lead the discussion of possible "catastrophes," another should take notes, and another should report the "story" to the class.

6   Activité • Les vacances de Jacques

Have the students describe what is happening in each picture in the present tense. Then have them do the same thing using the **passé composé.**

SLOWER-PACED LEARNING   Have students relate the story in English. Have them write down the **passé composé** of each verb in the proper person, gender, and number. Finally, have them write the story in French.

CHALLENGE   Invite students to say what they have done to meet someone new who was very attractive to them.

7   Activité • C'était comment, les vacances?

Brainstorm with the students some possible questions they might ask about the vacations suggested by the ads. Write the questions on a transparency. Then have students pair off to ask each other the questions. Circulate to spot-check and give assistance where needed. Finally, call on a few students to tell what they did and on others to tell what their partners did.

SLOWER-PACED LEARNING   On the board or on a transparency, write questions that students can use to ask each other:

> Tu es content(e) de tes vacances?   Qu'est-ce que tu as fait?
> Où est-ce que tu es allé(e)?   Est-ce que ça t'a plu?

8   Activité • Où est-ce qu'ils sont allés en vacances?

First have students recall all the countries whose French names they know. Write the countries on the board and review the prepositions used with them. Have students look at the pictures, name the purchases, and discuss their possible origins. Afterward, ask students to pretend they went to a particular country and have them tell what they brought back.

9   Activité • C'était comment?

Before having students pair off to do the activity, ask several students questions suggested in the directions, and have them respond.

SLOWER-PACED LEARNING   Have students suggest questions to be used in this activity; write them on the board: **Tu es sorti(e) pendant le week-end? Où est-ce que tu es allé(e)?** and so on. Then have them identify the places represented by the ticket stubs.

10   Activité • Récréation

These activities are optional. Number 1 can be done by teams who compete to see who can solve the puzzle first. The winning team must also be able to name each numbered object. Number 2 can be done by the whole class. If students can't guess the answer, make a hangman game **(le pendu)** of it on the board, allowing students to guess the letters. Number 3 can also be done by teams who compete to see who can finish first.

PRONONCIATION

The rhythm of French

Open your book to page 45. *(pause)* Refer to this page as you listen to this section.

1   **Ecoutez bien et répétez.**

French is spoken not in words, but in syllables. The syllables flow in a chain of steady beats, with pauses for making sense or taking a breath. This produces a sort of staccato (rat-tat-tat) typewriter-like rhythm. It's so different from English that most Americans have difficulty keeping it up in French, even though they might fully understand how it works. Expect it to take a lot of practice.

Remember, if you don't get the rhythm, you'll never—but never—sound French. Okay, it's nice to be able to practice your r's all the way to the **bistro** on the **rue de Rivoli,** but if you don't have the rhythm, you're already out of the running. So, if you've not yet got the beat, get it now. Work on it. Don't let go till you have it. Use it every time you open your mouth to say something in French. Keep in mind that it's the syllable that gives the French language its special beat.

In French, all syllables are created equal. That's the notion you get when you listen to the language. This is the fundamental difference between French and English speech. In English, syllables of different lengths and loudness, full or swallowed, give it its uneven, loud-soft rhythm, which you must definitely avoid when you speak French.

For starters, try saying these names in French, syllable by syllable: **Chi-ca-go, To-ron-to, Ca-na-da.** Give each syllable its share of your breath—equal time and equal opportunity to be heard. Now try it out with the next group: **A-la-ska, Ma-ni-to-ba, To-ky-o, O-tta-wa.** Don't rush and don't try to talk fast until you're really good at the rhythm; you'll only fumble. Now try the third group: **Ca-sa-blan-ca, mi-ssion im-po-ssible, nou-velle ad-mi-ni-stra-tion.** From here on, keep checking on your syllable-by-syllable delivery, especially in long words like those in the fourth group: **ad-mi-ni-stra-tion, a-é-ro-port Ke-nne-dy, départs in-ter-na-tio-naux.**

How syllables are created and divided into breath groups are questions you'll tackle later. If you can get the staccato beat down pat, you'll already be half way to sounding more French than English. But remember to say each syllable distinctly. Get used to moving your lips more than you do in English.

2   **Ecoutez et lisez.**

Now let's try some easy groups. Word groups are cut, not into words, but into syllables of equal length, regardless of where one word stops and the other begins. Repeat these words and phrases:

pa-re-exmple	un-be-lé-té	a-ve-cu-na-mie
ce-té-té	i-la-rrive	pa-ra-vion

I-la-rri-va-ve-cu-na-mie pa-ra-vion.

Notice that, when possible, French speakers try to end each syllable with a vowel sound, even though the syllable contains nothing but the vowel. Remember you said **a-é-ro-port.**

3 **Copiez les phrases suivantes pour préparer une dictée.**

Write the following sentences from dictation. First listen to the sentence as it is read to you. Then you will hear the sentence again in short segments, with a pause after each segment to allow you time to write. Finally you will hear the sentence a third time so that you may check your work. Let's begin.

1. Cette année, j'ai fait du camping avec Anatole. Cette année, *(pause)* j'ai fait du camping *(pause)* avec Anatole. *(pause)* Cette année, j'ai fait du camping avec Anatole.
2. C'était un bel endroit au bord de la mer. C'était *(pause)* un bel endroit *(pause)* au bord de la mer. *(pause)* C'était un bel endroit au bord de la mer.
3. C'était le même endroit qu'il y a quatre ans. C'était *(pause)* le même endroit *(pause)* qu'il y a quatre ans. *(pause)* C'était le même endroit qu'il y a quatre ans.
4. Nous avons pris le même avion. Nous avons pris *(pause)* le même avion. *(pause)* Nous avons pris le même avion.
5. Mon oncle a tout arrangé. *(pause)* Mon oncle *(pause)* a tout arrangé. *(pause)* Mon oncle a tout arrangé.
6. Il nous a montré comment faire. Il nous a montré *(pause)* comment faire. *(pause)* Il nous a montré comment faire.
7. A notre âge il faut apprendre. A notre âge *(pause)* il faut apprendre. *(pause)* A notre âge il faut apprendre.

VERIFIONS!

SECTION A

Review the **passé composé,** expressions of opinion, and phrases that indicate agreement and disagreement. You might ask volunteers to do the activities at the board, while others call out suggestions. Then have students do them as a homework assignment. Correct in class the next day.

SECTION B

Review the verbs conjugated with **être** in the **passé composé: aller, arriver, sortir, partir, descendre, rester...** Have students write these exercises as you circulate, observe, and assist.

SECTION C

Have students work in pairs. For the first activity, students should take turns making the statement and explaining. For the second activity, one student will make the statement, and the other will give the required response (action to take place in the future); students again take turns.

VOCABULAIRE

Have students play a word association game with this list. Have them write **Les vacances** and **L'école** at the top of two columns on sheets of paper; then have them list ten words they can find that they associate with each of these categories.

ETUDE DE MOTS

After finding or changing the verbs as indicated, students should use each in a sentence to make certain they understand the meaning. For example, although **rentrer** does mean literally *to re-enter*, its principal meaning is *to return* or *to go back*. Students should understand that they would use **rentrer** to indicate that they were returning to the United States from a trip abroad, but that they would use **retourner** if they wanted to say that they would like to return to France someday.

A LIRE

OBJECTIVE   To read for practice and pleasure

SOUVENIRS DE VACANCES

Before playing the cassette or reading the selection, have students look at the drawings and write their answers to the five questions in **Avant de lire.** Play the cassette as students read along in their books. Then have students revise their answers to the questions. Review the story by asking some simple comprehension questions. Then ask several that require analysis:

> Est-ce que Nicolas exagère quelquefois? Donnez un exemple.
> Est-ce que Nicolas aime les filles en général? Expliquez.
> Comment Marie-Edwige a-t-elle ennuyé Nicolas?

Activité • Devinez

Have students find the sentences in the text where the three words appear. Discuss how meaning can be derived from context. Give other examples from the reading, using words the students don't know.

Activité • Répondez

You might have students write out the answers in class or for homework.

Activité • Avez-vous bien lu?

For cooperative learning, have students form groups of three and prepare a description of one of the adventures that Nicolas bragged about.

Activité • Réfléchissez

Have the students write down the adjectives that describe Nicolas. Then have them search the text for statements made by Nicolas that indicate these personality traits and write them below the appropriate adjective.

CHAPITRE 1

Nous revoilà

C'est la rentrée. In early September French students return to their *collège* or *lycée* after the long summer vacation, *les grandes vacances.* The disappointment at seeing the vacation end gives way to the enthusiasm of seeing old friends, sharing vacation experiences, and making resolutions for the new school year.

In this unit you will:

PREMIER CONTACT	get acquainted with the topic
SECTION A	greet old and new friends . . . express an opinion, agree, and disagree . . . ask how others are
SECTION B	ask others how they spent the summer . . . express satisfaction, indifference, or dissatisfaction
SECTION C	talk about the last school year . . . make excuses . . . make resolutions for the new year
TRY YOUR SKILLS	use what you've learned
A LIRE	read for practice and pleasure

11

PREMIER CONTACT | getting acquainted with the topic

The authentic material in Premier Contact introduces the theme of the unit and is to be used for global comprehension only.

1 Retour de vacances 📼

Alors? Content(e) de rentrer au lycée ou triste? Faites le bilan de vos vacances et préparez la rentrée.

1 Vos vacances ont été... ?
a. passionnantes
b. agréables
c. pas terribles
d. carrément ennuyeuses
e. autre

5 Vous avez apprécié vos vacances?
a. Oui, c'était fantastique!
b. Oui, je me suis bien amusé(e)!
c. C'était pas mal.
d. Non, je me suis ennuyé(e)!
e. Non, c'était mortel!
f. autre

2 Vous avez passé vos vacances à... ?
a. téléphoner à des copains
b. faire du sport
c. lire
d. faire de la bicyclette
e. jouer au ping-pong
f. autre

6 Le jour de la rentrée, vous êtes... ?
a. joyeux(se)
b. calme
c. légèrement inquiet (inquiète)
d. vraiment ennuyé(e)
e. triste
f. autre

3 Vous avez passé vos vacances... ?
a. chez vous
b. à l'étranger
c. aux Etats-Unis
d. à la campagne
e. au bord de la mer
f. autre

7 Comment allez-vous au lycée?
a. en autobus
b. à pied
c. en patin à roulettes
d. en métro
e. en bicyclette
f. autre

4 Vous avez fait quel(s) sport(s) pendant vos vacances?
a. du foot
b. du basket
c. de la planche à voile
d. du surf
e. du tennis
f. autre

8 Et pour terminer par l'essentiel, avez-vous déjà fait des projets pour les prochaines vacances?
a. Non, pas du tout.
b. Vaguement, mais ce n'est pas précis.
c. Oui, évidemment.
d. autre

Photos on pp. 10–11: Collège Alphonse Daudet and Lycée Masséna are located in Nice. Alphonse Daudet (1840–1897) was a famous French novelist. André Masséna (1756–1817) was a French military hero.

2 Activité • Trouvez d'autres réponses Possible answers are given.

Pouvez-vous trouver d'autres réponses pour chaque question? Faites une liste.

1. courtes 2. regarder la télé 3. à la montagne 4. de la natation 5. Oui, c'était super! 6. content(e) 7. en voiture 8. Oui, beaucoup de projets.

3 Activité • Sondage

Faites une enquête parmi vos camarades de classe pour savoir qui a fait quoi pendant ses vacances, où chaque élève a passé ses vacances et qui est joyeux(se) ou triste de rentrer à l'école.

The capital of Honduras is Tegucigalpa.

Charlemagne (742–814 A.D.): King of the Franks; emperor of the Holy Roman Empire; the first "palace school" was established in 782.

Le budget de l'écolier

Pour les élèves entrant en sixième cette année, le coût de cette rentrée scolaire est de 1 800 francs minimum par écolier (près de $300). En effet, à partir de la sixième, les fournitures ne sont plus offertes par l'école. Cette somme peut varier de 40%; cela dépend si on fait les achats en hypermarchés, en grands magasins ou en magasins spécialisés. Les achats comprennent les livres de classe, les fournitures scolaires et les vêtements de sport obligatoires.

Vous avez des doutes sur la capitale du Honduras?

Atlas 2000   159 F

Charlemagne, il a inventé l'école, dit-on. Mais en quelle année?

Atlas historique   135 F

Le stylomine, vital pour les indécis qui <u>raturent</u> beaucoup. Un peu cher, mais tellement beau.

195 F

Le compas dans la trousse, c'est utile.

154 F

Ça ressemble à un journal intime, ce sera peut-être votre cahier de physique.

34,50 F

5   Activité • Trouvez les mots

Trouvez dans «Shopping rentrée» des mots de la même famille.

1. école   **2.** an   **3.** coûter   **4.** histoire   **5.** acheter

écolier   année   coût   historique   achats

6   Activité • Le budget de la rentrée

Qu'est-ce que vous allez acheter pour la rentrée? Faites une liste et ensuite faites un budget.

Article	Prix
un compas	154 f

Nous revoilà   13

Eh oui! Les vacances sont terminées! Une nouvelle année scolaire commence! Comment est-ce que vous débutez cette année? Vous êtes content(e) de rentrer ou vous regrettez vos vacances?

A1   Nous revoilà

Remind the students that "J'ai pas..." is often used by young people instead of "Je n'ai pas..." in spoken French.

Comme chaque année au mois de septembre, c'est la rentrée. Dans la cour du lycée Masséna à Nice, des jeunes discutent. Certains sont heureux de reprendre l'école; d'autres, au contraire, rêvent de repartir en vacances.

MARTIN   Eh! Alexandre!
ALEXANDRE   Tiens, salut Martin!
MARTIN   Comment ça va?
ALEXANDRE   Pas terrible, et toi?
MARTIN   Bof. J'ai pas envie de recommencer l'école.
ALEXANDRE   Moi non plus.
MARTIN   Oh là là! Vive les prochaines vacances!
ALEXANDRE   Tu as raison!...

ISABELLE   Alors, tu es contente de rentrer, Claire?
CLAIRE   Oui, très. Moi, je m'ennuie en vacances. Je trouve qu'elles sont trop longues.
ISABELLE   Pas moi! Au contraire! Elles sont trop courtes. A mon avis, il faut six mois de vacances!

bédés: bandes dessinées

ISABELLE   Qu'est-ce que tu as fait pendant tes vacances?
PHILIPPE   J'ai lu des bédés sur la plage. Et toi?
ISABELLE   Moi, j'ai passé deux semaines en Angleterre.
PHILIPPE   Eh bien, tu as bronzé!
ISABELLE   Tu trouves?
PHILIPPE   Oui, ça te va bien.

MARTIN   Alexandre! Regarde! Isabelle est avec une nouvelle.
ALEXANDRE Où ça?
MARTIN   Là-bas!
ALEXANDRE Super! Et elle est très mignonne! Viens, on va leur dire bonjour.

ISABELLE   Bonjour... Tu es nouvelle?
EMILIE   Oui.
ISABELLE   Je m'appelle Isabelle. Et toi?
EMILIE   Emilie. Je suis de Marseille. Tu connais Marseille?
ISABELLE   Non, je suis d'ici... Oh, voilà Martin et Alexandre, deux amis de l'année dernière. Fais attention, ils sont très sympa mais un peu dragueurs.

Have students locate Nice and Marseille on the map of France in the Reference section, p. 434.

Nous revoilà   15

Activité • Vrai ou faux?

1. La rentrée, c'est le premier jour des vacances.
2. Martin et Alexandre sont d'accord.
3. Isabelle trouve que les vacances sont trop longues.
4. Claire a envie de recommencer l'école.
5. Alexandre trouve Emilie jolie.
6. Isabelle connaît bien Emilie.

1. C'est faux. C'est le premier jour de classe.   2. C'est vrai.   3. C'est faux. Elle trouve que les vacances sont trop courtes.
4. C'est vrai.   5. C'est vrai.   6. C'est faux. Emilie est la nouvelle.

A3   Activité • Et vous?

1. Etes-vous content(e) de rentrer?
2. Trouvez-vous que les vacances sont trop longues ou trop courtes?
3. Combien de mois de vacances faut-il, à votre avis?
4. Rêvez-vous des prochaines vacances?
5. Quand sont les prochaines vacances?

Inversion questions will be presented in Unit 3, page 113.

A4   **COMMENT LE DIRE**
Expressing an opinion, agreeing, and disagreeing

OPINION	AGREEING	DISAGREEING
A mon avis,...	Je suis d'accord avec toi.	Je ne suis pas d'accord avec toi.
Je trouve que...	Moi aussi.	Pas moi.
		Au contraire,...
	Tu as (Vous avez) raison.	Tu as (Vous avez) tort.
Je n'ai pas envie de...	Moi non plus.	Moi, je...

A5   Activité • Et vous?   Possible answers are given.

Dans la cour de l'école, les élèves expriment *(express)* leurs opinions. Qu'est-ce que vous leur dites?
Etes-vous d'accord?

1. A mon avis, les vacances sont trop longues!

Je ne suis pas d'accord avec toi.

2. Moi, je trouve l'école fantastique!

Pas moi!

3. Il y a beaucoup à faire pendant les vacances d'été!

Je suis d'accord avec toi.

4. Il faut six mois de vacances!

Tu as raison!

5. Ah, les vacances, c'est horrible!

Au contraire! Les vacances, c'est super!

Activité • Exprimez votre opinion   Possible answers are given.

Qu'est-ce que vous pensez des actions de ces personnages? Trouvez-vous que ces jeunes ont raison ou qu'ils ont tort? Exprimez votre opinion.

1. Denis n'a pas invité Frédéric à son anniversaire. Deux semaines plus tard, Frédéric lui téléphone pour l'inviter à une boum. Je trouve que Frédéric a raison, et que Denis a tort.
2. Marie et Florence ont une interro de maths demain. Mais il y a un film de Clint Eastwood à la télé. «Qu'est-ce qu'on fait?» demande Marie. «On regarde le film!» répond Florence. Florence a tort.
3. Rachelle est l'amie de Marie-Claire. Hier soir, Rachelle a demandé à Marie-Claire de lui montrer son devoir d'anglais. Marie-Claire a refusé. Marie-Claire a raison.
4. Yasmine a reçu de l'argent pour son anniversaire. Qu'est-ce qu'elle va faire? Acheter un disque ou des vêtements? Aller au concert? Finalement, elle invite ses parents au cinéma.
   A mon avis, Yasmine a raison.

A7   Activité • Ecrivez   Possible answers are given.

Ecrivez votre opinion sur vos professeurs, vos vacances et vos cours. Voici quelques adjectifs pour vous aider. Je trouve que mes professeurs sont sévères. A mon avis, les vacances sont toujours trop courtes.
Le français, c'est difficile, mais les maths, c'est facile.

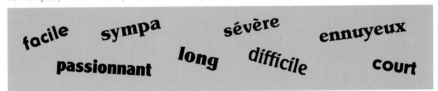

facile   sympa   sévère   ennuyeux
passionnant   long   difficile   court

A8   Activité • A vous maintenant!

Trouvez-vous les vacances trop longues? Trop courtes? Bien? Et la rentrée des classes, à votre avis, c'est sympa? Discutez avec un(e) camarade de classe. Après, exprimez vos opinions aux autres.

A9   NOUS REVOILA (SUITE) 📼

Dans la cour de l'école, les anciens retrouvent leurs amis. Mais il y a aussi des nouveaux et des nouvelles. On fait connaissance. On raconte ses vacances.

ISABELLE   Bonjour, madame. Comment allez-vous?
LE PROFESSEUR   Très bien, merci. Tu as passé de bonnes vacances?
ISABELLE   Excellentes!
LE PROFESSEUR   Il a fait beau en Angleterre?
ISABELLE   Un temps splendide! J'ai attrapé des coups de soleil. Et vos vacances, madame?
LE PROFESSEUR   Chez moi à la campagne, il a plu tout le temps.

Activité • Avez-vous compris?

Répondez aux questions suivantes, d'après A9 et A1.

1. Qui a passé ses vacances à la campagne? Le professeur a passé ses vacances à la campagne.
2. Où est-ce qu'Isabelle a passé ses vacances? Isabelle a passé ses vacances en Angleterre.
3. Qui est bronzé? Pourquoi? Isabelle est bronzée, parce qu'elle a attrapé des coups de soleil.
4. Qu'est-ce que Philippe a fait pendant les vacances? Il a lu des bédés sur la plage.
5. Qui est Emilie? C'est la nouvelle.
6. Pourquoi est-ce que Martin et Alexandre veulent parler aux filles? Parce qu'ils trouvent Emilie très mignonne.

A11 COMMENT LE DIRE
Asking how someone is

Comment allez-vous?	Très bien, merci. Et vous?
Comment vas-tu?	Pas mal (terrible). Et toi?
Ça va?	Drôlement bien!
Tu es en forme?	En pleine forme!

A12 Activité • A vous maintenant! Possible answers are given.

Dites bonjour…   et…

1. à un(e) camarade   demandez-lui comment il/elle va.
2. au professeur   demandez-lui comment il/elle va.
3. à deux camarades   demandez-leur comment ils/elles vont.

1. Salut! Comment vas-tu? 2. Bonjour, monsieur (madame, mademoiselle)! Comment allez-vous? 3. Bonjour, les copines! Comment allez-vous?

A13 Activité • Discussion en classe Possible answers are given.

Le premier jour de classe, le prof de français, avant de commencer son cours, pose quelques questions à ses élèves. On discute des vacances. Complétez le dialogue suivant avec des camarades de classe. Ensuite, changez de rôles.

LE PROFESSEUR	Alors, Isabelle, où est-ce que tu as passé tes vacances?
ISABELLE	…En Angleterre.
LE PROFESSEUR	Tu es bronzée!
ISABELLE	…Oui, j'ai attrapé des coups de soleil.
LE PROFESSEUR	Et toi, Philippe? Qu'est-ce que tu as fait pendant les vacances?
PHILIPPE	…J'ai lu des bédés sur la plage.
LE PROFESSEUR	Martin, toujours dragueur? Comment s'appelle la nouvelle?
MARTIN	…Elle s'appelle Emilie.
LE PROFESSEUR	Tu es d'où, Emilie?
EMILIE	…Je suis de Marseille.

VOUS EN SOUVENEZ-VOUS?
The passé composé *with* avoir

The "passé composé" was first introduced in Unit 10 of
Nouveaux copains. The "passé composé" with "être" will
be introduced in Section B of this unit.

1. As you already know, one way to express past time in French is to use the **passé composé.** You remember that this verb tense is composed of two parts: (a) a present-tense form of the auxiliary verb; (b) a past participle. **Avoir** is the auxiliary used most often. The past participle of most verbs consists of a stem plus a participle ending: **pass + é, fin + i, répond + u.**

Subject	Auxiliary	Past Participle
J'	ai	
Tu	as	
Il/Elle	a	**passé** de bonnes vacances.
Nous	avons	**fini** les devoirs.
Vous	avez	**répondu.**
Ils/Elles	ont	

2. In negative constructions, **ne** comes after the subject and **pas** immediately follows the auxiliary verb: Il **n'**a **pas** passé de bonnes vacances. Other adverbs that follow the auxiliary are "souvent, toujours, bien, beaucoup, encore, ensuite, presque."
3. Some adverbs usually come before the past participle: Il a **déjà** fini le devoir.
4. Here are the past participles of some irregular verbs that form the **passé composé** with **avoir.** You have seen these verbs before.

Infinitive	Past Participle	
être	**été**	Elle **a été** en Angleterre.
avoir	**eu**	Elle **a eu** de la chance.
faire	**fait**	Il **a fait** un temps splendide.
prendre	**pris**	Ils **ont pris** le bateau.
vouloir	**voulu**	Tu n'**as** pas **voulu** venir?
pouvoir	**pu**	Vous n'**avez** pas **pu** venir?
lire	**lu**	J'**ai lu** des livres anglais.
voir	**vu**	Elle **a vu** des films anglais.
mettre	**mis**	Elles **ont mis** leur imperméable.
savoir	**su**	Tu **as su** son adresse?
connaître	**connu**	Nous **avons connu** des gens sympa.
offrir	**offert**	Ils **ont offert** un cadeau à Anne.
ouvrir	**ouvert**	Elle **a ouvert** le cadeau.

Activité • A-t-elle passé de bonnes vacances?

Isabelle a passé ses vacances en Angleterre. Elle raconte ses vacances à son amie. Mettez les verbes au passé composé.

1. Il (faire) un temps splendide en Angleterre!
2. Nous (passer) beaucoup de temps à la plage.
3. Je (attraper) un coup de soleil.
4. Les professeurs (organiser) des excursions.
5. Nous (danser) dans des discothèques.
6. Je (rencontrer) un Anglais super mignon!
7. Mes amies (prendre) le train à Avon.
8. Moi, je (choisir) de rester à Londres.
9. Mon copain (avoir) de la chance.
10. Il (voir) la reine Elizabeth.
11. Je (perdre) mon appareil-photo.
12. Nous (apprendre) beaucoup.

1. a fait 2. avons passé 3. ai attrapé 4. ont organisé 5. avons dansé 6. ai rencontré
7. ont pris 8. ai choisi 9. a eu 10. a vu 11. ai perdu 12. avons beaucoup appris

Regardez les photos de vos copains. Qu'est-ce qu'ils ont fait pendant leurs vacances?

1.

Il a attrapé un coup de soleil.

2.

Ils ont lu des bédés sur la plage.

3.

Il a travaillé dans un supermarché.

4.

Ils ont passé leurs vacances à Londres.

A 17 Activité • A vous maintenant!   Possible questions are given. Answers will vary.

Demandez à un(e) camarade de classe s'il (si elle) a fait ces choses pendant les vacances. Posez les questions au passé composé. Ensuite, changez de rôle et répondez à ses questions.

1. lire un livre? quel livre?
2. voyager? où?
3. étudier une autre langue? quelle langue?
4. gagner de l'argent? comment?

5. voir un film français? quel film?
6. attraper un coup de soleil? où?
7. pratiquer un sport? quel sport?
8. organiser une boum? pourquoi?

1. Tu as lu un livre? Quel livre? 2. Tu as voyagé? Où? 3. Tu as étudié une autre langue? Quelle langue?
4. Tu as gagné de l'argent? Comment? 5. Tu as vu un film français? Quel film? 6. Tu as attrapé un coup de soleil? Où?
7. Tu as pratiqué un sport? Quel sport?
8. Tu as organisé une boum? Pourquoi?

A 18 Activité • Sondage

Dans la classe, trouvez une personne qui a déjà fait chaque chose.

goûter à la cuisine française   — Tu as déjà goûté à la cuisine française?
                                  — Oui, j'ai déjà... (Non, je n'ai pas encore...)

1. voyager au Canada
2. étudier l'espagnol
3. faire de la planche à voile

4. prendre l'avion
5. organiser une boum
6. faire de la photo

1. ... voyagé au Canada? 2. ... étudié l'espagnol? 3. ... fait de la planche à voile?
4. ... pris l'avion? 5. ... organisé une boum? 6. ... fait de la photo?

Vous êtes reporter pour
le journal de l'école.
Interviewez cinq
camarades de classe.
Posez-leur les questions
écrites dans votre cahier.
Ecrivez leurs réponses
et ensuite, racontez les
réponses à la classe.

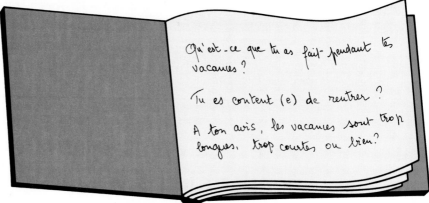

Qu'est-ce que tu as fait pendant tes vacances?

Tu es content (e) de rentrer?

A ton avis, les vacances sont trop longues, trop courtes ou bien?

A 20 Activité • Les achats de la rentrée

Qu'est-ce que vous avez acheté pour la rentrée? Des livres? Des cahiers? Des vêtements?
Faites une liste et ensuite demandez à un(e) camarade ce qu'il/elle a acheté.
Moi, j'ai acheté... Et toi, qu'est-ce que tu as acheté?

A 21 Savez-vous que... ?

Le lycée idéal existe-t-il? Les lycéens du lycée
Balzac à Paris ont de la chance parce que le
lycée est entouré d'arbres et de pelouses. Au
lycée Balzac il y a, comme dans la plupart des
lycées, une bibliothèque, un ciné-club et une
salle d'audio-visuel pour apprendre les langues.
De plus, il y a des ordinateurs ultra-sophistiqués
à la disposition des élèves. Et chose rare, une
piscine à l'intérieur même du lycée. Le rêve,
quoi!

Construire un lycée idéal, un lycée «cool»?
Voici quelques suggestions proposées par des
architectes amateurs, les lycéens eux-mêmes.
— L'aspect extérieur du lycée, ça compte.
— Un beau lycée, ça redonne le moral.
— Faire des couloirs larges.
— Mettre les sanitaires à tous les étages.
— Penser aux handicapés, avoir des rampes
    d'accès.
— Une piscine, c'est super!
— Une infirmerie, c'est indispensable.
— Faire quatre ou cinq sorties pour éviter les
    bousculades.

Honoré de Balzac (1799–1850) was one of the most
influential writers of the 19th century. His most important
work was "La Comédie Humaine."

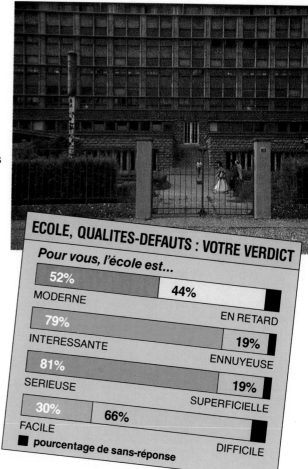

ECOLE, QUALITES-DEFAUTS : VOTRE VERDICT

Pour vous, l'école est...

52%	**44%**	
MODERNE		EN RETARD
79%		**19%**
INTERESSANTE		ENNUYEUSE
81%		**19%**
SERIEUSE		SUPERFICIELLE
30%	**66%**	
FACILE		DIFFICILE

■ **pourcentage de sans-réponse**

A 22 Activité • Ecoutez bien For script and answers, see p. T31.

Ecoutez ces élèves. Sont-ils contents de recommencer l'école? Oui ou non?

asking others how they spent the summer . . . expressing satisfaction, indifference, or dissatisfaction

Qu'est-ce que vous avez fait pendant vos vacances? Où êtes-vous allés? Avez-vous passé de bonnes vacances?... Les jeunes français ont eu le choix entre de nombreuses possibilités. Est-ce que c'est pareil aux Etats-Unis?

B1

Où est-ce qu'ils sont allés pendant leurs vacances? 📼

L'Ardèche: a mountainous region in south central France

Emilie veut faire un reportage pour le journal de l'école. Elle demande à ses camarades où ils sont allés cet été.

— Tu es allée où, Claire?
— Je suis allée dans un centre de vacances en Ardèche.
— Ça t'a plu?
— Enormément. J'ai rencontré des tas de gens sympathiques et j'ai fait du canoë-kayak et de la spéléologie... Je me suis beaucoup amusée!

— Et toi, Marc, tu es parti en vacances?
— Non. Au mois de juillet je suis resté chez moi. Ensuite, au mois d'août, j'ai travaillé dans une station-service pour gagner un peu d'argent.
— C'était bien?
— Drôlement bien. Ça m'a beaucoup plu. Moi, j'adore travailler. Les vacances, ça m'ennuie.

— Et toi, Marie, tu es aussi restée chez toi?
— Non, mes parents ont loué une villa à Arcachon au bord de la mer. J'y ai passé le mois d'août.
— Ça t'a plu?
— Bof, c'était pas génial. Je me suis ennuyée. Tu sais, la mer, c'est toujours la même chose.

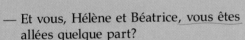

— C'était bien, tes vacances, Isabelle?
— Drôlement bien! J'ai fait un séjour linguistique en Angleterre. J'ai fait des progrès en anglais et mes parents sont satisfaits.

— Et vous, Hélène et Béatrice, vous êtes allées quelque part?
— Oui, nous sommes allées faire de la bicyclette dans les Pyrénées.
— C'était comment?
— C'était merveilleux! On a campé, on a pris des photos. Quelle magnifique région!

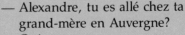

— Alexandre, tu es allé chez ta grand-mère en Auvergne?
— Oui.
— Tu t'es amusé?
— Mouais. La première semaine j'ai dormi jusqu'à midi. Mais la deuxième semaine j'ai rencontré une fille vraiment bien. Nous sommes sortis deux fois au cinéma. J'ai beaucoup aimé.

Les Pyrénées: the mountain range on the border between France and Spain
The Auvergne is an agricultural region in central France, known for its mineral springs. The Marquis de La Fayette (1757–1834), who helped the Americans in the American revolution, was from the Auvergne.

Nous revoilà 23

B2 Activité • Pourquoi?

Donnez des raisons. Pourquoi est-ce que... Possible answers are given.

1. Claire a choisi l'Ardèche? ...pour faire du canoë-kayak et de la spéléologie.
2. Isabelle est allée en Angleterre? ...pour faire un séjour linguistique.
3. Marc a travaillé dans une station-service? ...pour gagner de l'argent.
4. Marie n'a pas aimé ses vacances à Arcachon? Parce que la mer, c'est toujours la même chose.
5. Hélène et Béatrice sont allées dans les Pyrénées? ...pour faire de la bicyclette.
6. Alexandre a préféré la deuxième semaine chez sa grand-mère? Parce qu'il a rencontré une fille vraiment bien.

B3 Activité • Trouvez les synonymes

Remplacez les mots soulignés par des synonymes.

1. Claire a rencontré beaucoup de gens sympathiques. des tas
2. Les parents d'Isabelle sont contents de ses progrès en anglais. satisfaits
3. Les parents de Marie ont loué une maison. villa
4. Hélène et Béatrice ont fait du vélo. de la bicyclette
5. Elles ont fait des photos dans les Pyrénées. pris

B4 COMMENT LE DIRE
Inquiring and expressing satisfaction, indifference, or dissatisfaction

INQUIRING	SATISFACTION	INDIFFERENCE	DISSATISFACTION
C'était... comment? bien?	C'était... merveilleux! chouette! génial! super! drôlement bien! bien!	C'était... assez bien. comme ci, comme ça. pas mal. pas terrible.	C'était... triste. mortel.
Tu t'es amusé(e)?	Je me suis beaucoup amusé(e)! J'ai adoré!	Assez bien.	Je me suis ennuyé(e). J'ai détesté!
Ça t'a plu?	Ça m'a beaucoup plu. Ça m'a plu énormément.	Mouais! Bof!	J'ai pas aimé.

C'était, *it was*, is most often used as the past tense of **c'est**, *it is*. The "imparfait" will be introduced in Unit 9, p. 304. Reflexive pronouns will be introduced in Unit 7, p. 242.

B5 Activité • Ça vous a plu?   Possible answers are given.

Vous avez passé deux semaines dans un camp de vacances au bord de la mer. Vous rentrez chez vous et votre mère vous pose des tas de questions. Répondez.

1. C'était bien, le camp?
2. Et la cuisine, tu as aimé?
3. Tu as rencontré de nouveaux copains?
4. Comment tu as trouvé le cours de voile?
5. Tu t'es amusé(e)?

1. Oui, c'était chouette! 2. Bof! 3. Oui, j'ai rencontré des tas de gens sympathiques. 4. J'ai adoré! 5. Oui, beaucoup!

Demandez à un(e) camarade de classe s'il (si elle) a fait ces activités cet été. Ensuite, demandez-lui si ça lui a plu. Changez de rôle.

Tu as fait... ? Ça t'a plu?

l'équitation

la voile

la pêche

le camping

le ping-pong

le canoë

STRUCTURES DE BASE
The passé composé *with* être

The use of reflexive pronouns with the "passé composé" will be presented in Unit 7, p. 242.

1. You form the **passé composé** of some verbs with the auxiliary verb **être** instead of **avoir.** Compare these sentences: J'**ai téléphoné** à Emilie. Je **suis sorti** avec elle.

Masculine Subject			Feminine Subject		
Je	suis	rentré.	**Je**	suis	rentrée.
Tu	es	rentré.	**Tu**	es	rentrée.
Il	est	rentré.	**Elle**	est	rentrée.
Nous	sommes	rentrés.	**Nous**	sommes	rentrées.
Vous	êtes	rentré(s).	**Vous**	êtes	rentrée(s).
Ils	sont	rentrés.	**Elles**	sont	rentrées.

2. In general, when you form the **passé composé** with **être,** the past participle agrees in gender and number with the subject, in the same way that an adjective agrees with the noun it refers to. Compare these two structures.

> adjective agreement: **Anne** est heur**euse.**
> **passé composé** with **être:**   **Elle** est all**ée** à la boum.

Remind students that agreement has to be made with all subject pronouns, not only 3rd person pronouns.

3. In negative constructions, you place **ne** after the subject and **pas** after the auxiliary verb: Elle n'est **pas** restée à la maison.
4. Some adverbs, like **déjà, beaucoup,** and others, occur most often before the past participle: Ils sont **déjà** partis.
5. **Liaison** is often made between the forms of **être** and the past participle, especially with **est** and **sont.**

> Il est⌃^t⌃ allé à Rouen.   Ils sont⌃^t⌃ allés à Rouen.

Liaison may also be made between a negative construction and the past participle.

> Il n'est pas⌃^z⌃ allé à Paris.

6. The following is a list of verbs you already know that form the **passé composé** with **être: aller, arriver, descendre, entrer, partir, rentrer, rester, sortir, tomber.**
7. The verb **venir** and its compound **revenir,** *to return,* also form the **passé composé** with **être. (Re)venir** has an irregular past participle, **(re)venu:** Ils sont **(re)venus** en voiture.

B8
Activité • Le dernier jour des vacances

Qu'est-ce qu'ils ont fait le dernier jour des vacances? Mettez les verbes au passé composé.

1. Philippe (aller) au cinéma.
2. Isabelle (sortir) avec des amies.
3. Martin et Alexandre (rentrer) à minuit.
4. Emilie et Sylvie (descendre) en ville.
5. Marc (rester) à la maison.
6. Jérôme (revenir) d'Allemagne.

1. est allé 2. est sortie 3. sont rentrés 4. sont descendues 5. est resté 6. est revenu

B9
Activité • Où est-ce qu'ils sont allés?

Possible answers are given.

Où est-ce que vos amis dans B1 sont allés en vacances? Qu'est-ce qu'ils y ont fait?

1. Marie
2. Claire
3. Alexandre
4. Marc
5. Hélène et Béatrice
6. Isabelle

Marie est allée à Arcachon. Ses parents ont loué une villa. 2. Claire est allée en Ardèche. Elle a fait du canoë-kayak et de la spéléologie. 3. Alexandre est allé chez sa grand-mère en Auvergne. Il est sorti avec une fille. 4. Marc est resté chez lui. Il a travaillé. 5. Hélène et Béatrice sont allées dans les Pyrénées. Elles ont campé. 6. Isabelle est allée en Angleterre. Elle a fait un séjour linguistique.

Pendant les vacances d'été Sylvie a voyagé aux Etats-Unis. Racontez son voyage au passé composé.

1.

partir à New York le
dix août

2.

aller voir sa tante, son oncle,
ses cousins Bill et Debbie

3.

arriver à sept heures
du soir

4.

venir à l'aéroport

5.

y rester une semaine

6.

sortir souvent

7.

rentrer en France le dix-sept août

Sylvie est partie à New York le dix août. Elle est allée voir sa tante, son oncle, et ses cousins, Bill et Debbie. Elle est arrivée à sept heures du soir. Son oncle et sa tante sont venus à l'aéroport. Sylvie est restée une semaine à New York. Elle est sortie souvent. Sylvie est rentrée en France le dix-sept août.

Nous revoilà   **27**

Sylvie a écrit une lettre à son amie en France. Elle raconte son voyage aux Etats-Unis. Complétez sa lettre. Mettez les verbes au passé composé. Attention! Certains verbes se conjuguent avec **être**, d'autres avec **avoir**.

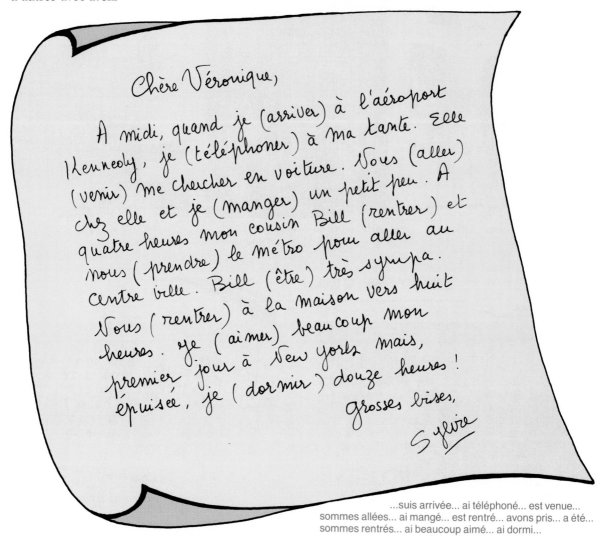

Chère Véronique,

A midi, quand je (arriver) à l'aéroport Kennedy, je (téléphoner) à ma tante. Elle (venir) me chercher en voiture. Nous (aller) chez elle et je (manger) un petit peu. A quatre heures mon cousin Bill (rentrer) et nous (prendre) le métro pour aller au centre ville. Bill (être) très sympa. Nous (rentrer) à la maison vers huit heures. Je (aimer) beaucoup mon premier jour à New York mais, épuisée, je (dormir) douze heures!

grosses bises,
Sylvie

...suis arrivée... ai téléphoné... est venue...
sommes allées... ai mangé... est rentré... avons pris... a été...
sommes rentrés... ai beaucoup aimé... ai dormi...

B12 Activité • A vous maintenant!

Vous discutez avec un(e) camarade de classe de vos vacances d'été. Vous lui demandez s'il (si elle) est parti(e) en vacances, où il/elle est allé(e), ce qu'il/elle a fait, si ça lui a plu. Ensuite, répondez à ses questions. Tu es parti(e) en vacances?
Tu es allé(e) où?
Qu'est-ce que tu as fait?

B13 Activité • Ecrivez

L'été dernier, vous êtes allé(e) à Paris voir votre correspondant(e) français(e). Décrivez votre visite imaginaire. Dites quand vous êtes parti(e), comment vous êtes allé(e) à Paris, ce que vous avez fait avec votre correspondant(e), combien de temps vous y êtes resté(e) et quand vous êtes rentré(e) aux Etats-Unis.

En France, tous les salariés ont droit à cinq semaines de vacances payées. Beaucoup de Français ont six semaines.

Les élèves des collèges et lycées ont des vacances à la Toussaint, à Noël, en février, à Pâques. En été, ils ont deux mois. Ce sont les grandes vacances. Qu'est-ce qu'ils font? Ils restent en famille ou vont chez des copains. Ils reçoivent de jeunes étrangers (*foreigners*) chez eux ou ils partent en séjour linguistique pour apprendre une autre langue. De nombreuses associations organisent également des séjours sportifs et culturels. Les jeunes travaillent souvent en juillet pour partir en août.

The hot air balloon was invented in 1783 by two French brothers, Joseph and Etienne Montgolfier.

Londres Séjours linguistiques Février, Pâques et été

Londres Informations

Population : 7.000.000 habitants
Situation géographique : capitale de la Grande-Bretagne
Baignade : piscines couvertes et découvertes
Possibilités sportives : nombreux choix possibles
Cinéma : des centaines
Théâtre : une multitude
Discothèques : un grand choix
Fêtes et manifestations : le grand prix de tennis à Wimbledon, des festivals, des rencontres sportives de toutes sortes

INCLUS DANS LE PRIX
Visite de Londres : visite guidée de Londres
Excursions dans la région : une journée à Brighton et une journée dans la ville universitaire d'Oxford
Visites éducatives : la Bourse, London Bridge, Piccadilly, Soho, Mayfair, Marble Arch, British Museum, Buckingham Palace
Type de cours : cours général, trois cours par jour, cinq jours par semaine
Niveau des cours : de la quatrième à la terminale
Professeurs et animateurs : deux professeurs-animateurs français et un professeur-animateur anglais
Hébergement : en pension complète, dans une famille soigneusement sélectionnée

Excursions non comprises : le Planetarium, le zoo Kew Gardens, Madame Tussaud's, la cathédrale de Canterbury, Cambridge, Hampton Court, le château de Windsor, promenade en bateau sur la rivière Thames, la ferme du parc Loseley, le zoo de Chessington, le Vidéo-Café près de Regent Street, la cathédrale St. Paul et la visite de la Cité Tower Bridge... Vous pouvez également proposer toutes les excursions que vous voulez. Londres est une ville aux ressources inépuisables!

For script and answers, see p. T35.

Ont-ils passé de bonnes vacances? Ecoutez la conversation. Ensuite, complétez ce tableau.

	Où?	Temps?	Activités?	Content(e)?
Sylvie				
Guillaume				

SECTION C talking about the last school year . . . making excuses . . . making resolutions for the new year

Maintenant les vacances sont loin. Les premiers cours ont commencé et il faut déjà penser à reprendre le travail. Il est temps de faire le bilan de l'année passée et de prendre des résolutions pour la nouvelle année.

C1 Les résolutions

 Point out that the verb "prendre" is used with "résolutions" and "décisions."

C'est la récréation. Emilie, Isabelle, Alexandre et Martin prennent des résolutions pour l'année scolaire.

ISABELLE · MARTIN · ALEXANDRE · EMILIE

ALEXANDRE	J'ai pris une grande décision cette année : je vais travailler.
EMILIE	Pourquoi? Tu n'as pas travaillé l'année dernière?
ALEXANDRE	Non, très peu… Je suis beaucoup sorti. Mes parents sont furieux. Je n'ai pas intérêt à redoubler l'année prochaine. Cette année, plus de sorties! Je vais travailler tous les soirs jusqu'à minuit! Le week-end! Pendant les vacances! Et à cinq heures, tous les matins, je vais faire de la gymnastique. C'est excellent pour commencer la journée.
ISABELLE	Tu vas tomber malade.
ALEXANDRE	Il faut souffrir pour réussir…
ISABELLE	Moi, je n'ai pas besoin de travailler. Je suis bonne dans toutes les matières.
ALEXANDRE	Ah oui? En anglais aussi?
ISABELLE	En anglais surtout… après mon séjour en Angleterre.

The verb "souffrir" follows the same pattern as "offrir."
plus de sorties: no more going out

ALEXANDRE	Comment on dit «Il pleut» en anglais?
ISABELLE	Je ne sais pas, mais c'est inutile : il fait toujours beau en Angleterre.
ALEXANDRE	Emilie, tu as des projets?
EMILIE	Oui. Je suis nulle en maths. Mes notes sont très mauvaises et je veux être architecte plus tard. Mais je n'y comprends rien!
ISABELLE	Ne t'inquiète pas, le prof de maths est très bon. Tu vas voir, il explique bien. A la fin de l'année, tu vas trouver ça facile.
ALEXANDRE	Et toi, Martin, qu'est-ce que tu vas faire cette année?
MARTIN	En bien, moi, cette année, je vais aller au cinéma.
EMILIE	Mais… ton avenir?
MARTIN	Justement, plus tard je veux faire des films. Le cinéma, c'est mon fort!

C2 Activité • Avez-vous compris?

Répondez aux questions suivantes.

1. Pourquoi est-ce qu'Alexandre va travailler cette année? Parce qu'il n'a pas intérêt à redoubler l'année prochaine.
2. Pourquoi est-ce qu'il n'a pas travaillé l'année dernière? Parce qu'il est beaucoup sorti.
3. Pourquoi est-ce qu'il va «souffrir» le matin? Parce qu'il faut souffrir pour réussir.
4. Pourquoi est-ce qu'Isabelle n'a pas besoin de travailler, à son avis? Parce qu'elle est bonne dans toutes les matières.
5. Quels sont les projets d'Emilie? Elle veut être architecte.
6. En quelle matière est-ce que Martin est bon? Le cinéma, c'est son fort.

Activité • Qu'est-ce que vous en pensez? Possible answers are given.

Exprimez votre opinion sur les idées, les désirs et les décisions de ces gens.

1. Alexandre dit : «Il faut souffrir pour réussir.» Je suis d'accord avec lui.
2. Alexandre va faire sa gymnastique tous les matins cette année. A mon avis, ce n'est pas une bonne idée.
3. Isabelle trouve qu'elle n'a pas besoin de travailler. Je trouve qu'elle a tort.
4. Emilie veut étudier les maths pour être architecte. Elle a raison.
5. Martin a envie de faire des films à l'avenir. C'est une bonne idée.
6. Les parents d'Alexandre sont furieux. Je suis d'accord avec eux. Ils ont raison.

C4 Activité • Et vous?

1. En quelles matières est-ce que vous êtes bon(ne)? Mauvais(e)?
2. Avez-vous eu de bonnes notes l'année dernière? En quelles matières?
3. Avez-vous eu de mauvaises notes? En quelles matières?
4. Quelles décisions est-ce que vous avez prises pour cette année?
5. Avez-vous des projets pour l'avenir?

C5 Activité • Ecrivez Possible answers are given.

Comment trouvez-vous l'école? Complétez le paragraphe suivant.

          génial   bon(ne)   bonnes   intéressants
    L'école, c'est… ! Généralement, je suis… élève. Mes notes sont… Je trouve les cours…, sauf… l'histoire
Je suis… en… L'année dernière, je… Mes parents… Cette année… je vais travailler.
      fort(e)   maths.   n'ai pas travaillé   ont été furieux.

C6 Activité • Enquête

Faites une enquête dans votre classe. Qui… ?

1. a des projets pour l'avenir
2. veut faire des films
3. veut être architecte
4. fait de la gymnastique le matin
5. travaille jusqu'à minuit
6. a fait un séjour en Angleterre

C7 **COMMENT LE DIRE**
Making excuses

Here are some common excuses for poor performance in school.

Je suis nul (nulle) en maths.	I'm hopeless in math.
Je n'y comprends rien.	I don't understand anything about it.
Ce n'est pas mon fort.	It's not my strong point.
Le prof ne m'aime pas.	The teacher doesn't like me.
Je suis mauvais(e) en informatique.	I'm bad in computer studies.
Le prof explique mal.	The teacher explains poorly.

The negative "ne… rien" is presented in Unit 6, p. 209.

Activité • Quelle est votre excuse? Possible answers are given.

Vous avez des difficultés. Expliquez pourquoi.

1. Vous n'avez pas réussi à l'examen d'anglais.   Je suis nul(le) en anglais.
2. En histoire vous ne comprenez rien.   Le prof explique mal.
3. Vous comprenez tout et vous travaillez bien, mais vous avez eu une mauvaise note à la dernière interrogation de maths.   Je suis mauvais(e) en maths.
4. Vous ne savez pas comment on dit «réussir» en espagnol.   Ce n'est pas mon fort.
5. Le professeur explique trois fois, mais vous ne comprenez toujours pas.   Je n'y comprends rien.
6. Vous avez eu trois colles *(detentions)* cette semaine.   Le prof ne m'aime pas.

C9   Activité • A vous maintenant!   The French grading system is based on a scale of 20. Normally, the highest score is 17 or 18. Ten is considered passing, with 6 or 7 failing.

Voici votre bulletin trimestriel *(report card)*. Vous montrez le bulletin à vos parents. Un(e) camarade de classe joue le rôle de votre père ou de votre mère. Préparez le dialogue.

— Dix-huit en anglais! Très bien! Je suis content(e)!
— Merci, papa (maman). J'ai beaucoup travaillé!

Nom:	Année Scolaire 19 ——	Classe
Notes	Matières	Appréciations des professeurs
18	Anglais	Très bon (bonne) élève !
11	Gymnastique	Un peu paresseux (paresseuse)
9	Géographie	Montre peu d'enthousiasme
10	Histoire	Travail moyen
5	Français	Comprend avec difficulté.
8	Mathémathiques	Assez mauvais travail
12	Sciences	A fait beaucoup de progrès
13	Informatique	Élève sérieux (sérieuse)

VOUS EN SOUVENEZ-VOUS?
Aller + *infinitive*

"Aller" plus infinitive was first introduced in Unit 5, p. 153, of <u>Nouveaux copains.</u>

You've already learned one way to express future time by using the verb **aller** with an infinitive.

Je	**vais**	**travailler** cette année.
Elle	**va**	**trouver** les maths faciles.

You remember that in a negative construction, **ne** precedes the verb **aller** and **pas** immediately follows it : Il **ne** va **pas** redoubler.

C11 Activité • **Qu'est-ce qu'ils vont faire?**

Connaissez-vous bien vos nouveaux amis? Qu'est-ce qu'ils vont faire dans ces situations?

1. Isabelle veut perfectionner son anglais. Elle va faire un séjour linguistique en Angleterre.
2. Martin veut faire des films. Il va souvent aller au cinéma.
3. Alexandre ne veut pas redoubler. Il va travailler cette année.
4. Emilie veut être architecte. Elle va travailler en maths.
5. Alexandre veut être en forme pour commencer la journée. Il va faire de la gymnastique tous les matins.
6. Martin et Alexandre veulent rencontrer la nouvelle élève. Ils vont lui dire bonjour.

C12 Activité • **On prend des résolutions**

On va mieux faire cette année. Quelles résolutions est-ce qu'on prend? Employez le verbe **aller** et l'infinitif. Par exemple :

Je n'ai pas travaillé.   L'année dernière, je n'ai pas travaillé.
                          Mais cette année, je vais beaucoup travailler.

1. Je n'ai pas bien écouté le professeur. Mais cette année, je vais bien écouter le professeur.
2. Alexandre est beaucoup sorti. ... il ne va pas sortir.
3. Mon amie a redoublé. ... elle ne va pas redoubler.
4. Emilie et Isabelle n'ont pas fait attention en classe. ... elles vont faire attention en classe.
5. Philippe n'a pas beaucoup lu. ... il va beaucoup lire.

C13 Activité • **En dehors de l'école** Possible answers are given.

Allez-vous uniquement travailler cette année, ou allez-vous aussi faire autre chose? Posez des questions à un(e) camarade pour savoir s'il (si elle) va faire ces choses cette année.

1. aller au cinéma
2. partir en vacances
3. lire des bandes dessinées
4. faire du sport
5. chercher un job
6. aller au concert

1. —Tu vas aller au cinéma cette année? — Oui, je vais y aller. 2. — Cette année, tu vas partir en vacances? — Non, cette année je vais travailler. 3. —Tu vas lire des bandes dessinées cette année? — Non, je vais lire des livres. — Oui, je vais faire du basket. 5. —Tu vas chercher un job cette année? — Oui, je vais travailler dans une station-service. 6. —Tu vas aller au concert? — Non, je ne vais pas aller au concert. 4. — Tu vas faire du sport?

C14 Activité • **Ecrivez**

Ecrivez cinq résolutions pour la nouvelle année scolaire.

Le Carnet de correspondance est un cahier officiel. Il permet aux professeurs de communiquer avec les parents par écrit. Chaque élève a son carnet et il doit y inscrire ses notes et certaines informations destinées aux parents. Les professeurs écrivent des commentaires s'il y a un problème. Les parents regardent le carnet chaque semaine et signent. Ils peuvent aussi faire des remarques ou poser des questions par écrit aux professeurs. L'élève est responsable de ce carnet et ne doit pas le perdre.

E.P.S.: Education Physique et Sportive

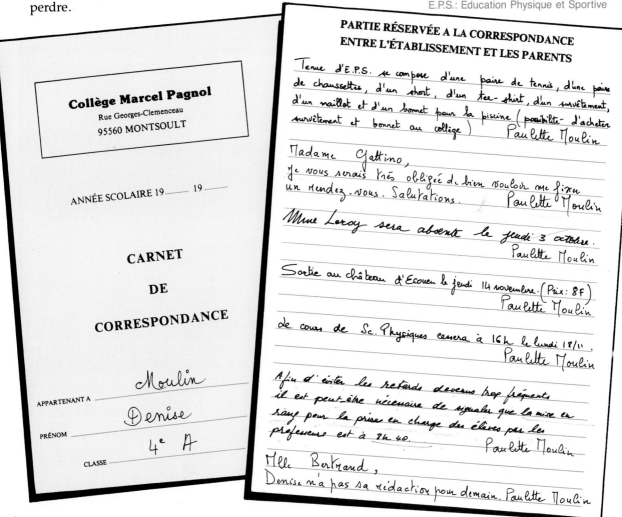

Collège Marcel Pagnol
Rue Georges-Clemenceau
95560 MONTSOULT

ANNÉE SCOLAIRE 19 ____ 19 ____

CARNET

DE

CORRESPONDANCE

APPARTENANT A ___ *Moulin*

PRÉNOM ___ *Denise*

CLASSE ___ *4ᵉ A*

**PARTIE RÉSERVÉE A LA CORRESPONDANCE
ENTRE L'ÉTABLISSEMENT ET LES PARENTS**

Tenue d'E.P.S. se compose d'une paire de tennis, d'une paire de chaussettes, d'un short, d'un tee-shirt, d'un survêtement, d'un maillot et d'un bonnet pour la piscine (possibilité d'acheter survêtement et bonnet au collège) Paulette Moulin

*Madame Gattino,
Je vous serais très obligée de bien vouloir me fixer un rendez-vous. Salutations.* Paulette Moulin

Mme Leroy sera absente le jeudi 3 octobre. Paulette Moulin

Sortie au château d'Ecouen le jeudi 14 novembre. (Prix: 8F) Paulette Moulin

Le cours de Sc. Physiques cessera à 16h le lundi 18/11. Paulette Moulin

Afin d'éviter les retards devenus trop fréquents il est peut-être nécessaire de signaler que la mise en rang pour la prise en charge des élèves par les professeurs est à 8h 40. Paulette Moulin

*Mlle Bertrand,
Denise n'a pas sa rédaction pour demain.* Paulette Moulin

C16 Activité • Ecoutez bien 📼 For script and answers, see p. T38.

1. Mettez les activités d'Emilie dans le bon ordre.
   a. Elle va préparer sa leçon d'histoire.
   b. Elle va étudier son anglais.
   c. Elle va faire ses maths.

2. Complétez. Isabelle veut…
   a. travailler avec Emilie.
   b. sortir.
   c. rester chez elle.

3. Vrai ou faux?
   a. Emilie a redoublé l'année dernière.
   b. Emilie et Isabelle vont aller au cinéma ce week-end.
   c. Emilie est très bonne élève.

4. Quel jour est-ce aujourd'hui?
   a. jeudi
   b. vendredi
   c. mardi

1 Des cartes postales 📟

Cet été, Marc est resté chez lui. Ses amis sont partis en vacances. Ils lui ont envoyé des cartes postales.

Salut !
C'est pas génial, Arcachon.
Je vais tous les jours à
la plage et je bronze.
Je fais aussi de la planche
à voile. Toujours la même
chose ! Et toi, qu'est-ce
que tu fais ?
                Amitiés
        Marie

Marc !
Je suis chez ma grand-mère
en Auvergne. On s'amuse
beaucoup. Il fait très beau.
Je fais de longues
promenades.
Qu'est-ce que tu fais ?
Raconte !
                Alexandre

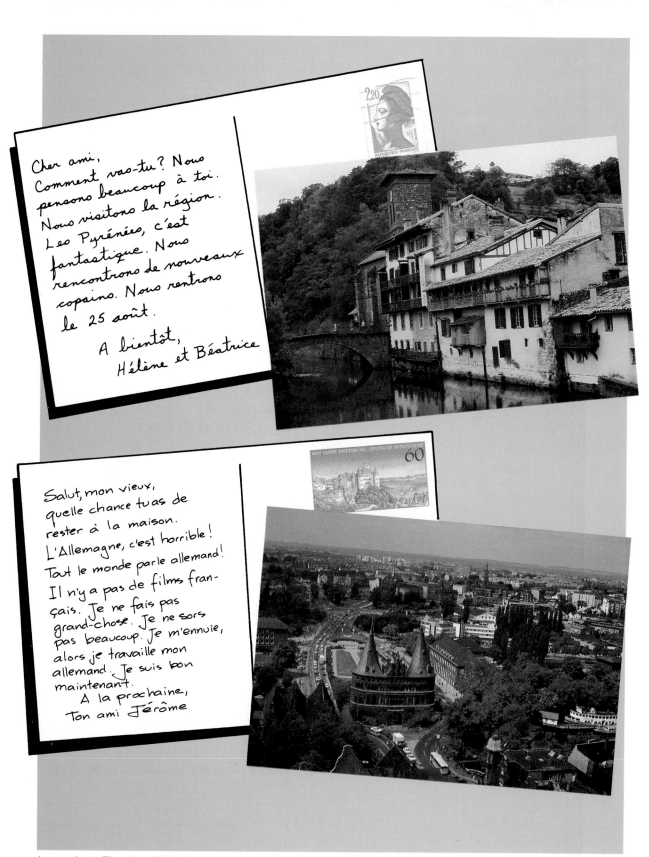

Cher ami,
Comment vas-tu ? Nous
pensons beaucoup à toi.
Nous visitons la région.
Les Pyrénées, c'est
fantastique. Nous
rencontrons de nouveaux
copains. Nous rentrons
le 25 août.

    A bientôt,
      Hélène et Béatrice

Salut, mon vieux,
quelle chance tu as de
rester à la maison.
L'Allemagne, c'est horrible !
Tout le monde parle allemand !
Il n'y a pas de films français. Je ne fais pas
grand-chose. Je ne sors
pas beaucoup. Je m'ennuie,
alors je travaille mon
allemand. Je suis bon
maintenant.

    A la prochaine,
      Ton ami Jérôme

Lower photo: The city of Lübeck is located northeast of Hamburg in the Federal Republic of Germany.

2   Activité • Racontez

Vous êtes Marc. Racontez les vacances de vos amis. Employez le passé composé.

1. Marie / aller / faire   Marie est allée à Arcachon. Elle a fait de la planche à voile.
2. Hélène et Béatrice / visiter / rentrer   Hélène et Béatrice ont visité les Pyrénées. Elle sont rentrées le 25 août.
3. Alexandre / être / faire   Alexandre a été chez sa grand-mère. Il a fait de longues promenades.
4. Jérôme / ne pas aimer / ne pas sortir   Jérôme n'a pas aimé l'Allemagne. Il n'est pas beaucoup sorti.

3   Activité • Ecrivez

C'est toujours la même chose! A la rentrée, le professeur de français vous demande de décrire vos vacances d'été. Ecrivez ce que vous avez fait cet été en quatre ou cinq phrases. Ensuite, imaginez ce que vous allez faire l'été prochain. Rêvez un peu; tout est possible. Ecrivez encore quatre ou cinq phrases. Employez le verbe **aller** et l'infinitif.

Reprinted by permission of UFS, Inc.

In this comic strip, "les maîtresses" refers to elementary school teachers.

Activité • Ecrivez   Possible answer is given.

Emilie, la nouvelle élève, a reçu une carte postale de son amie de Marseille. Ecrivez sa réponse.

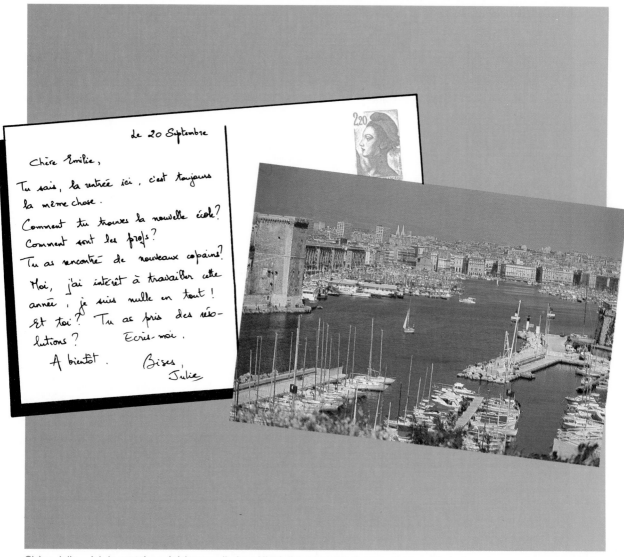

le 20 Septembre

Chère Emilie,

Tu sais, la rentrée ici, c'est toujours la même chose.

Comment tu trouves la nouvelle école? Comment sont les profs?

Tu as rencontré de nouveaux copains?

Moi, j'ai intérêt à travailler cette année, je suis nulle en tout! Et toi? Tu as pris des résolutions?   Ecris-moi.

A bientôt.   Bises,
                            Julie

Chère Julie,   Ici, la rentrée a été bonne. J'adore Nice! J'ai rencontré des tas d'amis, et le lycée est super. Les cours sont difficiles, mais les profs sont sympa! Je ne vais pas sortir, et je vais étudier tous les jours.

A bientôt,
Emilie

5   **Activité • Catastrophe!**   Possible answers are given.

Travaillez en groupe avec deux ou trois camarades de classe. Il faut inventer une catastrophe pour finir ces anecdotes.

1. Je suis parti(e) en Angleterre pour deux semaines en séjour linguistique. J'ai pris l'avion à Orly, et nous sommes arrivés à Londres en une heure.

2. Avec trois amis, nous avons décidé de faire une boum chez moi pour célébrer la fin des vacances. Nous avons téléphoné à une douzaine de copains et copines. Nous avons passé toute la journée de samedi à préparer des sandwiches, ranger le salon et choisir des disques. Enfin, tout a été prêt. 1. Il a plu tout le temps. J'ai oublié mon parapluie! 2. Puis, toutes les filles ont téléphoné. Elles ont toutes dit la même chose: «Demain, il y a une interro de maths. Je vais étudier.» Alors, les garçons sont venus à la boum, mais pas de filles! On ne s'est pas bien amusés.

Voici l'histoire en images de Jacques et d'une jolie fille qui travaille dans une pâtisserie. Jacques ne connaît pas la fille, mais il veut faire sa connaissance. Racontez l'histoire. Employez tous les verbes indiqués au passé composé.

1. voir

2. entrer (dans)

3. ne pas parler / acheter

4. rentrer

5. penser (à)

6. sortir

7. choisir

8. revenir

9. partir

10. offrir

1. Jacques a vu une jolie fille dans la pâtisserie.   2. Il y est entré.   3. Il n'a pas parlé à la fille, mais il a acheté un gâteau au marchand.   4. Il est rentré à son hôtel.   5. Il a pensé à elle.   6. Il est sorti de l'hôtel.   7. Il a choisi des fleurs.   8. Il est revenu à la pâtisserie.   9. La jeune fille est partie avec un garçon anglais.   10. Jacques a offert les fleurs à une vieille dame.

Regardez cette publicité. Pendant les vacances d'été, vous avez choisi de partir en Belgique. Votre camarade est allé(e) en Irlande. Posez des questions à votre camarade sur ses vacances. Vous lui demandez s'il (si elle) est content(e) de ses vacances, ce qu'il/elle a fait, si ça lui a plu, ce qu'il/elle n'a pas aimé… Ensuite, répondez à ses questions sur vos vacances.

The Ardennes mountains and forest extend from northern France into western Belgium and Luxembourg.

Séjours Linguistiques

Apprenez une langue étrangère pendant vos vacances.
La méthode? L'immersion totale dans un bain d'anglais.
La meilleure façon d'apprendre l'anglais, c'est de le «vivre».

Vous… **parlez anglais   pensez anglais
mangez anglais   vivez anglais
et même dormez anglais!**

Fortifiez votre anglais chez les Irlandais.
Sous l'amicale protection d'une famille irlandaise
Les familles irlandaises sont très accueillantes et vous allez apprécier leur mode de vie. Vous pouvez également séjourner en ferme.

Dans un climat de vacances
En Irlande vous pouvez faire de l'équitation, de la voile, du golf, des randonnées à bicyclette.
Cours d'anglais dans une école spécialisée

CORK   DUBLIN   LISMORE
Pour tous renseignements, écrire ou téléphoner à :

SEJOURS CULTURELS ET LINGUISTIQUES
62, Boulevard Raspail
75000 Paris
Tél. 45.76.90.43

VACANCES ACTIVES EN ARDENNE BELGE

EXPEDITION EN CANOË

Nouveauté qui plaît aux amoureux de la nature sauvage et du camping sportif. Vivez l'aventure au fil de la rivière Semois. Comme les trappeurs canadiens sur le Saint-Laurent, vous vous embarquez avec bagages sur votre canoë; les réserves de nourriture et d'eau, la tente et l'équipement minimum pour cette randonnée. Vous retrouvez une liberté perdue dans notre monde trop civilisé, le goût des bonheurs simples et le contact authentique avec la nature.

La randonnée : ± 20 km par jour
Retour :
Vers 18 heures, on recherche les bateaux aux points de rendez-vous. Les chauffeurs sont ramenés au point de départ pour reprendre leur voiture.

Accompagnement :
Un guide peut être mis à la disposition de votre groupe (10 pers.) pour accompagner la randonnée. Seulement en mai, en juin et en septembre. Supplément de 110 FB par pers. par jour. Réserver le guide 4 semaines à l'avance.

Randonnée libre

Vous partez sur la rivière 2, 3 ou 4 jours, en solitaire, en famille ou en groupe pour une randonnée de 40, 60 ou 80 km entre Moyen et Bouillon.
Périodes : de mai à septembre.
Equipement fourni :
- un canoë canadien 2 pers.;
- 2 tonneaux pour bagages.

Equipement à emporter (1) :
- matériel de camping : tente, sac de couchage, matelas mousse, vêtements, chaussures pour marcher dans l'eau;
- ravitaillement : nourriture, boissons, gamelle, couverts, camping gaz.

Camping :
Camping sauvage ou dans les campings installés au bord de la Semois.

■ **PRIX PAR CANOE 2 PLACES :**
2 jours : 900 FB par jour.
3 jours : 850 FB par jour.
4 jours et plus : 800 FB par jour.

Possibilité de louer de l'équipement sur place (à payer sur place)
- tente de 2 pers. : 200 FB par jour;
- matelas de mousse : 50 FB par jour;
- réchaud : 50 FB par jour + la bonbonne;
- gamelle : 30 FB par jour;
- gilet de sauvetage (taille enfant, junior et adulte) : 50 FB par jour;
- La Semois Touristique : carte vendue : 135 FB.

matelas de mousse: foam pad
réchaud: camping stove
gamelle: camping cookware
gilet de sauvetage: life jacket

Regardez ce qu'ils ont rapporté et dites où ils ont été en vacances.

1.

Ils ont été en France.

2.

Elles ont été en Suisse.

3.

Ils ont été en Angleterre.

4.

Elle a été à Québec.

5.

Il a été en Espagne.

6.

Ils ont été à New York.

Vous êtes sorti(e) pendant le week-end. Voici les talons *(stubs)* de vos billets. Pour chaque billet, préparez un dialogue avec un(e) camarade de classe. Votre camarade vous demande si vous êtes sorti(e) pendant le week-end, où vous êtes allé(e), ce que vous avez fait, ce que vous avez vu, comment c'était… Changez de rôle.

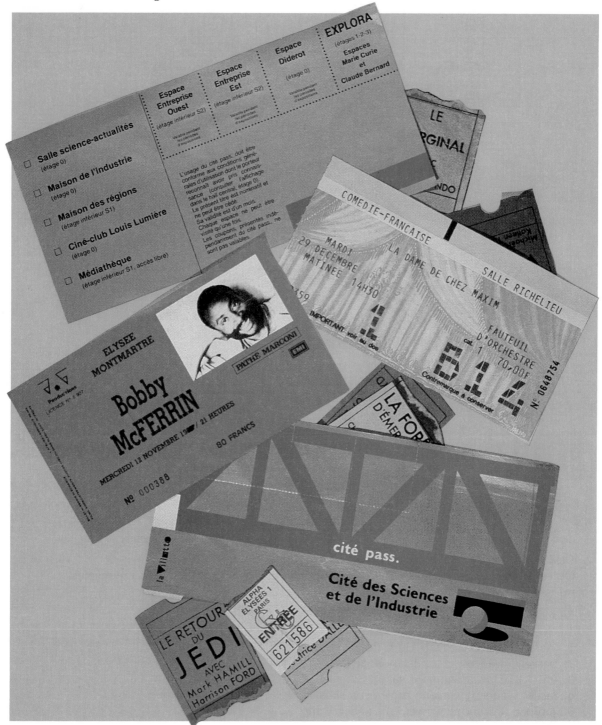

La Comédie Française (1792) is located near the Louvre in Paris. It is famous for its traditional theatre and the quality of its productions.
La Villette is a large complex located in northeast Paris. It encompasses a park, an exposition hall, a concert hall (le Zénith), a spherical cinema (la Géode), a museum of science and industry, and an institute of music.

1. Trouvez les mots

Vous avez recommencé l'école. Une nouvelle année de travail commence.

Vous dites *(say)* : — — — — — — — — — — — — — ! Vive la rentrée!

Pour trouver ces trois mots, écrivez la première lettre de chaque chose représentée par le dessin.

valise   île   veste   escalier

lit   avion

radio   enfant   nuages   tasse   règle   étagère   eau

2. Devinette

Qu'est-ce que nous ne voyons *(see)* pas et qui est toujours devant nous? La réponse est un mot de six lettres qui commence par *A*. avenir

3. Le mot qui manque.

Trouvez la logique dans chaque série de mots et complétez la série.

1. Washington, D.C., Etats-Unis; Paris, France; ____, Angleterre Londres
2. passer, vacances; ____, décision; attraper, coup de soleil prendre
3. être, ____; avoir, eu; faire, fait été
4. facile, vraiment; content, drôlement; satisfait, ____ énormément/très/bien
5. monter, descendre; arriver, ____; aller, venir partir

For script, see pp. T41–42.

PRONONCIATION

The rhythm of French

 1   Ecoutez bien et répétez.

French is spoken, not in words, but in syllables. Repeat these words after your teacher or after the recording.

Chi-ca-go   Ca-sa-blan-ca
To-ron-to   Mi-ssion im-po-ssible
Ca-na-da   nou-velle ad-mi-ni-stra-tion

A-la-ska   ad-mi-ni-stra-tion
Ma-ni-to-ba   a-é-ro-port Ke-nne-dy
To-ky-o   dé-parts in-ter-na-tio-naux
O-tta-wa

 2   Ecoutez et lisez.

Word groups are cut, not into words, but into syllables of equal length, regardless of where one word stops and the other begins. Repeat these words and phrases after your teacher or after the recording.

par exemple   pa-re-xemple
cet été   ce-té-té
un bel été   un be-lé-té
il arrive   i-la-rrive
avec une amie   a-ve-cu-na-mie
par avion   pa-ra-vion
Il arrive avec une amie par avion. I-la-rri-va-ve-cu-na-mie pa-ra-vion.

 3   Copiez les phrases suivantes pour préparer une dictée.

French speakers try to end each syllable with a vowel sound, even though the syllable contains nothing but a vowel. Try this with the following sentences, saying each syllable as you write it.

1. Cette année, j'ai fait du camping avec Anatole.
2. C'était un bel endroit au bord de la mer.
3. C'était le même endroit qu'il y a quatre ans.
4. Nous avons pris le même avion.
5. Mon oncle a tout arrangé.
6. Il nous a montré comment faire.
7. A notre âge, il faut apprendre.

VERIFIONS!

SECTION A

Do you know how to say what happened in the past?
Rewrite these sentences, putting the verbs in the **passé composé.**
1. Il (pleuvoir) tout le temps.
2. Mon frère (perdre) son portefeuille.
3. Moi, je (oublier) mon maillot de bain.
4. Nous (ne pas bronzer).
5. Maman (attraper) un coup de soleil.

1. a plu 2. a perdu 3. ai oublié 4. n'avons pas bronzé 5. a attrapé

Have you learned to express your opinion?
Using different expressions, restate the following sentences as your opinion.
1. Les vacances sont trop courtes.
2. Les maths sont faciles.

1. Je trouve que les vacances sont trop courtes. 2. A mon avis, les maths sont faciles.

Can you agree or disagree with someone?
Agree or disagree with the following statements.
1. Je suis content(e) de recommencer l'école. *(agree)*
2. Les bédés sont super! *(disagree)*
3. Les vacances d'été sont trop longues! *(agree)*
4. Le nouveau prof est sympa. *(agree)*

1. Moi aussi. 2. Je ne suis pas d'accord.
3. Je suis d'accord. 4. Tu as raison.

SECTION B

Can you ask a friend how things went?
Ask your friend as many questions as you can about the following:
1. les vacances Les vacances, c'était bien?
2. la plage Tu t'es amusé(e) à la plage?
3. la cuisine La cuisine, c'était comment?
4. les activités Les activités, ça t'a plu?

Have you learned how to express satisfaction, indifference, or dissatisfaction?
Express your feelings about the following items. Vary your responses.
1. le camp de vacances *(satisfaction)*
2. le séjour en Angleterre *(dissatisfaction)*
3. le concert *(dissatisfaction)*
4. l'excursion *(indifference)*

1. C'était merveilleux! 2. Je me suis ennuyé(e). 3. C'était mortel. 4. C'était pas terrible.

Do you know whether to use *avoir* or *être* in forming the *passé composé*?
Say and then write the sentence, using the **passé composé.**
1. Marie et Anne (sortir) samedi soir.
2. Elles (aller) au cinéma.
3. Elles (voir) un film américain.
4. Sylvie (rester) chez elle.
5. Elle (regarder) la télé.

1. sont sorties 2. sont allées 3. ont vu 4. est restée 5. a regardé

SECTION C

Can you make excuses for difficulties? 1. Le prof explique mal. 2. Ce n'est pas son fort.
Explain why these students have difficulties. Vary your responses.
1. Sylvie ne comprend rien aux maths.
2. Philippe a eu 8 en anglais.
3. Aude a de mauvaises notes.
4. Martin est nul en géographie.
5. Alexandre n'aime pas la physique.

3. Elle ne travaille pas. 4. Il n'y comprend rien. 5. Il est nul en physique.

Do you recall how to express future time?
You and your friends have not done these things yet. Say that you are going to do them later **(plus tard),** using **aller** plus the infinitive.
1. Claire n'a pas encore fini son devoir. Elle va...
2. Martin et Alexandre n'ont pas encore parlé à la nouvelle.
3. Hélène et Béatrice ne sont pas encore rentrées.
4. Moi, je n'ai pas encore lu ce livre.
5. Sylvie et moi n'avons pas encore étudié notre histoire.

1. Elle va finir son devoir plus tard. 2. Ils vont lui parler plus tard. 3. Elles vont rentrer plus tard.
4. Je vais lire ce livre plus tard. 5. Nous allons étudier notre histoire plus tard.

VOCABULAIRE

SECTION A

aller : Comment allez-vous? *How are you?*
les **anciens** (m.) *old friends*
l' **Angleterre** (f.) *England*
attention : faire attention *to be careful*
attraper *to catch*
au contraire *on the contrary*
une **bédé** *comic book*
bronzé, -e *tanned*
bronzer *to get a tan*
certains *certain ones*
chaque *each*
comme *like*
la **connaissance : faire (la) connaissance** *to get acquainted*
content, -e *happy, glad*
un **coup de soleil** *sunburn*
la **cour** *courtyard*
débuter *to begin*
un **dragueur** *flirt*
ennuyer : Je m'ennuie. *I get (am) bored.*
ennuyeux, -euse *boring*
la **forme : en (pleine) forme** *in (great) shape*
horrible *horrible*
long, longue *long*
moi aussi *me too*
moi non plus *neither do I*
passionnant, -e *exciting*
plu : Il a plu. *It rained.*
prochain, -e *next*
raconter *to tell*
raison : avoir raison *to be right*
recommencer *to start again*
regretter *to regret, miss*
repartir *to leave again*
reprendre *to start again*
retrouver *to meet (again)*
scolaire *school (adj.)*
sévère *strict*
splendide *splendid*
terminé, -e *finished, ended*
tort : avoir tort *to be wrong*
tout : tout le temps *all the time*

SECTION B

amuser : Je me suis amusé(e). *I had a good time.* **Tu t'es amusé(e)?** *Did you have a good time?*
Arcachon *town south of Bordeaux*
l' **Ardèche** (f.) **département** *in southeast France*
l' **Auvergne** (f.) *region in the center of the Massif Central*
la **bicyclette** *bicycle, bicycling*
bord : au bord de la mer *at the seashore*
camper *to camp*
le **camping** *camping*
le **canoë** *canoeing*
le **canoë-kayak** *kayaking*
un **centre de vacances** *vacation resort, camp*
le **choix** *choice*
ennuyé : Je me suis ennuyé(e). *I got (was) bored.*
énormément *enormously*
l' **équitation** (f.) *horseback riding*
était *was*
gagner *to earn, win*
le **journal** *newspaper*
jusqu'à *until*
louer *to rent*
merveilleux, -euse *marvelous*
pareil, pareille *similar*
la **pêche** *fishing*
le **ping-pong** *ping pong*
plu : Ça t'a plu? *Did you like it?* **Ça m'a plu.** *I liked it.*
la **possibilité** *possibility*
des **progrès** (m.) *progress*
les **Pyrénées** (f.) *mountains separating France from Spain*

quelque part *somewhere*
une **région** *region*
rencontrer *to meet*
satisfait, -e *satisfied*
un **séjour** *stay;* **un séjour linguistique** *stay to learn a language*
la **spéléologie** *cave exploring*
une **station-service** *gas station*
une **villa** *country house*
la **voile** *sailing*

SECTION C

un **architecte** *architect*
l' **avenir** (m.) *future*
le **bilan : faire le bilan** *to assess, take stock of*
comprendre *to understand*
une **décision** *decision;* **prendre une décision** *to make a decision*
expliquer *to explain*
la **fin** *end*
un **fort** *strong point*
furieux, -euse *furious*
inquiéter : Ne t'inquiète pas. *Don't worry.*
intérêt : avoir intérêt à *to be in one's interest to*
inutile *useless*
une **journée** *day*
justement *exactly*
loin *far (off)*
mal *poorly, badly*
malade *sick*
une **matière** *school subject*
moyen, moyenne *average*
la **note** *grade*
nul, nulle *hopeless, useless*
passé, -e *last*
peu *little, not much*
un **projet** *project, plan*
redoubler *to repeat a grade*
une **résolution** *resolution;* **prendre une résolution** *to make a resolution*
réussir *to succeed*

ETUDE DE MOTS

In French, as in English, the prefix **re-** before a verb indicates that the action is repeated. In French, if the verb begins with a vowel, just the letter **r-** is added. (1) Find some examples in the list above of the use of the prefix **re-**. (2) Copy the following verbs and rewrite them, adding the prefix **re-: entrer, venir, tourner, attraper.** (3) Write the meaning of each verb.

---

recommencer, repartir, reprendre, retrouver, redoubler
rentrer: to return (home);   revenir: to come back;   retourner: to return;   rattraper: to catch again

A LIRE

Souvenirs de vacances

This selection is taken from *Les Vacances du petit Nicolas* (1962), one of a series of five books written by René Goscinny and illustrated by Jean-Jacques Sempé, a famous French cartoonist. Goscinny, who died in 1977, is noted for several books, in particular *Astérix* and *Lucky Luke.*

Avant de lire

D'abord, regardez le titre de l'histoire et les dessins. Maintenant, qu'en pensez-vous?

1. Quel âge ont le garçon et la fille?   10 ans
2. De qui parle le garçon?   De Marie-Edwige.
3. A votre avis, est-ce que le garçon est modeste?   Non.
4. Pensez-vous qu'il aime la fille?   Oui.
5. C'est une histoire sérieuse ou comique?   Comique.

(C'est Nicolas qui parle.)

Marie-Edwige, c'est la fille de M. et Mme Courteplaque, nos voisins. Marie-Edwige, elle est très chouette, même si c'est une fille. Tiens, c'est une veine°! La voilà.

— Bonjour, Marie-Edwige, j'ai dit, tu vas dans le jardin?

— Oui, a dit Marie-Edwige. Et elle est passée par le trou dans la haie°. Marie-Edwige est devenue toute bronzée. Et avec ses yeux bleus et ses cheveux blonds, ça fait très joli. Non, vraiment, même si c'est une fille, elle est très chouette, Marie-Edwige.

— T'as passé de bonnes vacances? m'a demandé Marie-Edwige.

— Terrible! je lui ai dit. Je suis allé dans une colo°, il y avait° des équipes, et mon équipe, c'était la meilleure. Elle s'appelait «Œil-de-Lynx» et c'était moi le chef.

— Les chefs dans les colos, ce n'est pas des grands? a dit Marie-Edwige.

— Oui, j'ai dit, je vais t'expliquer : moi, j'étais l'aide du chef et il ne faisait rien sans me demander. Celui qui commandait vraiment, c'était moi.

— Et il y avait des filles dans la colo? a demandé Marie-Edwige.

— Peuh! j'ai répondu, bien sûr que non, c'était trop dangereux pour les filles. On faisait des choses terribles, et puis moi, j'ai sauvé deux filles qui se noyaient°.

— Tu racontes des blagues°, a dit Marie-Edwige.

— Comment des blagues? j'ai crié. C'est pas deux mais trois. J'en avais oublié un. Et puis, je vais te dire, à la pêche°, c'est moi qui ai gagné le concours. J'ai sorti un poisson comme ça! Et j'ai écarté les bras autant que je pouvais et Marie-Edwige a commencé à rigoler comme si elle ne me croyait pas. Et ça ne m'a pas plu; c'est vrai, avec les filles on ne peut pas parler.

---

c'est une veine *what luck;*   **haie** *hedge;*   **colo** = **colonie de vacances** *summer camp;*
il y avait *there were;*   **se noyaient** *were drowning;*   **blagues** *jokes;*   **pêche** *fishing*

— Moi, a dit Marie-Edwige, je suis allée à la plage avec mes parents, et j'ai rencontré Jeannot, et on est devenu copains.

— Marie-Edwige! a crié Mme Courteplaque, reviens tout de suite. Le déjeuner est servi.

— Je te raconterai plus tard, a dit Marie-Edwige, je vais rentrer. Et elle est partie en courant par le trou de la haie. Moi, je suis monté en courant dans ma chambre et j'ai donné un coup de pied° dans la porte de l'armoire. C'est vrai, quoi, à la fin, qu'est-ce qu'elle a Marie-Edwige à me raconter des tas de blagues sur ses vacances? D'abord, ça ne m'intéresse pas. Et puis Jeannot, c'est un imbécile et un laid°! haie: hedge

Activité • Devinez

Choisissez le bon équivalent anglais des mots suivants, d'après *(according to)* le texte.

1. voisins :
  a. *friends*
  b. *neighbors* (encerclé)
  c. *relatives*

2. devenu(e) :
  a. *became* (encerclé)
  b. *came back*
  c. *came from*

3. chef :
  a. *cook*
  b. *leader* (encerclé)
  c. *assistant*

Activité • Répondez

1. Où habite Marie-Edwige? Elle habite à côté de chez Nicolas.
2. Décrivez Marie-Edwige. Elle est blonde avec les yeux bleus.
3. Où est-ce que Nicolas a passé ses vacances? Nicolas a passé ses vacances dans une colonie de vacances.
4. Et Marie-Edwige? Où est-elle allée en vacances? Marie-Edwige a passé ses vacances à la plage avec ses parents.
5. A votre avis, est-ce que Nicolas raconte des blagues ou des histoires vraies? Nicolas raconte des blagues.

Activité • Avez-vous bien lu? Possible answers are given.

Nicolas a raconté ses aventures dans la colonie de vacances à Marie-Edwige. Décrivez trois aventures qu'il lui a racontées.
Il a aidé le chef de son équipe. Il a sauvé trois filles. Il a gagné le concours de pêche.

Activité • Réfléchissez Possible answers are given.

Voici cinq adjectifs. Choisissez ceux qui décrivent Nicolas. Donnez des raisons pour votre choix.

vantard *(boastful)*   méchant   jaloux *(jealous)*   paresseux   timide
Vantard, parce qu'il raconte des histoires. Jaloux, parce qu'il trouve Jeannot imbécile et laid.

---

coup de pied *kick*; **laid** *ugly boy*

CHAPITRE 2 Après l'école

	BASIC MATERIAL	COMMUNICATIVE FUNCTIONS
PREMIER CONTACT	**La Maison des Jeunes et de la Culture (1)** **Voulez-vous apprendre à jouer d'un instrument? (5)**	Reading for global comprehension and cultural awareness
SECTION A	**Après-midi libre (A1)**	**Exchanging information** • Answering a negative question affirmativ~~e~~ • Talking about recreational activities **Socializing** • Inviting friends
SECTION B	**A la Maison des Jeunes (B1)** **Autres activités (B4)**	**Exchanging information** • Choosing leisure activities **Persuading** • Offering encouragement
SECTION C	**Comment monter un groupe de rock? (C1)** **Ça marche! (C11)** **Autres instruments (C17)** **Une chanson (C27)**	**Exchanging information** • Talking about forming a rock group • Asking and telling how long something has been going on **Socializing** • Asking for, giving, and refusing permiss~~ion~~
TRY YOUR SKILLS	**Devant la Maison des Jeunes (1)**	

■ **Prononciation** (the vowel sound /ə/; dictation) **83**
■ **Vérifions!** **84** ■ **Vocabulaire** **85**

A LIRE	**Une chanson :** *En sortant du lycée* (A French girl tells about the best time of her day.) **Jazz et Rock** (famous jazz and rock musicians)

WRITING   A variety of controlled and open-ended writing activities appear in the Pupil's Edition. The Teacher's Notes identify other activities suitable for writing practice.

COOPERATIVE LEARNING   Many of the activities in the Pupil's Edition lend themselves to cooperative learning. For guidelines, see page T14.

Scope and Sequence

GRAMMAR	CULTURE	RE-ENTRY
	Local recreation center offerings	
The independent pronouns **moi, toi, lui, elle, nous, vous, eux, elles** (A8)	Leisure activities of French young people	Leisure activity vocabulary Extending, accepting, and refusing invitations The **passé composé**
The verbs **apprendre** and **comprendre** (B9)	Activities at the **Maison des Jeunes** Music preferences of French teenagers	The verb **prendre**
The verb **devoir** (C4) The pronoun **en** (C15)	Forming music groups	The verb **vouloir** Making a phone call Numbers

Recombining communicative functions, grammar, and vocabulary

Reading for practice and pleasure

UNIT RESOURCES **Cahier d'Activités, Cahier d'Exercices,** Unit 2 Cassettes, Transparencies 4–6, Quizzes 4–6, Unit 2 Test

TEACHER-PREPARED MATERIALS **Premier Contact** Pictures of **MJC** activities; **Section A** Pictures of leisure activities and food items; **Section B** Photos and recordings of French singers and rock groups; pictures of people learning; **A lire** Jazz and rock recordings

PREMIER
CONTACT

The authentic material in **Premier Contact** introduces the theme of the unit. Concentrate only on the general content of these documents. A detailed treatment of the grammar and vocabulary is not intended. Since students should be reading for global comprehension, they need not know the meaning of every word. For this reason, new words in **Premier Contact** have been omitted from the unit vocabulary list and the French-English Vocabulary at the end of the book.

OBJECTIVES To read for global comprehension and cultural awareness; to get acquainted with the topic

1   La Maison des Jeunes et de la Culture

Have students read the **MJC** bulletin to themselves. Ask questions to check comprehension: **Qu'est-ce qu'on peut faire à la MJC? Qu'est-ce qu'on fait à un bal? A la piscine? Dans un gymnase? Quels genres de danse est-ce qu'on peut faire? Il faut payer combien pour être membre de la MJC?** Explain any key words that students can't guess from the context.

2   Activité • Complétez

SLOWER-PACED LEARNING On the board or on a transparency, write the answers at random. Have students choose the correct ones to complete the sentences.

CHALLENGE Have individuals read the sentence beginnings and complete them orally. Then have students prepare one or two additional sentence beginnings for classmates to complete.

3   Activité • Qu'est-ce qu'ils vont choisir à la MJC?

Before class, gather pictures that represent possible **MJC** activities. Have students identify what is pictured. Then ask a series of simple questions to help students conclude what everyone will do at the **MJC.** For number 1, you might show a picture of a camera and ask the following questions:

> Qu'est-ce que c'est?
> Qu'est-ce que Pierre a reçu pour son anniversaire?
> Qu'est-ce que Pierre aime faire?
> Alors, qu'est-ce qu'il va choisir à la MJC?

4   Activité • Et vous?

Have students pick out an activity, workshop, or course that would interest them. Provide a model by telling what you prefer and why: **Moi, je choisis la cuisine d'été. J'aime manger!** If students have difficulty explaining why they chose an activity, have them imagine that they are one of the people in **Contact 3.**

5   VOULEZ-VOUS APPRENDRE A JOUER D'UN INSTRUMENT?

Call on several students to answer the question in the title. Refer them to C17 on page 72 for the names of other musical instruments to use in their answers. Then have students take a survey of four or five of their classmates, asking if they would like to study guitar, on what level, with which age group, and when. Have them prepare the questions first: **Tu veux apprendre la guitare? A quel niveau? Dans quel groupe d'âge? Quand?** Ask several students to report the results of their surveys.

6 ## Activité • Et vous?

Have students pair off to take turns asking and answering the questions.

7 ## Activité • Ecrivez

Begin by asking students what kinds of courses they could teach. Have students refer to the ads in **Contact 1** and **5** for ideas and phrases they might use. Since they are writing ads, students do not have to use complete sentences. As a homework assignment, you might have them print their ads on large sheets of paper or poster board and surround them with their own drawings or with pictures from magazines.

SECTION A

OBJECTIVES **To exchange information:** answer a negative question affirmatively; talk about recreational activities; **to socialize:** invite friends

CULTURAL BACKGROUND Students in France do not have as much leisure time as American students, so few of them can get part-time jobs. Most do not leave school until four, five, or even six o'clock, except on Wednesdays and Saturdays, when they are free at noon. They have a lot of homework in all subjects. France is still a family-oriented society; dinner is late and lengthy, and chores must be done. Therefore, students are able to go to the **Maison des Jeunes** primarily on Wednesdays and weekends. The **MJC** is all the more important to them because French **lycées** do not usually sponsor games, dances, or parties for students.

MOTIVATING ACTIVITY Have students talk in French about how they like to spend a free afternoon, a Saturday, or a holiday. As individuals mention various activities, list them on the board. Encourage students to copy them into their notebooks for use in later activities in this unit.

A1 # Après-midi libre!

Bring to class pictures that illustrate the various leisure activities mentioned in the dialogues. Use the pictures to teach new vocabulary: **un groupe de rock, un entraînement de foot, faire des achats/de la danse/de la gym/du judo/du théâtre.** Ask students to recall ways to accept and refuse invitations. Then ask them in French if they want to do the activities represented by the pictures. Next have them ask you; give some of the excuses they will encounter in the dialogues.

List the names of the people in the dialogues who are invited to do something, and have students copy the list. As they listen to the cassette, have them indicate whether each person accepts or refuses the invitation. Then have students work with a partner to read aloud and role-play one of the dialogues.

A2 ## Activité • Vrai ou faux?

Read the sentences; then ask volunteers to correct them orally. Students may phrase their corrections in two ways, as shown on the next page.

1. Laure va répéter avec un groupe de rock.
   Romain a un entraînement de foot.
2. Julien va au cinéma avec une copine.
   Emmanuelle va à la piscine.

A3 Activité • A vous maintenant!

Go over the example carefully so that students know how to ask about the previous day's activities. Have students pair off; each pair assumes the roles of one of the pairs named in the activity. After all have had sufficient time to practice, ask volunteers to role-play the dialogues.

CHALLENGE Have students re-create their dialogues, substituting their own responses.

A4 Savez-vous que... ?

Remind students that in a French **lycée,** classes for a course do not meet every day of the week but are scheduled more like college courses (Monday-Wednesday-Friday or Tuesday-Thursday-Saturday). This is why a **lycéen** studies more subjects at a time than an American high school student. It is also one of the reasons behind the heavy homework load of French students.

To make this a listening comprehension activity, prepare a list of questions and distribute them to students. After they've had a chance to read the questions, play the cassette and have them jot down brief answers.

A5 COMMENT LE DIRE

Practice with **Mais oui!** and **Mais si!** first. Tell students that you're going to ask some questions and that you want a "Yes!" answer to all of them. If they hear you ask a negative question, they should answer with **Mais si!**

Vous n'aimez pas les sports?   (Mais si!)
Vous êtes tous de bons élèves?   (Mais oui!)
Vous n'allez pas sortir après la classe?   (Mais si!)
Vous allez parler français avec moi?   (Mais oui!)

Now practice in a similar way with **Si, je veux bien** and **Oui, je veux bien:**

Marie, vous voulez jouer au tennis?   (Oui, je veux bien.)
Robert, vous ne voulez pas sortir maintenant?   (Si, je veux bien.)

CHALLENGE Give students a few moments to prepare two affirmative and two negative questions of their own. Then have them pair off and practice with each other as you circulate and listen.

A6 Activité • Si ou oui?

After students have completed the activity as instructed in their books, have them invite each other to do two things that evening: **Tu veux étudier chez moi ce soir? Tu ne veux pas sortir ce soir?** If students do not want to do something, they may answer with **Non, je ne veux pas.**

SLOWER-PACED LEARNING You might make this a listening comprehension activity. Have students make two columns on their papers: **Oui, je veux bien** and **Si, je veux bien.** Point out that when they see or hear the **ne... pas,** their chosen response is going to be **Si, je veux bien.** Then read them the invitations in the activity, and have them write the number of the invitation below the response of their choice. Go over the answers with them; then have them pair off to do the activity as instructed in their books.

A 7 ## Activité • A vous maintenant!

As students work in pairs, circulate among them and spot-check responses. After they've had a chance to practice in pairs, call on volunteers to give the questions and responses.

SLOWER-PACED LEARNING Allow the pairs to write out their questions and responses; then call on volunteers to read them to the class.

A 8 # STRUCTURES DE BASE

Demonstrate the use of independent pronouns by pointing to yourself **(moi)**, to students in front of you **(toi, vous)**, and to others at a distance **(lui, elle, eux, elles).** Point to various students and ask **Qui est-ce?** Have students respond **C'est moi,** and so on.

To practice using independent pronouns after prepositions, tell a student to come with you: **Paul, viens avec moi.** Take the student to the door. At the door, ask **Paul est avec Jacques? Non? Alors, avec qui est-il?** Leave Paul at the door and select a student on the other side of the room. Ask **Carole est près de lui ou loin de lui?** as you point to Paul. Repeat the procedure with other students. Place another student between you and Paul. Ask **Qui est entre lui et moi?** as you point to Paul. Say **Oui! Angèle est entre nous.** Repeat with other students.

To reinforce the use of independent pronouns in compound subjects, write several compounds on the board or on a transparency. Help students decide which verb forms should follow them. Then have students copy the compound subjects and write complete sentences using them. Call on several students to read their sentences aloud.

A 9 ## Activité • Qu'est-ce qu'ils font après l'école?

As students do the activity in pairs, circulate among them and spot-check by asking the questions yourself. As a variation, have the partners ask each other if they do the activities listed.

SLOWER-PACED LEARNING Ask students which pronoun they will use in each response; write these on the board or on a transparency as reminders. Help them with the verb forms they're going to need.

A 10 ## Activité • A la cafeteria

Bring in pictures of the food items mentioned. Hand them to students, asking questions: **C'est pour qui, les frites? Pour toi? Non, c'est pour eux,** and so on. Then have students pair off to do the activity, taking turns asking and answering the questions. As a quick check, have students close their books, and as you ask each question, have them write **C'est pour... ,** completing it with the appropriate pronoun.

A 11 ## Activité • Ecrit dirigé

You might assign this writing activity for homework.

SLOWER-PACED LEARNING Go through the letter, helping students to select the appropriate pronouns. Then have them write out the letter.

CHALLENGE   Give the letter as a **dictée** with books closed. When students hear you say "blank," they write in the correct pronoun. Then have students exchange papers, open their books, and correct each other's work.

A 12   COMMENT LE DIRE

For cooperative learning, have students form groups of four. Each member of the group invents a situation—a party, a movie, a sports event—and invites the others in the group to participate. The others respond with one of the phrases in the box.

A 13   Activité • A vous maintenant!

First do the exercise with the entire class. Propose each activity with a different expression from A12, and call on students at random for a response. Then have students propose the activities to you. Finally, have the students do the activity in pairs.

A 14   Activité • Ecrivez

Have students read the announcement first. Review time by asking **A quelle heure commence le cours? Il finit à quelle heure?** Then ask other questions: **Qui donne le cours? Quelle est la date du premier cours?** Next have students read the instructions; make certain they understand what they are to do. Begin the note to Damien on the board or on a transparency. Have students make suggestions. One student at a time might come up and add a sentence.

SLOWER-PACED LEARNING   On the board or on a transparency, complete the whole composition using students' ideas. Have them copy it into their notebooks. They should refer to this model as they write their own compositions.

CHALLENGE   Assign this as a composition to be collected the next day.

A 15   Activité • A vous maintenant!

Review telephone expressions: **Allô? Qui est à l'appareil? Ne quittez pas!** and so on. Have students read the announcements silently. Check comprehension by asking questions: **Jastro et le New Look, c'est un film? Quand est-ce que le groupe donne un concert? C'est où? A quelle heure? C'est combien?** Now have students pair off to discuss these events "over the phone."

SLOWER-PACED LEARNING   Review A1, A5, and A12, helping students to select phrases they can use in their telephone conversations. Write these on the board or on a transparency as prompters. To demonstrate how the responses might go, have a student "call" you.

CHALLENGE   After everyone has practiced in pairs, select two students who have not been working together; have them do a spontaneous conversation.

A 16   Activité • Ecoutez bien

You will hear six short dialogues in which one person invites another to do something. Does that person accept or refuse? On a separate sheet of paper, number from 1 to 6 and be prepared to indicate your answers. *(pause)*
Ecoutez bien.

1. —Eh, Marc, je vais à la MJC. Tu veux venir avec moi?
   —Je te remercie, mais je n'ai pas le temps. J'ai un devoir de maths.
   Il refuse.
2. —Tu n'as pas envie de passer l'après-midi avec moi?
   —Si. Qu'est-ce que tu veux faire? *Elle accepte.*
3. —Ça te dit de faire une balade, Aline?
   —Je veux bien si on ne rentre pas trop tard. *Elle accepte.*
4. —Je rentre chez moi. Tu ne veux pas prendre le bus avec moi?
   —Je dois attendre mon frère. Il sort à midi et demi. *Il refuse.*
5. —Qu'est-ce qu'on peut faire cet après-midi?
   —Je ne sais pas.
   —J'ai une idée : on va à la MJC!
   —Bof. Non, moi, je vais faire des achats. *Elle refuse.*
6. —Si tu veux, on peut aller au cinéma.
   —Quand ça?
   —Maintenant. Tu ne veux pas?
   —Si, c'est une bonne idée. *Il accepte.*

Et maintenant, vérifions. *Read each dialogue again and give the correct answer.*

OBJECTIVES **To exchange information:** choose leisure activities; **to persuade:** offer encouragement

CULTURAL BACKGROUND Most towns have a **Maison des Jeunes.** These establishments are similar to YMCAs. They are well-run and have a young, energetic, and sympathetic staff. Teenagers are encouraged to become involved in recreational and/or cultural activities. Often the activities lead to a competitive event or to a performance that parents and friends may attend.

MOTIVATING ACTIVITY Take a poll among the students as to the popularity of activities other than sports. Convey the meaning of new French terms through pantomime and pictures.

B1   A la Maison des Jeunes

You might use Overhead Transparency 5 to present this section. As students view the transparency, talk about the situation in French, emphasizing new vocabulary. Use some of the expressions of encouragement listed in B15 as you pretend to talk to the young people engaged in the different activities.

   This material lends itself well to TPR activities (see page T7). (1) Play the part of a theater director. Have two or three students play actors to whom you give commands: **Regardez droit devant vous! Parlez plus fort!** (2) Play the part of a judo instructor. Have two students stand facing each other; give them instructions: **Regardez votre adversaire! Mettez votre main droite sur son épaule gauche!** (3) Play the part of a dance instructor. Have three students form a chorus line and have them carry out your instructions: **Plus haut la jambe droite! Plus vite maintenant!** Use the appropriate terms of encouragement as students carry out your commands.

SLOWER-PACED LEARNING Present the material using the TPR activities described above. Then give students a list of the activities mentioned in the dialogues, or write the activities on the board: **la danse, le théâtre, le judo, la trompette.** Play the cassette recording of each dialogue and have students guess which activity is involved.

CHALLENGE   Have students form groups to role-play the dialogues. Ask volunteers to perform one of the dialogues in front of the class.

B2   Activité • Ce n'est pas vrai!

You might have students do this activity as a timed competition. Pair or group the students. The first group to produce a written list of correct sentences wins.

SLOWER-PACED LEARNING   On the board or on a transparency, write at random words that students will need in order to make the statements true.

CHALLENGE   Invite students to rewrite these statements as questions and then to answer them correctly.

B3   Activité • Et vous?

Have students work with a partner to ask and answer the questions. Call on a few students to report their answers to the class. For homework, students might write a paragraph based on their answers.

B4   AUTRES ACTIVITES

After students have examined the pictures and captions, ask **Qui fait de la... ?** or **Qui joue... ?** Students use the independent pronoun **moi** in responding.

B5   Activité • Ecoutez bien

> You're going to hear a conversation between Romain and one of the instructors at the rec center. Open your book to page 62. *(pause)* Read the incomplete sentences and the suggested completions in B5 silently. *(pause)* Be prepared to indicate your answers on a separate sheet of paper. Ready? **Ecoutez bien.**
>
> —Bonjour, monsieur. Je voudrais faire du sport. Qu'est-ce que vous avez comme cours?
> —Ça dépend de ce que vous aimez. Si vous voulez, vous pouvez faire du ping-pong, du tennis, du karaté, du judo...
> —C'est quel jour, le judo?
> —Tous les soirs, sauf le dimanche, le mercredi après-midi et le samedi toute la journée.
> —C'est cher?
> —Sept cents francs par mois.
> —Oh là là!
> —Le ping-pong, c'est moins cher.
> —Ah oui? C'est combien?
> —Cinq cents francs.
> —Et c'est quand?
> —Le lundi et le vendredi de six heures à huit heures, et le samedi tout l'après-midi.
> —Bon. Inscrivez-moi!

Et maintenant, vérifions.
1. **c** faire du sport.   4. **b** cher.
2. **a** du karaté.   5. **a** ce n'est pas cher.
3. **b** sept cents francs.

B 6   ### Activité • Savez-vous que... ?

Few words in this activity will need explanation—perhaps only **branchés.**
Read the paragraph aloud or play the cassette. Go on to the survey questions.
First have students respond by a show of hands; then call on individuals. Ask
volunteers to total the results and to figure the percentages. If you have any
photos of popular French singers or rock groups, bring them in to show the
class. Students would enjoy hearing any recordings you might have of these
performers.

     As an extra credit project, students might conduct their own surveys of
friends and classmates and report back to the class. For survey question 4,
students should substitute their own preferred singers and rock groups. Encourage them to bring in pictures to supplement their reports.

B 7   ### Activité • Et vous?

Have students pair off to ask each other the questions. Then call on a
volunteer to answer each one.

SLOWER-PACED LEARNING   Answers need not be in complete sentences.

B 8   ### VOUS EN SOUVENEZ-VOUS?

Review the verb **prendre** by asking simple questions using the verb:

     Vous prenez le petit déjeuner?   Votre mère prend du café le matin?
     Vous prenez des notes en classe?   Vous avez pris le car ce matin?

B 9   ### STRUCTURES DE BASE

Before having students look at the forms of **apprendre** and **comprendre** in their
books, model each form several times. Then, as students look at their books,
ask questions that require the use of different forms.

SLOWER-PACED LEARNING   Bring in pictures of people learning to do
things, and practice **apprendre à** plus infinitive with the class. Write some
model sentences on the board or on a transparency, and have students copy
them. For the verb **comprendre,** teach the phrase **Je ne comprends pas,** which
might be a useful classroom expression!

CHALLENGE   Have students write original sentences using these verbs. Select
some of the statements and dictate them to the class.

B 10   ### Activité • Complétez

Have students read the dialogue silently and write their completions on a sheet
of paper. Call on volunteers to read the completed dialogue aloud.

CHALLENGE   Encourage students to change the dialogue by using the names
of different courses or musical instruments.

B 11 Activité • Ils ne sont pas très bons

Have students bring in magazine pictures that show people learning to do different things. Have them show and describe these pictures to the class. You might have them make a collage of the pictures.

B 12 Activité • Ecrit dirigé

Students might copy this paragraph into their notebooks, filling in the blanks as they go. After they have finished, ask volunteers to write the correct completions on the board so that students can check their work.

SLOWER-PACED LEARNING Tell students to close their books. Read the completed paragraph aloud to the students. Then have them open their books and write the paragraph, filling in the verb forms as they go.

B 13 Activité • A vous maintenant!

For cooperative learning, have students pair off to talk about the things they are learning in school this year. Circulate among them, encouraging them to keep talking. Have them use the verb **comprendre** to ask each other if they understand various subjects, teachers, and so on.

B 14 Activité • Ecrivez

Work with the class to make up a model dialogue. As students make suggestions, write them on the board or on a transparency. Students should copy the final dialogue into their notebooks. Then have them pair off to make up similar dialogues.

SLOWER-PACED LEARNING Prepare a transparency with sample questions that might be used in this dialogue. Allow the students to work on it in class as you circulate and offer assistance.

CHALLENGE Have pairs of students present their dialogues to the class.

B 15 COMMENT LE DIRE

Have the students repeat the phrases several times after you. Then tell them that you're going to make a series of negative statements and that they should try to encourage you:

Je ne peux pas le faire!
C'est trop difficile!
Mais non, je suis fatigué(e)!

Je n'en peux plus!
Je n'y arrive pas!
C'est impossible!

B 16 Activité • Encouragez votre ami

First you might want to ask what the boy is doing—if he's learning to ski or if he skis well, if he's making progress—what his feelings are **(avoir peur),** and so on. Then do the activity with the entire class. Ask students to call out phrases of encouragement for each situation.

B 17 Activité • A vous maintenant!

After the pairs have practiced with the six statements in this activity, have students close their books and try to continue: one will say something discouraging, and the other will try to boost morale with a brief exclamation. Have them liven up their dialogues with expressive gestures and exaggerated tones of despair and good cheer.

OBJECTIVES   To exchange information: talk about forming a rock group; ask and tell how long something has been going on; **to socialize:** ask for, give, and refuse permission

CULTURAL BACKGROUND   Forming their own rock groups has become a popular activity among young French rock fans. Finding a place to practice, however, can be a problem. In the country, one can usually find a convenient barn or garage, but such things are rare in the cities. In Paris there are a few music studios that can be rented for a fairly reasonable sum (about $7.00 per hour plus a quarterly or yearly membership fee).

MOTIVATING ACTIVITY   Ask students to say what they have to do to form a rock group (find musicians, find a place to rehearse, and so on). Ask how many members they would need, which instruments they would play, when they would practice, and what they would call themselves.

C1

Comment monter un groupe de rock?

Introduce new vocabulary **(ambitieux, tu dois, monter)** by asking simple questions: **Vous avez déjà monté une équipe de softball? Vous devez faire vos devoirs après l'école?** Tell students that they're going to hear a dialogue between Laure and her mother. Laure is going to ask her mother's permission to do something. Tell students that they should note what Laure asks and whether her mother consents or refuses. Then play the cassette or read the dialogue aloud. Call on volunteers to tell you what Laure asked permission to do and what her mother said. Then have students read the dialogue aloud.

C2

Activité • Répondez

On the board or on a transparency, write at random phrases that students will need in order to answer the questions:

monter un groupe	étudier
depuis quatre ans	un groupe de rock
passer le bac	faire un disque

Allow students to consult this list as they answer.

C3

Activité • Et vous?

Give students time to think about their answers, especially to questions 2, 4, and 6. For question 4, you might allow students to talk about *anyone* they may have persuaded. You might omit question 5 if you feel that it could cause some embarrassment.

SLOWER-PACED LEARNING   You may want students to write out short answers to these questions before responding orally.

CHALLENGE   Have students write a four-line dialogue to illustrate their answers to question 4.

C4 **STRUCTURES DE BASE**

Practice **devoir** with the class. Tell students some things you have to do at home. Ask them what they have to do in school. Use all the forms of the verb, present and **passé composé,** in the discussion. Write the conjugation of **devoir** on the board. Students should copy the forms into their notebooks.

C5 **Activité • Vouloir ou devoir?**

Have students work in groups of three or four to find the answers. Then make two columns on the board, headed **Elle veut...** and **Elle doit...** Write the infinitives suggested by students.

C6 **Activité • Et vous?**

Have students make two columns on their papers, one headed **Je veux...** and the other **Je dois...** After they have had time to list a few verbs, have individuals give examples in complete sentences: **Je veux rester, mais je dois partir.**

C7 **Activité • Ecrit dirigé**

SLOWER-PACED LEARNING You may need to help students by pointing out that the conjugated verb in the first sentence **(fait)** will become the infinitive in the second **(faire).** Ask students to give the infinitive they will use in each sentence. Remind them that they must omit the negative words **(ne... pas)** from the second sentence.

C8 **COMMENT LE DIRE**

Practice by asking students permission to do various things: **Je peux ouvrir la fenêtre (montrer des photos, chanter)?** Have students respond with expressions from C8. Then have them pair off to practice asking for permission and responding. Suggest that they ask for permission to do the things they listed for C6 in the column headed **Je veux...**

C9 **Activité • A la place des parents**

Have students pair off to do the dialogue between Laure and one of her parents. The "parent" may select a response from C8 or make up one of his or her own.

C10 **Activité • A vous maintenant!**

Encourage students to be original, asking permission to do activities in addition to those listed. To explain their refusals, they might give reasons other than those shown in the box.

C11 **ÇA MARCHE!**

Play the cassette or read the dialogue aloud. Then have pairs of students take turns reading it aloud.

CHALLENGE Invite students who play instruments to respond to Laure's announcement themselves, making appropriate substitutions in the dialogue. Other students should volunteer to respond as Laure.

C 12 **Activité • Complétez**

Have students cover C11 with a sheet of paper. Tell students to pretend that they are Laure taking notes. Play the cassette again; students complete the sentences as they listen.

C 13 **Activité • Qu'est-ce qu'il faut faire?**

Use this activity as a competitive game. Have the students either write the phrases in the correct order or copy them as is and renumber. The first one to finish, with the correct sequence, wins.

C 14 **Activité • Ecrit dirigé**

Review C1 by playing the cassette. Go over the activity orally, asking volunteers to give a corrected version of each sentence. Then assign the paragraph to be written for homework.

C 15 **STRUCTURES DE BASE**

On the board or on a transparency, write a dialogue similar to the following one:

> —Tu as parlé à Bernard hier soir?
> —Oui, je lui ai parlé.
> —Il habite toujours à Nice?
> —Non, il n'y habite plus. Sa famille a déménagé pour aller à Arles.
> —Bernard est content d'habiter à Arles?
> —Oui, il en est content, je pense.
> —Il a déjà des amis là-bas?
> —Je crois qu'il en a.

Ask volunteers to tell how the pronouns **lui** and **y** are used. Then have students find another object pronoun in the dialogue. See if they can explain how it works. If not, point out that **en** replaces **du, de la, de l', des, de,** or **d'** and the word or phrase that follows it. Add that **en** is positioned in French sentences just as **lui** and **y** are. Have students open their books to read the explanation on page 71. You might provide additional examples.

C 16 **Activité • Répondez**

Play the cassette, pausing after each item to call on volunteers to respond. After drilling the correct response orally, assign the activity to be written.

SLOWER-PACED LEARNING   First ask students to identify the phrase that **en** would replace. Then continue as above.

C 17 **AUTRES INSTRUMENTS**

Ask individuals if they like one or more of these instruments and if they play one. Students should respond first with the noun and then with **en: J'aime la batterie; j'en joue souvent** or **Je n'aime pas le trombone; je n'en joue pas.**

C18 **Activité • Interrogez vos camarades**

Have students circulate and ask four or five classmates if they play the in-struments pictured in C17.

C19 **COMMENT LE DIRE**

Work with **depuis** until students feel comfortable with it. Don't insist on complete-sentence responses at first:

> Vous étudiez le français depuis combien de temps?   (Depuis deux ans.)
> Vous habitez cette ville depuis combien de temps?   (Depuis cinq ans.)

Then, using the same questions, have students respond in complete sentences: **J'étudie le français depuis deux ans. J'habite cette ville depuis cinq ans.** Now change the questions so that students will need to use **en** in their answers:

> Vous jouez de la guitare depuis combien de temps?
>   (J'en joue depuis trois ans.)
> Vous prenez des leçons de français depuis combien de temps?
>   (J'en prends depuis deux ans.)

Have students practice asking questions using **depuis.** Tell them some of your activities and have them ask you how long you have been doing them: **Je fais du jogging. (Depuis combien de temps?)**

C20 **Activité • Ça fait combien de temps?**

After students have paired off and worked out the questions and answers, call on different pairs to recite the dialogues for the class.

C21 **Activité • A vous maintenant!**

To help students prepare for this exercise, ask what their leisure activities are. Write some of their activities on the board and then add other possibilities. Have students refer to this list as they follow the model in their books.

C22 **Activité • Et vous?**

First ask individuals the questions; repeat two or three times. Then have students pair off to ask each other the questions. For homework, have students combine their answers into a written paragraph about their experience, real or imaginary, with musical instruments.

SLOWER-PACED LEARNING   Allow students to respond with short answers instead of complete sentences.

C23 **Activité • Ecrit dirigé**

Work with the class to write a model paragraph. Select a music group and call on volunteers to answer the questions. On the board or on a transparency, compose a paragraph from their answers. Have students copy the model into their notebooks. Then assign the activity as written homework.

C 24 **Savez-vous que... ?**

Read the paragraph aloud or play the cassette. Ask a series of brief questions:

> Comment peut-on apprendre à jouer d'un instrument?
> Pour monter un groupe, qu'est-ce qu'il faut faire?
> Qu'est-ce qui est le plus difficile?

For cooperative learning, students might pair off, choose one of the ads, and prepare a phone conversation between the writer of the ad and a respondant.

CHALLENGE Invite students to write their own ads to be posted on the classroom bulletin board. If they don't play instruments, they may write ads about other activities for which they would like to form groups.

C 25 **Activité • Qu'est-ce qu'on doit faire?**

Review the conjugation of **devoir** in a quick oral drill. Then have students do the activity both orally and in writing.

C 26 **Activité • Ecoutez bien**

> You're going to hear Guy and Benjamin talk about forming a rock group. Open your book to page 74. *(pause)* Read the incomplete sentences and the suggested completions in C26 silently. *(pause)* Be prepared to indicate your answers on a separate sheet of paper. Ready? **Ecoutez bien.**
>
> GUY Salut, Benjamin! Dis, j'ai une idée! Tu joues de la basse, non?
> BENJAMIN Oui. Pourquoi?
> GUY Tu en joues depuis longtemps?
> BENJAMIN Trois ans.
> GUY Tu en joues bien?
> BENJAMIN Pas mal.
> GUY Voilà : j'en ai marre de jouer de la musique tout seul. Tu n'as pas envie de monter un groupe de rock avec moi?
> BENJAMIN Si! C'est une excellente idée! Mais tu connais d'autres musiciens?
> GUY Oui. Mireille joue de la guitare. Paul joue de la batterie. Avec toi comme bassiste et moi comme deuxième guitariste, on peut faire un groupe.
> BENJAMIN Super! Quand est-ce qu'on répète?
> GUY Eh bien, on peut répéter le week-end. Il y a des soirs où tu es libre?
> BENJAMIN Oui, le mardi et le vendredi. Les autres soirs, je fais du foot.
> GUY OK. Moi aussi, je suis libre. Mais on doit demander aux autres s'ils peuvent venir.
> BENJAMIN Et l'année prochaine, on fait un disque!
> GUY Ne rêve pas trop! C'est pas facile, tu sais, de faire un disque! Et on n'a pas beaucoup de temps pour répéter.
> BENJAMIN Moi, je suis optimiste!
>
> Et maintenant, vérifions.
>
> 1. **c** bassiste.
> 2. **b** trois ans.
> 3. **c** monter un groupe.
> 4. **c** faire un disque.
> 5. **a** de la guitare.
> 6. **a** le week-end et deux soirs par semaine.

C 27 UNE CHANSON

Students should read this simple and easy-to-understand song and be permitted to enjoy it without comment. Let it inspire them to write poems in French themselves. Encourage them in French: **C'est possible! Allez-y!** Post their poems on the classroom bulletin board. Perhaps a musically talented student might write a melody for one of these poems, and the class could sing it.

C 28 Activité • Le personnage de Laure

Brainstorm with the students. On the board or on a transparency, write down their recollections of Laure. Then have them copy this list and write, in class or for homework, a well-organized paragraph about her.

TRY YOUR SKILLS

OBJECTIVE To recombine communicative functions, grammar, and vocabulary

CULTURAL BACKGROUND The **MJCs** are popular places to learn to dance, but those students who are serious about dancing attend conservatories. The conservatories teach classical, folk, and modern dance, including tap. In addition, there are numerous private dance studios.

MOTIVATING ACTIVITY Have students discuss dancing: the different types, whether they have taken (or are taking) dance lessons, and what kind of dancing they especially like.

1 Devant la Maison des Jeunes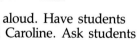

Play the cassette or have volunteers read the dialogues aloud. Have students pair off to practice, alternating the roles of Damien and Caroline. Ask students to find and read aloud different expressions for inviting friends.

2 Activité • Qui est-ce?

Students might answer with the name or practice the independent pronouns by answering **C'est lui** or **C'est elle.**

3 Activité • Et vous?

Have students pair off to ask each other the questions. Then ask volunteers to report their partners' responses to the class.

4 Activité • Choisissez un cours

For cooperative learning, divide the class into pairs or groups of four. After practicing, students should present their dialogues to the class.

SLOWER-PACED LEARNING Have students look at each announcement and think about what they might ask about that particular activity. They might take notes each time and then pair off to prepare their dialogues.

5 Activité • Ecrivez

Brainstorm with the class what a note of encouragement might say. Then assign this as written homework.

6 **Activité • Sondage**

To form the groups for this activity, write the letters *A, B, C, D,* and *E* on slips of paper. Have as many slips of paper as there are students in the class. Fold the papers and have each student pick one. The *A*'s form one group, the *B*'s another, and so on.

7 **Activité • Jeu**

Before playing this game, students should take blank sheets of paper and copy the phrases in squares as shown in their books. They should then cross each phrase off as they receive an affirmative response. They might also write in the square the name of the person who gave the affirmative response. In verifying the winner's results, ask the students whose names are written in the squares if they do indeed participate in the activities: **Vous jouez de la trompette?**

8 **Activité • Le cours de claquettes**

Before pairing off, have students brainstorm phrases of encouragement, invitation, and refusal. Write them on the board or on a transparency for reference.

9 **Activité • Projet**

You might allow students to work on their posters at home. Display the posters on a classroom bulletin board and have students ask the creator of each for more information.

10 **Activité • Qu'est-ce qu'on doit faire?**

For cooperative learning, have students work in groups to prepare responses to the letters. Then have each group present its answers to the class. Students might do this as a "television program," with one student acting as the moderator to read the letters and a panel of students responding with advice.

11 **Activité • Ecrivez**

Since students may be embarrassed to write about their real problems, let them make up imaginary problems and compose the letters. You might put a "Mademoiselle Boncoeur mailbox" in the classroom. Students place their letters in the box. Distribute the letters and ask the students to write responses. You might then select some to read aloud or to post on the bulletin board.

12 **Activité • Et vous?**

Have students write down their answers. Call on volunteers to read their responses to the class. Take a poll to discover the most common activities.

13 **Activité • Récréation**

This is an optional activity. If time allows and if students enjoy word games, have them expand on these by challenging classmates with items of their own making.

PRONONCIATION

The vowel sound /ə/

> Open your book to page 83. *(pause)* Refer to this page as you listen to this section.

1

Ecoutez bien et répétez.

You may not have noticed it, but in English you don't always say the same word in the same way. You change the sound of the word to fit the rhythm of the sentence. Listen to the sound of the word *was* in these two sentences: *It was nothing very important* and *What did you say it was?* Notice that it sounds like /wz/ in the first and that the same word comes out as /wəz/ in the second. See if you can catch the two pronunciations of the word *had* in these two sentences: *He had always wanted to see it* and *Yes, he had.* You see, the place of a word in an English sentence can change the way you say it.

The same is true for letters within words: the place of a letter in a word can change the way you say it. Listen to the o-sounds in these words: *photo, photography,* and *photographic.* The first *o* in the word *photo* sounds like /o/. In the word *photography,* the first *o* sounds very much like the vowels in the words *but* and *the.* Yet in the word *photographic,* it's the second *o* that sounds like the vowel in *but.* Vowel sounds like these, which tend to be neutralized into something that sounds like "uh, uh," allow you to give more importance to other vowels and to stress those within words. This is what helps English sound like English; if you don't do it, your English doesn't sound right.

1. In French, you can't do this; if you do, your French won't sound right. In French, don't slur or swallow any sound. Say each syllable distinctly and use your lips to form sounds more than you do in English. Listen now to the English and French ways of saying these words and repeat the French: *photo/* **photo,** *photography/* **photographie,** *photographic/* **photographique.** Do the same with the next group of words: *minute/* **minute,** *attitude/* **attitude,** *latitude/* **latitude,** *collection/* **collection,** *government/* **gouvernement,** *administration/* **administration.**

Did you notice that one of two things happens to a vowel sound in French? Either it's given its complete value or it's completely left out so that you skip a syllable. You skip syllables in English all the time. You can say *She is here* in three syllables or *She's here* in two; *They have arrived* in four syllables or *They've arrived* in three.

2. In French, if a vowel is to be given less importance, you completely leave it out and drop a syllable. Listen to these pairs of sentences and repeat the second one in each pair. Instead of saying **Je dois venir,** you say **Jé dois vénir.** *(pause)* Instead of saying **Je ne sais pas,** you say **Jé ne sais pas.** *(pause)* Instead of saying **Au revoir,** you say **Au révoir.** *(pause)* And instead of saying **A demain,** you say **A démain.** *(pause)* Did you hear the sound of the remaining syllables? All were fully pronounced.

3. What is this vowel sound that's sometimes pronounced and sometimes not? It sounds a bit like the unstressed vowel you heard in *photography* and *photographic,* the vowel sound in the English words *but* and *the.* But there are two important differences. First, it's longer and louder than in English, and second, you say it not with a smile, as in English, but with a kiss—that is, with your lips rounded and pushed forward. Try it: **me, te, se, le, je.** Feel the difference from English? It's worth working on now, since it's the sound that betrays most Americans trying to sound French after they've mastered everything else. So listen to both sounds and repeat the French: *the train/* **le train,** *the bus/* **le bus,** *premier/* **premier,** *the government/* **le gouvernement,** *probably/* **probablement.**

4. Not surprisingly, the vowel sound /ə/ is the sound most often left out in French. Again, it's the sound you hear in small words like **je, le, ce,** and **ne.** Like most things in French, leaving out sounds and syllables is governed by rules. So when do you and when don't you leave out a sound? It all depends on where you find it.

It's best to start with a rule of thumb that you can sharpen up later. Start by remembering the difference between *after* and *between.* Between what? Consonants, of course. Remember, you're talking about a shy, little vowel sound, the /ə/ in words like **je, me, te, ce,** and **le.** As a rule, you leave it out between two consonant sounds. Listen to these words and repeat them: **certainément, boulévard, ennémi, rapidément, samédi, pétite, achéter, lentément.**

Between any two consonants? Not exactly. It depends on where they are. The ones you just heard were somewhere in the middle of a word. But since you don't speak French in words, but in syllables within sense-groups, consonants that begin words, like the **d** in **demain,** sometimes find themselves in the middle of a meaning-group. Remember, you heard **A démain.** But if the word were alone, it would be pronounced **demain.** A few examples will clear this up. Repeat these pairs of words and phrases: **demain—à démain, le train—dans lé train, le jour—et lé jour, le dentiste—chez lé dentiste.** There are a few cases, however, where you don't have to worry very much about where the word happens to be. The most frequent is with the word **je** at the beginning of a sentence. Remember you heard **Jé dois vénir.** Now listen to the way the **je** sounds in these sentences and try to imitate it: **Jé dois venir. Jé vous en prie. Jé t'en prie. Jé le sais bien. Jé t'écoute.**

5. Now that you know when to leave out the vowel sound /ə/, all that remains is to find out when to pronounce it. When? Not *between* two consonants. Remember, you did pronounce it in the words **probablement** and **gouvernement.** That's it! *After* two consonants; after the **bl** and the **rn.** Notice that these are two consonant sounds, not consonant letters. In the **cl** in **oncle,** for example, there are two letters and two sounds, so it's **oncle.**

2 Ecoutez et lisez.

1. By now, you're probably in the habit of leaving out a lot of letters, especially the **e,** which is written but never or seldom pronounced as in the following phrases. Repeat them after me: **il aimé, il est maladé, ils disént, tu parlés.** There should be no problem here. The problem comes when the written letters are sometimes pronounced and sometimes not, depending on the rules that you just heard. You're tempted to be influenced by what you see, and you need practice in making the difference between the written and the spoken word, between what you see and what you hear. For example, repeat these phrases as you look at them in your book. You see two

syllables, but you say one: **Jє dois.** You see three syllables, but you say two: **Je lє sais.** And you see four syllables, but you say three: **Jє ne dois pas.**

2. Try reading the following half of a phone conversation. I'll say each word or phrase after you.

Allô?... Je t'écoute... Vendredi après-midi? Impossible... Samedi midi, alors... Certainement... Au Boulevard Saint-Michel?... Je sais... Au revoir. A demain.

3   **Copiez les phrases suivantes pour préparer une dictée.**

Write the following sentences from dictation. First listen to the sentence as it is read to you. Then you will hear the sentence again in short segments, with a pause after each segment to allow you time to write. Finally you will hear the sentence a third time so that you may check your work. Let's begin.

1. Moi aussi, je suis libre. Moi aussi, *(pause)* je suis libre. *(pause)* Moi aussi, je suis libre.
2. Tu veux faire de la musique? Il y a des petites guitares pour les jeunes. Tu veux faire *(pause)* de la musique? *(pause)* Il y a *(pause)* des petites guitares *(pause)* pour les jeunes. *(pause)* Tu veux faire de la musique? Il y a des petites guitares pour les jeunes.
3. Combien de fois par semaine? Combien de fois *(pause)* par semaine? *(pause)* Combien de fois par semaine?
4. On y va deux soirs par semaine et le samedi après-midi. On y va *(pause)* deux soirs par semaine *(pause)* et le samedi après-midi. *(pause)* On y va deux soirs par semaine et le samedi après-midi.
5. Je ne peux pas le faire. Je dois travailler. Je ne peux pas le faire. *(pause)* Je dois travailler. *(pause)* Je ne peux pas le faire. Je dois travailler.

VERIFIONS!

Review with students how to invite friends, to answer a negative question affirmatively, and to use independent pronouns. Then, for cooperative learning, have students pair off to work through the exercises.

For the first exercise, you might read the situations aloud and ask students to call out words of encouragement. For the second exercise, add more sentences, if needed:

Je n'____ pas ____ la question.
Tu n'____ pas ____ la leçon.
Il ____ ____ trop de café; il ne va pas dormir.

SECTION C

For cooperative learning, have students form pairs to complete the exercises. You might ask volunteers to role-play for the class the situations in the first exercise. Have other volunteers report to the class their partners' answers for the third exercise.

VOCABULAIRE

Divide the class into four groups and have each group make flashcards for a given section of the vocabulary list. Have two groups at a time test each other; then rotate the groups. You may want to create a competition and keep score.

ETUDE DE MOTS

Have two students write the pairs of words on a transparency while the others write them on their papers. Use the transparency to correct the work with the entire class.

A LIRE

OBJECTIVE   To read for practice and pleasure

UNE CHANSON : EN SORTANT DU LYCEE

Have students read the title of the song and look at the illustrations. Ask them to describe what the singer does after school, according to what they see. Then, for cooperative learning, have students work in groups to find answers to the questions in **Avant de lire.** Ask a volunteer to summarize the theme of the song. Next play the cassette as students follow along in their books. To check comprehension, write on the board or on a transparency several sentence beginnings and endings:

Elle va	de ses projets du soir.
Elle prend	de la moto.
Elle parle	une glace.
Elle écoute	de la musique.
Elle fait	au café.

Have volunteers match up the beginnings and endings to tell what the singer does after school. Then ask them what problem the singer has at the end of the song. **(Son père attend.)** Why has this happened? **(Elle rentre à la maison à sept heures. Elle est en retard.)** What will be the consequence of this? **(Elle ne peut pas aller à la patinoire.)**

Activité • Devinez

Have students begin a list of **faux amis,** if they have not already done so, with the word **pressé.** Have them brainstorm others. Suggest that they keep a special page in the vocabulary section of their notebooks for **faux amis.**

Activité • Après le lycée

As students tell the various after-school activities mentioned in the song, have them quote the line(s) where they found them.

Activité • Et vous?

Have students pair off to ask each other the questions. Call on volunteers to report to the class.

Activité • A vous maintenant!

First brainstorm with students what questions the singer's father might ask her. Write these on the board or on a transparency; have students copy them into their notebooks. Then have students reread the song lyrics, looking for answers the singer could give to these questions. Now have the students begin working in pairs. Each pair should decide what the father's reaction will be. If he is angry, students should come up with a fitting punishment other than the one the singer predicts in her song. After students have had sufficient time to practice, ask volunteers to present their dialogues to the class.

JAZZ ET ROCK

CULTURAL BACKGROUND   Today jazz has a thriving audience in France; however, interest in this form of music developed slowly in Europe at the beginning of the twentieth century. By the 1920s American jazz struck Europeans as fresh and direct. In 1932 several students, who wanted to educate the public about true jazz, founded the Hot Club in Paris, which became the most famous jazz club in history. In 1933 the Hot Club gave a series of concerts featuring lesser-known black American musicians. In 1934 its concerts featured European jazz musicians, among them Django Reinhardt, who was to have a major influence on American jazz. The popularity of jazz steadily grew in Europe. It reached its height during World War II, especially in France, where it came to represent freedom and opposition to the Nazis.

To introduce this reading selection, play recordings made by these jazz and rock musicians. Have students open their books and look at the photos of the musicians. Ask students to share with their classmates anything they might know about these men. Then read aloud the first paragraph as students follow along in their books. Next, with books closed, have students tell what they remember about Reinhardt. Go on to the second paragraph; have students read it silently. Ask several questions to check comprehension: **Charlie Christian a été d'où? Il a joué de quel instrument? Qui est Benny Goodman?** Go on to the last paragraph; ask a volunteer to read it aloud as the rest of the class follows along. With books closed, have individuals tell what they recall about Hendrix. You might write a list of words on the board or on a transparency for students to use in their summary: **noir, rock, guitare, composé, poète, Londres.**

Activité • Trouvez les dates

You might make a contest of this activity. Allow students to work in pairs. The first pair to put the events in their correct chronological order wins.

Activité • Vous avez bien lu?

Begin by reviewing numbers. Have students practice giving years in French. For additional practice, mention other years of historical importance and ask students to tell what happened.

Activité • Et vous?

CHALLENGE   Have students develop their answers to the questions into presentations for the class. Extra credit could be given.

CHAPITRE 2

Après l'école

Yes, there's life outside school! Some students would even say that life begins after school. Around the age of 15, young people in France turn from television to other interests. Music and friends take up more of their time. They like to read, go to the movies, and take part in sports.

In this unit you will:

PREMIER CONTACT	get acquainted with the topic
SECTION A	talk about recreational activities . . . invite friends
SECTION B	choose activities at a rec center . . . offer encouragement
SECTION C	talk about forming a rock group . . . ask for, give, and refuse permission
TRY YOUR SKILLS	use what you've learned
A LIRE	read for practice and pleasure

PREMIER CONTACT **getting acquainted with the topic**

The authentic material in Premier Contact introduces the theme of the unit and is to be used for global comprehension only.

1 La Maison des Jeunes et de la Culture

LA MJC ORGANISE PENDANT L'ANNEE POUR LES ADHERENTS ET LEURS AMIS :

— SPECTACLES   — COURS   — SORTIES
— CONCERTS   — BIBLIOTHEQUE   — DEBATS
— PIQUE-NIQUES   — BALS   — EXPOSITIONS
— CAFETERIA

**ASSEMBLEE GENERALE : JEUDI 19 MARS
BAL : SAMEDI 28 MARS**

SANTE PHYSIQUE

Aérobic
Un conditionnement physique sur musique avec chorégraphies

En gymnase et en piscine
45 minutes de mise en forme en gymnase
45 minutes d'exercices en piscine

DANSES

Ballet
Initiation aux techniques de base du ballet classique

Danse créative
Découverte des dominantes corps, temps, espace et mouvement par différentes techniques de danse

LANGUES

Conversation anglaise et espagnole
Niveau I : Débutant   Niveau III : Avancé
Niveau II : Intermédiaire   Niveau IV : Perfectionnement

GENERAL

Bande dessinée
Apprentissage des techniques de dessin, développement de scénario, composition des textes, etc.

Cuisine d'été
Idées originales pour la préparation de pique-nique : barbecues, salades et punchs rafraîchissants

Atelier photo
Connaissance du développement en noir et blanc
Contrôle de la lumière en prise de vues

Informatique
Cours d'initiation, atelier de perfectionnement
Programmation en basic et intelligence artificielle

> **CARTE JEUNE :**
> Aux possesseurs de la Carte Jeune, la MJC propose une réduction de 10 % sur les cours payés au trimestre et 10 % sur toutes les animations qui se déroulent au cours de l'année (Bal, soirée, Ciné, spectacles...)

**INSCRIPTION ANNUELLE : 55 FRANCS
VALABLE POUR TOUTES LES ACTIVITES**

You may wish to point out that the "MJC" is similar to American youth centers. For additional background on the "MJC", see p. T51.

2 Activité • Complétez   Possible answers are given.

1. Cette MJC est située... à Paris.
2. Les membres peuvent inviter... leurs amis.
3. La MJC organise... des spectacles, des concerts.
4. Les possesseurs de la Carte Jeune... ont une réduction de 10%.
5. Dans l'atelier photo on peut... apprendre à développer les photos en noir et blanc.
6. Le samedi 28 mars... il y a un bal.
7. Il faut payer 55 F pour... l'inscription annuelle.

3 Activité • Qu'est-ce qu'ils vont choisir à la MJC?

1. Pierre a reçu un nouvel appareil-photo.
2. Valérie et Nancy vont en Espagne cet été.
3. Pauline aime faire de la natation.
4. Les frères Dumont ont un nouvel ordinateur.
5. Nous aimons faire la cuisine.
6. Catherine est sportive.
7. Thomas aime discuter.

1. Atelier photo 2. Conversation espagnole 3. Exercices en piscine 4. Informatique
5. Cuisine d'été 6. Aérobic 7. Débats

4 Activité • Et vous? Possible answer is given.

Quelle activité choisissez-vous à la MJC? Pourquoi? Je choisis le ballet parce que j'aime danser.

5 VOULEZ-VOUS APPRENDRE A JOUER D'UN INSTRUMENT?

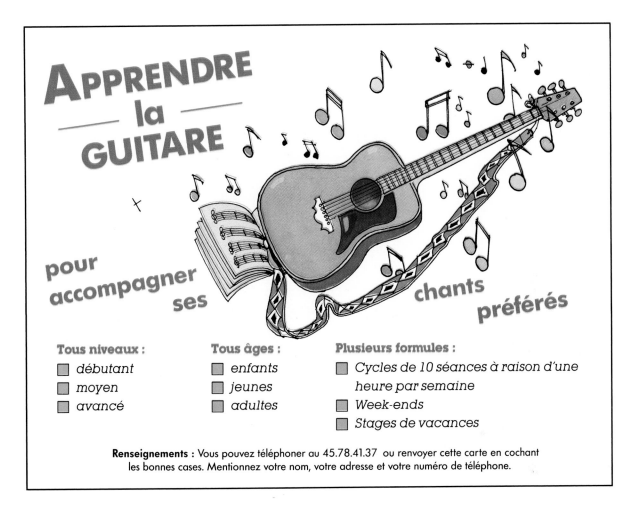

APPRENDRE la GUITARE

pour accompagner ses chants préférés

Tous niveaux :
☐ débutant
☐ moyen
☐ avancé

Tous âges :
☐ enfants
☐ jeunes
☐ adultes

Plusieurs formules :
☐ Cycles de 10 séances à raison d'une heure par semaine
☐ Week-ends
☐ Stages de vacances

Renseignements : Vous pouvez téléphoner au 45.78.41.37 ou renvoyer cette carte en cochant les bonnes cases. Mentionnez votre nom, votre adresse et votre numéro de téléphone.

6 Activité • Et vous? Possible answers are given.

Vous voulez apprendre la guitare. Relisez la publicité et répondez aux questions suivantes.

1. Quel est votre niveau? moyen
2. Dans quel groupe d'âge êtes-vous? jeunes
3. Quelle formule choisissez-vous? Pourquoi?
   Week-ends, parce que j'étudie pendant la semaine.

4. Vous voulez des renseignements.
   Qu'est-ce que vous faites? Je téléphone./
   J'envoie la carte.

7 Activité • Ecrivez Possible answer is given.

Vous voulez donner des cours pour gagner un peu d'argent. Qu'est-ce que vous pouvez donner comme cours? Des cours de guitare? De trompette? De maths? D'anglais? De danse? Ecrivez une petite annonce. Cours d'anglais. Tous niveaux. Offerts le week-end.
Renseignements : téléphoner au 38.63.01.08

talking about recreational activities . . . inviting friends

Le lycée, ce n'est pas tout. Il y a aussi une vie en dehors de l'école, une vie passionnante. Quand ils n'ont pas de devoirs, les jeunes français sortent, font du sport ou pratiquent de nombreuses activités. Il y a toujours quelque chose à faire.

A1   Après-midi libre! 📼

C'est mercredi et il est midi. Dans toute la France, les jeunes ont l'après-midi libre. Qu'est-ce qu'ils vont faire?

ROMAIN	Qu'est-ce que tu fais maintenant?
LAURE	Je vais répéter avec mon groupe de rock. Ça te plairait de venir écouter?
ROMAIN	Je ne peux pas. J'ai un entraînement de foot.

| EMMANUELLE | Tu veux venir avec nous à la piscine? |
| JULIEN | Impossible, je vais au cinéma avec une copine. |

| CÉCILE | Je vais faire des achats. Tu ne veux pas venir avec moi? |
| MARIE | Si, je veux bien. J'ai justement besoin d'acheter une paire de chaussures. |

In France, most students are free on Wednesday afternoon and have classes on Saturday morning.

CLAUDE   Ça te dit de venir regarder un film chez moi? On a un nouveau magnétoscope.

NICOLE   Non, il fait trop beau. Je vais faire une balade et prendre des photos.

CAROLINE   Ça t'intéresse de venir avec moi à la MJC?

DAMIEN   Qu'est-ce qu'on peut y faire?

CAROLINE   Des tas de choses. De la danse, de la gym, du judo… Moi, je fais du théâtre.

DAMIEN   OK, je veux bien. Mais d'abord, on va déjeuner.

THOMAS   Je ne sais pas quoi faire aujourd'hui. Tu n'as pas une idée?

ERIC   Si, viens avec nous. On fait un petit film vidéo avec des copains.

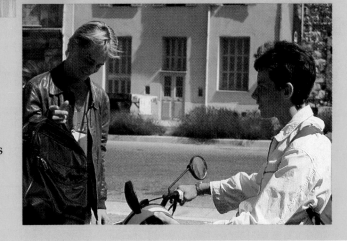

A2   Activité • Vrai ou faux?

Corrigez les phrases incorrectes d'après A1.

1. Laure et Romain vont répéter avec un groupe de rock.
2. Julien va au cinéma avec Emmanuelle.
3. Cécile et Marie vont faire des achats.
4. Claude et Nicole vont prendre des photos.
5. Caroline et Damien vont déjeuner après le théâtre.
6. Thomas et Eric n'ont pas d'idée.

1. C'est faux. Romain a un entraînement de foot. 2. C'est faux. Julien va au cinéma et Emmanuelle va à la piscine. 3. C'est vrai. 4. C'est faux. Claude va regarder un film, et Nicole va prendre des photos. 5. C'est faux. Ils vont déjeuner avant le théâtre. 6. C'est faux. Ils vont faire un petit film vidéo.

1. T. — J'ai fait un film vidéo avec des copains. Et toi? C. — Je suis allée à la MJC. 2. Cécile — J'ai fait des achats. Et toi? Claude — J'ai regardé un film. 3. E. — Je suis allée à la piscine. Et toi? M. — J'ai fait des achats. 4. L. — J'ai répété avec mon groupe rock. Et toi? J. — Je suis allé au cinéma. 5. J. — Je suis allé au cinéma. Et toi? R. — J'ai eu un entraînement de foot. 6. N. — J'ai fait une balade et j'ai pris des photos. Et toi? D. — Moi, je suis allé à la MJC avec Caroline.

A3 **Activité • A vous maintenant!**

C'est jeudi matin. Les jeunes dans A1 parlent dans la cour du lycée. Ils racontent ce qu'ils ont fait hier. Relisez A1 et préparez les dialogues avec un(e) camarade de classe.

Damien et Eric	D. — Qu'est-ce que tu as fait hier après l'école?
	E. — J'ai fait un film vidéo avec des copains. Et toi?
	D. — Moi, je suis allé à la MJC avec Caroline.

1. Caroline et Thomas **3.** Emmanuelle et Marie **5.** Julien et Romain
2. Claude et Cécile **4.** Laure et Julien **6.** Nicole et Damien

A4 **Savez-vous que... ?**

Les jeunes Français ont beaucoup d'heures de cours : de 25 à 30 heures par semaine. De plus, ils ont souvent des devoirs à faire à la maison. Ils sont donc très occupés. Mais ils trouvent quand même le temps de faire ce qui les intéresse hors de l'école. Qu'est-ce qu'ils font? Ça dépend. Ils peuvent faire du sport, mais aussi de la musique, du théâtre, du cinéma, de la photo, de l'informatique... Pour cela, ils vont au club sportif ou à la MJC. Ils veulent oublier l'ambiance de l'école, voir d'autres jeunes, faire autre chose.

A5 **COMMENT LE DIRE**
Answering a negative question affirmatively

There are two ways to say *yes* in French, **oui** and **si. Si** is used when you answer *yes* to a negative question.

Tu ne veux pas venir avec moi?	Si, je veux bien.
Tu veux venir avec moi?	Oui, je veux bien.

A6 **Activité • Si ou oui?**

Travaillez avec un(e) camarade de classe. Vous lui proposez des activités. Posez vos questions à la forme indiquée entre parenthèses. Il/Elle répond par **si** ou par **oui.** Changez de rôle.

faire une balade

— Tu veux faire une balade? *or* — Tu ne veux pas faire une balade?
— Oui, je veux bien. — Si, je veux bien.

1. prendre des photos (*affirmative*) **4.** regarder un film vidéo (*négative*)
2. faire un film vidéo (*négative*) **5.** aller au cinéma (*affirmative*)
3. faire des achats (*affirmative*) **6.** aller à la piscine (*négative*)

1. — Tu veux... ? — Oui, je veux bien. 2. — Tu ne veux pas... ? — Si, je veux bien. 3. — Tu veux... ? — Oui, je veux bien. 4. — Tu ne veux pas... ? — Si, je veux bien. 5. — Tu veux... ? — Oui, je veux bien. 6. — Tu ne veux pas... ? — Si, je veux bien.

A7 Activité • A vous maintenant! 🔲

Travaillez avec un(e) camarade de classe. Posez les questions suivantes à la forme négative. Répondez affirmativement.

1. Nous allons à la MJC cet après-midi?
2. Elle est ouverte?
3. On prend le métro?
4. On attend Philippe?
5. Tu vas faire de la gym?
6. Tu veux faire du théâtre?

1. — Nous n'allons pas à la MJC cet après-midi? — Si, allons-y!
2. — Elle n'est pas ouverte? — Si, elle est ouverte.
3. — On ne prend pas le métro? — Si, on prend le métro.
4. — On n'attend pas Philippe? — Si, on attend Philippe.
5. — Tu ne vas pas faire de gym? — Si, je vais faire de la gym.
6. — Tu ne veux pas faire de théâtre? — Si, je veux faire du théâtre.

A8 STRUCTURES DE BASE
The independent pronouns

1. You've already been using the independent pronouns **moi, toi, elle,** and **lui.** The following chart shows you all the independent pronouns and their corresponding subject pronouns. You'll notice that some are the same.

Independent Pronouns	moi	toi	lui	elle	nous	vous	eux	elles
Subject Pronouns	je	tu	il	elle	nous	vous	ils	elles

2. Independent pronouns are used . . .
   a. when there is no verb in the response. Qui? **Moi? Lui** aussi? **Elles,** non.
   b. to emphasize a noun or a pronoun. **Moi, je** fais du théâtre. **Sylvie, elle,** fait de la danse. **Eux, ils** font de la photo.
   c. after **c'est.** Qui est-ce? C'est **moi.** C'est **nous.** C'est (Ce sont) **eux.**
   d. after prepositions (**pour, sans, entre, chez, avec, loin de,** and so on). Viens **avec moi. Sans toi,** je n'y vais pas.
   e. in a compound subject. **Philippe et moi** allons au cinéma. **Jean et lui** sont au théâtre.

3. The pronoun **eux** may refer to a group of all males or a mixed group of males and females.

A9 Activité • Qu'est-ce qu'ils font après l'école? 🔲

Demandez à un(e) camarade de classe ce que vos amis font après l'école. Il/Elle répond avec les pronoms indépendants. Changez de rôle.

— Paul fait du sport? — Non, lui, il prend des photos.

Paul	faire du sport	prendre des photos
Caroline	faire des achats	faire du théâtre
Damien	faire une balade	aller à la MJC
Laure	aller au cinéma	répéter avec son groupe
Les garçons	aller à la piscine	faire de la gymnastique
Tu	faire du judo	avoir un entraînement de foot
Les filles	faire de la danse	faire une balade

— Caroline fait des achats? — Non, elle, elle fait du théâtre. / — Damien fait une balade? — Non, lui, il va à la MJC. / — Laure va au cinéma? — Non, elle, elle répète avec son groupe. /—Les garçons vont à la piscine? — Non, eux, ils font de la gymnastique. /
— Tu fais du judo? — Non, moi, j'ai un entraînement de foot. /
— Les filles font de la danse? — Non, elles, elles font une balade.

Activité • A la cafeteria 🎞️

Vous êtes à la MJC, à la cafeteria. Vous allez, avec un(e) camarade, chercher ce que vos copains ont commandé (*ordered*). Préparez les dialogues. Employez les pronoms corrects dans vos réponses.

    — C'est pour qui, la limonade? Pour Caroline?
    — Oui, c'est pour elle.

1. Oui, c'est pour lui.
2. Oui, c'est pour nous.
3. Oui, c'est pour eux.

1. Et l'eau minérale, c'est pour Damien?
2. C'est pour Philippe et toi, les sandwiches?
3. Les glaces sont pour Caroline et Damien?

4. Et les frites, c'est pour les filles?
5. C'est pour qui, le jus de fruits? Pour Anne?
6. C'est pour toi, la salade?

4. Oui, c'est pour elles. 5. Oui, c'est pour elle. 6. Oui, c'est pour moi.

A 11 Activité • Ecrit dirigé

Anne écrit un petit mot à son amie Caroline. Complétez sa lettre avec les pronoms **moi, toi, lui, elle, nous, vous, eux** ou **elles.**

```
Devine où je suis, __moi__ ! Devant un ordinateur! Brigitte et
Chantal font de l'informatique et je suis venue avec __elles__ à
la Maison des Jeunes. Je suis nulle, mais l'animateur, __lui__ ,
est très fort. Sans __lui__ , je n'y comprends rien! Il y a cinq
autres lycéens. A côté d'__eux__ je suis un vrai amateur, mais
je compose cette lettre pour __toi__ sur l'ordinateur.
Comment ça va, __toi__ ? Ecris-moi vite.
```

A 12 COMMENT LE DIRE
Inviting friends

Tu veux		Oui, je veux bien.
Tu ne veux pas		Si, je veux bien.
Ça te dit de	venir avec moi?	D'accord.
Ça t'intéresse de		Bonne idée!
Ça te plairait de		Oui, mais je ne peux pas.

A 13 Activité • A vous maintenant! 🎞️ Possible answers are given.

Vous avez envie de faire des millions de choses! Proposez à un(e) ami(e) de venir avec vous. Préparez les dialogues avec un(e) camarade de classe. Changez de rôle et variez les questions et les réponses.

    aller à la MJC   — Ça te dit d'aller à la MJC?
                         — D'accord. Bonne idée.

1. — Ça te dit de faire une balade? — Oui, mais je ne peux
2. — Ça te dit de regarder un film vidéo? — Bonne idée!
3. — Ça te dit de faire des achats? — Oui, d'accord.

1. faire une balade
2. regarder un film vidéo
3. faire des achats
4. aller au cinéma
5. venir à la piscine
6. sortir
7. prendre des photos
8. faire un film vidéo

4. — Ça te dit d'aller au cinéma? — Je veux bien. 5. — Ça te dit de venir à la piscine? — Non, je n'aime pas nager.
6. — Ça te dit de sortir? — Oui, je veux bien. 7. — Ça te dit de prendre des photos? — D'accord.
8. — Ça te dit de faire un film vidéo? — Bof!

A 14 Activité • Ecrivez Possible answer is given.

Caroline voit cette annonce à la porte du
théâtre dans la MJC. Elle écrit un petit mot à
Damien. Elle lui propose de prendre ce cours
avec elle. Qu'est-ce qu'elle écrit?
Damien, ça t'intéresse de faire du théâtre à la MJC?
C'est le mercredi et le samedi. Ça commence le
18 septembre.

ACTEURS! ACTRICES!
Vous aimez le théâtre?
Venez nombreux
le mercredi de 14 h à 16 h
le samedi de 15 h à 17 h.
Premier cours le mercredi
18 septembre.
Animateur : Jacques Blanc

A 15 Activité • A vous maintenant!

Vous téléphonez à un(e) ami(e) pour lui demander de sortir avec vous. Vous lui parlez de ces
trois spectacles et vous lui demandez s'il (si elle) veut venir avec vous. Avant de choisir, votre
ami(e) vous pose des questions : C'est à quelle heure? C'est où? C'est combien?... Commencez
par : «Tu veux sortir samedi?»

CONCERT!
EN PLEIN AIR
Place du Vieux
Marché
Groupe de
rock :
Jastro et le
New Look

Entrée gratuite — tout
le monde est invité —
surtout les lycéens.

SAMEDI 17 MAI
19h.30

MJC
de Paris
Notre aventure
en Inde
en photos
2 frères, de 18 et 19 ans,
ont réalisé un

superbe reportage-
photo en Inde

*Soirée projection, suivie
d'une réception amicale*

GRATUIT   17 MAI 20h.30

Cinéma Odéon
12, rue de la
Vieille Horloge

Soirée Jeunes 10 F
L'Extra-Terrestre
précédé de 3
nouveaux dessins
animés.

BOISSONS GRATUITES
*Invitez tous
vos copains*

SAMEDI 17 MAI
20 h. 00

A 16 Activité • Ecoutez bien   For script and answers, see pp. T50–51.

Vous allez écouter des dialogues. Une personne propose à une autre de faire quelque chose.
Dites si la deuxième personne accepte ou refuse.

Après l'école   59

Dans une Maison des Jeunes et de la Culture (MJC), on peut faire du théâtre, de la danse, de la musique, du judo et surtout rencontrer des jeunes. Il y a toujours une bonne ambiance.

B1

A la Maison des Jeunes

enrolled

Damien et Caroline sont maintenant inscrits. Ils ont commencé leur cours. Entrons dans la MJC et observons.

(A l'accueil) *reception desk*

PHILIPPE	Bonjour, mademoiselle. Qu'est-ce que vous avez comme cours de musique? J'ai envie d'apprendre à jouer d'un instrument.
L'ANIMATRICE *activity leader*	Nous avons d'excellents cours de trompette pour débutants, le mardi et le jeudi soir.
PHILIPPE	C'est combien?
L'ANIMATRICE	Deux cent cinquante francs par mois.
PHILIPPE	Il faut aussi acheter sa trompette?
L'ANIMATRICE	Bien sûr.
PHILIPPE	Oh, ça va faire cher! Vous n'avez pas plutôt des cours de flûte?

La MJC est ouverte toute la journée de 10 h 00 à 22 h 00.

Damien et Caroline répètent une pièce de théâtre.

(Au cours de théâtre)

DAMIEN	«Hélas, madame, je dois partir…
CAROLINE	Monsieur! Déjà? Vous ne m'aimez plus?
DAMIEN	Si, madame, énormément, mais j'ai un train à deux heures pour la Russie.»

Point out that in the verb "répéter," the second é sometimes changes to è. Compare to "préférer."

L'ANIMATRICE Non, Damien, non! Ne regarde pas Caroline. Regarde le public, droit devant toi. Et toi, Caroline, parle plus fort. Recommencez, s'il vous plaît.

CAROLINE Mais, mademoiselle, c'est la cinquième fois!

L'ANIMATRICE Encore un petit effort!

Roland fait une prise à son adversaire.

(Au cours de judo)

L'ANIMATEUR Non, non, ce n'est pas bien! Regarde-moi. Comme ça. Mets la main gauche sur son épaule droite. Tu comprends? Reprends maintenant.

Mireille va au cours de danse deux soirs par semaine et le samedi après-midi.

(Au cours de danse)

L'ANIMATRICE Plus haut, la jambe, plus haut!… Plus vite!… Mais non! Ecoute la musique.

MIREILLE Je n'y arrive pas!

L'ANIMATRICE Mais si!

MIREILLE Non, c'est trop rapide pour moi!

L'ANIMATRICE Allez! Tu y es presque! On reprend. Encore une fois!

D'après B1, ces phrases ne sont pas vraies. Corrigez les erreurs.

1. Caroline et Damien pratiquent un sport.
2. Philippe veut faire du théâtre.
3. Philippe va prendre des cours de trompette.
4. L'animateur de judo est content de Roland.
5. Mireille ne danse pas souvent.
6. Mireille danse très bien.

1. Ils font du théâtre.   2. Il veut faire de la trompette.   3. Il va prendre des cours de flûte.   4. L'animateur de judo n'est pas content de Roland.   5. Elle danse trois jours par semaine.   6. C'est trop rapide pour elle.

B3 Activité • Et vous?   Possible answers are given.

1. Quand est-ce que vous êtes libre pour faire ce que vous aimez?   Je suis libre...
2. Qu'est-ce que vous faites en dehors de l'école?   Je fais... / Je joue...
3. Est-ce qu' il y a un centre de jeunes dans votre ville?   Oui, il y a...
4. Quelles activités est-ce qu'on y propose?   On y propose...
5. Est-ce que vous y allez? Souvent? Avec des amis?   J'y vais... / Je n'y vais pas.

B4 AUTRES ACTIVITES 🎞

Les maisons des jeunes de la ville de Paris offrent une variété d'activités. Qu'est-ce que vous voulez faire?

1.
Faites de la philatélie!

2.
Faites de la peinture!

3.
Jouez aux échecs!

4.
Faites de la musculation!

5.
Faites de la poterie!

6.
Jouez aux dames!

Remind students of the correct prepositions: "faire + de" and "jouer + à."

B5 Activité • Ecoutez bien 🎞   For script and answers, see pp. T52–53.

Ecoutez la conversation et ensuite complétez les phrases suivantes.

1. Le garçon a envie de…
   a. faire du théâtre.
   b. apprendre la guitare.
   c. faire du sport.
2. Il peut faire…
   a. du karaté.
   b. du foot.
   c. du basket.
3. Le judo coûte…
   a. six cent francs.
   b. sept cent francs.
   c. cinq cent francs.
4. Le garçon trouve que le judo est…
   a. génial.
   b. cher.
   c. difficile.
5. Il choisit le ping-pong parce que…
   a. ce n'est pas cher.
   b. il est libre le soir.
   c. il aime mieux le ping-pong.

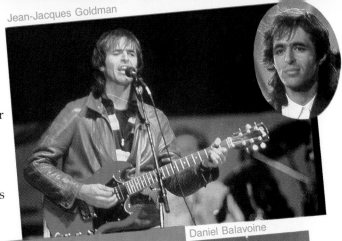
Jean-Jacques Goldman

B6 Savez-vous que… ?

De la musique avant toute chose! C'est le passe-temps favori des jeunes français. Branchés sur leur radio FM, leur stéréo ou leur baladeur *(Walkman),* ils écoutent toutes sortes de musique : funk, new-wave, chanson, classique. Ils apprécient le rock anglo-saxon, mais ils aiment aussi bien les chanteurs (Renaud, Jean-Jacques Goldman) et les groupes (Indochine, Carte de Séjour) français.

Daniel Balavoine

1

Parmi les activités suivantes, quelle est celle que, personnellement, vous préférez?

	%		%
Ecouter de la musique chez vous	24	Faire du sport	17,5
Aller écouter des concerts	12	La lecture	11
Jouer de la musique	10	La télévision	1,5
Le cinéma	22,5	Autres	1,5
		Total musique	**46**

2

Ecoutez-vous de la musique classique?

	%
Parfois	**60**
Régulièrement	**22**
Jamais	18

3

Quelle somme consacrez-vous chaque mois à la musique?

	%
Moins de 50 F	**43,5**
50 F à 100 F	**45**
100 F à 150 F	7,5
Plus de 150 F	4

Jean-Michel Jarre

4

Vous devez passer une année sur une île déserte et vous avez le droit d'emporter un disque (un seul). Lequel choisissez-vous?

GARÇONS	%	FILLES	%
Dire Straits	**7,8**	**Goldman**	**8,1**
Cure	6,7	Renaud	6,1
Renaud	5,8	Balavoine	5,8
Indochine	3,1	Indochine	3,5
Goldman	3,1	Cure	3,1
Sade	2,5	Sting	2,7
Balavoine	2,5	Sade	2
Jean-Michel Jarre	2,5	Jean-Michel Jarre	2
Pink Floyd	2,5	Dépêche Mode	1,9
Sting	2,2		

Indochine

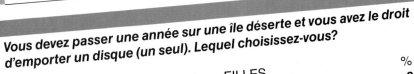

Activité • Et vous? Possible answers are given.

Aimez-vous la musique? Répondez aux questions suivantes. Ensuite posez les questions à un(e) camarade de classe.

1. Quel est le dernier disque que vous avez acheté? Ou la dernière cassette? C'est le...
2. Combien d'argent dépensez-vous *(spend)* chaque mois en musique (disques, cassettes, concerts, etc.)? Je dépense...
3. Quel est le dernier concert que vous êtes allé(e) écouter? Je suis allé(e) écouter...
4. Regardez-vous des émissions musicales à la télévision? Quelles émissions préférez-vous? Je regarde... Je préfère...
5. Trouvez-vous votre information musicale dans un journal ou dans un magazine? Quel journal? Quel magazine? Je trouve mon information dans...
6. Ecoutez-vous de la musique classique? Régulièrement? Quelquefois? Jamais? J'écoute... / Je n'écoute pas...
7. Vous devez passer une année sur une île déserte et vous avez le droit *(the right)* d'emporter un seul disque. Quel disque choisissez-vous? Je choisis...

Have the students compare their answers to the polls in B6.

B 8 VOUS EN SOUVENEZ-VOUS?

You've already learned the irregular verb **prendre.**

prendre	*to take*					
Je	**prends**	du lait.	Nous	**prenons**	du lait.
Tu	**prends**	l'autobus.	Vous	**prenez**	l'autobus.
Il/Elle/On	**prend**		Ils/Elles	**prennent**	

The past participle of **prendre** is **pris: Elles ont pris l'autobus.**

Note that "prendre des cours" may be used when talking about taking non-academic courses, which are commonly spoken of in the plural: "Je prends des cours de musique." "Suivre" may be used with academic or non-academic courses, either singular or plural: "Je suis un cours de maths." The verb "suivre" is presented in Unit 7, p. 249.

B 9 STRUCTURES DE BASE
The verbs apprendre *and* comprendre

1. **Apprendre,** *to learn,* and **comprendre,** *to understand,* are compounds of the verb **prendre.** They follow the same pattern as **prendre.**

apprendre	*to learn*				
J'	**apprends**	la trompette.	Nous	**apprenons**	la trompette.
Tu	**apprends**		Vous	**apprenez**	
Il/Elle/On	**apprend**		Ils/Elles	**apprennent**	

comprendre	*to understand*				
Je	**comprends**	bien.	Nous	**comprenons**	bien.
Tu	**comprends**		Vous	**comprenez**	
Il/Elle/On	**comprend**		Ils/Elles	**comprennent**	

2. As you might expect, the past participles of **apprendre** and **comprendre** resemble that of **prendre: appris, compris. Tu as appris la danse? Je n'ai pas bien compris.**
3. The verb **apprendre** is followed by the preposition **à** before the infinitive of another verb: **J'apprends à danser.**

Activité • Complétez

Complétez cette conversation avec les formes correctes de **prendre, apprendre** ou **comprendre**.

— Vous ____ des cours de musique? prenez
— Oui, nous ____ à jouer de la trompette. apprenons
— Et toi, Roland, tu ____ quels cours? prends
— Je ____ des cours de judo. prends
— C'est difficile?
— Quelquefois, je ne ____ pas très bien l'animateur. comprends
— L'année dernière, j'ai ____ le judo. Mais j'ai tout oublié. pris

B 11 Activité • Ils ne sont pas très bons 📼

Vos amis prennent des cours. Qu'est-ce qu'ils apprennent à faire?

1.

Elle apprend à jouer de la flûte.

2.

Ils apprennent à danser.

3.

Il apprend à faire de la planche à voile.

B 12 Activité • Ecrit dirigé

L'animateur de judo à la MJC parle de ses élèves. Complétez le texte en employant les formes correctes des verbes **apprendre** ou **comprendre**.

                    apprendre   comprennent
        «Mes élèves veulent ____ le judo, mais ils ne ____ pas mes instructions. Sauf une fille,
comprend Sophie! Elle ____ tout! Elle est vraiment extraordinaire! Hier, en deux minutes, elle ____ la a appris
nouvelle prise. Les autres ont mis une heure pour ____. Roland, lui, n' ____ pas ____!»
                              apprendre   a   compris

B 13 Activité • A vous maintenant!

Demandez à un(e) camarade de classe ce qu'il/elle apprend à l'école. Dites-lui ce que vous y apprenez. Demandez-lui aussi ce qu'il/elle a envie d'apprendre.
— Qu'est-ce que tu apprends à l'école?   — Moi, j'apprends...
— Qu'est-ce que tu as envie d'apprendre?

B 14 Activité • Ecrivez

Vous voulez inscrire votre petite sœur à un cours de musique. Ecrivez votre dialogue avec l'animateur ou l'animatrice de la MJC. Vous voulez savoir quels cours on propose, les heures, les jours et le prix, si on peut louer ou s'il faut acheter son instrument. Commencez par demander :
«Qu'est-ce que vous avez comme cours de musique?»   Other questions: C'est offert à quelle heure? Et quels jours? C'est combien? Il faut acheter l'instrument? Vous avez des cours pour les débutants?

COMMENT LE DIRE
Offering encouragement

Vas-y!	Go for it!
C'est bien!	Yes, that's fine!
Mais si, ça vient!	Of course, it's coming along!
Tu y es presque!	You're almost there!
Mais oui, tu y arrives!	OK, you're getting there!
Continue!	Keep going!
Encore un petit effort!	A little more effort!

B16 Activité • **Encouragez votre ami** Possible answers are given.

Jean-Pierre fait du ski pour la première fois. Encouragez-le.

1.

Continue!

2.

Vas-y!

3.

Encore un petit effort!

4.

C'est bien!

B17 Activité • **A vous maintenant!** Possible answers are given.

Votre ami(e) est découragé(e). Encouragez-le(la). Travaillez avec un(e) camarade de classe. L'un(e) de vous lit une des phrases; l'autre répond par une phrase d'encouragement.

1. Je n'y arrive pas!
2. Je n'ai pas compris!
3. C'est trop compliqué pour moi!
4. Je suis trop fatigué(e)!
5. Je suis nul(le)!
6. C'est trop difficile!

1. Mais si, ça vient!   2. Tu y es presque!   3. Continue!
4. Encore un petit effort!   5. Mais non, tu y arrives!   6. Tu y es presque!

talking about forming a rock group . . . asking for, giving, and refusing permission

Avez-vous déjà rêvé de former votre propre groupe de rock et de faire un disque? Laure, une jeune fille de 15 ans, a le même rêve.

C1 Comment monter un groupe de rock?

Laure joue de la guitare depuis quatre ans. Elle a déjà écrit des chansons. Elle est ambitieuse et elle rêve de faire un disque. Cette année, elle a décidé de monter un groupe de rock. Elle essaie de persuader sa mère.

LAURE — Maman, je voudrais monter un groupe de rock. Tu es d'accord?

MAMAN — Quelle idée! Comment est-ce que tu vas avoir le temps de faire tes études et de monter un groupe?

LAURE — Tu vas voir, maman, je peux faire les deux.

MAMAN — Fais attention; tu dois passer ton bac. L'année dernière tes notes n'ont pas été brillantes. Tu peux répéter avec ton groupe pendant les vacances et peut-être un week-end par mois. Ça, je veux bien.

LAURE — Mais nous devons répéter deux fois par semaine, au moins!

MAMAN — Pas question. Tu dois d'abord étudier.

LAURE — C'est ton dernier mot?

MAMAN — Oui.

LAURE — Les Rolling Stones n'ont pas demandé la permission à leurs mères pour jouer!

The Rolling Stones: a popular English rock band, formed in 1962.

C2 Activité • Répondez

1. Est-ce que Laure apprend à jouer de la guitare?
2. Qu'est-ce qu'elle rêve de faire?
3. Qu'est-ce qu'elle a décidé?
4. Quelles sont les objections de sa mère?
5. Quel est le dernier mot de sa mère?
6. Qui sont les Rolling Stones?

1. Non, elle joue de la guitare depuis quatre ans.
2. Elle rêve de faire un disque.
3. Elle a décidé de monter un groupe de rock.
4. Elle doit faire ses études parce qu'elle doit passer son bac.

5. Elle doit d'abord étudier.
6. Les Rolling Stones, c'est un groupe anglais très célèbre.

Après l'école   67

Activité • Et vous?   Possible answers are given.

1. Etes-vous ambitieux/ambitieuse? Je suis...
2. Qu'est-ce que vous rêvez de faire? Je rêve de...
3. Est-ce que vous jouez de la guitare? Oui, je joue... /Non, je ne joue pas...
4. Est-ce que vous avez déjà essayé de persuader votre mère?
   Pour quoi faire? Qu'est-ce qu'elle a répondu? Oui, j'ai essayé de... /Non, je n'ai pas encore...
5. L'année dernière, vos notes ont-elles été bonnes ou mauvaises? Elles ont été...
6. Est-ce que vous avez le temps de faire vos études et aussi de faire autre chose?
   Qu'est-ce que vous faites? J'ai le temps de... /Je n'ai pas le temps de...

C4   STRUCTURES DE BASE
The verb devoir

The following chart gives you the present-tense forms of the irregular verb **devoir.**

devoir		*to have to, must*		
Je	**dois**		Nous	**devons**	
Tu	**dois**	étudier.	Vous	**devez**	étudier.
Il/Elle/On	**doit**		Ils/Elles	**doivent**	

The past participle of devoir is **dû: J'ai dû acheter une guitare.** The verb **devoir** is often followed by the infinitive of another verb: **Tu dois passer ton bac.**

Point out that "devoir" follows the same pattern as "recevoir" in the present tense.

C5   Activité • Vouloir ou devoir?

Laure et sa mère ne sont pas d'accord. Qu'est-ce que Laure veut faire? Qu'est-ce qu'elle doit faire? Trouvez au moins deux choses dans C1.

   Laure veut… mais elle doit…

C6   Activité • Et vous?

Qu'est-ce que vous voulez faire? Qu'est-ce que vous devez faire? Faites des listes. Trouvez au moins six choses.

   Je veux…   Je dois…

C7   Activité • Ecrit dirigé   You may wish to remind students that d' will change to un in 3.

Qu'est-ce qu'ils doivent faire? Ecrivez des phrases complètes avec le verbe **devoir.**

   Laure ne fait pas d'études.   1. Ils doivent regarder le public.
   Elle doit faire des études.   2. Elle doit parler assez/plus fort.
                                     3. Nous devons faire un effort.

1. Damien et Caroline ne regardent pas le public.   4. Vous n'écoutez pas la musique.
2. Caroline ne parle pas assez fort.   5. Tu ne répètes pas.
3. Nous ne faisons pas d'effort.   6. Je n'étudie pas.

4. Vous devez écouter la musique.   5. Tu dois répéter.   6. Je dois étudier.

COMMENT LE DIRE
Asking for, giving, and refusing permission

ASKING	GIVING	REFUSING
Je peux . . . , s'il vous (te) plaît? Je voudrais . . . Vous êtes (Tu es) d'accord?	Oui, si vous voulez (tu veux). Je veux bien. Oui, pourquoi pas? D'accord. Bonne idée. Oui, bien sûr.	Quelle idée! Non, c'est mon dernier mot. C'est impossible. Non, je ne veux pas. Non, je refuse. (Il n'en est) pas question.

C9   Activité • A la place des parents   Possible answers are given.

Un(e) camarade de classe joue le rôle de Laure. Vous êtes son père ou sa mère. Donnez votre permission ou refusez. Changez de rôle.

1. Maman, le groupe peut répéter dans ma chambre? Oui, si vous voulez.
2. Je peux inviter cinq copains à la répétition? Non, c'est impossible.
3. Papa, nous pouvons laisser nos instruments dans le garage? Pas question!
4. Je voudrais offrir des boissons aux musiciens. Vous êtes d'accord? Oui, bien sûr.
5. Nous pouvons écouter des cassettes dans le living? Oui, pourquoi pas?
6. Je peux téléphoner aux Etats-Unis à un producteur américain? Quelle idée!

C10   Activité • A vous maintenant!   Possible answers are given.

Travaillez avec un(e) camarade. Votre camarade joue le rôle de votre mère ou de votre père. Faites un dialogue pour demander et donner la permission.
1. — Je peux... — Oui, si tu veux.
2. — Je peux... — Oui, pourquoi pas?

    monter un groupe de rock   — Je peux monter un groupe de rock?
                                   — Oui, je veux bien.

3. — Je peux... — D'accord. Bonne idée.   4. — Je voudrais... Tu es d'accord?—Oui, bien sûr.

1. sortir jeudi soir   4. répéter avec mon groupe
2. faire du théâtre   5. écouter des cassettes dans le living
3. prendre des cours de judo   6. téléphoner aux Etats-Unis

5. — Je peux... — Oui, bien sûr.   6. — Je voudrais... Vous êtes d'accord? — Oui, pourquoi pas?

Ensuite, demandez la permission et refusez. Utilisez les raisons suivantes pour justifier votre refus.

Ta mère regarde la télévision.

Tu dois faire tes devoirs.

Tu dois passer ton bac.

C'est trop dangereux.

Ta grand-mère vient dîner.

C'est trop cher.

1. — Non, ta grand-mère vient dîner.   2. — Non, tu dois faire tes devoirs.   3. — Non, c'est trop dangereux.
4. — Non, tu dois passer ton bac.   5. — Non, ta mère regarde la télévision.   6. — Non, c'est trop cher.

Laure a mis une annonce dans son lycée pour trouver des musiciens.

BERNARD   Allô? Je suis bien au 45.65.34.42?
LAURE   Oui.
BERNARD   Bonjour. Je m'appelle Bernard Dufour. Je téléphone au sujet de l'annonce.
LAURE   Tu es musicien?
BERNARD   Je suis bassiste.

Guitariste et chanteuse, 15 ans, cherche bon(ne)s musiciens (nes) pour monter un groupe de rock.

Tél. : 45.65.34.42

LAURE   Merveilleux! Ça fait longtemps que tu joues de la basse?
BERNARD   J'en joue depuis deux ans.
LAURE   Bon. Quand est-ce que tu peux répéter?
BERNARD   Pendant le week-end seulement.
LAURE   Ça va, moi aussi.
BERNARD   Où est-ce qu'on répète?
LAURE   J'ai un local au 44, rue Lafayette. C'est le garage d'une amie. Samedi à dix heures, ça va?
BERNARD   C'est d'accord.

C12 Activité • Complétez

Laure prend des notes en répondant au téléphone. Complétez les phrases.

1. Le garçon s'appelle... Bernard.
2. Il est... bassiste.
3. Il joue... depuis... de la basse... 2 ans.
4. Il peut répéter... le week-end.
5. On va répéter... samedi à dix heures, dans un garage au 44, rue Lafayette.

C13 Activité • Qu'est-ce qu'il faut faire?

Pour monter un groupe de rock, il y a beaucoup de choses à faire. Mettez ces choses dans le bon ordre.

Il faut...

3 1. chercher un local
2 2. persuader sa mère
6 3. faire un disque

4 4. mettre une annonce
1 5. apprendre à jouer d'un instrument
5 6. répéter très souvent

Activité • Ecrit dirigé

Ce texte n'est pas entièrement vrai. Faites les changements nécessaires.

de la guitare   rock   n'est pas

Laure joue ~~du piano~~ depuis trois ans. Elle rêve de monter un groupe de ~~jazz~~. Sa mère ~~est~~

ne peut pas d'accord. Laure ~~peut~~ répéter tous les soirs de la semaine. Elle met une annonce dans son

lycée/Un/Ils ~~immeuble~~. ~~Une~~ bassiste lui téléphone. ~~Elles~~ prennent rendez-vous pour le ~~dimanche~~ à ~~neuf~~

heures. ~~Elles~~ vont répéter dans ~~la chambre de Laure~~.   samedi   dix

Ils   un garage

C15 STRUCTURES DE BASE
The pronoun en

1. The object pronoun **en** is used to refer to things. It stands for a phrase beginning with **de, du, de la, de l',** or **des.**

Laure joue	**de la guitare.**	Elle	**en**	joue.
Elle prend	**des cours.**	Elle	**en**	prend.
Elle rêve	**de faire un disque.**	Elle	**en**	rêve.
Elle a envie	**de monter un groupe.**	Elle	**en**	a envie.
Elle a déjà écrit	**des chansons.**	Elle	**en**	a déjà écrit.

2. **En** comes immediately before the verb to which its meaning is tied. In an affirmative command, however, it immediately follows the verb and, in writing, is separated from it by a hyphen.

Elle	**en** prend.			
Elle n'	**en** prend	pas.		
Elle	**en** a pris.		*but,*	**Prends-en!**
Elle n'	**en** a pas pris.			**Prenez-en!**
Elle veut	**en** prendre.			
N'	**en** prends	pas.		

3. **Liaison** is obligatory . . .

   a. when **en** follows an affirmative command: **Prends-en.** Note the **liaison** in **Parles-en: -er** verbs, which normally have no final **-s** in the singular command, take one before **en.**

   b. when **en** is followed by a verb form beginning with a vowel sound: **J'en ai pris.**

C16 Activité • Répondez 📼

Répondez aux questions en employant le pronom **en.**

1. Est-ce que les jeunes prennent des cours à la MJC? Oui, ils en prennent.
2. Est-ce que Philippe veut jouer de la trompette? Non, il ne veut pas en jouer.
3. Est-ce que Roland fait du judo?
   Non, il n'en fait pas.
4. Est-ce que Mireille fait de la danse? Oui, elle en fait.
5. Est-ce que Bernard joue de la basse? Oui, il en joue.
6. Est-ce que Damien et Caroline font du théâtre? Oui, ils en font.

Vous jouez de quels instruments?

De la batterie?

De la guitare électrique?

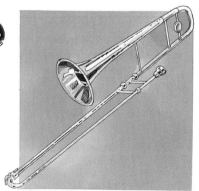

Du trombone?

De la clarinette?

Du piano?

Du saxophone?

C18 Activité • Interrogez vos camarades

Regardez les instruments dans C17. Posez des questions à vos camarades.

— Tu joues de la batterie?
— Oui, j'en joue. (Non, je n'en joue pas.)

C19 COMMENT LE DIRE
Asking and telling how long something has been going on

QUESTION	ANSWER
Tu joues de la basse depuis combien de temps?	Depuis deux ans. J'en joue depuis deux ans.
Ça fait combien de temps que tu joues de la basse?	Ça fait deux ans. Ça fait deux ans que j'en joue.

French uses the present tense where English uses the present perfect tense: **Je joue depuis...,** **Ça fait... que je joue.** *I have been playing for . . .*

Note that you may also use the "passé composé" in the French: "Ça fait deux mois que je n'ai pas vu mon copain." "Je n'ai pas vu mon copain depuis deux mois." I have not seen my friend for two months.

C20 Activité • Ça fait combien de temps?

Laure reçoit plusieurs réponses à son annonce. Elle veut avoir des renseignements sur les musiciens. Qu'est-ce qu'elle leur demande? Qu'est-ce qu'ils répondent? Préparez les questions et les réponses avec un(e) camarade de classe. Remind students that en replaces de expressions.

— Ça fait combien de temps que tu joues de la basse?
— Ça fait deux ans que j'en joue.

1. jouer de la basse / deux ans
2. être musicien / quatre ans
3. jouer de la guitare / six ans

1. ...tu joues... ? / ...que j'en joue.
2. ...tu es... ? / ...que je suis musicien.
3. ...tu joues... ? / ...que j'en joue.

4. rêver de monter un groupe / longtemps
5. apprendre à jouer de la trompette / un an
6. être bassiste / deux ans

4. ...tu rêves... ? / ...que j'en rêve.
5. ...tu apprends... ? / ...que j'apprends à en jouer.
6. ...tu es... ? / ...que je suis bassiste.

C21 Activité • A vous maintenant!

Demandez à un(e) camarade de classe ce qu'il/elle fait comme passe-temps. Ensuite, demandez-lui depuis combien de temps il/elle fait ça.

— Qu'est-ce que tu fais comme passe-temps?
— …
— Tu… depuis combien de temps?
(Ça fait combien de temps que tu… ?)

C22 Activité • Et vous?

1. Jouez-vous d'un instrument ou rêvez-vous d'en jouer?
2. De quel instrument?
3. Depuis combien de temps en jouez-vous ou rêvez-vous d'en jouer ?
4. Avez-vous un(e) ami(e) qui joue d'un instrument?
5. De quel instrument joue-t-il/elle?
6. Depuis combien de temps?

C23 Activité • Ecrit dirigé
Possible answers are given.

Répondez aux questions suivantes pour décrire votre groupe favori. Ecrivez vos réponses en forme de paragraphe.

1. Comment s'appelle votre groupe favori?
2. Depuis combien de temps est-ce que ces musiciens jouent ensemble?
3. Depuis combien de temps aimez-vous ce groupe?
4. Pourquoi est-ce que vous aimez ce groupe?
5. Êtes-vous déjà allé(e) à un de leurs concerts?
6. Est-ce que vos parents aiment aussi ce groupe? Pourquoi? Pourquoi pas?

Un groupe francophone des Antilles : KASSAV

Mon groupe favori s'appelle Kassav. Ils jouent ensemble depuis 12 ans. Ça fait un an que j'aime ce groupe. C'est un groupe antillais, et j'adore la musique des Antilles. Je suis allé(e) à deux de leurs concerts. Mes parents n'aiment pas Kassav. Ils préfèrent Mozart et Beethoven.

Savez-vous que... ? 📼

En France, beaucoup de jeunes jouent d'un instrument. Ils peuvent apprendre dans un conservatoire (pour le classique), dans une MJC ou avec un professeur privé. Certains montent des groupes. Ils commencent avec des amis, ou bien ils mettent une petite annonce dans leur lycée ou dans une revue musicale. Le plus difficile, c'est de trouver un local pour répéter, surtout en ville. Après, on peut jouer pour le plaisir ou pour faire un disque. Mais il faut travailler dur; la concurrence est rude!

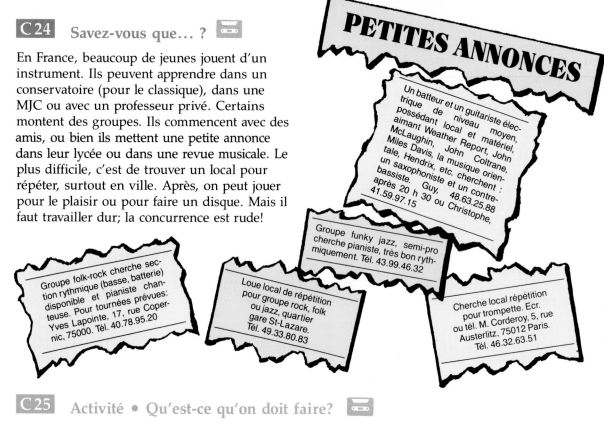

PETITES ANNONCES

Un batteur et un guitariste électrique de niveau moyen, possédant local et matériel, aimant Weather Report, John McLaughin, John Coltrane, Miles Davis, la musique orientale, Hendrix, etc. cherchent : un saxophoniste et un contrebassiste. Guy, 48.63.25.88 après 20 h 30 ou Christophe, 41.59.97.15

Groupe funky jazz, semi-pro cherche pianiste, très bon rythmiquement. Tél. 43.99.46.32

Groupe folk-rock cherche section rythmique (basse, batterie) disponible et pianiste chanteuse. Pour tournées prévues: Yves Lapointe, 17, rue Copernic, 75000. Tél. 40.78.95.20

Loue local de répétition pour groupe rock, folk ou jazz, quartier gare St-Lazare. Tél. 49.33.80.83

Cherche local répétition pour trompette. Ecr. ou tél. M. Corderoy, 5, rue Austerlitz, 75012 Paris. Tél. 46.32.63.51

C25 **Activité • Qu'est-ce qu'on doit faire?** 📼

Laure a écrit une liste des choses à faire. Faites des phrases complètes avec le verbe **devoir.**

> moi – chercher un local
> Bernard – trouver un autre guitariste
> Philippe et moi – écrire des chansons
> Bernard et Marie-Hélène – faire de la publicité
> Marie-Hélène – téléphoner à un producteur

Je dois chercher un local. Bernard doit trouver un autre guitariste. Phillippe et moi, nous devons écrire des chansons. Bernard et Marie-Hélène doivent faire de la publicité. Marie-Hélène doit téléphoner à un producteur.

C26 **Activité • Ecoutez bien** 📼 For script and answers, see p. T59.

Ecoutez le dialogue et choisissez la bonne réponse.

1. Benjamin est **a.** guitariste **b.** chanteur **c.** bassiste.
2. Il joue d'un instrument depuis **a.** longtemps **b.** trois ans **c.** trois mois.
3. Guy a envie de **a.** faire un disque **b.** jouer de la basse **c.** monter un groupe.
4. Benjamin rêve de **a.** monter un groupe **b.** faire du foot **c.** faire un disque.
5. Guy joue **a.** de la guitare **b.** de la batterie **c.** de la basse.
6. Guy et Benjamin peuvent répéter **a.** le week-end et deux soirs par semaine
   b. les autres soirs **c.** le week-end.

Voici une chanson composée par Laure.

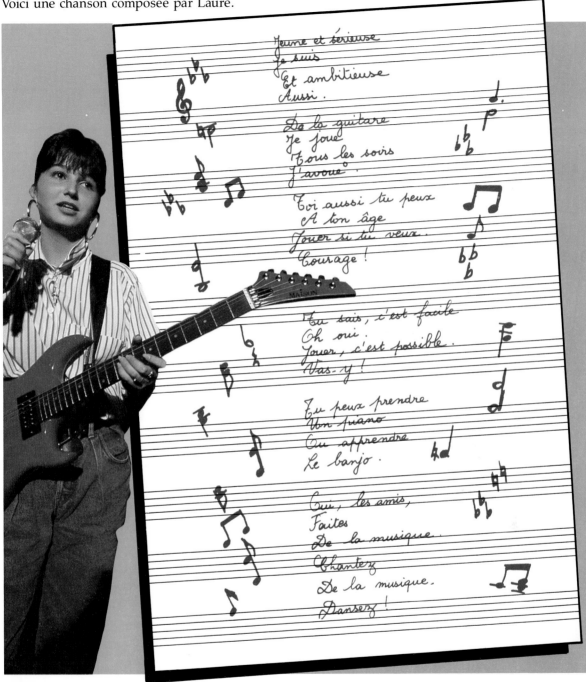

Jeune et sérieuse
Je suis
Et ambitieuse
Aussi.

De la guitare
Je joue
Tous les soirs
J'avoue.

Toi aussi tu peux
À ton âge
Jouer si tu veux.
Courage !

Tu sais, c'est facile
Oh oui.
Jouer, c'est possible.
Vas-y !

Tu peux prendre
Un piano
Ou apprendre
Le banjo.

Oui, les amis,
Faites
De la musique.
Chantez
De la musique.
Dansez !

C28   Activité • Le personnage de Laure   Possible answer is given.

Maintenant, vous connaissez Laure. En quelques phrases, décrivez-la. Dites ce qu'elle fait
et quels sont ses rêves.   Laure est jeune, sérieuse et ambitieuse. Elle joue de la guitare.
Elle rêve de monter un groupe de rock et de faire un disque.

avoue *admit*

Après l'école   75

1 Devant la Maison des Jeunes

Ts : tous

Caroline et Damien regardent le programme de la MJC. Quels cours choisir?

GYM-DANSE

Christine Boudreau

De la danse
De la gymnastique

Horaires :

Lundi 17h45 – 18h30 Ts niveaux
18h30 – 19h15 Ts niveaux

Jeudi 17h45 – 18h30 Ts niveaux
18h30 – 19h15 Ts niveaux

DAMIEN   Ça t'intéresse de faire de la gym-danse?
CAROLINE   Qu'est-ce que c'est, la gym-danse?
DAMIEN   Je ne sais pas. De la gymnastique avec de la danse.
CAROLINE   On peut essayer, non?

CLAQUETTES° AMÉRICAINES

Sarah Antonio

Horaires :

Lundi	18h00 – 19h30	Moyens
	19h30 – 21h00	Débutants/Moyens
Mardi	18h00 – 19h30	Avancés
	19h30 – 21h00	Débutants
Jeudi	14h00 – 15h30	Débutants
	18h00 – 19h30	Moyens/Avancés
Samedi	10h00 – 11h30	Moyens
	11h30 – 13h00	Débutants

CAROLINE   Ça te plairait d'aller au cours de claquettes américaines?
DAMIEN   Quelle différence il y a avec les claquettes françaises?
CAROLINE   Il n'y a pas de différence. Mais claquettes américaines, ça fait mieux.

claquettes   *tap-dancing*

DANSE CLASSIQUE

Jane Wicks   Arthur Maquis

La danse classique est la base de toute forme de danse.

Horaires :

Mardi 12h00 – 13h30
Avancé avec piano
Vendredi 12h00 – 13h30
Débutant
Samedi 10h30 – 12h00
Intermédiaire avec piano

DANSE MODERNE

Sandrine Raina

Horaires :

Mercredi	10h00 – 11h00		
	11h00 – 12h00	6–7	ans
	12h30 – 13h30	8–10	ans
	14h00 – 15h00	11–13	ans
		14–17	ans

CAROLINE Tu ne veux pas faire des percussions?

DAMIEN Si, mais je ne suis pas libre ces soirs-là.

DAMIEN Tu as envie de faire de la danse moderne ou de la danse classique?

CAROLINE Pour moi, danse classique.

DAMIEN Pas pour moi! Je veux être moderne!

PERCUSSIONS

Anatole Dubois

Chaque étudiant doit apporter son propre instrument : tam-tam, bongo, . . .

Horaires :

Lundi	18h00 – 19h30	Débutants
Mercredi	18h00 – 19h30	Inter
Vendredi	18h00 – 19h30	Avancés

THEATRE

Blanche Sarlat

Horaires :

Lundi	18h00 – 21h00
Mardi	13h45 – 18h00
	18h00 – 21h00
Mercredi	13h45 – 18h00
Jeudi	18h00 – 21h00

Niveaux : Débutant/Intermédiaire Avancé/Professionnel

DAMIEN Ça te dit de faire du théâtre?

CAROLINE Oui, je veux bien. Et toi?

DAMIEN Pourquoi pas? Quand ça?

CAROLINE Eh bien, le mardi et le jeudi soir, par exemple.

2 Activité • Qui est-ce?

C'est Caroline ou c'est Damien qui… ?

1. préfère la danse classique 1. C'est Caroline.
2. veut essayer la gym-danse 2. C'est Caroline.
3. n'a pas le temps de faire des percussions 3. C'est Damien.
4. préfère les claquettes américaines 4. C'est Caroline.
5. veut bien faire du théâtre 5. C'est Caroline.

3 Activité • Et vous?

1. Faites-vous de la danse? Classique? Moderne? Des claquettes?
2. Quel genre de danse préférez-vous?
3. Connaissez-vous un danseur ou une danseuse de claquettes célèbre?
4. Avez-vous votre propre instrument?
5. Faites-vous du théâtre? Où? Avec qui?
6. Qu'est-ce que vous faites pour garder la forme? Des exercices? Du jogging? De la danse?

4 Activité • Choisissez un cours   Possible questions are given.

Regardez les annonces de la MJC dans 1. Travaillez avec un(e) camarade de classe. Préparez une conversation entre un animateur ou une animatrice de la MJC et un(e) client(e). Posez des questions sur les cours et puis choisissez-en un. Changez de rôle. Ensuite, racontez vos choix à la classe.
C'est pour quel niveau? C'est quand? Où? C'est combien? Il faut avoir un instrument?

5 Activité • Ecrivez

Un(e) musicien(ne) de votre groupe de rock est découragé(e). Il/Elle a l'impression de jouer mal et a envie d'abandonner le groupe. Ecrivez-lui un petit mot d'encouragement.   Possible answer: Cher/Chère… ,
Tu joues très bien de la batterie. Tu es très important(e) pour notre groupe! La nouvelle chanson est difficile, mais tu y es presque. Continue! Encore un petit effort! N'abandonne pas, s'il te plaît! Courage!

6 Activité • Sondage

Voici le résultat d'un sondage récent fait parmi les jeunes français. Travaillez en groupes de quatre. Faites la même enquête dans votre groupe. Comparez vos résultats à ceux des Français.

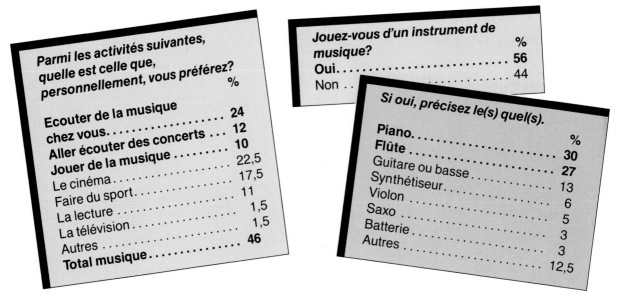

Circulez dans la classe et posez des questions aux autres élèves : «Tu joues de la trompette?»
Jouez comme au «loto». Vous devez trouver cinq réponses affirmatives en ligne droite ou
en diagonale. Qui… ?

joue de la trompette	fait des claquettes	aime la musique classique	fait du théâtre	joue du piano
est déjà allé (e) à un concert de rock	joue au football	va au cinéma trois fois par mois	a une collection de disques de rock	fait de l'informatique
joue au volley-ball	doit partir tout de suite après l'école	regarde la télé tous les jours	fait du judo	a déjà vu une pièce de théâtre
essaie de monter un groupe de rock	prend des cours de danse	essaie d'entrer dans un groupe de rock	va à une boum ce week-end	n'aime pas la musique rock
connaît les Rolling Stones	est fort(e) en maths	apprend à jouer d'un instrument	doit travailler vendredi soir	fait de l'aérobic

Activité • Le cours de claquettes

Avec un(e) camarade, complétez ces conversations. Ajoutez une invitation, un mot d'encouragement, une permission ou un refus. Possible answers are given.

               Ça te dit de prendre
— *(invitation)* des cours de claquettes?
— Des cours de claquettes? Non, je suis nulle!
— *(encouragement)* Mais non, tu es bonne!

— Madame Antonio, je peux partir? J'ai un rendez-vous à cinq heures.
— *(refus)* Non. C'est impossible.

               Ça te plairait d'aller au
— *(invitation)* cinéma après le cours?
— Après le cours? Je veux bien. Ça fait deux mois que je n'ai pas vu de film.

— Je n'arrive pas à marcher avec ces chaussures!
— *(encouragement)* Mais si, tu y arrives.

— Je n'y arrive pas! C'est trop compliqué pour moi!
— *(encouragement)* Mais si, tu y es presque!

Activité • Projet

Vous travaillez dans une MJC. Faites une affiche pour annoncer une activité. Indiquez les horaires, les niveaux, les prix, le local et le nom de l'animateur/animatrice.

Mademoiselle Boncœur est animatrice à la télévision. Les jeunes lui écrivent et lui parlent de leurs problèmes. Elle trouve toujours une solution. Vous êtes mademoiselle Boncœur. Travaillez avec un(e) camarade de classe. Trouvez des solutions à ces problèmes. Employez le verbe **devoir** et l'infinitif : «Vous devez…, Vous ne devez pas… »

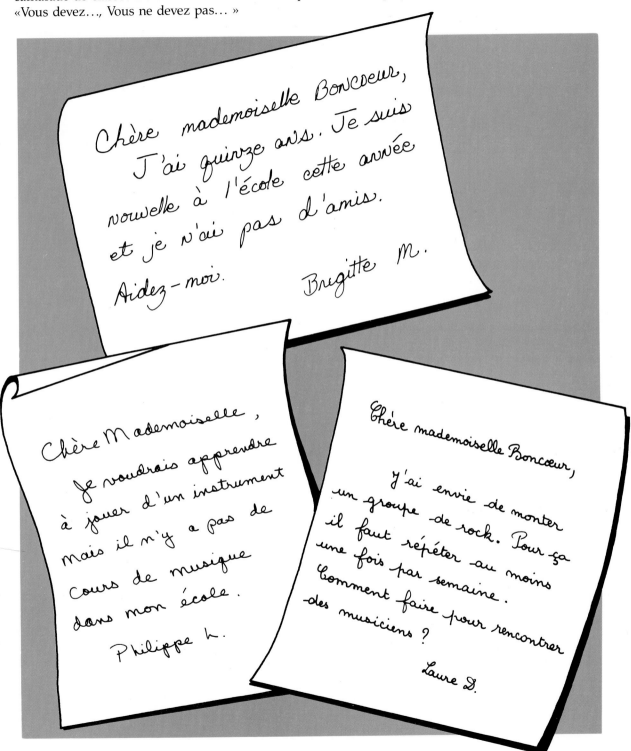

Chère mademoiselle Boncœur,
J'ai quinze ans. Je suis nouvelle à l'école cette année et je n'ai pas d'amis.
Aidez-moi.
Bregitte M.

Chère Mademoiselle,
Je voudrais apprendre à jouer d'un instrument mais il n'y a pas de cours de musique dans mon école.
Philippe L.

Chère mademoiselle Boncœur,
J'ai envie de monter un groupe de rock. Pour ça il faut répéter au moins une fois par semaine. Comment faire pour rencontrer des musiciens ?
Laure D.

Activité • Ecrivez

Et vous, avez-vous un problème?
Avez-vous besoin de conseils?
Ecrivez à mademoiselle
Boncœur.

Reprinted by permission of UFS, Inc.

12   **Activité • Et vous?**

Il y a des choses qu'on doit faire ou qu'on veut faire, d'autres qu'on apprend à faire, et d'autres encore qu'on oublie de faire.

Dites…

1. deux choses que vous devez faire.
2. deux choses que vous voulez faire.
3. deux choses que vous apprenez à faire.
4. deux choses que vous oubliez souvent de faire.

13   **Activité • Récréation**   (optional)

1. **Que de mots!**

   En utilisant les seules lettres du mot **voudrais,** formez le plus possible de mots de trois et de quatre lettres.   oui—dis—voir—vis—vrai—vais—roi—sou—soi—vous—vas—avis—dois—vois

2. **Le mot commun**

   Essayez de trouver un mot pour accompagner chacun de ces groupes de mots.

   _____ arriver $\left\{\begin{array}{l}\text{à danser}\\\text{en retard}\\\text{ce soir}\end{array}\right.$ _____ avoir/oublier $\left\{\begin{array}{l}\text{l'heure du cours}\\\text{le nom du prof}\\\text{son parapluie}\end{array}\right.$

   _____ répéter $\left\{\begin{array}{l}\text{une chanson}\\\text{une pièce de théâtre}\\\text{une phrase}\end{array}\right.$ _____ apprendre $\left\{\begin{array}{l}\text{l'alphabet}\\\text{à danser}\\\text{la guitare}\end{array}\right.$

   _____ pièce $\left\{\begin{array}{l}\text{de théâtre}\\\text{de la maison}\\\text{d'un franc}\end{array}\right.$ _____ monter $\left\{\begin{array}{l}\text{un groupe de jazz}\\\text{une valise}\\\text{à la tour Eiffel}\end{array}\right.$

PRONONCIATION

The vowel sound /ə/

1 Ecoutez bien et répétez.

1. In French, don't slur or swallow any sound.

photo	minute	collection
photographie	attitude	gouvernement
photographique	latitude	administration

2. In French, the vowel sound is given its complete value, or else it's completely left out and the syllable is dropped.

Je dois venir. / Jé dois vénir.   Au revoir. / Au révoir.

Je ne sais pas. / Je né sais pas.   A demain. / A démain.

3. The vowel sound /ə/ is made with the lips rounded and pushed forward: **me, te, se, le, je.**

the train / le train   the government / le gouvernement

the bus / le bus   probably / probablement

the premier / le premier

4. The sound most often left out in French is /ə/, as you hear it in **je, le, ce,** and **ne.**

a. It is left out *between* two consonant sounds near the middle of a word.

certainément	ennémi	samédi	achéter
boulévard	rapidément	pétite	lentément

b. It is left out between two consonant sounds in the middle of a meaning-group.

demain / à démain   le jour / et lé jour

le train / dans lé train   le dentiste / chez lé dentiste

5. The sound /ə/ is pronounced with full value *after* two consonant sounds: **probablement, gouvernement, oncle.**

2 Ecoutez et lisez.

1. il aimé — il est maladé — ils partént — tu parlés

Je dois / Jé dois   Je le sais / Je lé sais   Je ne dois pas / Je né dois pas

2. Try reading the following half of a phone conversation.

Allô?… Je t'écoute… Vendredi après-midi? Impossible… Samedi midi, alors…
Certainement… Au boulevard Saint-Michel… Je sais… Au revoir… A demain.

3 Copiez les phrases suivantes pour préparer une dictée.

1. Moi aussi, je suis libre.
2. Tu veux faire de la musique? Il y a de petites guitares pour les jeunes.
3. Combien de fois par semaine?
4. On y va deux soirs par semaine et le samedi après-midi.
5. Je ne peux pas le faire. Je dois travailler.

VERIFIONS!

SECTION A

Have you learned how to invite a friend to do something?
Suggest the following activities to a friend three different ways.
1. aller au cinéma   **2.** faire de l'aérobic   **3.** venir à la piscine
Ça te dit d'... ?   Ça t'intéresse de... ?   Ça te plairait de... ?

Do you know how to answer a negative question affirmatively?
Answer your friend's questions, beginning your replies with either **oui** or **si**.
1. Tu es libre? Oui, je suis...   **3.** Tu ne veux pas y aller? Si, je veux...
2. La MJC n'est pas ouverte?   **4.** Tu as une guitare? Oui, j'ai...
    Si, elle est...

Have you learned how to use the independent pronouns?
Answer affirmatively with the appropriate pronoun.   Oui, c'est pour toi/vous.
1. C'est Philippe? Oui, c'est lui.   **3.** C'est pour moi, le téléphone?
2. C'est ses copains?   **4.** Tu viens avec nous à la MJC?
    Oui, c'est eux.   Oui, je viens avec vous.

SECTION B

Can you offer encouragement to someone?
What would you say in each of these situations? Vary your expressions.
1. Your friend is having trouble moving a heavy object. Tu y es presque!
2. You're teaching your friend to dance. Encore un petit effort!
3. Your friend is running a race against a rival school. Vas-y!

Did you learn the forms of the verbs *prendre,* *apprendre,* **and** *comprendre*?
Complete the following sentences with the correct form and tense of the appropriate verb.
1. Je ____ des cours de judo le mercredi. prends
2. Mercredi dernier, je n' ____ le professeur. ai pas compris
3. Aujourd'hui, nous ____ une nouvelle prise. apprenons
4. Le judo, c'est difficile à ____ . apprendre

SECTION C

Do you know how to ask for, give, and refuse permission?
Ask for permission in this situation. Je peux voir tes photos, s'il te plaît?
   Votre amie fait de la photo. Vous voulez voir ses photos.
Give and then refuse permission in the following situation.
   Votre ami(e) veut voir votre devoir. Oui, pourquoi pas?
                    Pas question!

Can you ask and tell how long people have been doing something?
Ask in two different ways how long these people have been doing their activity.
1. Philippe joue de la trompette.   **2.** Damien et Caroline font du théâtre.
Answer the following question two different ways. Tu joues... depuis combien de temps?
Depuis combien de temps étudiez-vous le français? Ça fait combien de temps que tu... ?
Depuis deux ans. Ça fait deux ans.

Do you know how to use the pronoun *en*?
Answer the following questions, using the pronoun **en**.
1. Prenez-vous des cours de musique? Oui, j'en prends.
2. Jouez-vous d'un instrument? Oui, j'en joue.
3. Faites-vous de la photo? Oui, j'en fais.
4. Avez-vous fait du judo? Non, je n'en ai pas fait.

VOCABULAIRE

SECTION A

les **achats** (m.) *purchases;*
    faire des achats *to go shopping*
la **danse** *dance*
dehors : en dehors de *outside of, beyond*
déjeuner *to have lunch*
dit : Ça te dit... ? *Do you want to . . . ?*
un **entraînement** *practice, training*
la **gym** *gymnastics*
intéresser : Ça t'intéresse de... ? *Are you interested in . . . ?*
le **judo** *judo*
justement *as a matter of fact*
plairait : Ça te plairait de... ? *Would it please you to . . . ?*
pratiquer *to take part in*
répéter *to rehearse*
théâtre : faire du théâtre *to take part in a theater group*
tout *all, everything*

SECTION B

l' **accueil** (m.) *reception, registration desk*
un(e) **adversaire** *opponent*
l' **animateur, -trice** *activity leader*
apprendre *to learn*
arriver à *to manage;*
    Je n'y arrive pas! *I can't manage to do it!*
comme *in the way of*
dames : jouer aux dames *play checkers*

un(e) **débutant(e)** *beginner*
droit *straight*
échecs : jouer aux échecs *play chess*
un **effort** *effort*
encore *another*
l' **épaule** (f.) *shoulder*
la **flûte** *flute*
fort *loudly;* **plus fort** *louder*
haut, -e *high*
hélas *alas*
inscrit, -e *enrolled*
un **instrument** *instrument*
la **jambe** *leg*
journée : toute la journée *all day long*
la **main** *hand*
la **musculation** *body building*
observer *to observe*
la **peinture** *painting*
la **philatélie** *stamp collecting*
une **pièce : une pièce de théâtre** *play*
la **poterie** *pottery*
une **prise** *hold*
le **public** *audience*
rapide *fast*
la **Russie** *Russia*
la **trompette** *trumpet*

SECTION C

ambitieux, -euse *ambitious*
une **annonce** *announcement, ad*
attention : Fais attention. *Be careful. Pay attention.*
au moins *at least*
le **bac(calauréat)** *exam taken upon completion of secondary school*

la **basse** *bass guitar*
un(e) **bassiste** *bass player*
la **batterie** *set of drums*
brillant, -e *brilliant*
une **chanson** *song*
la **clarinette** *clarinet*
depuis *for*
devoir *to have to, must*
électrique *electric*
essayer *to try*
les **études** (f.) *studies*
étudier *to study*
former *to form*
le **garage** *garage*
un **local** *place*
longtemps *a long time*
marcher *to get started, to function*
moins : au moins *at least*
monter *to assemble, to organize*
un(e) **musicien, -ienne** *musician*
par : un week-end par mois *one weekend a month*
passer *to take (a test)*
la **permission** *permission*
persuader *to persuade*
peut-être *perhaps, maybe*
le **piano** *piano*
propre *own*
le **saxophone** *saxophone*
seulement *only*
sujet : au sujet de *regarding, concerning, about*
le **trombone** *trombone*
voudrais : je voudrais *I would like*

ETUDE DE MOTS

1. The feminine forms of several masculine nouns ending in **-teur** end in **-trice**: **animateur→animatrice.** You should recognize the following words. Copy them and then write their feminine forms.

    directeur   **acteur**   **aviateur**   **dessinateur**
    directrice   actrice   aviatrice   dessinatrice

2. In French, a person who plays the **guitare** is a **guitariste**. What are the French words for the players of the following instruments?

    clarinette   **saxophone**   **basse**   **violon**   **piano**
    clarinettiste   saxophoniste   bassiste   violoniste   pianiste

A LIRE

Une chanson :
En sortant du lycée

Patricia Lavila, a French singer, made this song a hit several years ago. In the song a young French girl tells about the best time of her day.

Avant de lire

Before you read all the lyrics, scan the first stanza for the answers to the following questions:
1. How does the girl feel about school? She's happy when school is out for the day.
2. What are the key words and phrases that reveal her feelings? respirer, la liberté, le meilleur moment

Le café est un lieu de rencontres très important dans la vie des jeunes Français. Qu'est-ce qu'ils font au café? Trouvez trois réponses. Ils prennent une glace. Ils s'amusent en se moquant des gens qui passent. Ils se posent des questions. Ils écoutent de la musique.

En sortant du lycée,
Je commence à respirer
A la seconde où la cloche° a sonné.
En sortant du lycée,
A nous deux la liberté.
C'est le meilleur moment de la journée.
Je ne suis jamais pressée, oh non,
D'aller m'enfermer° à la maison.

Vite, vite, vite
Je rejoins mes amis au café d'en face.
Vite, vite, vite
Je te paye un café, tu m'offres une glace.
On se retrouve à la terrasse,
Et l'on s'amuse en se moquant° un peu des gens qui passent.

Vite, vite, vite
On se pose des questions: «Que fais-tu ce soir?»
Vite, vite, vite
«Est-ce que tu es d'accord pour la patinoire?»
En attendant, va mettre un disque.
Les Rolling Stones, eh bien, d'accord,
Ça, c'est de la musique.

---

cloche *bell;* **m'enfermer** *shut myself up;* **se moquant... des** *making fun of*

En sortant du lycée,
Je retrouve Jean-Marie.
J'adore faire de la moto avec lui.
En sortant du lycée,
Nous roulons, cheveux° au vent.
Sur l'autoroute on s'offre du bon temps.
Mais il va pleuvoir et la nuit descend.
Faisons demi-tour, on nous attend.

Vite, vite, vite
On rejoint nos amis au café d'en face.
Vite, vite, vite
Je te paye un café, tu m'offres une glace.
Quelle heure est-il? Plus de sept heures.
J'en connais une° qui va passer un bien mauvais quart d'heure.

Vite, vite, vite
Je rentre à la maison. Je suis en retard.
Vite, vite, vite
Ne comptez plus sur moi pour la patinoire.
Ça va sûrement être ma fête.
Depuis longtemps mon père sûrement me guette° à la fenêtre.

Activité • Devinez

Choisissez les équivalents anglais.

1. pressée
   a. *ironed*
   b. *free*
   c. *rushed*

2. Ça va sûrement être ma fête.
   a. *I'm really going to be in trouble.*
   b. *It's going to be my birthday.*
   c. *There's going to be a party.*

Activité • Après le lycée

Faites une liste de tout ce que la chanteuse fait après le lycée. Elle retrouve ses amis au café, mange une glace, s'amuse en se moquant des gens, met un disque, écoute de la musique, fait de la moto avec Jean-Marie, et rentre à la maison.

Activité • Et vous?

1. Qu'est-ce que vous faites après l'école?
2. Où est-ce que vous rencontrez vos copains?
3. Sortez-vous le soir pendant la semaine?
4. Allez-vous à la patinoire? Avec qui?

Activité • A vous maintenant!

Imaginez le dialogue entre la chanteuse et son père quand elle rentre chez elle. Son père lui demande où elle a été, avec qui, ce qu'elle a fait... Préparez le dialogue avec un(e) camarade de classe.

---

cheveux *hair;* **j'en connais une** *I know one person;* **guette** *wait impatiently*

The French are very fond of American jazz, and over the years many musicians have adopted Paris as their home. The French movie, Round Midnight, depicts the Parisian life of an American saxophonist.

Jazz Jazz Jazz Jazz et

Il y a eu de merveilleux guitaristes de jazz et de rock tout au long du XX\ :sup:`e` siècle.

Django Reinhardt (1910–1953), né en Belgique dans une famille de Gitans°, est le créateur d'un style de jazz unique qui reflète le tempérament tzigane°. Django Reinhardt a perdu à la suite d'un accident l'usage de trois doigts de la main gauche; il a inventé avec seulement deux doigts une technique guitaristique. Il est devenu un merveilleux virtuose, improvisant sur scène des compositions extraordinaires. Il a travaillé avec différents musiciens de jazz dont° Stéphane Grapelli, violoniste français. Ses compositions sont devenues des classiques du jazz.

Jean-Baptiste (dit Django) Reinhardt

L'Américain Charlie Christian est né en 1919 à Dallas (Texas). Il a imposé la guitare électrique dans les formations de jazz. Sous ses doigts, la guitare rivalise° soudain avec les autres instruments de jazz. En 1939, il a travaillé avec le célèbre clarinettiste Benny Goodman. Sa carrière est brusquement interrompue par sa mort en 1942.

Charlie Christian et Benny Goodman

Gitans *Gypsies;* **tzigane** *gypsy;* **dont** *among them;* **rivalise** *rivals*

Rock Rock Rock Rock

Avec le musicien noir Jimi Hendrix, on quitte°
le domaine du jazz pour pénétrer dans celui
du rock. Jimi Hendrix est né à Seattle
(Washington) en 1942. Travaillant uniquement
sur la guitare électrique, il a fait profondément
évoluer la technique guitaristique de la
musique rock. Jimi Hendrix est devenu un
guitariste de rock hors du commun °, sans
doute le plus grand de son temps. Sa guitare a
eu sur les spectateurs un effet magique. Après
avoir accompagné B. B. King, il a composé sa
propre musique qui a suscité° une immense
émotion chez les auditeurs de rock. Virtuose
de la guitare, il a été aussi chanteur, poète et
homme de spectacle. Il est devenu, à la fin
des années soixantes, l'un des personnages
mythiques de la jeunesse passionnée de
musique rock. Il est mort à Londres en 1970,
à l'âge de 28 ans.

Jimi Hendrix

Activité • Trouvez les dates

Arrangez ces événements par ordre chronologique.

4. **1.** Django Reinhardt est mort. (1953)   1. **3.** Django Reinhardt est né. (1910)   3. **5.** Charlie Christian a travaillé avec

5. **2.** Jimi Hendrix est mort. (1970)   2. **4.** Charlie Christian est né. (1919)   Benny Goodman. (1939)

Activité • Avez-vous bien lu?

D'après le texte, qu'est-ce qui est arrivé *(happened)* en... ?

1. 1970   **2.** 1939   **3.** 1942   **4.** 1919   1. Jimi Hendrix est mort.
2. Charlie Christian a travaillé avec Benny Goodman.   3. Jimi Hendrix est né.   4. Charlie Christian est né.

Activité • Et vous?

Répondez aux questions suivantes.

1. Aimez-vous mieux le jazz ou le rock?   **3.** Connaissez-vous d'autres instruments de jazz?

2. Connaissez-vous d'autres genres de musique?   **4.** Connaissez-vous d'autres guitaristes?

---

quitte *leaves;* **hors du commun** *out of the ordinary;* **suscité** *created*

CHAPITRE 3 Amusons-nous!

	BASIC MATERIAL	COMMUNICATIVE FUNCTIONS
PREMIER CONTACT	**Le Carnaval de Québec (1)** **Le 14 Juillet (4)**	Reading for global comprehension and cultural awareness
SECTION A	**Bienvenue au Carnaval (A1)** **Au défilé (A11)**	**Exchanging information** • Talking about Carnival in Quebec **Expressing feelings, emotions** • Exclaiming, expressing admiration and surprise
SECTION B	**A Zygofolis (B1)** **Que d'émotions! (B9)**	**Socializing** • Talking about carnival rides • Asking for agreement **Expressing feelings, emotions** • Expressing fear, pain, hunger, thirst, discomfort **Expressing attitudes, opinions** • Expressing indecision, indifference
SECTION C	**La fête commence. (C1)**	**Socializing** • Making arrangements **Expressing feelings, emotions** • Expressing regret
TRY YOUR SKILLS	**Après le défilé (1)**	

■ **Prononciation** (liaison; dictation) **121**
■ **Vérifions!** **122** ■ **Vocabulaire** **123**

A LIRE	**La Marseillaise** (the story of the French national anthem) **Bonhomme Carnaval** (**Bonhomme Carnaval:** symbol of joy) **La Chanson du Carnaval** (the **Carnaval** song)

WRITING A variety of controlled and open-ended writing activities appear in the Pupil's Edition. The Teacher's Notes identify other activities suitable for writing practice.

COOPERATIVE LEARNING Many of the activities in the Pupil's Edition lend themselves to cooperative learning. For guidelines, see page T14.

Scope and Sequence

GRAMMAR	CULTURE	RE-ENTRY
	Activities during **Carnaval** in Quebec Celebrations of July 14	
Adjectives ending in **-al** and **-if** (A8)	**Carnaval** festivities	Adjectives Answering negative questions affirmatively
The verb **vivre** (B4) The formation and position of adverbs (B13)	A French amusement park	Inviting friends Adjectives The verb **avoir**
Asking questions using **est-ce que** and inversion (C8)	Bastille Day in France	Making a phone call Inviting friends Asking questions
Recombining communicative functions, grammar, and vocabulary		
Reading for practice and pleasure		

UNIT RESOURCES **Cahier d'Activités, Cahier d'Exercices,** Unit 3 Cassettes, Transparencies 7–9 (also 31, 31A, 32, 32A), Quizzes 7–9, Unit 3 Test

TEACHER-PREPARED MATERIALS **Section A** Magazines; **Section B** Pictures of roller coaster and fun house, index cards; **Section C** Map of Paris, toy telephones; **A lire** Map of France, recording of the «**Marseillaise**»

PREMIER
CONTACT

The authentic material in **Premier Contact** introduces the theme of the unit. Concentrate only on the general content of these documents. A detailed treatment of the grammar and vocabulary is not intended. Since students should be reading for global comprehension, they need not know the meaning of every word. For this reason, new words in **Premier Contact** have been omitted from the unit vocabulary list and the French-English Vocabulary at the end of the book.

OBJECTIVES   To read for global comprehension and cultural awareness; to get acquainted with the topic

1   Le Carnaval de Québec

Read the **Carnaval** schedule aloud or play the cassette as students read along in their books. Ask a few questions to assess global comprehension: **Quels sports fait-on pendant le Carnaval? Qui joue au hockey? Est-ce qu'il y a un bal?**

2   Activité • Cherchez des renseignements

Have students pair off to ask each other the questions. Do not insist on complete sentences for answers. Then have students prepare other comprehension questions to ask their classmates.

3   Activité • Réfléchissez

Students might search for answers to question 1 in **Contact 1,** competing to find the maximum number of activities within a specified period of time. For question 2, you may need to remind students what the historical connection is between French Canada and Louisiana. See **Aperçu culturel 2** in **Nouveaux copains.**

4   LE 14 JUILLET

Ask students to scan the newspaper article and schedule to find out what two events will take place **(le défilé** and **le feu d'artifice).** Play the cassette and have students follow along in their books. Ask simple questions about the fireworks display: **Le feu d'artifice est à quelle heure? Faut-il y aller en métro ou en voiture? Pourquoi?**

5   Activité • Complétez

First have students copy the five sentence beginnings. Then have them look in the article and schedule for the information needed to complete the sentences. Circulate to spot-check. Then have volunteers write their completions on a transparency that you've prepared in advance.

6   Activité • Et vous?

SLOWER-PACED LEARNING   Help students answer question 3 by writing a sample answer on the board: **J'ai déjà participé à un défilé. J'ai porté un pantalon bleu et un veston rouge. J'ai joué du saxophone.** Encourage them to bring in photos of their experiences.

CHALLENGE   Using their answers to the questions, students might prepare brief oral presentations for the class. Encourage them to use pictures or photos to enhance their talks.

SECTION A

OBJECTIVES   **To exchange information:** talk about Carnival in Quebec; **to express feelings, emotions:** exclaim, express admiration and surprise

CULTURAL BACKGROUND   You might point out to students that Canadian French has evolved differently than the French of France. Some American expressions have crept into the language: **avoir du fun** for **s'amuser, beurre de pinottes** for **beurre de cacahouètes, un(e) chum** for **un copain/une copine.** In other cases French words are used, but with the meanings that they have in English: **anxieux** for **désireux, opportunité** for **occasion, corporation** for **société commerciale.** Still more common, however, are expressions that are simply peculiar to Canadian French. If students travel to Quebec, they should know, for example, that the names of the meals are different: **le petit déjeuner** is **le déjeuner** in Quebec, **le déjeuner** is **le dîner,** and **le dîner** is **le souper.**

MOTIVATING ACTIVITY   Ask students to imagine what people might do in Quebec to celebrate **Carnaval.**

A 1

Bienvenue au Carnaval

Have students listen to the cassette, or ask them to read the monologues quickly to themselves. Pause after each monologue and ask students if the speaker(s) like Carnival or not. Students should support their answers by reading appropriate lines from the monologues.

CHALLENGE   Have students role-play the different speakers. Pretend that you're a reporter and ask **Pourquoi est-ce que vous aimez le Carnaval?** Students should answer according to what they recall the speakers said. They might give other reasons as well.

A 2   **Activité • Ajoutez une phrase**

SLOWER-PACED LEARNING   Form cooperative learning groups of four students each to find and to write down as many responses as they can, both from the text and of their own making. Then have them compete as explained below.

CHALLENGE   Say each statement and invite students to add as many logical phrases as possible. You might even make it a competition. Divide the class into teams. A team gains one point for each sentence it adds to the original; the team loses its turn if it doesn't have any sentences to add.

A 3   **Activité • Le pour et le contre**

Write the headings on the board. Brainstorm with students the advantages and disadvantages. Write their suggestions on the board. Or, for cooperative learning, have students work in pairs or small groups to make up their own lists.

A4 Activité • A vous maintenant!

Students might record their phone conversations. Listen to their recordings in private, making note of errors to summarize and correct in class the next day. You might then play a few of the recordings for the class.

A5 Activité • Ecrit dirigé

Read through the letter with students. Have them identify which verb and tense they will use to fill in each blank.

A6 Savez-vous que... ?

Carnaval takes place just before the 40 days of Lent **(le Carême)**. It begins on January 6, Epiphany **(le jour des Rois)**, and ends on Shrove Tuesday **(Mardi Gras)**, the day before Ash Wednesday **(le mercredi des Cendres)**. During this period of **Carnaval**, and especially during the final week, there are parades, masquerades, pageants, street dancing, and other forms of revelry. There is a final major celebration on **Mardi Gras**, sometimes ending with revelers dancing around a huge bonfire into which they throw the papier-mâché figures from the parades.

    Bonhomme Carnaval is a person dressed as a snowman wearing a red hat and red sash. He leads all the parades and festivities and goes through the streets shaking hands and dancing with the girls. There are papier-mâché imitations of him to be seen everywhere. In times past, Queen Carnival was the girl who sold the most tickets; now she doesn't have to sell tickets, but she must win a beauty contest.

A7 VOUS EN SOUVENEZ-VOUS?

Have the students recall what they know about adjectives in French—formation, position, and irregularities. As students bring up different points, ask them to provide examples. Then have them look at the chart in the book and read the example sentences aloud. Remind them that they cannot always know the spelling of an adjective by its sound; they must look at the subject pronoun, verb, or noun for a clue. Finally, discuss the information given below the chart.

A8 STRUCTURES DE BASE

Read aloud the examples in the chart and have students repeat them after you. Practice the adjectives in number 3 with a fill-in-the-blank exercise: **(actif)** **Raymond et Monique sortent souvent. Ils sont ——.**

A9 Activité • Décrivez les gens au Carnaval

Do this activity orally with the entire class. Then have students write two sentences about each picture: one giving the nationality; the other describing the people.

CHALLENGE Have students tell and write as much as they can about each picture. They might also role-play the people in the drawings.

A10 Activité • Ecrit dirigé

Have students brainstorm adjectives to fill in the blanks. Write their suggestions on the board or on a transparency. Then assign the activity for homework; students do not have to use the adjectives suggested in class.

A 11   **AU DEFILE** 🔲

Hold up your book, point to the pictures, and make an exclamation about each one. Then have students exclaim as you point to each picture again. Play the cassette or read the dialogue aloud. Have students pair off to practice the dialogue as you circulate and listen. Finally, ask volunteers to role-play Lucie and Robert for the class.

A 12   **Activité • Complétez**

For listening practice, have students copy the six sentence beginnings, close their books, and listen to the recording of A11 to find the completions. You may have to play the cassette twice.

A 13   **Activité • A vous maintenant!** 🔲

SLOWER-PACED LEARNING   First have students write down each noun and the adjective they would use to describe it. Go over the choices with the entire class. Then decide together what form each adjective should take. Finally, have students pair off to make up dialogues as instructed in their books.

A 14   **COMMENT LE DIRE**

After studying the examples in the box, students should practice with each other, exclaiming over the pictures in A11 or in magazines that you've provided. Have them take the information in one exclamation and use it in the other expressions:

> Ce qu'elles sont belles, les Duchesses!
> Qu'elles sont belles, les Duchesses!
> Qu'est-ce qu'elles sont belles, les Duchesses!
> Quelles belles Duchesses!

A 15   **Activité • Faites des exclamations** 🔲

You might point out that number 4 should be **Ce qu'il neige!** or **Qu'est-ce qu'il neige!** because **Qu'il neige!** would mean *Let it snow!*

A 16   **Activité • Quel beau défilé** 🔲

When students have completed the activity, call on different pairs to present their dialogues to the class.

A 17   **Activité • Qu'est-ce qu'ils disent?**

For cooperative learning, have students pair off or form small groups to role-play the people in the photos. Students should imagine what the people are saying and prepare the monologues or dialogues. Call on volunteers to present theirs to the class.

A 18   **Activité • A vous maintenant!**

For cooperative learning, have students form groups of three. One student in each group should serve as "director" as the other two make up the dialogue. For each dialogue, change "directors." Circulate and assist students. Allow volunteers to choose their best dialogue and to perform it for the class.

A 19
Activité • Ecoutez bien

> You're going to hear a recorded message for the schedule of events at the Winter Carnival in Quebec. Open your book to page 101. *(pause)* Copy the chart in A19 on a separate sheet of paper. *(pause)* As you listen to the message, fill in the chart, telling the day and time for each event that you want to attend. **Ecoutez bien.**
>
> Voici le programme des activités du Carnaval de Québec pour le week-end du 14 et 15 février.
>
> **Samedi 14**
> A 9h   petit déjeuner western de Calgary—rue Ste-Thérèse
> A 12h30   Fête des Enfants : un défilé des enfants en costume—rue Ste-Thérèse
> A 13h   Pièce de théâtre : *Un Ami dans le frigo*—palais Montcalm
> A 20h   Souper canadien—château Frontenac
> A 22h   Feu d'artifice—place Carnaval
> A 22h30   Bal de la Reine—château Frontenac
>
> **Dimanche 15**
> A 12h30   Championnat de patinage artistique—colisée de Québec
> A 14h30   Gala folklorique : 70 musiciens jouent de la musique canadienne—Cap Santé
> A 15h   Exposition des chars—place Carnaval
> A 20h   Fin du tournoi de hockey—colisée de Québec
> A 22h   Départ du Bonhomme—place du Palais
>
> Et maintenant, vérifions.
>
> **1.** dimanche, 20h   **3.** samedi, 20h
> **2.** samedi, 13h   **4.** samedi, 22h30

SECTION B

OBJECTIVES   **To socialize:** talk about carnival rides; ask for agreement; **to express feelings, emotions:** express fear, pain, hunger, thirst, discomfort; **to express attitudes, opinions:** express indecision, indifference

CULTURAL BACKGROUND   **Nice** is the so-called "capital" of the French Riviera **(la Côte d'Azur),** and **Zygofolis** is an amusement park on its outskirts. In addition to the attractions mentioned in the text, **Zygofolis** boasts a 3000-seat amphitheater with shows every day and evening, a swimming pool with man-made waves **(une piscine à vagues),** giant water slides **(les toboggans d'eau géants),** bumper cars **(les autos tamponneuses),** and numerous rides **(les manèges).**

MOTIVATING ACTIVITY   Ask students whether they like amusement parks and why or why not, what they like to do there, and whether there are any nearby.

B 1

A Zygofolis

Using gestures, play the role first of a **fonceur/fonceuse,** then of a person who is **réservé(e),** describing yourself each time in French. Ask students if they are **un fonceur/une fonceuse** or **réservé(e)** Next draw a roller coaster and a fun house on the board, or bring in pictures to illustrate them. Play the cassette or read the dialogue aloud as students follow along in their books. Ask them to find all the expressions that reveal how Simon feels about the attractions. Ask volunteers to present the dialogue, using dramatic gestures and facial expressions, for the class.

B2   Activité • Répondez

Students should work individually or in pairs to find answers to the questions.

SLOWER-PACED LEARNING   On a transparency or on the board, write the answers at random and letter them from *a* to *e.* Have students match the answers to the questions.

B3   Activité • Devinez

To make this a listening activity, have students write **Nicole** and **Simon** at the top of a sheet of paper and below, the numbers 1 to 6. As you read each description twice, have them place a check mark in the appropriate column.

CHALLENGE   Ask students to imagine other activities in which Nicole, the **fonceuse,** and Simon, the reserved one, might engage.

B4   STRUCTURES DE BASE

Have students repeat as you model the present-tense and **passé composé** forms of **vivre** and the exclamations with **Vive... !** Write the conjugation on the board and have students copy it. Contrast **vivre** with **habiter.** Have students express their feelings by making up other exclamations with **Vive... !**

B5   Activité • Comment vivent-ils?

To make this a listening activity, have students write **Rapidement** and **Tranquillement** at the top of a sheet of paper and below, the numbers 1 to 6. As you read each item, students should place a check mark in the proper column to indicate how the people live.

CHALLENGE   When students tell how they lead their lives, ask them to give examples or reasons why.

B6   COMMENT LE DIRE

Have students make suggestions followed by one of the questions in the left-hand column. Their classmates respond with the expressions on the right.

B7   Activité • A vous maintenant!

SLOWER-PACED LEARNING   To make a game of this, have each pair of students copy the questions onto one set of index cards and the possible responses onto another set of cards. Have the students hold one set in their hands so that their partners cannot read them. One student picks a question card from the other's hand and reads it; the second student picks an answer card from the other's hand and responds. Encourage them to add their own suggestions.

B 8 Activité • Insistez

For each pair of students, you might designate one drawing. Then have them prepare their dialogues and present them to the class.

SLOWER-PACED LEARNING   Help students identify the places in the drawings. Then brainstorm different ways to make suggestions for each.

B 9 QUE D'EMOTIONS!

Act out the expressions **être fatigué(e), avoir faim, avoir soif, avoir peur, avoir mal au cœur,** and **avoir le vertige.** Use them in question-and-answer practice. Play the cassette or read the dialogue, with pauses for repetition. Then call on pairs of students to read the dialogue aloud to the class.

B 10 Activité • Quelles sont leurs réactions?

Replay the cassette recording of B9, stopping after each part of the dialogue. Students should tell what is going on and then state the reactions and feelings of Nicole and Simon.

B 11 Activité • Qui parle? De qui? De quoi?

You might use a TPR technique for this activity. Have each student write **Nicole, Simon, le train fantôme, les montagnes russes,** and **la cafeteria** on separate index cards. Then read the five quotes. After each one ask **Qui parle?** and then **De qui?** or **De quoi?** Students should hold up the appropriate cards to indicate their responses each time. If some students choose an inappropriate card, have them look at the other cards being held up as you repeat the quote.

B 12 Activité • Ecrit dirigé

SLOWER-PACED LEARNING   Prepare two lists of questions in French: one list addressed to Nicole and the other to Simon. Form cooperative learning groups of three or four students each. Give a list of questions to each group. The members of the group should write down the answers and then rework them into a letter from Nicole or Simon.

B 13 STRUCTURES DE BASE

Explain the function of an adverb, making sure students understand that adverbs modify verbs, adjectives, and other adverbs. Then show students a list of masculine adjectives, including some that change form in the feminine **(continuel, joyeux, principal, vif, froid, lent)** and some that end in **-e (rapide, drôle, agréable).** Ask students to give the feminine forms of the adjectives. Show students how to form adverbs by adding **-ment** to the feminine forms of adjectives. Use each adverb in a sentence or question to reinforce the usage. Go over the exceptions (adverbs like **vraiment** and **intensément**) and adverbs that are not formed from adjectives. Finally, have students open their books and read the summary.

B 14 Activité • Découvrez les adjectifs et les adverbes

Have students copy each adverb and adjective and then write the form(s) required. When they've finished, show a transparency with the answers.

B 15 **Activité • Ajoutez un adverbe**

SLOWER-PACED LEARNING Project a transparency showing a list of adverbs. Have students read each sentence aloud, adding the adverb that they've chosen from the list.

B 16 **Activité • Trouvez des adverbes**

Have students write a complete sentence for each picture. Then call on individuals to read their sentences aloud. Finally, have students say as much as they can about each illustration.

B 17 **Activité • Et vous?**

SLOWER-PACED LEARNING First elicit the first-person-singular verb forms that students need: **vis, mange, parle, réponds, prends, fais.** Then write them on the board for students to refer to.

B 18 **COMMENT LE DIRE**

Review the conjugation of the verb **avoir.** Act out the various expressions dramatically and ask **J'ai peur ou j'ai mal au cœur?** and so on. Then have a student act out an expression, exaggerating the emotion. The rest of the class describes how the student is feeling, using the appropriate **avoir** expression.

B 19 **Activité • Qu'est-ce qu'ils ont?**

CHALLENGE Have students tell why the people feel the way they do.

B 20 **Activité • A vous maintenant!**

Encourage students to extend the dialogues by adding two more lines. The first speaker suggests another activity to which the other then agrees.

B 21 **Savez-vous que... ?**

Pictured on the brochure for **Mirapolis** is the giant Gargantua, a figure from medieval French folklore. In the sixteenth century the writer Rabelais made him the hero of a famous satirical novel by the same name. Ask students what English word comes from the name Gargantua.

On the board or on a transparency, write **Zygofolis, Mirapolis,** and Disneyland. Tell students to listen carefully to the cassette and find one thing to say about each. They may take notes.

B 22 **Activité • Ecoutez bien**

You're going to hear a conversation between Eric and Muriel. Open your book to page 109. *(pause)* Read the sentences in B22 silently. *(pause)* On a separate sheet of paper, number from 1 to 5 and be prepared to indicate whether the sentences are true or false. Ready? **Ecoutez bien.**

C'est lundi matin. Eric parle à Muriel devant le lycée.
ERIC	Qu'est-ce que tu as fait hier, Muriel? Tu es allée au cinéma?
MURIEL	Non, je suis allée au parc d'attractions.
ERIC	Ah oui? C'était bien? Tu t'es bien amusée?
MURIEL	Non, pas tellement.

ERIC	Qu'est-ce que tu as fait?
MURIEL	Mon frère m'a entraînée sur les montagnes russes.
ERIC	Tu aimes ça, toi?
MURIEL	Pas beaucoup. Et toi?
ERIC	Moi, pas du tout!
MURIEL	Pourquoi? Tu as peur?
ERIC	Je n'ai pas peur, mais ça me donne le vertige. Je ne trouve pas ça amusant du tout.
MURIEL	Et le train fantôme, alors? Tu n'aimes pas? Ça ne te donne pas le vertige quand même!
ERIC	Je trouve ça bête! C'est pas particulièrement amusant!
MURIEL	Tu sais ce que j'ai préféré?
ERIC	Non.
MURIEL	Les frites! Il y avait des frites formidables!

Et maintenant, vérifions.
1. Muriel a accompagné Eric au parc d'attractions. *faux*
2. Muriel a trouvé le parc drôlement bien. *faux*
3. Les montagnes russes donnent le vertige à Eric. *vrai*
4. Eric a peur du train fantôme. *faux*
5. Muriel aime manger. *vrai*

OBJECTIVES **To socialize:** make arrangements; **to express feelings, emotions:** express regret

CULTURAL BACKGROUND Bastille Day is colorful and exciting! In Paris festivities start the evening before **(la veille du 14 Juillet)** with music and dancing in the streets, especially at the **place de la Bastille, Montmartre, Montparnasse,** and in the Tuileries Gardens near the Louvre. Food stands are set up to provide refreshments. Indoor balls are organized around the city; everyone goes dancing!

MOTIVATING ACTIVITY Invite students to discuss the Fourth of July and how it is celebrated in their community. Ask what they did last July 4.

 # La fête commence.

Explain in French the festivities of July 13, pointing out **Montmartre, Montparnasse,** the **place de la Bastille,** and the **île St-Louis** on a map of Paris. Have students write the names Laure, Fabienne, Jean, and Henri on a sheet of paper. Tell them that they're going to hear Corinne invite her friends to the festivities. As students listen to the cassette, they should indicate on their paper whether or not Corinne's friends are going. Finally, have students form groups of five to practice the phone conversations. You might want to bring toy telephones to class for them to use.

C2 ## Activité • Pourquoi?

On the board or on a transparency, write at random the reasons for the situations. Have students match each reason to the appropriate situation.

C3   Activité • Présentez-vous

Students should look at the first line of each dialogue to find Corinne's way of identifying herself. Then have students pair off and practice phoning to invite each other to go out on July 13.

C4   Activité • A vous maintenant!

SLOWER-PACED LEARNING   Brainstorm with the class different scenarios: (1) Stéphanie accepts, and she and Henri arrange a time; (2) Stéphanie refuses and gives an excuse. Have students suggest words and sentences appropriate to each scenario; write them on the board or on a transparency. Then have students pair off and choose one of the scenarios to prepare, using the vocabulary on the board or transparency as a guide.

C5   Activité • Ecrivez

SLOWER-PACED LEARNING   Students may look back at the dialogues in C1 and compose a message by copying appropriate lines.

CHALLENGE   After students have made up their messages, they might record their messages on cassettes. The next day students exchange cassettes, listen to the recorded messages, and respond to them by calling the sender on the phone.

C6   Savez-vous que... ?

July 14—also known as Bastille Day—commemorates the day in 1789 when an angry Parisian mob stormed the Bastille, at that time a fortress guarding one of the gates of Paris and also a prison for political prisoners. It was hated as a symbol of absolute monarchy.

A new opera house has been constructed on the **place de la Bastille** amid heated controversy. Many Parisians revere the old Paris **Opéra.** The old **Opéra** is to be devoted to the dance.

C7   VOUS EN SOUVENEZ-VOUS?

For a review of number 1, take a series of statements, such as those in C2, and have students repeat them as questions, using rising intonation. Review numbers 2, 3, and 4 by writing the phrases below on the board or on a transparency; have students add appropriate interrogative words to make them into information questions.

Tu as payé...   Ils ont dit...
Il est venu...   Elle a téléphoné...
Vous êtes allés...

Finally, say a series of questions using **quoi** and have students restate them, using **qu'est-ce que.**

C8   STRUCTURES DE BASE

Take the yes/no questions you used in C7 and show how they work with **est-ce que**. For example, **Jean sort avec les autres?** would become **Est-ce que Jean sort avec les autres?** Then take the examples of information questions given in C7 above and have students restate them using **est-ce que:**

Tu as payé combien? ⟶ Combien est-ce que tu as payé?
Il est venu avec qui? ⟶ Avec qui est-ce qu'il est venu?

Next demonstrate inversion. Practice should be with pronoun subjects first. Tell students not to use inversion with **je,** however.

As-tu le temps de venir?   Dansent-ils dans les rues?
Voulez-vous aller au bal?   Est-elle d'accord pour le défilé?

Then have students practice inversion in questions with interrogative words.

Quand veux-tu partir?
A quelle heure veux-tu manger?
Comment vont-ils à Montmartre?

As you say questions and students repeat them, call attention to **liaison** where it occurs. Be sure to show the insertion of the **t** to make pronunciation easier where, otherwise, two vowels would come together: **Va-t-il au pique-nique? Prépare-t-elle les sandwiches?**

When students understand the principles using only pronouns, go back and demonstrate each of the points, using questions with noun subjects:

Est-ce que Laure a téléphoné?
A quelle heure est-ce que Laure a téléphoné?
Laure a-t-elle téléphoné?
A quelle heure Laure a-t-elle téléphoné?

Finally, explain that inversion is not used much in informal conversation, but that it should be used in writing. Now have students open their books and read the explanation carefully.

C9 Activité • Posez des questions

As students phrase each question, call on other individuals to play the role of the friend who phones and to answer the question.

C10 Activité • Encore des questions

For cooperative learning, have students pair off to complete the dialogue. Then have them practice saying it, exchanging roles each time.

C11 Activité • Ecrit dirigé

As the students read the questions they have written, call on others to make up answers to them.

C12 Activité • A vous maintenant!

As students work in pairs to prepare the dialogue, circulate and listen. On the board or on a transparency, write corrections of common errors you may have overheard. Go over them with the class. Ask a pair of volunteers to present their dialogue to the class. Have them do it a second time, pausing after each utterance for you to elicit variations created by other pairs.

C13 COMMENT LE DIRE

Have students extend invitations and make suggestions. For each invitation or suggestion, have other students respond with various expressions of regret.

To elicit **Quel dommage!** and **C'est dommage,** have students describe an unfortunate situation: **J'ai eu un petit accident ce matin** or **Tiens! J'ai perdu mon cahier!**

SLOWER-PACED LEARNING   You, rather than students, should present suggestions, invitations, and descriptions of unfortunate situations.

C14 Activité • Exprimez le regret

CHALLENGE   Have students make up their own situations to which other students respond.

C15 Activité • A vous maintenant!

SLOWER-PACED LEARNING   Before having students pair off, help them determine the **passé composé** forms they will need. Then brainstorm with students how they will express regret in each case.

C16 Activité • Complétez le dialogue

Have students work individually to decide which expression of regret and which reason to use in response to each suggestion. Then have them pair off to role-play the dialogue twice, switching roles the second time.

CHALLENGE   Encourage students to make up their own reasons instead of using the ones given in the box.

C17 Activité • Ecoutez bien

You're going to hear a radio broadcast direct from the Bastille Day parade. Open your book to page 115. *(pause)* Read the incomplete sentences and the suggested completions in C17 silently. *(pause)* Be prepared to indicate your answers on a separate sheet of paper. Ready? **Ecoutez bien.**

Mesdames, Mesdemoiselles, Messieurs, bonjour. Il est dix heures dix. Le ciel est complètement bleu, et quelle foule il y a aujourd'hui sur les Champs-Elysées pour assister au traditionnel défilé militaire du 14 Juillet!... Le président de la République est arrivé à la place Charles-de-Gaulle il y a dix minutes; il a été très applaudi. Et maintenant arrivent... les majorettes! Ce qu'elles sont merveilleuses, les majorettes!... Elles sont accompagnées par les musiciens de l'orchestre militaire... Ensuite viennent les troupes à pied... puis les troupes motorisées. Qu'ils sont énormes, les chars! *(noise of aircraft)* Entendez-vous ce bruit? Ce sont les hélicoptères et les avions de l'armée de l'air... Mais voilà les sympathiques pompiers dans leur uniforme rouge! Tout le monde applaudit très fort. Bravo, messieurs les Pompiers!... Mesdames, Mesdemoiselles, Messieurs, je vous remercie. Je vais maintenant laisser l'antenne à mon confrère Yves Danzac qui attend à la place de la Concorde. Au revoir et bon 14 Juillet!

Et maintenant, vérifions.

1. a	le matin	4. a	beaucoup
2. c	beau	5. c	en dernier
3. b	Paris	6. b	en avion

TRY YOUR SKILLS

OBJECTIVE To recombine communicative functions, grammar, and vocabulary

CULTURAL BACKGROUND On July 14, from 9:00 A.M. until noon, the traditional military parade takes place on the **Champs-Elysées** in Paris. There is an air show going on overhead at the same time: planes flying fast and in formation trail streaks of red, white, and blue smoke. The various uniforms of the soldiers, national guard, and police are impressive, as are the huge tanks and pieces of military equipment. Fireworks displays are held at 10:30 P.M. The bridges, the Eiffel Tower, the steps near the **palais de Chaillot,** and the steps from **Sacré Cœur** in **Montmartre** are excellent places from which to watch.

MOTIVATING ACTIVITY Have students share their observations on the differences between July 14 in France and July 4 in the United States.

1 ## Après le défilé

Show the questions in Skills 2 on transparency. Play the cassette or have two students read the dialogue aloud. Students listen with books closed to find the answers to the questions. They may take notes as they listen.

2 ### Activité • Répondez

Use this activity as suggested above in Skills 1.

3 ### Activité • Au défilé

For cooperative learning, have students form groups of four to compose questions based on the illustration. One person in the group should write them down. Then another member of the group should ask the rest of the class the questions. If students are unable to answer, other group members should respond.

4 ### Activité • Célébrez le 14 Juillet

First work with the entire class. Ask individuals if they would like to go to the museum, see the fireworks, or watch TV. Have students give reasons for their preferences. Then have students work in pairs to plan the way they will spend the day. They might make a schedule of their activities for the morning, afternoon, and evening. Using their schedules and notes, they should then tell the class what they've planned to do.

CHALLENGE Have pairs of students do the same activity, using the program for Carnival in Quebec shown on page 92.

5 ### Activité • Situations

Brainstorm with the students expressions of admiration, surprise, indecision, indifference, and regret. Write these on the board as reminders. Then have students work together in pairs either on all four situations or on one assigned situation. Volunteers might present their dialogues to the class.

6 ### Activité • Au Carnaval

SLOWER-PACED LEARNING First work with the entire class to elicit the verbs that will be needed.

CHALLENGE   After the activity, have students write a paragraph describing the party and what went on.

7   Activité • A vous maintenant!

Begin by eliciting from students activities in which they might have participated during **Mardi Gras** and how they might have dressed.

8   Activité • Bon appétit!

For cooperative learning, form groups of three, one member to be the waiter or waitress. Groups should present their skits to the class.

9   Activité • Ecrit dirigé

SLOWER-PACED LEARNING   Construct a sample "diary entry" with the students. Ask each question and elicit an answer. Write the answers on the board or on a transparency, and have the students copy the completed sample to use as a model when they write their own entries. As you correct papers, put some of the common errors on a transparency and correct them with the entire class.

10   Activité • Récréation

This activity is optional. You might make it a contest. See who can write the five words most quickly. Have students make up other sets of three words that suggest a fourth and use them to challenge their classmates.

PRONONCIATION

Liaison

Open your book to page 121. *(pause)* Refer to this page as you listen to this section.

1   Ecoutez bien et répétez.

Now that you know how to speak French in syllables and sense-groups, the next thing to learn is how to link the syllables together. You did this before when you cut the word sequences into syllables. Remember: **Il arrive avec une amie. I-la-rri-va-ve-cu-na-mi.** Notice that each syllable after the first begins with a consonant and ends with a vowel.

But what happens if the next syllable begins with a vowel, not with a consonant? First listen to how you would handle this sort of linking in English. You say things like *Not the pear, but the apple.* Notice that the linking between *the* and *pear*—*the pear*—is different from the one between *the* and *apple*—*the apple.* Did you hear the little y-sound? Listen again: *the apple.*

In French, this sort of thing is much more common than it is in English. Listen to this: **Lundi après-midi.** Did you hear the **y**-sound in **yaprès** as you did in *yapple*—the same sort of glide? It's as if the language wants to start the syllable with some sort of consonant, even if it's only a little one. It's simply the sound produced by the most natural position of your lips and tongue when you pass from one sound to the next. Try saying these word groups with the right glide: **midi et demi, samedi à midi, samedi ou dimanche, Je sais où il est.**

Sometimes you don't have to change the position of your lips or tongue when gliding from one vowel to another. Why? Because they may be the same vowel. Listen to this: **Il a acheté du pain.** What did you hear? Simply a double **a** which could sound like one long **aaaa.** These glides help you say each sense-group as if it were one word.

2   Ecoutez et lisez.

1. In linking French syllables together, you have to watch for the words that end in a consonant that is not pronounced. In fact, most final consonants in written French are hardly ever pronounced. Compare just a few words you already know by reading aloud the first group in your book. I'll repeat the words after you: *(pause)* **est,** *(pause)* **les,** *(pause)* **nos,** *(pause)* **chez,** *(pause)* **projets.**

2. You do tend to hear, however, the final **l**- and **r**-sounds, but not the consonants that follow them. Read aloud the next group of words: *(pause)* **ils,** *(pause)* **elles,** *(pause)* **hôtels,** *(pause)* **tard,** *(pause)* **fort,** *(pause)* **vers.**

3. Even though you seldom hear final written consonants, it's important to know that they're there, because you pronounce them when you have to link one word to another. This makes it possible to start the next syllable with a consonant, making it fit nicely into the basic French speech pattern. Listen to these examples and repeat them: **Il est là. I-lé-la.** *(pause)* **Il est ici. I-lé-ti-ci.** *(pause)*

The most common linking sound is /z/, which you often write as an **s.** Listen to these meaning groups and repeat them: **nos amis, no-za-mi** *(pause),* **les amies, lé-za-mi** *(pause),* **les Etats-Unis, lé-zé-ta-zu-ni.** *(pause)*

Another frequent linking sound is /t/. Remember, you always say **il est** and **elle écoute,** but you ask **est-il?** and **écoute-t-elle?** The **t**-linker appears in many common expressions that you should learn to say fluently, as if each were a single word. Try these: **tout à l'heure, tou-ta-l'heure** *(pause),* **Comment allez-vous? Co-men-ta-lé-vous?** *(pause)*

This linker is so popular that sometimes a final **d** is changed to the sound /t/. Listen to these: you say **elle vend** and **il prend,** but you ask **vend-elle?** and **prend-il?**

The **t**-linker may even be added when no other linker is around. You say **il y a,** but you ask **y a-t-il;** you say **Elle a un frère,** but you ask **A-t-elle un frère?**

The third popular linker is the sound /n/, possibly because so many words end with a nasal vowel, as in **mon, ton, son.** Listen to and repeat the following word groups, making the linking /n/ in the second half of each phrase: **mon frère et mon ami** *(pause),* **ton père et ton oncle** *(pause).*

4. In some cases, a stop is needed instead of a linkage. Listen: **Ils sont arrivés le onze... le onze.** You hear this most often before certain words written with an **h.** It helps make their meanings clear. Compare **les zéros,** which means *zeros,* with **les héros,** meaning *heros.*

Read aloud the pairs of words in *4b.* Remember, don't use any linkages. I'll repeat after you: *(pause)* **haricot—les haricots,** *(pause)* **Hollande—**

la Hollande, *(pause)* **homard**—le homard, *(pause)* **haut**—en haut.
You say many numerals with stops, as in **le onze.** You also use a stop when you say **cent onze** and **le huit.** The same thing happens before certain words, like **oui** or **alors.** You say **mais oui** and **et alors.** Read aloud the numbers and expressions in 4c and *d: (pause)* **le onze,** *(pause)* **cent onze,** *(pause)* **le huit,** *(pause)* **mais oui,** *(pause)* **et alors.**
5. Now try a few of these types of stops with some of the linkers you already know. Read aloud the dialogue. I'll say each line after you.

—Tu pars quand? Le onze?
—Mais oui. Samedi à midi et demi avec mon oncle Albert. Et toi?
—Lundi après-midi. Nous arrivons chez eux vers six heures.

3 **Copiez les phrases suivantes pour préparer une dictée.**

Write the following sentences from dictation. First listen to the sentence as it is read to you. Then you will hear the sentence again in short segments, with a pause after each segment to allow you time to write. Finally you will hear the sentence a third time so that you may check your work. Let's begin.

1. On est arrivé le onze. On est arrivé *(pause)* le onze. *(pause)* On est arrivé le onze.
2. C'est chouette d'être en haut. C'est chouette *(pause)* d'être en haut. *(pause)* C'est chouette d'être en haut.
3. Quand est-ce que Laure a téléphoné? Quand est-ce que *(pause)* Laure a téléphoné? *(pause)* Quand est-ce que Laure a téléphoné?
4. A-t-elle un frère? A-t-elle *(pause)* un frère? *(pause)* A-t-elle un frère?
5. Comment allez-vous? Comment allez-vous? *(pause)* Comment allez-vous?

VERIFIONS!

SECTION A Review A7, A8, and A14. Have students write out the two exercises; circulate and check their papers as they write. If you spot common errors, correct them on the board for all to see; call on students to explain proper forms and usage.

SECTION B Review B4, B6, and B13. Have students write out the three exercises. You might have three volunteers write their answers on a transparency. When students have completed the exercises, project the transparency. Correct any errors. Students refer to the transparency to correct their own work.

SECTION C Review C8 and C13. Read the four sentences in the first part aloud, and call on students to express their regret. The four questions, restated to use **est-ce que,** might be written on the board by individuals, after all students have had a chance to write them out at their desks.

VOCABULAIRE

Divide the class in half for a game of Charades. Ahead of time, write out on small pieces of folded paper those words that you feel can be acted out. One member of a team stands in front of his or her team, picks a word at random, and acts it out. If the team guesses the word correctly, it is a point for their side (usually 30 to 60 seconds is enough time). Teams alternate in picking and acting out words.

ETUDE DE MOTS

Students might also create adverbs from the adjectives **regrettable, froid, ouvert, joyeux,** and **rude.** For additional practice, students might make verbs from these nouns: **le défilé, un chant, un cri,** and **la résistance.**

A LIRE

OBJECTIVE To read for practice and pleasure

LA MARSEILLAISE

Start with **Avant de lire**. Ask students what **Alsace** is and what **Marseille** is. Point them out on a map of France. Ask a student to look up *paradox* in an English dictionary and to read the definition to the class. Allow students to explain in English the paradox of the «**Marseillaise**».

Before students begin to read, prepare multiple-choice items like the ones below. With books closed, have the students indicate what they think the answers are. Tell them that you will not see their answers—the point of the exercise is simply to focus their attention.

  1. L'hymne national de la France a été composé vers
     a. 1850.
     b. 1790.
  2. Rouget de Lisle était
     a. président de la France.
     b. dans l'armée.
  3. «La Marseillaise» a son titre parce que
     a. les soldats de Marseille l'ont chantée à Paris.
     b. les Parisiens l'ont introduite à Marseille.

Play the cassette or ask volunteers to read the text aloud. Have students go back to the multiple-choice items and mark the correct answers. Finally, play a recording of the «**Marseillaise**» (Unit Cassette 22, **Nouveaux copains**) and conduct a sing-along.

Activité • Connaissez-vous votre hymne national?

"The Star-Spangled Banner" was written in 1814 by Francis Scott Key, during the War of 1812. The poem was inspired by the sight of the American flag still flying at dawn over Fort McHenry after an unsuccessful night attack by the British.

Activité • Ecrit dirigé

Ask a volunteer to write his or her paragraph on a transparency. Project the paragraph and correct any errors. The other students may use the model to correct their own paragraphs.

BONHOMME CARNAVAL

Before they begin reading, ask students to summarize what they've already learned about **Carnaval.** Have them identify the characters in the illustrations. Then play the cassette or have volunteers read aloud as students follow along in their books. Pause at the end of each passage to ask questions: **Quel est le rôle du Bonhomme Carnaval à Québec? Dans le monde?**

Activité • Devinez

If students have difficulty, tell them to examine for clues the sentence in which the word was used. You might choose other words in the selection for further practice in guessing from context.

Activité • Qui est-ce? Qu'est-ce que c'est?

You might use this chart in a competition. Students should copy and complete it, referring back to the selection, or not, as you wish. The first individual or team to complete it correctly wins.

Activité • La leçon d'histoire

Jacques Cartier discovered the St. Lawrence River and explored the area surrounding it. Samuel de Champlain established a colony at Quebec and discovered Lake Champlain. General Louis Joseph de Montcalm was defeated by the English in the battle for Quebec.

LA CHANSON DU CARNAVAL

Play the cassette and have students sing along. If students are reluctant to sing, have the song playing as they come into class. In this way they hear the words and music in a relaxed frame of mind and may pick up the song on their own.

CHAPITRE 3

Amusons-nous!

Winter or summer, the French-speaking world enjoys itself. *Carnaval* in Quebec is a winter spectacle not to be missed. July in France is alive with festivities celebrating Bastille Day. Entertainment, though, isn't just for special occasions. Amusement parks provide everyday pleasure.

In this unit you will:

PREMIER CONTACT	get acquainted with the topic
SECTION A	talk about Carnival in Quebec . . . exclaim, express admiration and surprise
SECTION B	talk about rides at an amusement park . . . express feelings, indecision, and indifference
SECTION C	make arrangements to celebrate France's national holiday . . . express regret
TRY YOUR SKILLS	use what you've learned
A LIRE	read for practice and pleasure

PREMIER CONTACT getting acquainted with the topic

The authentic material in Premier Contact introduces the theme of the unit and is to be used for global comprehension only.

1

Le Carnaval de Québec 📼

Amusons-nous au Carnaval de Québec. Il y a des activités pour tous. Voici le programme.

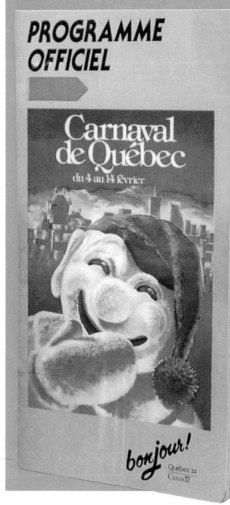

PROGRAMME OFFICIEL

Carnaval de Québec
du 4 au 14 février

bonjour!
Québec ::
Canada

SAMEDI 7 FEVRIER
19h00 DEFILE DE NUIT DU CARNAVAL
Variété de chars allégoriques tous illuminés, fanfares, personnages loufoques et animation.
Parcours : départ coin boulevard Henri-Bourassa, 1re avenue, 41e rue est, 4e avenue est, 22e rue, boul. des Alliés, Avenue du Colisée.

MERCREDI 11 FEVRIER
19h00 SOUPER CANADIEN
Lieu : Château Frontenac.
Réservations : 612-9120

20h00 PREMIER MATCH LNH/URSS
Partie de hockey opposant les joueurs étoiles de la Ligue nationale de hockey aux membres de l'équipe nationale d'Union Soviétique.
Lieu : Colisée de Québec.
Match télévisé.

DIMANCHE 8 FEVRIER
10h00 FETE POPULAIRE DE L'HIVER
Ouvert à la participation populaire. Ski de fond, patin, raquette, glissade, marche en plein-air.
Lieu : St-Frédéric, St-Simon-des-Mines, St-Théophile, St-Prosper, Ste-Justine.

MARDI 10 FEVRIER
21h00 SOIREE DU MARDI-GRAS
Super soirée costumée et dansante aux rythmes de la Louisiane et de l'Acadie.
Groupes invités : EXPRESSO S.V.P. de l'Acadie et WAYNE TOUPS de la Louisiane. Artiste spécial invité : MICHAEL DOUCET du groupe Beausoleil.
Lieu : Centre Durocher, 290, rue Carillon.
Admission : 6 $.

VENDREDI 13 FEVRIER
21h00 LA NUIT NOIRE
Inspirée du célèbre vidéo-clip de Michael Jackson, «Thriller», cette soirée thématique où l'humour noir sera à l'honneur vous promet des sensations de toutes sortes. Vidéos, animation et présence des Zoo-boys. Plusieurs prix à gagner.
Lieu : Centre municipal des congrès.
Admission : 6 $.

21h00 SOIREE FAIS DODO
Soirée de danse dans la tradition. de la Louisiane. Les enfants sont les bienvenus. Avec WAYNE TOUPS. Artiste invité : MICHAEL DOUCET du groupe Beausoleil.
Lieu : Théâtre du Grand Dérangement, 30 St-Stanislas.
Admission : 6 $.

chars: floats   personnages loufoques: costumed characters
glissade: sledding   souper: dîner   fais dodo: go night-night

2   Activité • Cherchez des renseignements

Lisez le programme pour trouver ces renseignements sur le Carnaval.

1. En quelle saison est le Carnaval? *En hiver.*
2. Dans quel pays? *Au Canada.*
3. Dans quelle ville? *A Québec.*
4. Quand? *Du 4 au 14 février.*
5. Combien de jours dure-t-il? *Onze jours.*

3   Activité • Réfléchissez

1. Qu'est-ce qu'on peut faire pendant le Carnaval? *1. On peut danser, voir des animations, des vidéos ou un match de hockey et faire du ski de fond, du patin ou des glissades.*
2. Pourquoi est-ce qu'il y a des danses et de la musique de Louisiane?
2. Les gens de l'Acadie et de la Louisiane ont un héritage français en commun.

4   **LE 14 JUILLET**

The French national holiday commemorates the taking of the Bastille prison on July 14, 1789. This marked the outbreak of the French Revolution, which eventually changed France's system of government from a monarchy to a republic.

Le 14 Juillet est la fête nationale en France. Tous les journaux en parlent!

MARDI 14 JUILLET

LA VIE POLITIQUE

De la place Charles-de-Gaulle à la place de la Concorde

Plus de 6000 hommes participent au défilé

Dès 7 heures, sont appliquées des restrictions au stationnement et à la circulation.

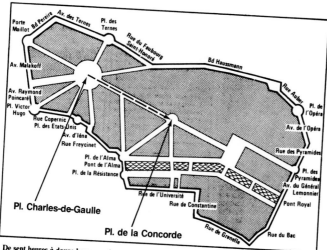

De sept heures à douze heures environ, la circulation et le stationnement seront interdits à l'intérieur de ce périmètre.

Sous le double thème de la tradition et de la technologie, se déroulera ce matin le défilé du 14 Juillet. Plus de six mille hommes participeront à la revue de la place Charles-de-Gaulle à la place de la Concorde, où a été édifiée la tribune présidentielle.

Voici la chronologie générale du défilé :

— 8 h 30 : Animation musicale jusqu'à 9 h 30.
— 9 heures : Mise en place des troupes.
— 10 heures : Arrivée du président de la République place Charles-de-Gaulle.
— 10 h 20 : Arrivée du président de la République place de la Concorde.

— 10 h 30 : Défilé aérien.
— 10 h 35 : Défilé des troupes à pied.
— 11 heures : Défilé des troupes montées et motocyclistes.
— 11 h 05 : Défilé des troupes mécanisées.
— 11 h 35 : Fin du défilé.

Il coûte 900.000 F

Un feu d'artifice jamais vu à Paris !

La mairie de Paris offre ce soir, à 22 h 30, aux habitants de la capitale et aux visiteurs le plus gigantesque feu d'artifice jamais tiré à l'occasion d'un 14-Juillet.

Sept cent cinquante tonnes d'explosifs, des fusées éclatant à cinq cents mètres d'altitude, quatre cent mille spectateurs attendus, le tout pour un coût de 900.000 francs, dont 450.000 pour la seule pyrotechnie. Pour l'illustration musicale, les artificiers de la maison Lacroix ont puisé dans les œuvres de vingt et un grands compositeurs classiques.

Un bon conseil : pour vous y rendre, préférez le métro à la voiture, les places seront rares et éloignées. C'est vu du Champs-de-Mars ou des bords de la Seine que le spectacle sera le plus beau.

le défilé: parade   le stationnement: parking   la circulation: traffic   le feu d'artifice: fireworks display

---

5   Activité • Complétez

Relisez l'article sur le défilé et complétez ces phrases.

1. Le défilé commence… à la place Charles-de-Gaulle.
2. Il finit… à la place de la Concorde.
3. Les deux thèmes du défilé sont… la tradition et la technologie.
4. Avant le défilé il y a… une animation musicale.
5. Les avions défilent à… 10h30.

6   Activité • Et vous?

1. Aimez-vous regarder les défilés? Et les feux d'artifice?
2. Quand est-ce qu'il y a un défilé et un feu d'artifice dans votre ville?
3. Avez-vous déjà participé à un défilé? Racontez votre expérience.

L'hiver est long et rude au Canada. Au début de février, les Québécois sont fatigués de la neige, de la glace et du froid. Ils sont prêts à s'amuser.

Carnival traditionally is a period of feasting and merrymaking immediately preceding Lent—a Christian holiday. It is celebrated worldwide, with major events occurring in New Orleans, Quebec, Rio de Janeiro, Nice, and Venice.

A1

Bienvenue au Carnaval

Rendez-vous à Québec pour le Carnaval! Venez nombreux, jeunes et vieux! C'est formidable, c'est fantastique! Tout le monde est joyeux… enfin, presque tout le monde.

«Chaque année, je viens exprès de Montréal pour assister au Carnaval. Pourquoi? Parce que l'ambiance est merveilleuse! Les gens sont gais, ouverts, sympathiques. On est ami avec tout le monde. On peut parler à tout le monde. C'est vraiment spécial.»

(Marie)

«Le Carnaval, nous, on adore! La ville est pleine de couleurs et de musique! Il y a des compétitions sportives et artistiques, des tournois de hockey, des défilés de chars… Dommage que ça ne dure pas toute l'année!»

(Raymond et Monique)

«J'ai soixante-huit ans et je suis une fan de Bonhomme Carnaval. Je ne cours pas les rues avec les jeunes mais je danse au Carnaval tous les ans avec mon mari.»

(Mme Gagné)

bonhomme (de neige): snowman

«Le Carnaval, j'en ai assez! Déjà le Saint-Laurent est gelé, les rues sont enneigées, c'est difficile de circuler en voiture; mais en plus, avec les défilés et les danses, on ne peut plus avancer. Et la nuit, comme j'habite la place Carnaval, j'entends le bruit, la musique, les cris, les chants; je n'arrive pas à dormir!»

(M. Côté)

A2 Activité • Ajoutez une phrase

Possible answers are given.

Parlez du Carnaval. Ajoutez une ou deux phrases.

Le Carnaval est une fête.   Tout le monde est joyeux.

1. Il fait froid à Québec.   1. Les gens sont fatigués de la neige.
2. Marie vient de Montréal pour assister au Carnaval.   2. Elle adore le Carnaval.
3. Il y a des compétitions et des défilés.   3. C'est fantastique à voir!
4. Mme Gagné aime le Carnaval.   4. Elle danse avec son mari.
5. C'est difficile de circuler.   5. Les rues sont enneigées.
6. M. Côté n'aime pas le Carnaval.   6. Il y a beaucoup de bruit!

A3 Activité • Le pour et le contre

Possible answers are given.

Faites une liste des avantages et des inconvénients (*disadvantages*) du Carnaval.

Les gens sont gais et sympathiques. On peut parler à tout le monde. La ville est pleine de couleurs et de musique. Il y a des compétitions sportives et artistiques.

Avantages	Inconvénients
Tout le monde est joyeux.	C'est difficile de circuler en voiture.

On ne peut plus avancer. Il y a trop de bruit. On n'arrive pas à dormir.

A4 Activité • A vous maintenant!

Vous assistez au Carnaval à Québec avec votre classe de français. Votre ami(e) français(e) vous téléphone de Paris. Préparez la conversation avec un(e) camarade de classe. Parlez de la ville de Québec, du temps, de l'ambiance, des gens et des activités du Carnaval.

Activité • Ecrit dirigé

Vous êtes à Québec. Vous écrivez une lettre à votre ami(e) français(e). Choisissez les verbes pour compléter ce paragraphe. Mettez-les à la forme correcte. Attention au temps des verbes!

participer — avancer — durer — circuler — neiger — être

Hier soir il ____ *a neigé*! Ce matin, toute la ville ____ *est* blanche! C'est très joli. Les voitures ____ *circulent* *avancent* avec difficulté et les gens ____ lentement dans les rues. Le Carnaval ____ dix jours. Il y a *dure* beaucoup de choses à faire; nous allons ____ à presque toutes les activités!
participer

A 6 Savez-vous que... ?

Le Carnaval de Québec a lieu chaque année en février. Pendant dix jours, Bonhomme Carnaval est partout. Bonhomme Carnaval a sa rue — la rue Carnaval, sa place — la place Carnaval, son palais — le Palais de Glace, sa Reine et ses Duchesses, sept jolies filles qui représentent sept divisions de la ville de Québec. Tous les Québécois participent joyeusement à la fête, et des milliers de visiteurs viennent de toute la province pour célébrer le Carnaval.

Le Palais de Glace

You may wish to introduce this poem as a mnemonic device for adjectives that usually precede the noun: petit, grand, gros
vilain, joli, beau
autre, long,
mauvais, bon,
jeune, vieux, nouveau.

A 7 VOUS EN SOUVENEZ-VOUS?
Adjectives

Here's a review of what you've learned about French adjectives.

Masculine		Feminine	
Singular	*Plural*	*Singular*	*Plural*
Il est **grand**.	Ils sont **grands**.	Elle est **grande**.	Elles sont **grandes**.
Il est **joyeux**.	Ils sont **joyeux**.	Elle est **joyeuse**.	Elles sont **joyeuses**.
Il est **joli**.	Ils sont **jolis**.	Elle est **jolie**.	Elles sont **jolies**.
Il est **immense**.	Ils sont **immenses**.	Elle est **immense**.	Elles sont **immenses**.
Il est **canadien**.	Ils sont **canadiens**.	Elle est **canadienne**.	Elles sont **canadiennes**.

1. Adjectives agree in gender and number with the nouns they refer to.
2. Most adjectives follow the nouns they refer to: **une rue étroite, une fête joyeuse**. A few common, short adjectives come before the nouns: **grand, petit, bon, mauvais, jeune, joli, autre, beau, vieux,** and **nouveau**.
3. **Beau, vieux,** and **nouveau** have a special form that is used before a masculine singular noun beginning with a vowel sound: **un bel enfant, un vieil homme, un nouvel ami.**

STRUCTURES DE BASE
Adjectives ending in -al *and* -if

Masculine		Feminine	
Singular	*Plural*	*Singular*	*Plural*
Il est **spécial.**	Ils sont **spéciaux.**	Elle est **spéciale.**	Elles sont **spéciales.**
Il est **sportif.**	Ils sont **sportifs.**	Elle est **sportive.**	Elles sont **sportives.**

1. To form the masculine plural of most adjectives that end in **-al,** change **-al** to **-aux:** **spécial→spéciaux. Banal** is an exception: **banal→banals.**
2. To make the feminine forms of adjectives that end in **-if,** change **f** to **v** and then add **-e** or **-es:** **sportif(s)→sportive(s).**
3. You've already seen several adjectives that make their plural and feminine forms in this way: **original, principal, familial, actif, naïf,** and **vif.**   Also: normal, génial
4. In familiar language, the masculine singular form of adjectives is used after **c'est: C'est spécial!**

Activité • Décrivez les gens au Carnaval   Possible answers are given.

Au carnaval de Québec, il y a des gens de toute nationalité : des Américains, des Canadiens, des Français, des Mexicains… Décrivez-les avec les adjectifs **américain, canadien, français, mexicain, sportif, créatif, grand, joli** et **joyeux.** Par exemple : Ils sont américains. Ils sont…

1.

Ils sont américains. Ils sont sportifs.

2.

Ils sont canadiens. Ils sont créatifs.

3.

Elles sont françaises. Elles sont jolies.

4.

Ils sont mexicains. Ils sont joyeux.

Activité • Ecrit dirigé   Possible answers are given.

Continuez la lettre que vous avez commencée dans A5. Voici un autre paragraphe. Complétez la description du Carnaval par des adjectifs à la forme correcte.

> fantastique · sympathique · heureux gais
>
> Le Carnaval est ____ ! Tout le monde est ____ . Jeunes et vieux sont ____ et ____ .
> spéciale L'ambiance est ____ . Avec la neige la ville de Québec est ____ . Dans les rues j'entends
> les cris ____ de·la foule. C'est vraiment ____ !   très jolie
> joyeux · extra

Samedi soir, tout le monde va au défilé. Les Québécois attendent le long de l'avenue du Colisée pour voir passer le défilé. Lucie et Robert expriment leur joie.

LUCIE   Quelle foule! C'est à quelle heure, le défilé?

ROBERT   A sept heures, je crois. Les voilà! Ils arrivent!

LUCIE   Qu'il est drôle, Bonhomme Carnaval! Tu ne trouves pas?

ROBERT   Si, très drôle!

LUCIE   Eh! Regarde ce char! Ce qu'elle est belle, la Reine! Mais qu'est-ce qu'elle doit avoir froid!

ROBERT   Vive la Reine! Vive les Duchesses!

LUCIE   Quel froid! Moi, je rentre.

ROBERT   Mais non, reste! Ce n'est pas encore fini. Maintenant il y a un superbe feu d'artifice.

A12 Activité • Complétez

1. Samedi soir... il y a le défilé.
2. Le défilé... commence à 7h.
3. Lucie et Robert... regardent le défilé.
4. Dans le défilé il y a... Bonhomme Carnaval, la Reine et les Duchesses.
5. La Reine... est belle.
6. Après le défilé... il y a un feu d'artifice.

Activité • A vous maintenant! 🔲 Possible answers are given.

Répétez ce dialogue avec un(e) camarade. Changez le nom et les adjectifs pour créer des dialogues différents. Changez de rôle.
—Qu'elles sont jolies, les Duchesses! Tu ne trouves pas?
—Si, très jolies!

— Qu'il est grand, Bonhomme Carnaval! Tu ne trouves pas?
— Si, très grand!
—Qu'elle est belle, la Reine! Tu ne trouves pas?
—Si, très belle!

—Qu'il est fantastique, le défilé! Tu ne trouves pas?
—Si! Il est fantastique!

—Qu'elle est grande, la foule! Tu ne trouves pas?
—Si, très grande!

—Qu'il est superbe, le feu d'artifice! Tu ne trouves pas?
—Si! Il est superbe!

A14 **COMMENT LE DIRE**
Exclaiming

Here are some ways to express admiration and surprise.

Ce qu'elles sont belles, les Duchesses!	How beautiful the Duchesses are!
Qu'il est drôle, Bonhomme Carnaval!	How funny Bonhomme Carnaval is!
Qu'est-ce qu'elle doit avoir froid!	How cold she must be!
Quelle foule!	What a crowd!

Ce que, que, qu'est-ce que, or a form of the adjective **quel** may be used to mean *how* or *what a*.

A15 Activité • Faites des exclamations 🔲 Possible answers are given.

Vous parlez à votre ami(e). Changez vos remarques en exclamations. Variez les expressions d'exclamation.

Il fait beau.   Qu'il fait beau!

1. J'ai faim. Qu'est-ce que j'ai faim!
2. La foule est immense. Quelle foule!
3. C'est une idée originale. Quelle idée originale!
4. Il neige. Ce qu'il neige!
5. Le défilé est long. Qu'il est long, le défilé!
6. Le feu d'artifice est beau. Qu'est-ce qu'il est beau, le feu d'artifice!

A16 Activité • Quel beau défilé! Possible answers are given.

Vous regardez le défilé du Carnaval avec un(e) ami(e). A tour de rôle, utilisez des exclamations pour exprimer votre joie. Variez les expressions. Attention à la forme de l'adjectif.

la neige / beau   Ce que la neige est belle!

1. les Duchesses / beau
2. la foule / joyeux
3. le Bonhomme / drôle
4. les chars / beau
5. la fête / génial
6. l'ambiance / gai
7. les rues / enneigé
8. la Reine / joli

1. Que les Duchesses sont belles! 2. Quelle foule joyeuse! 3. Ce qu'il est drôle, le Bonhomme! 4. Qu'est-ce qu'ils sont beaux, les chars! 5. Quelle fête géniale! 6. Qu'est-ce que l'ambiance est gaie! 7. Ce qu'elles sont enneigées, les rues! 8. Quelle jolie Reine!

Possible answers are given.

Activité • Qu'est-ce qu'ils disent?

1. Qu'est-ce que j'ai faim!
2. Qu'est-ce qu'ils sont drôles!
3. Ce qu'ils sont bons!
4. Quelle foule!
5. Qu'il est bon, le gâteau!
6. Qu'est-ce que les rues sont enneigées!

Activité • A vous maintenant!

Travaillez avec un(e) camarade de classe. Lisez les situations suivantes et préparez des dialogues.

1. (Vous regardez le programme.)
   Proposez une activité à votre camarade. Employez les expressions dans A12 au Chapitre 2. Il/Elle refuse. Vous discutez et vous choisissez ensemble une autre activité.
2. (Vous assistez au spectacle.)
   Exprimez votre joie. Employez les exclamations dans A14.
3. (Le spectacle est terminé.)
   Vous sortez et vous discutez. Vous avez beaucoup aimé. Employez le passé composé et aussi les expressions dans A4 et B4 au Chapitre 1.

FÊTONS LE CARNAVAL

MERCREDI 11 FEVRIER
19h00 SOUPER CANADIEN
Lieu : Château Frontenac.
Réservations : 612-9120

20h00 PREMIER MATCH LNH/URSS
Partie de hockey opposant les joueurs étoiles de la Ligue nationale de hockey aux membres de l'équipe nationale d'Union Soviétique.
Lieu : Colisée de Québec.
Match télévisé.

VENDREDI 13 FEVRIER
21h00 LA NUIT NOIRE
Inspirée du célèbre vidéo-clip de Michael Jackson, «Thriller», cette soirée thématique où l'humour noir sera à l'honneur vous promet des sensations de toutes sortes. Vidéos, animation et présence des Zoo-boys. Plusieurs prix à gagner.
Lieu : Centre municipal des congrès.
Admission : 6 $.

21h00 SOIREE FAIS DODO
Soirée de danse dans la tradition de la Louisiane. Les enfants sont les bienvenus. Avec WAYNE TOUPS. Artiste invité : MICHAEL DOUCET du groupe Beausoleil.
Lieu : Théâtre du Grand Dérangement, 30 St-Stanislas
Admission : 6 $.

Le Château Frontenac

Grand Dérangement: the deportation of the Acadians

Activité • Ecoutez bien   For script and answers, see p. T74.

Vous téléphonez pour savoir le programme du Carnaval pour le week-end. Ecoutez bien le message et choisissez vos activités.

Vous voulez. . .	Quel jour?	A quelle heure?
1. voir un match sportif.		
2. aller au théâtre.		
3. dîner.		
4. aller danser.		

talking about rides at an amusement park . . . expressing feelings, indecision, and indifference

Pour s'amuser, on peut toujours aller passer l'après-midi dans un parc d'attractions. Qu'est-ce que vous préférez? Le palais des Glaces ou les montagnes russes?

B1   A Zygofolis 📼

For information on Zygofolis, see p. 109.

Un parc d'attractions, ça peut être drôlement amusant! Demandez à Nicole et à son ami Simon.

Moi, je suis une fonceuse. Je veux vivre rapidement, intensément. Pour moi, les attractions, c'est fabuleux!

Fonceur? Pas moi. Je suis plus réservé. Je suis passionné d'ordinateurs. J'aime vivre tranquillement.

Mais, pour lui faire plaisir, Simon accompagne Nicole à Zygofolis, près de Nice.

NICOLE   Par quoi est-ce que tu veux commencer?
SIMON   Euh…
NICOLE   Par les montagnes russes ou par le train fantôme?
SIMON   Je ne sais pas trop.
NICOLE   Bon! Commençons par le train fantôme. D'accord?
SIMON   Comme tu veux.

NICOLE	Ou par les montagnes russes?
SIMON	Ce que tu préfères.
NICOLE	Tu n'as pas de préférence?
SIMON	Non, ça m'est égal.
NICOLE	Alors, commençons par le palais des Glaces. Ça te va?
SIMON	Oui, oui... Dis, on mange à quelle heure?

B2 Activité • Répondez

1. Comment est Nicole? Elle est fonceuse. Elle aime vivre intensément.
2. Quelle est la passion de Simon? Sa passion, c'est les ordinateurs.
3. Pourquoi est-ce que Simon accompagne Nicole au parc? Il y va pour lui faire plaisir.
4. Par où est-ce qu'ils commencent? Ils commencent par le palais des Glaces.
5. Qui a pris la décision? Pourquoi? Nicole a pris la décision parce que Simon n'a pas de préférence.

B3 Activité • Devinez

Maintenant, vous connaissez un peu Nicole et Simon. A votre avis, quels sont leurs goûts? C'est Nicole ou c'est Simon qui... ?

1. fait du canoë-kayak C'est Nicole qui...
2. aime beaucoup lire C'est Simon qui...
3. adore la musique classique C'est Simon qui...
4. va souvent à des concerts de rock C'est Nicole qui...
5. regarde les documentaires à la télé C'est Simon qui...
6. fait du judo C'est Nicole qui...

B4 STRUCTURES DE BASE
The verb vivre

vivre	*to live*				
Je	**vis**	} tranquillement.	Nous	**vivons**	} tranquillement.
Tu	**vis**		Vous	**vivez**	
Il/Elle/On	**vit**		Ils/Elles	**vivent**	

1. The past participle of **vivre** is **vécu: Il a vécu intensément.**
2. The verb **vivre** and the verb **habiter** both mean *to live*. **Habiter** means *to reside, to have one's home somewhere:* **J'habite à Paris. Vivre** means *to be alive, to live one's life:* **Elle vit rapidement.**
3. A special form of **vivre** is used in exclamations: **Vive le roi!** *Long live the king!* **Vive les vacances!** *Hurray for vacation!*

B5 Activité • Comment vivent-ils?

Est-ce que ces gens vivent rapidement ou tranquillement?

1. Nicole 1. Elle vit rapidement.
2. Simon 2. Il vit tranquillement.
3. Les jeunes 3. Ils vivent rapidement.
4. Les Américains 4. Ils vivent rapidement.
5. Vos grands-parents 5. Ils vivent tranquillement.
6. Vous 6. Moi, je vis...

COMMENT LE DIRE
Asking for agreement and expressing indecision and indifference

These expressions will help you when you're neither for nor against an action.

ASKING		RESPONDING
D'accord?	Je ne sais pas trop.	I don't really know.
Ça va?	Ça m'est égal.	It's all the same to me.
Ça te va?	Comme tu veux.	Whatever you want.
	Ce que tu préfères.	Whatever you want.
	Je n'ai pas de préférence.	I don't have any preference.

B7   Activité • A vous maintenant!

Travaillez avec un(e) camarade de classe. Proposez-lui de faire quelque chose. Votre camarade est indécis(e).

— On va au parc d'attractions? D'accord?
— Comme tu veux.

Ça te dit de…	aller au parc d'attractions	Je ne sais pas trop.
Ça te plairait de…	commencer par le palais des Glaces	Ça m'est égal.
Ça t'intéresse de…	prendre le train fantôme	Comme tu veux.
Tu veux…	manger	Ce que tu préfères.
… D'accord?	monter sur les montagnes russes	
… Ça te va?	rentrer	

B8   Activité • Insistez   Possible answers are given. Note that "Allez!" is used to encourage someone wh using either "vous" or "tu."

Proposez à un(e) camarade d'aller à l'endroit suggéré par le dessin. Il/Elle est indécis(e) mais vous insistez. Voici quelques arguments pour vous aider : Allez! C'est drôlement bien! C'est Marseille contre Bordeaux! Il y a de bons cours!

—Ça te dit d'aller au cinéma?

1.

—Je ne sais pas trop.
—Allez! C'est un bon film!

—Ça t'intéresse d'aller à la MJC?

2.

—Ça m'est égal.
—Il y a de bons cours!

3.

—On va au match de foot, d'accord?
—Je ne sais pas trop.
—Allez! C'est Marseille contre Bordeaux!

4.

—Ça te plairait d'aller à la tour Eiffel?
—Comme tu veux.
—Allez! C'est drôlement bien!

Nicole et Simon sont prêts pour le train fantôme.

NICOLE	Ça va drôlement lentement... Tu n'as pas peur?
SIMON	Non, j'ai faim.
NICOLE	Au secours! Un squelette!
SIMON	Tu es vraiment incompréhensible! Pourquoi tu viens si tu as peur?
NICOLE	J'adore avoir peur!

Nicole emmène Simon sur les montagnes russes.

NICOLE	Yaouh!... Ça te plaît?
SIMON	Pas tellement, non. J'ai mal au cœur, j'ai faim et j'ai soif... Eh, ne bouge pas continuellement! J'ai le vertige!
NICOLE	Ah, tu n'apprécies pas les émotions fortes, toi! Attention, une nouvelle descente!... Yaouh!

Enfin, les deux amis s'arrêtent à la cafeteria.

NICOLE	Ouf! Quelle émotion!
SIMON	Tu n'es pas fatiguée?
NICOLE	Pas du tout!
SIMON	Quelle résistance! Tu vis à deux cents à l'heure et tu as l'air en pleine forme!... Où vas-tu?
NICOLE	Faire un dernier tour de montagnes russes!

Other rides, "les manèges," include "les autos tamponneuses," bumper cars, and "la grande roue," Ferris wheel. A booth is "un stand."

B10   Activité • Quelles sont leurs réactions?

Qu'est-ce que Nicole et Simon font dans les endroits suivants? Quelles sont leurs réactions?

1. Dans le train fantôme
2. Sur les montagnes russes
3. A la cafeteria
4. Au parc d'attractions

1. Nicole a peur. Simon a faim.   2. Simon a mal au cœur et le vertige. Nicole bouge continuellement.   3. Simon est fatigué. Nicole veut faire un dernier tour de montagnes russes.   4. Nicole s'amuse. Simon est fatigué.

Activité • Qui parle? De qui? De quoi?

C'est Nicole qui parle? Ou Simon? De quoi ou de qui est-ce qu'elle/il parle?

1. Ça te plaît? Nicole/du parc d'attractions.
2. Au secours! Nicole/du squelette dans le train
3. Quelle résistance! Simon/de l'énergie de Nicole.

fantôme.

4. Tu es incompréhensible! Simon/de Nicole.
5. Ça va drôlement lentement! Nicole/du train fantôme.

B 12 Activité • Ecrit dirigé

Nicole et Simon racontent leur visite à Zygofolis dans une lettre à leurs amis. Ecrivez la description du point de vue de Nicole. Ensuite écrivez la description du point de vue de Simon.

B 13 STRUCTURES DE BASE
The formation and position of adverbs

1. Words like **lentement,** *slowly,* and **rapidement,** *quickly,* are called adverbs.
2. Many adverbs are formed by adding the suffix **-ment** to the feminine singular form of an adjective: **continuel→continuelle→continuellement; agréable→agréablement.**
3. Some adverbs are made by adding **-ment** to the masculine singular form of an adjective, but only if that form ends in **i** or **u: vrai→vraiment, absolu→absolument. Gai→gaiement** is an exception.
4. A few of the adverbs formed from adjectives whose masculine and feminine forms both end in a silent **e** are written with an **accent aigu** above the **e** before the suffix **-ment: intense→intensément, énorme→énormément.**

Adjective		Adverb
Masculine	*Feminine*	
continuel	**continuelle**	**continuellement**
intense	**intense**	**intensément**
vrai	vraie	**vraiment**

5. Many adverbs are not formed from an adjective: **beaucoup, bien, d'habitude, déjà, quelquefois, souvent, toujours, très, trop,** and **vite** are some you've already seen.
6. An adverb is most frequently placed after a verb: Elle bouge **continuellement.**
7. When the verb is in the **passé composé,** some adverbs immediately follow the auxiliary verb: Elle est **déjà** rentrée.

Generally, a short adverb of 1–3 syllables follows the auxiliary verb. An adverb of 3 or more syllables normally follows the past participle.

B 14 Activité • Découvrez les adjectifs et les adverbes

Voici quelques adverbes. Découvrez l'adjectif de base et donnez les deux formes, masculine et féminine.

1. lentement lent/lente
2. complètement complet/complète
3. tranquillement tranquille
4. rapidement rapide
5. drôlement drôle
6. intensément intense

Voici quelques adjectifs. Formez des adverbes.

1. heureux
2. passionné
3. agréable
4. énorme
5. chaud
6. parfait
7. juste
8. froid
9. vif
10. gai

1. heureusement
2. passionnément
3. agréablement
4. énormément
5. chaudement
6. parfaitement
7. justement
8. froidement
9. vivement
10. gaiement

Activité • Ajoutez un adverbe Possible answers are given.

Répétez les phrases suivantes en ajoutant un adverbe.

1. Nicole est vraiment incompréhensible.
2. Elle aime vivre intensément.

1. Nicole est incompréhensible.
2. Elle aime vivre.
3. Simon aime vivre.
4. Simon prend des décisions.

5. Les parcs d'attractions sont amusants.
6. Simon n'aime pas les montagnes russes.
7. Nicole bouge sur les montagnes russes.

3. Simon aime vivre tranquillement.   4. Simon prend mal les décisions.
5. Les parcs d'attractions sont drôlement amusants.   6. Simon n'aime pas beaucoup les montagnes russes.
7. Nicole bouge continuellement sur les montagnes russes.

B 16 Activité • Trouvez des adverbes Possible answers are given.

1.

Elle avance… lentement

2.

Il mange… rapidement

3.

Il aime… intensément (tristement)

4.

Elle lit… tranquillement

B 17 Activité • Et vous?

Comment est-ce que vous faites ces choses? Employez un adverbe dans votre phrase.

1. vivre Je vis…
2. manger Je mange…

3. parler français Je parle…
4. répondre en classe Je réponds…

5. prendre une décision Je prends…
6. faire du sport Je fais…

B 18 COMMENT LE DIRE
Expressing feelings

The verb **avoir** is used in many expressions of emotion and feeling. Here are a few.

FEAR	PAIN	HUNGER	THIRST	DISCOMFORT
J'ai peur. J'ai le vertige.	J'ai mal au cœur.	J'ai faim.	J'ai soif.	J'ai chaud. J'ai froid.

Comment est-ce qu'ils se sentent (feel)?

1.

Ils ont le vertige.

2.

Elle a peur.

3.

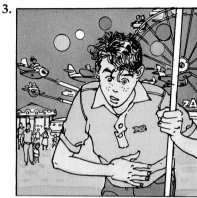

Il a mal au cœur.

4.

Ils ont soif.

5.

Il a chaud.

6.

Elle a froid.

Un(e) camarade vous propose ces activités. Vous refusez en employant les expressions dans B18.

— Ça te dit de monter sur les montagnes russes?
— Euh non, j'ai le vertige.

1.

2.

—On prend un sandwich?
D'accord?
—Non, je n'ai pas faim.

3.

—Tu veux une boisson?
—Non, merci. Je n'ai pas soif.

4.

—Ça t'intéresse de faire du
canoë-kayak?
—Non, j'ai peur.

—Tu veux faire du jogging?
—Non, j'ai chaud.

Zygofolis a ouvert à Nice en 1987. En 1987 aussi, le maire de Paris a inauguré le grand parc d'attractions de Mirapolis, à 50 km à l'ouest de Paris. Le thème choisi est les contes et légendes d'Europe. La figure symbole du parc est la statue de Gargantua.

A Marne-la-Vallée, à l'est de Paris, la compagnie Walt Disney va construire un immense parc d'attractions, comme Disneyland aux Etats-Unis. Il va ouvrir en 1992. On va naturellement donner des noms français aux personnages célèbres, sauf à Mickey Mouse et à Donald Duck. Cinderella va devenir Cendrillon, Goofy va devenir Dingo et Dopey va devenir Simplet. Pouvez-vous deviner les noms français pour Happy et pour Snow White? Dingue = crazy, hence Dingo, the French name for Goofy.

Solution : Joyeux et Blanche Neige

B22 Activité • Ecoutez bien 🎞️ For script and answers, see pp. T77–78.

Ecoutez la conversation et puis décidez si les phrases suivantes sont vraies ou fausses.

1. Muriel a accompagné Eric au parc d'attractions.
2. Muriel a trouvé le parc drôlement bien.
3. Les montagnes russes donnent le vertige à Eric.
4. Eric a peur du train fantôme.
5. Muriel aime manger.

making arrangements to celebrate France's national holiday . . .
expressing regret

Les Français célèbrent leur fête nationale le quatorze juillet. Les quartiers de Paris, théâtres de la Révolution de 1789, sont aujourd'hui des endroits où on danse et où on fait la fête.

For background on Bastille Day, see page T79.

C1   La fête commence. 📼

Have students locate the various places on the map of Paris, p. 435.

La veille du 14 Juillet, dans chaque quartier de Paris, il y a des bals... à Montmartre, à Montparnasse, à la Bastille, sur l'île Saint-Louis. Quand une bande de jeunes Parisiens veut sortir, le téléphone fonctionne toute la journée.

(9 h 10 — Corinne téléphone à Laure.)

CORINNE   Laure? Où veux-tu aller danser ce soir?

LAURE   Je ne sais pas. Et toi?

CORINNE   J'ai bien envie d'aller à Montmartre. Il y a un très bon orchestre.

LAURE   Moi, ça me va. Mais appelle les autres.

(10 h 45 — Corinne appelle Fabienne.)

CORINNE   Salut, Fabienne! J'ai eu Laure au téléphone. On est d'accord pour aller au bal de Montmartre.

FABIENNE   Je regrette, mais c'est trop loin pour moi.

CORINNE   Je suis désolée. Tu es toujours d'accord pour le défilé demain?

FABIENNE   Bien sûr!

CORINNE   Eh bien, à demain.

(11 h 20 — Corinne rappelle Laure.)

CORINNE   Oui, c'est encore moi. Fabienne ne peut pas venir.

LAURE   Quel dommage!

CORINNE   Quand est-ce que tu veux y aller?

LAURE   Ça m'est égal.

CORINNE   Vers neuf heures, ça te va?

LAURE   Parfait.

Montmartre is located in the 18th arrondissement. The Basilica of Sacré-Cœur dominates the butte and can easily be seen from most parts of Paris. Montparnasse, to the south, is a popular neighborhood for young people to meet and socialize. La Place de la Bastille is located to the east. This large traffic circle is dominated by the Column of July. It was the scene of important events in the French Revolution. The Ile Saint-Louis is a small island in the Seine. Located at the center of town, it contains some of the oldest buildings in Paris.

(13 h 40 — Corinne parle à Jean.)

CORINNE	Jean? Corinne à l'appareil. Qu'est-ce que tu fais ce soir? Ça t'intéresse d'aller au bal de Montmartre?
JEAN	Malheureusement, je ne peux pas. Je dois aller vendre des sandwiches et des boissons avec mon frère. J'ai absolument besoin de fric. *money*
CORINNE	C'est bien dommage!
JEAN	A quelle heure y allez-vous? Je peux peut-être venir après minuit?
CORINNE	Si tu veux. Il y a un café à l'angle de la place du Tertre. Rendez-vous à minuit et quart là-bas?
JEAN	D'accord. A ce soir!

(16 h 05 — Corinne appelle Henri.)

CORINNE	Coucou, Henri, c'est moi! Ça te dit de venir danser avec nous ce soir?
HENRI	Qui vient?
CORINNE	Laure, Jean et moi.
HENRI	Où est-ce que vous allez?
CORINNE	Au bal de Montmartre.
HENRI	Montmartre? Ah non! Il y a toujours plein de touristes! Allons à la Bastille. C'est beaucoup mieux.
CORINNE	Ecoute, je veux bien. Mais tu organises! Moi, j'abandonne! Décide avec les autres et rappelle-moi! Bonne chance!

La place du Tertre is a quaint village-like square popular with tourists. It is at the center of Montmartre.

C2 Activité • Pourquoi? Possible answers are given.

Expliquez pourquoi...

1. Il doit aller vendre des sandwiches et des boissons.
2. C'est trop loin pour elle.
4. Il y a un très bon orchestre.

1. Jean ne sort pas avec les autres à neuf heures.
2. Fabienne ne va pas au bal.
3. Henri ne veut pas aller à Montmartre.
3. Il y a trop de touristes.

4. Corinne a envie d'aller à Montmartre.
5. Henri doit téléphoner aux autres.
5. Il doit téléphoner aux autres parce que Corinne abandonne.

C3 Activité • Présentez-vous (*Introduce yourself*) Possible answers are given.

Pouvez-vous trouver dans C1 plusieurs expressions pour vous présenter au téléphone?
Salut! / C'est moi. / ...à l'appareil!

Amusons-nous! 111

C4 Activité • A vous maintenant! Possible answer is given.

Henri doit téléphoner aux autres. Il commence par appeler Stéphanie. Préparez le dialogue avec un(e) camarade de classe. Présentez-vous, proposez quelque chose, demandez l'avis de votre ami(e), fixez un rendez-vous, choisissez l'heure et l'endroit.

—Stéphanie? Henri à l'appareil. Ça te dit de venir avec nous à la Bastille? —Oui, je veux bien. A quelle heure?
—Vers 10h, devant la colonne.

C5 Activité • Ecrivez Possible answer is given.

Corinne a aussi téléphoné à Olivier. Elle a laissé un message sur le répondeur *(telephone answering machine)*. Ecrivez le message. Allô, Olivier. C'est moi, Corinne. Dis, tu veux aller avec moi et les autres à Montmartre

pour danser? Il y a un bon orchestre! On veut y aller
vers 9h. Rappelle moi vite, s'il te plaît!

C6 Savez-vous que... ?

Le 14 Juillet est la fête nationale française. Elle commémore la prise de la Bastille — une ancienne prison — le 14 juillet 1789. La prise de la Bastille symbolise le début de la Révolution française. La Bastille a été détruite en 1790. C'est aujourd'hui une vaste place, la place de la Bastille. Au centre, il y a une colonne en bronze. Elle commémore une autre révolution française, celle de juillet 1830. En haut de la colonne, une petite statue représente la Liberté.

The place de la Bastille is the site of a new opera house in Paris. The modern structure was completed despite the protests of those who revered the old Opéra, which will now focus on dance.

La place de la Bastille

C7 VOUS EN SOUVENEZ-VOUS?
Asking questions

1. You've already learned that in informal conversation you ask a yes/no question simply by raising your voice at the end of a statement.

> Tu as rappelé Laure?   Oui. / Non.

2. You also know that you can ask for information by placing an interrogative word or phrase at the end of a statement.

> Elle a téléphoné **à quelle heure?**

3. Interrogative words that you've already seen include **quoi, quand, comment, où, combien, qui, avec qui, à qui, pourquoi,** and **à quelle heure.**
4. Remember that **qu'est-ce que**, instead of **quoi**, is placed at the beginning of a statement to ask *what* in writing and more formal conversation.

C8 STRUCTURES DE BASE

Asking questions using **est-ce que** *and inversion*

1. You may use the phrase **est-ce que** to ask yes/no questions.

Yes/no questions	**Est-ce que** Laure a téléphoné? **Est-ce qu'**elle va rappeler Corinne?

To ask a yes/no question with **est-ce que**, place the phrase before a statement and raise your voice at the end. **Est-ce que** tu vas au bal? **Elision** occurs when the word following **est-ce que** begins with a vowel: **Est-ce qu'elles** vont sortir?

2. You may also use **est-ce que** in questions asking for information. These questions usually follow this pattern:

interrogative word or phrase + **est-ce que** + (pro)noun + verb

Your voice starts at a high pitch on the question word(s) and gradually falls as it goes on.

A quelle heure **Où**	est-ce que est-ce qu'	Laure a téléphoné? elle va ce soir?

  a. When **qui** is the subject of the question, **est-ce que** is not used: **Qui a téléphoné?**
  b. When **où, comment,** or **à quelle heure** is followed by a form of the verb **être, est-ce que** is not used: **Où sont les téléphones? Comment est Nicole?**

3. You may form questions in another way, using inversion instead of **est-ce que**. Inversion means that the subject pronoun and the verb are reversed, or inverted. In writing, a hyphen is placed between the verb and the pronoun that follows it. Inversion may be used in both yes/no and information questions.

Viens-tu avec moi? Quand **allons-nous** partir?

  a. When the verb ends in a vowel and the subject pronoun following it begins with a vowel, you make a **t**-sound between the two words. This makes the pronunciation easier. In writing, you add the letter **t** surrounded by hyphens:

Comment s'appelle-**t**-elle? A-**t**-elle un frère? Parle-**t**-il anglais?

  b. When the verb is in the **passé composé**, the subject pronoun and the auxiliary verb are inverted: **As-tu parlé avec Corinne?**

  c. When the subject of the question is a noun, use the following pattern of inversion: noun subject + verb + subject pronoun. **Jean vient-il avec nous?**

  d. **Liaison** occurs when you use inversion. When the verb ends with the letter **d,** you pronounce the **d** as a **t.**

  Ecoutent - ils des disques?   A quelle heure prend - elle le métro?

  e. The way you choose to ask questions depends on the situation you're in — formal or informal, speaking or writing — and the people you're talking to — young people or adults, acquaintances or strangers.

Amusons-nous!   113

Activité • Posez des questions

Votre ami(e) téléphone. Il/Elle vous invite à une soirée pour célébrer le 14 Juillet. Posez-lui des questions. Vous voulez savoir…

1. où est la soirée.
2. à quelle heure elle commence.
3. quand vous devez partir.

    1. Où est la soirée?
    2. A quelle heure est-ce qu'elle commence?
    3. Quand est-ce que je dois partir?

4. si vous devez prendre le métro.
5. comment vous pouvez rentrer.
6. qui vient.

    4. Est-ce que je dois prendre le métro?
    5. Comment est-ce que je peux rentrer?
    6. Qui vient?

C10 **Activité • Encore des questions**   Possible answers are given.

Vous allez au défilé du 14 Juillet avec des amis. Votre mère veut quelques renseignements. Devinez ses questions.

— Dis, maman, on va sortir. C'est d'accord?

— … ? Vous allez où?

— Au défilé.

— … ? Comment est-ce que vous y allez?

— On va prendre le métro tous ensemble.

— … ? A quelle heure est-ce que vous rentrez?

— Oh, vers 13 h 00.

— … ? Avec qui est-ce que tu y vas?

— Laure, Corinne, Henri et peut-être Jean.

— … ? Est-ce que tu as de l'argent?

— Oui, j'ai cinquante francs.

La Garde Républicaine défile le 14 Juillet.

C11 **Activité • Ecrit dirigé**

Pour célébrer le 14 Juillet, Laure et son frère Didier préparent une petite surprise pour leur mère. Laure pose des questions à Didier. Ecrivez ses questions en employant **est-ce que**.

1. Tu as acheté le cadeau, Didier?
2. Grand-mère arrive comment?
3. On va dîner dans quel restaurant?
4. Papa a réservé une table?
5. Tu vas prendre quelques photos?
6. Combien tu as payé les fleurs?

1. Est-ce que tu as acheté le cadeau? 2. Comment est-ce que Grand-mère arrive? 3. Dans quel restaurant est-ce qu'on va dîner? 4. Est-ce que Papa a réservé une table? 5. Est-ce que tu vas prendre quelques photos? 6. Combien est-ce que tu as payé les fleurs?

C12 **Activité • A vous maintenant!**
Possible answers are given.

Votre ami(e) français(e) a vu cette annonce dans le journal. Il/Elle vous invite au bal. Demandez des renseignements en posant cinq questions avec **est-ce que**. Préparez le dialogue avec un(e) camarade de classe.

— Ça te plairait d'aller au bal?

Grand Bal du 14 Juillet
Lundi   **13 Juillet**
Montparnasse
Venez tous!   **Gratuit°**
A partir de 20 h 00
Feu d'artifice à minuit

gratuit *free*

—Où est-ce que tu veux aller?
—A Montparnasse.
—Est-ce que c'est cher? —Non, c'est gratuit.
—A quelle heure est-ce que ça commence?
—A 20h.
—Qu'est-ce que tu vas mettre?
—Oh, des jeans, et un blouson.
—Qu'est-ce qu'on va voir?
—Un feu d'artifice.

COMMENT LE DIRE
Expressing regret

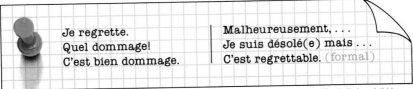

Je regrette.	Malheureusement, . . .
Quel dommage!	Je suis désolé(e) mais . . .
C'est bien dommage.	C'est regrettable. (formal)

"Zut!" is a common way of expressing regret for a personal action: Zut! J'ai oublié!

C14 **Activité • Exprimez le regret** Possible answers are given.

Vos amis vous parlent. Qu'est-ce que vous leur dites? Employez les expressions de regret.

1. Pierre ne peut pas venir au bal. Quel dommage!
2. Il pleut. Il n'y a pas de feu d'artifice.
3. Tu vas voir le défilé? 2. C'est bien dommage.
   3. Malheureusement, je ne peux pas.

4. Quelle foule! Je ne vois pas le défilé!
5. Fabienne ne peut pas sortir ce soir.
   4. C'est dommage.
   5. C'est regrettable.

C15 **Activité • A vous maintenant!** Possible answers are given.

Travaillez avec un(e) camarade de classe. A tour de rôle, composez une phrase négative au passé composé et exprimez le regret.

1. —Je n'ai pas vu le défilé. —Quel dommage!
2. —Malheureusement, Laure n'a pas rappelé. —C'est dommage!

Catherine / venir — Catherine n'est pas venue.
— C'est bien dommage.

3. —On n'a pas répondu au téléphone.
   —C'est regrettable.

4. —Malheureusement, nous ne sommes pas allés à Montmartre. —Quel dommage!
1. Je / voir le défilé
2. Laure / rappeler

3. On / répondre au téléphone
4. Nous / aller à Montmartre

5. Jean / trouver ses copains
6. Tu / téléphoner

5. —Jean n'a pas trouvé ses copains. —C'est bien dommage.
6. —Tu n'as pas téléphoné. —Je suis désolé(e), mais j'ai oublié.

C16 **Activité • Complétez le dialogue**

Vous avez une conversation avec un(e) camarade. Il/Elle vous propose d'aller au bal. Vous avez une raison pour ne pas venir. Votre camarade insiste. Exprimez vos regrets.

— Ça te dit de venir au bal avec moi?
— *(regrets) (raison)* Je regrette, mais...
— Viens après minuit!
— *(regrets) (raison)* Je ne peux pas.
— Prends un taxi!
— *(regrets) (raison)* Je veux bien, mais...
— Demande de l'argent à ton père!
— *(regrets) (raison)* Malheureusement,...
— Ben, fais comme tu veux. Moi, j'y vais!

Voici des raisons :

— Il ne veut pas.
— Je n'ai pas d'argent.
— Je dois vendre des boissons.
— J'ai peur de prendre le métro la nuit.

C17 **Activité • Ecoutez bien** For script and answers, see p. T81.

Choisissez la bonne réponse.

1. C'est **a.** le matin **b.** l'après-midi **c.** le soir.
2. Il fait **a.** mauvais **b.** froid **c.** beau.
3. Le défilé est à **a.** Marseille **b.** Paris **c.** Lyon.
4. Des spectateurs, il y en a **a.** beaucoup
   b. peu **c.** plusieurs.

5. Les pompiers défilent **a.** en premier **b.** en troisième **c.** en dernier.
6. L'armée de l'air est **a.** en moto **b.** en avion **c.** à pied.

1   Après le défilé 📼

Laure est allée voir le défilé du 14 Juillet. Sa mère veut savoir comment c'était.

SA MÈRE	C'était comment, le défilé?
LAURE	Oh, merveilleux! J'ai vraiment beaucoup aimé!
SA MÈRE	Tu as vu le président de la République?
LAURE	Non. Malheureusement, je suis arrivée trop tard.

SA MÈRE	Dommage. Alors, comment sont nos avions, nos militaires?
LAURE	Pas mal. Mais j'ai surtout aimé les pompiers°!

pompiers *firemen*

Pictured above is the marching band of the French Foreign Legion.

2   Activité • Répondez

1. Où est-ce que Laure est allée?
2. Qu'est-ce que sa mère veut savoir?
3. Comment était le défilé?
4. Pourquoi est-ce que Laure n'a pas vu le président?
5. Qu'est-ce qu'elle a surtout aimé?

1. Elle est allée au défilé.   2. Sa mère veut savoir comment c'était.   3. C'était merveilleux!   4. Elle est arrivée trop tard.
5. Elle a surtout aimé les pompiers.

Possible questions: A quelle heure commence le défilé? Est-ce qu'il y a des chevaux? Des chiens? Y a-t-il des jeunes? Dans quel groupe? Il y a des avions? Le défilé commence où? Où et quand finit-il? C'est sur quelle avenue?

Regardez cette illustration. Quelles questions est-ce que vous pouvez poser à un(e) camarade?

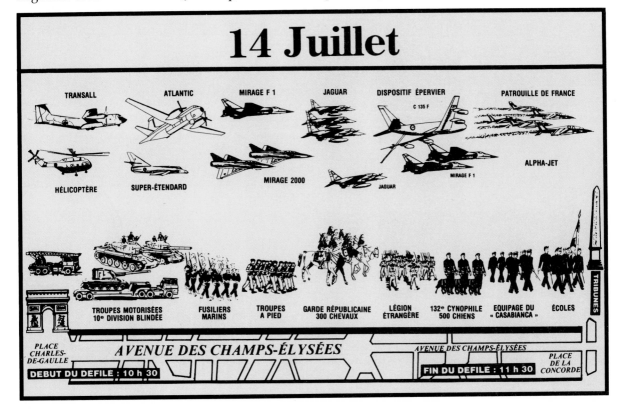

4 Activité • Célébrez le 14 Juillet   Possible answer is given.

Vous êtes à Paris avec votre correspondant(e) français(e). Qu'est-ce que vous allez faire? Regardez ce programme et faites vos plans pour la journée. Allez-vous assister au défilé ou préférez-vous le regarder à la télé? Il y a une cérémonie à l'Hôtel des Invalides. N'oubliez pas le feu d'artifice! Travaillez avec un(e) camarade et préparez le dialogue.

—Ça te dit d'aller au musée de l'Armée?
—Bof. Tu sais, moi, les militaires...

14 JUILLET
Le 14 Juillet au Musée de l'Armée

Les musées de l'Hôtel national des Invalides (musée de l'Armée, dôme royal, tombeau de l'Empereur, église Saint-Louis) sont ouverts le mardi 14 juillet, de 10h à 18h.

Le public a accès au tombeau de Napoléon jusqu' à 19 heures.

La projection permanente de documentaires et de grands films sur les guerres de 1914–1918 et 1939–1945 a lieu dans la salle de cinéma du musée de l'Armée à partir de 14 heures.

10 Ans — 100.000 Etoiles

grand spectacle pyrotechnique présenté par la mairie de Paris mardi 14 juillet, à 22 h 30, devant le Palais de Chaillot, d'une durée de 25 minutes.

Sélection Télévision

9.45 | A2 | Défilé du 14 Juillet

—Mais non, c'est génial le musée! Il y a une cérémonie à l'Hôtel, puis on peut voir le tombeau de Napoléon...
—Bon, mais d'abord je veux voir le défilé à la télé.
—Oui, bien sûr! Dis, tu ne veux pas aller voir le feu d'artifice?
—Si! Ça commence à quelle heure?
—A 22h30. C'est bien! Ça fait une bonne journée!

Activité • Situations   Possible dialogues are given.

Travaillez avec un(e) camarade de classe. Préparez un dialogue pour chaque situation.

1.

Votre ami(e) vous propose de monter à la tour Eiffel. Vous ne voulez pas. Vous refusez en exprimant vos regrets.

1. —Dis, on monte à la tour Eiffel?
—Non, je regrette, j'ai peur.
—C'est facile, ferme les yeux!
—Non, je refuse.

2.

Vous êtes sur les montagnes russes à un parc d'attractions. Vous aimez, mais votre ami(e) n'aime pas. Il/Elle donne une raison.

2. —Super! Ça te plaît?
—Non, j'ai mal au cœur.
—Courage!

3.

Vous êtes au Carnaval à Québec. Vous admirez les sculptures de neige.

3. —Qu'est-ce qu'elles sont belles, ces sculptures!
—Oui, elles sont fantastiques!

4.

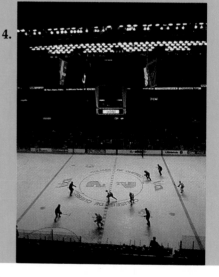

4. —Ça te dit de voir le feu d'artifice?
—Non, je n'aime pas le bruit. Je regrette.
—Tu aimes danser? Il y a un bal.

Vous êtes au Carnaval à Québec. Votre ami(e) canadien(ne) vous propose plusieurs choses : un match de hockey, un bal, un concert, le feu d'artifice. Vous n'arrivez pas à prendre une décision. Pour finir, votre ami(e) vous emmène voir un match de hockey.

—Comme tu veux. Ça m'est égal.
—Tu aimes la musique? Il y a un concert de rock ce soir.
—Oui, j'aime le rock, mais je n'ai pas de préférence.
—Dis, il y a aussi un match de hockey si tu préfères.
—D'accord.

Activité • Au Carnaval 🔲 Possible answers are given.

Vous avez organisé une soirée le dernier jour du Carnaval à Québec. Votre ami(e) veut savoir comment était la soirée. Il/Elle vous demande ce que vous avez fait. Répondez en employant l'adverbe suggéré par l'adjectif.

— Vous avez discuté?
— Ah oui, nous avons discuté vivement!

—Bernard a joué de la trompette?
—Oui, il en a joué longuement.

—Vous n'avez pas dansé?
—Si, on a dansé continuellement!

ous avez chanté?
ui, nous avons chanté
aiement!

(vif)

1.

(gai)

2.

(long)

3.

(continuel)

4.

(joyeux)

—Vous avez mangé?
—Oui, nous avons mangé joyeusement!

5.

(triste)

—Quand est-ce que vous êtes partis?
—Vers minuit, nous sommes partis tristement.

Activité • A vous maintenant!

Vous avez assisté à la Soirée du Mardi Gras au Carnaval de Québec. Votre ami(e) veut savoir comment c'était. Préparez le dialogue avec un(e) camarade de classe.

MARDI 10 FEVRIER
21h00 SOIREE DU MARDI-GRAS

Super soirée costumée et dansante aux rythmes de la Louisiane et de l'Acadie.

Groupes invités : EXPRESSO S.V.P. de l'Acadie et WAYNE TOUPS de la Louisiane. Artiste spécial invité : MICHAEL DOUCET du groupe Beausoleil.
Lieu : Centre Durocher, 290, rue Carillon.
Admission : 6 $

Amusons-nous! 119

—Bonjour, monsieur/mademoiselle.
Qu'est-ce que vous voulez?
—Je voudrais une coquille de fruits
de mer.
—Et avec ça?

8 Activité • Bon appétit! Possible dialogue is given.

Vous êtes au Carnaval à Québec avec des ami(e)s. Il est midi et vous avez faim. Alors, vous entrez dans un petit restaurant québécois pour déjeuner.

Regardez la carte, choisissez les plats et commandez votre repas.

Un(e) camarade va jouer le rôle du serveur/de la serveuse.

PATRIMOINE TERRASSE

entrées

Frites (French fries)	1.00
Frites avec sauce hot chicken (French fries with hot chicken sauce)	1.95
Oignons français (Onion rings)	1.95
Fondue Parmesan (Parmesan Fondue)	2.75
Salade du chef (Chef's salad)	2.50
Frites avec sauce à spaghetti (French fries with spaghetti sauce)	2.75
Poutine maison (French fries with sauce and cheese)	3.50
Poutine maison à l'italienne	3.95
Escargots de Bourgogne (Snails with garlic butter)	3.50
Coquille de fruits de mer	4.25

soupes (soups)

Jus de tomates ou V-8 (Tomato juice or V-8)	1.00
Deux choix de soupe du jour (Two choices of today's soup)	1.25
Soupe à l'oignon gratinée (Onion soup with cheese)	3.25

sandwichs
(servis avec frites et salade de choux)
(served with french fries and cole slaw)

Aux tomates (Tomatoes)	3.25
Jambon (Ham)	3.25
Fromage grillé (Grilled cheese)	3.25
Tomates et fromage (Tomatoes and cheese)	4.25
Poulet (Chicken)	4.25
Tomate et bacon (Tomatoes and bacon)	4.25
Western	4.25

club sandwich

Poulet (Chicken)	6.50
Fromage (Cheese)	5.50
Jambon (Ham)	5.75

mets italiens (Italian)
(choix sauce tomate ou viande)
(choice of tomato or meat sauce)

Spaghetti à la viande ou tomate (Spaghetti with meat or tomato sauce)	5.50
Spaghetti aux champignons (Spaghetti with mushrooms)	6.25
Spaghetti au pepperoni (Spaghetti with pepperoni)	6.25
Hamburger Caruso (Caruso hamburger)	5.75
Spaghetti à la viande gratiné (Spaghetti with meat sauce)	6.95
Lasagne (Lasagna)	6.50

pizzas

	6"	9"
Fromage (Cheese)	3.00	4.50
Champignons et piment	3.25	4.95
Pepperoni	3.50	5.25
Garnie (All dressed)	4.25	5.75
Patrimoine	4.75	6.95

poissons

Fish & Chips	4.75
Filet de sole au beurre (Filet of sole cooked in butter)	6.75

salades

Spécial du Chef (Chef's special salad)	4.75
Jambon (Ham)	6.50
Du Patrimoine	7.50
De poulet (Chicken)	7.50
Mimosa	6.95
César	8.50

sous-marins
(servis avec frites et salade de choux)
(served with french fries and cole slaw)

Végétarien (Fromage, salade, tomate, piments, champignons) (Cheese, salad, tomato, green peppers, mushrooms)	4.25
Pepperoni (Pepperoni, fromage, salade, tomate, piments, champignons) (Pepperoni, cheese, salad, tomato, green peppers, mushrooms)	4.95

hamburger
(servis avec frites et salade de choux)
(served with french fries and cole slaw)

Hamburger	3.50
Cheeseburger	3.75
Hot hamburger	4.95

biftecks

Bifteck haché (Chopped sirloin)	5.25
Bifteck minute (Minute steak)	6.50
Brochette (Sirloin brochette)	7.50
Filet mignon	8.95
Surlonge	14.95
Rib	16.95
T-Bone	16.95

desserts

Dessert du jour	1.00
Tartes (Pies)	1.25
Gâteau moka	2.25
Chocolat	2.25

TABLE D'HÔTE

Fondue Parmesan ou Salade César
(Fondue Parmesan or Cesar salad)

Soupe maison (Home soup)

Au choix (Your choice)

Lasagne (Lasagna)

Filet de sole au beurre (Filet of sole in butter)

Bifteck minute (Minute steak)

Dessert du jour (Dessert of the day)

Café ou Thé (Coffee or Tea)

10,99

FESTIVAL DU BIFTECK

Salade du Chef ou Salade César
(Chef's salad or Cesar salad)

Soupe maison (Home soup)

Au choix (Your choice)

Surlonge
Rib
T-Bone

Tartes assorties (Assorted pies)

Café ou Thé (Coffee or Tea)

19,95

Remind the students that the "entrée" is only the appetizer.

9 Activité • Ecrit dirigé Possible answer is given.

Il est dix heures du soir. Vous avez passé la journée au parc d'attractions avec des amis. Vous voulez raconter cette journée dans votre journal. Répondez aux questions suivantes et écrivez un paragraphe au passé composé.

1. Où êtes-vous allé(e) aujourd'hui? Avec qui?
2. A quelle heure y êtes-vous arrivé(e)s?
3. Avez-vous commencé par le palais des Glaces?
4. Etes-vous monté(e)s sur les montagnes russes?
5. Avez-vous eu le vertige?
6. Avez-vous pris le train fantôme?
7. Comment avez-vous trouvé le parc?
8. A quelle heure êtes-vous rentré(e)s?

Je suis allé(e) au parc d'attractions avec des copains.
On y est arrivé à 9h du matin.

MAI
JEUDI **19**

VENDREDI **20**

MAI
SAMEDI **21**

Aujourd'hui, j'ai passé une journée extra au parc d'attractions avec...

DIMANCHE **22**

On a commencé par le train fantôme.
Après, on est monté sur les montagnes russes.
Moi, j'ai eu le vertige. On a fini par le palais des Glaces.

J'ai trouvé le parc fantastique!
Je suis rentré(e) à 5h du soir très fatigué(e).

10 Activité • Récréation
(optional)

Jeu d'association

Quel mot est suggéré par chaque groupe de trois mots?

rue
marcher
gens

rapidement
vertige
descente

homme
froid
blanc

équipe
rondelle
glace

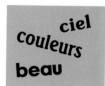
ciel
couleurs
beau

le défilé   les montagnes russes   Bonhomme Carnaval   le hockey   le feu d'artifice

For script, see pp. T83—85.

PRONONCIATION 📼

Liaison

1 Ecoutez bien et répétez.

Linking two vowels
    midi et demi   samedi à midi   samedi ou dimanche   Je sais où il est.

2 Ecoutez et lisez.

1. Most of the final consonants of written French are not sounded.
    es~~t~~ / es~~t~~   les / le~~s~~   nos / no~~s~~   chez / che~~z~~   projets / proje~~ts~~

2. You do hear the final **l** and **r** sounds but not the consonants that follow them.
    ils / il~~s~~   elles / elle~~s~~   hôtels / hôtel~~s~~   tard / tar~~d~~   fort / for~~t~~   vers / ver~~s~~

3. Final consonants, usually not heard, are sometimes pronounced to link words.
    Il est là. I-lé-la.   *but*   Il est ici. I-lé-ti-ci.
    a. The most often heard linking sound is /**z**/, even though it may be written as an **s.**
        nos amis   no-za-mi   les amis   lé-za-mi   les Etats-Unis   lé-zé-ta-zu-ni
    b. Another frequent linking sound is /**t**/.
        tout à l'heure   tou-ta-l'heur~~e~~   comment allez-vous   co-men-ta-lé-vou~~s~~
    c. Sometimes a final **d** is pronounced as **t** when linking occurs.
        vend-elle ven-tell~~e~~   prend-il pren-til
    d. A **t** may even be added to make pronunciation easier.
        il y a y a-t-il?   Elle a un frère.   A-t-elle un frère?
    e. The third most frequent linking sound is /**n**/.
        mon frère et mon ami   ton père et ton oncle

4. In some cases a stop is needed rather than a linkage.
    a. This happens before certain words beginning with **h,** often to keep meanings clear.
        les zéros   lé-zé-ro   les héros   lé-é-ro
    b. Repeat these pairs, being careful not to link the words.
        haricot / les haricots   Hollande / la Hollande   homard / le homard   haut / en haut
    c. Many numerals also contain stops.
        le onze   cent onze   le huit
    d. A stop occurs before certain words like **oui** and **alors.**
        mais oui   et alors

5. Read this dialogue, making the correct linkages and stops.
        — Tu pars quand? Le onze?
        — Mais oui. Samedi à midi et demi avec mon oncle Albert. Et toi?
        — Lundi après-midi. Nous arrivons chez eux vers six heures.

3 Copiez les phrases suivantes pour préparer une dictée.

1. On est arrivé le onze.
2. C'est chouette d'être en haut.
3. Quand est-ce que Laure a téléphoné?
4. A-t-elle un frère?
5. Comment allez-vous?

VERIFIONS!

Answers are given. Some answers will vary.

Do you know how to express excitement and amazement in French?
Transform these statements into exclamations in different ways.

1. Qu'est-ce qu'ils jouent bien!   2. Ce qu'il fait beau!

1. Les musiciens jouent bien.
2. Il fait beau.
3. La foule est immense.
4. La reine est belle.
5. Ce char est drôle.

3. Quelle foule immense!
4. Que la reine est belle!
5. Qu'est-ce qu'il est drôle, ce char!

Do you know all the patterns of adjective agreement?
Complete these noun phrases by putting the adjective in parentheses in its correct form and position.

1. des chars originaux   2. une couleur vive
3. une foule joyeuse

1. des chars (original)
2. une couleur (vif)
3. une foule (joyeux)
4. des filles (sportif)   4. des filles sportives
5. un feu d'artifice (beau)   5. un beau feu d'artifice
6. une compétition (spécial)   6. une compétition spéciale

Can you express indecision and indifference in French?
React to each of these suggestions in an indecisive or indifferent manner. Vary your remarks.

1. Ça te dit d'aller au parc d'attractions? Ça m'est égal.
2. Tu veux commencer par le train fantôme? Comme tu veux.
3. On va dans le palais des Glaces. D'accord? Je ne sais pas trop.
4. Montons sur les montagnes russes. Ce que tu préfères.
5. On va manger maintenant? Je n'ai pas de préférence.

Have you learned the forms of the verb _vivre_?
How do these people live their lives? Complete each sentence with the correct form of **vivre**.

1. Moi, je ___ tranquillement. vis
2. Mes copains ___ rapidement. vivent
3. Nicole ___ à deux cents à l'heure. vit
4. Vous ___ intensément. vivez
5. Tu ___ bien. vis
6. Nous ___ passionnément. vivons

Do you know how to make adverbs from certain adjectives?
Change the adjective in parentheses to an adverb and place it in the correct position in the sentence.

1. Les voitures circulent lentement dans la neige.
2. Le défilé avance rapidement.   3. Ils jouent drôlement bien.

1. Les voitures circulent dans la neige. (lent)
2. Le défilé avance. (rapide)
3. Ils jouent bien. (drôle)
4. La foule crie. (gai)
5. Les jeunes dansent. (joyeux)

4. La foule crie gaiement.   5. Les jeunes dansent joyeusement.

Can you express regret in French?
React to your friends' statements and questions. Use a different expression of regret each time.

C'est dommage!
Je suis désolé(e).

1. Je ne peux pas aller voir le défilé.
2. Tu n'as pas téléphoné à Fabienne?
3. Tu ne vas pas au bal? Je regrette.
4. Les rues sont bloquées!
Quel dommage!

Do you know how to ask questions using _est-ce que_?
Ask these questions using **est-ce que**.

1. Nous allons voir le feu d'artifice?
2. Le défilé commence à quelle heure?
3. Vous y allez avec qui?
4. On va danser?

1. Est-ce que nous allons voir le feu d'artifice?   2. A quelle heure est-ce que le défilé commence?   3. Avec qui est-ce que vous y allez?   4. Est-ce qu'on va danser?

VOCABULAIRE

SECTION A

assez : J'en ai assez! *I'm fed up!*
assister (à) *to attend*
avancer *to advance*
un **bonhomme (de neige)** *snowman*
le **bruit** *noise*
le **carnaval** *carnival*
ce que *how*
un **chant** *song*
un **char** *float*
circuler *to circulate*
une **compétition** *contest*
cours : Je cours *I run*
un **cri** *shout*
crois : Je crois *I believe*
un **défilé** *parade*
dommage *pity, too bad*
drôle *funny*
la **duchesse** *duchess*
durer *to last*
enfin *well*
enneigé, -e *snow-covered*
en plus *in addition*
entendre *to hear*
exprès *purposely*
exprimer *to express*
un(e) **fana(tique)** *fan*
fantastique *fantastic*
un **feu d'artifice** *fireworks*
formidable *great*
une **foule** *crowd*
le **froid** *cold (weather)*
gai, -e *gay, happy*
gelé, -e *frozen*
la **joie** *joy*
joyeux, -euse *joyous, happy*
le long de *along*
ouvert -e *open*
plein, -e (de) *full (of)*
les **Québécois** *inhabitants of Quebec*
la **reine** *queen*
rude *harsh*

le **Saint-Laurent** *Saint Lawrence River*
spécial, -e (m. pl. -aux) *special*
sportif, -ive *athletic*
un **tournoi** *tournament*
vive *long live . . . , hurrah for . . .*

SECTION B

accompagner *to accompany*
amusant, -e *fun, amusing*
apprécier *to appreciate*
arrêter (s') *to stop*
une **attraction** *attraction*
bouger *to move, budge*
le **cœur : mal au cœur** *stomach ache, nausea*
commencer par *to begin with (by)*
continuellement *continually*
une **descente** *descent*
drôlement *pretty, very*
égal, -e (m.pl. -aux) *equal; Ça m'est égal. I don't care.*
emmener *to take (someone somewhere)*
une **émotion** *emotion*
fabuleux, -euse *fabulous*
un **fantôme** *ghost*
un(e) **fonceur, -euse** *bold, courageous person*
la **forme : être en forme** *to be in good shape*
fort, -e *strong*
une **glace** *ice, mirror*
incompréhensible *incomprehensible*
intensément *intensely*
lentement *slowly*
les **montagnes russes (f.)** *roller coaster*
un **parc d'attractions** *amusement park*
passionné, -e (de) *enthusiastic (about)*

plaisir : faire plaisir à *to please*
plaît : Ça te plaît? *Do you like it?*
une **préférence** *preference*
rapidement *rapidly*
réservé, -e *reserved*
la **résistance** *resistance, endurance*
secours : Au secours! *Help!*
un **squelette** *skeleton*
tellement *so much*
un **tour** *spin, tour, ride*
tranquillement *quietly, peacefully*
le **vertige** *vertigo, fear of heights*
vivre *to live*

SECTION C

abandonner *to give up*
absolument *absolutely*
l' **angle (m.)** *angle, corner*
appeler *to call, to phone*
un **bal** *dance*
une **bande** *group*
la **chance** *luck*
coucou *hi*
dommage : C'est dommage! *That's too bad!*
fonctionner *to function, work*
le **fric (slang)** *money*
malheureusement *unfortunately*
un **orchestre** *orchestra*
parfait, -e *perfect*
rappeler *to call again, to call back*
regrettable *regrettable*
regretter *to regret*
un(e) **touriste** *tourist*
la **veille** *eve*
vendre *to sell*
vers *about, toward*

ETUDE DE MOTS

1. If **malheureusement** means *unfortunately,* can you guess the French word for *fortunately*? heureusement
   Now you should be able to form the two adjectives *fortunate* and *unfortunate* in French. heureux(se)/malheureux(se)
2. Can you find a pattern in the following pairs of words?

   abandon / abandonner   **fonction / fonctionner**   Double the -n and add -er to form the verb from the noun.

   Now apply the same pattern to make verbs of these nouns.
   collection   station   don   mention   bouton

collectionner/stationner/donner/mentionner/boutonner

A LIRE

La Marseillaise

You're going to read the story of how the French national anthem was born and how it got its name.

Avant de lire

Before you read the entire story, skim the first paragraph. Then explain the meaning of the word **paradoxe** and how it applies to the anthem.

Voilà le paradoxe de l'hymne national de la France : il a été composé en Alsace et il a finalement été appelé «La Marseillaise». La plus grande chanson de l'histoire de France a donné naissance° à une belle légende.

Nous sommes au début de la Révolution française. Le 20 avril 1792, la France a déclaré la guerre° à l'Autriche. Le 25 au soir, le maire de Strasbourg, M. Dietrich, invite à dîner quelques militaires. Claude Rouget de Lisle, un jeune officier de l'armée du Rhin, est triste. Il a passé des semaines heureuses à Strasbourg. Il y a rencontré de vrais amis, des amoureux des arts et de la musique.

Au cours du dîner on entend chanter des soldats dans la rue.

Ça ira by Ladré and Bécourt: Written in 1790 at the height of the revolution, this popular song called for the violent overthrow of the aristocracy in France.

Le maire dit : Vous entendez cette chanson révolutionnaire? Il faut trouver quelque chose de mieux pour nos soldats! Un chant aux paroles simples! Une musique capable d'émouvoir°! Puis il demande à Rouget de Lisle : Pourquoi ne leur écrivez-vous pas un chant, Monsieur de Lisle?

Rentré chez lui, le jeune officier prend son violon et sa plume. Il fait nuit. Le silence est total… Rouget de Lisle cherche… cherche… et compose finalement son «Chant de guerre pour l'armée du Rhin».

Le lendemain, il court montrer son chant à Dietrich. Le maire regarde longtemps la feuille de papier. Puis il appelle sa femme. Elle joue l'hymne nouveau au piano. Soudain, le maire lui dit : Allez chercher nos amis d'hier soir!

---

naissance *birth*; **guerre** *war*; **émouvoir** *move*

Before this century it was common for family members to refer to each other in the "vous" form. Since 1900, this practice has been declining. Today it is very rare to find a husband and wife who say "vous" to each other.

Bientôt, tout le monde est là. Sans un mot, Dietrich conduit ses amis près du piano. Le maire commence à chanter :

> — Allons enfants de la patrie,
> Le jour de gloire est arrivé…

Un tonnerre d'applaudissements° salue la note finale. Avec ce chant, dit Dietrich, nous allons gagner toutes les batailles, vaincre° tous nos ennemis!

Dans la ville de Marseille, un groupe de volontaires organise un banquet avant de partir en guerre. Au cours du banquet, un certain Manier reprend le chant de Rouget de Lisle. Le lendemain, le journal publie le texte; il est distribué aux soldats. En allant à Paris, les soldats marseillais répètent le «Chant de guerre pour l'armée du Rhin». Quand les Parisiens entendent chanter les soldats marseillais, ils appellent leur chanson le «Chant des Marseillais». Plus tard, elle devient «La Marseillaise».

Allons enfants de la patrie,°
Le jour de gloire est arrivé
Contre nous de la tyrannie
L'étendard sanglant° est levé (bis)
Entendez-vous dans nos campagnes
Mugir° ces féroces soldats?
Ils viennent jusque dans nos bras
Egorger° nos fils, nos compagnes
    Aux armes citoyens!
  Formez vos bataillons
    Marchons! Marchons!
  Qu'un sang impur°
  Abreuve° nos sillons!°

Activité • Connaissez-vous votre hymne national?

Connaissez-vous l'hymne national de votre pays? Répondez aux questions suivantes.

1. Comment s'appelle l'hymne national de votre pays? The Star-Spangled Banner
2. Qui a composé la chanson? Francis Scott Key
3. Quand? Le 14 septembre 1814

4. C'est une chanson de guerre? Oui, de la guerre de 1812.
5. Votre pays était en guerre avec quel autre pays à ce moment? Mon pays était en guerre avec l'Angleterre.

Francis Scott Key a composé The Star-Spangled Banner pendant la guerre de 1812. A ce moment, les Etats-Unis étaient en guerre avec l'Angleterre. The Star-Spangled Banner est maintenant l'hymne national des Etats-Unis.

Activité • Ecrit dirigé

Le paragraphe suivant parle de «La Marseillaise». Ecrivez le paragraphe en faisant les changements nécessaires pour qu'il parle de l'hymne national de votre pays.

Claude Rouget de Lisle a composé «La Marseillaise» en 1792. A ce moment, la France était en guerre avec l'Autriche. «La Marseillaise» est maintenant l'hymne national de la France.

---

tonnerre d'applaudissements *thunderous applause;* **vaincre** *defeat;* **patrie** *fatherland;* **étendard sanglant** *bloody flag;* **mugir** *roar;* **égorger** *to cut the throats of;* **sang impur** *impure blood;* **abreuve** *water;* **sillons** *plowed fields*

Bonhomme Carnaval

Février à Québec n'est pas un mois ordinaire, un mois d'hiver sombre. C'est au contraire un mois de gaieté, un mois de plein air et de bonne humeur. C'est la période du Carnaval!

Bonhomme Carnaval est le symbole de cette joyeuse période de l'année. Habillé en blanc, il porte une tuque° rouge et une ceinture fléchée°. Environ un mois avant le début du Carnaval, il fait une entrée spectaculaire dans la ville. Lors de° son arrivée dans la capitale, le maire de Québec lui offre les clés de la ville.

Bonhomme est un personnage important. En dehors de° son rôle de Roi du Carnaval, c'est un véritable diplomate de son pays. Il voyage à travers° le monde : dans toutes les provinces canadiennes et en Nouvelle Angleterre; en Europe et aux Bahamas; dans les Alpes françaises et à Paris. On a même vu Bonhomme au Carnaval de Nice et au Tournoi de roses de Pasadena. Il représente les Québécois et leur hospitalité légendaire.

Durant le Carnaval, Bonhomme est le Roi de la fête. Entouré de sa cour d'honneur, composée de la Reine et de six Duchesses, il préside à tous les grands événements : activités culturelles et sportives, défilés… Tous ses sujets lui montrent une joyeuse affection.

La Reine est un symbole de charme, de grâce et de majesté. Le couronnement de la Reine du Carnaval est un spectacle en plein air ouvert à tous, suivi de° danses et de feux d'artifice. La foule enthousiaste acclame la Reine. L'heureuse élue° représente l'un des sept duchés de la ville de Québec. Les duchés portent les noms glorieux des grands personnages de l'histoire du Canada : Cartier, Champlain, Laval, Frontenac, Lévy, Montcalm et Montmorency. The seven "duchés" (dukedoms) of Quebec exist only for Carnaval.

Une fois le nom de la principale héroïne du Carnaval de Québec divulgué°, la fête commence vraiment… Dix jours de rêve et de joie! Jacques Cartier (1491–1557): French sailor and explorer; discovered the St. Lawrence River. Samuel de Champlain (1567–1635): French explorer; founded the city of Quebec 1608

---

tuque *woolen cap;* **fléchée** *decorated with arrows;* **lors de** *at the time of;* **en dehors de** *apart from;* **à travers** *throughout;* **suivi de** *followed by;* **élue** *chosen one;* **divulgué** *revealed*

Marquis de Montcalm (1712–1759): French general; killed in the battle of the Plains of Abraham against the British
François de Montmorency-Laval (1623–1708): the first Roman Catholic bishop of Quebec city; a major figure in the religious and civil affairs of New France (Canada)
Comte de Frontenac (1620–1698): Governor general of New France in the late 1600's
François de Lévis (1719–1787): French general; fought the British at the battle of Sainte-Foy

Activité • Devinez

Choisissez l'équivalent anglais.

début beginning	**en plein air** outside	*outside*	*court*
clés keys	**cour** court	*beginning*	*keys*

Activité • Qui est-ce? Qu'est-ce que c'est?

Vous avez vu les adjectifs suivants dans l'histoire du Bonhomme Carnaval. Qu'est-ce que chaque adjectif décrit? Une personne? Une chose? Un événement? Complétez le tableau.

Adjectif	Qui?	Quoi?
joyeuse		période
sportives		activités
légendaire		l'hospitalité québécoise
glorieux	les grands personnages de l'histoire canadienne	
heureuse	l'élue	
spectaculaire		l'entrée de/ Bonhomme Carnaval/
enthousiaste	la foule	

Activité • La leçon d'histoire

Trouvez dans le texte les noms de deux explorateurs et d'un général célèbres.
Cartier and Champlain were explorers. Montcalm and Lévis were generals.

La Chanson du Carnaval

Les Québécois aiment chanter, surtout au moment du Carnaval. Voici une chanson populaire.

A Québec, ça commence royalement
Par le grand et joyeux déploiement°
Des tambours, des trompettes, des brillants°
Que l'on voit dans les vrais couronnements.

Carnaval, Mardi Gras, Carnaval
A Québec, c'est tout un festival.
Carnaval, Mardi Gras, Carnaval
Chantons tous le joyeux Carnaval.

---

déploiement *display;* **brillants** *diamonds*

CHAPITRE **4** # Week-end en Belgique

Chapitre de révision

UNIT RESOURCES **Cahier d'Activités, Cahier d'Exercices,** Unit 4
Cassette, Transparency 10 (also 1–9), Review Test 1
TEACHER-PREPARED MATERIALS **Review 1–26** Map of Belgium,
map of Europe

Unit 4 combines functions, grammar, and vocabulary that the students have
studied in Units 1–3. This unit provides communicative and writing practice in
different situations; some of the activities lend themselves to cooperative learning. If your students require further practice, you will find additional review
exercises in Unit 4 of the **Cahier d'Activités** and the **Cahier d'Exercices.** On the
other hand, if your students know how to use the material in Units 1–3, you
may wish to omit parts of Unit 4.

OBJECTIVE To review communicative functions, grammar, and vocabulary
from Units 1–3

CULTURAL BACKGROUND Belgium is a small country to the north-
northeast of France. The land is low-lying except for the Ardennes Mountains
in the southeast. Belgium is one of the most densely populated and highly
industrialized nations in Europe. The headquarters for both the European
Common Market and the North Atlantic Treaty Organization (NATO) are
located in Brussels **(Bruxelles),** the Belgian capital.

MOTIVATING ACTIVITY Have students locate Belgium on a map of
Europe. Ask them what they know about Belgium: **Qu'est-ce que vous savez
de la Belgique? C'est un grand pays? Où est-elle située? Quelle est la capitale?
Quelles langues parle-t-on en Belgique?**

1 Projets de week-end

CULTURAL BACKGROUND The Formula One Grand Prix championship is
the World Series of auto racing. There are 17 races on five continents, taking
place over eight months. Each race is televised throughout the world. Because
of the high speeds involved and the nature of the Formula One cars, the races
are very dangerous; several drivers have lost their lives. A top driver, in
addition to becoming an international celebrity, can earn a lot of money. Alain
Prost, a French driver who has won more Grand Prix races than anyone in
history, earns approximately $5 million a year.
  Spa, a town in the Ardennes Mountains, has long been famous for its mineral springs. The English word *spa* derives from the name of the town.

  Play the cassette or read aloud the introductory paragraph about Jérôme.
Then ask comprehension questions:

  Où habite Jérôme? Où est Valenciennes?
  Quel est son projet pour le week-end?
  Quel est son problème?
  Qu'est-ce qui peut être la solution?
  Pourquoi cette idée n'est-elle pas tout à fait bonne?

Next tell the students to listen carefully to the dialogue between Jérôme and Antoine. They should find out why Jérôme doesn't want to take the train, why he doesn't want to watch the race on TV, and two reasons why Antoine finally agrees to go. Students might jot down answers to these questions as they listen. Finally, have students pair off to practice reading the dialogue, changing roles. You might ask volunteers to role-play the situation for the class.

2 Activité • Répondez

For question 5, have students trace the boys' itinerary on a map. Encourage them to describe the journey in French, orally or in writing.

3 Activité • Les préparatifs

Before beginning this activity, review the present-tense forms of **devoir**. Students may do the activity in two ways. (1) They might talk about Antoine and Jérôme; therefore, their statements will begin with **Il doit** or **Ils doivent**. (2) They might role-play Antoine; their statements will begin with **Je dois** or **Nous devons.**

CHALLENGE   Have students pair off to make up a dialogue between Antoine and Jérôme. They ask each other if they've done the things listed. Tell students to use the **passé composé** and **pas encore.**

> —Jérôme, tu as fait des sandwiches?
> —Non, pas encore.
> —Et alors, quand est-ce que tu vas en faire?
> —Dans deux minutes!

4 Activité • Projetez le week-end

Cite each time given in the two-day schedule and ask what the brothers are going to do then: **Samedi, à 11 heures, qu'est-ce que Jérôme et Antoine vont faire?** You might vary your questions: **A quelle heure vont-ils dîner?**

5 Activité • A vous maintenant!

CULTURAL BACKGROUND   **Bruges** and **Ypres** are in West Flanders. **Bruges** is a quiet city known for its medieval architecture and its picturesque canals, narrow streets, and windmills. The **Fête des Chats** at **Ypres** takes place each May. It dates back to the Middle Ages when cats, then considered to be instruments of the devil, were thrown from the belfry tower. Today toy stuffed cats are thrown. The **Grand-Place** in Brussels is the cultural and historical heart of the city. It's surrounded by beautiful, centuries-old buildings. Waterloo, a village in southern Belgium, was the scene of Napoleon's definitive defeat by the British in June 1815.

For cooperative learning, have students work in pairs. They might alternate asking each other questions or making suggestions and responding with expressions of enthusiasm, indecision, indifference, or regret. Circulate among students as they practice.

SLOWER-PACED LEARNING   Before students work in pairs, review with them how to express indecision and indifference (Unit 3, B6, page 104), how to express regret (Unit 3, C13, page 115), and how to accept invitations (Unit 2, A12, page 58).

6 Savez-vous que... ?

Linguistic differences in regions of many countries cause trouble because they emphasize or reinforce ethnic and cultural differences, which are then reflected in politics and economics. This has been true in Belgium, where long-standing tensions between the Flemish- and French-speaking citizens erupted in a series of political crises in the 1960s. Although the constitutional reform of 1980 created autonomous regions with equal political power, Belgium remains linguistically and culturally divided. The nation's major unifying factors are the monarchy and the Roman Catholic church.

7 Activité • Un jeune Flamand parle

Play the cassette for the students. Then have them form cooperative learning groups of three or four students each. Group members should work together to understand the gist of the passage. Have one member from each group report to the class.

SLOWER-PACED LEARNING Distribute to students a French translation of the passage, with the sentences out of order. Have students match the French sentences to their Flemish equivalents and then rewrite the French in the correct order.

8 PREMIERE ETAPE

Have students look at the photos and tell in French what the boys are doing in each. Then play the cassette or read the dialogue aloud. Ask students to confirm whether their earlier statements about the photos were accurate. Next have the students read aloud and role-play the dialogue.

9 Activité • Situations

To review, ask volunteers to explain how to form questions in French using **est-ce que** and inversion. Then have students work in pairs: one should ask an appropriate question for each item and the other should respond. Students should then switch roles.

CHALLENGE Have students pair off to develop brief dialogues for each situation. Afterward, for each situation, call on a different pair to present what they prepared to the class.

10 Activité • A vous maintenant!

SLOWER-PACED LEARNING First establish the identity of each place pictured. Then role-play the **agent de police.** Call on individuals to ask you for directions to the places pictured.

CHALLENGE Have students draw maps of several city blocks, labeling streets and showing the places pictured in the activity. Then have them exchange maps and ask each other directions to get to each place.

11 Activité • Visitons Bruxelles

CULTURAL BACKGROUND Although Brussels was occupied during both world wars, it managed to survive relatively unscathed. There are therefore many fine examples of medieval and Renaissance architecture still standing. Although there has been much modern construction, especially on the outskirts, the city makes a deliberate effort to preserve its beautiful old buildings.

First play the cassette as students look at the photos and read the text. Ask questions about the photos. Ask students which activity they prefer to do and why. Then have students form groups of four to prepare the dialogues.

SLOWER-PACED LEARNING   Before students form groups, read the brochure aloud or play the cassette. Then review the functions and structures students will need to use: forming questions; extending, accepting, and refusing invitations; forming the **passé composé.**

12   ## AU CIRCUIT DE SPA-FRANCORCHAMPS

CULTURAL BACKGROUND   Alain Prost was born in 1955 near Lyons. He began racing professionally while still in his teens and made his Formula One debut in 1980. He was Grand Prix champion in 1985 and 1986, the first driver in more than 25 years to win the championship two years in a row.

Before playing the cassette or reading the dialogue aloud, tell students to listen for Jérôme's and Antoine's general reactions as they watch the race. Are the boys pleased? Disappointed? Excited? Uninterested? After the students have listened to the dialogues, have them suggest other ways Jérôme could have exclaimed about the speed of the cars and offered encouragement to Prost.

13   ## Activité • Encouragez les pilotes

Review with students expressions of encouragement (Unit 2, B15, page 66). Assign a different driver's name to each row and have students, in turn, cheer him on with different phrases.

14   ## Activité • Ecrivez

Review the **passé composé** with the students before they begin this activity.

SLOWER-PACED LEARNING   Before students begin writing, elicit oral answers to the questions in the instructions. Then have students offer various opinions.

15   ## Activité • Interview

Ask individuals to read aloud the article about Prost. You might then play the role of an interviewer, asking questions of the entire class and calling on volunteers to suggest answers. Finally, have the students pair off to prepare their interviews.

16   ## Activité • Jeu : Pilote de course

As the game progresses, a **pilote** who is not scoring well may choose to make a "pit stop" to "change drivers." As an extension of this game, you might have the class play Twenty Questions. One person pretends to be a famous person. The students try to guess who he or she is by asking questions.

17   ## TU AS PASSE UN BON WEEK-END?

CULTURAL BACKGROUND   During World War I, the city of **Ypres** was the scene of three bloody battles in which some 300,000 Allied soldiers lost their lives. Almost entirely destroyed, the city was rebuilt after the war.

Play the cassette or read the dialogue aloud. Ask the class **Qu'est-ce que Jérôme essaie de faire? Pourquoi a-t-il des difficultés?** Then, to re-enter the passé composé with avoir and être, have students open their books and tell what Patrice did last weekend and the weekend before last. Next have students imagine how Jérôme would have answered Patrice's questions if he had had the chance!

18 | **Activité • Faux, mais pourquoi?**

Make a timed contest of this activity. Students pair off and rewrite the sentences correctly. The first pair that finishes and makes the fewest mistakes wins.

19 | **Activité • Encore des questions**

Review the pronoun **en** (Unit 2, C15, page 71). Then have students complete the activity as instructed in the text.

SLOWER-PACED LEARNING Before students begin working in pairs, go through the items and have students identify which words in each will be replaced by **en.**

20 | **Activité • Ecrit dirigé**

SLOWER-PACED LEARNING Before they begin to write, brainstorm with students possible responses to the questions. Assign this to be written in class so that you can offer assistance. Students might work in pairs and read their dialogues to the class after they've completed them.

21 | **Activité • Ecrivez**

You might do this activity with the entire class. Write the first sentence of the composition on the board. Then go around the room, asking each student to add a sentence. If a student is at a loss, suggest a phrase that gives the main idea of the next sentence.

22 | **Activité • A la Fête des Chats**

First review how to express admiration and surprise (Unit 3, A14, page 99). Then have students look at the photos and describe what they see. Finally, have them make as many exclamations as they can about each photo.

23 | **Activité • A vous maintenant!**

For each item, brainstorm with students reasons why one might not have done the activity. For number 3, for example, reasons might include **Je n'ai pas pu trouver la rue des Bouchers, Je n'ai pas visité ce quartier de la ville,** or **Je n'ai pas aimé les restaurants là-bas.** Write suggestions on the board or on a transparency for students to refer to as they work in pairs.

24 | **Activité • Et vous?**

As a model, you might tell of a trip you took. Instead of talking about a trip they've taken, some students might prefer to talk about an imaginary one.

CHALLENGE Have students use these questions as a guide to prepare brief presentations. Allow a day or two for preparation so that they can gather photos or items to illustrate their talks.

25 ## Activité • Conversation

Give students a few moments to think of additional questions they might wish to ask. As students work in pairs, circulate and listen. To spot-check, ask several individuals to report their partners' answers to the class.

26 ## Activité • Ecrivez

After the students have written their messages, have them "mail" their postcards by dropping them into a "mailbox" in the classroom. The next day, after you've corrected their work, "deliver" the postcards to friends, and have individuals read aloud the messages they've received.

SLOWER-PACED LEARNING Before class, prepare a message about **Bruges.** Scramble the words in each sentence. Then, in class, distribute copies of the scrambled message to students. They should rewrite each sentence, putting the words in the correct order.

CONSULTONS LE DICTIONNAIRE

Up to now, many of the French texts that you've read are the same as the ones that you find in French newspapers, books, and magazines. In fact that's where some of the reading selections in your book came from! You may not have understood all the words in them, but the meanings of the most important ones were given at the bottom of each page. Maybe there were other words that you would have liked to know. Well, now you're going to learn how to find those meanings on your own. You're going to see, with the knowledge of French that you already have, how to pick up almost any text in everyday French and get the gist of it. How? By using the right dictionary in the right way. You'll find out what words mean— and much more! After you've seen what you can get out of a reliable, user-friendly dictionary, you might even be tempted to buy one!

If you expect to continue studying French until you really know the language and are able to use it, you're bound to need a dictionary sooner or later. And the sooner you get into the habit of using this tool intelligently, the better you'll be able to master the language. It's the same as anything else you decide to do. You need the tools to do the job. If you're going to be a serious biker, you'll probably need a ten-speed. If you're into photography, you need a reliable camera.

Whether you buy your own dictionary or use the ones in school, you've got to pick the right one for the job you want to do. First you should know that there are different types of French dictionaries—some big, some small; some with pictures, some without; some confusing, some inviting; some with too much information about each word and others without enough. Pick the one that suits you best, the one that you feel you can work with. Here are a few pointers on what you can get out of each type of dictionary.

1. Open your book to page 142. Let's start with the type of dictionary that gives the English meanings of French words, the so-called French-English bilingual dictionary. This is the sort of dictionary you may need to make out that French newspaper report you want to read or that magazine article, TV guide, or calendar of events that interests you. Look, for example, at page 93. Read the caption below the map. Can you make out all the words? Do you have an idea what's going on between the hours of seven and twelve inside the perimeter? What about the **stationnement**?

Is the caption saying that parking is permitted or prohibited? Turn back to page 142 and look up the word **interdit**. It says here: **interdit** *banned, forbidden*. So now you know that the map on page 93 shows a no-parking zone.

You can get French-English dictionaries in many shapes and sizes. Some are made to fit nicely into your pocket—great for traveling. Any of them are really handy to have around when you're reading French, provided they don't slow you down too much. Of course, the bigger they are the more they explain and the more words they contain.

The entry in your book for **interdit** comes from one of these French-English dictionaries. But there's another place where you could look for this word—in a French-French dictionary, the same sort of dictionary that French teenagers use every day. These dictionaries have a lot going for them. They're more up-to-date than French-English dictionaries, and they come in a wider variety of shapes and sizes. Now look up the word **interdit** on page 142 to see the entry in a French-French dictionary. Here it is: **interdit   non autorisé.** If you understand this, you'll probably like working from a French-French dictionary. It might help keep you thinking in French as you read!

2. Giving the meanings of words is only part of what dictionaries can do. Some help you learn to speak the language by telling you how words sound. They do this by assigning each sound a letter—only one letter to a sound and one sound to a letter. Simple, isn't it? But you'll need to be careful—this is not always the way a sound is *spelled*. Many sounds in French are spelled with two letters, like the **in** and the **it** in **interdit,** where eight letters are used to represent six sounds. Check this out in your dictionary on page 142. It says here: **interdit** /ɛ̃terdi/. Just what you expected? You'll do more of this later so that you can see the difference between the way a word is spelled and the way it sounds.

You may know a lot of French words and how to spell them, but if you want to say them, this may not be of much help to you. Look at page 142. You see how the word for *finger* looks in French there. It's spelled **doigt,** isn't it? How do you pronounce the final **gt**? Do you pronounce one letter, both, or neither one? Your friendly dictionary will tell you, if you only ask. Look it up and you'll find /**dwa**/. You don't pronounce the last two letters. You can have a lot of fun doing this; you'll do more later. But for the time being, let's see what else you can get out of your dictionary.

3. Suppose that you know what you want to say, but you can't say it in French. Will the dictionary be of any help? Well, it all depends. To begin with, you'll need another type of dictionary, one that starts not from the French, but from the English: an English-French bilingual dictionary. It may even be bound together in the same volume as the French-English dictionary that you've already used. But how do you use an English-French dictionary? Let's take an example. Suppose that you get an invitation by letter or postcard from a French family you've already met. They're polite enough, by the way, to compliment you on your French and ask if you know any other foreign languages, which you don't. You write back, saying that your French is not that good and that you don't think you have a gift for languages. What's the word for *gift* in French? Let's look it up on page 142. Under *gift* you find *(a)* **cadeau,** *(b)* **donation,** and *(c)* **don.** You pick the first French equivalent and write **Je n'ai pas de cadeau.** What will the family think? Well, they may take you for a cheapskate, because you're telling them in advance that you won't bring a gift. You should have picked the last equivalent, *(c)* **don,** and written **Je n'ai pas le don des langues.** But how could you have known in advance which one to select? You couldn't. Unless you already knew enough French to figure out which one made the most sense, or unless you checked out each equivalent in a French-French dictionary. If you leave it up to chance, your English-French dictionary could become more of a hindrance than a help.

Of course the big dictionaries, those that supply a lot of information about each word, may give you more help. Here is what you find in one of the latest and largest bilingual English-French dictionaries under *gift:* *(a) (present)* **cadeau.** *(b) (New Year's gift)* **étrennes.** *(c) (talent)* **don.** He has a . . . for math **Il a le don des maths.** So, because you're telling about your talent, rather than about the present you're not going to bring, you must pick *(c)* **don.** The moral of all this is be careful how you use your English-French dictionary. Use it for reference to look up words, but pay particular attention to explanations and example sentences that tell you how to use the words.

4. Now look back at the other side of the coin—the French-English side. Is there anything else you can see in it? Yes, indeed. The most obvious use. What people use dictionaries for most of the time. To find out how a word is spelled. You'll need to look up spellings if you're going to write French correctly. Most French people do. They're always looking up words in their **Larousse,** their **Robert,** or whatever. Of course, if you're only looking up the spelling, you don't need any of these big desk dictionaries. All you need is a French spelling dictionary. And this also has a lot going for it. It doesn't give you long columns of explanations that you have to skip over. Instead, you find thousands of words—one word per line—in a little book that fits nicely into your pocket. Some of these dictionaries give you a bonus by listing the conjugations of the main French verbs. Of course, if you don't want or need to spell a lot of words, your bilingual pocket French-English dictionary will serve as well. So will your big desk dictionary, if you don't mind carrying it around. So try them out for size and choose the one that works best for you.

Now, think of all the new words you've seen in the past three units. Are you sure you can say all of them out loud? Let's take some of them, group them together, and play a few games with them. You'll get the answers from your dictionary. Do exercises *a* through *f* on page 142 in your book.

APERÇU CULTUREL 2

Bonjour de Québec

OBJECTIVE   To read in French for cultural awareness

CULTURAL BACKGROUND   *Page 143*   The city of Quebec is the capital of the province of Quebec. It was founded in 1608 by Samuel de Champlain and captured by the British in 1759. The city lies at the top of a high bluff overlooking the St. Lawrence River. The old walled city has many buildings dating back to the seventeenth and eighteenth centuries. Its narrow, winding streets are paved with cobblestones. The modern part of Quebec city lies outside the walls.

Page 144   Laval University is the oldest French-language university in North America. It grew out of the **Séminaire de Québec** founded in the seventeenth century by François-Xavier de Montmorency Laval. Today the university has an enrollment of 20,000 students. The very modern University of Quebec, founded in 1969, is also located in Quebec city.

Grands-pères are swirls of rich, creamy dough that are cooked and then covered with maple syrup. They are a popular wintertime dessert.

Page 145   The **vieux port** lies at the foot of the cliff on which Quebec city is perched. This part of the city is called the **basse ville.** From the **basse ville** one can get to the **haute ville** by **funiculaire.**

Page 146   The **pastèque** that Héloïse refers to is watermelon. Robert Charlebois, a Canadian singer, is known for his pop and soft rock songs.

Page 149   **Le méchoui** is an Arab dish adopted by the French. It's lamb roasted over an open wood fire.

Page 150   **Une tourtière** is a meat pie. It's made with ground meat, such as pork or a mixture of pork and beef, mixed with seasonings and baked in a pie crust.

SUGGESTED TEACHING PROCEDURE

Show a map of Canada and have students locate the province of Quebec and the city of Quebec. Tell them they're going to hear a letter from a girl who lives in Quebec city. Have the students look at the photos, text, and captions as you play the cassette or read the text aloud. To check comprehension, stop after every page or two and ask simple questions: **Stéphane Desmarest a quel âge? Où habite-t-il? Dans quel magazine a-t-il mis son annonce? Qui lui écrit?** Students may look in their books to answer. When you come to the expressions **Mais chacun ses goûts!** (page 146) and **Plus on est de fous, plus on rit!** (page 148), ask students to give the English equivalents.

SLOWER-PACED LEARNING   Do not try to cover the entire photo essay at once. Do two or three pages each day. To help students keep track of the family members, draw Heloïse's family tree on the board or on a transparency, labeling her brother, parents, uncle, and maternal grandparents. To one side write **Amis**, and list Eric and Anne-Sophie.

CHALLENGE   Have the students read the text a second time, silently. Divide the class into teams of four or five students. Have team members write as many facts as they can recall about Héloïse and her family. The team that recalls the most facts wins.

Suggested Activity

Have the students reread the text for homework. The next day, read aloud to the class multiple-choice statements such as the following:

1. Les «grands-pères» sont
   a. des professeurs au collège.
   b. un dessert québécois.
   c. des vendeurs de fleurs.

2. Robert Charlebois est
   a. l'oncle d'Héloïse.
   b. un cycliste canadien.
   c. un chanteur québécois.

On a sheet of paper, students should write the letters of the correct answers.

Suggested Activity

CHALLENGE   Have students pretend that they're Stéphane and that they've just received the letter from Héloïse. Ask them to compose a reply to her. They should give Héloïse some information about themselves (the information may be fictitious), and they should ask her questions about some of the things she mentioned in her letter.

Suggested Activity

Ask students to scan the reading for words and expressions that gave them cultural clues. Discuss those clues and then compare Canada with France.

Climate: **deux saisons**
Sports: **le hockey**
Architecture: **une maison toute en briques**
Catholic influence: **collège des Jésuites,**
 l'hôpital de l'Enfant Jésus,
 le petit séminaire de Québec

Week-end en Belgique

Chapitre de révision

1   Projets de week-end

Qu'est-ce que vous faites généralement le week-end? Jérôme Loup habite à Valenciennes, en France, pas loin de la frontière belge. Il a un projet formidable pour le week-end. Il veut aller au Grand Prix de Formule 1 à Spa-Francorchamps en Belgique. Mais il y a 200 kilomètres et il n'a pas son permis de conduire *(driver's license)*. Son frère Antoine a une voiture, mais lui, il n'est pas passionné de sport automobile. Comment faire?

JÉRÔME	Tu sais, dimanche, il y a le Grand Prix de Belgique.
ANTOINE	Ah oui?
JÉRÔME	Avec Alain Prost.
ANTOINE	Pourquoi tu n'y vas pas? Il y a certainement des trains.
JÉRÔME	Oui, mais c'est pas pratique. Il faut changer à Bruxelles et après, à Spa, il faut prendre un bus jusqu'à Francorchamps.
ANTOINE	Ah, mon vieux, c'est ça le sport!
JÉRÔME	Et puis c'est ennuyeux d'y aller seul.
ANTOINE	Ça passe pas à la télévision?
JÉRÔME	Si, mais c'est différent… Ça te dit d'y aller?
ANTOINE	Où?
JÉRÔME	Eh bien, au Grand Prix!

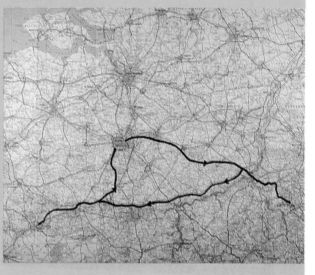

ANTOINE	Mmmm… Ça te plairait?
JÉRÔME	Enormément!
ANTOINE	Ça commence à quelle heure?
JÉRÔME	A quatorze heures trente.
ANTOINE	Bon, c'est d'accord. Mais on part samedi, comme ça on passe par Bruxelles. Ça fait longtemps que je rêve de visiter la ville.
JÉRÔME	Génial! Je prends mon appareil-photo!

ANTOINE	Ah, je vois! Tu veux y aller en voiture, et moi, je dois venir avec toi pour conduire.
JÉRÔME	Voilà! Tu as compris!
ANTOINE	Ça ne m'intéresse pas beaucoup, les courses de voitures.
JÉRÔME	Allez! Sois sympa. Et puis, il faut aller applaudir Prost, notre champion national!

Photo above: Alain Prost, French race car driver

Photos on page 128: The Hôtel de Ville in Ypres; the race track for the Spa-Francorchamps Grand Prix; A float from the "Fête des Chats" parade in Ypres. Also pictured is the Belgian flag.

Week-end en Belgique   129

Students may need to refer to the map on P. 434 to locate Belgium.

2   Activité • Répondez

1. La Belgique est au nord-est de la France.
2. Le Grand Prix de Belgique, a lieu à Spa-Francorchamps. C'est une course de voitures.

1. Où est la Belgique, par rapport (*in relation to*) à la France?
2. Où a lieu le Grand Prix de Belgique? Qu'est-ce que c'est? 3. Antoine doit conduire.
3. Pourquoi Antoine doit-il accompagner Jérôme à Francorchamps?
4. Qui est Alain Prost? 4. C'est le champion national de France. 5. Ils vont partir de Valenciennes samedi matin.
5. Racontez l'itinéraire que vont suivre Jérôme et Antoine.
Ils vont visiter Bruxelles. Dimanche, ils vont aller voir la course à Francorchamps.

1. Nous devons demander la permission aux parents.
2. Je dois prendre les billets.
3   Activité • Les préparatifs   3. Nous devons changer de l'argent.
4. Nous devons faire nos valises.

Pour ne rien oublier, Antoine fait une liste. Qu'est-ce que Jérôme et lui doivent faire avant de partir?

1. demander la permission aux parents — Jérôme et moi
2. prendre les billets — moi
3. changer de l'argent — Jérôme et moi
4. faire les valises — Jérôme et moi
5. emporter l'appareil-photo — Jérôme
6. faire des sandwiches — Jérôme

5. Jérôme doit emporter l'appareil-photo.
6. Il doit aussi faire des sandwiches.

4   Activité • Projetez le week-end   Possible answer is given.

Pour bien profiter du week-end, il faut faire des projets détaillés. Qu'est-ce que les frères Loup vont faire? Aidez Jérôme à projeter son week-end. Employez le verbe **aller** plus l'infinitif.
Nous allons partir à onze heures. A midi et demi, nous allons déjeuner à Bruxelles. Puis nous allons visiter la ville de 14h à

Samedi		Dimanche	
11h	départ	10h	en route!
12h30	déjeuner à Bruxelles	12h	arrivée à Francorchamps
14h_19h	visite de la ville	14h30	Grand Prix
19h	dîner	18h	départ de Francorchamps
21h	hôtel	20h	arrivée à Valenciennes

19h. Après ça, nous allons dîner. Après le dîner, nous allons chercher un hôtel. Dimanche, on va partir à dix heures. On va arriver à Francorchamps à midi. Le grand prix va commencer à deux heures et demie. Nous allons partir de Francorchamps à 18h. On va arriver à Valenciennes à 20h.

Vous habitez à Valenciennes. Vous voulez passer le week-end en Belgique. Proposez ces activités à un(e) camarade. Votre camarade accepte, refuse ou il/elle est indécis(e). Variez les expressions: Ça te dit de... ? Tu veux... ?

1.

—Ça t'intéresse de... ? visiter Bruges
—Ça m'est égal.

2.

—Tu veux... ? voir la Grand-Place à Bruxelles
—D'accord. Bonne idée!

3.

—Tu veux... ? aller au bord de la mer
—Oui, je veux bien.

4.

—Ça te dit de... ? passer le dimanche à Waterloo
—Non, je n'en ai pas envie.

5.

aller à la Fête des Chats à Ypres
—Ça te plairait d'... ?
—Je n'ai pas de préférence.

6.

—Tu ne veux pas... ? faire une balade en Belgique
—Si. Volontiers.

Week-end en Belgique   131

6 Savez-vous que... ? 🔊

En 1971, quatre régions linguistiques ont été constitutionnellement établies en Belgique : Flandre dans le nord, Wallonie dans le sud, les régions de langue allemande dans l'est, et Bruxelles. Les Flamands parlent flamand, ou néerlandais. Les Wallons sont francophones; ils parlent français. Bruxelles est bilingue. Dans l'est près de la frontière allemande, on parle allemand.

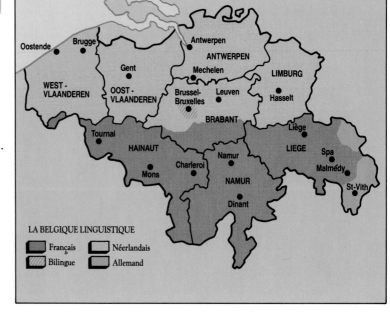

LA BELGIQUE LINGUISTIQUE

▨ Français ☐ Néerlandais
▨ Bilingue ☐ Allemand

carmes: Carmelite monks

Chaque ville en Belgique porte deux noms : son nom en français et son nom en flamand. En Flandre, les noms sont indiqués sur les routes en flamand. En Wallonie, ils sont indiqués en français. A Bruxelles, les deux noms sont indiqués. Quelques noms de villes sont presque les mêmes : Anvers en français est Antwerpen en flamand. D'autres sont différents : Ypres en français est Ieper en flamand. Je m'appelle Mark Vander Linden. Je suis belge et j'ai 15 ans. J'habite à Anvers, la capitale de la Flandre. Anvers est connue pour son industrie diamantaire. Chez moi, je parle néerlandais avec mes parents et mes amis, mais j'apprends le français à l'école. Je parle un peu anglais, et ça me plaît. Je veux visiter l'Amérique. Pour obtenir un bon travail en Belgique, il faut savoir le néerlandais, le français et l'anglais. Est-ce que vous comprenez mon néerlandais?

7 Activité • Un jeune Flamand parle 🔊

Ecoutez ce jeune Flamand parler néerlandais. Est-ce que vous comprenez? Racontez en français ce qu'il dit.

«Mijn naam is Mark Vander Linden. Ik ben Belg en 15 jaar oud. Ik woon in Antwerpen, de hoofdstad van Vlaanderen. Antwerpen is gekend voor zijn diamantindustrie. Ik spreek thuis Nederlands met mijn ouders° en mijn vrienden, maar ik leer Frans op school. Ik spreek een betje° Engels en dat doe ik graag. Ik zou graag Amerika bezoeken. Om een goede betrekking° in België te kunnen hebben moet ik Nederlands, Frans en Engels kennen. Verstaat u mijn Nederlands?» In English: My name is Mark Vander Linden. I'm Belgian and am 15 years old. I live in Antwerp the capital of Flanders. Antwerp is known for its diamond industry. At home I speak Dutch with my

ouders *parents*; **een betje** *un peu*; **betrekking** *travail* parents and my friends, but I'm learning French in school. I speak a little English and I like it. I'd like to visit America. In order to get a good job in Belgium, you must know Dutch, French and English. Do you understand my Dutch?

La frontière est à quelques kilomètres de Valenciennes. Jérôme et Antoine sont maintenant en Belgique.

(Sur la route)

JÉRÔME   C'est encore loin, Bruxelles?
ANTOINE   Non, on y est dans une heure.

(A Bruxelles)

ANTOINE   Pardon, monsieur, où est-ce qu'on peut trouver un bureau de change?
L'AGENT   Il y en a un dans la petite rue, là.

JÉRÔME   Combien est-ce que j'en prends?
ANTOINE   Fais le plein.   = Fill it up.

JÉRÔME   Combien d'argent est-ce que tu as changé?
ANTOINE   Cent francs. Ça fait six cents francs belges.

ANTOINE   Elle est drôlement impressionnante, cette place!
JÉRÔME   Oui... Dis, quelle heure est-il?
ANTOINE   Trois heures et demie.
JÉRÔME   Tu n'as pas faim?
ANTOINE   Si, un peu. Viens, on va prendre un sandwich dans un de ces cafés.

Activité • Situations Possible answers are given.

Vous êtes en Belgique et vous êtes dans les situations suivantes. Quelles questions posez-vous?
Utilisez l'inversion ou **est-ce que**. Travaillez avec un(e) camarade. 1. Est-ce qu'il y a un bureau de change près d'ici?
2. Quelle heure est-il? 3. Est-ce que tu veux aller au restaurant? 4. Combien est-ce que ça coûte?

1. Vous avez besoin de changer de l'argent.
2. Vous voulez connaître l'heure.
3. Vous avez faim.
4. Vous demandez le prix d'un sandwich.

5. Vous avez soif.
6. Vous voulez savoir le temps qu'il fait à Francorchamps.

5. Où est-ce qu'on peut prendre de l'eau minérale?
6. Quel temps fait-il à Francorchamps?

10 **Activité • A vous maintenant!**   Possible answers are given.

Ça y est, vous êtes à Bruxelles! Mais c'est la première fois et vous avez besoin de renseignements.
Demandez des renseignements à un agent de police pour savoir où vous pouvez trouver :

1.

Où est-ce que je peux trouver un bon restaurant, s'il vous plaît?

2.

Pour aller à la Grand-Place, s.v.p.?

3.

Où est Francorchamps, s.v.p.?

4.

Où est-ce que je peux changer de l'argent, s.v.p.?

5.

Est-ce qu'il y a un bon hôtel près d'ici?

6.

Où est l'Office du tourisme, s.v.p.?

Possible answers are given.

1. — Qu'est-ce que c'est l'atomium?
2. — Ça te dit d'aller manger rue des Bouchers?
3. — Hier j'ai passé une journée fantastique! J'ai vu...

Vous et votre ami(e) allez à l'Office de tourisme et vous trouvez cette publicité touristique. Lisez-la attentivement et faites des dialogues avec un(e) camarade.

1. Votre camarade joue le rôle de l'employé de l'Office de tourisme. Posez-lui des questions.
2. Proposez à votre camarade chacune des activités.

3. C'est le soir. Vous racontez votre journée à d'autres camarades et vous donnez votre opinion personnelle.

BRUXELLES VOUS INVITE!

Visitez la Grand-Place : l'élégant Hôtel de Ville (1402); les belles maisons des Corporations (1695); les illuminations; les marchés aux fleurs. Une cassette, votre «guide personnel», explique tout!

Allez voir l'Atomium, depuis l'exposition de 1958 le symbole de l'âge atomique en forme de molécule de fer°. Circulez dans les neuf sphères, reliées par des tubes. Visitez l'exposition de l'emploi non violent de l'énergie atomique.

Dînez dans un des nombreux restaurants de la rue des Bouchers. Goûtez le plat national de moules° et frites.

Venez goûter du chocolat! En pralines ou en tablettes, la variété est infinie! Emportez-en avec vous; c'est le cadeau le plus agréable.

Achetez de la dentelle°. La dentelle de Bruxelles est connue dans le monde entier. Choisissez des cols°, des blouses, des nappes°.

---

fer *iron;* **moules** *mussels;* **dentelle** *lace;* **cols** *collars;* **nappes** *tablecloths*

12   AU CIRCUIT DE SPA-FRANCORCHAMPS

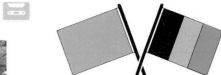

JÉRÔME   Qu'elles sont rapides, ces voitures! Elles vont trop vite! On n'a pas le temps de voir les pilotes!

ANTOINE   On voit mieux à la télévision.

The green flag is used to start the race.

Jérôme et Antoine arrivent à Francorchamps.

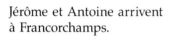

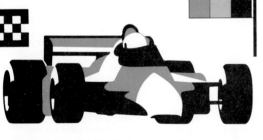

JÉRÔME   Allez Prost!

ANTOINE   Il est dans quelle voiture?

JÉRÔME   La blanche et rouge. Il va gagner!

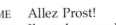

13 · Activité • Encouragez les pilotes

Vous assistez au Grand Prix de Belgique. Encouragez chaque pilote avec une phrase différente.

1. **Johansson**
   Allez, Johansson!

2. **de Cesaris**
   Plus vite, de Cesaris!

3. **Fabre**
   Vous y êtes presque, Fabre!

4. **Prost**
   Encore un petit effort, Prost!

5. **Cheever**
   Continue, Cheever!

S P O R T S

WEEK-END RESULTATS

Automobile
Grand Prix de Belgique
Classement
1. Alain Prost (Fra-Marlboro McLaren TAG) les 298,420 km en 1h27'03"217 (moyenne 205,680 km/h); **2. Stefan Johansson** (Suè-Marlboro McLaren TAG) à 24"764; **3. Andrea de Cesaris** (Ita-Brabham BMW) à un tour; **4. Eddie Cheever** (E-U-Arrows BMW) à un tour; **5. Satoru Nakajima** (Jap-Lotus Honda) à un tour; **6. René Arnoux** (Fra-Ligier Gitanes) à deux tours; **7. Piercarlo Ghinzani** (Ita-Ligier Gitanes) à trois tours; **8. Philippe Alliot** (Fra-Larrousse/Calmels) à trois tours; **9. Philippe Streiff** (Fra-Tyrrell Ford Cosworth) à quatre tours; **10. Pascal Fabre** (Fra-AGS Ford Cosworth) à cinq tours **Les autres concurrents n'ont pas été classés.**

14 · Activité • Ecrivez

Vous êtes journaliste pour la *Page Sportive Belge*. Ecrivez un paragraphe pour votre journal sur le Grand Prix de Belgique. Faites attention. Un bon reportage répond aux questions : où? qui? quoi? pourquoi? et comment? Vous pouvez terminer par une opinion ou une expression personnelle.

The use of "ne... que" is explained in Unit 6, p.209.

15 · Activité • Interview

Vous êtes journaliste. Vous avez interviewé Alain Prost. Voici votre article. Quelles questions est-ce que vous lui avez posées?

Un(e) camarade joue le rôle d'Alain Prost. Posez-lui les questions. Il/Elle répond d'après l'article.

IL N'Y EN A QU'UN, C'EST PROST!

5 Juillet 1981 : Grand Prix de France. Prost remporte° ce jour-là à Dijon le premier Grand Prix de sa carrière.
20 Septembre 1987 : Grand Prix du Portugal. Aujourd'hui, à Estoril, Prost est le roi, le seul. Vingt-huit succès en Grands Prix. Le record.
Pour dépasser Jackie Stewart, le précédent recordman des victoires en Formule 1, Alain Prost a eu besoin de six ans.

Alain Prost court pour gagner. Avec deux titres mondiaux°, le record de victoires en Grands Prix, Alain Prost est incontestablement un «super». A trente-deux ans, Alain n'a plus grand-chose à prouver. Mais il veut rester le meilleur. Alors, un troisième titre lui plairait bien. Prost ne pense pas prendre sa retraite° à quarante ans.

remporte *wins;* **titres mondiaux** *world titles;* **retraite** *retirement*

Quand est-ce que vous avez gagné votre premier Grand-Prix? Combien de titres mondiaux avez-vous? Allez-vous prendre votre retraite?

16 · Activité • Jeu : Pilote de course

Formez deux équipes. Chaque équipe choisit un de ses membres pour être son «pilote de course». Le «pilote» quitte la salle. L'équipe prépare des questions à poser à son «pilote» : des questions simples (Quel est votre nom?) et des questions un peu compliquées (Depuis combien de temps est-ce que vous participez à des courses?). A tour de rôle, chaque équipe pose une question à son «pilote». L'équipe gagne un point pour une bonne question et un point pour une bonne réponse.

Quel âge avez-vous? Ça fait combien de temps que vous êtes pilote? Pourquoi aimez-vous les courses? Combien de victoires avez-vous déjà eues?

Au retour de Belgique, Jérôme essaie de raconter son week-end à son copain Patrice, mais ce n'est pas facile.

Bienvenue (Welkom) à la Fête des Chats.

PATRICE   Salut, Jérôme! Tu as passé un bon week-end?

JÉRÔME   Excellent! Tu sais où je suis allé? Je…

PATRICE   Moi, je suis resté à la maison. Samedi, je suis allé au cinéma et dimanche, on a regardé le Grand Prix de Belgique à la télé.

JÉRÔME   Je sais, je…

PATRICE   C'était drôlement chouette. Prost a gagné devant Johansson. Toi aussi, tu as regardé la télé?

JÉRÔME   Non, je…

PATRICE   Dommage, tu as raté quelque chose! Tu as vraiment de la chance d'être parti! J'adore partir de Valenciennes, ça change. Moi, le weekend dernier, je suis allé à Ypres en Belgique, pour la Fête des Chats. Tu connais la Belgique?

For background on the "Fête des Chats," see p. T89.

historische stad: ville historique

JÉRÔME   Oui, justement je…

PATRICE   C'est pas mal. Les gens sont sympa. Ils ont un drôle d'accent, les Belges. Vas-y un jour, c'est pas loin… Tu as pris des photos?

JÉRÔME   Oui, pl…

PATRICE   Moi, j'en ai pris plein. Si tu veux, viens chez moi un soir de la semaine, on peut regarder mes photos.

JÉRÔME   D'ac…

PATRICE   Et si tu en as, bien sûr, tu peux venir avec!… Au fait, qu'est-ce que tu as fait ce week-end?

Le grand défilé des chats à Ypres (Ieper)

18 Activité • Faux, mais pourquoi?

Avez-vous bien compris le monologue de Patrice? Corrigez les phrases suivantes.

1. Patrice est parti lui aussi pour le week-end. Patrice est resté à la maison.
2. Patrice a vu la Fête des Chats à la télévision. Patrice a vu le Grand Prix de Belgique à la télé.
3. Valenciennes est une ville belge près de la frontière française. Valenciennes est une ville française
   près de la frontière belge.
4. Les Belges parlent français exactement comme les Français.
5. Patrice écoute attentivement les autres. Les Belges parlent français avec un accent.
   Il n'écoute pas. Il parle tout le temps.

19 Activité • Encore des questions 🔲

Patrice veut tout savoir sur le séjour en Belgique de Jérôme. Répondez-lui en utilisant le pronom **en** et une expression de quantité, si possible. Faites les dialogues avec un(e) camarade.

prendre des photos — Tu as pris des photos?
1. —Tu as changé de l'argent? — Oui, j'en ai pris beaucoup.
   —Oui, j'en ai changé un peu.

3. —Tu as rencontré des Belges?
   —Oui, j'en ai rencontré quelques-uns.
4. —Tu as mangé des frites?
   —Oui, j'en ai mangé beaucoup.

1. changer de l'argent
2. voir des voitures de course
3. rencontrer des Belges

4. manger des frites
5. trouver un hôtel
6. envoyer des cartes postales

5. —Tu as trouvé un hôtel?
   —Oui, j'en ai trouvé un.

2. —Tu as vu des voitures de courses?
   —Oui, j'en ai vu plein.

6. —Tu as envoyé des cartes postales?
   —Oui, j'en ai envoyé trois.

20 Activité • Ecrit dirigé

Enfin c'est le tour de Jérôme. Il va raconter son week-end. Ecrivez ses réponses aux questions de Patrice.

P. Au fait, Jérôme, tu n'as pas encore raconté ton week-end. Où est-ce que tu es allé?
J. ... Je suis allé à Spa-Francorchamps.
P. C'est vrai? Au Grand Prix! Pourquoi tu n'as rien dit?
J. ... Je n'ai pas pu.
P. Tu y es allé seul?
J. ... Non, j'y suis allé avec mon frère Antoine.
P. Quand est-ce que vous êtes partis?
J. ... Nous sommes partis samedi matin.
P. Samedi? Mais c'était dimanche, le Grand Prix.
J. ... On a visité Bruxelles samedi.
P. C'est bien, Bruxelles?
J. ... Oui, Bruxelles, c'est fantastique!
P. Qu'est-ce que vous avez mangé? Où avez-vous dormi?
J. ... Nous avons mangé des moules et des frites. Nous sommes restés dans un hôtel.
P. A la télé j'ai vu une foule énorme. C'était difficile de trouver une place?
J. ... Non, mais il était difficile de voir.
P. Tu as pris des photos de quoi?
J. ... J'ai pris des photos de Bruxelles et du Grand Prix.
P. Super! On va faire une séance photo!

21 Activité • Ecrivez

Racontez le week-end de Jérôme et Antoine. Dites où ils habitent, à quelle heure ils sont partis, où ils sont allés... Jérôme et Antoine habitent à Valenciennes. Ils sont partis samedi matin. Ils sont d'abord allés à Bruxelles pour visiter la ville. Ils ont vu l'Atomium et la Grand-Place. Ils ont bien mangé : des moules, des frites et du chocolat. Dimanche, ils sont allés à Francorchamps voir le Grand-Prix de Belgique. Quel bon week-end!

Vous êtes à la Fête des Chats à Ypres en Belgique. Vous regardez le défilé avec des amis. Exprimez votre opinion avec des exclamations : Ce qu'elle est belle! Qu'ils sont beaux!…

1. Quels beaux chars!

2. Que les chats sont drôles!

3. Ce qu'elles sont jolies, les filles!

4. Qu'ils jouent bien, ces garçons!

5. Qu'est-ce qu'elle est horrible, cette femme!

6. Quelle grande chatte!

Possible answers: 1. —Vous avez mangé des moules et des frites?
—Oui, le plat national de la Belgique est superbe!
2. —Vous avez acheté des chocolats?
—Oui, j'en ai acheté des tablettes.

23 Activité • **A vous maintenant!**

Vous avez passé le week-end à Bruxelles avec un(e) ami(e). De retour, vous répondez aux questions de votre camarade de classe. Variez vos réponses et changez de rôle.

3. —Vous avez dîné dans la rue des Bouchers?
—Bien sûr, on a bien mangé.
4. —Vous avez parlé avec des Belges.
—Oui, ils sont sympa.
5. —Vous êtes allé(e)s voir l'Atomium?
—Oui, c'était fantastique!
6. —Vous avez vu la Grand-Place?
—Non, on n'a pas eu assez de temps.
7. —Vous avez pris un tram?
—Non, on a pris la voiture.

prendre des photos — Vous avez pris des photos?
— Non, j'ai oublié mon appareil-photo.

1. manger des moules et des frites
2. acheter des chocolats
3. dîner dans la rue des Bouchers
4. parler avec des Belges
5. aller voir l'Atomium

6. voir la Grand-Place
7. prendre un tram
8. passer devant le palais Royal
9. visiter le musée de la Dentelle
10. descendre dans un hôtel

8. —Vous êtes passé(e)s devant le palais Royal?
—Oui, c'est très beau!

9. —Vous avez visité le musée de la Dentelle?
—Non, on n'a pas voulu.
10. —Vous êtes descendu(e)s dans un hôtel?
—Non, on est resté chez des amis.

24 Activité • **Et vous?**

Racontez un week-end où vous avez quitté votre ville.   Possible answer is given.

1. Où êtes-vous allé(e)?
2. Pourquoi?
3. Avec qui avez-vous voyagé?

4. Comment y êtes-vous allé(e)? En voiture? En train?
5. Qu'est-ce que vous y avez fait?
6. Comment était votre week-end?

Je suis allé(e) à Boston avec ma famille. On y est allé pour voir des cousins. Nous y sommes allés en voiture. C'était un très bon week-end. On a vu d'abord le Musée des beaux arts. Puis on est monté à la tour John Hancock. C'était extra!

25 Activité • **Conversation**

Travaillez avec un(e) camarade. Posez-lui des questions sur un week-end où il/elle a quitté sa ville. Employez les questions dans l'activité 24. Ensuite changez de rôle.

26 Activité • **Ecrivez**   Possible answer is given.

Pendant votre week-end en Belgique vous avez acheté cette carte postale pour envoyer à un(e) ami(e). Ecrivez un message. Cher Jacques, Bonjour de Bruges! C'est une jolie ville. On y fait de la dentelle. Les Belges parlent français et ils sont très sympathiques! Il y a beaucoup à voir et à faire. On a mangé des moules pour la première fois. Le chocolat est formidable!
J'en ai acheté une tablette pour toi.
A bientôt, Chantal

Bruges
Festival médiéval

Sophie Leblanc
7, rue Gauguin
91 600 Savigny
FRANCE

For script, see pp. T93–95.

CONSULTONS LE DICTIONNAIRE 🔲

A dictionary helps you . . .

1. find the meanings of words.

French-English dictionary

> **interdit** *adj* banned, forbidden.

French-French dictionary

> **interdit** *adj* non autorisé.

2. find out how a French word sounds.

> **interdit** [ɛ̃terdi] *adj* banned, forbidden.

> **doigt** [dwa] *nm* finger.

3. find out the French equivalents of English words.

> **gift** *n* **(a)** cadeau **(b)** donation **(c)** don.

Je n'ai pas de cadeau.
Je n'ai pas le don des langues.

> **gift** *n* **(a)** *(present)* cadeau **(b)** *(New Year's gift)* étrennes **(c)** *(talent)* don.
> **he has a . . . for math**   il a le don des maths.

4. find out how a word is spelled.   The "que" ending is pronounced [k]: [disk(ə)];   [myzik];
  a. Look up these words to find out how **-que** is pronounced. [klasik];   [fãtastik];
     disque   musique   classique   fantastique   artistique [artistik]
  b. Look up these words and write them in two groups, one where the final consonant is
     sounded, the other where it isn't.
        chaud   sportif   trop   beaucoup   club
  c. Use your dictionary to find out in which of these words the final **-s** is pronounced.
     Rewrite the words, underlining each **-s** that is sounded and crossing out each **-s** that is
     not.   The s in plus is sometimes pronounced, depending on the meaning.
        dos   plus   repas   ours   avis
     Do the same for these words that end in **-r** . . .
        arriver   hiver   ouvrir   aimer   char
     for these words that end in **-t** . . .
        chat   objet   tout   direct   respect
     for these that end in **-l** . . .
        sol   bol   ciel   pareil   spécial
     and for these that end in **-c.**
        parc   porc   blanc   chic   donc
  d. Write these words in three groups, according to whether the **x** is sounded or how it is
     pronounced. Use your dictionary.
        deuxième [z]   prix   choix   Bruxelles [s]   six [s]
  e. Look up these words to find out which **e**'s are sounded and which are not. Rewrite the
     words, crossing out each **e** that is not heard and underlining each **e** that is sounded. In
     the dictionary the sounded letter **e** will appear as /ə/.
        maintenant   cheval   samedi   développement
        devoir   partenaire   besoin   poissonnerie
  f. Use your dictionary to find out whether or not the **e** before **-ment** is sounded in these
     adverbs. Rewrite them in two groups.
        drôlement   éventuellement   seulement   exactement
        tranquillement   probablement   tristement   finalement

APERÇU CULTUREL 2

Bonjour de Québec

Salut, Stéphane !

La semaine dernière, j'ai lu ton annonce dans le magazine Okapi, et j'ai pensé : « Quelle coïncidence ! » Moi aussi, j'ai 15 ans. J'habite à Québec, et les maths, c'est la barbe ! Alors, tu veux bien correspondre avec moi ? Oh, j'ai oublié : je m'appelle Héloïse Dufour ! Je t'envoie dans cette lettre quelques photos pour te donner une petite idée de ma famille, mes copains et aussi mon pays...

Ça, c'est notre quartier. Nous habitons dans une maison toute en briques très ancienne, rue des Érables, dans la vieille ville.

Portrait de famille devant l'entrée : papa et maman au fond, et mon grand frère Paul à droite. Celle avec la chemise blanche, c'est moi. Zut, j'ai fermé les yeux !

A droite, je pose, très studieuse, devant mon école. Je vais au collège des Jésuites. C'est une école privée pour filles et garçons. Beaucoup de devoirs, et les profs sont super sévères, mais l'ambiance est sympa.

Papa est un gourmet ! Là, il montre avec fierté les champignons qu'il a achetés au marché. Quand il n'est pas dans la cuisine, papa est médecin à l'hôpital de l'Enfant Jésus.

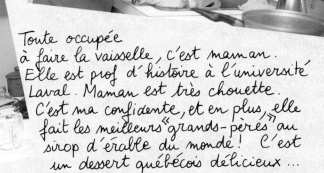

Toute occupée à faire la vaisselle, c'est maman. Elle est prof d'histoire à l'université Laval. Maman est très chouette. C'est ma confidente, et en plus, elle fait les meilleurs "grands-pères" au sirop d'érable du monde ! C'est un dessert québécois délicieux …

Au-dessus, c'est Paul. Sur la photo, il a l'air très travailleur, mais en vérité, quel paresseux ! Paul va au collège dans une des plus vieilles écoles du Canada, le petit séminaire de Québec. Je crois qu'il préfère le hockey à la géométrie, mais chut !

La fille à ma droite, c'est Anne-Sophie, ma meilleure amie. On est dans la même classe. C'est sympa quand on est tous réunis à table pour un souper aux chandelles !

Pendant l'été, je vends des fleurs sur le marché découvert du Vieux Port (regarde à gauche : j'aide une cliente ...). C'est un petit boulot super !

Mais travailler dehors toute la journée, ça donne faim et soif ! Alors, après le boulot, j'aime bien aller au café du coin (ça, c'est la photo en haut, à droite !).

En bas, à gauche, c'est encore moi, à la marina du Vieux Port. Des fois, avant de rentrer chez moi, je fais une petite balade. Moi, j'adore bronzer et rêver au soleil. Et puis, on a une vue magnifique sur la baie de québec.

Après le travail, la détente ! Moi, j'aime bien quand Anne-Sophie vient à la maison. On lit, on écoute des disques, on parle du collège, des copains, de tout et de rien ! Et toi, qu'est-ce que tu fais pendant tes loisirs ?

Paul, lui, n'a pas travaillé cet été. Il préfère se balader dans le parc et discuter avec ses copains. Pas fou, mon frère !
Sur la photo du dessous, toute la bande est en train de dévorer une délicieuse pastèque de Floride.
Celui sur la gauche, c'est Eric. Il vient de Paris !

Paul adore bricoler. Cet été, il a décidé de repeindre la vieille porte de sa chambre... en orange criard ! Il n'a pas demandé la permission à mes parents, et maman était furieuse. Quand papa a vu le résultat, il a dit : « Quelle horreur, mon fils ! Mais chacun ses goûts ! »

Mon frère est super bon en musique.
Quand il invite les copains à la maison, il aime bien écouter du rock ou des disques du fameux chanteur québécois Robert Charlebois.
Mais quand il est tout seul, il fait du piano. Qu'est-ce qu'il joue bien !

Nous, on a une maison de campagne à Notre-Dame-du-Rosaire (quel nom difficile à écrire !).

Notre-Dame-du-Rosaire, c'est un petit village génial à 60 milles à l'est de Québec. On y passe une partie des vacances et presque tous les week-ends. Après la ville, vive le calme de la nature ! Moi, j'aime...

Et voilà notre maison. Pas mal, hein ? Tu as vu le jardin ? Il est immense ! Alors, tu ne trouves pas ça chouette ?

Moi, ce que je préfère, c'est le porche. C'est de là que j'ai pris cette photo de Paul. On a une belle vue sur la campagne !

Tu peux voir sur la photo de droite que tout le reste de la maison est assez rustique. Beaucoup de meubles, comme le vaisselier massif au fond de la salle à manger, ont plus de cent ans ! Et chez toi, c'est comment ? Vous aussi, vous avez une maison de vacances ?

Tonton André (à gauche, avec le chapeau et les moustaches) a passé une semaine avec nous. C'est le frère de papa. Quel rigolo !

Là, il nous donne une leçon de pêche (dommage, sur la photo, on ne voit pas la rivière !). C'était un désastre ! Imagine, pour souper, on a dû acheter du poisson congelé au supermarché de la ville voisine...

Cet été, Paul a découvert la passion des oiseaux. Le voilà qui les observe avec ses jumelles. Il a l'air inspiré ! Lui qui a peur des chiens, il dit maintenant qu'il veut être vétérinaire. Avant, c'était président. Paul change toujours d'avis ! Maman dit que c'est l'âge...

Ici, on dit : « Au Canada, il y a deux saisons : l'hiver et juillet. » Après le froid, nous apprécions beaucoup le soleil, crois-moi ! Que c'est agréable de faire les clowns dans la rivière d'à côté. Plus on est de fous, plus on rit ! Mais après toute une journée en plein air, c'est chouette de retrouver l'ambiance sympa de notre maison...

Dans ma famille, on aime faire du vélo! Là, à gauche, on se prépare à aller à un pique-nique à 2 milles de la maison.

Et en route! Le champion en tête, maman au milieu, et puis moi. Papa et tonton André sont en retard, comme d'habitude! Ils ne gagneront jamais le Tour de France, c'est sûr...

Regarde comme c'est joli, la campagne québécoise!

Enfin arrivés!
Nous avons très faim après tant d'effort.
Il y a déjà beaucoup de monde au pique-nique, des amis de vacances. A droite, c'est la star du pique-nique. Mais non, pas Paul! Le mouton en train de cuire, bien sûr! On appelle ça un «méchoui.»

Mes grands-parents maternels
sont venus passer deux
jours avec nous. Ils habitent à
Montréal, et je ne les vois pas souvent, mais je les
adore! Quand ils sont repartis, j'étais très
triste...
A la fin des vacances, nous avons fait un
souper extra. Celui qui examine les
saucisses d'un air expert, c'est papa bien sûr!
Pour ce repas très spécial, nous avons mangé
une tarte à la viande. Ici, ça s'appelle
une "tourtière." Miam!

Anne-Sophie a
passé les derniers
jours de vacances
à Notre-Dame-
du-Rosaire. Là,
à droite, c'est
elle, Paul et moi,
en train de
discuter autour
d'un feu de camp.
La nuit est belle,
mais nous sommes
un peu nostalgiques.
Adieu, les vacances! Bientôt, la rentrée scolaire, les devoirs, les copains...
Bon, Stéphane, c'est tout! J'espère que maintenant, tu me connais
un petit peu mieux. Alors, à ton tour de m'écrire!
Ta nouvelle copine, Héloïse

CHAPITRE 5 **En famille**

	BASIC MATERIAL	COMMUNICATIVE FUNCTIONS
PREMIER CONTACT	**Quels sont vos rapports avec vos parents? (1)** **Aimeriez-vous avoir un confident? (4)**	Reading for global comprehension and cultural awareness
SECTION A	**Impossible, je suis pris! (A1)** **Qu'est-ce qu'ils n'ont pas le droit de faire chez eux? (A8)** **Vous voulez bien... ? (A20)**	**Socializing** • Refusing invitations • Asking permission **Expressing attitudes, opinions** • Expressing obligation
SECTION B	**C'est à qui de faire les courses? (B1)** **Autres responsabilités (B5)**	**Exchanging information** • Talking about family responsibilities • Assigning responsibility **Expressing attitudes, opinions** • Complaining
SECTION C	**Une affaire de cœur (C1)**	**Expressing feelings, emotions** • Sharing confidences • Asking for advice **Persuading** • Giving advice and encouragement
TRY YOUR SKILLS	**La boum d'anniversaire (1)**	

- **Prononciation** (the French r-sound /R/; dictation) **183**
- **Vérifions! 184** ■ **Vocabulaire 185**

A LIRE   **Pierre et Djemila** (impossible love for a French boy and his immigrant girlfrien)
Ah, les parents! (French friends discuss family restrictions.)
Ma famille (a French girl's poem in praise of her family)
Il faut que ma mère soit heureuse. (a boy's struggle in Burkina Faso)

WRITING   A variety of controlled and open-ended writing activities appear in the Pupil's Edition. The Teacher's Notes identify other activities suitable for writing practice.

COOPERATIVE LEARNING   Many of the activities in the Pupil's Edition lend themselves to cooperative learning. For guidelines, see page T14.

Scope and Sequence

GRAMMAR	CULTURE	RE-ENTRY
	Sharing confidences with parents and friends	
The present subjunctive with **il faut que...** and **vouloir que...** (A11) The present subjunctive of **faire** (A11)	The French family Family responsibilities	The verbs **devoir, vouloir, pouvoir** The present indicative of regular and irregular verbs
The direct-object pronouns **le, la, les** (B10)	Chores in the French household	Independent pronouns
The verb **voir** (C5) Object pronouns with the **passé composé** (C17)	The role of family and friends in the lives of French young people	Object pronouns with the present

Recombining communicative functions, grammar, and vocabulary

Reading for practice and pleasure

UNIT RESOURCES **Cahier d'Activités, Cahier d'Exercices,** Unit 5 Cassettes, Transparencies 11–13, Quizzes 10–12, Unit 5 Test

TEACHER-PREPARED MATERIALS **Section A** Index cards; **Section B** Pictures of household tasks; **Section C** Index cards

PREMIER
CONTACT

The authentic material in **Premier Contact** introduces the theme of the unit. Concentrate only on the general content of these documents. A detailed treatment of the grammar and vocabulary is not intended. Since students should be reading for global comprehension, they need not know the meaning of every word. For this reason, new words in **Premier Contact** have been omitted from the unit vocabulary list and the French-English Vocabulary at the end of the book.

OBJECTIVES To read for global comprehension and cultural awareness; to get acquainted with the topic

1 Quels sont vos rapports avec vos parents?

Play the cassette or read the letters aloud as students follow along in their books. Have a volunteer summarize the main idea of each letter. Ask a few questions to provoke a discussion: **Est-ce que vous parlez à vos parents de vos problèmes? Vos parents comprennent-ils vos idées?**

2 Activité • Avez-vous compris?

Students might work in pairs to find answers to the questions.

SLOWER-PACED LEARNING Give the students clues and ask them to name the person:

Cette personne a peur de parler à ses parents.
Cette personne raconte ses petits problèmes à sa mère.
Cette personne a décidé de parler à sa mère.
Cette personne n'a pas toujours le courage de parler à ses parents.

3 Activité • Et vous?

SLOWER-PACED LEARNING Ask volunteers to read aloud the letter or the part of a letter in **Contact 1** that best expresses their own feelings.

CHALLENGE Brainstorm with the class reasons young people might have for not confiding in parents. Write these on the board or on a transparency. They may suggest reasons such as:

Les parents sont trop occupés.
Ils n'ont pas le temps d'écouter mes problèmes.
Ils ne comprennent pas mes problèmes.
Ils disent toujours la même chose.
Leurs idées sont différentes.

Then make up an additional list of possible reasons in favor of confiding in parents.

4 AIMERIEZ-VOUS AVOIR UN CONFIDENT?

Play the cassette or read the letters aloud as students follow along in their books. Then ask students to read aloud those parts of the letters that give a definition of a confidant. For homework, you might ask students to make up their own definitions of a confidant.

5 Activité • Avez-vous compris?

After students have named the confidants that Catherine, Frédéric, and Myriam have found, ask them to suggest other confidants: **Mon chien! Mon chat! Mon prof!** and so on. For question 2, write on the board the feelings that students identify in the letters. Then have students classify the feelings as either happy or sad.

6 Activité • Et vous?

If students are reluctant to answer this question orally, have them write out their answers for you or have them make up an imaginary confidant. Another option would be to change the question to **Quelles sont les qualités d'un(e) confident(e) parfait(e)?**

SECTION A

OBJECTIVES **To socialize:** refuse invitations; ask permission; **to express attitudes, opinions:** express obligation

CULTURAL BACKGROUND   French teenagers don't have as much time for going out as do Americans, especially during the week. Household chores are one reason. Another reason is that French **lycée** students devote a lot of time to their studies. They attend classes for longer hours and are given more homework than their American counterparts. French parents tend to put pressure on their children to succeed in school. In a recent survey, 78 percent of French parents said they were **très attentifs** when it came to their children's grades. The same survey revealed that 72 percent believed it would be harder for their children to be successful in life than it had been for them. Consequently, a good education would be all the more valuable for the doors it could open.

MOTIVATING ACTIVITY   Ask students if they're allowed to go out on school nights. If they are, ask them what time they have to be home. You might want to conduct an anonymous poll and write the results on the board.

A1

Impossible, je suis pris!

Play the cassette or read the dialogues aloud, pausing after each one to check comprehension. For example, after the first dialogue you might ask **Qu'est-ce que Jean-Marc invite Patrice à faire? Pourquoi Patrice ne peut-il pas faire cela?** After students have demonstrated their understanding of the dialogues, they should practice reading them aloud. Then ask volunteers to role-play for the class.

A2 Activité • Avez-vous compris?

You might use a TPR technique for this activity. Tell the students that you're going to call out names of the people in A1. If the person is busy **(pris)**, students should raise their *right* hands. If the person is free **(libre)**, they should raise their *left* hands.

1. Jean-Marc *(left)*
2. Caroline *(left)*
3. Damien *(right)*
4. Xavier *(left)*
5. Hélène *(right)*
6. Isabelle *(right)*

If there is disagreement, select students to justify their responses by finding appropriate passages in the text.

A3 Activité • Pourquoi?

First review the present-tense forms of **devoir.** Then have students work in pairs to find the reasons for the refusals. They should write down their findings in complete sentences. Work with the entire class to correct, writing the responses on the board or on a transparency for all to see.

CHALLENGE   Ask students which of these reasons they might use. Can they think of others that would be useful?

A4 Activité • Imaginez

You might turn the activity into a game of Charades. Have students act out what they think Jean-Marc, Caroline, Xavier, and Muriel will do this evening. Their classmates call out guesses in French.

A5 Activité • Et vous?

Have the students pair off. Each pair writes the six commands on separate index cards or slips of paper. Taking turns, each partner picks a card and the two students engage in a dialogue:

—Qu'est-ce que tu dois faire? *(one student picks card)*
—Je dois… Et toi? *(partner picks card)*
—Moi, je dois…

A6 COMMENT LE DIRE

To practice these expressions, extend invitations to individuals: **On va au café? Voulez-vous jouer au tennis?** and so on. Have students choose expressions from the box to refuse your invitations.

A7 Activité • A vous maintenant!

Before students pair off, you might brainstorm with the class invitations to make and various ways to make them (Unit 2, A12, page 58).

A8 QU'EST-CE QU'ILS N'ONT PAS LE DROIT DE FAIRE CHEZ EUX?

Play the cassette or read the sentences aloud as students look at the illustrations. Then ask individuals whether they themselves have the right to do these things: **Avez-vous le droit de fumer chez vous? A l'école?** You might want to have students help you make a list on the board or on a transparency of what they may and may not do at school.

A9 Activité • Et vous?

Have students volunteer to say what they may or may not do, using the phrases given. They should first choose responses from the box but then continue by giving original responses. If some students do not wish to talk about themselves, they might pretend to be one of their favorite TV characters and answer accordingly.

A 10   **Savez-vous que... ?**

The age of majority, or legal age, is 18 in France. The voting age was lowered in 1976 from 21 to 18. The legal driving age is 18. France has recently passed a law permitting young people to drive at the age of 16 provided they are accompanied by a licensed driver. However, they must still wait until they're 18 to get a license.

    You might first convey the information in very simple French terms, writing key words on the board as you proceed. Then play the cassette as students read along in their books. Consider discussing, in English if necessary, the problems of an aging society, both in France and in the United States. Ask students why a government would pay its people to have more children. Point out the effect of two world wars on the French population.

A 11   **STRUCTURES DE BASE**

To avoid confusing and overwhelming students, confine your discussion of the subjunctive to the specific uses indicated here: expressing obligation and telling what one person wishes another would do.

    After discussing the formation of the subjunctive, as explained in number 2, have students practice writing the subjunctive forms of other verbs that you suggest: **finir, écouter, répondre,** and so forth.

    Ask students to repeat after you the subjunctive forms of the verbs they wrote out. Point out that there are three spoken forms for each verb. Ask students to give the three spoken forms of the verbs in the chart in number 2.

    Teach the subjunctive of **faire** and encourage students to use it in sentences: **Il faut que tu fasses tes devoirs? Il faut que tu fasses du baby-sitting?** and so on.

A 12   **COMMENT LE DIRE**

Emphasize that both the expressions (**devoir** + infinitive and **il faut que** + subjunctive) are French equivalents of the English *to have to:*

> Je dois partir.
> Il faut que je parte. } *I have to leave.*

Say sentences using **devoir** and ask students to restate them using **il faut que...**

> Je dois sortir. → Il faut que je sorte.
> Tu dois choisir. → Il faut que tu choisisses.
> Vous devez rester. → Il faut que vous restiez.

Reverse the procedure. Then ask students to tell one thing that they have to do that day: **Il faut que je rentre chez moi avant cinq heures.**

A 13   **Activité • Organisez une soirée**

After students have practiced saying what Arnaud has to do, have them pretend that they are the ones giving the party. They tell what they must do. Suggest that they add items to the list of things they have to do.

    CHALLENGE   Have students organize an imaginary picnic. They tell what they have to do.

A 14 Activité • La liste des parents

Students might work in pairs and take turns telling each other what they both have to do. You might have students write a similar list, containing different activities, that their parents might leave for them.

SLOWER-PACED LEARNING   Remind students that they will need to change **votre** and **vos** to **notre** and **nos**. For additional practice, students might pretend to be Hélène or Jacques. They go through the items a second time, beginning their sentences with **Maman et papa veulent que je...**

CHALLENGE   Imagine that Hélène and Jacques' parents come home and ask if they've done these things. Students role-play this situation, using the **passé composé.**

A 15 Activité • Ecrit dirigé

To personalize the activity, suggest that students write down a list of things they have to do today. Supply any additional vocabulary they may need, but encourage them to use what they've already learned.

A 16 Activité • Trouvez des excuses

As students work in pairs, they should take turns asking the questions and answering them.

SLOWER-PACED LEARNING   Before students pair off, work with the entire class to establish the correct subjunctive forms of the verbs in the box.

A 17 Activité • A vous maintenant!

SLOWER-PACED LEARNING   Have each pair of students write their lists in class and bring them to you for correction. Then have each pair do their dialogues orally. Finally, call for volunteers to present one of their dialogues to the class.

A 18 Activité • Tu peux venir avec moi?

Students work in pairs. As they look at the drawings, one invites the other: **Tu viens avec moi?** The partner, taking a cue from the drawing, refuses and gives an excuse. Exchange roles and repeat.

A 19 Activité • Jamais libre

You might make this activity a contest between two individuals or between two teams. The winner is the individual or the team that can carry on the longest.

A 20 VOUS VOULEZ BIEN... ?

Explain the influence of the word **bien** on the meaning of the word **vouloir.** **Je veux le faire** means *I want to do it*. **Je veux bien le faire** means *I'm willing to do it*. Therefore, **Vous voulez bien... ?** implies *Are you willing to let me do it?* It's a way of asking permission. Play the cassette or read the dialogue aloud as students listen with books closed. Tell them to listen for the following information: (1) what Julien wants to do, (2) whether or not his father agrees and under what conditions.

A 21 ## Activité • Et vous?

Using the questions given, students might act as "roving reporters," gathering data about each other. Have them report the results; then make a compilation.

SLOWER-PACED LEARNING To make a survey out of the activity, rephrase the questions slightly to require **oui** or **non** as an answer:

1. Est-ce que les parents de Julien sont trop sévères?
2. Le meilleur moment de demander la permission aux parents, c'est avant le dîner?
3. Est-ce que vos parents sont stricts?
4. Avez-vous le droit de sortir le soir?
5. Est-ce qu'il faut que vous rentriez avant huit heures?

Have students number on a sheet of paper from 1 to 5. As you ask the questions, students write **oui** or **non** next to the numbers. Collect students' papers; ask a volunteer to compile the results.

A 22 # COMMENT LE DIRE

First practice with **pouvoir** + infinitive: going around the room, have students ask permission to do something. Then, as one student responds, turn to another and ask him or her to rephrase the question using **vouloir bien** + subjunctive.

A 23 ## Activité • Demandez la permission

The student asking the question must change the infinitive to the first-person singular subjunctive form. Have the entire class decide what that form should be for all the verbs. Then have students pair off to practice, alternating roles.

A 24 ## Activité • A vous maintenant!

CHALLENGE The second student might add a reason for his or her parents' disapproval.

A 25 ## Activité • Ecoutez bien

> Your mother has left some instructions for you on the telephone answering machine. Listen carefully to what she and your father want you to do. On a separate sheet of paper, take notes as you listen, jotting down the different chores. Then write the information in complete sentences, beginning with **Il faut que je...** and **Ils veulent que je...** or **Il/Elle veut que je... Ecoutez bien.**
>
> Ton père et moi sommes invités chez des amis, et nous allons rentrer tard. Est-ce que tu peux garder ta petite sœur et lui donner à manger? Achète aussi du lait pour le petit déjeuner demain matin. Si tu

as le temps, passe l'aspirateur dans le salon. Il faut aussi que tu téléphones à ta grand-mère pour lui souhaiter un bon anniversaire... Ah, ton père veut que tu enregistres le match de foot à la télévision... Et n'oublie surtout pas de finir tes devoirs!... Bonne soirée!

Et maintenant, vérifions.

Ils veulent que je garde ma petite sœur. Ils veulent que je lui donne à manger. Il faut que j'achète du lait. Elle veut que je passe l'aspirateur. Il faut que je téléphone à ma grand-mère. Il veut que j'enregistre le match de foot. Il faut que je finisse mes devoirs.

SECTION B

OBJECTIVES   **To exchange information:** talk about family responsibilities; assign responsibility; **to express attitudes, opinions:** complain

CULTURAL BACKGROUND   One way French families have changed in recent years is that many married women work outside the home. Although not as many French mothers of school-age children have outside jobs compared to their American counterparts (35 percent versus 52 percent), the number is increasing. Another trend is the increasing mobility of French families. Like American families, French families are now more likely to move to a different part of the country in order to find or keep jobs. As a result, grandparents live far away and are no longer available for baby-sitting duties. French family members have adapted to these changes by sharing housework and child care responsibilities.

MOTIVATING ACTIVITY   Ask students if they help out at home: **Aidez-vous vos parents? Comment?** You may want to teach the French for some chores: **faire le ménage, sortir les poubelles, faire la vaisselle, faire la cuisine, faire les courses, mettre la table.**

B1   C'est à qui de faire les courses?

Bring to class pictures that depict household tasks. Hold these pictures up and describe each activity in French. Then put them in a box; have one student at a time pick a picture and describe it. Finally, using a TPR technique, tell individuals in French to do one of the tasks. Students act out what you told them to do. Then have students tell you to do these tasks. In response to their commands, introduce different complaints that students will hear in the dialogue. Have the students repeat these after you several times. Then give the commands again and see if the students can recall any complaints. Finally, play the cassette or read the dialogue aloud as the students follow along in their books. Have students form groups of three to practice reading the dialogue aloud.

B2   Activité • Avez-vous compris?

For this activity, you might have students respond in writing. As you ask each question, students should jot down the appropriate person's name.

B3   Activité • Donnez votre opinion

Begin this activity by asking **Qui trouve qu'Aurélie et Julien ont raison?** and then **Qui trouve qu'ils ont tort?** As students raise their hands, have those who share the same opinion pair off. Each pair should work together to write down their reasons. When all pairs have finished, call on them to read their reasons aloud. You might follow this up with a formal debate between two teams on the premise **Les jeunes doivent aider leurs parents à la maison.**

B4 ## Activité • Trouvez des excuses

Brainstorm possible excuses with the class. Write the suggestions on the board or on a transparency so that students may refer to them as they prepare their dialogues.

> Je fais mes devoirs.
> J'écris une lettre.
> Je finis mon travail.
> Je téléphone à...
> J'écoute de la musique.

Students might suggest all the common excuses they can think of and then use their imaginations to make up extraordinary excuses.

B5 ## AUTRES RESPONSABILITES

Have students look at the pictures as they listen to the cassette. Then have them talk about the pictures, using the phrases beneath. They might add who in their home does each of these chores. For writing practice, have students compose a paragraph about who does which domestic chores in their homes.

B6 ## Activité • A vous maintenant!

When lists are done, each student should turn to a neighbor. One student should begin by stating something he or she does at home: **Chez moi, je fais la vaisselle.** The student should then ask the other if he or she does the same chore: **Et toi, tu fais la vaisselle?** The second student responds, for example, **Non, je ne fais pas la vaisselle, mais je lave la voiture. Et toi, est-ce que tu laves la voiture?** They should continue this way for each item on their lists.

B7 ## Savez-vous que... ?

Give a brief summary in French of this cultural note, writing key words on the board as you speak. Then play the cassette and have the students listen with books open or closed, as you choose. Elicit their opinions about the roles of family members as presented in the poll. They should begin their responses with **Il est normal que...** Point out that they must use the subjunctive forms of verbs after this expression. Ask students to take a poll in school of the opinions of both students and faculty members concerning family responsibilities. They might make a chart of the results similar to the one shown in the book.

B8 ## COMMENT LE DIRE

You might give students other examples of this type of sentence, referring to their classroom situation:

C'est à vous de faire les devoirs.
C'est à moi de corriger vos devoirs.
C'est à moi de préparer les examens.

Then have them use this type of sentence to talk about their own family or an imaginary one:

C'est à ma mère de faire la cuisine.
C'est à mon père de faire la vaisselle.
C'est à moi de mettre la table.
C'est à ma sœur de sortir les poubelles.

B 9 **Activité • Donnez votre opinion**

Have students express their opinions by composing complete sentences from the elements given here.

CHALLENGE Ask students to give reasons for their opinions.

B 10 **STRUCTURES DE BASE**

Before beginning the presentation, you might have students recall what the direct object of a verb is in English.

You might use a TPR technique to teach direct-object pronouns. Tell a student **Fais la vaisselle,** and have him or her mime the action. Ask **Marc fait la vaisselle?** Students respond **Oui, il fait la vaisselle.** Ask the question again, this time modeling **Oui, il la fait.** Do the same with other expressions: **fais le ménage, lave la voiture, fais les courses, sors les poubelles.** Ask students questions that they can answer with direct-object pronouns: **Faites-vous la vaisselle chez vous? Mettez-vous la table? Faites-vous les lits? Faites-vous le ménage?**

Have the students open their books and look at the first chart. Read the sentence with the noun, and have the students read aloud the corresponding sentence with the pronoun. Then turn the first group of sentences into questions, and have students use the second group as answers: **Tu persuades ton frère? (Oui, je le persuade.)**

Now have students look at the second chart and repeat the four examples. For practice, give them the verbs **manger, chercher, regarder,** and **finir,** and have them restate the same four sentences using each new verb. Pay particular attention to the negative sentence. Give some sentences containing pronouns, and have students restate them, making them negative.

Go on to number 3 for practice with pronouns in affirmative commands. Ask students to change the verb in these commands to the informal form, **fais.** Have them think of other verbs and use them in this pattern. If they choose a verb that takes an indirect object, explain the difference.

Model the examples from numbers 4 and 5 to call attention to **élision** and **liaison.** Tell students that when using a verb that begins with a vowel, they only have two pronouns to worry about: **l'** and **les.** To reinforce **élision** and **liaison,** give sentences using a singular pronoun and have students restate them, making the pronoun plural, and vice versa: **Je l'aime ↔ Je les aime.**

SLOWER-PACED LEARNING Do not make your presentation all in one day. Take one part at a time. Give many examples. Have students copy the examples. Review the material covered each day before going on to the next point. Use short written check-ups to motivate and reinforce learning.

B 11   Activité • Chez les Legal

You might assign the activity as a written check-up. Have students write out the answers to the eight questions, replacing nouns with pronouns.

SLOWER-PACED LEARNING   Before doing the activity as recommended here, work with the entire class, first to identify the direct object in each sentence and then to decide which pronoun will replace it.

B 12   Activité • A votre avis

SLOWER-PACED LEARNING   Have students look at the drawings in B5, page 166, and decide which member of the Legal family does each task. They should give complete sentences in French. Then turn their sentences into questions, and have them practice answering with the correct direct-object pronoun. Finally, students may pair off to do the activity.

CHALLENGE   Have students say their dialogues in this manner:

> — C'est à M. Legal d'arroser le jardin?
> — Oui, c'est à lui de l'arroser.

B 13   Activité • A vous maintenant!

Begin by having students write down lists of household chores. Circulate among students as they work in pairs. Listen carefully to make sure they are using the direct-object pronouns correctly. Give help where needed.

B 14   Activité • Chacun sa tâche

SLOWER-PACED LEARNING   Before students work in pairs, have them identify an appropriate verb for each activity suggested in the note on the refrigerator: **la cuisine** → **faire la cuisine; la voiture** → **laver la voiture.** If students find the structure of the answer too difficult, they may simply respond to the question like this: **M. Ballard l'arrose.**

CHALLENGE   After students have done the activity as directed, have them go through the tasks again, using the model below:

> —C'est à qui d'arroser le jardin?
> —C'est à M. Ballard de l'arroser.
> —C'est à qui de faire la cuisine?
> —C'est à Mme Ballard de la faire.

B 15   Activité • Et chez vous?

If students ask why different forms of **faire** appear after **qui** in the example, explain that the true subject of **faire** here is the word before **qui.** Do not go into more detail at this time. The use of **qui** as a relative pronoun is presented in Unit 11, C14, page 406.

SLOWER-PACED LEARNING   If students find the sentence structure too complex, simplify the dialogue as follows:

> —Tu fais les courses chez toi?
> —Oui, je les fais. (Non, je ne les fais pas.)

B 16 COMMENT LE DIRE

You might want to replay the cassette of B1 and have the students identify all the complaints they can. Give students orders to do things; they should respond with appropriate complaints from the box. Encourage students to accompany their responses with appropriate gestures.

B 17 Activité • Elle n'est pas contente

Have students work in pairs, one giving the orders, and the other responding with complaints and gestures. They may continue the activity by adding other commands.

B 18 Activité • A vous maintenant!

Begin by having students write two lists of activities, those to use in asking permission and others to use in assigning tasks.

B 19 Activité • Ecoutez bien

You're going to hear Madame Lenoir and Madame Benoît compare notes about housework. Open your book to page 170. *(pause)* Read the questions in B19 to yourself. *(pause)* Listen to the conversation between the two women, and be prepared to indicate your answers on a separate sheet of paper. Ready? **Ecoutez bien.**

C'est Madame Lenoir qui commence. *(pause)*

MME LENOIR	C'est toi qui fais la cuisine chez toi?
MME BENOÎT	Non, c'est mon mari.
MME LENOIR	Et le ménage?
MME BENOÎT	C'est lui aussi. Il adore ça.
MME LENOIR	Quelle chance tu as! Moi, je dois tout faire chez moi. Mon mari ne fait rien.
MME BENOÎT	C'est pas normal! C'est un horrible macho! On est au vingtième siècle. Il faut que tu lui dises!
MME LENOIR	C'est inutile. Il n'écoute pas. Il passe son temps à regarder la télé et à lire le journal.
MME BENOÎT	Moi aussi.
MME LENOIR	Pendant que ton mari travaille?
MME BENOÎT	Bien sûr.
MME LENOIR	Mais c'est injuste! Pourquoi tu ne l'aides pas?
MME BENOÎT	Parce qu'à mon avis, c'est aux hommes de faire le ménage maintenant.

Et maintenant, vérifions.

1. Qui fait la cuisine et le ménage chez Madame Benoît?
   M. Benoît les fait.
2. Pourquoi est-ce que Monsieur Benoît fait tout à la maison?
   Parce qu'il adore faire ça.
3. Qui fait le travail chez Madame Lenoir? *Mme Lenoir le fait.*
4. A quoi est-ce que Monsieur Lenoir passe son temps?
   Il passe son temps à regarder la télé et à lire le journal.

5. Que fait Madame Benoît pendant que son mari travaille?
   Elle regarde la télé et lit le journal.
6. Pourquoi est-ce que Madame Benoît n'aide pas son mari?
   A son avis, c'est aux hommes de faire le ménage.

SECTION C

OBJECTIVES **To express feelings, emotions:** share confidences; ask for advice; **to persuade:** give advice and encouragement

CULTURAL BACKGROUND Friendships are very important to French young people, who tend to have a group of friends with whom they go out **(sortir en bande)** or with whom they get together at someone's home. Among young teenagers, dating as a means of getting to know someone isn't as common as it is in the United States, but it is increasing in popularity.

MOTIVATING ACTIVITY Ask students the following questions: **Où rencontrez-vous vos copains? Sortez-vous en groupe ou avec un(e) petit(e) ami(e)? Si vous voulez connaître quelqu'un, qu'est-ce que vous faites? A qui demandez-vous des conseils?**

C1

Une affaire de cœur

First write these questions on the board or on a transparency:

1. Quel est le problème de Sophie?
2. Qu'est-ce que son amie Mélanie lui propose?

Play the cassette as students listen with books closed. They should listen carefully, trying to find the answers to your questions. After playing the recording, elicit their findings. Then play the cassette again as students read along in their books. Ask students to find and read aloud those lines that reveal (1) Sophie's timidity and hesitancy, and (2) Mélanie's expressions of advice and encouragement.

C2 **Activité • Vrai ou faux?**

Ask a volunteer to read each sentence and to correct it if it is false. If a student says that a sentence is true, he or she should read the lines from the dialogue that substantiate the statement.

SLOWER-PACED LEARNING Have students keep their books closed. They make two columns on a sheet of paper, one headed **vrai** and the other **faux.** As you read the statements aloud, students place a check mark in the appropriate column.

C3 **Activité • Les conseils de Mélanie**

Form cooperative learning groups of four for this activity. Students might list the four things Mélanie tells Sophie to do, using **Il faut que...** + subjunctive: for example, **Il faut que Sophie organise une soirée.** Then they might rewrite the sentences using **devoir: Sophie doit organiser une soirée.**

Ask students if they can think of other ways in which Sophie might meet Julien: **Qu'est-ce que Sophie doit faire pour rencontrer Julien, à votre avis?** For writing practice, have students compose a letter that Sophie might write to ask the advice of "Dear Abby."

C4   Activité • Conversation téléphonique

After practicing each role once or twice, students could close their books and try to do the dialogue from memory, improvising when necessary. For writing practice, ask students to imagine that Sophie chose to write a note to Julien instead of phoning him.

C5   STRUCTURES DE BASE

Say sentences using **voir** in the present tense and have students restate the sentences, changing the verb to the **passé composé.** Then reverse the procedure. Point out the two different stems in the subjunctive forms.

For additional practice with **voir,** play a game of I Spy. One student says what he or she sees: **Je vois un crayon.** The next student in the row repeats what the first student said and adds another item: **Je vois un crayon et un livre.** Students continue in the same manner until someone is unable to remember the ever-growing list.

C6   Activité • Qu'est-ce qu'ils aiment voir?

You might assign this activity to be written in class or at home. Then follow up with personalized questions to be answered orally: **Voyez-vous souvent vos copains? Quel genre de film aimez-vous voir? Avez-vous déjà vu un film de Stephen King?**

C7   Activité • Ecrit dirigé

Prepare and project a transparency of the dialogues with the correct completions for students to use in correcting their papers. Then have students read aloud the projected dialogues; suggest substitutions that will require students to make changes in the direct-object pronouns.

C8   Activité • Et vous?

You might assign this activity to be written. Have students expand their answers to make a cohesive paragraph. Make a transparency of two or three of the paragraphs—with students' names deleted—for the class to read, comment on, and correct together.

C9   COMMENT LE DIRE

First go over all the phrases in the two boxes and have students repeat them after you. Then have them pair off and, using these phrases, compose several two-line dialogues. After they've had time to practice, volunteers might like to present theirs for the class.

C10 Activité • Ecoutez bien

You're going to hear six French friends ask some questions. Listen carefully and decide whether they're asking for permission or for advice. On a separate sheet of paper, number from 1 to 6. *(pause)* Be prepared to write **permission** or **conseils** after each number. **Ecoutez bien.**

1. Tu crois que je peux l'inviter? *(conseils)*
2. Tu veux bien que je sorte ce soir? *(permission)*
3. Qu'est-ce qu'il faut que je fasse? *(conseils)*
4. Vous voulez bien que je lui demande? *(permission)*
5. Tu crois que je peux lui écrire? *(conseils)*
6. Je peux sortir dimanche? *(permission)*

Et maintenant, vérifions. *Read each question again and give the correct answer.*

C11 Activité • Donnez des conseils

For cooperative learning, have students work in groups of three. For each question, they should choose appropriate ways of giving advice and encouragement from C9. Then they should make up two dialogues, one with Marie and the other with Laurent.

SLOWER-PACED LEARNING Have students copy each question and write down an appropriate response that they've selected from C9. Then have them work in pairs to make up a dialogue with either Marie or Laurent.

C12 Activité • A vous maintenant!

For cooperative learning, divide the class into groups of four. Assign each student in the group a different problem, selected from the six described. Each member of the group states his or her problem and asks for advice, which the others offer.

C13 Activité • Ecrivez

Work with the entire class to construct a sample letter to a guidance counselor, complaining about a grade received and asking for help and advice. Have students suggest sentences; write the letter on the board or on a transparency. Then ask students to write a similar letter to their counselor about a different problem. They may choose to write about a problem different from those suggested in C12. Remember to respect the privacy of individuals in any follow-up activity you may do.

C14 Savez-vous que... ?

Play the cassette and have the students follow along in their books. Then have them examine the survey. If you choose, you might take a similar survey of the class, being careful to respect individuals' privacy. Ask each student to write down in French the person (not by name) to whom they talk about their problems. Collect and shuffle the anonymous responses. Compile the results in a chart for the class, showing percentages.

C15 Activité • Sondage

Assign one student the task of preparing a chart. Make copies of it for the others in the class. Ask each student to interview five classmates. They might add a **Jamais** category to the choice of responses. Have students report their findings to the class: **On parle souvent de...**

C16 VOUS EN SOUVENEZ-VOUS?

As you read the chart with the students, give them additional sentences that they are to restate, using object pronouns. You might have students compose two or three sentences and write them on index cards. Have the students exchange cards and rewrite the sentences their classmates have composed, replacing nouns and phrases with appropriate pronouns.

C17 STRUCTURES DE BASE

Take the five sample sentences from the chart in the preceding activity, and tell students how to position the pronouns when the verbs are in the **passé composé**. Write these examples on the board for students to copy into their notebooks. Call attention to the agreement of the past participle where it is necessary. Have students repeat these examples several times. Then using the same sentences, make them negative.

Read the grammar presentation with the students; discuss the explanations and the examples with them. Give additional examples as you proceed. Make the point that in the spoken language, the choice of the third-person direct-object pronoun is only between **l'** and **les,** because the auxiliary verb **avoir** always begins with a vowel.

To practice the agreement of the past participle, dictate all the examples in number 5. For example, you say: **La boum? Elle l'a organisée.** Have students write only the second sentence in each pair.

C18 Activité • Sophie a tout fait?

You might make a contest of this activity. You give the vocabulary items, one team must phrase the question, and the other team must answer correctly.

SLOWER-PACED LEARNING For each item, prepare several index cards with the vocabulary on one side **(la date/fixer)** and the dialogue on the other **(—La date, tu l'as fixée? —Oui, je l'ai fixée.)** Distribute the cards to pairs of students. Tell them to refer to the written dialogue only if they need help. After a designated time period, tell pairs to exchange cards.

C19 Activité • Conversation à la boum

When students have finished this activity, have them invent more "party talk." Brainstorm with the class possible rejoinders, including object pronouns wherever possible.

C20 Activité • C'était bien, la soirée de Sophie?

Once students have completed the activity, have each pair make up a beginning and an end to the dialogue. An opening question might be **Qu'est-ce que tu as fait samedi?** The dialogue might close with **A quelle heure est-ce que tu es rentré(e)?**

C21 Activité • Ecrit dirigé

Have the correct completions ready on a transparency, or have them written on the board so that students can check their work. Then read the questions aloud and have students respond orally.

C22 Activité • Ecoutez bien

Your friend Agnès went to a party and called to tell you all about it. Since you weren't home, she left a message on your answering machine. Open your book to page 178. *(pause)* Read the six statements to yourself. *(pause)* On a separate sheet of paper, number from 1 to 6 and be prepared to indicate if the statements are true or false. *(pause)* Ready? **Ecoutez bien.**

Je rentre à l'instant d'une boum fantastique organisée chez Hélène. J'y ai rencontré un type super sympa, un ami d'Henri. Il s'appelle Francis, je crois… non, c'est François… Je ne sais même pas son nom! J'ai dansé plusieurs rocks avec lui. C'était drôlement chouette! J'ai envie de le revoir. Je ne sais pas si Catherine les a invités, lui et Henri, pour son anniversaire samedi prochain. J'ai envie de lui téléphoner pour savoir. Mais je n'ose pas. C'est drôle : d'habitude, je ne suis pas timide… Il a mon numéro de téléphone; peut-être qu'il va téléphoner demain?… Mais s'il ne téléphone pas? Qu'est-ce qu'il faut que je fasse? Que je l'appelle? Je ne sais pas… Bon, je vais dormir… Je crois que je suis un peu… amoureuse!

Et maintenant, vérifions.

1. Agnès est allée à l'anniversaire de Catherine. *faux*
2. Le garçon qu'elle a rencontré s'appelle Henri. *faux*
3. François est un ami d'Henri. *vrai*
4. D'habitude Agnès est timide. *faux*
5. Elle a le numéro de téléphone de François. *faux*
6. Elle a décidé de lui téléphoner demain. *faux*

TRY YOUR SKILLS

OBJECTIVE To recombine communicative functions, grammar, and vocabulary

CULTURAL BACKGROUND Birthdays are celebrated in France just as they are here, with a cake and presents. Gifts are also offered on a person's saint's day **(la fête)** if he or she happens to be named after a saint.

1   La boum d'anniversaire

Before students see these dialogues, have them open their books to page 180 and read Skills 2. Then tell the students to listen to the cassette that you're going to play and to write down the names of the people described in Skills 2. On the board write the names of all the people in the dialogues for students to refer to. Now play the cassette, twice or more if necessary.

2   Activité • Qui est-ce?

Use this activity as recommended above in Skills 1.

3   Activité • Qu'est-ce qu'ils disent?

For cooperative learning, form groups of two, three, or four students. They should read «La boum d'anniversaire» carefully and write down the statements from the dialogues that fulfill the functions described.

4   Activité • Ecrit dirigé

You may wish to assign this to be written for homework. Prepare a transparency of the text. The next day, project the text and call on volunteers to edit the text on the transparency. Students refer to the corrected transparency to check their work.

SLOWER-PACED LEARNING   Read the paragraph as it is to the entire class. Pause after each sentence and ask for volunteers to make any modifications. When you have finished correcting the paragraph orally, assign it to be written.

5   Activité • Qu'est-ce que vous répondez?

First have students work alone on responses to these stimuli; have them write down possible responses. Then make the statements or ask the questions, eliciting various oral responses. Collect the papers to check writing skills.

6   Activité • Changez tout

For cooperative learning, students work in pairs, first to practice the dialogue as it is, then to use it as a model for new dialogues.

SLOWER-PACED LEARNING   Before students work in pairs, brainstorm with the class possible substitutions for the underlined phrases. You might then require them to make up only one new dialogue.

7   Activité • Ecrivez

Elicit different statements of advice from students before you ask them to write their letters. Encourage them to use **il faut que tu..., tu dois,** and imperative verb forms to give advice.

CHALLENGE Have students write a letter similar to Julie's describing an imaginary problem and asking a friend for advice. Collect and distribute for others to answer.

8 Activité • Ecrivez

Tell students that the purpose of these questions is not to pry into their personal lives but to have them write French. They should feel free to give fictitious or imaginary information.

You might have students write this activity in class. Have them bring their compositions to you for assistance. Ask that they recopy their work and turn it in the next day.

9 Activité • Le (La) confident(e) idéal(e)

To prepare for this activity, students should reread the letters in **Premier Contact 4,** page 155.

10 Activité • A vous maintenant!

First look at the photos with the entire class. For each one, students should volunteer answers to the questions found in the instructions. Ask students to imagine the problem or secret the people are sharing. Then, for cooperative learning, pair off the students. Have each pair choose one photo (or assign a photo to each pair) and prepare the dialogue.

11 Activité • Récréation

This activity is optional. If students have difficulty, point out that clues are contained in the gender and the number of the object pronoun and/or in the past participle agreement. They will have to know the gender of the nouns.

PRONONCIATION

The French **r**-sound /**R**/

> Open your book to page 183. *(pause)* Refer to this page as you listen to this section.

1 Ecoutez bien et répétez.

> Wouldn't it be nice if you could just take a pill and wake up speaking French with a perfect accent? Too good to be true? How about one pill per sound? There are only about 40 in French, so it shouldn't take that

long. Suppose you start with one of the tough ones—the famous French r-sound. Here's the prescription for a popular brand of French r, the so-called Parisian r:

/R/ A voiced velar fricative
Indications: Air passes through a mild contraction in the upper pharynx or velum creating an audible friction.
Side effects: May cause a uvular trill /R/, which is not harmful and may even be beneficial.
Dosage: Gargle daily at frequent intervals without water.
Caution: Do not swallow. Do not curl tongue back. This may cause harmful retroflexion, or "English syndrome," which may become habit-forming. If this becomes habitual, stop treatment and call for help.

So there's the medicine. All you have to do now is follow the treatment. The medicine may or may not be of help, but the right exercise may work wonders. Take the pill and then do the work.

If there's a French sound worth working on, this is it, because the alternative just won't do. An English r-sound in French grates on the French ear. In fact, it's the sound someone will try to do when imitating Americans trying to speak French. So, if you haven't already mastered the French r-sound, do it now.

The fashionable Parisian /R/, which you're going to master, is not rolled or trilled. It is, in fact, closer to the hard h-sound, the one you hear in the name of the famous German composer Bach or in a Spanish name like Jaime. So start by thinking of it as a sort of singing h-sound. But how do you make this unusual sound?

Here's how. For starters, take a deep breath, open your mouth, and say "aaaaa" as you do when the doctor looks down your throat. *(pause)* Now do it again, but this time put your fingers on your throat, under your chin, and after you've started your "aaaaa," press them upward. You'll hear a friction-like sound in your "aaaaa" and when you do, ease the pressure and finish your "aaaaa." *(pause)* You've just said "aaaaraaa," or something like it. Repeat the "aaaaraaa" until you get the feel of it. *(pause)*

1. Now let's blend this "ara" of yours into a few French words. Try going from "ara" to **arabe** *(pause)*, **arracher** *(pause)*, **arrêt** *(pause)*, **arriver** *(pause)*. Fine. You may not have gotten it exactly right, but you will in time. Just keep at it. Two weeks is par for the course. Now let's go on. Try it all over again with the o-sound. Say "oooorooo" a few times. Blend it into these French words: **oraux, oral, horrible, orange.** Now round your lips and say **heureux, amoureux, durer, purée.**

2. Now let's see if you can keep the motor running by giving your /R/ more gas. Instead of cutting off the r-sound, just keep it going. You just said **amoureux,** so try to say **amour** *(pause)*. You said **oral,** now say **or** *(pause)*. Try repeating these pairs: **purée—pur, durée—dur, heureux—heure, carré—car.**

If this doesn't scare you, go on to repeat these: **par, père, pire, port, pour, peur; sur, sort, soir; tard, tort, tire; faire, fort, four; mer, mort, mur.**

3. Now that you've mastered the final **r,** it's time to do some combining. You know how to say **pour.** Now say **pourquoi** *(pause)*. You should also be able to say these pairs: **par—parfait, jour—journée, sort—sortir, sur—surtout, mer—merci.**

4. If you've held up so far, you can take a deep breath and look back at what you've achieved. You're now past the half-way mark. What's left is to start saying the **r**-sound at the beginning of words. Why not start with some consonants to lean on? Try these to begin with: **après, adresse, c'est trop, très bien, ouvrier, ouvrage, en gros, c'est grand.** Okay? Now go on to some pairs: **après—près, en gros—gros, c'est trop—trop, c'est froid—froid.** Now repeat these: **froid, franc; vrai, vrac; très, triste; grand, brun.**

Now you're almost ready for the beginning **r**-sound. If you can say **froid, trois,** and **crois,** you should be able to say **roi.** Try it: **froid, trois, crois, roi** *(pause).* Now go on: **grand, prend, cran, rang** *(pause);* **front, tronc, prompt, rond.**

If you can begin words with the famous Parisian /R/, you've arrived. To prove it to yourself, try these: **rat, riz, rêve, rose, rouge, riche, rigide, repas, réaction, répéter.** As a send-off, let's try words with the r's in different places. Listen to these and say them with your newly found skill: **rire, rare, regard, retard, retour,** and of course, **au revoir.**

2 | **Ecoutez et lisez.**

For a little more practice with the Parisian /R/, read aloud the dialogues. I'll say each line after you.

—La porte est fermée.
—Pourtant, l'adresse est correcte.
—Il est déjà trois heures. Nous sommes arrivés trop tard.
—Tu as raison. Voilà. C'est écrit. «Fermé le mardi après-midi.»
—On retourne demain?
—D'accord.
—Très bien.

3 | **Copiez les phrases suivantes pour préparer une dictée.**

Write the following sentences from dictation. First listen to the sentence as it is read to you. Then you will hear the sentence again in short segments, with a pause after each segment to allow you time to write. Finally you will hear the sentence a third time so that you may check your work. Let's begin.

1. Pourquoi tu es triste, alors? Pourquoi tu es triste, *(pause)* alors? *(pause)* Pourquoi tu es triste, alors?
2. Je suis malheureuse. Je suis *(pause)* malheureuse. *(pause)* Je suis malheureuse.
3. Des affaires de cœur? Des affaires *(pause)* de cœur? *(pause)* Des affaires de cœur?
4. Oui, je suis amoureuse. Oui, *(pause)* je suis amoureuse. *(pause)* Oui, je suis amoureuse.
5. Quoi, encore? Quoi, *(pause)* encore? *(pause)* Quoi, encore?

VERIFIONS!

Review how to express obligation, to refuse an invitation, and to ask permission. Have students write their answers, according to the instructions. Check work as they write, and call for volunteers to give their responses orally when all have finished.

Review object pronouns in B10 and how to complain in B16. Have students rewrite their answers to the first exercise, making the sentences negative. Tell students to use a different complaint for each item in the second exercise.

Review **voir** in C5 and pronouns with the **passé composé** in C17, as well as the communicative functions in C9. Students should rewrite their answers to the first exercise, making the sentences negative. Have a transparency with answers ready for the first and last exercises that students can check their work.

VOCABULAIRE

Point out the relationship between **conseil** and **conseiller.** Ask students to find words they have had that are in the same family, such as **discuter (discussion), dangereux (danger), amoureux (aimer, ami(e), amour),** and **sortir (sortie).**

ETUDE DE MOTS

Have the students practice saying these words, paying attention to the pronunciation of the initial **in-: intérêt, instant, inégal, indirect, inexploré, influence,** and **initial.**

A LIRE

OBJECTIVE To read for practice and pleasure

PIERRE ET DJEMILA

Have students scan the film description silently, picking out and writing down the five pieces of information requested in **Avant de lire.** They should not write complete sentences. Ask the students why they think love is impossible, as indicated in the subtitle. They should be able to answer in French. Tell them to scan the reading selection once more and call out the cognates. Finally, play the cassette as students follow along in their books.

Activité • Trouvez les mots

You might have the students work in pairs to do this activity. Have them write down their findings.

AH, LES PARENTS!

Read the introduction aloud to the students and be sure they understand the situation. Then play the cassette as students follow along in their books. Ask students to read aloud statements with which they can empathize.

CHALLENGE For cooperative learning, form groups of four. Assign the role of one of the characters in the reading selection to each member of the group. Students should read silently, very carefully, the role assigned to them. Then each group, with books closed, should try to reconstruct the conversation in their own words, assuming their new identities.

Activité • Trouvez les synonymes

Prepare a transparency of these sentences, leaving out the key words. After students have found the synonyms, ask individuals to write in the new words on the transparency for all to see.

Activité • Et vous?

You may want to make this a writing assignment to ensure individual privacy. If you do this activity orally, tell students they may talk of an imaginary situation and exaggerate.

MA FAMILLE

Play the cassette as students read along in their books.

CHALLENGE Ask students to rewrite the poem, adapting it to fit a favorite sitcom or comic strip family.

IL FAUT QUE MA MERE SOIT HEUREUSE.

Have students locate Burkina Faso on the map. Older maps may identify it by its former name, Upper Volta **(Haute Volta)**. Play the cassette as students read the story silently. First let them hear the entire story without interruption. Then ask what information they gathered about the boy. Play the cassette again, pausing after each paragraph to ask several questions. Finally, play the cassette a third time without interruption.

Activité • Devinez

Form several small groups. Assign a section of the story to each group. Have them construct similar test items for two or three words from their assigned sections. Compile the items composed by each group and have the entire class practice the new "test."

Activité • Vrai ou faux?

For listening practice, read the sentences aloud. As students listen with their books closed, they write **vrai** or **faux** on their papers. You might have students compose their own true-or-false statements based on the story.

CHAPITRE 5

En famille

Do French young people help out at home?
What chores do they do? What are they
allowed to do and not allowed to do? Do they
complain? Do they talk over their problems
with their family, or do they share confidences
with a special friend?

In this unit you will:

PREMIER CONTACT	get acquainted with the topic
SECTION **A**	refuse invitations . . . express obligation . . . ask permission
SECTION **B**	talk about family responsibilities . . . complain
SECTION **C**	share confidences and ask for advice . . . give advice and encouragement
TRY YOUR SKILLS	use what you've learned
A LIRE	read for practice and pleasure

PREMIER CONTACT getting acquainted with the topic

The authentic material in Premier Contact introduces the theme of the unit and is to be used for global comprehension only.

1

Quels sont vos rapports avec vos parents?

Béatrice a envoyé une lettre à un magazine. Dans sa lettre, elle pose une question. Les lecteurs écrivent leurs réponses.

Est-ce que vous parlez à vos parents de vos problèmes? Moi, je n'en parle pas avec ma mère. Je n'ose pas, ça m'embarrasse. Je voudrais savoir quels sont vos rapports avec vos parents.

Béatrice

Chère Béatrice, un jour j'ai décidé de faire le premier pas et de parler à ma mère de mes problèmes. Je lui ai posé des questions : elle m'a écouté et répondu. Maintenant, je suis mieux dans ma peau.

Xavier

Quand j'ai le cafard, quand j'ai eu une dispute avec une amie ou quand je pense à un garçon... ma mère le voit bien. Alors, elle demande ce qui se passe, et je lui raconte mes problèmes. Tu es timide? Alors, fonce! Et aie confiance. N'oublie pas que ta mère, elle aussi, a eu ton âge!

Marianne

Pour être honnête, Béatrice, non, je ne me confie jamais à mes parents, car j'ai peur de leur réaction. Moi, je me confie à des copains et copines, à des filles plus âgées que moi! Pour moi, le grand problème de l'adolescence, c'est d'être compris par ses parents. Moi, mes parents ne comprennent pas mes idées, et je ne peux donc pas me confier à eux!

Emma

Béatrice, tu sais, moi aussi je ne dis pas tout, c'est vrai, à mes parents, car je n'ose pas trop. Mais il faut avoir le courage de leur dire tes problèmes. Ils sont là pour ça, pour les résoudre et en parler avec toi.

Didier

"avoir le cafard": to have the blues

2 Activité • Avez-vous compris? Possible answers are given.

1. Qui parle à ses parents de ses problèmes? Qui ne leur parle pas?
Marianne, Xavier, et Didier leur en parlent;
Emma et Béatrice ne leur en parlent pas.

2. Pourquoi ne parlent-ils pas à leurs parents? Trouvez deux raisons.
Emma a peur de leur réaction.
Ça embarrasse Béatrice.

3 Activité • Et vous? Possible answer is given.

Avec qui êtes-vous d'accord? Avec Didier? Avec Emma?... Pourquoi?
Je suis d'accord avec Marianne : quand j'ai le cafard, je parle avec ma mère.

AIMERIEZ-VOUS AVOIR UN CONFIDENT? 📼

C'est la question posée aux jeunes français par un magazine. Voici quelques-unes de leurs réponses.

Je crois que chaque être humain trouve, un jour ou l'autre, un ami capable de comprendre les sentiments les plus profonds. Par exemple, moi, mon grand confident, c'est mon journal. C'est, je crois, le moyen idéal pour conserver mes petits secrets, mes regrets, mes chagrins, et mes joies.

Catherine

J'ai un copain que je ne voudrais perdre pour rien au monde. On se comprend parfaitement, et, quand on a un problème, on en parle. On partage beaucoup de choses : des sentiments, des ennuis....

Frédéric

Chacun rêve de soulager son coeur ou de partager ses joies. Il faut un ami qui écoute, qui donne ses impressions sans mentir, et surtout qui ne répète rien. Moi, ce confident exemplaire, je l'ai trouvé. C'est ma correspondante. Je lui dis tout et elle, elle me fait confiance.

Myriam

C'est très difficile de trouver l'ami confident; c'est une chose rare. Parfois mes amies répètent mes secrets, et ça ne me fait pas plaisir.

Marie

5 **Activité • Avez-vous compris?** Possible answers are given.

1. Catherine, Frédéric, Myriam et Marie ont-ils tous trouvé un(e) confident(e)? Qui est-ce? Qu'est-ce que c'est? Catherine a son journal; Frédéric a un copain; Myriam a sa correspondante; Marie n'a pas trouvé de confident.
2. Trouvez dans les lettres au moins deux «sentiments».
   des regrets, des chagrins, des joies, des ennuis, le plaisir

6 **Activité • Et vous?** Possible answer is given.

Avez-vous un(e) confident(e)? Qui est-ce? Qu'est-ce que vous lui racontez?
Ma confidente, c'est ma sœur. Je lui raconte tous mes ennuis.

Vivre en famille, c'est sympathique, mais ça crée aussi des obligations. Chaque famille a ses propres règles. Comment est-ce que c'est chez vous? Est-ce qu'il faut que vous aidiez vos parents, que vous gardiez votre petit frère ou votre petite sœur, ou encore que vous rentriez à une certaine heure? Qu'est-ce que vous avez le droit ou pas le droit de faire?

A1   Impossible, je suis pris! 📼

Quand on vit en famille, on doit souvent refuser des invitations.

JEAN-MARC	Tu ne veux pas venir regarder un film vidéo chez moi?
PATRICE	Désolé, je garde mon petit frère.
JEAN-MARC	Jusqu'à quelle heure?
PATRICE	Je ne sais pas. Il faut que j'attende mes parents.

CAROLINE DAMIEN	Ça te dit de jouer au tennis? Je suis pris. Il faut que j'aide ma mère. Mais si tu es libre, on peut jouer demain après l'école.
CAROLINE	Je ne peux pas. Il faut que je finisse mes devoirs.

XAVIER	Vous n'avez pas envie d'aller faire des jeux vidéo?
JACQUES	Non, il faut qu'on rentre à six heures.
MURIEL	Allez, vous pouvez bien rentrer à sept heures!
HÉLÈNE	Impossible, nos parents sont très stricts.

MURIEL	On y va ce soir?
ISABELLE	Non, mes parents ne veulent pas que je sorte pendant la semaine. Je dois rester à la maison.
MURIEL	Eh bien, ils sont sévères! Moi, je peux faire ce que je veux.
ISABELLE	Tu as le droit de sortir tous les soirs?
MURIEL	Euh, non, de temps en temps seulement… Il faut que je demande la permission.

A2 Activité • Avez-vous compris?

Sont-ils pris ou libres? Remind students that the feminine form of "pris" is "prise" and that the s is pronounced like [z].

1. Jean-Marc   **2.** Caroline   **3.** Damien   **4.** Xavier   **5.** Hélène   **6.** Isabelle

Il est libre.   Elle est libre.   Il est pris.   Il est libre.   Elle est prise.   Elle est prise.

A3 Activité • Pourquoi? Possible answers are given.

Patrice, Damien, Jacques, Caroline et Isabelle refusent les invitations de leurs amis. Pour quelles raisons? Qu'est-ce qu'ils doivent faire? Répondez avec le verbe **devoir**. Patrice doit garder son frère. Damien doit aider sa mère. Jacques doit rentrer à 6h. Caroline doit finir ses devoirs. Isabelle doit rester à la maison.

A4 Activité • Imaginez Possible answers are given.

A votre avis, maintenant que leurs amis ont refusé leurs invitations, qu'est-ce que Jean-Marc Caroline, Xavier, et Muriel vont faire ce soir? Trouvez le maximum d'activités.

Jean-Marc va regarder un film vidéo.   Caroline va jouer au tennis.   Xavier va faire des jeux vidéo.   Muriel va sortir.

A5 Activité • Et vous?

Qu'est-ce que vous devez faire chez vous? Répondez en employant le verbe **devoir**.

1. **Rentre à six heures!**
Je dois rentrer à 6h.

2. **Garde ton petit frère!**
Je dois garder mon petit frère.

3. **Aide ta mère!**
Je dois aider ma mère.

4. **Fais tes devoirs!**
Je dois faire mes devoirs.

5. **Mets la table!**
Je dois mettre la table.

6. **Range ta chambre!**
Je dois ranger ma chambre.

A6 COMMENT LE DIRE
Refusing invitations

Désolé(e).	Je suis occupé(e).
Impossible.	Je ne suis pas libre.
Je regrette.	Je ne peux pas.
Je suis pris(e).	Je n'ai pas le droit de...

Proposez quelque chose à un(e) camarade. Il/Elle refuse en utilisant les expressions dans A6, le verbe **devoir** et les activités dans A5.

— Ça te dit de jouer au tennis?
— Je ne peux pas. Je dois aider ma mère.

—Tu veux faire des jeux vidéo? —Je dois garder mon frère.
—Ça te dit d'aller à la MJC? —Je dois aider ma mère.
—On sort? —Je dois faire mes devoirs.

A8   QU'EST-CE QU'ILS N'ONT PAS LE DROIT DE FAIRE CHEZ EUX?

1.

Ils n'ont pas le droit de fumer. C'est mauvais pour la santé.

2.

Il n'a pas le droit de regarder la télévision après dix heures. C'est trop tard.

3.

Elle n'a pas le droit de faire de la mobylette en ville. C'est trop dangereux.

4.

Elle n'a pas le droit de téléphoner trop longtemps. Ça coûte cher.

In France, all telephone calls are charged per call and by length of time.

Activité • Et vous?   Possible answers are given.   J'ai le droit de sortir le soir / organiser des boums / conduire une mobylette / aller dans des discothèques.

Qu'est-ce que vous avez le droit ou pas le droit de faire chez vous?

J'ai le droit de...   Je n'ai pas le droit de... Je n'ai pas le droit de manger entre les repas / regarder la télévision après dix heures / fumer / téléphoner trop longtemps.

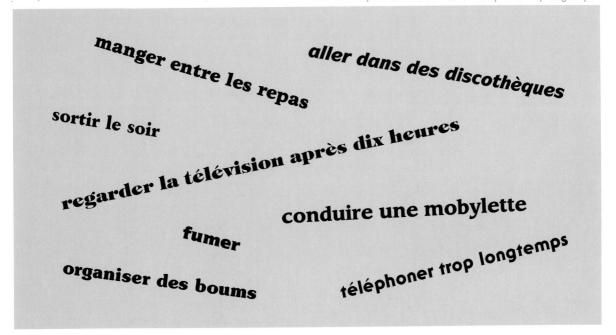

manger entre les repas

aller dans des discothèques

sortir le soir

regarder la télévision après dix heures

conduire une mobylette

fumer

organiser des boums

téléphoner trop longtemps

Et à l'école? Dans la classe de français?   Je n'ai pas le droit de faire du patin à l'école. Je n'ai pas le droit de parler anglais dans la classe de français, mais j'ai le droit de parler français.

A10   Savez-vous que... ?

La France vieillit. Le nombre de jeunes dans la population diminue; le nombre de personnes âgées augmente.

Les familles nombreuses sont l'exception aujourd'hui. La famille française a en moyenne deux enfants.

Pour encourager la natalité, le gouvernement offre aux familles nombreuses des allocations familiales : une certaine somme d'argent qui dépend du revenu de la famille et du nombre d'enfants. Les familles nombreuses ont aussi droit à des déductions fiscales.

Les jeunes français sont majeurs à dix-huit ans. A partir de cet âge, ils peuvent voter.. vivre leur vie. Enfin, en théorie, parce qu'en moyenne ils vivent encore longtemps dans leur famille, souvent jusqu'à vingt-cinq ans.

"Vieillir," to grow old, is conjugated like "finir."

La France vieillit...

Evolution démographique de la France (1850–2000).

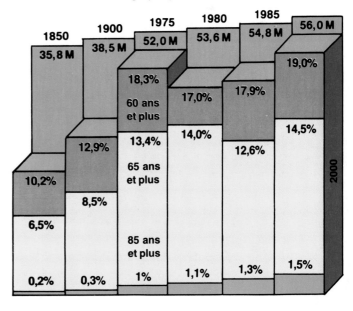

STRUCTURES DE BASE

The subjunctive with il faut que... *and* vouloir que...
The subjunctive of faire

1. The verb forms you have been using so far are called indicative forms. However, if you want to say that someone must do something, using **il faut que...,** or that someone wants or doesn't want someone else to do something, using **vouloir que,** then you have to use special verb forms called subjunctive forms. Look at these examples.

INDICATIVE	SUBJUNCTIVE
J'**attends** mes parents.	Il faut que j'**attende** mes parents.
Je **sors.**	Ils ne veulent pas que je **sorte.**

Remind the students that when the subject of the sentence wants to do something, "vouloir" is followed by the infinitive: "Je veux sortir."

2. To make the present subjunctive forms of all regular verbs and many irregular verbs, you drop the verb ending of the **ils/elles** form of the present indicative. Then you add to the stem the endings **-e, -es, -e, -ions, -iez,** and **-ent.**

Present Subjunctive		
Stem	*Endings*	
rest~~ent~~	**-e**	Il faut que je **reste** ici.
rentr~~ent~~	**-es**	Ils veulent que tu **rentres.**
attend~~ent~~	**-e**	Il faut qu'il **attende.**
choisiss~~ent~~	**-ions**	Il faut que nous **choisissions.**
sort~~ent~~	**-iez**	Ils veulent que vous **sortiez.**
mett~~ent~~	**-ent**	Il faut qu'ils **mettent** la table.

3. As you might expect, some irregular verbs have irregular subjunctive forms. **Venir, prendre (apprendre, comprendre),** and **recevoir** form their subjunctive stem for the **je, tu, il(s),** and **elle(s)** forms from the **ils/elles** forms of the present indicative: **vienn~~ent~~→je vienne, prenn~~ent~~→tu prennes, reçoiv~~ent~~→il reçoive.** The stem for the **nous** and **vous** forms comes from the first-person plural of the present indicative: **ven~~ons~~→nous venions, pren~~ons~~→vous preniez, recev~~ons~~→nous recevions.**

   To make the subjunctive forms of **faire,** you have to add the regular subjunctive endings to the stem **fass-: fasse, fasses, fasse, fassions, fassiez, fassent.** The subjunctive forms of "aller," "avoir", and "être" are presented in Unit 7, p. 260.

4. There are only three spoken forms of the present subjunctive: the **je, tu, il(s),** and **elle(s)** verb forms are pronounced alike; the **nous** and **vous** forms are sounded differently.

COMMENT LE DIRE

Expressing obligation

DEVOIR + infinitive	IL FAUT QUE + subjunctive
Je dois rester à la maison.	Il faut que je reste à la maison.
Nous devons partir.	Il faut que nous partions.

"Il faut que nous partions" is the same as "Il faut partir".

Activité • Organisez une soirée

Arnaud veut organiser une soirée. Qu'est-ce qu'il doit faire d'abord? Et ensuite?
Employez **Il faut que…**

ranger le salon

demander la permission aux parents

acheter de la nourriture

téléphoner aux copains

choisir les cassettes

fixer la date

Il faut d'abord qu'il demande la permission aux parents, et qu'il fixe la date. Ensuite, il faut qu'il téléphone aux copains, qu'il achète de la nourriture, qu'il range le salon et qu'il choisisse des cassettes.

A 14 Activité • La liste des parents

Les parents d'Hélène et de Jacques sont partis et ils leur ont laissé une liste de choses à faire.
Hélène regarde la liste et elle dit à Jacques ce qu'ils doivent faire. Qu'est-ce qu'elle lui dit?
Employez **Il faut que…** Even though Hélène and Jacques have their own bedrooms, Hélène would say, "Il faut que nous rangions notre chambre."

> N'oubliez surtout pas de
> 1. ranger votre chambre. 4. déjeuner avec votre tante.
> 2. passer l'aspirateur. 5. téléphoner à vos grands-parents.
> 3. finir vos devoirs. 6. acheter des fruits.
> Bonne journée! A ce soir!

1. Il faut que nous rangions notre chambre. 2. Il faut que nous passions l'aspirateur. 3. Il faut que nous finissions nos devoirs.
4. Il faut que nous déjeunions avec notre tante. 5. Il faut que nous téléphonions à nos grands-parents.
6. Il faut que nous achetions des fruits.

Vous vivez intensément; vous n'avez pas le temps de tout faire. Pour ne pas oublier, vous faites une liste de quelques affaires pendantes (*unfinished business*). Ecrivez votre liste en employant **Il faut que…**

1. regarder le reportage sur la Une
2. téléphoner à Julien
3. organiser une soirée
4. faire du jogging
5. répondre à la lettre de Corinne
6. acheter de nouvelles chaussures

à faire
Il faut que je regarde
le reportage …

1. Il faut que je regarde le reportage sur la Une.   2. ...téléphone à Julien   3. ...organise une soirée
4. ...fasse du jogging   5. ...réponde à la lettre de Corinne   6. ...achète de nouvelles chaussures.

Travaillez avec un(e) camarade. Votre camarade vous propose de faire ces choses. Malheureusement, vous ne pouvez pas. Choisissez une excuse. Employez **Il faut que…**

venir dîner demain   — Tu peux venir dîner demain?

2. —Tu peux jouer au foot?
    —Non, je ne peux pas. Il faut que je travaille.

3. —Tu peux aller à la MJC?
    —Non, je ne peux pas. Il faut que je finisse mes devoirs.

— Non, je ne peux pas. Il faut que je dîne chez ma tante.

1. venir dîner demain
2. jouer au foot
3. aller à la MJC
4. venir au cinéma
5. faire une balade
6. sortir samedi soir

rester à la maison
travailler
garder son petit frère
dîner chez sa tante
finir ses devoirs
rentrer à sept heures
attendre ses parents

4. —Tu peux venir au cinéma?   —Non, je ne peux pas. Il faut que j'attende mes parents.
5. —Tu peux faire une balade?   —Non, je ne peux pas. Il faut que je garde mon petit frère.

6. —Tu peux sortir samedi soir?
    —Non, je ne peux pas. Il faut que je reste à la maison.

Vous avez certainement des projets pour ce soir. Ecrivez au moins cinq choses que vous avez envie de faire. Votre camarade écrit cinq choses qu'il/elle doit faire. Ensuite, faites un dialogue. Vous lui proposez de venir avec vous et il/elle refuse en employant **Il faut que…** Changez de rôle.

Vous :
aller au cinéma
— Ça te dit d'aller au cinéma?

Votre camarade :
finir mes devoirs
— Je ne peux pas. Il faut que je finisse mes devoirs.

Vous avez envie de sortir. Vous allez chez tous vos amis et vous leur proposez de venir avec vous. Malheureusement, ils sont tous occupés. Regardez les dessins. Quelles excuses donnent-ils? Faites des dialogues avec un(e) camarade.

1.

2.

3.

—Ça te dit d'aller au cinéma?
—Non, malheureusement, il faut que je
finisse mes devoirs.
—Dommage.

—Tu veux regarder un match de foot-ball?
—Oui, je veux bien, mais il faut que je range ma chambre.
—D'accord.

—Tu veux aller à la piscine?
—Désolé(e), il faut que je garde mon petit frère.
—Je peux rester avec toi, si tu veux.
—Ah, super!

Activité • Jamais libre

Votre camarade veut absolument faire quelque chose avec vous, mais vous n'êtes jamais libre.
Trouvez le plus d'expressions possibles. Faites un dialogue sans fin.

baby-foot: table soccer

— Ça te plairait de jouer au baby-foot ce soir?
— Malheureusement, je ne suis pas libre. Il faut que je… travaille.
— Et demain matin?
— Ah, je suis pris(e). Il faut que je… finisse mes devoirs.
— Alors, jeudi à cinq heures?
— … Impossible, il faut que j'attende mes parents.

A20   VOUS VOULEZ BIEN… ?

Julien Legal demande la permission à ses parents de sortir.

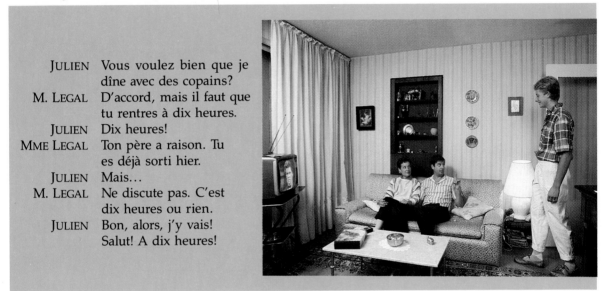

JULIEN Vous voulez bien que je dîne avec des copains?
M. LEGAL D'accord, mais il faut que tu rentres à dix heures.
JULIEN Dix heures!
MME LEGAL Ton père a raison. Tu es déjà sorti hier.
JULIEN Mais…
M. LEGAL Ne discute pas. C'est dix heures ou rien.
JULIEN Bon, alors, j'y vais! Salut! A dix heures!

A21   Activité • Et vous?   Possible answers are given.

1. Trouvez-vous que les parents de Julien sont trop sévères? Non, pas du tout.
2. Quel est le meilleur moment de demander la permission aux parents? C'est pendant le dîner.
3. Vos parents sont-ils stricts? Oui, mes parents sont très stricts.
4. Avez-vous le droit de sortir le soir? J'ai le droit de sortir le samedi soir.
5. Faut-il que vous rentriez à une certaine heure? Oui, il faut que je rentre à dix heures.

A22   COMMENT LE DIRE
Asking permission

POUVOIR + infinitive	VOULOIR BIEN QUE + subjunctive
Est-ce que je peux sortir?	Vous voulez bien que je sorte?

Point out that the adverb "bien" is the key word in asking permission with "vouloir." Without "bien," the question has a different meaning: Do you want me to go out?

En famille   163

Possible answers are given:
— Tu veux bien que je sorte au café?
— Non, tu es déjà sorti(e) hier.

Un(e) camarade joue le rôle de votre père ou de votre mère. Vous lui demandez la permission de faire certaines choses. Il/Elle refuse et donne une raison.

— Tu veux bien que je fasse de la mobylette?
— Non, c'est trop dangereux.

— Tu veux bien que je téléphone aux Etats-Unis.
— Non, c'est trop cher.
— Tu veux bien que je regarde la télévision?
— Non, il faut que tu finisses tes devoirs.

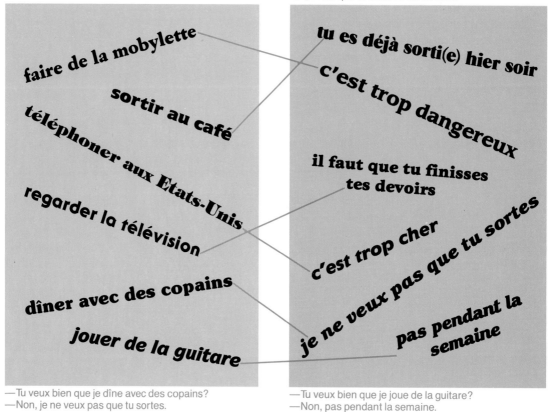

faire de la mobylette

sortir au café

téléphoner aux Etats-Unis

regarder la télévision

dîner avec des copains

jouer de la guitare

tu es déjà sorti(e) hier soir

c'est trop dangereux

il faut que tu finisses tes devoirs

c'est trop cher

je ne veux pas que tu sortes

pas pendant la semaine

—Tu veux bien que je dîne avec des copains?
—Non, je ne veux pas que tu sortes.

—Tu veux bien que je joue de la guitare?
—Non, pas pendant la semaine.

A 24 Activité • A vous maintenant! Possible answers are given.

Demandez à un(e) camarade si ses parents veulent bien qu'il/elle fasse ces choses.

faire de la mobylette — Tes parents veulent bien que tu fasses de la mobylette?
— Non, ils ne veulent pas.
(Oui, ils veulent bien.)

1. fumer   Tes parents veulent bien que tu fumes?
2. faire de la mobylette ...que tu fasses...?
3. écouter du rock dans le salon ... que tu écoutes...?

4. organiser une boum chez vous ...que tu organises...?
5. sortir le soir pendant la semaine ...que tu sortes...?
6. regarder la télévision après dix heures
...que tu regardes...?

A 25 Activité • Ecoutez bien   For script and answers, see pp. T105–106.

Votre mère a téléphoné et elle a laissé un message sur le répondeur. Ecoutez le message et écrivez ce que vous devez faire. Employez **Il faut que je...** et **Ils veulent que je...** ou **Il/Elle veut que je...**

Quand on vit en famille, il faut souvent participer aux tâches domestiques. Qui fait les courses chez vous? Le ménage? La vaisselle? A votre avis, c'est normal?

B1   ## C'est à qui de faire les courses? 📼

Chez les Legal, tout le monde participe.

Un jour Mme Legal fait la cuisine…   …et M. Legal fait la vaisselle.

Le lendemain c'est le contraire. Aurélie et Julien ont aussi des choses à faire mais ce soir ils n'ont pas envie de bouger.

MME LEGAL	Tiens, Aurélie, voilà la liste pour les courses.
AURÉLIE	J'écoute de la musique, maman.
MME LEGAL	Dépêche-toi, ça ferme à sept heures.
AURÉLIE	Tu ne peux pas demander à Julien d'y aller?
JULIEN	Moi, je lis.
AURÉLIE	Je fais les courses tous les jours! C'est à toi de les faire ce soir.
MME LEGAL	Allez, Aurélie.
AURÉLIE	C'est injuste! Pourquoi c'est toujours moi qui travaille ici?
JULIEN	J'ai passé l'aspirateur hier.
AURÉLIE	Et moi, j'ai fait la vaisselle.
JULIEN	C'est normal.
AURÉLIE	Non, c'est pas normal!
JULIEN	Si, c'est aux filles de la faire…
AURÉLIE	Macho!
JULIEN	Féministe!
MME LEGAL	Arrêtez de dire des bêtises! Aurélie, va faire les courses! Et toi, Julien, va mettre la table!
JULIEN	Mais je lis, maman!
MME LEGAL	Allez, pas de discussion!

Aurélie fait les courses.

Julien met la table.

shopping cart: un chariot

Activité • Avez-vous compris?

Chez les Legal, qui… ?

1. fait la cuisine   Mme Legal
2. fait la vaisselle   M. Legal
3. doit aller faire les courses   Aurélie

4. a passé l'aspirateur hier   Julien
5. a fait la vaisselle hier   Aurélie
6. va mettre la table maintenant   Julien

B3   Activité • Donnez votre opinion   Possible answer is given.

Aurélie et Julien ne veulent pas faire les courses. Trouvez-vous qu'ils ont raison ou tort?
Pourquoi? Commencez votre réponse par **Je trouve qu'Aurélie a raison parce que…**
Je trouve qu'Aurélie et Julien ont tort parce qu'il faut que les enfants aident leurs parents.

B4   Activité • Trouvez des excuses   Possible answers are given.
Commands were first presented in Nouveaux copains, Unit 6, p. 170.

Votre mère ou votre père vous demande de faire ces choses. Trouvez des excuses. Faites des
dialogues avec un(e) camarade. Changez de rôle.

— Fais les courses, s'il te plaît.
— Je lis, maman (papa).

1. faire les courses
2. faire la vaisselle
3. mettre la table
5. —Passe l'aspirateur, s'il te plaît!
   —Mais je veux sortir.

2. —Fais la vaisselle, s'il te plaît!
   —Mais j'écoute de la musique.
3. —Mets la table, s'il te plaît!
   —Je regarde la télé, maman (papa).

4. ranger ta chambre   4. —Range ta chambre, s'il te plaît!
5. passer l'aspirateur   —Mais je fais mes devoirs.
6. aider ta mère (ton père)
6. —Aide ta mère, s'il te plaît!
   —Je joue de la guitare, papa.

B5   **AUTRES RESPONSABILITES**

1.

laver la voiture

2.

arroser le jardin

3.

sortir les poubelles

4.

tondre la pelouse

5.

faire le ménage

6.

donner à manger au chat

Activité • A vous maintenant!   Possible answers are given.

Qu'est-ce que vous faites chez vous? Faites une liste et ensuite demandez à un(e) camarade s'il (si elle) fait aussi ces choses chez lui/elle.

Je fais...   Je range...   Je mets...   Est-ce que tu...?

B7   Savez-vous que… ?

La plupart des familles françaises n'ont pas de femme de ménage *(cleaning woman)* et les tâches domestiques sont souvent partagées par tous les membres de la famille. D'habitude, le père participe au travail de la maison, surtout si sa femme travaille. Mais bien sûr, ça dépend des familles et du milieu : beaucoup de Français sont encore très traditionnels et, par exemple, dans les campagnes, c'est généralement la mère qui s'occupe de la maison. Les enfants doivent souvent aider leurs parents. Ils font les «petits travaux». Parfois, en échange, ils reçoivent de l'argent de poche, par exemple, pour laver la voiture.

A la maison, ce n'est pas encore l'égalité. «Etes-vous d'accord ou non?»

	Filles	Garçons
Dans la famille, il est normal que la mère fasse les travaux ménagers.	OUI : 58% NON : 42%	OUI : 68% NON : 32%
Dans la famille, il est normal que le père fasse le bricolage.	OUI : 75% NON : 25%	OUI : 83% NON : 17%
En rentrant de son travail le soir, il est normal que le père aide la mère à la maison.	OUI : 76% NON : 24%	OUI : 71% NON : 29%

Monsieur, est-ce que vous faites… ?

	Souvent	Parfois	Jamais
la vaisselle	34%	42%	23%
le ménage	20	47	33
la lessive	9	14	76
la toilette des enfants	10	24	39
les courses	53	37	10
les repas	22	41	37

les travaux ménagers: household chores
le bricolage: home improvements; repairs
la lessive: laundry

B8   **COMMENT LE DIRE**
Assigning responsibility

C'est à Julien de faire les courses.	It's up to Julien to do the shopping.
C'est aux filles de faire les courses.	Girls are supposed to do the shopping.

B9   Activité • Donnez votre opinion   Possible answers are given.

A votre avis, c'est à qui de faire quoi?

C'est {
aux garçons
aux filles
à la mère
au père
à tout le monde
} de {
faire la vaisselle.
faire les courses.
faire la cuisine.
faire le ménage.
laver la voiture.
sortir les poubelles.
donner à manger au chien.
garder les enfants.
}

C'est aux garçons de faire la vaisselle.
C'est aux filles de laver la voiture.
C'est à la mère de faire les courses.
C'est au père de faire la cuisine.
C'est à tout le monde de garder les enfants.

STRUCTURES DE BASE ✓
The direct-object pronouns le, la, les

1. The pronouns **le,** *him* or *it,* **la,** *her* or *it,* and **les,** *them,* may stand for people or things.

Singular	Je persuade	**mon frère.**	Je	**le**	persuade.
	Il fait	**le ménage.**	Il	**le**	fait.
	Je persuade	**ma sœur.**	Je	**la**	persuade.
	Elle fait	**la vaisselle.**	Elle	**la**	fait.
Plural	Je persuade	**mes copains.**	Je	**les**	persuade.
	Ils font	**les courses.**	Ils	**les**	font.

2. In most cases, a direct-object pronoun comes immediately before the verb of which it is the object.

Je	la fais.	
Je vais	la faire.	
Je ne	la fais	pas.
Ne	la fais	pas!

3. In an affirmative command, the direct-object pronoun immediately follows the verb. In writing, it is separated from the verb by a hyphen.

> Faites-**le!**
> Faites-**la!**
> Faites-**les!**

4. **Elision** occurs when **le** or **la** comes before a verb that begins with a vowel.

J'aide mon père.	**Je l'aide.**
J'aide ma mère.	**Je l'aide.**

5. **Liaison** occurs when **les** comes before a verb that begins with a vowel.

J'écoute mes parents.	**Je les écoute.**

Activité • Chez les Legal 📼 Possible answers are given.

Chez les Legal, tout le monde participe. Répondez aux questions suivantes avec un pronom, **le, la** ou **les.** Travaillez avec un(e) camarade.

— M. Legal fait la cuisine?   — Oui, il la fait.

1. M. Legal fait la cuisine?
2. Il fait aussi la vaisselle?
3. Mme Legal fait la cuisine?
4. Elle fait la vaisselle aussi?
5. M. Legal fait les courses?
6. Aurélie met la table?
7. Elle prépare le dîner?
8. Julien passe l'aspirateur?

1. Oui, il la fait.   2. Non, Mme Legal la fait.   3. Oui, elle la fait.   4. Non, M. Legal la fait.   5. Non, Aurélie les fait.
6. Non, Julien la met.   7. Non, M. Legal le prépare.   8. Oui, il le passe.

Activité • A votre avis 📼 Possible answers are given.

Imaginez la famille Legal et donnez votre avis. Est-ce que les membres de la famille font les choses représentées par les dessins 1–5 dans B5? Travaillez avec un(e) camarade. Employez les pronoms **le, la** et **les** dans vos réponses.

— A ton avis, M. Legal arrose le jardin?   — Oui, il l'arrose. (Non, il ne l'arrose pas.)

—A ton avis, Mme Legal lave la voiture?   —Non, elle ne la lave pas.
—A ton avis, Julien sort les poubelles?   —Oui, il les sort.
—A ton avis, Aurélie tond la pelouse?   —Non, elle ne la tond pas.
—A ton avis, M. Legal fait le ménage?   —Oui, il le fait.

Vous voulez savoir ce que vos amis font chez eux. Vous leur posez des questions. Ils répondent avec un pronom. Changez de rôle.

— Tu passes l'aspirateur chez toi?
— Oui, je le passe. Et toi, tu laves la voiture?
— Non, je ne la lave pas.

B 14   Activité • Chacun sa tâche

On est bien organisé chez les Ballard. Madame Ballard a mis une liste de tâches domestiques sur le réfrigérateur. Qui fait quoi?

Travaillez avec un(e) camarade. Posez des questions et répondez avec un pronom.

— Qui arrose le jardin chez les Ballard?
— C'est M. Ballard qui l'arrose.

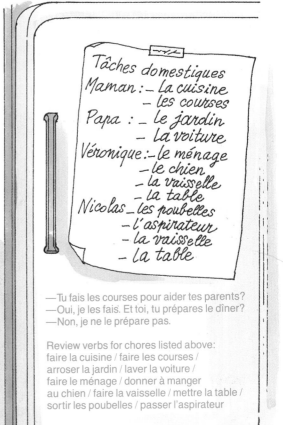

Tâches domestiques
Maman : – La cuisine
– les courses
Papa : – Le jardin
– La voiture
Véronique : – le ménage
– le chien
– la vaisselle
– la table
Nicolas – les poubelles
– l'aspirateur
– la vaisselle
– La table

—Tu fais les courses pour aider tes parents?
—Oui, je les fais. Et toi, tu prépares le dîner?
—Non, je ne le prépare pas.

Review verbs for chores listed above:
faire la cuisine / faire les courses /
arroser la jardin / laver la voiture /
faire le ménage / donner à manger
au chien / faire la vaisselle / mettre la table /
sortir les poubelles / passer l'aspirateur

B 15   Activité • Et chez vous?

Faites une liste de choses que vous faites chez vous. Demandez ensuite à un(e) camarade si c'est lui/elle qui les fait chez lui/elle.

— C'est toi qui fais les courses chez toi?
— Oui, c'est moi qui les fais.
    (Non, c'est ma sœur qui les fait.)

B 16   COMMENT LE DIRE
Complaining

C'est injuste!	C'est moi qui fais tout ici!
C'est pas juste!	C'est toujours moi qui...
C'est pas normal!	Tu ne fais rien, toi!

Agreement between qui and the verb in a relative clause is presented in Unit 11, p. 406: ... moi qui fais...; nous qui faisons..., etc.
The negative "ne...rien" is presented in Unit 6, p. 209.

B17 Activité • Elle n'est pas contente

Cette fille doit tout faire chez elle. Qu'est-ce qu'elle dit? Possible answers are given.

Ce week-end, il faut que tu passes l'aspirateur!
C'est pas juste!

Il faut que tu arroses le jardin!
C'est injuste!

Va sortir les poubelles!
C'est pas normal!

N'oublie pas de faire le ménage!
C'est moi qui fais tout ici!

Donne à manger a chien!
Tu ne fais rien, toi!

Tiens, voilà la liste des courses!
C'est toujours moi qui fais les courses!

B18 Activité • A vous maintenant! Possible answer is given.

Travaillez avec un(e) camarade. Il/Elle joue le rôle de votre père ou de votre mère. Vous demandez la permission de faire des choses. Il/Elle refuse et vous demande de faire une tâche domestique. Ensuite, vous vous plaignez *(complain)*.

— Je peux sortir ce soir?
— Non, il faut que tu arroses le jardin.
— C'est injuste! C'est toujours moi qui l'arrose!
— …

—Vous voulez bien que je fasse une balade avec des copains?
—Impossible! Il faut que tu passes l'aspirateur.
—C'est injuste! C'est moi qui fais tout ici!

B19 Activité • Ecoutez bien For script and answers, see pp. T110–11.

Ecoutez Madame Lenoir et Madame Benoît parler du travail à la maison et répondez aux questions suivantes.

1. Qui fait la cuisine et le ménage chez Madame Benoît?
2. Pourquoi est-ce que Monsieur Benoît fait tout à la maison?
3. Qui fait le travail chez Madame Lenoir?
4. A quoi est-ce que Monsieur Lenoir passe son temps?
5. Que fait Madame Benoît pendant que son mari travaille?
6. Pourquoi est-ce que Madame Benoît n'aide pas son mari?

sharing confidences and asking for advice . . . giving advice and encouragement

En dehors de sa famille, Sophie a de nombreux amis. Elle passe beaucoup de temps avec eux, surtout avec Mélanie, sa meilleure amie. C'est sa confidente et elle lui raconte tout.

C1   Une affaire de cœur 📼

Sophie est un peu amoureuse de Julien. Mélanie lui donne des conseils.

SOPHIE   J'ai besoin de te parler. Tu connais Julien?
MÉLANIE   Oui, je l'ai rencontré à l'anniversaire d'Aurélie.
SOPHIE   Comment tu le trouves?
MÉLANIE   Pas mal.
SOPHIE   Super mignon, tu veux dire! Tu le vois souvent?
MÉLANIE   Non, je l'ai vu une seule fois. Pourquoi?

SOPHIE   J'ai bien envie de le rencontrer. Tu ne sais pas comment je peux faire?
MÉLANIE   Si, c'est facile. Il faut absolument que tu organises une soirée et que tu l'invites.
SOPHIE   Mais je ne le connais pas!
MÉLANIE   Et alors? Il ne faut pas être timide. Tu l'appelles ou tu lui envoies une invitation.
SOPHIE   Je n'ose pas.

MÉLANIE   Allez! Un peu de courage!
SOPHIE   Tu crois vraiment que je peux l'inviter?
MÉLANIE   Pourquoi pas? Il adore danser.
SOPHIE   Bon, eh bien, je vais organiser une soirée samedi soir.
MÉLANIE   Euh non, pas samedi, mes grands-parents viennent dîner et mes parents veulent que je reste à la maison.

C2   Activité • Vrai ou faux?

1. Sophie est amoureuse de Julien.
2. Elle connaît Julien.
3. Mélanie voit Julien tous les jours.
4. Mélanie écoute les conseils de son amie.
5. Sophie est timide.
6. Mélanie est libre samedi soir.

1. C'est vrai.
2. C'est faux. Elle ne le connaît pas.
3. C'est faux. Elle l'a vu une seule fois.
4. C'est faux. Mélanie lui donne des conseils.
5. C'est vrai.
6. C'est faux. Elle doit rester à la maison parce que ses grands-parents vont dîner chez elle.

Activité • Les conseils de Mélanie

Qu'est-ce que Mélanie conseille à Sophie? Trouvez quatre choses que Sophie doit faire, d'après Mélanie, pour rencontrer Julien.

Elle doit organiser une soirée et inviter Julien. Elle ne doit pas être timide. Elle doit appeler Julien ou lui envoyer une invitation.

C4 Activité • Conversation téléphonique

Finalement, Sophie a décidé de téléphoner à Julien pour l'inviter à une soirée. Travaillez avec un(e) camarade et reconstituez leur conversation en choisissant les mots.

SOPHIE   ...Bonjour. C'est Julien?
JULIEN   ... Oui
SOPHIE   Je m'appelle... Sophie Je suis une... amie de Mélanie.
JULIEN   Ah oui!
SOPHIE   Voilà. J'ai envie d'organiser une... soirée Ça te dit de... ? venir
JULIEN   Bien sûr!
SOPHIE   Quand est-ce que tu es... ? libre
JULIEN   ... soir. Samedi
SOPHIE   Ah, c'est... ! impossible / prise Mélanie est... Elle doit dîner avec ses... grands-parents Qu'est-ce que tu penses de... ? dimanche
JULIEN   Dimanche? C'est... ! parfait

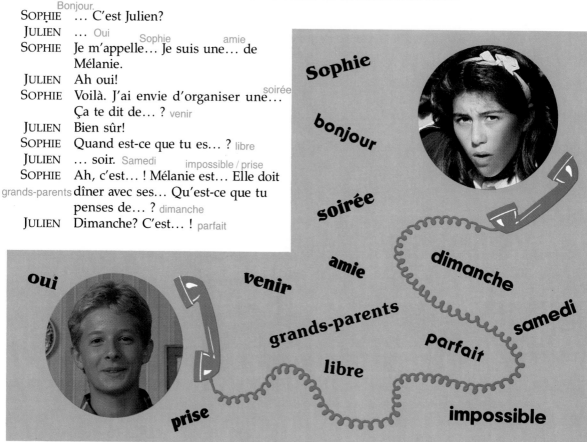

C5   STRUCTURES DE BASE
The verb voir

voir *to see*					
Je	**vois**	souvent les copains.	Nous	**voyons**	souvent les copains.
Tu	**vois**		Vous	**voyez**	
Il/Elle/On	**voit**		Ils/Elles	**voient**	

The past participle of **voir** is **vu**: **J'ai vu Julien une seule fois.**
The subjunctive forms of **voir** are: **voie, voies, voie, voyions, voyiez, voient.**
The verb **croire**, *to believe, think*, follows the same patterns as **voir**.

Point out that the singular forms of "voir" and the third-person plural form sound alike.

Activité • Qu'est-ce qu'ils aiment voir?

Complétez les phrases avec le verbe **voir.**

1. Je ____ souvent mes copains. vois
2. Nous aimons ____ des films d'horreur. voir
3. Sauf Sophie. Elle, elle ____ toujours les films d'amour avec plaisir. voit

4. Samedi dernier nous ____ le nouveau film de Stephen King. avons vu
5. Est-ce que vous ____ souvent des films à la télévision? voyez

C7 Activité • Ecrit dirigé

Complétez ces dialogues avec les formes correctes du verbe **voir.**

1.

— Tu ____ vois souvent Mélanie?
— Oui, je la ____ vois tous les jours.

2.

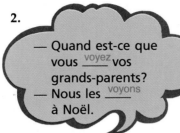
— Quand est-ce que vous ____ voyez vos grands-parents?
— Nous les ____ voyons à Noël.

3.

— Sophie a ____ vu Julien?
— Non, elle le ____ voit dimanche.

C8 Activité • Et vous?   Possible answers are given.

1. Est-ce que vous voyez souvent vos copains?
2. Où est-ce que vous les voyez d'habitude?
3. Est-ce que vous voyez souvent des films?

4. Est-ce que vos parents ne veulent pas que vous voyiez certains films?

1. Oui, je les vois souvent.   2. D'habitude, je les vois à l'école.
3. Oui, j'en vois souvent.   4. Mes parents ne veulent pas que je voie certains films.

C9 COMMENT LE DIRE
Sharing confidences and asking for advice

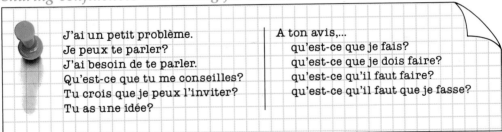

J'ai un petit problème.
Je peux te parler?
J'ai besoin de te parler.
Qu'est-ce que tu me conseilles?
Tu crois que je peux l'inviter?
Tu as une idée?

A ton avis,...
qu'est-ce que je fais?
qu'est-ce que je dois faire?
qu'est-ce qu'il faut faire?
qu'est-ce qu'il faut que je fasse?

Giving advice and encouragement

ADVICE	ENCOURAGEMENT
Invite-la.	Bien sûr!
Il faut que tu l'invites.	Sûrement!
Téléphone-lui.	Pourquoi pas?
Il faut que tu lui téléphones.	Il faut oser.
Oublie-le.	Un peu de courage!
Il faut que tu l'oublies.	N'hésite pas.

"Oublie-le" means forget <u>him</u>, not forget <u>it</u>.

C10 Activité • Ecoutez bien For script and answers, see p. T113.

Est-ce qu'on demande des conseils ou la permission?

C11 Activité • Donnez des conseils Possible answers are given.

Vos amis Marie et Laurent vous demandent des conseils. Aidez-les.

1. Tu crois que je peux lui téléphoner?

2. A ton avis, il faut que je l'invite?

3. Qu'est-ce qu'il faut que je fasse pour le rencontrer?

4. Est-ce que je peux lui envoyer une invitation?

5. Tu crois que je peux lui parler?

6. J'ai envie de la voir. Qu'est-ce qu'il faut que je fasse?

1. Sûrement! Téléphone-lui. 2. Il ne faut pas être timide. Invite-le. 3. Il faut que tu lui téléphones.
4. N'hésite pas, invite-la. 5. Oublie-la! 6. Un peu de courage, invite-la!

Activité • A vous maintenant!

Travaillez avec un(e) camarade. Vous êtes dans les situations suivantes. Demandez et donnez des conseils. Changez de rôle.

1. Vous avez besoin d'argent.
2. Vous voulez avoir une mobylette.
3. Vous avez envie de rencontrer un garçon/une fille.
4. Vous voulez être invité(e) à la boum de Sophie.
5. Vous êtes invité(e) à une boum, mais vous ne voulez pas y aller.
6. Vous trouvez votre note en maths injuste. Vous hésitez à en parler à votre professeur.

C13 **Activité • Ecrivez**   Possible answer is given.

Choisissez une des situations dans C12. Vous n'osez pas discuter de votre problème avec le conseiller ou la conseillère *(counselor)*. Alors, vous lui écrivez un petit mot. Dans la lettre, vous décrivez le problème et lui demandez des conseils.   Voilà mon problème : Je voudrais rencontrer Florence, mais je suis trop timide. Elle est très sympa. Elle a beaucoup d'amis, et moi, je suis seul. Qu'est-ce que je dois faire?

C14 **Savez-vous que… ?**

Les copains, c'est une autre famille. Les jeunes français passent beaucoup de temps entre eux, à l'école à la récréation, après l'école, le week-end et souvent pendant les vacances. Ils forment une «bande» de copains. Toute la bande va au café. Là, ils jouent au baby-foot, au flipper *(pinball)* ou aux jeux vidéo. Les filles préfèrent souvent rester entre elles et parler à leurs confidentes.

Interlocuteurs privilégiés : les copains et la mère
En général, avec qui parlez-vous de vos problèmes?

copains ou copines	51%
mère	48%
frères ou sœurs	24%
père	18%
un des grands-parents	4%
un ou une adulte ami(e)	3%
certains professeurs	2%
autres	1%
je n'ai personne à qui parler	-
ne se prononcent pas	1%

interlocuteur: listener

Activité • Sondage

Quand vous êtes avec des copains, de quoi parlez-vous? Faites ce sondage dans votre classe. Demandez à vos camarades : «Quand vous êtes avec des copains, parlez-vous souvent ou pas souvent des sujets suivants?» On parle souvent de...
On ne parle pas souvent de...

1. Des devoirs, des cours, des professeurs
2. De votre famille
3. De musique
4. De vos lectures (*reading*)
5. De vos sorties (boums, cinéma)
6. De sport
7. Des histoires entre filles et garçons
8. De vos vacances
9. De vos copains et de vos copines
10. Des vedettes de la télévision, du cinéma et de la chanson
11. Des programmes de télévision
12. De l'actualité politique
13. De la faim dans le monde
14. De religion
15. De la drogue
16. Du SIDA (*AIDS*)
17. De ce que vous voulez faire plus tard

Point out that when "parler" is negative, du, de la, de l', and des do not change to de:
Nous ne parlons pas du SIDA.

Sujet	Souvent	Pas souvent
1. Des devoirs, des cours		
2. De vos professeurs		

C16 VOUS EN SOUVENEZ-VOUS?
Object pronouns

Let's review the pronouns you've seen so far that have been used as the objects of verbs.

lui	*Replaces phrase:* **à** + *one person*	Elle parle **au professeur**. Elle **lui** parle.
leur	*Replaces phrase:* **à** + *more than one person*	Nous téléphonons **aux copains**. Nous **leur** téléphonons.
en	*Replaces phrase:* **de** + *object or place*	Il joue **de la guitare**. Il **en** joue.
y	*Replaces phrase:* *preposition* + *location*	Ils vont **en France**. Ils **y** vont.
le, la, les	*Replaces nouns:* *objects or people*	Ils font **la vaisselle**. Ils **la** font.

The object pronouns me, te, nous, and vous are presented in Unit 6, p. 199.

You remember that an object pronoun comes immediately before the verb to which its meaning is tied, except in an affirmative command or request form.

Parle-**lui**.   Prenez-**en**.   Faites-**la**.
Téléphonez-**leur**.   Restes-**y**.

STRUCTURES DE BASE
Object pronouns with the passé composé

1. In the **passé composé,** an object pronoun immediately precedes the auxiliary verb.

Nous	**lui** avons	parlé.
Nous	**en** avons	pris.
Nous	**l'** avons	trouvé(e).

2. Elision takes place when the pronoun **le** or **la** precedes the auxiliary verb **avoir.**

   (le) Nous **l'avons** trouvé.   (la) Tu **l'as** invitée?

3. Liaison occurs when the plural pronoun **les** appears before the auxiliary verb **avoir.**

   Ils **les** ont trouvés.

4. When the words **ne... pas** are used to make the verb negative, **ne** is placed before the object pronoun and **pas** is placed after the auxiliary verb.

   Je **ne lui ai pas** téléphoné.

5. The past participle of a verb used with **avoir** may change its spelling. Just as an adjective agrees with the noun it modifies, the past participle of a verb in the **passé composé** must agree in gender and number with the direct object that comes before it. If the preceding direct object is feminine singular, **-e** is added to the past participle. If the preceding direct object is masculine plural, **-s** is added to any past participle that doesn't already end in **-s**. If the direct object is feminine plural, **-es** is added.

Son ami?	Elle **l'**a rencontré.	**Les copains?**	Elle **les** a invité**s**.
La boum?	Elle **l'**a organisé**e**.	**Les copines?**	Elle **les** a vu**es** au café.

If the past participle of a verb ends with a consonant, the addition of **-e** or **-es** to make it agree with a preceding direct object will cause you to pronounce the consonant.

Le ménage?	Nous **l'**avons fai**t**. (**t** is not pronounced)
La vaisselle?	Nous **l'**avons fai**te**. (**t** is pronounced)
Les courses?	Nous **les** avons fai**tes**. (**t** is pronounced)

The spelling change in the past participle must not be made when the preceding object of the verb is an indirect object or the pronouns **y** or **en**.

Sophie?	Je **l'**ai invité**e**.	*But,*	Je **lui** ai téléphoné.
Julien et Didier?	Je **les** ai rencontré**s**.	*But,*	Je **leur** ai parlé.
La tour Eiffel?	Je **l'**ai vu**e**.	*But,*	J'**y** suis monté.
Les légumes?	Je **les** ai acheté**s**.	*But,*	J'**en** ai mangé.

Point out that verbs conjugated with être in the passé composé generally do not take a direct object.
Use of the reflexive pronoun with the passé composé is presented in Unit 7, p. 242.

Use of the reflexive pronoun with the passé composé is presented in Unit 7, p. 242.

C18   Activité • Sophie a tout fait?

Travaillez avec une camarade. Votre camarade joue le rôle de Sophie. Vous lui demandez si elle a fait les préparatifs pour sa soirée. Elle répond avec un pronom.

   la date / fixer   — La date, tu l'as fixée?
                     — Oui, je l'ai fixée.

1. la date / fixer
2. la permission / demander
3. les copains / appeler

4. Julien / inviter
5. les boissons / acheter
6. les sandwiches / faire

7. la musique / choisir
8. le salon / ranger

1. ...tu l'as fixée?
2. ...tu l'as demandée?
3. ...tu les as appelés?

4. ...tu l'as invité?
5. ...tu les as achetées?
6. ...tu les as faits?

7. ...tu l'as choisie?
8. ...tu l'as rangé?

En famille   177

Activité • Conversation à la boum

A la boum de Sophie vous entendez des conversations variées. Choisissez les remarques qui vont ensemble et faites les dialogues avec un(e) camarade.

1. Ils sont nouveaux, tes bracelets?
2. C'est ta cassette?
3. La mousse est délicieuse!
4. Véronique ne vient pas?
5. Tu as toujours ta mob?

"Emprunter à," to borrow from, is active vocabulary in Unit 6.

Oui, je les ai achetés hier.
1.

Non, je l'ai empruntée à Guy.
2.

Non, je l'ai vendue.
5.

Tu trouves? Ma mère l'a faite.
3.

Non, Sophie ne l'a pas invitée.
4.

C20 Activité • C'était bien, la soirée de Sophie?

Vous êtes allé(e) à la soirée chez Sophie. Votre camarade vous demande ce que vous y avez fait. Répondez avec un pronom. 1. Je (ne) l'ai (pas) rencontrée. 2. Je (ne) l'ai (pas) vu. 3. Je (ne) l'ai (pas) aimée.

1. Tu as rencontré Mélanie?
2. Tu as vu Julien?
3. Tu as aimé la musique?
4. On a fini les sandwiches?

5. Julien a invité Sophie à danser?
6. Tu as aidé Sophie à ranger le salon après la soirée?

4. On (ne) les a (pas) finis. 5. Il (ne) l'a (pas) invitée à danser. 6. Je (ne) l'ai (pas) aidée à ranger le salon.

C21 Activité • Ecrit dirigé

Qui a fait quoi après la soirée? Complétez les réponses avec le pronom correct. Faites l'accord du participe, s'il le faut.

1. Qui a fait la vaisselle?
   C'est Sophie et Mélanie qui __l'__ ont fait __e__ .

2. Qui a rangé la pièce?
   C'est nous qui __l'__ avons rangé __e__ .

3. Qui a sorti la poubelle?
   C'est Julien qui __l'__ a sorti __e__ .

4. Qui a passé l'aspirateur?
   C'est Arnaud qui __l'__ a passé ____ .

5. Qui a mis les sandwiches dans le frigo?
   C'est Sylvie qui __les__ a mis ____ dans le frigo.

6. Qui a fini les gâteaux?
   C'est moi qui __les__ ai fini __s__ .

C22 Activité • Ecoutez bien   For script and answers, see p. T115.

Votre amie Agnès est rentrée d'une boum. Elle a téléphoné pour tout vous raconter. Elle a laissé un message sur votre répondeur. Ecoutez le message et dites ensuite si les phrases suivantes sont vraies ou fausses.

1. Agnès est allée à l'anniversaire de Catherine.
2. Le garçon qu'elle a rencontré s'appelle Henri.
3. François est un ami d'Henri.

4. D'habitude Agnès est timide.
5. Elle a le numéro de téléphone de François.
6. Elle a décidé de lui téléphoner demain.

1

La boum d'anniversaire 📼

Sylvain fête son anniversaire. Il y a la famille, mais aussi quelques amis.

— Jacques et Fabrice ne viennent pas ?
— Non, Sylvain ne les a pas invités ;
il y a déjà trop de monde.

    — Qu'est-ce que tu as, Fabienne ?
    — Oh, Anne... j'ai besoin de te
    parler. Je suis amoureuse de Julien.
    Qu'est-ce que je dois faire, à ton avis ?
    — Invite-le un soir, au cinéma !

— Allô ? Sylvain ? C'est Emmanuel.
Je suis désolé, je ne peux pas venir.
Mes parents ne veulent pas que je sorte.
— Quel dommage !

— C'est toi qui as fait la
mousse, Claire ?
    — Non, c'est ma mère.
    — Elle est drôlement bonne !
      — Ma mère ?
      — Non, sa mousse !

        — Tu la connais ?
        — Bien sûr ! Je l'ai rencontrée
        chez ma cousine.

— Qui est-ce qui va faire la vaisselle, Sylvain ?
C'est tes parents ?
    — Non, c'est toujours moi qui la fais !

      — Je dois partir : il faut que je
      rentre avant dix heures.
        — Au revoir, Sophie.

En famille 179

2   Activité • Qui est-ce?   Possible answers are given.

Identifiez ces gens d'après «La boum d'anniversaire».   1. Jacques et Fabrice n'ont pas été invités.
2. Emmanuel refuse l'invitation à regret.

1. Deux personnes n'ont pas été invitées.
2. Quelqu'un refuse l'invitation à regret.
3. Quelqu'un est amoureux.

4. Quelqu'un donne un conseil.
5. Quelqu'un a fait une mousse.
6. Quelqu'un fait toujours la vaisselle.

3. Fabienne est amoureuse de Julien.   4. Anne donne un conseil à Fabienne.
5. La mère de Claire a fait une mousse.   6. Sylvain fait toujours la vaisselle.

3   Activité • Qu'est-ce qu'ils disent?   Possible answers are given.

Trouvez les phrases dans «La boum d'anniversaire».   1. Invite-le un soir au cinéma.
2. C'est toi qui as fait la mousse?

1. Someone is giving advice.
2. Someone is asking for information.
3. Someone is expressing obligation.

4. Someone is politely refusing.
5. Someone is giving an excuse.
6. Someone is complaining.

3. Je dois partir : il faut que je rentre avant 10 h.   4. Je suis désolé, je ne peux pas venir.
5. Mes parents ne veulent pas que je sorte.   6. C'est toujours moi qui la fais!

4   Activité • Écrit dirigé   Possible answer is given.

Le paragraphe suivant parle de la boum de Sylvain. Mais quelques phrases ne sont pas «vraies». Recopiez le paragraphe. Faites les changements nécessaires. Il y a beaucoup de monde à la boum de Sylvain. Il n'a pas invité Jacques et Fabrice. Emmanuel ne peut pas venir parce que ses parents ne veulent pas qu'il sorte.

> Il n'y a pas beaucoup de monde à la boum de Sylvain. Il a invité tous ses amis. Jacques et Fabrice sont là. Emmanuel est venu aussi : ses parents lui laissent faire tout ce qu'il veut. Il y a de bons sandwiches sur la table. C'est la mère de Sylvain qui les a faits. Tout le monde a l'air content. Il est presque dix heures et une des invitées doit partir... Dommage! Une jeune fille, Fabienne, est amoureuse de Sylvain. Elle demande conseil à Anne. Anne ne veut pas que Fabienne parle à Sylvain.

Il y a de la mousse sur la table. C'est la mère de Claire qui l'a faite. Tout le monde a l'air content. Il est presque 10 heures et Sophie doit partir ... Dommage! Une jeune fille, Fabienne, est amoureuse de Julien. Anne conseille à Fabienne d'inviter Julien au cinéma.

5   Activité • Qu'est-ce que vous répondez?   Possible answers are given.

Vous êtes à la boum de Sylvain. Différentes personnes vous parlent. Qu'est-ce que vous leur répondez?

1. Quel dommage!   2. Oui, ils sont sympa!   3. C'est dommage, il danse bien.
4. Oui, c'est Marc. Il est mignon.   5. Oui, elle est délicieuse!   6. Il faut que tu l'invites à danser.

Activité • Changez tout
Possible dialogue is given.

Travaillez avec un(e) camarade. Répétez ce dialogue deux fois. Changez les phrases soulignées chaque fois.

— Salut! <u>Ça te dit d'aller au cinéma?</u>
— <u>Impossible. Je suis pris(e).</u>
— Qu'est-ce que tu fais?
— <u>Mes parents veulent</u> que je <u>garde ma petite sœur.</u>
— <u>C'est toujours toi qui la gardes!</u>

—Salut! Tu veux aller à la MJC?
—Désolé(e), je ne suis pas libre.
—Qu'est-ce que tu fais?
—Maman ne veut pas que je sorte.
—C'est pas juste!

Activité • Ecrivez
Possible answer is given.

Vous avez reçu cette lettre de votre amie Julie. Elle est élève dans une école privée. Elle a un petit problème. Répondez à sa lettre en lui donnant des conseils. Chère Julie, Tu peux rencontrer des garçons à la MJC. N'aie pas peur. Tu dois faire un effort. Il faut que tu présentes tes amis à tes parents. Bonne chance!

Cher (Chère)...

J'ai envie de sortir avec des garçons. Mes parents ne veulent pas. Qu'est-ce que je dois faire pour que mes parents changent d'avis? Mon école n'est pas mixte. Qu'est-ce qu'il faut que je fasse pour rencontrer des garçons? Au secours!
Ton amie
Julie

Activité • Ecrivez
Possible answer is given.

Répondez aux questions suivantes et ensuite, écrivez quelques lignes sur vos relations avec votre ami(e) ou vos copains.

1. Vous lui / leur racontez tout?
2. Vous lui / leur demandez des conseils? Sur quoi?
3. Vous l' / les aidez? A faire quoi?
4. Ils / Elles vous aident? A faire quoi?
5. Vous aimez être avec lui / eux / elle(s)?

Ma confidente s'appelle Héloïse. Je lui raconte tout. Elle me donne toujours des conseils sur les parents, la famille et les amis. Moi, je l'aide avec ses problèmes; je lui donne des conseils. On est toujours ensemble, Héloïse et moi.

Activité • Le(La) confident(e) idéal(e) Possible answer is given.

Formez un groupe de quatre avec trois autres camarades. Préparez ensemble une description d'un(e) confident(e) idéal(e). Ecrivez votre description et puis lisez-la à la classe.

Le confident idéal est toujours là quand on a un problème. On peut lui parler des problèmes.
Il écoute bien et donne des conseils. Il garde les secrets.

10

Activité • A vous maintenant!

Regardez les gens sur ces photos. A qui parlent-ils? De quoi? Demandent-ils des conseils? Racontent-ils un secret? Discutent-ils d'un problème? Imaginez leurs conversations et préparez les dialogues avec un(e) camarade.

1.

2.

3.

4.

11

Activité • Récréation optional

Jeu des pronoms

Devinez ce que les pronoms **le, l', les** représentent dans les phrases suivantes.

1. C'est ma mère qui le prépare.
2. Je les ai écoutés.
3. Tu les as invitées?
4. C'est mon frère qui l'a faite.
5. Nous l'avons mise.
6. C'est elle qui les a achetées.
7. Anne les a faits après l'école.

déjeuner   table   Anne et Caroline
Alain et Pierre   disques
vaisselle
devoirs   cassettes   ménage

1. le déjeuner 2. les disques 3. Anne et Caroline 4. la vaisselle 5. la table 6. les cassettes 7. les devoirs

PRONONCIATION 📼

The French **r**-sound /R/

1 Ecoutez bien et répétez.

1. In the middle of a word

arabe	arracher	arrêt	arriver
oraux	oral	horrible	orange
heureux	amoureux	durer	purée

2. At the end of a word

purée→pur   heureux→heure
durée→dur   carré→car

par, père, pire, port, pour, peur   faire, fort, four
sur, sort, soir   mer, mort, mur
tard, tort, tire

3. Combining

pour→pourquoi   sort→sortir
par→parfait   sur→ surtout
jour→journée   mer→merci

4. At the beginning of a word

après	c'est trop	ouvrier	en gros
adresse	très bien	ouvrage	c'est grand

après→près   c'est trop→trop
en gros→gros   c'est froid→froid

froid	vrai	très	grand
franc	vrac	triste	brun

froid→trois→crois→roi   grand→prend→cran→rang   front→tronc→prompt→rond

rat	rêve	rouge	rigide	réaction
riz	rose	riche	repas	répéter

rire, rare, regard, retard, retour, au revoir

2 Ecoutez et lisez.

— La porte est fermée.
— Pourtant, l'adresse est correcte.
— Il est déjà trois heures. Nous sommes arrivés trop tard.
— Tu as raison. Voilà. C'est écrit. «Fermé le mardi après-midi.»
— On retourne demain?
— D'accord.
— Très bien.

3 Copiez les phrases suivantes pour préparer une dictée.

1. Pourquoi tu es triste, alors?
2. Je suis malheureuse.
3. Des affaires de cœur?
4. Oui, je suis amoureuse.
5. Quoi, encore?

VERIFIONS!

Answers are given. Some answers will vary.

SECTION A

Do you know how to express obligation? 1. Il doit téléphoner... / Il faut qu'il téléphone...

Tell what these people have to do, first using **devoir** and then **Il faut que...**

1. Marc / téléphoner à ses grands-parents
2. Je / finir mes devoirs
2. Je dois finir... / Il faut que je finisse...
3. Vous / attendre chez votre oncle
4. Elles / faire les courses
3. Vous devez attendre... / Il faut que vous attendiez...
4. Elles doivent faire... / Il faut qu'elles fassent...

Can you refuse an invitation?

Refuse the following invitations in different ways.

1. On va au parc d'attractions dimanche? Désolé(e), je dois garder mon frère.
2. Ça te dit de sortir ce soir? Je ne peux pas. Mon père ne veut pas que je sorte.

Do you know how to ask permission? 1. Est-ce que je peux aller au cinéma?
Je veux aller au cinéma. Tu es d'accord?

Ask permission to do each of the following things in two different ways.

2. Je peux faire de la moto? Tu veux bien que je fasse de la moto?

1. Vous voulez aller au cinéma samedi.
2. Vous voulez faire de la moto.

SECTION B

Do you know how to use the direct-object pronouns *le, la,* and *les*?

Replace the direct objects in these sentences with **le, la,** or **les.**

Nathalie l'aide.
1. Nathalie aide sa mère.
2. Marc connaît les parents de Julien.
Marc les connaît.

Appelle-les!
3. Appelle tes grands-parents.
4. Mon père fait la vaisselle.
Mon père la fait.

Can you complain about something in French?

Complain about each of the following situations.

1. Vous faites la vaisselle tous les jours. C'est injuste! C'est toujours moi qui fais la vaisselle.
2. Vos parents ne veulent pas que vous sortiez. C'est pas normal!
3. Votre frère n'aide pas votre mère. Tu ne fais rien, toi!
4. Votre mère veut que votre père fasse tout. C'est aux femmes de faire le ménage!

SECTION C

Do you know how to use direct-object pronouns with the *passé composé*?

Replace the nouns with pronouns in these sentences.

Tu les as revues?
1. Tu as revu Nadine et Corinne?
2. Vous avez fait la vaisselle?
Vous l'avez faite?

Tu les as apportés?
3. Tu as apporté les disques?
4. Je n'ai pas rencontré le blond.
Je ne l'ai pas rencontré.

Can you ask for advice?

In French, explain your problem to a friend and ask for advice.
Je veux sortir, mais mes parents veulent que je reste à la maison et que je garde ma petite sœur.
1. You want to go out, but your parents won't let you.
2. You want to meet a certain person.
J'ai envie de rencontrer Marc. Qu'est-ce que je dois faire?

Do you know how to give advice or encouragement to a friend?

Offer advice or encouragement to these friends.

1. Je suis amoureuse de lui. Je fais une boum samedi soir. Tu crois que je peux l'inviter? Pourquoi pas? Invite-le!
2. Je la trouve belle, mais je suis trop timide. Je n'ose pas lui parler.
Il faut oser. Un peu de courage!

Did you learn the forms of the verb *voir*?

Make a complete sentence, using the correct form and tense of **voir.**

1. Je / voir / souvent / copains.
2. Nous / voir / déjà / film.
3. Vous / voir / voiture / là-bas?
4. Anne / voir / toujours / westerns.

1. Je vois souvent mes copains. 2. Nous avons déjà vu ce film.
3. Vous voyez la voiture là-bas? 4. Anne voit toujours des westerns.

VOCABULAIRE

SECTION A

aider *to help*
ce que *what*
créer *to create*
dangereux, -euse *dangerous*
désolé, -e *sorry*
discuter *to discuss, argue*
le **droit** *right*
fumer *to smoke*
garder *to take care of*
une **obligation** *obligation*
pris, -e *busy, occupied*
refuser *to refuse*
la **règle** *rule*
la **santé** *health*
strict, -e *strict*
tard *late*
temps : de temps en temps *from time to time*

SECTION B

Allez! *Come on!*
arroser *to water*

les **bêtises** (f.) *nonsense*
bouger *to move, budge*
le **contraire** *opposite*
les **courses** (f.) *shopping*
la **cuisine** *cooking*
Dépêche-toi! *Hurry!*
une **discussion** *discussion*
domestique *domestic, household*
Féministe! *Feminist!*
fermer *to close*
injuste *unfair, unjust*
la *it, her*
laver *to wash*
le *it, him*
le **lendemain** *the next day*
les *them*
lis : je lis *I'm reading*
Macho! *Male chauvinist!*
le **ménage** *housework*
normal, -e *normal*
participer *to take part, participate*
la **pelouse** *lawn*
la **poubelle** *garbage can*

la **responsabilité** *responsibility*
sortir *to take out*
la **tâche** *task*
tiens *here*
tondre *to mow*
la **vaisselle** *dishes*

SECTION C

une **affaire de cœur** *love affair*
amoureux, -euse (de) *in love (with)*
un(e) **confident(e)** *confidant*
un **conseil** *advice*
conseiller *to advise*
le **courage** *courage*
hésiter *to hesitate*
meilleur, -e *best*
oser *to dare*
une **soirée** *party, evening*
sûrement *certainly*
timide *shy, timid*
vouloir dire *to mean*

ETUDE DE MOTS

In French, as in English, the prefix **in-** is sometimes used to make the base word negative. Find a French word in the list above that contains the prefix **in-**. Write the word and its English meaning. Then write the French word without the prefix **in-**. What is the base word? What does it mean in English? Now do the same for these French words: **invisible, inexact, inactif, incorrect,** and **inattentif.** If the base word begins with a consonant, the French prefix **in-** represents the nasal sound [ɛ̃], as in **invisible.** If the base word begins with a vowel, the letters **i** and **n** are sounded separately, as in **inutile.** Practice pronouncing the words that you wrote on your paper.

injuste: unfair, unjust; juste: fair, just   invisible: invisible; visible: visible   inexact: not exact; exact: exact
inactif: inactive; actif: active   incorrect: incorrect; correct: correct   inattentif: inattentive; attentif: attentive.

A LIRE

Pierre et Djemila

Avant de lire

1. Pierre et Djemila
2. Pierre a 17 ans. Djemila a 14 ans.
3. Pierre est français. Djemila est algérienne.
4. C'est un film d'amour.
5. Il finit mal.

Before you dash out to the movies with your friends, you scan, or look over very quickly, the following description of a new film that's playing nearby. You want to find out the following information:

1. The name of the film
2. The names and ages of the two heroes
3. The nationalities of the heroes
4. What kind of film it is
5. Whether or not it has a happy ending

Impossible amour

Un film de Gérard Blain avec Jean-Pierre André, Nadja Reski, Abdelkader.

C'est un très beau film, très actuel que nous propose Gérard Blain, acteur et auteur, réalisateur depuis 1970. Un excellent film sélectionné pour le 40ᵉ Festival de Cannes où, espérons-le, il obtiendra un prix. Une histoire simple, sans star, mais avec beaucoup d'émotion et une interprétation parfaite des deux jeunes héros. Pierre a dix-sept ans. Djemila, quatorze ans, vient d'une famille algérienne. Ils vivent tous deux dans une cité populaire° de Roubaix où les affaires de cœur entre Français et immigrés sont une source permanente de conflits. Cependant, la pureté et l'innocence de ces deux ados sont une réponse lumineuse à ce racisme et cette intolérance. L'amour de Pierre pour Djemila porte un degré de violence telle que° cette histoire si simple, si belle, si naïve finit très mal. *Pierre et Djemila* concerne sûrement de très nombreux spectateurs, sensibles° aux problèmes de racisme.

ados: adolescents

Activité • Trouvez les mots

1. Trouvez deux mots qui donnent le thème du film. innocence, intolérance, racisme

2. Trouvez trois adjectifs qui décrivent l'histoire. simple, belle, naïve

---

cité populaire *low-cost housing development;* **telle que** *so that;* **sensibles** *sensitive*

Ah, les parents! 📼

Alexandra, Isabelle, Patrice et Laurent sont allés au café. Ils parlent des problèmes qu'ils ont avec leurs parents, se plaignent *(complain)* de leur sévérité, des permissions qu'ils sont obligés de demander chaque fois qu'ils ont envie de faire quelque chose.

ALEXANDRA C'est simple, ils me laissent rien faire.

ISABELLE Moi, c'est pas terrible non plus. Ils doivent savoir où je vais, qui je vois, ce que je fais…

PATRICE Moi, c'est pareil. Défense de° faire de la moto, d'inviter les copains quand les parents ne sont pas à la maison, de les inviter plus d'une fois par mois même quand ils sont à la maison. Défense de dépenser° de l'argent… Défense par-ci, défense par-là. Mais toi, Laurent, tes parents sont moins sévères!

LAURENT Ah, pas du tout! Ils sont beaucoup plus sévères avec moi que ne l'étaient leurs parents avec eux!

PATRICE Comment ça?

LAURENT C'est simple. A quinze ans, mon père avait le droit d'inviter qui il voulait à la maison. Il avait les plus chouettes parents de la terre. Modernes, et tout. Maintenant, c'est pas pareil. Le week-end, mon père est fatigué. Il récupère°. On ne doit surtout pas faire de bruit. C'est pas marrant°, je vous assure. Pendant les vacances, il ne veut pas que mes copains viennent chez nous, mettent du rock, fassent du bruit. Je les envie, moi, les copains qui sont libres de faire ce qu'ils veulent.

ALEXANDRA C'est pas plus brillant chez nous. Mes deux parents travaillent. Alors, les samedis-dimanches, ils veulent la paix. Regarder la télé, lire les journaux au lit. Résultat, c'est mortel! Toi, Isabelle, c'est vrai que tu dois demander la permission à tes parents, mais, au moins, tu peux faire des programmes! Tes parents sont d'accord! L'important, c'est de savoir leur demander la permission.

ISABELLE Leur demander la permission!… Tu me fais rire°! Tu crois que c'est drôle de devoir demander des permissions du matin au soir?

PATRICE Eh, les filles, vous ne croyez pas que vous exagérez un peu? Heureusement qu'on a des parents qui s'inquiètent à notre sujet°. Ça veut dire qu'ils nous aiment.

LAURENT Eh bien moi, j'aimerais qu'ils m'aiment moins, mais qu'ils me laissent faire un peu plus ce que je veux.

PATRICE On ne peut pas tout avoir! Aujourd'hui, la vie est plus dangereuse. Alors, les parents sont plus sévères!

ALEXANDRA Suffit de philosopher! On va au cinéma?

TOUS On n'a pas la permission des parents!

---

défense de *forbidden;* **dépenser** *to spend* **récupère** *recovers;* **marrant** *fun;* **rire** *laugh;* **s'inquiètent à notre sujet** *worry about us*

Activité • Trouvez les synonymes

Trouvez dans la lecture l'équivalent des mots soulignés.

1. C'est pas <u>drôle</u>. marrant
2. Tes parents sont moins <u>stricts</u>. sévères
3. Il a les plus chouettes parents <u>du monde</u>. de la terre
4. Les <u>week-ends</u>, ils veulent récupérer. les samedis-dimanches
5. Elle doit demander des permissions <u>toute la journée</u>. du matin au soir

Activité • Et vous?

Maintenant, vous connaissez la situation chez Alexandra, Isabelle, Patrice et Laurent. Est-ce que c'est pareil chez vous?

Ma famille

Voici un poème écrit par Camille, une jeune Française. Lisez son poème pour savoir pour qui elle écrit le poème et pourquoi elle l'écrit.

Mon nom est Camille,
Et je suis une fille.
J'écris ce poème
Pour ceux que j'aime,
Ma mère, mon père,
Mes sœurs et mes frères.
Je veux leur dire
Que je suis heureuse
De vivre
Dans une famille nombreuse.

C'est vrai.
Vivre avec ses parents,
C'est pas toujours marrant.
Moi, je n'ai pas le droit
De sortir le soir.
Je dois faire mes devoirs
Et rentrer à six heures.
Il faut que je garde ma sœur,
Mon petit frère
Et que j'aide ma mère.
Mais ça ne fait rien
Parce que je suis bien
Dans ma famille.
Tout le monde est sympa,
Et même si on ne peut pas
Faire ce qu'on veut,
On est tous heureux
D'être si nombreux.

Elle écrit le poème pour sa famille pour leur dire qu'elle est heureuse de vivre dans une famille nombreuse.

Burkina Faso, formerly Upper Volta, is a country in western Africa. The name, Burkina Faso, means "land of the honest people." France governed the country until 1960.

Il faut que ma mère soit heureuse.

Ibrahim, un jeune lycéen, parle de sa famille et de sa vie au Burkina Faso, un pays d'Afrique.

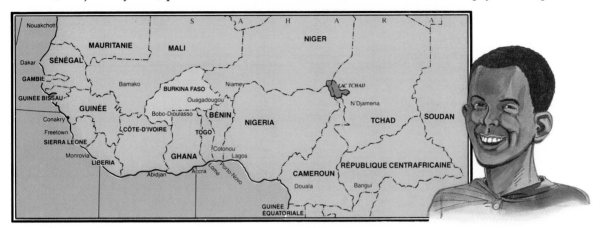

Je suis d'une famille pauvre. Ma mère est veuve°. Elle touche une pension de 8 000 F° par an. Quelquefois, sa petite sœur qui travaille à Dakar lui envoie 1 000 F. J'ai neuf frères et sœurs et je suis l'aîné des garçons. Je vais à l'école tous les jours. Je suis le seul à faire des études. Je dois aider ma mère. Je le veux. Ma mère n'a qu'une petite case° avec le sol en terre, une natte° et des jarres où elle garde des provisions. Il n'y a pas l'électricité et on doit aller aux toilettes chez les voisins.

Dans mon village, on marie les jeunes à 15 ou 16 ans. Moi, je n'ai pas de copines. Il y avait une fille qui me plaisait bien l'année dernière, mais elle a redoublé, et on n'est plus dans la même classe. Elle n'est pas venue me voir, et je n'ai pas insisté. Peut-être aussi parce qu'elle est d'une famille plus riche que la mienne. Ici, pour sortir avec filles, il faut de l'argent.

---

veuve *widow;* **8 000 F** *approx. $1,300;* **case** *hut;* **natte** *mat*

A Ouaga, les filles rêvent de boutiques chères comme «Au chic parisien». Elles veulent des robes, pas des pagnes°. Et de belles chaussures. Pour acheter un jean, j'ai dû économiser l'argent de ma bourse° pendant un mois. Les filles des familles pauvres veulent aussi être bien habillées.

Je suis au lycée technique, et on m'envie à cause de ça. Mais j'aurais préféré° faire des études littéraires : je voudrais écrire un roman qui parle de l'Afrique. L'Afrique a beaucoup de problèmes. Ici, il y a beaucoup d'enfants scolarisés, mais au niveau des résultats, c'est zéro. On est souvent 100 par classe. La plupart ne peuvent pas continuer au-delà du° primaire. Et même ceux qui vont à l'école tous les jours, et qui réussissent, n'arrivent pas à trouver de travail. Je vois les enfants de la rue, les petits mendiants° qui gardent les vélos, qui portent les paniers°. Je me dis qu'ils sont innocents. Ils n'ont jamais rien à manger, et ils ne vont jamais à l'école.

Parfois je me sens° contraint. J'accepte la souffrance. Seul, je médite, je regarde le ciel. J'ai des copains, des fils de commerçants, qui ne pensent qu'à sortir et à s'amuser.

---

pagnes *African skirt;*   **bourse** *scholarship;*   **aurais préféré** *would have preferred;*   **au-delà du** *beyond;*   **mendiants** *beggars;*
paniers *baskets;*   **me sens** *feel*

Je peux travailler pendant l'été. Toute la journée, pendant un mois chez un commerçant, pour 100 F seulement. Je dois réussir pour aider ma mère, un jour. Pour qu'elle soit° heureuse, pour que mes petits frères puissent° aussi aller à l'école tous les jours. Je suis le premier responsable de ma famille. Tout le monde me regarde. Et moi, toute la journée, je pense à cela. J'ai dit à maman qu'elle ne s'inquiète° pas. Je suis un bon fils et je vais réussir.

Activité • Devinez

Choisissez l'équivalent anglais du mot souligné dans chaque phrase.

1. Elle touche une pension de 8 000 F par an.
       a. *touches*   **b.** *pays into*   **c.** *receives*
2. J'ai neuf frères et sœurs. Je suis l'aîné des garçons.
       a. *the best*   **b.** *the oldest*   **c.** *the friend*
3. Elle est d'une famille plus riche que la mienne.
       a. *me*   **b.** *my*   **c.** *mine*
4. Je voudrais écrire un roman qui parle de l'Afrique.
       a. *Roman*   **b.** *novel*   **c.** *romance*
5. Ici, il y a beaucoup d'enfants scolarisés.
       a. *in school*   **b.** *sick*   **c.** *scolded*

Activité • Vrai ou faux? Possible answers are given.

Dites si les phrases suivantes sont vraies ou fausses, d'après la lecture. Si la phrase est fausse, corrigez-la. 1. C'est vrai. 2. C'est faux. Pour acheter un jean il doit économiser pendant un mois.

1. Ibrahim vient d'une famille nombreuse.
2. Ibrahim ne peut pas acheter de jean.
3. La majorité des enfants continuent leurs études au lycée.
4. Les filles préfèrent les vêtements africains.
5. Ibrahim et ses frères vont à l'école.
6. Ibrahim fait des études littéraires au lycée.
7. La tante d'Ibrahim travaille au Sénégal.

3. C'est faux. La plupart des enfants ne peuvent pas continuer au-delà du primaire.

---

soit (subjunctive) = *est;*   **puissent** (subjunctive) = *peuvent;*   **s'inquiète** *worry*
4. C'est faux. Les filles préfèrent les vêtements parisiens.   5. C'est faux. Il est le seul à faire des études.
6. C'est faux. Il est au lycée technique.   7. C'est vrai.

CHAPITRE 6 L'argent et les petits boulots

	BASIC MATERIAL	COMMUNICATIVE FUNCTIONS
PREMIER CONTACT	**Le bas de laine (1)** **Un compte bancaire (5)**	Reading for global comprehension and cultural awareness
SECTION A	**Murielle demande de l'argent à son père. (A1)**	**Persuading** • Asking a favor • Insisting **Socializing** • Refusing or granting a favor **Exchanging information** • Expressing a need
SECTION B	**Murielle cherche un job. (B1)** **Autres jobs (B7)** **Murielle trouve un job. (B17)**	**Persuading** • Giving advice **Exchanging information** • Inquiring about others' activities **Expressing feelings, emotions** • Expressing pleasure and disappointment
SECTION C	**Un petit boulot, pour quoi faire? (C1)**	**Exchanging information** • Talking about the advantages of working **Expressing attitudes, opinions** • Giving reasons for doing something
TRY YOUR SKILLS	**Nicole répond à une annonce. (1)**	

■ **Vocabulaire** (the sounds /y/, /œ/, and /ø/; dictation) **225**
■ **Vérifions!** **226**   ■ **Vocabulaire** **227**

A LIRE	**Le Katalavox** (A French girl's invention helps the handicapped.) **Les jeunes entrepreneurs** (French teenagers start their own businesses.) **Test : L'argent et vous** (money: a self-test)

WRITING   A variety of controlled and open-ended writing activities appear in the Pupil's Edition. The Teacher's Notes identify other activities suitable for writing practice.

COOPERATIVE LEARNING   Many of the activities in the Pupil's Edition lend themselves to cooperative learning. For guidelines, see page T14.

Scope and Sequence

GRAMMAR	CULTURE	RE-ENTRY
	French spending and saving habits	
Object pronouns **me, te, nous, vous** (A8)	Allowances and bank accounts	Object pronouns **le, la, les, lui, leur**
Other words used with **ne: plus, jamais, rien, que** (B13)	Jobs for French teenagers	Asking for advice The negative **ne... pas**
Object pronouns with the **passé composé: me, te, nous, vous** (C11)	How French teenagers spend their money	Adjectives Object pronouns with the **passé composé: le, la, les, lui, leur, y, en**

Recombining communicative functions, grammar, and vocabulary

Reading for practice and pleasure

UNIT RESOURCES **Cahier d'Activités, Cahier d'Exercices,** Unit 6 Cassettes, Transparencies 14–16 (31, 31A), Quizzes 13–15, Unit 6 Test, Midterm Test, Proficiency-Based Test 1

TEACHER-PREPARED MATERIALS **Try Your Skills** Classified ads, index cards, stop watch; **A lire** Map of France

PREMIER
CONTACT

The authentic material in **Premier Contact** introduces the theme of the unit. Concentrate only on the general content of these documents. A detailed treatment of the grammar and vocabulary is not intended. Since students should be reading for global comprehension, they need not know the meaning of every word. For this reason, new words in **Premier Contact** have been omitted from the unit vocabulary list and the French-English Vocabulary at the end of the book.

OBJECTIVES   To read for global comprehension and cultural awareness; to get acquainted with the topic

1

Le bas de laine

Have students look at the drawings of the piggy bank and the woolen sock. Explain that the French put their money in a **bas de laine** but **Les Américains mettent leur argent sous le matelas.** Draw this on the board to illustrate. Ask **Quel est votre «bas de laine», une tirelire ou un compte bancaire?** Play the cassette as students read along in their books. Have them read the two charts and then make as many statements about them as they can.

2   ## Activité • Devinez

The **bas de laine** is, of course, symbolic of money set aside. Ask students to suggest an accurate equivalent in English.

3   ## Activité • Et vous?

Students might pair off to take turns asking and answering these questions. Remind the students that they may invent imaginary or even fantastic situations if they would rather not talk about themselves.

4   ## Activité • Sondage

Have students compose survey sheets containing the questions they will ask their classmates, with space for tabulating responses:

Questions	Information
Tu reçois de l'argent de poche?	
Combien?	
Tu dépenses tout ton argent?	
Tu mets de l'argent de côté?	

Have them circulate and conduct their surveys. Then call for reports on results, without individuals being named.

5   ## UN COMPTE BANCAIRE

Play the cassette as students read along in their books. Ask questions to assess global comprehension: **Comment s'appelle ce compte bancaire? Pour qui est-ce? Nommez deux avantages d'un compte CrédiJeunes.**

6 Activité • Avez-vous compris?

For cooperative learning, form small groups and have each one find the answers to these questions. See which group can finish first with the most accurate information.

7 Activité • Imaginez

Call on volunteers to share their ideas. Have them use the verb **aller** + infinitive:

> Je vais acheter une Corvette.
> Ensuite, je vais faire le tour du monde.
> Je ne vais pas tout dépenser.
> Je vais beaucoup mettre sur un compte bancaire.

SECTION A

OBJECTIVES **To persuade:** ask a favor; insist; **to socialize:** refuse or grant a favor; **to exchange information:** express a need

CULTURAL BACKGROUND Only 36 percent of French teenagers receive a regular allowance, typically 80 to 200 francs per month, depending on their age. This doesn't mean, however, that the other 64 percent are without funds! Some find part-time jobs, and many do extra chores at home to earn money. For some students, it pays to study—half of all French parents use money as an incentive for getting good grades in school.

MOTIVATING ACTIVITY Ask students what they think the ideal allowance is: **A votre avis, l'argent de poche idéal, c'est combien?**

A1 ## Murielle demande de l'argent à son père.

Introduce the key verbs **prêter, emprunter,** and **rendre** by acting them out. Then ask students to lend you school supplies, using questions like those in the dialogue: **Vous n'avez pas un stylo à me donner? Vous pouvez me prêter un crayon?** Then have them ask you for something, using the same questions. Refuse some, saying **Impossible! Désolé, demande à... Pas question.** Accept others, saying **D'accord. Bon, voilà. Tiens, le/la/les voilà.** Reverse roles; have students refuse and accept as you ask them to lend you things. Now introduce **économe** and **dépensier/dépensière** by acting out the meanings. Ask **Etes-vous économe ou dépensier/dépensière?**

Tell the students they're going to hear Murielle and her father. Ask students to listen for the following information: how much money Murielle wants, for what purpose, whether or not she gets it, and what she must do in exchange. Then play the cassette of the first section of the dialogue. Students listen with books closed. Afterward, call for volunteers to give the information for which they were listening. Proceed in this manner for the next sections of the dialogue. Finally, replay the recording of the entire conversation as students follow along in their books.

A2 Activité • Avez-vous compris?

If you've already answered these questions orally in dealing with A1, you might assign the answers to be written for homework. Questions 4 and 5 lend themselves well to class discussion.

A3   Activité • Actes de parole

For cooperative learning, have students form groups of four to do this activity. Have each group draw the chart as suggested. Assign one category, or function, to each student. Group members should help each other.

A4   Activité • A vous maintenant!

Have students pair off. Before they begin their dialogues, have them write down the amount of money to be borrowed, a reason why, a refusal, an insistence, and a final concession or refusal. Students might use the charts that they made for A3 for some of their lines. As you listen to the dialogues, select several to be repeated for the class.

A5   Activité • Et vous?

SLOWER-PACED LEARNING   On a transparency, write the beginnings of the answers:

1. Je reçois… Je demande…
2. Je gagne… Je lave…
3. J'emprunte… Je n'emprunte pas… Je le rends…
4. Je suis…
5. Je le dépense pour…

Project the transparency so that students may refer to it as they answer the questions. Remind students that they may invent fictitious situations.

CHALLENGE   You might have students work in pairs to invent an imaginary person. Each pair should write a paragraph about that person's finances, using the questions as a guide.

A6   Savez-vous que… ?

The bank card pictured comes with **le Compte Jeans Epargne.** French young people from age 13 to 18 can open such an account only with their parents' permission. They have to make an initial deposit of 100 francs and then maintain a balance of 100 to 3000 francs. The **Jeans Club** card can be used in automatic teller machines to make deposits and withdrawals; it is not a credit card.

Write **Le budget** on the board as a heading. Underneath, draw two columns, one labeled **Dépenses quotidiennes,** the other **Dépenses exceptionnelles.** Explain **quotidienne** without using English. Ask for volunteers to suggest what they would put below each heading. Write their suggestions in the appropriate column. Then have students open their books. Have them look at the photo and the bank card as you describe each in French. Then play the cassette as students read along. As a follow-up, ask students to find out from a local bank how old one has to be to open a bank account and how much money is required to open it.

A 7 VOUS EN SOUVENEZ-VOUS?

Review the third-person direct-object pronouns by asking simple questions: **Tu vois Jacques? Tu connais Marianne? Tu connais ses parents? Tu vois le tableau?** Review **lui** and **leur**. Ask **Tu téléphones à tes amis? Tu téléphones à Marianne? A Jacques?** Then have students open their books; read with them the explanation and examples. Remind them of the correct position of the pronouns. Use only the present tense here. Object pronouns with the **passé composé** will be treated in Section C of this unit. As a check, say a few sentences that contain a direct- or indirect-object noun, and have students restate them using the appropriate pronoun. Follow this with written practice:

Jean-Luc dépense son argent.	Je comprends la question.
Marianne connaît Jacques.	Je téléphone à ma mère.
Ils aiment les pique-niques.	Tu réponds à tes parents?

Review these object pronouns in affirmative and negative commands also.

CHALLENGE You may wish to review, at the same time, the use of the pronouns **y** and **en: Il répond à la lettre. (Il y répond.) Il emprunte de l'argent. (Il en emprunte.)**

A 8 STRUCTURES DE BASE

Call attention to the first chart, making the point stated in number 1. After students have read the explanation and chart in number 2, have them repeat the sentences in the box, substituting the appropriate form of other verbs such as **accompagner, téléphoner, attendre.**

When you discuss number 3, have the students recall other verbs they might substitute for **téléphonez** in the sentence **Téléphonez-moi!**

To practice **élision** in number 4, give students a pair of verbs, one beginning with a consonant, the other with a vowel. Have them make sentences with the verbs:

chercher / aider	répondre / écouter
Elle me cherche. Elle m'aide.	Elle me répond. Elle m'écoute.

To practice **liaison** in number 5, use the pronoun **te** in sentences with a verb that begins with a vowel, and have students restate the sentences, changing the pronoun to **vous: Elle t'aide. → Elle vous aide.** Then do the same drill, changing **me** to **nous. Elle m'aide. → Elle nous aide.** Use only the present tense here. Object pronouns with the **passé composé** will be treated in Section C of this unit.

A 9 Activité • Les parents vous aident

Once again, remind students that they need not reveal their personal situation; they may invent an imaginary situation for the sake of practicing their French. You may want to have students write this activity and do the following one orally. Ask students to think of other verbs or verb phrases that they might use in this activity.

A 10 Activité • Vos ami(e)s vous aident

Rather than have students respond to each item in order, allow anyone to make an affirmative or negative statement, using an item of their choice. One student might begin: **Mes ami(e)s ne me prêtent pas d'argent.**

CHALLENGE   One student turns to another and asks **Tes amis te comprennent?** The other answers **Oui, ils (elles) me comprennent** or **Non, ils (elles) ne me comprennent pas,** and asks, in turn, of a third student **Tes ami(e)s t'aident?** The third student answers **Oui, ils (elles) m'aident** or **Non, ils (elles) ne m'aident pas.** The activity proceeds in this manner around the room.

A 11 Activité • Qu'est-ce que vous lui offrez?

After students have practiced the dialogue in pairs, reversing roles, call on volunteers to read it aloud, using the appropriate pronouns. You might choose to assign this activity to be written for homework and call on volunteers to read it aloud the following day.

A 12 Activité • Qu'est-ce que je fais?

SLOWER-PACED LEARNING   First have students make the **je** form of each verb preceded by the object pronoun **te.** Write the phrases on the board. Then have students give the appropriate request form with **-moi.** Write these on the board also. Then have students pair off to practice orally.

A 13 COMMENT LE DIRE

Have students pair off and proceed as follows. One student reads a request from the first box. The other refuses by choosing and reading an appropriate expression. The first student chooses and reads a statement to insist, and finally the second student grants the request with an expression chosen from the second box. The pair should then change roles and repeat the dialogue, choosing different sentences this time.

—Tu peux me prêter dix francs?
—Ah non! Cette fois, c'est fini!
—S'il te plaît!
—Bon, ça va pour cette fois.

A 14 Activité • A vous maintenant!

Before having students pair off, ask volunteers to identify the items on the desk in the drawing. Have students proceed as in A13, substituting items on the desk for money. Then tell them to close their books. They should recreate the same situation by placing several school supplies on their desks and make up similar dialogues.

A 15 Activité • Demandez de l'aide

You might first brainstorm excuses to complete the incomplete statements in the box on the right.

SLOWER-PACED LEARNING   First ask students to read aloud from the box on the right those expressions they would use to accept and then those they would use to refuse. You might distribute a list of possible excuses they might use to complete the refusal statements.

A 16 **COMMENT LE DIRE**

Model these sentences for the students. Then ask them to think of something they need. They should choose one of these sentences to tell you what it is. Call on volunteers until most students have expressed a need for some item.

A 17 Activité • Le lèche-vitrine

Have students practice the model for the activity, exchanging roles. Tell them that the last line might be a refusal. Students should refer to A13 and A16 and vary the expressions they use.

A 18 Activité • Qu'est-ce qu'il vous faut?

Give students time to think of their answers and to jot them down before you call on volunteers to share their thoughts.

A 19 Activité • Ecrit dirigé

Make a contest of this. Students pair off, agree on how to complete the message, and write down only the words they would add. The first pair to finish with the most accurate completions wins.

CHALLENGE   Have students respond to Murielle's request by writing a message to leave on her telephone answering machine.

A 20 Activité • Ecrivez

Read the model letter aloud to the students and check comprehension with a few questions. Students might choose an object from A17 and ask their grandparents to lend them its cost.

A 21 Activité • Ecoutez bien

Your friend Paul calls you on the phone. How do you respond to what he says? Open your book to page 203. *(pause)* Copy the suggested responses in A21 on a separate sheet of paper. *(pause)* As you listen to Paul, number the responses in the order that you would make them. Ready? **Ecoutez bien.**

—Allô? C'est Paul. Comment vas-tu?
—...
—On va au cinéma?
—...
—Il y a un bon film près de chez moi.
—...
—*L'Argent*. C'est un film français. Alors, on y va?
—...
—Demande quelques francs à tes parents.
—...
—Alors, qu'est-ce qu'on fait?

—...

—Je veux bien, mais je n'en ai pas assez. Eh bien, à bientôt.

Et maintenant, vérifions.

  __2__   Bonne idée. Qu'est-ce qu'il y a à voir?
  __1__   Ça va très bien.
  __5__   Pas question. J'ai déjà eu mon argent de poche.
  __6__   Tu ne peux pas me prêter 30 francs?
  __3__   Comment il s'appelle?
  __4__   Je veux bien, mais j'ai besoin d'argent.

SECTION B

OBJECTIVES **To persuade:** give advice; **to exchange information:** inquire about others' activities; **to express feelings, emotions:** express pleasure and disappointment

CULTURAL BACKGROUND French teenagers can earn money by baby-sitting, mowing lawns, distributing flyers, and so on. However, the practice of teenagers' working part-time is not as widespread in France as it is in the United States. Among the reasons for this difference are the longer school day in France and the pressure of lengthy homework assignments and difficult examinations. In addition, French young people don't feel the need that some Americans do for expensive items such as cars and proms.

MOTIVATING ACTIVITY Ask students about their part-time jobs: **Avez-vous un job? Où travaillez-vous? Pourquoi avez-vous un job?**

B1

Murielle cherche un job.

Tell students that Murielle is **désespérée** (act out the meaning) and that she is going to call her friend Nathalie. Then play the cassette recording of the first half of the dialogue only. Students may have books open or closed, as you choose. Pause to ask questions 1, 2, and 3 in A2. Now tell the students in French that Nathalie is going to propose four jobs to Murielle. Tell them to try to identify the four jobs and Murielle's reaction to each. Play the cassette recording of the rest of the dialogue. Ask questions 4 and 5 in A2. Finally, play the cassette again and have students role-play the dialogue.

B2

Activité • Avez-vous compris?

If you've elicited oral responses to these questions as suggested in B1, have students write the answers.

SLOWER-PACED LEARNING If students have difficulty phrasing answers to these questions, have them simply read aloud the line(s) from the dialogue that give(s) the answer.

CHALLENGE Have students write a summary of the situation in B1, using the questions in B2 as a guide.

B3   Activité • Ecrit dirigé

For cooperative learning, form small groups to complete this paragraph. One member of each group should write out the completed paragraph. Then call on the recorder from each group to read aloud the paragraph. Select the best completions and write them on a transparency for all to see. Assign the paragraph to be written for homework.

B4   Activité • Qu'est-ce qu'il faut?

First read the ads aloud to the students as they follow along in their books. Then have students pair off to prepare answers to the questions in this activity. Tell them that some answers are found in the dialogue and in the ads, but that they may need to make up their own responses. Encourage them to add to the answers they find in the book. When they've finished, ask volunteers to share their responses with the class.

B5   Activité • Vous ne pouvez pas prêter de l'argent

Remind students that they must use subjunctive forms after **il faut que.** Review the formation of the subjunctive before students pair off to do this activity.

B6   Activité • Demandez des conseils

To expand the dialogue, suggest that the first student play the "Yes, but..." game: to every suggestion from the "counselor," he or she must say «**Oui, mais...** » and explain why that idea won't work.

B7   AUTRES JOBS

Students might not understand the concept of **au pair** work, although it's becoming more common in the United States. Elicit student comments about these jobs by asking questions:

> Quel job préférez-vous? Pourquoi?
> Connaissez-vous quelqu'un qui travaille comme… ?
> Que fait un animateur/une animatrice?
> Que fait une fille qui travaille au pair?

B8   Activité • Et vous?

You might have each student ask a classmate these questions and take notes. Afterward, have him or her tell about the other's job. Finally, assign the answers to be written in the form of a paragraph for homework.

B9   Savez-vous que… ?

The **CIDJ** provides information about jobs, training, vacations, sports, and leisure activities. French young people consult the **CIDJ** primarily about job-related matters. The **CIDJ** circulates announcements for temporary jobs, teaches young people how to write résumés and letters of application, and arranges interviews for them with prospective employers.

Briefly summarize in French the main ideas of this cultural note, writing key words on the board as you go. Then play the cassette as students read along in their books. Finally, discuss the photos. Have students tell what the students in the photos are doing.

B 10 COMMENT LE DIRE

To practice the phrase, students might enjoy the challenge of giving *you* advice. Invite them to do so, but they will have to use the **vous** form. For example, you might say **Je cherche un appartement** or **Des amis viennent dîner chez nous ce soir et je ne sais pas quoi préparer.** Be sure to respond appropriately to any advice they give you.

B 11 Activité • A vous maintenant!

Students pair off. The first selects any suggestion from the first box. The second student chooses an appropriate response from the box below. Then the two students exchange roles.

B 12 VOUS EN SOUVENEZ-VOUS?

Before students open their books, ask them to recall what they've learned about the use of **ne... pas.** When they've exhausted their memories, have them open their books and read the generalizations. Pay particular attention to number 4: the use of **de.** You may want to give students more oral and written practice on each of the four points.

B 13 STRUCTURES DE BASE

To teach the negative expressions, their position, and their use, begin with **rien** and **jamais** only. Ask questions that students may answer with short negative responses using **rien** and **jamais: Qu'est-ce que vous avez dit? (Rien!) Ecoutez-vous de la musique classique? (Jamais!)**

Then practice **rien, jamais,** and **plus** in complete sentences by asking questions such as these:

> Vous travaillez toujours dans le fast-food? (Non, je ne travaille plus dans le fast-food.)
> Vous prenez quelquefois du café? (Non, je ne prends jamais de café.)

Establish **toujours** and **quelquefois** as opposites of **plus** and **jamais.**

To practice **ne... jamais** with the **passé composé,** have students tell something that they've never done: **Je n'ai jamais voyagé en France.** To practice **ne... rien** with the **passé composé,** ask questions such as **Qu'est-ce que vous avez dit (mangé, trouvé, fait, vu)?**

Practice **ne... que** first with verbs in the present tense: **Avez-vous beaucoup d'argent? (Non, je n'ai que deux dollars.)** Contrast **beaucoup** and **ne... que.** To practice **ne... que** with the **passé composé,** have students complete these sentences:

> Je n'ai demandé...   Je n'ai acheté...
> Je n'ai mangé...   Je n'ai emprunté...
> Je n'ai reçu...   Je n'ai lu...

B 14 **Activité • Travaillent-ils toujours?**

SLOWER-PACED LEARNING First point out the position of the adverb **toujours** in the question. Ask volunteers to phrase the question for each item; write it on a transparency. Do the same for the responses, using **ne... plus.** Project both transparencies as students pair off to practice the dialogues.

CHALLENGE Suggest that the student answering the question add a sentence explaining why:

— Hélène travaille toujours au pair?
— Non, elle ne travaille plus au pair. Elle doit rentrer
à l'école maintenant.

B 15 **Activité • Déjà ou jamais?**

Ask volunteers to tell which activities they've already done and which they've never done. You might then have students pair off and repeat the following dialogue for each drawing:

— Tu as déjà fait du baby-sitting?
— Oui, j'ai déjà fait du baby-sitting. (Non, je n'ai jamais
fait de baby-sitting.)

B 16 **Activité • Pas assez d'argent**

Review the numbers in French from 1 to 200 before students pair off to do this activity.

B 17 **MURIELLE TROUVE UN JOB**

First direct students' attention to the ad. Identify it by saying **C'est une petite annonce.** Read the ad aloud. Then have students look at the pictures. Describe each one in French, telling what is happening. Have the students read the phone conversation silently. Then ask them **Est-ce que Murielle a toujours son job?** Elicit **ne... plus** in the answer. Read the dialogue aloud to the students, dramatizing the verbs.

It might be fun to use a TPR technique to reinforce new vocabulary. Give commands to individuals using the new verbs: **Aboyez! Miaulez! Griffez! Tapez! Payez!**

B 18 **Activité • Avez-vous compris?**

Have students pair off, find answers to the questions, and write them down. Then call on volunteers to read their answers aloud. Write the best answers on a transparency for all to see. Continue with related personal questions:

Avez-vous déjà écrit une petite annonce? Pour quoi?
Aimez-vous les animaux, ou est-ce qu'ils vous embêtent?
Avez-vous déjà gardé des chiens?

B 19 **Activité • Qu'est-ce que Murielle peut répondre?**

Students have to think about Murielle's personality and her probable reaction to each of the five suggestions given here. Begin by replaying the cassette recordings of A1, B1, and B17 or by rereading the dialogues.

SLOWER-PACED LEARNING Tell students to reread the dialogues in A1, B1, and B17 and to pick out the lines that Murielle might say in answer to each suggestion.

B 20 Activité • Le personnage de Murielle

For cooperative learning, form groups of four. Students should refer to A1, B1, and B17 as they prepare their lists. Write a definitive list on a transparency as the groups share their results.

B 21 COMMENT LE DIRE

Ask students questions from the first column, and have them select answers from the other two columns. Continue asking various students until all the responses have been practiced.

B 22 Activité • Répondez à Murielle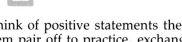

Have students take a few moments to think of positive statements they might make in each case. Then have them pair off to practice, exchanging roles. When students have finished, make each negative statement to several individuals, eliciting positive responses.

SLOWER-PACED LEARNING Play the role of Murielle yourself at first, and have students respond to you with various positive or negative statements.

B 23 Activité • Ça boume?

Students pair off. One student prepares a question for the odd-numbered items and a response for the even-numbered items. The other student does the opposite. Then the two practice their dialogues. Call on several pairs to repeat their dialogues for selected items for the class.

B 24 Activité • A vous maintenant!

SLOWER-PACED LEARNING First brainstorm with students possible substitutions for the underlined segments of the model dialogue. Then have them practice in pairs.

B 25 Activité • Et vous?

Encourage students to try to respond spontaneously and rapidly to these questions. Ask the same questions several times to different students.

CHALLENGE Students should respond to each item with a statement of pleasure or disappointment and then add at least one more statement to explain their attitude: **Les études, ça m'embête! J'ai trop de devoirs!**

B 26 **Activité • Ecrivez**

Begin by choosing one of the want ads and telling the students about the
job in French, as if you were writing a letter. This will serve as a model for
them. Or, in advance, write a model letter on a transparency. Project it and
read it to the class. Then ask students to select the ad for the job that appeals
to them. Have them work on the letter in class, using their dictionaries
and asking you for help, if necessary. Make transparencies of three or four
of the best letters and project them (without names) for all to read. Prepare
another transparency containing a selection of common errors and correct
them with the class.

B 27 **Activité • Ecoutez bien**

You're going to hear six short dialogues in which one person asks another
about his or her job. For each dialogue, decide whether the second
person likes or dislikes the job. On a separate sheet of paper, number
from 1 to 6. *(pause)* Be prepared to write **On aime** or **On n'aime pas** after
each number. **Ecoutez bien.**

1. —Alors, ce job, il est bien?
   —Bof, tu sais, moi, les animaux, ça m'embête. *(On n'aime pas.)*
2. —Tu as trouvé un job?
   —Oui, un job super! Je vends des bonbons! *(On aime.)*
3. —Tu fais toujours du baby-sitting?
   —Oui, mais j'en ai marre! *(On n'aime pas.)*
4. —C'est bien, la vente de glaces sur la plage?
   —C'est extra! Il y a la mer, il fait chaud, c'est les vacances… *(On aime.)*
5. —Tu aimes travailler dans un fast-food?
   —J'adore! Je mange des hamburgers toute la journée! *(On aime.)*
6. —Tu gardes des chiens?
   —Oui, c'est l'enfer! Ça aboie et ça casse tout! *(On n'aime pas.)*

Et maintenant, vérifions. *Read each dialogue again and give the correct answer.*

SECTION C

OBJECTIVES **To exchange information:** talk about the advantages of
working; **to express attitudes, opinions:** give reasons for doing something

CULTURAL BACKGROUND From 1950 to 1980, the buying power of the
average French person doubled. Owning a home, car, TV set, and major
household appliances came within the reach of most French people. Instead
of saving in order to buy these goods, the French learned to buy on credit,
with the result that saving money became less popular. The 1980s have seen
the growth in buying power come to a halt, and the French are finding that
they must spend a greater portion of their income in order to maintain their
standard of living. In spite of efforts by the government to encourage
saving, less and less money is being set aside for the future.

MOTIVATING ACTIVITY Ask students how they feel about jobs for
teenagers: **Est-ce que c'est important, un job? Pourquoi?**

Un petit boulot, pour quoi faire?

Play the cassette or read the letters aloud as the students follow along in their books. Pause after each letter to ask the related questions in C2 and to explain vocabulary, in French if possible.

CHALLENGE   Ask students to write their own responses to Murielle's letter.

C2   Activité • Avez-vous compris?

If you have not proceeded as suggested in C1, then form four groups. Assign each group one of the letters in C1 and have them prepare the answers to the appropriate questions. One member of the group should write down the answers. Another member should report them to the class.

C3   Activité • Comment sont-ils?

Review the gender of adjectives. Point out word families such as **travailleur—travailler—travail,** and so on. Next have students select an adjective to describe each of the letter-writing students in C1. They may select more than one adjective if they think several apply. They may also wish to add other appropriate adjectives that they recall. Ask volunteers to tell which adjectives apply to them: **Moi, je suis paresseux. Je ne suis pas travailleur.**

C4   Savez-vous que... ?

Play the cassette as students read along in their books. Then have them read the chart. Teach them how to say percentages in French. You will also want to teach them the distinction between the use of the decimal point and the comma in numbers in English and French. Where we use a decimal point, the French use a comma. Note that they say **virgule** for the decimal.

> 10% = dix pour cent
> 3.8% (English) = 3,8% (French) = trois virgule huit pour cent
> *But:* 17,5% = dix-sept et demi pour cent

Have individuals read each expenditure item and the percentage after it. Have each student write down the percentage of money he or she would like to spend for the items in the chart. Collect the papers and compile a chart for the entire class.

CHALLENGE   Have students do a similar survey and chart on how their friends and classmates spend their money. They might limit the number of those surveyed to 10 or 20 so that the percentage is easier to calculate. Ask them to make a chart, in French, that can be posted in the classroom. They should also report orally on the results.

C5   COMMENT LE DIRE

Have students repeat after you the three basic expressions shown in the box. Have them substitute a different infinitive phrase before and after each expression:

> Travailler en été, c'est un moyen de gagner de l'argent pour l'année scolaire.
> Voyager à l'étranger, c'est une occasion d'apprendre une autre langue.
> Mettre de l'argent sur un compte bancaire, c'est une façon d'économiser.

C6   **Activité • Vive les petits boulots!**

Students should complete the sentence using the pictures as cues.

C7   **Activité • Pour quoi faire?**

Point out that the three expressions on the left are not exactly interchangeable; one is more appropriate than another in certain instances:

> Avoir un job, c'est une occasion (*opportunity*) de voyager (économiser).
> Avoir un job, c'est un moyen (*a means*) de payer ses études (être indépendant).

Students might work individually to rank the reasons for having a job according to their own priorities and values.

C8   **Activité • Donnez votre avis**

Have students work in pairs. They should make a complete sentence for each item: **Aller à l'ecole, c'est une occasion d'apprendre.** Call on volunteers to share their sentences with the class.

SLOWER-PACED LEARNING   Distribute a list of possible infinitive phrases for students to choose from as they construct their sentences.

C9   **Activité • Conversation**

Students might refer to the phrases in the box in C7 and to those in C8 for possible substitutions in the dialogue.

C10   **VOUS EN SOUVENEZ-VOUS?**

Say several sentences in the present tense and ask students to restate them using an appropriate object pronoun, **y,** or **en.** Next practice with verbs in the **passé composé** by asking a question and having students respond using an appropriate pronoun: **Avez-vous téléphoné à Murielle? (Oui, je lui ai téléphoné.)** To practice the agreement of the past participle, dictate several sentences containing a verb in the **passé composé** and an object pronoun. Have these on a transparency and project each one after students have had time to write it so they may correct their work immediately.

C11   **STRUCTURES DE BASE**

After reading the grammar explanation with the students, practice using these pronouns with the **passé composé** both orally and in writing. Ask individuals questions using **vous** and have them respond with **me:**

> Pierre vous a téléphoné? (Oui, il m'a téléphoné.)
> Il vous a invité(e) à sa boum? (Oui, il m'a invité(e) à sa boum.)
> Il vous a donné son adresse? (Non, il ne m'a pas donné son adresse.)

After you ask each question of a student, have another student ask the same question of the same student, using **te** instead of **vous.** Then ask the same question of two students, using **vous** and having them both answer using **nous.** Finally, have students ask you the same question using **vous.**

Practice the agreement of the past participle by dictating two sentences and having students write only the second one. They should listen carefully to the first sentence, which gives a clue to the identity of the person to whom the pronoun refers.

> Pourquoi est-ce que tu es venue, Marie? Je t'ai invitée?
> Nous sommes les Dupont. Vous nous avez appelés?

C12 Activité • Qu'est-ce que Murielle répond?

Students respond orally to the questions as if they were Murielle. Have them first reread A1, B1, and B17 to reacquaint themselves with Murielle. They might answer in this way:

> 1. Oui, ils me donnent de l'argent de poche. (Oui, ils m'en donnent.)
> 2. Mon père m'a prêté de l'argent.

C13 Activité • Ecrit dirigé

Have students work together in pairs to prepare Murielle's statements. As students volunteer their answers, write them on a transparency for all to see.

C14 Activité • Qu'est-ce que les lycéens répondent?

Assign the roles of Marianne, Patrice, Nicole, and Marc to pairs of students who prepare the answer(s) together. Each pair should give their answer(s) orally to the entire class.

C15 Activité • Ecrit dirigé

Students should write the answers they prepared and those their classmates gave in C14.

C16 Activité • Conversation

Have students work in pairs to complete the dialogue. Then have them write a summary of the situation in the third person to practice other pronouns. They should give a name to the boy or girl in the dialogue.

C17 Activité • A vous maintenant!

CHALLENGE Students might rephrase their answers to use the same structure as the question: **Non, ce n'est pas moi qui t'ai téléphoné.** Or, they might give the name of another friend who did the activity: **Non, c'est Marie qui t'a téléphoné.**

C18 Activité • Ecrit dirigé

SLOWER-PACED LEARNING First read the letter aloud as students follow along in their books. Next distribute copies of the letter and have students underline all the words they believe will have to change. Then ask them which words they underlined; confirm or correct their decisions. Once everyone knows which words will change, have students suggest how they would change the words. Finally, assign the letter to be rewritten.

C 19 **Activité • Ecrivez**

SLOWER-PACED LEARNING As you read aloud each sentence of the directions that tells what must be said, have students compose the sentence at their desks; then ask a volunteer to write his or her version on the board or on a transparency. Proceed in the same way through the letter. For homework, have students recopy their work, to be handed in the following day.

C 20 **Activité • Ecoutez bien**

> François and Jérôme are having a friendly disagreement over money. Open your book to page 220. *(pause)* Copy the incomplete sentences in C20 on a separate sheet of paper. *(pause)* Listen to François and Jérôme's conversation and be prepared to complete the sentences. Ready? **Ecoutez bien.**
>
> | FRANÇOIS | Salut, Jérôme! Ça va? |
> |---|---|
> | JÉRÔME | Ça va... Tiens, tu t'es acheté une nouvelle chemise? |
> | FRANÇOIS | Oui. Elle est jolie, non? |
> | JÉRÔME | Et un nouveau pantalon! Eh bien, mon vieux!... Mais, on t'a offert une mobylette? |
> | FRANÇOIS | Non, je l'ai payée avec mon argent. |
> | JÉRÔME | Tes parents ne t'ont pas aidé? |
> | FRANÇOIS | Si, un peu, mais j'ai aussi travaillé pendant les vacances de Pâques. |
> | JÉRÔME | Tu as gagné beaucoup d'argent? |
> | FRANÇOIS | Oui, mais j'ai déjà tout dépensé! |
> | JÉRÔME | Et moi, tu m'as oublié? |
> | FRANÇOIS | Toi? |
> | JÉRÔME | Oui, moi... Je t'ai prêté 300 francs le mois dernier. |
> | FRANÇOIS | C'est vrai! Tu as été drôlement sympa! |
> | JÉRÔME | Trop! Quand est-ce que tu vas me rembourser? |
> | FRANÇOIS | Euh, je ne sais pas... bientôt... Mais, pour l'instant, c'est pas facile, je n'ai plus un centime. |
> | JÉRÔME | Pourquoi tu ne m'as pas remboursé avant? |
> | FRANÇOIS | J'y ai pensé, mais... |
> | JÉRÔME | Je comprends!... Tu sais, j'ai une excellente idée : tu peux me prêter ta mobylette? |
> | FRANÇOIS | Bien sûr! Essaie-la! |
> | JÉRÔME | Merci... Alors, voilà : je la prends et je te la rends quand tu me rends mon argent! Salut! |
> | FRANÇOIS | Oh, Jérôme! Attends!... Ma mobylette! *(noise of moped leaving)* |
>
> Et maintenant, vérifions.
>
> Jérôme n'est pas content parce que François ne lui a pas remboursé son argent. Alors, il prend la mobylette de François et il la rend quand François lui rend son argent.

TRY
YOUR
SKILLS

OBJECTIVE To recombine communicative functions, grammar, and vocabulary

CULTURAL BACKGROUND Announcement for **petits boulots** are often posted in the windows of the neighborhood **boulanger-pâtissier, boucher,** or **libraire.**

MOTIVATING ACTIVITY Bring in an ad for a job from the classified section of the local newspaper. Read it to the students and have them suggest the questions they would ask over the phone and the things they would say to recommend themselves for the job.

1   Nicole répond à une annonce.

Play the cassette or read the dialogue aloud as students read along in their books. You might then ask several questions to check comprehension:

> Quel âge a Nicole?
> Quel job est-ce qu'elle cherche?
> Il faut travailler combien d'heures par semaine?
> Est-ce que Nicole accepte le job?
> Quand est-ce qu'elle commence ce nouveau travail?

2   Activité • Qu'est-ce que Nicole dit?

Students might write these special information-gathering phrases in their notebooks.

3   Activité • Ecrit dirigé

You might have students copy the questions in the box. Then play the cassette recording of the dialogue. As students listen with books closed, they should write down the desired information.

4   Activité • Répondez à une annonce

For cooperative learning, divide the class into groups of three or four. They help each other prepare the questions they will ask: (1) as the person applying for the job and (2) as the employer. The answers given should clue the right questions. Students should then practice, exchanging roles.

5   Activité • Jeu de rôle

SLOWER-PACED LEARNING You should work with the entire class at first. Choose one ad and have students brainstorm questions they would ask. Then have them pair off to make up questions that they would ask as applicants. You play the role of the employer for each group.

6   Activité • Ecrivez

Students might use Murielle's ad in B17 as a guide.

CHALLENGE Have students write their ads on index cards. Collect, shuffle, and redistribute them to the students. Each student should then play the role of a prospective employer who has the desired job available and discuss the job possibilities with the writer of the ad.

7 Activité • Situations

Have students pair off. Assign one situation to each pair. After students have practiced, call on the pairs to present their dialogues.

8 Activité • A vous maintenant!

CHALLENGE Make this a competition. Have students present their extemporaneous dialogues for the class. The pair that can keep going the longest wins. Someone who has a watch with a timer should serve as contest judge.

9 Activité • Récréation

These activities are optional. Form groups and have a contest to see who can guess the correct answers in the shortest time. Students with an artistic bent might prepare similar drawings for additional contests.

PRONONCIATION

The sounds /y/, /œ/, /ø/

Open your book to page 225. *(pause)* Refer to this page as you listen to this section.

1 Ecoutez bien et répétez.

When you speak English, you don't have to use your lips very much. Some people just open and close their mouths. It's quite natural if your lips are on the lazy side, but they'll have to come alive if you're going to sound French. For nearly all French vowels, you'll have to move your lips, and more often than not, to round them.

A second thing to keep in mind is that, unlike English, French is spoken mostly in the front of the mouth. That is where most of the vowel action is. If you combine these two features of French speech—rounding and fronting—you get three sounds never heard in English: /y/, /œ/, and /ø/.

1. After the French **r**-sound, the sound most worth working on is the sound /y/ as you hear it in **Une rue sans issue.** Although the sound /y/ is spelled with a **u,** it's not pronounced like one. That's the first thing to keep in mind. It doesn't even belong to the same family as the **u,** that is, the family of back vowels. In fact, your friendly dictionary draws your attention to this fact by writing the sound, not with a **u,** but with a **y,** placing it in the family of front vowels along with /e/ and /i/. So think of it as a sort of rounded /i/. That's the best way to start getting a handle on this exotic vowel.

Let's try it. Take a deep breath and say /i/ as in *we*, as long and as tightly as you can. *(pause)* Now do this again, but this time gradually push your lips forward: round them tightly while keeping the sound /i/ going.

You'll hear it being transformed into a different sound. If you hear a whistling sound, that's okay. You're on the right track. Do this until you get the feel of the new sound. *(pause)*

Now try out your new sound in some word series going from /i/ to /y/. Listen to them and repeat word for word: **si, su, sur; dit, du, dure; riz, rue, rhume; fit, fut, fume.** So far, so good.

You've probably noticed that many words spelled with the letter **u** look the same in English as they do in French. But they do sound different. Be careful to pronounce them the French way when speaking French. Listen to the English and the French pronunciations of these words, and repeat the French: *tube*/**tube**, *cube*/**cube**, *pure*/**pure**, *cure*/**cure**, *humid*/**humide**, *bureau*/**bureau**, *volume*/**volume**, *ridicule*/**ridicule**. Did you hear the /iu/ or the /u/ in the English and the /y/ you said in French? But sometimes in English, for the same spelling you say /ə/ as in *nerve*. Listen to these and repeat the French: *surface*/**surface**, *subtle*/**subtil**, *buffet*/**buffet**, *minute*/**minute**.

2. Seeing that your lips are still rounded or at least in shape, you might as well go on to another important sound that is basic for learning to say the masculine article **un** correctly. You'll first have to learn to say /œ/. How do you do it?

Start with your newly acquired sound /y/. First take a deep breath and say a long /yyyyy/. *(pause)* Do it again, this time gradually opening your mouth as wide as possible, lips still rounded as if you were trying to hold a ping-pong ball. *(pause)* Once you've got this sound, try saying **œuf** and **bœuf.** *(pause)* Remember, this is a rounded vowel like an open /ɔ/ and a front vowel like an open /ɛ/. In fact, your dictionary writes it that way, combining both sounds as in the word **œuf.** Try this out with some common words. Repeat these: **œuf, neuf, seul, peuvent, fleuve, jeune.** In some words, the sound /œ/ is spelled **œ**; in others, it is spelled **eu**, as in **fleuve.** But no matter. You'll also find this sound in many words ending in an **r**-sound. Since you already know how to say the final **r**-sound, try these words: **sœur, cœur, beurre, fleur, peur, pleure, erreur, valeur.**

3. You now have two of the most important and most typical sounds of French. All you need is one more to complete the set of front rounded French vowels. It should be easy from here on. Start with the last sound, the /œ/. Make a long one /œœœœ/. While you're doing this, gradually close your mouth a little, pushing your lips even farther forward, and you'll get a /øøøø/. *(pause)* You'll hear a sound that is pretty close to the sound /ə/ as in **le, me, ce, te.** Once again: /œœœ/—/øøøø/. *(pause)*

Now try these pairs: **œuf—œufs, bœuf—bœufs, un œil—des yeux.** The sound /ø/ appears in words you'll be using often. Try some: **peu, deux, ceux, veut, mieux, monsieur.**

2 | **Ecoutez et lisez.**

Now try these three sounds all together. Read aloud the dialogues. I'll say each line after you.

— Tu as vu la lune. — Qui est venu? — Qu'est-ce que tu as bu?
— Ça t'a plu? — Tu l'as vu? — Du jus pur.

— Tu es seule? Où est ta sœur?
— Chez le coiffeur.

— Pourquoi tu pleures? Tu as peur de faire des erreurs?
— Non, c'est une affaire de cœur.

Now read the two sentences aloud. I'll repeat each after you.

Le vieux monsieur n'a que deux cheveux.
Il ne pleut pas quand le ciel est bleu.

3

Copiez les phrases suivantes pour préparer une dictée.

Write the following sentences from dictation. First listen to the sentence as it is read to you. Then you will hear the sentence again in short segments, with a pause after each segment to allow you time to write. Finally you will hear the sentence a third time so that you may check your work. Let's begin.

1.—Je n'ai pas reçu d'argent. Mes parents ont refusé. Je n'ai pas reçu *(pause)* d'argent. *(pause)* Mes parents *(pause)* ont refusé. *(pause)* Je n'ai pas reçu d'argent. Mes parents ont refusé.

2.—Trouve-toi un job. Voici : «On cherche une jeune fille sérieuse pour garder deux enfants le jeudi soir au vingt-deux, rue du Cherche-Midi.» Trouve-toi un job. *(pause)* Voici : *(pause)* «On cherche *(pause)* une jeune fille sérieuse *(pause)* pour garder deux enfants *(pause)* le jeudi soir *(pause)* au vingt-deux, *(pause)* rue du Cherche-Midi.» *(pause)* Trouve-toi un job. Voici : «On cherche une jeune fille sérieuse pour garder deux enfants le jeudi soir au vingt-deux, rue du Cherche-Midi.»

3.—Ah non. Pas d'enfants. J'ai déjà gardé mes neveux. Ça suffit. Ah non. *(pause)* Pas d'enfants. *(pause)* J'ai déjà gardé *(pause)* mes neveux. *(pause)* Ça suffit. *(pause)* Ah non. Pas d'enfants. J'ai déjà gardé mes neveux. Ça suffit.

4.—Voilà, on cherche des serveuses. Tu peux téléphoner à Monsieur Durand au Bœuf sur le Toit. Voilà, *(pause)* on cherche des serveuses. *(pause)* Tu peux téléphoner *(pause)* à Monsieur Durand *(pause)* au Bœuf sur le Toit. *(pause)* Voilà, on cherche des serveuses. Tu peux téléphoner à Monsieur Durand au Bœuf sur le Toit.

5.—Surtout pas. Je déteste l'odeur des frites. Surtout pas. *(pause)* Je déteste *(pause)* l'odeur des frites. *(pause)* Surtout pas. Je déteste l'odeur des frites.

6.—Toi, tu es paresseuse. Tu ne sais pas ce que tu veux. Toi, tu es paresseuse. *(pause)* Tu ne sais pas *(pause)* ce que tu veux. *(pause)* Toi, tu es paresseuse. Tu ne sais pas ce que tu veux.

VERIFIONS!

Have students work individually and write down the expressions for the first five exercises. Then have students work in pairs to make up several different dialogues using the expressions. After students have completed the sixth exercise as instructed in their books, you might have them reverse the subject and object. For example, **Elle me prête quinze francs** would become **Je lui prête quinze francs.**

SECTION B

Elicit several extemporaneous responses from volunteers for each exercise before assigning them to be written. For additional practice with the negative expressions, provide items similar to those in the second exercise, including or omitting the English equivalents, as you choose.

SECTION C

As a variation on the first exercise, you might ask students to give different reasons for going to school, for traveling, and so on. Call for volunteers to write their answers to the last exercise on the board in order to direct attention to the agreement of the past participle.

VOCABULAIRE

Give the students a time limit. They may work individually or in small groups. See who can make up the greatest number of sentences using vocabulary from this list within the time allotted. Award the maximum number of points for sentences containing no errors.

ETUDE DE MOTS

You might make a speed-and-accuracy contest of this activity. Once again, students may work individually or in small groups.

A LIRE

OBJECTIVE   To read for practice and pleasure

LE KATALAVOX

Have students locate **Alsace** on a map of France. If they have difficulty finding the answers to the questions in **Avant de lire,** the answers to the first two questions are in the first line of the story. For the answer to the third question, students should begin scanning at the top of page 229.

Next play the cassette or read the article aloud as students follow along in their books. Ask students to find at least three applications of Martine's invention.

Activité • Qu'est-ce que c'est?

Tell students to locate the sentences in the reading selection that contain these words and to try to make an intelligent guess as to their meanings according to the context.

Activité • Imaginez

Students could either (1) write a paragraph or (2) prepare a brief oral presentation about their inventions. Encourage the use of drawings or designs to accompany their reports.

Activité • Ecrivez

Students should refer to the paragraph in the article which describes the person they choose.

CHALLENGE   Students select a major French inventor, such as Montgolfier, Curie, Pasteur, or Pascal. They research the inventor's contribution and write a thank-you note in French.

LES JEUNES ENTREPRENEURS

Form several small groups. Assign one **entrepreneur** to each group. Students should read the paragraph and listen to the cassette. Each group must then plan a presentation for the class.

Activité • Avez-vous compris?

Have students reread the selection to find the information indicated and to complete their charts.

Activité • Qu'en pensez-vous?

Students might choose their favorite entrepreneur(s) and work in pairs or small groups to write brief paragraphs, using these questions as a guide.

Activité • Et vous?

Encourage students to think back to their early childhood. Many may have made lemonade to sell, offered to rake leaves for the neighbors, and so on. They may even have photos at home of their **entreprise**, which they can show while reporting to the class or use to accompany a written account, as you choose.

TEST : L'ARGENT ET VOUS

Explain to students that this questionnaire offers an opportunity to examine their attitudes toward money. They should listen to the cassette first. Then they should read through the test silently, selecting their answers as they go. Then they determine their totals and their classification, as directed under **Résultats du test**. Ask students to rewrite the description of their classification from their own point of view, changing the subject from **vous** to **je.** They might change sentences in the description of their classification if they feel the sentences do not apply to them.

Activité • Donnez votre opinion

Have volunteers answer the first question orally. Ask all students to think seriously about the second question and then to write down at least one complete sentence. Call on volunteers to read their sentences to the class.

L'argent et les petits boulots

French young people have a language all their own. *Les petits boulots* are jobs. How do French teenagers get their money? Do they receive an allowance? Do they have part-time jobs? And when they earn money, do they tend to spend it or save it?

In this unit you will:

PREMIER CONTACT	get acquainted with the topic
SECTION A	ask a favor . . . insist . . . refuse or grant a favor . . . express a need
SECTION B	give advice . . . inquire about others' activities . . . express pleasure and disappointment
SECTION C	talk about the advantages of working . . . give reasons for doing something
TRY YOUR SKILLS	use what you've learned
A LIRE	read for practice and pleasure

PREMIER CONTACT getting acquainted with the topic

The authentic material in Premier Contact introduces the theme of the unit and is to be used for global comprehension only.

1   Le bas de laine 📼

Beaucoup de jeunes français ont leur «bas de laine». Ils mettent leur argent de poche dans leur tirelire ou sur leur compte bancaire. D'autres dépensent tout leur argent.

Une tirelire

Le bas de laine

L'argent de poche
(en moyenne)

	par semaine	par mois
5–11 ans	11 F	
12–14 ans		60 F
15–18 ans		150 F

Le bas de laine des 15–20 ans
«Mettez-vous de l'argent de côté?»

	Dépense tout	En met de côté	Ne peut pas dire
Ensemble	26 %	64 %	10 %
Hommes	29 %	63 %	8 %
Femmes	24 %	65 %	11 %
15–16 ans	20 %	69 %	11 %
17–18 ans	20 %	70 %	10 %
19–20 ans	40 %	52 %	8 %

2   Activité • Devinez

Bien sûr, les jeunes français ne mettent pas leur argent dans un vrai bas de laine. Qu'est-ce que le «bas de laine» signifie?   bas de laine: (lit.) wool stocking; (fig.) nest egg

3   Activité • Et vous?

1. Recevez-vous de l'argent de poche? Combien? Par semaine? Par mois?
2. Dépensez-vous tout votre argent ou mettez-vous de l'argent de côté?
3. Avez-vous déjà ouvert un compte bancaire?
4. Mettez-vous de l'argent dans une tirelire? Pourquoi?

4   Activité • Sondage   Possible questions are given.

Demandez à vos camarades de classe s'ils reçoivent de l'argent de poche et combien, s'ils dépensent tout leur argent ou s'ils mettent de l'argent de côté.
Est-ce que tu reçois de l'argent de poche? Combien reçois-tu?
Est-ce que tu dépenses le tout ou est-ce que tu mets de l'argent de côté?

5 UN COMPTE BANCAIRE

En France, de nombreuses banques essaient d'attirer les jeunes de 13 ans.

CrédiBank annonce :

CrédiJeunes

Un compte bancaire réservé à vous, les jeunes! Faites comme plus d'un million de vos copains! Protégez vos économies!
Placez votre argent de poche sur le compte bancaire

CrédiJeunes!
De vraies économies

- Versez votre premier dépôt (minimum 200 F).
- Touchez 6,5% d'intérêts.

Des avantages uniques

- Le Club CrédiJeunes
- Un bulletin spécialement édité pour vous
- Des places de cinéma gratuites

Des opérations faciles

- Faites vos retraits et vos versements librement

au guichet

dans plus de 10 000 succursales
ou
au distributeur automatique

grâce à une carte magnétique.

6 Activité • Avez-vous compris?

Répondez aux questions suivantes d'après la publicité.

1. Pour ouvrir un compte bancaire les jeunes français ont besoin de combien d'argent? *1. Ils ont besoin de 200 F au minimum.*
2. Combien d'intérêts touchent-ils dans cette banque? *2. Ils touchent 6,5% d'intérêts.*
3. Où peuvent-ils faire des retraits et des dépôts? *3. Ils peuvent faire des retraits et des dépôts au guichet ou au distributeur automatique.*

7 Activité • Imaginez   *Possible answer is given.*

Vous avez reçu beaucoup d'argent. Qu'est-ce que vous faites de l'argent? Dépensez-vous le tout? Qu'est-ce que vous achetez? Mettez-vous de l'argent de côté? Combien? Mettez-vous de l'argent sur un compte bancaire ou achetez-vous des valeurs *(stocks)*?
J'ai reçu 500 dollars. J'ai mis 250 dollars de côté sur un compte bancaire. Je vais acheter des vêtements et un vélo avec le reste.

asking a favor . . . insisting . . . refusing or granting a favor . . . expressing a need

Comment faites-vous quand vous avez besoin d'argent? En empruntez-vous à vos parents ou cherchez-vous un job? Les parents de Murielle lui donnent un peu d'argent de poche par semaine, mais elle le dépense très vite.

A1

Murielle demande de l'argent à son père.

Il y a des personnes économes et d'autres dépensières. Murielle fait plutôt partie de la deuxième catégorie.

(Vendredi soir)

MURIELLE   Papa, tu n'as pas 30 francs à me donner?
SON PÈRE   Pour quoi faire?
MURIELLE   Pour aller au cinéma avec Nathalie.
SON PÈRE   Et ton argent de poche?
MURIELLE   Il est déjà dépensé.
SON PÈRE   Eh bien!
MURIELLE   Allez, papa, c'est la dernière fois!
SON PÈRE   Tu as demandé à ta mère?
MURIELLE   Oui.
SON PÈRE   Qu'est-ce qu'elle a dit?
MURIELLE   «Demande à ton père.»
SON PÈRE   Bravo! Voilà une femme économe! Tiens, les voilà. Mais, en échange, je veux que tu me laves la voiture.
MURIELLE   D'accord!

(Le week-end suivant)

MURIELLE   Papa, tu peux me prêter de l'argent?
SON PÈRE   Encore!
MURIELLE   Oui, il faut que je m'achète une jupe.
SON PÈRE   Mais tu en as des centaines dans ton placard!
MURIELLE   Elles sont démodées.
SON PÈRE   Désolé, mais c'est impossible.
MURIELLE   Allez, papa, sois gentil! C'est pas cher, une jupe!
SON PÈRE   Combien tu veux?
MURIELLE   Oh, juste 150 F.
SON PÈRE   Bon, voilà 100 F.
MURIELLE   Merci, papa!

(Quinze jours plus tard)

MURIELLE	Tiens, papa, je te rends tes 100 F.
SON PÈRE	Déjà!
MURIELLE	J'ai reçu de l'argent de grand-mère pour ma fête.
SON PÈRE	Félicitations. Tu lui as dit merci?
MURIELLE	Bien sûr... Je suis ravie... Mais... euh... J'ai besoin de 50 F... Tu ne peux pas me...
SON PÈRE	Ah non! Cette fois-ci, c'est fini!
MURIELLE	S'il te plaît, papa! C'est pour la fête des Pères. C'est pour t'offrir un cadeau!

"La Fête des Pères" is celebrated on the third Sunday in June.

A2 Activité • Avez-vous compris? Possible answers are given.

Répondez aux questions suivantes d'après les dialogues dans A1.

1. Pourquoi est-ce que Murielle veut emprunter de l'argent à son père? Pouvez-vous trouver trois raisons?
2. Murielle demande de l'argent à son père. Quelles autres sources d'argent a-t-elle?
3. Qu'est-ce que Murielle a fait en échange des 30 francs?
4. Trouvez-vous Murielle économe ou dépensière?
5. Murielle demande de l'argent à son père pour lui acheter un cadeau. Trouvez-vous que c'est normal? 1. Murielle veut emprunter de l'argent pour aller au cinéma, pour acheter une jupe et pour acheter un cadeau. 2. Ses autres sources sont sa mère, sa grand-mère et son argent de poche. 3. Elle a lavé la voiture de son père. 4. Elle est dépensière. 5. Non, ce n'est pas normal.

A3 Activité • Actes de parole

Trouvez dans les dialogues entre Murielle et son père deux façons (ways) de demander de l'argent, deux façons de refuser de l'argent, deux façons de persuader quelqu'un et deux façons de donner de l'argent.

Demander	Refuser	Persuader	Donner
—Tu n'as pas... F à me donner? —Tu peux me prêter... ? —J'ai besoin de...	—Désolé, c'est impossible. —Ah non, cette fois-ci, c'est fini.	—Allez, sois gentil! —C'est la dernière fois! —S'il te plaît...	—Bon, voilà... —Tiens, les voilà...

A4 Activité • A vous maintenant!

Travaillez avec un(e) camarade de classe. Votre camarade joue le rôle de votre père ou de votre mère. Vous lui demandez de l'argent. Vous essayez de le/la persuader. Il/Elle refuse ou accepte de donner de l'argent. Changez de rôle.

A5 Activité • Et vous? Possible answers are given.

1. Recevez-vous de l'argent de poche ou demandez-vous de l'argent à vos parents chaque fois que vous en avez besoin? 1. Je reçois 20 dollars d'argent de poche par mois.
2. Gagnez-vous de l'argent? Comment faites-vous? Quand?
3. Empruntez-vous de l'argent à vos amis? Le rendez-vous tout de suite?
4. Etes-vous économe ou dépensier/dépensière?
5. Qu'est-ce que vous faites avec votre argent? Le dépensez-vous? Pour quoi faire?

2. Je gagne de l'argent de temps en temps quand je garde des enfants.
3. Oui, j'emprunte quelquefois de l'argent à mes amis. Je le rends tout de suite.
4. Je suis économe.
5. J'en mets un peu de côté. J'achète quelquefois des vêtements, et je vais souvent au cinéma.

L'argent et les petits boulots 197

En général, les jeunes français reçoivent un peu d'argent de poche chaque semaine pour leurs dépenses quotidiennes *(daily)*. Avec cet argent, ils peuvent prendre le bus ou déjeuner à midi s'ils ne mangent pas à la cantine de l'école. Pour les dépenses exceptionnelles : sortir, acheter des vêtements ou partir en vacances, ils demandent à leurs parents de les aider. Souvent, ils doivent faire quelque chose en échange : laver la voiture ou tondre la pelouse. Quand ils ont vraiment besoin d'argent, ils cherchent un job.

On peut ouvrir un compte en banque à l'âge de treize ans. On a alors une carte bancaire pour retirer de l'argent dans des distributeurs automatiques. On apprend ainsi à faire un budget.

For more information on French savings accounts, see p. T126.

BNP: Banque Nationale de Paris

You've already seen the direct-object pronouns **le, la,** and **les** and the indirect-object pronouns **lui** and **leur.**

Object Pronouns		
	Direct	*Indirect*
Singular	**le, la**	**lui**
Plural	**les**	**leur**

You remember that the direct-object pronouns **le, la,** and **les** may represent people or objects.
   Elle persuade **son père.** Elle **le** persuade.
   Elle dépense **son argent.** Elle **le** dépense.

Do you recall that the indirect-object pronouns **lui** and **leur** only represent people?
   Elle emprunte de l'argent **à son père.** Elle **lui** emprunte de l'argent.
   Elle téléphone **à ses amies.** Elle **leur** téléphone.

STRUCTURES DE BASE
The object pronouns me, te, nous, *and* vous

1. The object pronouns **me,** *me,* **te,** *you,* **nous,** *us,* and **vous,** *you,* can be used as either direct or indirect objects.

Object Pronouns		
	Direct	Indirect
Singular	me te le, la	me te lui
Plural	nous vous les	nous vous leur

2. The object pronouns **me, te, nous,** and **vous** come before the verb to whose meaning they are most closely related. In the affirmative command, the pronoun follows the verb and, in writing, is separated from it by a hyphen.

Elle	**nous** aide.			
Elle ne	**nous** aide	pas.		
Elle ne peut pas	**nous** aider.		*But,*	Aidez-**nous!**
Ne	**nous** aidez	pas!		

3. In an affirmative command, **moi** is used instead of **me.**
    Ne **me** téléphonez pas. *But,* Téléphonez-**moi.**

4. **Elision** occurs when **me** or **te** is used before a verb that begins with a vowel.
    Elle m'écoute.   **Elle t'écoute.**

5. **Liaison** occurs when **nous** or **vous** comes before a verb that begins with a vowel.
    Elle nous͡ aide.   **Elle vous͡ aide.**

Object agreement with the past participle is discussed in C11, p. 218.

A9   Activité • **Les parents vous aident**   Possible answers are given.

Est-ce que votre père ou votre mère fait ces choses pour vous ou pour vous et vos frères et sœurs?

préparer le petit déjeuner   — Ma mère me (nous) prépare le petit déjeuner.
                         (Ma mère ne me (nous) prépare pas le petit déjeuner.)

1. Ma mère m' (nous) achète...   3. Mon père m' (nous) aide à...   5. Mon père et ma mère m' (nous) écoutent...
1. acheter les vêtements   **3. aider à faire les devoirs**   **5. écouter**
2. donner de l'argent de poche   **4. offrir des cadeaux**   **6. donner des conseils**
2. Ma mère me (nous) donne...   4. Mon père m' (nous) offre...   6. Ma mère et mon père me (nous) donnent...

A10   Activité • **Vos ami(e)s vous aident**

Est-ce que vos ami(e)s font ces choses pour vous?

écouter   — Ils/Elles m'écoutent.   Point out that "d'" and "de" must be used
          (Ils/Elles ne m'écoutent pas.)   in negative answers to items 5 and 7.

1. comprendre   **3. inviter**   **5. prêter de l'argent**   **7. envoyer des lettres**
2. aider   **4. téléphoner**   **6. raconter leurs secrets**   **8. conseiller**

1. Ils/Elles (ne) me comprennent (pas).   2. Ils/Elles (ne) m'aident (pas).   3. Ils/Elles (ne) m'invitent (pas).   4. Ils/Elles (ne) me téléphonent (pas).   5. Ils/Elles (ne) me prêtent (pas d') de l'argent.   6. Ils/Elles (ne) me racontent (pas) leurs secrets. 7. Ils/Elles (ne) m'envoient (pas de) des lettres.   8. Ils/Elles (ne) me conseillent (pas).

L'argent et les petits boulots   199

A11 Activité • Qu'est-ce que vous lui offrez?

Travaillez avec un(e) camarade. Répétez le dialogue suivant en employant les pronoms **me** et **te**.

— C'est bientôt ton anniversaire. Qu'est-ce que je peux __t'__ offrir?
— Je ne sais pas. Tu peux peut-être __m'__ acheter un disque.
— Bonne idée! Tu peux __me__ prêter de l'argent?
— Combien veux-tu? Je ne peux pas __te__ prêter beaucoup.
— Oh, pas beaucoup. C'est pour __t'__ offrir un disque.
— Ah bon! Tiens, voilà 100 F. Comme ça tu peux __m'__ offrir un très bon disque!

1. —Je te prête le disque de jazz? —Non, prête-moi plutôt le disque de rock.   2. —Je t'achète des fleurs?
                                                                      —Non, achète-moi plutôt des bonbons.

A12 Activité • Qu'est-ce que je fais?

3. —Je t'offre un cadeau?
    —Non, offre-moi plutôt de l'argent.

Travaillez avec un(e) camarade. Votre camarade offre de faire quelque chose pour vous, mais vous préférez autre chose.   4. —Je te donne 100 F? —Non, donne-moi plutôt 200 F.

                                   5. —Je t'aide à faire la vaisselle?

offrir un livre (un disque)   — Je t'offre un livre?   —Non, aide-moi plutôt à faire les courses.

7. —Je te téléphone ce soir?   — Non, offre-moi plutôt un disque. 6. —Je t'attends au café?
  —Non, téléphone-moi plutôt demain matin.   —Non, attends-moi plutôt à la patinoire.

1. prêter le disque de jazz (le disque de rock)
2. acheter des fleurs (des bonbons)
3. offrir un cadeau (de l'argent)
4. donner 100 F (200 F)
5. aider à faire la vaisselle (faire les courses)
6. attendre au café (à la patinoire)
7. téléphoner ce soir (demain matin)
8. envoyer une lettre (une carte postale)

    8. —Je t'envoie une lettre?
      —Non, envoie-moi plutôt une carte postale.

A13 COMMENT LE DIRE

Asking a favor and insisting

ASKING	INSISTING
Tu peux me prêter 10 francs?	S'il te (vous) plaît!
Tu ne peux pas me prêter 100 francs?	Sois (Soyez) sympa!
Tu as 100 francs à me prêter?	Sois (Soyez) gentil(le)!
Tu n'as pas 100 francs à me prêter?	Allez!
Prête-moi 100 francs, s'il te plaît.	

Refusing or granting a favor

REFUSING	GRANTING
Ah non! Cette fois, c'est fini!	Bon, ça va pour cette fois.
Pas question!	D'accord.
Demande à ta mère!	Bon, voilà.
Désolé(e), c'est impossible.	Tiens, le/la/les voilà.

Activité • A vous maintenant!

Regardez ce qu'il y a sur la table de votre
camarade de classe. Demandez-lui de vous
prêter quelque chose. Il/Elle refuse. Vous
insistez. Enfin, il/elle vous donne ce que
vous demandez.

—Tu peux me prêter ta calculette?
—Pas question, tu l'empruntes tout le temps.
—S'il te plaît, sois gentil(le).
—Je dois faire mes devoirs de maths.
—Allez, juste pour 15 minutes...
—Tiens, voilà, mais rends-la moi
dans 15 minutes.
—Merci.

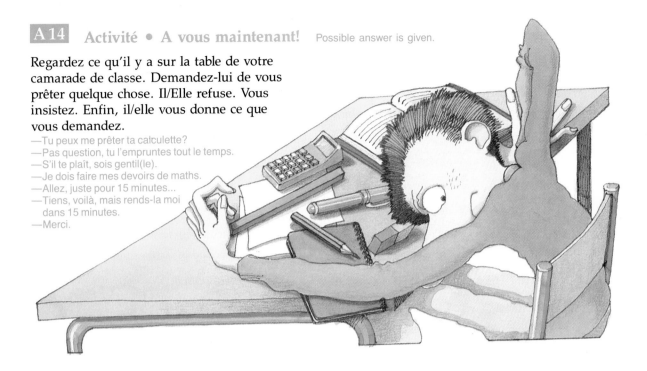

Activité • Demandez de l'aide

Demandez à votre ami(e) s'il (si elle) peut faire ces choses pour vous. Il/Elle accepte ou refuse.
Changez de rôle.

aider à faire les devoirs — Tu peux m'aider à faire mes devoirs?
— Bien sûr! (Désolé(e), je ne peux pas.)

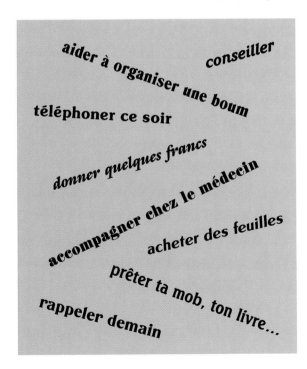

aider à organiser une boum
conseiller
téléphoner ce soir
donner quelques francs
accompagner chez le médecin
acheter des feuilles
prêter ta mob, ton livre...
rappeler demain

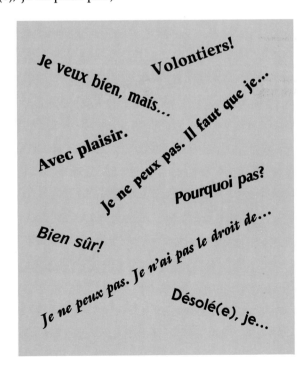

Je veux bien, mais...
Volontiers!
Avec plaisir.
Je ne peux pas. Il faut que je...
Pourquoi pas?
Bien sûr!
Je ne peux pas. Je n'ai pas le droit de...
Désolé(e), je...

L'argent et les petits boulots 201

COMMENT LE DIRE
Expressing a need

Il me faut (absolument) un livre de maths.
Il faut que je m'achète une jupe.
J'ai (vraiment) besoin de 50 F.

A 17 Activité • **Le lèche-vitrine** Possible answers are given.

—Tu peux me prêter 200 F?
—Pour acheter quoi?
—Il faut que je m'achète un jean.
—Tiens, les voilà.

Vous êtes dans un centre commercial avec votre ami(e). Vous avez envie de tout acheter, mais vous n'avez pas assez d'argent. Vous lui demandez qu'il/elle vous en prête. Faites un dialogue et changez de rôle.

— Tu peux me prêter 100 F?
— Pour quoi faire?
— J'ai besoin d'un tee-shirt.
— Tiens, les voilà.

—Prête-moi 120 F, s'il te plaît.
—Pour acheter quoi?
—Il me faut une calculatrice (calculette).
—Demande à ta mère!

—Tu ne peux pas me prêter 3500 F?
—Pour quoi faire?
—Il faut que je m'achète une mobylette.
—Demande à tes parents.

Activité • **Qu'est-ce qu'il vous faut?** Possible answers are given.

Avez-vous absolument besoin de quelque chose? Qu'est-ce qu'il vous faut pour... ?

1. votre chambre
2. l'école
3. être heureux/heureuse
4. être indépendant(e)

1. Pour ma chambre, il me faut absolument... **2.** Pour l'école, il me faut absolument...
3. Pour être heureux(se), il me faut absolument... **4.** Pour être indépendant(e), il me faut absolument...

A 19 Activité • **Ecrit dirigé**

Murielle a laissé un message sur le répondeur d'une amie pour lui demander quelque chose. Mais le répondeur marche mal et le message est pratiquement inaudible. Pouvez-vous l'écrire?

Salut. Je... téléphone pour... demander quelque chose. Est-ce que tu peux... prêter ton livre de maths? J'en ai... besoin pour l'examen jeudi. Merci. Murielle.
te *te* *me* *absolument*

A 20 Activité • **Ecrivez**

Vous avez encore dépensé votre argent de poche. Mais cette fois-ci, vos parents ne veulent pas vous en donner. Vous écrivez alors une lettre à vos grands-parents. Vous leur demandez de vous prêter un peu d'argent. Expliquez-leur pourquoi vous en avez besoin.

lundi 23 janvier

Chers grands-parents,

Devinez! J'ai eu 18 à mon interro d'anglais. C'est bien, non? Pourtant, papa ne veut pas me prêter d'argent pour acheter le dernier disque de Dire Straits. Quelle barbe! C'est très bon pour mon anglais, les disques ... Mais papa ne comprend pas très bien. Est-ce que vous pouvez me prêter 50 francs?

Grosses bises de Françoise

A 21 Activité • **Ecoutez bien** [cassette icon] For script and answers, see pp. T129–30.

Votre ami vous téléphone. Choisissez vos réponses dans la liste suivante. Indiquez l'ordre de vos réponses en écrivant les numéros de 1 à 6 à côté.

_____ Bonne idée. Qu'est-ce qu'il y a à voir?
_____ Ça va très bien.
_____ Pas question. J'ai déjà eu mon argent de poche.

_____ Tu ne peux pas me prêter 30 francs?
_____ Comment il s'appelle?
_____ Je veux bien, mais j'ai besoin d'argent.

giving advice . . . inquiring about others' activities . . . expressing pleasure and disappointment

Murielle n'arrive pas à faire un budget. Elle est toujours à court d'argent. Comment est-ce qu'elle peut faire pour acheter ce qui lui plaît? Il y a deux solutions.

B1 ## Murielle cherche un job.

Murielle n'a plus d'argent. Sur les conseils de son amie Nathalie, elle va chercher un job.

MURIELLE   Je suis désespérée. J'ai envie d'offrir un cadeau à mes grands-parents, mais je n'ai rien sur mon compte.

NATHALIE   Désolée, mais cette fois-ci je ne peux rien te prêter. Je n'ai que 30 francs et il faut que je les garde pour prendre le bus. Tu n'as jamais d'argent! Pourquoi est-ce que tu n'économises pas?

MURIELLE   J'ai essayé, je ne peux pas.

NATHALIE   Alors pourquoi est-ce que tu ne cherches pas un job?

MURIELLE   Tu as raison. Un job! Voilà la solution!

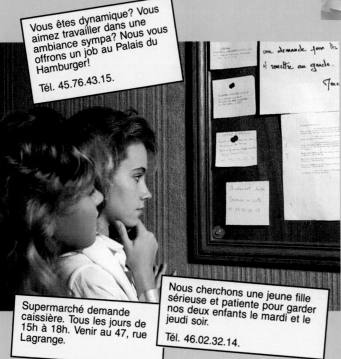

Vous êtes dynamique? Vous aimez travailler dans une ambiance sympa? Nous vous offrons un job au Palais du Hamburger!

Tél. 45.76.43.15.

Supermarché demande caissière. Tous les jours de 15h à 18h. Venir au 47, rue Lagrange.

Nous cherchons une jeune fille sérieuse et patiente pour garder nos deux enfants le mardi et le jeudi soir.

Tél. 46.02.32.14.

NATHALIE   Tiens! Ça ne t'intéresse pas de travailler dans un fast-food?

MURIELLE   Surtout pas! Je déteste l'odeur des hamburgers!

NATHALIE   Oh, regarde! Caissière dans un supermarché!

MURIELLE   Je ne sais pas compter.

NATHALIE   Voilà ce qu'il te faut : baby-sitter!

MURIELLE   Ah non! Pas d'enfants! Ça m'énerve! J'ai déjà gardé mes neveux. Ils crient, ils cassent tout! Je préfère mille fois les animaux!

NATHALIE   Eh bien, pourquoi tu ne mets pas une annonce pour garder des chiens?

MURIELLE   Excellente idée! Moi, les animaux, j'adore!

Activité • **Avez-vous compris?** Possible answers are given.

Répondez aux questions suivantes d'après la conversation entre Murielle et Nathalie.

1. Quel est le problème de Murielle?   1. Elle est toujours à court d'argent.
2. Quels sont les deux solutions que son amie lui propose?   2. Elle lui propose d'économiser et de trouver un job.
3. Pourquoi est-ce que son amie ne peut pas lui prêter d'argent?   3. Elle a 30 F, et il faut qu'elle les garde pour
4. Pourquoi est-ce que Murielle ne veut pas travailler dans un fast-food? Comme caissière? prendre le bus.
   Comme baby-sitter?   4. Elle déteste l'odeur des hamburgers. Elle ne sait pas compter. Ça l'énerve.
5. Enfin, qu'est-ce que Murielle décide de faire?   5. Elle décide de mettre une annonce pour garder des chiens.

B 3   Activité • **Ecrit dirigé**

Complétez ce paragraphe d'après B1.
       acheter un cadeau   n'a pas d'argent   lui prêter   prendre le bus
   Murielle veut... mais elle... Son amie ne peut pas... d'argent parce qu'elle doit...
Murielle a essayé d'économiser mais... Son amie lui propose deux solutions : il faut
que Murielle... ou qu'elle...   elle ne peut pas
       économise   trouve un job

B 4   Activité • **Qu'est-ce qu'il faut?**   Possible answers are given.

Regardez les annonces et relisez le dialogue dans B1. Qu'est-ce qu'il faut pour être caissière?
Pour travailler dans un fast-food? Pour garder les enfants?   Pour être caissière, il faut savoir compter.
Pour travailler dans un fast-food, il faut être dynamique.
Pour garder les enfants, il faut être sérieux(se) et patient(e).

B 5   Activité • **Vous ne pouvez pas prêter d'argent**   Possible answers are given.

Murielle vous demande de lui prêter de l'argent. Vous refusez. Choisissez une raison.
Pouvez-vous penser à d'autres raisons? Travaillez avec un(e) camarade et changez de rôle.

— Tu peux me prêter... ?   —Tu peux me prêter un franc? Je dois téléphoner à mes parents.
— Désolé(e), il faut que je...   —Désolé(e), il faut que je garde de l'argent pour le bus.
                                —... 100 francs? Je veux offrir un cadeau à Nicolas.
                                —... mette de l'argent en banque.

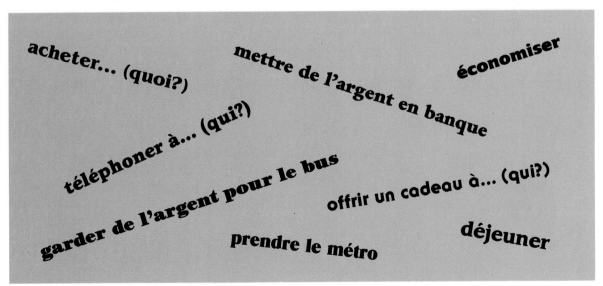

acheter... (quoi?)   mettre de l'argent en banque   économiser
téléphoner à... (qui?)
garder de l'argent pour le bus
offrir un cadeau à... (qui?)
prendre le métro   déjeuner

—...5 francs? Je veux prendre le métro.   —...75 francs? Je veux acheter ce disque.
—...déjeune à midi.   —...économise.

L'argent et les petits boulots   205

Activité • **Demandez des conseils** Possible answers are given.

Formez un groupe de quatre. Un(e) camarade joue le rôle d'un conseiller/d'une conseillère. Les autres lui racontent leurs problèmes et lui demandent des conseils. Il/Elle leur donne des conseils. Changez de rôle.

Vous avez un problème…   Vous demandez des conseils…

> **Je n'arrive pas à faire un budget.**
> **Je suis toujours à court d'argent.**
> **Je n'ai rien sur mon compte.**
> **Je n'ai plus d'argent.**

> **Qu'est-ce que je dois faire?**
> **Qu'est-ce qu'il faut que je fasse?**
> **Vous avez une idée?**
> **Qu'est-ce que vous me conseillez?**

Il faut que tu… économises. / demandes à tes parents. / mettes une annonce. / fasses des économies. / cherches un job. / ne dépenses pas.

> **économiser**   **demander à tes parents**   **mettre une annonce**
> **faire des économies**   **chercher un job**   **ne pas dépenser**

B7   **AUTRES JOBS**

Vous cherchez un job? Vous pouvez…

travailler comme animateur/ animatrice.

être serveur/serveuse dans un restaurant.

travailler au pair dans un pays étranger.

travailler dans une ferme.

vendre des glaces sur la plage.

distribuer des prospectus.

B8   Activité • Et vous?   Possible answers are given.

1. Est-ce que vous avez (avez déjà eu) un job?   1. Oui, j'ai un job.   2. Je travaille le week-end.
2. Est-ce que vous travaillez (avez travaillé) pendant l'année scolaire? Le week-end? Le soir?
3. Combien d'heures par jour et combien de jours par semaine travaillez-vous (avez-vous travaillé)?   3. Je travaille 10 heures par semaine.
4. Est-ce que vous aimez (avez aimé) le job?   4. Oui, je l'aime.
5. Si vous n'avez jamais travaillé, est-ce que vous avez envie d'avoir un job? Quel job? Pourquoi?   5. J'ai envie de travailler au pair dans un pays étranger parce que j'adore voyager.

B9   Savez-vous que… ? 🖥

Officiellement, les jeunes français doivent avoir seize ans minimum pour travailler, mais certains ont un petit job, ou boulot, par exemple aide-pompiste *(service station attendant).* Ils n'ont pas beaucoup de temps pendant l'année scolaire et ils travaillent surtout pendant les mois de juillet ou d'août pour payer leurs vacances. La plupart du temps, ils trouvent leur job par l'intermédiaire de leur famille ou grâce à des amis. Ils peuvent

aussi mettre une petite annonce dans leur immeuble ou dans leur école. Parfois, on trouve également des petites annonces dans les magasins, dans les CIDJ (Centres d'information et de documentation jeunesse) et dans des magazines pour jeunes. Pour trouver un petit boulot, c'est souvent plus facile si vous connaissez une langue étrangère. Mais surtout, il faut être patient et courageux : trouver un job n'est jamais facile!

The Centre d'information et documentation jeunesse provides information to young people on all areas of interest. While most inquiries regard career opportunities and job possibilities, the CIDJ also provides information on education, sports, vacations, travel, and so on.

B10   COMMENT LE DIRE
Giving advice

Pourquoi (est-ce que) tu ne cherches pas un job?
Pourquoi (est-ce que) tu ne mets pas une annonce?

In some circumstances in spoken French, such as negative questions, the indefinite article may be kept:
Pourquoi tu ne mets pas <u>une</u> (ou: d') annonce dans le journal? Tu ne vends pas <u>des</u> (ou: de) glaces sur la plage?

L'argent et les petits boulots   207

Votre ami(e) cherche un job. Vous lui donnez des idées mais il/elle a une attitude négative. Il/Elle choisit une réponse. Travaillez avec un(e) camarade et changez de rôle.

— Pourquoi tu ne mets pas une annonce dans le journal?
— Je n'ai pas assez d'argent!

Pourquoi tu ne... ?

faire le ménage dans un hôtel   répondre à cette annonce

garder les chiens   mettre une annonce

vendre des glaces sur la plage

arroser les plantes des voisins qui partent en vacances   faire du baby-sitting

travailler dans un fast-food

Parce que...

Il fait trop chaud sur la plage!   Les enfants, ça m'énerve!

Je déteste l'odeur des hamburgers!   Ça ne m'intéresse pas!

Mes parents ne veulent pas.

J'en ai assez des chiens!

J'ai déjà mis 50 annonces!   C'est la barbe!

B12 VOUS EN SOUVENEZ-VOUS?
The negative ne... pas

You've already learned to use **ne... pas** to make a sentence negative. Do you remember these points?

1. You place **ne (n')** before the verb and **pas** after it.
Nous **ne** sommes **pas** économes. Nous **n'**économisons **pas**.

2. In the **passé composé** the words **ne... pas** surround the auxiliary verb.
Elle **n'a pas** économisé son argent.

3. Object pronouns are placed between **ne** and the verb form that follows it.

— Tu as **de l'argent?**   — Non, je **n'en** ai pas.
— Tu as dépensé **ton argent de poche?**   — Non, je **ne** l'ai pas dépensé.

4. In a negative construction **de** is used instead of **un, une, des, du, de la,** or **de l'.**
Elle n'a pas **d'**argent. Elle n'a pas **de** job.
See note in B10, p. 207 regarding exceptions to this rule.

STRUCTURES DE BASE
Other words used with **ne**: **plus, jamais, rien,** *and* **que**

1. Several other negative expressions are used in the same way as **ne... pas.** Some of these are **ne... plus,** *no longer,* **ne... jamais,** *never,* and **ne... rien,** *nothing.*

Present	Elle **ne** garde **pas** les enfants. Elle **ne** les garde **plus.** Elle **ne** les garde **jamais.** Elle **n'**a **rien** sur son compte.	She does *not* take care of children. She *no longer* takes care of them. She *never* takes care of them. She has *nothing* in her account.
Passé composé	Ils **n'**ont **pas** lavé la voiture. Ils **ne** l'ont **jamais** lavée. Ils **n'**ont **rien** fait.	They did *not* wash the car. They *never* washed it. They did *nothing.*

2. In a short negative remark without a verb form, **ne** is not used.

    — Tu fais souvent de petits jobs?   — Non, **jamais.** *(No, never.)*
    — Qu'est-ce que tu as?   — **Rien.** *(Nothing.)*

3. The word **que** is used with **ne** to mean *only.* **Ne** is placed before the verb; **que** precedes the noun it limits.

Je **n'**ai **que** 30 francs. Elle **n'**achète **que** des vêtements. Elle **n'**aime acheter **que** des vêtements.	I *only* have 30 francs. She *only* buys clothes. She likes to buy *only* clothes.

Point out that <u>du</u>, <u>de la</u>, <u>de l'</u>, and <u>des</u> do not change to <u>de</u> after <u>que</u>: Je ne garde que <u>des</u> chiens.

In the **passé composé, ne** comes before the auxiliary verb, as you might expect, but **que** follows the past participle.

Je **n'**ai **pas** demandé beaucoup d'argent. Je **n'**ai demandé **que** 30 francs.	I did *not* ask for a lot of money. I *only* asked for 30 francs.

B 14   Activité • Travaillent-ils toujours?

Un(e) camarade vous demande si vos copains font toujours *(still)* leurs jobs. Répondez avec **ne... plus.**

    1. —Murielle garde toujours les chiens?   2. —Hélène travaille toujours au pair?
       —Non, elle ne garde plus les chiens.   —Non, elle ne travaille plus au pair.

   Pierre / être serveur   — Pierre est toujours serveur?   3. —Guy garde toujours les enfants?
                 — Non, il n'est plus serveur.   —Non, il ne garde plus les enfants.

1. Murielle / garder les chiens   **4.** Les frères Duclos / distribuer des prospectus
2. Hélène / travailler au pair   **5.** Nathalie et Emilie / être animatrices
3. Guy / garder les enfants   **6.** Fabienne / vendre des glaces sur la plage

4. —Les frères Duclos distribuent toujours des prospectus?   6. —Fabienne vend toujours des glaces sur la plage?
   —Non, ils ne distribuent plus de prospectus.   —Non, elle ne vend plus de glaces sur la plage.

5. —Nathalie et Emilie sont toujours animatrices?
   —Non, elles ne sont plus animatrices.   **L'argent et les petits boulots**

Dites quelles activités vous avez déjà faites et quelles activités vous n'avez jamais faites.
Répondez au passé composé avec **déjà** ou **ne... jamais.**

— J'ai déjà fait du baby-sitting.
   (Je n'ai jamais fait de baby-sitting.)

1.

Je n'ai jamais fait de judo.

2.

J'ai déjà fait du théâtre.

3.

Je n'ai jamais fait de canoë-kayak.

4.

J'ai déjà fait de la gymnastique.

5.

Je n'ai jamais joué aux échecs.

6.

J'ai déjà fait de la peinture.

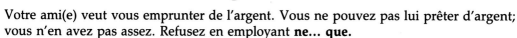

Votre ami(e) veut vous emprunter de l'argent. Vous ne pouvez pas lui prêter d'argent;
vous n'en avez pas assez. Refusez en employant **ne... que.**

    100 F / 50 F — Tu me prêtes cent francs?
                        — Désolé(e), je n'ai que cinquante francs.

1. ... trente francs?   ... dix francs.
2. ... soixante-cinq francs?   ... vingt-cinq francs.
3. ... vingt francs?   ... cinq francs.
4. ... deux cents francs?   ... cent francs.
5. ... soixante-quinze francs?   ... soixante francs.
6. ... cinq francs?   un franc.

1. 30 F / 10 F   **3.** 20 F / 5 F   **5.** 75 F / 60 F
2. 65 F / 25 F   **4.** 200 F / 100 F   **6.** 5 F / 1 F

Murielle écrit une petite annonce et la met dans les boutiques de son quartier.

Murielle a tapé l'annonce à la machine.

Vous avez des chiens à garder ou à promener? Téléphonez-moi au 42.22.20.00. Je suis une jeune fille sérieuse et j'adore les animaux!

Elle a trouvé un job.
Elle promène le chien.

Quinze jours plus tard, Nathalie lui téléphone pour avoir des nouvelles.

NATHALIE   Alors, ton job? Ça boume?
MURIELLE   J'ai arrêté hier.
NATHALIE   Pourquoi? Ça ne te plaît plus?
MURIELLE   Non, ça m'embête. Les chiens, c'est l'enfer! Ça aboie et ça mange tout!
NATHALIE   Pourquoi tu ne gardes pas les chats?
MURIELLE   Ne me parle plus d'animaux! Les chats, ça miaule et ça griffe! J'en ai assez des animaux! En plus, c'est mal payé! Maintenant, c'est décidé : j'économise!

B18   Activité • Avez-vous compris?   Possible answers are given.

Répondez aux questions suivantes d'après le dialogue entre Murielle at Nathalie.

1. Est-ce que Murielle travaille toujours?
2. Pourquoi a-t-elle arrêté?
3. Pendant combien de temps a-t-elle travaillé?
4. Aime-t-elle toujours les animaux?
5. Qu'est-ce que Murielle a décidé de faire?
6. Comment trouvez-vous Murielle?

1. Non, elle ne travaille plus.   2. Elle n'aime pas les chiens.   3. Elle a travaillé pendant 14 jours.
4. Non, elle n'aime plus les animaux.   5. Elle a décidé d'économiser.   6. Je ne la trouve pas sérieuse.
Je la trouve impatiente.

L'argent et les petits boulots   211

Activité • Qu'est-ce que Murielle peut répondre? Possible answers are given.

Connaissez-vous Murielle? A votre avis, qu'est-ce qu'elle répond aux conseils de ses amis?

1. *Cherche un petit boulot.*

Je n'aime pas travailler.

3. **Pourquoi tu ne gardes pas les enfants?**

Les enfants, ne m'en parle pas!

2. **N'achète plus rien.**

J'ai essayé et je ne peux pas.

4. **Garde les chiens.**

Je n'aime pas les chiens.

5. **Mets une annonce.**

J'en ai déjà mis 50.

B20 Activité • Le personnage de Murielle Possible answers are given.

Maintenant que vous connaissez bien Murielle, pouvez-vous faire une liste de ce qu'elle aime et de ce qu'elle n'aime pas? Elle aime dépenser de l'argent.
Elle n'aime pas les enfants, les animaux et l'odeur des hamburgers.

B21 COMMENT LE DIRE
Inquiring about others' activities
Expressing pleasure and disappointment

INQUIRING	PLEASURE	DISAPPOINTMENT
Ça va, ton job?	Super, c'est très bien payé!	Non, c'est mal payé.
Ça marche, ton job?	Je trouve ça super!	Non, j'en ai assez.
		J'en ai marre. (fam.)
Ça boume, ton job? (fam.)	(Je trouve que) c'est passionnant (intéressant).	Non, c'est l'enfer.
Ça t'intéresse, ton job?	J'adore!	Non, je déteste.
Ça te plaît, ton job?	Ça me plaît beaucoup.	Non, ça m'ennuie.
Ça t'amuse, ton job?	Je suis ravi(e).	Non, ça m'embête (m'énerve).

B22 Activité • Répondez à Murielle Possible answers are given.

Murielle a une attitude négative. Vous, vous avez une attitude positive. Qu'est-ce que vous dites à Murielle? Trouvez des expressions positives dans B21. Travaillez avec un(e) camarade et changez de rôle.

MURIELLE   Les enfants, c'est l'enfer!
VOUS   Moi, j'adore les enfants!

1. J'en ai marre de faire du baby-sitting!
2. Travailler dans un fast-food, j'en ai assez!
3. Les chiens, ça m'énerve!
4. J'ai déjà travaillé; c'est mal payé!
5. J'en ai assez de faire des économies!
6. Les animaux, ça m'embête!
7. Travailler comme caissière, c'est l'enfer!

1. Je trouve ça super!   2. Ça me plaît beaucoup!   3. Moi, j'adore les chiens!
4. J'aime beaucoup travailler.   5. Je trouve ça intéressant.
6. Les animaux, moi, j'adore!   7. Je trouve ça super et c'est bien payé!

Activité • Ça boume? 🔲 Possible answers are given.

Travaillez avec un(e) camarade. Vous lui demandez si ça marche. Il/Elle répond avec une expression positive ou négative. Changez de rôle.

le job — Alors, ça boume, le job?
— Non, j'en ai marre d'arroser les plantes!

2. —Ça boume, les études?
   —Non, c'est l'enfer.
3. —Ça te plaît, l'informatique?
   —Oui, je trouve que c'est passionnant!

1. le job   3. l'informatique   5. les enfants   7. les économies
2. les études 4. les amours   6. les animaux   8. le budget

4. —Ça va, les amours? —Non, j'en ai marre.   5. —Ça t'amuse, les enfants? —Oui, j'adore!   6. Ça t'intéresse, les animaux?
—Non, ça m'embête.   7. —Ça va, les économies? —Non, j'ai essayé, je ne peux pas.   8. —Ça va, le budget? —Non, je suis
désespéré(e).

B24 Activité • A vous maintenant! Possible answers are given.

Faites une conversation avec un(e) camarade. Suivez le modèle. Choisissez une attitude positive ou négative. Variez les phrases soulignées. Changez de rôle.

— Je n'ai jamais d'argent! _plus_
— Cherche un job.
— Je ne sais rien faire.
— Pourquoi tu ne fais pas du baby-sitting? _mets pas une annonce_

        (Positive)   *ou*   *(Négative)*
— Bonne idée! Je vais mettre des   — Ah non! Les enfants, j'en ai marre!
annonces dans mon quartier.   J'en ai déjà mis 50.
Je vais faire ça cet après-midi.

B25 Activité • Et vous?

1. Ça marche, les études?   4. Ça vous amuse de donner des conseils aux amis?
2. Ça vous plaît, les petits jobs?   5. Les amours, ça boume?
3. Ça vous intéresse, l'informatique?   6. Les enfants, ça vous intéresse? Et les animaux?

Possible answer: Cher... J'ai trouvé un job. Je travaille dans un hôtel international. Je fais du baby-sitting. Je rencontre
B26 Activité • Ecrivez des étrangers intéressants. La semaine dernière, j'ai gardé des enfants français. Je trouve
ça passionnant! Je gagne 5 dollars de l'heure. C'est super!

Regardez les petites annonces suivantes. Imaginez. Vous avez trouvé un de ces jobs. Vous travaillez depuis un mois. Ecrivez une lettre à votre correspondant(e) français(e). Parlez-lui de votre job, des heures, de la paie… Dites-lui si vous aimez le job ou si vous ne l'aimez pas et pourquoi.

Car washer - Mon.-Fri., week nights, rain/shine, $4.50/hr. 2-4 hrs /night. Airport Taxi Co. 555-2680

Fast-Food Workers - Full and part time, days or evenings. $4.35/hr. Apply Quick Chow opp. RR station.

Cashier - French restaurant. Florida theme park - Knowledge of French asset. Sat. + Sun. hours. $4.25/hr. 555-8200.

Kennel Help - Animal hospital. Bathe, walk animals. $3.35/hr. Sat. + Sun. hours. AniKare Clinic, 72 Fliene Blvd.

Waiters/Waitresses - $3.34/hour + tips. Full or part time. Flexible hours. Uniforms provided. Center Restaurant.

Sitters - earn $5 an hour. Meet intn'l guests. Days or evenings. Apply in person. Ritts Hotel.

Housekeeper - Eve. or wknds. $3.75-$4/hr. Uniforms provided. Apply in person. Outside Inn, 1600 Main St.

B27 Activité • Ecoutez bien 🔲 For script and answers, see p. T135.

Ecoutez les dialogues et dites si les personnes aiment ou n'aiment pas leurs jobs.

Murielle a voulu trouver un job pour gagner un peu d'argent et le dépenser. Est-ce qu'il y a d'autres raisons pour avoir un job? Qu'en pensez-vous?

C1 Un petit boulot, pour quoi faire? 📼

Murielle est inquiète. Elle adore dépenser, elle ne peut pas économiser et elle est trop paresseuse pour garder un job. Est-ce qu'elle est normale? Elle a écrit au journal de son lycée pour avoir l'opinion d'autres lycéens.

Est-ce que vous avez travaillé? Moi, je suis dépensière, mais dès que je commence un job pour gagner de l'argent, j'ai envie d'arrêter. Qu'est-ce qu'il faut faire? Répondez-moi.

Murielle

Tu sais, Murielle, un job, ça peut être sympa. Pour moi, c'est une occasion d'aider mes parents. A Noël je les ai aidés au restaurant et ils m'ont payée. C'est aussi un apprentissage, une façon d'apprendre un métier. Ça me plaît beaucoup.

Marianne

Moi, je n'ai pas de job et je suis heureux. Je suis d'accord avec toi: le travail, c'est la barbe! Quand j'ai vraiment besoin d'argent, je propose mes services. La semaine dernière par exemple, j'ai lavé la voiture de nos voisins. Ils m'ont donné 50 F. Pour être heureux, il faut travailler un minimum. Donc dépenser le minimum!

Patrice

Je trouve que tes désirs sont incompatibles, Murielle. Moi, j'ai une passion, la planche à voile. L'année dernière, j'ai fait un stage en Bretagne. Mes parents m'ont aidée et m'ont offert la moitié du stage, mais j'ai dû trouver le reste. J'ai travaillé et j'ai économisé. Voilà!... Toi, ta passion, c'est dépenser. Pour dépenser, il te faut de l'argent. Si tu ne changes pas, il n'y a pas de solution.

Nicole

L'important, Murielle, c'est d'être indépendant. Mes parents ne me donnent pas beaucoup d'argent de poche mais je n'aime pas leur en demander plus: alors je cherche des jobs. Au mois d'août, j'ai travaillé comme réceptionniste dans un hôtel. Ce n'est pas difficile, mais il faut parler anglais. On gagne pas mal et c'est aussi un moyen de rencontrer des gens. Après, j'ai acheté des disques. C'est ça, l'indépendance!

Marc

Activité • **Avez-vous compris?** Possible answers are given.

Répondez aux questions d'après les réponses à la lettre de Murielle.

(La réponse de Marianne)   1. Elle a aidé ses parents au restaurant.
2. C'est une occasion d'aider ses parents.
C'est aussi un apprentissage.

1. Quel job est-ce que Marianne a eu?
2. Pourquoi est-ce que ce job lui plaît? Donnez deux raisons.

(La réponse de Patrice)   3. Il n'a pas de job.   4. Le travail, c'est la barbe!
5. Quand il a vraiment besoin d'argent, il propose ses services.

3. Pourquoi est-ce que Patrice est heureux?
4. Comment est-ce qu'il trouve le travail en général?
5. Comment est-ce qu'il fait pour avoir de l'argent?

(La réponse de Nicole)   6. Ses parents lui ont offert la moitié
d'un stage de planche à voile.
7. Pour le reste elle a travaillé et économisé.

6. Qu'est-ce que ses parents ont fait pour elle?
7. Comment est-ce qu'elle a trouvé le reste de l'argent?
8. A son avis, qu'est-ce qu'il faut faire quand on aime dépenser?

(La réponse de Marc)   8. Quand on aime dépenser, il faut avoir de l'argent.
9. Il cherche un job pour être indépendant.

9. Pourquoi est-ce qu'il cherche un job?   10. Il a travaillé comme réceptionniste
dans un hôtel.
10. Quel job est-ce qu'il a trouvé?   11. Avec l'argent, il a acheté des disques.
11. Qu'est-ce qu'il a fait avec l'argent gagné?

MARIANNE

PATRICE

NICOLE

MARC

Activité • **Comment sont-ils?** Possible answers are given.

D'après leurs réponses, comment trouvez-vous Murielle et les lycéens?

Murielle — Marianne — Patrice — Nicole — Marc

travailleur/travailleuse
Marc est travailleur.

paresseux/paresseuse
Patrice est paresseux.

dépensier/dépensière
Murielle est dépensière.

sérieux/sérieuse
Marianne est sérieuse.

sportif/sportive
Nicole est sportive.

économe
Marc est économe.

L'argent et les petits boulots   215

Savez-vous que… ?

Qu'est-ce que les jeunes français font de leur argent? Beaucoup d'entre eux adorent acheter des vêtements. Pour être à la mode, il faut en changer souvent! Ils achètent aussi des disques et des bandes dessinées. La plupart mettent cependant de l'argent de côté pour sortir avec des copains, aller au cinéma ou au concert. Pour les gros achats, leurs parents les aident et ils économisent, par exemple pour acheter une planche à voile, une chaîne stéréo, une petite moto ou passer leur permis de conduire. Les petits boulots, ça leur permet de gagner un peu d'argent et d'acheter ce qui leur plaît. C'est une façon d'être indépendant.

Qualifying for a driver's license in France requires private instruction, which can cost as much as 6,000 F.

Que font-ils de leur argent?	
15 ans	
Garçons	**Filles**
1. Sorties ciné, restau: 32,5 %	Vêtements : 30 %
2. Cigarettes : 22,5 %	Sorties ciné, restau: 30 %
3. Café, jeux : 20 %	Disques : 30 %
4. Essence : 20 %	Café, jeux : 30 %
5. Nourriture : 17,5 %	Livres, journaux : 20 %
6. Livres, journaux : 15 %	Cigarettes : 20 %
7. Disques : 12,5 %	Cadeaux : 20 %
8. Vêtements : 7,5 %	Nourriture : 17,5 %

N.B. : La rubrique café, jeux indique les dépenses effectuées dans les cafés pour boire et jouer aux jeux électroniques (flipper…).

C5 **COMMENT LE DIRE**
Giving reasons for doing something

Avoir un job,	c'est un moyen de (d')	être indépendant(e).
	c'est une façon de (d')	aider les parents.
	c'est une occasion de (d')	apprendre un métier.
Having a job	is a means of	being independent.
	is a way to	help your parents.
	is an opportunity to	learn a trade.

C6 *omit* Activité • Vive les petits boulots!

Trouvez dans C1 trois raisons de travailler.

Travailler,…

1. c'est un moyen de(d')…

apprendre un métier.

2. c'est une façon de(d')…

faire des économies.

3. c'est une occasion de(d')…

d'aider les gens.

Activité • **Pour quoi faire?** Possible answers are given.

Voici plusieurs raisons d'avoir un job. A votre avis, quel est leur ordre de préférence?

Avoir un job,...

c'est un moyen de (d')...

c'est une façon de (d')...

c'est une occasion de (d')...

être indépendant(e)   apprendre un métier   voyager

changer sa vie   acheter quelque chose   aider ses parents

s'amuser

offrir des cadeaux

faire comme les autres   rencontrer des gens

économiser   payer ses études

Avoir un job, c'est un moyen d'apprendre un métier.
Avoir un job, c'est une occasion de payer ses études.
Avoir un job, c'est une façon de changer sa vie.

C8 *ou* **Activité • Donnez votre avis**   Possible answers are given.

1. Aller à l'école, c'est une occasion de rencontrer des amis.   2. Faire les devoirs, c'est un moyen d'apprendre.

Pouvez-vous donner des raisons pour ces autres activités?

1. aller à l'école   **3.** faire un voyage   **5.** avoir un(e) correspondant(e)
2. faire les devoirs   **4.** faire du sport   **6.** apprendre le français

3. Faire un voyage, c'est un moyen de voir un autre pays.   4. Faire du sport, c'est un moyen de garder la forme.   5. Avoir un(e) correspondant(e), c'est un moyen d'avoir un(e) confident(e).   6. Apprendre le français, c'est un façon de connaître une autre culture.

C9 *ou* **Activité • Conversation**   Possible answers are given.

Faites une conversation avec un(e) camarade. Suivez le modèle. Vous pouvez varier les phrases soulignées.

— Tu es content(e) d'avoir un job?   de travailler
— Ah oui, c'est une occasion de rencontrer des gens.   un moyen / d'être indépendante
   (Non, ça m'ennuie.)   ça m'énerve

C10 VOUS EN SOUVENEZ-VOUS?
Object pronouns with the passé composé

You've learned that when a verb is in the **passé composé**, object pronouns come before the auxiliary verb. In a negative sentence, object pronouns are placed between **ne** and the auxiliary verb.

Nous **lui** avons parlé.   Nous **ne lui** avons **pas** parlé.

You may also recall that the spelling of the past participle of a verb in the **passé composé** may change to agree in gender and number with a preceding direct-object pronoun. Remember that the spelling of the past participle does not change when the preceding pronoun is an indirect object, **y,** or **en.**

Elle a appelé **Marie.**   Elle a téléphoné **à Marie.**
Elle **l'**a appelé**e.**   *But,*   Elle **lui** a téléphon**é.**

Object pronouns with the passé composé: me, te, nous, vous

1. The object pronouns **me, te, nous,** and **vous** appear in the same position in the sentence as the object pronouns **le, la, les, lui, leur, y,** and **en.**

Present	Tu **me** prêtes de l'argent?
Passé composé	Il **m'**a prêté de l'argent.

2. **Me, te, nous,** and **vous** may be either direct objects or indirect objects of a verb. **Me** may mean *me* or *to (for) me;* **nous** may mean *us* or *to (for) us;* **te** and **vous** may mean *you* or *to (for) you.*

3. With few exceptions, when you speak, you don't have to know whether **me, te, nous,** and **vous** are direct or indirect objects. Only when you write will you have to know for sure, and then only when you write a sentence in which **me, te, nous,** or **vous** is used with a verb in the **passé composé.** Why? Because you may have to change the spelling of the past participle if **me, te, nous,** or **vous** is a direct object of the verb. Once you have decided that the pronoun is the direct object, you must then know to whom the pronoun refers. To one person? To more than one? To a male? To a female? Look at these examples.

	Direct-Object Pronoun	*Indirect-Object Pronoun*
Masculine Singular	Il **m'**a invité. Il **t'**a invité? Il **vous** a invité?	Il **m'**a téléphoné. Il **t'**a téléphoné? Il **vous** a téléphoné?
Masculine Plural or Mixed Group	Il **nous** a invité**s**. Il **vous** a invité**s**?	Il **nous** a téléphoné. Il **vous** a téléphoné?
Feminine Singular	Il **m'**a invité**e**. Il **t'**a invité**e**? Il **vous** a invité**e**?	Il **m'**a téléphoné. Il **t'**a téléphoné? Il **vous** a téléphoné?
Feminine Plural	Il **nous** a invité**es**. Il **vous** a invité**es**?	Il **nous** a téléphoné. Il **vous** a téléphoné?

4. How can you tell whether **me, te, nous,** or **vous** is a direct object or an indirect object? Unfortunately, there is no single, fixed rule that you can apply. The best way to tell is to try to remember which verbs take an indirect object. Here are a few verbs of this type that you've already seen.

téléphoner	**répondre**	**prêter**	**envoyer**
montrer	**donner**	**emprunter**	**écrire**
parler	**offrir**	**acheter**	

The reflexive pronouns with the "passé composé" are presented in Unit 7, p. 242.

C12 Activité • Qu'est-ce que Murielle répond? Possible answers are given.

Vous connaissez bien Murielle. Répondez pour elle à ces questions. Employez le pronom **me** dans les réponses.

1. Est-ce que vos parents vous donnent de l'argent de poche?
2. Comment est-ce que vous avez fait pour acheter cette jupe?
3. Qu'est-ce que vos grands-parents vous ont donné pour votre fête?
4. Qu'est-ce que votre amie Nathalie vous a conseillé de faire?
5. Pourquoi est-ce que vous ne gardez pas d'enfants ou de chiens?

1. Oui, ils me donnent de l'argent de poche; mais ce n'est pas assez.
2. Mon père m'a prêté de l'argent.
3. Ils m'ont donné 100 F.
4. Elle m'a conseillé de mettre une annonce pour garder les chiens.
5. Ça ne me plaît pas.

 C13 *omit* Activité • Ecrit dirigé   See C12 for answers.

Maintenant, écrivez les réponses aux questions dans C12. Faites attention à l'accord du participe passé.

C14 Activité • Qu'est-ce que les lycéens répondent?

Relisez C1. Ensuite répondez aux questions suivantes pour les camarades de Murielle. Travaillez avec un(e) camarade. Posez les questions et répondez. Changez de rôle.

(Marianne)
1. Travailler dans le restaurant de vos parents, ça vous a plu? Oui, ça m'a plu.
2. Est-ce que vos parents vous ont payée? Oui, ils m'ont payée.

(Patrice)
3. Combien d'argent est-ce que vos voisins vous ont donné pour laver leur voiture?
Ils m'ont donné 50 F.

(Nicole)
4. Comment est-ce que vous avez fait pour payer votre stage en Bretagne l'été dernier?
Mes parents m'ont donné la moitié de l'argent, et j'ai travaillé pour le reste.

(Marc)
5. Comment est-ce que vous faites pour avoir de l'argent? Quand j'ai besoin d'argent, je cherche des jobs.
6. Est-ce que votre job comme réceptionniste vous a intéressé? Oui, ça m'a intéressé.

C15 Activité • Ecrit dirigé   See C14 for answers.

Ecrivez les réponses aux questions dans C14.

C16 Activité • Conversation

Lisez ce dialogue avec un(e) camarade en employant les pronoms **me, te,** ou **lui.**

— Tes parents __t'__ ont offert de l'argent?
— Non, j'ai lavé la voiture des voisins.
— Ils __t'__ ont payé(e)?
— Oui, ils __m'__ ont donné 50 F.
— Et ton frère, il __t'__ a aidé(e)?
— Oui, un peu.
— Et tu __lui__ as donné de l'argent?
— Mais non, il __m'__ a arrosé(e) tout le temps! Ça __m'__ a embêté(e)!

1. —C'est toi qui m'as donné ce livre?
—Non, je ne t'ai pas donné ce livre.

Vous avez mauvaise mémoire. Vous demandez à votre ami(e) si c'est lui/elle qui a fait quelque chose. Il/Elle répond que non. Travaillez avec un(e) camarade. Employez les pronoms **me** et **te** dans vos dialogues.

2. —C'est toi qui m'as appelé(e) ce matin?
—Non, je ne t'ai pas appelé(e) ce matin.

téléphoner hier soir — C'est toi qui m'as téléphoné hier soir?
— Non, je ne t'ai pas téléphoné. 3. —C'est toi qui m'as envoyé cette carte postale?
—Non, je ne t'ai pas envoyé cette carte postale.

1. donner ce livre
2. appeler ce matin
3. envoyer cette carte postale

4. emprunter une cassette
5. téléphoner cet après-midi
6. prêter 100 francs

4. —C'est toi qui m'as emprunté une cassette?
—Non, je ne t'ai pas emprunté de cassette.

5. —C'est toi qui m'as téléphoné cet après-midi? —Non, je ne t'ai pas téléphoné cet après-midi.
6. —C'est toi qui m'as prêté 100 francs? —Non, je ne t'ai pas prêté 100 francs.

C18 Activité • Ecrit dirigé

Murielle parle de ses vacances dans une lettre à son amie Nathalie.

> Chère Nathalie,
> Très gentiment, mon oncle et ma tante m'ont invitée pour les vacances. Malheureusement, je n'ai pas eu le temps d'aller à la plage; je les ai aidés tous les jours au magasin. Ça m'a intéressée, mais ils ne m'ont pas bien payée! Et toi, on t'a bien payée pour ton travail?
> Grosses bises
> Murielle

Maintenant, réécrivez la lettre. Cette fois, c'est Marc et sa sœur Anne qui écrivent à leurs amis Célia et Jean-Luc. Faites tous les changements nécessaires. Chers Célia et Jean-Luc, Très gentiment, notre oncle et notre tante nous ont invités pour les vacances. Malheureusement, nous n'avons pas eu le temps d'aller à la plage, nous les avons aidés tous les jours au magasin. Ça nous a intéressés, mais ils ne nous ont pas bien payés! Et vous, on vous a bien payés pour votre travail? Grosses bises, Marc et Anne

C19 Activité • Ecrivez

Vous êtes en vacances dans un centre de loisirs au bord de la mer. Vous écrivez un petit mot à vos parents pour leur demander de l'argent. Vous leur expliquez qu'un copain ou une copine vous a emprunté de l'argent, mais qu'il/elle ne vous a pas encore rendu l'argent. Dites que votre copain/copine a écrit à ses parents, mais qu'ils ne lui ont pas encore envoyé d'argent. Possible answer: Cher papa et chère maman, Ça va bien ici, mais je n'ai pas assez d'argent. Malheureusement, j'ai prêté 200 F à un ami. Il a déjà écrit à ses parents, mais ils n'ont pas encore répondu. Donc, il ne m'a pas encore rendu mes 200 F. Pouvez-vous m'envoyer de l'argent? Merci et grosses bises, ...

C20 Activité • Ecoutez bien For script and answers, see p. T139.

Ecoutez la conversation entre François et Jérôme. Ensuite complétez les phrases suivantes.

Jérôme n'est pas content parce que… Alors, il prend… et il la rend quand…

1   Nicole répond à une annonce.

NICOLE	Allô? Je suis bien au 42.43.21.30?
M. PERROT	Oui, mademoiselle.
NICOLE	Bonjour, monsieur. Je vous téléphone au sujet de l'annonce.
M. PERROT	Oui. Bonjour. Vous avez quel âge?
NICOLE	Quinze ans.
M. PERROT	Vous avez déjà gardé des enfants?
NICOLE	Non, je n'ai jamais gardé d'enfants, mais je les aime bien. C'est combien d'heures par semaine?
M. PERROT	Six. Le mardi, le jeudi et le vendredi. Deux heures par jour de six à huit. Ça vous va?
NICOLE	Oui. C'est combien de l'heure?
M. PERROT	Vingt-cinq francs.
NICOLE	Bon, d'accord. Je commence quand?
M. PERROT	Demain à six heures, si vous voulez.
NICOLE	Oui, ça va. Vous pouvez me donner votre adresse?
M. PERROT	Bien sûr. Vingt-deux, rue du Cherche-Midi, dans le 6ᵉ. C'est au deuxième étage à droite. Monsieur et Madame Perrot. Vous pouvez me donner votre nom?
NICOLE	Nicole. Nicole Sinclair.
M. PERROT	Eh bien, à demain, Nicole.
NICOLE	Au revoir, monsieur.

> Couple cherche jeune fille sérieuse pour garder des enfants le soir.
> Téléphonez au : 42.43.21.30.

2   Activité • Qu'est-ce que Nicole dit?

Trouvez dans la conversation téléphonique ce que Nicole dit pour…

1. vérifier le numéro de téléphone.
2. donner la raison de son appel (call).

3. demander l'adresse.
4. demander combien les Perrot vont la payer.

1. Je suis bien au 42. 43. 21. 30?
2. Je vous téléphone au sujet de l'annonce.

3. Vous pouvez me donner votre adresse?
4. C'est combien de l'heure?

L'argent et les petits boulots   221

3 Activité • Ecrit dirigé

Nicole a préparé une feuille de papier pour noter les renseignements. Pouvez-vous les noter pour elle?

> Combien d'heures par semaine? six
> Quels jours? le mardi, le jeudi et le vendredi
> Je commence quand? demain à 6 h
> Où? 22, rue du Cherche-Midi, dans le 6ᵉ, au 2ᵉ étage à droite
> Combien est-ce qu'ils me paient?
> Nom de la famille? Perrot   25 F de l'heure

4 Activité • Répondez à une annonce Possible answers are given.

Vous cherchez un job. Vous lisez cette annonce et vous téléphonez au Palais du Hamburger pour demander des renseignements. Voici les réponses du directeur du Palais. Quelles sont vos questions?

> jeune fille
> Vous êtes dynamique? Vous aimez travailler dans une ambiance sympa? Nous vous offrons un job au Palais du Hamburger!
> Tél. 45.76.43.15.

1. — ... Je suis bien au 45.76.43.15?
   — Oui, mademoiselle (monsieur).

2. — ... Pouvez-vous me donner votre adresse?
   — Rue de Rennes, à cent mètres de Saint-Germain-des-Prés.

3. — ... C'est combien d'heures par semaine?
   — C'est un travail à mi-temps, de neuf heures à treize heures ou de dix-sept heures à vingt et une heures, tous les jours, samedi compris.

4. — ... C'est combien de l'heure?
   — Quarante francs de l'heure.

Maintenant, c'est le directeur du Palais du Hamburger qui vous demande des renseignements. Voici vos réponses. Trouvez ses questions.

1. — ... Vous avez quel âge?
   — J'ai seize ans.

2. — ... Vous avez déjà travaillé?
   — Oui, j'ai été serveur (serveuse) dans un restaurant.

3. — ... Dans quel restaurant?
   — Au Bœuf sur le Toit. Vous pouvez téléphoner au 47.36.29.12.

4. — ... Comment s'appelle votre patron là-bas?
   — Il s'appelle Monsieur Durand.

5. — ... Quand est-ce que vous pouvez commencer?
   — Quand vous voulez, monsieur. Samedi prochain, si vous voulez.

6. — ... Vous pouvez me donner votre nom?
   — (Votre nom)

Activité • Jeu de rôle

Choisissez une de ces annonces et répondez-y par téléphone. Faites la conversation téléphonique avec un(e) camarade. Vous faites d'abord une liste de renseignements que vous voulez demander. Votre camarade fait une liste de questions qu'il/elle veut vous poser. Puis, choisissez une autre annonce et changez de rôle.

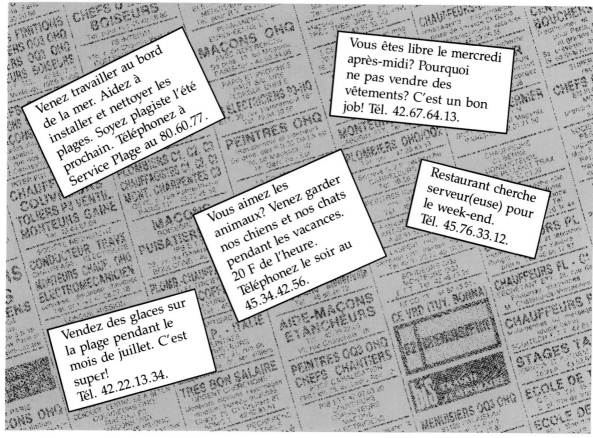

Venez travailler au bord de la mer. Aidez à installer et nettoyer les plages. Soyez plagiste l'été prochain. Téléphonez à Service Plage au 80.60.77.

Vous êtes libre le mercredi après-midi? Pourquoi ne pas vendre des vêtements? C'est un bon job! Tél. 42.67.64.13.

Vous aimez les animaux? Venez garder nos chiens et nos chats pendant les vacances. 20 F de l'heure. Téléphonez le soir au 45.34.42.56.

Restaurant cherche serveur(euse) pour le week-end. Tél. 45.76.33.12.

Vendez des glaces sur la plage pendant le mois de juillet. C'est super! Tél. 42.22.13.34.

Jeune fille sérieuse et patiente peut garder votre chien ou votre chat pendant les vacances.
25 F de l'heure.
Tél. 42.34.46.20.

6

Activité • Ecrivez   Possible answer is given.

Vous avez besoin d'argent. Vous mettez une annonce dans votre quartier pour trouver un job. Ecrivez votre annonce. Dites quel job vous cherchez, quand, combien vous voulez gagner... N'oubliez pas d'indiquer un moyen d'entrer en contact avec vous.

Possible dialogues are given.

7

Activité • Situations

1. —Dis, tu as 20 F à me prêter?
   —Pour quoi faire?
   —Pour aller au cinéma?
   —Tiens, les voilà.

Vous êtes dans ces situations. Préparez trois dialogues avec un(e) camarade.

1. Vous demandez de l'argent à un(e) ami(e). Il/Elle vous demande pourquoi. Vous répondez. Il/Elle accepte.

2. Vous voulez aller à un concert de rock. Vous demandez à votre père ou à votre mère de vous donner 100 francs. Il/Elle refuse. Vous lui demandez alors de vous prêter 100 francs. Il/Elle accepte.

3. Vous demandez à votre sœur ou à votre frère de vous prêter 50 francs. Elle/Il demande quand vous allez lui rendre son argent. Vous répondez. Elle/Il vous donne 50 francs.

2. —Maman, je voudrais voir le concert de Sting.
   Tu as 100 F à me donner?
   —Non, c'est trop cher.
   —Tu peux me prêter les 100 F?
   —Bon, d'accord, et demain tu me laves la voiture.
   —D'accord! Merci, maman!

3. —Tu peux me prêter 50 F, s'il te plaît?
   —Quand est-ce que tu me rends l'argent?
   —Demain. Maman va me donner mon argent de poche!
   —D'accord.

L'argent et les petits boulots   223

Vous n'avez pas d'argent. Vous allez voir quelqu'un. Vous lui demandez de vous prêter de l'argent. Vous lui dites combien et vous lui expliquez pourquoi vous en avez besoin. Il/Elle refuse. Vous insistez. Il/Elle refuse encore! Vous trouvez une autre raison. Il/Elle refuse encore une fois! Vous continuez. Bonne chance!

—Tu peux me prêter 45 F pour acheter un disque?
—Je veux bien, mais je ne peux pas.
—Sois gentil!
—Non, c'est impossible.

9 Activité • **Récréation** (optional)

1. **Devinez**

   Nous avons demandé à un artiste de dessiner des jeunes qui travaillent. Malheureusement, il n'a pas fini ses dessins. Pouvez-vous deviner ce que ces jeunes font?

a. Elle promène un chien.

b. Il est serveur.

c. Elle garde un enfant.

2. **Devinettes**

   Voici des phrases célèbres qui parlent d'argent ou de travail. Choisissez le dessin qui illustre chaque phrase.

   1. L'argent est une troisième main.
   2. Si vous voulez savoir la valeur de l'argent, essayez d'en emprunter.
   3. L'abeille laborieuse n'a pas le temps d'être triste.

a. 3   b. 1   c. 2

PRONONCIATION

The sounds /y/, /œ/, /ø/

1 Ecoutez bien et répétez.

1. The sound /y/

tube	tube	*humid*	humide	*surface*	surface
cube	cube	*bureau*	bureau	*subtle*	subtil
pure	pure	*volume*	volume	*buffet*	buffet
cure	cure	*ridicule*	ridicule	*minute*	minute

2. The sound /œ/

œuf	bœuf		

œuf	seul	fleuve	
neuf	peuvent	jeune	

sœur	beurre	peur	erreur
cœur	fleur	pleure	valeur

3. The sound /ø/

œuf	/	œufs	peu	veut
bœuf	/	bœufs	deux	mieux
un œil	/	des yeux	ceux	monsieur

2 Ecoutez et lisez.

— Tu as vu la lune?   — Qui est venu?   — Qu'est-ce que tu as bu?
— Ça t'a plu?   — Tu l'as vu?   — Du jus pur.

— Tu es seule? Où est ta sœur?   — Pourquoi tu pleures? Tu as peur de faire des erreurs?
— Chez le coiffeur.   — Non, c'est une affaire de cœur.

Le vieux monsieur n'a que deux cheveux.
Il ne pleut pas quand le ciel est bleu.

3 Copiez les phrases suivantes pour préparer une dictée.

1. — Je n'ai pas reçu d'argent. Mes parents ont refusé.
2. — Trouve-toi un job. Voici : «On cherche une jeune fille sérieuse pour garder deux enfants le jeudi soir au vingt-deux, rue du Cherche-Midi.»
3. — Ah non. Pas d'enfants. J'ai déjà gardé mes neveux. Ça suffit.
4. — Voilà, on cherche des serveuses. Tu peux téléphoner à Monsieur Durand au Bœuf sur le Toit.
5. — Surtout pas. Je déteste l'odeur des frites.
6. — Toi, tu es paresseuse. Tu ne sais pas ce que tu veux.

VERIFIONS!

Answers are given. Some answers will vary.

Do you know how to ask someone to lend you something?

Ask your friend to lend you 100 francs in three different ways.
Tu peux me prêter 100 F?   Tu as 100 F à me donner?   Tu peux me donner 100 F?

Can you insist if your first request is refused?

Give two different expressions to accomplish this.
Allez!   Sois gentil!

Have you learned how to refuse a request for a favor?

Refuse your friend's request, using two different expressions.
Non, cette fois, c'est fini.   Pas question!

Do you know what to say as you grant a request?

Your friend has asked to borrow a few francs. What two different expressions
might you use as you lend the money?   Bon, voilà.   Tiens.   Ça va pour cette fois.

Can you express a need?

Say that you need a certain amount of money. Say that you need to buy
something.   J'ai besoin de 200 F. Il faut que j'achète une nouvelle robe.

Have you learned how to use the object pronouns *me, te, nous,* and *vous*?

Restate each sentence, adding the French equivalent of the English pronoun in
parentheses.   1. Elle me prête 15 F.   3. Il nous téléphone à 8 h.
1. Elle prête quinze francs. *(me)*   3. Il téléphone à huit heures. *(us)*
2. J'attends là-bas. *(you, pl.)*   4. Nous allons aider. *(you, sing.)*
   2. Je vous attends là-bas.   4. Nous allons t'aider.

Do you know how to give advice?

Ask your friend why he/she doesn't do each of the following things.
1. chercher un job   2. mettre une annonce
Pourquoi est-ce que tu ne cherches pas un job?   Pourquoi est-ce que tu ne mets pas une annonce?

Have you learned to use *plus, jamais, rien,* and *que* with *ne*?

Restate each sentence, adding the French equivalent of the English given in
parentheses.   Je n'ai jamais gardé les chiens.   Nous n'avons rien mangé.
1. J'ai gardé les chiens. *(never)*   3. Nous avons mangé. *(nothing)*
2. Elle est serveuse. *(no longer)*   4. Tu as huit francs. *(only)*
   Elle n'est plus serveuse.   Tu n'as que huit francs?

Can you ask people how they feel about their activities?

Ask your friend how he/she likes his/her job. Use three different expressions.
Ça te plaît, ton job?   C'est intéressant, ton job?   Ça va, ton job?

Do you know how to express pleasure and disappointment?

Tell your friend in at least two different ways how much you like your new job.
Now express disappointment with your new job three different ways.
J'adore! C'est passionnant.   Ça m'énerve.   Ça m'embête.   C'est mal payé.

Do you know how to give reasons for doing something?

Give three different reasons for having a job, using **moyen, façon,** and
occasion.   C'est un moyen d'être indépendant(e). C'est une occasion d'apprendre un métier.
C'est une façon de gagner de l'argent.

Have you learned to use the object pronouns *me, te, nous,* and *vous* with the
passé composé?

Rewrite each sentence, changing the verb to the **passé composé.** Make any
necessary spelling changes in the past participle.
   Il nous a invités, Pierre et moi?   Nathalie! Anne! Je vous ai attendues!
1. Il nous invite, Pierre et moi?   3. Nathalie! Anne! Je vous attends.
2. Paul t'offre un cadeau, Marie?   4. Tes parents te paient, Marianne?
   Paul t'a offert un cadeau, Marie?   Tes parents t'ont payée, Marianne?

VOCABULAIRE

SECTION A

l' **argent de poche** (m.)
spending money,
allowance
Bravo! *Well done!*
la **catégorie** *category*
une **centaine** *hundred*
démodé, -e *out of style*
dépenser *to spend*
dépensier, -ière
spendthrift
dit : Qu'est-ce qu'elle a
dit? *What did she say?*
échange : en
échange *in exchange*
économe *economical,*
thrifty
emprunter (à) *to borrow*
(from)
encore *again*
Félicitations! *Congratulations!*
juste *just, only*
partie : faire partie
de *to belong to*
une **personne** *person*
prêter *to lend*
ravi, -e *delighted*
rendre *to give back,*
return
vraiment *really*

SECTION B

aboyer *to bark*
arrêter *to stop*
boume : Ça
boume? *How's it*
going?
un **budget** *budget*
un(e) **caissier, -ière** *cashier*
casser *to break*
un **centre de loisirs**

vacation camp, resort
un **compte** *bank account;*
sur mon compte
in my account
compter *to count*
court : à court de
short of
crier *to shout*
décidé *decided*
désespéré, -e
discouraged
distribuer *to distribute*
dynamique *dynamic*
économiser *to economize*
embêter *to annoy*
énerver *to upset*
l' **enfer** (m.) *hell*
étranger, -ère *foreign*
un **fast-food** *fast-food*
restaurant
une **ferme** *farm*
garder *to keep*
griffer *to claw, scratch*
intéresser *to interest*
jamais *never*
marcher : Ça marche?
Is it going well?
miauler *to meow*
un **neveu** (pl. **-x**) *nephew*
des **nouvelles** (f.) *news*
l' **odeur** (f.) *odor*
pair : travailler au pair
to work as a mother's
helper
patient, -e *patient*
payé *paid*
un **pays** *country*
promener *to walk (an*
animal)
un **prospectus** *handbill,*
flier
sérieux, -se *serious*

un(e) **serveur, -euse** *waiter,*
waitress
une **solution** *solution*
taper à la machine *to*
type

SECTION C

un **apprentissage** *apprenticeship*
un **boulot** (fam.) *job*
changer *to change*
un **désir** *desire*
dès que *as soon as*
donc *therefore*
écrit : elle a écrit *she*
wrote
une **façon** *way*
l' **important** (m.)
important thing
incompatible *incompatible*
l' **indépendance** (f.) *independence*
indépendant, -e
independent
inquiet, -ète *worried*
un **métier** *trade, craft*
un **minimum** *minimum*
la **moitié** *half*
un **moyen** *means*
une **occasion** *opportunity*
payer *to pay*
proposer *to propose,*
suggest
la **raison** *reason*
un(e) **réceptionniste** *receptionist,*
desk clerk
le **reste** *rest, remainder*
les **services** (m.) *services*
un **stage** *training course*
travailleur, -euse
hardworking
un(e) **voisin, -ine** *neighbor*

ETUDE DE MOTS

Can you find the following words in the list above?
1. Find one word to illustrate the rule that nouns ending in **-ion** are feminine.
2. Find four adjectives that are also past participles of verbs.
3. Find one verb that requires an indirect-object pronoun.
4. Find the word that has the opposite meaning of **prêter**.
5. Find three words that add an **accent grave** in the feminine form.

---

1. une solution, une occasion   2. démodé, ravi, décidé, désespéré, payé   3. prêter, emprunter   4. emprunter
5. dépensière, étrangère, inquiète, caissière

A LIRE

Le Katalavox 📼

Quand on a une passion et qu'on aime travailler, il y a toujours moyen de réussir. Voici l'histoire de Martine Kempf, une jeune Alsacienne.

Avant de lire

Ceci est l'histoire d'une jeune femme française qui a inventé un appareil extraordinaire. Avant de lire l'histoire, pouvez-vous trouver rapidement :
— le nom de son invention? Le Katalavox
— la description de l'invention? C'est un petit ordinateur. Il reconnaît la voix de son maître et lui obéit très vite.
— la raison de cette invention? C'est utile et ça rend service.

Une invention française pleine d'avenir...

Le Katalavox, c'est une petite boîte, un peu plus grande qu'un walkman. Installé sur une chaise roulante, il ne reconnaît que la voix° de son maître° et lui obéit au 10ᵉ de seconde. La chaise avance, recule, tourne à droite ou à gauche sur un seul mot de son utilisateur. Adapté sur une voiture, la porte s'ouvre, le rétroviseur° s'ajuste, la radio s'allume, le moteur se met en marche à la voix. En salle d'opération, le micro-chirurgien° peut, avec l'ordinateur à commande vocale, utiliser toutes les fonctions de son microscope ou contrôler la lumière° de la salle d'opération.

Aujourd'hui, dans son local de Sunnyvale dans la Silicon Valley aux Etats-Unis, Martine Kempf explique : «Mon père a depuis 30 ans une entreprise qui adapte des voitures pour les handicapés physiques. Lorsqu'il a voulu développer un système pour aider les gens sans bras°, nous avons pensé à la commande vocale.»

Nous sommes en 1981. Martine Kempf est alors étudiante en astronomie à Bonn en Allemagne. Son père et elle se renseignent°. Partout, la réponse est la même : l'ordinateur à commande vocale existe au stade expérimental, mais il n'y a pas de produit commercialisable. Qu'à cela ne tienne°! Martine Kempf décide de chercher. «J'ai obtenu mon premier ordinateur, j'ai appris à l'utiliser et sept mois plus tard, j'ai fabriqué mon premier prototype du Katalavox.»

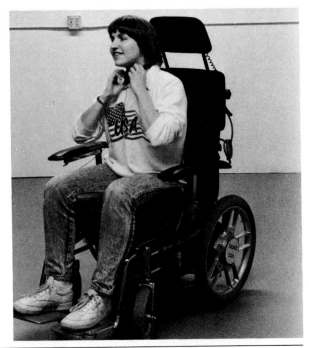

---

voix *voice;* **maître** *master;* **rétroviseur** *rear-view mirror;* **micro-chirurgien** *micro-surgeon;* **lumière** *light;* **bras** *arms;* **se renseignent** *inquire;* **Qu'à cela ne tienne!** *That doesn't matter!*

Martine Kempf a été surprise par le succès de son Katalavox. «Quand j'ai fait le prototype, dit-elle, je l'ai fait parce que c'est très utile et que ça rend service.» Des applications «pour rendre service», Martine Kempf en fait encore beaucoup aujourd'hui. «J'ai fait une application pour un ingénieur qui est totalement paralysé à l'âge de 42 ans. Je lui ai fait des lunettes avec un capteur infrarouge. Quand il cligne de l'œil°, il envoie un signal. J'ai adapté une stéréo pour lui. Maintenant il peut écouter des livres enregistrés. C'est une belle application qui me fait plaisir.»

Après deux ans aux Etats-Unis, l'entreprise Kempf va bien. Pourtant Martine Kempf ne veut pas faire carrière° dans l'électronique. «J'ai beaucoup d'idées sur ce que je vais faire mais je ne le dis pas. C'est une surprise. Le principal, c'est d'avoir une passion et de beaucoup travailler.»

Aujourd'hui, en Alsace, dans le village où Martine est née, il y a une rue Martine Kempf. Les villageois sont fiers° de cette jeune femme connue dans le monde entier pour sa merveilleuse invention, le Katalavox.

Abridgment of "Scandale en France, succès aux Etats-Unis" (Retitled: "Le Katalavox") by Dominique Brémond from *Journal Français d'Amérique*, October 1987. Reprinted by permission of Journal Français d'Amérique.

Activité • Qu'est-ce que c'est?

Choisissez la bonne définition.

1. prototype
2. reculer
3. une entreprise
4. rendre service
5. villageois

a. aider
b. les habitants d'un village
c. modèle
d. le contraire d' «avancer»
e. une compagnie

Activité • Imaginez

Vous êtes inventeur/inventrice. Qu'est-ce que vous allez inventer? Donnez des raisons.

Activité • Ecrivez   Possible answers are given.

Martine Kempf reçoit beaucoup de lettres de remerciements envoyées par les gens qu'elle a aidés. Imaginez une lettre de remerciements envoyée par une des personnes suivantes.

1. Une personne handicapée qui peut maintenant conduire une voiture
2. Un micro-chirurgien   1. Chère Mlle Kempf, Merci beaucoup pour votre invention. Je suis handicapé(e). Maintenant avec le Katalavox, je peux conduire ma voiture. C'est un moyen d'être indépendant.

cligne de l'oeil *winks;* **carrière** *career;* **fiers** *proud*   2. Chère Mlle Kempf, Je suis micro-chirurgien. Votre invention, le Katalavox, m'aide beaucoup dans la salle d'opération. C'est formidable! Vous avez aidé beaucoup de gens. Merci beaucoup!

Les jeunes entrepreneurs

Avez-vous l'esprit d'entreprise? Voici des jeunes français qui ont créé une entreprise. Ils fabriquent pour revendre avec un bénéfice°.

Avant de lire

Lisez rapidement ces histoires pour trouver les réponses aux questions suivantes. 1. Stéphanie fait et revend des confitures.   Laura et Capucine fabriquent et revende des bracelets. Valérie fabrique et revend des vêtements.   Dimitri et Aurélien revendent des objets

1. Qui fabrique et revend un produit? Quel produit? qu'ils trouvent dans les
greniers ou les caves.

2. Qui offre ses services? Quels services?

2. Jean-François a monté un club de vacances pour les animaux.
Dimitri et Aurélien ont une entreprise de débarras de caves et greniers.

Stéphanie, 15 ans, fait des confitures. Elle adore l'odeur des fruits qui éclatent° dans le sirop. Pour faire baisser son prix de revient°, elle a différents moyens. Les fraises, elle va les cueillir° directement chez les producteurs. Les myrtilles, elle les ramasse° chez sa tante Christine, qui habite dans les Vosges. Les pêches et les abricots, elle les achète au marché. Elle vend sa production à des amis de sa mère et à des voisins. Ses prix? Ceux de supermarché, mais avec la qualité en plus. Seule obligation pour sa clientèle, lui rendre les pots vides. Prix : 13 F les 250 grammes.

Laura et Capucine, 12 ans et 14 ans, fabriquent avec beaucoup de dextérité° de petits bracelets de coton noué°. Elles font des concours°, à celle qui va le plus vite. Leur production, les bons jours : 3 à 4 chacune. Elles les vendent aux copines de classe et espèrent trouver un petit marchand de gadgets ou de souvenirs qui leur en prendrait en dépôt-vente°. Le bracelet vaut 50 F.

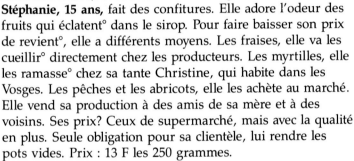

Valérie, 17 ans, veut plus tard être styliste. Elle a commencé par se bricoler des tenues° bien à elle. Ses copines de terminale ont craqué pour ses mini-jupes et pour ses vestes courtes et cintrées°… Elle a commencé à leur fabriquer des vêtements à la demande. Même les garçons de sa classe lui commandent maintenant des tee-shirts teints ou imprimés au pochoir°. Elle s'est fait une véritable clientèle. La jupe vaut 70 F, le tee-shirt teint 40 F. Plus elle fait de vêtements, plus elle va vite et plus sa cagnotte° augmente.

---

bénéfice *profit;*   **éclatent** *burst;*   **prix de revient** *cost price;*   **cueillir** *pick;*   **ramasse** *gather;*   **dextérité** *manual skill;*
noué *knotted;*   **concours** *race;*   **en dépôt-vente** *on consignment;*   **tenues** *clothes;*   **craqué** *went wild;*   **cintrées** *gathered at the waist;*   **imprimés au pochoir** *stenciled;*   **cagnotte** *nest egg*

Jean-François, 15 ans, lui, a la chance de vivre dans une maison avec un grand jardin. Un copain sympa lui a donné l'idée de monter un club de vacances pour les animaux. Seule condition posée par ses parents : que tous ces hôtes° ne mettent pas les «pattes» dans la maison. Avec un peu de grillage, Jean-François a construit dans un coin° du jardin un chenil°. Le soir, les chiens sont rentrés dans la cave°, les chats dans le garage. Les hamsters et les souris° blanches en pension sont installées dans leur cage, dans un coin du grenier°. Ses tarifs : pour un chien, 500 F par mois; pour un chat, 300 F par mois; pour un hamster, 100 F par mois; la nourriture n'est pas comprise.

Dimitri et Aurélien, 15 et 16 ans, vont sans doute être antiquaires° plus tard. L'été dernier, ils ont décidé de monter une «entreprise» de débarras° de caves et greniers. Ils ont préparé, à l'aide de la photocopieuse du père d'Aurélien, un petit prospectus proposant leurs services et l'ont distribué dans le quartier. Les copains recherchent surtout les objets qui ont un peu de valeur. Ils les nettoient°, les réparent, mettent un petit coup de peinture. Ils ont un véritable trésor de guerre, qu'ils comptent vendre à la braderie° municipale. Ils n'ont pas encore osé pour l'instant s'installer au marché aux puces° en *squatters*; les marchands officiels ont tendance à vous chasser° ou à vous dénoncer à la police.

Activité • Avez-vous compris?

Trouvez dans «Les jeunes entrepreneurs» les renseignements nécessaires pour compléter ce tableau.

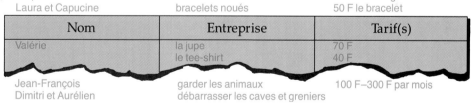

Nom	Entreprise	Tarif(s)
Stéphanie	la confiture	13 F les 250 g
Laura et Capucine	bracelets noués	50 F le bracelet
Valérie	la jupe	70 F
	le tee-shirt	40 F
Jean-François	garder les animaux	100 F–300 F par mois
Dimitri et Aurélien	débarrasser les caves et greniers	

Activité • Qu'en pensez-vous?   Possible answers are given.

1. Quel(s) entrepreneur(s) admirez-vous? Pourquoi? J'admire Valérie parce que j'aime les vêtements.
2. Quelle entreprise vous intéresse? Faire de la confiture, ça m'intéresse.
3. A votre avis, est-ce que ces jeunes vont avoir du succès? Pourquoi?
   Oui, parce qu'ils ont de très bonnes idées.

Activité • Et vous?

1. Avez-vous déjà fabriqué quelque chose pour revendre? Expliquez.
2. Avez-vous déjà essayé d'offrir vos services pour gagner de l'argent? Expliquez.

---

hôtes *guests;* **coin** *corner;* **chenil** *kennels;* **cave** *cellar;* **souris** *mice;* **grenier** *attic;* **antiquaires** *antique dealers;* **débarras** *cleaning out;* **nettoient** *clean;* **braderie** *rummage sale;* **marché aux puces** *flea market;* **chasser** *chase*

Test : L'argent et vous

Est-ce que l'argent est important pour vous? Le gardez-vous ou le dépensez-vous? Etes-vous économe ou dépensier/dépensière? Pour savoir, passez d'abord ce test. Ensuite, interprétez vos résultats.

1.

Pour avoir de l'argent de poche,...
a. vous faites de petits travaux chez vous.
b. vous demandez à vos parents quand vous avez besoin.
c. vous demandez chaque mois une augmentation.

2.

Vos parents vous donnent cinq dollars.
a. Vous dépensez tout immédiatement.
b. Vous mettez l'argent dans une tirelire.
c. Vous économisez pour acheter quelque chose.

3.

Pour vous, l'argent c'est...
a. superflu.
b. merveilleux.
c. pratique.

4.

Il y a une pièce de cinq *cents* sur le trottoir.
a. Vous continuez votre chemin sans un regard.
b. Vous hésitez. Finalement vous ne prenez pas la pièce : cinq *cents,* ce n'est pas assez pour vous.
c. Vous ramassez les cinq *cents.*

5.

Vous rêvez d'être riche...
  a. tous les jours.
  b. jamais.
  c. quelquefois.

6.

Vous avez hérité d'une fortune°.
  a. Vous pleurez de joie.
  b. Vous invitez vos parents dans un restaurant chic et cher.
  c. Vous comptez le nombre de maisons que vous allez pouvoir acheter.

7.

Vous voulez recevoir...
  a. un peu d'argent tous les mois.
  b. tout l'argent tout de suite.
  c. beaucoup d'argent tous les ans.

8.

Ensuite...
  a. vous organisez une grande fête.
  b. vous n'allez plus à l'école.
  c. vous donnez un million de dollars aux gens qui ont faim.

---

hérité d'une fortune *inherited a fortune*

9.

Vous achetez…
a. une voiture rapide et confortable.
b. une petite maison de campagne.
c. un billet d'avion pour des pays exotiques.

10.

Votre rêve, c'est de…
a. faire pleuvoir en Afrique.
b. construire Manhattan sur la Lune.
c. dépenser tout votre argent.

11.

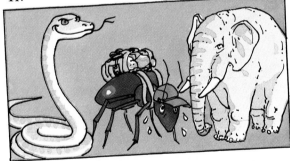

A votre avis, l'argent c'est…
a. un serpent rusé.
b. une fourmi travailleuse.
c. un éléphant puissant.

12.

Maintenant que vous êtes riche, vous voulez…
a. devenir célèbre.
b. être encore plus riche.
c. avoir une vie tranquille et merveilleuse.

Résultats du test

Dans ce tableau, regardez, pour chaque question, la lettre qui correspond à votre réponse. Comptez combien vous avez de réponses par ligne (quand la lettre est *soulignée*, comptez deux points). Vous avez beaucoup de points à la première ligne? Vous êtes «Carte de crédit».

VOUS ÊTES...	1	2	3	4	5	6	7	8	9	10	11	12
Carte de crédit	c	a	b	a	a	c	b	a	a	b	c	a
Porte-monnaie	a	b	a	b	b	b	a	c	c	a	a	c
Tirelire	b	c	c	c	c	a	c	b	b	c	b	b

Carte de crédit

Vous aimez dépenser, vous ne pouvez pas économiser. Pour vous, c'est impossible de garder de l'argent. Vous adorez acheter. Dès que vous avez de l'argent, vous courez au centre commercial, au magasin de disques, vous invitez des amis... C'est si facile de payer avec une carte de crédit! Une petite signature et ça y est! Vous achetez tout et n'importe quoi, simplement pour le plaisir d'acheter. A ce rythme, il faut être milliardaire!

Porte-monnaie°

Pour vous, l'argent c'est un moyen de rendre les autres heureux. Vous aimez offrir, faire des cadeaux à vos amis, aider vos parents. Vous êtes content(e) avec un minimum d'argent. Vous ne voulez pas être riche, ça ne vous intéresse pas. Non, vous désirez être tranquille, à l'abri du° besoin, c'est tout. Un peu d'argent pour vous, le reste pour les autres, c'est votre seule ambition.

Tirelire

Pour vous, l'argent c'est l'argent. Vous savez faire des économies. Vous connaissez la valeur de l'argent. Vous réfléchissez beaucoup avant de dépenser. Vous n'êtes pas égoïste° ou avare°, et vous pouvez dépenser de l'argent pour offrir un beau cadeau. Mais vous êtes sage°, vous ne gaspillez° jamais.

Activité • Donnez votre opinion   Possible answers are given.

1. Etes-vous d'accord avec le résultat de votre test?   Oui, je suis d'accord. (ou) Non, je ne suis pas d'accord.
2. Pour vous, qu'est-ce que l'argent représente? Et pour vos camarades? Complétez la phrase suivante de différentes façons.   Pour moi, l'argent représente l'indépendance. Les copains sont d'accord avec moi.

   L'argent, c'est un moyen de...   être indépendant(e).

---

porte-monnaie *change purse;*   **à l'abri du** *sheltered from;*   **égoïste** *selfish;*   **avare** *greedy;*   **sage** *wise;*   **gaspillez** *waste*

CHAPITRE 7 En pleine forme

	BASIC MATERIAL	COMMUNICATIVE FUNCTIONS
PREMIER CONTACT	**Un sport pour l'été (1)** **Ne sautez pas le petit déjeuner! (4)**	Reading for global comprehension and cultural awareness
SECTION A	**Fabrice n'est pas en forme. (A1)** **Où est-ce qu'ils vont quand ils ont mal? (A14)**	**Exchanging information** • Talking about health **Expressing feelings, emotions** • Complaining about health **Socializing** • Expressing concern
SECTION B	**Début de la remise en forme (B1)** **Le nouveau régime de Fabrice (B13)**	**Persuading** • Talking about eating well • Giving and justifying advice **Expressing attitudes, opinions** • Expressing doubt, uncertainty, dislikes
SECTION C	**La remise en forme (suite) (C1)** **La remise en forme (fin) (C5)** **Autres exercices (C7)**	**Persuading** • Talking about fitness • Assuring and reassuring • Encouraging **Expressing feelings, emotions** • Expressing fatigue • Expressing pity
TRY YOUR SKILLS	**Fabrice n'arrive plus à dormir. (1)**	

- **Prononciation** (the nasals; dictation) **265**
- **Vérifions!** **266**   ■ **Vocabulaire** **267**

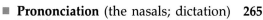

A LIRE	**Bibi : le fana de la forme** (A health fanatic pens a poem about his problems.) **Comment soigner les petits maux?** (a French doctor's diagnosis) **La Chromogym** (a colorful gym class in France)

WRITING   A variety of controlled and open-ended writing activities appear in the Pupil's Edition. The Teacher's Notes identify other activities suitable for writing practice.

COOPERATIVE LEARNING   Many of the activities in the Pupil's Edition lend themselves to cooperative learning. For guidelines, see page T14.

Scope and Sequence

GRAMMAR	CULTURE	RE-ENTRY
	Health benefits of sports French breakfast habits	
The reflexive pronouns 　with verbs in the 　present tense and in the 　**passe composé** (A7) The verb **se sentir** (A10)	Sleeping habits of French 　teenagers	**Il faut que** + subjunctive Inviting friends
The verb **boire** (B5) The verb **suivre** (B11)	Fast food in France	Food vocabulary Offering, accepting, and 　refusing food or drink Giving reasons for doing 　something
The verb **courir** (C10) Irregular subjunctives: 　**aller, avoir,** and 　**être** (C13)	Health clubs in France	Numbers The present subjunctive: 　regular forms

Recombining communicative functions, grammar, and vocabulary

Reading for practice and pleasure

UNIT RESOURCES　**Cahier d'Activités, Cahier d'Exercices,** Unit 7 Cassettes,
Transparencies 17–19, Quizzes 16–18, Unit 7 Test

TEACHER-PREPARED MATERIALS　**Section A**　Illustrations of reflexive
actions; **Section B**　Pictures of food and drink; artificial fruits and vegetables;
pictures of unappetizing foods; **Try Your Skills**　French magazines

PREMIER
CONTACT The authentic material in **Premier Contact** introduces the theme of the unit. Concentrate only on the general content of these documents. A detailed treatment of the grammar and vocabulary is not intended. Since students should be reading for global comprehension, they need not know the meaning of every word. For this reason, new words in **Premier Contact** have been omitted from the unit vocabulary list and the French-English Vocabulary at the end of the book.

OBJECTIVES   To read for global comprehension and cultural awareness; to get acquainted with the topic

1   Un sport pour l'été

Students are not responsible for learning the names of the parts of the body as indicated in the drawing. Say the words aloud as students look at the drawing of the athlete. Then, using a TPR technique, have students point to the part of their body as you mention the French name: **Montrez-moi le coude! Voici le coude!** The game Simon Says **(Jacques a dit)** also makes practice fun. Now have students follow along in their books as you play the cassette or read aloud the article about summer activities. Pause at the end to ask a few questions:

> Quelle est la bonne saison pour commencer une activité sportive?
> Quelles parties du corps utilisez-vous quand vous marchez?
> Quelles parties du corps le golf fait-il travailler?
> Quel sport est bon pour le cœur et les poumons?
> Quel sport est excellent pour la respiration et la circulation?
> Le vélo est bon pour quelles parties du corps?
> Quel sport n'est pas bon pour tout le monde?

2   Activité • Trouvez des renseignements

For cooperative learning, students might work in pairs or small groups. Have them make a table for themselves as shown. They should work with their classmate(s) to find the required information in the article. Verify the data by calling on individuals.

3   Activité • Et vous?

Encourage students to skim the article to find reasons for choosing a certain sport: **pour entretenir la forme, pour garder la ligne, pour dépenser des calories, pour fortifier les muscles et les jambes,** and so on.

SLOWER-PACED LEARNING   Prepare lists of reasons for selecting a sport and reasons for beginning in the summer. Have students select answers from these.

CHALLENGE   Students may wish to argue for winter as the ideal season to start sports. Encourage a discussion to include names of winter sports and their benefits to the body.

4   NE SAUTEZ PAS LE PETIT DEJEUNER!

Before reading the article, have students tell what they know about breakfast in France. Have them guess what percentage of French people don't eat breakfast and, among those who do, what percentage have a balanced breakfast, a hot beverage and a **tartine,** or a hot beverage only. Then play the cassette or read the article aloud as students follow along in their books. They should compare their predictions to the figures mentioned in the article.

5 ### Activité • Avez-vous compris?

SLOWER-PACED LEARNING   Prepare multiple-choice answers to the questions and distribute them to the class. Read the questions aloud and have students circle the letter of their choice. Reread the questions and have students volunteer their answers, repeating the sentence they chose. The choices for the first question might be as follows: *(a)* **Ils sont nutritionnistes.** *(b)* **Ils n'ont pas le temps.** *(c)* **Ils ont besoin de calories et de protéines.**

6 ### Activité • Et vous?

For question 2, provide some specialized vocabulary:

des œufs *eggs*	le pain grillé *toast*
du lard *bacon*	des crêpes *pancakes*
des saucisses *sausage*	des céréales *cereal*
un jus d'orange *orange juice*	

7 ### Activité • Sondage

Have students make up a survey form with columns headed **Tu sautes le petit déjeuner? Tu prends le petit déjeuner?** and **Qu'est-ce que tu prends?** Have students circulate among their classmates to conduct their surveys. Then have them report their findings.

OBJECTIVES   **To exchange information:** talk about health; **to express feelings, emotions:** complain about health; **to socialize:** express concern

CULTURAL BACKGROUND   The French have become much more health conscious in the past decade. This trend has affected French young people in some ways more than others. According to a recent survey, approximately 65 percent of French teenagers say that they get some physical exercise. Of these, about one third do so on a regular basis. On the other hand, many show little interest in developing good eating habits. They choose to skip breakfast so that they can spend a few minutes more getting ready in the morning. They then often eat a rushed lunch at school. Few schools have modern, cafeteria-style lunch rooms that offer a variety of dishes. In most a set menu is prepared in large quantities and served at one sitting. If given the choice, French teenagers would much rather eat fast foods than a balanced meal.

MOTIVATING ACTIVITY   Have students answer the questions in the introduction to Section A: **Vous avez du mal à vous lever le matin? Vous n'arrivez pas à dormir? Vous êtes en forme? Vous manquez de tonus?**

A1 ## Fabrice n'est pas en forme.

First have students look at the pictures and read the captions. Ask one or two volunteers to describe the situation briefly in English. Then ask students to suggest in French or in English what Fabrice should do to feel better:

Fabrice se sent mal. Que doit-il faire pour se sentir mieux? If a student answers **Fabrice doit bien manger,** confirm the response with **C'est vrai. Il doit bien se nourrir.** Or, if a student says **Fabrice doit faire du sport,** confirm with **Oui, il doit s'entraîner.** Emphasize the similarity in meaning between **manger/se nourrir** and **faire du sport/s'entraîner.** Continue introducing new reflexive verbs in this way. Next play the cassette or read the dialogue aloud. Have students imagine Fabrice's answer to the last question in the dialogue. Finally, have students read aloud and role-play the dialogue.

A2 Activité • Parlons de Fabrice

You might ask these questions orally of the entire class and call on volunteers to answer. Or, have students work in pairs to find the answers and write them down.

SLOWER-PACED LEARNING Prepare answers to these questions on the board or on a transparency. Students may then match each answer to the appropriate question.

A3 Activité • Actes de parole

On the board or on a transparency, write the expressions the students find. Then have them pair off and use these expressions to make up their own brief dialogues.

A4 Activité • Choisissez

Have students identify the two habits that are not beneficial, beginning their sentences with **Il ne faut pas.** Ask students what other good habits they can think of. As a project, students might create posters to illustrate their sentences, using magazine pictures or original drawings.

A5 Activité • Qu'est-ce qu'il faut faire?

Call attention to the subjunctive form **fasse** after **il faut que.** Explain the difference between the use of the infinitive and the use of a clause after **il faut.** You might want to give students a few practice items on this point, such as changing **Il faut travailler** to **Il faut que tu travailles.**

SLOWER-PACED LEARNING Have students suggest what activity is illustrated in each picture. Then have them give the subjunctive form of the appropriate verb. Finally, have students answer with complete sentences.

A6 Activité • Et vous?

First ask volunteers to rephrase the questions, using **tu** instead of **vous.** For cooperative learning, have students pair off to ask each other these questions. After they have practiced, call on individuals to report their partners' answers to the class.

A7 STRUCTURES DE BASE

Ask students if they noticed something different about the new verbs in A1. The small words that precede these verbs are there for a reason. Demonstrate with **La mère couche son enfant** and **Le garçon se couche.** Use visuals to show the difference between these two statements. Have students guess how the **je, tu, ils** forms would be constructed, based on what they observed in A1. Present the **nous** and **vous** forms. To confirm understanding of the reflexive concept, show visuals that depict **La mère nourrit son enfant, Le garçon se nourrit bien, La fille promène le chien, La fille se promène.** Have students then vary the subjects of the sentences that have reflexive verbs: **Je me nourris bien, Tu te nourris bien,** and so on. Next have students open their books to page 242 and read the explanation about reflexive pronouns.

Use a TPR technique to reinforce the meanings and to practice the imperative forms. Direct individuals to perform the action of the verb: **Couchez-vous, Levez-vous, Entraînez-vous.** Students should dramatize the actions as they tell what they're doing: **Je me couche, Je me lève, Je m'entraîne.** Next have students direct others to perform by giving the same commands: **Couche-toi, Lève-toi.** Then have them give the same commands to a couple of students, using the **vous** form. The students respond using the **nous** form. Have other students tell what their classmates are doing, using the third-person forms.

To practice infinitive forms, have students tell what they're going to do: **Je vais me coucher tard ce soir, Je vais me lever à six heures demain.** To practice the **passé composé** orally, give sentences using a reflexive verb in the present tense, and have students restate them in the **passé composé.** To practice past participle agreement, dictate several sentences.

A 8 Activité • Qu'est-ce qu'on fait?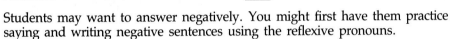

Students should look at each picture and respond, first in the present tense and then in the **passé composé.** After they've done the activity orally, assign it to be written; check for correct spellings of past participles.

A 9 Activité • A vous maintenant!

Students may want to answer negatively. You might first have them practice saying and writing negative sentences using the reflexive pronouns.

CHALLENGE Encourage students to expand their answers with additional or more precise information. Also, have them expand the dialogues by adding **Et toi?** to the first response.

A10 STRUCTURES DE BASE

Have students repeat after you the forms of the reflexive verb **se sentir,** both affirmative and negative. Explain the difference between **Je ne me sens pas bien** and **Je me sens mal.** The latter is much stronger. It implies that you're on the verge of collapse. Then ask questions of and about members of the class: **Vous vous sentez bien, Anne? Jacques, est-ce qu'Anne se sent bien?**

A11 Activité • Complétez le dialogue

For cooperative learning, have students pair off to decide on the appropriate verb forms. They should have you check their work, and then practice the dialogue together, exchanging roles. Call on volunteers to dramatize the dialogue for the class.

CHALLENGE Have the students continue the dialogue between Fabrice and his mother for three additional exchanges.

A 12 Activité • Faites des excuses

Tell students that they will have to change the reflexive pronoun **se** to **me** in their responses. Students should pair off to do this activity and take turns asking and answering the questions.

A13 ## Activité • Et vous?

You might invite students to ask you the questions and you give them appropriate answers; this will suggest possible responses to them. Finally, have them pair off to ask each other the questions.

A 14 ## OU EST-CE QU'ILS VONT QUAND ILS ONT MAL?

Tell students that the verb **avoir** is used in many expressions of feeling. Ask them to recall any **avoir** expressions that they can (Unit 3, B18, page 107).

Play the cassette as students look at the illustrations and repeat the captions. Use the new vocabulary in personalized questions: **Vous allez souvent chez le dentiste (docteur)? Vous aimez y aller?** Explain the difference between a **pharmacie** in France and an American drugstore. Have students refer to the drawing in **Premier Contact** of this unit. They might use the parts of the body with **avoir du mal à** in a game. Students indicate a part of their body and classmates respond with **Tu as mal (au genou).**

A15 ## COMMENT LE DIRE

Have students read to themselves the expressions of concern. Then pretend that you're not feeling well and encourage them to show their concern for you, using the expressions in the box with **vous.** Respond to their concern with different complaints. Use gestures and facial expressions to make your meaning clear. Then reverse roles: you express concern for the students and they complain.

A16 ## Activité • Donnez des conseils

Read the "complaints" aloud, using body language; have students repeat and imitate. Then have students do the activity in pairs, taking turns complaining and advising. Encourage students to suggest additional advice.

A17 ## Savez-vous que... ?

Play the cassette or have a volunteer read the paragraph aloud as students follow along in their books. Ask several questions to assess comprehension: **En général, combien d'heures est-ce que les Français dorment chaque nuit? Combien d'heures est-ce que les adolescents doivent dormir? Et combien d'heures est-ce que les adolescents français dorment en réalité? Pourquoi?** As a follow-up activity, have students conduct a survey of adults and other young people. They should arrange their findings in a chart entitled **Le sommeil des Américains** and report them to the class. If they find any great differences between French and American sleeping habits, students might try to suggest reasons why this is so.

A18 ## Activité • Ecoutez bien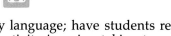

You're going to hear six of your French friends complain about their health. What advice would you give them? Open your book to page 245.

(pause) Copy the chart in A18 on a separate sheet of paper. *(pause)* As you listen to each complaint, make a check mark in the appropriate box. Ready? **Ecoutez bien.**

1. Je n'arrive jamais à me lever le matin. *Il faut te coucher plus tôt.*
2. J'ai drôlement mal aux dents. *Va chez le dentiste.*
3. J'ai mal à la tête. *Pourquoi tu ne vas pas chez le pharmacien?*
4. Je ne me sens pas bien; j'ai mal partout. *Va chez le docteur.*
5. Je ne suis pas en forme. *Fais des exercices.*
6. J'ai mal au cœur. *Il faut que tu manges mieux.*

Et maintenant, vérifions. *Read each statement again and give the correct answer.*

SECTION B

OBJECTIVES **To persuade:** talk about eating well; give and justify advice; **to express attitudes, opinions:** express doubt, uncertainty, dislikes

CULTURAL BACKGROUND As a result of increasing prosperity since World War II, the diet of the French people has changed. Meat, rather than grain products, is now the staple. The French are the largest consumers of meat in Europe, and their diet is getting steadily closer to that of a typical American. Consumption of sugar is also very much on the increase. The French still consume less sugar than the Americans and the English, but the gap is narrowing. The French still drink very little milk, but they get their calcium by eating a lot of cheese. Fresh fruit is also popular. The consumption of bread is down by half from 40 years ago, but bread is still typically served with every meal. The ills that accompany a rich diet—heart disease, increased risk of cancer, obesity—have contributed to making the French more diet and health conscious in recent years.

MOTIVATING ACTIVITY Discuss students' eating habits, favorite snacks, and favorite places to eat out: **Est-ce que vous vous nourrissez bien? Prenez-vous un goûter après l'école? Mangez-vous souvent dans un fast-food?**

B1   Début de la remise en forme

Use pictures to present the new vocabulary from the first dialogue: **des céréales, une tartine, un verre.** Teach the verb **peser** and show the students how to calculate their weight in kilos (divide their weight in pounds by 2.2). Then play the cassette or read the dialogue aloud for the students. Call on students to summarize the exchange. Follow the same procedure for the second dialogue, asking comprehension questions afterward. Continue in the same way with the third dialogue. Have students listen for what Fabrice wants to eat and what Sandrine suggests he eat. After all three dialogues have been presented, students working in pairs should choose one dialogue to read aloud and role-play for the class.

B2   Activité • Complétez

Allow students time to skim the dialogues for the words that they will need to complete the sentences; they should jot down the words as they find them.

Then call on individuals to read aloud the completed sentences. Assign the sentences to be written for homework.

SLOWER-PACED LEARNING Prepare and distribute a list of possible completions from which students may choose.

B3 Activité • Expliquez

Have students look for the reasons in the text. You might have them pair off and do this activity as a dialogue between Fabrice (who asks **Pourquoi... ?)** and Sandrine (who says **Parce que...**).

SLOWER-PACED LEARNING For each item, play the recording of the dialogue where the answer is to be found. Tell students to listen carefully for an adjective that tells why these things are beneficial.

B4 Activité • A vous maintenant!

Students should find these expressions to offer advice: **Il faut que tu..., Tu devrais...,** and **Il vaut mieux que tu...** You may also wish to review the expressions in Unit 5, C9, page 173.

SLOWER-PACED LEARNING As students find the three expressions, write them on the board. Point out the two that are followed by subjunctive forms. Next to each expression, write the numbers of two of the activities. Have students pair off and write out the sentences.

CHALLENGE For cooperative learning, have students pair off and make up mini-dialogues:

—Tu devrais manger des céréales.
—Mais je ne les aime pas! C'est infect!

They might keep the dialogues going as long as possible.

—Tu devrais manger des céréales.
—Mais je ne les aime pas!
—C'est plus fortifiant qu'une tartine.
—C'est infect!
—Ça donne du tonus!
—Ça me donne mal au cœur!

B5 STRUCTURES DE BASE

Cut out pictures of various drinks from magazines. Hand a picture to each student; keep one yourself. Call on volunteers to identify the pictures. Use these pictures to teach the forms of **boire**. Show your cup of coffee and say **Je bois du café.** Point to a student who has a picture of milk and ask **Qu'est-ce que tu bois?** The student answers **Je bois du lait.** Point to another student and ask **Qu'est-ce qu'il/elle boit?** Continue in this way with the other forms of **boire**. To teach the past participle, put the picture of the coffee down and say **J'ai bu mon café.** Take a picture from one of the students and ask **Qu'est-ce que tu as bu?** Have the student answer in the **passé composé.** Continue taking back the pictures as students practice saying **J'ai bu...** or **Nous avons bu...** Have students open their books to look at the spelling of the present-tense forms of **boire**. Note the different stem in the first- and second-person plural forms. Point out the change in the stem of the subjunctive forms. To practice the subjunctive forms, tell students what you drink and have them advise a better drink: **Je bois du café. (Il vaut mieux que vous buviez du lait.)**

B 6 **Activité • Qu'est-ce qu'ils boivent?**

Students should look at the pictures and tell what the people are drinking. Ask students which of the drinks pictured they drink. Then have them ask you if you drink these beverages. Finally, assign this activity to be written.

B7 **Activité • Sondage**

Have students duplicate the chart shown in the book. Then have them circulate and interview five of their classmates. Call on individuals to report one or two of their findings: **Janine boit quelquefois du soda, Paul ne boit jamais de café.** Then ask students to write one sentence about each of their interviewees.

B8 **Activité • Et vous?**

Have students choose one of the breakfasts offered at this restaurant. They might describe their breakfast to their classmates and give a reason for their choice.

CHALLENGE Have students role-play the ordering of breakfast in the restaurant.

B9 **Activité • A vous maintenant!**

Have students pair off to practice the dialogue, exchanging roles after each variation. If someone offers them something and they want it, they should say **Oui, s'il vous plaît** or **Je veux bien.** Remind students that **Merci** used alone in this context means *No, thank you.*

CHALLENGE Students repeat the activity. This time, one offers the other something to drink. The other would rather have something to eat.

B10 **Savez-vous que... ?**

Before 1960, there were no restaurant chains in France. All restaurants were independent and were usually family-owned. It took a long time for chains to catch on with the French, but in recent years they've gained tremendous popularity. The American chains such as McDonald's and Burger King are popular with people who have had an opportunity to travel abroad and be exposed to the fast-food chains.

Take-out food is popular among the French, and not just from fast-food restaurants. There are take-out shops that sell excellent, elaborate cooked dishes for those who don't have the time to prepare them themselves. Such shops, however, are rather expensive.

First write the following words on the board: **McDonald's, Quick, Freetime, Burger King, un longburger.** Tell the students that they should be able to identify these in French after they read the text. Then play the cassette as students read along in their books. Call on volunteers to identify the words, or have students work in pairs to do so. Ask students to tell how McDonald's in France differs from its American counterpart.

Referring to the receipt from Freetime, students might role-play the customer and counterperson in the restaurant. The customer might ask how much each item costs.

B11 STRUCTURES DE BASE

Say the forms of **suivre** and have students repeat them after you. Point out that **suivre** follows a pattern close to that of **partir, sortir,** and **dormir:** it has one stem for the singular forms and another for the plural forms. The singular forms are all pronounced alike; the consonant of the infinitive is heard in all the plural forms. Ask personalized questions of the students, using the verb in both its meanings: **Suivez-vous un régime? Avez-vous déjà suivi un régime? Suivez-vous des cours de maths? Avez-vous déjà suivi des cours de musique?** When talking about taking a course in school, the French always use **cours** in the plural: **Je suis des cours de...**

Elicit the subjunctive forms of **suivre.** They follow the regular pattern. Tell students that you want to be an architect. They tell you which courses you have to take: **Je veux être architecte. (Il faut que vous suiviez des cours de maths.)**

B12 Activité • Et vous?

Respect the privacy of individuals by asking volunteers to answer these questions. You might prefer to have students write the answers.

B13 LE NOUVEAU REGIME DE FABRICE

Have students study the diet prepared for Fabrice by Sandrine. Have them learn the fruits and vegetables by looking at the pictures. Bring in artificial fruits and vegetables or pictures of food cut from magazines, and test students' knowledge by asking them to name them. For a TPR exercise, place the artificial food or the pictures on a table. Ask students to come up to the table and give you a certain item: **Venez ici... Donnez-moi une pomme, s'il vous plaît.** As students hand you the picture or artificial food, they should say **Voilà une pomme.**

Ask different students what Fabrice can have on Monday, Tuesday, and so on. Next ask students which meal they like most, which they like least, and why. Finally, ask students to make up a balanced meal that Fabrice might eat on a holiday.

B14 Activité • Avez-vous compris?

After students have answered according to Fabrice's diet, personalize these questions: **Combien de fois par semaine mangez-vous du poulet?** and so on.

B15 Activité • Ecrit dirigé

After students have written down what they ate and drank the previous day, they might write one or two sentences summarizing or drawing conclusions about their eating habits. They might also make resolutions for changes: **Je ne vais plus manger de glace. Je ne vais manger que des fruits et des légumes.**

B16 COMMENT LE DIRE

Read aloud the sentences in the boxes and have students repeat them. Then suggest that students look around the room at their classmates and write down one or two bits of advice they would give them. Have them pass these notes to their classmates, who should write appropriate responses from among those in the second box. Walk around the room checking the notes.

CHALLENGE Have students keep the notes going back and forth as long as they can write meaningful, relevant French. Have volunteers read their final exchanges to the class. Collect the papers and correct them.

CHAPITRE 7 / B17–22

B17 Activité • Il faut que Fabrice mange mieux

Encourage students to suggest other foods and drinks, in addition to those pictured.

CHALLENGE Have students work in pairs. One plays the role of Fabrice, who expresses doubt about some suggestions and agrees with others.

B18 Activité • Donnez des conseils

Have students pair off and exchange roles for each complaint. After this practice, you might ask individuals what is wrong with their partners, and what they advised them to do.

> —Qu'est-ce qu'il a, votre ami?
> —Il ne se sent pas bien.
> —Vous lui avez donné des conseils?
> —Oui, je lui ai conseillé de se reposer.

B19 Activité • A vous maintenant!

After practicing with the ideas given here, students should state their real desires and try to give each other good advice.

CHALLENGE Some students might like to role-play advisors, counselors, or amateur psychologists (Madame or Monsieur Sait-Tout). Have other students go to them for guidance and counseling.

B20 COMMENT LE DIRE

Model these negative expressions with appropriate facial expressions and gestures, and have students repeat and imitate. Hold up pictures of various unappetizing foods clipped from magazines, and invite students to react. Review ways to express likes, and add pictures of popular, appetizing foods.

B21 Activité • Il faut bien se nourrir

After students have practiced in pairs, have them role-play one of the situations for the class. For further practice, students may substitute foods and beverages not shown here.

B22 Activité • Ecoutez bien

Imagine you're listening to a talk show on French radio. The subject? Nutrition. Docteur Leblanc answers questions from teenagers who call in. Open your book to page 253. (pause) Read the questions in B22 to yourself. (pause) Now listen to the teenagers' questions and to the doctor's advice. Be prepared to indicate your answers on a separate sheet of paper. Ready? **Ecoutez bien.**

JULIEN   Bonjour, monsieur. Je m'appelle Julien. J'adore les hamburgers et les frites, mais ma mère ne veut pas que je mange dans les fast-foods. A votre avis, est-ce qu'elle a raison?

DOCTEUR   Oui, l'alimentation «fast-food» est vraiment déséquilibrée.
LEBLANC   Dans les frites, le soda et les hamburgers, il y a beaucoup trop de graisses et de sucre. Et ça manque de vitamines. Si vous déjeunez dans les fast-foods, prenez des légumes, un fruit et du lait le soir.

DELPHINE   Bonjour, monsieur. Je m'appelle Delphine. Je mange des kilos de chocolat. Est-ce que c'est mauvais?

DOCTEUR   Le chocolat, c'est bon si vous en mangez une ou deux fois
LEBLANC   par an, au moment de Noël, par exemple. Mais si vous en prenez trop souvent, c'est mauvais. Parce que le chocolat, ce n'est que du sucre et de la graisse.

XAVIER   Bonjour, monsieur. Je m'appelle Xavier. Je suis un fana de tennis. J'y joue tout le temps. Qu'est-ce que les champions de tennis mangent le jour du match?

DOCTEUR   Le jour du match, les joueurs de tennis, comme Yannick
LEBLANC   Noah et Henri Leconte, déjeunent avant onze heures du matin. Ils prennent un bol de céréales avec du lait, une ou deux biscottes avec de la confiture, un steak, une salade et un ou deux fruits. Ensuite, toutes les demi-heures avant le match, ils boivent du jus de fruits avec de l'eau.

Et maintenant, vérifions

1. Qu'est-ce que la mère de Julien ne veut pas qu'il fasse? *Elle ne veut pas qu'il mange dans les fast-foods.*
2. En général, qu'est-ce que le docteur Leblanc pense du fast-food? *Il pense qu'il y a trop de graisses et de sucre et que ça manque de vitamines.*
3. Quel est le problème de Delphine? *Elle mange trop de chocolat.*
4. D'après le docteur, quand est-ce que le chocolat peut être un problème? *Ça peut être un problème si on en prend souvent.*
5. Qui sont Yannick Noah et Henri Leconte? *Ce sont des joueurs de tennis.*
6. Qu'est-ce qu'ils boivent le jour du match? *Ils boivent du jus de fruits avec de l'eau.*

SECTION C

OBJECTIVES   **To persuade:** talk about fitness; assure and reassure; encourage; **to express feelings, emotions:** express fatigue; express pity

CULTURAL BACKGROUND   As a part of their increasing health awareness, the French are exercising more today. Health clubs are opening, and jogging has become popular. Even the spas, which the French have always patronized as places to "take a cure" and drink the mineral waters, have added physical activities to their programs. Probably the most popular physical activity of all, though, is going out dancing, which the French do more often than Americans.

MOTIVATING ACTIVITY   Ask students what exercises they do at home or in gym class: **Qu'est-ce que vous faites comme exercices chez vous? Aux cours d'éducation physique?**

C1   La remise en forme (suite)

Before students listen to the dialogue, tell them that they should try to discover how Fabrice feels since his meal with Sandrine; what he wants to do about it; and why he feels that way, according to Matthieu. Then play the cassette or have two students read the dialogue aloud. Next students should report what they discovered. Finally, have students read aloud and role-play the dialogue.

C2   Activité • Avez-vous compris?

You might make a speed-and-accuracy contest of this activity. Form small groups. They compete to find and write down the answers as quickly and accurately as possible. Establish a point scale for various finish times and levels of accuracy.

C3   Activité • Trouvez d'autres raisons

The student who inquires how the other feels should vary the question for each situation. The response should suit the various situations in the pictures.

SLOWER-PACED LEARNING   Discuss each picture with the class. Have students tell how each person in the picture feels. Then they should rephrase the sentences as if they were talking about themselves. Next brainstorm ways of asking how others are feeling. Refer to A15 in this unit for assistance. Finally, have students pair off to prepare their dialogues.

CHALLENGE   Students might extend their conversations by giving their partners advice, using the expressions presented in B16, page 251.

C4   Activité • Ecrivez

Before writing, students should review what Sandrine has done that she might report to Matthieu. Divide the class into two teams. Have a student from the first team go to the board and write Matthieu's opening words. If he or she has difficulty, suggest **Ça marche, le régime?** Then have a student from the second team go to the board and write Sandrine's reply. Allow the rest of the team to give suggestions to the representative at the board. Continue until the telephone conversation is complete. Ask volunteers to read the conversation aloud. Then erase it; do not allow students to copy it. Assign a similar dialogue to be written for homework.

C5   LA REMISE EN FORME (FIN)

Begin presentation of this dialogue by reading it aloud to the students, who listen with books closed. As you read, use appropriate gestures and intonation, especially when reading Fabrice's expressions of discouragement **(Je craque! Je suis mort! Je n'en peux plus! Je suis crevé!)** and Matthieu's expressions of encouragement **(Force-toi! Courage! Allez, continue!)**. Then have students open their books and read the dialogue silently as they listen to the cassette. Ask for volunteers to read aloud the statements of discouragement and encouragement, with appropriate expression.

C6 **Activité • Avez-vous compris?**

Have students write the answers to these questions; then ask volunteers to read their answers aloud. Write the correct answers on a transparency for all to use in correcting their papers.

C7 **AUTRES EXERCICES**

After students read the descriptions of the pictures, ask them if they do any of these exercises, how many, how often, when, where, and so on. As a check-up, prepare a transparency of the pictures without captions. Describe each picture and have students write the number of the picture you're talking about.

C8 **Savez-vous que... ?**

Play the cassette as students read along in their books. Call attention to the following vocabulary: **une carte d'abonnement à l'année** (*a one-year membership card*). Ask the students to find a word of the same family as **corps**. You might also ask them to guess the verb form of **abonnement**.

Discuss celebrities and their publications: **Qu'est-ce que Sylvie Vartan a fait? Connaissez-vous des célébrités américaines qui aient fait un beauty book ou une beauty vidéo?**

Start a discussion about health clubs by asking **Allez-vous à un centre sportif? Avez-vous un abonnement? Qu'est-ce que vous y faites comme activités?** If students do not have an association with a health club, have them imagine that they have a membership in the **Gymnase Club** and answer questions according to the schedule in their books.

C9 **Activité • Et vous?**

If students do not exercise or go to a health club, tell them to imagine that they do or to answer as an acquaintance, a relative, or a celebrity who does. Students might use these questions to take a survey of their classmates.

C10 **STRUCTURES DE BASE**

As students look at the conjugation in their books, say the forms of **courir** aloud and have them repeat after you. Include the **passé composé** and present subjunctive forms. Additional oral and written practice might include changing both affirmative and negative sentences from the present to the past.

CHALLENGE Ask students to use **courir** to give a command, to make a suggestion, to give advice, to ask for information, to say how long someone has been running, to encourage someone, to express a liking for the activity, or to express a need.

C11 **Activité • La course**

Students should give the results of the race first in the present and then in the past, using the **passé composé**. Ask them how they would cheer and shout encouragement in French as they watched these runners. To personalize, have a volunteer bring in the results from your school's last track meet. Have students tell how fast the winner of each race ran.

C12 VOUS EN SOUVENEZ-VOUS?

With books closed, elicit from students their understanding of the subjunctive: its formation and the uses that they've learned so far. Illustrate their commentary by writing examples on the board. Ask them to recite the subjunctive forms of **faire**. Then have them open their books and read the explanation silently. Answer any questions they may have.

SLOWER-PACED LEARNING   Proceed as suggested above. However, you might want to have students substitute different subjects that you propose in the example sentences that you've written on the board.

C13 STRUCTURES DE BASE

Introduce the subjunctive of **être** by telling students what they have to be in order to succeed in school: **Il faut que vous soyez sages (polis, travailleurs).** Ask them what a good teacher must be: **Il faut qu'il soit...** Write the sentences on the board.

Use a TPR technique to introduce the subjunctive of **aller**. Tell a student **Je veux que tu ailles à la porte.** Stop the student midway and ask the class **Qu'est-ce que je veux?** Elicit **Vous voulez qu'il/elle aille à la porte.** Repeat with two students, and elicit the other forms of **aller**.

Have students open their books and read the explanation. Practice by writing the following infinitive phrases on the board; have students tell what their parents want them to do, using **Ils veulent que je...**

| aller à l'école tous les jours | être sage |
| avoir de bonnes notes | être attentif/attentive |

Do not spend a lot time on the subjunctive forms of **vouloir, pouvoir,** and **savoir** in numbers 3 and 4; they are rarely used after the expressions that students have learned so far.

C14 Activité • Donnez des raisons

Encourage students to suggest reasons in addition to those given in parentheses.

SLOWER-PACED LEARNING   First have the students phrase each question and ask you. Give the expected answer. Then you ask the questions and have students answer as they heard you do. Finally, have students pair off to do the activity.

C15 Activité • Donnez des conseils

For practice with other subject pronouns, have students form groups of four. Two students ask the questions of the other two, using **vous,** and the other two respond with **nous.** You might then tell the students about other people and have them respond with **il(s)** or **elle(s): Sylvie a mal partout. (Il faut qu'elle aille chez le docteur.)**

C16 COMMENT LE DIRE

Have students pair off. One student expresses fatigue; the other expresses pity and offers encouragement. Students should repeat the activity until they have practiced most of the expressions. Then they should exchange roles.

C17 Activite • Ils n'en peuvent plus

When students have finished this activity, have them close their books. Then address each of the statements to individuals. Students should respond extemporaneously with any expression of fatigue they recall. Then you express your fatigue in different ways to students. They should recall an expression of encouragement for you.

C18 COMMENT LE DIRE

Explain to students that they're going to learn how to reassure someone who has expressed concern for them. Make appropriate statements of concern that will elicit each of these assurances from students. For example, to elicit the first one, you might say **Ça va? Vous êtes sûr(e)?** Students should respond **Je vous assure que ça va.** To practice the two ways of saying each sentence, you say a sentence one way and have the students look at the chart in their books and say it the other way. Make up additional statements of assurance, using different vocabulary after the word **que.**

C19 Activité • Rassurez-le

SLOWER-PACED LEARNING   Before students pair off to do this activity, brainstorm with the class various opening remarks that the first speaker might make. Among the possibilities are **Tu as mauvaise mine. Tu es malade? Tu ne manges pas bien?** Write these on the board or on a transparency as students suggest them. Then have students turn these concerns into statements of reassurance. Finally, brainstorm substitutions for **Tu es sûr(e)?** Now have students pair off. Leave all their suggestions in view for reference.

CHALLENGE   Have students adapt the dialogue to a parent-child situation. Students should think of concerns that parents have, such as, **Tu ne fumes pas? Tu fais tes devoirs?** and so forth. After students have worked in pairs, have them engage you in the same dialogue so that they practice using **vous** as well as **tu.**

C20 Activité • Vous n'êtes pas d'accord

Encourage students to expand their statements of assurance. For example, in the model dialogue the second speaker might say **Si, je t'assure que je fais assez d'exercices. Je fais quinze pompes tous les matins.**

C21 Activité • Ecoutez bien

You're going to hear a radio ad for a health club. You want to encourage one of your friends to go there, so you note down as much information about it as you can. Open your book to page 262. *(pause)* Copy the chart in C21 on a separate sheet of paper. *(pause)* As you listen to the ad, fill in the chart with the name of the health club, the days and times it's open, its telephone number, and the activities it offers. Ready? **Ecoutez bien.**

Vous n'êtes pas en forme? Vous êtes fatigué? Vous n'avez pas envie de travailler et vous n'arrivez pas à vous lever le matin? Un conseil : il faut que vous fassiez de la gymnastique. Un endroit : le Gymnase Club! Vous pouvez y aller le matin avant de partir à l'école ou au travail, le soir, le week-end, quand vous voulez! Nous sommes ouverts tous les jours, du lundi au vendredi de sept heures à vingt-deux heures, le samedi de neuf heures à vingt heures et le dimanche de neuf heures à dix-sept heures. Ici, vous pouvez faire de la musculation, de l'aérobic, du stretching, du yoga, de la danse! Vous aimez nager? Nous avons des piscines! Vous êtes un ou une fana de tennis? Nous avons des courts de tennis! Alors, vous hésitez encore? Téléphonez-nous pour avoir des renseignements sur les prix et pour connaître nos adresses : 45.62.99.76. Nous vous attendons. Ici, c'est la super forme!

Et maintenant, vérifions.

Nom : *Gymnase Club* Jours : *Tous les jours* Heures : *L–V: 7h–22h* *S: 9h–20h* *D: 9h–17h* Tél. : *45.62.99.76*	Activités : *musculation,* *aérobic, stretching, yoga,* *danse, tennis, natation*

TRY
YOUR
SKILLS

OBJECTIVE To recombine communicative functions, grammar, and vocabulary

CULTURAL BACKGROUND Adolescents have long been notorious for neglecting their health: eating unbalanced meals, not getting enough exercise, and staying up too late. The French have expressed their concern by creating an institute to study the special medical problems of adolescents. It is called **IRMA (l'Institut de recherche sur la médecine des adolescents).**

MOTIVATING ACTIVITY Students might imagine that they are **animateurs** or **animatrices** at a summer camp for overweight children. What kind of advice or encouragement would they give to their charges?

1   **Fabrice n'arrive plus à dormir.**

Before reading these excerpts from Fabrice's dream, review or call attention to the use of **drôle** in the expression **un(e) drôle de...,** as in:

C'est un drôle de garçon.
C'est une drôle de fille.
Ce sont de drôles de rêves.

Have students think of other statements using this expression.
   Play the cassette or read the excerpts aloud. Have students repeat. To dramatize, you might have one willing "victim" sit in the center of a circle and play Fabrice, while his friends surround him to give advice.

2   **Activité • Répondez**

Have students answer these comprehension questions orally or in writing. You might first present and explain the use of the phrase

conseiller à quelqu'un de faire quelque chose. Students will need to use this in their answer to question 3.

For cooperative learning, have students work in small groups to prepare answers to these questions orally. As groups are ready, meet with them and hear their answers. Make suggestions for corrections and then have the groups prepare written answers.

3 Activité • Chez le docteur

Before students pair off to role-play, brainstorm with the class complaints that the patient might have, and questions and advice that a doctor might give. When students have prepared their dialogues, choose one or two and have students dramatize them for the class.

4 Activité • Donnez des conseils

Begin by discussing the smoking issue with students in French. Have those who are for and those who are against smoking give their reasons in a debate. As a follow-up activity, students might prepare anti-smoking posters in French for the classroom or for a hallway bulletin board.

5 Activité • Réfléchissez

For cooperative learning, have students form groups of three or four to discuss Fabrice's plans for getting into shape and his chances of succeeding. Circulate among students as they talk to stimulate discussion where it may have stalled. Each group should write down in two columns reasons for their optimism or pessimism.

6 Activité • Projet

Students might get ideas for slogans and illustrations by browsing through advertisements in French magazines.

CHALLENGE Students might show their posters to their classmates, accompanied by a brief speech in French on the topic. Display as many of these posters as possible in the classroom, and place the most attractive on school bulletin boards or display cases.

7 Activité • Ecrivez

First read Fabrice's letter aloud to the students. Then they must decide whether or not they're going to sympathize with him. Once they've taken a position, but before they begin writing their letters, they should jot down expressions of pity, expressions of commiseration such as **Ce n'est pas juste/C'est injuste, Ils ont tort,** or expressions of agreement such as **Je suis d'accord, Ils ont raison.** They should add statements that they might make about exercising and nutrition. Then they should weave their notes into a cohesive letter. Read several aloud to the class and circulate all letters among the students for them to read.

8 Activité • Récréation

This activity is optional. You might first have the students name the activity and then make up a sentence about each illustration.

PRONONCIATION 🔲

The nasals

> Open your book to page 265. *(pause)* Refer to this page as you listen to this section.

1 Ecoutez bien et répétez.

Did you ever hear someone talking through the nose? Maybe you too are able to do it. If you can, you've already got an edge on what's coming up. Nasals. Those little vowels that sound so very, very French, which English speakers never seem to get exactly right. But you will. Just keep on trying.

By now you must have heard these nasal sounds hundreds of times in little words like **un, bon, pain,** and **blanc.** Let's check now to see if you're saying them right. Mind you, you just can't avoid them. You find them in the most common words: in the article **un;** in the pronoun **en;** in the possessives **mon, ton, son;** in basic adjectives like **bon, brun, blanc;** and in hundreds of common and proper nouns. In fact, it's hard to say very much in French without using nasal vowels. So work on them until you get them to sound French.

1. One problem is that these nasal sounds don't exist in English. Or do they? Did you ever hear someone say "Gimmie a san'wich"? Maybe you might say it that way when you're tired or not too careful about your speech. Listen again, especially to the last word, *sandwich.* Hear the first syllable /sɛ̃/ in *sandwich?* It sounds like the French word **saint** as in **Saint-Paul, Saint-Pierre, Saint-Germain,** or any of the hundreds of saints' names that identify the towns and streets of France and Quebec. Try them: **Saint-Paul, Saint-Pierre.**

If you can say **saint,** you can say a lot of important words. Try these: **saint, pain, bain, faim, main, train. J'ai faim. Un pain, s'il vous plaît.** Now you can say things like this. Repeat after me: **J'ai tellement faim. Je vais manger tout un pain. A quelle heure est le prochain train pour Saint-Germain? A cinq heures vingt.**

2. Now go back to the sandwiches. This time you'll order a French one, the kind that's made with a roll, something like a submarine. You know, the ones where you have to open your mouth wide. So do just that to begin with: open wide and say /aaaaa/. *(pause)* That's it. Now let it all out through your nose as you did with the English sandwich sound. Do it again, going from /aaaaa/ to /ãããã/. Try it a couple of times until you get it. Don't bite into it. You haven't got your sandwich yet. *(pause)* Now try this: /aaaa/, /ãããã/, /ssãããã/. Then /sãd/ and /witʃ/ **sandwich.** *(pause)* That's the way to order one in French. You can even say **Des sandwiches au pain blanc.** Now sink your teeth into these words: **dent, blanc, plan, temps, vent, gant, grand, franc, pense, banque, langue, jambe.** Now you can go on and repeat things like these: **Les sandwiches au pain blanc sont à vingt francs. Sa tante a de l'argent à la banque.**

3. Good, **Bon.** Yes. **Bon.** That's what you're going to try now. How to say things like **bonbon,** and **bon ton,** the French way. Start by opening your mouth, rounding your lips and putting an **o**-sound—not through your throat—but right through the nose until you can feel it sizzle. Say: **bon** *(pause)* **bon,** *(pause)* **Des bonbons.** *(pause)* **J'aime les bonbons.** *(pause)*

C'est bon. *(pause)*

Good! Now repeat all the other good things you can say. You can talk about your girl friend, **ma blonde** *(pause)*, your uncle, **mon oncle** *(pause)*, and much more, including the lyrics of a famous old song: **"Sur le pont d'Avignon, on y danse tout en rond."** *(pause)* So far you've already got enough nasal vowels to order a variety of sandwiches—ham, salmon, or tuna: **Deux sandwiches au jambon, trois sandwiches au saumon et quatre sandwiches au thon.** *(pause)*

4. Bon! Just one more nasal sound to go and you've got the complete set. You can't speak French without it. It's the sound of the indefinite article, or noun marker, of more than half the nouns in the language, the number-one sound, **le numéro un.** You can already say the feminine article as in **une fille.** For the masculine, you need **un** to be able to say **un garçon.** How do you do it? Take a deep breath, say /œœœ/ and direct the air through your nose till it begins to sound like /œ̃œ̃œ̃/. *(pause)* So now you can say **un garçon.** *(pause)* You should be able to count one thing at a time **(un à un)**, borrow something **(emprunter)**, give it back on Monday **(lundi)**, and even get sandwiches on brown bread **(du pain brun).**

5. Now that you've got all the nasals, try them all together and see how they sound. Listen to these and repeat: **Chacun monte dans le train et prend sa place.** *(pause)* **Ça fait cinq cent cinquante et un francs onze.** Now for the famous French test sentence. Listen and repeat: **Un bon pain blanc.** Can you say it? You can? Well, you've arrived. You're beginning to sound French.

2 **Ecoutez et lisez.**

Just to be sure you have all the nasals under control, read the dialogue aloud. I'll say each line after you.

—Tu prends des vacances en septembre?
—Bien sûr, à la campagne, chez mon oncle et ma tante.
—C'est où?
—A vingt kilomètres d'ici. En train, ça ne prend pas très longtemps. On arrive juste à temps pour le dîner.
—On mange bien?
—Oui, mais ce n'est pas abondant. Tu sais, mon oncle Armand n'est pas gourmand. Pour lui, du pain blanc frais et un bon camembert, ça suffit!

3 **Copiez les phrases suivantes pour préparer une dictée.**

Write the following sentences from dictation. First listen to the sentence as it is read to you. Then you will hear the sentence again in short segments, with a pause after each segment to allow you time to write. Finally, you will hear the sentence a third time so that you may check your work. Let's begin.

1. Bonjour, Francine. Depuis quand tu es au régime? Bonjour, Francine. *(pause)* Depuis quand *(pause)* tu es au régime? *(pause)* Bonjour, Francine. Depuis quand tu es au régime?

2. Depuis le vingt septembre. Ça fait un an que je fais des exercices. Depuis *(pause)* le vingt septembre. *(pause)* Ça fait un an *(pause)* que je fais *(pause)* des exercices. *(pause)* Depuis le vingt septembre. Ça fait un an que je fais des exercices.

3. Comment tu te sens? Comment tu te sens? *(pause)* Comment tu te sens?

4. J'ai mal à la tête le matin, au ventre après manger et aux jambes toute la journée. Et toi? J'ai mal à la tête *(pause)* le matin, *(pause)* au ventre après manger *(pause)* et aux jambes *(pause)* toute la journée. *(pause)* Et toi? *(pause)* J'ai mal à la tête le matin, au ventre après manger et aux jambes toute la journee. Et toi?

5. Moi, ça va, je fais de la natation. Chaque matin je fais de nombreuses longueurs de bassin. C'est excellent pour la santé. Moi, ça va, *(pause)* je fais de la natation. *(pause)* Chaque matin *(pause)* je fais *(pause)* de nombreuses longueurs *(pause)* de bassin. *(pause)* C'est excellent *(pause)* pour la santé. *(pause)* Moi, ça va, je fais de la natation. Chaque matin je fais de nombreuses longueurs de bassin. C'est excellent pour la santé.

VERIFIONS!

SECTION A

You might give the first part of this review—forms of reflexive verbs—as a written check-up. Have students exchange papers and correct each other's work immediately, as you show the correct forms on a transparency. Make up additional items if students need more practice.

For the next two exercises, have students write down the expressions they recall. Then call the class together and ask individuals to read their lists aloud until all possible expressions have been given. Individuals should add to their own lists expressions suggested by others that they may not have thought of.

SECTION B

Have students write out the sentences in the first exercise. Correct them immediately.

Once students have written five foods and beverages for the second exercise, have them scramble the letters and give their lists to classmates to unscramble.

Once the students have written down the expressions they recall for the last three exercises and you have verified them, tell the students to think of and write down the statements or questions that might have provoked the sentences that they've written.

SECTION C

When students have written down five exercises, play a game of Charades in which students make their teammates guess the exercise that they act out.

The six sentences using the subjunctive should be written out for all to see and self-check.

Students should write down their responses to the third and fourth exercises. Call on an individual to read his or her response for the third exercise, and ask a volunteer to respond to the first student with an appropriate response he or she wrote for the fourth exercise. Proceed in this manner until the supply of different expressions is exhausted.

VOCABULAIRE

Divide the class into two teams. A student on one team chooses and calls out two words from the list. Two members of the opposing team must prepare extemporaneously a two-line, meaningful dialogue, using the two words, one in each line. After an appropriate number of points are awarded, the second team challenges the first in the same way.

ETUDE DE MOTS

For additional practice, use **se forcer (à)** and **se lever** from this vocabulary list. You may wish to introduce **se laver** and **se réveiller**.

A LIRE

OBJECTIVE   To read for practice and pleasure

BIBI : LE FANA DE LA FORME

One of the skills that enables students to read well is the ability to recognize cognates. Begin by having the students identify those in **Avant de lire.** Then have students look at the illustrations and scan the poem for the answer to the question **Qu'est-ce que Bibi fait pour être en pleine forme?** Now play the cassette as students read the poem silently. Follow up with a few questions to check comprehension: **Qu'est-ce qu'il mange? Qu'est-ce qu'il ne mange pas?**

Activité • Réfléchissez

Opinions may vary. Bibi is happy about his shape but unhappy at having to watch his diet. It is important that students justify their opinions. Differences of opinion may prompt a debate in French.

Activité • Donnez des conseils

Have students decide whether they will play the devilish role of the tempter or the encouraging role of the advocate. Then they should prepare remarks for each stanza of the poem. Read the poem aloud, pausing after each stanza to hear their comments.

COMMENT SOIGNER LES PETITS MAUX?

Before students open their books, talk about the three illnesses, **la grippe, le rhume,** and **l'angine,** in French, using gestures and dramatics to convey meaning. Pretend to be sick, saying **Oh, je suis malade! J'ai une maladie! J'ai un rhume.** Ask students if they often have these ailments: **Avez-vous souvent la grippe? Un rhume? Une angine? Qu'est-ce que vous faites pour vous soigner?**

Next have students scan the reading selection to find the information requested in **Avant de lire,** that is, what causes or transmits these diseases. Tell them to look for cognates for *cause* and *transmit.*

Now play the cassette as students read along in their books. Ask several questions to assess comprehension.

Activité • Complétez

You might make a contest of this activity to see which individual, which pair, or which group can find and write down the correct words the most quickly and accurately.

Activité • A vous maintenant!

To prepare for this activity, have students draw two columns on their papers, one headed **Symptômes** and the other **Conseils.** They should find and write down in the appropriate columns the symptoms and advice for the flu and a sore throat. Check the results by calling on individuals to read their lists. Keep calling on students until all symptoms and advice have been suggested. Then have students work in pairs to prepare their dialogues. Volunteers might dramatize their dialogues in front of the class, using props.

LA CHROMOGYM

Play the cassette as students read along in their books. Ask a volunteer to summarize the selection in one English sentence.

Activité • Cherchez des renseignements

Have students make the chart as shown. Students may wish to make a large poster, illustrating the chart with different colors and with cut-outs or drawings of people exercising.

Activité • Choisissez les couleurs

Students' opinions will vary. You might take a poll of the class, or have students do so, to arrive at a consensus.

CHALLENGE   You might share with an advanced group Arthur Rimbaud's poem, «**Les Voyelles**», in which he attributes colors to sounds.

Activité • Et vous?

Begin by telling students what your favorite color is, how it reflects your personality, and how and when you use it. This will give them a model to follow in preparing their own responses.

CHAPITRE 7

En pleine forme

Working out and eating right have become goals of many Americans. Body-building, aerobics, and health foods are gradually taking hold in France, too. Another imported life-style, *le fast-food*, is slowly changing the eating habits of the French, especially those of young people.

In this unit you will:

PREMIER CONTACT	get acquainted with the topic
SECTION A	talk about health . . . express concern for someone's health . . . complain about one's health
SECTION B	talk about eating well . . . give and justify advice . . . express doubt, uncertainty, and dislikes
SECTION C	talk about getting into shape . . . express fatigue . . . pity, encourage, and reassure others
TRY YOUR SKILLS	use what you've learned
A LIRE	read for practice and pleasure

PREMIER CONTACT getting acquainted with the topic

The authentic material in the Premier Contact introduces the theme of the unit and is to be used for global comprehension only.

1

Un sport pour l'été 📼

Voulez-vous commencer une activité sportive? L'été est la saison idéale.

LES PARTIES DU CORPS

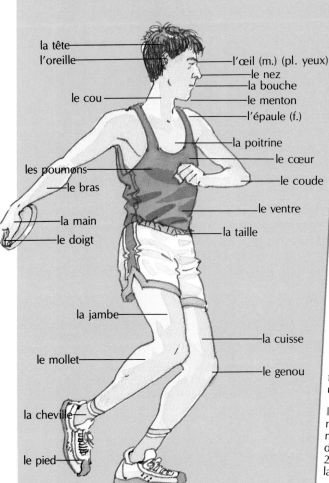

- la tête
- l'oreille
- le cou
- les poumons
- le bras
- la main
- le doigt
- la jambe
- le mollet
- la cheville
- le pied
- l'œil (m.) (pl. yeux)
- le nez
- la bouche
- le menton
- l'épaule (f.)
- la poitrine
- le cœur
- le coude
- le ventre
- la taille
- la cuisse
- le genou

L'été est une bonne période pour commencer une activité sportive. Ce coup de "starter" de la forme sera votre assurance anti-kilos pour l'hiver prochain. Quel sport choisir?

La marche : pour entretenir la forme. Lorsque vous marchez, vous utilisez plus de la moitié des muscles du corps... Marchez d'un pas vif, et sur des distances de plus en plus longues. Le golf est un sport d'adresse qui relève également de la marche. Il fait travailler plus spécialement les bras et les épaules, affine la taille. Promenade en forêt ou golf, en une heure, vous perdez 300 calories!

Le jogging : pour garder la ligne. Déconseillé aux personnes d'un certain âge et à celles qui n'ont jamais fait de sport, le jogging est particulièrement bon pour le cœur et les poumons. Il aide également à conserver la ligne. Au début, arrêtez-vous dès que vous vous sentez fatigué car il ne faut jamais forcer. Vous dépensez 350 à 420 calories en une heure.

La natation : pour se muscler en douceur. Sport excellent pour la respiration et la circulation sanguine, la natation raffermit tous les muscles. Comme pour la marche, il n'est pas nécessaire de nager vite. Mieux vaut parcourir de nombreuses longueurs de bassin. La dépense en calories est de 300 à 350 par heure.

La bicyclette : pour les jambes et les cuisses. Ce sport remodèle cuisses et mollets. Pour que l'exercice soit utile, il faut le pratiquer au moins 30 minutes, trois fois par semaine. 300 à 350 calories dépensées en une heure.

Le tennis : pour les abdominaux et les jambes. Le tennis donne de la souplesse, fortifie les muscles abdominaux et amincit les jambes. A pratiquer une ou deux fois par semaine. La dépense énergétique est de 270 à 400 calories, selon le rythme adopté pendant la partie.

2 Activité • Trouvez des renseignements

Trouvez dans l'article les renseignements pour compléter ce tableau.

Sport	Excellent pour :	Calories dépensées
La marche	entretenir la forme	300 calories en une heure
La natation	se muscler en douceur, la respiration, la circulation	300 à 350 calories en une heure
Le jogging	garder la ligne, le cœur, les poumons	350 à 420 calories en une heure
La bicyclette	les jambes et les cuisses	300 à 350 calories en une heure
Le tennis	les abdominaux et les jambes	270 à 400 calories en une heure

1. Imaginez. Vous voulez commencer une activité sportive. Quel sport
choisissez-vous? Pourquoi? Je choisis... parce que...

2. A votre avis, est-ce que l'été est la saison idéale pour commencer
une activité sportive? Pourquoi? A mon avis, l'été (n')est (pas) la saison idéale parce que...

4 NE SAUTEZ PAS LE PETIT DEJEUNER!

Sautez-vous le petit déjeuner? C'est un repas important. Prenez le temps de manger!

'Breakfast food' à la française

Depuis longtemps, les nutritionnistes français
dénoncent l'insuffisance ou l'absence du petit
déjeuner. D'après les chiffres, ils ont raison* :

- 2,5% des Français ne prennent pas de petit
  déjeuner.
- 27% prennent seulement une boisson chaude.
- 49% prennent une boisson chaude et des tartines.
- 21,5% seulement prennent un petit déjeuner
  complet.

Le manque de temps est sans doute le principal
responsable, puisque 32,6% des Français prennent leur
petit déjeuner debout dans la cuisine, 22,5% au bistrot
et 8% en arrivant au bureau. Ceux qui ont du temps
en profitent : 5,5% le prennent dans leur lit et 1%
dans la baignoire.

Même si leurs connaissances en matière diététique
ont progressé, trop de Français ignorent encore que
le petit déjeuner doit apporter à l'organisme le quart
des calories et protéines dont il aura besoin au cours
de la journée.

*Sondage effectué dans la région parisienne.

5 Activité • Avez-vous compris?

Répondez aux questions suivantes d'après «Breakfast food à la française».

1. Quelle est la raison principale que donnent les Français pour sauter le petit
déjeuner ou pour manger un petit déjeuner insuffisant? Le manque de temps.

2. Pourquoi est-ce que le petit déjeuner est un repas important?
Le petit déjeuner doit apporter à l'organisme le quart des calories et protéines dont il aura besoin au cours de la journée.

6 Activité • Et vous?

1. Sautez-vous le petit déjeuner ou le prenez-vous? Je le prends/Je le saute.

2. Qu'est-ce que vous prenez d'habitude au petit déjeuner? Je prends...

3. Prenez-vous quelquefois le petit déjeuner au lit? Quand?
Oui, je le prends au lit quand...

7 Activité • Sondage

Faites une enquête dans votre classe pour trouver qui saute le petit déjeuner, qui
prend le petit déjeuner, et ce qu'ils prennent.

SECTION A

talking about health . . . expressing concern for someone's health . . . complaining about one's health

Vous avez du mal à vous lever le matin? Vous n'arrivez pas à dormir? Vous n'êtes jamais en forme et vous manquez de tonus?... Il faut prendre des mesures énergiques!

A1 Fabrice n'est pas en forme.

Sandrine, Matthieu et Fabrice passent l'après-midi ensemble. Ils se promènent et ils discutent. Mais Fabrice n'a pas l'air en forme.

MATTHIEU	Qu'est-ce que vous voulez faire maintenant?
FABRICE	Bof.
MATTHIEU	Mais qu'est-ce que tu as, Fabrice? Tu n'as rien envie de faire aujourd'hui!
FABRICE	Je ne me sens pas très bien. J'ai mal partout.

Sandrine et Matthieu s'inquiètent pour Fabrice. Ils trouvent qu'il n'est pas en forme.

Fabrice s'est couché tard parce qu'il a travaillé jusqu'à minuit.

SANDRINE	C'est parce que tu t'es couché trop tard. Tous les soirs, tu travailles jusqu'à minuit. Il faut te reposer. Tu te nourris bien au moins?
FABRICE	Non, très mal.
MATTHIEU	Et tu fais des exercices?
FABRICE	Quels exercices?
SANDRINE	Bon, ça ne va pas du tout. On va s'occuper de toi et te soigner. A partir de demain, tu fais un régime.
MATTHIEU	Et tu t'entraînes! Dimanche, on se lève à six heures pour faire du jogging.
FABRICE	Ah, désolé, mais dimanche, je suis pris. Je fais la grasse matinée.
MATTHIEU	Pas question! Tu veux être en forme ou pas?

«Tu n'as rien envie de faire.» is more commonly used than «Tu as envie de ne rien faire.»

Activité • Parlons de Fabrice

Est-ce que vous connaissez Fabrice? Répondez aux questions suivantes d'après A1.

1. Qu'est-ce que Fabrice a envie de faire aujourd'hui?
2. A quelle heure est-ce qu'il se couche d'habitude?
3. Pourquoi est-ce qu'il se couche tard?
4. Qu'est-ce qu'il aime faire le dimanche?
5. Qu'est-ce qu'il va faire demain avec Sandrine?
6. Et dimanche avec Matthieu?

1. Il n'a rien envie de faire.   2. Il se couche d'habitude à minuit.   3. Il travaille jusqu'à minuit.   4. Le dimanche, il aime faire la grasse matinée.   5. Il va faire un régime.   6. Il va faire du jogging/s'entraîner.

A3 Activité • Actes de parole

Pouvez-vous trouver dans A1 au moins deux expressions pour dire que quelqu'un n'est pas en forme?   Il manque de tonus.   Il n'a pas l'air en forme.   Je ne me sens pas très bien.   J'ai mal partout.

A4 Activité • Choisissez 📼

Qu'est-ce qu'il faut faire pour être en forme? D'après Sandrine et Matthieu, pour être en forme il faut…   bien se nourrir.   faire un régime.   faire des exercices.   s'entraîner.

> **bien se nourrir**   **se coucher à minuit**
> **faire un régime**   **faire la grasse matinée**
> **faire des exercices**   **s'entraîner**

Avoid using the negative form with «Il faut que…»

A5 Activité • Qu'est-ce qu'il faut faire? 📼   Possible answers are given.

Pour être en forme, qu'est-ce qu'il faut que Fabrice fasse?

Il faut qu'il se lève tôt.

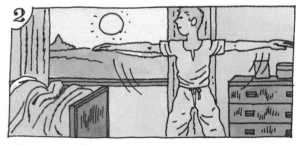

Il faut qu'il s'entraîne.

Il faut qu'il fasse un régime.

Il faut qu'il se couche avant minuit.

1. Jusqu'à quelle heure travaillez-vous le soir?
2. Avez-vous le droit de regarder la télévision jusqu'à minuit?
3. Faites-vous la grasse matinée? Tous les jours?
4. Est-ce qu'il y a des jours où vous n'êtes pas en forme? Quand?
5. Qu'est-ce que vous faites d'habitude pour être en forme?

A7   STRUCTURES DE BASE
The reflexive pronouns

1. Sometimes the subject of a sentence is both the doer and receiver of the action of the verb. This is shown in French by a special group of pronouns called reflexive pronouns.

Reflexive Pronouns	me	te	se	se	nous	vous	se	se
Subject Pronouns	je	tu	il	elle	nous	vous	ils	elles

2. The reflexive pronouns represent the subject of the verb and, like all object pronouns, are placed before the verb they refer to.

Je	me	couche		Nous	nous	couchons	
Tu	te	couches	tard.	Vous	vous	couchez	tard.
Il/Elle/On	se	couche		Ils/Elles	se	couchent	

3. In a negative construction, **ne** precedes the reflexive pronoun and **pas, plus, rien,** or **jamais** follows the verb: Il **ne** s'entraîne **pas.** Tu **ne** te reposes **jamais.** The negative command «Ne te repose pas!»

4. In an affirmative suggestion or a command, the reflexive pronouns **nous** and **vous** follow the verb and are separated from it in writing by a hyphen. **Toi** is used, rather than **te.**
    Reposons-nous!   Levez-vous!   Soigne-toi!

5. When the infinitive of a reflexive verb is used in a sentence, the reflexive pronoun must agree with the subject it refers to.
    Je vais **me coucher.   Elles** vont **se promener.   Nous** voulons **nous reposer.**

6. **Elision** occurs with the reflexive pronouns **me, te,** and **se** when the verb begins with a vowel sound. Je **m'**inquiète. Tu **t'**inquiètes? Elle **s'**inquiète.

7. The English equivalent of a French reflexive construction sometimes includes a reflexive pronoun: **Je me soigne bien,** *I take good care of myself.* Most of the time, however, it does not: **Je me lève,** *I get up,* **Ils se promènent,** *They take a walk.*

8. The **passé composé** of verbs taking a reflexive pronoun is always formed with the auxiliary verb **être.** If the reflexive pronoun is the direct object of the verb, the past participle agrees with it and changes its spelling accordingly. If the reflexive pronoun is the indirect object, there is no change in the past participle.

Je	me	suis	couché(e)		Nous	nous	sommes	couché(e)s	
Tu	t'	es	couché(e)	tard.	Vous	vous	êtes	couché(e)(s)	tard.
Il	s'	est	couché		Ils	se	sont	couchés	
Elle	s'	est	couchée		Elles	se	sont	couchées	

A8 Activité • Qu'est-ce qu'on fait? Possible answers are given.

Regardez ces dessins. Dites ce qu'on fait et ensuite, ce qu'on a fait.

1. Elle se lève.
Elle s'est levée.

2. Il se repose.
Il s'est reposé.

3. Il se couche.
Il s'est couché.

4. Ils s'entraînent.
Ils se sont entraînés.

A9 Activité • A vous maintenant! Possible answers are given.

Demandez à un(e) camarade s'il (si elle) fait ces choses. Ensuite, répondez à ses questions.

s'entraîner tous les jours
— Tu t'entraînes tous les jours?
— Oui, je m'entraîne tous les jours.

1. se coucher tard
2. se lever tôt
3. bien se nourrir
4. bien se soigner
5. se promener avec des amis
6. se reposer après l'école

1. Je (ne) me couche (pas) tard. 2. Je (ne) me lève (pas) tôt. 3. Je (ne) me nourris (pas) bien. 4. Je (ne) me soigne (pas) bien. 5. Je (ne) me promène (pas) avec des amis. 6. Je (ne) me repose (pas) après l'école.

A10 STRUCTURES DE BASE
The verb se sentir

The forms of the reflexive verb **se sentir** follow the same pattern as those of **sortir**. There is one stem for the singular forms and another for the plural forms.

se sentir *to feel*			
je me	sen	-s	Je **me sens** bien.
tu te		-s	Tu **te sens** bien?
il/elle/on se		-t	Elle **se sent** bien.
nous nous	sent	-ons	Nous **nous sentons** bien.
vous vous		-ez	Vous **vous sentez** bien?
ils/elles se		-ent	Ils **se sentent** bien.

A11 Activité • Complétez le dialogue

La mère de Fabrice lui demande de se lever, mais il ne peut pas parce qu'il se sent mal. Complétez leur dialogue en mettant les verbes à la forme correcte.

SA MÈRE (Se lever)! Il est huit heures! *Lève-toi!*
FABRICE Je sais, mais je dois (se reposer). *me reposer*
SA MÈRE Pourquoi?
FABRICE Je (se sentir) mal. *me sens*
SA MÈRE Qu'est-ce que tu as? *t'inquiète/me soigner*
FABRICE Ne (s'inquiéter) pas! Je vais (se soigner).
SA MÈRE Oui, et ce soir, tu (se coucher) à neuf heures!
te couches

En pleine forme 243

Activité • Faites des excuses Possible answers are given.

Votre camarade vous propose de faire quelque chose, mais vous refusez. Choisissez
une raison. 1. Non, je dois me lever tôt demain.
2. Non, je dois m'occuper de mon petit frère.
3. Non, je dois m'entrainer. 4. Non, je dois me
coucher à 9 h. 5. Non, je dois me lever tôt demain.
6. Non, je dois me reposer.

Non, je dois...

1. Tu vas regarder la télévision ce soir?
2. Tu peux venir à mon anniversaire?
3. Tu viens dîner avec nous?
4. Ça te dit d'aller au fast-food?
5. Tu es libre pour aller au cinéma?
6. Tu ne peux pas sortir avec moi?

se coucher à neuf heures

s'entraîner

se lever tôt demain

s'occuper de son petit frère

se reposer

A 13 Activité • Et vous?

1. A quelle heure est-ce que vous vous levez d'habitude? Et ce matin?
2. A quelle heure est-ce que vous vous couchez? Et hier soir?
3. Est-ce que vous vous couchez tard? Pourquoi?
4. Qu'est-ce que vous faites quand vous ne vous sentez pas bien? Des exercices? Un régime?
Vous vous reposez?

1. D'habitude, je me lève à...   Ce matin, je me suis levé(e) à...
2. D'habitude, je me couche à...
   Hier soir, je me suis couché(e)...
3. Je me couche tard/tôt parce que...
4. Quand je ne me sens pas bien, je...

A 14 OU EST-CE QU'ILS VONT QUAND ILS ONT MAL?

Il a mal aux dents. Il va chez
le dentiste.

Elle a mal à la tête. Elle va
acheter des médicaments chez
le pharmacien.

Elle a mal partout. Elle va chez
le docteur.

A 15 COMMENT LE DIRE
Expressing concern for someone's health
Complaining about one's health

EXPRESSING CONCERN	COMPLAINING
Qu'est-ce que tu as?	Je me sens mal.
Qu'est-ce qui t'arrive?	Je ne me sens pas bien.
Tu n'as pas l'air en forme.	J'ai du mal à dormir.
Ça n'a pas l'air d'aller.	J'ai mal à la tête, au cœur...
Tu as mauvaise mine.	

A16 Activité • Donnez des conseils Possible answers are given.

Votre camarade n'est jamais en forme. Vous lui suggérez quelque chose pour se soigner.

— Oh là là, je me sens mal!   — Va chez le docteur.
                                           (Pourquoi tu ne vas pas chez le docteur?)

1. Oh là là, je me sens mal!
2. J'ai drôlement mal dormi!
3. Je n'arrive jamais à me lever!
4. J'ai très mal aux dents!
5. Depuis hier, j'ai mal partout!
6. En cours de maths, j'ai toujours mal à la tête!

aller chez le docteur   *se coucher tôt*
aller chez le pharmacien   *se reposer*
faire un régime   *aller chez le dentiste*

2. Pourquoi tu ne te reposes pas?   5. Va chez le docteur!
3. Pourquoi tu ne te couches pas tôt?   6. Va chez le docteur!
4. Va chez le dentiste!

A17 Savez-vous que… ?

D'habitude, combien d'heures dormez-vous chaque nuit? Les Français dorment souvent moins qu'ils ne le désirent : 7 heures 30 en moyenne (1982). La durée du sommeil varie bien sûr selon les individus : Napoléon, par exemple, ne dormait que de 3 à 5 heures pour récupérer. On dit que les adolescents ont besoin d'environ 9 heures de sommeil par jour pour être «bien dans leur peau» *(to feel great)*. Pourtant, un sondage réalisé en Lorraine en 1982 indique qu'à peine 20% des garçons et 17% des filles de 14 à 18 ans satisfont ce besoin vital. Pire, 1 adolescent sur 20 dort même moins de 7 heures par jour. Le coupable *(the guilty one)*? La télévision monopolise sans doute la majeure partie de ces heures volées *(stolen)* au sommeil.

Le sommeil des Français	
Nombres d'heures	**100%**
Plus de 10 heures	1
10 heures	3
9 heures	8
8 heures	31
7 heures	27
6 heures	19
5 heures et moins	11

Sofres (mai 1982)

A18 Activité • Ecoutez bien For script and answers, see pp. T152–53.

Ecoutez ces jeunes qui ne sont pas en forme. Quels conseils pouvez-vous leur donner?

	1	2	3	4	5	6
Fais des exercices.						
Va chez le docteur.						
Il faut que tu manges mieux.						
Pourquoi tu ne vas pas chez le pharmacien?						
Il faut te coucher plus tôt.						
Va chez le dentiste.						

En pleine forme   245

talking about eating well . . . giving and justifying advice . . . expressing doubt, uncertainty, and dislikes

Pour être en forme, il faut bien se nourrir. C'est essentiel. Avec une bonne alimentation, équilibrée et variée, Fabrice va certainement retrouver des couleurs.

B1 Début de la remise en forme 📼

Fabrice a pris de mauvaises habitudes. Sandrine veut qu'il suive un nouveau régime.

(Sur le chemin de l'école)

(A l'heure du déjeuner)

SANDRINE	Combien tu pèses?
FABRICE	Cinquante-deux kilos.
SANDRINE	Ce n'est pas assez. Il faut absolument que tu manges plus et mieux. Qu'est-ce que tu prends d'habitude au petit déjeuner?
FABRICE	Une tartine et un bol de café.
SANDRINE	C'est très mauvais! Tu devrais boire un grand verre de jus d'orange et manger des céréales. C'est plus fortifiant et ça donne du tonus.

FABRICE	Tu veux que je t'offre un hamburger?
SANDRINE	Merci. Aujourd'hui on déjeune à la cantine.
FABRICE	«On»?
SANDRINE	Toi et moi. Il vaut mieux que tu manges un repas équilibré, avec des légumes, de la salade et du fromage.
FABRICE	Mais c'est mauvais à la cantine!
SANDRINE	Peut-être, mais c'est nourrissant.

(Le soir à la sortie de l'école)

FABRICE	Lâche-moi!
SANDRINE	Non, je ne veux pas que tu entres dans cette boulangerie.
FABRICE	Mais j'ai faim!
SANDRINE	Je te conseille d'acheter des fruits. C'est meilleur, et il y a plus de vitamines.
FABRICE	Allez! Juste un petit éclair au chocolat!
SANDRINE	Pas question... Maintenant, on va aller dans un restaurant végétarien.
FABRICE	Au secours!

1 kilogram = 2.2 pounds; 52 kilograms = 114.4 pounds

B2 Activité • Complétez

Trouvez des mots dans B1 pour compléter ces phrases.

1. Fabrice ne se soigne pas bien; il a pris…
2. Il ne se nourrit pas bien; il faut qu'il mange…
3. Le café est mauvais; le jus d'orange est plus…
4. Il vaut mieux que Fabrice mange un repas… et…
5. Acheter un éclair, c'est mauvais. Acheter des fruits, c'est…

1. de mauvaises habitudes. 2. plus et mieux. 3. nourrissant, fortifiant.
4. équilibré, nourrissant. 5. meilleur.

B3 Activité • Expliquez

D'après Sandrine, ces choses sont importantes. Pourquoi?

1. Il faut manger un repas équilibré. 1. C'est nourrissant.
2. Il faut acheter des fruits. 2. Il y a plus de vitamines.
3. Il faut prendre du jus d'orange et des céréales au petit déjeuner. 3. C'est fortifiant et ça donne du tonus.
4. Il vaut mieux déjeuner à la cantine. 4. C'est nourrissant.

B4 Activité • A vous maintenant! Possible answers are given.

Pouvez-vous trouver trois expressions dans B1 pour conseiller à quelqu'un de faire quelque chose? Ensuite, utilisez les expressions pour conseiller à un(e) camarade de faire ces choses.

1. manger des céréales
2. faire du sport
3. acheter des fruits
4. prendre un repas équilibré
5. faire un nouveau régime
6. se remettre en forme

1. Mange des céréales, c'est fortifiant. 2. Fais du sport, c'est bien pour la ligne. 3. Achète des fruits, il y a des vitamines.
4. Prends un repas équilibré, c'est bien nourrissant. 5. Fais un nouveau régime, tu vas retrouver des couleurs. 6. Il vaut mieux que tu te remettes en forme.

B5 STRUCTURES DE BASE
The verb boire

boire	*to drink*				
Je	bois		Nous	buvons	
Tu	bois	de l'eau.	Vous	buvez	de l'eau.
Il/Elle/On	boit		Ils/Elles	boivent	

The past participle of **boire** is **bu: Il a bu du jus d'orange.**
The subjunctive forms of **boire** are **boive, boives, boive, buvions, buviez, boivent.**

B6 Activité • Qu'est-ce qu'ils boivent?

Je… bois
1.

Nous… buvons
2.

Sandrine… boit
3.

Vous… buvez
4.

Sandrine et Matthieu boivent
5.

du lait

du chocolat

du jus de fruits

du soda

de l'eau

Faites un sondage dans votre classe. Demandez à vos camarades s'ils (si elles) boivent les boissons dans B6, et quand ils/elles les boivent : «Tu bois du lait? Quand est-ce que tu en bois?»

Elève	Lait	Eau	Jus	Soda	Chocolat
Janine	jamais	tous les jours	jamais	quelquefois	tous les matins

B8 Activité • Et vous?

Qu'est-ce que vous mangez au petit déjeuner? Qu'est-ce que vous buvez?

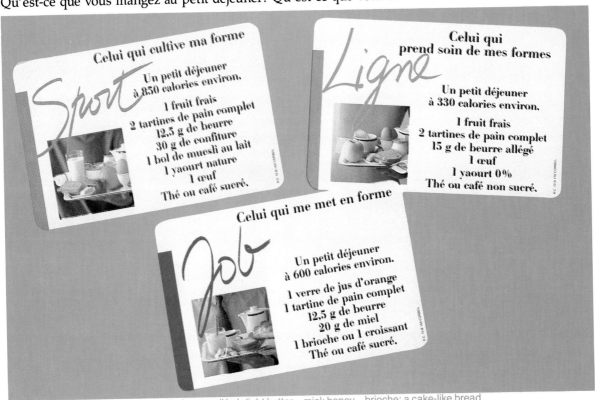

Celui qui cultive ma forme

Sport

Un petit déjeuner à 850 calories environ.

1 fruit frais
2 tartines de pain complet
12,5 g de beurre
30 g de confiture
1 bol de muesli au lait
1 yaourt nature
1 œuf
Thé ou café sucré.

Celui qui prend soin de mes formes

Ligne

Un petit déjeuner à 330 calories environ.

1 fruit frais
2 tartines de pain complet
15 g de beurre allégé
1 œuf
1 yaourt 0%
Thé ou café non sucré.

Celui qui me met en forme

Job

Un petit déjeuner à 600 calories environ.

1 verre de jus d'orange
1 tartine de pain complet
12,5 g de beurre
20 g de miel
1 brioche ou 1 croissant
Thé ou café sucré.

muesli: a multi-grain breakfast cereal   beurre allégé: light butter   miel: honey   brioche: a cake-like bread

B9 Activité • A vous maintenant!

Vous êtes chez un(e) ami(e). Il/Elle vous offre quelque chose à manger et à boire. Faites ce dialogue avec un(e) camarade. Employez les boissons dans B6.

— Tu as faim? Tu veux quelque chose à manger?
— Non merci, mais je veux bien quelque chose à boire.
— Qu'est-ce que tu bois?
— Donne-moi du... , s'il te plaît.

Savez-vous que... ?

En 1988, la compagnie américaine McDonald's a ouvert son 67ᵉ fast-food en France, un nouveau restaurant sur l'avenue des Champs-Elysées à Paris. Pour plaire aux Français, McDonald's a décidé de mettre moins de sucre et plus de moutarde dans les sauces pour la salade. On sert aussi de l'eau minérale et de la bière dans ces restaurants. Le dimanche, on offre des cadeaux aux enfants.

Chose étonnante, c'est une compagnie française avec un nom anglais, Quick, qui a le plus de fast-foods en France. Freetime est le nom d'un autre fast-food français. Chez Freetime, on sert le longburger; c'est un hamburger rectangulaire dans un petit pain rectangulaire. La compagnie américaine Burger King a aussi des restaurants en France.

Ce sont surtout les jeunes qui vont dans les fast-foods. Les adultes, eux, préfèrent les cafeterias dans les centres commerciaux et sur les grandes routes, ou les cantines là où ils travaillent. Mais en général, le fast-food devient de plus en plus populaire en France.

In France, young people refer to McDonald's as «McDo.»

B 11 STRUCTURES DE BASE
The verb suivre

suivre *to follow*					
Je	**suis**	} un régime.	Nous	**suivons**	} un régime.
Tu	**suis**		Vous	**suivez**	
Il/Elle/On	**suit**		Ils/Elles	**suivent**	

The past participle of **suivre** is **suivi**: **Ils ont suivi un régime.** The verb **suivre** may also mean *to take* when you talk about courses: **Je suis des cours de musique,** *I'm taking a music course.*

B 12 Activité • Et vous? Possible answers are given.

Répondez aux questions suivantes.

1. Avez-vous déjà suivi un régime? Et votre ami(e)? 1. Oui, j'ai déjà suivi.../Non, je n'ai jamais suivi...
2. Qui suit maintenant un régime chez vous? Vous? Votre sœur? Votre mère? 2. ...suit un régime chez moi.
3. Pourquoi? Pour être en forme? Pour perdre des kilos? Pour prendre des kilos? 3. Il/Elle le suit pour...
4. Suivez-vous toujours les conseils de vos ami(e)s? 4. Oui, je les suis toujours./Non, je ne les suis jamais.

Sandrine a écrit pour Fabrice son régime de la semaine.

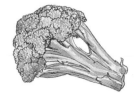

des brocolis (m.)

Lundi	Mardi	Mercredi
tomates poisson riz pomme	pamplemousse poulet carottes fromage	salade viande pommes de terre orange

une carotte

Jeudi	Vendredi	Samedi
tomates viande brocolis yaourt	salade poisson haricots verts banane	tomates poulet pâtes poire

du riz

Dimanche	
salade viande riz gâteau (petit !)	Ça, c'est un régime bien équilibré ! Encore un petit effort, et tu vas retrouver tes couleurs …

une poire

une orange

un pamplemousse

une banane

un yaourt

des pâtes (f.)

une pomme de terre

une tomate

des haricots verts

une pomme

Activité • **Avez-vous compris?** Possible answers are given.

Répondez aux questions suivantes d'après B13.

deux fois   deux fois   cinq fois

1. Combien de fois par semaine est-ce que Fabrice mange du poulet? Du poisson? Des fruits?
2. Est-ce qu'il ne mange absolument pas de dessert?   Si, le dimanche, il mange un petit gâteau.
3. Comment trouvez-vous le régime de Fabrice? Equilibré? Fortifiant? Nourrissant?   Je le trouve...
4. A votre avis, est-ce que Fabrice va avoir de la difficulté à suivre le régime? Pourquoi?
    Il va avoir de la difficulté parce qu'il n'a jamais suivi de régime.

B15   Activité • **Ecrit dirigé**

Qu'est-ce que vous avez mangé hier? Faites une liste et dites si la nourriture est nourrissante ou pas.

Nourriture	Nourrissant
Du gâteau	Non
Une pomme	Oui

B16   COMMENT LE DIRE
Giving and justifying advice

Tu devrais Je te conseille de } boire du lait. Il vaut mieux que tu boives du lait.	C'est excellent pour la santé. C'est bon pour toi. C'est ce qu'il te faut. C'est nourrissant. C'est meilleur.

Expressing doubt, uncertainty   Point out that when advising more than one person, the expression «Tu devrais...» becomes «Vous devriez...»

Tu crois?	Vraiment?
Tu es sûr(e)?	C'est vrai?

B17   Activité • **Il faut que Fabrice mange mieux**   Possible answers are given.

Qu'est-ce que vous conseillez à Fabrice de manger ou de boire? Dites pourquoi.

1.    **2.** 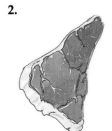   **3.**    **4.**    **5.**

Il vaut mieux que tu manges des fruits. C'est excellent pour la santé.

Tu devrais manger de la viande. C'est bon pour toi.

Je te conseille de manger du poisson. C'est ce qu'il te faut.

Tu devrais boire du lait. C'est nourrissant.

Il vaut mieux que tu manges des légumes. C'est meilleur.

Vos camarades se plaignent *(complain).* Donnez-leur des conseils.

1. Tu devrais aller chez le dentiste!   2. Il vaut mieux que vous mangiez des fruits.   3. Vous devriez aller chez le docteur.
4. Je te conseille de te coucher tôt.   5. Pourquoi tu ne manges pas des fruits?

B19   Activité • A vous maintenant!   Possible answers are given.

Votre ami(e) exprime ses envies. Vous lui donnez des conseils, mais il/elle a des doutes.
Faites les dialogues avec un(e) camarade. Changez de rôle.

— J'ai envie d'apprendre l'anglais.
— Tu devrais aller aux Etats-Unis.
— Tu crois?
— Oui, c'est un bon moyen d'apprendre l'anglais.

2. Il vaut mieux que tu cherches un job.   3. Tu devrais organiser une soirée.
4. Je te conseille d'apprendre la guitare.   5. Tu devrais aller dans un
restaurant.   6. Il vaut mieux que tu voyages.

1. apprendre l'anglais
2. gagner de l'argent
3. voir mes copains
4. jouer de la musique
5. bien manger
6. connaître d'autres pays

aller en Angleterre
aller dans un bon restaurant
organiser une soirée   voyager
chercher un job   apprendre la guitare

The subjunctive of the verb "aller" is presented in Section C of this unit.

COMMENT LE DIRE
Expressing dislike for foods and beverages

Je n'aime pas ça.	I don't like it.
C'est pas bon.	It's not good.
C'est mauvais.	It's bad.
Ça n'a pas de goût.	It's tasteless.
C'est infect.	It's disgusting.

B21 Activité • **Il faut bien se nourrir**

Votre ami(e) ne se nourrit pas bien. Vous lui conseillez de manger de la nourriture fortifiante et nourrissante. Faites les dialogues avec un(e) camarade. Employez les expressions dans B16 et B20. Changez de rôle. des légumes; une pomme; un yaourt; du poisson; des haricots verts; du riz

— Tu devrais manger des céréales.
— Je n'aime pas ça.
— Mais c'est excellent pour la santé.
— Tu crois?

B22 Activité • **Ecoutez bien**   For script and answers, see pp. T157–58.

Vous écoutez la radio. Il y a une émission pour les jeunes sur la nourriture. Des garçons et des filles téléphonent au docteur Leblanc pour lui demander des renseignements et des conseils. Ecoutez leurs questions et les réponses du docteur. Ensuite, répondez aux questions.

1. Qu'est-ce que la mère de Julien ne veut pas qu'il fasse?
2. En général, qu'est-ce que le docteur Leblanc pense du fast-food?
3. Quel est le problème de Delphine?
4. D'après le docteur, quand est-ce que le chocolat peut être un problème?
5. Qui sont Yannick Noah et Henri Leconte?
6. Qu'est-ce qu'ils boivent le jour du match?

SECTION
C

talking about getting into shape . . . expressing fatigue . . . pitying, encouraging, and reassuring others

Bien se nourrir, d'accord, mais il faut faire des exercices. Qu'est-ce que vous faites pour conserver la forme?

C1 ## La remise en forme (suite) 📼

C'est maintenant au tour de Matthieu de s'occuper de Fabrice.

MATTHIEU Alors, ça va mieux?
FABRICE Non, je me sens mal. Il faut que j'aille chez le docteur.
MATTHIEU Qu'est-ce qui t'arrive?
FABRICE Je suis allé au restaurant végétarien avec Sandrine vendredi, et depuis, j'ai mal au cœur. Ça ne marche pas, son régime!

MATTHIEU Mais non! C'est parce que tu n'es pas habitué. Il faut que tu sois patient. Ce n'est que le début de ton rétablissement. Demain, on va s'entraîner. Je t'assure que tu vas être un autre homme!

J'ai mal au cœur: I feel nauseous.   J'ai mal au ventre: My stomach hurts.

C2 Activité • Avez-vous compris?

Répondez aux questions suivantes d'après la conversation entre Matthieu et Fabrice.

1. Comment est-ce que Fabrice se sent?
2. D'après Fabrice, pourquoi est-ce qu'il ne se sent pas bien?
3. D'après Matthieu, pourquoi est-ce que Fabrice a mal au cœur?
4. Quels conseils est-ce que Matthieu lui donne?
5. Qu'est-ce que Matthieu et Fabrice vont faire demain?

1. Il se sent mal.   2. C'est parce qu'il est allé au restaurant végétarien.
3. Matthieu croit que c'est parce que Fabrice n'est pas habitué.   4. Il lui conseille d'être patient.   5. Ils vont s'entraîner.

Fabrice n'est pas en forme parce qu'il est allé au restaurant végétarien avec Sandrine. Pouvez-vous trouver d'autres raisons? Faites de courts dialogues avec un(e) camarade d'après les dessins. Changez de rôle.
1. Je suis fatigué.   2. J'ai mal à la tête.   3. J'ai mal au cœur.
4. J'ai mal partout.

— Ça va mieux?
— Non, je n'arrive pas à dormir.

1.

2.

3.

4.

Imaginez. Avant de téléphoner à Fabrice, Matthieu a téléphoné à Sandrine pour savoir comment marche le régime de Fabrice. Ecrivez leur conversation téléphonique.

— Allô, Sandrine? C'est Matthieu. Le régime de Fabrice, ça marche?
— Oui, ça va bien. On est allé dans un restaurant végétarien. C'était très bon.
— Bon, nous allons nous entraîner demain. Il va être un autre homme.

En pleine forme   255

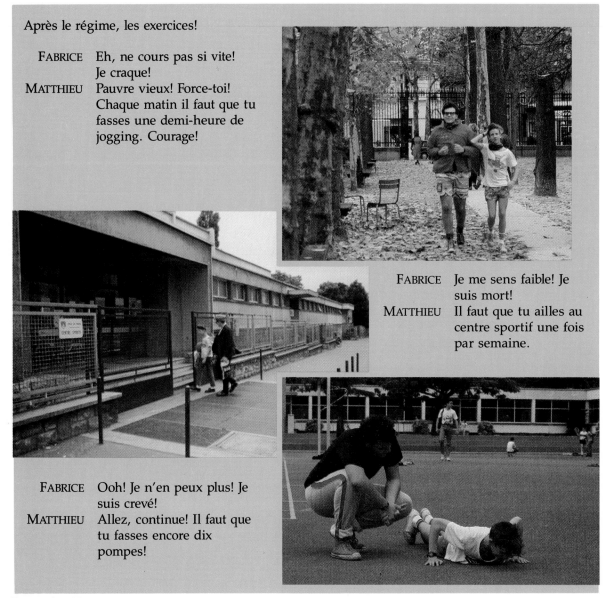

Après le régime, les exercices!

FABRICE Eh, ne cours pas si vite! Je craque!

MATTHIEU Pauvre vieux! Force-toi! Chaque matin il faut que tu fasses une demi-heure de jogging. Courage!

FABRICE Je me sens faible! Je suis mort!

MATTHIEU Il faut que tu ailles au centre sportif une fois par semaine.

FABRICE Ooh! Je n'en peux plus! Je suis crevé!

MATTHIEU Allez, continue! Il faut que tu fasses encore dix pompes!

Pauvre vieux!/Pauvre vieille!: You poor thing!

C6 Activité • Avez-vous compris?

Répondez aux questions suivantes d'après les dialogues entre Matthieu et Fabrice.

1. Qu'est-ce que Matthieu dit pour encourager Fabrice? Trouvez au moins deux expressions dans les dialogues. Force-toi! Allez, continue! Courage!
2. Fabrice est fatigué. Qu'est-ce qu'il dit? Trouvez au moins deux expressions dans les dialogues. Je craque! Je suis crevé! Je me sens faible. Je suis mort. Je n'en peux plus!
3. Qu'est-ce que les garçons font le matin? Pendant combien de temps? Ils font du jogging pendant une demi-heure
4. Est-ce que Matthieu et Fabrice vont aller au centre sportif tous les jours? Non, ils vont y aller une fois par semaine
5. Qu'est-ce qu'ils font au centre sportif? Ils s'entraînent.

Qu'est-ce qu'on fait comme exercices?

1.

des pompes

2.

de l'aérobic

3.

de la musculation

4.

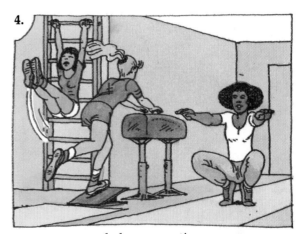

de la gymnastique

5.

de la natation

6.

de la relaxation

Comme aux Etats-Unis, mais avec quelques années de retard, les Français font de plus en plus attention à leur corps. Le mouvement est venu des Etats-Unis, et les mots aussi : aérobic, body-building, stretching font maintenant partie du langage courant. La télévision et les éditeurs suivent la mode, et des vedettes comme Sylvie Vartan, célèbre chanteuse des années soixante, ont écrit leur *Beauty Book*.

De nombreux centres proposent des activités corporelles. Le plus important est le Gymnase Club, créé en 1979. Avec une carte d'abonnement à l'année, on peut y faire ce qu'on veut : de la musculation, du judo, de la natation ou du tennis. Il existe aussi un Gymnase Club réservé aux jeunes, le Gymnase Club Junior.

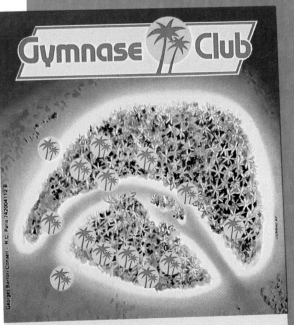

Le forfait :
21 Gymnases - 9 piscines
62 activités - 7 jours sur 7
• AUTEUIL • DENFERT • GRENELLE • LA DEFENSE • LAFAYETTE • MAILLOT • MONCEAU • MONTSOURIS • NATION • PLACE D'ITALIE • REPUBLIQUE • SALLE DES CHAMPS • VAUGIRARD (JUNIOR) • VELIZY.

GYMNASE CLUB SALLE DES CHAMPS

Heures d'ouverture : du lundi au vendredi de 7 h à 22 h
Samedi 9 h à 20 h - Dimanche 9 h à 17 h
Musculation aux appareils, plan d'entraînement personnalisé aux heures d'ouverture du gymnase.

Activités	Lundi	Mardi	Mercredi	Jeudi	Vendredi	Samedi	Dimanche
Musculation Séance de 30 mn	12h/12h30 13h/13h30 17h/17h30 18h/18h30 19h/19h30	12h/12h30 13h/13h30 17h/17h30 18h/18h30 19h/19h30	12h/12h30 13h/13h30 17h/17h30 18h/18h30 19h/19h30	12h/12h30 13h/13h30 17h/17h30 18h/18h30 19h/19h30	12h/12h30 13h/13h30 17h/17h30 18h/18h30 19h/19h30	11h 11h30 12h 12h30	11h 11h30 12h 12h30
Culture physique stretching* séance de 45 mn	7h30 8h15* 11h*/12h15* 13h45 16h30* 17h* 18h30 19h15*/20h 20h45*	7h30/9h* 10h/11h* 12h15/13h* 13h45 16h30* 17h*/17h45 18h30* 20h* 20h45	7h30 8h15* 11h/12h15 13h*13h45 16h30* 17h/17h45 19h15* 20h 20h45*	8h15/9h* 10h/11h* 12h15*/13h 13h45 16h30* 17h* 18h30* 19h15/20h* 20h45	7h30 8h15/9h 11h* 13h*/13h45 16h30* 17h* 17h45* 19h15 20h	9h30 11h30* 12h15 13h15 14h* 15h 16h* 17h 18h	9h30 11h* 12h15 13h15* 14h30 15h15
Préparation au ski séance de 45 mn	10h		10h		10h		
Rubber band séance de 30 mn	9h/13h	8h15 19h15	9h 18h30	7h30 17h45	12h15 18h30	10h15	10h15
Aérobic séance de 45 mn * séance de 60 mn	10h*/12h15 13h/15h30* 17h15/18h 18h45 19h30	10h*/12h15 13h/15h30* 17h15/18h 18h45 19h30	10h*/12h15 13h/15h30* 17h15/18h 18h45 19h30	10h*/12h15 13h/15h30* 17h15/18h 18h45 19h30	10h*/12h15 13h/15h30* 17h15/18h 18h45 19h30	10h 12h15 13h 15h 16h	10h 11h 12h15
Yoga séance de 60 mn		20h	20h		20h30		
Judo séance de 90 mn	14h30		14h30				
Modern jazz séance de 90 mn	20h15		20h15		20h15	17h	14h
Rock séance de 90 mn	14h	14h 20h15	14h	14h	14h	10h	
Danse orientale séance de 90 mn		20h15		20h15			
Danse de salon séance de 90 mn	9h	9h 14h30	9h	9h	9h 14h30	9h	9h

The names at the bottom of the left-hand page of realia are metro stops.

Musculation aux appareils: weight training
Danse de salon: ballroom dancing
Le forfait: total price includes:

C9 Activité • Et vous?

1. Est-ce que vous faites des exercices? Quel genre d'exercices?
2. Quand est-ce que vous les faites? Tous les jours? Une fois par semaine? Trois fois par jour? Le dimanche?
3. Pourquoi est-ce que vous faites des exercices?
4. Est-ce qu'il y a un centre de musculation près de chez vous? Est-ce que vous y allez? Avec qui? Quand?

STRUCTURES DE BASE
The verb courir

courir	*to run*					
Je	**cours**	} vite.	Nous	**courons**	} vite.	
Tu	**cours**		Vous	**courez**		
Il/Elle/On	**court**		Ils/Elles	**courent**		

The past participle of **courir** is **couru: Je n'ai pas couru vite.**

Activité • La course *The race*

Vous êtes bon(ne) à la course? Au centre sportif, vous avez couru le 100 mètres contre des copains. Vous avez noté les temps. Dites les temps de tous les coureurs.

— Corinne court le 100 mètres en treize secondes deux.

Course: 100 m

Corinne	13"2
Philippe	13"5
Jean-Paul	13"5
Claire	13"8
* Moi	14"3
Matthieu	14"2
Fabrice	16"2

VOUS EN SOUVENEZ-VOUS?
The subjunctive

You recall that you generally use the subjunctive forms of a verb if you want to say that activities must take place, that someone wants or doesn't want them to take place, or that it's better that they do.

> Il faut que tu **manges** mieux.
> Je veux que tu te **nourrisses** bien.
> Il vaut mieux que tu **prennes** un jus de fruit.

Do you remember how to make the subjunctive forms of a verb? First, you find the stem by dropping the verb ending from the regular **ils/elles** form. Then you add these endings: **-e, -es, -e, ions, -iez,** or **-ent.**

Present Subjunctive		
Stem	*Endings*	
rest~~ent~~	**-e**	Il faut que je **reste** ici.
rentr~~ent~~	**-es**	Ils veulent que tu **rentres.**
attend~~ent~~	**-e**	Il vaut mieux qu'il **attende.**
choisiss~~ent~~	**-ions**	Il faut que nous **choisissions.**
sort~~ent~~	**-iez**	Ils ne veulent pas que vous **sortiez.**
mett~~ent~~	**-ent**	Il faut qu'ils **mettent** la table.

Remember that the verb **faire** has an irregular stem in all the subjunctive forms: **fasse, fasses, fasse, fassions, fassiez, fassent.** Some verbs have two different stems: **boive, boives, boive, buvions, buviez, boivent.**

STRUCTURES DE BASE
Irregular subjunctive forms: aller, avoir, *and* être

1. **Aller, avoir,** and **être** have two different irregular stems in the present subjunctive: one for the **je, tu, il(s),** and **elle(s)** forms, and another for the **nous** and **vous** forms.

aller	avoir	être
Il faut...	Il faut...	Il faut...
que j' **aille**	que j' **aie**	que je **sois**
que tu **ailles**	que tu **aies**	que tu **sois**
qu'il/elle/on **aille**	qu'il/elle/on **ait**	qu'il/elle/on **soit**
que nous **allions**	que nous **ayons**	que nous **soyons**
que vous **alliez**	que vous **ayez**	que vous **soyez**
qu'ils/elles **aillent**	qu'ils/elles **aient**	qu'ils/elles **soient**

2. You use the subjunctive forms of **avoir** and **être** in commands.

N'**aie** pas peur!   **Sois** patient(e)!
N'**ayez** pas peur!   **Soyez** patient(e)(s)!

3. **Vouloir** also has two different irregular stems in the present subjunctive: **veuille, veuilles, veuille, voulions, vouliez, veuillent.**

4. **Pouvoir** and **savoir,** like **faire,** have one irregular stem for all forms of the present subjunctive: **puiss-, sach-.**

Activité • Donnez des raisons

Pourquoi est-ce qu'il faut que ces gens fassent ces choses? Donnez des raisons. Employez **Il faut que...** et le subjonctif du verbe **être.** Travaillez avec un(e) camarade. Changez de rôle.

Fabrice fait du jogging. (en forme)
1. Il faut qu'ils soient beaux.
2. Il faut que je sois en bonne santé.
1. Ils font de la musculation. (beau)
2. Tu suis un régime. (en bonne santé)
3. Nous faisons de l'aérobic. (en forme)
3. Il faut que vous soyez (nous soyons) en forme.

— Pourquoi est-ce que Fabrice fait du jogging?
— Il faut qu'il soit en forme.

4. Vous courez si vite. (prêt pour le match)
5. Murielle cherche un job. (indépendant)
4. Il faut que je sois (nous soyons) prêt(e)(s) pour le match.
5. Il faut qu'elle soit indépendante.

Activité • Donnez des conseils

Donnez des conseils à votre ami(e). Dites-lui où il faut qu'il/elle aille. Employez **Il faut que...** et le subjonctif du verbe **aller.** Changez de rôle.

avoir mal au cœur   — J'ai mal au cœur.
               — Il faut que tu ailles chez le docteur.

1. avoir mal partout
2. avoir mal aux dents
3. avoir envie d'être en forme
4. vouloir faire du théâtre
5. devoir acheter des médicaments
6. manger trop de viande

au centre sportif	chez le docteur
chez le pharmacien	à la Maison des Jeunes
dans un restaurant végétarien	chez le dentiste

1. Il faut que tu ailles chez le docteur.   2. Il faut que tu ailles chez le dentiste.   3. Il faut que tu ailles au centre sportif.
4. Il faut que tu ailles à la Maison des Jeunes.   5. Il faut que tu ailles chez le pharmacien.
6. Il faut que tu ailles dans un restaurant végétarien.

COMMENT LE DIRE
Expressing fatigue

Je n'en peux plus!	Je suis mort(e)! (fam.)
Je suis fatigué(e).	Je suis crevé(e)! (fam.)
Je suis épuisé(e).	Je craque! (fam.)
J'abandonne.	

Pitying and encouraging

PITYING	ENCOURAGING
(Mon) Pauvre vieux!	Allez!
(Ma) Pauvre vieille!	Vas-y!
Pauvre Fabrice!	Encore un effort!
Pauvre petit(e)!	Courage!
	Force-toi!

Point out that "Allez!" may be used as an encouragement even when addressing someone as "tu".

C17 Activité • **Ils n'en peuvent plus** Possible answers are given.

Vous proposez à un(e) camarade de faire quelque chose. Il/Elle refuse parce qu'il/elle est fatigué(e). Vous l'encouragez. Variez les expressions et changez de rôle.

— Tu viens avec moi faire du jogging?
— Non, je suis fatigué(e).
— Allez, force-toi!

1. — Non, je suis épuisé(e) — Force-toi!
2. — Je n'en peux plus! — Allez, vas-y!
3. — Non, ça n'a pas de goût. — Allez!
4. — J'abandonne. — Courage!
5. — Je suis mort(e)! — Encore un effort!

1. Tu viens avec moi faire de la musculation?
2. Allez, encore des pompes!
3. Mange encore un peu de riz!
4. On va voir un troisième film?
5. Tu devrais faire du vélo maintenant.
6. Fais de la natation. C'est excellent!

6. — Je craque! — Force-toi!

C18 ## COMMENT LE DIRE
Assuring and reassuring someone

Je t' (vous) assure que ça va.	Ça va, je t' (vous) assure.
Je te (vous) promets que je me sens mieux.	Je me sens mieux, je te (vous) promets.
Je te (vous) garantis que je me nourris bien.	Je me nourris bien, je te (vous) garantis.

The verb "assurer" takes the indirect-object pronoun when followed by a clause introduced by "que": Je <u>lui</u> assure que ça va bien.

C19 Activité • **Rassurez-le** Possible answers are given.

Votre camarade vous trouve mauvaise mine. Vous lui assurez que vous êtes en pleine forme. Travaillez avec un(e) camarade et changez de rôle. Variez les expressions soulignées. Employez les expressions dans A15, B16 et C18.

— Tu n'as pas l'air en forme.
— Si, ça va. Ça n'a pas l'air d'aller. Qu'est-ce qui t'arrive?

— Tu es sûr(e)? Tu crois? Vraiment? C'est vrai?
— Oui, je t'assure que ça va mieux.
  je te promets que...
  je te garantis que...

Vos amis ont constaté *(noticed)* plusieurs choses chez vous *(about you)*. Mais vous n'êtes pas d'accord avec eux. Vous les assurez du contraire. Variez les expressions. Changez de rôle.

— Tu ne fais pas assez d'exercices.
— Si, je t'assure que je fais assez d'exercices.

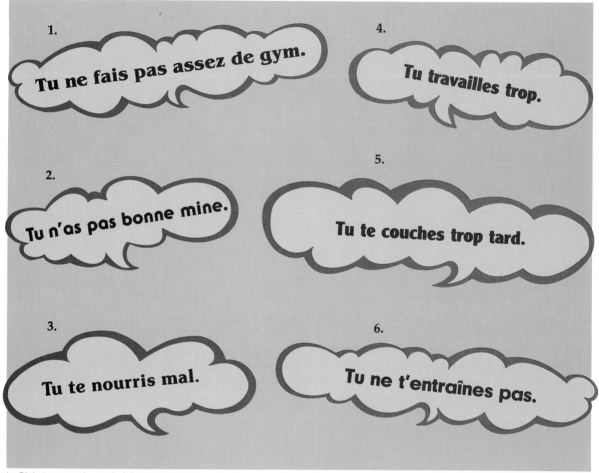

1. Tu ne fais pas assez de gym.

4. Tu travailles trop.

2. Tu n'as pas bonne mine.

5. Tu te couches trop tard.

3. Tu te nourris mal.

6. Tu ne t'entraînes pas.

1. Si, je te garantis que je fais assez de gym.   2. Je me sens bien, je t'assure.   3. Je me nourris bien, je te promets.   4. Ça va, je t'assure.   5. Non, je me couche tôt, je t'assure.   6. Si, je te garantis que je m'entraîne.

Ecoutez cette publicité radiophonique pour le Gymnase Club. Vous voulez encourager un(e) de vos ami(e)s à y aller. Ecrivez le maximum de renseignements pour pouvoir le/la renseigner.

Nom : Jours : Heures : Tél.	Activités :

1 · Fabrice n'arrive plus à dormir.

Depuis quelques jours, Fabrice fait de drôles de rêves : ses parents, ses amis, tout le monde lui donne des conseils pour être en forme.

> Tu as drôlement mauvaise mine! Tu devrais aller chez le médecin!

> Pourquoi tu ne fais pas de jogging tous les matins?

> Mais non, il faut que tu manges mieux!

> Mange des fruits. C'est meilleur que les bonbons!

> Pas du tout! A mon avis, tu devrais boire du jus d'orange. C'est excellent pour la santé!

> Tu n'as pas l'air en forme. Je te conseille de faire de la gym!

2 · Activité • Répondez

Répondez aux questions suivantes d'après 1.

1. Parce qu'il fait de drôles de rêves.   2. Il rêve que tout le monde lui donne des conseils pour être en forme.   3. D'aller chez le médecin, de mieux manger, de boire du jus d'orange, de faire du jogging, de manger des fruits, et de faire de la gym.
4. Ils trouvent qu'il a mauvaise mine et qu'il n'est pas en forme.   5. Parce que c'est excellent pour la santé.

1. Pourquoi est-ce que Fabrice n'arrive plus à dormir?
2. Décrivez ses rêves.
3. Quels conseils est-ce que les autres lui donnent dans ses rêves?
4. Comment est-ce que les autres trouvent Fabrice?
5. Pourquoi est-ce qu'il devrait boire du jus d'orange?

3 · Activité • Chez le docteur

Imaginez. Vous allez chez le docteur. Vous lui dites que vous ne vous sentez pas bien. Il vous donne des conseils. Préparez le dialogue avec un(e) camarade.   Refer students to A15, p. 244 for expressions of complaining, and to B16, p. 251 for expressions of justifying and giving advice.

4 · Activité • Donnez des conseils

Votre ami(e) ne se sent pas bien. Il/Elle fume des cigarettes depuis longtemps. Vous lui conseillez de ne plus fumer, de se remettre en forme. Il/Elle vous promet d'abandonner ses mauvaises habitudes. Préparez le dialogue avec un(e) camarade.

Helpful expressions:
Arrête de fumer: Stop smoking.   Ça sent mauvais: It smells bad.   C'est mauvais pour la santé: It's bad for your health.

5 — Activité • Réfléchissez   Possible answer is given.

Maintenant vous connaissez bien Fabrice. A votre avis, est-ce que la réforme de Fabrice
va réussir ou non? Exprimez votre opinion et donnez vos raisons.

A mon avis, Fabrice va réussir parce que ses amis insistent. Il va abandonner ses mauvaises habitudes. Il va être un autre homme.

6 — Activité • Projet

Comme devoir, votre professeur vous a demandé de dessiner une affiche. Il vous a donné
le choix : (1) une affiche qui conseille aux gens de bien se nourrir ou (2) une affiche qui
conseille aux gens de faire des exercices. Choisissez un sujet et dessinez l'affiche.

7 — Activité • Ecrivez   Possible answer is given.

Fabrice vous a écrit une lettre. Il vous parle de sa remise en forme. Avez-vous pitié de lui
ou êtes-vous d'accord avec les efforts de Sandrine et de Matthieu? Répondez à la lettre en
exprimant votre opinion.   Cher Fabrice, mon pauvre vieux! Tes amis sont vraiment sympa. Ils s'occupent de toi, et ils vont
t'aider. Il faut absolument que tu suives leurs conseils. Tu vas voir, dans quelques jours, tout va aller

> Cher / Chère...
>   Comment vas-tu? Moi, ça va pas terrible. Je
> t'écris de mon lit. J'ai passé une journée horrible.
> J'ai deux amis, Matthieu et Sandrine; tu les as vus,
> je crois, quand tu es venu(e) en France en juillet. Je
> ne sais pas ce qu'ils ont, mais depuis quinze jours,
> ils veulent absolument que je fasse des exercices et
> que je me nourrisse mieux. Ils disent que j'ai
> mauvaise mine, que j'ai l'air faible. C'est vrai, je
> ne suis pas très en forme, mais ils exagèrent. Maintenant,
> je suis malade! Imagine: moi qui ne suis pas
> sportif, je dois faire de la musculation, du jogging,
> de la gymnastique...! Je suis épuisé! Moi qui aime
> les pâtisseries, il faut que je suive un régime et que
> je mange de la nourriture infecte dans les restaurants
> végétariens!
>   Bon, je te quitte parce qu'il faut que je me couche:
> demain matin, il faut que j'aille faire du jogging
> avec Matthieu au jardin du Luxembourg à sept
> heures! Salut!
>   Amitiés,
>   Fabrice

mieux, et moi, je vais t'appeler Mr. Muscles! Envoie-moi une photo!

8 — Activité • Récréation (optional)

Devinez

Qu'est-ce que ces symboles représentent?

1.   2.   3.   4.

la musculation   l'aérobic   la relaxation   la danse

For script, see pp. T165–67.

PRONONCIATION

The nasals

1 Ecoutez bien et répétez.

1. The sound /ɛ̃/

Saint-Paul	saint	bain	main
Saint-Pierre	pain	faim	train

J'ai faim. Un pain, s'il vous plaît.
J'ai tellement faim. Je vais manger tout un pain.
A quelle heure est le prochain train pour Saint-Germain?
A cinq heures vingt.

2. The sound /ã/

dent	temps	grand	banque
blanc	vent	franc	langue
plan	gant	pense	jambe

Les sandwiches au pain blanc sont à vingt francs.
Sa tante a de l'argent à la banque.

3. The sound /ɔ̃/

bon, bon   des bonbons   J'aime les bonbons.   C'est bon.
ma blonde   mon oncle   Sur le pont d'Avignon, on y danse tous en rond.
Deux sandwiches au jambon, trois sandwiches au saumon et quatre sandwiches
au thon.

4. The sound /œ̃/

un garçon   un à un   emprunter   lundi   du pain brun

5. The sounds /ɛ̃/, /ã/, /ɔ̃/, and /œ̃/ together

Chacun monte dans le train et prend sa place.
Ça fait cinq cent cinquante et un francs onze.
Un bon pain blanc.

2 Ecoutez et lisez.

— Tu prends des vacances en septembre?
— Bien sûr, à la campagne, chez mon
oncle et ma tante.
— C'est où?
— A vingt kilomètres d'ici. En train, ça ne prend
pas longtemps. On arrive juste à
temps pour le dîner.

— On mange bien?
— Oui, mais ce n'est pas abondant. Tu
sais, mon oncle Armand n'est pas
gourmand. Pour lui, du pain blanc
frais et un bon camembert, ça suffit.

3 Copiez les phrases suivantes pour préparer une dictée.

1. Bonjour, Francine. Depuis quand tu es au régime?
2. Depuis le vingt septembre. Ça fait un an que je fais des exercices.
3. Comment tu te sens?
4. J'ai mal à la tête le matin, au ventre après manger et aux jambes toute la journée. Et toi?
5. Moi, ça va, je fais de la natation. Chaque matin je fais de nombreuses longueurs de bassin.
C'est excellent pour la santé.

VERIFIONS!

SECTION A

Have you learned to make the forms of reflexive verbs?
1. Il se couche tôt.
2. Nous nous levons tard.
3. Je me sens mieux.
Make complete sentences, using the correct verb forms.
1. Il / se coucher / tôt
2. Nous / se lever / tard
3. Je / se sentir / mieux
4. Vous / se soigner / bien
5. Tu / se nourrir / mal
6. Elles / se reposer / maintenant
4. Vous vous soignez bien.   5. Tu te nourris mal.   6. Elles se reposent maintenant.

Can you express concern for someone's health?
What would you say if you noticed that your friend didn't look well? Use three different expressions. Ça n'a pas l'air d'aller.   Tu as mauvaise mine.   Tu n'as pas l'air en forme.

Do you know how to complain about your health?
Say that you're not feeling well. Then tell what's wrong with you.
Je ne me sens pas très bien.   J'ai mal partout.

SECTION B

Have you learned the verbs *boire* and *suivre*?
1. Ils boivent du jus de fruit.
2. Elle suit un régime.
Make complete sentences, using the correct forms of the verbs.
1. Ils / boire / jus de fruit
2. Elle / suivre / régime
3. Elle / ne / boire / pas / café
4. Nous / suivre / même / régime
5. Vous / boire / lait   3. Elle ne boit pas de café.
6. Je / suivre / conseils
4. Nous suivons le même régime.   5. Vous buvez du lait.   6. Je suis ses conseils.

Do you know the French names of some nourishing food?
Suggest five foods or beverages that are good for you.
les fruits, les légumes, le lait, l'eau, le jus de fruit.

Can you give advice in French and give reasons for it?
Give advice and reasons to these people.
1. Ton ami ne boit jamais de lait.   Tu devrais boire du lait. C'est nourrissant.
2. Ton amie ne mange pas de fruit. Elle mange des éclairs.
Je te conseille de manger des fruits. C'est meilleur.

Do you know how to express uncertainty or doubt?
What three different questions would you ask if you weren't certain that what your friend said was true or appropriate?
Tu es sûr(e)?   Tu crois?   Vraiment?   C'est vrai?

Have you learned how to express dislike for foods or beverages?
Say that you don't like something in two different ways.
C'est mauvais.   Ça n'a pas de goût.   C'est infect.   Je n'aime pas ça.   C'est pas bon.

SECTION C

Have you learned the French names for various exercises?
Tell five different things that you or your friends do for exercise.
la natation, le jogging, l'aérobic, les pompes, la musculation

Can you make regular and some irregular subjunctive verb forms?
Advise your friend to do the following, using **Il faut que...** and the subjunctive.   1. ...tu manges mieux.   2. ...tu te nourrisses bien.   3. ...tu perdes des kilos.
1. manger mieux
2. bien se nourrir
3. perdre des kilos
4. faire des exercices
5. aller chez le docteur
6. être patient(e)
4. ...tu fasses des exercices.   5. ...tu ailles chez le docteur.   6. ...tu sois patient(e).

Do you know how to express fatigue?
Say that you can't go on, that you're exhausted, and that you're giving up.
Je n'en peux plus.   Je suis mort(e).   Je suis crevé(e).   J'abandonne.   Je craque.

Can you pity and encourage others?
Express pity and offer encouragement in two different ways to your friend.
Pauvre vieux, allez!   Pauvre petit, courage!   Pauvre ..., force-toi!

Have you learned how to assure or reassure someone?
React to your friends' remarks, giving assurance in three different ways.
1. Tu n'as pas l'air d'être en forme!
Mais si, je te garantis que je suis en forme.
2. Tu te sens mieux? Vraiment?
Je me sens mieux, je t'assure!

arrive : Qu'est-ce qui t'arrive? *What's wrong with you?*
avoir : Qu'est-ce que tu as? *What's wrong with you?*
coucher (se) *to go to bed*
une **dent** *tooth*
énergique *energetic*
entraîner (s') *to train, work out*
un **exercice** *exercise*
inquiéter (s') *to worry*
lever (se) *to get up*
mal : avoir du mal à *to have difficulty;* **avoir mal à** *to hurt, ache*
manquer (de) *to lack*
matinée : faire la grasse matinée *to sleep late*
une **mesure** *measure*
mine : avoir mauvaise mine *to look sick*
nourrir (se) *to feed, nourish*
occuper (s') (de) *to take charge (of)*
partir : à partir de from . . . on(ward)
partout *everywhere*
un(e) **pharmacien, -ienne** *pharmacist*
promener (se) *to walk*
un **régime : faire un régime** *to go on a diet*
reposer (se) *to rest*
sentir (se) *to feel*
soigner (se) *to take care of*

la **tête** *head*
le **tonus** *muscle tone*

l' **alimentation** (f.) *food*
une **banane** *banana*
boire *to drink*
le **brocoli** *broccoli*
la **cantine** *cafeteria*
une **carotte** *carrot*
des **céréales** (f.) *cereal*
certainement *undoubtedly*
le **chemin** *way*
le **début** *beginning*
devrais *should*
un **éclair** *eclair*
équilibré, -e *balanced*
essentiel, -elle *essential*
fortifiant, -e *fortifying*
une **habitude** *habit*
un **haricot vert** *string bean*
infect, -e *disgusting, rotten*
lâcher *to let go, release*
meilleur, -e *better, best*
nourrissant, -e *nourishing*
une **orange** *orange*
un **pamplemousse** *grapefruit*
les **pâtes** (f.) *pasta*
peser *to weigh*
une **poire** *pear*
une **pomme** *apple*
une **pomme de terre** *potato*
la **remise en forme** *remaking*
un **restaurant** *restaurant*
retrouver : retrouver des couleurs *to get your color back*

le **riz** *rice*
suivre *to follow, take*
une **tartine** *slice of bread and butter*
une **tomate** *tomato*
vaut : il vaut mieux que... *it's better that . . .*
végétarien, -ienne *vegetarian*
un **verre** *glass*
une **vitamine** *vitamin*
le **yaourt** *yogurt*

assurer *to assure*
conserver *to keep, preserve*
courir *to run*
craquer (fam.) *to be about to collapse*
crevé, e *exhausted*
depuis *(ever) since*
le **docteur** *doctor*
épuisé, -e *exhausted*
faible *weak*
forcer (se) *to force oneself*
garantir *to guarantee*
habitué, -e *used to, accustomed*
mort, -e *dead*
pauvre *poor*
peux : Je n'en peux plus! *I can't continue!*
une **pompe** *push-up*
promettre *to promise*
le **rétablissement** *restoration*
le **tour** *turn*

ETUDE DE MOTS

You've learned that reflexive pronouns may be used with many verbs to show that the subject is performing the action of the verb on itself; the subject and the reflexive pronoun refer to the same person or thing. You may often use the same verbs without the reflexive pronoun to show that the subject is acting upon someone or something else.

Je me couche. *I go to bed. (I put myself to bed.)*
La mère couche les enfants. *The mother puts the children to bed.*

Make up pairs of sentences similar to those above using the following verbs, first with a reflexive pronoun, then without.

se promener   s'inquiéter   se soigner   se nourrir

Je me promène.   Je promène le chien.   Je m'inquiète.   J'ai perdu 5 kilos.   Ça inquiète ma mère.   Elle se soigne.
Sa mère la soigne quand elle est malade.   Il faut bien se nourrir.   Les parents doivent bien nourrir leurs enfants.

A LIRE

Bibi : le fana de la forme

Connaissez-vous des fanatiques de la forme? Alors, vous connaissez déjà Bibi. Il a écrit ses pensées intimes. Est-il heureux?

Avant de lire

Reconnaissez-vous ces mots? Pouvez-vous deviner leurs équivalents anglais?

additif additive   **graisse** fat   **kiwis** kiwi fruit
cholestérol cholesterol **s'exercer** to exercise **vanille** vanilla

Lisez le poème rapidement. Qu'est-ce que Bibi fait pour être en pleine forme?

Je me regarde
Et je me trouve beau.
Cuisine régime,
Cuisine bonne mine.
Additifs?
Jamais.
Cholestérol?
Je ne me laisse pas tenter°.
Je ne mange aucune graisse,
Aucun sucre.
Pas de sel.
Je me regarde
Et je me trouve beau.

Je ne mange rien
Mais j'ai envie de tout.
D'habitude, je me couche
Sans rien manger,
Ou presque.
Une pomme,
Un verre de lait écrémé°.
De bon matin je fais du jogging.
Je me muscle le ventre.
Après, j'ai mal aux genoux.
L'après-midi,
Je fais de la bicyclette.
Je ne mange rien
Mais j'ai envie de tout.

---

me laisse tenter *let myself be tempted;* **écrémé** *skimmed*

Il vaut mieux que ça change.
Il vaut mieux que je mange.
Mais j'avale des corn flakes,
Du lait écrémé,
Du jus d'orange,
Du kasha°, des kiwis,
Du yaourt aux myrtilles°.
Je me fais des muscles.
Je cultive le body-building.
Je cours,
Je dors,
Je rêve de manger.
Il vaut mieux que ça change.
Il vaut mieux que je mange.

Je meurs° de faim,
Je dépéris°.
J'ai mal aux genoux,
Je cours trop!
Quand je me regarde,
Je me trouve beau.
Beau mais affamé°!
J'ai mal de ne rien manger!
Il vaut mieux que ça change.
Il vaut mieux que je mange
Des gâteaux,
Du chocolat,
De la glace à la vanille.
Je ne veux plus m'exercer!
Je meurs de faim,
Je dépéris!

Activité • Réfléchissez   Possible answers are given.

A votre avis, est-ce que Bibi est content? Pourquoi? Citez *(quote)* des vers *(lines)* du poème
pour justifier votre opinion.   A mon avis, Bibi n'est pas content. Il dit : «Je meurs de faim. Il vaut mieux que ça change.»

Activité • Donnez des conseils   Possible answer is given.

Donnez des conseils à Bibi. Encouragez-le ou déconseillez-le.   Allez, Bibi! Il faut souffrir pour réussir! Si tu veux
rester beau, tu dois t'entraîner tout le temps. En plus, il faut que tu suives un régime très strict.

---

kasha *crushed wheat;*   **myrtilles** *blueberries;*   **meurs** *die;*   **dépéris** *fade away;*   **affamé** *starved*

Comment soigner les petits maux°? 📼

Comment vous sentez-vous? Avez-vous souvent la grippe°? Un rhume°? Une angine°? Le docteur Bonsoin vous donne des conseils utiles pour soigner les petits maux.

Avant de lire

La grippe et l'angine sont des maladies°. Lisez le texte rapidement pour trouver ce qui cause ou transmet ces maladies.

Dr Jean Bonsoin
7, rue de l'Hôpital
96102 Guéri, France

LA GRIPPE : COMMENT S'EN DEBARRASSER°?

Tiens, une maladie qui fait voyager! Asiatique ou espagnole, venue de Bangkok ou du Texas, c'est toujours la grippe. Mais est-ce à chaque fois tout à fait la même maladie? Oui et non. La grippe est transmise par un virus, un microbe minuscule qui a le pouvoir de se transformer au fil du temps°, pour infester les hommes, femmes ou enfants qui ont la santé affaiblie.
La grippe est généralement sans gravité, surtout si l'on est jeune. On s'en tire° avec quelques jours de fièvre°, des frissons°, des courbatures°. Que faire? Se reposer, boire beaucoup, prendre de la vitamine C et de l'aspirine si la fièvre est trop désagréable. Ne pas surchauffer sa chambre, et penser même à l'aérer de temps en temps.
En cas de doute ou de fièvre prolongée, appelez votre médecin.

L'ANGINE : POURQUOI VAUT-IL TOUJOURS MIEUX APPELER UN MEDECIN?

Vous avez 40° de fièvre le matin! Impossible d'avaler° quoi que ce soit! Vous avez la sensation d'avoir des boules° dans la gorge°...
Si vous regardez votre gorge dans une glace, vous découvrez vos amygdales très rouges ou couvertes de petits points blancs.
Cette douleur de gorge peut être accompagnée de maux de ventre.
Pas de doute : c'est bien une angine, causée par un redoutable° microbe qu'on appelle «streptocoque».
Il ne faut jamais laisser traîner° une angine.
Elle est susceptible d'entraîner des complications, comme des rhumatismes ou une maladie du rein°.
Une angine doit être prise au sérieux. Appelez votre médecin sans hésiter.

Activité • Complétez

1. Un virus, c'est un ____ . microbe minuscule
2. Un virus ____ la grippe. transmet
3. Le streptocoque, c'est un ____ . microbe

4. Les amygdales sont dans la ____ . gorge
5. L'angine et la grippe sont des ____ . maladies

Activité • A vous maintenant!

Vous vous sentez mal. Votre ami(e) vous demande ce que vous avez. Vous lui décrivez vos symptômes. Il/Elle vous donne des conseils. Faites le dialogue avec un(e) camarade. Employez les renseignements dans «La grippe... » et dans «L'angine... ».

---

maux (pluriel de mal) *illnesses;* **grippe** *flu;* **rhume** *cold;* **angine** *sore throat;* **maladies** *illnesses;* **s'en débarrasser** *to get rid of it;* **au fil du temps** *in the course of time;* **s'en tire** *pulls through;* **fièvre** *fever;* **frissons** *chills;* **courbatures** *aches;* **avaler** *swallow;* **boules** *lumps;* **gorge** *throat;* **redoutable** *fearsome;* **laisser traîner** *neglect;* **rein** *kidney*

La Chromogym

Est-ce que les couleurs exercent une influence sur vos émotions? Sur vos actions? Lisez cet article sur un cours de gymnastique unique.

A Paris, deux professeurs d'éducation physique offrent un cours de gymnastique en couleur. Ils ont étudié l'influence des couleurs sur les émotions des gens, surtout la chromothérapie pratiquée aux Etats-Unis et en Grande-Bretagne. Ils ont décidé d'introduire les couleurs dans leurs cours de gymnastique. Voici les résultats de leurs recherches.

Le rouge augmente° le rythme cardiaque.
Il est parfait pour les exercices de tonicité.

Le bleu crée une sensation de bien-être.
Il est recommandé pour les exercices d'assouplissement°.

Le jaune et l'orange sont les couleurs de l'harmonie.
Ils conviennent° aux mouvements difficiles et lents, à la coordination.

Le vert facilite la respiration.
Il est bon pour l'échauffement° et la récupération.

Activité • Cherchez des renseignements

Préparez un résumé de cet article en complétant ce tableau.

Couleur	Influence	Exercice
le rouge	le rythme cardiaque	tonicité
le bleu	sensation de bien-être	les exercices d'assouplissement
le jaune et l'orange	l'harmonie	la coordination
le vert	la respiration	l'échauffement et la récupération

Activité • Choisissez les couleurs   Possible answers are given.

A votre avis, quelles couleurs conviennent à ces activités?
1. le yoga le bleu
2. la musculation le rouge
3. l'aérobic le vert
4. la danse classique le jaune et l'orange
5. le jogging le vert
6. la natation le rouge

Activité • Et vous?

Quelle est votre couleur favorite? Reflète-t-elle votre personnalité? Comment et quand l'utilisez-vous?

---

augmente *increases;*   **assouplissement** *relaxation;*   **conviennent** *are suitable;*   **échauffement** *warming-up, limbering*

CHAPITRE 8 **Rendez-vous en Suisse**

Chapitre de révision

> **UNIT RESOURCES**   **Cahier d'Activités, Cahier d'Exercices,** Unit 8
> Cassette, Transparency 20 (also 11–19), Review Test 2
> **TEACHER-PREPARED MATERIALS**   **Review 1–27**   Map of Switzerland,
> map of Europe, toy telephones

Unit 8 combines functions, grammar, and vocabulary that the students have
studied in Units 5–7. This unit provides communicative and writing practice in
different situations; some of the activities lend themselves to cooperative learning. If your students require further practice, you will find additional review
exercises in Unit 8 of the **Cahier d'Activités** and the **Cahier d'Exercices.** On
the other hand, if your students know how to use the material in Units 5–7,
you may wish to omit parts of Unit 8.

OBJECTIVE   To review communicative functions, grammar, and vocabulary
from Units 5–7

CULTURAL BACKGROUND   Switzerland **(la Suisse)** is a small, mountainous
country on France's eastern border. It is separated from France by the Jura
Mountains **(le Jura),** Lake Geneva **(le lac de Genève** or **le lac Léman),** and
the Alps **(les Alpes).** The capital is Bern. In addition to French, German,
and Italian, Romansh is one of Switzerland's national languages.

MOTIVATING ACTIVITY   On a map of Europe, have students locate
Switzerland. Then ask students what they know about Switzerland. They
might mention cities, products, sports, or anything else they associate with
this country. List their suggestions on the board or on a transparency. As
you progress through the unit, add to the list started here. When you reach
the end of the unit, use this to review what students have learned.

1 Premier rendez-vous

CULTURAL BACKGROUND   Lake Geneva is 45 miles (72.4 kilometers) long
and from 2 to 9 miles (3.2 to 14.5 kilometers) wide. Its southern shore is in
France and its northern shore in Switzerland. Geneva is at its western end,
where the **Rhône** flows out of the lake. The city is built on both sides of the
river and the end of the lake. Its two sections are connected by several bridges.
It is a cosmopolitan city, with elegant shops and buildings, in a picturesque
location. **Lausanne,** farther east along the lake shore, is set into the hillsides
that rise from the lake. It is both a business center and a resort city.

On the map in the text, have students locate **Genève, Lausanne,** and **le lac
Léman.** Then, in French, tell students they're going to hear about a French girl's
visit to Switzerland. Students should listen for her name, where she's staying,
and the name of her new friend. Play the cassette or read the introduction
aloud. After students have identified the girl and her friend, tell them to listen
for two interesting comments about language in Switzerland. Play the cassette
or have two students who have already prepared the dialogue read it aloud
for the class. Ask students what the Swiss equivalents are for **soixante-dix,
quatre-vingts,** and **quatre-vingt-dix.** Then have students name the four
languages spoken in Switzerland. Next, as students listen to the remainder

of the dialogue, they should try to discover the one drawback to Isabelle's visit and what Bruno suggests to overcome it. Finally, have students read the dialogue aloud.

2 Activité • Avez-vous compris?

Have students write the answers to these questions. Then have volunteers read their answers aloud to the class.

3 Activité • Et vous?

Have students work in pairs to answer these questions. They should be prepared to report their partners' answers to the class.

CHALLENGE Have students prepare a brief talk about a trip they've taken. They might bring in photos, slides, or postcards and say something about each one in French.

4 Activité • Une journée à Genève

First review reflexive pronouns and how to use them. Then have students tell what they would do in Geneva, using **nous** and the phrases provided. Next brainstorm with them other things they might do there. Write these on the board or on a transparency, and have students write them in their notebooks. For homework, have students write a postcard to a friend, using the **passé composé** and the lists in their books and notebooks to tell what they did in Geneva.

5 Activité • Que faire?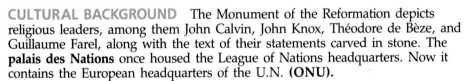

CULTURAL BACKGROUND The Monument of the Reformation depicts religious leaders, among them John Calvin, John Knox, Théodore de Bèze, and Guillaume Farel, along with the text of their statements carved in stone. The **palais des Nations** once housed the League of Nations headquarters. Now it contains the European headquarters of the U.N. **(ONU).**

Review with students how to form the subjunctive of regular verbs, **aller,** and **faire.** Next have students suggest ways to accept or refuse an invitation that would be appropriate in this situation. Then have students work in pairs to complete the activity.

SLOWER-PACED LEARNING On the board or on a transparency, list ways to accept an invitation (Unit 2, A12, page 58) and ways to refuse one (Unit 5 A6, page 157). Students may refer to these while working in pairs.

6 Activité • A vous maintenant!

Brainstorm with students which sights of their town or city they would want to show to a foreign guest. Once again, review ways to accept or refuse an invitation. You might also review how to express indifference or lack of interest (Unit 3, B6, page 104). Then have students work in pairs, one role-playing the Swiss guest and the other, the American host.

CHALLENGE Encourage students role-playing the American host to vary their invitations and suggestions (Unit 2, A12, page 58).

7   Activité • Avant le rendez-vous

Bring toy telephones to class. After students have had time to practice, have them present their conversations, using the telephones, to the class.

CHALLENGE   Review with students other ways to ask for and give advice (Unit 5, C9, page 173) to use in their conversations.

8   Activité • A votre avis

Have students use the expressions in the box to complete the three statements. Then divide the class into groups of four students each and conduct a speed-and-accuracy contest. See how many additional benefits of going to a foreign country each group can list. The group with the greatest number of logical statements wins.

9   Activité • Ecrivez

Review vocabulary from Unit 6 relating to jobs. Working at the board or on a transparency, help students develop and write the first ad. Then have them write two more as you circulate. Collect papers and return the next day with errors circled. Have students rewrite their ads, making the necessary corrections. Collect and post on a classroom bulletin board.

10   Savez-vous que... ?

Read aloud the cultural information given here, or play the cassette. Have individuals summarize each paragraph. For homework, you might have students look through magazines for ads featuring Swiss products. Have them write in French some brief copy to convince a consumer to buy that product: **Vous ne voulez jamais être en retard? Achetez une montre Swatch!**

11   VISITE DE LA SUISSE EN PHOTOGRAPHIE

CULTURAL BACKGROUND   Bern was founded in the twelfth century on the Aare River. It is famous for the arcades that cover its sidewalks and for fountains topped by brightly painted statues. **Neuchâtel** is celebrated for its beauty and for the purity of the French spoken by its inhabitants, said to be the best French in Switzerland. **Crans-Montana** is in the part of the Alps called the **Valais,** which is also home to the Matterhorn. The resort is popular year round. In the summer, one can ski the **Plaine Morte Glacier** or play golf. **Montreux,** a resort town on the shore of Lake Geneva, is known for its mild climate and beautiful gardens.

Have students look at the photos as you read the dialogue aloud or play the cassette. Pause after the description of each photo to ask questions: **Comment s'appelle la capitale de la Suisse? Quelle langue est-ce qu'on y parle?** After students have heard the entire dialogue, have them tell what Bruno says to invite Isabelle, how Isabelle expresses an obligation, and how Bruno gives advice to Isabelle.

12   Activité • Vrai ou faux?

CHALLENGE   Have students number sheets of paper from 1 to 8. Read the eight statements to them. They should write **vrai** or **faux** after each number. Have them exchange papers and check each other's work as you go through the statements again, asking for an oral response. Ask for false statements to be made true.

13 Activité • **Faites le guide**

Review with students how to ask for advice (Unit 5, C9, page 173) before they begin working in pairs.

SLOWER-PACED LEARNING Brainstorm with students possible advice for each item. Write the phrases suggested on the board or on a transparency. Allow students to refer to these phrases as they work in pairs.

CHALLENGE Encourage students to incorporate into their conversations expressions of doubt and uncertainty (Unit 7, B16, page 251).

> —Moi, je parle bien allemand. Alors, à ton avis, qu'est-ce qu'il faut que je fasse en Suisse?
> —Tu devrais visiter Berne.
> —Tu crois?
> —Oui, parce qu'on y parle allemand.

14 Activité • **Faites le touriste**

Ask students how they might express fatigue and offer encouragement. Write their suggestions on the board or on a transparency. Or, if you prefer, have students refer to Unit 7 (C16), page 261, and Unit 2 (B15), page 66, for these expressions. Then, for cooperative learning, divide the class into groups of four students; have one member of each group play the role of a tour-group leader, encouraging the "student travelers" to see this and that, while they complain.

15 Activité • **A vous maintenant!**

Students will probably want to talk about the same places of interest that they mentioned in Activity 6. As they give advice, they should justify their suggestions: **Je te conseille d'aller à... Si tu aimes les parcs d'attractions, c'est vraiment formidable! Il y a des montagnes russes, un palais des Glaces...**

16 Activité • **Encore à vous!**

First review with students how to invite friends (Unit 2, A12, page 58) and how to refuse an invitation (Unit 5 A6, page 157). Then brainstorm with students vacation activities they might want to talk about. As students work in pairs, encourage them to give creative reasons for refusing.

17 Activité • **Et vous?**

First review how to ask for and give advice (Unit 5, C9, page 173). Then have students think about what they would like to do, where they would like to go on vacation, how much money they would need, and how they might earn the money. Have them pair off to do the activity. After they've had time to talk, ask individuals to report their partners' plans to the class.

18 **LES ADIEUX**

CULTURAL BACKGROUND Swiss railroads are famous for their efficiency and punctuality. In addition to the trains operated by the **CFF (Chemins de fer fédéraux),** there are numerous local lines and small mountain railways.

Have students look at the photos as you play the cassette or have two students read the dialogue aloud. As students listen, they should discover how Isabelle felt about her stay in Switzerland, what Bruno gives her before she leaves, and whether or not Isabelle will return for the jazz festival.

19 Activité • Avez-vous compris?

SLOWER-PACED LEARNING Allow students to refer to the dialogue; help them find the right lines to give them the answers they need.

20 Activité • Répondez

Review object pronouns, position of object pronouns, and agreement of the past participle with a preceding direct-object pronoun. Give several examples on the board, using boxes and arrows, for visual reinforcement.

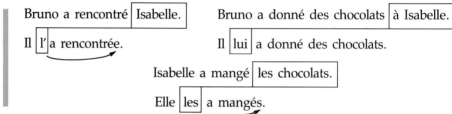

Have students answer the questions orally and then write out their answers.

21 Activité • Jeu des renseignements

Divide the class into groups of four students each. Students can compete within the group, or groups can compete against one another. The object is to find the most information about Isabelle and Bruno. Students might make three lists, as below:

Isabelle	Bruno	Tous les deux
française	suisse	jeunes
Bordeaux	Genève	parlent français

The above answers are abbreviated; you might have students write complete sentences: **Isabelle vient de Bordeaux. Bruno habite la ville de Genève.**

22 Activité • Jeu de rôle

Review with students how to ask for, give, and refuse permission and how to insist. After students have practiced, ask groups to present their conversations to the class.

CHALLENGE Have students make this a three-part conversation. Isabelle asks one of her parents for permission to go to the jazz festival; that parent refuses. She then asks her other parent, who gives permission. Next the two parents tell one another about their conversations with Isabelle, and they come to an agreement about Isabelle's request.

23 Activité • Coup de téléphone

If possible, pair girls with boys to prepare a phone conversation between Isabelle and Bruno. If this is not possible, change the characters or the situation slightly to make them more appropriate.

24 Activité • Ecrivez

To prepare students, review the story of Bruno and Isabelle. Have students suggest possible outcomes. Then have them begin to write down their ideas, developing the story. Or, you might assign this for homework. Collect students' papers the next day, indicate where corrections need to be made, and return to students for revision. After students have made the required corrections, post their story completions on a bulletin board in the classroom.

25 Activité • Ecrivez

Have a volunteer read Isabelle's letter aloud as students follow along in their books. Ask another student to summarize the letter. Ask others to suggest what Bruno's letter to a friend might contain. Students may take notes as things that Bruno might say are suggested. Have students begin to write his letter in class and complete it at home.

26 Activité • Ecoutez bien

You're going to hear a radio ad from the Swiss Tourist Office. Open your book to page 283. *(pause)* Copy the chart in 26 on a separate sheet of paper. *(pause)* As you listen to the ad, fill in the chart with information about Switzerland. You don't have to write complete sentences. Ready? **Ecoutez bien.**

Vous vous ennuyez? Vous ne savez pas quoi faire pendant vos vacances de Pâques? Pourquoi ne pas venir nous voir en Suisse? Nous sommes sympathiques, chaleureux, accueillants, et nous parlons plusieurs langues. Eh oui, plus de problèmes pour vous faire comprendre!... Vous aimez le ski? Nous avons des dizaines de stations de sports d'hiver. Vous aimez faire du cheval? Nous organisons de nombreuses randonnées. Vous aimez vous promener? Nos paysages sont superbes. Nous avons des montagnes, des lacs et de très jolies villes. Vous pouvez visiter Genève, Lucerne, Zurich, Bâle. Alors, si vous êtes amateur de photographie, n'hésitez pas! La Suisse est le pays pour vous. Et si vous voulez offrir des cadeaux à votre famille, à vos amis ou à votre fiancé(e), nous avons ce qu'il vous faut. Vous avez déjà entendu parler des chocolats suisses? Des montres suisses? Des chaussures suisses? Bien sûr! Alors pourquoi ne pas les acheter ici?... Vous voulez savoir maintenant comment venir chez nous? C'est facile. La plupart de nos grandes villes ont un aéroport. Le prix? Le billet aller-retour New York-Zurich coûte approximativement six cents dollars... Si vous avez besoin de plus de renseignements, adressez-vous à votre agence de tourisme... Bon voyage!

Et maintenant, vérifions. *Read the information in the chart.*

Sports et Activités	Paysages (Scenery)	Cadeaux/ Souvenirs	Transport	Prix du Voyage
ski, cheval, promenades, photographie	*montagnes, lacs, jolies villes*	*chocolats, montres, chaussures*	*avion*	*$600*

27 Activité • A vous maintenant!

For additional information about Switzerland, students may wish to refer to the

the dialogues between Isabelle and Bruno or to the list started during the motivating activity of this unit.

CONSULTONS LE DICTIONNAIRE

Open your book to page 284. *(pause)* Refer to this page as you listen to this section. By now you should be able to say nearly all the vowel sounds of French, including the famous /y/, /ø/, and /œ/, as in **tu, ceux,** and **œuf,** coming from the front of your mouth, and also those typical, very French, nasal sounds, /œ̃/, /ɔ̃/, /ɛ̃/, and /ã/, as in **un bon pain blanc.**

1. But how do you know when to say each sound? Can you tell from the way they're written? Well, there may be a problem. At least the French language has one. All these French vowels you've been twisting over and around your tongue —yes, all 16 of them—have to be written with only a few letters. How do you write 16 vowel sounds with only 5 vowel letters—*a, e, i, o, u*? By the magic of combinations, as you do in English. Think of the combinations with the letter *u* as in *mauve, neutral, suit,* and *mouse,* or with the letter *o* as in *boot, bought, about,* and *boat.* This would be fine if there were one combination for each sound. But the system is not that good. Think of the different sounds of the combination *ol* in *golf* and in *wolf.*

French is a bit more systematic, but not that much. In the combination **er,** the r is pronounced in **fer** but not in **acier.** Why? Because French, just like English, isn't always pronounced the way it's spelled. So how do you know how to pronounce new words that you come across while you're reading?

2. You can put together a good set of combinations that can really help—combinations of letters that make single sounds. They're not all foolproof, but they cover most words. You probably already know more of them than you think.

Let's begin with the sound /y/. How is it spelled in the words in *2a*? Listen and repeat them: **tu, étude, revenu, suffit, jupe, refus, discute, salut.** *(pause)* That's right: it's always spelled with the letter **u.** So does this mean that every time you see the letter **u,** you can say the sound /y/? Not at all. The letter **u** is used in combination with other letters to show different sounds. Which ones?

Look at the box in *2b*. Inside the brackets after each word is the way the word sounds, just as you'll find it in your dictionary. All of these words have the letter **u,** either alone or combined with another vowel or a consonant to make a single sound. You can see by looking at the bracketed words here that the **u**-combinations make five different vowel sounds: **tu, vous, eux, un, leur, faut.**

Get your dictionary ready now. Use it to look up the words listed in *2c*. Put them in separate columns according to the way the letter **u** is pronounced, alone or in combinations. You should have a column for the sound /y/ as in **une,** for the sound /u/ as in **vous,** for /ø/ as in **eux,** for /œ̃/ as in **un,** for /œ/ as in **leur,** and for /o/ as in **faut.** *(long pause)*

Now let's see what this all means. When does the /œ̃/ sound of **un** become the /y/ sound of **tu**? Look at the pairs you can extract from your list: **un/une, brun/brune, chacun/chacune, parfum/parfumé.** That's right: /œ̃/ becomes /y/ when followed by a vowel. You can check this with other words you know. While the letter **u** is pronounced /œ̃/ in **lundi** and **chacun,** it's pronounced /y/ in **prune** and **lune.**

Next take a look at the words in the /œ/ column. What have you got? You must have the singular forms **œuf** and **bœuf** as well as **neuf, cœur,** and **chanteur.** And where did you put the plural forms **œufs** and **bœufs**? No, not under /œ/, but under /ø/ along with the word **eux.** Now pair them off and what do you get? Singular is /œ/ and plural is /ø/: **un œuf/des œufs, un bœuf/des bœufs.** But what about **chanteur** and **chanteuse**? Yes, masculine is /œ/: **un chanteur, un serveur,** and feminine is /ø/: **une chanteuse, une serveuse.** Note also that many /œ/ words end in **r,** as in **sœur** and **cœur,** or in **l,** as in **seul.** Others end in **f,** like **neuf,** but not in **v,** as in **neuve.** The rest have the sound /ø/: **jeu, deux, cheveux.**

Now what's left? Yes, there are all those words under the sound /u/, as in **vous, nous, cousin, rouge, pourtant, gourmand, souvent.** No problem. They're all spelled with **ou.** At least that's something you can count on.

Now what have you got under the sound /o/? You have **auto, autre, jaune,** all written as **au.** But that's not all. You have **beau** and **manteau.** So you've got the letter **u** helping to spell the sound /o/, with the backup of the letters **e** and **a.**

3. Of course the sound /o/ can also be spelled with the letter **o** as in **mot.** But that doesn't mean that every time you see the letter **o** in a word, it's pronounced /o/. The letter **o,** like the letter **u,** is used in combination with other letters to show different sounds. What about the words written with **on, oin,** and **ion**? You've seen a lot of them. Now look up the words in 3. Put them in six separate columns according to the way the letter **o** is pronounced. You'll have one column for the sound /o/ as in **moto** and **rôle,** another for the sound /ɔ/ as in **note,** one for the sound /ɔ̃/ as in **bon,** one for the sound /wa/ as in **toi,** one for the sound /wɛ̃/ as in **coin,** and one for the sound /sjɔ̃/ as in **nation.** You'll find them all in your dictionary (*long pause*).

How many columns do you have for words written with **oi**? You should have two, one for /wa/ as in **toi** and one for /wɛ̃/ as in **coin.** But where did you put **Antoine** and **moine**? You noticed that with words ending in **n,** the **n** is generally not pronounced. But if the word ends in an **e,** the **n** is pronounced. Think of **bon** and **bonne.** Yes, you put **Antoine** and **moine** under **toi,** not under **coin.**

Finally compare these words with **oin** to those with **ion.** To avoid confusion, let's take only those with **tion** as in **nation.** Where did you list these words, words like **question, addition,** and **option**? Not along with **coin** or **Antoine.** Not if you looked them up. If you did, you found they end in /sjɔ̃/, all sounded with a little /j/ sound (as in *yes*) in front of them. Fine.

Now recheck your lists and read off all the words, saying them with the right sounds—thanks to your friendly dictionary. Give it a pat on the back and say "That's all for now."

APERÇU CULTUREL 3

Amitiés de France

OBJECTIVE   To read in French for cultural awareness

CULTURAL BACKGROUND   *Page 285*   **Marly-le-Roi** is a small town of less than 18,000 people. The inhabitants are called **Marlychois. Marly** was the site of Louis XIV's country retreat built by the architect Mansart. It consisted of 13 pavilions around magnificent formal gardens and fountains. The dominant royal pavilion represented the sun, and the satellite pavilions represented the 12 signs of the Zodiac. Besides the royal family, only favored guests could come to **Marly.** The proximity of each one's assigned pavilion to that of the king was an indication of rank or favor. Today nothing remains of the seventeenth-century splendor of **Marly-le-Roi** except the park and the forest where Louis XIV used to hunt; the buildings were destroyed during the Revolution.

Page 286   ***Paris-Match*** is a large-format photo-and-news magazine similar to *Life* or *Look.*

Page 287   The **café au lait** Stéphane has for breakfast is made half of strong coffee and half of hot milk, plus two or three lumps of sugar. At home, bowls are used, but in a coffee shop **café au lait** is served in a very large cup.

Jean-Luc's 4L is a small Renault. It has a small, fuel-efficient engine similar in size to that of a 2CV. **Décapotable** means that it has a canvas sun-roof that can be rolled back.

Page 289   Not all municipal libraries have a children's department or a section for young people, although such departments are becoming more common. In Paris, for example, there is at least one library in each **arrondissement** that has a **secteur jeunesse.** Some libraries attempt to attract young readers by stocking **bédés** and by organizing discussion clubs **(clubs de lecture).**

Page 290   There are three open-broadcast television stations in France: TF1, A2, and FR3. Of the three, TF1 is privately owned and the other two are managed by the government. Other channels are available on cable.

Page 291   The cartoonist and screenwriter Marcel Gotlib (born 1934) began his career drawing cartoons for young people before going on to cartoons for adults. He is the creator of the character **Superdupont,** a sort of comic French Superman.

SUGGESTED TEACHING PROCEDURE

Remind students of Héloïse's letter from Quebec **(Aperçu culturel 2).** Tell them they're now going to hear Stéphane's reply. Play the cassette or read the text aloud as students look at the photos and follow along. To check comprehension, pause after every page or two and ask simple questions. Students can look in their books to answer.

Have the students reread the letter silently. Then read a series of true-or-false statements, such as the following:

> Marly-le-Roi est près de Paris.
> Stéphane prend un bus jaune pour aller à l'école.
> Stéphane adore les maths.

Students should mark their answers on a sheet of paper. Go over the statements again, having students correct the false statements. If you wish, the second reading of the letter might be assigned for homework and the true-or-false statements read the next day.

SLOWER-PACED LEARNING You may wish to take two or three days to cover this photo essay. Then give the students a list of incomplete sentences, such as the following:

Stéphane habite dans la ville de _____.
Le père de Stéphane travaille comme _____.
Stéphane prend un bol de _____ au petit déjeuner.

Have the students pair off to find the completions in the text. Call on volunteers to read their completed sentences.

CHALLENGE After students have reread the text, have them form groups of three. They should compose a list of six questions based on Stéphane's letter. Have the groups exchange the lists and answer each other's questions.

Suggested Activity

Have students find the places where Stéphane expresses enthusiasm about something, and have them note the expressions he uses **(Qu'est-ce que... ! C'est le pied! Fantastique! C'est chouette! J'adore!)**. Have students suggest other exclamations of pleasure or enthusiasm that he might have used. Next have them look for expressions of displeasure or dislike **(Je trouve ça infect, J'en ai marre, Berk)**. Have them suggest similar phrases.

Suggested Activity

Have students look for insights into French culture through words or phrases in the text.

American influence: **un tee-shirt,**
            Deux flics à Miami
Life style: **on dîne à sept heures,**
        sa baguette
School: **j'ai eu un 18,**
        la meilleure note

Have students make a comparative culture chart in which they list contrasts between French and American culture. On a second sheet of paper, have them make a chart of similarities between French and American culture.

CHAPITRE **8**

Rendez-vous en Suisse

Chapitre de révision

1 Premier rendez-vous 📼

Visiter un pays étranger, c'est l'occasion de connaître une autre culture et, très souvent, de rencontrer de nouveaux amis.

Isabelle Velley passe ses vacances de Pâques chez ses cousins en Suisse, un joli pays où on parle français. A Genève, elle a rencontré un garçon, Bruno Tessin. Aujourd'hui, elle a rendez-vous avec lui au bord du lac Léman. Pour ce premier rendez-vous, elle se lève tôt.

Isabelle et Bruno sont timides et la conversation commence difficilement.

BRUNO Bonjour, comment vas-tu?
ISABELLE Bien. Et toi?
BRUNO Moi aussi… On se promène un peu?
ISABELLE Si tu veux.

ISABELLE Il est drôlement joli, le lac Léman.
BRUNO Oui… Ici, on l'appelle le lac de Genève mais à Lausanne, à septante kilomètres, ils l'appellent le lac de Lausanne… Pourquoi est-ce que tu ris?
ISABELLE Septante! Vous parlez un drôle de français en Suisse!
BRUNO Pourquoi? Nous sommes logiques : après soixante nous disons septante, octante, nonante. C'est mieux que soixante-dix, quatre-vingts et quatre-vingt-dix!
ISABELLE C'est vrai, tu as raison.

ISABELLE On parle aussi français à Lausanne?
BRUNO Oui, dans l'ouest jusqu'à Sierre. Après, dans le nord, on parle allemand. Vers l'Italie, on parle italien et dans l'est, on parle romanche.
ISABELLE Quatre langues!
BRUNO Eh oui!

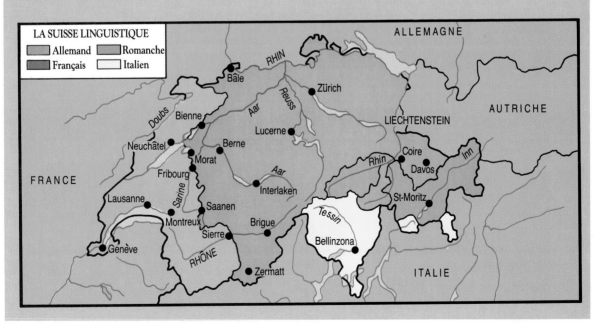

LA SUISSE LINGUISTIQUE
Allemand Romanche
Français Italien

ALLEMAGNE
AUTRICHE
LIECHTENSTEIN
FRANCE
ITALIE

RHIN
Reuss
Aar
Doubs
Rhin
Inn
Aar
Sarine
RHÔNE
Tessin

Bâle
Zürich
Bienne
Lucerne
Neuchâtel
Berne
Coire
Morat
Davos
Fribourg
Interlaken
St-Moritz
Lausanne
Saanen
Montreux
Brigue
Bellinzona
Sierre
Genève
Zermatt

Romanche: A romance language closely related to Latin
Lac Léman, Lac de Lausanne: Lake Geneva
Photos on p. 206: street scenes in Geneva (top left) and Lausanne (bottom right)

(suite page suivante)

Rendez-vous en Suisse 273

ISABELLE	Tu connais la France?
BRUNO	Non, je n'y suis jamais allé. Et toi, tu viens ici pour la première fois?
ISABELLE	Oui, et malheureusement je n'ai pas le temps de tout visiter. Je pars déjà la semaine prochaine.
BRUNO	Tu veux que je te montre des photos de la Suisse? J'en ai toute une collection. Ça va te donner une idée. Ça te dit?
ISABELLE	Bien sûr! C'est un bon moyen de connaître ton pays!

2 Activité • Avez-vous compris?

Répondez aux questions suivantes d'après «Premier rendez-vous».

1. Pourquoi est-ce qu'Isabelle se lève tôt? 1. Elle se lève tôt parce qu'elle a rendez-vous avec Bruno.
2. Où est-ce qu'Isabelle et Bruno se promènent? 2. Ils se promènent au bord du lac.
3. Quelles langues est-ce qu'on parle en Suisse? 3. En Suisse on parle allemand, français, italien et romanche.
4. Est-ce qu'Isabelle a déjà visité la Suisse? 4. Non, c'est la première fois.
5. Est-ce que Bruno est déjà allé en France? 5. Non, il n'y est jamais allé.
6. Pourquoi est-ce que Bruno propose de montrer ses photos à Isabelle?
6. Il lui montre ses photos pour lui donner une idée du pays.

3 Activité • Et vous?

1. Etes-vous déjà allé(e) dans un autre pays ou dans un autre état des Etats-Unis? Je suis déjà allé(e) en/à/au(x)
Où ça? Quand? (For a complete list of states with appropriate prepositions, see the Teacher's Resource Materials.
2. Connaissez-vous d'autres pays où on parle plusieurs langues? Quels pays? Qu'est-ce qu'on y parle comme langues?

4 Activité • Une journée à Genève Possible answers are given.

Vous visitez Genève avec des copains. Imaginez votre journée typique. Dites ce que vous faites avec vos copains.

Le matin :	L'après-midi :	Le soir :
se lever à sept heures	se reposer	se coucher très tôt
se promener partout	se forcer à ressortir	

Le matin, on se lève à sept heures pour pouvoir se promener partout. Puis, l'après-midi, on se repose un peu. Vers trois heures, on se force à ressortir pour faire les boutiques. Le soir, on est vraiment crevés, et on se couche tôt.

A Genève, vous proposez à votre copain/copine de faire ces choses. Il/Elle accepte ou refuse et donne des raisons. Changez de rôle. Commencez par «Tu veux qu'on… ?» + **le subjonctif.**
... fasse les boutiques?   ... aille voir le Monument de la Réformation?   ... se promène dans le parc de la Grange?   ... visite le palais de Nations?   ... fasse le tour du lac en bateau?   ... aille au musée de l'Horlogerie?

faire les boutiques

aller voir le Monument de la Réformation

se promener dans le parc de la Grange

visiter le palais des Nations

faire le tour du lac en bateau

aller au musée de l'Horlogerie

La Réformation: a religious movement of the 1500's that gave birth to Protestantism
Guillaume Farel (1489–1565) French leader of the Reformation; brought John Calvin to Geneva
Théodore de Bèze (1519–1605) French theologian; leader of the Reformation in France
John Knox (1505–1572) Scottish reformer, writer and statesman; briefly exiled in Geneva
John Calvin (1509–1564) French theologian and reformer; leader of the Reformation in Switzerland

Activité • A vous maintenant!

Maintenant, votre ami(e) suisse vient vous voir chez vous. Qu'est-ce que vous lui proposez? Il y a des choses à faire dans votre ville? Commencez par «Tu veux qu'on... ?».

7 **Activité • Avant le rendez-vous**   Possible answers are given.

Vous avez rencontré un garçon/une fille suisse. Vous avez envie de le/la revoir, mais vous êtes timide et vous hésitez. Vous demandez conseil à votre ami(e). Faites le dialogue avec un(e) camarade.

Vous :
Tu crois que je peux... ?
A ton avis, qu'est-ce qu'il faut que je fasse?

lui donner rendez-vous?
lui téléphoner?
l'inviter?

Votre ami(e) :
Bien sûr!
Non, il vaut mieux que tu...
Il faut que tu... t'habilles bien.

l'oublies.
lui envoies une lettre.

lui offres un cadeau.

Pour vous aider :

donner rendez-vous   **inviter**   **envoyer**
oublier   **offrir**   **bien s'habiller**
téléphoner

8 **Activité • A votre avis**

Aller dans un pays étranger, c'est une occasion de faire ou d'apprendre beaucoup de choses. Qu'est-ce que c'est pour vous? Employez les expressions suivantes et trouvez le maximum de réponses.

C'est un moyen de...   C'est une occasion de...   C'est une façon de...

prendre des photos   **goûter à une nouvelle cuisine**
apprendre une autre langue   **rencontrer de nouveaux amis**   **s'amuser**
connaître une autre culture

9 **Activité • Ecrivez**   Possible answer is given.

Pour payer son voyage en Suisse, il faut qu'Isabelle trouve un travail. Elle met des annonces chez les commerçants et dans son lycée. Ecrivez trois annonces différentes pour elle.

Vous avez des enfants à garder? Téléphonez-moi au 45.38.81.20. Je suis une jeune fille sérieuse qui adore les enfants. 30 francs de l'heure.

La Suisse est un pays de 6 500 000 habitants à l'est de la France. Sa capitale est Berne. On y parle officiellement quatre langues, l'allemand, (69,3%), le français (18,9%), l'italien (9,5%) et le romanche (0,9%). C'est principalement un pays de montagnes, et ses stations de sports d'hiver des Alpes sont mondialement connues.

Elle accueille tous les ans 6 000 000 de touristes. Ils viennent pour skier, visiter le pays ou faire les vitrines de Genève et de Zurich où ils trouvent des spécialités suisses, comme le chocolat, les montres, les chaussures et les produits de luxe.

La Suisse est un pays neutre, et elle accueille de nombreuses conférences internationales. Certaines associations humanitaires, comme l'OMS (l'Organisation Mondiale pour la Santé) et la Croix Rouge, ont leur siège à Genève. C'est un petit pays (les Etats-Unis sont 227 fois plus grands) mais son influence est importante.   siège: headquarters

The European headquarters of the United Nations is also located in Geneva.

Quand on n'a pas le temps de visiter un pays, il y a une solution pour s'en faire une idée : regarder des photos.

Bruno a sorti sa collection de photos pour les montrer à Isabelle.

— Voici Berne, la capitale. On y parle allemand.

— Ça, c'est Neuchâtel, une ville pittoresque au bord du lac de Neuchâtel.

— Tu devrais vraiment aller visiter Lausanne. On parle français à Lausanne et à Neuchâtel.

— Tu vois, là c'est Crans-Montana, une station de sports d'hiver très connue. Si tu aimes le ski, je te conseille d'y aller. Tu peux faire des kilomètres!

— Et cette photo, qu'est-ce que c'est?
— C'est le festival de jazz de Montreux. J'y vais tous les ans… Tu aimes le jazz?
— Oui, beaucoup.
— Qu'est-ce que tu fais en juillet?
— Je n'ai pas de projets. Pourquoi?
— Parce que… euh… J'ai bien envie d'y retourner. Tu ne veux pas venir avec moi? Je t'invite.

— C'est gentil mais… Tiens, qui est-ce, la fille, là, avec toi? Elle est drôlement jolie!
— Tu trouves?
— C'est une copine?
— Pas du tout! C'est ma sœur. C'est un copain qui nous a pris en photo… Alors, pour Montreux, c'est d'accord?
— Je ne sais pas… Il faut que je demande à mes parents.
— Ça ne t'intéresse pas?
— Si, mais…
— Quoi? Qu'est-ce qu'il y a?
— Il faut que j'y réfléchisse… Je ne peux pas te répondre tout de suite.
— OK, je suis patient!

12 Activité • Vrai ou faux?

Ces phrases sont-elles vraies ou fausses d'après «Visite de la Suisse en photographie»?

1. Bruno n'aime pas prendre des photos.
2. Lausanne est la capitale de la Suisse.
3. On parle allemand à Berne.
4. On peut faire du ski à Crans-Montana.
5. Il y a un festival à Montreux tous les ans.
6. Isabelle est prise en juillet.
7. Bruno a une sœur.
8. Isabelle est d'accord pour venir à Montreux.

1. C'est faux. Bruno a toute une collection de photos. 2. C'est faux. Berne est la capitale de la Suisse. 3. C'est vrai.
4. C'est vrai. 5. C'est vrai. 6. C'est faux. Elle n'a pas de projets. 7. C'est vrai. 8. C'est faux. Il faut qu'elle réfléchisse.

13 Activité • Faites le guide   Possible answers are given.

Vous connaissez un peu la Suisse? Votre ami(e) veut y aller mais il/elle ne sait pas quoi faire ou quoi voir. Donnez-lui des conseils. Commencez par «Tu devrais... », «Je te conseille de... » ou «Il faut absolument que tu... ». Variez les expressions.   Pour parler allemand, tu devrais aller dans le nord.

Pour parler italien, il faut absolument que tu ailles dans le sud.   Pour faire du ski, je te conseille d'aller à

Votre ami(e)...   Crans-Montana.   Tu devrais aller à Neuchâtel. C'est une ville pittoresque.   Pour faire des achats, il faut

parle allemand.   veut faire des achats.   absolument que tu fasses les boutiques à Genève.

parle italien.   aime faire des excursions en bateau.   Je te conseille de faire le tour du lac

aime skier.   est intéressé(e) par les capitales.   Léman en bateau.   Si tu es intéressé(e)

aime les jolies villes.   veut visiter des musées.   par les capitales, tu devrais aller à Berne.

Je te conseille d'aller au musée de l'Horlogerie.

14 Activité • Faites le touriste   Possible answers are given.

Vous et votre ami(e), vous êtes touristes à Genève. Votre ami(e) ne veut plus visiter la ville; il/elle se plaint; il/elle est fatigué(e). Vous, vous avez toujours beaucoup d'énergie. Vous voulez continuer la visite. Vous encouragez votre ami(e) à continuer.

Allez! Force-toi! Il faut aller faire les boutiques et visiter les musées. Encore un petit effort!

15 Activité • A vous maintenant!

Un(e) ami(e) suisse vient vous voir chez vous. Il/Elle a envie de visiter votre ville. Qu'est-ce que vous lui conseillez d'aller voir ou faire? Y a-t-il de vieux monuments? Une jolie église? Un bon restaurant? Un lac?...

16 Activité • Encore à vous

Proposez à un(e) camarade de faire quelque chose pendant les vacances. Il/Elle refuse parce qu'il faut qu'il/elle fasse autre chose.

— Tu ne veux pas... ?
— Désolé(e), il faut que je...

17 Activité • Et vous?

Qu'est-ce que vous allez faire pendant les vacances? Vous avez des projets? Est-ce qu'il y a quelque chose que vous avez envie de faire mais vous n'avez pas assez d'argent? Faites une conversation avec un(e) camarade. Il/Elle vous pose des questions. Vous lui répondez. Il/Elle vous donne des idées ou des conseils. Changez de rôle.

C'est le dernier jour. Il faut qu'Isabelle rentre chez elle, à Bordeaux. Bruno l'a accompagnée à la gare. Ils sont tous les deux un peu tristes, mais ils vont peut-être bientôt se revoir.

BRUNO	A quelle heure part ton train?
ISABELLE	A trois heures. Tu m'accompagnes sur le quai?
BRUNO	Bien sûr!

BRUNO	Tiens, je t'offre un cadeau.
ISABELLE	Qu'est-ce que c'est?
BRUNO	Ouvre.
ISABELLE	Une boîte de chocolats suisses!
BRUNO	C'est une spécialité.
ISABELLE	C'est très sympa, je te remercie.

BRUNO	Alors, tu es contente de ton séjour? Ça t'a plu, la Suisse?
ISABELLE	Enormément. Malheureusement, je ne suis restée que dix jours. Je n'ai presque rien vu.
BRUNO	Si, tu l'as visitée en photographie.

BRUNO	Tu m'écris une carte postale de France?
ISABELLE	Oui.
BRUNO	Tu penses revenir pour le festival de jazz?
ISABELLE	Peut-être...
BRUNO	Allez! J'ai tellement envie que tu viennes! On va s'amuser, je te garantis.
ISABELLE	Je t'écris.
BRUNO	Non, téléphone-moi!... Je t'attends!
ISABELLE	Salut!
BRUNO	Bon voyage!

19 Activité • Avez-vous compris?

Corrigez ces phrases d'après «Les adieux».

1. Isabelle est contente de partir.
2. Elle part en avion.
3. Bruno l'accompagne à l'aéroport.
4. Elle n'a pas aimé la Suisse.
5. Bruno ne lui a rien offert.
6. Il n'a pas envie qu'elle revienne.

1. Elle est un peu triste de partir.   2. Elle prend le train.   3. Il l'accompagne à la gare.   4. Elle a beaucoup aimé la Suisse.
5. Il lui a offert des chocolats suisses.   6. Il a tellement envie qu'elle revienne!

20 Activité • Répondez 🔲

Répondez aux questions suivantes en employant les pronoms **le, la, les** ou **lui**.

1. Est-ce que Bruno a accompagné Isabelle à la gare?
2. Est-ce que la Suisse a plu à Isabelle?
3. Est-ce qu'Isabelle a pris le train pour rentrer en France?
4. Est-ce que Bruno a invité Isabelle à venir à Montreux?
5. Est-ce qu'Isabelle et Bruno ont mangé les chocolats?
6. Est-ce qu'Isabelle va écrire à Bruno?

1. Oui, il l'a accompagnée à la gare.   2. Oui, la Suisse lui a plu.   3. Oui, elle l'a pris.   4. Oui, il l'a invitée.
5. Non, ils ne les ont pas mangés.   6. Oui, elle va lui écrire.

21 Activité • Jeu des renseignements   Possible answers are given.

Maintenant vous connaissez bien Isabelle et Bruno. Trouvez le maximum de renseignements sur eux : où ils habitent, dans quel pays, dans quelle ville, s'ils ont de la famille, ce qu'ils aiment... Travaillez en groupe. Celui/Celle qui trouve le plus de renseignements gagne le jeu.

Isabelle Velley est de Bordeaux. Elle est française. Elle habite avec ses parents. Elle a des cousins en Suisse.   Bruno Tessin est
suisse. Il habite à Genève. Il parle français. Il a une sœur. Il aime skier. Il va tous les ans au festival de jazz de Montreux. Il aime faire
de la photo.

22 Activité • Jeu de rôle   Possible dialogue is given.

Isabelle demande à ses parents la permission d'aller au festival de jazz de Montreux. Ils refusent. Elle insiste. Ils lui demandent pourquoi elle veut y aller, comment elle va payer son voyage, combien de temps elle va rester... Finalement... Est-ce qu'ils acceptent ou refusent? Organisez une discussion avec deux autres camarades de classe : le père, la mère et Isabelle.

— Vous voulez bien que... ? j'aille en Suisse pour le festival de jazz?
— Non, il faut que tu... restes ici. C'est trop cher.
— ... C'est injuste! Je peux payer! Je vais faire du baby-sitting.
— Bon, d'accord, mais tu vas aller avec ton frère.
— Ah non! Ça, c'est impossible!

23 Activité • Coup de téléphone   Possible dialogue is given.
—Allô, Bruno? C'est moi, Isabelle. J'ai de bonnes nouvelles. Je viens pour le festival de jazz!
Isabelle téléphone à Bruno pour lui dire qu'elle peut venir avec lui au festival de jazz de Montreux. Préparez la conversation téléphonique avec un(e) camarade.
—Chouette! Je vais acheter les billets demain. Quand est-ce que tu arrives?
—Samedi matin, vers 9 heures. Oh, mon frère vient aussi...
—Ah oui? Bon, ça va. Je vais vous chercher à 9 heures, samedi.

24 Activité • Ecrivez   Possible answer is given.

Vous voulez devenir écrivain et vous avez envie de continuer l'histoire d'Isabelle et de Bruno. A votre avis, qu'est-ce qu'Isabelle va faire maintenant? Elle va aller à Montreux? Elle va trouver un job pour payer le voyage? Elle va écrire à Bruno? Et Bruno, qu'est-ce qu'il va faire? Il va écrire à Isabelle? Il va lui envoyer un cadeau? Il va parler d'elle à ses copains? Imaginez et écrivez une suite *(continuation)* à leur histoire.   Isabelle a fait du baby-sitting pendant deux mois. Avec l'argent
qu'elle a gagné, elle est allée au festival de jazz de Montreux avec Bruno. Les deux jeunes se sont bien amusés. Maintenant, Isabelle
et Bruno s'écrivent. Bruno est amoureux. Il parle tout le temps d'Isabelle à ses copains. Il veut même lui envoyer un cadeau pour son
anniversaire!

Cher... Cette année, les vacances ont vraiment été super! J'ai rencontré une Française très jolie, sympa et intéressante.
Elle s'appelle Isabelle, et elle est de Bordeaux. Je l'ai invitée à venir au festival de jazz de Montreux en juillet.
Elle va me téléphoner pour me dire si elle peut venir. J'attends sa réponse avec impatience.

25 Activité • Ecrivez

Isabelle et Bruno ont écrit à leurs amis pour leur raconter ce qu'ils ont fait pendant les vacances de Pâques. Voici la lettre d'Isabelle. Pouvez-vous écrire la lettre de Bruno?

> Chère Sabine,
>
> Je suis rentrée hier de vacances. Tu sais où je suis allée? A Genève, en Suisse. J'ai fait la connaissance d'un garçon drôlement sympa. Il s'appelle Bruno. Je l'ai rencontré chez mes cousins. Ensuite, il m'a donné rendez-vous au bord du lac Léman. Il m'a raconté sa vie, et il m'a donné quelques renseignements sur la Suisse. Sais-tu qu'on y parle quatre langues? Le lendemain, il m'a montré de très jolies photos de son pays. Il m'a aussi invitée à venir avec lui au festival de jazz de Montreux au mois de juillet. Mais je ne sais pas si je vais y aller. Il faut d'abord que je demande la permission à mes parents et que je trouve de l'argent pour le voyage. Mais je vais essayer... Oh, et il m'a aussi offert une boîte de chocolats suisses! Ne le répète pas: je suis amoureuse!
>
> Bises, Isabelle

26 Activité • Ecoutez bien 🔲 For script and answers, see p. T175.

Ecoutez ce message publicitaire radiophonique produit par l'Office du tourisme suisse.
Notez le maximum de renseignements.

Sports et Activités	Paysages (Scenery)	Cadeaux/ Souvenirs	Transport	Prix du Voyage

27 Activité • A vous maintenant!

Proposez à un(e) camarade de venir avec vous en Suisse. Il/Elle vous demande comment vous allez y aller, ce que vous allez y faire, combien de temps vous allez y rester, combien coûte le voyage... Vous répondez et vous essayez de le/la persuader de vous accompagner. Employez les renseignements que vous avez appris dans 26.

For script, see pp. T176–77.

CONSULTONS LE DICTIONNAIRE

1. Neither English nor French is written as it is spoken.
   u *mauve, neutral, suit, mouse*   fer *(iron)*   acier *(steel)*
   o *boot, bought, about, boat*
        golf/wolf

2. The vowel **u** and its combinations
   a. tu   étude   revenu   suffit   jupe   refus   discute   salut
   b. In your dictionary you'll find the sound of the word within brackets.

   > **tu** [ty]   **vous** [vu]   **eux** [ø]   **un** [œ̃]   **leur** [lœr]   **faut** [fo]

   c. Now look up these words and list them in six separate columns, according to the sound of the letter **u,** alone or in combination.

   For answers, see Unit Cassette Guide, p. 107.

/y/ une	/u/ vous	/ø/ eux	/œ̃/ un	/œ/ leur	/o/ faut

   deux, jeu, œuf, jupe, jaune, brun, cou, rouge, beau, nous, chevaux, bœuf, chacun, pourtant, parfum, un, jeune, sœur, poumon, serveuse, nombreuse, prune, souvent, peux, oublie, bouche, bœufs, sucre, lundi, une, cours, chanteur, cousin, gourmand, parfumé, manteau, cheveux, monsieur, chacune, sûr, serveur, où, brune, neuve, autre, auto, cœur, truc, revenu, Etats-Unis, uniforme, neuf, œufs, chanteuse, emprunt

   d. [œ̃] → [y]
   un/une   chacun/chacune   lundi   prune
   brun/brune   parfum/parfumé   chacun lune
   e. [œ] → [ø]
   un œuf/des œufs   un chanteur/une chanteuse   neuf/neuve
   un bœuf/des bœufs   un serveur/une serveuse

3. The vowel **o** and its combinations
   The letter **o,** like the letter **u,** is used in combination with other letters to show different sounds: **on, oin, ion.** Look up these words and list them in six separate columns, according to the way the letter **o** is sounded.
   For answers, see Unit Cassette Guide, p. 107.

/o/ moto, rôle	/ɔ/ note	/ɔ̃/ bon	/wa/ toi	/wɛ̃/ coin	/jɔ̃/ nation

   mode, fois, selon, question, moi, votre, monnaie, salon, orange, lorsque, copain, dos, soigner, opération, mollet, nombre, moins, sport, produit, comment, coquette, côté, poche, addition, coiffure, indigestion, montagne, bonne, postale, prochain, loin, canton, pompiste, mot, école, monde, voilà, option, propose, gestion, doit, objet, offrir, drôle, jolie, alors, accord, moine, adore, compte, quoi, voyage, téléphone, chocolat, offert, invitation, Antoine, rapport, comme, stylo, rocher, patrimoine, choque, profit, avoir, avoine, voiture, boulot, voile, aboie, mois

APERÇU CULTUREL 3 📼

Amitiés de France

Chère Héloïse,

Tu es vraiment une correspondante super sympa! Mille bises pour ta lettre, et surtout pour les photos. Ta famille, elle a l'air très chouette. Et puis, dis donc, le Canada français, qu'est-ce que c'est joli! Il faut que j'économise assez d'argent de poche pour te rendre visite, un jour! Bon, à moi de te montrer ma vie en France...

Nous, on habite à Marly-le-Roi, dans la banlieue parisienne.

Le charmant jeune homme, cartable à la main, devant l'entrée de son immeuble... Tu l'as deviné, c'est moi, en route pour l'école!

Marly-le-Roi, c'est à vingt-quatre kilomètres au sud-ouest de Paris. A peine une demi-heure en train, et on est en plein cœur de la capitale!

A Marly, il y a pas mal de quartiers modernes, mais aussi de vieilles petites rues assez typiques de l'Ile-de-France.

La ville tire son nom du célèbre Louis XIV. Avant, il y avait un château. Maintenant, il ne reste qu'un immense parc, en vert sur la carte du haut.

Faisons vite le tour de la famille. D'abord, papa. Il est photographe pour le magazine Paris-Match, et il voyage partout dans le monde. Qu'est-ce qu'il a de la chance!

Papa adore me battre aux échecs. Je crois que ça l'amuse!

Mal au cœur, mal à la tête? Ça ne fait rien, maman est là. Elle est infirmière à l'hôpital Necker à Paris, et elle sait tout guérir! Les fleurs, c'est sa passion. Il y en a partout dans notre salon, même sur les rideaux et le canapé!

En train de récupérer le courrier, c'est mon frère, Jean-Luc. Il va à l'université à Paris, et son rêve, c'est d'être prof de français. Quelle drôle d'idée! Moi, la littérature, à part les bédés... Tu crois que tous les frères sont bizarres?

Ça, c'est notre chatte Mimine!

N'oublions pas grand-père (on l'appelle tous papi Jeannot)! Il habite à deux minutes de chez nous, dans un pavillon typiquement banlieusard. On s'arrête souvent lui dire un petit bonjour ou lui apporter sa baguette pour le dîner.

Ah, l'école... Tous les matins c'est la panique, et je suis toujours en retard! Mais je ne pars jamais sans avoir pris un bon petit déjeuner. Ce que je préfère, c'est un bol de café au lait et des biscottes avec du beurre ou de la confiture. Moi, les corn-flakes, je trouve ça infect!

D'habitude, je vais à la gare à cinq minutes de chez nous.

En général, les trains sont à l'heure, sauf bien sûr, quand il y a des grèves!

Je fais souvent le trajet avec Céline, une camarade de classe qui habite dans mon immeuble. C'est pratique, on descend juste au prochain arrêt.

Des fois, Jean-Luc est sympa, et il m'accompagne au collège en voiture. Lui, c'est un fana de la mécanique! Il faut vraiment que tu voies sa 4L décapotable. C'est le pied! Moi, mon rêve, c'est d'avoir une mobylette.(J'ai un copain qui a une Peugeot rouge vraiment géniale!) J'ai demandé la permission à mes parents, mais ils trouvent que c'est dangereux...

J'ai vu à la télé qu'en Amérique, les enfants vont souvent à l'école dans de drôles de bus jaunes!

Nous, en France, on n'a presque pas de cars de ramassage scolaire. Mais si on veut, on peut prendre le bus de la RATP, c'est-à-dire le bus public. Comme moyens de transport, j'ai vraiment le choix!

Oh, j'ai oublié de t'expliquer. Je suis en troisième au collège mixte public de Marly-le-Roi. Là, sur les marches, en train d'attendre que la cloche sonne, c'est moi, une copine et Sébastien. Lui, c'est mon meilleur ami depuis l'école maternelle!

« Salut, mon vieux, ça va? » Le matin, c'est tout un rituel: entre copains, on se serre la main...

Mais n'oublions surtout pas de faire la bise aux copines! Tu vois la fille à droite? Elle, c'est un génie en maths. Elle est sympa, elle me dit toujours: « Allons, courage! Tu vas y arriver! » Mais moi, les fractions... je n'y comprends rien!

Les devoirs, j'en ai marre! Je dois étudier tous les soirs, et après, j'ai du mal à dormir. Maman trouve que j'ai mauvaise mine. Pas étonnant!

Quand il faut que je fasse une rédaction, je vais souvent à la bibliothèque municipale.

Quelle collection impressionnante de livres et de magazines!

Après les devoirs, il me reste parfois assez de temps pour me détendre.

J'en profite souvent pour écouter des disques sur ma chaîne compacte (merci, Papa Noël).

Mon autre jouet préféré est très à la mode en ce moment: c'est le fameux Minitel! Grâce à un terminal branché sur une ligne téléphonique, tu peux faire un tas de choses sans bouger de chez toi: obtenir les programmes de cinéma ou des tickets de concert, par exemple. Fantastique, non?

Corvée quotidienne... Aller chercher le pain. C'est pas juste! Jean-Luc, lui, il ne fait rien!

Corvée numéro deux: mettre la table. Qu'est-ce que ça m'embête! Je n'arrive jamais à mettre les couteaux du bon côté!

Chez nous, on dîne à sept heures précises. J'aime bien, c'est une occasion de discuter en famille. Mais quand on parle de mes notes... Pourtant, la semaine dernière, j'ai eu un 18 en histoire-géo. C'était la meilleure note de la classe! Qu'est-ce que j'étais content... ☺

Et bien sûr, après la vaisselle, il y a la télé. Papa et maman adorent regarder les informations de huit heures sur TF1 ou A2, nos deux plus grandes chaînes. C'est trop sérieux pour moi! Je préfère les séries comme «Deux flics à Miami» avec, euh..., Don Jainssont? (zut, j'ai oublié son nom!)

Moi, je vais à l'école le samedi matin, mais heureusement, j'ai le mercredi après-midi de libre. J'en profite pour me balader avec Sébastien...

moi   Sébastien

Ou bien lire les dernières bédés de Gotlib, mon dessinateur favori. Qu'est-ce qu'il est drôle !

Dans notre immeuble, c'est chouette, on peut utiliser le sous-sol pour les loisirs. Alors, souvent, je joue au ping-pong avec Jean-Luc. Après une heure d'exercice, je te garantis que je suis mort ! Mais c'est bon pour la santé...

Souvent, on répète ensemble un morceau de guitare, moi, mon frère et deux copines. Tu devrais nous voir ! On fait du bruit, mais qu'est-ce qu'on s'amuse ! Moi, la musique, c'est mon fort. Et toi, tu joues d'un instrument ?

Le samedi, je t'ai déjà dit, il y a les cours, et puis la visite traditionnelle au supermarché. Berk!

Mais après ça, le week-end commence enfin! Je vais de temps en temps voir un film avec les copains. Mon frère a un petit job à la caisse du Fontenelle, le ciné du coin.

Moi, j'adore les comédies et les films de science-fiction. Est-ce que tu as vu E.T.?

Souvent, après le ciné ou juste pour le plaisir, on aime bien discuter au café autour d'une menthe à l'eau ou d'une limonade.

Mais faire une boum le samedi, c'est une façon de finir la semaine en beauté, tu ne trouves pas?

Et voilà! Ça, c'est ma vie en huit pages... Sois sympa, réponds-moi vite!

Oh, est-ce que tu peux m'envoyer un tee-shirt avec écrit « J'♡ Québec »?

Stéphane

CHAPITRE 9 Un dépaysé à Lyon

	BASIC MATERIAL	COMMUNICATIVE FUNCTIONS
PREMIER CONTACT	**Visite de Lyon (1)** **Les fameuses marionnettes de Lyon (4)**	Reading for global comprehension and cultural awareness
SECTION A	**Antoine se plaint. (A1)**	**Exchanging information** • Comparing city and country life **Expressing feelings, emotions** • Saying you miss something **Persuading** • Consoling someone
SECTION B	**Les retrouvailles (B1)**	**Socializing** • Renewing old acquaintances **Exchanging information** • Talking about past experiences
SECTION C	**Par où commencer? (C1)** **A Fourvière (C12)**	**Exchanging information** • Making comparisons • Reporting a series of events **Persuading** • Making suggestions
TRY YOUR SKILLS	**Que de déménagements! (1)**	

■ **Prononciation** (glides with /j/, /w/, and /ɥ/; dictation)   **329**
■ **Vérifions!   330**   ■ **Vocabulaire   331**

A LIRE	**Vive la grève!** (Parisians cope with strikes.) **L'Embouteillage** (a Parisian traffic jam in verse) **Les Charpentier déménagent** (A French family moves from the country to Pari〈

WRITING   A variety of controlled and open-ended writing activities appear in the Pupil's Edition. The Teacher's Notes identify other activities suitable for writing practice.

COOPERATIVE LEARNING   Many of the activities in the Pupil's Edition lend themselves to cooperative learning. For guidelines, see page T14.

Scope and Sequence

GRAMMAR	CULTURE	RE-ENTRY
	Tours of **Lyon** The **Guignol** theater	
Making comparisons with nouns (A9) The imperfect (A15)	**Lyon** and its cultural life Country life in **Bourgogne**	Expressing agreement and disagreement Independent pronouns Household chores vocabulary
The uses of the **passé composé** and the imperfect (B12) The use of **être en train de** (B12)	Transportation to and within **Lyon** Weekend activities in France	Expressing past time
Making comparisons with adjectives and adverbs (C5)	The sights of **Lyon**	Adjective agreement Making suggestions Expressing agreement and disagreement Prepositions of location Refusing and accepting an invitation

Recombining communicative functions, grammar, and vocabulary

Reading for practice and pleasure

UNIT RESOURCES **Cahier d'Activités, Cahier d'Exercices,** Unit 9 Cassettes, Transparencies 21–23 (also 31, 31A), Quizzes 19–21, Unit 9 Test

TEACHER-PREPARED MATERIALS **Premier Contact** Puppets; **Section A** Farm pictures, map of France, 4 × 6 index cards; **Section B** Index cards; **Section C** Index cards

The authentic material in **Premier Contact** introduces the theme of the unit. Concentrate only on the general content of these documents. A detailed treatment of the grammar and vocabulary is not intended. Since students should be reading for global comprehension, they need not know the meaning of every word. For this reason, new words in **Premier Contact** have been omitted from the unit vocabulary list and the French-English Vocabulary at the end of the book.

OBJECTIVES To read for global comprehension and cultural awareness; to get acquainted with the topic

1

Visite de Lyon

Play the cassette or read the brochure aloud as students follow along in their books. Students should discover the two ways in which they might tour Lyons **(visites commentées pour les groupes, visites audio-guidées pour les individuels).** If they were in Lyons, which might they choose? Why?

2 ## Activité • Vrai ou faux?

As you read these statements aloud, have students look for the correct information in the brochure about Lyons. Have them change statements 1 and 2 to make them true.

3 ## Activité • A vous maintenant!

For cooperative learning, divide the class into groups of four students each. The groups should brainstorm what areas or attractions in their city or town they would want to show off. They should then organize the visit, deciding what should be seen on which day. Call for reports from group leaders after five to ten minutes.

4 ## LES FAMEUSES MARIONNETTES DE LYON

Bring puppets or marionettes to class. Use them to demonstrate **donner des coups de bâton, frapper, applaudir,** and **rire.** Then play the cassette or read the passage aloud as students follow along in their books. Next give the puppets to volunteers and have them demonstrate what Guignol, Madelon, and the police officer do. Their classmates should react as suggested in the text, with applause and laughter. Try to elicit expressions of encouragement from the "audience:" **Allez, Guignol, encore un petit effort! Courage, Madelon!**

5 ## Activité • Avez-vous bien lu?

Have students work in pairs to answer the questions. After they've completed the activity, ask volunteers to share their answers with the class.

6 ## Activité • Avez-vous compris?

Call on volunteers to answer the questions. Then you might ask **A quoi est-ce que ces pièces ressemblent aux Etats-Unis?** Students should see the resemblance between such puppet plays and slapstick movies or cartoons.

7 ## Activité • Et vous?

Have students work in pairs to answer the questions. Have volunteers report their partners' answers to the class.

SECTION A

OBJECTIVES **To exchange information:** compare city and country life; **to express feelings, emotions:** say you miss something; **to persuade:** console someone

CULTURAL BACKGROUND French young people, like people everywhere, enjoy the countryside for its green spaces and uncrowded conditions, and the city for its entertainment possibilities. In a national poll, it was found that only in Paris do the majority (75 percent) of people feel that there is enough entertainment available to them near where they live. That number drops to 50 percent for other cities and to 10 percent for rural areas. But when it comes to the idea of moving, most young people would like to stay where they are: 61 percent of young people in the Paris region would like to remain there, and the same percentage of young people in the country want to stay in the country.

MOTIVATING ACTIVITY Many students may know what it means to be **dépaysé(e).** Invite only those who are willing to talk about moves they've made to share their impressions with their classmates. What did they miss most, initially? What adjustments did they have to make? How do they feel now about where they live?

A1

Antoine se plaint.

Before class, gather pictures of **une ferme, une vache, un lapin, une poule,** and **un oiseau.** Use them to present farm vocabulary. Demonstrate or give examples for **déménager, se plaindre, le mal du pays.** Then play the cassette or read Antoine's monologue aloud as students listen with books closed. Ask students for their general impression of Antoine's attitude: **A votre avis, est-ce qu'Antoine est heureux ou triste?** Next give students several minutes to read Antoine's statements to themselves. They should find one reason why Antoine likes the country and one reason why he dislikes Lyons. Now play the cassette or read aloud Didier's and Nadine's replies. Once again, ask students what their general impression is: **D'après Didier et Nadine, est-ce qu'Antoine a tort ou raison?** Finally, allow students to read Didier's and Nadine's statements to themselves. Have them tell why Lyons is a great place to live.

A2 ### Activité • Décrivez la vie d'Antoine

Give students several minutes to look back at A1 for descriptions of Antoine's life in Lyons. The descriptions should correspond to the information in the chart. For the first item, students might say **Antoine habite dans un petit appartement.** If students ask why the verbs in the left-hand column end in **-ait,** tell them that this is a past-tense ending they will soon learn. Do not explain the imperfect at this time.

SLOWER-PACED LEARNING On the board or on a transparency, write at random sentences that describe Antoine's life in the country and in the city. Have students decide which sentences belong in each category.

A3 ### Activité • Complétez

After students have completed the sentences with the words in the box, see how many other completions they can come up with for numbers 1, 2, 4, and 6. They might suggest **poules, lapins,** or **chevaux** for number 1. Remind students of changes to be made in the sentences: for example, **au** might become **à la** in number 4 if the completion is **à la piscine.** This could be a contest done in pairs or small groups. The group with the greatest number of logical completions wins.

A 4 Activité • Actes de parole

As students identify the expressions of regret or consolation in A1, write them on the board or on a transparency. Then have students suggest ways to vary the expressions. For example, **C'était si bien à la campagne** could become **C'était si bien en Floride.**

A 5 Activité • A votre avis

As students work in pairs, one should list the advantages and disadvantages of life in the city, and the other, the advantages and disadvantages of life in the country. See which pair of students can come up with the most complete lists.

A 6 Activité • Débat

Before students begin this activity, ask which expressions in the box indicate agreement and which indicate disagreement. Make sure that students use these expressions as they develop their debates.

SLOWER-PACED LEARNING   Simplify the model for students:

> —Moi, j'aime la campagne!
> —Et moi, je préfère la ville!
> —La campagne, c'est joli.
> —La ville, c'est fascinant.
> —Mais en ville, il y a de la pollution. J'aime pas!

A 7 Activité • Et vous?

Model possible answers by having students ask you the questions. Then have students pair off to ask each other the questions. After they've practiced together, call on individuals to tell what they found out about their partners.

A 8 Savez-vous que... ?

Lyons was founded by the Romans in 43 B.C., at which time it was called Lugdunum. The Romans developed it as a trade center, and it became the principal city of Gaul. It was in Lyons that Christianity was introduced to Gaul, and the city was ruled by archbishops until 1307, when it was annexed to the French kingdom.

Today Lyons is famous for its silk industry, its chemical industry, its river port, its university, and its cuisine. In fact, Lyons is considered to be the gastronomic capital of France. On its outskirts are the restaurants of Paul Bocuse and the Troisgros brothers, of **nouvelle cuisine** fame.

Vieux Lyon contains many beautiful old buildings from the Middle Ages and the Renaissance, set in narrow, picturesque streets. In **vieux Lyon** one can find many of the traditional Lyonnais restaurants called **bouchons,** which serve a variety of **charcuteries.**

On a wall map of France, ask a student to point out the places mentioned in the first paragraph. Then play the cassette or read the paragraphs aloud as students follow along in their books.

A 9 STRUCTURES DE BASE

Have students open their books and read the explanation and examples in number 1. You might want to emphasize that **du, de la,** and **des** are *not* used with comparative constructions. Ask students to make up one or two variations for each sentence in the chart.

Remind students that the independent pronouns in number 2 represent people. To practice, have them work in pairs, comparing the school supplies they have with them: **J'ai autant de cahiers que toi, mais tu as plus de classeurs que moi.**

A 10 Activité • Faites des comparaisons

You might have students go through these items three times, making comparisons with the places Didier and Nadine have both gone and with the places each has gone separately, so that students use **eux, elle,** and **lui.**

SLOWER-PACED LEARNING First have students decide whether **moins** or **plus** would be appropriate with each item. Then have them make the comparisons.

A 11 Activité • Comparez la ville et la campagne

Students should make logical comparative statements. They may use **autant** as well as **plus** and **moins.**

SLOWER-PACED LEARNING On the board or on a transparency, make two columns, one headed **En ville** and the other **A la campagne.** Have students decide in which column each item should appear. List each item as students suggest; then ask which comparison word would be most logical. As they answer, write +, =, or − beside the word. Your lists might look something like this:

En ville		A la campagne	
+	cinémas	−	bruit
+	pollution	−	appartements
−	espace	=	terrains de sport

Allow students to refer to these lists as they make complete comparative statements.

A12 Activité • Conversation

Students may agree as well as disagree with their partners' preferences. Circulate as they talk, prompting and correcting.

A13 Activité • Quelle maison aimez-vous mieux?

Ask students to bring to class two pictures clipped from magazines: one for their "old" house and another for their "new" one. They should show the pictures to a classmate, compare the two houses, and indicate their preferences.

A14 Activité • Ecrivez

If students do not wish to write about a vacation spot that they've visited, they might use the brochures shown in their books for inspiration. First have students think about what they might compare: air quality, attractions, activities, and so on. They might list these before writing. Then supervise as they write their postcards. To make it more realistic, you might distribute 4 × 6 index cards and encourage students to turn them into actual postcards, with the message and address on one side, and a picture, sketch, or amusing slogan—in French—on the back. Collect, correct, and display on a classroom bulletin board.

STRUCTURES DE BASE

Have students open their books to page 298 and read to themselves the paragraph at the bottom of the page. Ask if the paragraph describes Antoine's past or present life. Tell students to look at the verbs in the paragraph. What do these verbs have in common? Explain that the endings **-ais** and **-ait** belong to a past tense called the imperfect. List the imperfect endings on the board or on a transparency. Have students substitute different subject pronouns in the sentence **J'avais des amis.** Continue practicing with regular verbs. Return to the paragraph on page 298; ask if it describes Antoine's life or tells what he did once or twice in the past. At this time students need only have a general impression that the imperfect is a descriptive tense. The differences between the **passé composé** and the imperfect are treated in B12 of this unit. Finally, have students read the explanation on page 304 of their books.

Activité • Quand nous habitions à la campagne...

Remind students that they will be using the imperfect in this activity because they are expressing repeated past actions (numbers 1–6) and descriptions of something in the past (number 7).

SLOWER-PACED LEARNING You might first ask students to identify the subject in each sentence and tell what ending they will add to the stem of the verb. Then call on individuals to read the complete sentences. You may want to write the verb form they've used on the board.

Activité • Que faisait Antoine quand il était plus jeune?

Students may refer to A1 for the answers to these questions.

CHALLENGE Have students answer without referring to A1.

Activité • Comment est-ce que c'était?

As students role-play Antoine, encourage them to add descriptive comments: **C'était tellement bien! C'était amusant! C'était difficile.**

Activité • Et vous?

For cooperative learning, have students pair off to ask each other the questions. If students do not wish to talk about their own childhood, they might answer as a favorite TV star or character might do.

Activité • A vous maintenant!

Students should work in pairs, taking turns initiating the dialogues.

COMMENT LE DIRE

Model the expressions in both categories—complaining about missing something and consoling someone—as students repeat after you. Then, personalizing the expressions on the left, talk about missing something, and have students call out to you expressions of consolation.

A22 Activité • La ville, c'était si bien!

Have students work on their own to develop responses that someone who has just moved to the country and is still unhappy might make. After several minutes, have students pair off to do the dialogue.

A23 Activité • Ecrivez

If students do not wish to write about places they've lived, allow them to choose other places that interest them. You might wish to establish a minimum number of advantages that students must include. Specify also whether the lists should consist of phrases or complete sentences. If you choose to have students write complete sentences, remind them to use the imperfect when listing advantages of the place where they used to live.

A24 Activité • Jeu de rôle

As students work in pairs, circulate and listen. You might ask several pairs to present their dialogues to the class.

A25 Activité • Le bon vieux temps

Be sure that students use the present tense with the phrases in the left-hand box and the imperfect with those in the right-hand box. Encourage them to personalize the activity, mentioning things they really do now and really used to do when they were small. Or, if students would rather not talk about themselves, they might role-play a character from a book or movie.

A26 Activité • Ecoutez bien

> You're going to hear six short dialogues in which people talk about their homes. Where are they living *now*? Open your book to page 307. *(pause)* Copy the chart in A26 on a separate sheet of paper. *(pause)* As you listen to each dialogue, make a check mark in the appropriate box. Ready? **Ecoutez bien.**
>
> 1. —Je regrette drôlement la ville. Il y avait plus de concerts, de cinémas, de distractions…
>   —Ne regrette rien. C'est bien de vivre à la campagne. *à la campagne*
> 2. —Tu avais un appartement avant?
>   —Oui, mais j'habite une maison maintenant. *dans une maison*
> 3. —Vous avez vendu votre appartement à Lyon?
>   —Oui, nous n'aimions pas Lyon. Nous avons acheté une maison en Bourgogne. *dans une maison*
> 4. —J'adore ton appartement!
>   —Moi, je le trouve trop petit. Il y a deux ans, j'habitais dans une maison immense. C'était si bien. *dans un appartement*
> 5. —La campagne me manque. C'était tellement mieux là-bas.
>   —T'en fais pas. C'est bien de vivre en ville. *en ville*
> 6. —Tu n'habitais pas avec ta sœur l'année dernière?
>   —Si, mais j'ai déménagé. Maintenant j'habite en ville. *en ville*
>
> Et maintenant, vérifions. *Read each dialogue again and give the correct answer.*

SECTION B

OBJECTIVES **To socialize:** renew old acquaintances; **to exchange information:** talk about past experiences

CULTURAL BACKGROUND In France, as in the United States, strikes are sometimes called by unions in order to force management to come to terms. French unions are very unlike American unions, however. They are organized by political philosophy rather than by trade. The largest union, the **CGT (Confédération générale du travail),** is pro-communist. The next largest is the **CFDT (Confédération française démocratique du travail),** which is pro-socialist. The third largest is the **FO (Force ouvrière),** which is anti-communist. Workers in France don't have to belong to any union if they don't want to, and most don't, although they agree that the unions do represent them. Most strikes are directed against a single factory or company, but since the unions cut across trade lines, it is possible for a general strike to be called, affecting an entire region or even the entire country. Such strikes are infrequent, but they are very disruptive when they occur.

MOTIVATING ACTIVITY Ask students if they have ever traveled alone, perhaps to visit relatives or an old friend who has moved away. How was the trip? How did they travel? Any complications or delays? If they were to do it again, how would they travel?

B1

Les retrouvailles

As students look at the photos on page 308, tell them briefly, in French, what is going on. Use vocabulary with which students are already familiar. Then have students look at the picture on page 309 and describe what Philippe is thinking about. Since this depicts a past event, encourage students to use the imperfect: **Il pleuvait. La famille se promenait.** Continue your summary of the situation, filling in details that students may have missed. Next play the cassette or have two students (who have previously practiced the dialogue) read aloud as students follow along in their books. Students should discover what friends who haven't seen each other for a long time might say upon meeting again. Finally, have students read aloud and role-play the dialogue.

B2 ## Activité • Avez-vous compris?

For cooperative learning, have students work in pairs to answer the questions. Afterward, have volunteers share their answers with the class.

B3 ## Activité • Comparez les visites

For cooperative learning, divide the class into groups of four students each. Two students in each group act as recorders: one writes the list for Philippe's first visit, and the other, the list for his second visit. Remind groups that as they add events and descriptions to the ones given in their books, they should use past tenses for the first visit and the present tense for the second visit. Note that at this point the distinction between past and present is more important than correct usage of the **passé composé** and the imperfect. After groups have completed their lists, the group members who were not recorders should report their results to the class.

B4 ## Activité • Que dit Antoine?

Model Antoine's exclamations for students. Then have students identify their communicative function by selecting from the list on the left. See if students can suggest other ways in which Antoine could have expressed himself within these functions: for example, he might have said **Facilement!** or **Je vois bien!** instead of **Parfaitement!**

B5 ## Activité • Imaginez

Since students will be naming actions—what the family did—direct them to use only the **passé composé.** As students work in pairs, circulate and listen. Then ask several volunteers to describe to the class the family's visit.

B6 ## Activité • Chaîne de phrases

Have students continue the activity started in their books. Tell them to describe the day, using the imperfect. After students have added five or six sentences, ask them to tell what happened, using the **passé composé.** Repeat the activity, using a different theme suggested by students. You might want to write this series of sentences on a transparency for use in presenting the **passé composé** and the imperfect in B12.

B7 ## Savez-vous que... ?

Young people who plan to do a lot of traveling by train in France during the summer can purchase a discount card called a **carte Jeune** from the **SNCF.** The card entitles them to a 50 percent discount on tickets for all French trains, as long as their trips don't begin during peak travel times (holidays and the beginning and end of weekends).

Play the cassette or have a volunteer read the paragraphs about transportation aloud. Then have students look at the train schedule and tell which trains take only two hours to go from Paris to Lyons. At which train station do they arrive? Which trains take a bit more than two hours for the trip? Why?

B8 ## COMMENT LE DIRE

Have students repeat the expressions after you. Tell them that you are a friend or relative whom they haven't seen for several years. They should use the expressions to say that they're glad to see you and to say how long it's been since your last meeting.

B9 ## Activité • Conversation brouillée

Have students work in pairs. One student in each pair copies Laurence's lines onto separate index cards or slips of paper. The other copies Antoine's lines. Then, together, the two students work to put the cards in order so that the dialogue makes sense. Finally, partners practice reading the dialogue aloud.

CHALLENGE Instead of using the sentences given in the box, students make up what Antoine might say.

B10 ## Activité • Situations

For cooperative learning, students pair off. Assign one of the situations to each pair. As students practice, circulate to listen and assist. Call on volunteers to present dialogues to the class.

SLOWER-PACED LEARNING Before class, prepare lists of helpful phrases and vocabulary for each situation. Distribute to each pair the list for their assigned situation. Circulate as students work in pairs.

VOUS EN SOUVENEZ-VOUS?

On the board or on a transparency, write several examples that illustrate the formation of the **passé composé.** As students look at these, ask them to summarize what they've learned about this past tense. Follow a similar procedure for the imperfect. To summarize, have students read silently the explanation on page 312 of their books.

B12 **STRUCTURES DE BASE**

Have volunteers read aloud the explanation on page 313 of their books. Then show them the series of sentences generated for B6 or a passage from B1 that illustrates the uses of the imperfect and the **passé composé.** Ask volunteers to explain why each tense was used.

Next choose a story, perhaps a fairy tale, with which most students are familiar. Ask them to relate, in English, only *what happened* in the story: for example, Little Red Riding Hood's mother asked her to take a basket to her grandmother. Little Red Riding Hood went into the forest with the basket. She met a wolf. They spoke to each other and so on. Students should see how uninteresting a story consisting only of isolated actions can be. Show them how to expand it by adding actions in progress and descriptions. Once the story is complete, have students give the French equivalents for all the verbs, using the **passé composé** and the imperfect as appropriate.

SLOWER-PACED LEARNING You might want to give the students these general rules of thumb for when to use the **passé composé** and when to use the imperfect. (1) If, in English, you use *was* or *were* and the *-ing* form of the verb or *used to* and the infinitive of the verb, then you will use the imperfect in French: **Nous lisions** = *We were reading; We used to read.* (2) If you use the *-ed* form of the verb in English, you will use the **passé composé** in French: **Elle est arrivée** = *She arrived.* As with all rules, however, there are exceptions.

B13 **Activité • Que faisaient-ils quand... ?**

Have students suggest what four actions might be depicted by the two photos. Remind them that one action was already going on when the other happened. Students should decide which actions should be expressed by the imperfect and which by the **passé composé.**

B14 **Activité • Une journée à Lyon**

Have students read the paragraph to themselves. Then, for each verb, ask which tense should be used. If students make an error, explain why the other tense should be used. Next go back and call on individuals to read the sentences aloud and to make the necessary changes.

SLOWER-PACED LEARNING Have students copy these sentences into their notebooks, leaving blanks where there are infinitives. Then do the activity as indicated above. Students fill in the conjugated verbs as they're given.

B15 **Activité • Ecrit dirigé**

Before students begin working in pairs, tell them that they should add the phrases to their paragraph in the order that they're given in the box. To get students started, have a volunteer pick out one or two verbs that are going to to be used to express a single past action: verbs that will be in the **passé composé.** As students work together, they should discuss their choice of tenses. When they've finished, go through the activity, writing answers as suggested by students on the board or on a transparency. Clarify the use of tenses when necessary.

SLOWER-PACED LEARNING   Use the phrases in the box to prepare a paragraph like the one in B14, with the infinitives in parentheses. Then have students work in pairs as suggested above.

CHALLENGE   Have students continue the story of what Antoine did last evening.

B16   Activité • Et vous?

Assign this activity for homework so that students will have time to think about their answers. You could then ask for answers to be given orally, or you could call for answers to be written in the form of a composition.

B17   Activité • La colonie de vacances

Have students look at the pictures and identify the series of actions taking place. Then have volunteers suggest what might serve as background (or description). Have students pair off to do the activity as instructed in their books. For homework, they might write a paragraph about Didier and his friends at summer camp.

SLOWER-PACED LEARNING   Write phrases on the board or on a transparency. Go through these with students and classify them as actions or descriptions. As students work in pairs, allow them to refer to these lists.

B18   Activité • Conversation

If students do not wish to talk about what they did last weekend, they might use one of the attractions pictured in their books for inspiration. As students work in pairs, circulate, listen, and prompt. Call for some students to present their conversations to the class.

B19   Activité • Racontez

To safeguard the privacy of individuals, you might wish to make this a written assignment. If you prefer to use this as an oral activity, allow students who do not wish to talk about their own childhood to make up an anecdote or borrow one from the life of a favorite TV character.

B20   Activité • Ecoutez bien

A journalist is preparing a report on visitors to Lyons. Open your book to page 315. *(pause)* Read the questions in B20 to yourself. *(pause)* Listen to the journalist as she interviews a visitor, and be prepared to indicate your answers on a separate sheet of paper. Ready? **Ecoutez bien.**

—Bonjour, madame.
—Bonjour, mademoiselle.
—Vous êtes déjà venue à Lyon?
—Oui, plusieurs fois quand j'étais plus jeune.
—Et maintenant, vous venez souvent?

—Non, pas vraiment.
—Pourquoi?
—Parce que je déteste Lyon!
—Ah oui?
—Je n'aime pas les grandes villes. Vous savez, quand je suis venue ici pour la première fois, il y a trente-deux ans, le métro n'existait pas, il y avait moins de voitures, et on pouvait marcher tranquillement dans les rues. Vous avez vu maintenant? Les voitures, le bruit, la pollution, les grèves... En plus, il pleut toujours! Avant, il ne pleuvait jamais!
—Vous en êtes sûre?
—Oui, il faisait toujours très beau... C'était le bon temps!
—Alors, pourquoi est-ce que vous venez à Lyon si vous n'aimez pas?
—Parce qu'à la campagne, je m'ennuie!

Et maintenant, vérifions.
1. Est-ce que la dame est déjà venue à Lyon? *Oui (elle y est déjà venue).*
2. Y vient-elle souvent maintenant? *Non, pas vraiment.*
3. Quand est-ce qu'elle est venue pour la première fois? *Elle est venue pour la première fois il y a trente-deux ans.*
4. Qu'est-ce qui est différent maintenant? *Maintenant il y a le métro, les voitures, le bruit, la pollution, les grèves...*
5. Quel temps faisait-il avant? *Avant, il ne pleuvait jamais.*
6. Pourquoi est-ce que la dame vient à Lyon? *Parce qu'elle s'ennuie à la campagne.*

SECTION C

OBJECTIVES **To exchange information:** make comparisons; report a series of events; **to persuade:** make suggestions

CULTURAL BACKGROUND The basilica of **Notre-Dame-de-Fourvière** was built after the Franco-Prussian War of 1870. The archbishop of Lyons had promised to build a church if the enemy didn't reach the city during the war. The exterior resembles a fortress, with octagonal towers and crenelated walls. The interior is richly decorated with colorful mosaics. An observation post at the top of the basilica offers a panoramic view of the area.

MOTIVATING ACTIVITY Have students imagine that their pen pal from France is visiting them and that they want to show him or her the closest large city. Where would they go? What city transportation would they use? How much do they think it would cost to show someone the sights? Would they go there more than once?

C1 ## Par où commencer?

Play the cassette or have two volunteers (who have previously prepared the dialogue) read aloud as students look at the photos. While listening, students should discover where Philippe and Antoine decide to go first and what means of transportation they'll use. Then have students read the dialogue aloud.

C2 ### Activité • Vrai ou faux?

Call on volunteers to read the statements aloud. Call on others to indicate whether the statements are true or false. Have students correct those that are false.

C3   Activité • Actes de paroles

Give students several minutes to reread C1 to look for a way to make suggestions. Ask students to remember another way to make suggestions (**nous** verb form) and to restate the suggestions made in C1: **Commençons par monter à Fourvière! Prenons le métro!**

C4   Activité • Trouvez des mots

Have students make a chart as shown below and fill it in with appropriate adjectives and adverbs from C1.

	la marche	le funiculaire	le métro	le bus
avantages		*vite*	*moderne*	*pratique*
inconvénients	*fatigante*			

Which form of transportation do students prefer?

C5   STRUCTURES DE BASE

Ask students to recall what words they used in making comparisons with nouns. Tell them that **plus** and **moins** are also used with adjectives and adverbs, and that **aussi** replaces **autant**. Have students consult the charts they prepared as suggested in C4 above. As they compare these means of transportation, write their suggestions on the board or on a transparency. Use **fatigant(e)** to explain adjective agreement. Then have students open their books to page 318 to read the explanation to themselves.

C6   Activité • Comparez

Write the nouns on separate slips of paper and place them in a container. Do the same for the adjectives. Have students take two nouns at a time, along with one adjective, and compare the nouns using **plus, moins,** or **aussi** to make a logical statement.

C7   Activité • Quel moyen de transport?

In their questions, students should suggest destinations appropriate for the means of transportation they name. With **l'avion** and **le train,** the destination might be **Montréal,** while with **la moto** and **la bicyclette,** it might be **le centre commercial.**

C8   Activité • A vous maintenant!

Since students will need to use feminine adjectives to describe the landmarks pictured, review the feminine forms of the adjectives listed. Then have students compare the landmarks to one another.

CHALLENGE   As a speed-and-accuracy contest, see how many sentences students can write comparing these places, using adjectives other than the ones suggested.

C9   **Activité • Ecoutez bien**

You're going to hear some young people deciding which means of transportation to use. Open your book to page 320. *(pause)* Copy the chart in C9 on a separate sheet of paper. *(pause)* Fill in the chart by listing the advantages and inconveniences of each form of transportation. **Ecoutez bien.**

ALAIN   Alors, on prend le bus ou le métro?
MARC   Oh, le métro, c'est plus rapide.
PIERRE   Mais le bus est plus tranquille.
ANNE   Moi, je préfère prendre le taxi. C'est plus confortable.
MARC   Le métro, c'est moins cher.
SYLVIE   La marche à pied aussi.
PIERRE   Mais c'est plus fatigant.
SYLVIE   C'est plus fatigant, mais c'est plus agréable.
MARC   Mais moins rapide.
PIERRE   A mon avis, le bus c'est plus pratique!
ALAIN   Bon! Pourquoi on ne prend pas le funiculaire? On a une belle vue!

Et maintenant, vérifions. *Read the information in the chart.*

le métro	le bus	le taxi	la marche à pied	le funiculaire
rapide *pas cher*	*tranquille* *pratique*	*confortable*	*pas chère* *agréable* *fatigante* *pas rapide*	*belle vue*

C10   **Activité • Jeu de rôle**

If students prefer, allow them to discuss pastimes rather than sports. Have volunteers role-play their conversations for the class.

C11   **Activité • Ecrivez**

Have students think of two American cities, one that a French student might want to visit and another that they would recommend more highly. Ask them why they would prefer the second, and have them jot down their ideas. They should then write their letters as you circulate and assist. The letters can be completed and/or recopied as a homework assignment.

CHALLENGE   After you have corrected the letters and returned them, students should exchange letters with a classmate and respond as they think the French pen pal would.

C12   **A FOURVIERE**

Write phrases on the board that describe the events out of order, and have students copy them on a sheet of paper.

Antoine et Philippe	déjeunent	regardent Lyon
	montent à Fourvière	visitent la ville
	vont à la librairie	

Play the cassette or read the dialogue aloud. Have students write the phrases in the correct order. Play the cassette again; students confirm and correct their answers. Then ask volunteers to read the phrases aloud in the correct order to check their understanding of the dialogue. Finally have students work in pairs to read aloud and role-play the dialogue.

C13 Activité • Suivez la carte

Before students begin the activity, review the prepositions of location, using examples with people and objects in the classroom. Help students locate **Fourvière** on the map; then have them complete the activity in pairs as directed.

SLOWER-PACED LEARNING Ask the students to say where a specific place is in relation to another: **l'hôtel de ville et la place Bellecour** (**L'hôtel de ville est à gauche de la place Bellecour**).

C14 COMMENT LE DIRE

Present the words that are needed in reporting a series of events: **d'abord, ensuite, après, enfin.** Have students refer to the list of events they made for C12. Have them state the sequence of events, using these words. Next ask students to invent a simple series. You might suggest various contexts: what they do to get ready for school in the morning and so on.

C15 Activité • A votre avis

Have students reread silently the dialogue in C12. Then, either orally or in writing, students should arrange the boys' activities in the proper order, according to their plans and time schedule.

C16 Savez-vous que... ?

Construction of the **cathédrale Saint-Jean** was begun in the twelfth century and completed in the fifteenth. It has beautiful stained-glass windows and an astronomical clock that announces the hours of noon, 1 P.M., 2 P.M., and 3 P.M. with the sound of a rooster crowing and the movement of mechanical angels.

The **place Bellecour** is one of the largest (310 by 200 meters) and most picturesque squares in France. The statue of Louis XIV in its center is the second one to appear on that spot, the first having been broken up and melted down during the Revolution.

The **place des Terreaux** contains a fountain with statues of horses designed by the sculptor Frédéric Bartholdi, who designed the Statue of Liberty.

The **parc de la Tête d'Or** has a lake, a zoo, and botanical gardens. There are **son-et-lumière** shows in the park during the summer.

C17 Activité • Ecrivez

Give students 4 × 6 index cards and ask them to make postcards, with sentences on one side and a sketch and/or slogan on the back. Collect and display the cards on a classroom bulletin board.

C18 Activité • Jeu de rôle

Have students form groups of three, one in each group playing Philippe and the other two his parents. The parents ask Philippe as many questions as they can about his trip to Lyons and about Antoine. They might ask him, for example, how much money he spent and if he met any girls. Encourage students to use their imaginations and to continue as long as possible.

C19 Activité • Et vous?

If students do not wish to talk about a friend of their own, they might select a fictional character from a different world, such as E.T., who comes to visit them. Encourage students to be imaginative in their answers.

C20 COMMENT LE DIRE

Have students repeat after you the sentences in both boxes. Ask them to make suggestions with **si** about things they would like to be doing at that moment: **Si on allait à la cafeteria? Si on quittait l'école?** Have classmates respond to their suggestions with enthusiasm: **Quelle bonne idée! Allons-y!** and so forth. Then have volunteers relate the suggestions according to the model sentences in the second box.

C21 Activité • Antoine fait des suggestions

SLOWER-PACED LEARNING Students convert each of the seven items into a suggestion, choosing any of the six ways illustrated in C20 each time.

CHALLENGE Have students convert *each* item into the six different ways of suggesting the activity, as shown in C20:

> Si on faisait le tour de Lyon?
> Faisons le tour de Lyon!
> On va faire le tour de Lyon?
> Pourquoi on ne fait pas le tour de Lyon?
> Tu n'as pas envie de faire le tour de Lyon?
> Tu veux qu'on fasse le tour de Lyon?

C22 Activité • Faites des suggestions

Encourage students to be creative in the excuses they invent for this activity. After they've practiced, ask each pair to select one item and present the dialogue to the class.

C23 Activité • Philippe est difficile!

Have students suggest some of the missing lines in the dialogue. Practice with them, giving Philippe's responses yourself. Then have students practice in pairs, taking turns as Antoine.

C24 Activité • A vous maintenant!

Students make up dialogues similar to the one in C23, but with subjects of their own choosing. After pairing off, they may need to spend a few minutes sharing ideas, perhaps even making a few notes or cue cards. As they practice their dialogues, circulate among them and listen.

TRY YOUR SKILLS

OBJECTIVE   To recombine communicative functions, grammar, and vocabulary

CULTURAL BACKGROUND   **Arcachon** is a resort on the Atlantic coast south of **Bordeaux.** Since trains run frequently from **Bordeaux** to **Arcachon,** and since the trip takes only half an hour, the resort is very popular with the **Bordelais** in the summer.

MOTIVATING ACTIVITY   Ask students what they would miss about the town or city where they live if they had to move to a different place with a different climate.

1 Que de déménagements!

Play the cassette or read aloud Sylvie's monologue. As students listen, they should discover as much as they can about the activities of Sylvie and her family: **Ils se promenaient à la campagne, Sylvie allait au théâtre avec sa mère,** and so on. If students cannot remember an activity of note, direct them to the paragraph in which it is mentioned and have students read the paragraph to themselves.

2 Activité • Complétez

CHALLENGE   Students complete these sentences orally as they glance back at the material in Skills 1. Call on a volunteer to complete each one.

3 Activité • Devinez

Call on individuals to answer the questions. They may refer back to Skills 1 as needed.

4 Activité • D'habitude...

Review the formation of the imperfect with students. Play the cassette of Skills 1 again and have students complete the chart on a separate sheet of paper. To correct, they open their books to Skills 1, exchange papers, and compare the charts to the information in the paragraphs.

5 Activité • Jeu de rôle

Divide the class into two teams: one asks the questions and the other gives Sylvie's answers. Team members may confer with one another to come up with logical questions and answers. See how long they can keep the conversation going.

6 Activité • Ecrivez

Review how to make comparisons with nouns, adjectives, and adverbs. You might have students do this activity in class or for homework.

7 Activité • Sylvie accueille Florence

Brainstorm with students expressions to use when renewing old acquaintances. Write these on the board or on a transparency for students to refer to as they work in pairs.

8 **Activité • Sylvie console Florence**

Review the expressions for saying how much you miss something and for consoling someone. Start the conversation between Sylvie and Florence with the entire class; have the students continue in pairs. Ask pairs to present their dialogues to the class.

9 **Activité • Ecrivez**

Suggest that students reread **Contact 4,** A8, and C16 before they begin their diary entries. If you assign this activity for homework, collect the entries and indicate where corrections need to be made. Return work to students for revision. Suggest that they rewrite the entries, making them into a booklet that looks like a diary. Collect students' corrected entries and display them in the classroom.

10 **Activité • Souvenir, souvenir...**

Review the uses of the **passé composé** and the imperfect with students. Before students begin to work in pairs, suggest a fictional past situation and develop the details of it with the class. Then, as students work in pairs, they may use a situation from their own past or they may make one up. As students listen, they might take brief notes on the memories their partners describe. For homework, they should consult their notes and write a short summary of their partners' anecdotes to hand in.

11 **Activité • Situation**

Brainstorm with students different ways to make suggestions; write examples on the board or on a transparency for students to consult as they work in pairs. You might suggest that students use the expressions from the boxes in C22 to accept and refuse. As students talk, circulate and listen. Ask volunteers to role-play the situation for the class.

12 **Activité • Récréation**

These activities are optional. For the first one, you might ask students to identify the first picture **(vache)** and then use letters from that word to figure out what the other pictures are.

PRONONCIATION

Glides with /j/, /w/, and /ɥ/

> Open your book to page 329. *(pause)* Refer to this page as you listen to this section.

1 **Ecoutez bien et répétez.**

> **1.** If you've been listening carefully to the samples of French you've heard up to now, you might have noticed some fast little sounds reminding

you of the first sound in *yes, yet,* and *you.* For instance, you heard one in **monsieur/msjo/—/sjo/**—a bit like when you say *It's you* in English. It's something between a consonant and a vowel; it's called a glide. That's because it glides you into the next sound. Take for instance the French word for *diamond.* It's written almost the same as in English, but its sound is /**djamā**/. Listen to the first syllable: /**dja**/. Can you say it? Repeat: /**dja**/, /**dja**/, **diamant.** Like the English syllable *d'ya* in *What d'ya say?*, only faster and tenser. In fact, /**ja**/ is sometimes spelled *ya*, as in **y a-t-il.** Repeat: **y a-t-il.** Now try these words: **voyage, payer, pierre, pied, papier, panier, cahier, collier, soulier.**

But you've got to try this glide with those typical French sounds with which it is heard most often. Try these: **vieux, monsieur, les yeux, adieu.** And don't forget the nasals. Say these: **bien, sien, lien, viande, lion, nous avions, savions.** Did you notice that this gliding sound is often written with the letter **i**, although the sound section of your dictionary will code it as **j**, since that is the international code for this sound, **y** having already been taken up for the sound /**y**/. It sometimes is the only sound that separates the present tense from the past, as it does in the imperfect. Listen to and repeat these: **nous allons—nous allions, vous allez—vous alliez.**

This glide often appears written **ill** as in **bouillon** and **Marseillaise.** Try these: **brouillard, maillot, ailleurs, accueillant.** Learn to say it at the end of words like **fille.** Continue now: **travaille, vieille, paille, feuille, Antilles.**

Many common words you've seen written with a final **il** also end in this sound. Try some: **soleil, œil, travail.**

How about some French sentences: **Le vieux monsieur travaille à Marseille.** *(pause)* **Quand il se sent bien et qu'il fait du soleil, il y va à pied.** So far so good. But just one more thing. There are a few words with **ille** and **ill** that are actually pronounced with an l-sound. So few, however, that you can remember them all. The most common are **ville** and **village.**

2. Another vowel sound that often serves as a consonant or syllable maker is the **w**-sound you hear in **quoi, moi, toi, soi, choix, bois.** This is pronounced like the **w**-sound in the English *west wind* and is often written **ou**, as in **Louis, Louise, souhait, jouer.** Repeat these: **Louis, Louise, souhait, jouer.** Now try some more: **boire, voir, droit, soir.** It may be more tricky with the nasals, but you've got to get it. Try these: **loin, coin, point, soin.**

You also need this little glide sound for words starting with **ou** as in **ouest** or sentences like **Où est-ce que c'est?** Both sound somewhat like the English word *west.* But don't be fooled by appearances. This little glide can quickly transform itself into a full-fledged consonant when it finds itself up against another vowel. And then all of a sudden syllables disappear. Look what happens here. You see an **ou** and you say it as a single sound. Listen: **C'est où?** You can write the same thing in five written syllables as **Où est-ce que c'est?** But what happens when you say it? How many syllables do you have left? Listen: /**wɛs kə se**/. Three. Your **où** has become a /**w**/ to form a syllable with **est** and **ce.** So you get /**wɛs**/. Neat, isn't it?

Let's try this one out in a few sentences: **Moi, j'ai soif, et toi?** *(pause)* **Oui, allons voir ce qu'il y a à boire à la cantine.** *(pause)* **Où est-ce que c'est? C'est loin?** *(pause)* **Non, là-bas. Juste au coin de la rue.**

3. Finally, here is a gliding sound that comes only from the famous French sound /**y**/ as in **tu.** Its sound is like this vowel sound and the sound /**i**/ at the same time. It's often written **ui** as in **nuit** but sometimes **ue** as in **duel** or **ua** as in **nuage!** Try it out by saying /**yi**/, /**yi**/, /**yi**/ rapidly. *(pause)* Now try these words: **puis, nuit, lui, cuir, suivi, huit, juillet, pluie, bruit, saluer, nuage, juin.**

Don't get this mixed up with the other glide, the /w/ as in **Où est-ce que c'est?** Listen to the difference between them and repeat: **deux joints— deux juin, enfoui—enfui, avec Louis—avec lui.** Let's put some of these into sentences to remember: **Les nuages sont suivis par la pluie.** *(pause)* **Louis a passé un mois avec lui, du huit juin au huit juillet.**

2 **Ecoutez et lisez.**

For a little more practice with glides, read the dialogue aloud. I'll say each line after you.

—Tu as vu ces nuages?
—Oui, le temps est à la pluie.
—On ne peut pas rester sur la plage toute la nuit.
—Puis la gare Saint-Louis, c'est loin d'ici. Vite!
—Dépêche-toi. Prends le panier et allons-y!

3 **Copiez les phrases suivantes pour préparer une dictée.**

Write the following sentences from dictation. First listen to the sentence as it is read to you. Then you will hear the sentence again in short segments, with a pause after each segment to allow you time to write. Finally you will hear the sentence a third time so that you may check your work. Let's begin.

1. Le village où habitait Antoine n'est pas loin de Lyon. Le village *(pause)* où habitait Antoine *(pause)* n'est pas loin de Lyon. *(pause)* Le village où habitait Antoine n'est pas loin de Lyon.
2. Lyon, c'est bruyant et pollué par les voitures. Mais je suis habitué. Lyon, c'est bruyant *(pause)* et pollué par les voitures. *(pause)* Mais je suis habitué. *(pause)* Lyon, c'est bruyant et pollué par les voitures. Mais je suis habitué.
3. Ici, on peut voir les voisins deux ou trois fois par mois, on peut sortir après le travail, et les gens sont gentils. Ici, on peut voir les voisins *(pause)* deux ou trois fois par mois, *(pause)* on peut sortir *(pause)* après le travail, *(pause)* et les gens sont gentils. *(pause)* Ici, on peut voir les voisins deux ou trois fois par mois, on peut sortir après le travail, et les gens sont gentils.
4. Oui, je suis bien ici. Je ne regrette rien. Oui, je suis bien ici. *(pause)* Je ne regrette rien. *(pause)* Oui, je suis bien ici. Je ne regrette rien.

VERIFIONS!

Have students write their answers to the first activity; call on individuals to read their answers. You might ask students to supply different nouns for their sentences: **A la campagne, il y a plus d'oiseaux qu'en ville. Il y a plus de cinémas en ville qu'à la campagne.**

After students have written their answers to the second activity, have them exchange papers and correct each other's work.

Have students write their answers to the third activity; then call on individuals to read their answers. Students should add to their own lists those expressions suggested by others.

Have students work in pairs for the fourth activity, exchanging roles as consoler and consoled. Circulate among them, giving help where needed. Then call on volunteers to present their dialogues to the class.

Have students reread B1 before doing the first activity. Call on volunteers to read the expressions to the class.

Have students do the second activity individually. Prepare a transparency with the answers so that students can check their work. Ask students why they used the **passé composé** or the imperfect in each case.

Have students write their answers to the first two activities and submit them to you to check.

Have students work in pairs to do the next two activities. They might think of other activities to suggest. Call on volunteers to write their answers on the board.

VOCABULAIRE

Divide the class into groups of four. Each group must compose four logical sentences using as many of the vocabulary words as possible. Group members should take turns writing the sentences on a sheet of paper. The group that uses the most words wins.

ETUDE DE MOTS

Have the students write sentences using the **-ant** adjectives formed from the verbs listed in their books. For additional practice with adjectives, have students locate other adjectives in the vocabulary list and use them to describe nouns from the list.

A LIRE

OBJECTIVE   To read for practice and pleasure

VIVE LA GREVE!

For **Avant de lire,** you might wish to brainstorm advantages and disadvantages of strikes with the entire class rather than have students work in pairs.

Play the cassette as students read along. Pause after each of the five parts to check comprehension. Ask students to summarize the reaction of each person to the strike, in English if necessary.

Write sentences like these on the board or on a transparency:

1. Cette personne apprécie la bonne humeur des Parisiens.
2. Cette personne a perdu de l'argent à cause de la grève.
3. Cette personne pense que la campagne est trop calme.

Have the students read the story again, matching each sentence with the appropriate person.

Activité • Qui est-ce?

Allow students to glance back at the paragraphs as needed in order to answer the questions.

Activité • Imaginez

Brainstorm with students things that one can and cannot do during a power outage. List these on the board or on a transparency. Students may select from these lists as they tell what they would or could not do.

L'EMBOUTEILLAGE

Play the cassette or read the poem aloud. The poem contains very colorful visual images. You might ask the students to illustrate it; display the illustrations in the classroom.

Activité • Vrai ou faux?

Read the statements; have students correct the two that are false.

Activité • Avez-vous compris?

As students answer the questions, they should justify their answers.

Activité • Ecrivez

Have students work in pairs to do this activity. Call on volunteers to read their sentences to the class.

LES CHARPENTIER DEMENAGENT

After students have answered the questions in **Avant de lire,** describe briefly the five members of the Charpentier family. Tell students that the family is going to move from **Yerres** to Paris. Ask them to jot down their prediction of how each person is going to react to the move, and whether the person prefers **Yerres** or Paris. Then play the cassette as students read along in their books. As they read, they should confirm their predictions or adjust their perception of each family member's attitude.

Activité • Devinez

Have students locate the phrases in the story and choose their meanings from the context.

Activité • Complétez

Have students work individually to skim the reading and to find the answers to complete the sentences. Have them write down only the missing words. When all have finished, call on individuals to complete the sentences aloud.

Activité • Avez-vous bien lu?

Have students pair off to discuss the feelings of the different members of the family. Why are they happy or unhappy? Are those feelings likely to change? Why or why not?

Activité • A votre avis

Have students make three lists: (1) possible reasons for the grandmother accompanying the family to Paris; (2) advantages for her; 3) advantages for the family. Call on volunteers to read their lists.

Activité • Jeu de rôle

Brainstorm with the students how to console someone. Begin the dialogue with the entire class before having the students break into groups.

CHAPITRE 9

Un dépaysé à Lyon

Moving to a different city or town can be an overwhelming experience. Leaving behind friends, relatives, and favorite places is always difficult. But moving to a new place and making new friends can also be exciting. A city like Lyons offers many attractions to newcomers.

In this unit you will:

PREMIER CONTACT	get acquainted with the topic
SECTION A	compare city life and country life . . . say how much you miss something . . . console someone
SECTION B	renew old acquaintances . . . talk about past experiences
SECTION C	explore Lyons . . . report a series of events . . . make comparisons . . . make suggestions
TRY YOUR SKILLS	use what you've learned
A LIRE	read for practice and pleasure

PREMIER CONTACT · getting acquainted with the topic

The authentic material in Premier Contact introduces the theme of the unit and is to be used for global comprehension only.

1 Visite de Lyon 🎞

VISITEZ LYON
AVEC LES GUIDES
DE L'OFFICE DU TOURISME

Toute l'année, l'Office du Tourisme organise pour les groupes de dix personnes au minimum des visites commentées sur des thèmes nombreux et variés :

LYON ANCIEN
LYON MODERNE
LES MUSEES ET LEURS EXPOSITIONS
LA CROIX ROUSSE
LE LYON TECHNIQUE

Pilotage et commentaires assurés en toutes langues par des guides interprètes professionnels.

BUREAU DES GUIDES :
5, PLACE SAINT-JEAN
Tél. (7) 248.45.76

Pour les individuels : Visite audio-guidée. Location de l'appareil : au Pavillon du Tourisme Place Bellecour, au Centre d'Echanges de Perrache et 5, Place Saint-Jean.

Le quartier de la Croix-Rousse: a beautiful old section of Lyons, originally known for its silk weavers.

2 Activité • Vrai ou faux?

1. Il y a des visites organisées de Lyon seulement au printemps et en été.
2. Les visites sont toutes pareilles.
3. Si vous ne parlez pas français, vous pouvez demander un guide qui parle anglais.
4. Si vous visitez Lyon tout(e) seul(e), vous pouvez visiter la ville sans guide et simplement écouter une cassette. 1. C'est faux. Il y a des visites pendant toute l'année. 2. C'est faux. Il y a des visites sur des thèmes nombreux et variés. 3. C'est vrai. 4. C'est vrai.

3 Activité • A vous maintenant!

Vous organisez des visites de votre ville (ou village) pour des élèves français qui passent quinze jours chez vous. Quels thèmes est-ce que vous choisissez pour les visites?

Photo on page 295: the coat of arms of Lyons

Pendant votre séjour à Lyon, ne manquez pas de venir au théâtre de Guignol. Là, on applaudit aux coups de bâton que Guignol donne à sa femme Madelon ou à l'agent de police. On tremble quand il rentre chez lui et se fait frapper par sa femme. Et on rit aux exploits de son joyeux camarade, Gnafron.

Les amateurs de couleur locale ne doivent pas quitter Lyon sans avoir vu Guignol.

Des représentations sont données les mercredis, dimanches et fêtes à 14 h 15 et 16 h 30. Le théâtre est fermé en été.

5 Activité • Avez-vous bien lu?

Répondez aux questions suivantes d'après «Les fameuses marionnettes de Lyon».

1. Comment s'appelle le théâtre?
2. Quels jours est-il ouvert?
3. Quel genre de théâtre est-ce?

4. Comment s'appelle le personnage principal?
5. Qui est Madelon? Gnafron?

1. Le théâtre s'appelle le nouveau Guignol de Lyon. 2. Il est ouvert les mercredis, dimanches et fêtes. 3. C'est un théâtre de marionnettes. 4. Il s'appelle Guignol. 5. Madelon est sa femme; Gnafron est son joyeux camarade.

6 Activité • Avez-vous compris?

Répondez aux questions suivantes d'après «Les fameuses marionnettes de Lyon».

1. Les pièces montées dans ce théâtre sont-elles comiques ou sérieuses?
2. Quelles sont les réactions des spectateurs en regardant ces pièces?

1. Les pièces sont comiques. 2. Les spectateurs rient et applaudissent.

7 Activité • Et vous?

1. Est-ce que vous êtes déjà allé(e) au théâtre?
2. Quelle pièce est-ce que vous avez vue?
3. C'était quel genre de pièce? Comique? Tragique?

4. Est-ce que vous avez déjà vu des marionnettes? Où?

comparing city life and country life . . . saying how much you
miss something . . . consoling someone

Est-ce que vous avez déjà eu l'occasion de déménager, de changer de maison, de ville ou de région? Avez-vous eu du mal à vous adapter à votre nouvelle vie? Est-ce que vous vous sentiez un peu dépaysé(e)? Antoine Blonet a déménagé à Lyon à cause du travail de ses parents. Il se plaint à ses cousins lyonnais, Nadine et Didier.

A1

Antoine se plaint.

Quand il était plus jeune, Antoine habitait à la campagne, en Bourgogne. Quand il est arrivé à Lyon, il avait le mal du pays.

C'était si bien à la campagne!

C'était tellement mieux là-bas!

(Antoine parle.)
Je regrette drôlement la campagne. Là-bas, nous avions une jolie maison avec un jardin et de l'espace.

J'avais beaucoup d'amis. On prenait le car ensemble pour aller à l'école; on jouait au foot. Tous les week-ends, j'allais voir ma grand-mère à une vingtaine de kilomètres. Elle a une ferme avec quelques vaches, des lapins, des poules... Cette vie me manque beaucoup.

La Bourgogne (Burgundy), a region in east-central France, is noted for its wine.

Ici, à Lyon, nous avons un petit appartement au troisième étage d'un immeuble. Il n'y a pas beaucoup de vue. A la campagne, c'était calme, il y avait moins de bruit. On entendait les oiseaux. En ville, je suis réveillé par les voitures. Avant, je marchais beaucoup, je profitais de la nature. Maintenant, il faut que je prenne le métro ou le bus. Et puis, il y a de la pollution : à la campagne, je respirais l'air pur.

Fais-toi une raison. make the best of it

(Didier le console.)
Regretter, ça ne sert à rien. Fais-toi une raison. A la campagne, tu voyais toujours les mêmes gens, et pour aller au cinéma, il fallait faire des kilomètres!

T'en fais pas! Tu vas te plaire ici.

(C'est Nadine qui parle.)
Tu vas voir. Lyon est une ville merveilleuse, active et très riche culturellement. Ici, il y a beaucoup de films et de concerts, et on rencontre souvent de nouvelles personnes. C'est fascinant!... Moi, je trouve que c'est bien de vivre en ville!

Activité • Décrivez la vie d'Antoine

Complétez le tableau pour décrire la vie d'Antoine à Lyon.

En Bourgogne	A Lyon
Antoine habitait une jolie maison.	Il habite un appartement.
Il marchait beaucoup.	Il prend le bus ou le métro.
Il respirait l'air pur.	Il y a de la pollution.
Il voyait toujours les mêmes gens.	On rencontre souvent de nouvelles personnes.
Il entendait les oiseaux.	Il est réveillé par les voitures.

 A3 Activité • Complétez

Complétez les phrases avec ces mots.

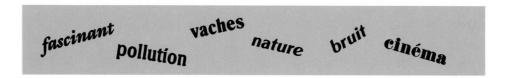

fascinant   vaches   nature   bruit   cinéma   pollution

1. Normalement, dans une ferme il y a des <u>vaches</u> .
2. A la campagne, il y a moins de <u>bruit</u> qu'en ville.
3. En ville, on profite rarement de la <u>nature</u> .
4. Pour aller au <u>cinéma</u> à la campagne, il faut faire des kilomètres.
5. En ville, il y a souvent de la <u>pollution</u> .
6. Vivre en ville, c'est <u>fascinant</u> .

A4 Activité • Actes de parole   Possible answers are given.

Pouvez-vous trouver dans A1 trois expressions pour exprimer le regret et trois expressions pour consoler quelqu'un? C'était si bien à la campagne!   C'était tellement mieux là-bas!   Je regrette drôlement la campagne! Cette vie me manque beaucoup.

Regretter, ça ne sert à rien.   Fais-toi une raison.   T'en fais pas!   Tu vas te plaire ici.   Tu vas voir.

A5 Activité • A votre avis   Possible answers are given.

Quels sont les avantages et les inconvénients de la ville et de la campagne d'après Antoine et ses cousins? Faites une liste avec un(e) camarade. Est-ce que vous êtes d'accord avec eux? Est-ce que vous voyez d'autres avantages et d'autres inconvénients? Essayez d'en trouver le maximum.

La ville		La campagne	
avantages	inconvénients	avantages	inconvénients
On rencontre de nouvelles personnes. C'est très riche culturellement. Il y a beaucoup de films et de concerts.	On a un petit appartement. On entend le bruit des voitures. On prend toujours le métro ou le bus.	On a une maison avec jardin. On entend les oiseaux. On marche beaucoup. On profite de la nature.	On voit toujours les mêmes gens. Il faut faire des kilomètres pour aller au cinéma.

Activité • Débat

Il est temps de choisir : décidez-vous maintenant pour la ville ou la campagne. Ensuite, trouvez un(e) camarade de classe qui a un avis différent. Employez la liste que vous avez préparée dans A5 et ces expressions. Préparez un débat et faites-le devant la classe.

— A mon avis, il faut habiter à la campagne. Là, on peut voir souvent ses amis.
— Au contraire! Il n'y a pas de bus ou de métro. Alors, c'est difficile d'aller les voir.
— Mais...

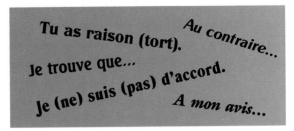

Tu as raison (tort). Au contraire...
Je trouve que...
Je (ne) suis (pas) d'accord.
A mon avis...

A7 Activité • Et vous?

1. Où habitez-vous? Depuis combien de temps?
2. Etes-vous content(e) d'habiter là où vous êtes? Pourquoi?
3. Avez-vous déjà déménagé? Pour aller où?
4. Avez-vous envie d'habiter ailleurs? Où? Pourquoi?

A8 Savez-vous que... ?

Lyon est la deuxième ville de France après Paris. Elle est située sur la route Paris-Marseille, à une centaine de kilomètres de la Suisse, et elle est traversée par deux fleuves, le Rhône et la Saône : elle est au carrefour des routes commerciales.

C'est aussi une ville culturelle : le Théâtre National Populaire et l'Opéra de Lyon sont célèbres dans le monde entier... et n'oublions pas le personnage de Guignol, introduit à Lyon en 1795 par le marionnettiste Laurent Mourguet. Guignol est un personnage très populaire, optimiste et joyeux, qui a souvent des ennuis avec la police. Le théâtre de Guignol est dans le vieux Lyon.

Un dépaysé à Lyon   301

STRUCTURES DE BASE Comparisons with adjectives and adverbs are presented in C5, p. 318.
Making comparisons with nouns

1. To make comparisons with nouns, you use **plus, autant,** or **moins** + **de (d')** + a noun + the word **que (qu').** Some French people pronounce the s in "plus" when making a comparison with nouns. When "plus" is at the end of a sentence, the s is always pronounced: Moi, j'en ai plus.

plus/autant/moins + de (d')	*Noun*	que (qu')	
En ville, il y a **plus de**	concerts	**qu'**	à la campagne.
En ville, on a **autant d'**	amis	**qu'**	à la campagne.
A la campagne, il y a **moins de**	monde	**qu'**	en ville.

2. The independent pronouns **moi, toi, lui/elle, nous, vous,** and **eux/elles** may follow **que (qu').**
Je vais à autant de concerts que **toi.**
Il a vu plus de films que **nous.**

3. Sometimes you may make comparisons without the **que.** In this case, what you've said or written before the comparison should make clear what the comparison refers to.
En ville, on entend partout les voitures, les bus,... Heureusement, il y a **moins de bruit à la campagne.**

A10 Activité • Faites des comparaisons 🔲

Comme Antoine n'habite pas Lyon depuis longtemps, il est allé dans moins d'endroits en ville que Didier et Nadine et dans plus d'endroits à la campagne. Faites des comparaisons en employant **lui/elle** et **eux.**

Antoine est allé dans moins d'endroits en ville que Didier et Nadine. Il est allé dans moins de parcs qu'eux...

1. parcs   3. boutiques   5. cafés   7. fermes
2. cinémas   4. musées   6. discothèques

2. ...moins de cinémas qu'eux.   3. ...moins de boutiques qu'eux.   4. ...moins de musées qu'eux.   5. ...moins de cafés qu'eux.
6. ...moins de discothèques qu'eux.   7. ...plus de fermes qu'eux.

A11 Activité • Comparez la ville et la campagne 🔲   Possible answers are given.

Comparez les avantages et les inconvénients de la ville et de la campagne.

En ville, il y a plus de cinémas qu'à la campagne. En ville, il y a plus de cinémas, de bruit, de pollution,
A la campagne, il y a moins de bruit qu'en ville.   d'appartements, de voitures qu'à la campagne.

1. cinémas   4. espace   7. voitures   10. jardins
2. bruit   5. appartements   8. arbres (*trees*)   11. air pur
3. pollution   6. terrains de sport   9. maisons   12. lapins

A la campagne, il y a plus d'espace, d'arbres, de jardins, d'air pur, de lapins qu'en ville. A la campagne, il y a moins de terrains de sport, de maisons, de voitures qu'en ville.

A12 Activité • Conversation

Demandez à un(e) camarade s'il (si elle) aime mieux vivre en ville ou à la campagne. Il/Elle vous répond et vous pose la même question. Trouvez des arguments et employez les comparatifs.

— Tu préfères vivre en ville ou à la campagne?
— Je préfère vivre en ville parce qu'il y a plus de cinémas. Et toi?
— Moi, je préfère vivre à la campagne. Il y a moins de pollution.

jardins   bruit   concerts
voitures   espace   cinémas

Activité • Quelle maison aimez-vous mieux?

Imaginez que vous venez de *(have just)* vous installer dans cette nouvelle maison. Est-ce que vous l'aimez mieux que votre ancienne maison ou non? Pourquoi? A-t-elle autant de pièces que l'ancienne? De chambres? De salles de bains? D'étages? Comparez la nouvelle et l'ancienne pour expliquer votre préférence.

A 14 Activité • Ecrivez   Possible answer is given.

Ecrivez à votre ami(e) une carte postale pour lui dire où vous passez les vacances. Dites-lui pourquoi vous aimez ou vous n'aimez pas cet endroit. Employez les comparatifs.

Cher (Chère)…
Je passe les vacances à Savine-le-Lac. J'aime beaucoup parce que … il y a plus de jeunes qu'en ville, et j'ai autant d'amis ici que chez moi. A la campagne, c'est calme et il y a moins de bruit.

A 15   STRUCTURES DE BASE
The imperfect

1. You've already learned that the **passé composé** expresses past time in French. Another way of expressing past time is by using the imperfect. To form the imperfect, begin with the present-tense **nous** form; drop the **-ons;** then add the imperfect endings. They are the same for all verbs.

	-er Verbs	*-ir Verbs*	*-re Verbs*
Present-tense **nous** *Forms*	habit**ǿńś**	choisiss**ǿńś**	entend**ǿńś**
Imperfect	j' habit**ais** tu habit**ais** il/elle/on habit**ait** nous habit**ions** vous habit**iez** ils/elles habit**aient**	je choisiss**ais** tu choisiss**ais** il/elle/on choisiss**ait** nous choisiss**ions** vous choisiss**iez** ils/elles choisiss**aient**	j' entend**ais** tu entend**ais** il/elle/on entend**ait** nous entend**ions** vous entend**iez** ils/elles entend**aient**

2. The verb **être** is an exception: its imperfect stem is **ét-**. However, it uses the same imperfect endings as other verbs: **j'étais, tu étais,** and so on.
3. The verbs **falloir, pleuvoir,** and **neiger** each have only one imperfect form. They are **il fallait, il pleuvait,** and **il neigeait.**
4. For verbs that end in **-ger,** like **manger** and **ranger,** add an **e** before the imperfect endings for the **je, tu, il/elle,** and **ils/elles** forms of the verb: je mang**eais**, tu mang**eais**, il rang**eait**, elles rang**eaient**.
5. For verbs that end in **-cer,** like **commencer,** place a cedilla below the **c** in the **je, tu, il/elle,** and **ils/elles** forms of the verb: je commen**çais**, tu commen**çais**, elle commen**çait**, ils commen**çaient.**
6. You may be wondering why there's more than one way to express past time in French. You'll learn the reasons a little later on, but for now, you should keep in mind these uses of the imperfect.
   a. Use the imperfect to describe past circumstances or conditions.
   > L'an dernier, ils **habitaient** près de chez moi. On **était** très contents.
   b. Use the imperfect to tell what *used to* happen.
   > Tous les week-ends j'**allais** voir ma grand-mère.

A 16   Activité • Quand nous habitions à la campagne...

Antoine vous parle de l'emploi du temps de sa famille à la campagne l'année passée. Mettez les verbes à l'imparfait.

> Je (se réveiller) tous les matins à 6 h.   Je me réveillais tous les matins à 6 h.

1. Mon père et ma mère (se lever) très tôt, à 5 h 30.
2. Ma sœur (préparer) le petit déjeuner.
3. Moi, je (promener) notre chien dans la forêt.
4. Ma sœur et moi (prendre) le bus de 7 h 45.
5. Nous ne (rentrer) pas à la maison pour déjeuner. Moi, je (jouer) au foot, et ma sœur (se promener) avec ses amis.
6. Le soir, des voisins (venir) nous voir.
7. Nous (être) très contents.

1. se levaient   2. préparait   3. promenais   4. prenions   5. rentrions / jouais / se promenait   6. venaient   7. étions

A 17   Activité • Que faisait Antoine quand il était plus jeune?

1. Où habitait-il?
2. Comment était sa maison?
3. Comment allait-il à l'école?
4. Quand allait-il voir sa grand-mère?
5. Qu'est-ce qu'il devait faire pour aller au cinéma?
6. Qu'est-ce qu'il faisait à la campagne?

1. Il habitait à la campagne, en Bourgogne.   2. Sa maison était jolie avec un jardin et de l'espace.   3. Il prenait le car pour aller à l'école.   4. Il allait voir sa grand-mère tous les week-ends.   5. Il faisait des kilomètres pour aller au cinéma.   6. A la campagne, il respirait de l'air pur, il marchait beaucoup, il profitait de la nature, il entendait les oiseaux.

Activité • Comment est-ce que c'était? 🔲 Possible answers are given.

Antoine a fait ce dessin pour vous montrer sa vie à la campagne. Mettez-vous à sa place et décrivez ce qu'on y faisait, comment c'était… Employez l'imparfait.

1. avoir des lapins et des poules
2. aider à soigner les animaux
3. s'occuper du jardin

4. arroser les légumes
5. faire le ménage
6. jouer ensemble

7. travailler beaucoup
8. vivre tranquillement
9. être heureux

1. On avait des lapins et des poules.   2. Ma sœur aidait mon père à soigner les animaux.   3. Mon père s'occupait du jardin.
4. Moi, j'arrosais les légumes.   5. Ma mère faisait le ménage.   6. D'habitude, ma sœur et moi, on jouait ensemble.
    7. Mes parents travaillaient beaucoup.   8. Nous vivions tranquillement.   9. J'étais heureux.

A19 Activité • Et vous?

1. Où habitiez-vous quand vous aviez dix ans?
2. Aviez-vous beaucoup d'amis? Comment s'appelaient-ils?

3. Qu'est-ce que vous faisiez pendant la semaine? Le week-end?
4. Etiez-vous heureux/heureuse? Pourquoi?

A20 Activité • A vous maintenant!

Demandez à un(e) camarade ce qu'il/elle faisait à l'école quand il/elle était plus jeune. Posez une question chacun(e) à tour de rôle.

— Tu faisais des maths?
— Pas souvent.
— Pourquoi?
— J'étais nul(le) en maths!

déjeuner à la cantine (à quelle heure?)

pratiquer un sport (quel sport?)

faire des maths (pourquoi?)

regarder des bédés en classe (pourquoi?)

passer des examens (quand?)

être membre d'un club (quel club?)

recevoir de bonnes notes (dans quels cours?)

Tu déjeunais… ?   Tu pratiquais… ?   Tu faisais… ?   Tu regardais… ?   Tu passais… ?   Tu étais… ?   Tu recevais… ?

COMMENT LE DIRE
Saying how much you miss something
Consoling someone

SAYING HOW MUCH YOU MISS SOMETHING	CONSOLING SOMEONE
Je regrette (drôlement) la campagne.	Ne regrette rien. C'est bien de vivre en ville.
Qu'est-ce que je regrette!	Tu as tort de regretter. Ça ne sert à rien.
C'était si bien!	Tu vas voir. Lyon est une ville merveilleuse.
C'était tellement mieux!	N'y pense plus.
Il y avait moins de (plus de)...	(Ne) t'en fais pas! Tu vas te plaire ici.
La campagne me manque.	Fais-toi une raison.

A 22   Activité • La ville, c'était si bien!   Possible answers are given.

Votre famille a quitté la ville pour aller vivre à la campagne. Un(e) camarade vous demande si vous êtes content(e) d'habiter à la campagne. Qu'est-ce que vous lui répondez?

— Tu es content(e) d'habiter à la campagne?
— ... Non, je regrette drôlement la ville.
— Mais pourquoi est-ce que tu regrettes? C'est bien ici, non?
— ... Il y a moins de choses à faire.
— Il y a aussi des avantages à la campagne.
— ... On voit toujours les mêmes gens; il y a beaucoup moins de variété.
— Oui, mais ici il y a moins de pollution.
— ... C'était tellement mieux!
— A mon avis, tu as tort.
— ... Qu'est-ce que je regrette la ville!
— Allez, n'y pense plus!

A 23   Activité • Ecrivez   Possible answers are given.

Où avez-vous habité avant? A la campagne? En ville? A la montagne? Près de la plage? Faites une liste des avantages de cet endroit-là. Ensuite, faites une liste des avantages de là où vous habitez maintenant. Quel endroit a le plus d'avantages?

Avant	Maintenant
Je profitais de la nature.	Il y a de la pollution.
Il y avait plus d'espace.	Il y a plus de bruit.
C'était joli.	Il faut prendre le métro.
C'était calme.	Il y a plus de gens.

A 24   Activité • Jeu de rôle

Un(e) de vos camarades vient de déménager. Il/Elle exprime ses regrets d'avoir quitté son ancienne vie. Vous le/la consolez. Indiquez-lui les avantages de sa nouvelle vie. Changez de rôle. Employez la liste que vous avez préparée dans A23.

— Je regrette beaucoup...
— Ne regrette rien. Tu vas voir, ici, c'est pas mal.
   Il y a...

Quand vous étiez petit(e), est-ce que votre vie était plus amusante, plus facile qu'elle est actuellement *(now)*? Dites à un(e) camarade que vous regrettez votre ancienne vie. Il/Elle vous demande pourquoi. Vous comparez votre ancienne vie à votre vie actuelle. Votre camarade essaie de vous consoler. Puis changez de rôle.

— C'était tellement mieux quand j'étais petit(e).
— Pourquoi?
— Maintenant...   Mais quand j'étais petit(e),...

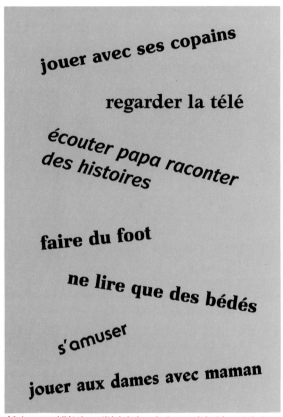

Maintenant, j'ai / arrose / fais / tonds / sors / promène...

Mais quand j'étais petit(e), je jouais / regardais / écoutais / faisais / lisais / m'amusais . . .

For script and answers, see p. T187.

Ecoutez les dialogues et dites où les personnes habitent maintenant.

	1	2	3	4	5	6
Dans un appartement						
Dans une maison						
En ville						
A la campagne						

Quand on déménage, le plus dur, c'est souvent de quitter ses amis. Depuis qu'il habite à Lyon, Antoine n'a pas revu son ami Philippe. Il lui a écrit plusieurs fois, mais Philippe n'aime pas écrire et ne lui a jamais répondu. Enfin, Philippe a décidé de venir passer la journée à Lyon.

B1

Les retrouvailles 📼

Antoine vient chercher son ami à la gare de Lyon-Perrache. Il est ravi de le revoir.

ANTOINE	Philippe!
PHILIPPE	Eh, Antoine! Ça me fait plaisir de te revoir!
ANTOINE	Moi aussi! Tu as fait un bon voyage?
PHILIPPE	Oui, pas de problèmes.
ANTOINE	Dis donc, ça fait longtemps que je ne t'ai pas vu!
PHILIPPE	Eh, oui! Presque un an!...

ANTOINE	Alors, raconte : comment va ta famille?
PHILIPPE	Ça va. Tout le monde t'embrasse.
ANTOINE	Et l'école, quoi de neuf?
PHILIPPE	J'ai redoublé.
ANTOINE	C'est pas vrai!
PHILIPPE	Si!...

ANTOINE   Dis, tu es déjà venu à Lyon?

PHILIPPE   Oui, il y a longtemps, pour voir une exposition… Mais j'en garde un très mauvais souvenir.

ANTOINE   Vraiment? Pourquoi?

PHILIPPE   Ecoute, quand nous sommes descendus du train, il pleuvait et il y avait une grève des transports en commun. Plus de métro, plus de bus, pas de parapluie, impossible de trouver un taxi! Nous avons été obligés de marcher sous la pluie. L'enfer! Ma petite sœur pleurait, moi, j'avais mal aux pieds, mon père râlait, et ma mère était furieuse parce que son nouveau chapeau était trempé!

ANTOINE   Eh bien!

PHILIPPE   Attends, ce n'est pas fini! Quand nous sommes enfin arrivés à l'exposition, c'était fermé, il était trop tard! Tu imagines la scène?

ANTOINE   Parfaitement! Mais ne t'inquiète pas : aujourd'hui, il ne pleut pas, il n'y a pas de grève, et tu vas voir, Lyon est une ville passionnante!

GARE DE LYON PERRACHE

B2 Activité • Avez-vous compris?

Répondez aux questions suivantes d'après la conversation entre Antoine et Philippe.

1. Où est-ce qu'Antoine et Philippe se rencontrent? Ils se rencontrent à la gare.
2. Depuis combien de temps est-ce qu'Antoine n'a pas vu Philippe? Depuis presqu'un an.
3. Est-ce que Philippe a eu de bons résultats à l'école cette année? Non, il a redoublé.
4. Pour quelle raison est-ce que Philippe est déjà venu à Lyon? Pour voir une exposition avec sa famille.
5. Pourquoi est-ce qu'il n'a pas apprécié sa journée à Lyon? Parce qu'ils ont été obligés de marcher sous la pluie.
6. Qu'est-ce qui est différent cette fois? Il ne pleut pas. Il n'y a pas de grève.

B3 Activité • Comparez les visites

Dans B1, pouvez-vous distinguer les deux visites de Philippe à Lyon? Avec un(e) camarade de classe, choisissez les phrases qui décrivent la première visite, et celles qui décrivent la deuxième. Ensuite, ajoutez d'autres événements et descriptions.

1. Philippe rend visite à Antoine. 2ème
2. Il pleuvait. 1ère
3. Philippe est arrivé à Lyon avec toute sa famille.
4. Il fait beau. 2ème
5. Philippe est venu voir une exposition. 1ère
6. Philippe voyage tout seul. 2ème
7. Il y avait une grève des transports en commun. 1ère

La première visite	La deuxième visite
1ère	

B4 Activité • Que dit Antoine?

Dans B1, Antoine encourage Philippe, lui montre qu'il écoute attentivement. Que dit Antoine pour… ?

1. exprimer la curiosité Quoi de neuf?
2. exprimer le doute C'est pas vrai!
3. exprimer l'étonnement (surprise)
4. dire qu'il comprend bien   Vraiment?
   Parfaitement!

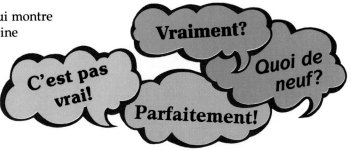

B5 Activité • Imaginez   Possible answer is given.

Philippe et sa famille ont passé une excellente journée à Lyon. Pas de grève, beaucoup de soleil, visite d'une exposition. Toute la famille est heureuse… Racontez cette journée à un(e) camarade de classe. Dites où ils voulaient aller, où ils sont allés, à quelle heure, comment, ce qu'ils ont fait, ce qu'ils ont vu, à quelle heure ils sont repartis…

Ils voulaient voir une exposition à Lyon. Ils sont arrivés en train à neuf heures du matin. Il faisait très beau! Il y avait du soleil et il faisait chaud. Ils ont pris un taxi pour aller au musée. Sa mère portait un nouveau chapeau, et elle était contente. Ils ont vu la belle exposition. Ils se sont promenés à pied. C'était fantastique! Ils sont repartis à huit heures du soir.

B6 Activité • Chaîne de phrases

Chacun dit une phrase à tour de rôle pour raconter une mauvaise journée.

ÉLÈVE 1   Nous étions à la plage.
ÉLÈVE 2   Il pleuvait.

ÉLÈVE 3   Ma petite sœur était malade.
ÉLÈVE 4   …

Remind students to use the imperfect for description and the passé composé for events of a specific duration.

Pour aller à Lyon, c'est très facile.
Vous pouvez prendre l'avion et arriver
à l'aéroport de Satolas, ou prendre le
train et descendre à l'une des deux
gares, Perrache ou la Part-Dieu. Si
vous êtes très pressé, prenez le TGV
(Train à Grande Vitesse). Pour faire les
450 kilomètres entre Paris et Lyon,
il ne met que deux heures!

Pour circuler dans Lyon, c'est aussi
très facile! Le métro existe depuis
1978. Il a trois lignes et fonctionne de
cinq heures du matin à minuit. Il est
propre, rapide, moderne... et
accueillant, à l'image de la ville.

PARIS   LYON   ST-ETIENNE

N° du TGV		651	603	701/605	653 ◀	609	613	615	617	625	677	679	681 ■
		🔲	🔲		🔲	8.00	10.00	11.00	12.00	14.00	15.25	16.25	17.27
Restauration									13.25				
Paris-Gare de Lyon	D	6.15	6.45	7.00	7.30	9.26							19.31
Le Creusot TGV	A	7.41				10.08	12.02	13.00	14.08	16.02	17.27	18.27	19.41
Lyon-Part-Dieu	A	8.23	8.45	9.02	9.30	10.18	12.12	13.10	14.18	16.12	17.37	18.36	b
Lyon-Perrache	A	8.33	8.55	9.12	9.40	a	b	b	b	a	b		
Saint-Etienne	A			9.49									

A Arrivée
D Départ
a Correspondance à Perrache.
b Correspondance à Part-Dieu.

◀ Ce TGV ne comporte que des voitures 1ʳᵉ classe.
■ Ce TGV ne comporte des voitures 2ᵉ classe que les vendredis.
🔲 Service restauration à la place en 1ʳᵉ classe, en réservation.

Have students locate St. Etienne on the map, p. 434.

COMMENT LE DIRE
Renewing old acquaintances

During normal commercial service, the TGV
travels at a speed of 260 kmh (162 mph).

Ça me fait plaisir
J'avais vraiment envie } de te (re)voir!
Je suis content(e)
Je suis heureux (heureuse) que tu sois (re)venu(e)!
Ça fait longtemps que je ne t'ai pas vu(e)!
Il y a si longtemps!

Activité • Conversation brouillée

A Lyon, Antoine retrouve Laurence, une copine de Bourgogne. Réunissez les deux parties de la conversation.

LAURENCE Ah, ça me fait vraiment plaisir de te revoir!
ANTOINE …
LAURENCE J'ai plein de choses à te dire.
ANTOINE …
LAURENCE Alors la ville, c'est comment?
ANTOINE …
LAURENCE Oui, mais je déménage l'année prochaine.
ANTOINE …
LAURENCE Ma famille vient à Lyon. L'année prochaine, je vais au lycée avec toi!
ANTOINE …

— **C'est vrai? Raconte.**
— **Moi aussi. Il y a si longtemps... depuis que j'habite à Lyon!**
— **Ah, super!**
— **Au début je détestais, je ne supportais pas le bruit, les odeurs, mais maintenant, ça va. Et toi, toujours à la campagne?**
— **Et moi donc! Je voulais vraiment te voir aussi!**

B 10   Activité • Situations

Vous êtes dans ces situations. Faites les dialogues avec un(e) camarade.

1. Vous rendez visite à un(e) ami(e) que vous n'avez pas vu(e) depuis longtemps. Il/Elle a l'air en forme. Parlez de votre santé, de ce que vous faites, vous deux, pour vous soigner et bien vous nourrir. See Unit 7, pp. 244 and 251 for expressing concern and advising.

2. Dans un café, vous rencontrez un(e) ami(e) qui a déménagé dans une autre ville il y a trois ans. Vous vous posez mutuellement des questions sur votre vie, votre famille…

3. Après les grandes vacances, vous êtes content(e) de retrouver votre ami(e) à l'école. Parlez de ce que vous avez fait depuis que vous vous êtes vu(e)s — vos petits boulots, vos responsabilités chez vous… See Unit 2, p. 72 for expressing how long something has been going on. See Unit 5, pp. 160, 167, and 169 for expressing obligation, responsibility, and complaining. See Unit 6, pp. 212 and 216 for inquiring about activities and giving reasons.

B 11   **VOUS EN SOUVENEZ-VOUS?**
Expressing past time

1. You recall that the **passé composé** and the imperfect both express past time in French.
2. The **passé composé** is composed of two parts: (a) a present-tense form of the auxiliary verb **avoir** or **être;** (b) a past participle.
   a. You use the auxiliary verb **être** with **aller, arriver, descendre, entrer, partir, rentrer, rester, revenir, sortir, tomber,** and **venir.** The past participle agrees in gender and number with the subject: Ma **sœur** est **arrivée** en retard.
   b. You also use **être** with verbs that have a reflexive pronoun. When the reflexive pronoun is a direct object, the past participle agrees with it: Les enfants **se sont couchés.** If the pronoun is an indirect object, there is no agreement: Elle s'est **acheté** une jupe.
   c. You also remember that for verbs conjugated with **avoir,** the past participle agrees in gender and number with a direct object that comes before it: J'aime bien ta jupe! Où est-ce que tu **l'as achetée?**
3. To form the imperfect, you begin with the present-tense **nous** form of the verb, drop the **-ons,** and add the appropriate imperfect ending: **-ais, -ais, -ait, -ions, -iez,** or **-aient.**
   a. You also recall that you use the imperfect to describe past circumstances or conditions: Ma mère **était** furieuse parce que son chapeau était trempé.
   b. In addition, you use the imperfect to tell what *used to* happen: Le matin, on **prenait** le car pour aller à l'école.

STRUCTURES DE BASE

The uses of the passé composé *and the imperfect*
The use of être en train de

1. Although the **passé composé** and the imperfect both express past time in French, each has specific uses. You choose between them, depending on how you wish to present what happened.

Circumstances/ Conditions	Completed Actions	Actions in Progress	Habitual Actions
Il **était** huit heures du soir. Il **faisait** très froid.	Ma sœur **est sortie** avec ses amies.	Mon père **râlait** et ma mère **pleurait**.	D'habitude, ma sœur **restait** à la maison le soir et **faisait** ses devoirs.

2. When you want to tell *what happened* in the past, you use the **passé composé**. Completed actions are expressed in the **passé composé**.

3. If you want to *describe* circumstances or conditions that existed in the past, you use the imperfect. Actions that were in progress also describe past circumstances, so you use the imperfect to express them.

4. If you want to say that an action was in progress when another action happened, you use the imperfect to express the action that was going on and the **passé composé** to tell that the other action occurred: Philippe **décrivait** sa première visite à Lyon quand Antoine lui **a posé** une question.

5. The phrase **être en train de** followed by an infinitive is often used to emphasize that an action was going on in the past: Nous **étions en train de lire** des B.D. It's the French equivalent of *to be busy doing* something. Point out that when "être en train de" is used to express a past action, it is implied or expressed that another action interrupted: Nous étions en train de lire des B.D. quand il est arrivé. This expression is used in the present to talk about an action that is in progress: Je suis en train de finir mes devoirs.

Activité • Que faisaient-ils quand... ?

Qu'est-ce que ces gens faisaient? Qu'est-ce qui les a interrompus?

Le garçon lisait un livre et sa sœur écoutait des cassettes quand leur mère est entrée dans le salon.

 1.

 2.

Le garçon faisait la vaisselle quand la fille est arrivée.

Activité • Une journée à Lyon

Laurence raconte ce qu'elle a fait hier. Mettez les verbes entre parenthèses à l'imparfait ou au passé composé.

Hier, ma mère et moi, nous (visiter) la ville de Lyon. Quand nous y (arriver), il (faire) très beau. Nous (prendre) un taxi pour aller dans la vieille ville. Mon copain Antoine nous (attendre). Il (être) déjà au restaurant. Nous (déjeuner) là. Le repas (être) très bon. Ensuite, Antoine nous (accompagner) ma mère et moi chez sa tante. Avant, elle (habiter) dans notre village. Quand nous (entrer), elle (préparer) des confitures avec les fruits de son jardin. Elle (être) heureuse de nous revoir. Hier, ma mère et moi, nous avons visité la ville de Lyon. Quand nous y sommes arrivées, il faisait très beau. Nous avons pris un taxi pour aller dans la vieille ville. Mon copain Antoine nous attendait. Il était déjà au restaurant. Nous avons déjeuné là. Le repas était très bon. Ensuite, Antoine nous a accompagnées ma mère et moi chez sa tante. Avant, elle habitait dans notre village. Quand nous sommes entrées, elle préparait des confitures avec les fruits de son jardin. Elle était heureuse de nous revoir.

Un dépaysé à Lyon 313

Activité • Ecrit dirigé   Possible answer is given.

Qu'est-ce qu'Antoine a fait hier soir? Avec un(e) camarade de classe, choisissez entre le passé composé et l'imparfait. Ensuite, racontez l'histoire sous forme de paragraphe.

> Hier, Antoine voulait voir un film au cinéma… Il avait 50 F. Il est parti de chez lui à six heures. Malheureusement, il pleuvait. Il est entré dans un magasin. Là, il a acheté un parapluie. Le parapluie lui a coûté 45 F. Après, il est

avoir 50 F	**acheter un parapluie**
partir de chez lui à six heures	*coûter 45 F*
pleuvoir	**rentrer chez lui**
entrer dans un magasin	**n'avoir plus d'argent pour aller au cinéma**

rentré chez lui parce qu'il n'avait plus d'argent pour aller au cinéma.

B16 Activité • Et vous?

1. Etes-vous déjà allé(e) vous promener en ville ou à la campagne?
2. Comment y êtes-vous allé(e)? Avec qui?
3. Qu'est-ce que vous avez fait?
4. Quel temps faisait-il?
5. Est-ce qu'il y avait du monde?
6. Avez-vous retrouvé des amis? De la famille? Que faisaient-ils quand vous êtes arrivé(e)?

B17 Activité • La colonie de vacances   Possible answers are given.

Quand Didier et ses amis avaient 10 ans, ils sont allés en colonie de vacances. Regardez ces dessins, et décrivez à un(e) camarade de classe ce que les garçons y ont fait, comment c'était… Employez le passé composé et l'imparfait.

1. Didier et ses amis ont pris le train.

2. Le voyage était long, et ils se sont ennuyés.

3. Quand les enfants sont arrivés à la colonie de vacances, le moniteur les attendait.

4. Les enfants se promenaient tous les matins dans la forêt avec leur moniteur.

5. La cuisine de la colo était infecte, mais le moniteur l'aimait.

6. Tous les après-midi, ils nageaient dans le lac.

Avec un(e) camarade de classe, parlez de ce que vous avez fait le week-end dernier. Vous lui posez des questions et il/elle vous répond.

> Qu'est-ce que tu as fait ce week-end?
> Où est-ce que tu es allé(e)?
> Tu y es allé(e) en voiture?
> Il faisait quel temps?
> … ?

B19 **Activité • Racontez**   Possible answers are given.

Choisissez un événement mémorable de votre enfance. C'était triste? Joyeux? Amusant? Dangereux? Racontez cet événement et ses circonstances à un(e) camarade de classe.
C'était en 1981. Je n'avais que 6 ans quand on a quitté la grande ville. C'était triste.

B20 **Activité • Ecoutez bien**   For script and answers, see pp. T191–92.

Une journaliste prépare un reportage sur les gens qui visitent Lyon. Ecoutez cette interview et répondez aux questions.

1. Est-ce que la dame est déjà venue à Lyon?
2. Y vient-elle souvent maintenant?
3. Quand est-ce qu'elle est venue pour la première fois?
4. Qu'est-ce qui est différent maintenant?
5. Quel temps faisait-il avant?
6. Pourquoi est-ce que la dame vient à Lyon?

exploring Lyons . . . reporting a series of events . . . making comparisons . . . making suggestions

Une journée pour visiter Lyon, ce n'est pas beaucoup. Mais on a tout de même le temps de voir certaines choses et de se faire une idée de la ville.

C1

Par où commencer?

Philippe et Antoine commencent la visite de la ville.

PHILIPPE   Alors, le Lyonnais, qu'est-ce que tu proposes?

ANTOINE   Si on commençait par monter à Fourvière?

PHILIPPE   Qu'est-ce que c'est?

ANTOINE   Tu vois la basilique, là-haut? Eh bien, c'est là. C'est l'endroit idéal pour avoir une vue générale de Lyon.

PHILIPPE   Comment on y va? A pied?

ANTOINE   Non, en funiculaire, ça va plus vite, et c'est moins fatigant que la marche! Mais d'abord, il faut prendre le bus.

Photo above: la basilique Notre-Dame de Fourvière

PHILIPPE Et si on prenait le métro? Il est drôlement moderne, il paraît.

ANTOINE Oui, mais il ne va pas jusqu'au funiculaire. C'est plus pratique d'y aller en bus.

PHILIPPE Ça ne fait rien. J'ai envie d'essayer le métro.

ANTOINE Comme tu veux.

Un carnet de six tickets, ça fait vingt francs. C'est pas trop cher!

Cet appareil rend la monnaie: This machine makes change.

C2 Activité • Vrai ou faux?

1. Antoine a envie de commencer la visite par la basilique.
2. De Fourvière, on a une belle vue.
3. Pour monter à Fourvière, il faut prendre le métro.
4. Le métro va jusqu'au funiculaire.
5. Six tickets de métro coûtent vingt francs.
6. Antoine et Philippe prennent le bus pour aller au funiculaire.

1. C'est vrai. 2. C'est vrai. 3. C'est faux. Il faut prendre le funiculaire.
4. C'est faux. Le bus va jusqu'au funiculaire. 5. C'est vrai. 6. C'est faux. Ils prennent le métro.

C3 Activité • Actes de parole

Pouvez-vous trouver dans C1 une façon de proposer quelque chose?
Si on... ?

C4 Activité • Trouvez des mots   Possible answers are given.

Pouvez-vous trouver dans C1 les avantages et les inconvénients de ces moyens de transport pour aller à Fourvière?

1. la marche
C'est trop fatigant.

2. le funiculaire
Ça va plus vite et c'est moins fatigant.

3. le métro
Il ne va pas jusqu'au funiculaire.

4. le bus
C'est plus pratique.

STRUCTURES DE BASE
Making comparisons with adjectives and adverbs

1. To make comparisons with adjectives or adverbs, you use **plus, aussi,** or **moins** + an adjective or adverb + **que (qu').**

plus/aussi/moins	*Adjective / Adverb*	que (qu')	
Le bus est **plus**	pratique	**que**	le métro.
Le bus est **aussi**	cher	**que**	le métro.
Le bus est **moins**	rapide	**que**	le métro.
Le métro va **plus**	vite	**que**	le bus.

2. You remember that adjectives agree in gender and number with the nouns that they modify. This is true in comparisons as well.

Le bus est aussi **cher** que le métro.　　　**Une moto** est plus **chère** qu'un vélo

Les vélos sont moins **chers** que les mobylettes.　　**Les voitures** sont moins **chères** que les avions.

3. The adjective **bon(ne)** is an exception. It cannot be used with **plus** and instead becomes **meilleur(e)** *(better)*: Le vélo est **meilleur** pour la santé que la marche à pied.

4. Like **bon,** the adverb **bien** cannot be used with **plus.** Its comparative form is **mieux. Mieux** is often used after **être** to describe a noun: La moto, c'est **mieux** que le vélo. Although **mieux** *acts as* an adjective, it does not agree with the noun it modifies.

 C6　Activité • Comparez　　Possible answers are given.

Voici des moyens de transport. Est-ce que vous pouvez les comparer entre eux? Utilisez les adjectifs donnés.

Le métro est moins cher que l'avion.

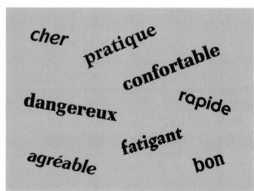

Le métro est meilleur que le bus.　L'avion est plus confortable / cher / rapide / pratique que le train.　La moto est plus dangereuse / agréable que la voiture.　La bicyclette est moins fatigante que la marche à pied.

C7　Activité • Quel moyen de transport?　Possible answers are given.

Vous sortez avec un(e) camarade. Il/Elle propose deux moyens de transport possibles. Choisissez un moyen et donnez la raison de votre choix. Utilisez les moyens de transport dans C6 et les adverbes **lentement** et **vite.** Changez de rôle.

— On prend le métro ou le bus pour aller au ciné?　—On prend la moto ou la voiture pour aller à l'école?
— Prenons le métro. Il va plus vite.　　　　　　　—Prenons la voiture. Elle va plus vite.
— Tu as raison. Le métro, c'est mieux.　　　　　—Tu as raison. La voiture, c'est mieux.

Regardez ces photos. Pouvez-vous comparer ces sites entre eux? Utilisez les adjectifs donnés.

joli   vieux   moderne   beau   ancien   grand   petit

La basilique de Notre-Dame-de-Fourvière

La cathédrale Saint-Jean

La place Bellecour

La gare de la Part-Dieu

La place des Terreaux

La place Bellecour est plus grande que la place des Terreaux.
La basilique Notre-Dame de Fourvière est moins ancienne que la cathédrale Saint-Jean.
La gare de la Part-Dieu est plus moderne que la basilique Notre-Dame de Fourvière.

Un dépaysé à Lyon   319

Activité • Ecoutez bien 🔊 For script and answers, see p. T194.

Plusieurs personnes discutent des moyens de transport à Lyon. Ecoutez leur conversation, et complétez le tableau avec les avantages et les inconvénients de chaque moyen.

le métro	le bus	le taxi	la marche à pied	le funiculaire

C10 Activité • Jeu de rôle   Possible completions are given.

Avec un(e) camarade, jouez les rôles d'Antoine et Philippe. Essayez de vous persuader l'un l'autre que votre sport préféré est mieux. Employez les expressions dans A4 du Chapitre 1 et le comparatif des adjectifs donnés.

— La musculation, j'adore! C'est intéressant et... c'est bon pour la santé, etc.
— Tu plaisantes! Le football, c'est mieux. C'est plus amusant que la musculation et moins dangereux.
— Mais je ne suis pas d'accord... Le foot, c'est fatigant.

> facile   difficile   dangereux
> fatigant   passionnant
> bon pour la santé
> ennuyeux   amusant

C11 Activité • Ecrivez   Possible comparisons are given.

Votre correspondant(e) français(e) va passer plusieurs semaines aux Etats-Unis. Il/Elle compte *(is planning)* visiter une ville que vous trouvez ennuyeuse. Dans une lettre, vous lui proposez de visiter une ville plus intéressante. Comparez les deux villes pour persuader votre correspondant(e) de visiter la ville que vous préférez.

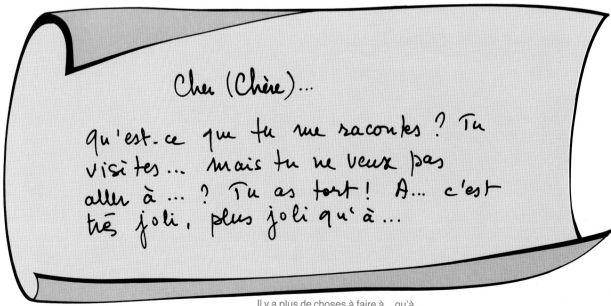

Cher (Chère)...

Qu'est-ce que tu me racontes? Tu visites... mais tu ne veux pas aller à...? Tu as tort! A... c'est très joli, plus joli qu'à...

Il y a plus de choses à faire à... qu'à...
C'est moins dangereux à... qu'à...
On s'amuse plus à... qu'à...
... est aussi cher que...

Antoine et Philippe sont montés à Fourvière.

ANTOINE   Voilà, nous y sommes! D'ici, on voit très bien Lyon!... La grande
tour, là-bas, c'est le quartier de la Part-Dieu où il y a la gare...
Les deux fleuves, c'est la Saône et le Rhône... En bas, tu as le
quartier Saint-Jean, c'est le vieux Lyon... Pas mal, hein?

PHILIPPE   Oui!

ANTOINE   Si on allait se promener?

PHILIPPE   Bonne idée, mais avant de partir, il faut que
j'aille dans une librairie acheter des bandes
dessinées. A la campagne, on ne trouve rien.

ANTOINE   Ton train part à quelle heure?

PHILIPPE   Vers huit heures.

ANTOINE   Oh, on a le temps!... Allons d'abord déjeuner
et après, en route pour la visite!

Vous êtes sur la colline de Fourvière avec un(e) ami(e). Il/Elle demande où se trouvent les endroits ou les monuments intéressants. Regardez le plan du centre de Lyon et répondez. Utilisez les expressions comme **à gauche (de)**, **à droite (de)**, **en face (de)**, **au fond (de)**, **devant**.

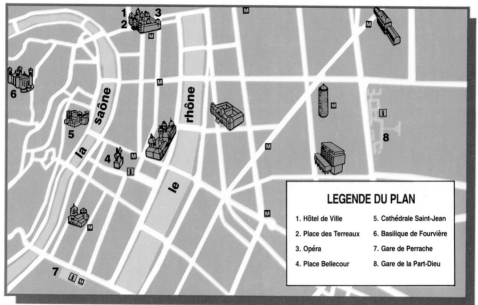

LEGENDE DU PLAN

1. Hôtel de Ville   5. Cathédrale Saint-Jean
2. Place des Terreaux   6. Basilique de Fourvière
3. Opéra   7. Gare de Perrache
4. Place Bellecour   8. Gare de la Part-Dieu

La Gare de Perrache se trouve à gauche de la Gare de la Part-Dieu. La Place Bellecour se trouve à droite de la cathédrale Saint-Jean. L'Hôtel de Ville se trouve à côté de la place des Terreaux. L'Opéra se trouve en face de la place des Terreaux.

C14   COMMENT LE DIRE
Reporting a series of events

D'abord, Antoine et Philippe décident où aller.
Ils choisissent ensuite un moyen de transport.
Après, Philippe achète des tickets de métro.
Les garçons arrivent enfin à Fourvière.

C15   Activité • A votre avis   Possible answer is given.

D'après leur conversation dans C12, qu'est-ce que vous pensez que Philippe et Antoine vont faire cet après-midi? Mettez les activités suivantes dans l'ordre chronologique.

aller au café   *visiter le vieux Lyon*
prendre le funiculaire
        aller à la gare
    acheter des bandes dessinées
se dire au revoir

Ils vont d'abord… Ensuite…
Après… Vers la fin de l'après-midi…
A sept heures et demie… Enfin…

Ils vont d'abord aller au café. Ensuite, ils vont prendre le funiculaire. Après, ils vont visiter le vieux Lyon. Vers la fin de l'après-midi, ils vont acheter des bandes dessinées. A sept heures et demie, ils vont aller à la gare. Enfin, ils vont se dire au revoir.

Il y a beaucoup de vieux monuments à voir à Lyon, la cathédrale Saint-Jean (XIe siècle), Notre-Dame-de-Fourvière (XIXe siècle), les maisons anciennes du vieux Lyon ou la place Bellecour avec sa statue du roi Louis XIV. Si vous préférez le Lyon moderne, allez au centre commercial de la Part-Dieu ou dans le quartier piétonnier *(pedestrian)*, autour de la place des Cordeliers.

Et si vous en avez assez de la ville, du bruit et de la pollution, allez vous promener au parc de la Tête d'Or, flânez *(stroll)* sur les quais de la Saône, ou allez vous détendre *(relax)* et faire de la planche à voile au parc de loisirs de Miribel-Jonage, à la sortie de Lyon.

A Lyon, il y a…

la cathédrale Saint-Jean

le quartier piétonnier

la place des Terreaux

la basilique de Notre-Dame-de-Fourvière

la place Bellecour

le parc de la Tête d'Or

le parc de loisirs de Miribel-Jonage

La cathédrale Saint-Jean or la primatiale Saint-Jean dates from the 11th century.
La basilique de Notre-Dame-de-Fourvière, built after the war of 1870, is the site of many pilgrimages.
La place Bellecour is one of the largest open plazas in France.
La place des Terreaux, the center of city life in Lyons, features a famous fountain.

Un dépaysé à Lyon   323

C17 Activité • Ecrivez

Avant de prendre le train, Philippe envoie une carte postale à sa sœur. Il raconte en quelques mots ce qu'il a fait et le temps qu'il faisait. Ecrivez sa carte. Possible answer: Chère... Lyon est une ville fantastique! Antoine est un très bon guide. Il connaît bien la ville. On a visité le vieux quartier. On a pris le métro et on est monté à Fourvière. De là-bas, on peut voir tout Lyon. Il a fait un temps splendide! Grosses bises, Philippe

C18 Activité • Jeu de rôle   Possible answers are given.

Philippe est rentré chez lui. Ses parents lui posent des questions sur Lyon et sur ce qu'il a fait. Faites le dialogue avec deux camarades de classe. Utilisez C1 et C10, mais aussi votre imagination.

LE PÈRE	Alors, tu as revu Antoine? Comment va-t-il?
PHILIPPE	... Il va bien.
LA MÈRE	Où est-ce qu'il habite?
PHILIPPE	... Il habite dans un appartement.
LA MÈRE	Est-ce que ses parents vont bien?

PHILIPPE	... Oui, ils vont bien aussi.
LA MÈRE	Qu'est-ce que vous avez fait, Antoine et toi?
PHILIPPE	... Nous avons beaucoup fait! Nous avons vu toute la ville.
LE PÈRE	... ? Est-ce que vous avez pris le métro? —Ah oui. Il est rapide et moderne.

C19 Activité • Et vous?

1. Avez-vous déjà reçu un(e) ami(e) chez vous?
2. Est-ce qu'il y a longtemps que vous ne l'avez pas vu(e)?
3. Combien de temps a-t-il/elle passé chez vous?
4. Pourquoi est-il/elle venu(e)?
5. Qu'est-ce que vous avez fait?

C20 COMMENT LE DIRE
Making suggestions

Si + the imperfect is used to make suggestions.

Si on allait se promener?	What if we went for a walk?
Si on prenait le métro?	What if we took the subway?
Si on allait au cinéma?	What if we went to the movies?

Do you recall these other ways to make suggestions?

Prenons le funiculaire!
On va acheter des bandes dessinées?
Pourquoi on ne va pas au centre ville?
Tu n'as pas envie d'acheter des vêtements?
Tu veux qu'on aille dans le vieux Lyon?

For expressions of indecision or indifference when responding to a suggestion, see Unit 3, p. 104. For refusing and giving reasons, see Unit 5, p. 157.

Activité • **Antoine fait des suggestions** Possible answers are given.

Antoine propose que vous fassiez les activités suivantes. Que dit-il?

visiter le quartier Saint-Jean — Si on visitait le quartier Saint-Jean?

1. faire le tour de Lyon
2. aller voir la place Bellecour
3. monter à Fourvière
4. prendre le métro

5. visiter le musée des Beaux Arts
6. acheter des bandes dessinées
7. aller au théâtre après le dîner

1. On va faire le tour de Lyon? 2. Allons voir la place Bellecour! 3. Pourquoi on ne monte pas à Fourvière? 4. Tu n'as pas envie de prendre le métro? 5. Et si on visitait le musée des Beaux Arts? 6. Allons acheter des bandes dessinées. 7. Ça te dit d'aller au théâtre après le dîner?

C22 Activité • **Faites des suggestions** Possible dialogue is given.

Proposez une activité à un(e) camarade. Il/Elle refuse. Puis vous proposez la même activité pour une heure ou un jour différent. Il/Elle accepte. Ensuite, changez de rôle.

aller à un concert — Pourquoi on ne va pas à un concert vendredi?
—Ça te dit de faire les boutiques ce soir? — Désolé(e). Je ne peux pas. Je travaille jusqu'à neuf heures.
—Je ne peux pas, je dois finir mes devoirs. — Si on y allait samedi soir?
—Et si on les faisait demain après-midi? — Oui, pourquoi pas?
—D'accord. Bonne idée!

1. faire les boutiques
2. se promener le long du Rhône
3. s'acheter une glace

4. visiter le vieux Lyon
5. prendre des photos
6. aller au parc d'attractions

Pour refuser

Désolé(e)... Je suis occupé(e)... Je ne peux pas... Je ne suis pas libre Je regrette mais...

Pour accepter

Si tu veux. Oui, pourquoi pas? Volontiers! D'accord. Bonne idée! Génial!

C23 Activité • **Philippe est difficile!** Possible answers are given.

Avec un(e) camarade de classe, complétez ce dialogue entre Antoine et Philippe.

ANTOINE … Ça te dit d'aller au théâtre de Guignol?
PHILIPPE Les marionnettes, c'est pour les enfants!
ANTOINE … Si on allait dans un restaurant?
PHILIPPE Non, vraiment, je n'ai pas faim.
ANTOINE … Pourquoi on ne visite pas le jardin Botanique?
PHILIPPE Je n'aime pas les jardins.

ANTOINE … Si on montait à Fourvière?
PHILIPPE Je suis fatigué; je n'en peux plus!
ANTOINE … Il y a un bon western au cinéma.
PHILIPPE Le ciné, encore!
ANTOINE Bon alors, qu'est-ce que tu proposes?
PHILIPPE … Je voudrais aller au parc d'attractions.
ANTOINE Bon, si tu veux. Je t'invite…

C24 Activité • **A vous maintenant!**

Vous avez envie de faire des tas de choses. Proposez à un(e) camarade de faire quelque chose avec vous. Il/Elle n'a pas l'air intéressé(e). Faites-lui des suggestions jusqu'à ce qu'il/elle accepte de venir. Changez de rôle.

1   Que de déménagements!

Sylvie Brunetière a été obligée de déménager plusieurs fois. Elle a vraiment fait le tour de la France! Elle nous montre des photos des endroits où elle a vécu, et elle nous raconte.

Je viens d'un petit village de Champagne. J'y ai habité jusqu'à l'âge de douze ans. J'aimais énormément vivre à la campagne. Le dimanche, nous allions nous promener avec mes parents. J'avais beaucoup d'amis, et j'en garde un très bon souvenir.

Ensuite, nous avons habité deux ans à Strasbourg, dans l'est. L'hiver, il faisait drôlement froid, il neigeait, et je faisais du ski de fond... Ma mère adore le théâtre, et nous allions souvent au TNS, un théâtre national où il y avait de merveilleux spectacles.

Quand j'ai passé mon bac, nous habitions à Bordeaux. Mon père était ingénieur et ma mère était professeur. Moi, j'étudiais... L'été, j'allais au bord de la mer à Arcachon. C'était super sympa! Nous sommes restés quatre ans dans le sud-ouest.

Maintenant, je suis à l'université à Lyon. Quand je suis arrivée il y a six mois, je ne connaissais pas et je me sentais un peu dépaysée. C'était difficile — Lyon est une grande ville pleine de voitures. Mais aujourd'hui, je suis habituée. C'est une ville tellement excitante!

Activité • Complétez

Complétez les phrases suivantes d'après «Que de déménagements!»

1. Sylvie vient d'un village de… Champagne.
2. Elle y a vécu jusqu'à l'âge de… douze ans.
3. Il y a un… à Strasbourg. théâtre national
4. Strasbourg est dans… de la France. l'est   professeur
5. Les parents de Sylvie travaillaient tous les deux à Bordeaux. Sa mère était… et son père était… ingénieur.
6. Quand elle habitait à Bordeaux, Sylvie passait ses vacances… au bord de la mer à Arcachon.
7. Sylvie a commencé ses études universitaires à… Lyon.
8. Elle trouve cette ville… excitante.

3 Activité • Devinez

Répondez aux questions suivantes.

1. Sylvie est plus ou moins âgée que vous?
2. A quel âge est-elle allée à Bordeaux?
3. Dans quelle région de France se trouve Strasbourg? Bordeaux?

4. Où faisait-il froid l'hiver?
5. Quelle ville était près de la mer?

1. Elle est plus âgée que moi.   2. Elle est allée à Bordeaux à l'âge de quatorze ans.   3. Strasbourg est dans l'est. Bordeaux est dans le sud-ouest.   4. Il faisait froid à Strasbourg en hiver.   5. Bordeaux était près de la mer.

4 Activité • D'habitude…

D'habitude, que faisait Sylvie dans chaque endroit où elle a vécu? Complétez le tableau avec ses activités habituelles.

Champagne	Strasbourg	Bordeaux	Lyon
Le dimanche, elle se promenait avec ses parents.	Elle faisait du ski du fond; elle allait au TNS.	L'été, elle allait au bord de la mer.	Maintenant, elle est à l'université.

5 Activité • Jeu de rôle   Possible questions are given.

Un(e) camarade joue le rôle de Sylvie. Vous lui posez des questions sur sa vie. Votre camarade répond d'après «Que de déménagements!» Si vous posez une question sans réponse dans le texte, votre camarade doit inventer une réponse logique. Ensuite, changez de rôle.

Tu viens d'où?
Pendant combien de temps est-ce que tu y as vécu?
Ça te plaisait ou pas?
C'était comment, Strasbourg? Où est-ce que tu as passé ton bac? Tu aimes Lyon? Où est-ce que tu habitais quand tu avais 13 ans?

6 Activité • Ecrivez   Possible answer is given.

Avec un(e) camarade de classe, choisissez un endroit où Sylvie a vécu. Imaginez son ancienne vie à cet endroit, et sa vie maintenant à Lyon. Comparez ses ami(e)s, ses vêtements, ses sorties, ses goûts et ses projets avec ceux de sa vie actuelle.

Quand Sylvie avait 14 ans, elle habitait à Strasbourg. En hiver, elle faisait du ski de fond. Elle portait des vêtements chauds. Maintenant, elle a 20 ans. Elle est étudiante à l'université à Lyon. Il fait beau, et elle porte des vêtements confortables. Elle a beaucoup d'amis, et ils sortent souvent ensemble.

Activité • **Sylvie accueille Florence**   Possible dialogue is given.

Florence, une amie d'enfance de Sylvie, a déménagé de Champagne à Lyon. Sylvie est contente de la revoir. Elles se donnent des nouvelles. Faites le dialogue avec un(e) camarade.

— Salut, Sylvie.
— Florence! Ça me fait plaisir de te voir! Ça fait longtemps que je ne t'ai pas vue.
— Presque neuf ans!...   —Comment ça va, tes parents?
—Ils vont très bien. Tu vas les voir. Ils t'ont invitée à dîner chez nous ce soir. Et ta famille?
—Mes parents vont bien aussi.

8   Activité • **Sylvie console Florence**

La vie en Champagne manque beaucoup à Florence. Elle en parle à Sylvie, et Sylvie essaie de la consoler. Faites le dialogue avec un(e) camarade. Ensuite, changez de rôle.
Refer students to A21, p. 306 for appropriate expressions.

9   Activité • **Ecrivez**

Vous avez passé une semaine à Lyon. Au retour, vous écrivez votre journal tous les jours. Inscrivez la date, les endroits où vous êtes allé(e), ce que vous avez fait, si ça vous a plu ou si vous n'avez pas aimé.

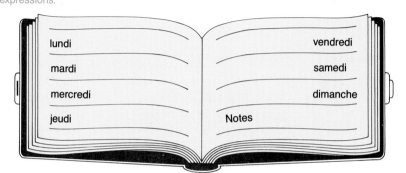

lundi	vendredi
mardi	samedi
mercredi	dimanche
jeudi	Notes

10   Activité • **Souvenir, souvenir...**   Possible answer is given.

Racontez un souvenir — bon ou mauvais — à un(e) camarade de classe. Dites avec qui vous étiez et décrivez le lieu, la situation, ce que vous avez fait...   Quand j'avais dix ans, je suis allé(e) à Chicago avec ma famille. C'était super! C'était en juin, et il faisait très beau. D'abord, nous avons visité la ville. Ensuite, nous sommes allés au musée. Ça m'a beaucoup plu. Après, nous sommes allés à un match de base-ball à Wrigley Field. Nous sommes enfin partis le lendemain.

11   Activité • **Situation**

Votre correspondant(e) français(e) passe huit jours chez vous. Vous décidez de ce que vous allez faire ensemble pendant son séjour. Faites-lui des suggestions. Il/Elle refuse quelques suggestions mais en accepte d'autres. Faites le dialogue avec un(e) camarade.
Refer students to C20, p. 324 for vocabulary for making, refusing, and accepting suggestions.

12   Activité • **Récréation**   (optional)

1. **Quel est cet animal?**
   Pour connaître le nom de cet animal de la ferme, prenez l'initiale de chacun des objets, et mettez ces lettres l'une après l'autre.   vache

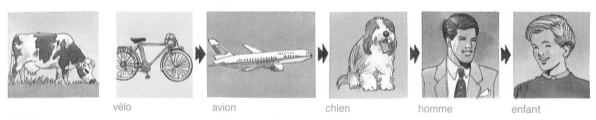

vélo   avion   chien   homme   enfant

2. **Enigme**
   Antoine demande à Philippe combien pèse sa valise. Philippe répond «sept kilos plus une demi-valise». Combien pèse la valise de Philippe?

   Solution : Dix kilos et demi.

For script, see pp. T198–200.

PRONONCIATION

Glides with /j/, /w/, and / ɥ /

1 Ecoutez bien et répétez.

1. Glides with /j/

diamant	voyage	pierre	papier	cahier	soulier
y a-t-il	payer	pied	panier	collier	

vieux	bien	lion	nous allons→nous allions
monsieur	sien	nous avions	vous allez→vous alliez
les yeux	lien	savions	
adieu	viande		

brouillard	fille	paille	soleil
maillot	travaille	feuille	œil
ailleurs	vieille	Antilles	travail
accueillant			

Le vieux monsieur travaille à Marseille.
Quand il se sent bien et qu'il fait du soleil, il y va à pied.

2. Glides with /w/

Louis	boire	loin	— Moi, j'ai soif. Et toi?
Louise	voir	coin	— Oui, allons voir ce qu'il y a à boire à la cantine.
souhait	droit	point	— Où est-ce que c'est? C'est loin?
jouer	soir	soin	— Non, là-bas. Juste au coin de la rue.

3. Glides with / ɥ /

puis	cuir	juillet	saluer	deux joints→deux juin
nuit	suivi	pluie	nuage	enfoui→enfui
lui	huit	bruit	juin	avec Louis→avec lui

Les nuages sont suivis par la pluie.
Louis a passé un mois avec lui, du huit juin au huit juillet.

2 Ecoutez et lisez.

— Tu as vu ces nuages?
— Oui, le temps est à la pluie.
— On ne peut pas rester sur la plage toute la nuit.
— Puis la gare Saint-Louis, c'est loin d'ici. Vite!
— Dépêche-toi. Prends le panier et allons-y!

3 Copiez les phrases suivantes pour préparer une dictée.

1. Le village où habitait Antoine n'est pas loin de Lyon.
2. Lyon, c'est bruyant et pollué par les voitures. Mais je suis habitué.
3. Ici, on peut voir les voisins deux ou trois fois par mois, on peut sortir après le travail, et les gens sont gentils.
4. Oui, je suis bien ici. Je ne regrette rien.

Answers are given. Some answers will vary.

SECTION A

Do you know how to make comparisons with nouns?
Complete these sentences. See A9, p. 302.
1. A la campagne, il y a _____ de chiens qu'en ville. autant
2. Il y a _____ de gens en ville qu'à la campagne. plus
3. En ville, il y a _____ de jardins qu'à la campagne. moins
4. On a _____ d'amis en ville qu'à la campagne. autant

Do you know how to form the imperfect of different verbs?
Complete this sentence by putting the following phrases in the imperfect.
    Quand j'habitais à la campagne,…
1. je (voir) mes copains tous les soirs. voyais
2. mes parents (inviter) nos voisins toutes les semaines. invitaient
3. ma sœur et moi, nous (se promener) en forêt. nous promenions
4. toute la famille (manger) dans le jardin en été. mangeait

Do you know how to say how much you miss something?
You've just moved to a new city. What are three expressions you might use to
say how much you miss your home town? See A21, p. 306. Je regrette...
C'était tellement mieux! C'était si bien!

Do you know how to console someone?
What might you say in these situations?
1. Votre ami(e) d'enfance, que vous n'avez pas vu(e) depuis trois ans, s'est
   installé(e) dans votre quartier. Il/Elle a le mal du pays. Ne regrette rien.
   Fais-toi une raison.
2. Votre ami(e), qui habite depuis toujours la même ville, va déménager à Paris.

SECTION B

Do you know how to renew old acquaintances?
What are two expressions you might use to greet a friend whom you haven't
seen for a long time. J'avais vraiment envie de te revoir!   Je suis content(e) de te revoir!

Do you know how to use the imperfect and the *passé composé*?
Complete this paragraph with the imperfect and the **passé composé**.

                                                                    étions
    C'est fini! Adieu, la ferme, la nature! Hier, nous (être) encore à la campagne.
voulions Nous (vouloir) profiter de cette dernière journée. Nous (se lever) à sept heures. nous sommes le
brillait Le soleil (briller) pour mieux nous dire au revoir. Nous (préparer) un pique-nique. avons prépa
est venu Tout le monde (venir). Nous (danser) jusqu'au soir. Vers huit heures, le car nous avons dansé
attendait (attendre). Nous (dire) au revoir. Puis nous (monter) dans le car et il (partir). est parti
                   avons dit   sommes montés

SECTION C

Do you know how to make comparisons with adjectives and adverbs?
Compare these means of transportation. See C5, p. 318.
le métro   le bus   la marche à pied   l'avion   la bicyclette   le taxi

Do you know how to report a series of events?
Tell four things that you did after school yesterday. Which was first? Next?
Afterward? Last? See C14, p. 322.

Do you know how to make suggestions using *si* + the imperfect?
Make these suggestions to a friend. Si on allait au théâtre? / prenait le métro? / achetait des livres?
1. aller au théâtre   2. prendre le métro   3. acheter des livres

Do you know other ways to make suggestions? See C20, p. 324.
Make the three suggestions above in different ways to a friend.

VOCABULAIRE

SECTION A

à cause de *because of*
actif, -ive *active*
adapter (s') *to get used to*
l' **air** (m.) *air*
la **Bourgogne** *Burgundy*
calme *calm*
consoler *to console*
culturellement *culturally*
déménager *to move*
dépaysé, -e *uprooted*
l' **espace** (m.) *room, space*
faire : (Ne) t'en fais pas!
  Don't worry!
fascinant, -e *fascinating*
un **lapin** *rabbit*
lyonnais, -e *from Lyon*
le **mal : avoir le mal du pays**
  to be homesick
manque : ... me manque
  I miss . . .
moins de *fewer, less*
la **nature** *nature*
occasion : avoir l'occasion
  de *to have the*
  opportunity
un **oiseau** (pl. -x) *bird*
plaindre (se) *to complain*
plaire (se) : Tu vas te
  plaire ici. *You're going to*
  like it here.
la **pollution** *pollution*
une **poule** *chicken*
profiter (de) *to take*
  advantage (of)
pur, -e *pure*
quelques *some*

raison : Fais-toi une raison.
  Make the best of it.
respirer *to breathe*
réveillé, -e *awakened*
riche *rich*
sert : Ça ne sert à rien. *It*
  doesn't do any good.
une **vache** *cow*
une **vingtaine** *about twenty*

SECTION B

un **chapeau** *hat*
depuis que *since*
dur, -e *hard, difficult*
embrasse : Tout le monde
  t'embrasse. *Everyone*
  sends you their love.
une **exposition** *show, exhibit*
une **grève** *strike;* **une grève des**
  transports en commun
  public transportation strike
imaginer *to imagine*
longtemps : Ça fait
  longtemps que je ne t'ai
  pas vu! *It's been a long*
  time since I've seen you; **Il**
  y a si longtemps!
  It's been such a long time!
neuf : Quoi de neuf?
  What's new?
obligé, -e *obliged*
parfaitement *perfectly*
pleurer *to cry*
la **pluie** *rain*
quitter *to leave*
râler *to complain, fume*

les **retrouvailles** (f.) *reunion*
la **scène** *scene*
un **souvenir** *memory*
trempé, -e *soaked*

SECTION C

la **basilique** *basilica*
un **carnet** *booklet (of tickets,*
  stamps, etc.)
certain, -e *certain*
comme : Comme tu
  veux. *If you want.*
en bas *down below*
fatigant, -e *tiring*
un **funiculaire** *cable car*
général, -e *general*
idéal, -e *ideal*
idée : se faire une idée de
  to get a feel for
là-haut *up there* (en hout)
un(e) **Lyonnais(e)** *person who*
  lives in Lyon
la **marche** *walking*
moderne *modern*
paraît : il paraît (que) *it*
  seems (that)
pratique *practical*
proposer *to propose,*
  suggest
rapide *fast*
route : En route! *Let's get*
  going!
tout de même *anyway*
vite *quickly*

ETUDE DE MOTS   fatigant, fascinant

Find two adjectives in the list above that contain the suffix **-ant**. What is the English -ing equivalent of **-ant**? Adjectives with the suffix **-ant** are often formed from verbs. What are the **-ant** adjectives that come from these verbs?

amuser	**exciter**	**fortifier**	**nourrir**	**passionner**
amusant	excitant	fortifiant	nourrissant	passionnant

A LIRE

Vive la grève! ▭

Avant de lire

Pouvez-vous imaginer la ville de Paris sans électricité, sans métro? Comment va-t-on à l'école? Au travail? Avec un(e) camarade de classe, faites une liste des avantages et des inconvénients de cette situation.

Possible advantages: Il n'y a pas d'école, pas de travail. On peut rester à la maison. On peut se reposer, jouer avec des amis.

Une grève du métro et de l'électricité peut paralyser la ville. Qu'en pensent les Parisiens? Certains prennent les choses du bon côté! D'autres…

Possible disadvantages: On ne peut pas regarder la télé. On ne peut pas écouter des disques. Il n'y a pas de métro, on doit rester à la maison. On doit prendre un repas froid.

(Nadine Tanière, juriste)
Habituellement, je suis calme et réservée; tranquille, comme ma province natale. Mais en réalité, ma nature profonde est agressive et râleuse°. Avec la grève, je me défoulais°! Je rouspétais° pour un oui ou pour un non. Ça m'amusait. Je ne suis pas faite pour la tranquillité de la province.

(Fabienne Dumont, télépromotrice°)
Paris, c'est une ville bruyante, d'accord. Mais je me suis rendue compte qu'à cause de la grève, les Parisiens se parlaient! En province, les gens sont plus râleurs que les Parisiens. Ils se plaignent, ils rouspètent. Les Parisiens, au contraire, essayaient toujours de prendre les choses du bon côté. Ils avaient de l'humour. J'aime bien la province, mais je préfère Paris, même si c'est bruyant!

juriste: legal expert, not necessarily a practicing lawyer

---

râleuse *complaining;* **défoulais** *let off steam;* **rouspétais** *griped;* **télépromotrice** *property developer who works over the phone*

(Gilles Leroy, agent de voyage)

A Paris, je marchais tout le temps pendant la grève du métro pour faire les courses, pour aller à un rendez-vous, au restaurant. Tout le monde marchait. J'aimais bien la ville un peu désorganisée, le bruit, les embouteillages°, les klaxons°. Les feux étaient en panne°, on se bousculait° partout. A cause des coupures d'électricité°, nous organisions avec des amis des petits dîners tranquilles aux chandelles. Ça me plaisait beaucoup.

(Jean-Pierre Moreau, garçon de café)

Notre patron a perdu 70 000 F en trois semaines de grève. C'est trois ans de vacances en moins pour lui. Notre chiffre d'affaires° était de 30 pour cent inférieur à la normale pendan la grève du métro! Le café était très calme, les clients rares. Le patron perdait de l'argent, et moi, j'en perdais aussi! Je suis payé au pourcentage. J'ai perdu 3 000 F. C'est la vie!

(Dominique Péric, employé à la RATP°)

Pendant la grande grève à Paris, j'étais là, je renseignais les gens. Ils me demandaient pourquoi le métro ne marchait pas. Je leur expliquais qu'il y avait une grève. Ils étaient furieux. Ils disaient, «En province ça n'arrive jamais!» «C'est vrai, je répondais, mais en province il n'y a pas de métro. La vie est trop calme là-bas! Même les oiseaux s'y ennuient! Alors qu'ici...»

Activité • Qui est-ce?

Répondez aux questions suivantes d'après «Vive la grève!»

Gilles Leroy

1. Qui préparait des dîners aux chandelles?
2. Qui renseignait les gens? Dominique Péric
3. Qui était râleur et agressif? Nadine Tanière

4. Qui a perdu de l'argent? Jean-Pierre Moreau
5. Qui a remarqué que les Parisiens étaient gentils? Fabienne Dumont

Activité • Imaginez

Possible answer is given.

Je suis rentré(e). J'ai fait mes devoirs aux chandelles. J'ai mangé un sandwich

Il y avait une panne d'électricité chez vous hier soir. Qu'est-ce que vous avez fait? Qu'est-ce que vous n'avez pas pu faire? froid.Le frigo ne marchait pas. J'ai téléphoné aux amis, mais je ne pouvais pas les voir parce qu'il n'y avait pas de métro. Je n'ai pas pu regarder la télé. Je voulais écouter des disques, mais c'était impossible! Je me suis couché(e) tôt.

---

les embouteillages *traffic jams;* **les klaxons** *horns;* **les feux étaient en panne** *the traffic lights were out of order;* **se bousculait** *jostled;* **des coupures d'électricité** *power cuts;* **chiffre d'affaires** *sales figures;* **RATP = Régie autonome des transports parisiens** *Parisian transportation authority*

L'Embouteillage°

Feu vert Feu vert Feu vert!
Le chemin est ouvert!
Tortues° blanches, tortues grises, tortues noires.
Tortues têtues Tintamarre°!
Les autos crachotent°,
Toussotent°, cahotent°
Quatre centimètres
Puis toutes s'arrêtent.

Feu rouge Feu rouge Feu rouge!
Pas une ne bouge!
Tortues jaunes, tortues beiges, tortues noires,
Tortues têtues Tintamarre!
Hoquettent° s'entêtent°,
Quatre millimètres,
Pare-chocs à pare-chocs
Les voitures stoppent.

Blanches, grises, vertes, bleues,
Tortues à la queue leu leu°,
Jaunes, rouges, beiges, noires,
Tortues têtues Tintamarre!
Bloquées dans vos carapaces
Regardez-moi bien : je passe!

Activité • Vrai ou faux?

1. Les voitures s'avancent quand il y a le feu rouge.
2. Les voitures roulent lentement dans un embouteillage.
3. Il y a peu de bruit pendant un embouteillage.

1. C'est faux. Elles s'arrêtent au feu rouge.   2. C'est vrai.
3. C'est faux. Il y a beaucoup de bruit pendant un embouteillage.

Activité • Avez-vous compris? Possible answers are given.

Répondez aux questions suivantes d'après le poème.

1. A quoi est-ce que l'auteur compare les voitures?
2. A votre avis, est-ce que cette comparaison est juste? Pourquoi?
3. D'après vous, quel moyen de transport est-ce que l'auteur emploie?

1. L'auteur les compare aux tortues.   2. A mon avis, la comparaison est juste. Dans un embouteillage, les voitures avancent aussi lentement que les tortues.   3. Il est à pied parce que lui, il passe.

Activité • Ecrivez Possible answer: Il y a beaucoup de voitures de toutes les couleurs. Elles vont lentement.

C'est un embouteillage. Quand le feu est vert, quelques voitures passent, mais ça
Pouvez-vous résumer *(summarize)* en quelques phrases ce qui se passe dans le poème?
n'avance pas très vite. L'auteur est à pied. Il/elle va plus vite que les voitures.

---

l'embouteillage *traffic jam;*   **tortues** *turtles;*   **tintamarre** *racket, noise;*   **crachotent** *sputter;*   **toussotent** *cough slightly;*   **cahotent** *bump along;*   **hoquettent** *hiccup;*   **s'entêtent** *persist;*   **à la queue leu leu** *single file;*   **carapaces** *shells*

Les Charpentier déménagent

Dans cette histoire, une famille de cinq enfants, père, mère et grand-mère, a quitté la province pour déménager à Paris. Ils expriment des sentiments mixtes devant ce déménagement.

Avant de lire

Dans une famille de trois générations, qui s'adapte facilement à un changement de domicile *(home)*? Qui a du mal à s'y adapter?

Un véritable spectacle : le père, la mère, la grand-mère et les cinq enfants. Ils ont débarqué hier. Ils venaient de Yerres, près de Paris, où ils vivaient depuis des générations. Le père est représentant en tissus. Sa firme l'a muté° à Paris. La mère est institutrice. Au début, elle n'était pas contente. Elle disait :

— Paris, c'est l'enfer, le bruit, les lycées surpeuplés. C'est les mauvaises fréquentations pour les enfants. On se fait attaquer dans la rue, dans le métro. J'aime bien mieux Yerres. C'est plus propre°, plus humain.

Les enfants, eux, étaient contents de déménager à Paris. Ils en avaient assez de l'ennui de la province, du manque de distractions. Rémy, l'aîné, disait :

— On peut rien faire quand il pleut à Yerres. Et quand on a regardé la télé pendant une demi-journée, on a vraiment envie d'autre chose. A Paris, au moins, il y a la ville, les gens, le rythme d'une grande cité! Le spectacle est dans la rue, quoi! Moi, j'aime.

---

muté *transferred*; **propre** *clean*
représentant en tissus: cloth (fabric) salesman
Yerres: a small town 23 km. south of Paris

Sa sœur, Yvette, treize ans, aime aussi.

— Je m'ennuyais à mourir à Yerres! Où j'étais, il n'y avait pas moyen de rencontrer des jeunes intéressants. Tous banlieusards°, ennuyeux comme la pluie. Mes meilleures copines sont à Paris. Elles vont et viennent, elles rencontrent des copines, elles vont au ciné, au café. Demain, avec Chantal, nous allons écouter un groupe de rock. C'est ça, Paris!

Le père, lui, est très heureux aussi. Ce déménagement est une véritable promotion. Il a toujours aimé la ville, l'action, la compétition.

— Ah, oui. Je suis très heureux. Je ne regrette absolument pas Yerres. A mon avis, la vie n'est pas plus dure à Paris qu'en province. C'est vrai, ce n'est pas toujours facile de trouver un bon logement. Mais une fois trouvé, je préfère encore l'excitation et le bruit de la ville à l'ennui profond de la province. Entre ville bruyante et province tranquille, moi, j'ai enfin choisi la ville. Et cette ville, c'est Paris!

Grand-mère, elle, ne dit rien. Elle finit de ranger la cuisine dans le nouvel appartement. Elle écoute, hoche la tête. Maintenant, elle est en train de faire du café. Elle dit à mi-voix°, en regardant les trois plus jeunes enfants commencer une partie de Monopoly :

— Moi, on ne m'a pas demandé mon avis. Alors, je ne dis rien.

Et elle va s'installer près de la fenêtre qui donne sur le parc. Sylvie, la petite dernière, trois ans à peine, voulait savoir à quoi pensait sa grand-mère. Celle-ci pensait au joli pavillon° de Yerres. Elle rêvait aux petites collines couvertes de coquelicots au printemps, à l'Essonne° qui rejoint la Seine, aux bals musette° qu'elle ne verra° plus. Elle pensait aux rives de l'Yerres.

---

banlieusards *suburbanites*; **à mi-voix** *in a soft voice*; **pavillon** *small house*; **l'Essonne** *river that feeds into the Seine*; **bals musette** *popular dance with accordion music*; **verra** (future) = *voit*

Activité • Devinez

Choisissez l'équivalent anglais des mots soulignés dans chaque phrase.

1. Ils ont débarqué hier.
   - **a.** *climbed in*
   - **b.** *arrived*

2. Les lycées sont surpeuplés.
   - **a.** *overcrowded*
   - **b.** *inferior*

3. C'est les mauvaises fréquentations pour les enfants.
   - **a.** *bad company*
   - **b.** *bad frequencies*

4. Elle écoute, hoche la tête.
   - **a.** *lifts her head*
   - **b.** *shakes her head*

5. Les trois plus jeunes enfants commencent une partie de Monopoly.
   - **a.** *a party*
   - **b.** *a game*

Activité • Complétez

1. Les Charpentier ont vécu longtemps…
2. Ils ont déménagé à Paris parce que…
3. D'après…, la vie en ville était dangereuse.
4. Rémy a dit qu'on… en province.
5. Yvette trouvait les jeunes en province…
6. D'après le père, Paris était… et la province était…

1. à Yerres. 2. la firme de M. Charpentier l'a muté à Paris. 3. Mme Charpentier 4. ne peut rien faire quand il pleut
5. très ennuyeux. 6. une ville bruyante/tranquille.

Activité • Avez-vous bien lu?

Répondez aux questions suivantes d'après «Les Charpentier déménagent».

1. Pourquoi est-ce que Rémy, Yvette et leur père sont contents d'être à Paris?

   Ils trouvent que la province est ennuyeuse. Ils préfèrent la ville où il y a beaucoup à faire, beaucoup de gens différents.

2. Pourquoi est-ce que leur mère et leur grand-mère ne sont pas contentes?

   Elles préfèrent la vie tranquille. La mère pense que la ville est trop dangereuse pour les enfants. La grand-mère aime beaucoup les jolies fleurs et les collines de la campagne. Elle aime les bals musette de la province.

Activité • A votre avis   Possible answer is given.

Pourquoi est-ce que la grand-mère est venue à Paris avec la famille? Quels en sont les avantages pour elle? Pour les autres membres de la famille?

La grand-mère ne voulait pas rester seule à Yerres. Chez ses enfants, elle prépare la cuisine et elle fait le ménage.

Activité • Jeu de rôle

Un soir, après quelques mois à Paris, M. Charpentier rentre chez lui avec une mauvaise nouvelle. Il annonce à Rémy, Yvette, sa femme et la grand-mère que sa firme le mute encore — il faut retourner à Yerres. Que dit chaque membre de la famille? Faites la conversation avec quatre camarades de classe.

CHAPITRE 10 Voyage à Arles

	BASIC MATERIAL	COMMUNICATIVE FUNCTIONS
PREMIER CONTACT	Arles—Monuments et Musées (1) En Camargue (3)	Reading for global comprehension and cultural awareness
SECTION A	Projet de voyage (A1) Rendez-vous manqué? (A5) Arrêt à Berre (A21) Pour le pique-nique (A23)	**Exchanging information** • Making preparations for a trip **Expressing feelings, emotions** • Expressing impatience **Socializing** • Making excuses
SECTION B	Visite d'Arles (B1)	**Exchanging information** • Talking about sightseeing • Making comparisons **Expressing feelings, emotions** • Expressing relief and regret
SECTION C	Dernières heures (C1) Le matériel photo (C7)	**Exchanging information** • Telling about past events **Expressing attitudes, opinions** • Expressing lack of interest
TRY YOUR SKILLS	La séance diapo (1)	

■ **Prononciation** (the ghost **h**; **l** and **gn**; dictation)   371
■ **Vérifions!** 372 ■ **Vocabulaire** 373

A LIRE	**Alerte au château de Rambouillet** (adventure in the **Château de Rambouillet**)

WRITING   A variety of controlled and open-ended writing activities appear in the Pupil's Edition. The Teacher's Notes identify other activities suitable for writing practice.

COOPERATIVE LEARNING   Many of the activities in the Pupil's Edition lend themselves to cooperative learning. For guidelines, see page T14.

Scope and Sequence

GRAMMAR	CULTURE	RE-ENTRY
	History of **Arles** The **Camargue** region	
The interrogative pronouns **qui est-ce qui, qui est-ce que, qu'est-ce qui** (A12)	School trips and government-sponsored educational projects The city of **Berre** and its industry	Asking permission Giving advice Asking questions Interrogative pronouns
Making comparisons: superlatives of adjectives and adverbs (B6)	The sights of **Arles** **Provence** Van Gogh and Cézanne	Making comparisons with nouns, adjectives, and adverbs
The past infinitive (C10)	**Arles:** the national center of photography	The **passé composé** Inviting friends

Recombining communicative functions, grammar, and vocabulary

Reading for practice and pleasure

UNIT RESOURCES **Cahier d'Activités, Cahier d'Exercices,** Unit 10 Cassettes, Transparencies 24–26 (also 31, 31A), Quizzes 22–24, Unit 10 Test

TEACHER-PREPARED MATERIALS **Premier Contact** Books of Van Gogh's paintings; pictures of ancient peoples, plants, birds, rice, horses, bulls; **Section A** Map of France; pictures of a chemical factory, solvents, pesticides, picnic; **Section B** Picture of a bullfight; reproductions of works by Cézanne and Van Gogh; **Section C** Toy camera, photographic equipment

PREMIER CONTACT

The authentic material in **Premier Contact** introduces the theme of the unit. Concentrate only on the general content of these documents. A detailed treatment of the grammar and vocabulary is not intended. Since students should be reading for global comprehension, they need not know the meaning of every word. For this reason, new words in **Premier Contact** have been omitted from the unit vocabulary list and the French-English Vocabulary at the end of the book.

OBJECTIVES To read for global comprehension and cultural awareness; to get acquainted with the topic

1   Arles—Monuments et Musées

Obtain books from the library that show Van Gogh's paintings. Gather pictures of ancient Greeks, Romans, and Gauls. Showing the pictures, tell students about the history of **Provence** and **Arles;** use the information given in the introductory paragraph.

Then play the cassette as the students look at the photos and read along in their books. Ask students to find one word in each caption to identify the photo: **C'est un théâtre, C'est des bains,** and so on. Ask them which place they would like to visit.

2   Activité • Cherchez des renseignements

As students scan the photos and captions in **Contact 1,** read each question aloud. Call on individuals as they find the answers.

3   EN CAMARGUE

Gather pictures of plants, birds, rice, horses, and bulls. Point out the **Camargue** region on a wall map of France. Give students a brief commentary in French about the **Camargue,** using your pictures to illustrate your talk. Refer to your picture of a horse or draw one on the board to illustrate **le crin,** the coarse hair of the mane and tail of a horse. Before you have students open their books, write on the board or on a transparency a few words from the text that students are likely to recognize: **pénètre, réserve, plantes, paradis, située, triangle, forme, désertique, troupeaux sauvages.** Ask students to guess their English equivalents. Then write **location** and **caravane;** explain that these are **faux amis.** Tell students that **location** means *rental* and **caravane** a *camper* or *recreational vehicle.*

Now have students read along as you play the cassette. They should look at the map and identify in French what they see.

4   Activité • La visite continue

Have students pair off to take turns asking and answering the questions. Then call for a volunteer to answer each question.

5   Activité • Faisons du camping

Ask students **Qui fait du camping? Est-ce que vous aimez faire du camping? Où est-ce que vous allez?** Then tell them that they're going camping in the **Camargue.** For cooperative learning, have students pair off, read the ad for the **Crin-Blanc** campground, and find the answers to the questions.

CHALLENGE   Ask students to pair off and prepare a dialogue about their planned camping trip to the **Camargue.**

SECTION
A

OBJECTIVES   **To exchange information:** making preparations for a trip; **to express feelings, emotions:** express impatience; **to socialize:** make excuses

CULTURAL BACKGROUND   **Arles** nestles by the Rhône River, about 55 miles (88.5 kilometers) inland from the Mediterranean Sea and approximately 450 miles (724 kilometers) south of Paris. **Arles** is a very old city, with many ancient works in stone: Roman aqueducts, monuments, and theaters. One would expect an artist to be fascinated by these antiquities, but the artist who brought scenes of **Arles** to the art salons and museums of the world paid no attention to them. Instead, Vincent Van Gogh was thrilled by the light and color of **Arles.** He painted the bright southern sun above wheat fields, beautiful orchards, sunflowers, and the people of **Arles.**

MOTIVATING ACTIVITY   Initiate a discussion about school field trips **(des voyages scolaires).** Have students talk about one they're going to take or about those they've taken. Ask questions: **Allez-vous faire un voyage scolaire cette année? Avez-vous fait un voyage scolaire l'année dernière? Où allez-vous (êtes-vous allé(e)(s))? Avec qui? Pour quoi faire? Aimez-vous faire des voyages scolaires?** and so on.

Projet de voyage

On a wall map of France, trace the route Mme Leroy and her students will take as you read aloud the itinerary. Then play the cassette as students look at the photos and follow along in their books. Point out how the dates and times of day are written on the itinerary. Give some dates in English and have students practice saying or writing them in French. Then have students practice changing official time to conversational time and vice versa.

Have students close their books. Read aloud various activities planned by Mme Leroy **(arrêt à Berre)** and have students try to recall on which day each is scheduled **(le premier jour).**

A 2   **Activité • Avez-vous compris?**

SLOWER-PACED LEARNING   Students look at the itinerary in A1 as you ask the questions. They jot down on their papers a word or two that answers each question.

CHALLENGE   Students consult the itinerary in A1 to find the answers to the questions. They jot down a word or two in reply to each one. The student who finishes first and answers all the questions correctly wins.

A 3   **Activité • A vous maintenant!**

First brainstorm with the class ways of asking for, granting, and refusing permission (Unit 2, C8, page 69). Then have students suggest various questions their parents might ask about the planned field trip. Next role-play the situation with the class. You play the student who asks permission to go on the trip to **Arles.** The class assumes the role of the parents; individuals respond to your remarks. Finally, form groups of three students each and have them prepare their own scenarios. Call on volunteers to present their conversations to the class.

A4   Savez-vous que... ?

Play the cassette or read this cultural note aloud to students as they follow along in their books. Ask students to reread the selection and find as many reasons as they can to justify taking field trips. You might also ask students to propose their own ideas for a **Projet d'action educative.**

A5   RENDEZ-VOUS MANQUE?

Have students look at the photos first; ask individuals what Alexandra is doing in each one. Then read the dialogue aloud or play the cassette. Tell the students to listen carefully to find two reasons why Alexandra is late this morning. **(Elle cherche son pull rouge. Elle a oublié son appareil-photo.)** Ask volunteers to summarize the situation in simple French sentences.

A6   Activité • Vrai ou faux?

Call on individuals to read these sentences aloud, say whether they are true or false, and correct them if they are false.

SLOWER-PACED LEARNING   You might use this as a listening comprehension activity. With books closed, students write **vrai** or **faux** on their papers as you read the sentences aloud.

A7   Activité • Complétez

For several of these sentences, there is more than one possible completion. Accept meaningful variations.

SLOWER-PACED LEARNING   Write a list of choices on the board or on a transparency from which students may select appropriate completions.

A8   Activité • Et vous?

Tell students first to imagine their destination and then to list five things they would take on their field trip. When students have completed their lists, individuals read their lists aloud. Their classmates try to guess the destination of the trip and the activity planned.

SLOWER-PACED LEARNING   Prepare in advance a list including things that one would and would not take on a field trip. Identify the destination of the trip. Pass out copies of the list and have students cross out those objects that would be inappropriate.

A9   Activité • Quelques recommandations

You may want to review the present subjunctive forms of verbs before students begin this activity (Unit 5, A11, page 160).

CHALLENGE   To re-enter the function of assuring someone and the use of **aller** + infinitive, have "Michel" answer his "mother" or "father" **(Il ne faut pas que tu manges trop!)** by saying **Je t'assure que je ne vais pas trop manger.**

A10   Activité • A vous maintenant!

For cooperative learning, form groups of four. Have the students in each group brainstorm as many logical completions as they can for the incomplete sentences in the boxes. Then have each group split up into pairs to prepare dialogues. Ask volunteers to present their dialogues in front of the class.

CHALLENGE   Tell the class to pretend to be students on the waiting bus and to call out either expressions of encouragement or irritation to Alexandra.

A 11   VOUS EN SOUVENEZ-VOUS? 🔊

Review interrogative pronouns as students keep their books closed. First read aloud the sample questions in the box. Ask students to listen for and repeat the "question word," or the interrogative pronoun. Then have them tell what information the question asks for. Next have students answer each question. Finally, elicit additional questions using the same interrogative pronouns. Tell students to open their books; read the summary together.

A 12   STRUCTURES DE BASE

Continue the discussion of interrogative pronouns begun in A11. Ask students what function the pronouns serve. (They ask for information.) Ask how you can tell if someone is asking about people or things. (**Qui** refers to people; **que, qu'est-ce que,** and **quoi** refer to things.) Now tell students that **qui** has two longer forms, one when it is the subject and the other when it is the object.

Subject	**Object**
Qui a dit ça?	Qui appelez-vous?
Qui est-ce qui a dit ça?	Qui est-ce que vous appelez?
(Who said that?)	*(Whom are you calling?)*

You may wish to explain that the longer form calls more attention to itself, adding greater emphasis.

Now tell students that **que** also has two longer forms, one used as a subject and the other used as an object.

Subject	**Object**
Qu'est-ce qui arrive?	Que voulez-vous?
(What is happening?)	Qu'est-ce que vous voulez?
	(What do you want?)

Draw students' attention to the use of **qui est-ce que** and **qu'est-ce que** to avoid inverting the subject and verb.

Remind students about the interrogative forms that they've been using after prepositions: **qui** for *whom* (people) and **quoi** for *what* (things).

Avec qui vas-tu au cinéma?	De quoi parlez-vous maintenant?
Pour qui as-tu acheté ces fleurs?	A quoi penses-tu?

Finally, have students open their books and read silently the explanation in A12. Respond to any questions.

A 13   Activité • Trouvez les réponses 🔊

Be sure students working in pairs change roles so that each one asks and answers the questions.

CHALLENGE   Have each pair continue the discussion by asking additional questions: **Que fait ton oncle? Combien de temps vas-tu passer chez eux? Quand allez-vous rentrer?**

A 14   Activité • Trouvez les questions 🔊

SLOWER-PACED LEARNING   Ask the appropriate questions at random. Students read the answers and write the number of the appropriate one.

A 15 Activité • Encore des questions

SLOWER-PACED LEARNING Ask students to tell you the English equivalent for **quelque chose.** Then ask them what interrogative pronouns they would use to ask questions about **quelque chose (que, qu'est-ce que, qu'est-ce qui).** Write these on the board. Then do the same for **quelqu'un.** Now, for cooperative learning, have students work in pairs or small groups to compose the questions. When all have finished, ask volunteers to give each question; encourage others to give an appropriate answer.

CHALLENGE Have students pair off and prepare dialogues, using the sentences as cues. They read the statements and ask questions relating to them:

—Pierre lit quelque chose.
—Qu'est-ce qu'il lit?
—Je ne sais pas, peut-être une bédé.

A 16 Activité • Et vous?

To emphasize the use of the prepositions, have students give brief answers to these questions, beginning their answers with the preposition: **A quoi est-ce que vous vous intéressez? (Aux jeux vidéo.)**

A 17 COMMENT LE DIRE

Dramatize the expressions of impatience as you model them for students. Insist that students use appropriate expression as they repeat. Have them express their impatience. **(Vite! On est en retard!)** Give appropriate responses. **(Attendez! Je cherche mon pull!)** Then reverse roles; you urge them to hurry, and they respond appropriately.

Present the expressions for making excuses in the same manner. Make suggestions or extend invitations and have students respond with an appropriate excuse. Then reverse roles.

A 18 Activité • Alexandra est toujours en retard

SLOWER-PACED LEARNING Before students work in pairs, ask volunteers to change the five statements to the first person, as if Alexandra were saying them. Tell students that they might make three-line dialogues beginning with **Mais qu'est-ce que tu fais?**

A 19 Activité • Alexandra n'a pas le temps

First have students work by themselves, reading Bernard's lines and writing down some hurried responses that Alexandra might give. Then read aloud Bernard's lines and call on several volunteers to respond as Alexandra. Finally, have students work in pairs to practice the telephone conversation.

A 20 Activité • Jeu de rôle

Tell students to write down as many completions as they can for the sentences in the model. Call on volunteers to read their suggestions aloud. Then brainstorm with the class ways of insisting: **Allez! Sois gentil(le)! Tu as assez de temps!** Have volunteers act out their skits for the class.

A 21 ARRET A BERRE

Review Mme Leroy's itinerary by tracing it, with a stopover at **Berre,** on a wall map of France. Bring in pictures of a chemical factory, solvents, pesticides, and a picnic to use in teaching new vocabulary. Using the map and the pictures, tell students about the stopover in **Berre** in French. Then play the cassette as students follow along in their books. Ask questions to check comprehension. Ask students to read aloud the sentences that express Eric's reaction to the factory tour and Julie's reaction to the trip.

A 22 Activité • Répondez

Have students pair off to take turns asking and answering the questions. Remind students that they will have to use the preposition from the question in their answer.

A 23 POUR LE PIQUE-NIQUE

Play the cassette as students look at the illustration and repeat the vocabulary. Have them work in pairs, quizzing each other on the vocabulary. Bring in a picnic basket containing all the items shown. Students should ask what you have in the basket:

> —Est-ce qu'il y a une baguette dans le panier?
> —Oui, il y a une baguette. *(Take out the bread and put it on the table.)*
>   (Non, il n'y a pas de baguette.)

After you've placed all the items on the table, use a TPR technique to direct students to replace the items in the basket: **Pierre, mettez les biscuits dans le panier, s'il vous plaît.** The student follows instructions and then says what he or she has done: **J'ai mis les biscuits dans le panier.**

A 24 Activité • A vous maintenant!

For cooperative learning, divide the class into groups of four. Each group plans a picnic, and a leader is chosen by each group to direct the planning. Another student acts as recorder, writing down the time, the meeting place, the picnic spot, and who is bringing what. The group should also plan activities for the day such as a game of volleyball, a boat ride on a nearby lake, a walk in the woods, and so on. These should be written down also. A reporter from each group should report the group's plans to the class.

A 25 Activité • Et vous?

For homework, you might have students organize their answers to the questions in a paragraph.

A 26 Activité • Ecrivez

Review A1, A5, and A21 with students, or brainstorm with them the information their messages might include. Give students several minutes to write their messages. Collect and correct them. The next day, have students pair off to role-play a mother and father. Distribute half the messages, one to each pair. The "parents" should read the message and react to it, with either approval or disapproval.

A 27 **Activité • Ecoutez bien**

On the morning of the class trip to **Arles,** nothing seems to be going right for Mme Leroy. Open your book to page 351. *(pause)* Read the incomplete sentences and the suggested completions in A27 silently. *(pause)* Listen as Mme Leroy takes care of some annoying last-minute problems. Be prepared to indicate your answers on a separate sheet of paper. **Ecoutez bien.**

Allez, dépêchez-vous! Nous ne sommes pas en avance!... Tiens, le car n'est pas encore arrivé? Que fait le chauffeur? Il est déjà dix heures et demie!... Ah, le voilà! Mettez vite vos bagages dans le car!... Très bien, on peut partir!... Mais où est Alexandra?... Alexandra!... C'est pas possible, qu'est-ce qu'elle fait? Elle est toujours en retard! Florence, va lui téléphoner pour savoir si elle arrive!... On ne va jamais être à Arles à cinq heures!... Zut, je n'ai pas pensé au pique-nique! Chloé! Eric! Voici de l'argent : allez nous acheter du pain et du fromage. On vous attend, faites vite!... Eh, François, où vas-tu?... Qu'est-ce que tu dis? Chercher quoi?... Ton appareil-photo? Où l'as-tu oublié?... Bon, vas-y, mais dépêche-toi!... Ça y est, il pleut! Ah, ça commence bien! Quelqu'un a un parapluie à me prêter?... Ah, te voilà, Alexandra. Monte dans le car... Bon, tout le monde est là, Florence, Alexandra, Chloé, Eric?... En route! Mais... Chauffeur! Où êtes-vous?... Notre chauffeur a disparu!... Ah, vous êtes là! Nous sommes prêts, on peut y aller!... Comment?... Non, c'est pas vrai! Le car est en panne et ne veut pas partir?... Ah, ces départs, je déteste ça!

Et maintenant, vérifions.

1. **b** en retard.
2. **c** à Alexandra.
3. **a** au pique-nique.
4. **b** son appareil-photo.
5. **c** acheter du pain et du fromage.
6. **b** en retard.
7. **a** ne veut pas partir.
8. **a** pleuvoir.

SECTION B

OBJECTIVES **To exchange information:** talk about sightseeing; make comparisons; **to express feelings, emotions:** express relief and regret

CULTURAL BACKGROUND The one thing Van Gogh did not like about living and painting in **Provence** was the **mistral,** a cold, dry, violent wind from the north that blows down the valley of the Rhône to the Mediterranean. **Mistral,** a **provençal** word, means **"vent maître"** in French. It shook Van Gogh's easel and canvas; at times he laid his canvas on the ground and painted on his knees.

The **provençal** poet Frédéric Mistral (1830–1914) described **Provence** as **l'empire du soleil.** His last name is a fairly common family name in the region but has no relation to the wind.

Bullfights are popular in **Provence.** Unlike bullfights in Spain, the bull is not killed. He wears a **cocarde** (a rosette, a rose made of colored cloth) attached between his horns, which are often covered by leather balls to protect the bullfighter, who tries to snatch the rosette.

MOTIVATING ACTIVITY Invite students to talk about historical places they have visited by asking **Qui est-ce qui a déjà visité un endroit ou un site historique? Avec qui? Quand? C'était intéressant? Voulez-vous y retourner?**

Visite d'Arles

B 1

Borrow from a history teacher pictures of a combat in the Roman Coliseum between gladiators and lions. Talk about the pictures in French, describing the combat and its usual outcome. Do the same with a picture of a Spanish bullfight, contrasting this bullfight with those in **Provence.** Use as much of the vocabulary of B1 as you can in your presentation. You might write some of the new words you use on the board as you proceed.

Play the cassette as students follow along in their books. Reread the introductory paragraph to them and explain (in French, if possible) that many French **lycées** accept boarding students and therefore have a dormitory, so Mme Leroy and her students were able to stay overnight in a **lycée.**

Have the students look at the photos and say as much about them as they can, using the new vocabulary. Ask questions about the photos if students' comments are not forthcoming.

B 2 Activité • Avez-vous compris?

For cooperative learning, students might work in groups to find and write down the answers to these questions. Then ask each group one of the questions. When all questions have been answered, collect the papers and correct them.

B 3 Activité • Faites le guide

Encourage students to bring in photos, slides, or pictures of the historical sites in order to illustrate the "guided tour" they will give their classmates. When students give their oral presentations, allow them to use notes. Each pair should divide the commentary between them.

SLOWER-PACED LEARNING Choose a historical site and give the students an illustrated "guided tour" of it in French to model the activity. Keep it simple so as not to discourage them. You might then have pairs of students bring in a picture of a site they have chosen and write down what they can about it in French. Correct their papers; then they can prepare their oral presentations for the class.

B 4 Savez-vous que... ?

Bring to class reproductions of paintings by Cézanne and Van Gogh. Or, you might ask the art teacher to show reproductions of the paintings and to talk about them.

Play the cassette and have students read along in their books. Ask students to describe what they see in the two paintings and to tell which one they prefer. Encourage them to give reasons for their preferences.

B 5 VOUS EN SOUVENEZ-VOUS?

Have students read the explanation silently. Say the model sentences aloud and have students repeat them. Tell students to restate the sentences, replacing the nouns in the first chart and the adjectives and adverb in the second chart. Continue to review comparisons by using classroom examples: **Il y a plus (moins) de garçons que de filles. Sur la table il y a moins de crayons que de stylos,** and so on. Give students other things to compare, using adjectives: **un cheval/un taureau (beau), une course de taureaux en Espagne/une course de taureaux en France (intéressante),** and so on.

B 6   STRUCTURES DE BASE

Read the grammar presentation together with the students, having them repeat the model sentences after you. Direct students' attention to those sentences in B1 and B4 that contain superlatives. Ask students to make up new sentences, replacing parts of the models. Then have them complete this sentence: **Le français, c'est le cours le...** They might adapt the sentence **Alexandra arrive le plus tard** to their own class.

Point out and practice the repetition of the article in sentences where the adjective follows the noun: **C'est la ville la plus ancienne.** Students will need writing practice with superlatives. They might like to tell which of their school subjects is the most or least **ennuyeux, amusant,** or **intéressant.**

B 7   Activité • Pouvez-vous les comparer?

Remind students that the article and the adjective must agree with the subject; this may mean some changes: **Alexandra est plus petite qu'Eric. Alexandra est la plus petite. Eric est le moins petit.** Have students do the activity orally; then assign it to be written.

B 8   Activité • Exagérez un peu

Students might pair off to complete these dialogues, alternating roles.

SLOWER-PACED LEARNING   Point out that the indefinite article in **une jolie ville** becomes the definite article in the superlative **la plus jolie ville.** Call on volunteers to change the noun phrase in each sentence (**une vaste réserve**) to the superlative (**la plus vaste réserve**). Write the superlative phrases on the board. Then remind students that they are singling out one person, place, or thing from a larger group, region, or country when they use the superlative. If they mention the larger group or area, then they must use **de, du, de la, de l',** or **des** before it: **C'est la plus jolie ville de Provence.** Go back and have volunteers add to each superlative the appropriate **de** phrase: **la plus vaste réserve de la région.** Write these on the board. Now say the first sentence in each item and call on volunteers to construct the entire response, referring to the phrases on the board. Finally, have students pair off to practice the dialogues, changing roles each time.

CHALLENGE   Prepare similar statements or questions about local sites and celebrities to elicit superlatives from students: **Il y a une montagne près d'ici? (Oui, c'est la plus grande montagne de l'état.)**

B 9   Activité • Qui fait quoi, et comment?

SLOWER-PACED LEARNING   You might turn each item into a question to ask the class: **Qui arrive le plus tard?** Students answer **Alexandra arrive le plus tard.** Then have students pair off, one asking the questions you asked, the other answering.

B 10   Activité • Ecrit dirigé

SLOWER-PACED LEARNING   Have students write on their papers only the superlative phrases that replace the adjectives in parentheses. When everyone has finished, have students correct their papers as you go over the answers orally. If there are questions, write the correct phrases on the board or on a transparency. Then assign the entire paragraph to be written as homework.

B 11 COMMENT LE DIRE

Present the expressions as students listen with books closed. Go to the window and look out. (Pick a nice day!) Begin by giving a reason for your relief about the weather: **Nous allons faire un pique-nique aujourd'hui. Heureusement...** Have students repeat the expressions of relief after you. Present the expressions of regret in the same way. Express regret over something that has already happened locally, real or imaginary: **Nous avons fait un pique-nique hier. Malheureusement, il a plu!** Then have students open their books to read the expressions and the note. Review with the class which expressions are followed by the subjunctive and which are not. Students may need additional practice with the past subjunctive. Supply other activities about which students can express relief or regret (**réussir à l'examen, rater le train,** and so on) or have them compose their own sentences.

B 12 Activité • Actes de parole

For cooperative learning, form pairs or small groups of students who work together to locate the expressions and write them down. You might make this a contest.

B 13 Activité • Remettez le dialogue dans le bon ordre

Have students work in pairs. You might suggest that one student copy Eric's lines on separate cards or slips of paper and that his or her partner copy Chloé's lines. After the students have put the dialogue in order, they practice it, exchanging roles once or twice. Call on a few volunteers to recite their dialogues for their classmates.

B 14 Activité • Regret ou soulagement?

Form groups of three for this activity. One student reads the statements from the book. The other two listen to what is said and take turns relating to each other their regret or relief. Students should exchange roles.

SLOWER-PACED LEARNING Prepare a transparency of possible rejoinders to each statement or distribute copies to students. Groups proceed as described above, selecting appropriate responses from the list.

B 15 Activité • A vous maintenant!

For situation 1, students might make up this statement of relief: **C'est une bonne chose qu'il ait plu!** Then they might prepare a dialogue like this:

—Tu es allé(e) à la campagne dimanche?
—Non, il a plu.
—C'est dommage.
—Mais non, c'est une bonne chose qu'il ait plu!
—Pourquoi?
—Je déteste la campagne!

B 16 Activité • Organisez un voyage scolaire

For cooperative learning, students might work in small groups to plan a class trip. They report their plans to the class. Encourage other students in the class to ask questions or make comments.

To help students organize their thoughts, prepare a chart for each group or pair to fill in, with columns headed **Où? Pourquoi? Quand? Comment? Activités? Retour?** The recorder for each group fills in the chart. After the group's presentation to the class, have the members write a paragraph telling about their plans.

B 17   **Activité • Ecrivez**

Before students begin to write, conduct a discussion in French with the entire class about field trips that students have taken.

Students should first make an outline to organize their thoughts, using the questions in the instructions as a guide. Have students show you their outlines before they begin to write their compositions. Make suggestions concerning content and remind students of certain expressions or grammar points they might want to consider. Students should then prepare a rough draft and have a classmate read it and comment on it. Finally, they should write and hand in their completed compositions.

B 18   **Activité • Ecoutez bien**

You're going to hear Julie and Eric talk about their impressions of **Arles.** Open your book to page 358. *(pause)* Copy the headings in B18 on a separate sheet of paper. As you listen to Julie and Eric, write down what each one liked, did not like, and regretted. You don't have to write complete sentences. Ready? **Ecoutez bien.**

ERIC   Qu'est-ce que tu as aimé le plus?
JULIE   La Camargue! Quelle belle région! C'est une des plus jolies de la France... Et puis j'adore l'équitation... Ces chevaux sauvages, c'était merveilleux! Dommage qu'on ne fasse pas plus de sport dans ces voyages!
ERIC   Moi, en Camargue, je me suis drôlement ennuyé... Les chevaux, ça ne m'intéresse pas! Ce n'était pas amusant... Mais j'ai bien aimé Arles. Malheureusement, j'ai oublié mon appareil-photo.
JULIE   Moi aussi, je voulais prendre des chevaux en photo.
ERIC   Au fait, ça t'a plu, Arles?
JULIE   Non, pas trop. Les vestiges romains, j'en ai marre.
ERIC   Oui, c'est dommage qu'il n'y ait pas eu de courses de taureaux!
JULIE   C'est vrai, il doit y avoir une super ambiance!
ERIC   En tout cas, heureusement qu'il a fait beau!
JULIE   Oui, nous avons vraiment eu de la chance!

Et maintenant, vérifions.

Julie :
Ce qu'elle a aimé : *la Camargue, l'équitation, les chevaux sauvages*
Ce qu'elle n'a pas aimé : *Arles, les vestiges romains*
Ce qu'elle regrette : *d'avoir oublié son appareil-photo; qu'on ne fasse pas de sport; qu'il n'y ait pas eu de courses de taureaux*

Eric :
Ce qu'il a aimé : *Arles*
Ce qu'il n'a pas aimé : *la Camargue, les chevaux*
Ce qu'il regrette : *d'avoir oublié son appareil-photo; qu'il n'y ait pas eu de courses de taureaux*

SECTION

C

OBJECTIVES   **To exchange information:** tell about past events; **to express attitudes, opinions:** express lack of interest

CULTURAL BACKGROUND   The **Rencontres Internationales de la Photographie** are held each summer in **Arles.** The month-long activities include workshops, expositions, shows, lectures, and debates. Admission is charged for most events. Several evening shows are held in the ancient Roman arena.

France has a prominent place in the history of photography. Nicéphore Niepce (1765–1833) invented a process of photography perfected later by Louis Daguerre (1787–1851). The Lumière brothers, Louis (1864–1948) and Auguste (1862–1954), invented the cinematograph in 1895, the first mechanism to project moving pictures on a screen. The French photographer Henri Cartier-Bresson is world-renowned.

MOTIVATING ACTIVITY   When they go on a field trip, students may have as much fun on the bus and during free moments as they do at the event. Is that the case with your students? Ask them **Qu'est-ce que vous faites pour vous amuser en route? Qu'est-ce que vous faites pendant votre temps libre?**

C1   Dernières heures

Bring a toy camera to class. Tell students in French that Mme Leroy's students took a lot of photos on the trip, especially the last day. Then pretend to take pictures of students, using expressions from the text: **Souriez un peu! Ne faites pas de grimaces! Soyez naturels! Attention, le petit oiseau va sortir.** Do this several times. Have students repeat the expressions. Give the camera to individuals and have them pretend to take pictures of classmates, making appropriate remarks.

Then draw a postcard on a transparency. Write **Chers parents,...** Turn to the class and say **Je n'ai plus d'idées. Qu'est-ce que je peux mettre?** Have students pretend to be Mme Leroy's group and tell you what to write. Write their suggestions or have individuals write what they propose.

Play the cassette and have students read along in their books. Call on volunteers to summarize the last hours of the field trip to **Arles.**

C2   Activité • Avez-vous compris?

Assign one question to one student until all students have been assigned a question. Tell students to each find the answer to his or her question and to write it down. When all have finished, elicit the response to each question. Those who have written the response to the same question might suggest their own refinements to the answer.

C3   Activité • Actes de parole

Have students pair off, find the answers, and jot them down. After you have elicited all the answers orally, tell each pair to find and write down another expression the person could have said to accomplish the same communicative function. For example, instead of saying **Fais un effort,** Florence might have said **Force-toi!**

C4   Activité • Ecrivez

SLOWER-PACED LEARNING   On separate slips of paper, write several things students saw in **Arles,** places they visited, and activities they did.

Do not write complete sentences. Place these slips of paper in three boxes, one for each of the categories. Students each choose one slip of paper from each box and write their postcards using that information.

C5 Activité • A vous maintenant!

For cooperative learning, divide the class into groups of four. Students should first review the conversations of the young people they're going to portray. They might also make notes on the characters' interests and attitudes. Once they have the characters fixed in their minds, they should try to make their conversations as spontaneous as possible. Allow some time for practice and then have each group present its dialogue for the class.

SLOWER-PACED LEARNING Prepare four transparencies, one for each character. In English, write a summary of what each person might say in the conversation. Students form groups; each group assumes the role of one of the characters and formulates remarks in French according to the transparency.

C6 Savez-vous que... ?

Read the cultural note aloud as students follow along in their books. Then ask questions, such as the following, to check comprehension:

> Pourquoi est-ce qu'on appelle Arles «la capitale de la photographie»?
> Combien de temps doit-on étudier pour devenir photographe professionnel?
> Qu'est-ce qu'il y a à Arles au mois de juillet?
> Qu'est-ce qu'on peut faire pendant les Rencontres Internationales?

CHALLENGE Students keep their books closed. Tell them that they're going to hear about a photography festival in **Arles.** They are to listen carefully and then be able to say (1) what they would do at the festival as a professional photographer, and (2) what they would do there as a tourist. Students may take notes as you play the cassette or read the selection aloud. Elicit oral answers.

C7 LE MATERIEL PHOTO

If possible, bring to the class this photographic equipment. Students keep books closed as you describe each item and its function. Have students repeat after you. Use a TPR technique by asking students to show you the different pieces: **Montrez-moi l'objectif.**

C8 Activité • Qu'est-ce qu'il vous faut?

Have students work individually to find and jot down just the names of the appropriate equipment. Then read the situations aloud and have students volunteer answers. Encourage the use of both ways to express need: **Il me faut...** and **J'ai besoin de...**

C9 Activité • Le photographe débutant

Have students pair off to practice this dialogue, supplying the missing words for the photographic equipment. They should exchange roles. Call on some pairs to read the dialogue aloud for the others.

CHALLENGE After students have practiced in pairs, have them close their books. Then call on volunteers to recreate the situation in their own words.

C 10 STRUCTURES DE BASE

Write the following phrases on the board: **avant de quitter Arles, après avoir quitté Arles.** Give the English equivalents: *before leaving Arles, after having left Arles.* Explain the difference between the present and past infinitives. Stress that both the activity in the infinitive form and the subsequent activity in the sentence must be performed by the same person(s). Use the examples in complete sentences: **Avant de quitter Arles, ils ont acheté des cartes postales. Après avoir quitté Arles, ils sont retournés à Nice.**

Read the explanation in the book together with the students. Point out the agreement of the past participle. Have them repeat the model sentences and practice restating them, substituting the past infinitives of other appropriate verbs.

Give students both oral and written practice in changing **avant de** + present infinitive to **après** + past infinitive: **avant de sortir** → **après être sorti(e)(s).**

Tell students that the past infinitive is useful in recounting a series of past events, particularly in writing. In conversation they may choose to avoid this structure by using two sentences.

C 11 Activité • Qu'est-ce qu'ils ont fait? Et après?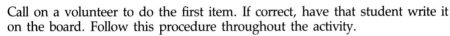

Call on a volunteer to do the first item. If correct, have that student write it on the board. Follow this procedure throughout the activity.

SLOWER-PACED LEARNING Have the students dictate the sentences to you as you write them on the board so that you can make all the agreements of the past participles. Then erase the board and assign the sentences to be written for homework.

C 12 Activité • A vous maintenant!

For cooperative learning, form pairs or small groups. Tell students to write down the activities in the correct chronological order, one below the other. Then, starting with the first two activities, they combine every two activities into one sentence, the first activity stated in the past infinitive form.

SLOWER-PACED LEARNING Prepare a transparency of the sentences, grouping them in pairs. Project the transparency and have students tell which activity in each pair happened first. Then have students combine the sentences in each pair, using the past infinitive.

C 13 COMMENT LE DIRE

Students listen with their books closed as you dramatize these expressions of disinterest. Seated at your desk, holding a stack of papers to correct, say **Corriger ces copies, ça ne me dit rien. Je n'ai pas le courage de corriger ces copies. Ça m'embête de...** and so on. Then have students open their books and repeat the expressions after you. Ask students to give other examples, following these models, of things in which they have no interest.

To practice the expression **Tu parles!,** have individuals suggest that their classmates do something: **Pourquoi est-ce que vous ne faites pas vos devoirs?** They respond **Tu parles!** Students might pair off to make up similar two-line dialogues.

C 14 Activité • Et vous?

SLOWER-PACED LEARNING Brainstorm with the students as many activities as they can think of. Write the suggestions in the infinitive form on the board or on a transparency. Then have students choose those that don't interest them and express, in French, their lack of interest.

C15 Activité • A vous maintenant!

For cooperative learning, students pair off to practice inviting, refusing, indicating lack of interest, and giving excuses. Point out that they can find their cues in each sentence:

> —Tu veux aller faire des courses?
> —Ça m'ennuie de faire des courses.
> —Allez, pourquoi?
> —Il fait trop chaud.

Students should take turns initiating the dialogues.

SLOWER-PACED LEARNING Students prepare only two-line dialogues, as in the first two lines shown above.

C16 Activité • Ecoutez bien

Alexandra wrote a letter to your French class about her trip to **Arles.** Before reading the letter to the class, your teacher gives you a list of things that Alexandra did during her trip and asks you to indicate on which day she did each. Open your book to page 363. *(pause)* Copy the list of activities in C16 on a separate sheet of paper. *(pause)* As you listen to the letter, write a number 1 next to what Alexandra did on the first day of the trip, a 2 next to what she did the second day, and a 3 next to what she did the third day. Ready? **Ecoutez bien.**

> Nous sommes arrivés ici avant-hier. Sur la route, nous nous sommes arrêtés pour visiter une usine à Berre. C'était assez ennuyeux, mais après, nous avons pique-niqué au bord de l'étang. Il faisait très beau! La nuit, nous avons dormi dans un lycée. Le matin, après avoir pris le petit déjeuner au lycée, nous avons fait le tour d'Arles : nous avons vu le théâtre et les arènes romaines où il y a des courses de taureaux, mais sans mise à mort, heureusement! Après avoir déjeuné, nous sommes allés en Camargue faire de l'équitation. C'était génial! Aujourd'hui, nous sommes libres. On prend des photos et on écrit des cartes postales et des lettres. Bientôt, on va tous ensemble prendre un dernier verre au café avant de monter dans le car. Voilà, je n'ai pas le courage de vous écrire plus longuement; il fait trop chaud! Je vais aller acheter un timbre et mettre cette lettre à la poste.
>
> Je vous embrasse tous bien fort,
Alexandra

Et maintenant, vérifions. *Read each sentence and the number before it.*

_1_	Elle arrive à Arles.	_3_	Elle écrit la lettre.
_2_	Elle monte à cheval.	_2_	Elle prend le petit déjeuner au lycée.
_3_	Elle achète un timbre.	_2_	Elle visite le théâtre antique.
_3_	Elle revient chez elle.	_1_	Elle visite l'usine.
_1_	Elle pique-nique.		

OBJECTIVE   To recombine communicative functions, grammar, and vocabulary

CULTURAL BACKGROUND   **Saintes-Maries-de-la-Mer** is a small fishing port and seaside resort on the Mediterranean coast in the **Camargue** region. According to legend, Marie-Jacobé, sister of the Virgin Mary, Marie-Salomé, and their servant, Sara, a black woman, were driven from Judea and took refuge on this site. Two pilgrimages are made in May and October of each year to **Saintes-Maries,** especially by gypsies, who revere Sara as their patron saint.

MOTIVATING ACTIVITY   Have volunteers bring in slides, photos, or mementos of a field trip they've taken and tell the class about them.

1

La séance diapo

Play the cassette or read the dialogues aloud as students look at the photos and read the text. Review vocabulary and structures presented in this unit by asking students to read aloud from these dialogues examples of interrogative pronouns, superlatives, past infinitives, exclamations, suggestions, expressions of annoyance and impatience, and so forth. You may also wish to ask a few questions to check comprehension:

> Qui est-ce qui a pris les photos que Mme Leroy est en train de montrer?
> Qu'est-ce qu'il faut que les élèves fassent après avoir regardé les photos?
> Comment vont-ils choisir la meilleure photo?

2

Activité • A votre avis

Have students pair off to study the photos and formulate their opinions. Tell them to write down the numbers of the photos and their opinions next to them. After students have had a chance to express their opinions, take a poll of the entire class through a show of hands.

3

Activité • Que faire?

As students examine the announcements, you might ask some questions to check their comprehension of the information presented. Then have them pair off to prepare their dialogues.

4

Activité • Vous n'êtes pas enthousiaste

For cooperative learning, students might work in pairs. They will want to review the expressions of lack of interest in C13 and decide on three reasons for not wanting to write a report.

5

Activité • Ecrivez

First review orally the expressions of relief and regret in B11, and have students recall some highlights of the trip to **Arles.** Before students write their compositions, have them make an outline for you to check, followed by a rough draft, which a classmate should read.

SLOWER-PACED LEARNING   On a transparency, write your own composition as if you were one of Mme Leroy's students. Project it for the class. Point out various communicative functions and ask students to suggest other ways to say the same thing or ways to express an opposite reaction.

6 ## Activité • A vous maintenant!

You might begin by telling students about a trip you've taken. Encourage them to ask you questions about it and also to comment on it. You may wish to have individuals relate their trips to their classmates, who then question and comment. Some students may prefer to record their talks for the class to listen to.

7 ## Activité • Ecrivez

Students should reread Mme Leroy's itinerary in A1. Encourage students to be imaginative; they might organize a voyage in space or in time.

8 ## Activité • Ecrivez

Students might write about the photos on the postcards in their messages. A typical salutation on the postcard might be **Bonjour d'Arles!** or **Un petit bonjour d'Arles!**

9 ## Activité • Si on allait... ?

First read the schedule aloud to the students as they follow along in their books. Explain in French anything they don't understand. Ask them to tell which events they would like to see and which they would not. Review the use of **si** + the imperfect to make a suggestion (Unit 9, C20, page 324). Students should give free play to their imaginations, yet react according to their own likes and dislikes, as they work in pairs to make up dialogues.

10 ## Activité • Visite des Saintes-Maries

Have students describe the photos, particularly what activities are taking place. Note these activities on the board or on a transparency. Then students pair off and decide what to do during their visit to **Saintes-Maries.** You might suggest that they plan a two-day stay in the town. As a writing assignment, students might write postcards to their French class.

11 ## Activité • Jeu de rôle

You may want to make a contest of this activity. Form groups of three or four. Two groups will compete against each other. Students work together to make up situations that will elicit expressions of regret and relief. Then one group describes a situation to the other group. The second group must decide whether the situation calls for an expression of relief or regret and make an appropriate remark in French. The two groups take turns describing situations and expressing relief or regret. Points are awarded for appropriate responses.

12 ## Activité • Quelles sont ces photos?

You might extend the scope of this activity to include pictures in some or all of the preceding units. For writing practice, have students write their descriptions of photos on index cards and exchange the cards.

13 ## Activité • Créez votre projet

For cooperative learning, form groups of four for this activity. You might first brainstorm with the entire class ideas for projects. Write all suggestions on the board. Each group may choose one idea to develop or think of still another on their own. The group prepares a written program for their project including goals, times, places, dates, participants, activities, and so on. Groups should report orally and in writing to their classmates, who decide which projects to pursue.

14   Activité • Récréation

This activity is optional. Make a contest of this to see who can succeed first in finding and writing down the five inconsistencies in the drawing.

PRONONCIATION

The ghost **h; l** and **gn**

Open your book to page 371. *(pause)* Refer to this page as you listen to this section.

1   Ecoutez bien et répétez.

1. Have you ever been told that there's no **h**-sound in French? Well, it's true, there isn't. It's an English sound that you can't use. But if there's no **h**-sound in French, why are words like **heure, hôtel,** and **dehors** spelled with an **h**? Well, once upon a time, there was an **h**-sound, but they went and lost it. So don't say the **h.** Just drop it when you speak French. Try it out: **heure, hôtel, dehors.**

Wonderful! You don't have to worry about **h**'s. You can pretend they're not even there. Right? Right, that is, unless you see a ghost. Yes, some **h**'s have ghosts that can stop traffic. In fact, that's about all they do. They stop you from linking one French sound with another. So where are you going to come face to face with one of these ghost **h**'s? You really can't tell in advance. It may be in that **hôtel** in Nice, in the lobby, **le hall.** In English, you say *hall* and *hotel.* In French, you leave out the **h** to say **hall** and **hôtel.** So where's the ghost? Surprise! Just ask someone to meet you in the lobby of the hotel and you'll see. . . **dans le hall de l'hôtel.** Before you say **hall,** stop short, but don't before **hôtel.** Say it: **le... hall.** Now try the whole thing: **dans le hall de l'hôtel.**

Okay for **hall** and **hôtel.** But how about the other words? How do you know when to link and when to stop? Why, you'll have to see your friendly dictionary, of course.

But if the dictionary shows you how a word is pronounced by assigning each sound a letter, how does it show this non-sound that you have to watch out for? Look at the box in *1b.* If you look up words like **hall** and **héros,** you'll find instead of an **h** a little stop sign that looks like an apostrophe, as in /'ol/ and /'ero/. This little sign is to the flow of French speech what a red light is to the flow of traffic. It says stop. So you don't say *the zeros,* /le ze ro/, when you mean *the heroes,* /le'ero/. Try these stops: **les haricots, les hors-d'œuvre, des harengs, en haut, le hasard, Ils ont hâte.**

Now that you know how to make the stop, all you need to find out is when to make it. To start you on your way, play a game with your dictionary. On page 371 in *1c,* there are 14 words that are the same in English as in French. Half of them have no **h**-sound and half have a ghost **h.** What you need to do is look them up in your dictionary and put the article **le, la,** or **l'** in front of each word. Put **l'** before the no-**h** words and list them together in one column. Put the article **le** or **la** in front of the stop-**h** words and arrange them in another column. Let's start with an example of each: **l'hôtel** would go in the no-**h** column and **le hall** in the stop-**h** column. Ready? Got your dictionary? Go on with the words in *1c (long pause)*

Let's check your list. Do you have 7 words in each column? Good. Repeat the words in the no-**h** column: **l'horizon, l'hypocrite, l'hélicoptère, l'herbicide, l'héritage, l'humour, l'hydrogène.** Now say the words in the stop-**h** column: **le handicap, le hamburger, le halo, le hamster, le héros, le hippy, la harpe.**

Of course, you won't be able to look in your dictionary for every word spelled with an **h** whenever you open your mouth. Just remember the ones you learn. There aren't all that many. Be sure to remember them with an article or a noun marker in front. Remember, it's **la Hollande, un hangar, le hasard,** and **deux harengs.**

2. Okay, you don't say the **h** in French. But what about the **th** in words like **thermomètre?** It's simple. Imagine the **h** isn't there. Just say the **t.** But in words that are about the same in French as in English, be careful not to slip into the English *th.* Try these—all pronounced with a **t**-sound, no **th:** **thermomètre, théâtre, thé, thème, thermos, mathématiques, mythe.** Fine.

3. Now what about the combination **ch?** Well, that too is pronounced differently than it is in English. But it's not hard to say. If you think of it as an *sh* as in *show,* you've got it about right. The **ch** in **la Chine** is pronounced not as in *chin* but rather as in the word *shin.* In fact, it's the same sound that you find in the English words *machine, chef, chauffeur,* and *Chicago.* Compare these English and French **ch**-words and repeat the French: *chat/* **chatte,** *chant/* **chante,** *change/* **change,** *chocolate/* **chocolat.**

Now that was easy. That must cover the words with **ch.** Sorry, not all. Someone had to go and mess up the system. With the **ch** it was the ancient Greeks. Instead of leaving well enough alone, some learned Frenchmen had to bring in words from Old Greek and pronounce them **à la grecque.** Of course, the English did the same thing, the one trying to outdo the other in sounding learned—and ancient. So let's see how English and French match up. Listen to both and repeat the French: *choral/* **choral,** *choir/* **chœur,** *chaos/* **chaos,** *Christine/* **Christine.**

This doesn't mean that all **ch**-words pronounced with a **k**-sound in English are said that way in French. That would be just too easy. There are a few misleading pairs that you have to watch. Here are a few. Listen to them and repeat the French words: *architect/* **architecte,** *chemistry/* **chimie,** *archives/* **archives.** There are not many. When in doubt, once again, go see your dictionary for help. Well, that's enough for the **h**'s.

4. Let's turn to a couple of other sounds that are something like the English ones, but not quite. First there's the l-sound. It's different from the English. Listen: *sell,* **sel,** *fill,* **fil.** The American and French l-sounds are different because American and French speakers do not do the same things when they pronounce these sounds. The difference is essentially in the position of the tongue. American speakers tend to curve the tongue backward. French speakers don't. In producing an American l, the tip of the tongue touches the roof of the mouth at a higher point than that for a French l. When producing a French l, French speakers press the tip of the tongue against the ridge at the base of the upper front teeth. Now try these: **elle, quelle, celle, ville, ciel, bel, glace, place, classe, clé.**

5. Another sound to watch out for is **gn,** like the English sound /nyə/ as in the words *onion* and *companion*. Listen and you'll hear a close match: *onion*/**oignon,** *companion*/**compagnon.** Now, continue with the French: **mignon, magnifique, signer, ligne.** Fine. **C'est magnifique.**

2 **Ecoutez et lisez.**

For a little more practice with the ghost **h, l,** and **gn,** read the dialogue aloud. I'll say each line after you.

—On joue de la musique de chambre tous les soirs de six à dix heures dans le hall de l'hôtel.
—Moi, je préfère le chant solo ou bien les chœurs sans accompagnement.
—Pour moi, c'est l'orchestre symphonique, le théâtre et l'opéra.
—J'ai même des billets pour *Le Lac des Cygnes*. C'est la nouvelle compagnie. J'ai hâte de les voir. Il paraît que le spectacle est magnifique.

3 **Copiez les phrases suivantes pour préparer une dictée.**

Write the following sentences from dictation. First listen to the sentence as it is read to you. Then you will hear the sentence again in short segments, with a pause after each segment to allow you time to write. Finally you will hear the sentence a third time so that you may check your work. Let's begin.

1. Le restaurant dans cet hôtel est célèbre pour ses haricots. Le restaurant *(pause)* dans cet hôtel *(pause)* est célèbre *(pause)* pour ses haricots. *(pause)* Le restaurant dans cet hôtel est célèbre pour ses haricots.
2. Moi, je n'aime pas les oignons dans mon hamburger. Moi, je n'aime pas *(pause)* les oignons *(pause)* dans mon hamburger. *(pause)* Moi, je n'aime pas les oignons dans mon hamburger.
3. Hier, Christine et Charles ont pris du thé avec leurs compagnons. Hier, Christine et Charles *(pause)* ont pris du thé *(pause)* avec leurs compagnons. *(pause)* Hier, Christine et Charles ont pris du thé avec leurs compagnons.
4. Signez sur la ligne, s'il vous plaît. Signez sur la ligne, *(pause)* s'il vous plaît. *(pause)* Signez sur la ligne, s'il vous plaît.
5. Le théâtre est près de la cathédrale. Le théâtre *(pause)* est près de la cathédrale. *(pause)* Le théâtre est près de la cathédrale.

VERIFICONS!

SECTION A

Students might work in pairs to do all the exercices for this section. For the first part of the exercise on interrogative pronouns, you might also ask students to provide answers. They should write down their responses and submit them to you for correction.

SECTION B

Have students work individually and write their answers for this section. Call on volunteers to read aloud their statements for the first activity.

Prepare a transparency of the answers to the second exercise. You might compose additional practice items to review the superlatives.

SECTION C

Review the expressions of disinterest in C13. Allow students to refer to them as they do the first exercise.

Then have students write out the second exercise on past infinitives. Finally, ask students to write their own sentences using the past infinitive.

VOCABULAIRE

Form two teams. Going down the vocabulary lists, the teams, in turn, must use the words in complete sentences. You might set a theme to which all sentences must relate. For example, you say **Nous allons à Arles.** The first team, using **s'amuser,** might say **Nous allons nous amuser.** The second team might continue with **Nous faisons un arrêt à Berre.** If a team cannot use a word, the turn goes to the other team.

To review pronunciation, ask students to find and write down those words in the list that contain a certain sound.

ETUDE DE MOTS

When students have found the past participles used as adjectives, have them use each one in noun phrases to show the four possible spellings: **un livre interdit, des films interdits, une région interdite, les recherches interdites.**

A LIRE

OBJECTIVE To read for practice and pleasure

ALERTE AU CHATEAU DE RAMBOUILLET

You might offer extra credit to those students interested in doing research on the famous people and places listed in **Avant de lire.** The student assigned to each topic should give a brief report to the class, in French if possible.

For each of the four parts of the story, read aloud the italicized question. Then play the cassette recording of the part and have students read along in their books to find the answer to the question.

Play the cassette again as students read along. Pause after each part to check comprehension. Your questions should not only probe for details but should also require students to synthesize information and find reasons why.

Activité • Avez-vous compris?

Students should complete each sentence, using the past infinitive construction. Students might compose additional items of this type based on the story for their classmates to complete.

SLOWER-PACED LEARNING   Provide a list of possible events with the verbs in the present infinitive forms.

Activité • Commentez

You might make a contest of this activity. Divide the class into groups of three or four students each. The group that comes up with the greatest number of logical completions for the three sentences wins.

Activité • Téléphonez

Review expressions used in making a phone call: **Allô, je suis bien au... ? Qui est à l'appareil?** and so on. Reread with the class the relevant part of the story. Brainstorm with the class things that M. Laroche might say and things the police officer might say. Then have students pair off to prepare their phone conversations.

Activité • Faites le guide

Students should make notes for their guided tours as they study the photos and illustrations. Call on volunteers to present theirs to the class. Classmates pretend they are part of the tour group and ask the "guide" questions.

CHAPITRE 10

Voyage à Arles

In France, as in the United States, teachers take their students on field trips to extend and enrich their schoolwork. Museums, historical landmarks, and industries are common destinations. On long trips, a group might stay in the dormitory of a nearby *lycée,* since many *lycées* accommodate boarding students. Students look forward to the new experiences that the *voyages scolaires* provide.

In this unit you will:

PREMIER CONTACT	get acquainted with the topic
SECTION A	prepare to take a field trip . . . ask for information . . . express impatience . . . make excuses
SECTION B	explore the city of Arles . . . make comparisons . . . express relief and regret
SECTION C	talk about the trip . . . tell about past events . . . express lack of interest
TRY YOUR SKILLS	use what you've learned
A LIRE	read for practice and pleasure

PREMIER CONTACT getting acquainted with the topic

The authentic material in Premier Contact is meant to introduce the theme of the unit and to be used for global comprehension only.

1 ## Arles—Monuments et Musées

Arles, fondée par les Grecs au VIᵉ siècle avant J.-C. (Jésus-Christ), a connu des siècles de gloire et de prospérité sous les Romains. Elle a été la plus grande ville de Provence et la capitale des Gaules. Au Moyen-Age, Arles était un grand centre religieux. C'est à Arles que Van Gogh a peint 300 de ses plus belles toiles.

Les arènes romaines (fin du 1ᵉʳ siècle)

L'amphithéâtre mesure 136 m sur 107 m. Il peut contenir 12 000 spectateurs.

Le théâtre antique (fin du 1ᵉʳ siècle avant J.-C.)

Le théâtre de style augustéen est consacré au Festival d'Arles (juin-juillet), et aux Rencontres Internationales de la Photographie.

Le Musée Réattu (XVᵉ–XVIᵉ–XVIIᵉ siècles)

Dans ce musée, il y a des peintures et des dessins de l'école provençale des XVIIIᵉ et XIXᵉ siècles. Plusieurs de ses salles sont aussi consacrées à l'art contemporain.

Les Alyscamps

Cette allée romantique de tombeaux est le vestige d'un vaste cimetière qui entourait la cité du IIIᵉ au XIIᵉ siècle. Vincent Van Gogh (novembre 1888) et Paul Gauguin ont peint chacun un tableau de ce site merveilleux.

La Cathédrale et le Cloître Saint-Trophime (XIIᵉ–XIVᵉ siècles)

A côté de la cathédrale romane avec son magnifique portail, ce cloître est l'un des plus raffinés de l'occident.

Les thermes de Constantin (IVᵉ siècle)

Malgré les ravages du temps, la grande salle des bains chauds est bien conservée.

Le Musée Arlaten

Il a été fondé par le poète Frédéric Mistral. Ce musée présente différents aspects de la vie traditionnelle en Provence.

Vincent Van Gogh (1853–1890) Dutch-born artist; lived much of his life in France
Paul Gauguin (1848–1903) French artist; well-known for the paintings he did while living in Tahiti
Frédéric Mistral (1830–1914) French writer; wrote in "provençal," the dialect of southern France
Le style augustéen: classic Roman style; the Augustan Age (27 B.C.–180 A.D.) was the period of greatest peace and prosperity for the Roman Empire.

Activité • Cherchez des renseignements   Possible answers are given.

Vous, vous connaissez bien Arles. Mais c'est la première visite de votre ami(e). Répondez à ses questions.

1. C'est une vieille ville, Arles? Oui, Arles est une vieille ville; elle date du VIe siècle.
2. La cathédrale de Saint-Trophime est-elle très vieille? Oui, elle est très vieille.
3. Qu'est-ce qui est le plus vieux, les arènes ou le théâtre antique? Le théâtre antique est le plus vieux.
4. J'ai envie de voir des peintures modernes. Où est-ce qu'on va? On va au Musée Réattu.
5. Où est-ce que les Romains prenaient leur bain? Les Romains prenaient leur bain aux thermes de Constantin.
6. Van Gogh habitait à Arles, non? Oui, il a peint 300 de ses plus belles toiles à Arles.

3 EN CAMARGUE

Dès qu'on quitte Arles vers le sud, on pénètre en Camargue — pays de traditions, réserve naturelle de plantes et d'oiseaux, terre à riz, paradis des chevaux et des taureaux — située dans le triangle formé par les deux bras du Rhône.

Au Sud de la France,
Là où le Rhône
Se jette dans la mer,
Est un pays,
Presque désertique
Appelé la Camargue
Où vivent encore
Des troupeaux de chevaux sauvages.
Crin-Blanc était le chef de l'un de ces troupeaux.
C'était un cheval fort et redoutable.

– Extrait de *Crin-Blanc* par Albert Lamorisse

CRIN-BLANC
—CAMPING-CARAVANING—
Au cœur de la Camargue !
Sanitaires grand confort, piscines, tennis, restaurant, équitation, libre-service..., locations de caravanes

Activité • La visite continue   Possible answers are given.

Vous et votre ami(e), vous quittez Arles pour aller en Camargue. Avant de partir, vous étudiez la carte de la région et vous lisez le petit extrait d'Albert Lamorisse. Maintenant, pouvez-vous répondre à ces questions?

1. Où se trouve la Camargue?
2. La Camargue est près de quel fleuve?
3. Quels animaux est-ce qu'on y voit?
4. Qu'est-ce qu'on peut y faire?

1. La Camargue se trouve au sud de la France.   2. La Camargue est près du Rhône.   3. On y voit des chevaux sauvages et des taureaux.   4. On peut voir des plantes et des oiseaux. On peut nager et on peut faire de l'équitation et du camping.

5 ## Activité • Faisons du camping   Possible answers are given.

Vous allez faire du camping en Camargue. Vous trouvez de la publicité pour un camping, le Crin-Blanc. Répondez aux questions de votre ami(e).

1. Pourquoi a-t-on choisi le nom «Crin-Blanc» pour le camping?
2. Où est-ce que le camping se trouve?
3. Qu'est-ce qu'on peut y faire comme sports?
4. Où est-ce qu'on peut manger?
5. Est-ce qu'il y a des toilettes?

1. C'était le nom du chef d'un des troupeaux de chevaux. C'était un cheval fort et redoutable.   2. Le camping se trouve au cœur de la Camargue.   3. On peut jouer au tennis, faire de l'équitation ou nager.   4. On peut manger au restaurant.
5. Oui, il y a des toilettes.

Souvent, en France, pour illustrer un cours, un professeur décide d'organiser un voyage éducatif.
Avez-vous déjà participé à des voyages organisés par votre école? Où êtes-vous allé(e)?

A1

Projet de voyage

Cette année, Mme Leroy, professeur d'histoire-géographie au collège Alphonse Daudet
de Nice, a choisi d'emmener sa classe de troisième visiter Arles, en Provence.

Voyage scolaire du lundi
13 mai au mercredi 15 mai

Premier jour:
10h00 - Rendez-vous au collège
Départ (Soyez à l'heure)
Arrêt à Berre
- Visite de l'usine
- Pique-nique au bord
de l'étang

17h00 - Arrivée à Arles

Deuxième jour:
- Activités culturelles
- Visite d'Arles
- Activités sportives
- Équitation en
Camargue

Troisième jour:
- Journée libre à Arles
16h00 - Départ pour Nice

Mme Leroy parle du voyage avec ses élèves.

Le trajet

Alphonse Daudet (1840–1897) French writer from Nîmes

Activité • Avez-vous compris?

Avez-vous bien lu le programme? Répondez à ces questions.

1. Combien de temps va durer le voyage?
2. D'où partent-ils?
3. Qu'est-ce que Mme Leroy veut que les élèves fassent?
4. Qu'est-ce qu'ils vont faire après la visite de l'usine?

5. Quel jour arrivent-ils à Arles? A quelle heure?
6. Quels types d'activités sont prévus (planned) pour le deuxième jour?
7. Où vont-ils faire du cheval?
8. Qu'est-ce qui est au programme du mercredi?

1. Le voyage va durer trois jours. 2. Ils partent du collège. 3. Elle veut qu'ils soient à l'heure. 4. Ils vont faire un pique-nique au bord de l'étang. 5. Ils arrivent à Arles lundi à 17h. 6. Les activités culturelles et sportives sont prévues pour le deuxième jour. 7. Ils vont faire du cheval en Camargue. 8. Rien. C'est une journée libre à Arles.

A3 Activité • A vous maintenant!   Possible dialogue is given.

Vous êtes un(e) élève de Mme Leroy. Quelques jours avant le voyage scolaire à Arles, vous en parlez avec vos parents. Vous leur demandez la permission d'y aller. Ils vous demandent des renseignements. Organisez la discussion avec deux camarades de classe : le père, la mère et vous.
—Maman, papa, Mme Leroy va emmener les élèves à Arles. Vous voulez bien que j'y aille?   —Qu'est-ce que vous allez faire là-bas?
—On va visiter une usine, pique-niquer au bord d'un étang, et visiter la ville. Après, on va faire de l'équitation en Camargue.

A4 Savez-vous que... ?

Vous en avez assez de tout apprendre dans les livres? Vous voulez sortir de l'école? Vous avez envie de connaître la réalité sociale et culturelle? Une solution : préparez avec votre professeur un P.A.E. (Projet d'Action Educative). En France, c'est une activité scolaire financée par le gouvernement : le but est d'ouvrir l'école au monde extérieur. Vous pouvez organiser un voyage en France ou à l'étranger, créer un club de sport ou d'informatique, réaliser (create) un spectacle... Proposez vos idées!

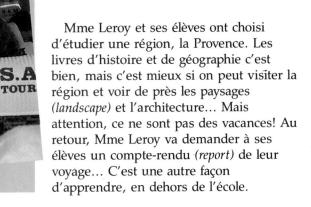

Mme Leroy et ses élèves ont choisi d'étudier une région, la Provence. Les livres d'histoire et de géographie c'est bien, mais c'est mieux si on peut visiter la région et voir de près les paysages (landscape) et l'architecture... Mais attention, ce ne sont pas des vacances! Au retour, Mme Leroy va demander à ses élèves un compte-rendu (report) de leur voyage... C'est une autre façon d'apprendre, en dehors de l'école.

Alexandra Gastaldi se dépêche. Comme d'habitude, elle est en retard.

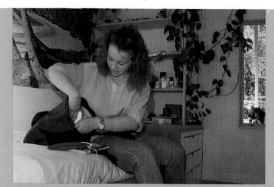

Alexandra fait ses bagages.

Elle met ses boucles d'oreilles.

MME GASTALDI	Dépêche-toi, Alexandra! Il est déjà dix heures et quart! Tu vas rater le car!
ALEXANDRA	Je sais!
MME GASTALDI	Qu'est-ce que tu fais?
ALEXANDRA	Je cherche mon pull rouge. Qui est-ce qui l'a pris? Il était là hier!
MME GASTALDI	C'est peut-être ta sœur.
ALEXANDRA	Bon, ça ne fait rien, j'en ai d'autres. A ton avis, qu'est-ce qui va avec mon tee-shirt rose?
MME GASTALDI	Le bleu.
ALEXANDRA	D'accord... Voilà, je suis prête!
MME GASTALDI	Tu n'as rien oublié?
ALEXANDRA	Ah, si, mon appareil-photo!... OK, j'y vais! Salut, maman!
MME GASTALDI	Tu ne manges rien?
ALEXANDRA	Je n'ai pas le temps; il faut que je me dépêche. Je suis en retard.
MME GASTALDI	Emporte au moins une pomme!... Amuse-toi bien!
ALEXANDRA	Merci!... A mercredi!

Elle embrasse sa mère.

Enfin, elle part.

Est-ce que les phrases suivantes sont vraies ou fausses d'après A5?

1. Alexandra est toujours en retard.
2. Alexandra ne pouvait pas trouver son pull rouge hier.
3. Elle ne trouve pas son pull bleu.
4. Elle ne prend pas son appareil-photo.
5. Elle prend un bon petit déjeuner avant de partir.
6. Sa mère lui donne un fruit.

1. C'est vrai.   2. C'est faux. Il était là hier.   3. C'est faux. Elle trouve son pull bleu.   4. C'est faux. Elle prend son appareil-photo.
5. C'est faux. Elle ne mange pas de petit déjeuner.   6. C'est vrai. Sa mère lui donne une pomme.

Complétez les phrases suivantes d'après A5.

se dépêche
1. Si Alexandra ne ____ pas, elle va rater le car.
2. Il est déjà dix heures et quart! Elle est ____ !
en retard
3. Son pull bleu _va_ très bien avec son tee-shirt rose.

prend (a oublié)
4. Alexandra ____ son appareil-photo.
5. Sa mère veut qu'Alexandra ____ son petit déjeuner. prenne, mange
6. Elle veut aussi qu'Alexandra ____ . s'amuse

A8 Activité • Et vous? Possible answers are given.

Vous partez avec votre classe en voyage scolaire. Vous emportez cinq objets utiles. Dites quels sont ces objets et pourquoi vous les emportez. Je prends un cahier et un stylo pour écrire / des timbres pour envoyer les cartes postales / un appareil-photo pour prendre des photos.

A9 Activité • Quelques recommandations

Michel ne se sent pas bien. Il a mal au ventre et mal à la tête, mais il veut tout de même partir en voyage avec la classe de Mme Leroy. Qu'est-ce que ses parents lui conseillent avant son départ? Employez **Il faut que...** ou **Il ne faut pas que...** Point out that a negative recommendation should begin with "Il ne faut pas que..."

1. ne pas trop manger
2. bien se soigner
3. ne pas faire de sport
4. mettre son pull

5. emporter son blouson
6. dormir dans le car
7. prendre ses médicaments
8. se coucher tôt

1. Il ne faut pas que tu manges trop. 2. Il faut que tu te soignes bien. 3. Il ne faut pas que tu fasses de sport. 4. Il faut que tu mettes ton pull. 5. Il faut que tu emportes ton blouson. 6. Il faut que tu dormes dans le car. 7. Il faut que tu prennes tes médicaments. 8. Il faut que tu te couches tôt.

A10 Activité • A vous maintenant!

Alexandra arrive en retard au rendez-vous. Tout le monde l'attend depuis plus d'une demi-heure. Mme Leroy, le professeur, est furieuse. Imaginez le dialogue entre Mme Leroy et Alexandra. Faites le dialogue avec un(e) camarade. Voici quelques expressions pour vous aider.

Mme Leroy...

Tu ne pourrais pas... ?
Mais qu'est-ce que tu fais?
Qu'est-ce qui t'est arrivé?
Il faut que tu...
Tu devrais...

Alexandra...

Désolée...
Je regrette, mais...
Je ne pouvais pas...
Je me suis levée...
J'ai oublié...

VOUS EN SOUVENEZ-VOUS?
Interrogative pronouns

You've been using several interrogative pronouns to ask for information. Look at these examples. You recall that **qui** refers to people; **que** or **qu'est-ce que** and **quoi** refer to things.

Qui a téléphoné?	*Who phoned?*
Avec qui est-ce que vous sortez?	*Who are you going out with?*
Que font-ils?	*What are they doing?*
Qu'est-ce que tu fais?	*What are you doing?*
De quoi parlent-ils?	*What are they talking about?*

A 12 STRUCTURES DE BASE
Interrogative pronouns

1. You use interrogative pronouns to ask for information. There are several pronouns, and some of them have different forms. The pronoun and the form you use depend on (1) whether you refer to people or things, (2) whether you use the pronoun as the subject or the object of the verb in your question, and (3) whether you use the pronoun as the object of a preposition in your question.

2. As the subject of a verb, **qui** has two forms and **que** has one. Note that "qui" is more commonly used than "qui est-ce qui."

People	**Qui** a téléphoné? **Qui est-ce qui** a téléphoné?	*Who phoned?*
Things	**Qu'est-ce qui** t'intéresse?	*What interests you?*

As the subject of a verb, **que** must be followed by **est-ce qui: qu'est-ce qui**. **Qui** may be used alone or with **est-ce qui**.

3. As the object of a verb, both **qui** and **que** have two forms.

People	**Qui** cherches-tu? **Qui est-ce que** tu cherches?	*Who are you looking for?*
Things	**Que** cherches-tu? **Qu'est-ce que** tu cherches?	*What are you looking for?*

When using "que," you may say either "Que cherche-t-il?" (inversion) or "Que cherche Pierre?" (reversal), but you may
When **qui** or **que** is used alone as the object of a verb in a question, the subject and the verb must be inverted, or reversed. To avoid inversion, **est-ce que** may be used after **qui** or **que**.
not use both the subject noun and subject pronoun in the same question.

4. As the object of a preposition (such as **de, à, pour, avec**), **qui** may be used, but **que** becomes **quoi**.

People	**De qui** parlez-vous? **De qui** est-ce que vous parlez?	*Who are you talking about?*
Things	**De quoi** parlez-vous? **De quoi** est-ce que vous parlez?	*What are you talking about?*

Here again, inverting the subject and verb of the question can be avoided by using **est-ce que**.

Activité • Trouvez les réponses

Vous allez faire un voyage. Votre ami(e) vous pose des questions. Trouvez des réponses convenables. Travaillez avec un(e) camarade.

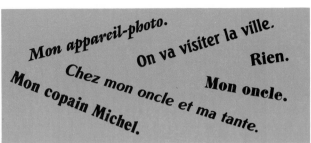

1. Chez qui est-ce que tu vas passer les vacances?
2. Qu'est-ce que tu vas leur offrir?
3. Qu'est-ce que tu emportes?
4. Qui est-ce qui va t'accompagner?
5. Qui est-ce qui va vous retrouver à la gare?
6. Qu'est-ce que vous allez faire là-bas?

1. Chez mon oncle et ma tante.   2. Rien.   3. Mon appareil-photo.   4. Mon copain Michel.   5. Mon oncle.   6. On va visiter la ville.

A 14   Activité • Trouvez les questions   *Possible questions are given.*

directions on type nat the same as these —

Voici des réponses. Est-ce que vous pouvez trouver les questions?

Mes amis viennent avec nous.   Qui est-ce qui vient avec vous?
(Qui vient avec vous?)

1. C'est Mme Leroy qui accompagne les élèves.
2. Ce sont les élèves du collège Alphonse Daudet qui vont visiter Arles.
3. Elle a oublié son appareil-photo.
4. C'est sa sœur qui a pris son pull rouge.
5. Alexandra emporte une pomme.
6. Ils vont faire un pique-nique.

1. Qui accompagne les élèves?   2. Qui va visiter Arles?
3. Qu'a-t-elle oublié?   4. Qui a pris son pull rouge?   5. Qu'est-ce qu'Alexandra emporte?   6. Qu'est-ce qu'ils vont faire?

A 15   Activité • Encore des questions   *Possible answers are given.*

Enfin, Mme Leroy et ses élèves sont en route. Dans le car, il y a beaucoup de bruit. Vous posez des questions aux autres. Trouvez une question pour chacune des situations suivantes.

Luc mange quelque chose.   Qu'est-ce que tu manges?
(Que manges-tu?)

Quelqu'un a crié.   Qui est-ce qui a crié?
(Qui a crié?)

1. Qu'est-ce que tu lis?   2. De qui parles-tu?
3. Qu'est-ce que Mme Leroy a dit?   4. A qui est-ce que le chauffeur a parlé?   5. Qu'est-ce que tu as trouvé?   6. Qu'est-ce que tu veux que je fasse?
7. Qu'est-ce qui a fait ce bruit?   8. Qui a pris mon sac?
9. Qu'est-ce qui est tombé?   10. Qu'est-ce qu'Eric a demandé?   11. Que cherchent Chloé et Isabelle?

1. Pierre lit quelque chose.
2. Claire parle de quelqu'un.
3. Mme Leroy a dit quelque chose.
4. Le chauffeur a parlé à quelqu'un.
5. Votre ami(e) a trouvé quelque chose.
6. Un(e) camarade veut que vous fassiez quelque chose.
7. Quelque chose a fait un grand bruit.
8. Quelqu'un a pris votre sac.
9. Quelque chose est tombé.
10. Eric a demandé quelque chose.
11. Chloé et Isabelle cherchent quelque chose.

A 16 Activité • Et vous?

1. A quoi est-ce que vous vous intéressez?
2. Avec qui est-ce que vous aimez parler?
   1. Je m'intéresse à...
   2. J'aime parler avec...

3. De quoi est-ce que vous aimez parler?
4. De quoi est-ce que vous avez envie?
   3. J'aime parler de...
   4. J'ai envie de...

A 17 COMMENT LE DIRE
Expressing impatience

Vite! On est en retard!
Dépêche-toi! On va rater le train!
Tu vas être en retard!

Tu peux te dépêcher?
Mais qu'est-ce que tu fais?

Making excuses

Je suis pressé(e).
Je suis déjà en retard.

Je n'ai pas le temps.
Il faut que je sois à l'école dans cinq minutes.

A 18 Activité • Alexandra est toujours en retard

Vous êtes venu(e) chercher Alexandra pour prendre le car. Elle n'a pas fini de se préparer. Qu'est-ce que vous lui dites? Faites les dialogues avec un(e) camarade. Employez les expressions dans A17.

Alexandra veut téléphoner à un copain.   — Attends. Je veux téléphoner à un copain.
                                          — Tu n'as pas le temps. On va être en retard!

1. Alexandra veut mettre ses boucles d'oreille.
2. Elle ne trouve pas son pull rouge.
3. Elle veut prendre son petit déjeuner.

4. Elle cherche son appareil-photo.
5. Elle n'a pas préparé son sac.

A 19 Activité • Alexandra n'a pas le temps   Possible answers are given.

Alexandra est prête à partir. Elle est pressée. Le téléphone sonne. C'est son copain Bernard. Il est gentil, mais qu'est-ce qu'il aime parler! Trouvez les réponses d'Alexandra. Employez les expressions dans A17.

— Allô, Alexandra, c'est Bernard. Ça va?
— ... Oui, ça va, mais il faut que je sois à l'école dans cinq minutes.
— Je ne vais pas te déranger longtemps. C'est au sujet des maths. Tu peux m'aider?
— ... Pas maintenant. On part pour Arles et je vais rater le car.
— Tu vas à Arles? Je ne savais pas. Qu'est-ce que vous allez faire?
— ... Je ne sais pas, Bernard. Excuse-moi, mais je suis pressée.
— Bon, d'accord. Mais tu rentres quand?
— ... Dans deux jours. Je suis en retard, au revoir!
— Attends, attends... Tu peux me rapporter un souvenir?
— ... Oui, d'accord. Alors, à mercredi!
— Bon, bon, si tu ne veux pas me parler... Bon voyage!

Activité • Jeu de rôle Possible dialogue is given.

Vous partez en pique-nique avec des copains. Il faut que vous vous dépêchiez pour ne pas rater le train. Un(e) ami(e) arrive au moment où vous partez et vous propose de faire quelque chose. Vous ne pouvez pas parce que vous êtes pressé(e). Il/Elle insiste et vous perdez du temps.

— Tiens, tu ne veux pas… ?
— Désolé(e), mais je suis pressé(e)…

—Ça ne prend pas longtemps.
—Non, je n'ai pas le temps. Je dois prendre le train.
—Mais tu peux prendre un train plus tard!

A 21 **ARRET A BERRE**

Sur la route d'Arles, le groupe s'arrête pour visiter le complexe chimique de Berre.

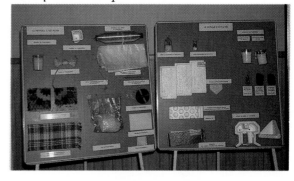

Le complexe chimique de Berre est une usine où on fait de la recherche…

… et où on produit des solvants, des pesticides et des matières plastiques.

ERIC De quoi est-ce qu'il parle, le guide? J'y comprends rien!
CHLOÉ De l'usine.
ERIC Ça t'intéresse, toi? Moi, ça me barbe. J'ai faim!… Elle doit drôlement polluer, cette usine!

Après la visite de l'usine, Mme Leroy et ses élèves pique-niquent au bord de l'étang de Berre.

JULIE Ah, c'est bien, le pique-nique!… A quoi est-ce que tu penses?
FLORENCE A l'école. C'est sympathique d'être ici, non?
JULIE Oui, ça change.
FLORENCE Moi, ça me donne envie de faire de longs voyages.

Répondez aux questions suivantes d'après A21. Choisissez des mots dans la boîte de droite pour répondre.

1. Avec quoi est-ce qu'on produit des pesticides?
2. Avec qui est-ce qu'Eric parle?
3. De qui est-ce qu'Eric parle?
4. De quoi est-ce que le guide parle?
5. Avec qui est-ce que les jeunes pique-niquent?
6. A quoi est-ce que Florence pense?

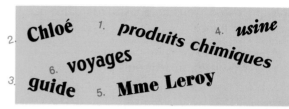

Chloé   1. produits chimiques   4. usine
2.   6. voyages
guide   3.   5. Mme Leroy

A 23   POUR LE PIQUE-NIQUE

Voici ce qu'il vous faut pour pique-niquer.

une baguette

du fromage

une thermos

des biscuits

des boissons

du saucisson

des fruits

des verres et des assiettes en papier

un panier

une nappe

A 24 Activité • A vous maintenant!

Vous avez envie d'organiser un pique-nique. Vous avez choisi un joli endroit, et maintenant vous voulez savoir qui veut venir et qui apporte quoi. Vous interrogez vos camarades, et vous répondez à leurs questions. Travaillez en groupes de quatre ou cinq.

Vous :	Vos camarades :
Qui est-ce qui veut faire un pique-nique?	Où est-ce que c'est?
Qui est-ce qui apporte… ?	Quand? Avec qui?…

A 25 Activité • Et vous?

1. Faites-vous des pique-niques? Avec qui? Quand?
2. Où pique-niquez-vous d'habitude? Dans un parc? Dans votre jardin?
3. Qu'est-ce que vous mangez?
4. Qu'est-ce que vous buvez?
5. Qui apporte quoi?
6. Qu'est-ce que vous faites comme activités?

A 26 Activité • Ecrivez   Possible answer is given.

Vous allez partir en voyage avec Mme Leroy et ses élèves. Vos parents ne sont pas chez vous, et ils ne vont pas rentrer avant votre départ. Vous leur écrivez un petit mot. Vous leur dites où vous allez, avec qui, ce que vous allez faire et quand vous allez rentrer.

Chers Maman et Papa, Je pars pour Arles avec Mme Leroy et la classe. D'abord, on va visiter la ville et ensuite, on va aller en Camargue. Je rentre mercredi soir. A mercredi. Bises, . . .

A 27 Activité • Ecoutez bien 🔲   For script and answers, see p. T212.

Avant un départ en voyage, il y a souvent des problèmes. Ecoutez Mme Leroy, et ensuite, choisissez la bonne réponse.

1. Alexandra est…
   a. malade.   **b.** en retard.   **c.** là.

2. Florence téléphone…
   a. à sa mère.   **b.** au chauffeur.   **c.** à Alexandra.

3. Mme Leroy n'a pas pensé…
   a. au pique-nique.   **b.** aux bagages.   **c.** à son appareil-photo.

4. François va chercher…
   a. ses bagages.   **b.** son appareil-photo.   **c.** le pique-nique.

5. Mme Leroy demande à Chloé et Eric d'…
   a. acheter un parapluie.   **b.** aller chercher Alexandra.   **c.** acheter du pain et du fromage.

6. Le chauffeur est arrivé…
   a. à dix heures.   **b.** en retard.   **c.** en avance.

7. Le car…
   a. ne veut pas partir.   **b.** est prêt à partir.   **c.** est trop petit.

8. Il commence à…
   a. pleuvoir.   **b.** neiger.   **c.** faire froid.

Voyage à Arles   351

exploring the city of Arles . . . making comparisons . . . expressing relief and regret

Il y a aujourd'hui des villes provençales plus importantes qu'Arles, comme Avignon ou Aix-en-Provence, mais à une époque lointaine, Arles était la plus grande ville de Provence. Maintenant encore, quand on se promène, on peut voir des vestiges de ce merveilleux passé.

Have students locate Arles, Avignon, and Aix-en-Provence on the map on p. 354.

B1

Visite d'Arles

Le groupe est arrivé à Arles. Les élèves ont dormi dans le dortoir d'un lycée, et après le petit déjeuner, Mme Leroy les a emmenés faire le tour de la ville.

MME LEROY   Arles est une ancienne cité romaine. Il reste encore de très nombreux vestiges. Ici, nous sommes dans les arènes. Au temps des Romains, il y avait des combats de gladiateurs. Parfois, on lâchait les lions. Les gladiateurs devaient se défendre. Le plus souvent, malheureusement, ils étaient dévorés. Tout Arles assistait à ces jeux!

MME LEROY	Maintenant, on organise des courses de taureaux. Heureusement que les taureaux ne sont pas mis à mort!... C'est interdit... C'est plus civilisé.
ERIC	Dommage!
CHLOÉ	Quoi?
ERIC	Qu'il n'y ait pas de mise à mort! J'étais en Espagne l'année dernière. On tuait les taureaux! C'était super!
CHLOÉ	Barbare!

MME LEROY	Voici le théâtre... probablement le mieux conservé de la région. Dommage qu'on ne soit pas en été! Au moment du festival, on y donne d'excellentes pièces de théâtre et de très bons opéras.
ALEXANDRA	Eh bien, heureusement qu'on n'est pas en été! Je déteste l'opéra!
FRANÇOISE	Chut! Elle va t'entendre!
MME LEROY	En juillet, on y organise aussi les Rencontres Internationales de la Photographie, la plus importante manifestation consacrée à la photographie en France.

ALEXANDRA	Madame, qu'est-ce qu'on fait cet après-midi?
MME LEROY	Pourquoi? Vous vous ennuyez?
ALEXANDRA	Pas du tout!
MME LEROY	On va faire de l'équitation en Camargue. Là-bas, on trouve les plus beaux chevaux de la région.
FRANÇOISE	Et à quelle heure on revient?
MME LEROY	Le plus tard possible!

B2   Activité • Avez-vous compris?

Répondez aux questions suivantes d'après B1.

1. Dans quelle région de France se trouve Arles?
2. Comment sait-on que les Romains habitaient Arles?
3. Qu'est-ce qu'on organisait dans les arènes au temps des Romains?
4. Quelle est la différence entre les courses de taureaux à Arles et celles en Espagne?
5. Qu'est-ce qu'on donne maintenant dans le théâtre antique?
6. Quelle est la saison la plus touristique à Arles?

1. Arles se trouve en Provence.   2. On le sait parce qu'on peut y voir des vestiges romains.   3. Il y avait des combats de gladiateurs.   4. En Espagne, on tue les taureaux.   5. Au moment du festival, on y donne d'excellentes pièces de théâtre et de très bons opéras.   6. L'été est la saison la plus touristique à Arles.

Choisissez un site ou un monument historique de votre ville, de votre état ou de votre pays. Travaillez avec un(e) camarade et préparez un commentaire. Ensuite, faites le guide pour votre classe. Washington est la capitale des Etats-Unis. Elle est située au bord du Potomac. Nous sommes maintenant devant le Capitole. C'est le siège du Sénat et de la Chambre des Représentants. Derrière nous, vous pouvez admirer le Smithsonian. Allons visiter le musée!

B4   Savez-vous que... ?

La Provence est une des régions les plus jolies et les plus touristiques de France. Elle a inspiré de nombreux peintres, attirés (*attracted*) par sa belle lumière (*light*). Les plus connus sont l'impressionniste français Paul Cézanne (1839–1906) et le Néerlandais Vincent Van Gogh (1853–1890).

Cézanne est né à Aix-en-Provence. Il est célèbre pour ses recherches en peinture et pour sa série de tableaux sur la montagne Sainte-Victoire, près d'Aix.

Voici le vrai pont de Langlois, un pont-levis (*drawbridge*). Mais ce n'est pas celui que Van Gogh a peint : c'est une reproduction de l'ancien pont qui n'existe plus. Van Gogh aimait ce vieux pont parce qu'il ressemblait à ceux de Hollande, son pays natal.

Van Gogh a vécu à Arles en 1888. Pauvre, malade et en proie à une crise de folie (*prey to madness*), il s'est coupé l'oreille et a été hospitalisé à Saint-Rémy-de-Provence en 1889. Une de ses œuvres, *Le Pont de Langlois*, est un des tableaux les plus connus du monde.

VOUS EN SOUVENEZ-VOUS?
Making comparisons

You recall that you make comparisons with nouns by using **plus, autant,** or **moins** + **de (d')** + a noun + **que (qu').**

En ville, il y a	**plus de concerts qu'**	à la campagne.
En ville, il a	**autant d'amis qu'**	à la campagne.
A la campagne, il y a	**moins de monde qu'**	en ville.

You also remember that you make comparisons with adjectives or adverbs by using **plus, aussi,** or **moins** + an adjective or an adverb + **que (qu').**

Le bus est	**plus pratique que**	le métro.
Le bus est	**aussi cher que**	le métro.
Le bus va	**moins vite que**	le métro.

Remember that adjectives always agree in gender and number with nouns, even in comparisons.

B6   STRUCTURES DE BASE
Making comparisons: superlatives of adjectives and adverbs

1. When you compare one person or thing to others, you may use the superlative: the most, the least. To form the superlative in French, you use the appropriate article, **le, la,** or **les,** followed by **plus,** *most*, or **moins,** *least.*

2. Superlatives of adjectives are formed with the appropriate article, **le, la,** or **les.** The adjectives agree with the nouns they refer to. To express *in* or *of* after the superlative, you use **de.**

Person/Thing	le/la/les	plus/moins	Adjective	de	Group/Place
C'est la ville	la	plus	ancienne	de	Provence.
Les chevaux de Camargue sont	les	plus	beaux *ch.*	de	la région.
Eric est	le	moins	sérieux	du	groupe.

^le garçon

3. The adjective **bon(ne)** cannot be used with **le plus.** Instead, you must use **le (la) (les) meilleur(e)(s),** *the best.*

    Le pique-nique était **le meilleur** moment du voyage.

4. Superlatives of adverbs are always formed with **le.**

Person/Thing	le	plus/moins	Adverb
Alexandra arrive	le	plus	tard.
Elle court	le	moins	vite.

5. The adverb **bien** cannot be used with **le.** Instead, you must use **le mieux:** C'est le monument **le mieux** conservé.   Remind the students that adverbs are also used to modify verbs: Elle travaille le mieux.

6. **Ce,** rather than **il, elle, ils,** or **elles,** is normally used before **être** when followed by a superlative. **Eric? C'est le moins sérieux.**
    Point out the difference in placement between adjectives that usually appear before the noun and those that usually follow it: Nous avons visité les plus vieux vestiges de la région. Nous avons visité les vestiges les plus intéressants de la région. For a list of adjectives that occur before the noun, see Unit 3, p. 96.

Activité • **Pouvez-vous les comparer?** Possible answers are given.

Vous avez fait la connaissance de certains membres du groupe, et vous pouvez imaginer leur caractère. Comparez-les deux à deux.

Chloé est plus sérieuse qu'Eric.   Chloé est la plus sérieuse (des deux).

Eric est le moins sérieux (des deux).

1. Florence est plus sensible qu'Alexandra.
2. Alexandra est plus petite qu'Eric.
3. Eric est moins âgé que François.

4. Chloé est plus organisée qu'Eric.
5. Julie est moins économe que Florence.
6. Mme Leroy est plus intéressée que ses élèves.

1. Florence est la plus sensible.   2. Alexandra est la plus petite.   3. Eric est le moins âgé.   4. Chloé est la plus organisée. 5. Julie est la moins économe.   6. Mme Leroy est la plus intéressée.

B8   Activité • **Exagérez un peu**

Mme Leroy et ses élèves aiment beaucoup Arles, sa région et son passé. Complétez leurs conversations avec le superlatif des adjectifs.

— Arles est une jolie ville!   — Arles est une jolie ville!

— Oui, c'est... Provence.   — Oui, c'est la plus jolie ville de Provence.

1. — Saint-Trophime, c'est une ancienne église?
   — Oui, c'est... Arles. la plus ancienne d'
2. — Qu'est-ce qu'il est bien conservé, ce théâtre! le mieux conservé de
   — Oui, c'est... tous les vestiges romains.
3. — Il y a une importante manifestation de photos à Arles?
   — Oui, c'est... France. la plus importante de

4. — Van Gogh est un très bon peintre. Tu trouves pas? le meilleur de
   — Si, c'est... tous les peintres flamands.
5. — La Camargue a une vaste réserve d'oiseaux.
   — Oui, c'est... région. la plus vaste de la
6. — Il y a de beaux chevaux en Camargue.
   — C'est vrai. Ce sont... région. les plus beaux de la

B9   Activité • **Qui fait quoi, et comment?**

Comparez les membres du groupe avec le superlatif des adverbes.

Françoise écoute bien.   C'est Françoise qui écoute le mieux.

Julie ne parle pas beaucoup.   C'est Julie qui parle le moins.

1. Alexandra arrive tard. Alexandra arrive le plus tard.
2. Françoise arrive tôt. Françoise arrive le plus tôt.
3. Eric mange vite. Eric mange le plus vite.

4. Mme Leroy parle fort. Mme Leroy parle le plus fort.
5. Eric n'écoute pas attentivement. Eric écoute le moins attentivement.
6. Julie a bien dormi. Julie a dormi le mieux.

B10   Activité • **Ecrit dirigé**

De retour au lycée, Alexandra a écrit une rédaction (*composition*) sur Arles. Recopiez sa rédaction et complétez-la avec les superlatifs des adjectifs et des adverbes entre parenthèses.

Au temps des Romains, Arles était (grand) la plus grande ville de Provence et (beau) la plus belle. On y donnait les jeux (célèbre) les plus célèbres dans le grand amphithéâtre. Les gladiateurs (fort) tuaient quelquefois les lions, mais les plus fo (souvent) le plus souvent l'homme était dévoré. Aujourd'hui, l'amphithéâtre s'appelle les arènes, parce qu'on y donne les jeux (populaire) les plus populaires sans mise à mort. Le théâtre antique est le monument (bien) le mieux conservé conservé de la région. C'est aussi le monument ancien (joli) le plus joli d'Arles. Il est utilisé pour les Rencontres Internationales de la Photographie, (important) la plus importante manifestation consacrée à la photographie. Si vous allez en France, ne manquez pas de visiter Arles, une des villes (intéressant) les plus intéressantes de Provence!

COMMENT LE DIRE
Expressing relief and regret

RELIEF	REGRET
Heureusement qu'il fait beau!	Malheureusement, elle est arrivée en retard!
Nous avons de la chance qu'il fasse beau!	C'est dommage qu'elle soit arrivée en retard!
Ouf! Il n'a pas plu!	Quel dommage! Elle est arrivée en retard!
C'est une bonne chose qu'il n'ait pas plu!	

Note that the past subjunctive is composed of the present subjunctive of the auxiliary verb **avoir** or **être** and the past participle of the main verb. C'est une bonne chose qu'il n'**ait** pas **plu**! C'est dommage qu'elle **soit arrivée** en retard! Point out that the subjunctive is used only in certain expressions.

B12 Activité • Actes de parole

Pouvez-vous trouver dans les dialogues de B1 deux expressions de regret et deux expressions de soulagement *(relief)*?
Le plus souvent, malheureusement, ils étaient dévorés. / Dommage! / Dommage qu'on ne soit pas en été!
Heureusement que les taureaux ne sont pas mis à mort. / Eh bien, heureusement qu'on n'est pas en été!

B13 Activité • Remettez le dialogue dans le bon ordre

Eric et Chloé parlent des courses de taureaux et de l'exposition de photo à Arles. Travaillez avec un(e) camarade et remettez leur conversation dans le bon ordre.

Eric

Chloé

3
Moi, j'aime regarder les courses de taureaux, mais c'est dommage qu'il n'y ait pas de mise à mort.

8
C'est vrai, nous avons de la chance qu'il fasse beau!

7
Ne nous disputons pas. Reposons-nous et profitons du soleil.

2
Oh non, heureusement! Moi, je déteste les expositions de photo!

1
C'est dommage qu'on ne soit pas en juillet, j'adore la photo.

4
Heureusement qu'il n'y a pas de mise à mort. C'est si cruel!

5
En Espagne, on tue les taureaux dans l'arène.

6
Oui, et moi, je trouve que c'est une bonne chose qu'on ne soit pas en Espagne!

Activité • **Regret ou soulagement?** Possible answers are given.

Vous visitez Arles avec des amis. Pendant votre visite, on répond à vos questions à l'Office de tourisme, au restaurant, à la gare, dans la rue… Pour chaque réponse, exprimez votre regret ou votre soulagement à vos amis. Variez les expressions. 1. C'est dommage! Ils n'ont plus de plans.

2. Malheureusement, tous les hôtels sont complets.

Les taxis sont juste en face. — Nous avons de la chance que les taxis soient juste en face!

1. Je n'ai plus de plans de la ville.

2. Tous les hôtels sont complets.

3. Le festival? Il a fini hier.

4. J'ai une seule table libre.

5. Nous n'avons plus de gâteau.

6. Il n'y a pas de courses de taureaux.

7. Le musée n'est pas ouvert aujourd'hui.

8. Les étudiants ont droit à un tarif réduit.

9. Le bus passe devant le théâtre.

10. Le train est déjà parti.

3. Quel dommage! Le festival a fini hier. 4. Nous avons de la chance qu'ils aient une table libre. 5. Malheureusement, il n'y a plus de gâteau. 6. Quel dommage! Il n'y a pas de courses de taureaux. 7. C'est dommage que le musée ne soit pas ouvert aujourd'hui. 8. Heureusement que les étudiants ont droit à un tarif réduit. 9. Nous avons de la chance que le bus passe devant le théâtre. 10. Malheureusement, le train est déjà parti.

B15 Activité • **A vous maintenant!**

Travaillez avec un(e) camarade. D'abord, trouvez une expression de regret ou de soulagement pour chacune des situations suivantes. Variez les expressions. Ensuite, préparez un dialogue pour chaque situation. Possible answers are given.

1. Vous détestez la campagne. Des copains vous ont invité(e). Vous n'êtes pas parti(e) parce qu'il pleuvait. Tell the students the subjunctive for "il pleut" is "il pleuve."

2. Votre classe organise un voyage. Vous avez envie d'y participer, mais vous êtes malade.

3. Vous avez invité votre amie à sortir avec vous ce week-end, mais elle a du travail et elle ne peut malheureusement pas venir.

1. C'est une bonne chose qu'il pleuve! 2. Malheureusement, je suis malade! 3. C'est dommage qu'elle ne puisse pas venir.

B16 Activité • **Organisez un voyage scolaire** Possible answer is given.

Votre classe d'histoire ou de français va faire un voyage. Le professeur vous a demandé de faire des projets pour le voyage. Travaillez avec un(e) camarade. Décidez où vous allez, pourquoi, quand, comment, ce que vous allez faire là-bas, quand vous allez rentrer… Présentez vos projets à la classe.

Nous allons à Washington, D.C. parce que nous voulons voir les monuments. On va y aller dans deux semaines. On va prendre un avion et ensuite, on va visiter la ville en bus et à pied. Nous allons partir dimanche et rentrer mercredi.

B17 Activité • **Ecrivez** Possible answer is given.

Décrivez un voyage scolaire que vous avez fait. Dites où, avec qui, pourquoi, quand, comment vous y êtes allé(e)s, ce que vous avez fait là-bas, quand vous êtes rentré(e)s… Donnez aussi vos impressions sur le voyage et dites ce que vous avez appris.

Je suis allé(e)… avec ma classe de… pour… On est parti le… On a pris… pour y aller. On a vu… et on a visité… parce que… J'ai aimé… Je n'ai pas aimé… J'ai appris que…

B18 Activité • **Ecoutez bien** For script and answers, see p. T216.

Julie et Eric échangent leurs impressions sur la visite d'Arles. Ecoutez leur conversation et dites ensuite ce qu'ils ont aimé, ce qu'ils n'ont pas aimé et ce qu'ils regrettent.

Julie :	Eric :
Ce qu'elle a aimé :	Ce qu'il a aimé :
Ce qu'elle n'a pas aimé :	Ce qu'il n'a pas aimé :
Ce qu'elle regrette :	Ce qu'il regrette :

talking about the trip . . . telling about past events . . .
expressing lack of interest

Tout a une fin, même les bonnes choses! Le temps a passé très vite et il faut déjà songer à partir. Mais avant de quitter Arles, tout le monde profite des derniers instants.

C1   Dernières heures

Le rendez-vous est fixé à 16h00 au car. C'est le moment de prendre des photos et d'écrire des cartes postales, car après, ce n'est plus possible.

Avant de partir, Françoise prend le plus de photos possible. C'est la meilleure façon de garder des souvenirs.

— Allez, souriez un peu!... Qu'est-ce que vous avez l'air bêtes!... Mais arrêtez de faire des grimaces! Soyez naturels! Cette photo va être exposée aux Rencontres Internationales d'Arles!... Attention, le petit oiseau va sortir!

Florence et Julie vont acheter des cartes postales.

JULIE   Je n'ai pas le courage d'écrire à mes parents.

FLORENCE   Fais un effort. Ça fait toujours plaisir, une petite carte!

JULIE   «Chers parents... Euh... Quand nous sommes arrivés, il faisait beau...» Je n'ai plus d'idées. Qu'est-ce que je peux mettre?

FLORENCE   Je ne sais pas, invente!

Enfin, après avoir pris des photos, écrit des cartes postales et pris un dernier verre dans un café, les élèves sont montés dans le car.

En route! Adieu, Arles!

"Adieu" is used to say goodbye when one is never going to see the person or place again, or at least not for a long time.

Activité • Avez-vous compris?

Répondez aux questions suivantes d'après C1.

1. Qu'est-ce que Françoise fait avant de partir? Pourquoi?
2. Qu'est-ce qu'elle veut que le groupe fasse?
3. Qu'est-ce que Julie est allée acheter?
4. Avec qui y est-elle allée?
5. Pourquoi faut-il envoyer une carte postale?
6. A qui Julie écrit-elle?
7. De quoi est-ce qu'elle parle?
8. Qu'est-ce qu'on fait avant de monter dans le car?

1. Elle prend le plus de photos possible, parce que c'est la meilleure façon de garder des souvenirs. 2. Elle veut que le groupe sourie. 3. Elle est allée acheter des cartes postales. 4. Elle y est allée avec Florence. 5. Ça fait toujours plaisir 6. Julie écrit à ses parents. 7. Elle parle de l'arrivée à Arles et du temps qu'il faisait. 8. Avant de monter dans le car, on prend des photos, on écrit des cartes postales et on prend un dernier verre dans un café.

C3 Activité • Actes de parole

Relisez les dialogues dans C1. Qui est-ce qui dit quoi? Et pourquoi?

1. Qui est-ce qui encourage quelqu'un? Qu'est-ce qu'elle dit?
2. Qui est-ce qui demande des conseils? Qu'est-ce qu'elle dit?
3. Qui est-ce qui donne une raison de faire quelque chose? Qu'est-ce qu'elle dit?
4. Qui est-ce qui s'exclame? Qu'est-ce qu'elle dit?

1. Florence encourage Julie. Elle lui dit : Fais un effort. 2. Julie demande des conseils. Elle dit : Qu'est-ce que je peux mettre? 3. Florence donne une raison. Elle dit : Ça fait toujours plaisir, une petite carte! 4. Françoise s'exclame. Elle dit : Attention, le petit oiseau va sortir!

C4 Activité • Ecrivez   Possible answers are given.

Julie n'a plus d'idées. Aidez-la à écrire sa carte postale. Dites ce que vous avez vu à Arles, ce que vous avez visité, ce que vous avez fait… J'ai vu les arènes romaines / le théâtre antique / les Alyscamps / les chevaux de Camargue. J'ai visité le complexe chimique de Berre / le Musée Réattu / la Cathédrale et le Cloître Saint-Trophime / le Musée Arlaten / les thermes de Constantin. J'ai pique-niqué au bord de l'étang / fait le tour de la ville / fait de l'équitation.

C5 Activité • A vous maintenant!

Florence, Alexandra, Françoise et Eric sont au café devant un dernier verre. Vous les connaissez mieux maintenant. Vous savez ce qu'ils ont fait et ce qu'ils aiment ou n'aiment pas. Imaginez leurs commentaires et jouez la conversation. Travaillez en groupe.

C6 Savez-vous que… ?

Arles est la capitale de la photographie. Depuis 1982, il y a une école nationale de photographie. Les études durent trois ans. On y apprend la technique… et aussi à regarder.

En juillet, pendant un mois, il y a les Rencontres Internationales. C'est l'occasion pour les photographes de se rencontrer, d'échanger des idées et de montrer leur travail. Dans toute la ville, il y a des expositions de photographie. On peut aussi voir des projections de diapositives (slides) ou des reportages dans le théâtre antique… Quel curieux mélange (mixture)! Si les Romains voyaient leur théâtre!…

Alors, si vous êtes photographe amateur, venez à Arles! C'est fantastique!

Si vous êtes photographe amateur, qu'est-ce qu'il vous faut?

une pellicule couleur ou noir et blanc pour diapositives ou pour photos sur papier

un appareil-photo

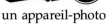

un objectif grand angle pour prendre des vues générales

un zoom pour prendre des gros plans

gros plans: close-ups

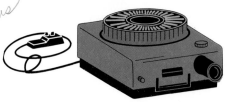

un projecteur avec carrousel

un flash électronique

un écran pour projeter les diapositives

C8 Activité • Qu'est-ce qu'il vous faut?

De quel matériel photographique avez-vous besoin dans les situations suivantes?

1. Vous voulez prendre des photos.
2. Vous voulez photographier un petit objet.
3. Vous avez envie de prendre une vue très large.
4. Vous allez organiser vos diapositives avant de les projeter.
5. Vous allez montrer vos diapositives à vos amis.

1. un appareil-photo, une pellicule   2. un zoom   3. un objectif grand angle   4. un carrousel   5. un projecteur et un écran

---

C9 Activité • Le photographe débutant

Vous voulez acheter du matériel photo. Vous allez dans une boutique spécialisée, et vous posez des questions au vendeur(à la vendeuse). Complétez la conversation. Travaillez avec un(e) camarade.

VENDEUR/VENDEUSE	Vous désirez?
VOUS	Bonjour, monsieur/madame. Je veux acheter un… appareil-photo.
VENDEUR/VENDEUSE	Quelle marque voulez-vous?
VOUS	La meilleure et la… chère! moins
VENDEUR/VENDEUSE	Ça, c'est difficile! Et si vous voulez faire des photos à l'intérieur, il faut que vous achetiez… un flash électronique.
VOUS	Et pour prendre un grand bâtiment de près?
VENDEUR/VENDEUSE	Vous avez besoin d'un… Pour photographier une objectif grand angle.

fleur ou un animal de loin, vous avez besoin d'un… Ça rapproche les objets. zoom.

VOUS Bon, je vais voir. Je n'ai pas assez d'argent pour tous les accessoires. Je crois que je ne vais appareil-photo. acheter que cet… et des.. pellicules.

VENDEUR/VENDEUSE Couleur ou noir et blanc?

VOUS … Couleur.

VENDEUR/VENDEUSE Pour… ou pour photos? diapositives

VOUS Pour… photos.

STRUCTURES DE BASE
The past infinitive

The preposition **après** may be followed by the past infinitive. The past infinitive of a verb is composed of two parts:

- **être** or **avoir,** depending on which auxiliary verb the main verb takes in the **passé composé;**
- the past participle of the main verb.

Infinitive	Passé Composé	Past Infinitive
arriver	Ils **sont arrivés.**	**Après être arrivés,** ils ont visité l'usine.
se reposer	Nous **nous sommes reposés.**	**Après nous être reposés,** nous avons continué la visite.
déjeuner	J'**ai déjeuné.**	**Après avoir déjeuné,** j'ai acheté des cartes postales.

Notice that the agreement of the past participle in the past infinitive follows the same rules as those you've learned for the **passé composé.**

C11 Activité • Qu'est-ce qu'ils ont fait? Et après?

Dites ce que Mme Leroy et ses élèves ont fait. Faites des phrases avec le passé de l'infinitif.

arriver au rendez-vous / monter dans le car   Après être arrivés au rendez-vous, ils sont montés dans le car.

1. déjeuner / se reposer
2. se promener dans Arles / aller en Camargue
3. arriver en Camargue / monter à cheval

4. faire du cheval / rentrer au lycée
5. prendre des photos / écrire des cartes postales
6. boire un dernier verre / monter dans le car

1. Après avoir déjeuné, ils se sont reposés. 2. Après s'être promenés, ils sont allés en Camargue. 3. Après être arrivés en Camargue, ils sont montés à cheval. 4. Après avoir fait du cheval, ils sont rentrés au lycée. 5. Après avoir pris des photos, ils ont écrit des cartes postales. 6. Après avoir bu un dernier verre, ils sont montés dans le car.

C12 Activité • A vous maintenant!
Possible answers are given.

Voici quelques activités que les élèves ont faites pendant le trajet. Dites ce qu'ils ont fait d'abord et ce qu'ils ont fait ensuite. Faites le maximum de phrases avec le passé de l'infinitif.

Ils sont arrivés à Berre.   Après être arrivés à Berre, ils ont visité l'usine.
Ils ont visité l'usine.

Après avoir vu les arènes...   Après avoir visité...   Après avoir fait le tour d'Arles...   Après avoir pique-niqué...

Ils ont vu les arènes.

Ils ont visité le théâtre antique.

Ils sont montés dans le car.

Ils ont fait le tour d'Arles.

Ils ont passé la nuit dans le dortoir d'un lycée.

Ils ont pique-niqué.

Ils se sont arrêtés à Berre.

Ils ont fait de l'équitation en Camargue.

Ils ont écrit des cartes postales.

Ils sont allés à l'étang.

Après avoir écrit...   Après être montés...   Après avoir passé la nuit dans le dortoir d'un lycée...   Après s'être arrêtés à Berre...
Après avoir fait de l'équitation...   Après être allés à l'étang...

COMMENT LE DIRE
Expressing lack of interest

> Ecrire des cartes postales, ça ne me dit rien.
> Je n'ai pas le courage d'écrire des cartes postales.
> Ça m'embête d'écrire des cartes postales.
> Ça m'ennuie d'écrire des cartes postales.
> Je n'ai pas (souvent) envie d'écrire des cartes postales.
> Ecrire des cartes postales? Tu parles!

C14 Activité • Et vous?

Qu'est-ce qui ne vous intéresse pas? Ecrire des cartes postales? Visiter des musées? Faire un voyage scolaire? Faites une liste d'au moins six choses qui ne vous intéressent pas, et exprimez votre manque d'enthousiasme *(lack of interest)*. Variez les expressions.

Students should use expressions from C13 above. Remind them to use the infinitive as shown.

C15 Activité • A vous maintenant!   *Possible answers are given.*

Votre camarade vous propose de faire plusieurs choses. Exprimez votre manque d'enthousiasme. Variez les expressions et changez de rôle.

Ça te dit de... ?   Tu veux... ?   Ça te plairait de... ?
Tu ne veux pas... ?   Ça t'intéresse de... ?

1. Il fait chaud, et on vous demande d'aller faire des courses.
2. Vous êtes fatigué(e), et on vous invite à faire 10 km de jogging.
3. Vous revenez de voyage, et on vous invite à sortir.
4. Vous avez très bien déjeuné, et on vous propose de manger.
5. Vous faites un voyage agréable, et on vous demande de rentrer à la maison.
6. On vous demande d'aller rendre visite à des gens. Vous ne les aimez pas.

1. Aller faire des courses, ça ne me dit rien.   2. Faire 10 km de jogging? Tu parles!   3. Je n'ai pas envie de sortir parce que je reviens d'un voyage.   4. Je n'ai pas envie de manger. J'ai déjà déjeuné.   5. Ça m'ennuie de rentrer à la maison. C'est un voyage très agréable.   6. Ça m'embête de leur rendre visite!

C16 Activité • Ecoutez bien   *For script and answers, see p. T220.*

Alexandra a écrit une lettre à votre classe de français. Dans sa lettre, elle décrit son voyage à Arles. Avant de vous lire la lettre, votre professeur vous donne une liste des principales activités d'Alexandra, et vous demande d'indiquer quel jour elle les a faites. Après avoir écouté la lettre, écrivez 1 (premier jour), 2 (deuxième jour) ou 3 (troisième jour) en face de chaque activité.

_____ Elle arrive à Arles.
_____ Elle monte à cheval.
_____ Elle achète un timbre.
_____ Elle revient chez elle.
_____ Elle pique-nique.

_____ Elle écrit la lettre.
_____ Elle prend le petit déjeuner au lycée.
_____ Elle visite le théâtre antique.
_____ Elle visite l'usine.

1

La séance diapo

Rentrée à Nice, la classe a repris les cours… Mais le voyage n'est pas complètement terminé. La semaine suivante, Mme Leroy rassemble toutes les photos prises par ses élèves et organise une séance diapo.

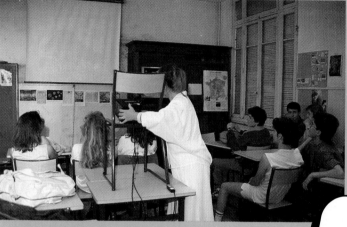

MME LEROY   Je vais vous projeter ces photos, mais attention! Après les avoir regardées, je veux que vous fassiez un compte-rendu° écrit sur le voyage. D'accord? Pas de questions? Bon, allons-y!

MME LEROY	Vous reconnaissez?
TOUS	Bien sûr!
MME LEROY	Qu'est-ce que c'est?
ERIC	Les arènes.
CHLOÉ	Mais non, idiot, c'est le théâtre!

MME LEROY	Et ça?
ERIC	C'est Paris!
MME LEROY	Eric, si tu continues, tu vas sortir!

Photo above: la Camargue

FRANÇOISE   Superbe, cette photo!
Qui est-ce qui l'a
prise?

ERIC   C'est moi!

FRANÇOISE   Bravo, c'est la plus
jolie!

JULIE   C'est pas vrai, c'est
pas lui, c'est moi!

MARC   Eh bien, Alexandra, tu fais une drôle de tête sur cette photo!
A quoi pensais-tu? Tu as l'air un peu idiote!

ALEXANDRA   Et toi? Tu t'es pas regardé? Quelle grimace!

MARC   Euh, si on passait à une autre photo?

MME LEROY   Voilà, c'est la fin. Maintenant, nous allons voter pour savoir
quelle est la meilleure!

---

compte-rendu *report*

sur cette photo: in this photo

Comparez ces photos prises par le groupe pendant le voyage scolaire. Donnez votre avis et
dites pourquoi. Students may also use comparatives as well as superlatives:
La numéro sept est plus amusante que la première.

Quelle est la plus (moins)… ?

    belle   originale   intéressante

    triste   amusante   sentimentale

1.

5.

2.

6.

3.

7.

4.

8.

Possible dialogue: —On prend le train? C'est pas cher.
—Bof. Prendre un petit train, ça ne me dit rien.
—Et si on allait au théâtre antique?
—D'accord, j'aime bien voir les vestiges romains.

3 **Activité • Que faire?**

Vous êtes à Arles avec votre ami(e). Vous ne savez pas quoi faire. Vous voyez ces deux publicités. Allez-vous prendre le train? Allez-vous visiter le théâtre antique? Décidez-vous. Préparez le dialogue avec un(e) camarade.

4 **Activité • Vous n'êtes pas enthousiaste**

Le professeur vous a demandé d'écrire un compte-rendu du voyage scolaire. Vous n'avez pas envie de l'écrire. Qu'est-ce que vous dites à votre ami(e)? Trouvez trois moyens d'exprimer votre manque d'enthousiasme et trouvez chaque fois une raison différente.

See C13, p. 363 for expressions of lack of interest.

5 **Activité • Ecrivez**   Possible answer is given.

Vous n'en avez pas envie, mais vous écrivez un compte-rendu de votre voyage à Arles avec Mme Leroy et ses élèves. Qu'est-ce que vous y avez fait? Qu'est-ce qui vous a plu le mieux? Qu'est-ce que vous n'avez pas aimé? Avez-vous envie d'y retourner? Pourquoi? Dans votre compte-rendu, exprimez le soulagement et le regret.

On a commencé par la visite de l'usine de Berre. C'était la visite la plus ennuyeuse! Le lendemain, on a visité Arles. Je n'aime pas les vestiges romains, mais le théâtre antique est moins nul que les arènes. Ce que j'ai le plus aimé, c'était la visite en Camargue. Après avoir déjeuné, on a fait de l'équitation, et moi, j'ai monté le plus beau cheval!

6 **Activité • A vous maintenant!**

Avec un(e) camarade, parlez d'un voyage que vous avez fait avec une classe, avec votre famille ou avec des amis. Posez des questions à votre ami(e) sur son voyage, et répondez à ses questions sur votre voyage.

7 **Activité • Ecrivez**

Vous avez organisé un voyage, et vous devez maintenant faire un programme pour le donner à tous les participants. Ecrivez-le, avec les dates, les horaires, les types d'activités.

Refer to program in A1, p. 342.

Programme du voyage scolaire du ... au ... à ...
Premier jour :

Pendant votre visite d'Arles, vous envoyez une carte postale à votre classe de français. Ecrivez le message; dites ce que vous avez fait et ce que vous avez vu à Arles. Chers amis, Arles est très jolie. C'est plus ancien que notre ville. J'ai visité la ville, vu des monuments et pris des photos. La Camargue est splendide. On y voit les plus beaux chevaux du monde. En équitation, j'étais le plus mauvais du groupe, mais ça m'a plu. A bientôt.

C'est l'été. Vous êtes à Arles pour les Rencontres Internationales de la Photographie. Le programme offre des spectacles et des expositions en grand nombre. Qu'est-ce que vous décidez d'aller voir? Préparez le dialogue avec un(e) camarade.

SPECTACLES

SPECTACLE MULTI-MÉDIA sur écran de 130 m² au Théâtre Antique.

5 JUILLET
"Un jour dans la vie aux USA"
200 photographes pendant un jour.

6 JUILLET
"Rock et Photo"
Les grands photographes de la scène Rock mondiale.

10 JUILLET
"Le Liban"
"Voyage au cœur de la merveilleuse catastrophe" Un sujet sur New York.

EXPOS

L'ATELIER DES FORGES, un espace spectaculaire pour la photographie. Dans une usine de 1850, une vingtaine d'expositions est proposée aux visiteurs.

"La mode des années 50"
"Célèbres portraits de la scène rock"
"Photos hollandaises de la scène punk"
"L'Asie d'un photographe australien"

"Portraits de rues à Haïti"

"Paris-Zürich"
17 photographies en plein vol.

"Portraits Officiels Chinois"
"Demain le tramway"
7 photographes, 72 affiches.

—Si on allait voir les photos des USA? Ça doit être bon.
—Les Etats-Unis? Ça ne me dit rien. Allons voir les photos de la scène punk.
—D'accord, mais ensuite je veux voir les photos de New York.

Pendant votre voyage en Camargue, vous visitez le village des Saintes-Maries-de-la-Mer. Il y a beaucoup à faire ici. Avec un(e) camarade, faites le projet de votre visite. A tour de rôle, proposez les activités suggérées par les photos; acceptez ou refusez les suggestions. Finalement, préparez votre programme d'activités.

Possible activities are given.

chercher des renseignements à l'Office du tourisme.

1.

2.

visiter le musée Baroncelli

3.

jouer au golf miniature

4.

prendre un verre

5.

faire les boutiques

6.

aller au cinéma / faire un tour de manège

Activité • Jeu de rôle Possible answer is given.

Avec un(e) camarade de classe, trouvez des situations qui vous amènent *(which cause you)* à exprimer un soulagement ou un regret. Par exemple :

— C'est l'anniversaire de votre mère. Vous avez oublié d'acheter un cadeau mais votre sœur en a acheté un pour vous.

— Heureusement que ma sœur a acheté un cadeau!

—Vous êtes invité à une boum, mais vous avez perdu l'adresse. Vous téléphonez aux autres amis qui sont invités, mais ils sont déjà partis pour la boum.
—C'est dommage qu'ils soient déjà partis!

12 **Activité • Quelles sont ces photos?** Possible dialogue is given.

Travaillez avec un(e) camarade. Votre camarade choisit une photo dans ce chapitre. Il/Elle vous la décrit. Vous devez identifier la photo. Vous avez droit à deux réponses. Si vous identifiez la photo, c'est à votre tour de choisir une photo, et ainsi de suite *(and so on)*.

—Je regarde une photo. Sur cette photo, il y a des gens à la terrasse d'un café. Ils boivent un dernier verre avant de partir en car.
—Est-ce que c'est la photo à la page 369, numéro 4?
—Non. Essaie encore. Fais un effort!

—C'est la photo à la page 359 dans C1?
—Oui, c'est ça!

13 **Activité • Créez votre projet**

Votre professeur veut réaliser un projet avec votre classe, mais il/elle a besoin de l'avis de tout le monde. Ecrivez quelques lignes pour proposer une idée. Justifiez-la. Cela peut être un voyage ou autre chose : la création d'un club, la réalisation d'un film vidéo ou d'un reportage… C'est à vous de trouver la meilleure idée.

14 **Activité • Récréation** (optional)

Au temps des Romains. Ce dessin contient cinq erreurs. Pouvez-vous les trouver?

les erreurs: le voilier moderne; le casque de moto; l'appareil-photo; le soldat parle français, pas latin; le poteau indique la distance en kilomètres (Le système métrique existe depuis 1795.)

For script, see pp. T223–25.

PRONONCIATION 📼

The ghost **h**; **l** and **gn**

1 Ecoutez bien et répétez.

1. The ghost **h**
   a. heure   hôtel   dehors   le hall   dans le hall de l'hôtel

   b. | **hall** [ˈol]   **héros** [ˈeʀo]   **dehors** [dəɔr] |

   les zéros   les héros
   les haricots   *green beans*   en haut   *upstairs*
   les hors-d'œuvre   *appetizers*   le hasard   *chance, fate, luck*
   des harengs   *herring*   Ils ont hâte.   *They're in a hurry.*

   c. Consultez le dictionnaire : **le, la,** ou **l'**? Lisez la liste et puis relisez-la avec **un** ou **une**.
   horizon, handicap, hamburger, hypocrite, hélicoptère, halo, herbicide,
   héritage, hamster, héros, humour, hydrogène, hippy, harpe

   d. la Hollande   un hangar   le hasard   deux harengs

2. The **th** combination
         thermomètre   théâtre   thé   thème   thermos   mathématiques   mythe
3. The **ch** combination
   a. /**sh**/ as in English
         la Chine   *chat*   chatte   *chant*   chante   *change*   change   *chocolate*   chocolat
   b. /**k**/ as in English
         choral   choral   *choir*   chœur   *chaos*   chaos   *Christine*   Christine
   c. Unlike English
         architect   architecte   *chemistry*   chimie   *archives*   archives
4. The sound /**l**/
         elle   quelle   celle   ville   ciel   bel   glace   place   classe   clé
5. The sound /**ɲ**/
         oignon   compagnon   mignon   magnifique   signer   ligne

2 Ecoutez et lisez.

— On joue de la musique de chambre tous les soirs de six à dix heures dans le hall de l'hôtel.
— Moi, je préfère le chant solo ou bien les chœurs sans accompagnement.
— Pour moi, c'est l'orchestre symphonique, le théâtre et l'opéra.
— J'ai même des billets pour *Le Lac des Cygnes*. C'est la nouvelle compagnie. J'ai hâte de les
   voir. Il paraît que le spectacle est magnifique.

3 Copiez les phrases suivantes pour préparer une dictée.

1. Le restaurant dans cet hôtel est célèbre pour ses haricots.
2. Moi, je n'aime pas les oignons dans mon hamburger.
3. Hier, Christine et Charles ont pris du thé avec leurs compagnons.
4. Signez sur la ligne, s'il vous plaît.
5. Le théâtre est près de la cathédrale.

VERIFIONS!

Can you express impatience in French? Refer students to A17, p. 348.

Urge your friend to hurry. Use a different expression for each situation.
1. Vous allez au concert avec votre ami(e). Le concert a déjà commencé.
2. Il est une heure. Vous prenez le train à une heure et quart.
3. Votre ami(e) a un rendez-vous chez le dentiste.
4. Vous êtes pressé(e). Votre ami(e) cherche quelque chose.

Have you learned to make excuses in French? Refer students to A17, p. 348.

You're in a hurry. Refuse your friend's requests. Vary your excuses.
1. Encore un jus de fruit?
2. Si on passait chez Philippe?
3. Tu peux m'aider?
4. Allons au café.

Have you learned the interrogative pronouns?

Fill in the blanks with **qui** or **que** in these questions.
1. _Qui_ est-ce _qui_ a déjà visité la Provence?
2. _Qu'_ est-ce _qui_ t'intéresse? Les arènes ou le théâtre?
3. _Qui_ est-ce _que_ tu appelles?
4. _Qu'_ est-ce _que_ tu manges?

Complete these questions with the preposition **à, avec,** or **de** and **qui** or **quoi.**
A quoi   **1.** — ____ penses-tu?   — Je pense au voyage qu'on va faire.
Avec qui **2.** — ____ part-on?   — On part avec Mme Leroy, notre prof d'histoire.
De quoi **3.** — ____ as-tu besoin?   — J'ai besoin de mon appareil-photo.

Do you know how to express relief and regret in French? Refer students to B11, p. 357.

Express your relief or regret in each of these situations.
1. Vous avez organisé un pique-nique pour samedi. Il a plu toute la semaine. Samedi il y a du soleil. Point out that the subjunctive of "peut" is "puisse."
2. Vous avez organisé une boum. Tout le monde peut venir.
3. Votre professeur favori va déménager dans une autre ville.

Have you learned to form and use the superlative of adjectives and adverbs?

Complete these sentences, using the superlative form of the adjective or adverb.
1. C'est ____ église. (+ beau) la plus belle
2. C'est le monument ____ . (- intéressant) le moins intéressant
3. C'est Sophie qui court ____ . (+ vite) le plus vite
4. Le printemps est ____ saison. (+ bon) la meilleure

Do you know how to express in French a lack of interest? Refer students to C13, p. 363.

Express your lack of interest in doing what your friend suggests.
1. J'ai envie d'aller prendre des photos cet après-midi. Tu viens avec moi?
2. Ça te dit d'aller en Camargue le week-end prochain?
3. Allez, écris à tes grand-parents. Ça va leur faire plaisir.
4. Accompagne-moi à la gare. Ce n'est pas très loin.

Have you learned to form and use the past infinitive?

Restate these sentences, using **après** + the past infinitive.
1. Ils ont étudié la Provence, et ils sont partis à Arles.
2. Ils ont visité les arènes, et ils sont allés voir le théâtre.
3. Ils sont allés dîner dans un petit restaurant, et ils ont dormi dans un lycée.

1. Après avoir étudié la Provence, ils sont partis à Arles.
2. Après avoir visité les arènes, ils sont allés voir le théâtre.
3. Après être allés dîner dans un petit restaurant, ils ont dormi dans un lycée.

VOCABULAIRE

(See A23: picnic supplies.)

SECTION A

amuser (s') *to have fun*
un arrêt *stop, stopover*
barber (fam.) *to bore*
chimique *chemical*
le complexe *complex*
le départ *departure*
dépêcher (se) *to hurry*
éducatif, -ive *educational*
un étang *pond*
heure : à l'heure *on time*
illustrer *to illustrate*
manquer *to miss*
la matière plastique *plastic*
un pesticide *pesticide*
un pique-nique *picnic*
pique-niquer *to picnic*
polluer *to pollute*
pressé, -e *in a hurry*
produire *to produce*
qu'est-ce qui *what*
qui est-ce que *whom*
qui est-ce qui *who*
rater *to miss*
la recherche *research*
un solvant *solvent*
le trajet *route, journey*
une usine *factory*

SECTION B

ancien, -ienne *ancient, old*
les arènes (f.) *arena*
barbare *barbarian, barbaric*
la Camargue *the Rhône delta*
Chut! *Shhh!*

civilisé, -e *civilized*
un combat *fight, battle*
consacré, -e (à) *devoted (to)*
conservé, -e *preserved*
une course de taureaux *bullfight*
défendre (se) *to defend
(oneself)*
dévoré, -e *devoured, eaten*
le dortoir *dormitory*
une époque *epoch, age, era*
un gladiateur *gladiator*
interdit *forbidden*
lâcher *to release*
lointain, -e *faraway, distant*
une manifestation *show,
demonstration*
la mise à mort *killing*
mis(e) à mort *put to death*
un opéra *opera*
parfois *sometimes*
le passé *past*
la photographie *photography*
probablement *probably*
provençal, -e *from Provence*
rester : il reste *there
remain(s)*
romain, -e *Roman*
les Romains *Romans*
le taureau (pl. -x) *bull*
temps : au temps de *at the
time of*
tuer *to kill*
un vestige *trace, relic*

SECTION C

adieu *farewell, goodbye*

amateur *amateur*
angle : grand angle *wide
angle*
bête *dumb, stupid*
car *because*
un carrousel *slide carrousel*
courage : Je n'ai pas le
courage de... *I don't feel
up to . . .*
une diapo(sitive) *slide*
dit : Ça ne me dit rien.
That doesn't appeal to me.
un écran *projection screen*
exposer *to exhibit*
fixer *to set*
un flash *flash*
une grimace : faire des grimaces
to make a (funny) face
un instant *instant, moment*
inventer *to invent*
naturel, -elle *natural*
un objectif *lens*
un oiseau (pl. -x) *bird*
pareil, pareille *such*
parler : Tu parles! (fam.)
You've got to be kidding!
une pellicule *film (for camera)*
profiter (de) *to take
advantage (of)*
un projecteur *projector*
projeter *to project*
songer (à) *to think (about)*
souriez *smile*
un zoom *zoom lens*

ETUDE DE MOTS

The past participle of some verbs may be used as adjectives. For example, **inventé**, *invented*, the past participle of **inventer**, *to invent*, may also be an adjective: **C'est une machine inventée par mon oncle.** Of course, a past participle used as an adjective follows the rules you have learned concerning adjectives and how they must agree with the nouns they modify.

In the list above, find four adjectives that are also past participles of verbs. Write them down and then write their infinitives next to them. pressé -e; civilisé -e; consacré -e; conservé -e; dévoré -e

Now complete the following sentences with the adjective forms of two verbs from the list above.

1. Le fleuve est ___ pollué ; on n'y nage plus.
2. J'ai acheté un beau livre ___ illustré pour ma petite nièce.

A LIRE

Alerte au château de Rambouillet

Un voyage scolaire pas comme les autres

Avant de lire

Les personnages et les endroits suivants sont mentionnés dans cette histoire. Les connaissez-vous? Sinon, faites des recherches pour mieux apprécier l'histoire suivante.

Rambouillet   Le Général de Gaulle
François 1er Le Maréchal Leclerc
Chartres
Versailles
Napoléon 1er

Vous souvenez-vous du système de notation (*grading*) dans les écoles françaises? Lisez le premier paragraphe. Quel est le rôle des notes dans cette histoire?

For background on the French grading system, see annotation on p. 33.

Préparatifs

Qui choisit la destination? Pourquoi?

Un jour, en classe d'histoire, Mme Lefrac a annoncé qu'elle nous emmènerait visiter le château de notre choix, quand la moyenne° de la classe aura dépassé dix sur vingt. Nous avons obtenu quatorze aux examens de fin d'année!

Un matin de juin, je suis parti avec ma classe pour Rambouillet, au sud-ouest de Paris. Nous étions vingt élèves, filles et garçons. Mme Lefrac, notre professeur d'histoire, nous accompagnait; il y avait aussi M. Laroche, qui organise régulièrement des visites guidées pour lycéens. Pour ceux que l'histoire intéresse, le château de Rambouillet a été construit au XIVe siècle. François 1er, le Roi-Chevalier, y est mort en 1547.

---

moyenne *average*

Rambouillet: a small town 54 km. southwest of Paris; known for its beautiful château and the expansive forest which surrounds it
François 1er (1497–1547): king of France; known for his interest in the arts

Avant le départ, nos accompagnateurs nous ont demandé de rester ensemble pendant la visite pour ne pas nous perdre. Il ne fallait pas traîner° derrière les autres. Si nous avions besoin de quitter notre groupe, nous devions avertir° M. Laroche ou Mme Lefrac. Nous savions qu'il fallait obéir aux consignes°. Mais si on s'écartait° du groupe sans faire attention, et qu'on n'arrivait plus à retrouver ses camarades, il fallait aller attendre au point de rendez-vous, Place de la Libération, devant l'hôtel de ville°, qui se trouve à l'est du château. Et si on était vraiment tout à fait perdu, il fallait aller au poste de gendarmerie le plus proche.

Ah! J'ai oublié de vous dire mon nom. Je m'appelle Didier. Philippe, c'est mon copain. Comme moi, il adore l'histoire. On ne se quitte jamais. C'est nous qui avons proposé la visite de Rambouillet à la classe. Pourquoi Rambouillet? Tout simplement parce que c'est à cinquante kilomètres de Paris, qu'on peut continuer à Chartres°, vers le sud-ouest, et que la forêt de Rambouillet est l'une des plus belles de France. On y chasse le chevreuil° et le sanglier°!

Visite du château et du parc
Qu'est-ce qui est arrivé dans la salle de bains de Napoléon 1er?
Mme Lefrac voulait que Philippe et moi commentions° la visite à tour de rôle. Le château de Rambouillet n'est pas grand comme Versailles; ses jardins à la française° sont plus petits. Je venais de distribuer à tout le monde le plan de Rambouillet, copié du guide de tourisme. Notez bien, à l'ouest du château, l'emplacement de la Chaumière des Coquillages° et, au nord de la Chaumière, la Laiterie de la Reine°.

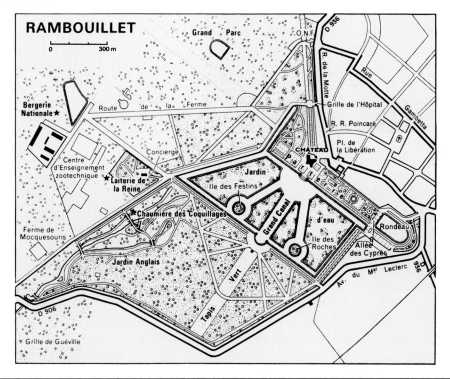

---

traîner *to lag behind;* **avertir** *to alert;* **obéir aux consignes** *to obey orders;* **s'écartait** *became separated;* **hôtel de ville** *town (city) hall;* **Chartres** *town southwest of Paris;* **chevreuil** *roebuck;* **sanglier** *boar;* **commentions** *give a commentary on;* **à la française** *in the French style;* **Chaumière des Coquillages** *Shellfish Cottage;* **Laiterie de la Reine** *the queen's dairy farm*

Chartres: a small city 87 km. southwest of Paris; known for its spectacular cathedral
Versailles: magnificent palace and grounds, located to the west of Paris; the residence of French kings from 1682 until the French Revolution

La classe a posé quelques questions sur la grosse tour, seul vestige du château fort° qu'était Rambouillet au temps du Roi-Chevalier. C'est par cette tour que nous sommes entrés dans la salle de bains que s'est fait construire Napoléon 1er. Je vous disais que Philippe et moi, on ne se quittait jamais. Jusqu'à la salle de bains de Napoléon, on était ensemble.

A ce moment, M. Laroche s'est écrié :
— Mais, il manque quelqu'un! Nous ne sommes plus que dix-neuf!

Ça a été la panique. On s'est mis à courir de tous côtés. On se bousculait. Tout le monde voulait redescendre au rez-de-chaussée. Peine perdue°. On ne trouvait pas l'escalier! On était désorientés. M. Laroche et Mme Lefrac criaient : «Restons groupés! Ne nous séparons pas!» Mais chacun n'en faisait qu'à sa tête°.

Finalement, on s'est retrouvé par miracle dans la salle de marbre du rez-de-chaussée.

---

château fort *fortified castle;* **peine perdue** *waste of time;* **n'en faisait qu'à sa tête** *went his own sweet way;*
Napoléon 1er (1769–1821): emperor of France; conquered most of Europe during his reign

Les recherches commencent.

D'après les filles, pourquoi est-ce que Philippe a disparu? Et d'après la police?

Pas de Philippe à l'horizon.

Une fille dit méchamment :

— C'est bien fait! Philippe s'est perdu parce qu'il n'a pas trouvé nécessaire de suivre les consignes comme tout le monde. Il n'a pas le sens de l'orientation°, le pauvre!

Un garçon rétorque :

— Comme si tu avais, toi, le sens de l'orientation! Tu t'es bien égarée°, l'année dernière au musée du Louvre! On t'a retrouvée dans les cabinets°!

Brouhaha, discussions, disputes. Je me demandais ce qu'il fallait faire. Et si on allait du côté de la Chaumière des Coquillages? Philippe nous avait peut-être devancés° là-bas... Mme Lefrac et M. Laroche sont d'accord.

La Chaumière des Coquillages est située dans la partie nord du parc arrangée en jardin anglais. On venait d'y tondre le gazon. La Chaumière est entièrement décorée de coquillages, d'éclats de marbre° et de nacre°. Superbe. Mais pas de Philippe!

— Il a été mangé par un sanglier dans la forêt de Rambouillet! s'exclame une fille.

— Les sangliers ne mangent pas les vrais hommes, répond Rémy, le cancre° de la classe. Les hommes ont la peau° dure, parce qu'ils réfléchissent. Les sangliers préfèrent les filles...

---

sens de l'orientation *sense of direction;* **Tu t'es bien égarée** *You got lost;* **cabinets** *toilets;* **devancé** *arrived ahead of;*
éclats de marbre *marble chips;* **nacre** *mother-of-pearl;* **cancre** *dunce;* **peau** *skin*

Re-disputes. Les filles crient : «Hou… le vilain! Hou… l'horrible!» M. Laroche essaie de calmer tout le monde, mais tous parlent à la fois.

— Un peu de silence, s'il vous plaît, dit M. Laroche. Nous perdons notre temps. Ce n'est pas comme ça que nous allons retrouver Philippe. Allons au rendez-vous devant l'hôtel de ville.

Pas de Philippe devant l'hôtel de ville. Il y avait un café sur la place; Philippe y était peut-être entré pour acheter des cartes postales. Personne dans le café, à part quelques vieux touristes allemands en train de dévorer des croissants au chocolat…

Je me demandais vraiment où pouvait bien être Philippe. Il n'avait pas l'habitude de disparaître comme ça, en cours de sortie. Lui était-il arrivé quelque chose? Philippe était-il en danger? Il s'était peut-être égaré dans la forêt de Rambouillet! Il fallait appeler les pompiers, la police! M. Laroche se précipite au téléphone. A son retour, il nous annonce qu'il vient d'avertir le poste de gendarmerie. Le préfet de police lui a suggéré d'aller voir dans l'entresol° du château, là où se trouvent les Appartements d'Assemblée. Il y avait, paraît-il, une équipe de télévision qui filmait quelque chose. Philippe était peut-être là-bas, mêlé° à la foule.

Le disparu retrouvé

Où est-ce qu'on a retrouvé Philippe?

Nous courons dans la direction du château, au milieu d'une foule de touristes. Tout le monde se dépêchait d'aller voir ce qui se passait dans les Appartements d'Assemblée.

---

entresol *mezzanine, between ground floor and first floor;* **mêlé** *mingled*

Eh bien, vous n'allez pas me croire. Arrivés à la porte des fameux Appartements, qu'est-ce qu'on voit? Notre Philippe, debout sous les projecteurs° d'une caméra de télévision! Il tenait à la main une feuille de papier, et s'apprêtait à° lire quelque chose. Il ne nous voyait pas. Silencieuse, la foule des touristes attendait. Voilà que le réalisateur° de l'émission de télévision fait un signe de la main. Et mon copain Philippe commence à lire, d'une voix haute et claire, l'ordre qu'avait donné le Général de Gaulle à la Division Leclerc de marcher sur Paris.

Plus tard, Philippe nous a expliqué que l'équipe de télévision faisait un film sur Rambouillet à l'intention des classes du cycle secondaire. L'élève qui devait lire l'ordre du Général de Gaulle s'était évanoui° sous la chaleur° des projecteurs. Philippe, qui se trouvait là par hasard, qui nous avait quittés sans faire attention, avait offert de remplacer l'élève. On l'avait pris tout de suite!

Après la prise de vue°, tout le monde a applaudi. Mme Lefrac a présenté notre groupe au réalisateur du film. Il a félicité Mme Lefrac pour le talent et l'intelligence de Philippe. Il a promis de nous inviter à voir le film en séance de projection privée! Nous étions contents d'avoir retrouvé Philippe. Il était devenu une grande vedette!

---

projecteurs *spotlights;* **s'apprêtait à** *was getting ready to;* **réalisateur** *director;* **s'était évanoui** *had fainted;* **chaleur** *heat;* **prise de vue** *filming, shooting*

Charles de Gaulle (1890–1970): general and president of France; dominated French political life for 30 years
Maréchal Leclerc (1902–1947): French army officer; hero of World War II; led French troops in liberation of Paris

Activité • Avez-vous compris?   Possible answers are given.

Complétez les phrases suivantes d'après «Alerte au château de Rambouillet».

1. Après… , Philippe et Didier ont commenté la visite.
2. Après… , le groupe est allé à l'hôtel de ville.
3. Après… , Philippe se trouvait dans les Appartements d'Assemblée.

1. être arrivés (avoir distribué des plans)
2. avoir cherché partout
3. s'être écarté du groupe

Activité • Commentez   Possible answers are given.

Commentez «Alerte au château de Rambouillet» en complétant ces phrases.

1. Heureusement que… on a trouvé Philippe.
2. Malheureusement,… les élèves n'ont pas obéi aux consignes.
3. C'est une bonne chose que M. Laroche… ait téléphoné au préfet de police.

Activité • Téléphonez   Possible dialogue is given.

Imaginez la conversation téléphonique entre M. Laroche et le préfet de police. Préparez la conversation avec un(e) camarade.

—Allô! Ici M. Laroche. Je viens d'emmener ma classe visiter le château de Rambouillet. Quelle catastrophe! J'ai perdu un élève! Qu'est-ce que je dois faire?
—Calmez-vous, monsieur! Il y a une équipe de télé qui fait un film dans les Appartements d'Assemblée. Je suis sûr que vous allez le retrouver là-bas, mêlé à la foule.   —Ah oui, il est sûrement là. Merci, monsieur l'agent.

Activité • Faites le guide
Possible answer is given.

Vous avez trouvé un job d'été comme guide au château de Rambouillet. Montrez le château à un groupe de touristes. Donnez-leur des renseignements sur le château.

Voilà les Appartements d'Assemblée. Ici, à la fin de la deuxième guerre mondiale, le Général de Gaulle a donné l'ordre à la Division Leclerc de marcher sur Paris. C'était un événement historique.

CHAPITRE 11 Bientôt l'avenir

	BASIC MATERIAL	COMMUNICATIVE FUNCTIONS
PREMIER CONTACT	Le minitel rend la vie plus facile. (1) Visite de la Cité des Sciences (3)	Reading for global comprehension and cultural awareness
SECTION A	Comment vivrons-nous en l'an 2010? (A1)	**Expressing attitudes, opinions** • Predicting what the future will be like • Expressing doubt and certainty
SECTION B	Votre avenir (B1)	**Expressing attitudes, opinions** • Imagining your future **Expressing feelings, emotions** • Expressing intentions, goals, wishes, and dreams
SECTION C	Est-ce que vous croyez que l'avenir sera meilleur? (C1)	**Expressing attitudes, opinions** • Discussing problems of the future • Expressing beliefs, hope, and doubt
TRY YOUR SKILLS	Un sondage (1)	

■ **Prononciation** (pure vowel and consonant sounds; dictation) **413**
■ **Vérifions!** **414** ■ **Vocabulaire** **415**

A LIRE	**Un Cours sur les lasers** (a science lesson in a French classroom) **Le Jour où la Terre s'est arrêtée de tourner** (an unusual day in France)

WRITING A variety of controlled and open-ended writing activities appear in the Pupil's Edition. The Teacher's Notes identify other activities suitable for writing practice.

COOPERATIVE LEARNING Many of the activities in the Pupil's Edition lend themselves to cooperative learning. For guidelines, see page T14.

Scope and Sequence

GRAMMAR	CULTURE	RE-ENTRY
	The **minitel** The **Explora** exhibit at **la Villette**	
The future tense (A8)	French technology	Household chores vocabulary Expressing an opinion Giving advice

The future of irregular
  verbs (B14)
The future with **quand**
  (B14)
	The French space program	Inviting friends

The relative pronouns
  qui and **que** (C14)
	A visit to the **Cité des
	  Sciences et de l'Industrie**
		Making suggestions
		Accepting or refusing an
		  invitation
		Expressing indifference
		The comparative
		Expressing past time

Recombining communicative functions, grammar, and vocabulary

Reading for practice and pleasure

UNIT RESOURCES **Cahier d'Activités, Cahier d'Exercices,** Unit 11 Cassettes, Transparencies 27–29, Quizzes 25–27, Unit 11 Test

TEACHER-PREPARED MATERIALS **Section B** Index cards, travel brochures; **Try Your Skills** Index cards in two colors

PREMIER CONTACT

The authentic material in **Premier Contact** introduces the theme of the unit. Concentrate only on the general content of these documents A detailed treatment of the grammar and vocabulary is not intended. Since students should be reading for global comprehension, they need not know the meaning of every word. For this reason, new words in **Premier Contact** have been omitted from the unit vocabulary list and the French-English Vocabulary at the end of the book.

OBJECTIVES   To read for global comprehension and cultural awareness; to get acquainted with the topic

1

Le minitel rend la vie plus facile.

Have students look at the pictures in this ad. Ask **Qu'est-ce que vous voyez sur tous ces dessins?** Tell students that the computer is called a **minitel** and that many French people have them in their homes. Play the cassette or read the text aloud as students follow along in their books. As students listen, they should discover several uses of the **minitel.**

2   Activité • Avez-vous compris?

Allow students to refer back to **Contact 1** to find answers to numbers 1 and 2. If students had a **minitel** or a similar service available to them, how might they use it?

3   VISITE DE LA CITE DES SCIENCES

Tell students that **la Cité des Sciences et de l'Industrie** is a museum near Paris. Have them look at the photo on page 380 and the photo of part of **Explora** on page 381. Play the cassette or read the passage about **Explora** aloud as students follow along in their books. Afterward, ask volunteers to summarize in very general terms the main idea of each of the two paragraphs **(les choses à voir à Explora; comment chercher les renseignements).**

4   Activité • Avez-vous bien lu?

You might turn these questions into multiple-choice items. On the board or on a transparency, write choices similar to these:

> **1.** Qui s'intéresse à visiter Explora?
>   **a.** Les enfants   **b.** Les adultes   **c.** Les enfants et les adultes

If you choose to do this, students should answer with their books closed. If you choose to have students answer the questions as they are in the text, allow them to refer back to **Contact 3** as they answer.

5   Activité • A vous maintenant!

On the board or on a transparency, write the following themes: **l'univers et la vie, la technologie, la communication.** Brainstorm with the students possible temporary exhibits that could be related to each theme.

SLOWER-PACED LEARNING   Provide names of some temporary exhibits and have students fit them into the above themes. Possible names might include **la Télévision a 50 ans, l'Homme réparé, le Sang des hommes, Portraits-Robots, une Aventure architecturale,** and **le Matin des molécules.**

SECTION A

OBJECTIVES **To express attitudes, opinions:** predict what the future will be like; express doubt and certainty

CULTURAL BACKGROUND France has been on the cutting edge of many technological areas. The French auto company Renault pioneered the use of industrial robots in the manufacture of automobiles. The French have installed thousands of microcomputers in the public schools to make sure that students become computer literate. The **minitel** has revolutionized everyday communications.

These days, the French are experimenting with voice-activated telephones that would eliminate the need to dial numbers. The intention is to use them in car phones and to aid the disabled. Two such voice-activated public telephones, called **Publivox,** have been installed in **Rennes.** So far, the experimental telephones have been able to recognize numbers spoken in a variety of accents.

MOTIVATING ACTIVITY Have students suggest briefly what they think the future might be like. How might life be different in the year 2010? What improvements do they hope to see?

A1 Comment vivrons-nous en l'an 2010?

Play the cassette or read aloud each section of the dialogue as students look at the accompanying pictures in their books. To verify students' comprehension and to clarify new vocabulary, ask questions after each section. For example, after the second section, you might say **Regardez le dessin. Qu'est-ce que la voiture peut faire? Qu'est-ce qui s'ouvre tout seul? Sur le dessin, montrez-nous les portières. Et où est le moteur?**

If students ask why the verbs are conjugated in a new way, tell them that the verbs express future actions. Do not explain how to form the future tense at this time.

A2 Activité • Faux, mais pourquoi?

Have volunteers read the statements aloud and then correct them. They might add whether they agree with Henri: **Je suis d'accord avec Henri** or **Je ne suis pas d'accord avec Henri parce que...**

A3 Activité • Comment est-ce que ça changera?

SLOWER-PACED LEARNING Before class, write on the board or on a transparency the changes that the items in the box will undergo. List them at random:

On les fera à la maison.
Les robots les feront.
Elles nous comprendront.

A leur place, on prendra des pilules.
On les fera sur l'ordinateur.

Have students match the items to these changes.

A4 Activité • Faites des phrases

SLOWER-PACED LEARNING Brainstorm with students vocabulary they can use to talk about future developments in these three areas. Then have them compose sentences. Ask volunteers to write sentences on the board. Correct any errors. Collect papers at the end of the activity.

A 5   Activité • Actes de parole

On the board write the following headings at the top of two columns:

Pour exprimer...

| le scepticisme   la certitude

Have students come to the board and write the expressions in the proper column as they find them in A1. They should copy the lists and keep them in their notebooks for reference.

A 6   Activité • A votre avis

Have students circulate and ask five of their classmates the questions. They should keep track of the answers and summarize them for the class.

SLOWER-PACED LEARNING   You might make this a listening activity by taking an opinion poll of the class. Ask **Qui pense qu'il y aura toujours des voitures en l'an 2010? Qui pense qu'il n'y aura plus de voitures?** Students indicate their answers by a show of hands.

A 7   Activité • Et vous?

Assign the questions for homework. Have students write answers in paragraph form. Encourage them to interview their parents on the use of the home computer. Students who do not have a home computer might interview a teacher in the business department or a salesclerk in a computer store.

A 8   STRUCTURES DE BASE

Have students open their books to A1 and scan for verbs that express future actions. On the board or on a transparency, make two lists of the examples students find: one for regular verbs and one for **avoir, être,** and **faire.** Students should look at the list of regular verbs. They should guess how to form future stems. Then use a model sentence, such as **On mangera différemment,** to model the forms of the future; have students repeat after you. Now have students open their books to page 387; have volunteers read numbers 1–5 aloud. Continue to practice the future by asking simple questions, perhaps about what students will do next year. Finally, present the future forms of **avoir, être,** and **faire.**

SLOWER-PACED LEARNING   Present the future of regular verbs on one day and that of **avoir, être,** and **faire** the next.

A 9   Activité • Henri donne des précisions

SLOWER-PACED LEARNING   Determine with students the verb form needed for each line of the dialogue; have a volunteer write each on the board. Leaving the forms on the board for reference, have students pair off to read the dialogue aloud.

A 10   Activité • Dans 30 ans...

SLOWER-PACED LEARNING   First help students determine the verb or expression that they will need in order to describe each picture. Then have them do a chain drill as suggested on the following page.

CHALLENGE   Do a chain drill by having the first student turn to his or her neighbor and state what the robot will do in his or her home. Then the first student asks what a robot will do in the other student's home:

ÉLÈVE 1   Mon robot passera l'aspirateur. Ton robot le fera chez toi?
ÉLÈVE 2   Non, mon robot fera la cuisine. Et chez toi? Que fera ton robot?
ÉLÈVE 3   Chez moi, il écrira des lettres...

Continue until most students have participated. After they've mentioned the activities pictured, students should suggest other things that a robot might do.

A 11   Activité • Ecrit dirigé

SLOWER-PACED LEARNING   Go through the paragraph, helping students decide which verb should be used where. Then have them copy the paragraph, adding the verbs in the appropriate form. Correct in class.

CHALLENGE   Have students use a sheet of paper to cover the list of verbs above the paragraph. Have them copy the paragraph, adding verbs in the future they think would be appropriate. Collect and correct.

A 12   Activité • Un message du XXIᵉ siècle

Have students read silently the message from the future. Since they are to recount the message in general terms (how people will live), point out that they'll need to use **nous** or **on** as they speak. You might go through the first few sentences with the class: **Plus tard, on habitera dans des maisons sous l'eau. On aura plusieurs robots : ils nous apporteront le petit déjeuner et feront la vaisselle.** Then have students work in pairs.

SLOWER-PACED LEARNING   Have students say what they will do in the future, using ideas from the message: **Moi, j'habiterai dans une maison sous l'eau. J'aurai plusieurs robots...** Encourage them to add their own ideas as well.

A 13   Activité • Ecrivez

Assign this activity for homework. Students may refer back to the activities in this section for ideas, but encourage them to be original. The next day, collect students' papers. Indicate where corrections are needed and return to students for revision. Collect and correct revised papers.

A 14   Savez-vous que... ?

There are 3.5 million **minitel** terminals in French households, representing 15 percent of telephone subscribers. The basic model of the terminal is distributed free; the only **minitel** service for which users do not pay is the electronic telephone directory.

   The Peugeot 505 communicates in French, English, and German. A male voice relays messages about the engine and other parts of the car: **Stop! Température d'eau anormale!** and **Attention! Charge de batterie anormale!** Messages about passenger safety and comfort are given by a female voice: **Attention! Porte non fermée!** and **Veuillez attacher votre ceinture!**

A 15   Activité • Ecoutez bien

You're going to hear a commercial for the **minitel.** As you listen, list on a separate sheet of paper six possible ways to use the **minitel.** You don't have to write complete sentences. Ready? **Ecoutez bien.**

Dépêchez-vous! Demandez votre minitel! Ce sera bientôt impossible de vivre sans lui. A quoi sert-il? A tout! Avec lui, vous communiquerez immédiatement avec votre banque, votre supermarché ou vos amis! Plus besoin de sortir de chez vous! Vous ferez vos courses et vous paierez par minitel! Vous pourrez savoir tous les programmes de cinéma, de théâtre ou de musique! Vous aurez le temps qu'il fait partout dans le monde! Vous pourrez aussi savoir les horaires des trains, réserver vos places d'avion, appeler un taxi, et mille autres choses! Alors, vous hésitez encore? Demandez vite votre minitel! Soyez moderne!

Et maintenant, vérifions. On peut utilisez le minitel pour...
- communiquer avec sa banque, son supermarché, ses amis
- faire ses courses
- avoir les programmes de cinéma, de théâtre, de musique
- écouter la météo
- savoir les horaires des trains
- réserver ses places d'avion
- appeler un taxi

A 16 Activité • Donnez des conseils

Before working in pairs, students may add other uses of the **minitel** they've learned about to the ones listed in A15.

A 17 COMMENT LE DIRE

Model the expressions and have students repeat after you. For practice, make a series of statements to the class and invite students to react, expressing certainty or doubt: **Il n'y aura plus de classes dans dix ans. Vous n'aurez plus d'examens cette année. Les profs n'aiment pas donner de bonnes notes.**

A 18 Activité • Vous êtes sceptique

After students have spoken about the four situations shown in their books, have them discuss two more that they make up themselves.

A 19 Activité • A vous maintenant!

Brainstorm with the class things that will have changed 50 years from now. List their ideas on the board or on a transparency. They may refer to these as they work in pairs. Invite some students to present their dialogues in front of the class after all have finished.

SECTION B

OBJECTIVES **To express attitudes, opinions:** imagine your future; **to express feelings, emotions:** express intentions, goals, wishes, and dreams

CULTURAL BACKGROUND What do young people look for in a job? Boys most often cite salary as the most important criterion, followed by time off to devote to family life. Girls name the same two criteria as most important, but in reverse order. Job security is third among both boys and girls. Possibility of promotion is fairly low on the list, being of interest to only 10 percent of boys and 5 percent of girls.

MOTIVATING ACTIVITY Have the class come up with a composite view of the perfect life. They should agree as a group whether this would include working; if so, what kind of work; and so on. Encourage discussion.

B1   **Votre avenir**

Before class, write on the board or on a transparency a multiple-choice item that will help students establish the context of the monologues: **C'était (a) des reportages à la télé (b) une émission de radio (c) des annonces dans un aéroport.** Play the cassette or read the introduction aloud as students listen with books closed. After students have indicated their choice, list the names of the young people who call in to the radio show and have students copy them. As they listen to the monologues, students should write one or two words beside each name to summarize that young person's goals. For example, they might write **musicien** next to Armand; **mariage** or **se marier** next to Stéphanie. Afterward, compare students' impressions. If there are any great discrepancies, have students open their books and read the appropriate passage to themselves to verify what the young person's major goal is. Then have students read each paragraph silently.

B2   Activité • Répondez

Allow students to refer back to B1 as they answer the questions.

B3   Activité • Complétez

SLOWER-PACED LEARNING   On the board, list words that students will need for this activity. They may use some words more than once.

B4   Activité • Et vous?

Students may need a few minutes to think about ideas for their own future. Have them refer to B1 for suggestions. After they've discussed their plans with a partner, have students write a paragraph about them for homework.

B5   Activité • Actes de parole

Return to B1; help students look for expressions to use when introducing their plans for the future. Have them list these in their notebooks for reference.

B6   Activité • Jeu de rôle

Divide the class into pairs of students. Assign two characters from B1 to each pair. Have students practice; they may refer to B1 as needed. Afterward, have volunteers present their dialogues to the class.

B7   Activité • Et vous?

Have students work in pairs, asking each other the questions. Ask volunteers to report their partners' answers to the class.

CHALLENGE   Turn this into a survey, with students circulating to ask each other the questions. They record answers and report results to the class.

B8   Savez-vous que... ?

While the **ASE (Agence spatiale européenne)** is developing its space shuttle Hermès, the French have been cooperating with both the American and Soviet space agencies in order to send their astronauts into space. In 1987 French astronaut Patrick Baudry spent several days in orbit aboard a United States space shuttle, and in December, 1988, Jean-Loup Chrétien completed the second joint French-Soviet space mission after having spent four weeks with his Soviet colleagues aboard the space station Mir.

B 9· **COMMENT LE DIRE**

Model the expressions and have students repeat. Then have each student use one of the expressions to state an intention, goal, wish, or dream.

B 10 **Activité • Qui a envie de faire quoi?**

Students pair off. One copies the reporter's questions onto separate index cards or slips of paper. The other copies the answers. Partners work together to match the questions to the answers. Then one takes back the cards with the questions, and the other, those with the answers. They read the conversation aloud.

B 11 **Activité • Interviewez un(e) camarade**

Brainstorm with students what they would do in order to be able to do the things listed in the box. Write their suggestions on the board or on a transparency. Using expressions from B9, students should vary the ways in which they state their goals, wishes, and dreams. Encourage students to state their real personal goals as well.

B 12 **Activité • Et vous?**

To safeguard individual privacy, you might have students write out their answers to only one of these questions to turn in to you the following day.

B 13 **Activité • Ecrivez**

Bring to class travel brochures describing trips that offer different activities. Distribute these to students who do not wish to write about their own plans. Review how to invite friends (Unit 2, A12, page 58). Once students have decided what summer plans to write about, have them list all the reasons why someone might want to participate in them. Then have students compose their letters, selecting from their lists of reasons only the most convincing.

B 14 **STRUCTURES DE BASE**

Have students tell how to form the future of regular verbs. Tell them that the future endings are used with all irregular verbs. Have students open their books and read aloud after you the sentences in the chart. Ask them to change the subjects of the sentences in order to practice the different forms.

Next, on the board or on a transparency, write several sentence beginnings with **quand: Quand j'aurai mon permis de conduire,... Quand je serai marié(e),... Quand j'aurai des enfants,...** Ask students to complete the beginnings, using verbs in the future. Have volunteers share their completions with the class. Point out that in sentences with **quand** that refer to the future, verbs in both parts of the sentence are conjugated in the future tense.

B 15 **Activité • Quel sera l'avenir de Philippe?**

SLOWER-PACED LEARNING Make this a written activity for students. Have them write only the needed forms of the future. Collect and correct.

CHALLENGE Have students pair off to do this activity orally. They should exchange roles and repeat.

B 16   Activité • Demain...

Have students look at the pictures and suggest what verbs they will need to use. You might write these on the board or on a transparency for reference. Then call on students to state the various things Nicolas will do tomorrow.

B 17   Activité • A vous maintenant!

Have students form pairs to tell each other what they will do tomorrow. Encourage them to continue as long as possible, naming all the activities they can think of. Have students report their partners' activities to the class.

B 18   Activité • Et vous?

Practice the sentences with the whole class, calling on individuals to complete them. Then have students interview several of their neighbors, asking **Qu'est-ce que tu feras quand... ?**

B 19   Activité • Dis-moi ce que tu aimes; je te dirai ce que tu feras

Allow students to take several minutes to think about their likes and dislikes. As they recite them to a partner, the partner notes key words and phrases on a sheet of paper. He or she then takes a few minutes to jot down predictions that correspond to the student's interests. Then the partner tells his or her predictions.

B 20   Activité • Ecrivez

Give students time to review the basic material in Unit 7 and to reacquaint themselves with Fabrice, Matthieu, and Sandrine. When ready, they should write three brief paragraphs predicting the future of each one.

B 21   Activité • Ecoutez bien

Open your book to page 399. *(pause)* Copy the chart in B21 on a separate sheet of paper. *(pause)* Listen as Patrice and Anne talk about what their lives will be like when they're 30 years old. Fill in the chart, telling what kind of work they'll be doing, whether or not they'll marry and have children, and where they'll be living. **Ecoutez bien.**

PATRICE	Tu peux t'imaginer à 30 ans?
ANNE	Très bien! Quand j'aurai 30 ans, je serai professeur d'anglais, je serai mariée, j'aurai quatre enfants, et j'habiterai à la campagne.
PATRICE	Eh bien, quelle précision! Et ton mari, il travaillera?
ANNE	Oui, il sera président de la République!
PATRICE	Pas mal!
ANNE	Et toi, qu'est-ce que tu feras?
PATRICE	Je serai pilote d'avion.
ANNE	Tu te marieras?
PATRICE	Jamais! Je préfère rester célibataire. On a plus de liberté.
ANNE	Alors, tu n'auras pas d'enfants?
PATRICE	Non, ça ne m'intéresse pas tellement.
ANNE	Tu habiteras où?

PATRICE Partout! J'irai à l'étranger. Je voyagerai beaucoup. Je ferai le tour du monde!

ANNE On ne se verra pas beaucoup!

PATRICE Non, mais on s'écrira!

Et maintenant, vérifions. *Read the information in the chart.*

	Anne	Patrice
Profession?	*professeur d'anglais*	*pilote d'avion*
Mariage?	*oui*	*non*
Enfants?	*quatre*	*non*
Résidence?	*à la campagne*	*à l'étranger*

SECTION C

OBJECTIVES **To express attitudes, opinions:** discuss problems of the future; express beliefs, hope, and doubt

CULTURAL BACKGROUND In a recent survey of French young people, unemployment was mentioned most often (by 62 percent of those surveyed) as one of the most serious problems facing society. Next on the list were world hunger (55 percent), racism (51 percent), the arms race (48 percent), drugs (44 percent), human rights violations (44 percent), insecurity (31 percent), and pollution (29 percent).

MOTIVATING ACTIVITY On the board or on a transparency, list **le racisme, la faim, le chômage, la pollution, la drogue, la course aux armements** from most to least important according to French young people (as indicated above). Take a poll of students to determine which of these problems most and least concern them. Are there other problems they would like to add to the list?

C1 # Est-ce que vous croyez que l'avenir sera meilleur?

Before class, prepare a list of world problems to distribute to students. Be sure to include **le racisme, la faim, le chômage, la pollution, la drogue, la course aux armements, la surpopulation, les maladies, l'alcoolisme,** and **la violence.** Tell students they are going to hear a conversation between two young people. As they listen, they should circle on their lists the problems these two young people discuss. Play the cassette or read the dialogue aloud. Then, by a show of hands, see if students have been able to discover which problems were discussed. Now have students open their books. They should read silently to find the solutions that Pierre has proposed for the problems that they've circled on their lists. Ask students if they agree with Pierre's solutions.

C2 ## Activité • Vrai ou faux?

After students have indicated whether the statements are true or false, according to Pierre, have them give their own opinions.

C3 ## Activité • Pierre a réponse à tout

Students skim the dialogue once more to find Pierre's solutions to the problems presented in the box. Ask students to suggest other solutions.

C4 ## Activité • Actes de parole

Return to C1; help students look for expressions of doubt, hope, certainty, and reassurance. Have them list these in their notebooks for reference.

C5 ## Activité • Ecrit dirigé

Have students read silently Roxane's paragraph about the future. Ask them to tell what problems she foresees. They should address each of these as they rewrite the paragraph from Pierre's point of view.

SLOWER-PACED LEARNING Rewrite the paragraph according to Pierre. Distribute to the students copies of it along with copies of Roxane's paragraph, but do not indicate whose point of view is expressed in each. Have students read to themselves both paragraphs. From what they have learned about Roxane and Pierre, they should be able to identify the author of each paragraph.

C6 ## Activité • Qu'est-ce qui existera ou n'existera plus?

You might also have students justify why or why not something will still exist in the future.

C7 ## Activité • Et vous?

CHALLENGE This activity might be handled as a debate between two teams representing political parties or perhaps scientists of opposing views. Divide the class into two groups, and have each group choose a leader and do some brainstorming. After about ten minutes, have the two teams take turns presenting their viewpoints.

C8 ## Savez-vous que... ?

The permanent exhibit at the **Cité des Sciences,** called **Explora,** is divided into four parts: (1) **De la Terre à l'Univers,** covering undersea and space exploration, mathematics, geology, and astrophysics; (2) **L'Aventure de la Vie,** which is concerned with meteorology, ecology, agriculture, philosophy, and biology; (3) **La Matière et le Travail de l'Homme,** including matter and energy, physics, transportation, robotics, economics, and industry; (4) **Langages et Communication,** covering sound transmission, human behavior, imaging, and computer science. Each area shows the latest advances in the subjects mentioned. In addition to **Explora,** there are changing temporary exhibits.

C9 ## Activité • Conversation

After students have practiced in pairs, you might ask several to present their dialogues to the class.

CHALLENGE Have students use a sheet of paper to cover the expressions in the boxes so that they will have to construct their conversations without consulting this information.

C10 ## COMMENT LE DIRE

Have students open their books to page 405 and repeat after you the expressions in the left-hand column of the chart. Ask students how the

expressions on the top differ from the ones on the bottom; make sure they understand when to use the present indicative and when to use the present subjunctive. Then make statements about present-day problems. Students use the expressions to say whether or not you're right:

> —La surpopulation est un problème grave.
> —Je pense que vous avez raison.
>   (Je ne pense pas que la surpopulation soit un problème grave.)

Teach the expressions in the right-hand column of the chart in a similar manner.

C11 Activité • Etes-vous d'accord?

Review with students the subjunctive forms of the verbs in the **Aujourd'hui** category. Then go through the sentences with the class, asking volunteers to state their opinions.

C12 Activité • A votre avis

First have students vary the model, substituting expressions from C10 for **je crois que.** Then have them work in pairs to complete the activity.

C13 Activité • Ecrivez

Review with students the comparative for adjectives and nouns. Then, for cooperative learning, form groups of four. They begin by brainstorming a list of ways in which schools in the future will differ from those of today. A student acting as recorder writes these down. Next, group members should work to compose complete sentences; another student might record these.

C14 STRUCTURES DE BASE

Have students open their books and follow along as you explain. Go over each part of the explanation, giving several additional examples for each part. Students should understand that relative clauses modify a noun. Make sure they know that **qui** is followed by a verb and **que** by a noun or pronoun. Write several sentence beginnings on the board and ask students to supply appropriate relative clauses:

> Je connais un professeur qui...   La pollution est un problème que...
> J'admire un étudiant qui...   M. Dupont est un professeur que...

SLOWER-PACED LEARNING   Give the students several examples in English of sentences containing relative clauses, to make sure they understand the concept. Do not insist on past participle agreement for the **passé composé.**

C15 Activité • Roxane est réaliste

Go through the sentences with students to see if they can determine whether **qui** or **que** will be needed to complete each one. Then have them read the sentences aloud, filling in the blanks.

C16 Activité • Toujours optimiste

Have students read the phrases silently. Then call on volunteers to read each complete sentence. Ask others if they agree or disagree.

C 17 **Activité • Pierre continue de rêver**

First help students decide which sentences from the box on the right go with the sentences in the box on the left. Then have students combine sentence pairs using **qui**. Be sure they drop the subject of the second sentence in each pair.

C 18 **Activité • Vos emplois futurs**

Give students several moments to decide which description might match each future profession. Then have students work in pairs, following the model. Encourage them to express doubt and predict an alternate future career. For example, instead of saying that Danielle will become an astronaut, students might say **Tu crois? Moi, je pense qu'elle sera pilote** or **Je pense qu'elle sera agent de voyages.**

C 19 **Activité • L'avenir en rose**

SLOWER-PACED LEARNING On the board or on a transparency, write the three parts of each sentence out of order: **nous mangerons/sera plus nourrissante/la nourriture.** Students unscramble the parts and add **que** to make complete sentences: **La nourriture que nous mangerons sera plus nourrissante.**

C 20 **Activité • Ecrivez**

Brainstorm with students a list of things about the present that might surprise someone from the future. Write these on the board or on a transparency, and have students copy them into their notebooks. Select several items and develop a model letter with the class, reviewing how to use the **passé composé** and the imperfect. Have students begin their letters in class and complete them for homework. Collect the next day and correct.

C 21 **Activité • Ecoutez bien**

You're going to hear a French boy talk about the future. According to him, what problems will have to be solved? As you listen, list the problems he mentions on a separate sheet of paper. You don't have to write complete sentences. Ready? **Ecoutez bien.**

> Je crois que dans le futur, il y aura de nombreux problèmes à résoudre. D'abord, la pollution. A mon avis, c'est un des problèmes les plus graves. Si on ne fait rien maintenant, il sera bientôt trop tard. Ensuite, comme on vivra plus longtemps, il y aura trop de monde sur la Terre et on n'aura pas assez à manger. On devra coloniser d'autres planètes pour survivre, mais je ne sais pas si ce sera possible. Par contre, je pense qu'on réussira à résoudre le problème du chômage : il y aura de nouveaux emplois, par exemple, réparateur de robots... En conclusion, j'espère qu'on trouvera vite des solutions, mais il faut se dépêcher car c'est urgent!

Et maintenant, vérifions.

    la pollution   la faim   la surpopulation   le chômage

OBJECTIVE   To recombine communicative functions, grammar, and vocabulary

CULTURAL BACKGROUND   Young people have been the subject of much scrutiny by the media and by business because people under 25 now make up 45 percent of the population of France. Young people are basically optimistic about their futures: a full 87 percent believing that their standard of living in the year 2000 will be equal to or superior to that of their parents. The overwhelming majority believe they will marry at some point in their mid-twenties and have two or three children. As to how long they will live, 24 percent believe to age 75, 34 percent to age 85, and 25 percent to age 95 or over.

MOTIVATING ACTIVITY   Ask students to peruse newspapers and magazines, and to bring in at least one article dealing with the future, especially as it pertains to young people. Have them present these items and ideas to the class for discussion.

1   Un sondage

Have students read the survey to themselves. Play the cassette or read the dialogue aloud. Return to the survey and ask students to write their responses on a separate sheet of paper. Collect and ask a volunteer to tabulate the results. Share the results with the class the following day.

2   Activité • Répondez

Have students skim the survey once more to respond to the questions. Ask a student to summarize the dialogue between Danielle and Vincent.

3   Activité • Contradictions

You might make the false statements and have class members contradict you.

4   Activité • Donnez des raisons

Students should be able to suggest logical reasons why Danielle is optimistic, as in the model. See if pairs of students can do so for all of Danielle's responses.

5   Activité • Et vous?

Students might ask the questions of each other, working in pairs.

6   Activité • Ecrivez

Students should draw on the answers they gave in **Premier Contact 1** and **5** as they write a paragraph about their futures. You might wish to review briefly the future tense before they begin.

7   Activité • Ecrivez et parlez

Students work in pairs to make up an original survey. When they've finished writing their questions with multiple-choice answers, have them work as a team, circulating among their classmates to administer their survey. Have them summarize results and then hand in both the survey and the report.

8 Activité • Dites votre opinion

Ask students to write an exchange similar to the model in their books. Collect these; choose the best half to make into a game. Write the future intentions on a set of index cards of one color. Write the opinions on a set of index cards of a different color. Distribute either an intention card or an opinion card to each student in class the next day. Students circulate, stating their intentions to each other. The first pair to logically match up an intention and an opinion wins.

9 Activité • D'accord, pas d'accord...

Have students prepare lists of advantages and disadvantages of having a **minitel.** Then have them pair off and exchange papers so that they can think about their own reactions to the other's reasoning. Finally, have them turn their ideas into a dialogue, working from their lists.

10 Activité • Faites une étude de marché

If you prefer, you might do this activity with the entire class. Brainstorm a list of possibilities with students. Then, by a show of hands, see which of the five possibilities are the most popular.

CHALLENGE   After discovering the five most popular ways to spend money, have students write a paragraph explaining the reasons for these choices.

11 Activité • Récréation

This activity is optional. You might make a contest of this by seeing who can match up the elements in the boxes first.

PRONONCIATION

Pure vowel and consonant sounds

> Open your book to page 413. *(pause)* Refer to this page as you listen to this section.

1 Ecoutez bien et répétez.

> **1.** Many French sounds are quite close to those of English, but few are exactly the same. This is especially true for the vowels. So much so that, many years ago, a famous French writer on a visit to England was moved to remark that English had only one vowel, but he couldn't figure out which one because it didn't keep still long enough. A gross exaggeration perhaps. But he was a good observer. English has very few pure sounds. French has practically nothing but pure sounds. So, if you're going to develop a good French accent, you've got to keep that in mind and pay attention to the quality of your French sounds until they become second nature. Listen carefully to the o-sound in this English sentence: *Oh no, don't go alone.* Hear the little w-sound at the end of each o-sound? In French, it would sound more like /o - o - o - o/. And no matter how long you hold the sound, it's always /o/ in French. Listen to how you say the month of May in English

and French: *May*/**mai.** Listen again to these English and French pairs and repeat the French: *quay*/**quai,** *gay*/**gaie,** *see*/**si,** *we*/**oui,** *too*/**tout,** *do*/**doux,** *doe*/**dos,** *mow*/**mot,** *foe*/**faux,** *sue*/**sous.**

Did you notice that the French vowels were not only purer than the English but also shorter? This is the case even in the middle of words. Listen to these pairs and repeat the French, paying special attention to the length. Be sure to keep your French vowels short: *peep*/**pipe,** *ball*/**bol,** *fool*/**foule,** *loop*/**loupe,** *feel*/**file,** *peak*/**pique,** *dawn*/**donne,** *league*/**ligue.** That's right, the French vowels are shorter; maybe that's why it's easier to keep them pure. But what happens if you stretch them?

You've already seen that neighboring sounds can change the quality of vowels in English—like the vowel of *was* in these two sentences: *He wasn't there. But I was.* Does this happen in French? Never. No matter what their companions, vowels always stay pure, even as their neighbors drag them out. Listen to these pairs of short and stretched vowels in French and repeat them: **cas—case, fait—fer, bouche—bouge, douce—douze, libre—livre, russe—ruse, creux—creuse, œuf—œuvre, lent—lente, grand—grande, craint—craindre, rond—ronde.** What makes these vowels longer than the others? Their neighbors. Did you notice that all the nasal vowels are short when they end a word and long when they don't? You just said **rond** but **ronde.** Watch out for all words ending in an **r;** it stretches out the vowel. You said **fait** but **fer.** Right? Same applies to the **z**-sound even though it's usually written with one **s.** Remember? **Russe** but **ruse.**

2. If you have any doubt, you can always look the word up. Your dictionary will show the stretch of the vowel by putting a colon after it, as in /**vi:v**/, but not after the short vowels, as in /**vif**/. Use your dictionary to look up the words in number 2 on page 413, and arrange them into long and short vowel groups. *(long pause)*

3. If French vowels are pure, so are French consonants. This means that they are not diluted by background noise. For instance, listen to the word *papa* in English and French: *papa*/**papa.** The **p**-sound in English comes out with a puff of air that could blow out a flame or clear the hair from your forehead. Not in French. Listen: **papa.** The French **p**-sound is more like the English *p* in *spat.* Listen: *spat*/**patte, à quatre pattes.** Compare these and repeat the French: *pat*/**patte,** *pair*/**père,** *peep*/**pipe,** *poor*/**pour.** The difference is the same for the two **k**-sounds. Again, repeat the French: *key*/**qui,** *cat*/**quatre,** *coat*/**côte.** And finally, you get the same difference in the two **t**-sounds. Try these, repeating the French: *type*/**type,** *tour*/**tour,** *ton*/**tonne,** *tore*/**tort.**

Let's hold on to the French **t**-sound for a while. What will really help you avoid the puff of air in the English **t**-sound is the correct position of the tongue. Your tongue is much farther forward in French than in English. The best thing to do is to press your tongue well against the back of your top teeth. Try it. Listen and repeat: **tout, tout à fait; tôt, tôt ou tard; ta, ta table; ton, ton thé; tête, tête à tête; tu, tu tires.**

It's worth getting this tongue position right because it's the same one for the **d-, n-, s-,** and **z**-sounds, as in the words **dos, nos, sot,** and **zone.** For all these French sounds, try saying them by putting more pressure on your teeth to stop the air. Try it with these expressions: **ton dos, tes dents, tout deux, très doux, dis donc, je t'ai dit.** Keeping the same tongue position, now try the French **n**-sound: **ton nez, ta nationalité, ton nom, ton numéro.** When you come to the **s**- and **z**-sounds, you keep this tongue position, but you've got to let the air out, as you do in English. Try it as you repeat these: **c'est dans son auto; deux cent soixante-dix; son sac à main est tout neuf; zone dangereuse.**

4. Now let's hold onto this **s**-sound for a while. You've probably already noticed that it's not always written with an **s**. In what you've just said, you found the sound in the words **cent, soixante** and **dix**. So what are three ways of spelling /s/? Let's see. There's **s**, of course, as in **son** and **sac**. There's **x**, as in **dix** and **soixante**, and there's **c**, as in **cent** and **c'est**. But there are other ways to spell /s/. There's **ç** in **ça** and **François**—that's only before an **a**, **o**, or **u**. There's also **sc**, as in **scène** and **science**—like in English. And then there's **ss**, as in **bassin** and **baisser**. Pay attention to this last word because a single **s** in the same position gives you a **z**-sound. You say **baisser** with an **s**-sound. Take away an **s** and you'd have to say **baiser** with a **z**-sound. Don't get words like this mixed up. **Baisser** means *to lower* and the other, **baiser**, means *a kiss*. Another thing to watch out for is when the grouping of your words into continuous sense groups places an **s** in the same position as in **baiser**, that is, between two vowels, as in **les autres** and **dix autres**, where the **s** and the **x** come out as a **z**-sound. Before leaving the **s** and **z**, let's go back to the **s**-sound being written as the letter **c**. Is the **c** always pronounced like an **s**? Use your dictionary to look up the words in number 4 on page 413 and find out when the **c** is not an **s**-sound and why.

5. As a fitting end to this inspection of quality control, let's take a look at the final consonants of French. Most final consonants, as you know, are not pronounced. So they're easy. Just don't say them. There are some very important ones, however, that you must say if you're going to be understood. You'll just have to learn them for yourself. If you can master which are pronounced and which are not, you might even end up by becoming a French poet. Don't think so? Well, try this. Look at the words ending in consonants in number 5. How many can you make rhyme? Look them up in your friendly dictionary and put them into rhyming pairs. Ready? Get started! *(long pause)*

---

2   **Ecoutez et lisez.**

For a little more practice with pure vowel and consonant sounds, read aloud the dialogue. I'll say each line after you.

—On ne peut pas sortir les livres.
—Si, pour deux semaines seulement. J'en ai sorti la semaine dernière.
—On peut en sortir deux à la fois?
—Mais oui, on peut en sortir autant qu'on veut.
—Où est-ce qu'on s'adresse?
—Dans la grande salle, à gauche. Il faut donner ton nom et ton numéro de téléphone.

---

3   **Copiez les phrases suivantes pour préparer une dictée.**

Write the following sentences from dictation. First listen to the sentence as it is read to you. Then you will hear the sentence again in short segments, with a pause after each segment to allow you time to write. Finally you will hear the sentence a third time so that you may check your work. Let's begin.

1. Vous pouvez déjà savoir combien vous pèserez quand vous serez sur la planète Mars. Vous pouvez déjà savoir *(pause)* combien vous pèserez *(pause)* quand vous serez *(pause)* sur la planète Mars. *(pause)*

Vous pouvez déjà savoir combien vous pèserez quand vous serez sur la planète Mars.

2. Ce sont les robots qui feront notre boulot. On aura une vie merveilleuse. Ce sont les robots *(pause)* qui feront notre boulot. *(pause)* On aura *(pause)* une vie merveilleuse. *(pause)* Ce sont les robots qui feront notre boulot. On aura une vie merveilleuse.

3. Si je réussis dans mes études, j'aurai un boulot intéressant. Si je réussis *(pause)* dans mes études, *(pause)* j'aurai un boulot *(pause)* intéressant. *(pause)* Si je réussis dans mes études, j'aurai un boulot intéressant.

4. Est-ce qu'il y aura encore des rêveurs? Est-ce qu'il y aura *(pause)* encore des rêveurs? *(pause)* Est-ce qu'il y aura encore des rêveurs?

VERIFIONS!

Review with students the future and expressions of doubt and certainty. Have them write out the verb forms needed to complete the first five sentences. Call on individuals to read the sentences aloud and on others to write the correct forms on the board.

For the second exercise, divide the class into groups of three students each. One should read the statements; another should respond with expressions of doubt; and the third should insist that he or she is certain the predictions will take place.

Review the future of irregular verbs. Then have students reread the expressions in B9. While they have their books open to B9, ask various individuals the four questions on page 414 until many have had a chance to participate. Next have students read aloud the sentences in the paragraph about the future. Have them write the correct verb forms on the board.

Have the students review C10; then have each student write a sentence about one of the topics mentioned. Have the students who wrote about the same topics form a group. They should discuss their beliefs and try to come up with a consensus statement: **La majorité pense que...**

Review relative pronouns before students begin the second exercise. After they have written their choices, ask volunteers to read the sentences aloud.

VOCABULAIRE

Mark off the classroom as if it were a baseball diamond with four bases: first, second, third, and home. Divide the class into two teams. Give each "batter" a word from the vocabulary list to translate. If the "batter" does so correctly, he or she goes to first base. If the same "batter" can give a synonym or definition *in French*, he or she goes to second base. If the "batter" fails, he or she is out. When the "batter" advances to second base, he or she becomes a "runner," who can be advanced if the next team member up scores a single or double. After three outs, the other team goes to bat. Continue and score as in baseball.

ETUDE DE MOTS

Have students use their dictionaries to look up additional words related to those underlined in the sentences. Have them explain how the words in each family are related in meaning.

A LIRE

OBJECTIVE   To read for practice and pleasure

UN COURS SUR LES LASERS

For **Avant de lire,** some students may want to mention other uses of the laser; see if they can do so in French. Allow a discussion to develop if time allows.

Have students read the selection for homework. The next day, they should be ready to summarize the teacher's lesson on lasers and to comment on Gérard's and Yvette's roles in the plot.

Activité • Choisissez l'équivalent anglais

Have students select the correct English equivalents and then use the French terms in complete sentences.

Activité • Vrai ou faux?

Have students read the statements aloud and correct those that are false.

LE JOUR OU LA TERRE S'EST ARRETEE DE TOURNER

Have students look at the title of the story and the illustrations. See what they can predict about the story; summarize the plot for them. Then have students read the story for homework. The next day, play the cassette for each section; stop to answer any questions; then continue playing the cassette until students have listened to the whole story.

Activité • Complétez

Students will need to skim the story again to find the words or phrases that complete the sentences. Call on volunteers to share their answers with the class.

Activité • Avez-vous compris?

See if students are able to answer the questions without referring back to the story.

Activité • Ecrivez

You might have students do this writing activity in cooperative learning groups in class or, if you prefer, individually for homework.

Bientôt l'avenir

French young people are excited about progress and by dreams of the future. Technological innovations, like the *minitel*, have made their way into everyday life. Places like the *Cité des Sciences et de l'Industrie* show what the future might hold. But young people are concerned about the future. They wonder what their lives will be like and how the world will solve its problems.

In this unit you will:

PREMIER CONTACT	get acquainted with the topic
SECTION **A**	predict what the future will be like . . . express doubt and certainty
SECTION **B**	imagine what your future will be like . . . express intentions, goals, wishes, and dreams
SECTION **C**	discuss problems of the future . . . express beliefs, hope, and doubt
TRY YOUR SKILLS	use what you've learned
A LIRE	read for practice and pleasure

getting acquainted with the topic

The authentic material in Premier Contact introduces the theme of the unit and is to be used for global comprehension only.

1 Le minitel rend la vie plus facile.

Un nouveau système de communication a fait ses débuts dans de nombreux domiciles français.

Le minitel vous offre un monde de services pour vous informer et communiquer. Il est vraiment très facile à utiliser : il faut un petit terminal — le minitel — qui se branche sur une ligne téléphonique. Vous appelez les services que vous désirez, et l'écran montre les informations demandées, sous forme de textes et de graphiques.

Vous pourrez ainsi utiliser des services différents : suivre un cours, passer des commandes, consulter votre compte bancaire, obtenir les programmes des spectacles… Tout cela sans sortir de chez vous! La vie sera plus facile, le monde plus proche!

Avec le minitel, on ne s'ennuie pas. On a tous les programmes de cinéma, la liste des matches, les activités du club photo…

Je peux même commander un nouveau chéquier à ma banque et me renseigner sur les conditions d'ouverture d'un compte épargne…

J'avais oublié le numéro de téléphone d'un ami. Je l'ai retrouvé tout de suite avec l'Annuaire Electronique. En quelques secondes, on obtient le renseignement qu'on veut.

On gagne beaucoup de temps avec le minitel. Je pars demain en province. Immédiatement, j'ai sur mon écran les horaires de tous les trains. Je peux même réserver ma place.

For additional background on the minitel, see p. T233.

Photo on pages 380 and 381: La Géode de la Cité des Sciences et de l'Industrie; the Ariane missile taking off; part of the "Explora" exhibit.

Activité ● **Avez-vous compris?**   Possible answers are given.

Répondez aux questions suivantes d'après «Le minitel rend la vie plus facile».

1. Qu'est-ce qu'on peut faire avec le minitel?

2. Pourquoi utiliser le minitel? Quels sont les avantages de son emploi?

3. Est-ce qu'il y a un service identique aux Etats-Unis?

1. On peut utiliser des services différents : suivre un cours, passer des commandes, consulter notre compte bancaire, obtenir les programmes des spectacles...   2. On gagne beaucoup de temps avec le minitel.
3. Il n'y a pas de système identique aux Etats-Unis.

3   VISITE DE LA CITÉ DES SCIENCES

A la Cité des Sciences et de l'Industrie, il y a beaucoup de choses à voir et à faire. Comme on ne peut pas tout visiter, le mieux, c'est de commencer par Explora, son exposition permanente.

la Villette
Cité des Sciences et de l'Industrie

30, avenue Corentin-Cariou
75019 Paris. Tél. : 40.22.15.71
Métro : porte de la Villette
Autobus : 150, 152, 250A, PC

HORAIRES D'OUVERTURE

samedi, dimanche et jours fériés	12h à 20h
mardi, jeudi, vendredi	10h à 18h
mercredi (nocturne)	12h à 21h
fermeture le lundi	

Explora

A Explora, vous entrerez dans la passionnante aventure de l'univers et de la vie, de la technologie et de la communication. Aussi bien pour les enfants que pour les adultes, Explora vous fera jouer à l'astronaute dans le fauteuil de l'espace, piloter un avion en simulation, assister au spectacle de la forêt et de ses habitants, et des centaines d'autres choses encore.

Explora occupe les trois étages supérieurs du bâtiment. Pour tout renseignement, une équipe d'agents d'accueil, parlant 18 langues étrangères, est à votre disposition aux banques d'accueil.

For additional background on the Cité des Sciences et de l'Industrie, see p. T239. Refer students to the map of Paris, p. 435.

4   Activité ● **Avez-vous bien lu?**   Possible answers are given.

Répondez aux questions suivantes d'après «Visite de la Cité des Sciences».

1. Qui s'intéresse à visiter Explora?

2. Que peut-on faire à Explora?

3. Si vous ne pouvez pas trouver le spectacle de la forêt, où vous renseignez-vous?

1. C'est aussi intéressant pour les enfants que pour les adultes.   2. On peut jouer à l'astronaute, piloter un avion, assister au spectacle de la fôret, et des centaines d'autres choses encore.   3. Pour tout renseignement, vous pouvez aller aux banques d'accueil.

5   Activité ● **A vous maintenant!**

La Cité des Sciences et de l'Industrie a des expositions temporaires liées *(related)* aux thèmes d'Explora. On vient dans votre lycée vous demander ce que vous aimeriez y voir. Qu'est-ce que vous suggérez comme exposition temporaire?

L'an 2010, c'est bientôt... Les nouvelles technologies sont déjà là : les robots, les ordinateurs, le laser. Qu'est-ce qui changera dans notre vie quotidienne? Est-ce que vous y pensez quelquefois?

A1 Comment vivrons-nous en l'an 2010?

Henri raconte à Charlotte comment il voit l'avenir.

HENRI   Bientôt, nous vivrons mieux. Nous aurons des robots. Ils feront la cuisine et toutes les tâches domestiques. Ils passeront l'aspirateur et rangeront la maison.

CHARLOTTE   Ça m'étonnerait!

HENRI   Je t'assure que c'est vrai! Et... très important... ils nous apporteront le petit déjeuner au lit.

Bonjour! Il est sept heures et il fait beau. Bon appétit!

C'est moi!

Désolé, je ne reconnais pas votre voix. Désolé,...

HENRI   Les voitures auront un pilotage automatique. On dira «C'est moi!», les portières s'ouvriront et le moteur démarrera. Ensuite, on programmera son itinéraire, comme sur les avions.

HENRI   On mangera aussi différemment. On achètera des pilules nutritives avec toutes les calories nécessaires.

CHARLOTTE   J'en doute! A mon avis, il y aura toujours des fruits et des légumes. C'est meilleur.

HENRI   Tu as peut-être raison. Qui sait?

Un kilo de tomates, s'il vous plaît.

HENRI   Les ordinateurs seront indispensables. Grâce à eux, on n'aura plus besoin d'aller tous les jours au lycée. On communiquera directement avec nos professeurs.

CHARLOTTE   Tu crois vraiment? Moi, je ne pense pas, je...

HENRI   Mais si! J'en suis convaincu! On fera aussi nos courses sans sortir. Les petites boutiques n'existeront plus. On fera son marché sur l'ordinateur.

Pourquoi est-ce que tu es en panne? J'ai faim, moi!

MME NOGUIER   Henri?
HENRI   Oui, maman?
MME NOGUIER   Tu peux aller m'acheter du jambon?
HENRI   Mais maman, je suis avec Charlotte!
MME NOGUIER   Ne discute pas!
HENRI   Tu vois, Charlotte. Plus tard, nous vivrons mieux!

A2 Activité • Faux, mais pourquoi?

D'après Henri, les phrases suivantes sont fausses. Pouvez-vous les corriger?

1. En l'an 2010, nous vivrons moins bien.
2. Il n'y aura plus de voitures.
3. Nous mangerons les mêmes choses qu'aujourd'hui.

4. On n'aura plus besoin d'ordinateurs.
5. Il y aura toujours de petites boutiques.
6. On fera son marché comme maintenant.

1. En l'an 2010, nous vivrons mieux.   2. Les voitures auront un pilotage automatique.   3. On achètera des pilules nutritives avec toutes les calories nécessaires.   4. Les ordinateurs seront indispensables.   5. Les petites boutiques n'existeront plus.   6. On fera son marché sur l'ordinateur.

Activité • **Comment est-ce que ça changera?** Possible answers are given.

D'après Henri, comment est-ce que ces choses changeront en l'an 2010? Travaillez avec un(e) camarade pour faire une liste.

les voitures   *les courses*   **les études**   *les repas*   **les tâches domestiques**

Les voitures auront un pilotage automatique. Les robots préparont nos repas et feront toutes les tâches domestiques. Nous ferons nos études et nos courses sur l'ordinateur.

A4 Activité • **Faites des phrases** Possible answers are given.

Dites à un(e) camarade quelques phrases sur le rôle de ces choses dans le futur. Utilisez le texte et votre imagination.

Les ordinateurs seront indispensables.

Les robots feront les tâches domestiques.

Les voitures auront un pilotage automatique.

A5 Activité • **Actes de parole** Scepticisme : Ça m'étonnerait. J'en doute. Tu crois vraiment? Je ne pense pas...

Pouvez-vous trouver dans A1 trois façons d'exprimer le scepticisme *(doubt)*? Deux façons d'exprimer la certitude?
Certitude : Je t'assure. Mais si! J'en suis convaincu.

A6 Activité • **A votre avis**

D'après vous, qu'est-ce qu'il y aura toujours et qu'est-ce qu'il n'y aura plus en l'an 2010? Un(e) camarade de classe vous demande votre opinion et vous répondez. Ensuite, changez de rôle.

    — Tu penses qu'il y aura des voitures en l'an 2010?
    — A mon avis, il y aura toujours des voitures.
      (... il n'y aura plus de voitures)

1. des vacances   3. de petites boutiques   5. des fruits   7. des villages
2. des avions   4. de l'argent   6. du travail   8. des cours à l'école

A7 Activité • **Et vous?**

1. Est-ce que vous avez un ordinateur chez vous?
2. Si oui, qu'est-ce qu'on peut faire avec? Vous l'utilisez pour quoi faire? Est-ce que vos parents l'utilisent? Pour quoi faire?
3. Est-ce qu'il y a un ordinateur dans votre école?
4. Si oui, pour quelles matières est-ce que vous l'utilisez? Combien de fois par semaine?

STRUCTURES DE BASE
The future

1. In French, there is a special tense that is used to express future actions. Take a look at the chart below to see how this tense, the future, is formed.

	-er Verbs	*-ir Verbs*	*-re Verbs*
Stem	**changer-**	**sortir-**	**vivr-**
Future	je changer**ai** tu changer**as** il/elle/on changer**a** nous changer**ons** vous changer**ez** ils/elles changer**ont**	je sortir**ai** tu sortir**as** il/elle/on sortir**a** nous sortir**ons** vous sortir**ez** ils/elles sortir**ont**	je vivr**ai** tu vivr**as** il/elle/on vivr**a** nous vivr**ons** vous vivr**ez** ils/elles vivr**ont**

2. The future endings are **-ai, -as, -a, -ons, -ez,** and **-ont.** They are the same for all verbs.

3. For most verbs that end in **-er** or **-ir,** the future stem is the same as the infinitive: **parler → je parlerai, finir → tu finiras.**

4. For verbs ending in **-re,** the future stem is formed by dropping the final **e** from the infinitive: **attendr̸e → il attendra.**

5. Some **-er** verbs have future stems that are slightly different from their infinitive forms. They follow the patterns shown in the chart below.

*Add **accent grave***		*Change **y** to **i***		*Double the consonant*	
acheter	**achèter-**	(s') ennuyer	**(s')ennuier-**	(s') appeler	**(s')appeller-**
amener	**amèner-**	essayer	**essaier-**		
emmener	**emmèner-**	payer	**paier-**		
(se) lever	**lèver-**				
peser	**pèser-**				

6. There are several irregular verbs that have special future stems. You'll learn many of them soon, but for the time being, you should know these three: **avoir → aur-, être → ser-,** and **faire → fer-.**

A 9 Activité • Henri donne des précisions

Charlotte demande à Henri des précisions *(details)* sur sa façon de voir l'avenir. Mettez les verbes entre parenthèses au futur.

CHARLOTTE	Tu crois que l'école (exister) encore dans 30 ans? <small>existera</small>
HENRI	Non, les enfants (apprendre) tout chez eux, avec un ordinateur. <small>apprendront</small>
CHARLOTTE	Et les adultes, ils (travailler) aussi à la maison? <small>travailleront</small>
HENRI	Bien sûr! Ils (rester) à la maison et ne (travailler) que cinq heures par jour. <small>resteront / travailleront</small>
CHARLOTTE	Alors, tu ne (sortir) plus de chez toi? <small>sortiras</small>
HENRI	Mais si, je (sortir)! On (avoir) beaucoup de temps libre. Moi, je le (passer) chez des copains. <small>sortirai / aura / passerai</small>
CHARLOTTE	On (être) plus heureux que maintenant? <small>sera</small>
HENRI	Bien sûr! On (travailler) moins et on (s'amuser) plus!
	<small>travaillera s'amusera</small>

Dans 30 ans, vous achèterez un robot. Regardez ces dessins et dites à un(e) camarade ce que le robot fera chez vous.

1.

Le robot passera l'aspirateur.

2.

Il fera les repas.

3.

Il écrira des lettres.

4.

Le robot chantera.

5.

Il sortira la poubelle.

6.

Il fera le ménage.

7.

Il tondra la pelouse.

8.

Il lavera la voiture.

9.

Il promènera le chien.

Activité • Ecrit dirigé

Henri imagine maintenant comment on vivra dans 100 ans. Aidez-le en ajoutant à ce paragraphe les verbes au futur.

travailler   faire   être   exister   acheter   avoir   apporter

Plus tard, les voitures ____ des moteurs électriques et la pollution n'____ plus. Le
auront   *existera*

métro ____ remplacé par des trottoirs roulants *(moving sidewalks)*. Les gens ____ chez
sera   *travailleront*

eux et il y ____ moins de monde dans les rues. Nous n'____ plus rien dans les
aura   *achèterons*

magasins, nous ____ notre marché sur l'ordinateur, et des robots nous ____ nos achats
ferons

à domicile *(home)*. Tout ____ très bien!
                   apporteront
                   sera

A 12 Activité • Un message du XXIᵉ siècle   Possible answer is given.

Vous êtes en communication avec une personne du XXIᵉ siècle. Elle vous a envoyé un
message par ordinateur où elle vous décrit sa vie. Lisez-le et ensuite, racontez à un(e)
camarade de classe comment on vivra plus tard.   *Là-bas, ça sera drôlement bien! On habitera dans des maisons sous l'eau.*
On aura plusieurs robots. L'un d'eux apportera le petit déjeuner et fera la vaisselle. Un autre s'occupera de la voiture aquatique.

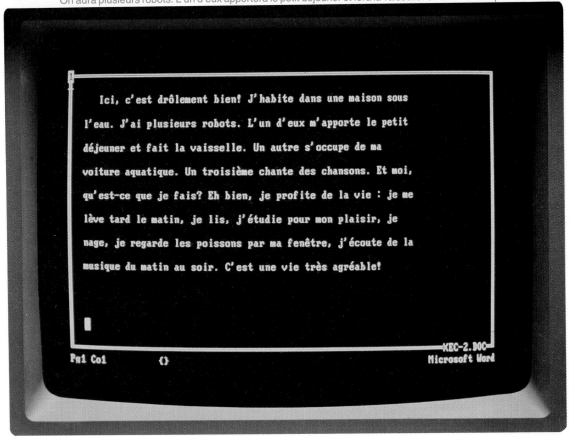

Ici, c'est drôlement bien! J'habite dans une maison sous l'eau. J'ai plusieurs robots. L'un d'eux m'apporte le petit déjeuner et fait la vaisselle. Un autre s'occupe de ma voiture aquatique. Un troisième chante des chansons. Et moi, qu'est-ce que je fais? Eh bien, je profite de la vie : je me lève tard le matin, je lis, j'étudie pour mon plaisir, je nage, je regarde les poissons par ma fenêtre, j'écoute de la musique du matin au soir. C'est une vie très agréable!

Pg1 Col   {}   KEC-2.DOC
                         Microsoft Word

Un troisième chantera des chansons. Et nous, qu'est-ce que nous ferons? Nous profiterons de la vie : On se lèvera tard le matin, on étudiera
pour son plaisir, on nagera, on regardera les poissons par la fenêtre, on écoutera de la musique du matin au soir. Ça sera une vie très agréable!

A 13 Activité • Ecrivez

A votre avis, comment vivrons-nous dans 50 ans? Est-ce qu'il y aura encore des voitures?
Aurons-nous des robots? Qu'est-ce qu'ils feront? A quoi serviront les ordinateurs? Qu'est-ce
qu'on mangera? Est-ce que la vie sera plus ou moins facile qu'aujourd'hui? Pourquoi?

Savez-vous que... ?

Dans le domaine des techniques nouvelles, la France est souvent bien placée pour répondre aux besoins de la société de l'an 2000. Elle a été, par exemple, le premier pays à introduire le système de communication minitel dans les foyers *(homes)* français. Grâce au minitel, on peut maintenant obtenir des informations sur tous les sujets (météo, horaires de trains...) ou communiquer avec sa banque ou son supermarché sans sortir de chez soi.

Le constructeur automobile français Peugeot-Citroën travaille actuellement *(presently)* sur la voiture du futur. Peugeot, par exemple, a été le premier constructeur du monde à présenter en 1982 une voiture qui parle, la 505 turbo à injection. Peugeot's talking car, which is no longer in production, said such things as «Attention! Niveau d'huile insuffisant.» and «Veuillez attacher vos ceintures.» For additional background on this car, see page T233.

A15   Activité • Ecoutez bien   For script and answers, see pp. T233–34.

Ecoutez ce texte publicitaire pour le minitel. Faites une liste de six utilisations *(uses)* possibles du minitel.

A16   Activité • Donnez des conseils   See answers to A15 on pp. T233–34.

Parlez des avantages du minitel avec un(e) camarade. Utilisez la liste que vous avez préparée dans A15. Ensuite, changez de rôle.

— Il faut que tu aies un minitel.
— Pourquoi?
— Parce qu'avec un minitel, tu...

COMMENT LE DIRE
Expressing doubt and certainty

DOUBT	CERTAINTY
Je ne (le) crois pas.	Je t'assure que c'est vrai.
Je ne (le) pense pas.	Mais oui (si)! C'est évident!
Ça m'étonnerait!	Evidemment.
Ça m'étonnerait que nous ayons des robots!	Je (J'en) suis convaincu(e).
J'en doute.	Je (J'en) suis persuadé(e).
	J'en suis sûr(e).

Note the use of the subjunctive after "Ça m'étonnerait que..."

A 18   Activité • **Vous êtes sceptique**

Un(e) camarade vous donne son avis sur comment il/elle voit l'avenir. Vous n'êtes pas convaincu(e). Il/Elle vous assure qu'il/elle a raison. Faites un dialogue. Variez les expressions.

— Plus tard, on vivra sur Mars.   Refer to expressions of doubt and certainty in A17.
— Je ne crois pas!
— Mais si! C'est évident!

1. On volera.

2. On vivra sous l'eau.

3. On remontera dans le temps.

4. On parlera une langue universelle.

A 19   Activité • **A vous maintenant!**   Possible dialogue is given.

Y a-t-il des choses qui existent maintenant qui n'existeront plus dans 50 ans? Des choses que vous faites que vous ne ferez plus? Dites-les à un(e) camarade. Il/Elle exprime son scepticisme. Vous confirmez ce que vous avez dit, et vous donnez une explication.

— Plus tard, on ne travaillera plus.   —En l'an 2010, il n'y aura plus de professeurs! Il n'y aura que des ordinateurs.
— Ça m'étonnerait!   —J'en doute.
— Moi, j'en suis convaincu!   —Je t'assure que c'est vrai!
— Qu'est-ce qu'on fera alors?
— On se reposera.

imagining what your future will be like . . . expressing
intentions, goals, wishes, and dreams

*Comment imaginez-vous votre avenir? Où habiterez-vous? Que ferez-vous? Travaillerez-vous?
Dans quoi? Serez-vous marié(e)? A votre avis, est-ce que vous serez très différent(e) de
maintenant?*

B1 Votre avenir

Un journaliste de l'émission de radio *A vous la parole!* a posé
cette question à ses auditeurs : «Comment est-ce que vous
voyez votre avenir?» Ecoutez les réponses qui ont été
diffusées. Est-ce que vous avez les mêmes idées ou les
mêmes souhaits que ces jeunes pour votre avenir?

Allô, c'est bien *A vous la parole*? Je m'appelle
Arnaud. Quand j'aurai 30 ans, je serai un musicien
célèbre. Je jouerai partout dans le monde. Des
millions de jeunes viendront m'écouter et chanteront
mes chansons. Mes parents seront fiers de moi, mes
copains m'envieront, et toutes les filles voudront se
marier avec moi!

Allô, bonjour, je m'appelle Stéphanie. Plus tard,
j'espère avoir quatre enfants. Nous habiterons à la
campagne, loin des villes et de la pollution. Mais je ne
me marierai pas avant 25 ans : je ne suis pas pressée!
Je m'entendrai bien avec mon mari, et on ne se disputera
jamais. Nous pourrons élever nos enfants dans le calme.
Ce sera pour moi la meilleure des vies.

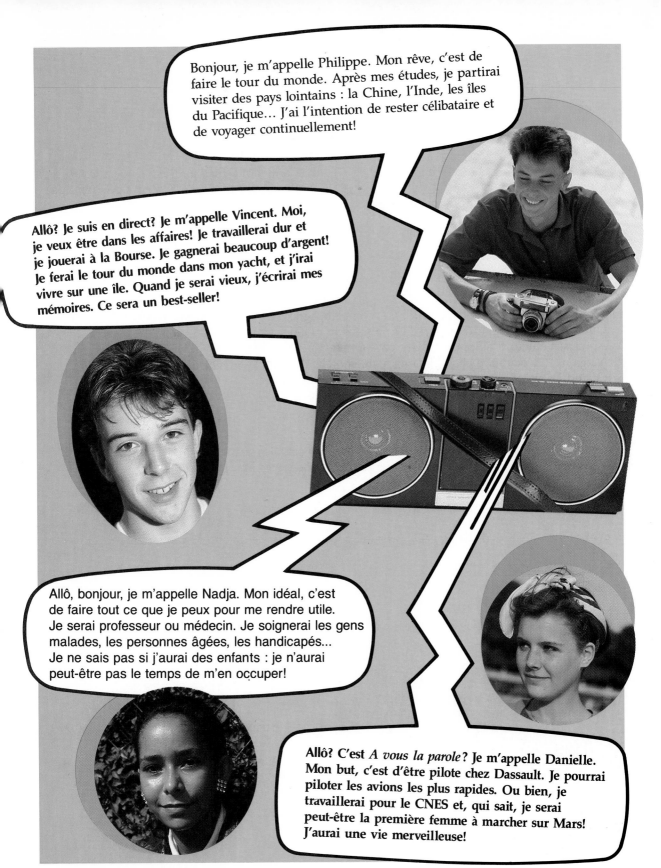

Bonjour, je m'appelle Philippe. Mon rêve, c'est de faire le tour du monde. Après mes études, je partirai visiter des pays lointains : la Chine, l'Inde, les îles du Pacifique… J'ai l'intention de rester célibataire et de voyager continuellement!

Allô? Je suis en direct? Je m'appelle Vincent. Moi, je veux être dans les affaires! Je travaillerai dur et je jouerai à la Bourse. Je gagnerai beaucoup d'argent! Je ferai le tour du monde dans mon yacht, et j'irai vivre sur une île. Quand je serai vieux, j'écrirai mes mémoires. Ce sera un best-seller!

Allô, bonjour, je m'appelle Nadja. Mon idéal, c'est de faire tout ce que je peux pour me rendre utile. Je serai professeur ou médecin. Je soignerai les gens malades, les personnes âgées, les handicapés… Je ne sais pas si j'aurai des enfants : je n'aurai peut-être pas le temps de m'en occuper!

Allô? C'est *A vous la parole*? Je m'appelle Danielle. Mon but, c'est d'être pilote chez Dassault. Je pourrai piloter les avions les plus rapides. Ou bien, je travaillerai pour le CNES et, qui sait, je serai peut-être la première femme à marcher sur Mars! J'aurai une vie merveilleuse!

CNES: Centre national d'études spatiales
Dassault: French aeronautics company

Activité • Répondez

Répondez aux questions suivantes d'après B1.

1. Pourquoi les parents d'Arnaud seront-ils fiers de lui?
2. Pourquoi est-ce que Stéphanie habitera à la campagne?
3. Est-ce que ses enfants seront heureux? Pourquoi?
4. Comment est-ce que Vincent gagnera de l'argent?

5. Qu'est-ce qu'il fera de cet argent?
6. Pourquoi est-ce que Philippe restera célibataire?
7. Où ira-t-il?
8. Comment est-ce que Nadja aidera les autres?
9. Pourquoi est-ce qu'elle n'aura peut-être pas d'enfants?
10. Qu'est-ce que Danielle fera?

1. Parce qu'il sera un musicien célèbre.   2. Parce que c'est loin des villes et de la pollution.   3. Oui, parce qu'ils pourront les élever dans le calme.   4. Il jouera à la Bourse.   5. Il fera le tour du monde.   6. Parce qu'il voyagera continuellement.   7. Il ira en Chine, en Inde, dans les îles du Pacifique.   8. Elle sera médecin ou professeur.

B3   Activité • Complétez

9. Elle n'aura pas le temps de s'en occuper.   10. Elle sera pilote chez Dassault.

Complétez les phrases suivantes avec des verbes appropriés au futur.

1. Quand Stéphanie __aura__ 30 ans, elle __vivra__ à la campagne.
2. Quand Vincent __aura__ un yacht, il __fera__ le tour du monde.
3. Après ses études, Philippe __visitera__ des pays étrangers.
4. Nadja n'__aura__ peut-être pas d'enfants, parce qu'elle __aidera__ les gens malades.
5. Quand Danielle __travaillera__ dans un centre d'études spatiales, elle __pilotera__ des avions.

B4   Activité • Et vous?

Pensez maintenant à vos projets pour l'avenir. Quelles activités dans B1 est-ce que vous ferez? Lesquelles (*which ones*) ne ferez-vous pas? Parlez-en avec un(e) camarade.

B5   Activité • Actes de parole

Pouvez-vous trouver dans B1 trois expressions pour exprimer ce qu'on compte faire à l'avenir?

Plus tard, j'espère... / J'ai l'intention de... / Mon rêve, c'est de... / Je veux... / Mon idéal, c'est de... / Mon but, c'est de...

B6   Activité • Jeu de rôle

Avec un(e) camarade de classe, utilisez le texte dans B1 et votre imagination pour faire des dialogues entre...

Arnaud et Danielle
Phílippe et Stéphanie
Stéphanie et Nadja
Arnaud et Vincent
Philippe et Nadja
Stéphanie et Danielle

— Arnaud, qu'est-ce que tu feras plus tard?
— Je serai musicien.
— Tu seras très célèbre?
— Bien sûr!
— Moi, je serai célèbre aussi...

Activité • Et vous?   Possible answers are given.

1. Continuerez-vous vos études? Où?
2. Est-ce que vous vous marierez? A quel âge?
3. Aurez-vous des enfants? Combien?
4. Où est-ce que vous habiterez?
5. Quel genre de travail est-ce que vous ferez?
6. Est-ce que vous voyagerez? Où?

1. Je continuerai mes études à... (Je ne continuerai pas mes études.)   2. Je me marierai quand j'aurai... ans. (Je ne me marierai jamais.)   3. J'aurai... enfants. (Non, je n'aurai pas d'enfants.)   4. J'habiterai...   5. Je ferai... (Je serai...)
6. Je voyagerai... (Non, je ne voyagerai pas.)

B8   Savez-vous que… ?

En France, la recherche spatiale est dirigée par le CNES (Centre national d'études spatiales), souvent en collaboration avec les pays membres de l'Agence spatiale européenne (France, République Fédérale d'Allemagne, Grande-Bretagne, Belgique, Italie, Pays-Bas, Espagne, Danemark, Suède et Suisse). La première fusée *(rocket)* européenne, Ariane, a été lancée *(launched)* à Kourou, en Guyane française, le 24 décembre 1979. L'ASE a maintenant l'intention de faire construire un avion spatial. Il s'appellera Hermès.

Have students locate "la Guyane Française" on the map in the Reference section, p. 436

B9   COMMENT LE DIRE
Expressing intentions, goals, wishes, and dreams

J'ai l'intention de J'ai envie de Je souhaite J'espère Je veux (bien) Je désire J'aimerais (bien)	me marier.	Mon idéal, c'est de Mon but, c'est de Mon rêve, c'est de J'ai pour projet de	vivre en ville.

Point out that many of these expressions use "de" and all of them are followed by the infinitive. Remind students that the reflexive pronoun must agree with the subject even when the reflexive verb is in the infinitive form: Mon rêve, c'est de me marier.

Activité • Qui a envie de faire quoi?

Un journaliste interroge un groupe de jeunes. Avec un(e) camarade de classe, réunissez ses
questions et leurs réponses.

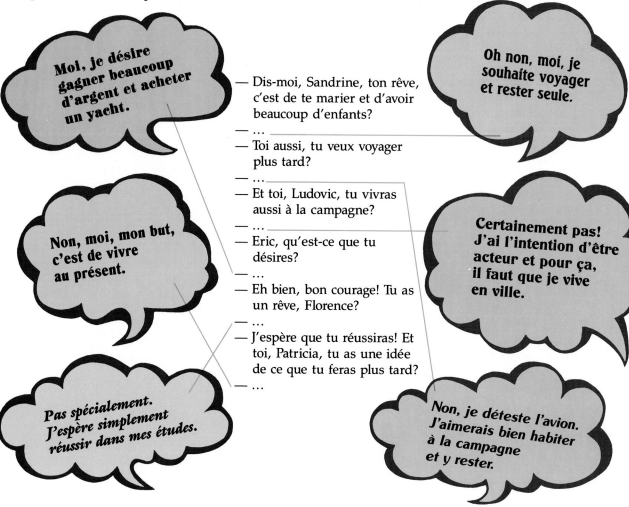

Moi, je désire gagner beaucoup d'argent et acheter un yacht.

Oh non, moi, je souhaite voyager et rester seule.

Non, moi, mon but, c'est de vivre au présent.

Certainement pas! J'ai l'intention d'être acteur et pour ça, il faut que je vive en ville.

Pas spécialement. J'espère simplement réussir dans mes études.

Non, je déteste l'avion. J'aimerais bien habiter à la campagne et y rester.

— Dis-moi, Sandrine, ton rêve, c'est de te marier et d'avoir beaucoup d'enfants?
— ...
— Toi aussi, tu veux voyager plus tard?
— ...
— Et toi, Ludovic, tu vivras aussi à la campagne?
— ...
— Eric, qu'est-ce que tu désires?
— ...
— Eh bien, bon courage! Tu as un rêve, Florence?
— ...
— J'espère que tu réussiras! Et toi, Patricia, tu as une idée de ce que tu feras plus tard?
— ...

B 11   Activité • Interviewez un(e) camarade

Posez des questions à un(e) camarade de classe pour
savoir ce qu'il/elle fera plus tard. Il/Elle vous interroge
à son tour.

— Tu as un rêve dans la vie?
— Oui, mon rêve, c'est de...
— Comment tu feras pour y arriver?
— Eh bien, je...

se promener sur Mars
devenir une star du rock
faire le tour du monde
se marier
avoir une maison à la campagne
gagner beaucoup d'argent
être célèbre
être champion(ne) cycliste

B 12   Activité • Et vous?

Qu'est-ce que vous voulez faire ce soir? Et l'année prochaine? Et dans l'avenir?

Refer to B9 for expressions of intentions, goals, wishes, and dreams.

Activité • Ecrivez

Est-ce que vous avez des projets pour l'été prochain? Ecrivez à un(e) ami(e) pour lui dire ce que vous avez l'intention de faire. Ensuite, invitez-le(la) à venir avec vous, et dites-lui ce que vous ferez. Donnez-lui envie de vous accompagner!

> Cher (Chère)...
> L'été prochain, j'ai
> l'intention de... Ça te dit
> de m'accompagner? Nous...

Cher... L'été prochain, j'ai l'intention de voyager en Europe en vélo.
Ça te dit de m'accompagner? Nous visiterons toutes les grandes villes.
On rencontrera des tas de gens sympa. On visitera tous les musées.
On mangera dans les meilleurs restaurants, et on sera en très bonne forme!

STRUCTURES DE BASE
The future of irregular verbs
The future with **quand**

1. In addition to **avoir, être,** and **faire,** there are several irregular verbs that have special future stems.

Infinitive	Future Stem	
aller	**ir-**	J'**irai** à la boum chez Luc samedi prochain.
devoir	**devr-**	Je **devrai** préparer un dessert.
envoyer	**enverr-**	Il t'**enverra** une invitation, je crois.
falloir	**faudr-**	Il **faudra** que nous y allions ensemble.
pleuvoir	**pleuvr-**	Il ne **pleuvra** pas ce soir.
pouvoir	**pourr-**	Tu **pourras** y amener ton frère.
recevoir	**recevr-**	Je sais qu'il **recevra** une invitation.
savoir	**saur-**	Vous **saurez** comment aller chez Luc?
venir	**viendr-**	Sinon, je **viendrai** vous chercher.
voir	**verr-**	Nous **verrons** tous nos copains chez lui.
vouloir	**voudr-**	Lui, il **voudra** bien danser avec moi!

"Falloir" has only one form, the third person singular: Il faudra…

2. When you use **quand** in a sentence that predicts the future, the verbs in the sentence should be in the future.

> Quand je **serai** vieux (vieille), j'**écrirai** mes mémoires.
> Je **serai** un(e) musicien(ne) célèbre quand j'**aurai** 30 ans.

Activité • Quel sera l'avenir de Philippe?

Stéphanie prétend *(claims)* connaître Philippe mieux qu'il ne se connaît. Complétez leur conversation en mettant les verbes entre parenthèses au futur.

PHILIPPE   Quand je (être) [serai] adulte, qu'est-ce que je (faire)? [ferai]

STÉPHANIE   Tu (aller) loin, très loin… Tu (faire) le tour du monde. [iras / feras]

PHILIPPE   Comme je (voyager) beaucoup, je ne me (marier) pas. [voyagerai / marierai]

STÉPHANIE   Mais si! Tu te (marier) à 25 ans. Ta femme (être) riche, et elle (adorer) voyager. Vous (voir) [marieras / sera / adorera] toutes les merveilles du monde ensemble. Tous les gens (vouloir) être à votre place. [verrez / voudront]

PHILIPPE   Et nous n'(avoir) pas d'obligations? [aurons]

STÉPHANIE   Si, une seule. Il (falloir) que vous veniez me voir une fois par an, et nous (rester) toujours amis. [faudra] [resterons]

Activité • **Demain…**   Possible answers are given.

Dites exactement à un(e) camarade ce que Nicolas fera demain. Décrivez sa journée d'après ces dessins.   For reporting a series of events, refer students to Unit 9 (C14), p. 322.

1. Il se lèvera tôt.

2. D'abord, il prendra son petit déjeuner.

3. Ensuite, il sortira les poubelles.

4. Puis, il partira de chez lui.

5. Il arrivera à la MJC.

6. Là, il s'entraînera.

7. Il fera du basket-ball.

8. Après, il déjeunera avec un copain.

9. Enfin, les garçons écouteront des cassettes.

Activité • A vous maintenant! Possible answer is given.

Pensez maintenant à ce que vous ferez demain. Décrivez à un(e) camarade la journée que vous imaginez. Soyez précis(e). Je me réveillerai. Je m'habillerai. Je prendrai mon petit déjeuner. Ensuite, j'irai chez des copains. On écoutera des cassettes, et après, on ira au cinéma.

Activité • Et vous?

Qu'est-ce que vous ferez… ?

1. quand vous sortirez du lycée
2. quand vous aurez 25 ans
3. quand vous gagnerez de l'argent
4. quand vous serez vieux (vieille)

Remind students that when they use "quand" in a complex sentence that predicts the future, the verbs in both clauses should be in the future.

Activité • Dis-moi ce que tu aimes; je te dirai ce que tu feras

Demandez à un(e) camarade de classe ce qu'il/elle aime ou n'aime pas. Prédisez (predict) son avenir d'après ses goûts. Puis changez de rôle.

— J'aime la ville. Je suis très indépendant(e), mais j'aime le contact avec les gens. J'aime le sport; je suis très actif(active), très organisé(e).
— Tu habiteras en ville. Tu seras probablement médecin, ou peut-être professeur. Tu sauras très bien t'occuper de tes affaires. Tu ne te marieras pas, ou alors quand tu auras 40 ans. Tu feras beaucoup de sports. Tu gagneras de l'argent, et tu pourras faire ce que tu voudras. Possible questions for the interview:
Qu'est-ce que tu préfères : la ville ou la campagne? Est-ce que tu aimes le contact avec les gens? Est-ce que tu es fonceur (fonceuse)? Où est-ce que tu préfères habiter? Est-ce que tu préfères une vie active ou une vie calme? Tu aimes faire du sport?

Activité • Ecrivez Possible answers are given.

D'après ce que vous savez de Fabrice, Matthieu et Sandrine dans le Chapitre 7, imaginez leur vie dans 20 ans. Ecrivez quelques phrases sur chacun d'entre eux. Dites où ils habiteront, avec qui, ce qu'ils feront comme travail… Fabrice ne sera jamais en forme, mais il sera un acteur célèbre. Matthieu sera probablement professeur de gymnastique. Sandrine sera médecin. Elle s'occupera de tout le monde!

Activité • Ecoutez bien For script and answers, see pp. T237–38.

Ecoutez ce dialogue entre Anne et Patrice. Ensuite, décrivez la situation d'Anne et celle de Patrice quand ils auront 30 ans.

	Anne	Patrice
Profession ?		
Mariage ?		
Enfants ?		
Résidence?		

L'avenir, c'est l'inconnu… Nous vivrons autrement, mais il y aura certainement de nombreux problèmes. Est-ce qu'on réussira à les résoudre? Qu'est-ce que vous en pensez?

C1   Est-ce que vous croyez que l'avenir sera meilleur?

Pierre et Roxane sont allés visiter la Cité des Sciences et de l'Industrie à Paris. A la sortie, ils discutent du futur… Etes-vous de l'avis de Roxane? Est-ce que Pierre est un rêveur?

ROXANE   Comment tu vois l'avenir? En rose ou en noir?

PIERRE   En rose, bien sûr! On vivra plus vieux. On travaillera moins. Des robots feront le travail que nous faisons actuellement. On aura beaucoup plus de loisirs. Plus tard, ce sera mille fois mieux!

ROXANE   Je ne crois pas que tu aies raison. Et le chômage? Comment est-ce qu'on gagnera de l'argent quand les robots prendront nos emplois?

PIERRE   Il y aura d'autres emplois : il faudra bien programmer les robots et les réparer.

ROXANE   Et le problème de la pollution qui est déjà si grave? On pourra le résoudre?

PIERRE   T'en fais pas, je suis certain qu'on trouvera une solution.

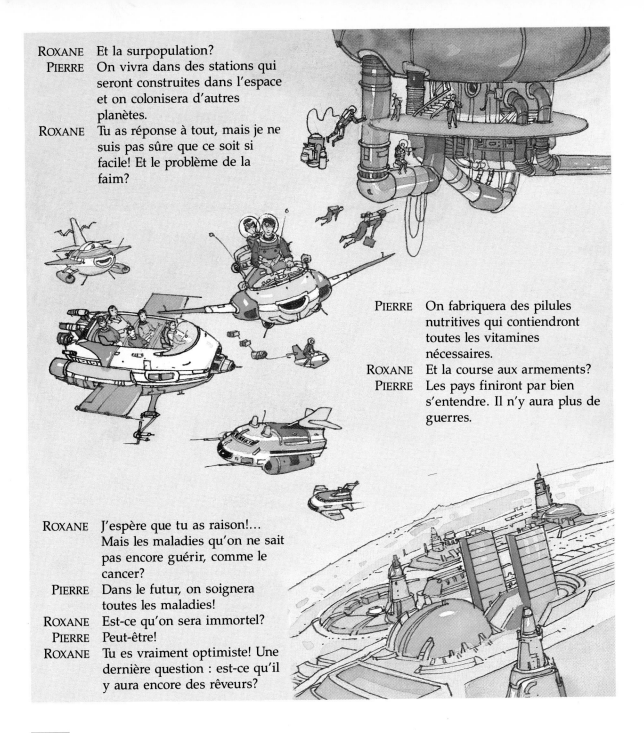

ROXANE   Et la surpopulation?

PIERRE   On vivra dans des stations qui seront construites dans l'espace et on colonisera d'autres planètes.

ROXANE   Tu as réponse à tout, mais je ne suis pas sûre que ce soit si facile! Et le problème de la faim?

PIERRE   On fabriquera des pilules nutritives qui contiendront toutes les vitamines nécessaires.

ROXANE   Et la course aux armements?

PIERRE   Les pays finiront par bien s'entendre. Il n'y aura plus de guerres.

ROXANE   J'espère que tu as raison!… Mais les maladies qu'on ne sait pas encore guérir, comme le cancer?

PIERRE   Dans le futur, on soignera toutes les maladies!

ROXANE   Est-ce qu'on sera immortel?

PIERRE   Peut-être!

ROXANE   Tu es vraiment optimiste! Une dernière question : est-ce qu'il y aura encore des rêveurs?

C2   Activité • Vrai ou faux?

D'après Pierre, dites si les phrases suivantes sont vraies ou fausses.

1. Pierre voit l'avenir en rose.
2. Dans l'avenir, on travaillera moins.
3. Il y aura beaucoup de chômage.
4. Il n'y aura plus de pollution.
5. On ne vivra plus sur la Terre (Earth).
6. Il n'y aura plus de guerres.
7. On ne sera plus jamais malade.

1. C'est vrai.   2. C'est vrai.   3. C'est faux, il y aura d'autres emplois.   4. C'est vrai.   5. C'est vrai.   6. C'est vrai.   7. C'est vrai.

Activité • Pierre a réponse à tout   Possible answers are given.

Quelles sont les solutions que trouve Pierre pour résoudre les problèmes... ?

Des robots feront le travail que nous faisons actuellement. Il y aura d'autres emplois : il faudra bien programmer les robots et les réparer. On vivra dans des stations qui seront

du travail	de la faim
du chômage	de la guerre
de la surpopulation	des maladies

construites dans l'espace, et on colonisera d'autres planètes. On fabriquera des pilules nutritives qui contiendront toutes les vitamines nécessaires. Les pays finiront par bien s'entendre. Il n'y aura plus de guerres.

C4   Activité • Actes de parole   Dans le futur, on soignera toutes les maladies.

1. Que dit Roxane pour exprimer le scepticisme? L'espoir *(hope)*?
2. Que dit Pierre pour exprimer la certitude?
3. Roxane s'inquiète de la pollution. Que dit Pierre pour la rassurer?

1. Je ne crois pas...   Je ne suis pas sûre...   2. Je suis certain...   3. T'en fais pas...

C5   Activité • Ecrit dirigé   Possible answer is given.

Roxane a écrit ce paragraphe sur l'avenir. Pouvez-vous le réécrire d'après Pierre?
Utilisez le dialogue dans C1, et aussi votre imagination.

Moi, je vois l'avenir en noir. Je crois que le travail sera plus difficile que maintenant. Il faudra que tout le monde sache utiliser les ordinateurs. Mais beaucoup de gens ne savent ni lire ni écrire. Alors, comment pourront-ils apprendre à utiliser les ordinateurs? Ou à lire et à écrire? Il n'y a pas assez de bons professeurs pour leur apprendre les choses qu'il faut savoir. Ces gens n'auront pas de choix, et le chômage sera pour eux un grand problème.

Moi, je vois l'avenir en rose. Je crois que le travail sera moins difficile que maintenant. Tout le monde saura lire, écrire et utiliser les ordinateurs. Il y aura de bons professeurs pour apprendre aux gens les choses qu'il faut savoir.

C6   Activité • Qu'est-ce qui existera ou n'existera plus? On aura beaucoup plus de loisirs.

Travaillez avec un(e) camarade à tour de rôle.
Dites si ces choses existeront encore ou n'existeront plus dans 100 ans. Continuez, en ajoutant vos propres idées.

— Le cinéma existera encore.
— Il n'y aura plus de restaurants.
— ...

cinéma
centre de vacances
fast-food   feu d'artifice
bal
parc d'attractions
restaurant

Note the plural: feux d'artifice.

C7   Activité • Et vous?

1. Est-ce que vous êtes optimiste ou pessimiste pour l'avenir?
2. A votre avis, quels seront les problèmes les plus importants à résoudre? Avez-vous des idées pour les résoudre?

La Cité des Sciences et de l'Industrie, ouverte en 1986 à Paris, est un musée consacré à la science et aux technologies nouvelles.

Il y a un planétarium pour voyager dans l'espace; une médiathèque *(multimedia library)*, l'un des plus grands centres de documentation scientifique du monde; des expositions temporaires et permanentes sur le futur; une salle de cinéma géante, la Géode. Vous pouvez voir la maquette *(model)* de la fusée Ariane, apprendre comment les astronautes vivent dans l'espace, connaître votre poids *(weight)* quand vous serez sur la planète Mars, visiter le «zoo des robots» ou essayer des centaines *(hundreds)* d'ordinateurs différents...

On peut passer des heures à la Cité des Sciences, pour s'amuser ou pour apprendre... On a alors l'impression de vivre dans le futur!

Imaginez que vous visitez la Cité des Sciences et de l'Industrie avec un(e) camarade.
Avant de commencer la visite, vous discutez des choses que vous voulez voir. Faites des
suggestions à un(e) camarade de classe. Il/Elle accepte, exprime son indifférence ou refuse.

Pour faire des suggestions

— Si on allait voir le spectacle de la forêt?
— Non, ça ne me dit rien. Tu n'as pas envie
de visiter le zoo des robots?
— Si tu veux. Et après,...

> *Allons voir... !*
> Sí on allait... ?
> Pourquoi on ne va pas... ?
> Tu n'as pas envie de... ?

Pour accepter	Pour exprimer l'indifférence	Pour refuser
Si tu veux. Je veux bien. Oui, pourquoi pas? D'accord. Bonne idée.	*Je n'ai pas de préférence.* Ça m'est égal. Comme tu veux. Ce que tu préfères.	*Je n'ai pas envie.* Non, je ne veux pas. Non, c'est ennuyeux. Non, ça ne me dit rien.

Le fauteuil de l'espace

Le spectacle de la forêt

Le zoo des robots

La médiathèque

La maquette d'Ariane

COMMENT LE DIRE
Expressing beliefs, hope, and doubt

	... about existing situations			... about future possibilities	
BELIEFS HOPE	Je crois Je pense Je suis sûr(e) Je suis certain(e) J'espère	que tu **as** raison.		Je crois Je pense Je suis sûr(e) Je suis certain(e) J'espère	que la vie **sera** meilleure.
DOUBT	Je ne crois pas Je ne pense pas Je ne suis pas sûr(e) Je ne suis pas certain(e) Je doute	que tu **aies** raison.		Je ne crois pas Je ne pense pas Je ne suis pas sûr(e) Je ne suis pas certain(e)	que la vie **sera** meilleure.

Note that the subjunctive is used after expressions of doubt about existing situations.
Note that the subjunctive, rather than the future tense, is normally used with "Je doute que..."

C11 Activité • Etes-vous d'accord? Possible answers are given.

Etes-vous d'accord avec ces opinions sur le présent et le futur? Mettez une expression de C10 devant chaque phrase pour exprimer ce que vous pensez.

Je crois que les solutions sont faciles à trouver.   Je pense que les gens s'entendront bien.

Aujourd'hui   **Dans le futur**

Les solutions sont faciles à trouver.

Tout va bien.

Les gens s'entendront bien.

La vie sera meilleure.

Les gens commencent à s'inquiéter.

On voyagera en voiture ou en bus.

Tout le monde aura de quoi manger.

Il y a trop de violence.

Les villes sont dangereuses.

Les gens souffriront de la faim.

Les gens visiteront d'autres planètes.

Nous avons beaucoup de problèmes à résoudre.

Je doute que tout aille bien.   Je ne suis pas sûr(e) que les gens visiteront d'autres planètes.

C12 Activité • A votre avis

Pensez-vous qu'il sera possible de vivre éternellement? De guérir toutes les maladies? De nourrir tout le monde? De faire disparaître la pollution? De résoudre le problème de la surpopulation? Faites un dialogue avec un(e) camarade. Utilisez les expressions dans C10.

— Moi, je crois qu'on vivra éternellement. Et toi, qu'est-ce que tu en penses?
— Je crois que tu as raison.
   (Je ne crois pas que tu aies raison.)

Le journal d'un lycée français va publier une enquête sur les écoles du futur vues par les Américains. Décrivez en quelques lignes comment vous voyez les écoles. Est-ce qu'on suivra autant de cours que maintenant? Quels cours? Croyez-vous que les écoles seront meilleures? Pourquoi? Exprimez vos doutes et vos espoirs. En l'an 2010, les écoles seront différentes. Je pense qu'elles seront meilleures. Il y aura moins de cours, et on ira à l'école deux ou trois jours par semaine seulement. Je suis sûr(e) qu'on aura beaucoup de travail, mais tous les élèves auront des ordinateurs chez eux, et ce sera plus facile de faire les devoirs.

C14 STRUCTURES DE BASE
The relative pronouns qui *and* que

1. You know that to modify a noun in French, you use an adjective. But sometimes you may have more to say about a person, place, or thing than an adjective can express. When this happens, you need to use a relative clause, a kind of sub-sentence that has its own subject and verb.

Noun + Adjective	*Noun + Relative Clause*
On fabriquera des pilules **nutritives**.	On fabriquera des pilules **qui contiendront des vitamines**.
La pollution est un problème **grave**.	La pollution est un problème **que nous voulons résoudre**.

2. A relative clause comes after the noun it modifies, and it begins with a relative pronoun. Two common relative pronouns in French are **qui** and **que.** Both of these relative pronouns can represent people, places, and things.

People	Pierre discute avec une fille **qui** s'appelle Roxane.	Roxane sort avec un garçon **que** je ne connais pas.
Places	J'ai visité une ville **qui** est près de Strasbourg.	La ville **que** j'ai visitée était intéressante.
Things	On vivra dans des stations **qui** seront construites dans l'espace.	Des robots feront le travail **que** nous faisons actuellement.

Notice that **qui** and **que** directly follow the nouns that they represent.

3. The pronoun **qui** acts as the subject of a relative clause and is followed by a verb. The form of the verb will vary, depending on the word that **qui** represents.

C'est moi qui **ai**		C'est nous qui **avons**	
C'est toi qui **as**	raison.	C'est vous qui **avez**	raison.
C'est Roxane qui **a**		C'est les copains qui **ont**	

For verbs conjugated with **être** in the **passé composé,** remember to make the past participle of the verb agree with whatever **qui** represents.

C'est **Laure** qui est **arrivée** en retard.

Je ne connais pas **les garçons** qui sont **entrés** après nous.

4. The pronoun **que** acts as the direct object of the verb in a relative clause. For verbs conjugated with **avoir** in the **passé composé,** make the past participle agree with whatever **que** represents.

La mobylette que tu as **achetée** est chouette!

J'aime bien **les disques** que tu m'a **offerts.**

C15 Activité • Roxane est réaliste

Complétez les idées de Roxane avec les pronoms **qui** et **que (qu')**.

1. La pollution est un problème _qui_ m'inquiète beaucoup.
2. C'est un problème _qui_ a changé notre monde pour toujours.
3. Les solutions _qu'_ on a proposées ne sont pas suffisantes.
4. Il faut trouver des solutions _que_ les gens prennent au sérieux.
5. Autrement, le monde _que_ nous connaissons aujourd'hui n'existera plus dans 100 ans.
6. Ce sera les générations futures _qui_ souffriront à cause de notre égoïsme.

C16 Activité • Toujours optimiste

Pierre continue de réfléchir sur le futur. Réunissez les deux parties de chaque phrase pour mieux connaître ses idées.

Les maisons qu'on habitera seront souterraines.

Les maisons
Il y aura des voitures
Les gens ne connaîtront plus les livres
On fera des maisons
Il existera des téléphones
Les générations futures vivront dans un monde

que nous avons du mal à imaginer
qui permettront de voir l'interlocuteur
qui seront transformables
qui rouleront à 500 kilomètres à l'heure
qu'on habitera seront souterraines
que nous lisons aujourd'hui

C17 Activité • Pierre continue de rêver Possible answers are given.

Faites une seule phrase à partir des deux phrases de Pierre. Utilisez le pronom **qui**.

Il y aura des voitures qui fonctionneront à l'électricité.

On construira des avions.
On utilisera des voitures.
Il y aura des ordinateurs.
On fabriquera des vêtements.
Il y aura des télévisions.
Bientôt, on aura tous des robots.
Il y aura des voitures.

Ils obéiront à notre voix.
Elles pourront changer de dimension.
Les robots feront les courses à notre place.
Elles fonctionneront à l'électricité.
Ils ne se déchireront (tear) pas.
Ces avions voleront (will fly) sans pilote.
Ces voitures fonctionneront automatiquement.

On construira des avions qui voleront sans pilote. On utilisera des voitures qui fonctionneront à l'électricité. Il y aura des ordinateurs qui obéiront à notre voix. On fabriquera des vêtements qui ne se déchireront pas. Il y aura des télévisions qui pourront changer de dimension. Bientôt, on aura tous des robots qui feront les courses à notre place. Il y aura des voitures qui fonctionneront automatiquement.

D'après les intérêts de vos camarades, pouvez-vous prédire *(predict)* la profession qu'ils choisiront? Parlez-en avec un(e) camarade de classe. Employez le pronom **qui** quand il convient.

— C'est Danielle qui voyage le plus possible en avion. Je pense qu'elle sera astronaute.
— Tu as raison.
(Tu crois?...)

> **Pierre aime jouer avec les ordinateurs.**
> **Nadja adore soigner les animaux.**
> *Fabrice fait des maquettes de fusées.*
> **Danielle voyage le plus possible en avion.**
> *Sandrine préfère les aliments nutritifs.*

C'est Danielle qui voyage le plus possible en avion. Je crois qu'elle sera astronaute.

C'est Fabrice qui fait des maquettes de fusées. Je crois qu'il sera ingénieur.

C'est Sandrine qui préfère les aliments nutritifs. Je pense qu'elle sera diététicienne.

astronaute

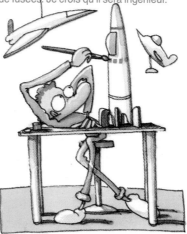

ingénieur

diététicienne

programmeur

vétérinaire

C'est Pierre qui aime jouer avec les ordinateurs. Je pense qu'il sera programmeur.

C'est Nadja qui adore soigner les animaux. Je crois qu'elle sera vétérinaire.

Activité • L'avenir en rose   Possible answers are given.

Avec un(e) camarade, faites des phrases sur l'avenir. Employez ces expressions et le pronom **que.**

Le monde que nous verrons en l'an 2100 sera meilleur.

Le monde	***nous ne savons pas guérir***	**iront plus vite**
Les moyens de transport	**nous mangerons**	**sera plus nourrissante**
Les voitures	***nous ferons en l'an 2100***	*sera plus intéressant*
La nourriture	**nous utiliserons**	**seront guérissables**
Le travail	**nous verrons en l'an 2100**	**sera meilleur**
Toutes les maladies	*nous conduirons*	*seront extrêmement rapides*

Les moyens de transport que nous utiliserons seront extrêmement rapides.   Les voitures que nous conduirons iront plus vite. La nourriture que nous mangerons sera plus nourrissante.   Le travail que nous ferons en l'an 2100 sera plus intéressant.   Toutes les maladies que nous ne savons pas guérir seront guérissables.

C20 **Activité • Écrivez**   Possible answer is given.

Imaginez que vous vivez en l'an 2200 et qu'il est possible de remonter dans le temps. Vous décidez de visiter le XXe siècle. Après la visite, vous écrivez une lettre à un(e) camarade pour lui dire ce que vous avez vu. Employez le passé composé et l'imparfait dans votre lettre. Utilisez les pronoms **qui** et **que** quand ils conviennent. N'oubliez pas de faire les accords nécessaires.

Cher (Chère)...
Me voilà revenu(e) d'un petit séjour au XXe siècle! Les gens qui vivaient à cette époque étaient vraiment primitifs! Savez-vous qu'ils voyageaient en voiture? Il y avait de la pollution et beaucoup de guerres dans le monde. En plus, les jeunes écoutaient de la musique démodée.

C21 **Activité • Écoutez bien**   For script and answers, see p. T241.

Écoutez ce garçon parler des problèmes du futur. A son avis, quels problèmes est-ce qu'on devra résoudre? Faites une liste de ces problèmes.

1   Un sondage

Danielle a répondu à un sondage sur l'avenir des jeunes.

1. Pensez-vous souvent à l'avenir?
 (a.) Oui, tout le temps
 b. Oui, souvent
 c. Oui, de temps en temps
 d. Non, jamais

2. Quel est le problème qu'il faudra résoudre en premier?
 (a.) La faim dans le monde
 b. Le cancer
 c. La course aux armements
 d. Le chômage
 e. Le racisme
 f. La surpopulation
 g. Autre _____

3. Quelle sera votre situation?
 (a.) Je serai marié(e).
 b. Je serai célibataire.

4. Aurez-vous des enfants? Combien?
 a. Pas d'enfants
 b. Un
 c. Deux
 d. Trois
 (e.) Quatre
 f. Plus

5. Où habiterez-vous?
 a. En ville
 b. A la campagne
 c. Au bord de la mer
 d. A la montagne
 (e.) A l'étranger

6. Quel sera votre travail?
 a. Médecin
 b. Professeur
 c. Ouvrier
 d. Artiste
 e. Informaticien
 (f.) Autre *astronaute*

7. Dans votre famille, qui est-ce qui... ?
 a. fera la vaisselle   *mon mari*
 b. fera les courses   *mon mari*
 c. lavera la voiture   *mon mari*
 d. s'occupera des enfants   *moi*
 e. travaillera   *tous les deux*

8. Pour fêter votre trentième anniversaire, qu'est-ce que vous vous offrirez?
 (a.) Un week-end dans l'espace
 b. Une voiture programmable
 c. Un robot
 d. Autre _____

9. Combien gagnerez-vous par mois?
 a. Entre 5 000 F et 8 000 F
 b. Entre 8 000 F et 10 000 F
 c. Entre 10 000 F et 15 000 F
 (d.) Plus de 15 000 F

10. Jusqu'à quel âge vivrez-vous?
 a. 75 ans
 b. 85 ans
 c. 95 ans
 d. Autre *150 ans*

DANIELLE	Vincent, tu veux regarder mes réponses au sondage?
VINCENT	Montre... Tu as l'intention de te marier?
DANIELLE	Bien sûr!
VINCENT	Avec moi?
DANIELLE	Certainement pas! On ne s'entend pas assez bien!
VINCENT	Et tu penses vivre jusqu'à 150 ans! Eh bien, tu es optimiste!
DANIELLE	J'espère vivre longtemps : j'aime tellement la vie!

Activité • Répondez

Répondez aux questions d'après les réponses de Danielle dans «Un sondage».

1. Est-ce que Danielle veut rester célibataire?
2. Où est-ce qu'elle a l'intention d'habiter?
3. Combien espère-t-elle gagner?
4. Combien d'enfants souhaite-t-elle avoir?
5. Quelle profession a-t-elle choisie?
6. Jusqu'à quel âge espère-t-elle vivre?

1. Non, elle veut se marier.   2. Elle a l'intention d'habiter à l'étranger.   3. Elle espère gagner plus de 15 000 F par mois.
4. Elle souhaite avoir quatre enfants.   5. Elle a choisi d'être astronaute.   6. Elle espère vivre jusqu'à 150 ans.

3 Activité • Contradictions   Possible answers are given.

Dites à un(e) camarade une phrase fausse sur ce que Danielle veut faire plus tard. Votre camarade doit donner la vraie réponse de Danielle.

— Danielle ne pense jamais à l'avenir.
— Mais si, elle y pense tout le temps!

—Elle veut être médecin.
—Mais non, elle veut être astronaute.
—Elle veut avoir un enfant.
—Mais non, elle veut avoir quatre enfants!
—Elle ne veut pas se marier.
—Mais si, elle veut se marier.

4 Activité • Donnez des raisons   Possible answer is given.

Vincent dit que Danielle est optimiste. Avec un(e) camarade, discutez pourquoi, d'après ce que vous savez de Danielle.

— Danielle veut devenir astronaute, mais il y a très peu de femmes dans cette profession. Il faut travailler dûr pour réussir.
— Oui, elle est très optimiste. Elle veut aussi… avoir quatre enfants. C'est très difficile d'avoir beaucoup d'enfants et une carrière.   Elle rêve parce qu'elle pense que son mari fera toutes les tâches domestiques, mais il n'y a pas beaucoup d'hommes qui feront ça!

5 Activité • Et vous?

1. Jusqu'à quel âge continuerez-vous vos études?
2. Dans quel genre de maison habiterez-vous?
3. Gagnerez-vous plus d'argent que votre mari (votre femme)?
4. Que ferez-vous de votre argent?
5. Vous restera-t-il assez de temps pour les autres?
6. Voyagerez-vous dans l'espace?

6 Activité • Ecrivez   Possible answer is given.

Ecrivez un paragraphe pour dire comment vous voyez votre avenir. Reportez-vous aux questions posées dans «Un sondage» et ajoutez d'autres éléments qui vous semblent importants.   Je pense souvent à l'avenir. Il faudra résoudre le problème de la course aux armements en premier. Je serai marié(e), et nous aurons deux enfants. Nous habiterons en ville. Je serai médecin et je gagnerai plus de 15 000 F par mois. Je vivrai jusqu'à 95 ans.

7 Activité • Ecrivez et parlez

Avec un(e) camarade, faites votre propre sondage sur l'avenir. Ecrivez de nouvelles questions qui concernent plus particulièrement les jeunes américains. Ensuite, posez vos questions à deux autres camarades de classe et répondez à leurs questions.   Possible questions are given.

Qu'est-ce que tu étudieras à l'université?
Dans quels pays veux-tu voyager?
Où penses-tu vivre?
A quel âge est-ce que tu prendras ta retraite?

Que feras-tu après avoir fini tes études au lycée?
a. Je chercherai un emploi.
b. J'irai dans une école technique.
c. J'irai à l'université.
d. Je ferai le tour du monde.
e. Autre.

8 Activité • Dites votre opinion

Un(e) camarade vous dit ce qu'il/elle veut faire plus tard. Vous lui donnez votre opinion. Puis changez de rôle.

— Plus tard, je souhaite avoir quatre enfants.
— Pour avoir quatre enfants, il faut que tu te maries jeune et que ton mari ait un bon emploi. Je doute que tu puisses travailler avec quatre enfants ou que…

9 Activité • D'accord, pas d'accord…   Possible answers are given.

Faites une liste des avantages et des inconvénients du minitel. Montrez votre liste à un(e) camarade. Il/Elle dit s'il (si elle) est d'accord ou pas d'accord, et pourquoi. Ensuite, changez de rôle.

Avantages	Inconvénients
Avec un minitel, on gagnera du temps.	On aura moins de contacts avec les gens.
… On peut obtenir des informations sur tous les sujets. On peut communiquer avec sa banque ou son supermarché. Ça sera très bon pour les gens qui ne peuvent pas sortir de chez eux.	… Ça peut se casser. Ça prend de la place. Je déteste les ordinateurs!

> Je suis d'accord avec toi : on gagnera du temps. Mais je pense qu'on aura autant de contacts avec les gens parce qu'on aura plus de temps libre…

10 Activité • Faites une étude de marché

Une agence de marketing vous a demandé de faire une enquête pour savoir ce que les jeunes achèteront en premier quand ils gagneront un peu d'argent. Posez cette question à vos camarades : «Qu'est-ce que tu achèteras quand tu auras un peu d'argent?» Ils ont droit à cinq réponses. Ensuite, faites une synthèse des résultats. Have students begin their responses with: Quand j'aurai un peu d'argent, j'achèterai . . .

Synthèse des résultats

Les articles les plus fréquemment mentionnés étaient …
1.
2.
3.

11 Activité • Récréation   (optional)

Jeu d'association

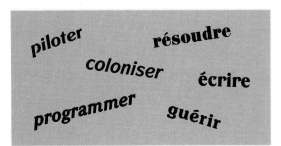

piloter des avions / résoudre des problèmes / coloniser des planètes / écrire des mémoires / programmer des ordinateurs / guérir des maladies

PRONONCIATION

Pure vowel and consonant sounds

1 Ecoutez bien et répétez.

1. Pure vowel sounds

quai   gaie   si   oui   tout   doux   dos   mot   faux   sous

pipe   bol   foule   loupe   file   pique   donne   ligue

cas/case	douce/douze	creux/creuse	grand/grande
fait/fer	libre/livre	œuf/œuvre	craint/craindre
bouche/bouge	russe/ruse	lent/lente	rond/ronde

2. Look up these words in your dictionary. Arrange them into long and short vowel groups.
membre, juge, fiche, fige, rive, peu, pas, rose, nom, zone, autre, faut, faute, sable
For answers, see Unit Cassette Guide, p. 146.

3. Pure consonant sounds

patte	qui	type	tout→tout à fait	ton→ton thé
père	quatre	tour	tôt→tôt ou tard	tête→tête à tête
pipe	côte	tonne	ta→ta table	tu→tu tires
pour		tort		

ton dos	ton nez	c'est dans son auto
tes dents	ta nationalité	deux cent soixante-dix
tous deux	ton nom	son sac à main est tout neuf
très doux	ton numéro	zone dangereuse
dis donc		
je t'ai dit		

4. Look up these words in your dictionary to find when the **c** is not an /**s**/ and why.
cire, car, celle, cygne, côte, curé, scandale, esclave
For answers, see Unit Cassette Guide, p. 146.

5. Look up these words in your dictionary and put them into rhyming pairs.
galop, gros, malin, noix, bref, parfum, banc, clerc, gentil, estomac, avril, mars, un, corps, Alain, farce, allô, sort, sot, doigt, chef, blanc, fusil, nerf, péril, Thomas
For answers, see Unit Cassette Guide, p. 146.

2 Ecoutez et lisez.

— On ne peut pas sortir les livres.
— Si, pour deux semaines seulement. J'en ai sorti la semaine dernière.
— On peut en sortir deux à la fois?
— Mais oui, on peut en sortir autant qu'on veut.
— Où est-ce qu'on s'adresse?
— Dans la grande salle, à gauche. Il faut donner ton nom et ton numéro de téléphone.

3 Copiez les phrases suivantes pour préparer une dictée.

1. Vous pouvez déjà savoir combien vous pèserez quand vous serez sur la planète Mars.
2. Ce sont les robots qui feront notre boulot. On aura une vie merveilleuse.
3. Si je réussis dans mes études, j'aurai un boulot intéressant.
4. Est-ce qu'il y aura encore des rêveurs?

Do you know how to form the future of verbs?
Complete these sentences with the future of the verbs in parentheses.

1. Dans 100 ans, nous (vivre) sur d'autres planètes. vivrons
2. En l'an 2100, nous n'(acheter) que par correspondance. achèterons
3. Je (travailler) chez moi et je ne (sortir) plus. travaillerai / sortirai
4. Tu (apprendre) à vivre avec des robots. apprendras
5. Les robots (faire) beaucoup de travail. feront

Do you know how to express doubt and certainty?
First say that you doubt that these things will happen. Then say that you're sure they will take place. See A17, p. 391.

1. En l'an 2100, nous vivrons sur Mars.
2. Nous ne travaillerons plus que 20 heures par semaine.
3. Les voitures n'existeront plus.
4. Nous prendrons des pilules nourrissantes.

Do you know how to express intentions, goals, wishes, and dreams?
Answer the following questions. See B9, p. 395.

1. Qu'est-ce que vous voulez faire plus tard?
2. Quel est votre but dans la vie?
3. Qu'est-ce que vous avez l'intention de faire demain?
4. Quel est votre rêve pour l'an 2000?

Do you know how to form the future of irregular verbs?
Complete this paragraph with the future of the verbs in parentheses.

serons ... irons
Quand nous (être) adultes, ma sœur et moi, nous (aller) à l'étranger. Ma
sera / fera   sœur (être) sûrement médecin. Elle (faire) tout pour aider les autres. Moi,
pourrai   j'adore les langues étrangères, alors je (pouvoir) travailler comme interprète.
Nos parents (venir) nous voir. Ils (être) contents de notre succès.
viendront ... seront

Do you know how to express beliefs, hope, and doubt?
Say what you think about . . . See C10, p. 405.

les loisirs   la pollution   la guerre   la surpopulation

Do you know how to use the relative pronouns *qui* and *que*?
Complete these sentences with **qui** and **que (qu')**.

1. Les robots _que_ nous utiliserons seront très intelligents.
2. Les avions _qu'_ on construira ressembleront à des fusées.
3. On fera des ordinateurs _qui_ traduiront toutes les langues.
4. Les villes _que_ nous habiterons seront souterraines.
5. On fabriquera des voitures _qui_ pourront voler.

VOCABULAIRE

SECTION A

bientôt *soon*
les **calories** (f.) *calories*
communiquer *to communicate*
convaincu : J'en suis convaincu. *I'm convinced of it.*
démarrer *to start (a car)*
différemment *differently*
directement *directly*
étonnerait : Ça m'étonnerait! *That would surprise me!*
être en panne *to be out of order*
évident : C'est évident! *That's obvious!*
exister *to exist*
faire son marché *to do one's grocery shopping*
grâce à eux *thanks to them*
indispensable *indispensable*
un **itinéraire** *itinerary, route*
le **laser** *laser*
le **moteur** *motor*
nécessaire *necessary*
nutritif, -ive *nutritive*
le **pilotage automatique** *automatic piloting*
des **pilules** (f.) *pills*
les **portières** (f.) *(car) doors*
programmer *to program*
quotidien, -ne *daily*
les **robots** (m.) *robots*
sans *without*
les **technologies** (f.) *technologies*
la **voix** *voice*

SECTION B

les **affaires** (f.) : **être dans les affaires** *to be in business*
âgé, -e *elderly*
les **auditeurs** (m.) *listeners*
un **best-seller** *bestseller*
la **Bourse : jouer à la Bourse** *to play the stock market*
un **but** *goal*
le **calme** *stillness*
célibataire *unmarried*
la **Chine** *China*
le **CNES (Centre national d'études spatiales)** *French center for space research*
Dassault *French aeronautics company*
diffusé, -e *broadcast*
disputer (se) *to argue, fight*
élever *to raise*
en direct *on the air*
entendre : s'entendre bien (avec) *to get along well (with)*
envier *to envy*
fier, fière *proud*
handicapé, -e *handicapped*
un **idéal** *ideal*
une **île** *island*
imaginer *to imagine*
l' **Inde** (f.) *India*
loin (de) *far (from)*
marié, -e *married*
marier (se) (avec) *to get married (to)*
les **mémoires** (m.) *memoirs*
des **millions** (m.) *millions*
le **monde** *world*
le **Pacifique** *Pacific*
la **parole** *word*

partout *everywhere*
un **pilote** *pilot*
piloter *to pilot*
poser *to ask*
un **projet** *plan*
un **rêve** *dream*
un **souhait** *wish*
utile : se rendre utile *to make oneself useful*
un **yacht** *yacht*

SECTION C

actuellement *currently*
autrement *differently*
le **cancer** *cancer*
le **chômage** *unemployment*
coloniser *to colonize*
construit, -e *built*
contenir *to contain*
la **course aux armements** *arms race*
croire *to believe*
un **emploi** *job*
l' **espace** (m.) *space*
fabriquer *to make*
la **faim** *hunger*
grave *serious, important*
guérir *to cure*
la **guerre** *war*
immortel, -elle *immortal*
l' **inconnu(e)** *unknown*
les **loisirs** (m.) *free time*
les **maladies** (f.) *diseases*
nombreux, -euse *numerous*
optimiste *optimistic*
une **planète** *planet*
réparer *to repair*
résoudre *to solve*
un(e) **rêveur(-euse)** *dreamer*
si *so*
la **surpopulation** *overpopulation*

ETUDE DE MOTS

In French, many words belong to word families. These words are related in spelling and meaning. In the list above, find words related to the following words: **connaître, différent(e), malade, un mari, une porte, un rêve.** Tell how their meanings are tied together.

In the following sentences, what do the underlined words mean? To help figure them out, find the words they are related to in the list above.

1. Les **actualités** passent à la télé à 20 h.
2. La **gravité** de la situation nous préoccupe.
3. Cette autoroute a besoin de **réparations.**
4. La pollution est un problème **mondial.**

connaître: l'inconnu(e);   différent: différemment;   malade: les maladies;   un mari: marié(e), se marier;   une porte: les portières;
un rêve: un(e) rêveur(-euse)
1. (actuellement) actualités: news 2. (grave) gravité: seriousness
3. (réparer) réparations: repairs 4. (monde) mondial: worldwide

Bientôt l'avenir   415

A LIRE

Un Cours sur les lasers

Avant de lire

1. Lisez rapidement l'histoire pour trouver la définition du laser.
2. Regardez les dessins pour trouver comment on utilise le laser.

Le laser est un rayon de lumière très puissant. Il est utilisé pour couper les métaux et pour mesurer la distance de la Terre à la lune.

M. Scientis donne un cours sur les lasers. Comme tous les professeurs, il a dans sa classe des élèves intelligents et d'autres qui sont un peu moins doués.

M. Scientis	Quelqu'un sait ce que c'est, le laser?
Gérard	Oui, moi, m'sieur!
M. Scientis	Bien, Gérard. On vous écoute.
Gérard	Eh bien… C'est une des réalisations scientifiques les plus intéressantes du XXᵉ siècle, m'sieur.
M. Scientis	D'accord, mais qu'est-ce que c'est?
Gérard	Aucune idée°, m'sieur.

M. Scientis	Bon, je vais vous expliquer… Les lasers sont des rayons de lumière° très puissants°. Vous connaissez la différence entre la lumière laser et la lumière ordinaire?
Gérard	Oui, m'sieur!
M. Scientis	Allez-y.
Gérard	La lumière laser est beaucoup plus puissante que la lumière ordinaire et… euh… la lumière ordinaire est beaucoup moins puissante que la lumière laser.

M. Scientis	Vous ne vous fatiguez pas trop, Gérard. Mais vous avez raison. La lumière laser est plus puissante parce que ses rayons sont concentrés… Le premier laser a été fabriqué par des savants californiens en…

---

aucune idée *no idea;* **des rayons de lumière** *light rays;* **puissants** *powerful*

GÉRARD	Je sais, m'sieur!
M. SCIENTIS	Oui?
GÉRARD	En… J'ai oublié.
M. SCIENTIS	1960!
GÉRARD	J'pouvais pas le savoir, m'sieur. J'suis né en 1975.

M. SCIENTIS	Ne faites pas l'idiot! Je continue… A quoi servent les lasers? Qui a une idée?
GÉRARD	Moi, m'sieur!
M. SCIENTIS	Vous n'allez pas dire une bêtise°?
GÉRARD	Bien sûr que non, m'sieur.
M. SCIENTIS	Ça m'étonnerait.
GÉRARD	Mais…
M. SCIENTIS	Laissez un peu parler les autres°. Yvette?
YVETTE	Les lasers servent dans l'industrie. Pour couper les métaux, par exemple.
M. SCIENTIS	Bien.
YVETTE	Et aussi en médecine. Pour la chirurgie° de l'œil ou pour détruire° les tumeurs.
M. SCIENTIS	Bien. Et encore?

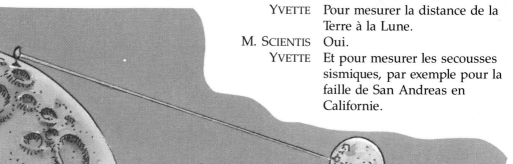

YVETTE	Pour mesurer la distance de la Terre à la Lune.
M. SCIENTIS	Oui.
YVETTE	Et pour mesurer les secousses sismiques, par exemple pour la faille de San Andreas en Californie.

---

dire une bêtise *to talk nonsense;* **Laissez un peu parler les autres.** *Give the others a chance to talk.* **la chirurgie** *surgery;* **détruire** *to destroy*

M. SCIENTIS   Parfait. Il y a également les disques laser et les vidéodisques qui marchent avec des rayons laser... A votre avis, qu'est-ce qu'on fera avec les lasers plus tard?

Allô? Il marche ton téléphone à fibres optiques?

Bien sûr, puisque je t'entends!

YVETTE   Je pense qu'ils seront de plus en plus importants. On les utilisera dans les réseaux téléphoniques. D'ailleurs, ça existe déjà. On appelle ça les réseaux à fibres optiques. Grâce à eux, on communiquera beaucoup plus que maintenant.

M. SCIENTIS   Merci, Yvette. Gérard?

GÉRARD   Oui, m'sieur?

M. SCIENTIS   Vous n'avez rien écouté?

GÉRARD   Si, m'sieur.

M. SCIENTIS   Vous en êtes sûr?

GÉRARD   Oui, m'sieur.

M. SCIENTIS   Alors venez ici et faites-nous un cours sur les lasers.

GÉRARD   Euh... Vous ne pouvez pas répéter, m'sieur? Je n'ai pas tout compris.

Activité • Choisissez l'équivalent anglais

un savant   une secousse sismique   *network*   *earth tremor*

un réseau   une réalisation   *creation*   *scientist*

Activité • Vrai ou faux?

1. La lumière ordinaire est plus puissante que la lumière laser. C'est faux.
2. On a inventé le premier laser aux Etats-Unis. C'est vrai.
3. Aujourd'hui, on emploie les lasers dans l'industrie, en médecine et dans les télécommunications. C'est vrai.
4. On n'emploie pas les lasers dans les sciences. C'est faux.

Le Jour où la Terre s'est arrêtée de tourner

Cela a commencé par un énorme grincement°. En un dixième de seconde, sans savoir comment, je me retrouve par terre°. Tous mes meubles° sont renversés, ma vaisselle est en mille morceaux. Je me relève et je me tâte° : je n'ai rien de cassé. Je regarde autour de moi : ma chambre est sens dessus-dessous°. Je pense tout d'abord à un tremblement de terre, vous savez, quand le sol° bouge et les murs s'effondrent°... Je me précipite dehors pour ne pas me faire écraser° par mon immeuble.

Dans la rue, il y a quantité de gens qui courent dans tous les sens, se bousculent°, crient...

— Que se passe-t-il?

— C'est un tremblement de terre!

— Une éruption volcanique! dit un homme au chapeau vert.

— Un raz-de-marée°!

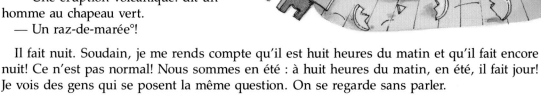

Il fait nuit. Soudain, je me rends compte qu'il est huit heures du matin et qu'il fait encore nuit! Ce n'est pas normal! Nous sommes en été : à huit heures du matin, en été, il fait jour! Je vois des gens qui se posent la même question. On se regarde sans parler.

— C'est une éruption volcanique, répète l'homme au chapeau vert. Elle a provoqué un gigantesque nuage de poussière° qui couvre le ciel et cache° le soleil.

C'est à ce moment qu'un homme accourt, terrifié.

— La Terre s'est arrêtée de tourner!

— Quoi!

— Ils ont dit ça à la télévision!

— Ce n'est pas possible! La Terre ne s'arrête pas de tourner comme ça, du jour au lendemain°! Il y a des lois° physiques!

— C'est ce qu'ils ont dit.

---

un grincement *grinding;*   **par terre** *on the floor;*   **les meubles** *furniture;*   **je me tâte** *I feel myself (for injuries);*   **sens dessus-dessous** *topsy turvy;*   **le sol** *the ground;*   **s'effondrent** *collapse;*   **écraser** *to crush;*   **se bousculent** *bump into one another;*   **un raz-de-marée** *tidal wave;*   **un nuage de poussière** *dust cloud;*   **cache** *hides;*   **du jour au lendemain** *from one day to the next;*   **des lois** *laws*

— Et vous les croyez? demande un petit homme tout chauve°. Moi, je vous dis que c'est de la pub°. Vous allez voir : maintenant, ils vont nous conseiller d'acheter les lampes de poche° ECLAIRE MIEUX!

— Vous dites n'importe quoi! Personne ne peut apporter la nuit, comme ça, sur toute la ville.

— Mais, si c'est vrai. Si la Terre s'est arrêtée de tourner, savez-vous ce que cela veut dire? Cela veut dire : plus de jour, plus de soleil. Toujours la nuit!

— Toujours la nuit? dit un autre. Moi, je suis veilleur de nuit°. Je dors le jour et je travaille la nuit. Ça va complètement changer ma vie. Plus de repos! Travail, travail, toujours travail!

A ce moment, arrive un vendeur de journaux : «Achetez les *Dernières Nouvelles d'Alsace!* Tout sur l'événement du jour!»

Tout le monde se précipite et s'arrache° les journaux... En effet, sur la première page, en gros caractères, on peut lire :

**LA TERRE S'EST ARRETEE
DE TOURNER**

et en dessous°, en plus petits caractères :

Les savants s'interrogent.

Je me pince pour m'assurer que je ne rêve pas. Puis, comme rien ne se passe, je remonte dans ma chambre pour me faire un café. En route, je croise° mes voisins avec leurs cinq enfants. Tous portent de gros sacs et des valises.

— Vous partez en vacances?

— Pas exactement. Mais nous quittons ce pays de ténèbres°! Vous ne pensez pas que nous allons rester ici, dans la nuit et le froid!

— Mais où irez-vous?

— De l'autre côté de la Terre. S'il fait toujours nuit ici, là-bas il fait toujours jour. Quand je pense à tous ces gens qui s'amusent sur les plages de Californie pendant que nous, en Alsace, nous grelottons° dans le noir, je n'ai plus envie de rester ici!... Excusez-nous, on se dépêche... on veut avoir une place dans un avion!

— Bon voyage!

---

chauve *bald;* **la pub** = **la publicité** *advertising;* **les lampes de poche** *flashlights;* **veilleur de nuit** *night watchman;* **s'arrache** *snatch;* **en dessous** *below;* **croise** *pass;* **ténèbres** *shadows;* **grelottons** *shiver*

Partout, il y a des gens avec des valises et des enfants sur les épaules. Il y a des embouteillages° monstres; il n'y a plus de policiers pour faire la circulation°. Des gens se disputent, se battent. Tout le monde s'en va°! Ils sont fous! Il y aura un problème de la surpopulation là-bas! Et si la Terre se remet en marche? Ils auront l'air malins°!... Je cours me réfugier dans ma chambre. J'allume la télévision : il n'y a plus de programme.

— Vous ne partez pas?
C'est mon concierge° qui est entré.
— Qui? Moi? Oh non, j'aime beaucoup trop cette ville pour partir! Je préfère rester ici, même dans le noir. D'ailleurs, la Californie sera bientôt surpeuplée. Et vous? Vous ne partez pas?
— Non. Ma femme a envie, mais nous n'avons pas l'argent pour le billet d'avion. Moi, ça ne me dérange° pas : je suis comme vous, j'aime bien notre ville... Vous êtes occupé pour l'instant?
— Non, pourquoi?
— Ça vous dit de faire une partie d'échecs?
— Volontiers! Vous prenez les blancs ou les noirs?

Activité • Complétez

Complétez les phrases suivantes d'après l'histoire.

1. Le jour où la Terre s'arrête de tourner, il fait... à huit heures du matin.   nuit
2. Si la Terre ne tourne plus,... en Alsace et... en Californie.   il fait toujours nuit / il fait toujours jour
3. Les voisins du jeune homme se dépêchent pour...   prendre l'avion.
4. Le jeune homme décide de rester en Alsace parce que...   il aime sa ville.
5. Son concierge a l'intention d'y rester aussi parce que...   il n'a pas assez d'argent pour le billet d'avion.

Activité • Avez-vous compris?

Répondez aux questions suivantes.

1. Au début, comment est-ce que les gens essaient d'expliquer ce qui se passe?
2. Comment est-ce qu'ils apprennent que la Terre s'est arrêtée de tourner?
3. En général, comment est-ce que les gens réagissent (react)? Que font-ils? Pourquoi?

1. Ils pensaient que c'était une éruption volcanique ou un tremblement de terre.   2. Ils ont dit ça à la télévision.   3. Ils ont peur. Ils se disputent et se battent. Tout le monde s'en va!

Activité • Ecrivez   Possible answer is given.

Imaginez une fin à cette histoire. Est-ce que la vie changera en Alsace? Qu'est-ce qu'on fera pour survivre?   L'Alsace sera très calme : il n'y aura plus de gens. Il fera très froid. Le jeune homme décidera de partir pour la Californie.

des embouteillages *traffic jams;*   faire la circulation *to direct traffic;*   s'en va *is leaving;*   Ils auront l'air malins! *They'll make complete fools of themselves!*   concierge *superintendent;*   dérange *bother*

CHAPITRE 12 **Vacances au Sénégal**

Chapitre de révision

UNIT RESOURCES   **Cahier d'Activités, Cahier d'Exercices,** Unit 12
Cassette, Transparency 30 (also 21–29, 33), Review Test 3, Final Test,
Proficiency-Based Test 2

TEACHER-PREPARED MATERIALS   **Review 1–26**   Map of the
world, map of Africa, map of Senegal, poems of Léopold Senghor,
pictures of Normandy

Unit 12 combines functions, grammar, and vocabulary that the students have
studied in Units 9–11. This unit provides communicative and writing practice in
different situations; some of its activities lend themselves to cooperative learning. If your students require further practice, you will find additional review
exercises in Unit 12 of the **Cahier d'Activités** and the **Cahier d'Exercices.** On
the other hand, if your students know how to use the material in Units 9–11,
you may wish to omit parts of Unit 12.

OBJECTIVE   To review communicative functions, grammar, and vocabulary
from Units 9–11

CULTURAL BACKGROUND   Senegal lies on the westernmost tip of Africa's
Atlantic coast. The capital is **Dakar,** a large modern port city. Most of the
country is savanna, which becomes semi-desert in the north and forest in the
south. Senegal, a former French colony, gained complete independence in
1960. French is the official language. **Le wolof,** the language of the majority of
the people, is the national language. The motto of Senegal is **Un peuple, un
but, une foi.**

   Léopold Sédar Senghor, Senegal's president from 1963 to 1980, is perhaps
better known to Americans than the country itself. Poet and statesman, Senghor
formulated the concept of **négritude,** which asserted the importance of the
black African heritage. His many excellent works proclaim black African cultural
values. Senghor was elected to the **Académie française** in 1983.

   Another Senegalese writer is Birago Diop. His tales of Amadou Koumba
tell of real or mythical people in the daily life of a village. Amadou Koumba
issues proverbs, such as, "Replying to a greeting never burns the tongue" and
"Sharing a hedge has never made two fields the same size."

MOTIVATING ACTIVITY   Tell students in French that in this unit they are
going to visit Senegal in Africa. Ask them if they are familiar with any other
countries in Africa and how they learned about them: **Connaissez-vous d'autres
pays d'Afrique? Que savez-vous de ces pays? Où avez-vous appris ça?** Students
will suggest the English names of African countries; give them the French names.

1   **Invitation au voyage**

CULTURAL BACKGROUND   The baobab tree is the symbol of Senegal (see
page 424 for illustration). It grows in all regions, and every part of it is useful.
The bark serves to make rope and the leaves may be eaten. They are a source
of ascorbic acid and are used to treat asthma, rheumatism, anemia, and
inflammations. The pulp of the fruit, the calabash, is eaten and its exterior is

used as a container or a musical instrument. The seeds of the calabash are also put to use to reduce swellings and to dry oil.

Before presenting the dialogue, tell students in French about Fabienne and her dilemma about what to do during her summer vacation. Mention her relatives and the places where they live; point out the places on a map of the world: **la Nouvelle-Calédonie, la Normandie,** and **la Corse.** Add that Angèle invites Fabienne to spend some time in her native land, Senegal. Point out Senegal on the map.

Play the cassette and have students read along in their books. Stop the recording after Fabienne's first speech. Ask the first three questions in Activity 2 and elicit oral responses. Then play the recording of the next two exchanges between Angèle and Fabienne. Pause to ask question 4 in Activity 2. Finally, play the recording of the remainder of the dialogue and ask the last three questions in Activity 2.

Have students pair off to practice the entire dialogue. When they have finished, call on volunteers to recreate the dialogue in their own words.

2   Activité • Avez-vous compris?

If you have not used these questions as suggested above, form small groups for cooperative learning. Students work together to formulate one answer to each question and then they write it down. After you have collected the papers, call on volunteers to summarize the situation: Fabienne's problem and Angèle's solution to it. Ask others why the solution is a good one.

3   Activité • Actes de parole

SLOWER-PACED LEARNING   For listening comprehension practice, read aloud at random the quotes from the dialogue that illustrate these communicative functions. Students choose the description of the function from their books and write the number of each of their choices in the order in which you read the quotes.

4   Savez-vous que... ?

Before you play the cassette, prepare a brief list of questions to check comprehension: **Pouvez-vous nommer quatre genres de paysage au Sénégal? Quelles langues parle-t-on au Sénégal?** Then play the cassette or read the cultural note aloud as students read along in their books. Answer any questions they may have. Now tell the students to scan the selection for the answers to your questions.

SLOWER-PACED LEARNING   Prepare a few multiple-choice statements instead of questions: **Au Sénégal, on parle** *(a)* **allemand** *(b)* **wolof** *(c)* **savane.** Follow the procedure suggested above.

CHALLENGE   You might want to choose some poems or verses by Senghor for the students to read and discuss.

5   Activité • Faites des comparaisons

For cooperative learning, have students form pairs to compare France and Senegal, as suggested, using the statistics given. Students might take turns asking questions **(Est-ce qu'il fait chaud au Sénégal?)** and answering them **(Oui, il fait plus chaud qu'en France).** Encourage them to use comparatives **(La France a plus d'habitants)** in their dialogues.

SLOWER-PACED LEARNING Brainstorm some questions that Fabienne might ask Angèle based on these figures.

6 **Activité • Exprimez des souhaits**

Once students have expressed wishes using **si** + the imperfect, encourage them to recall or find in the Summary of Functions, pages 437–43, other ways of expressing the same desires, such as **J'ai tellement envie d'aller en Nouvelle-Calédonie.**

7 **Activité • Préparatifs de voyage**

You might want to have students write this activity. Have students pair off. Tell them to list the activities in the order in which Fabienne might have done them and then to write an account of what she did. Ask a student from each pair to read their composition aloud for the class. If students disagree on the order of the activities as read, ask them to give reasons. For written homework, tell the students to describe the preparations they made for a trip that they've taken.

8 **Activité • Qu'en pensez-vous?**

Review with students the use of the subjunctive or the indicative after these expressions (Unit 11, C10, page 405). Then call on students to express their opinions about the statements. Follow up by asking students to write two or three sentences describing events they think will happen, using the future tense **(Il pleuvra demain).** As they read their statements aloud, have other students react to them, using the expressions of opinion in the box.

9 **Activité • Ecrivez**

Before students begin to write, brainstorm with the class remarks that Fabienne might make beyond relating the facts, such as expressions of regret, surprise, delight, need, and so on. For cooperative learning, groups of four students might compose one letter.

SLOWER-PACED LEARNING You might write the letter as a collective effort in class. Call for volunteers to write the letter on the board, sentence by sentence. Correct each sentence as it is written and have students copy the completed letter. The next day, have students work in pairs to write the letter in their own words, without referring to the model.

CHALLENGE Ask students to compose a short reply that Fabienne's grandmother might write. In the note, she would express her disappointment **(C'est dommage que...)** and then her happiness for Fabienne's new adventure **(C'est une bonne chose que...).**

10 **Activité • Ecrivez**

This second letter might be written following the procedures suggested for Activity 9. To vary the activity, distribute the letters to different individuals or groups and have them compose answers written by Angèle's uncle and aunt.

11 **C'ETAIT COMMENT AU SENEGAL?**

CULTURAL BACKGROUND **Thiès** is the capital of one of Senegal's regions. It is the hub of the country's railway system and a major commercial and industrial center. Industries located in **Thiès** include aluminum, phosphates, cement, and tanning. The city is also a major center of the peanut trade.

Point out that Angèle talks about what she used to do in Senegal before coming to France, so she uses the imperfect. You may want to review the formation of the imperfect. Then play the cassette or read the dialogue aloud as students look at the photos and follow along in the text. Have students pair off to practice reading the dialogue, exchanging roles. Write the following verbs on the board: **aller, apprendre, habiter, passer, parler, être.** Have students close their books; ask them to tell what Angèle used to do in Senegal, using the imperfect forms of the verbs on the board.

You might want to reinforce the use of **il y a** to mean *ago* by having students tell something they did or were doing in the past and how long ago it was: **J'ai appris à faire du vélo il y a dix ans. Il y a cinq ans je vivais à la campagne.**

12 Activité • Vrai ou faux?

For listening practice, read these statements aloud as students listen with their books closed. Tell them to write on their papers the number of each statement and **vrai** or **faux**. Call on volunteers to correct the false statements.

13 Activité • Fabienne est curieuse

Have students work in pairs, taking turns asking and answering questions.

CHALLENGE   When students have completed the activity, tell them to adapt the questions to ask of a partner who has moved here from another place, either real or imaginary.

14 Activité • Angèle manquait d'enthousiasme

SLOWER-PACED LEARNING   Have the students write down the imperfect form of the verb in each numbered item to agree with the subject **tu.** Then tell them to ask you the questions as if they were speaking to one of their school friends. Respond to each question by adapting one of the expressions in the box. Now reverse the procedure. Finally, have students pair off to practice asking and responding to the questions.

15 Activité • Jeu de rôle

In preparation, tell students to reread the dialogue between Angèle and Fabienne in 11. They should find and adapt Fabienne's questions so that Angèle might ask them of Fabienne: **Qu'est-ce que tu faisais là-bas? Qu'est-ce que tu apprenais à l'école? Tu habitais Caen? Pourquoi es-tu venue habiter ici?** and so on. They should also change the instructions of Activity 15 to direct questions: **Tu aimais y vivre? Tu t'es habituée à la ville?** and so on.

You might give students some background information on **Normandie** and show them pictures of the province. This would give them some insight as to what Fabienne's life there might have been like.

CHALLENGE   As a variation, students might "interview" a historical character about life at that moment in history.

16 Activité • Ecrivez

Brainstorm with students other aspects of their lives of five years ago that they might write about. If students' lives have not changed much in the last five years, tell them to go back farther in time. To provide listening practice and a model for what students will write, tell what you were doing (in reality or fictitiously) five years ago.

17 ### Activité • A vous maintenant!

Have students circulate and interview one another about last year's activities. Have them jot down notes and report their findings to the class. Then have them write their findings in a cohesive paragraph for homework.

18 ### QU'EST-CE QU'ON FERA AU SENEGAL?

CULTURAL BACKGROUND   **Dakar** enjoys an ideal temperature because of its location on the **Cap Vert** peninsula jutting into the Atlantic Ocean. The island of N'Gor, or **Gorée** in French, lies a short distance away. It provides a weekend getaway spot for many in **Dakar. Dakar** has a deepwater harbor protected from the sea. In 1902 **Dakar** was designated the capital of all French West Africa. **Dakar** gained attention when French aviation pioneer Mermoz set up an airmail route to Brazil.

You may wish to review the formation of the future tense in Unit 11, pages 387 and 397, before presenting this dialogue. Have students watch for these future forms as you play the cassette or read the dialogue aloud and as they read along in their books. Have them look at the photos; ask a question about each one. Finally, ask volunteers to tell what the two girls will do during their visit.

19 ### Activité • Avez-vous compris?

Read aloud, at random, short answers to these questions. As students identify the appropriate questions, they write down the numbers of the questions in the order in which you gave the answers. Read in the correct order the numbers they should have written. Then ask the questions and have students give oral answers. Assign the answers to be written for homework.

20 ### Activité • Actes de parole

Have students work silently to find the expressions called for. Ask individuals to read the quotes. As a student reads a quote, call on others to respond to it as Angèle or Fabienne might do. Then ask students to suggest other ways the speaker might have expressed the same feeling or idea.

21 ### Activité • C'est une bonne chose

SLOWER-PACED LEARNING   Students need not write complete sentences to express their relief or satisfaction. They may simply say **Nous avons de la chance! Heureusement! C'est une bonne chose!** or **Ouf!**

22 ### Activité • La réunion familiale

Angèle's family will have many questions to ask her about her three years in France. They will also remark on Angèle's changed appearance during that time. Brainstorm such questions and remarks with students before they pair off to prepare their dialogues. Remind students they may have to change **te** or **tu** to **vous** and **je** to **nous,** depending on the circumstances.

23   Activité • **Et vous?**

Encourage students to imagine activities other than those mentioned by Angèle. When all have finished, call on volunteers to read their lists aloud. Then collect the papers.

24   Activité • **A vous maintenant!**

Suggest that students review the **Comment le dire** sections for expressions they might use. They may work in pairs or in small groups. Some might like to present their dialogues to the class the following day.

SLOWER-PACED LEARNING   On a transparency, write a model dialogue with the lines out of order. Project the transparency and have students put the lines in the correct order. Underline phrases in the dialogue for giving advice and for inviting friends. Brainstorm with students other ways to express these functions. Finally, have students work in pairs, varying the underlined phrases to make up their own dialogues.

25   Activité • **Projets de voyage**

Begin by reading aloud to the students the information about Senegal. Next call on volunteers to phrase the questions suggested in the directions to the activity. As a student suggests a question, ask others to give answers the travel agent might give. Finally, have students pair off to prepare dialogues. When they've finished, you might ask individuals to report on their travel plans or ask pairs to dramatize their dialogues for the class.

26   Activité • **Ecoutez bien**

You're going to hear a radio news broadcast from Senegal. The announcer will be reporting the results of the last elections in that country. Open your book to page 431. *(pause)* Take a moment to read the statements in Activity 26 to yourself. *(pause)* On a separate sheet of paper, number from 1 to 6 and be prepared to indicate if the statements are true or false. *(pause)* Ready? **Ecoutez bien.**

Sénégal, le 28 février. Voici les dernières informations. Abdou Diouf a été réélu aujourd'hui président du Sénégal avec soixante-dix-sept pour cent des voix. Son principal opposant, Abdoulaye Wade, le candidat du parti démocratique sénégalais, a eu vingt et un pour cent des votes.

Durant ses sept premières années à la tête du gouvernement, M. Diouf a conservé des rapports très privilégiés avec la France et a notamment accentué les liens avec les Etats-Unis.

Abdoulaye Wade, le principal opposant, un avocat très populaire parmi les jeunes, a accusé M. Diouf et les membres du parti socialiste sénégalais de fraude électorale.

Et maintenant, vérifions.
1. Abdoulaye Wade est le nouveau président du Sénégal. *faux*
2. Abdou Diouf a eu vingt et un pour cent des votes. *faux*
3. Abdoulaye Wade est le candidat du parti socialiste. *faux*
4. Abdoulaye Wade est médecin. *faux*
5. Abdou Diouf est président du Sénégal depuis cinq ans. *faux*
6. M. Diouf a abandonné les relations avec la France. *faux*

PRONONCIATION

Review

> Open your book to page 432. *(pause)* Refer to this page as you listen to this section.

1 **Ecoutez, répétez et lisez.**

> By now you should know the main features of French pronunciation. Were you able to keep up your French sounds as you advanced? It's time to find out. Let's check!
>
> **1.** First we'll go over the sounds of the French vowels, how they're written, and how they're pronounced. Then you'll have a chance to test yourself. Let's start with the /i/.
>
> You hear this sound in the word **si.** It's spelled three ways: with an **i** as in **il,** with an **î** as in **île,** or with a **y** as in **gym.** The French /i/ is shorter, tenser, and purer than the vowel sound in the English word *eat.* Listen and repeat: **si, il, île, gym.** Now read aloud the self-check sentence in your book, and I'll repeat it after you. *(pause)* **Si, il y a des livres ici.**
>
> Let's go on to the sound /e/ that you hear in the word **thé.** It can be spelled with **é** as in **été, ai** as in **j'ai, er** as in **aller,** or **ez** as in **chez.** The sound /e/ is shorter, tenser, and purer than the vowel sound in the English word *ate.* Listen and repeat: **thé, été, j'ai, aller, chez.** Now read aloud the self-check sentence in your book; I'll repeat it after you. *(pause)* **J'ai étudié au cours d'été.**
>
> Take a look at the next sound, the sound /ɛ/, as in the word **sept.** The letter **e** spells this sound, as in **sel.** So do **è,** as in **père, ê** as in **fête, ais** as in **frais, aie** as in **haie, aient** as in **avaient,** and **ei** as in **peine.** The French sound /ɛ/ is a lot like the vowel sound in the English word *press.* Listen and repeat: **sept, sel, père, fête, frais, haie, avaient, peine.** Look at the self-check sentence in your book and read it aloud. I'll say it after you. *(pause)* **Qu'est-ce qu'elle fait avec mes lettres?**
>
> And now, how about the **a**-sound, the sound in the little word **la?** It has three spellings: **a** as in **patte, à** as in **là,** and **e** as in **femme.** You say it like the first part in the English word *pie,* not as in *man* or *far.* Listen and repeat: **la, patte, là, femme.** Now read aloud the self-check sentence in your book, and I'll repeat it. *(pause)* **Ça va, les bagages?**
>
> As for the next sound, the /ɔ/ that you hear in **fort,** it's spelled only one way, with an **o** as in **robe.** It sounds something like the vowel in the English *four,* but it's more rounded, open, and forward. Listen and repeat: **fort, robe.** Check yourself now by reading aloud the self-check sentence in your book. *(pause)* **Sonne encore, peut-être qu'il dort.**
>
> Let's go on to a related sound, the **o**-sound that you hear in the word **mot.** It can be spelled with an **o** as in **zone, ô** as in **rôle, au** as in **jaune, aux** as in **chevaux,** or **eau** as in **beau.** To say this sound correctly, you need to keep your lips tense at all times, just as you would in the first part of the English word *mow,* not as in *so* or *go.* Listen and repeat: **mot, zone, rôle, jaune, chevaux, beau.** Now read aloud the self-check sentence in your book. *(pause)* **L'auto est dans la mauvaise zone.**

Now take a look at the **u**-sound, as in the word **tout.** It has only one spelling, **ou** as in **vous.** The French **u**-sound is shorter, tenser, and rounder than the vowel sound in the English word *too.* Listen and repeat: **tout, vous.** Look at the self-check sentences in your book and read them aloud. I'll say them after you. *(pause)* **C'est pour nous? Merci beaucoup.**

And now, how about the **y**-sound, the sound in the word **tu?** The letter **u** spells this sound, as in **dur.** So does **û,** as in the word **sûr.** You say it like a pure /i/ but with your lips rounded, as though you're going to whistle. Listen and repeat: **tu, dur, sûr.** Now read aloud the self-check sentences in your book. *(pause)* **Tu es venu du sud? Ça t'a plu?**

You're halfway through your review of French vowel sounds. How are you doing? Let's continue with the sound /ø/. You hear it in the word **ceux** and spell it **eu,** as in **peu,** or **œu,** as in **vœux.** You say it like a pure /e/ but with your lips forward and well rounded. Listen and repeat: **ceux, peu, vœux.** Look at the self-check sentence in your book and read it aloud. *(pause)* **Veux-tu deux œufs?**

Are you ready to take a look at the next sound, the sound /œ/, as in the word **œuf?** It can be spelled **eu** as in **seul** or **œu** as in **sœur.** This sound also begins like a pure /e/, but you say it with your mouth more open. Listen and repeat: **œuf, seul, sœur.** Now read aloud the self-check sentence in your book. *(pause)* **Sa sœur a peur de rester seule.**

As for the next sound, the /ə/ that you hear in **le,** it's spelled only one way, with an **e** as in **je.** It sounds something like the vowel in the English word *the,* but you say it with your lips forward and rounded. Listen and repeat: **le, je.** Read aloud the self-check sentence in your book. *(pause)* **C'est ce que demande le monsieur.**

And now, how about the nasal sound /ɛ̃/, the sound in the word **pain?** It's spelled five ways: **ain** as in **train, ein** as in **plein, in** as in **fin, im** as in **timbre,** and **aim** as in **faim.** You say it like the vowel sound in the English *get,* but you exhale through your nose. Listen and repeat: **pain, train, plein, fin, timbre, faim.** Look at the self-check sentences in your book and read them aloud. *(pause)* **Le train est plein. Voilà le prochain.**

Let's go on to the sound /ã/ that you hear in the word **dans.** You spell it with **an** as in **plan, en** as in **vent, em** as in **temps,** or **am** as in **lampe.** Don't round your lips when you make this sound. Exhale through your nose and say it like the *a* in *father.* Listen and repeat: **dans, plan, vent, temps, lampe.** Now read aloud the self-check sentence in your book. *(pause)* **Les enfants de cinq ans rentrent.**

The third nasal vowel sound is /ɔ̃/ as in **mon.** It's spelled two ways: **on** as in **bon** and **om** as in **nombre.** You say it like the /o/ in **tôt** but through your nose and with your lips more closed and rounded. Make sure to keep it different from the /ã/ in **dans.** Listen and repeat: **mon, bon, nombre.** Look at the self-check sentence in your book and read it aloud. *(pause)* **Ils sont donc bons, vos bonbons.**

And last but not least there's the sound /œ̃/ that you hear in the word **un.** The letters **un** spell this sound, as in **brun.** So do **um,** as in **parfum.** You say it like the sound /ɛ̃/ in **fin** but with your lips well rounded. Listen and repeat: **un, brun, parfum.** Read aloud the self-check sentence in your book. *(pause)* **Aucun emprunt le lundi.**

Well, that's it for the basic vowels of French. If you got them all right, you can pat yourself on the back.

2. What remains are the three glides and a few unique French consonants. Let's go on with the glides, which you've heard in expressions like **y a-t-il, Où est-ce que c'est?** and **C'est à lui.**

You hear the first glide in the word **bien.** It's spelled four ways: with an **i** as in **viande, y** as in **il y a, ail** as in **travail,** and **eille** as in **oreille.** This glide sounds like the *y* in the English *yes* only it's more tense. Listen and repeat: **bien, viande, il y a, travail, oreille.** Now read aloud the self-check sentence in your book. *(pause)* **Il y a bien sûr du travail à la pièce.**

The second glide is the sound in **oui.** You can spell it two ways: **ou** as in **Louis** and **oi** as in **soir.** This glide sounds a lot like the *w* in the English *we* only it's tenser. Listen and repeat: **oui, Louis, soir.** Look at the self-check sentences in your book and read them aloud. *(pause)* **Où est Louis? Il est parti loin.**

The last glide is the one you hear in **huit.** It has three spellings: the letter **u** before an **a** as in **nuage, u** before an **i** as in **nuit,** and **u** before an **e** as in **saluer.** This glide is like the sounds /y/ and /i/ pronounced together rapidly. Listen and repeat: **huit, nuage, nuit, saluer.** Now read aloud the self-check sentence in your book. *(pause)* **J'ai vu les nuages et j'ai entendu la pluie.**

3. Finally, let's take a look at a couple of consonants that are typically French. The first is the sound /ɲ/ that you hear in the word **ligne.** It has only one spelling: **gn** as in **campagne.** It sounds something like the *ni* in the English *onion.* Listen and repeat: **ligne, campagne.** Look at the self-check sentences in your book and read them aloud. *(pause)* **C'est magnifique! Mon compagnon a gagné!**

And to finish up, the famous Parisian r-sound. You hear it in the word **rose** and spell it with an **r** as in **rire** or with two **r**'s as in **beurre.** To say it, you need to make a slight contraction in your upper throat or a little gargling sound. There's no similar sound in English. To check yourself, read aloud the last sentence in your book. *(pause)* **J'ai appris à prononcer le français. Merci!**

And with this, we say **au revoir** to you—with a few final pointers on keeping up what you've acquired. First don't forget that you're going to say all these sounds in syllables of equal importance, making sense groups and breath groups. Within each sense group, don't forget your linkers in groups like **de temps en temps, les autres, tout de suite,** and so forth.

Don't forget to drop syllables in words like **samedi** but to keep them in words like **vendredi.**

Keep up your French speech by listening to some French every day and, if possible, repeating as much as you can. If you're traveling to France or to some other French-speaking country, don't forget your friendly dictionary, even a small one. And a phrase book can be great to refresh your memory. With these little tools and what you know already, there's no reason why you shouldn't be able to say correctly every word you may need. So, **Bon voyage! Bon courage!** and, once again, **Au revoir!**

---

2   **Copiez les *Self-checks* pour préparer une dictée.**

First listen to the sentence as it is read to you. Then you will hear the sentence again in short segments, with a pause after each segment to allow you time to write. Finally you will hear the sentence a third time so that you may check your work. Let's begin.

    1. Si, il y a des livres ici. Si, *(pause)* il y a *(pause)* des livres ici. *(pause)* Si, il y a des livres ici.

2. J'ai étudié au cours d'été. J'ai étudié *(pause)* au cours d'été. *(pause)* J'ai étudié au cours d'été.

3. Qu'est-ce qu'elle fait avec mes lettres? Qu'est-ce qu'elle fait *(pause)* avec mes lettres? *(pause)* Qu'est-ce qu'elle fait avec mes lettres?

4. Ça va, les bagages? Ça va, *(pause)* les bagages? *(pause)* Ça va, les bagages?

5. Sonne encore, peut-être qu'il dort. Sonne encore, *(pause)* peut-être *(pause)* qu'il dort. *(pause)* Sonne encore, peut-être qu'il dort.

6. L'auto est dans la mauvaise zone. L'auto est *(pause)* dans la mauvaise zone. *(pause)* L'auto est dans la mauvaise zone.

7. C'est pour nous? Merci beaucoup. C'est pour nous? *(pause)* Merci beaucoup. *(pause)* C'est pour nous? Merci beaucoup.

8. Tu es venu du sud? Ça t'a plu? Tu es venu du sud? *(pause)* Ça t'a plu? *(pause)* Tu es venu du sud? Ça t'a plu?

9. Veux-tu deux œufs? Veux-tu *(pause)* deux œufs? *(pause)* Veux-tu deux œufs?

10. Sa sœur a peur de rester seule. Sa sœur a peur *(pause)* de rester seule. *(pause)* Sa sœur a peur de rester seule.

11. C'est ce que demande le monsieur. C'est ce que demande *(pause)* le monsieur. *(pause)* C'est ce que demande le monsieur.

12. Le train est plein. Voilà le prochain. Le train est plein. *(pause)* Voilà le prochain. *(pause)* Le train est plein. Voilà le prochain.

13. Les enfants de cinq ans rentrent. Les enfants de cinq ans *(pause)* rentrent. *(pause)* Les enfants de cinq ans rentrent.

14. Ils sont donc bons, vos bonbons. Ils sont donc bons, *(pause)* vos bonbons. *(pause)* Ils sont donc bons, vos bonbons.

15. Aucun emprunt le lundi. Aucun emprunt *(pause)* le lundi. *(pause)* Aucun emprunt le lundi.

16. Il y a bien sûr du travail à la pièce. Il y a bien sûr *(pause)* du travail *(pause)* à la pièce. *(pause)* Il y a bien sûr du travail à la pièce.

17. Où est Louis? Il est parti loin. Où est Louis? *(pause)* Il est parti loin. *(pause)* Où est Louis? Il est parti loin.

18. J'ai vu les nuages et j'ai entendu la pluie. J'ai vu les nuages *(pause)* et j'ai entendu *(pause)* la pluie. *(pause)* J'ai vu les nuages et j'ai entendu la pluie.

19. C'est magnifique! Mon compagnon a gagné! C'est magnifique! *(pause)* Mon compagnon *(pause)* a gagné! *(pause)* C'est magnifique! Mon compagnon a gagné!

20. J'ai appris à prononcer le français. Merci! J'ai appris *(pause)* à prononcer *(pause)* le français. *(pause)* Merci! *(pause)* J'ai appris à prononcer le français. Merci!

CHAPITRE 12

Vacances au Sénégal

Chapitre de révision

1 Invitation au voyage 📼

Le mois de juillet approche. Il faut penser aux grandes vacances. Qu'est-ce que Fabienne va faire? Elle a plusieurs possibilités, mais elle n'a pas encore pris de décision. Son amie Angèle a une merveilleuse idée. Elle est née au Sénégal et elle a de la famille là-bas. Elle propose à Fabienne de venir avec elle dans son pays natal.

FABIENNE Je ne sais pas quoi faire pendant mes vacances… Je souhaitais aller voir mes cousins en Nouvelle-Calédonie; malheureusement, le voyage est trop cher. Ma grand-mère veut que je vienne la voir en Normandie, mais ça ne me dit pas trop. Ma sœur m'invite en Corse, mais je connais déjà. J'ai envie de changer…

ANGÈLE Si tu venais avec moi?
FABIENNE Où?
ANGÈLE Au Sénégal.
FABIENNE En Afrique?
ANGÈLE Oui, je vais voir ma famille qui habite Dakar. Il y a longtemps que je ne l'ai pas vue. Tu peux venir avec moi si tu veux.

FABIENNE Tu crois que c'est possible? Ta famille… Tu es sûre que ça ne l'embêtera pas?
ANGÈLE Au contraire! Elle est très accueillante, et elle sera ravie de te voir!
FABIENNE Ça me tente!… Le voyage est cher?

ANGÈLE Ça va. Il y a des charters qui ne sont pas trop chers. Mais il faut réserver très vite.
FABIENNE Tu pars quand?
ANGÈLE Au mois d'août.
FABIENNE Parfait! Ça me donne le temps de trouver un job pour payer mon voyage!
ANGÈLE Et pour là-bas, ne t'inquiète pas! Tu n'auras pas besoin d'argent : tu seras notre invitée.

Photo on p. 422: Dakar, Senegal
Refer to maps on pp. 434–436 to locate "Sénégal, Nouvelle Calédonie, Normandie," and "Corse."

1. Elle ne sait pas quoi faire pendant les vacances. 2. Le voyage est trop cher.
3. La Normandie, ça ne lui dit pas trop. Elle connaît déjà la Corse.

2 Activité • Avez-vous compris?

Répondez aux questions suivantes d'après «Invitation au voyage».

1. Quel est le problème de Fabienne?
2. Pourquoi ne peut-elle pas aller en Nouvelle-Calédonie?
3. Pourquoi ne veut-elle pas aller en Normandie? En Corse?
4. Pourquoi est-ce que Fabienne hésite quand Angèle l'invite?
5. Quels sont les avions les moins chers?
6. Comment est-ce que Fabienne a l'intention de payer son voyage?
7. Pourquoi est-ce que Fabienne n'aura pas besoin d'argent au Sénégal?

4. Elle ne veut pas embêter la famille d'Angèle. 5. Les charters sont les avions les moins chers. 6. Elle va trouver un job. 7. Elle sera l'invitée de la famille d'Angèle.

3 Activité • Actes de parole

Qui est-ce qui parle? C'est Fabienne ou Angèle? Qu'est-ce qu'elle dit? Trouvez leurs paroles dans «Invitation au voyage». 1. Fabienne —Je souhaitais aller voir mes cousins... 2. Angèle —Si tu venais avec moi? 3. Angèle —Il y a longtemps que je ne l'ai pas vue.

1. Elle exprime un désir.
2. Elle propose de faire quelque chose.
3. Elle regrette quelqu'un.
4. Elle est indifférente.
5. Elle exprime un regret.
6. Elle invite son amie.
7. Elle n'est pas sûre.

4. Fabienne —...ça ne me dit pas trop. 5. Fabienne —...malheureusement, le voyage est trop cher.
6. Angèle —Tu peux venir avec moi si tu veux. 7. Fabienne —Tu crois que... Tu es sûre que...

4 Savez-vous que... ?

La République du Sénégal est située sur la côte occidentale *(west)* de l'Afrique. C'est un petit pays, mais il présente une grande variété de paysages : savane *(grassy plain)*, forêt tropicale, désert, plaine fertile. Le climat est doux et les gens sont très accueillants *(welcoming)*. La population se compose de différents groupes ethniques qui ont chacun leur langue. Le français est la langue officielle; le wolof est la langue nationale.

Le Sénégal est un pays en pleine expansion agricole et industrielle. L'économie repose essentiellement sur l'arachide *(peanut)*. De nouvelles industries sont nées, notamment celles de l'huile *(oil)* et des phosphates.

Au début du XVIIᵉ siècle, quelques marchands de Dieppe et de Rouen ont fondé la Compagnie du Sénégal et de la Gambie. Ils ont obtenu le monopole du commerce et ont établi les postes de Saint-Louis et de l'île de Gorée. Le Sénégal est devenu une république autonome en 1958. La Constitution de 1963 a institué une république présidentielle. Le premier président était Léopold Senghor, homme politique et poète célèbre qui a démissionné *(resigned)* en 1981. Son successeur, Abdou Diouf, a été réélu en 1988.

Have students find Dieppe and Rouen on the map on p. 434.
arachide: the name of the peanut plant

Activité • Faites des comparaisons   Possible answers are given.

Fabienne demande à Angèle de parler de son pays. Elle lui demande de le comparer à la France. Préparez un dialogue avec un(e) camarade.

Sénégal

Superficie (*area*) :	196 200 km²
Nombre d'habitants :	6 100 000
Capitale :	Dakar (800 000)
Climat :	Deux saisons : hiver, été
Température moyenne :	28°C
Langues :	français, wolof

France

550 000 km²
55 000 000
Paris (3 000 000)
Quatre saisons
14°C
français

La France est plus grande que le Sénégal.
Il y a plus de gens en France qu'au Sénégal.
Dakar est une ville plus petite que Paris.
Il fait moins chaud en France qu'au Sénégal.
On parle plus de langues au Sénégal qu'en France.

6 **Activité • Exprimez des souhaits**

Mettez-vous à la place de Fabienne et d'Angèle, et exprimez leurs souhaits. Employez : «Ah, si... » + l'imparfait.

Fabienne n'a pas assez d'argent pour aller en Nouvelle-Calédonie.
—Ah, si j'avais assez d'argent pour aller en Nouvelle-Calédonie!

1. Fabienne ne peut pas trouver un job.
2. Elle ne sait pas quoi faire pendant les vacances.
3. Elle ne parle pas wolof.
4. Angèle n'est pas au Sénégal.
5. Sa famille n'est pas en France.
6. Ses parents ne veulent pas revenir au Sénégal.

1. Ah, si je pouvais... 2. Ah, si je savais... 3. Ah, si je parlais... 4. Ah, si j'étais... 5. Ah, si ma famille était là... 6. Ah, si mes parents voulaient revenir...

7 **Activité • Préparatifs de voyage**   Possible answer is given.

Avant de partir pour le Sénégal, Fabienne avait beaucoup à faire. Racontez ce qu'elle a fait pour préparer son voyage. Employez **d'abord, ensuite, après** et **enfin.**

réserver les places   trouver un job   choisir des cadeaux
chercher un passeport
se faire vacciner   acheter des vêtements   changer de l'argent

Elle a d'abord réservé les places sur un charter. Ensuite, elle a trouvé un job pour payer son voyage. Elle a cherché un passeport, et elle s'est fait vacciner. Après, elle a acheté des vêtements et choisi des cadeaux. Enfin, elle a changé de l'argent.

Activité • Qu'en pensez-vous?   [icon]   Possible answers are given.

Dites ce que vous pensez de ces affirmations (statements). Variez les expressions et justifiez votre opinion.

1. Fabienne ira passer ses vacances en Normandie.
2. Elle acceptera l'invitation de sa sœur.
3. Elle se plaira au Sénégal.

4. Elle apprendra le wolof.
5. Angèle a assez d'argent pour payer son voyage.
6. Elle ne reviendra pas en France.

1. Je doute que Fabienne aille passer ses vacances en Normandie.   2. Je pense qu'elle n'acceptera pas l'invitation de sa sœur.

Je pense que...   Je suis sûr(e)/certain(e) que...   Je doute que...

Je crois que...

Je ne crois pas que...   Je ne pense pas que...

3. Je crois qu'elle se plaira au Sénégal.   4. Je ne pense pas qu'elle apprendra le wolof.   5. Je ne crois pas qu'Angèle ait assez d'argent pour payer son voyage.   6. Je suis certain(e) qu'elle ne reviendra pas en France.

9   Activité • Ecrivez   Possible answer is given.

Fabienne écrit à sa grand-mère pour lui dire pourquoi elle ne va pas passer ses vacances en Normandie cette année. Elle lui parle de son amie Angèle, lui dit comment elle l'a invitée au Sénégal, comment elles iront, quand elles partiront... Elle lui dit qu'elle pense aller la voir plus tard en Normandie.

Chère grand-mère,
Je regrette, mais ...

...je ne passerai pas mes vacances chez toi cette année. Je vais au Sénégal avec ma copine, Angèle. Elle m'a invitée à rester chez sa famille à Dakar pendant le mois d'août. Mais ne t'inquiète pas. Je vais t'envoyer plein de cartes postales. Après, je te verrai en septembre, avant la rentrée. Je t'embrasse bien fort.
                                    Fabienne

10   Activité • Ecrivez   Possible answer is given.

Angèle écrit à son oncle et à sa tante pour leur dire qu'elle a invité une copine. Elle parle de Fabienne, de son intention de travailler au mois de juillet...

Cher oncle, Chère tante,

Je vous ai déjà parlé de mon amie Fabienne.

Cher oncle, chère tante, Je vous ai déjà parlé de mon amie Fabienne. Elle est très sympa. Je l'ai invitée à aller avec moi au Sénégal, et elle a accepté. Elle va d'abord travailler au mois de juillet pour payer son voyage. Nous partirons début août. J'espère que ça ne vous embêtera pas. Ecrivez-moi. Bises, Angèle.

Angèle a quitté le Sénégal il y a trois ans. Fabienne lui demande comment était sa vie là-bas.

FABIENNE Qu'est-ce que tu faisais quand tu étais là-bas?

ANGÈLE J'allais à l'école.

FABIENNE Qu'est-ce que tu apprenais?

ANGÈLE Eh bien, comme ici, le français, les maths, la géo... J'avais des copains... On allait à la plage le week-end ou à un match de foot. Là-bas, c'est le sport le plus populaire, comme en France.

Thiès: city 70 km. east of Dakar; major center of the peanut trade.

FABIENNE Tu habitais Dakar?

ANGÈLE Oui, mais j'allais souvent à Thiès. Ma grand-mère y vivait. J'y passais presque toutes mes vacances. Je serai heureuse de la revoir.

FABIENNE Tu parlais français?

ANGÈLE Oui, mais dans ma famille, on parle wolof.

FABIENNE Tu sais le parler?

ANGÈLE Bien sûr!

FABIENNE Tu as de la chance. Mais pourquoi es-tu venue habiter ici?

ANGÈLE J'ai suivi mes parents qui venaient travailler en France.

FABIENNE Ça te plaisait là-bas?

ANGÈLE Enormément! J'étais drôlement heureuse!

FABIENNE Pas en France?

ANGÈLE Si, mais c'est différent... Je regrette un peu le Sénégal. C'est mon pays!

12 Activité • Vrai ou faux?

Ces phrases sont-elles vraies ou fausses d'après la conversation entre Fabienne et Angèle?

1. Angèle a quitté le Sénégal il y a plus de deux ans.
2. A l'école, elle n'apprenait pas la même chose qu'en France.
3. Le week-end, elle allait à la campagne.
4. Elle habitait Thiès.

5. Sa grand-mère n'habitait pas Dakar.
6. Angèle passait toutes ses vacances chez des cousins.
7. Elle était heureuse au Sénégal.
8. Au Sénégal, on ne parle que le français.

1. C'est vrai.   2. C'est faux. Elle apprenait la même chose.   3. C'est faux. Elle allait à la plage ou à un match de foot.   4. C'est faux. Elle habitait Dakar.   5. C'est vrai.   6. C'est faux. Elle passait toutes ses vacances chez sa grand-mère.   7. C'est vrai.   8. C'est faux. On parle aussi wolof.

13 Activité • **Fabienne est curieuse** 🔊 Possible answers are given.

Fabienne pose des questions à Angèle. Voilà les réponses d'Angèle. Trouvez les questions de Fabienne.

> J'habitais Dakar. — Où est-ce que tu habitais?

1. J'allais à l'école en bus.
2. Je jouais au volley-ball.
3. Je passais mes week-ends à la plage.
4. Je parlais wolof.
5. Mes parents sont venus en France pour travailler.
6. Je me sentais bien là-bas.

1. Comment allais-tu à l'école? 2. Qu'est-ce que tu faisais comme sports? 3. Où passais-tu les week-ends?
4. Quelle langue parlais-tu? 5. Pourquoi tes parents sont-ils venus en France? 6. Comment est-ce que tu te sentais là-bas?

14 Activité • **Angèle manquait d'enthousiasme** Possible answers are given.

Fabienne interroge Angèle sur ce qu'elle faisait à l'école, et Angèle exprime son manque d'enthousiasme à cette époque. Avec un(e) camarade, jouez les rôles de Fabienne et Angèle. Changez chaque fois d'expression.

> — Tu allais à l'école? — Oui, mais ça ne me plaisait pas beaucoup.

1. apprendre la géo
2. faire de la gym
3. prendre le bus
4. parler français
5. beaucoup travailler
6. avoir beaucoup de devoirs

1. —Tu apprenais... ? —Oui, mais, ça ne me disait rien d'apprendre la géo. 2. —Tu faisais... ? —Non, je n'avais pas

Ça ne me disait rien de... Je n'avais pas le courage de...

Ça m'embêtait de...

Tu parles!

Ça m'ennuyait de... Je n'avais pas envie de...

le courage de faire de la gym. 3. —Tu prenais... ? —Oui, mais ça m'embêtait de prendre le bus. 4. —Tu parlais... ?
—Oui, mais je n'avais pas envie de parler français. 5. —Tu travaillais... ? —Oui, mais ça m'ennuyait de travailler
beaucoup. 6. —Tu avais... ? —Tu parles! J'avais plein de devoirs!

15 Activité • **Jeu de rôle** Possible dialogue is given.

Il y a cinq ans, Fabienne habitait à la campagne en Normandie. Angèle lui demande ce qu'elle faisait, si elle aimait y vivre, si elle s'est habituée à la ville, ce qu'elle préfère maintenant... Imaginez la vie de Fabienne, et faites un dialogue avec un(e) camarade. Commencez par : «Et toi, où est-ce que tu habitais avant?» —J'habitais en Normandie.
—Qu'est-ce que tu faisais à la campagne?
—A l'école, j'apprenais les maths, l'histoire... comme ici. Le week-end, je faisais de l'équitation. J'étais très heureuse là-bas.
—Ça ne te plaît pas ici?

16 Activité • **Ecrivez** —Si, énormément! C'était bien d'être à la campagne quand j'étais petite.
Maintenant, je préfère l'excitation et le bruit de la ville.

Qu'est-ce que vous faisiez il y a cinq ans? Dites en quelques lignes où vous viviez, où vous alliez à l'école, ce que vous faisiez, où vous alliez en vacances...

17 Activité • **A vous maintenant!**

Demandez à un(e) camarade ce qu'il/elle faisait l'année dernière. Puis, changez de rôle.

Fabienne veut aussi savoir comment ce sera quand elles iront là-bas.

FABIENNE Alors, raconte! Qu'est-ce qu'on fera?

ANGÈLE On ira d'abord à Dakar. On dormira chez mon oncle et ma tante. Je te présenterai à mes cousins.

FABIENNE Ils sont mignons?

ANGÈLE Très!

FABIENNE Super!

ANGÈLE Ma petite cousine a deux ans et mon cousin a neuf ans.

FABIENNE Quel dommage!

FABIENNE On peut se baigner à Dakar?

ANGÈLE Oui, on ira sur l'île de Gorée. On partira le matin, on bronzera...

ANGÈLE A midi, on mangera une tieboudienne.

FABIENNE Qu'est-ce que c'est?

ANGÈLE Le plat national. C'est du riz avec du poisson.

ANGÈLE L'après-midi, on visitera la ville. Tu verras la Médina, c'est le quartier le plus commerçant... et le Village des Arts où tu pourras acheter des souvenirs typiquement africains...

FABIENNE Ça me fait rêver! Il faudra aussi que j'apprenne un peu de wolof!... Au fait, est-ce qu'il y a des discothèques à Dakar?

ANGÈLE Bien sûr! Tu veux aller danser?

FABIENNE Oui, et j'espère qu'on dansera sur de la musique africaine!

ANGÈLE T'en fais pas, on ne s'ennuiera pas! Je suis sûre qu'on passera d'excellentes vacances!

L'île de Gorée: island 3 km southeast of the port of Dakar; once the center of slave trade in west Africa

1. L'oncle et la tante d'Angèle recevront les filles à Dakar. 2. Sa cousine a deux ans, et son cousin a neuf ans.

Activité • Avez-vous compris?   Possible answers are given.

Répondez aux questions suivantes d'après «Qu'est-ce qu'on fera au Sénégal?»

1. Qui recevra Angèle et Fabienne à Dakar?
2. Quel âge ont les cousins d'Angèle?
3. Pourquoi Fabienne dit-elle «Quel dommage»?
4. Qu'est-ce que c'est, une «tieboudienne»?

5. Qu'est-ce que les filles feront pendant la journée?
6. Qu'est-ce que c'est, la Médina?
7. Qu'est-ce qui fait rêver Fabienne?

3. Parce que les cousins d'Angèle sont trop jeunes. 4. C'est du riz avec du poisson. 5. Elles iront à la plage. Elles visiteront la ville. 6. C'est le quartier le plus commerçant. 7. Les projets du voyage la font rêver.

20   **Activité • Actes de parole**   Possible answers are given.

Trouvez dans le dialogue ce que les filles disent dans les situations suivantes.

1. Fabienne exprime un regret.
2. Angèle fait des comparaisons.
3. Fabienne exprime un besoin.

4. Fabienne exprime un souhait.
5. Angèle rassure Fabienne.

1. Quel dommage! 2. ...c'est le quartier le plus commerçant.
3. Il faudra aussi que j'apprenne... 4. J'espère qu'on dansera... 5. T'en fais pas, on ne s'ennuiera pas!

21   **Activité • C'est une bonne chose**   Possible answers are given.

Angèle vous donne des informations sur le voyage au Sénégal. Vous exprimez votre soulagement et votre satisfaction. Préparez les dialogues avec un(e) camarade. Changez de rôle et variez les expressions.

— Nous irons d'abord à Dakar dans ma famille.
— C'est une bonne chose que ta famille puisse nous recevoir!

Nous avons de la chance (que)...

Heureusement (que)...

C'est une bonne chose (que)...

Ouf!...

1. Au Sénégal, il fait drôlement chaud.
2. On ira se baigner au bord de la mer.
3. Tu pourras acheter des souvenirs à la Médina.
4. On ira sur la Corniche pour avoir une vue générale de la ville.
5. Tu apprendras un peu de wolof; c'est facile.
6. On ira danser; il y a beaucoup de discothèques.

1. Heureusement que nous avons des shorts! 2. C'est une bonne chose que j'aie pris des cours de natation! 3. C'est une bonne chose! L'anniversaire de maman est en septembre. 4. Heureusement que j'ai un appareil-photo! 5. Ouf! On parle aussi français au Sénégal! 6. Heureusement! J'adore danser!

22   **Activité • La réunion familiale**

Il y a longtemps qu'Angèle n'a pas vu sa famille. Imaginez les conversations quand elle retrouvera sa famille à Dakar. Préparez les conversations avec un(e) camarade. Employez les expressions suivantes.

Ça me fait plaisir de te revoir!

Il y a si longtemps!

Je suis heureux (heureuse) que tu sois revenu(e)!

Je suis content(e) de te revoir!

Ça fait longtemps que je ne t'ai pas vu(e)!

23 Activité • Et vous? Possible answers are given.

Vous avez l'opportunité d'aller à Dakar. Nommez six choses que vous y ferez.
J'irai à l'île de Gorée. Je visiterai Dakar et Thiès. J'achèterai des souvenirs au Village des Arts. J'apprendrai le wolof. Je danserai
dans des discothèques. Je mangerai une tieboudienne. Je rencontrerai des jeunes.

24 Activité • A vous maintenant!

Qu'est-ce que vous avez l'intention de faire pendant vos vacances? Un(e) camarade écoute
vos projets, puis fait des objections ou vous donne des conseils. A la fin, il/elle finit par
vous inviter. Employez ces expressions :

J'aimerais... Je souhaite... Je désire... J'ai l'intention de...

Possible questions are given.
25 Activité • Projets de voyage

Vous avez l'intention de faire un
voyage au Sénégal. Vous allez à
une agence de voyages pour vous
renseigner. Vous posez des questions
à l'agent. Vous voulez savoir quels
documents il vous faudra, quel
temps il fait là-bas et de quels
vêtements vous aurez besoin, quelle
est la monnaie du Sénégal, combien
coûte le voyage, ce qu'il y a à faire et
à voir... Préparez le dialogue avec
un(e) camarade. Quels documents faudra-t-il?
Quel temps fait-il au Sénégal?

De quels vêtements est-ce que j'aurai besoin?
Quelle monnaie utilise-t-on au Sénégal?

- **FORMALITÉS**
Passeport en cours de validité. Certificat de vacci-
nation antiamarile.

- **HEURE LOCALE**
En hiver : 1 heure de moins qu'en France.
En été : 2 heures de moins.

- **CLIMAT**
Doux sur la côte, chaud et sec au nord, pluies au
centre, tropical humide au sud.

- **MONNAIE**
Le franc CFA°. 5 000 F CFA = 100 FF.

- **QUELQUES CONSEILS**
Emporter des vêtements légers et confortables, mais
aussi une veste pour les soirées, car la brise rafraîchit
l'atmosphère après le coucher du soleil. Ne pas
oublier des chaussures confortables pour les excursions, lunettes de soleil, chapeau de toile et une paire
de jumelles pour observer les oiseaux sur les rives du
fleuve Casamance.

- **VOLTAGE**
220 volts.

- **POUR EN SAVOIR PLUS**
Office du tourisme du Sénégal, 24, bd de l'Hôpital -
75005 Paris.

26 Activité • Ecoutez bien For script and answers, see p. T253.

Vous écoutez une émission radiophonique venant du Sénégal. Ce sont les informations. On
parle des dernières élections dans le pays. Ecoutez les informations, et dites si les phrases
suivantes sont vraies ou fausses.

1. Abdoulaye Wade est le nouveau président du Sénégal.
2. Abdou Diouf a eu vingt et un pour cent des votes.
3. Abdoulaye Wade est le candidat du parti socialiste.
4. Abdoulaye Wade est médecin.
5. Abdou Diouf est président du Sénégal depuis cinq ans.
6. M. Diouf a abandonné les relations avec la France.

CFA = Communauté Financière Africaine

PRONONCIATION

Review

1 Ecoutez, répétez et lisez.

1. Vowels

Vowel	Spelling	Self-check
/i/ as in **si**	il, île, gym	Si, il y a des livres ici.
/e/ as in **thé**	été, j'ai, aller, chez	J'ai étudié au cours d'été.
/ɛ/ as in **sept**	sel, père, fête, frais, haie, avaient, peine	Qu'est-ce qu'elle fait avec mes lettres?
/a/ as in **la**	patte, là, femme	Ça va, les bagages?
/ɔ/ as in **fort**	robe	Sonne encore, peut-être qu'il dort.
/o/ as in **mot**	zone, rôle, jaune, chevaux, beau	L'auto est dans la mauvaise zone.
/u/ as in **tout**	vous	C'est pour nous? Merci beaucoup.
/y/ as in **tu**	dur, sûr	Tu es venu du sud? Ça t'a plu?
/ø/ as in **ceux**	peu, vœux	Veux-tu deux œufs?
/œ/ as in **œuf**	seul, sœur	Sa sœur a peur de rester seule.
/ə/ as in **le**	je	C'est ce que demande le monsieur.
/ɛ̃/ as in **pain**	train, plein, fin, timbre, faim	Le train est plein. Voilà le prochain.
/ã/ as in **dans**	plan, vent, temps, lampe	Les enfants de cinq ans rentrent.
/ɔ̃/ as in **mon**	bon, nombre	Ils sont donc bons, vos bonbons.
/œ̃/ as in **un**	brun, parfum	Aucun emprunt le lundi.

2. Glides

Glide	Spelling	Self-check
/j/ as in **bien**	viande, il y a, travail, oreille	Il y a bien sûr du travail à la pièce.
/w/ as in **oui**	Louis, soir	Où est Louis? Il est parti loin.
/ɥ/ as in **huit**	nuage, nuit, saluer	J'ai vu les nuages et j'ai entendu la pluie.

3. Consonants

Consonant	Spelling	Self-check
/ɲ/ as in **ligne**	campagne	C'est magnifique! Mon compagnon a gagné!
/ʀ/ as in **rose**	rire, beurre	J'ai appris à prononcer le français. Merci!

2 Copiez les *Self-checks* pour préparer une dictée.

FOR REFERENCE

LA FRANCE

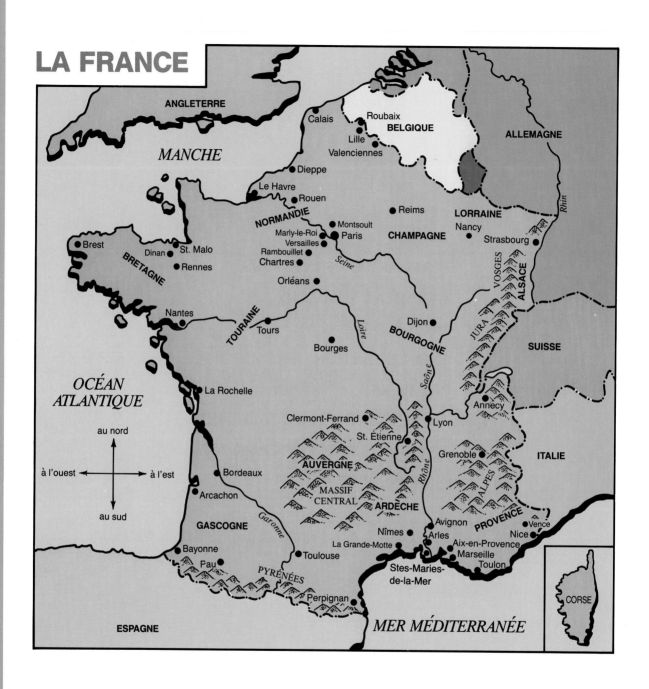

ANGLETERRE

MANCHE

Calais
Roubaix
BELGIQUE
Lille
Valenciennes

ALLEMAGNE

Dieppe
Le Havre
Rouen
Reims
LORRAINE
Nancy
NORMANDIE
Montsoult
Marly-le-Roi
Paris
CHAMPAGNE
Strasbourg
Versailles
Rambouillet
Chartres
Orléans

Brest
Dinan
St. Malo
Rennes
BRETAGNE

Seine

VOSGES
ALSACE

Nantes
TOURAINE
Tours

Loire

Dijon
BOURGOGNE

JURA

SUISSE

Bourges

OCÉAN
ATLANTIQUE

au nord

à l'ouest ← → à l'est

au sud

La Rochelle

Annecy

Clermont-Ferrand
St. Étienne

Lyon

Saône

Rhône

Grenoble

ITALIE

Bordeaux

AUVERGNE

Arcachon

MASSIF
CENTRAL
ARDÈCHE

ALPES

PROVENCE

Avignon
Vence
Nice

GASCOGNE

Garonne

Nîmes
Arles
Aix-en-Provence
La Grande-Motte
Marseille
Toulon

Bayonne
Pau
Toulouse

Stes-Maries-
de-la-Mer

PYRÉNÉES

Perpignan

ESPAGNE

MER MÉDITERRANÉE

CORSE

434

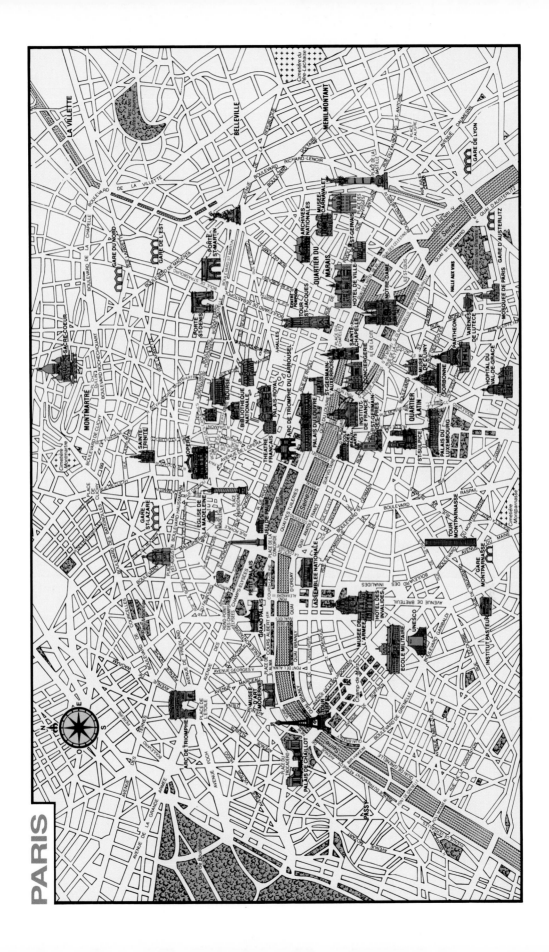

PARIS

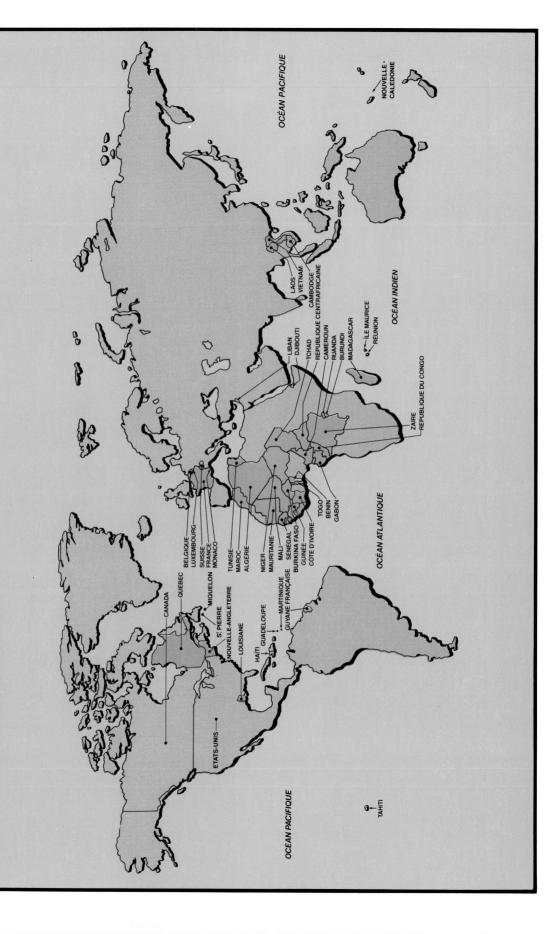

LA FRANCOPHONIE

OCÉAN PACIFIQUE

OCÉAN PACIFIQUE

OCÉAN ATLANTIQUE

OCÉAN INDIEN

NOUVELLE-CALEDONIE

LAOS
VIETNAM
CAMBODGE
TCHAD
RÉPUBLIQUE CENTRAFRICAINE
CAMEROUN
RUANDA
BURUNDI
MADAGASCAR
ÎLE MAURICE
REUNION

LIBAN
DJIBOUTI

ZAÏRE
REPUBLIQUE DU CONGO

TOGO
BENIN
GABON

CANADA
QUEBEC

BELGIQUE
LUXEMBOURG
SUISSE
FRANCE
MONACO

TUNISIE
MAROC
ALGÉRIE

NIGER
MAURITANIE

MALI
SENEGAL
BURKINA FASO
GUINÉE
CÔTE D'IVOIRE

MIQUELON
St PIERRE
NOUVELLE-ANGLETERRE

LOUISIANE

MARTINIQUE
GUYANE FRANÇAISE

HAITI
GUADELOUPE

ETATS-UNIS

TAHITI

SUMMARY OF FUNCTIONS

A *function* is what you do with language—what your purpose is when you speak. Here is a list of functions and some expressions you can use to accomplish them. The roman numeral **I** tells you that the expressions were introduced in **Nouveaux copains.** Roman numeral **II** lets you know that the expressions are found in **Nous, les jeunes.** Following the roman numerals, you'll see the number of the unit and the letter of the section where you learned the expression.

SOCIALIZING

Saying hello
I	1 (A4)	Bonjour!
		Bonsoir!
		Salut!

Saying goodbye
I	1 (A4)	Au revoir!
		Salut!
		A tout à l'heure!

Addressing people
I	1 (A5)	madame
		mademoiselle
		monsieur

Getting someone's attention
I	11 (B6)	Excusez-moi,...
		Pardon,...

Welcoming people
I	6 (A4)	Entrez. / Entre.
		Soyez le bienvenu. / Bienvenue.
		Faites comme chez vous.
		Fais comme chez toi.

Expressing good wishes
I	11 (C5)	Bonne fête!
		Joyeux Noël!
		Bonne année!
		Joyeuses Pâques! (Joyeuse Pâque!)
		Joyeux (Bon) anniversaire!
		Bonnes vacances!
		Bon voyage!
		Bonne route!
		Bonne santé!
		Meilleurs vœux (souhaits)!

Paying compliments
I	6 (C15)	Tu es un chef!
I	10 (C4)	Il / Elle te va bien.
		Ils / Elles te vont bien.
		C'est tout à fait ton style!
		Mes compliments pour la mousse.

Les sandwiches sont excellents!
Tu as bon goût!
Tu joues (danses) drôlement bien!

Acknowledging compliments
I	10 (C4)	Tu trouves?
		Oh, ce n'est rien.
		C'est gentil.

Expressing thanks
I	2 (C13)	Merci.

Responding to thanks
I	6 (A21)	De rien.

Making a phone call
I	5 (C4)	Allô.
		Je suis bien chez... ?
		C'est une erreur.
		C'est occupé.
		Ça ne répond pas.
		Qui est à l'appareil?
		Ne quittez pas.
		Vous demandez quel numéro?

Offering food / drink
I	6 (C18)	Encore du / de la... ?
		Vous prenez du / de la... ?

Accepting food / drink
I	6 (C18)	Oui, volontiers!
		Oui, avec plaisir!
		Oui, s'il vous plaît!
I	10 (C1)	J'ai soif!

Refusing food / drink
I	6 (C18)	Non, merci. Je n'ai plus faim.
		Merci. C'est bon, mais...

Inquiring about others' activities
II	1 (B4)	C'était comment,... ?
		C'était bien,... ?
		Ça t'a plu?
		Tu t'es amusé(e)?

II   6 (B21)   Ça va, ton / ta... ?
Ça marche, ton / ta... ?
Ça boume, ton / ta... ?
Ça t'intéresse, ton / ta... ?
Ça te plaît, ton / ta... ?
Ça t'amuse, ton / ta... ?

Sharing confidences
II   5 (C9)   J'ai un petit problème.
Je peux te parler?
J'ai besoin de te parler.

Asking how someone is feeling
I   1 (A4)   Ça va?

II   1 (A11)   Comment allez-vous?
Comment vas-tu?
Tu es en forme?

Telling how someone is feeling
I   1 (A4)   Ça va.
(Très) bien.

II   1 (A11)   Très bien, merci. Et vous?
Pas mal (terrible). Et toi?
Drôlement bien!
En pleine forme!

Asking for agreement
II   3 (B6)   D'accord?
Ça va?
Ça te va?

Inviting friends
I   9 (B1)   Tu peux... ?
Tu veux... ?

I   9 (B6)   Je t'invite à...

II   2 (A12)   Tu ne veux pas... ?
Ça te dit de... ?
Ça t'intéresse de... ?
Ça te plairait de... ?

Accepting an invitation
I   9 (B10)   Si tu veux.
D'accord!
Bonne idée!
Volontiers!
Avec plaisir!

II   2 (A12)   Oui, je veux bien.
Si, je veux bien.

Refusing an invitation
I   9 (B10)   Je n'ai pas envie.
Je ne peux pas.
Encore!
Je regrette, mais...
Impossible,...

II   2 (A12)   Oui, mais je ne peux pas.

II   5 (A6)   Désolé(e).
Je suis pris(e).
Je suis occupé(e).
Je ne suis pas libre.
Je n'ai pas le droit de...

Making excuses
I   10 (A16)   Non, pas encore.
J'ai oublié.
Je n'ai pas eu le temps.
Je n'ai pas pu.

II   1 (C7)   Je suis nul (nulle) en maths.
Je n'y comprends rien.
Ce n'est pas mon fort.
Le prof ne m'aime pas.
Je suis mauvais(e) en
informatique.
Le prof explique mal.

II   10 (A17)   Je suis pressé(e).
Je suis déjà en retard.
Je n'ai pas le temps.
Il faut que je sois à... dans...
minutes.

Asking for permission
II   2 (C8)   Je peux..., s'il vous (te) plaît?
Je voudrais... Vous êtes (Tu es)
d'accord?

II   5 (A22)   Est-ce que je peux... ?
Vous voulez bien que je... ?

Giving permission
II   2 (C8)   Oui, si vous voulez (tu veux).
Je veux bien.
Oui, pourquoi pas?
D'accord. Bonne idée.
Oui, bien sûr.

Refusing permission or a favor
II   2 (C8)   Quelle idée!
Non, c'est mon dernier mot.
C'est impossible.
Non, je ne veux pas.
Non, je refuse.
(Il n'en est) pas question.

II   6 (A13)   Ah non! Cette fois, c'est fini!
Pas question!
Demande à ta mère!
Désolé(e), c'est impossible.

Asking a favor
II 6 (A13) Te peux me prêter… ?
Tu ne peux pas me prêter… ?
Tu as… à me prêter?
Tu n'as pas… à me prêter?
Prête-moi…, s'il te plaît.

Granting a favor
II 6 (A13) Bon, ça va pour cette fois.
D'accord.
Bon, voilà.
Tiens, le / la / les voilà.

Expressing concern for someone's health
II 7 (A15) Qu'est-ce que tu as?
Qu'est-ce qui t'arrive?
Tu n'as pas l'air en forme.
Ça n'a pas l'air d'aller.
Tu as mauvaise mine.

Renewing old acquaintances
II 9 (B8) Ça me fait plaisir.
J'avais vraiment envie de te revoir!
Je suis content(e) de te revoir!
Je suis heureux (heureuse) que tu sois (re)venu(e)!
Ça fait longtemps que je ne t'ai pas vu(e)!
Il y a si longtemps!

EXCHANGING INFORMATION

Asking for information
I 5 (B16)

Comment?	Qui?
Combien?	Avec qui?
Quoi?	A qui?
Où?	Pourquoi?
Quand?	A quelle heure?

I 6 (C7) Qu'est-ce que… ?

I 11 (B9) Quel(s) / Quelle(s)… ?
Quel / Quelle est… ?
Quels / Quelles sont… ?

Asking and giving names
I 1 (B4) Tu t'appelles comment?
Je m'appelle…
Il / Elle s'appelle comment?
Il / Elle s'appelle…

Asking and saying where someone is from
I 1 (C1) Tu es d'où?
Je suis de…
Il / Elle est de…

I 1 (C4) Vous êtes d'où?
Nous sommes de…
Ils / Elles sont de…

Asking someone's age and telling yours
I 6 (B5) Tu as quel âge?
J'ai… ans.

Saying how often you do something
I 2 (A8) d'habitude
toujours
souvent
quelquefois

Saying what you're going to do
I 5 (C10) Je vais (+ infinitive)

Asking for directions
I 5 (B9) Les téléphones (la douane), s'il vous plaît?
Où sont les téléphones, s'il vous plaît?
Où est la douane, s'il vous plaît?

Giving locations
I 5 (B9)

juste là	devant
ici	en face (de)
là-bas	entre
à droite (de)	à côté (de)
à gauche (de)	près (de)
tout droit	

Asking prices
I 2 (C17) C'est combien?

I 11 (B6) Il / Elle coûte combien?
Ils / Elles coûtent combien?
Combien coûte / coûtent… ?

Answering a negative question affirmatively
II 2 (A5) Tu ne veux pas venir avec moi?
Si, je veux bien.

Expressing obligation to yourself and others
II 5 (A12) Je dois…
Il faut que je…

Assigning responsibility
II 5 (B8) C'est à... de...

Expressing a need
I 2 (C7) Il me faut (absolument)...
Il faut que je...
J'ai (vraiment) besoin de...

Giving reasons for doing something
II 6 (C5) Avoir un job,...
c'est un moyen de...
c'est une façon de...
c'est une occasion de...

Asking and telling how long
something has been going on
II 2 (C19) Tu... depuis combien de
temps?
Ça fait combien de temps que
tu... ?
Depuis...
Je... depuis...
Ça fait...
Ça fait... que je...

Reporting a series of events
II 9 (C14) D'abord,...
Ensuite,...
Après,...
Enfin,...

Expressing intentions, goals, wishes, and dreams
II 11 (B9) J'ai l'intention de...
J'ai envie de...
Je souhaite...
J'espère...
Je veux (bien)...
Je désire...
J'aimerais (bien)...
Mon idéal, c'est de...
Mon but, c'est de...
Mon rêve, c'est de...
J'ai pour projet de...

EXPRESSING FEELINGS AND EMOTIONS

Expressing annoyance
I 6 (C1) Quelle vie!

I 10 (A1) Zut!

Exclaiming to express admiration,
astonishment, and surprise
I 6 (C1) Quelle question!

I 11 (C12) Quelle surprise!

II 3 (A14) Ce qu'elles sont belles, les
Duchesses!
Qu'il est drôle, Bonhomme
Carnaval!
Qu'est-ce qu'elle doit avoir
froid!
Quelle foule!

Complaining about one's health
II 7 (A15) Je me sens mal.
Je ne me sens pas bien.
J'ai du mal à dormir.
J'ai mal à la tête, au cœur...

Expressing satisfaction
II 1 (B4) C'était...
merveilleux! super!
chouette! drôlement bien!
génial! bien!
Je me suis beaucoup amusé(e)!
J'ai adoré!
Ça m'a beaucoup plu.
Ça m'a plu énormément.

Expressing dissatisfaction
II 1 (B4) C'était triste.
C'était mortel.
Je me suis ennuyé(e).
J'ai détesté!
J'ai pas aimé.

Expressing feelings
II 3 (B18) J'ai peur.
J'ai le vertige.
J'ai faim.
J'ai soif.
J'ai chaud.
J'ai froid.
J'ai mal au cœur.

Expressing regret
I 9 (B10) Je regrette!

I 10 (TYS 1) Dommage!

II	3 (C13)	Quel dommage! C'est bien dommage. Malheureusement,… Je suis désolé(e) mais… C'est regrettable. (FORMAL)

II	10 (B11)	Malheureusement, elle est arrivée en retard! C'est dommage qu'elle soit arrivée en retard! Quel dommage! Elle est arrivée en retard!

Expressing pleasure

II	6 (B21)	Super, c'est très bien payé! Je trouve ça super! (Je trouve que) c'est passionnant (intéressant). J'adore! Ça me plaît beaucoup. Je suis ravi(e).

Expressing disappointment

II	6 (B21)	Non, c'est mal payé. Non, j'en ai assez. Non, j'en ai marre. (FAM.) Non, c'est l'enfer. Non, je déteste. Non, ça m'ennuie. Non, ça m'embête (m'énerve).

Expressing fatigue

II	7 (C16)	Je n'en peux plus! Je suis fatigué(e). Je suis épuisé(e). J'abandonne. Je suis mort(e)! (FAM.) Je suis crevé(e)! (FAM.) Je craque! (FAM.)

Expressing pity

II	7 (C16)	(Mon) pauvre vieux! (Ma) pauvre vieille! Pauvre Fabrice! Pauvre petit(e)!

Saying how much you miss something

II	9 (A21)	Je regrette (drôlement)… Qu'est-ce que je regrette! C'était si bien! C'était tellement mieux!

Il y avait moins (plus) de…
… me manque.

Expressing impatience

II	10 (A17)	Vite! On est en retard! Dépêche-toi! On va rater… Tu vas être en retard! Tu peux te dépêcher? Mais qu'est-ce que tu fais?

Expressing relief

II	10 (B11)	Heureusement que… Nous avons de la chance que… Ouf! … C'est une bonne chose que…

PERSUADING

Making requests or giving commands

I	6 (A6)	Entrez, s'il vous plaît. Entre, s'il te plaît. Venez / Viens avec moi.

Making suggestions

I	7 (B7)	Allons visiter Dinan! On va visiter Dinan?

II	9 (C20)	Si on allait… ? Si on prenait… ? Pourquoi on ne va pas… ? Tu n'as pas envie de… ? Tu veux qu'on aille… ?

Asking for advice

I	11 (A13)	A ton avis, qu'est-ce que je peux acheter (offrir) à… ? Tu as une idée? J'offre… à… Qu'est-ce que tu en penses?

II	5 (C9)	A ton avis,… qu'est-ce que je fais? qu'est-ce que je dois faire? qu'est-ce qu'il faut faire? qu'est-ce qu'il faut que je fasse? Qu'est-ce que tu me conseilles? Tu crois que je peux l'inviter? Tu as une idée?

Giving advice

I	11 (A13)	Achète-lui / leur… Tu peux lui / leur offrir… Bonne idée! Non, offre-lui / leur plutôt… Il / Elle a déjà plein de…

II	5	(C9)	Invite-la.

II 5 (C9) Invite-la.
Il faut que tu l'invites.
Téléphone-lui.
Il faut que tu lui téléphones.
Oublie-le.
Il faut que tu l'oublies.

II 6 (B10) Pourquoi (est-ce que) tu ne
cherches pas... ?
Pourquoi (est-ce que) tu ne
mets pas... ?

II 7 (B16) Tu devrais...
Je te conseille de...
Il vaut mieux que tu...

Justifying advice
II 7 (B16) C'est excellent pour la santé.
C'est bon pour toi.
C'est ce qu'il te faut.
C'est nourrissant.
C'est meilleur.

Insisting
II 6 (A13) S'il te (vous) plaît!
Sois (Soyez) sympa!
Sois (Soyez) gentil(le)!
Allez!

Offering encouragement
II 2 (B15) Vas-y!
C'est bien!
Mais si, ça vient!
Tu y es presque!
Mais oui, tu y arrives!
Continue!
Encore un petit effort!

II 5 (C9) Bien sûr!
Sûrement.
Pourquoi pas?
Il faut oser.
Un peu de courage!
N'hésite pas.

II 7 (C16) Allez!
Encore un effort!
Courage!
Force-toi!

Assuring someone
II 7 (C18) Je t' (vous) assure que ça va.
Je te (vous) promets que je me
sens mieux.
Je te (vous) garantis que je me
nourris bien.

Reassuring someone
II 7 (C18) Ça va, je t' (vous) assure.
Je me sens mieux, je te (vous)
promets.
Je me nourris bien, je te (vous)
garantis.

Consoling someone
II 9 (A21) Ne regrette rien. C'est bien
de...
Tu as tort de regretter. Ça ne
sert à rien.
Tu vas voir. ...
N'y pense plus.
(Ne) t'en fais pas! Tu vas te
plaire...
Fais-toi une raison.

EXPRESSING ATTITUDES AND OPINIONS

Expressing likes and preferences
I 3 (C12) J'aime...
J'aime mieux...

. . . about school subjects
I 2 (B19) C'est facile / chouette / génial /
extra / super!

. . . about films, plays, TV shows, books
I 9 (C11) C'est drôle / amusant /
émouvant / original / génial /
un bon film!
J'adore... !

. . . about food
I 6 (C15) C'est bon.
C'est délicieux / excellent /
super / extra!
J'adore!

. . . about gifts
I 11 (C18) Qu'il / Qu'elle est... !
Quel(le) joli(e)... !
Quelle surprise!
C'est très gentil!
C'est une excellente idée!
Tu as bien choisi!

Expressing dislikes
I 3 (C12) Je n'aime pas...

. . . about school subjects
I 2 (B19) C'est difficile / la barbe /
pas terrible / pas le pied!

. . . about films, plays, TV shows, books

I	9 (C11)	C'est (trop) violent!
		C'est bidon / un navet / pas original / un mauvais film / toujours la même chose!
		Je déteste… !

. . . about food

II	7 (B20)	Je n'aime pas ça.
		C'est pas bon.
		C'est mauvais.
		Ça n'a pas de goût.
		C'est infect.

Complaining

II	5 (B16)	C'est injuste!
		C'est pas juste!
		C'est pas normal!
		C'est moi qui fais tout ici!
		C'est toujours moi qui…
		Tu ne fais rien, toi!

Expressing indecision, indifference, or lack of interest

| I | 7 (B1) | Bof! |
| | | Mouais! |

II	1 (B4)	C'était…
		assez bien.
		comme ci, comme ça.
		pas mal.
		pas terrible.
		Assez bien.

II	3 (B6)	Je ne sais pas trop.
		Ça m'est égal.
		Comme tu veux.
		Ce que tu préfères.
		Je n'ai pas de préférence.

II	10 (C13)	…, ça ne me dit rien.
		Je n'ai pas le courage de…
		Ça m'embête de…
		Ça m'ennuie de…
		Je n'ai pas (souvent) envie de…
		… Tu parles!

Expressing an opinion

II	1 (A4)	A mon avis,…
		Je trouve que…
		Je n'ai pas envie de…

Expressing agreement

I	3 (C1)	Bon.
I	5 (B1)	OK.
I	9 (B10)	D'accord.
II	1 (A4)	Je suis d'accord avec toi.
		Moi aussi.
		Tu as (Vous avez) raison.
		Moi non plus.

Expressing disagreement

II	1 (A4)	Je ne suis pas d'accord avec toi.
		Pas moi.
		Au contraire,…
		Tu as (Vous avez) tort.
		Moi, je…

Expressing doubt and uncertainty

II	7 (B16)	Tu crois?
		Tu es sûr(e)?
		Vraiment?
		C'est vrai?

II	11 (A17)	Je ne (le) crois pas.
		Je ne (le) pense pas.
		Ça m'étonnerait!
		Ça m'étonnerait que nous ayons des robots!
		J'en doute.

II	11 (C10)	Je ne crois pas que…
		Je ne pense pas que…
		Je ne suis pas sûr(e) que…
		Je ne suis pas certain(e) que…
		Je doute que…

Expressing certainty

II	11 (A17)	Je t'assure que c'est vrai.
		Mais oui (si)! C'est évident!
		Evidemment.
		Je (J'en) suis convaincu(e).
		Je (J'en) suis persuadé(e).
		J'en suis sûr(e).

Expressing beliefs and hope

II	11 (C10)	Je crois que…
		Je pense que…
		Je suis sûr(e) que…
		Je suis certain(e) que…
		J'espère que…

GRAMMAR SUMMARY

ARTICLES

Singular		Plural
Masculine	Feminine	
un frère **un** ⌃ami	**une** sœur	**des** frères / sœurs **des** ⌃amis / amies
le frère **l'**ami	**la** sœur **l'**amie	**les** frères / sœurs **les** ⌃amis / amies
ce frère **cet** ⌃ami	**cette** sœur	**ces** frères / sœurs **ces** ⌃amis / amies

POSSESSIVE ADJECTIVES

Singular		Plural	Singular		Plural
Masculine	Feminine		Masculine	Feminine	
mon frère **mon** ⌃ami	**ma** sœur **mon** ⌃amie	**mes** frères / sœurs **mes** ⌃amis / amies	**notre** frère	**notre** sœur	**nos** frères / sœurs **nos** ⌃amis / amies
ton frère **ton** ⌃ami	**ta** sœur **ton** ⌃amie	**tes** frères / sœurs **tes** ⌃amis / amies	**votre** frère	**votre** sœur	**vos** frères / sœurs **vos** ⌃amis / amies
son frère **son** ⌃ami	**sa** sœur **son** ⌃amie	**ses** frères / sœurs **ses** ⌃amis / amies	**leur** frère	**leur** sœur	**leurs** frères / sœurs **leurs** ⌃amis / amies

INTERROGATIVE ADJECTIVES: QUEL

	Singular	Plural
Masculine	**quel**	**quels**
Feminine	**quelle**	**quelles**

ADJECTIVES: FORMATION OF FEMININE

	Masculine	Feminine
Most adjectives (*add* -e)	**Il est brun.**	**Elle est brune.**
Most adjectives ending in -é (*add* -e)	**Il est fatigué.**	**Elle est fatiguée.**
All adjectives ending in an unaccented -e (*no change*)	**Il est jeune.**	**Elle est jeune.**
Most adjectives ending in -eux (-eux → -euse)	**Il est généreux.**	**Elle est généreuse.**
All adjectives ending in -ien (-ien → -ienne)	**Il est italien.**	**Elle est italienne.**
All adjectives ending in -if (-if → -ive)	**Il est sportif.**	**Elle est sportive.**

ADJECTIVES AND NOUNS: FORMATION OF PLURAL

		Masculine	Feminine
Most noun and adjective forms (*add* -s)	Sing. Pl.	un pantalon vert des pantalons verts	une jupe verte des jupes vertes
Most noun and <u>masculine</u> adjective forms ending in -al (-al → -aux)	Sing. Pl.	le sport principal les sports princip<u>aux</u>	la rue principale les rues principales
All noun and <u>masculine</u> adjective forms ending in -eau (*add* -x)	Sing. Pl.	le nouveau bat<u>eau</u> les nouv<u>eaux</u> bat<u>eaux</u>	la nouvelle voiture les nouvelles voitures
All noun and <u>masculine</u> adjective forms ending in -s (*no change*)	Sing. Pl.	un autobu<u>s</u> gri<u>s</u> des autobu<u>s</u> gri<u>s</u>	une mobylette grise des mobylettes grises
All <u>masculine</u> adjective forms ending in -x (*no change*)	Sing. Pl.	un garçon paresseux des garçons paresseux	une fille paresseuse des filles paresseuses

ADVERBS: FORMATION

Adjective		Adverb
Masculine	Feminine	
continuel intense **vrai**	**continuelle** **intense** vraie	**continuellement** **intensément** **vraiment**

ADVERBS: NEGATIVE EXPRESSIONS

Elle **ne** garde **pas** les enfants.
Elle **ne** les garde **plus.**
Elle **ne** les garde **jamais.**
Elle **n'a rien** sur son compte.

NOUNS: COMPARATIVE

moins de **autant de**   +   noun   +   **que**   **plus de**

ADJECTIVES AND ADVERBS: COMPARATIVE AND SUPERLATIVE

Comparative	Superlative
moins **aussi** + adjective or + **que** **plus** adverb	**le/la/les** + **moins** **plus** + adjective or + **de** adverb

IRREGULAR COMPARATIVE AND SUPERLATIVE FORMS

	Comparative	Superlative
bon(s), bonne(s) **mauvais, -e, -es**	**meilleur (e)(s)** **plus mauvais, -e, -es**	**le/la/les meilleur(e)(s)** **le/la/les plus mauvais, -e, -es** **le/la/les pire(s)**
bien	**mieux**	**le mieux**

REGULAR VERBS: SIMPLE TENSES

	Stem	Ending	Stem	Ending	Stem	Ending
Infinitive	aim	**-er**	chois	**-ir**	attend	**-re**
PRESENT	aim	**-e** **-es** **-e** **-ons** **-ez** **-ent**	chois	**-is** **-is** **-it** **-issons** **-issez** **-issent**	attend	**-s** **-s** **—** **-ons** **-ez** **-ent**
REQUESTS, COMMANDS, SUGGESTIONS	écout	**-e** **-ons** **-ez**	chois	**-is** **-issons** **-issez**	attend	**-s** **-ons** **-ez**

IMPERFECT		FUTURE		PRESENT SUBJUNCTIVE	
Stem	Ending	Stem	Ending	Stem	Ending
Present tense **nous** form: habitǿnş finissǿnş entendǿnş	**-ais** **-ais** **-ait** **-ions** **-iez** **-aient**	Infinitive: habiter finir entendrę́	**-ai** **-as** **-a** **-ons** **-ez** **-ont**	Present tense **ils** form: habitę́nţ finissę́nţ entendę́nţ	**-e** **-es** **-e** **-ions** **-iez** **-ent**

REGULAR VERBS: COMPOUND TENSES

		Auxiliary		Past Participle	
PASSE COMPOSE	with **avoir**	ai avons as avez a ont		aim **-é** chois **-i** attend **-u**	
	with **être**	suis sommes es êtes est sont		arriv **-é(e)(s)** sort **-i(e)(s)** descend **-u(e)(s)**	

		Auxiliary		Past Participle	
PAST SUBJUNCTIVE	with **avoir**	aie ayons aies ayez ait aient		jou **-é** fin **-i** entend **-u**	
	with **être**	sois soyons sois soyez soit soient		retourn **-é(e)(s)** part **-i(e)(s)** descend **-u(e)(s)**	

PAST INFINITIVE: FORMATION

Infinitive		Auxiliary Verb	Past Participle
déjeuner arriver se reposer	après {	avoir être s'être	déjeuné arrivé(e)(s) reposé(e)(s)

PRONOUNS

Independent Pronouns	Subject Pronouns	Direct-Object Pronouns	Indirect-Object Pronouns	Reflexive Pronouns
moi	je (j')	me	me	me
toi	tu	te	te	te
lui	il	le	lui	se
elle	elle	la	lui	se
nous	nous	nous	nous	nous
vous	vous	vous	vous	vous
eux	ils	les	leur	se
elles	elles	les	leur	se

PRONOUNS

Pronoun replacing **de** + noun phrase	en
Pronoun replacing **à, dans, sur...** + noun phrase	y

INTERROGATIVE PRONOUNS

	People	Things
Subject of verb	qui qui est-ce qui	qu'est-ce qui
Object of verb	qui qui est-ce que	que qu'est-ce que
Object of preposition	de qui à qui	de quoi à quoi

RELATIVE PRONOUNS

	Qui Subject of verb in clause	**Que** Object of verb in clause
People	Pierre discute avec une fille **qui** s'appelle Roxane.	Roxane sort avec un garçon **que** je ne connais pas.
Places	J'ai visité une ville **qui** est près de Strasbourg.	La ville **que** j'ai visitée était intéressante.
Things	On vivra dans des stations **qui** seront construites dans l'espace.	Des robots feront le travail **que** nous faisons actuellement.

VERBS FOLLOWED BY AN INFINITIVE

aimer oser penser pouvoir préférer savoir vouloir	+ infinitive

aider s'amuser apprendre arriver commencer donner se forcer inviter réussir	à	+ infinitive

s'arrêter conseiller continuer décider demander se dépêcher dire essayer finir s'occuper oublier parler persuader proposer refuser	de	+ infinitive

EXPRESSIONS FOLLOWED BY AN INFINITIVE

avoir l'air avoir le courage avoir le droit avoir envie avoir l'occasion avoir raison avoir tort être obligé(e)	de	+ infinitive
avoir intérêt avoir du mal être habitué(e)	à	+ infinitive

VERB INDEX

Following is an alphabetical list of verbs with stem changes, spelling changes, or irregular forms. An infinitive appearing after the verb means that the verb follows one of the patterns shown on pages 449–57. Verbs like **sortir** have been included in the list. All verbs ending in **-ir** that have not been included are like **choisir**.

aboyer, like **essayer**, 450
acheter, 449
aller, 451
appeler, 450
apprendre, like **prendre**, 455
avancer, like **commencer**, 450
avoir, 451

boire, 451
bouger, like **manger**, 450

changer, like **manger**, 450
commencer, 450
comprendre, like **prendre**, 455
connaître, 452
contenir, like **venir**, 457
convaincre, 452
courir, 452
croire, 452

déménager, like **manger**, 450
devoir, 452
dire, 453
dormir, like **sortir**, 456

écrire, 453
élever, like **lever**, 450
ennuyer, like **essayer**, 450
envoyer, 453
espérer, like **préférer**, 451
essayer, 450
être, 453

faire, 453
forcer, like **commencer**, 450

inquiéter, like **préférer**, 451

lever, 450
lire, 454

manger, 450
mettre, 454

nager, like **manger**, 450
neiger, like **manger**, 450

offrir, 454
ouvrir, like **offrir**, 454

paraître, like **connaître**, 452
partir, like **sortir**, 456
payer, like **essayer**, 450
peser, like **lever**, 450
plaindre, 454
plaire, 454
pleuvoir, 455
plonger, like **manger**, 450
pouvoir, 455
préférer, 451
prendre, 455
produire, 455
projeter, 451
promener, like **lever**, 450
promettre, like **mettre**, 454

ranger, like **manger**, 450
rappeler, like **appeler**, 450
recevoir, 455
recommencer, like **commencer**, 450
repartir, like **sortir**, 456
répéter, like **préférer**, 451
reprendre, like **prendre**, 455
résoudre, 456
rire, 456

savoir, 456
sentir, like **sortir**, 456
servir, like **sortir**, 456
songer, like **manger**, 450
sortir, 456
soulever, like **lever**, 450
sourire, like **rire**, 456
suivre, 456

valoir, 457
venir, 457
vivre, 457
voir, 457
vouloir, 457

Verbs with Stem and Spelling Changes

Verbs listed in this section are not irregular, but they do show some stem and spelling changes. The forms in which the changes occur are printed in **boldface** type.

ACHETER

Present	**achète, achètes, achète,** achetons, achetez, **achètent**
Commands	**achète,** achetons, achetez
Passé Composé	*Auxiliary:* avoir *Past Participle:* acheté
Imperfect	achetais, achetais, achetait, achetions, achetiez, achetaient
Future	**achèterai, achèteras, achètera, achèterons, achèterez, achèteront**
Subjunctive	**achète, achètes, achète,** achetons, achetez, **achètent**
Past Subjunctive	*Auxiliary: present subjunctive of* avoir *Past Participle:* acheté

APPELER

Present	**appelle, appelles, appelle,** appelons, appelez, **appellent**
Commands	**appelle,** appelons, appelez
Passé Composé	*Auxiliary:* avoir *Past Participle:* appelé
Imperfect	appelais, appelais, appelait, appelions, appeliez, appelaient
Future	**appellerai, appelleras, appellera, appellerons, appellerez, appelleront**
Subjunctive	**appelle, appelles, appelle,** appelions, appeliez, **appellent**
Past Subjunctive	*Auxiliary: present subjunctive of* avoir *Past Participle:* appelé

COMMENCER

Present	commence, commences, commence, **commençons,** commencez, commencent
Commands	commence, **commençons,** commencez
Passé Composé	*Auxiliary:* avoir *Past Participle:* commencé
Imperfect	**commençais, commençais, commençait,** commencions, commenciez, **commençaient**
Future	commencerai, commenceras, commencera, commencerons, commencerez, commenceront
Subjunctive	commence, commences, commence, commencions, commenciez, commencent
Past Subjunctive	*Auxiliary: present subjunctive of* avoir *Past Participle:* commencé

ESSAYER

Present	**essaie, essaies, essaie,** essayons, essayez, **essaient**
Commands	**essaie,** essayons, essayez
Passé Composé	*Auxiliary:* avoir *Past Participle:* essayé
Imperfect	essayais, essayais, essayait, essayions, essayiez, essayaient
Future	**essaierai, essaieras, essaiera, essaierons, essaierez, essaieront**
Subjunctive	**essaie, essaies, essaie,** essayions, essayiez, **essaient**
Past Subjunctive	*Auxiliary: present subjunctive of* avoir *Past Participle:* essayé

LEVER

Present	**lève, lèves, lève,** levons, levez, **lèvent**
Commands	**lève,** levons, levez
Passé Composé	*Auxiliary:* avoir *Past Participle:* levé
Imperfect	levais, levais, levait, levions, leviez, levaient
Future	**lèverai, lèveras, lèvera, lèverons, lèverez, lèveront**
Subjunctive	**lève, lèves, lève,** levions, leviez, **lèvent**
Past Subjunctive	*Auxiliary: present subjunctive of* avoir *Past Participle:* levé

MANGER

Present	mange, manges, mange, **mangeons,** mangez, mangent
Commands	mange, **mangeons,** mangez
Passé Composé	*Auxiliary:* avoir *Past Participle:* mangé
Imperfect	**mangeais, mangeais, mangeait,** mangions, mangiez, **mangeaient**
Future	mangerai, mangeras, mangera, mangerons, mangerez, mangeront
Subjunctive	mange, manges, mange, mangions, mangiez, mangent
Past Subjunctive	*Auxiliary: present subjunctive of* avoir *Past Participle:* mangé

PREFERER

Present	**préfère, préfères, préfère,** préférons, préférez, **préfèrent**
Passé Composé	*Auxiliary:* avoir *Past Participle:* préféré
Imperfect	préférais, préférais, préférait, préférions, préfériez, préféraient
Future	préférerai, préféreras, préférera, préférerons, préférerez, préféreront
Subjunctive	**préfère, préfères, préfère,** préférions, préfériez, **préfèrent**
Past Subjunctive	*Auxiliary: present subjunctive of* avoir *Past Participle:* préféré

PROJETER

Present	**projette, projettes, projette,** projetons, projetez, **projettent**
Commands	**projette,** projetons, projetez
Passé Composé	*Auxiliary:* avoir *Past Participle:* projeté
Imperfect	projetais, projetais, projetait, projetions, projetiez, projetaient
Future	**projetterai, projetteras, projettera, projetterons, projetterez, projetteront**
Subjunctive	**projette, projettes, projette,** nous projetions, vous projetiez, **projettent**
Past Subjunctive	*Auxiliary: present subjunctive of* avoir *Past Participle:* projeté

Verbs with Irregular Forms

Verbs listed in this section are those that do not follow the pattern of verbs like **aimer,** verbs like **choisir,** or verbs like **attendre.**

ALLER

Present	vais, vas, va, allons, allez, vont
Commands	va, allons, allez
Passé Composé	*Auxiliary:* être *Past Participle:* allé
Imperfect	allais, allais, allait, allions, alliez, allaient
Future	irai, iras, ira, irons, irez, iront
Subjunctive	aille, ailles, aille, allions, alliez, aillent
Past Subjunctive	*Auxiliary: present subjunctive of* être *Past Participle:* allé

AVOIR

Present	ai, as, a, avons, avez, ont
Commands	aie, ayons, ayez
Passé Composé	*Auxiliary:* avoir *Past Participle:* eu
Imperfect	avais, avais, avait, avions, aviez, avaient
Future	aurai, auras, aura, aurons, aurez, auront
Subjunctive	aie, aies, ait, ayons, ayez, aient
Past Subjunctive	*Auxiliary: present subjunctive of* avoir *Past Participle:* eu

BOIRE

Present	bois, bois, boit, buvons, buvez, boivent
Commands	bois, buvons, buvez
Passé Composé	*Auxiliary:* avoir *Past Participle:* bu
Imperfect	buvais, buvais, buvait, buvions, buviez, buvaient
Future	boirai, boiras, boira, boirons, boirez, boiront
Subjunctive	boive, boives, boive, buvions, buviez, boivent
Past Subjunctive	*Auxiliary: present subjunctive of* avoir *Past Participle:* bu

CONNAITRE

Present	connais, connais, connaît, connaissons, connaissez, connaissent
Passé Composé	*Auxiliary:* avoir *Past Participle:* connu
Imperfect	connaissais, connaissais, connaissait, connaissions, connaissiez, connaissaient
Future	connaîtrai, connaîtras, connaîtra, connaîtrons, connaîtrez, connaîtront
Subjunctive	connaisse, connaisses, connaisse, connaissions, connaissiez, connaissent
Past Subjunctive	*Auxiliary: present subjunctive of* avoir *Past Participle:* connu

CONVAINCRE

Present	convaincs, convaincs, convainc, convainquons, convainquez, convainquent
Commands	convaincs, convainquons, convainquez
Passé Composé	*Auxiliary:* avoir *Past Participle:* convaincu
Imperfect	convainquais, convainquais, convainquait, convainquions, convainquiez, convainquaient
Future	convaincrai, convaincras, convaincra, convaincrons, convaincrez, convaincront
Subjunctive	convainque, convainques, convainque, convainquions, convainquiez, convainquent
Past Subjunctive	*Auxiliary: present subjunctive of* avoir *Past Participle:* convaincu

COURIR

Present	cours, cours, court, courons, courez, courent
Commands	cours, courons, courez
Passé Composé	*Auxiliary:* avoir *Past Participle:* couru
Imperfect	courais, courais, courait, courions, couriez, couraient
Future	courrai, courras, courra, courrons, courrez, courront
Subjunctive	coure, coures, coure, courions, couriez, courent
Past Subjunctive	*Auxiliary: present subjunctive of* avoir *Past Participle:* couru

CROIRE

Present	crois, crois, croit, croyons, croyez, croient
Commands	crois, croyons, croyez
Passé Composé	*Auxiliary:* avoir *Past Participle:* cru
Imperfect	croyais, croyais, croyait, croyions, croyiez, croyaient
Future	croirai, croiras, croira, croirons, croirez, croiront
Subjunctive	croie, croies, croie, croyions, croyiez, croient
Past Subjunctive	*Auxiliary: present subjunctive of* avoir *Past Participle:* cru

DEVOIR

Present	dois, dois, doit, devons, devez, doivent
Passé Composé	*Auxiliary:* avoir *Past Participle:* dû
Imperfect	devais, devais, devait, devions, deviez, devaient
Future	devrai, devras, devra, devrons, devrez, devront
Subjunctive	doive, doives, doive, devions, deviez, doivent
Past Subjunctive	*Auxiliary: present subjunctive of* avoir *Past Participle:* dû

DIRE

Present	dis, dis, dit, disons, dites, disent
Commands	dis, disons, dites
Passé Composé	*Auxiliary:* avoir *Past Participle:* dit
Imperfect	disais, disais, disait, disions, disiez, disaient
Future	dirai, diras, dira, dirons, direz, diront
Subjunctive	dise, dises, dise, disions, disiez, disent
Past Subjunctive	*Auxiliary: present subjunctive of* avoir *Past Participle:* dit

ECRIRE

Present	écris, écris, écrit, écrivons, écrivez, écrivent
Commands	écris, écrivons, écrivez
Passé Composé	*Auxiliary:* avoir *Past Participle:* écrit
Imperfect	écrivais, écrivais, écrivait, écrivions, écriviez, écrivaient
Future	écrirai, écriras, écrira, écrirons, écrirez, écriront
Subjunctive	écrive, écrives, écrive, écrivions, écriviez, écrivent
Past Subjunctive	*Auxiliary: present subjunctive of* avoir *Past Participle:* écrit

ENVOYER

Present	envoie, envoies, envoie, envoyons, envoyez, envoient
Commands	envoie, envoyons, envoyez
Passé Composé	*Auxiliary:* avoir *Past Participle:* envoyé
Imperfect	envoyais, envoyais, envoyait, envoyions, envoyiez, envoyaient
Future	enverrai, enverras, enverra, enverrons, enverrez, enverront
Subjunctive	envoie, envoies, envoie, envoyions, envoyiez, envoient
Past Subjunctive	*Auxiliary: present subjunctive of* avoir *Past Participle:* envoyé

ETRE

Present	suis, es, est, sommes, êtes, sont
Commands	sois, soyons, soyez
Passé Composé	*Auxiliary:* avoir *Past Participle:* été
Imperfect	étais, étais, était, étions, étiez, étaient
Future	serai, seras, sera, serons, serez, seront
Subjunctive	sois, sois, soit, soyons, soyez, soient
Past Subjunctive	*Auxiliary: present subjunctive of* avoir *Past Participle:* été

FAIRE

Present	fais, fais, fait, faisons, faites, font
Commands	fais, faisons, faites
Passé Composé	*Auxiliary:* avoir *Past Participle:* fait
Imperfect	faisais, faisais, faisait, faisions, faisiez, faisaient
Future	ferai, feras, fera, ferons, ferez, feront
Subjunctive	fasse, fasses, fasse, fassions, fassiez, fassent
Past Subjunctive	*Auxiliary: present subjunctive of* avoir *Past Participle:* fait

LIRE

Present	lis, lis, lit, lisons, lisez, lisent
Commands	lis, lisons, lisez
Passé Composé	*Auxiliary:* avoir *Past Participle:* lu
Imperfect	lisais, lisais, lisait, lisions, lisiez, lisaient
Future	lirai, liras, lira, lirons, lirez, liront
Subjunctive	lise, lises, lise, lisions, lisiez, lisent
Past Subjunctive	*Auxiliary: present subjunctive of* avoir *Past Participle:* lu

METTRE

Present	mets, mets, met, mettons, mettez, mettent
Commands	mets, mettons, mettez
Passé Composé	*Auxiliary:* avoir *Past Participle:* mis
Imperfect	mettais, mettais, mettait, mettions, mettiez, mettaient
Future	mettrai, mettras, mettra, mettrons, mettrez, mettront
Subjunctive	mette, mettes, mette, mettions, mettiez, mettent
Past Subjunctive	*Auxiliary: present subjunctive of* avoir *Past Participle:* mis

OFFRIR

Present	offre, offres, offre, offrons, offrez, offrent
Commands	offre, offrons, offrez
Passé Composé	*Auxiliary:* avoir *Past Participle:* offert
Imperfect	offrais, offrais, offrait, offrions, offriez, offraient
Future	offrirai, offriras, offrira, offrirons, offrirez, offriront
Subjunctive	offre, offres, offre, offrions, offriez, offrent
Past Subjunctive	*Auxiliary: present subjunctive of* avoir *Past Participle:* offert

PLAINDRE

Present	plains, plains, plaint, plaignons, plaignez, plaignent
Commands	plains, plaignons, plaignez
Passé Composé	*Auxiliary:* avoir *Past Participle:* plaint
Imperfect	plaignais, plaignais, plaignait, plaignions, plaigniez, plaignaient
Future	plaindrai, plaindras, plaindra, plaindrons, plaindrez, plaindront
Subjunctive	plaigne, plaignes, plaigne, plaignions, plaigniez, plaignent
Past Subjunctive	*Auxiliary: present subjunctive of* avoir *Past Participle:* plaint

PLAIRE

Present	plais, plais, plaît, plaisons, plaisez, plaisent
Commands	plais, plaisons, plaisez
Passé Composé	*Auxiliary:* avoir *Past Participle:* plu
Imperfect	plaisais, plaisais, plaisait, plaisions, plaisiez, plaisaient
Future	plairai, plairas, plaira, plairons, plairez, plairont
Subjunctive	plaise, plaises, plaise, plaisions, plaisiez, plaisent
Past Subjunctive	*Auxiliary: present subjunctive of* avoir *Past Participle:* plu

PLEUVOIR

Present	il pleut
Passé Composé	*Auxiliary:* avoir *Past Participle:* plu
Imperfect	il pleuvait
Future	il pleuvra
Subjunctive	il pleuve
Past Subjunctive	*Auxiliary: present subjunctive of* avoir *Past Participle:* plu

POUVOIR

Present	peux, peux, peut, pouvons, pouvez, peuvent
Passé Composé	*Auxiliary:* avoir *Past Participle:* pu
Imperfect	pouvais, pouvais, pouvait, pouvions, pouviez, pouvaient
Future	pourrai, pourras, pourra, pourrons, pourrez, pourront
Subjunctive	puisse, puisses, puisse, puissions, puissiez, puissent
Past Subjunctive	*Auxiliary: present subjunctive of* avoir *Past Participle:* pu

PRENDRE

Present	prends, prends, prend, prenons, prenez, prennent
Commands	prends, prenons, prenez
Passé Composé	*Auxiliary:* avoir *Past Participle:* pris
Imperfect	prenais, prenais, prenait, prenions, preniez, prenaient
Future	prendrai, prendras, prendra, prendrons, prendrez, prendront
Subjunctive	prenne, prennes, prenne, prenions, preniez, prennent
Past Subjunctive	*Auxiliary: present subjunctive of* avoir *Past Participle:* pris

PRODUIRE

Present	produis, produis, produit, produisons, produisez, produisent
Commands	produis, produisons, produisez
Passé Composé	*Auxiliary:* avoir *Past Participle:* produit
Imperfect	produisais, produisais, produisait, produisions, produisiez, produisaient
Future	produirai, produiras, produira, produirons, produirez, produiront
Subjunctive	produise, produises, produise, produisions, produisiez, produisent
Past Subjunctive	*Auxiliary: present subjunctive of* avoir *Past Participle:* produit

RECEVOIR

Present	reçois, reçois, reçoit, recevons, recevez, reçoivent
Commands	reçois, recevons, recevez
Passé Composé	*Auxiliary:* avoir *Past Participle:* reçu
Imperfect	recevais, recevais, recevait, recevions, receviez, recevaient
Future	recevrai, recevras, recevra, recevrons, recevrez, recevront
Subjunctive	reçoive, reçoives, reçoive, recevions, receviez, reçoivent
Past Subjunctive	*Auxiliary: present subjunctive of* avoir *Past Participle:* reçu

RESOUDRE

Present	résous, résous, résout, résolvons, résolvez, résolvent
Commands	résous, résolvons, résolvez
Passé Composé	*Auxiliary:* avoir *Past Participle:* résolu
Imperfect	résolvais, résolvais, résolvait, résolvions, résolviez, résolvaient
Future	résoudrai, résoudras, résoudra, résoudrons, résoudrez, résoudront
Subjunctive	résolve, résolves, résolve, résolvions, résolviez, résolvent
Past Subjunctive	*Auxiliary: present subjunctive of* avoir *Past Participle:* résolu

RIRE

Present	ris, ris, rit, rions, riez, rient
Commands	ris, rions, riez
Passé Composé	*Auxiliary:* avoir *Past Participle:* ri
Imperfect	riais, riais, riait, riions, riiez, riaient
Future	rirai, riras, rira, rirons, rirez, riront
Subjunctive	rie, ries, rie, riions, riiez, rient
Past Subjunctive	*Auxiliary: present subjunctive of* avoir *Past Participle:* ri

SAVOIR

Present	sais, sais, sait, savons, savez, savent
Commands	sache, sachons, sachez
Passé Composé	*Auxiliary:* avoir *Past Participle:* su
Imperfect	savais, savais, savait, savions, saviez, savaient
Future	saurai, sauras, saura, saurons, saurez, sauront
Subjunctive	sache, saches, sache, sachions, sachiez, sachent
Past Subjunctive	*Auxiliary: present subjunctive of* avoir *Past Participle:* su

SORTIR

Present	sors, sors, sort, sortons, sortez, sortent
Commands	sors, sortons, sortez
Passé Composé	*Auxiliary:* être *Past Participle:* sorti
Imperfect	sortais, sortais, sortait, sortions, sortiez, sortaient
Future	sortirai, sortiras, sortira, sortirons, sortirez, sortiront
Subjunctive	sorte, sortes, sorte, sortions, sortiez, sortent
Past Subjunctive	*Auxiliary: present subjunctive of* être *Past Participle:* sorti

SUIVRE

Present	suis, suis, suit, suivons, suivez, suivent
Commands	suis, suivons, suivez
Passé Composé	*Auxiliary:* avoir *Past Participle:* suivi
Imperfect	suivais, suivais, suivait, suivions, suiviez, suivaient
Future	suivrai, suivras, suivra, suivrons, suivrez, suivront
Subjunctive	suive, suives, suive, suivions, suiviez, suivent
Past Subjunctive	*Auxiliary: present subjunctive of* avoir *Past Participle:* suivi

VALOIR

Present	il vaut
Passé Composé	*Auxiliary:* avoir *Past Participle:* valu
Imperfect	il valait
Future	il vaudra

VENIR

Present	viens, viens, vient, venons, venez, viennent
Commands	viens, venons, venez
Passé Composé	*Auxiliary:* être *Past Participle:* venu
Imperfect	venais, venais, venait, venions, veniez, venaient
Future	viendrai, viendras, viendra, viendrons, viendrez, viendront
Subjunctive	vienne, viennes, vienne, venions, veniez, viennent
Past Subjunctive	*Auxiliary: present subjunctive of* être *Past Participle:* venu

VIVRE

Present	vis, vis, vit, vivons, vivez, vivent
Commands	vis, vivons, vivez
Passé Composé	*Auxiliary:* avoir *Past Participle:* vécu
Imperfect	vivais, vivais, vivait, vivions, viviez, vivaient
Future	vivrai, vivras, vivra, vivrons, vivrez, vivront
Subjunctive	vive, vives, vive, vivions, viviez, vivent
Past Subjunctive	*Auxiliary: present subjunctive of* avoir *Past Participle:* vécu

VOIR

Present	vois, vois, voit, voyons, voyez, voient
Commands	vois, voyons, voyez
Passé Composé	*Auxiliary:* avoir *Past Participle:* vu
Imperfect	voyais, voyais, voyait, voyions, voyiez, voyaient
Future	verrai, verras, verra, verrons, verrez, verront
Subjunctive	voie, voies, voie, voyions, voyiez, voient
Past Subjunctive	*Auxiliary: present subjunctive of* avoir *Past Participle:* vu

VOULOIR

Present	veux, veux, veut, voulons, voulez, veulent
Commands	veuille, veuillons, veuillez
Passé Composé	*Auxiliary:* avoir *Past Participle:* voulu
Imperfect	voulais, voulais, voulait, voulions, vouliez, voulaient
Future	voudrai, voudras, voudra, voudrons, voudrez, voudront
Subjunctive	veuille, veuilles, veuille, voulions, vouliez, veuillent
Past Subjunctive	*Auxiliary: present subjunctive of* avoir *Past Participle:* voulu

PRONUNCIATION

Pronunciation exercises are found in the following units.

1 NOUS REVOILA
The rhythm of French   (page 45)

2 APRES L'ECOLE
The vowel sound /ə/   (page 83)

3 AMUSONS-NOUS!
Liaison   (page 121)

5 EN FAMILLE
The French **r**-sound /ʀ/   (page 183)

6 L'ARGENT ET LES PETITS BOULOTS
The sounds /y/, /œ/, /ø/   (page 225)

7 EN PLEINE FORME
The nasals   (page 265)

9 UN DEPAYSE A LYON
Glides with /j/, /w/, and /ɥ/   (page 329)

10 VOYAGE A ARLES
The ghost **h; l** and **gn**   (page 371)

11 BIENTOT L'AVENIR
Pure vowel and consonant sounds   (page 413)

12 VACANCES AU SENEGAL
Review   (page 432)

NUMBERS

CARDINAL

0	zéro	14	quatorze	71	soixante et onze
1	un/une	15	quinze	72	soixante-douze
2	deux	16	seize	80	quatre-vingts
3	trois	17	dix-sept	81	quatre-vingt-un/une
4	quatre	18	dix-huit	90	quatre-vingt-dix
5	cinq	19	dix-neuf	91	quatre-vingt-onze
6	six	20	vingt	100	cent
7	sept	21	vingt et un/une	101	cent un/une
8	huit	22	vingt-deux	200	deux cents
9	neuf	30	trente	201	deux cent un/une
10	dix	40	quarante	1 000	mille
11	onze	50	cinquante	1 001	mille un/une
12	douze	60	soixante	1 920	mille neuf cent vingt
13	treize	70	soixante-dix	2 000	deux mille

ORDINAL

1st	premier, première	1er, 1ère	5th	cinquième	5e	8th	huitième	8e
2nd	deuxième	2e	6th	sixième	6e	9th	neuvième	9e
3rd	troisième	3e	7th	septième	7e	10th	dixième	10e
4th	quatrième	4e						

FRENCH-ENGLISH VOCABULARY

This vocabulary list includes all the active words (new words appearing in basic material, listed in the **Vocabulaire** section of each unit) presented in **Nous, les jeunes.** Also included are words for recognition only (new words, which may be understood from context, appearing in exercises, in optional material, in the Try Your Skills and **A Lire** sections, or in review units.) Omitted are the words in **Premier Contact,** a few close cognates, glossed words, and words explained in the **Savez-vous que… ?** sections.

Active vocabulary that was introduced in **Nouveaux copains** also appears in this list, followed by the roman numeral **I.** The vocabulary presented in **Nous, les jeunes** is followed by the roman numeral **II** and an arabic numeral that refers to the unit in which the word or phrase is introduced. When the arabic numeral is in light type, it indicates vocabulary for recognition only.

Verbs are given in the infinitive. Nouns are always given with a gender marker. If gender is not apparent, however, it is indicated by *m.* (masculine) or *f.* (feminine) following the noun. Irregular plurals are also given, abbreviated *pl.* An asterisk (*) before a word beginning with *h* indicates an aspirate *h.*

A

à *at, to, in, on,* **I**
abandonner *to give up,* **I**
aboyer *to bark,* **II, 6**
absolument *absolutely,* **II, 3**
à cause de *because of,* **II, 9**
accompagner *to accompany,* **II, 3**
un **accord** *agreement,* **II, 11**
accourir *to run up,* **II, 11**
l' **accueil** (m.) *reception, registration desk,* **II, 2**
accueillant, -e *welcoming,* **II, 1**
les **achats** (m.) *purchases,* **II, 2;**
   faire des achats *to go shopping,* **II, 2**
acheter *to buy,* **I**
actif, -ive *active,* **II, 9**
actuellement *currently,* **II, 11**
s' **adapter** *to get used to,* **II, 9**
adieu *farewell, goodbye,* **II, 10**
admirer *to admire,* **I**
adorer *to love,* **I**
une **adresse** *address,* **I**
un **adversaire** *opponent,* **II, 2**
un **aéroport** *airport,* **I**
les **affaires : être dans les affaires** (f.) *to be in business,* **II, 11**
une **affaire de cœur** *love affair,* **II, 5**
une **affiche** *poster,* **I**
âge : Tu as quel âge? *How old are you?* **I**
âgé, -e *elderly,* **II, 11**

agréable *pleasant,* **I**
aider *to help,* **II, 5**
aimer *to love,* **I; aimer mieux** *to prefer, like better,* **I**
l' **air** (m.) *air,* **II, 9; avoir l' air de** *to look like,* **I**
un **album** *album,* **I**
l' **alimentation** (f.) *food,* **II, 7**
aller *to go,* **I; Allez!** *Come on!* **II, 5; Allons-y!** *Let's go!* **I; Comment allez-vous?** *How are you?* **II, 1**
allô *hello (on phone),* **I**
alors *so, well, then,* **I**
alsacien, -ienne *Alsatian,* **I**
amateur *amateur,* **II, 10**
une **ambiance** *atmosphere,* **I**
ambitieux, -euse *ambitious,* **II, 2**
américain, -e *American,* **I**
un(e) **Américain(e)** *American,* **I**
un(e) **ami(e)** *friend,* **I**
amour : une histoire d'amour *love story,* **I**
amoureux, -euse (de) *in love (with),* **II, 5**
un(e) **amoureux, -euse** *lover,* **II, 3**
amusant, -e *fun, amusing,* **II, 3**
s' **amuser** *to have fun,* **II, 10; Je me suis amusé(e).** *I had a good time.* **II, 1; Tu t'es amusé(e)?** *Did you have a good time?* **II, 1**
un **an** *year,* **I**

ancien, -ienne *ancient, old,* **II, 10**
les **anciens** (m.) *old friends,* **II, 1**
l' **anglais** (m.) *English (language),* **I**
l' **angle** (m.) *angle, corner,* **II, 3; grand angle** *wide angle,* **II, 10**
l' **Angleterre** (f.) *England,* **II, 1**
un **animal** (pl. -aux) *animal,* **I**
l' **animateur, -trice** *activity leader,* **II, 2**
année : Bonne année! *Happy New Year!* **I**
un **anniversaire** *anniversary, birthday,* **I**
une **annonce** *announcement, ad,* **II, 2**
antiamaril,-e *anti-yellow fever,* **II, 12**
août (m.) *August,* **I**
un **appartement** *apartment,* **I**
appeler *to call, phone,* **II, 3; (s') appeler** *to call, be named,* **I**
appétit : Bon appétit! *Enjoy your meal!* **I**
applaudir *to applaud,* **II, 4**
apporter *to bring,* **I**
apprécier *to appreciate,* **II, 3**
apprendre *to learn,* **II, 2**
un **apprentissage** *apprenticeship,* **II, 6**
l' **aprèm = l'après-midi,** **I**
après *after,* **I**
l' **après-midi** (m.) *afternoon, in the afternoon,* **I**
un **arbre généalogique** *family tree,* **I**

Arcachon *town south of Bordeaux*, **II, 1**
un **architecte** *architect*, **II, 1**
l' **Ardèche** (f.) *department in southeast France*, **II, 1**
les **arènes** (f.) *arena*, **II, 10**
l' **argent** (m.) *money*, **I**; l' **argent de poche** (m.) *spending money, allowance*, **II, 6**
une **armoire** *wardrobe*, **I**
un **arrêt** *stop, stopover*, **II, 10**
(s') **arrêter** *to stop*, **II, 3**
l' **arrivée** (f.) *arrival*, **I**
arriver *to arrive*, **I**; **arriver à** *to manage*, **II, 2**; **Je n'y arrive pas!** *I can't manage to do it!* **II, 2**; **Ça n'arrive jamais!** *It never happens!* **II, 9**; **Qu'est-ce qui t'arrive?** *What's wrong with you?* **II, 7**
arroser *to water*, **II, 5**
l' **art** (m.) *art*, **I**; **les arts plastiques** *art (class)*, **I**
l' **aspirateur** (m.) *vacuum cleaner*, **I**; **passer l' aspirateur** *to vacuum*, **I**
un **assassin** *murderer*, **I**
assez *rather*, **I**; **assez (de)** *enough*, **I**; **J'en ai assez!** *I'm fed up!* **II, 3**
assister à *to attend*, **II, 3**
assurer *to assure*, **II, 7**
l' **athlétisme** (m.) *track and field*, **I**
attendre *to wait (for)*, **I**
attention : faire attention *to be careful*, **II, 1**; **Fais attention.** *Pay attention.* **II, 2**
une **attraction** *attraction*, **II, 3**
attraper *to catch*, **II, 1**
au contraire *on the contrary*, **II, 1**
les **auditeurs** (m.) *listeners*, **II, 11**
aujourd'hui *today*, **I**
au revoir *goodbye*, **I**
aussi *also, too*, **I**
l' **automne** (m.) *autumn, fall*, **I**; **en automne** *in the fall*, **I**
autre *other*, **I**
autrement *differently*, **II, 11**
l' **Auvergne** (f.) *region in the center of the Massif Central*, **II, 1**
avancer *to advance*, **II, 3**
avant (de) *before*, **I**
avec *with*, **I**
l' **avenir** (m.) *future*, **II, 1**
une **avenue** *avenue*, **I**
avertir *to inform*, **II, 10**
un **avion** *airplane*, **I**
avis : à mon avis *in my opinion*, **I**
un(e) **avocat(e)** *lawyer*, **I**
avoir *to have*, **I**; **avoir l'air (de)** *to look like*, **I**; **avoir... ans** *to be . . . years old*, **I**; **avoir besoin de** *to need*, **I**; **avoir de la chance** *to be lucky*, **II, 1**; **avoir droit à** *to have the right to*, **II, 1**; **avoir envie de** *to feel like*, **I**; **avoir faim** *to be hungry*, **I**; **avoir lieu** *to take place*, **II, 3**; **avoir peur de** *to*

be afraid of, **I**; **Qu'est-ce que tu as?** *What's wrong with you?* **II, 7**; **avoir soif** *to be thirsty*, **I**
avril (m.) *April*, **I**

B

bac(calauréat) *exam taken upon completion of secondary school*, **II, 2**
un **badge** *(slogan) button*, **I**
les **bagages** (m.) *luggage, baggage*, **I**; **aux bagages** *at the baggage claim area*, **I**
une **bague** *ring*, **I**
une **baguette** *long loaf of bread*, **II, 10**
un **bal** *dance*, **II, 3**
une **balade** *walk, stroll*, **I**
se balader *to go for a walk*, **II, AC1**
une **balle** *baseball, tennis ball*, **I**
un **ballon** *inflated ball, balloon*, **I**
banal, -e *banal, ordinary*, **I**
une **banane** *banana*, **II, 7**
une **bande** *group*, **II, 3**
des **bandes dessinées** (f.) *comic strips, comics*, **I**
la **banlieue** *suburbs*, **II, AC3**
une **banque** *bank*, **I**
barbare *barbarian, barbaric*, **II, 10**
la **barbe : C'est la barbe!** *It's boring!* **I**
barber (fam.) *to bore*, **II, 10**
le **base-ball** *baseball*, **I**
la **basilique** *basilica*, **II, 9**
le **basket(-ball)** *basketball*, **I**
des **baskets** (f.) *(high) sneakers*, **I**
la **basse** *bass guitar*, **II, 2**
un(e) **bassiste** *bass player*, **II, 2**
un **bateau** (pl. -x) *boat*, **I**
des **bâtons** (m.) *ski poles*, **I**
une **batte** *bat*, **I**
la **batterie** *set of drums*, **II, 2**
un **batteur** *drummer*, **II, 2**
se battre *to fight with one another*, **II, 11**; **La boum bat son plein.** *The party's in full swing.* **I**
beau, bel, belle, beaux, belles *beautiful*, **I**
beaucoup (de) *many, much, a lot (of)*, **I**
une **bédé** *comic book*, **II, 1**
la **Belgique** *Belgium*, **I**
besoin : avoir besoin de *to need*, **I**
un **best-seller** *best seller*, **II, 11**
bête *dumb, stupid*, **II, 10**
les **bêtises** (f.) *nonsense*, **II, 5**
le **beurre** *butter*, **I**; **le beurre de cacahouètes** *peanut butter*, **I**
une **bibliothèque** *library*, **II, 1**
le **bicross** *dirtbiking*, **I**
la **bicyclette** *bicycle, bicycling*, **II, 1**
bidon : C'est bidon! *It's trash!* **I**
bien *fine, well, nice*, **I**; **bien**

sûr *of course*, **I**; **eh bien** *well*, **I**; **ou bien** *or else*, **I**
bientôt *soon*, **II, 11**
bienvenu, -e : Bienvenue! *Welcome!* **I**; **Soyez le/la bienvenue!** *Welcome!* **I**
un **bijou** *jewel*, **I**; **des bijoux** *jewelry*, **I**
une **bijouterie** *jewelry store*, **I**
le **bilan : faire le bilan** *to assess, take stock of*, **II, 1**
un **billet** *ticket, bill (money)*, **I**
la **biolo(gie)** *biology*, **I**
un **biscuit** *cookie*, **II, 10**
Bises *Love and kisses*, **I**
une **blague** *joke*, **II, 1**
le **blanc** *white*, **I**; **blanc, blanche** *white*, **I**
le **bleu** *blue*, **I**; **bleu, -e** *blue*, **I**
un **blouson** *waist-length jacket*, **I**
le **blues** *blues (music)*, **I**
bof *aw (expression of indifference)*, **I**
boire *to drink*, **II, 7**
le **bois** *wood*, **I**; **en bois** *wooden*, **I**
une **boisson** *drink, beverage*, **I**
une **boîte** *box*, **I**
un **bol** *bowl*, **I**
bon, bonne *good, OK*, **I**; **Il fait bon.** *It's nice weather.* **I**
un **bonbon** *piece of candy*, **I**
une **bonbonne** *bottle of propane gas*, **II, 1**
le **bonheur** *happiness*, **II, 1**
un **bonhomme (de neige)** *snowman*, **II, 3**
bonjour *hello*, **I**
bonsoir *good evening*, **I**
bord : au bord de la mer *at the seashore*, **II, 1**
une **botte** *boot*, **I**
des **boucles d'oreilles** (f.) *earrings*, **II, 10**
bouger *to move, budge*, **II, 3**
une **bougie** *candle*, **I**
une **boulangerie** *bakery*, **I**
un **boulot** (fam.) *job*, **II, 6**
une **boum** *party*, **I**; **La boum bat son plein.** *The party's in full swing.* **I**
boume : Ça boume? *How's it going?* **II, 6**
la **Bourgogne** *Burgundy*, **I**
la **Bourse : jouer à la Bourse** *to play the stock market*, **II, 11**
une **bousculade** *crush*, **II, 1**
une **bouteille** *bottle*, **I**
une **boutique** *boutique, shop*, **I**
un **bowling** *bowling alley*, **I**
un **bracelet** *bracelet*, **I**
branché, -e *in the know, with it*, **II, 2**; **la mode branchée** *the latest style*, **I**
Bravo! *Well done!* **II, 6**
la **Bretagne** *Brittany*, **I**
bricoler *to tinker*, **II, AC2**
brillant, -e *brilliant*, **II, 2**
une **brioche** *brioche*, **I**
le **brocoli** *broccoli*, **II, 7**
bronzé, -e *tanned*, **II, 1**
bronzer *to get a tan*, **II, 1**
le **bruit** *noise*, **II, 3**

brun, -e *brown, brunet, brunette,* I

Bruxelles *Brussels,* I

un **budget** *budget,* II, 6

un **bureau** (pl. **-x**) *desk,* I; le **bureau de change** *currency (money) exchange,* I

un **bus** *bus (public),* I; **en bus** *by bus,* I

un **but** *goal,* II, 11

C

ça *it, that,* I; **Ça ne fait rien.** *That's all right.* I; **Ça va?** *Are things going OK?* I; **Ça va.** *Fine.* I

cacahouètes : le beurre de cacahouètes *peanut butter,* I

un **cadeau** (pl. **-x**) *gift,* I

le **café** *coffee,* I; **le café au lait** *coffee with milk,* I; **un café** *cafe,* I

une **cafeteria** *cafeteria,* I

un **cahier** *notebook,* I

un(e) **caissier, -ière** *cashier,* II, 6

une **calculette** *pocket calculator,* I

le **calme** *stillness,* II, 11

calme *calm,* II, 9

les **calories** (f.) *calories,* II, 11

la **Camargue** *the Rhône delta,* II, 10

la **campagne** *countryside,* I

camper *to camp,* II, 1

le **camping** *camping,* II, 1

le **Canada** *Canada,* I

un **canapé** *couch, sofa,* II, AC3

le **cancer** *cancer,* II, 11

le **canoë** *canoeing,* II, 1

le **canoë-kayak** *kayaking,* II, 1

la **cantine** *cafeteria,* II, 7

la **capitale** *capital,* I

car *because,* II, 10

le **carnaval** *carnival,* II, 3

un **carnet** *booklet (of tickets, stamps, etc.),* II, 9

une **carotte** *carrot,* II, 7

le **carrefour** *crossroads,* II, 9

un **carrousel** *slide carrousel,* II, 10

une **carte** *map, card,* I; **une carte postale** *postcard,* I; **une carte (de vœux)** *greeting card,* I

un **casque** *helmet,* I

casser *to break,* II, 6

une **cassette** *cassette,* I

une **catastrophe** *catastrophe,* I

la **catégorie** *category,* II, 6

une **cathédrale** *cathedral,* I

ce *this, that,* I

célèbre *famous,* I

célibataire *unmarried,* II, 11

celle(-là) (f.) *this/that one, the one,* I

celles(-là) (f.) *these, those, the ones,* I

celui(-là) (m.) *this/that one, the one,* I

une **centaine** *hundred,* II, 6

un **centimètre (cm)** *centimeter,* I

centre : un centre commercial *shopping center, mall,* I; **un centre de loisirs** *vacation camp, resort,* II, 6; **un centre de vacances** *vacation resort, camp,* II, 1

ce que *how,* II, 3; *what,* II, 5

des **céréales** (f.) *cereal,* II, 7

les **cérébraux** (m.) *intellectuals,* II, AC1

certain, -e *certain,* II, 9

certainement *undoubtedly,* II, 7

certains *certain ones,* II, 1

ces *these, those,* I

c'est *he's, it's, this is, that's, these/those are,* I

cet *this, that,* I

cette *this, that,* I

ceux(-là) (m.) *these, those, the ones,* I

chacun : Chacun va de son côté. *Each one goes his separate way.* I

les **chagrins** (m.) *sorrows,* II, AC1

une **chaîne stéréo** *stereo,* I

une **chaise** *chair,* I

une **chambre** *bedroom,* I; **une chambre d'amis** *guest room,* I

les **champignons** (m.) *mushrooms,* II, AC2

le **championnat** *championship,* I

la **chance** *luck,* II, 3

changer *to exchange,* I; *to change,* II, 6

une **chanson** *song,* II, 2

un **chant** *song,* II, 3

chanter *to sing,* I

un **chapeau** *hat,* II, 9; **un chapeau de toile** *canvas hat,* II, 12

chaque *each,* II, 1

un **char** *float,* II, 3

un(e) **chat(te)** *cat,* I

chaud, -e *warm,* I; **Il fait chaud.** *It's warm.* I

une **chaussette** *sock,* I

une **chaussure** *shoe,* I; **des chaussures de ski** *ski boots,* I

un **chef** *chef,* I

le **chemin** *way,* II, 7

une **chemise** *man's shirt,* I

un **chemisier** *woman's tailored shirt,* I

un **chèque** *check,* I; **un chèque de voyage** *traveler's check,* I

cher, chère *expensive,* I

chercher *to look for,* I

le **cheval** *horseback riding,* I; *horse* (pl. **-aux**), II, 10

les **cheveux**(m.) *hair,* I

chez *to/at someone's house,* I; **chez le disquaire** *record shop,* I; **chez le/la fleuriste** *the florist's,* I

un(e) **chien(ne)** *dog,* I

chimique *chemical,* II, 10

la **Chine** *China,* II, 11

le **chocolat** *chocolate, hot chocolate,* I; **un gâteau au**

chocolat *chocolate cake,* I; **une mousse au chocolat** *chocolate mousse,* I

choisir *to choose,* I

le **choix** *choice,* II, 1

le **chômage** *unemployment,* II, 11

une **chose** *thing,* I; **quelque chose** *something,* I

chouette *great,* I

Chut! *Shhh!* II, 10

le **ciel** *sky,* I

le **cinéma** *movie theater, movies,* I

circuler *to circulate,* II, 3

civilisé, -e *civilized,* II, 10

la **clarinette** *clarinet,* II, 2

une **classe** *grade,* I

un **classeur** *loose-leaf notebook,* I

le **classique** *classical music,* I

classique *classical,* I

un **club** *club,* I

le **CNES (Centre national d'études spatiales)** *French center for space research,* II, 11

le **cœur : mal au cœur** *stomach ache, nausea,* II, 3

une **coiffure** *hairdo,* I

col : un col roulé *turtleneck shirt,* I

collectionner *to collect,* I

un **collège** *middle or junior high school,* I

un **collier** *necklace,* I

coloniser *to colonize,* II, 11

un **combat** *fight, battle,* II, 10

combien (de) *how much, how many,* I

comique : un film comique *comedy,* I

comme *like, as,* I; *in the way of,* II, 2; **Comme tu veux.** *If you want.* II, 9

commencer *to start,* I; **commencer par** *to begin with (by),* II, 3

comment *how,* I

un(e) **commerçant(e)** *merchant,* I

communiquer *to communicate,* II, 11

une **compétition** *contest,* II, 3

le **complexe** *complex,* II, 10

un **compliment : Mes compliments pour...** *My compliments on...,* I

comprendre *to understand,* II, 1

un **compte** *bank account,* II, 6; **sur mon compte** *in my account,* II, 6

compter *to count,* II, 6; *to intend,* II, 11

un **concert** *concert,* I

la **concurrence** *competition,* II, 2

un(e) **confident(e)** *confidant,* II, 5

la **confiture** *jam,* I

la **connaissance : faire (la) connaissance** *to get acquainted,* II, 1

connaître *to know, be acquainted with,* I

consacré, -e (à) *devoted (to),* **II, 10**
un **conseil** *advice,* **II, 5**
conseiller *to advise,* **II, 5**
conservé, -e *preserved,* **II, 10**
conserver *to keep, preserve,* **II, 7**
les **consignes** (f.) *orders,* **II, 10**
consoler *to console,* **II, 9**
construit, -e *built,* **II, 11**
contenir *to contain,* **II, 11**
content, -e *happy, glad,* **II, 1**
continuellement *continually,* **II, 3**
continuer *to continue,* **I**
le **contraire** *opposite,* **II, 5**
le **contrôle des passeports**
  passport check, **I**
convaincu : J'en suis convaincu.
  I'm convinced of it. **II, 11**
convenir *to be appropriate, fit,*
  II, 11
un **copain, une copine** *pal, friend,* **I**
le **coquelicot** *poppy (flower),* **II, 9**
le **corps** *body,* **II, 7**
un(e) **correspondant(e)** *pen pal,* **I**
une **corvée** *chore,* **II, AC1**
côté : à côté (de) *next to, next*
  door to, **I; Chacun va de son**
  côté. *Each one goes his*
  separate way. **I**
se coucher *to go to bed,* **II, 7**
coucou *hi,* **II, 3**
une **couleur** *color,* **I**
le **couloir** *hall,* **I**
un **coup de soleil** *sunburn,* **II, 1**
la **cour** *courtyard,* **II, 1**
le **courage** *courage,* **II, 5; Je n'ai**
  pas le courage de... *I don't*
  feel up to..., **II, 10**
courir *to run,* **II, 7; Je cours** *I*
  run, **II, 3**
le **courrier** *mail,* **II, AC3**
un **cours** *course, class,* **I**
une **course de voitures** *auto race,*
  II, 4; la course aux
  armements *arms race,* **II, 11;**
  une course de taureaux
  bullfight, **II, 10**
les **courses** (f.) *shopping,* **II, 5**
court : à court de *short of,* **II, 6**
court, -e *short,* **I**
un(e) **cousin(e)** *cousin,* **I**
coûter *to cost,* **I**
le **couvert** *place setting,* **II, 1**
craquer (fam.) *to be about to*
  collapse, **II, 7**
un **crayon** *pencil,* **I**
créer *to create,* **II, 5**
crevé, -e *exhausted,* **II, 7**
un **cri** *shout,* **II, 3**
criard, -e *loud, garish,* **I**
crier *to shout,* **II, 6**
croire *to believe,* **II, 11; Je**
  crois *I believe,* **II, 3; Tu**
  crois? *Do you think so?* **I**
un **croissant** *croissant,* **I**
une **crosse** *hockey stick,* **I**
la **cuisine** *kitchen,* **I; cooking,* **II, 5**
culturellement *culturally,* **II, 9**
curieux, -euse *curious,* **I**

D

d'abord *first (of all),* **I**
d'accord *OK,* **I; être d'accord**
  to agree, **I**
dames : jouer aux dames *to*
  play checkers, **II, 2**
dangereux, -euse *dangerous,*
  II, 5
dans *in,* **I**
la **danse** *dance,* **II, 2**
danser *to dance,* **I**
Dassault *French aeronautics*
  company, **II, 11**
la **date** *date,* **I**
de *from, of,* **I; de la, de l'**
  some, any, **I**
le **débarras** *storeroom,* **I**
le **début** *beginning,* **II, 7**
un(e) **débutant(e)** *beginner,* **II, 2**
débuter *to begin,* **II, 1**
décapotable *convertible,* **II, AC3**
décembre (m.) *December,* **I**
décider *to decide,* **I**
une **décision** *decision,* **II, 1;**
  prendre une décision *to*
  make a decision, **II, 1**
déclarer *to declare,* **I**
décoré, -e *decorated,* **I**
(se) défendre *to defend*
  (oneself), **II, 10**
un **défilé** *parade,* **II, 3**
dehors *outside,* **II, 11; en**
  dehors de *outside of, beyond,*
  II, 2
déjà *already,* **I**
le **déjeuner** *lunch,* **I; le petit**
  déjeuner *breakfast,* **I**
déjeuner *to have lunch,* **II, 2**
délicieux, -euse *delicious,* **I**
demain *tomorrow,* **I**
demander (à) *to ask,* **I; Vous**
  demandez quel numéro?
  What number are you calling? **I**
démarrer *to start (a car),* **II, 11**
déménager *to move,* **II, 9**
demie : et demie *half past (the*
  hour), **I**
une **demi-heure** *a half-hour,* **I**
démodé, -e *out of style,* **II, 6**
une **dent** *tooth,* **II, 7**
un(e) **dentiste** *dentist,* **I**
le **départ** *departure,* **II, 10**
dépaysé, -e *uprooted,* **II, 9**
se dépêcher *to hurry,* **II, 10;**
  Dépêche-toi! *Hurry!* **II, 5**
dépendre (de) *to depend (on),* **I**
dépenser *to spend,* **II, 6**
dépensier, -ière *spendthrift,* **II, 6**
depuis *for,* **II, 2;** *(ever) since,*
  II, 7; depuis que *since,* **II, 9**
dernier, -ière *last,* **I**
des *some, any,* **I**
descendre *to go down,* **I**
une **descente** *descent,* **II, 3**
désespéré, -e *discouraged,* **II, 6**
un **désir** *desire,* **II, 6**
désolé, -e *sorry,* **I**

dès que *as soon as,* **II, 6**
le **dessert** *dessert,* **I**
un **dessin animé** *cartoon,* **I**
la **détente** *relaxation,* **II, AC2**
détester *to hate,* **I**
deuxième *second,* **I; au**
  deuxième étage *on the*
  second floor, **I**
devant *in front of,* **I**
devoir *to have to, must,* **II, 2**
les **devoirs** (m.) *homework,* **I**
dévoré, -e *devoured, eaten,* **II, 10**
devrais *should,* **II, 7**
une **diapositive** *slide,* **II, 10**
un **dictionnaire** *dictionary,* **I**
différemment *differently,* **II, 11**
différent, -e *different,* **I**
difficile *difficult, hard,* **I**
diffusé, -e *broadcast,* **II, 11**
dimanche (m.) *Sunday,* **I; le**
  dimanche *on Sunday(s),* **I**
diminuer *to decrease,* **II, 5**
le **dîner** *dinner, supper,* **I; l' heure**
  du dîner *dinnertime,* **I**
dîner *to eat dinner,* **I**
dire *to say,* **I; Ça ne me dit**
  rien. *That doesn't appeal to*
  me. **II, 10; Ça te dit... ?** *Do*
  you want to... ? **II, 2; Dis!**
  Say! **I; Qu'est-ce qu'elle a**
  dit? *What did she say?* **II, 6**
directement *directly,* **II, 11**
diriger *to direct,* **II, 11**
une **discothèque** *disco,* **I**
une **discussion** *discussion,* **II, 5**
discuter *to talk,* **I**
disparaître *to disappear,* **II, 11**
disponible *available,* **II, 2**
se disputer *to argue, fight,*
  II, 11
disquaire : chez le disquaire
  record shop, **I**
un **disque** *record,* **I**
distribuer *to distribute,* **II, 6**
le **docteur** *doctor,* **II, 7**
un **dollar** *dollar,* **I**
domestique *domestic,*
  household, **II, 5**
dommage *pity, too bad,* **II, 3;**
  C'est dommage! *That's too*
  bad! **II, 3**
donc *therefore,* **II, 6**
donner *to give,* **I; Ça donne**
  faim. *It makes you hungry.* **I**
dormir *to sleep,* **I**
le **dortoir** *dormitory,* **II, 10**
la **douane** *customs,* **I**
un(e) **douanier, -ière** *customs agent,* **I**
une **douzaine (de)** *dozen,* **I**
douzième *twelfth,* **I**
un **dragueur** *flirt,* **II, 1**
droit *straight,* **II, 2; tout**
  droit *straight ahead,* **I**
le **droit** *right,* **II, 5**
droite : à droite (de) *to the*
  right (of), **I**
drôle *funny,* **I**
drôlement *pretty, very,* **II, 3;**

drôlement bien *extremely well,* I
du = de + le *some, any,* I
la **duchesse** *duchess,* II, 3
dur, -e *hard, difficult,* II, 2
durer *to last,* II, 3
dynamique *dynamic,* II, 6

E

l' **eau** (f.) *water,* I; l' **eau minérale** *mineral water,* I
écarter les bras *to spread one's arms,* II, 1
échange : en échange *in exchange,* II, 6
une **écharpe** *scarf,* I
échecs : jouer aux échecs *to play chess,* II, 2
un **éclair** *eclair,* II, 7
une **école** *school,* I; l' **école maternelle** *pre-school,* II, AC3
économe *economical, thrifty,* II, 6
économiser *to economize,* II, 6
écouter *to listen (to),* I
un **écran** *projection screen,* II, 10
écrit : elle a écrit *she wrote,* II, 6
éducatif, -ive *educational,* II, 10
un **effort** *effort,* II, 2
égal, -e (m. pl. **-aux**) *equal,* II, 3; **Ça m'est égal.** *I don't care.* II, 3
égaler *to equal,* I
s' **égarer** *to get lost,* II, 10
une **église** *church,* I
égoïste *selfish,* I
électrique *electric,* II, 2
élégant, -e *elegant,* I
un(e) **élève** *pupil, student,* I
élever *to raise,* II, 11
elle *she, it,* I
elles *they, them,* I
embêter *to annoy,* II, 6
embrasser *to kiss,* II, 10; **Tout le monde t'embrasse.** *Everyone sends you their love.* II, 9
une **émission** *television program, show,* I
emmener *to take (someone somewhere),* II, 3
une **émotion** *emotion,* II, 3
émouvant, -e *touching,* I
l' **emplacement** (m.) *location,* I
un **emploi** *job,* II, 11; **un emploi du temps** *schedule,* I
un(e) **employé(e)** *employee,* I
emporter *to bring,* I
emprunter (à) *to borrow (from),* II, 6
en *in, by, on, to,* I; **en bas** *down below,* II, 9; **en direct** *on the air,* II, 11; **en plus** *in addition,* II, 3
encore *more, again,* I; **Encore!** *Not again!* I; **encore un(e) another,** I; **encore un peu** *a little more,* I; **pas encore** *not yet,* I

un **endroit** *place,* I
énergique *energetic,* II, 7
énerver *to upset,* II, 6
un **enfant** *child,* I
l' **enfer** (m.) *hell,* II, 6
enfin *in short, finally,* I; *well,* II, 3
enneigé, -e *snow-covered,* II, 3
des **ennuis** (m.) *troubles,* II, 9
s' **ennuyer : Je m'ennuie.** *I get (am) bored.* II, 1; **Je me suis ennuyé(e).** *I got (was) bored.* II, 1; **s'ennuyer à mourir** *to be bored to death,* II, 9
ennuyeux, -euse *boring,* II, 1
énormément *enormously,* II, 1
une **enquête** *inquiry,* II, 2
une **enseigne** *sign,* I
ensemble *together,* I
ensuite *then, next,* I
entendre *to hear,* II, 3; **s'entendre bien (avec)** *to get along well (with),* II, 11
entourer *to surround,* II, 1
un **entraînement** *practice, training,* II, 2
s'entraîner *to train, work out,* II, 7
entre *between,* I
l' **entrée** (f.) *entrance,* I
entrer *to come in, enter,* I
envie : avoir envie (de) *to feel like,* I
envier *to envy,* II, 11
envoyer *to send,* I
l' **épaule** (f.) *shoulder,* II, 2
une **épicerie** *grocery store,* I
une **époque** *epoch, age, era,* II, 10
épuisé, -e *exhausted,* II, 7
équilibré, -e *balanced,* II, 7
l' **équitation** (f.) *horseback riding,* II, 1
un **érable** *maple tree,* II, AC2
une **erreur** *error, wrong number,* I
un **escalator** *escalator,* I
un **escalier** *stairs,* I
l' **espace** (m.) *room, space,* II, 9
l' **espagnol** (m.) *Spanish (language),* I
espérer *to hope,* I
essayer *to try,* II, 2
essentiel, -elle *essential,* II, 7
et *and,* I
un **étage** *floor,* I; **au premier/ deuxième/troisième étage** *on the second/third/fourth floor,* I
une **étagère** *bookcase,* I
était *was,* II, 1
un **étang** *pond,* II, 10
les **Etats-Unis** (m.) *the United States,* I
l' **été** (m.) *summer,* I; **en été** *in the summer,* I
une **étoile** *star,* II, 3
étonnant, -e *surprising,* II, 7
étonnerait : Ça m'étonnerait! *That would surprise me!* II, 11

étranger, -ère *foreign,* II, 6
être *to be,* I; **être en panne** *to be out of order,* II, 11
étroit, -e *narrow, tight,* I
les **études** (f.) *studies,* II, 2
un(e) **étudiant(e)** *student,* I
étudier *to study,* II, 2
l' **Europe** (f.) *Europe,* I
eux *them, they,* I; **chez eux** *at, to their house,* I
évident : C'est évident! *That's obvious!* II, 11
éviter *to avoid,* II, 1
un **examen** *exam,* I
excellent, -e *excellent,* I
excusez-moi *excuse me,* I
un **exercice** *exercise,* II, 7
exister *to exist,* II, 11
expliquer *to explain,* II, 1
exposer *to exhibit,* II, 10
une **exposition** *show, exhibit,* II, 9
exprès *purposely,* II, 3
exprimer *to express,* II, 3
extra(ordinaire) *terrific, great,* I
extravagant, -e *extravagant, wild,* I

F

fabriquer *to make,* II, 11
fabuleux, -euse *fabulous,* II, 3
face : en face (de) *across (from),* I
facile *easy,* I
une **façon** *way,* II, 6
faible *weak,* II, 7
la **faim** *hunger,* II, 11; **avoir faim** *to be hungry,* I; **Ça donne faim.** *It makes you hungry.* I
faire *to do, make,* I; **Fais (Faites) comme chez toi (vous).** *Make yourself at home.* I; **faire (de)** *to take part in sports,* I; **faire demi-tour** *to turn around,* II, 2; **faire du baby-sitting** *to baby-sit,* I; **faire du lèche-vitrines** *to go window-shopping,* I; **faire l'idiot** *to act stupid,* I; **faire de la photo** *to take pictures,* I; **faire des rencontres** *to meet,* I; **faire son marché** *to do one's grocery shopping,* II, 11; **Ça fait joli.** *That looks pretty.* I; **Ça ne fait rien.** *That's all right.* I; **Il fait bon.** *It's nice weather.* I; **Il fait chaud/frais/ froid.** *It's warm/cool/cold.* I; **Il fait dix.** *It's ten (degrees).* I; **Il fait moins dix.** *It's ten below (zero).* I; **Il fait quel temps?** *What's the weather like?* I; **Il fait quelle température?** *What's the temperature?* I; **(Ne) t'en fais pas!** *Don't worry!* II, 9
une **famille** *family,* I; **en famille** *with one's family,* I
un(e) **fana(tique)** *fan,* II, 3

fantastique *fantastic*, **II, 3**
un **fantôme** *ghost*, **II, 3**
fascinant, -e *fascinating*, **II, 9**
un **fast-food** *fast-food restaurant*, **II, 6**
fatigant, -e *tiring*, **II, 9**
fatigué, -e *tired*, **I**
faut : il faut *it is necessary*, **I; il me/te faut** *I/you need*, **I**
Félicitations! *Congratulations!* **II, 6**
Féministe! *Feminist!* **II, 5**
une **femme** *wife, woman*, **I**
une **fenêtre** *window*, **I**
une **ferme** *farm*, **II, 6**
fermer *to close*, **I**
une **fête** *party, holiday, saint's day*, **I; Bonne fête!** *Happy holiday! (Happy saint's day!)* **I**
fêter *to celebrate*, **II, 11**
un **feu d'artifice** *fireworks*, **II, 3**
une **feuille** *sheet of paper*, **I**
un **feuilleton** *soap opera*, **I**
février (m.) *February*, **I**
fier, fière *proud*, **II, 11**
un **filet** *net*, **I**
une **fille** *girl, daughter*, **I**
un **film** *movie, film*, **I; un film comique** *comedy*, **I; un film d'horreur** *horror movie*, **I; un film policier** *detective film, mystery*, **I; un film de science-fiction** *science-fiction movie*, **I; un film vidéo** *videocassette*, **I**
un **fils** *son*, **I**
la **fin** *end*, **II, 1**
la **finale** *final game, finals*, **I**
finir *to finish, end*, **I**
fixer *to set*, **II, 10**
un **flash** *flash*, **II, 10**
une **fleur** *flower*, **I**
fleuriste : chez le/la fleuriste *the florist's*, **I**
un **fleuve** *river*, **I**
un **flic** (slang) *cop*, **II, AC3**
la **flûte** *flute*, **II, 2**
une **fois** *one time, once*, **I; à la fois** *at the same time*, **I**
le **folk** *folk music*, **I**
un(e) **fonceur, -euse** *bold, courageous person*, **II, 3**
fonctionner *to function, work*, **II, 3**
fond : au fond de *at the end of*, **I**
le **foot(ball)** *soccer*, **I**
se **forcer** *to force oneself*, **II, 7**
la **forme : en (pleine) forme** *in (great) shape*, **II, 1; être en forme** *to be in good shape*, **II, 3**
former *to form*, **II, 2**
formidable *great*, **II, 3**
un **fort** *strong point*, **II, 1**
fort *loudly*, **II, 2; plus fort** *louder*, **II, 2**
fort, -e *strong*, **II, 3**
fortifiant, -e *fortifying*, **II, 7**

une **foule** *crowd*, **II, 3**
une **fourmi** *ant*, **II, 6**
frais, fraîche *cool*, **I; Il fait frais.** *It's cool.* **I**
un **franc (F)** *franc*, **I**
le **français** *French (language)*, **I**
français, -e *French*, **I**
un(e) **Français(e)** *French person*, **I**
la **France** *France*, **I**
un **frère** *brother*, **I**
le **fric** (slang) *money*, **II, 3**
un **frigo** *fridge*, **I**
des **frites** (f.) *French fries*, **I**
le **froid** *cold (weather)*, **II, 3**
froid, -e *cold*, **I; Il fait froid.** *It's cold.* **I**
le **fromage** *cheese*, **I**
le **fruit** *fruit*, **I; le jus de fruit** *fruit juice*, **I**
fumer *to smoke*, **II, 5**
un **funiculaire** *cable car*, **II, 9**
furieux, -euse *furious*, **II, 1**

G

gagner *to earn, win*, **II, 1**
gai, -e *gay, happy*, **II, 3**
une **gamelle** *mess kit*, **II, 1**
un **gant** *(baseball) glove*, **I**
le **garage** *garage*, **II, 2**
garantir *to guarantee*, **II, 7**
un **garçon** *boy*, **I**
garder *to guard*, **I; to take care of*, **II, 5; to keep*, **II, 6; garder la forme** *to keep in shape*, **I**
la **gare** *railroad station*, **I**
un **gâteau** (pl. **-x**) *cake*, **I; un gâteau au chocolat** *chocolate cake*, **I**
gauche : à gauche (de) *to the left (of)*, **I**
géant, -e *giant*, **II, 11**
gelé, -e *frozen*, **II, 3**
la **gendarmerie** *police station*, **I**
général, -e *general*, **II, 9**
généreux, -euse *generous*, **I**
Genève *Geneva*, **I**
génial, -e *fantastic, great*, **I**
un **genre** *kind*, **I**
les **gens** (m.) *people*, **I**
gentil, gentille *nice*, **I**
la **géo(graphie)** *geography*, **I**
un **gilet de sauvetage** *life jacket*, **II, 1**
la **glace** *ice cream*, **I; ice, mirror*, **II, 3**
un **gladiateur** *gladiator*, **II, 10**
une **gomme** *eraser*, **I**
le **goût** *taste*, **I**
le **goûter** *afternoon snack*, **I**
grâce : grâce à eux *thanks to them*, **II, 11**
un **gramme (g)** *gram*, **I**
grand, -e *big, large*, **I**
une **grand-mère** *grandmother*, **I**
un **grand-père** *grandfather*, **I**
les **grands-parents** (m.) *grandparents*, **I**

grave *serious, important*, **II, 11**
une **grève** *strike*, **II, 9; une grève des transports en commun** *public transportation strike*, **II, 9**
griffer *to claw, scratch*, **II, 6**
grimace : faire des grimaces (f.) *to make a (funny) face*, **II, 10**
gris, -e *gray*, **I**
gros, grosse *big, thick*, **I**
guérir *to cure*, **II, 11**
la **guerre** *war*, **II, 11**
un **guide** *guide, guidebook*, **I; un guide touristique** *tour guide*, **I**
une **guitare** *guitar*, **I**
la **gym(nastique)** *gym, P.E.*, **I**

H

habiller *to dress*, **II, 3**
habiter *to live (in), reside*, **I**
une **habitude** *habit*, **II, 7; d' habitude** *usually*, **I**
habitué, -e *used to, accustomed*, **II, 7**
handicapé, -e *handicapped*, **II, 11**
un **haricot vert** *string bean*, **II, 7**
haut, -e *high*, **II, 2; en haut de** *at the top of*, **I**
hein *huh?, is it?, right?* **I**
hélas *alas*, **II, 2**
hésiter *to hesitate*, **II, 5**
une **heure (h)** *hour, time*, **I; à l'heure** *on time*, **II, 10; à quelle heure** *what time*, **I; Il est quelle heure?** *What time is it?* **I; Il est... heure(s).** *It's ...o'clock.* **I; l' heure du dîner** *dinnertime*, **I; tout à l'heure** *in a minute*, **I**
heureusement *luckily, fortunately*, **I**
heureux, -euse *happy*, **I**
hier *yesterday*, **I**
l' **histoire** (f.) *history*, **I; une histoire d'amour** *love story*, **I**
l' **hiver** (m.) *winter*, **I; en hiver** *in the winter*, **I**
le **hockey** *hockey*, **I**
un **homme** *man*, **I**
un **hôpital** (pl. **-aux**.) *hospital*, **I**
un **horaire** *schedule, timetable*, **I**
horreur : un film d'horreur *horror movie*, **I**
horrible *horrible*, **II, 1**
hors de *outside of*, **II, 2**
un **hors-d'œuvre** (pl. **hors-d'œuvre**) *hors d'œuvre*, **I**
un **hôtel** *hotel*, **I**

I

ici *here*, **I**
un **idéal** *ideal*, **II, 11**
idéal, -e *ideal*, **II, 9**
une **idée** *idea*, **I; se faire une idée de** *to get a feel for*, **II, 9**

idiot, -e *stupid*, I; **faire l'idiot** *to act stupid*, I
il *he, it*, I
une **île** *island*, II, 11
illustrer *to illustrate*, II, 10
ils *they*, I
il y a *there is, there are*, I; **Il y a du soleil/vent.** *It's sunny/windy.* I; **Qu'est-ce qu'il y a à la télé?** *What's on TV?* I
imaginer *to imagine*, II, 9
immense *immense, huge*, I
un **immeuble** *apartment house*, I
immortel, -elle *immortal*, II, 11
un **imperméable** *raincoat*, I
l' **important** (m.) *important thing*, II, 6
impossible *impossible*, I
impressionnant, -e *impressive*, I
incompatible *incompatible*, II, 6
incompréhensible *incompréhensible*, II, 3
l' **inconnu(e)** *unknown*, II, 11
l' **Inde** (f.) *India*, II, 11
l' **indépendance** (f.) *independence*, II, 6
indépendant, -e *independent*, II, 6
indispensable *essential, indispensable*, II, 11
inépuisable *inexhaustible*, II, 1
infect, -e *disgusting, rotten*, II, 7
un(e) **infirmier, -ière** *nurse*, I
les **informations** (f.) *news*, I
l' **informatique** (f.) *computer science*, I
un **ingénieur** *engineer*, I
injuste *unfair, unjust*, II, 5
inquiet, -ète *worried*, II, 6
s'inquiéter *to worry*, II, 7; **Ne t'inquiète pas.** *Don't worry.* II, 1
inscrit, -e *enrolled*, II, 2
un **instant** *instant, moment*, II, 10
un **instrument** *instrument*, II, 2
intensément *intensely*, II, 3
interdit *forbidden*, II, 10
intéresser *to interest*, II, 6; **Ça t'intéresse de... ?** *Are you interested in... ?* II, 2
intérêt : avoir intérêt à *to be in one's interest to*, II, 1
une **interro(gation)** *quiz*, I
interroger *to question*, II, 11
une **interview** *interview*, I
inutile *useless*, II, 1
inventer *to invent*, II, 10
une **invitation** *invitation*, I
inviter *to invite*, I
un **itinéraire** *itinerary, route*, II, 11

J

jamais *never*, II, 6
la **jambe** *leg*, II, 2
le **jambon** *ham*, I
janvier (m.) *January*, I
un **jardin** *garden*, I; **un jardin anglais** *informal garden*, I

le **jaune** *yellow*, I; **jaune** *yellow*, I
le **jazz** *jazz*, I
je *I*, I
un **jean** *jeans*, I
un **jeu** (pl. -x) *game, game show*, I; **les Jeux Olympiques** *Olympic Games, Olympics*, I
jeudi (m.) *Thursday*, I; **le jeudi** *on Thursday(s)*, I
jeune *young*, I; **les jeunes** (m.) *young people, the youth*, I; **la Maison des Jeunes** *Youth Recreation Center*, I
des **joggers** (m.) *running shoes*, I
le **jogging** *jogging*, I
la **joie** *joy*, II, 3
joli, -e *pretty, attractive*, I
jouer *to play*, I; **jouer à** *to play (a game)*, I; **jouer au baby-foot** *to play table soccer*, I; **jouer de** *to play (a musical instrument)*, I
un **jour** *day*, I; **tous les jours** *every day*, I
un **journal** (pl. -aux) *diary*, I; *newspaper*, II, 1
une **journaliste** *reporter*, I
une **journée** *day*, II, 1; **toute la journée** *all day long*, II, 2
joyeux, -euse *joyous, happy*, II, 3; **Joyeux anniversaire!** *Happy birthday!* I; **Joyeux Noël!** *Merry Christmas!* I; **Joyeuse Pâque!** *Happy Passover!* I; **Joyeuses Pâques!** *Happy Easter!* I
le **judo** *judo*, II, 2
juillet (m.) *July*, I
juin (m.) *June*, I
les **jumelles** (f.) *binoculars*, II, 12
une **jupe** *skirt*, I
le **jus** *juice*, I; **le jus de fruit** *fruit juice*, I
jusqu'à *until*, II, 1
juste *right*, I; **juste là** *right there*, I; *just, only*, II, 6
justement *exactly*, II, 1; *as a matter of fact*, II, 2

K

un **kilo (kg)** *kilo(gram)*, I
un **kilomètre** *kilometer*, I

L

la *the*, I
la *it, her*, II, 5
là *there, here*, I; **juste là** *right there*, I
là-bas *over there*, I
lâcher *to let go, release*, II, 7
là-haut *up there*, II, 9
laisser *to leave*, I
le **lait** *milk*, I
une **lampe** *lamp*, I
un **lapin** *rabbit*, II, 9
large *wide, loose*, I

le **laser** *laser*, II, 11
laver *to wash*, II, 5
le *the*, I
le *it, him*, II, 5
lèche-vitrines : faire du lèche-vitrines *to go window shopping*, I
un **légume** *vegetable*, I
le **long de** *along*, II, 3
le **lendemain** *the next day*, II, 5
lentement *slowly*, II, 3
les *the*, I
les *them*, II, 5
leur *(to or for) them*, I
leur, leurs *their*, I
se lever *to get up*, II, 7
un(e) **libraire** *bookseller*, I
une **librairie** *bookstore*, I
libre *free, unoccupied*, I
la **limonade** *lemon soda*, I
lire *to read*, I; **Je lis.** *I'm reading.* II, 5
une **liste** *list*, I
un **lit** *bed*, I
un **litre** *liter*, I
le **living** *living room*, I
un **livre** *book*, I
un **local** *place*, II, 2
un **logement** *housing*, II, 9
loin *far (off)*, II, 1; **loin (de)** *far (from)*, II, 11
lointain, -e *faraway, distant*, II, 10
les **loisirs** (m.) *free time*, II, 11
long, longue *long*, II, 1
longtemps *a long time*, II, 2; **Ça fait longtemps que je ne t'ai pas vu(e)!** *It's been a long time since I've seen you.* II, 9; **Il y a si longtemps!** *It's been such a long time!* II, 9
louer *to rent*, II, 1
lui *(to or for) him/her*, I
lundi (m.) *Monday*, I; **le lundi** *on Monday(s)*, I
un **lycée** *high school*, I
un(e) **lycéen(ne)** *high school student*, I
lyonnais, -e *from Lyon*, II, 9
un(e) **Lyonnais(e)** *person who lives in Lyon*, II, 9

M

ma *my*, I
Macho! *Male chauvinist!* II, 5
madame (Mme) *Mrs., madam, ma'am*, I
mademoiselle (Mlle) *miss*, I
un **magasin** *store*, I; **un grand magasin** *department store*, I
un **magazine** *magazine*, I
un **magnétoscope** *videocassette recorder, VCR*, I
magnifique *magnificent*, I
mai (m.) *May*, I

un **maillot de bain** *bathing suit*, I
la **main** *hand*, II, 2
maintenant *now*, I
la **mairie** *town hall*, I
mais *but*, I; **mais non** *of course not*, I
une **maison** *house, home*, I; **la Maison des Jeunes (MJC)** *Youth Recreation Center*, I
le **mal : avoir le mal du pays** *to be homesick*, II, 9; **avoir du mal à** *to have difficulty*, II, 7; **avoir mal à** *to hurt, ache*, II, 7
mal *poorly, badly*, II, 1; **pas mal** *not bad*, I
malade *sick*, II, 1
les **maladies** (f.) *diseases*, II, 11
malheureusement *unfortunately*, II, 3
malin, maligne *clever, smart*, I
maman *Mom*, I
manger *to eat*, I
une **manifestation** *show, demonstration*, II, 10
le **manque de distractions** *lack of amusement*, II, 9
manquer *to miss*, II, 10; **manquer (de)** *to lack*, II, 7; **... me manque** *I miss . . .*, II, 9
un **manteau** (pl. **-x**) *coat*, I
la **marche** *walking*, II, 9
marcher *to walk*, I; *to get started, function*, II, 2; **Ça marche?** *Is it going well?* II, 6
mardi (m.) *Tuesday*, I; **le mardi** *on Tuesday(s)*, I
un **mari** *husband*, I
le **mariage : l'anniversaire** (m.) **de mariage** *wedding anniversary*, I
marié, -e *married*, II, 11
se marier (avec) *to get married (to)*, II, 11
une **maroquinerie** *leather-goods shop*, I
marre : J'en ai marre! *I'm sick of it!* II, AC3
le **marron** *brown*, I; **marron** *brown*, I
mars (m.) *March*, I
un **match** (pl. **-es**) *game*, I; **un match de foot** *soccer game*, I
un **matelas de mousse** *foam mattress*, II, 1
les **maths** (**mathématiques**) (f.) *math*, I
une **matière** *school subject*, II, 1; **la matière plastique** *plastic*, II, 10
le **matin** *morning, in the morning*, I
matinée : faire la grasse matinée *to sleep late*, II, 7
mauvais, -e *bad*, I
méchant, -e *mean*, I
un **médecin** *doctor*, I
un **médicament** *medicine*, I
meilleur, -e *best*, I; *better*, II, 7; **Meilleurs vœux (souhaits)!** *Best wishes!* I

un **membre** *member*, I
même *even, same*, I
une **mémoire** *memory*, I; **un trou de mémoire** *memory lapse*, I; **les mémoires** (m.) *memoirs*, II, 11
le **ménage** *housework*, II, 5
une **menthe à l'eau** *mint-flavored water*, II, AC3
la **mer** *sea*, I
merci *thank you, thanks*, I
mercredi (m.) *Wednesday*, I; **le mercredi** *on Wednesday(s)*, I
une **mère** *mother*, I
merveilleux, -euse *marvelous*, II, 1
mes *my*, I
une **mesure** *measure*, II, 7
mesurer *to measure*, I
un **métier** *trade, craft*, II, 6
un **mètre** (m.) *meter*, I
le **métro** *subway*, I; **en métro** *by subway*, I
mettre *to put (on), wear*, I
miauler *to meow*, II, 6
midi (m.) *noon*, I
mieux *better*, I; **aimer mieux** *to prefer, like better*, I
mignon, -onne *cute*, I
le **milieu** *environment*, II, 5
un **millier** *about a thousand*, II, 3
des **millions** (m.) *millions*, II, 11
mine : avoir mauvaise mine *to look sick*, II, 7
un **minimum** *minimum*, II, 6
minuit (m.) *midnight*, I
mis(e) à mort *put to death*, II, 10
la **mise à mort** *killing*, II, 10
une **mob(ylette)** *moped*, I; **en mobylette** *by moped*, I
la **mode** *style*, I; **à la mode** *stylish*, I; **la mode branchée** *the latest style*, I; **la mode rétro** *the style of the Fifties*, I; **la mode sport** *the sporty style/look*, I
moderne *modern*, II, 9
moi *me*, I; **moi aussi** *me too*, II, 1; **moi non plus** *neither do I*, II, 1
moins *minus*, I; **Il fait moins dix.** *It's ten degrees below (zero).* I; **au moins** *at least*, II, 2; **moins de** *fewer, less*, II, 9
un **mois** *month*, I
la **moitié** *half*, II, 6
mon *my*, I
le **monde** *world*, II, 11; **tout le monde** *everybody*, I
monsieur (M.) *Mr., sir*, I
la **montagne** *mountain*, I; **à la montagne** *in the mountains*, I; **les montagnes russes** (f.) *roller coaster*, II, 3
monter *to take up*, I; *to assemble, organize*, II, 2
une **montre** *watch*, I

Montréal *Montreal*, I
montrer *to show*, I
un **monument** *monument*, I
un **morceau** (pl. **-x**) *number, piece*, I
mort, -e *dead*, II, 7
mot : un petit mot *note*, I; **un mot de remerciements** *thank-you note*, I
le **moteur** *motor*, II, 11
une **moto** *motorcycle*, I; **en moto** *by motorcycle*, I
mouais (expression of disinterest) *Who cares?* I
un **mouchoir** *handkerchief*, I
une **mousse** *mousse*, I; **une mousse au chocolat** *chocolate mousse*, I
un **moyen** *means*, II, 6
moyen, moyenne *average*, II, 1
la **musculation** *body building*, II, 2
un **musée** *museum*, I
un(e) **musicien, -ienne** *musician*, II, 2
la **musique** *music*, I
des **myrtilles** (f.) *blueberries*, II, 6

N

nager *to swim*, I
une **nappe** *tablecloth*, II, 10
natal, -e *native*, II, 12
la **natation** *swimming*, I
la **nature** *nature*, II, 9
naturel, -elle *natural*, II, 10
un **navet : C'est un navet!** *It's a dud!* I
ne : ne... pas *not*, I
nécessaire *necessary*, II, 11
neiger *to snow*, I; **Il neige.** *It's snowing.* I
neuf : Quoi de neuf? *What's new?* II, 9
un **neveu** (pl. **-x**) *nephew*, II, 6
un **niveau** *level*, II, 2
Noël : Joyeux Noël! *Merry Christmas!* I
le **noir** *black*, I; **noir, -e** *black*, I
un **nom** *name*, I
nombreux, -euse *numerous*, II, 11
non *no*, I; **non?** *isn't it?* I; **mais non** *of course not*, I
normal, -e *normal*, II, 5
nos *our*, I
la **note** *grade*, II, 1
notre *our*, I
se nourrir *to feed, nourish*, II, 7
nourrissant, -e *nourishing*, II, 7
nouveau, nouvel, nouvelle, nouveaux, nouvelles *new*, I
des **nouvelles** (f.) *news*, II, 6
novembre (m.) *November*, I
un **nuage** *cloud*, I
nul, nulle *hopeless, useless*, II, 1
un **numéro** *number*, I
nutritif, -ive *nutritive*, II, 11

O

un **objectif** *lens,* **II, 10**
les **objets trouvés** *lost and found,* **I**
une **obligation** *obligation,* **II, 5**
obligé, -e *obliged,* **II, 9**
observer *to observe,* **II, 2**
une **occasion** *opportunity,* **II, 6;**
avoir l'occasion de *to have the opportunity,* **II, 9**
occupé, -e *busy,* **I**
s' **occuper de** *to take charge of,* **II, 7**
octobre (m.) *October,* **I**
l' **odeur** (f.) *odor,* **II, 6**
un **œuf** *egg,* **I**
l' **Office de tourisme** (m.) *Tourist Office,* **I**
offrir *to offer, give,* **I**
un **oiseau** (pl. **-x**) *bird,* **II, 9**
une **omelette** *omelette,* **I**
on *one, we, you, they, people in general,* **I**
un **oncle** *uncle,* **I**
un **opéra** *opera,* **II, 10**
optimiste *optimistic,* **II, 11**
un **orage** *thunderstorm,* **I**
l' **orange** (m.) *orange (color),* **I;**
orange *orange,* **I; une orange** *orange,* **II, 7**
un **orchestre** *orchestra,* **II, 3**
un **ordinateur** *computer,* **I**
organiser *to organize, arrange,* **I**
original, -e (m. pl. **-aux**) *original,* **I**
oser *to dare,* **II, 5**
ou *or,* **I; ou bien** *or else,* **I**
où *where,* **I**
oublier *to forget,* **I**
oui *yes,* **I**
un **ouragan** *hurricane,* **I**
ouvert, -e *open,* **II, 3**
un(e) **ouvrier, -ière** *factory worker, blue collar worker,* **I**
ouvrir *to open,* **I**

P

le **Pacifique** *Pacific,* **II, 11**
le **pain** *bread,* **I**
pair : travailler au pair *to work as a mother's helper,* **II, 6**
une **paire** *pair,* **I**
un **pamplemousse** *grapefruit,* **II, 7**
un **panier** *basket,* **II, 10**
un **pantalon** *pants, slacks,* **I**
papa *Dad,* **I**
une **papeterie** *stationery store,* **I**
Pâque : Joyeuse Pâque! *Happy Passover!* **I**
Pâques : Joyeuses Pâques! *Happy Easter!* **I**
par *by, per,* **I; une fois par semaine** *once a week,* **I**
paraît : il paraît (que) *it seems (that),* **II, 9**
un **parapluie** *umbrella ,* **I**
un **parc d'attractions** *amusement park,* **II, 3**

parce que *because,* **I**
pardon *excuse me,* **I**
pareil, pareille *similar,* **II, 1; such,* **II, 10**
les **parents** (m.) *parents,* **I**
paresseux, -euse *lazy,* **I**
parfait, -e *perfect,* **I**
parfaitement *perfectly,* **II, 9**
parfois *sometimes,* **II, 10**
le **parfum** *perfume,* **I**
une **parfumerie** *perfume shop,* **I**
parler *to speak, talk,* **I; Tu parles!** (fam.) *You've got to be kidding!* **II, 10**
parmi *among,* **II, 2**
la **parole** *word,* **II, 11; les paroles** *lyrics (of song),* **II, 3**
participer *to take part, participate,* **II, 5**
une **partie** *game,* **II, 11; faire partie de** *to belong to,* **II, 6**
partir *to leave,* **I; à partir de from … on(ward),* **II, 7**
partout *everywhere,* **II, 7**
pas *not,* **I; pas cher** *inexpensive,* **I; pas mal** *not bad,* **I; pas le pied, pas terrible** *not so great,* **I; pas de problèmes** *no problem,* **I; pas encore** *not yet,* **I**
le **passé** *past,* **II, 10**
passé, -e *last,* **II, 1**
un **passeport** *passport,* **I**
passer *to go by/through, spend (time), be playing (a movie),* **I; to take (a test),* **II, 2; passer sur** *to go up on,* **I; passer l'aspirateur** *to vacuum,* **I**
un **passe-temps** *pastime,* **I**
une **passion** *passion,* **I**
passionnant, -e *exciting,* **II, 1**
passionné, -e (de) *enthusiastic (about),* **II, 3**
le **pâté** *pâté,* **I**
les **pâtes** (f.) *pasta,* **II, 7**
patient, -e *patient,* **II, 6**
le **patin à glace** *ice-skating,* **I; des patins** *skates* **I**
une **patinoire** *skating rink,* **I**
une **pâtisserie** *pastry shop,* **I**
pauvre *poor,* **II, 7**
un **pavillon** *house in the suburbs,* **II, AC3**
payé *paid,* **II, 6**
payer *to pay,* **II, 6**
un **pays** *country,* **II, 6**
la **pêche** *fishing,* **II, 1**
un **peintre** *painter,* **I**
la **peinture** *painting,* **II, 2; une peinture** *painting,* **II, 10**
une **pellicule** *film (for camera),* **II, 10**
la **pelouse** *lawn,* **II, 5**
pendant *during,* **I**
une **penderie** *closet,* **I**
penser *to think,* **I; Qu'est-ce que tu en penses?** *What do you think of that?* **I**
perdre *to lose,* **I**

un **père** *father,* **I**
la **permission** *permission,* **II, 2**
un **personnage** *character,* **II, 1**
une **personne** *person,* **II, 6**
persuader *to persuade,* **II, 2**
peser *to weigh,* **II, 7**
un **pesticide** *pesticide,* **II, 10**
petit, -e *little, small,* **II, 1; un peu (de)** *a little,* **I; encore un peu** *a little more,* **I**
peu *little, not much,* **II, 1; un peu (de)** *a little,* **I; encore un peu** *a little more,* **I**
peur : avoir peur de *to be afraid of,* **I**
peut-être *maybe,* **I**
une **pharmacie** *drugstore,* **I**
un(e) **pharmacien(ne)** *pharmacist,* **II, 7**
la **philatélie** *stamp collecting,* **II, 2**
la **photo (graphie)** *photography,* **I; faire de la photo** *to take pictures,* **I; une photo** *photo, picture,* **I**
un(e) **photographe** *photographer,* **I**
la **physique** *physics,* **I**
le **piano** *piano,* **II, 2**
une **pièce** *room,* **I; une pièce de théâtre** *play,* **II, 2**
un **pied** *foot,* **I; Il joue comme un pied!** *He plays like an idiot!* **I; à pied** *on foot,* **I; C'est le pied!** *It's fun!* **I; pas le pied** *not so great,* **I**
une **pierre** *stone,* **I; en pierre** *(made) of stone,* **I**
le **pilotage automatique** *automatic piloting,* **II, 11**
un **pilote** *pilot,* **II, 11; driver,* **II, 4**
piloter *to pilot,* **II, 11**
des **pilules** (f.) *pills,* **II, 11**
le **ping-pong** *ping pong,* **II, 1**
un **pique-nique** *picnic,* **II, 10**
pique-niquer *to picnic,* **II, 10**
une **piscine** *swimming pool,* **I**
une **place** *square,* **I**
une **plage** *beach,* **I**
se **plaindre** *to complain,* **II, 9**
plaire : s'il vous plaît *please,* **I; Ça te plaît?** *Do you like it?* **II, 3; Ça te plairait de…?** *Would it please you to…?* **II, 2; Ça t'a plu?** *Did you like it?* **II, 1; Ça m'a plu.** *I liked it.* **II, 1; Tu vas te plaire ici.** *You're going to like it here.* **II, 9**
plaisanter *to joke,* **I**
plaisir : avec plaisir *with pleasure,* **I; faire plaisir à** *to please,* **II, 3**
un **plan** *map (of a city),* **I**
la **planche à voile** *windsurfing,* **I**
une **planète** *planet,* **II, 11**
un **plat** *dish (part of a meal),* **II, 3**
plein, -e *full,* **I; plein (de)** *a lot (of),* **I**
pleurer *to cry,* **II, 9**
pleuvoir *to rain,* **I; Il pleut.** *It's raining.* **I; Il a plu.** *It rained.* **II, 1**

la **pluie** *rain,* **II, 9**
une **plume** *pen,* **II, 3**
plus *plus, more, most,* **I; au plus** *at most,* **I; en plus** *too,* **I; ne... plus** *not ...anymore,* **I; le plus simple** *the simplest thing,* **I; plus tard** *later (on),* **I**
plusieurs *several,* **I**
plutôt *more (of), rather, instead,* **I**
pointu, -e *pointed,* **I**
la **pointure** *size (shoes),* **I**
une **poire** *pear,* **II, 7**
le **poisson** *fish,* **I**
policier, -ière *detective,* **I**
polluer *to pollute,* **II, 10**
la **pollution** *pollution,* **II, 9**
un **polo** *polo shirt,* **I**
une **pomme** *apple,* **II, 7**
une **pomme de terre** *potato,* **II, 7**
une **pompe** *push-up,* **II, 7**
un **port de plaisance** *marina,* **I**
une **porte** *gate, door,* **I**
un **portefeuille** *wallet,* **I**
porter *to wear,* **I**
les **portières** (f.) *doors (car),* **II, 11**
poser *to ask,* **II, 11**
la **possibilité** *possibility,* **II, 1**
la **poste** *post office,* **I**
un **poster** *poster,* **I**
la **poterie** *pottery,* **II, 2**
la **poubelle** *garbage can,* **II, 5**
un **pouce** *inch,* **I**
une **poule** *chicken,* **II, 9**
le **poulet** *chicken,* **I**
pour *for, in order to,* **I**
pourquoi *why,* **I**
pouvoir *to be able to, can,* **I; Je n'en peux plus!** *I can't continue!* **II, 7**
pratique *practical,* **I**
pratiquer *to take part in,* **II, 2**
se précipiter *to dash, rush,* **II, 11**
une **préférence** *preference,* **II, 3**
préférer *to prefer,* **I**
premier, -ière : au premier étage *on the second floor,* **I**
prendre *to take, have (to eat or drink),* **I**
préparer *to prepare, make,* **I**
près (de) *near,* **I**
presque *almost,* **I**
pressé, -e *in a hurry,* **II, 10**
prêt, -e *ready,* **I**
prêter *to lend,* **II, 6**
principal, -e (m. pl. **-aux**) *main,* **I**
le **printemps** *spring,* **I; au printemps** *in the spring,* **I**
pris, -e *busy, occupied,* **II, 5**
une **prise** *hold,* **II, 2**
probablement *probably,* **II, 10**
un **problème** *problem,* **I; pas de problèmes** *no problems,* **I**
prochain, -e *next,* **II, 1**
produire *to produce,* **II, 10**
un **prof(esseur)** *teacher,* **I**

une **profession** *occupation,* **I**
profiter (de) *to take advantage (of),* **II, 9**
programmer *to program,* **II, 11**
une **programmeur, -euse** *computer programmer,* **I**
des **progrès** (m.) *progress,* **II, 1**
un **projecteur** *projector,* **II, 10**
un **projet** *project, plan,* **II, 1**
projeter *to project,* **II, 10**
promener *to walk (an animal),* **II, 6; se promener** *to walk,* **II, 7**
promettre *to promise,* **II, 7**
proposer *to propose, suggest,* **II, 6**
propre *own,* **II, 2**
un **prospectus** *handbill, flier,* **II, 6**
provençal, -e *from Provence,* **II, 10**
la **Provence** *Provence,* **I**
une **province** *province,* **I; en province** *in the provinces,* **I**
le **public** *audience,* **II, 2**
publicitaire *advertising,* **II, 11**
puis *then,* **I**
un **pull** *pullover,* **I**
pur, -e *pure,* **II, 9**
un **pyjama** *pajamas,* **I**
les **Pyrénées** (f.) *mountains separating France from Spain,* **II, 1**

Q

quand *when,* **I**
quand même *nevertheless,* **II, 2**
un **quart** *quarter,* **I; et quart** *quarter past (the hour),* **I; moins le quart** *quarter of/to (the hour),* **I; un quart d'heure** *a quarter-hour,* **I**
un **quartier** *neighborhood,* **I**
que *what,* **I; Qu'il/elle est** (+ adj.)**!** *It's so* (+ adj.)**!** **I**
les **Québécois** *inhabitants of Quebec,* **II, 3**
quel(s), quelle(s) *which, what,* **I; Quel (Quelle)...!** *What a... !* **I; Quelle question/vie!** *What a question/life!* **I**
quelques *some,* **II, 9; quelque chose** *something,* **I; quelque part** *somewhere,* **II, 1**
quelquefois *sometimes,* **I**
qu'est-ce que *what,* **I; Qu'est-ce que c'est?** *What is it/that?* **I**
qu'est-ce qui *what,* **II, 10**
une **question** *question,* **I; Quelle question!** *What a question!* **I**
qui *who, whom,* **I; qui est-ce qui** *who,* **II, 10; qui est-ce que** *whom,* **II, 10**
quitter *to leave,* **II, 9; Ne quittez pas.** *Hold on (telephone).* **I**
quoi *what,* **I**
quotidien, -ne *daily,* **II, 11**

R

raconter *to tell (about),* **II, 1**
une **radio** *radio,* **I**
rafraîchir *to cool, refresh,* **II, 12**
la **raison** *reason,* **II, 6; avoir raison** *to be right,* **II, 1; Fais-toi une raison.** *Make the best of it.* **II, 9**
râler *to complain, fume,* **II, 9**
une **randonnée** *hike,* **II, 1**
ranger *to tidy up,* **I**
rapide *fast,* **II, 2**
rapidement *rapidly,* **II, 3**
rappeler *to call again, call back,* **II, 3**
une **raquette** *(tennis) racket,* **I**
un **rasoir électrique** *electric razor,* **I**
rater *to miss,* **II, 10**
ravi, -e *delighted,* **II, 6**
un **rayon** *department (in a store),* **I**
une **réalisation** *accomplishment,* **II, 11**
une **réceptionniste** *receptionist, desk clerk,* **II, 6**
une **recette** *recipe,* **I**
recevoir *to receive,* **I**
un **réchaud** *camp stove,* **II, 1**
une **recherche** *search,* **I; research,* **II, 10**
recommencer *to start again,* **II, 1**
la **récré(ation)** *recess, break,* **I**
récupérer *to pick up,* **II, AC3**
une **rédaction** *composition,* **II, AC3**
redoubler *to repeat a grade,* **II, 1**
un **réfrigérateur** *refrigerator,* **I**
refuser *to refuse,* **II, 5**
regarder *to look at, watch,* **I**
un **régime : faire un régime** *to go on a diet,* **II, 7**
une **région** *region,* **II, 1**
une **règle** *ruler,* **I; rule,* **II, 5**
regrettable *regrettable,* **II, 3**
regretter *to be sorry,* **I; miss,* **II, 1**
la **reine** *queen,* **II, 3**
remerciements : un mot de remerciements *thank-you note,* **I**
remercier *to thank,* **I**
la **remise en forme** *remaking,* **II, 7**
les **remparts** (m.) *city walls,* **I**
une **rencontre : faire des rencontres** *to meet,* **I**
rencontrer *to meet,* **II, 1**
un **rendez-vous** *rendezvous,* **I**
rendre *to give back, return,* **II, 6**
se rendre compte *to realize,* **II, 11**
les **renseignements** (m.) *information,* **I; aux renseignements** *at the information desk,* **I**
rentrer *to return, come (go) home,* **I**
réparer *to repair,* **II, 11**
repartir *to leave again,* **II, 1**

un **repas** *meal*, **I**
répéter *to rehearse*, **II, 2**
une **répétition** *rehearsal*, **II, 2**
répondre (à) *to answer*, **I**; **Ça ne répond pas.** *There's no answer.* **I**
un **reportage** *news report, commentary*, **I**
un **repos** *rest*, **II, 11**
se reposer *to rest*, **II, 7**
reprendre *to start again*, **II, 1**
les **réseaux** (m.) *networks*, **II, 11**
réservé, -e *reserved*, **II, 3**
la **résistance** *resistance, endurance*, **II, 3**
une **résolution** *resolution*, **II, 1**; **prendre une résolution** *to make a resolution*, **II, 1**
résoudre *to solve*, **II, 11**
respirer *to breathe*, **II, 9**
la **responsabilité** *responsibility*, **II, 5**
un **restaurant** *restaurant*, **II, 7**
le **reste** *rest, remainder*, **II, 6**
rester *to stay*, **I**; **il reste** *there remain(s)*, **II, 10**
le **rétablissement** *restoration*, **II, 7**
retard : en retard *late*, **I**
retraite : à la retraite *retired*, **I**
rétro : la mode rétro *the style of the Fifties*, **I**
les **retrouvailles** (f.) *reunion*, **II, 9**
retrouver *to meet (again)*, **II, 1**; **retrouver des couleurs** *to get your color back*, **II, 7**
réussir *to succeed*, **II, 1**
un **rêve** *dream*, **II, 11**
réveillé, -e *awakened*, **II, 9**
rêver *to dream*, **I**
un(e) **rêveur,-euse** *dreamer*, **II, 11**
le **rez-de-chaussée** *ground floor*, **I**; **au rez-de-chaussée** *on the ground floor*, **I**
riche *rich*, **II, 9**
un **rideau** *drape*, **II, AC3**
rien *nothing*, **I**; **Ça ne fait rien.** *That's all right.* **I**; **Ce n'est rien.** *It's nothing.* **I**
un **rigolo** *joker*, **II, AC2**
une **rive** *river bank*, **II, 12**
le **riz** *rice*, **II, 7**
une **robe** *dress*, **I**
les **robots** (m.) *robots*, **II, 11**
le **rock** *rock music*, **I**
un **roi** *king*, **I**
romain, -e *Roman*, **II, 10**
les **Romains** *Romans*, **II, 10**
une **rondelle** *hockey puck*, **I**
rose *pink*, **I**
le **rouge** *red*, **I**; **rouge** *red*, **I**
route : Bonne route! *Have a good trip! (by car)* **I**; **En route!** *Let's get going!* **II, 9**
rude *harsh*, **II, 3**
une **rue** *street*, **I**
la **Russie** *Russia*, **II, 2**

S

sa *his, her*, **I**
un **sac** *bookbag, handbag, purse*, **I**; **un sac à dos** *backpack*, **I**
le **Saint-Laurent** *Saint Lawrence River*, **II, 3**
une **saison** *season*, **I**
une **salade** *salad*, **I**
une **salle : la salle de bains** *bathroom*, **I**; **la salle à manger** *dining room*, **I**
le **salon** *living room*, **I**
salut *hello, hi, bye, see you*, **I**
samedi (m.) *Saturday*, **I**; **le samedi** *on Saturday(s)*, **I**
une **sandale** *sandale*, **I**
un **sandwich** (pl. **-es**) *sandwich*, **I**
les **sanitaires** (m.) *toilets*, **II, 1**
sans *without*, **II, 11**
la **santé** *health*, **II, 5**; **Bonne santé!** *Get well soon!* **I**
satisfait, -e *satisfied*, **II, 1**
une **sauce** *sauce*, **I**
le **saucisson** *salami*, **I**
sauf *except*, **I**
sauter *to skip*, **II, 7**
un **savant** *scientist*, **II, 11**
une **savate** *clumsy idiot*, **I**
la **Savoie** *Savoy*, **I**
savoir *to know (how)*, **I**
le **saxophone** *saxophone*, **II, 2**
la **scène** *scene*, **II, 9**
la **science-fiction** *science fiction*, **I**
scolaire *school (adj.)*, **II, 1**
secours : Au secours! *Help!* **II, 3**
les **secousses sismiques** (f.) *earth tremors*, **II, 11**
un **séjour** *stay*, **II, 1**; **un séjour linguistique** *stay to learn a language*, **II, 1**
séjourner *to stay*, **II, 1**
une **semaine** *week*, **I**; **une fois par semaine** *once a week*, **I**
se sentir *to feel*, **II, 7**
septembre (m.) *September*, **I**
une **série** *series*, **I**
sérieux, -se *serious*, **II, 6**
sert : Ça ne sert à rien. *It doesn't do any good.* **II, 9**
un(e) **serveur, -euse** *waiter, waitress*, **II, 6**
les **services** (m.) *services*, **II, 6**
se servir de *to use*, **II, 11**
ses *his, her*, **I**
seul, -e *only*, **I**
seulement *only*, **II, 2**
sévère *strict*, **II, 1**
un **short** *shorts*, **I**
si *yes*, **I**; *if*, **I**; **s'il vous plaît** *please*, **I**; *so*, **II, 11**
un **siècle** *century*, **I**
un **site** *site, location*, **I**
situé-e *situated*, **I**
le **ski** *skiing, ski*, **I**; **le ski sur gazon** *grass skiing*, **II, AC1**
une **sœur** *sister*, **I**

soif : avoir soif *to be thirsty*, **I**
(se) soigner *to take care of, (oneself)*, **II, 7**
un **soir** *evening*, **I**; **le samedi soir** *on Saturday nights*, **I**; **tous les soirs** *every evening*, **I**
une **soirée** *party, evening*, **II, 5**
le **soleil** *sun*, **I**; **Il y a du soleil.** *It's sunny.* **I**
une **solution** *solution*, **I**
un **solvant** *solvent*, **II, 10**
son *his, her*, **I**
songer (à) *to think (about)*, **II, 10**
la **sortie** *exit*, **I**
sortir *to go out*, **I**; *to take out*, **II, 5**
souffler *to blow (out)*, **I**
un **souhait** *wish*, **II, 11**; **Meilleurs souhaits!** *Best wishes!* **I**
souple *flexible*, **I**
souriez *smile*, **II, 10**
souterrain, -e *underground*, **II, 11**
un **souvenir** *memory*, **II, 9**
souvent *often*, **I**
spécial, -e (m. pl. **-aux**) *special*, **II, 3**
un **spectacle** *performance*, **II, 2**
la **spéléologie** *cave exploring*, **II, 1**
splendide *splendid*, **II, 1**
un **sport** *sport*, **I**; **le sport** *sports*, **I**; **la mode sport** *the sporty style/look*, **I**
sportif, -ive *athletic*, **II, 3**
un **squelette** *skeleton*, **II, 3**
un **stade** *stadium*, **I**
un **stage** *training course*, **II, 6**
une **station-service** *gas station*, **II, 1**
stéréo : une chaîne stéréo *stereo*, **I**
strict, -e *strict*, **II, 5**
un **style** *style*, **I**
un **stylo** *pen*, **I**
le **sud** *south*, **I**
suffit : Ça suffit! *That's enough!* **I**
la **suite** *continuation*, **I**
suivre *to follow, take*, **II, 7**
sujet : au sujet de *regarding, concerning, about*, **II, 2**
super *super*, **I**
superbe *superb*, **I**
sûr : bien sûr *surely, of course*, **I**
sur *on, in (a photo)*, **I**
surchauffer *to overheat*, **II, 7**
sûrement *certainly*, **II, 5**
le **surf** *surfing*, **I**
la **surpopulation** *overpopulation*, **II, 11**
une **surprise** *surprise*, **I**
surtout *especially, mainly, mostly*, **I**
un **survêt** *jogging suit, sweatsuit*, **I**
swinguer : Ça va swinguer! *It's going to swing!* **I**
sympa(thique) *nice*, **I**

T

ta *your*, **I**
une **table** *table*, **I**; **mettre là table** *to set the table*, **I**; **une table de nuit** *night stand*, **I**

une **tablette** *bar (chocolate)*, **I**
la **tâche** *task*, **II, 5; les tâches**
    domestiques *chores*, **II, 11**
la **taille** *size*, **I**
une **tante** *aunt*, **I**
  taper à la machine *to type*, **II, 6**
  tard *late*, **II, 5; plus tard**
    later, **I**
une **tartine** *slice of bread and butter*,
    II, 7
un **tas (de)** *a lot (of)*, **I**
une **tasse** *cup*, **I**
le **taureau** (pl. **-x**) *bull*, **II, 10**
un **taxi** *taxi*, **I; les taxis** *taxi*
    stand, **I**
la **technologie** *technology*, **II, 11;**
    shop (class), **I**
un **tee-shirt** *T-shirt*, **I**
un **téléphone** *telephone*, **I**
  téléphoner (à) *to phone, call*, **I**
la **télé(vision)** *television, TV*, **I;**
    Qu'est-ce qu'il y a à la
    télé? *What's on TV?* **I**
tellement *so much*, **II, 3**
la **température** *temperature*, **I; Il**
    fait quelle température?
    What's the temperature? **I**
le **temps** *time, weather*, **I; au**
    temps de *at the time of*, **II,**
    10; combien de temps *how*
    long, **I; de temps en temps**
    from time to time, **II, 5; Il fait**
    quel temps? *What's the*
    weather like? **I**
le **tennis** *tennis*, **I**
des **tennis** (m.) *sneakers (low)*, **I**
terminé, -e *finished, ended*, **II, 1**
la **terrasse** *terrace*, **I**
terrible : pas terrible *not so*
    great, **I**
tes *your*, **I**
la **tête** *head*, **II, 7**
le **thé** *tea*, **I**
théâtre : faire du théâtre *to*
    take part in a theater group, **II, 2**
une **thermos** *thermos*, **II, 10**
tiens *hey, say*, **I; here**, **II, 5**
timide *shy, timid*, **II, 5**
le **tissu** *cloth, fabric*, **II, 9**
toi *you*, **I**
les **toilettes** (f.) *toilet, restroom*, **I**
un **toit** *roof*, **I**
une **tomate** *tomato*, **II, 7**
ton *your*, **I**
tondre *to mow*, **II, 5**
le **tonus** *muscle tone*, **II, 7**
tort : avoir tort *to be wrong*, **II, 1**
toujours *always*, **I**
une **tour** *tower*, **I**
un **tour** *spin, tour, ride*, **II, 3; turn,**
    II, 7
un(e) **touriste** *tourist*, **II, 3**
touristique : un guide
    touristique *tour guide*, **I**
une **tournée prévue** *scheduled tour*,
    II, 2
tourner *to turn*, **I**
un **tournoi** *tournament*, **II, 3**

tout *everything, all*, **I**
tout : tout à fait *totally*, **I; A**
  tout à l'heure. *See you*
    later. **I; tout de suite** *right*
    away, **I; tout de même**
    anyway, **II, 9**
tout, toute, tous, toutes *all,*
    entirely, **I; tout le monde**
    everybody, **I; tous les**
    ans *every year*, **I; tous les**
    jours *every day*, **I; tous les**
    soirs *every evening*, **I; tout le**
    temps *all the time*, **II, 1**
un **train** *train*, **I**
le **trajet** *route, journey*, **II, 10**
une **tranche** *slice*, **I**
tranquillement *quietly,*
    peacefully, **II, 3**
le **travail** *work, schoolwork*, **I; Au**
    travail! *Down to work!* **I**
travailler *to work*, **I**
travailleur, -euse *hardworking,*
    II, 6
trempé, -e *soaked*, **II, 9**
très *very*, **I**
triste *sad*, **I**
troisième *third*, **I; au**
    troisième étage *on the fourth*
    floor, **I**
le **trombone** *trombone*, **II, 2**
la **trompette** *trumpet*, **II, 2**
trop *too*, **I; trop (de)** *too*
    much, too many, **I**
un **trou** *hole*, **I; un trou de**
    mémoire *memory lapse*, **I**
une **trousse** *pencil case*, **I**
trouver *to find*, **I; Comment tu**
    trouves? *How is it?* **I; Tu**
    trouves? *Do you think so?* **I**
tu *you*, **I**
un **tube** *hit (song)*, **I**
tuer *to kill*, **II, 10**
un **type** *guy*, **I**

U

un, une *a, an, one*, **I**
une **usine** *factory*, **II, 10**
utile : se rendre utile *to make*
    oneself useful, **II, 11**

V

les **vacances** (f.) *vacation*, **I;**
    Bonnes vacances! *Have a*
    nice vacation! **I**
une **vache** *cow*, **II, 9**
la **vaisselle** *dishes*, **II, 5**
une **valise** *suitcase*, **I**
varié, -e *varied*, **I**
les **variétés** (f.) *variety show*, **I**
vaut : il vaut mieux que... *it's*
    better that..., **II, 7**
végétarien, -ienne *vegetarian*,
    II, 7
la **veille** *eve*, **II, 3**
un **vélo** *bicycle*, **I; en vélo** *by*

    bicycle, **I; le vélo** *cycling*, **I**
un(e) **vendeur, -euse** *salesman,*
    saleswoman, **I**
vendre *to sell*, **II, 3**
vendredi (m.) *Friday*, **I; le**
    vendredi *on Friday(s)*, **I**
venir *to come*, **I**
le **vent** *wind*, **I; Il y a du vent.**
    It's windy. **I; dans le vent**
    trendy, **I**
un **verre** *glass*, **II, 7**
vers *about, toward*, **II, 3**
le **vert** *green*, **I; vert, -e** *green*, **I**
le **vertige** *vertigo, fear of heights*,
    II, 3
une **veste** *jacket, blazer*, **I**
un **vestige** *trace, relic*, **II, 10**
un **vêtement** *article of clothing*, **I;**
    les vêtements *clothes*, **I**
un **viaduc** *viaduct*, **I**
la **viande** *meat*, **I**
une **vie** *life*, **I; Quelle vie!** *What a*
    life! **I**
vieillir *to grow older*, **II, 5**
vieux, vieil, vieille, vieux,
    vieilles *old*, **I**
vif, vive *bright (color)*, **I**
une **villa** *country house*, **II, 1**
un **village** *village*, **I**
une **ville** *city, town*, **I**
une **vingtaine** *about twenty*, **II, 9**
violent, -e *violent*, **I**
un **visage** *face*, **I**
une **visite** *visit*, **I**
visiter *to visit*, **I**
une **vitamine** *vitamin*, **II, 7**
vite *quickly, fast*, **I**
vive *long live..., hurrah for...*,
    II, 3
vivre *to live*, **II, 3**
un **vœu** (pl. **-x**) *wish*, **I; une carte**
    (de vœux) *greeting card*, **I;**
    Meilleurs vœux! *Best*
    wishes! **I**
voici *here is/are*, **I**
voilà *there is/are, here is/are,*
    here/there you are, **I; le voilà**
    there it is, **I**
la **voile** *sailing*, **II, 1**
voir *to see*, **I**
un(e) **voisin, -ine** *neighbor*, **II, 6**
une **voiture** *car*, **I; en voiture** *by*
    car, **I**
la **voix** *voice*, **II, 11**
un **vol** *flight*, **I**
le **volley(-ball)** *volleyball*, **I**
volontiers *of course, gladly*, **I**
vos *your*, **I**
votre *your*, **I**
vouloir *to want*, **I; Si tu**
    veux. *If you want to.* **I; je**
    voudrais *I would like*, **II, 2;**
    vouloir dire *to mean*, **II, 5**
vous *you*, **I; chez vous** *at, to*
    your house, **I**
un **voyage** *trip*, **II, 10; Bon**
    voyage! *Have a good trip! (by*
    plane, ship) **I**

vrai, -e *true,* **I**
vraiment *really,* **I**
une **vue** *view,* **I**

W

un **week-end** *weekend,* **I**
un **western** *western,* **I**

Y

y *there,* **I**
un **yacht** *yacht,* **II, 11**
le **yaourt** *yogurt,* **II, 7**

Z

un **zéro** *zero,* **I;** **Il fait zéro.** *It's zero (degrees).* **I**
un **zoom** *zoom lens,* **II, 10**
Zut! *Darn it!* **I**

ENGLISH-FRENCH VOCABULARY

In this vocabulary list, the English definitions of all active French words in **Nouveaux copains** and in **Nous, les jeunes** are given, followed by the French. The roman numeral after each entry refers to the book in which it is introduced; the arabic numeral refers to the unit in **Nous, les jeunes** in which it is presented. It is important to use a French word in its correct context. The use of a word can be checked easily by referring to the unit in which it appears.

French words and phrases are presented in the same way as in the French-English Vocabulary

A

a *par*, **II, 2; one weekend a month** *un week-end par mois*, **II, 2**
a, an, one *un, une*, **I**
able: to be able to, can *pouvoir*, **I**
about *vers*, **II, 3**; *au sujet de*, **II, 2**
absolutely *absolument*, **II, 3**
to **accompany** *accompagner*, **II, 3**
account: bank account *un compte*, **II, 6; in my account** *sur mon compte*, **II, 6**
to **ache** *avoir mal à*, **II, 7**
acquainted: to get acquainted *faire (la) connaissance*, **II, 1**
across (from) *en face (de)*, **I**
active *actif, -ive*, **II, 9**
activity leader *animateur, -trice*, **II, 2**
to **act stupid** *faire l'idiot*, **I**
to **adapt** *s'adapter*, **II, 9**
addition: in addition *en plus*, **II, 3**
address *une adresse*, **I**
to **admire** *admirer*, **I**
to **advance** *avancer*, **II, 3**
advantage: to take advantage of *profiter de*, **II, 9**
advice *un conseil*, **II, 5**
to **advise** *conseiller*, **II, 5**
affair: love affair *une affaire de cœur*, **II, 5**
afraid: to be afraid of *avoir peur de*, **I**
after *après*, **I**
afternoon, in the afternoon *l' après-midi* (m.), **I**
again *encore*, **II, 6; Not again!** *Encore!* **I**
air *l' air* (m.), **II, 9; on the air** *en direct*, **II, 11**
airplane *un avion*, **I**
airport *un aéroport*, **I**
alas *hélas*, **II, 2**
album *un album*, **I**
all (pron.) *tout*, **I**; (adj.) *tout, toute, tous, toutes*, **I**

all right: That's all right. *Ça ne fait rien.* **I**
almost *presque*, **I**
along *le long de*, **II, 3**
already *déjà*, **I**
Alsatian *alsacien, -ienne*, **I**
also, too *aussi*, **I**
always *toujours*, **I**
amateur *amateur*, **II, 10**
ambitious *ambitieux, -euse*, **II, 2**
American *américain, -e*, **I**; *un(e) Américain(e)*, **I**
amusements *les distractions* (f.), **II, 9; amusement park** *un parc d' attractions*, **II, 3**
amusing *amusant, -e*, **II, 3**
ancient, old *ancien, -ienne*, **II, 10**
and *et*, **I**
angle, corner *l' angle* (m.), **II, 3; wide angle** *grand angle*, **II, 10**
animal *un animal* (pl. *-aux*), **I**
anniversary, birthday *un anniversaire*, **I**
announcement, ad *une annonce*, **II, 2**
to **annoy** *embêter*, **II, 6**
another *encore un(e)*, **II, 2**
to **answer** *répondre (à)*, **I; There's no answer.** *Ça ne répond pas.* **I**
anyway *tout de même*, **II, 9**
apartment *un appartement*, **I; apartment house** *un immeuble*, **I**
appeal: That doesn't appeal to me. *Ça ne me dit rien.* **II, 10**
apple *une pomme*, **II, 7**
to **appreciate** *apprécier*, **II, 3**
apprenticeship *un apprentissage*, **II, 6**
April *avril* (m.), **I**
architect *un architecte*, **II, 1**
arena *les arènes* (f.), **II, 10**
to **argue, fight** *se disputer*, **II, 11**
arrival *l' arrivée* (f.), **I**
to **arrive** *arriver*, **I**
art *l' art* (m.), **I; art (class)** *les arts plastiques*, **I**

as *comme*, **I**
to **ask** *demander (à)*, **I; to ask a question** *poser une question*, **II, 11**
to **assemble, organize** *monter*, **II, 2**
to **assess, take stock of** *faire le bilan*, **II, 1**
to **assure** *assurer*, **II, 7**
at, to, in, on *à*, **I**
athletic *sportif, -ive*, **II, 3**
atmosphere *une ambiance*, **I**
to **attend** *assister à*, **II, 3**
attention: Pay attention. *Fais (Faites) attention.* **II, 2**
attraction *une attraction*, **II, 3**
audience *le public*, **II, 2**
August *août* (m.), **I**
aunt *une tante*, **I**
autumn, fall *l' automne* (m.), **I; in the fall** *en automne*, **I**
avenue *une avenue*, **I**
average *moyen, moyenne*, **II, 1**
aw (expression of disdain) *bof*, **I**
awakened *réveillé, -e*, **II, 9**

B

to **baby-sit** *faire du baby-sitting*, **I**
backpack *un sac à dos*, **I**
bad *mauvais, -e*, **I; (That's) too bad!** *(C'est) dommage!* **II, 3**
badly *mal*, **II, 1**
bakery *une boulangerie*, **I**
balanced *équilibré, -e*, **II, 7**
ball: baseball, tennis ball *une balle*, **I**
ball: inflated ball, balloon *un ballon*, **I**
banal, ordinary *banal, -e*, **I**
banana *une banane*, **II, 7**
bank *une banque*, **I**
bar (chocolate) *une tablette*, **I**
barbarian, barbaric *barbare*, **II, 10**
to **bark** *aboyer*, **II, 6**
baseball *le base-ball*, **I**

basilica   *la basilique*, **II, 9**
basket   *un panier*, **II, 10**
basketball   *le basket(-ball)*, **I**
bass guitar   *la basse*, **II, 2**
bass player   *un(e) bassiste*, **II, 2**
bat   *une batte*, **I**
bathing suit   *un maillot de bain*, **I**
bathroom   *la salle de bains*, **I**
battle   *un combat*, **II, 10**
to **be**   *être*, **I**
beach   *une plage*, **I**
bean: string bean   *un haricot vert*, **II, 7**
beautiful   *beau, bel, belle, beaux, belles*, **I**
because   *parce que*, **I**; *car*, **II, 10**; **because of**   *à cause de*, **II, 9**
bed   *un lit*, **I**
bedroom   *une chambre*, **I**
before   *avant (de)*, **I**
to **begin**   *commencer*, **I**; *débuter*, **II, 1**; **to begin with (by)**   *commencer par*, **II, 3**
beginner   *un(e) débutant(e)*, **II, 2**
beginning   *le début*, **II, 7**
Belgium   *la Belgique*, **I**
to **believe**   *croire*, **II, 11**; **I believe**   *Je crois*, **II, 3**
to **belong to**   *faire partie de*, **II, 6**
below: down below   *en bas*, **II, 9**
best   *meilleur, -e*, **I**; **Best wishes!**   *Meilleurs vœux (souhaits)!* **I**; **Make the best of it.**   *Fais-toi une raison.* **II, 9**
best seller   *un best-seller*, **II, 11**
better   *mieux*, **I**; **to prefer, like better**   *aimer mieux*, **I**; **It's better that...**   *Il vaut mieux que...*, **II, 7**
between   *entre*, **I**
beverage   *une boisson*, **I**
bicycle   *la bicyclette*, **II, 1**; *un vélo*, **I**; **by bicycle**   *en vélo*, **I**
big, large   *grand, -e*, **I**; *gros, grosse*, **I**
bill (money)   *un billet*, **I**
biology   *la biolo(gie)*, **I**
bird   *un oiseau (pl. -x)*, **II, 9**
birthday   *un anniversaire*, **I**; **Happy birthday!**   *Joyeux (Bon) anniversaire!* **I**
black   *le noir*, **I**; *noir, -e*, **I**
to **blow (out)**   *souffler*, **I**
blue   *le bleu*, **I**; *bleu, -e*, **I**
blues (music)   *le blues*, **I**
boat   *un bateau (pl. -x)*, **I**
body building   *la musculation*, **II, 2**
bold, courageous person   *un(e) fonceur, -euse*, **II, 3**
book   *un livre*, **I**
bookbag   *un sac*, **I**
bookcase   *une étagère*, **I**
booklet (of tickets, stamps)   *un carnet*, **II, 9**
bookseller   *un(e) libraire*, **I**
bookstore   *une librairie*, **I**
boot   *une botte*, **I**; **ski boots**   *des chaussures de ski*, **I**

to **bore**   *barber (fam.)*, **II, 10**; **I get (am) bored.**   *Je m'ennuie.* **II, 1**; **I got (was) bored.**   *Je me suis ennuyé(e).* **II, 1**
boring   *ennuyeux, -euse*, **II, 1**; **It's boring!**   *C'est la barbe!* **I**
to **borrow (from)**   *emprunter (à)*, **II, 6**
bottle   *une bouteille*, **I**
boutique, shop   *une boutique*, **I**
bowl   *un bol*, **I**
bowling alley   *un bowling*, **I**
box   *une boîte*, **I**
boy   *un garçon*, **I**
bracelet   *un bracelet*, **I**
bread   *le pain*, **I**; *une baguette*, **II, 10**
break   *la récré(ation)*, **I**
to **break**   *casser*, **II, 6**
breakdown: to be broken down   *être en panne*, **II, 11**
breakfast   *le petit déjeuner*, **I**
to **breathe**   *respirer*, **II, 9**
bright   *vif, vive*, **I**
brilliant   *brillant, -e*, **II, 2**
to **bring**   *apporter*, **I**; *emporter*, **I**
brioche   *une brioche*, **I**
Brittany   *la Bretagne*, **I**
broadcast   *diffusé, -e*, **II, 11**
broccoli   *le brocoli*, **II, 7**
brother   *un frère*, **I**
brown   *le marron*, **I**; *marron*, **I**
brunette   *brun, -e*, **I**
Brussels   *Bruxelles*, **I**
budget   *un budget*, **II, 6**
built   *construit, -e*, **II, 11**
bull   *le taureau (pl. -x)*, **II, 10**; **bullfight**   *une course de taureaux*, **II, 10**
Burgundy   *la Bourgogne*, **I**
bus (public)   *un bus*, **I**; **by bus**   *en bus*, **I**
business: to be in business   *être dans les affaires (f.)*, **II, 11**
busy   *occupé, -e*, **I**; *pris, -e*, **II, 5**
but   *mais*, **I**
butter   *le beurre*, **I**; **peanut butter**   *le beurre de cacahouètes*, **I**
button (slogan)   *un badge*, **I**
to **buy**   *acheter*, **I**
by, per   *par*, **I**; **once a week**   *une fois par semaine*, **I**

C

cable car   *un funiculaire*, **II, 9**
cafe   *un café*, **I**
cafeteria   *une cafeteria*, **I**; *la cantine*, **II, 7**
cake   *un gâteau (pl. -x)*, **I**; **chocolate cake**   *un gâteau au chocolat*, **I**
calculator: pocket calculator   *une calculette*, **I**
to **call: to be called, named**   *s'appeler*, **I**; **to call, phone**   *appeler*, **II, 3**; *téléphoner (à)*, **I**; **to call (phone) again**   *rappeler*, **II, 3**
calm   *calme*, **II, 9**

calories   *les calories (f.)*, **II, 11**
to **camp**   *camper*, **II, 1**
camp: vacation camp, resort   *un centre de loisirs*, **II, 6**
camping   *le camping*, **II, 1**
Canada   *le Canada*, **I**
cancer   *le cancer*, **II, 11**
candle   *une bougie*, **I**
candy: piece of candy   *un bonbon*, **I**
canoeing   *le canoë*, **II, 1**
capital   *la capitale*, **I**
car   *une voiture*, **I**; **by car**   *en voiture*, **I**
card   *une carte*, **I**; **postcard**   *une carte postale*, **I**; **greeting card**   *une carte de vœux*, **I**
care: I don't care.   *Ça m'est égal.* **II, 3**; **Who cares?**   *Mouais.* **I**; **to take care of**   *garder*, **II, 5**; *(se) soigner*, **II, 7**
careful: to be careful   *faire attention*, **II, 1**
carnival   *le carnaval*, **II, 3**
carrot   *une carotte*, **II, 7**
carrousel   *un carrousel*, **II, 10**
cartoon   *un dessin animé*, **I**
cashier   *un(e) caissier, -ière*, **II, 6**
cassette   *une cassette*, **I**
cat   *un(e) chat(te)*, **I**
catastrophe   *une catastrophe*, **I**
to **catch**   *attraper*, **II, 1**
category   *la catégorie*, **II, 6**
cathedral   *une cathédrale*, **I**
cave exploring   *la spéléologie*, **II, 1**
centimeter   *un centimètre (cm)*, **I**
century   *un siècle*, **I**
cereal   *des céréales (f.)*, **II, 7**
certain   *certain, -e*, **II, 9**
certainly   *sûrement*, **II, 5**; *certainement*, **II, 7**
certain ones   *certains*, **II, 1**
chair   *une chaise*, **I**
championship   *le championnat*, **I**
to **change**   *changer*, **II, 6**
check   *un chèque*, **I**; **traveler's check**   *un chèque de voyage*, **I**
checkers: to play checkers   *jouer aux dames*, **II, 2**
cheese   *le fromage*, **I**
chef   *un chef*, **I**
chemical   *chimique*, **II, 10**
chess: to play chess   *jouer aux échecs*, **II, 2**
chicken   *le poulet*, **I**; *une poule*, **II, 9**
child   *un enfant*, **I**
China   *la Chine*, **II, 11**
chocolate, hot chocolate   *le chocolat*, **I**; **chocolate cake**   *un gâteau au chocolat*, **I**; **chocolate mousse**   *une mousse au chocolat*, **I**
choice   *le choix*, **II, 1**
to **choose**   *choisir*, **II, 1**
chores   *les tâches domestiques (f.)*, **II, 11**
Christmas: Merry Christmas!   *Joyeux Noël!* **I**
church   *une église*, **I**
to **circulate**   *circuler*, **II, 3**

city, town une ville, I
civilized civilisé, -e, II, 10
clarinet la clarinette, II, 2
classical classique, I; **classical music** le classique, I
clever, smart malin, maligne, I
to **close** fermer, I
closet une penderie, I
clothing: article of clothing un vêtement, I; **clothes** les vêtements, I
cloud un nuage, I
club un club, I
clumsy idiot une savate, I
coat un manteau (pl. -x), I
coffee le café, I; **coffee with milk** le café au lait, I
cold froid, -e, I; le froid, II, 3; **It's cold.** Il fait froid, I
collapse: to be about to collapse craquer (fam.), II, 7
to **collect** collectionner, I
to **colonize** coloniser, II, 11
color une couleur, I; **to get your color back** retrouver des couleurs, II, 7
to **come** venir, I; **to come in,** entrer, I; **Come on!** Allez! II, 5
comedy un film comique, I
comic book une bédé, II, 1; **comic strips, comics** des bandes dessinées (f.), I
to **communicate** communiquer, II, 11
to **complain** se plaindre, II, 9
complex le complexe, II, 10
compliments: My compliments on ... Mes compliments pour..., I
computer un ordinateur, I
computer programmer un(e) programmeur, -euse, I
computer science l' informatique (f.), I
concerning au sujet de, II, 2
concert un concert, I
confidant un(e) confident(e), II, 5
Congratulations! Félicitations! II, 6
to **console** consoler, II, 9
to **contain** contenir, II, 11
contest une compétition, II, 3
continually continuellement, II, 3
continuation la suite, I
to **continue** continuer, I; **I can't continue!** Je n'en peux plus! II, 7
contrary: on the contrary au contraire, II, 1
convinced: I'm convinced of it. J'en suis convaincu(e). II, 11
cookie un biscuit, II, 10
cooking la cuisine, II, 5
cool frais, fraîche, I; **It's cool.** Il fait frais. I
to **cost** coûter, I
to **count** compter, II, 6
country un pays, II, 6
countryside la campagne, I
courage le courage, II, 5
course: of course bien sûr, volontiers, I; **of course not** mais

non, I
courtyard la cour, II, 1
cousin un(e) cousin(e), I
cow une vache, II, 9
cow une vache, II, 9
to **create** créer, II, 5
croissant un croissant, I
crowd une foule, II, 3
to **cry** pleurer, II, 9
culturally culturellement, II, 9
cup une tasse, I
to **cure** guérir, II, 11
curious curieux, -euse, I
currency (money) exchange le bureau de change, I
currently actuellement, II, 11
customs la douane, I
customs agent un(e) douanier, -ière, I
cute mignon, -onne, I
cycling le vélo, I

D

Dad papa, I
daily quotidien, -ne, II, 11
dance un bal, II, 3; la danse, II, 2
to **dance** danser, I
dangerous dangereux, -euse, II, 5
to **dare** oser, II, 5
Darn it! Zut! I
date la date, I
day un jour, I; **every day** tous les jours, I; une journée, II, 1; **all day long** toute la journée, II, 2; **the next day** le lendemain, II, 5
dead mort, -e, II, 7
death: put to death mis(e) à mort, II, 10
to **decide** décider, I
decision une décision, II, 1; **to make a decision** prendre une décision, II, 1
to **declare** déclarer, I
decorated décoré, -e, I
to **defend (oneself)** (se) défendre, II, 10
degrees: It's ten (degrees). Il fait dix. I; **It's ten below (zero).** Il fait moins dix. I
delicious délicieux, -euse, I
delighted ravi, -e, II, 6
demonstration une manifestation, II, 10
dentist un(e) dentiste, I
department (in a store) un rayon, I
departure le départ, II, 10
to **depend (on)** dépendre (de), I
descent une descente, II, 3
desire un désir, II, 6
desk un bureau (pl. -x), I; **desk clerk** un(e) réceptionniste, II, 6
dessert le dessert, I
detective policier, -ière, I
devoted (to) consacré, -e (à), II, 10
devoured dévoré, -e, II, 10
diary un journal (pl. -aux), I
dictionary un dictionnaire, I

diet: to go on a diet faire un régime, II, 7
different différent, -e, I
differently autrement, II, 11; différemment, II, 11
difficult difficile, I
difficulty: to have difficulty avoir du mal , II, 7
dinner le dîner, I; **dinnertime** l' heure du dîner, I
directly directement, II, 11
dirtbiking le bicross, I
disco une discothèque, I
discouraged désespéré, -e, II, 6
to **discuss, argue** discuter, II, 5
discussion une discussion, II, 5
diseases les maladies (f.), II, 11
disgusting, rotten infect, -e, II, 7
dishes la vaisselle, II, 5
distant lointain, -e, II, 10
to **distribute** distribuer, II, 6
to **do** faire, I
doctor un médecin, I; le docteur, II, 7
dog un(e) chien(ne), I
dollar un dollar, I
domestic, household domestique, II, 5
door la porte, I; **(car)** les portières (f.), II, 11
dormitory le dortoir, II, 10
dozen une douzaine (de), I
dream un rêve, II, 11
to **dream** rêver, I
dreamer un(e) rêveur,-euse, II, 11
dress une robe, I
to **drink** boire, II, 7
drink une boisson, I
drugstore une pharmacie, I
drums la batterie, II, 2
duchess la duchesse, II, 3
dud: It's a dud! C'est un navet! I
dumb, stupid bête, II, 10
during pendant, I
dynamic dynamique, II, 6

E

each chaque, II, 1
each one: Each one goes his separate way. Chacun va de son côté. I
to **earn** gagner, II, 1
earrings des boucles d'oreilles (f.), II, 10
Easter: Happy Easter! Joyeuses Pâques! I
easy facile, I
to **eat** manger, I; **to eat dinner** dîner, I
eaten dévoré, -e, II, 10
eclair un éclair, II, 7
economical économe, II, 6
to **economize** économiser, II, 6
educational éducatif, -ive, II, 10
effort un effort, II, 2
egg un œuf, I
elderly âgé, -e, II, 11
electric électrique, II, 2
elegant élégant, -e, I
else: or else ou bien, I

emotion *une émotion,* **II, 3**
employee *un(e) employé(e),* **I**
end *la fin,* **II, 1; at the end of** *au fond de,* **I**
endurance *la résistance,* **II, 3**
energetic *énergique,* **II, 7**
engineer *un ingénieur,* **I**
England *l' Angleterre (f.),* **II, 1**
English (language) *l' anglais (m.),* **I**
enjoy: Enjoy your meal! *Bon appétit!* **I**
enormously *énormément,* **II, 1**
enough *assez,* **I; That's enough!** *Ça suffit!* **I**
enrolled *inscrit, -e,* **II, 2**
enthusiastic (about) *passionné, -e (de),* **II, 2**
entrance *l' entrée (f.),* **I**
to **envy** *envier,* **II, 11**
epoch, age, era *une époque,* **II, 10**
equal *égal, -e (m. pl. -aux),* **II, 3**
to **equal** *égaler,* **I**
eraser *une gomme,* **I**
error *une erreur,* **I**
escalator *un escalator,* **I**
especially *surtout,* **I**
essential *essentiel, -elle,* **II, 7;** *indispensable,* **II, 11**
Europe *l' Europe (f.),* **I**
eve *la veille,* **II, 3**
even *même,* **I**
evening *un soir,* **I; on Saturday nights** *le samedi soir,* **I; every evening** *tous les soirs,* **I**
everybody *tout le monde,* **I**
everything, all *tout,* **I**
everywhere *partout,* **II, 7**
exactly *justement,* **II, 1**
exam *un examen,* **I**
excellent *excellent, -e,* **I**
except *sauf,* **I**
to **exchange** *changer,* **I; in exchange** *en échange,* **II 6**
exciting *passionnant, -e,* **II, 1**
excuse me *excusez-moi, pardon,* **I**
exercise *un exercice,* **II, 7**
exhausted *crevé, -e, épuisé, -e,* **II, 7**
exhibit *une exposition,* **II, 9**
to **exhibit** *exposer,* **II, 10**
to **exist** *exister,* **II, 11**
exit *la sortie,* **I**
expensive *cher, chère,* **I**
to **explain** *expliquer,* **II, 1**
to **express** *exprimer,* **II, 3**
extravagant, wild *extravagant, -e,* **I**
extremely: extremely well *drôlement bien,* **I**

F

fabulous *fabuleux, -euse,* **II, 3**
face *un visage,* **I; to make a (funny) face** *faire des grimaces (f.),* **II, 10**
factory *une usine,* **II, 10**
fair *juste,* **I**
family *une famille,* **I; with one's family** *en famille,* **I**

famous *célèbre,* **I**
fan *un(e) fan(atique),* **II, 3**
fantastic *fantastique,* **II, 3;** *génial, -e* **I**
far (off) *loin,* **II, 1; far from** *loin de,* **II, 11**
faraway, distant *lointain, -e,* **II, 10**
farewell, goodbye *adieu,* **II, 10**
farm *une ferme,* **II, 6**
fascinating *fascinant, -e,* **II, 9**
fast *rapide,* **II, 2;** *vite,* **I**
fast-food restaurant *un fast-food,* **II, 6**
father *un père,* **I**
February *février (m.),* **I**
fed: I'm fed up! *J'en ai assez!* **II, 3**
to **feed, nourish** *se nourrir,* **II, 7**
to **feel** *se sentir,* **II, 7; to get a feel for** *se faire une idée de,* **II, 9; to feel like** *avoir envie de,* **I; I don't feel up to...** *Je n'ai pas le courage de...,* **II, 10**
Feminist! *Féministe!* **II, 5**
fewer, less *moins de,* **II, 9**
fight, battle *un combat,* **II, 10**
film *un film,* **I; (for camera)** *une pellicule,* **II, 10**
final game, finals *la finale,* **I**
finally *enfin,* **I**
to **find** *trouver,* **I;**
fine *bien,* **I**
to **finish, end** *finir,* **I**
finished, ended *terminé, -e,* **II, 1**
fireworks *un feu d'artifice,* **II, 3**
first (of all) *d'abord,* **I**
fish *le poisson,* **I**
fishing *la pêche,* **II, 1**
flash *un flash,* **II, 10**
flexible *souple,* **I**
flight *un vol,* **I**
flirt *un dragueur,* **II, 1**
float *un char,* **II, 3**
floor *un étage,* **I; on the second/ third/fourth floor** *au premier/ deuxième/troisième étage,* **I; on the ground floor** *au rez-de-chaussée,* **I**
florist: the florist's *chez le/la fleuriste,* **I**
flower *une fleur,* **I**
flute *la flûte,* **II, 2**
folk music *le folk,* **I**
to **follow** *suivre,* **I**
food *l' alimentation (f.),* **II, 7**
foot *un pied,* **I; on foot** *à pied,* **I**
for *depuis,* **II, 2**
for, in order to *pour,* **I**
forbidden *interdit,* **II, 10**
to **force oneself (to)** *se forcer(à),* **II, 7**
foreign *étranger, -ère,* **II, 6**
to **forget** *oublier,* **I**
to **form** *former,* **II, 2**
fortifying *fortifiant, -e,* **II, 7**
fortunately *heureusement,* **I**
franc *un franc (F),* **I**
France *la France,* **I**
free, unoccupied *libre,* **I**

French *français, -e,* **I; (language)** *le français,* **I; (person)** *un(e) Français(e),* **I**
French center for space research *le CNES (Centre national d'études spatiales),* **II, 11**
French fries *des frites (f.),* **I**
Friday *vendredi (m.),* **I; on Friday(s)** *le vendredi,* **I**
fridge *un frigo,* **I**
friend *un(e) ami(e),* **I; old friends** *les anciens (m.),* **II, 1**
from, of *de,* **I; from... on(ward)** *à partir de,* **II, 7**
front: in front of *devant,* **I**
frozen *gelé, -e,* **II, 3**
fruit *le fruit,* **I; fruit juice** *le jus de fruit,* **I**
full *plein, -e,* **I; full of** *plein, -e de,* **I**
to **fume** *râler,* **II, 9**
fun: to have fun *s'amuser,* **II, 10; fun, amusing** *amusant, -e,* **II, 3; It's fun!** *C'est le pied!* **I**
to **function** *fonctionner,* **II, 3;** *marcher,* **II, 2**
funny *drôle,* **I**
furious *furieux, -euse,* **II, 1**
future *l' avenir (m.),* **II, 1**

G

game *un match (pl. -es), un jeu (pl. -x),* **I; soccer game** *un match de foot,* **I; game show** *un jeu (pl. -x),* **I; Olympic Games, Olympics** *les Jeux Olympiques,* **I**
garage *le garage,* **II, 2**
garbage can *la poubelle,* **II, 5**
garden *un jardin,* **I; informal garden** *un jardin anglais,* **I**
gas station *une station-service,* **II, 1**
gate, door *une porte,* **I**
gay, happy *gai, -e,* **II, 3**
general *général, -e,* **II, 9**
generous *généreux, -euse,* **I**
Geneva *Genève,* **I**
geography *la géo(graphie),* **I**
get: to get along well (with) *s'entendre bien (avec),* **II, 11; to get up** *se lever,* **II, 7; Get well soon!** *Bonne santé!* **I**
ghost *un fantôme,* **II, 3**
gift *un cadeau (pl. -x),* **I**
girl, daughter *une fille,* **I**
to **give** *donner, offrir,* **I; to give back, return** *rendre,* **II, 6; to give up** *abandonner,* **I**
gladiator *un gladiateur,* **II, 10**
gladly *volontiers,* **I**
glass *un verre,* **II, 7**
glove: (baseball) glove *un gant,* **I**
to **go** *aller,* **I; to go by/through, spend (time), be playing (a movie)** *passer,* **I; to go down** *descendre,* **I; to go out** *sortir,* **I; to go to bed** *se coucher,* **II, 7; to go up on** *passer sur,* **I; Is it going**

well? *Ça marche?* **II, 6; Let's get going!** *En route!* **II, 9; Let's go!** *Allons-y!* **I**
goal *un but*, **II, 11**
good, OK *bon, bonne*, **I; It doesn't do any good.** *Ça ne sert à rien.* **II, 9**
goodbye *au revoir, salut*, **I;** *adieu*, **II, 10**
good evening *bonsoir*, **I**
grade *une classe*, **I;** *la note*, **II, 1**
gram *un gramme (g)*, **I**
grandfather *un grand-père*, **I**
grandmother *une grand-mère*, **I**
grandparents *les grands-parents (m.)*, **I**
grapefruit *un pamplemousse*, **II, 7**
gray *gris, -e*, **I**
great *chouette, extra(ordinaire), génial, -e*, **I;** *formidable*, **II, 3; not so great** *pas terrible*, **I;** *pas le pied*, **I**
green *le vert*, **I;** *vert, -e*, **I**
grocery store *une épicerie*, **I**
ground floor *le rez-de-chaussée*, **I; on the ground floor** *au rez-de-chaussée*, **I**
group *une bande*, **II, 3**
to guarantee *garantir*, **II, 7**
to guard *garder*, **I**
guest: guest room *une chambre d'amis*, **I**
guide *un guide*, **I; tour guide** *un guide touristique*, **I; guidebook** *un guide*, **I**
guitar *une guitare*, **I**
guy *un type*, **I**
gym, gymnastics, P.E. *la gym(nastique)*, **I**

H

habit *une habitude*, **II, 7**
hair *les cheveux (m.)*, **I**
hairdo *une coiffure*, **I**
half *la moitié*, **II, 6; half past (the hour)** *et demie*, **I; a half-hour** *une demi-heure*, **I**
hall *le couloir*, **I**
ham *le jambon*, **I**
hand *la main*, **II, 2**
handbag *un sac*, **I**
handbill, flier *un prospectus*, **II, 6**
handicapped *handicapé, -e*, **II, 11**
handkerchief *un mouchoir*, **I**
happy *heureux, -euse*, **I;** *content, -e*, **II, 1;** *gai, -e*, **II, 3**
hard *dur, -e*, **II, 2; difficult** *dur, -e*, **II, 9**
hardworking *travailleur, -euse*, **II, 6**
harsh *rude*, **II, 3**
hat *un chapeau*, **II, 9**
to hate *détester*, **I**
to have *avoir*, **I; to have (to eat or drink)** *prendre*, **I; to have to** *il faut*, **I;** *devoir*, **II, 2**
he *il*, **I; he's** *c'est*, **I**
head *la tête*, **II, 7**

health *la santé*, **II, 5**
to hear *entendre*, **II, 3**
hell *l' enfer (m.)*, **II, 6**
hello *bonjour, salut*, **I; (on phone)** *allô*, **I**
helmet *un casque*, **I**
to help *aider*, **II, 5; Help!** *Au secours!* **II, 3**
her *la*, **II, 5; (to or for) her** *lui*, **I;** *son, sa, ses*, **I**
here *ici*, **I;** *tiens*, **II, 5; here is/are** *voici*, **I**
to hesitate *hésiter*, **II, 5**
hey, say *tiens*, **I**
hi *coucou*, **II, 3**
high *haut, -e*, **II, 2**
high school *un lycée*, **I; high school student** *un(e) lycéen(ne)*, **I**
him *le*, **II, 5; (to or for) him** *lui*, **I**
his *son, sa, ses*, **I**
history *l' histoire (f.)*, **I**
hit (song) *un tube*, **I**
hockey *le hockey*, **I; hockey puck** *une rondelle*, **I; hockey stick** *une crosse*, **I**
hold *une prise*, **II, 2; Hold on (telephone).** *Ne quittez pas.* **I**
hole *un trou*, **I**
holiday: Happy Holiday! *Bonne fête!* **I**
homesick: to be homesick *avoir le mal du pays*, **II, 9**
homework *les devoirs (m.)*, **I**
to hope *espérer*, **I**
hopeless, useless *nul, nulle*, **II, 1**
horrible *horrible*, **II, 1**
horror movie *un film d'horreur*, **I**
hors d'œuvre *un hors-d'œuvre (pl. hors-d'œuvre)*, **I**
horse *le cheval*, **I; horseback riding** *le cheval*, **I;** *l' équitation (f.)*, **II, 1**
hospital *un hôpital (pl. -aux.)*, **I**
hotel *un hôtel*, **I**
hour *une heure (h)*, **I**
house, home *une maison*, **I; to/at someone's house** *chez*, **I; country house** *une villa*, **II, 1**
housework *le ménage*, **II, 5**
how *comment*, **I;** *ce que*, **II, 3; How are you?** *Comment allez-vous?* **II, 1; How is it?** *Comment tu trouves?* **I; How's it going?** *Ça boume?* **II, 6; how much, how many** *combien (de)*, **I; How old are you?** *Tu as (Vous avez) quel âge?* **I**
huh? *hein?* **I**
hundred: about a hundred *une centaine*, **II, 6**
hunger *la faim*, **II, 11**
hungry: to be hungry *avoir faim*, **I; It makes you hungry.** *Ça donne faim.* **I**
hurrah: long live... , hurrah for ... *vive*, **II, 3**
hurricane *un ouragan*, **I**

to hurry *se dépêcher*, **II, 10; in a hurry** *pressé, -e*, **II, 10; Hurry!** *Dépêche-toi!* **II, 5**
to hurt *avoir mal à*, **II, 7**
husband *un mari*, **I**

I

I *je*, **I**
ice *la glace*, **I; ice cream** *une glace*, **II, 3; ice-skating** *le patin à glace*, **I; ice skates** *des patins*, **I**
idea *une idée*, **I**
ideal *un idéal*, **II, 11;** *idéal, -e*, **II, 9**
if *si*, **I**
to illustrate *illustrer*, **II, 10**
to imagine *imaginer*, **II, 9**
immense, huge *immense*, **I**
immortal *immortel, -elle*, **II, 11**
important *grave*, **II, 11; important thing** *l' important (m.)*, **II, 6**
impossible *impossible*, **I**
impressive *impressionnant, -e*, **I**
in *à, dans, en*, **I; in the know, with it** *branché, -e*, **II, 2**
inch *un pouce*, **I**
incompatible *incompatible*, **II, 6**
incomprehensible *incompréhensible*, **II, 3**
independence *l' indépendance (f.)*, **II, 6**
independent *indépendant, -e*, **II, 6**
India *l' Inde (f.)*, **II, 11**
information *les renseignements (m.)*, **I; at the information desk** *aux renseignements*, **I**
instant *un instant*, **II, 10**
instead *plutôt*, **I**
instrument *un instrument*, **II, 2**
intensely *intensément*, **II, 3**
to interest *intéresser*, **II, 6; to be in one's interest to** *avoir intérêt à*, **II, 1; Are you interested in... ?** *Ça t'intéresse de...?* **II, 2**
interview *une interview*, **I**
to invent *inventer*, **II, 10**
invitation *une invitation*, **I**
to invite *inviter*, **I**
island *une île*, **II, 11**
it *ça*, **I;** *il, elle*, **I;** *le, la*, **II, 5; It's so (+ adj.)!** *Qu'il/elle est (+ adj.)!* **I**
itinerary *un itinéraire*, **II, 11**

J

jacket: waist-length jacket *un blouson*, **I; blazer** *une veste*, **I**
jam *la confiture*, **I**
January *janvier (m.)*, **I**
jazz *le jazz*, **I**
jeans *un jean*, **I**
jewel *un bijou*, **I; jewelry** *des bijoux*, **I**
jewelry store *une bijouterie*, **I**
job *un boulot (fam.)*, **II, 6;** *un emploi*, **II, 11**
jogging *le jogging*, **I; jogging suit** *un survêt*, **I**

to **joke** *plaisanter,* **I**
journey *un voyage,* **II, 10;**
  (distance covered) *le trajet,*
  II, 10
joy *la joie,* **II, 3**
joyous, happy *joyeux, -euse,* **II, 3**
judo *le judo,* **II, 2**
juice *le jus,* **I; fruit juice** *le jus de*
  fruit, **I**
July *juillet* (m.), **I**
June *juin* (m.), **I**
just *juste,* **II, 6; to have just**
  venir de, **II, 11**

K

kayaking *le canoë-kayak,* **II, 1**
to **keep** *garder,* **II, 6;** *conserver,* **II, 7;**
  to keep in shape *garder la forme,* **I**
kidding: You've got to be kidding!
  Tu parles! (fam.) **II, 10**
to **kill** *tuer,* **II, 10**
killing *la mise à mort,* **II, 10**
kilo(gram) *un kilo (kg),* **I**
kilometer *un kilomètre,* **I**
kind *un genre,* **I**
king *un roi,* **I**
to **kiss** *embrasser,* **II, 10**
kisses: Love and kisses *Bises,* **I**
kitchen *la cuisine,* **I**
to **know (how)** *savoir,* **I**
to **know, be acquainted with**
  connaître, **I**

L

to **lack** *manquer (de),* **II, 7**
lamp *une lampe,* **I**
laser *le laser,* **II, 11**
last *dernier, -ière,* **I;** *passé, -e,* **II, 1**
to **last** *durer,* **II, 3**
late *en retard,* **I;** *tard,* **II, 5**
later, *plus tard,* **I; See you later.** *A*
  toute à l'heure, **I**
lawn *la pelouse,* **II, 5**
lawyer *un(e) avocat(e),* **I**
lazy *paresseux, -euse,* **I**
to **learn** *apprendre,* **II, 2**
least: at least *au moins,* **II, 2**
leather-goods shop *une*
  maroquinerie, **I**
to **leave** *laisser, partir,* **I;** *quitter,* **II, 9**
to **leave again** *repartir,* **II, 1**
left: to the left (of) *à gauche (de),* **I**
leg *la jambe,* **II, 2**
lemon soda *la limonade,* **I**
to **lend** *prêter,* **II, 6**
lens *un objectif,* **II, 10; zoom**
  lens *un zoom,* **II, 10**
let go *lâcher,* **II, 7**
life *une vie,* **I; What a life!**
  Quelle vie! **I**
to **like** *aimer,* **I; I would like** *je*
  voudrais, **II, 2; You're going to**
  like it here. *Tu vas te plaire ici.*
  II, 9; Do you like it? *Ça te plaît?*
  II, 3; Did you like it? *Ça t'a plu?*
  II, 1; I liked it. *Ça m'a plu.* **II, 1**
like *comme,* **I**

list *une liste,* **I**
to **listen (to)** *écouter,* **I**
listeners *les auditeurs* (m.), **II, 11**
liter *un litre,* **I**
little *petit, -e,* **I; a little** *un peu*
  (de), **I; a little more** *encore un*
  peu, **I; little, not much** *peu,* **II, 1**
to **live** *vivre,* **II, 3; to live (in),**
  reside *habiter,* **I**
living room *le living,* **I;** *le salon,* **I**
location *l'emplacement* (m.), **I;** *un*
  site, **I**
long *long, longue,* **II, 1**
longer: no longer *ne... plus,* **I**
to **look: to look at, watch** *regarder,* **I; to**
  look for *chercher,* **I; to look like**
  avoir l'air de, **I; to look sick** *avoir*
  mauvaise mine, **II, 7**
loose (clothing) *large,* **I**
to **lose** *perdre,* **I**
lost: lost and found *les objets*
  trouvés, **I**
lot: a lot (of) *beaucoup (de), un tas*
  (de), plein (de), **I**
loud, garish *criard, -e,* **I**
loudly *fort,* **II, 2; louder** *plus*
  fort, **II, 2**
to **love** *aimer, adorer,* **I**
love: in love (with) *amoureux, -*
  euse (de), **II, 5; love story** *une*
  histoire d'amour, **I; Love and**
  kisses *Bises,* **I**
luck *la chance,* **II, 3**
luckily *heureusement,* **I**
luggage *les bagages* (m.), **I**
lunch *le déjeuner,* **I; to have**
  lunch *déjeuner,* **II, 2**
Lyons: from Lyons *lyonnais, -e,* **II, 9**

M

magazine *un magazine,* **I**
magnificent *magnifique,* **I**
main *principal, -e* (m. pl. *-aux*), **I**
to **make** *faire, préparer,* **I;** *fabriquer,* **II,**
  11; Make yourself at home.
  Fais (Faites) comme chez toi (vous).
  I; It makes you hungry. *Ça*
  donne faim. **I**
Male chauvinist! *Macho!* **II, 5**
mall *un centre commercial,* **I**
man *un homme,* **I**
to **manage to** *arriver à,* **II, 2; I can't**
  manage to do it! *Je n'y arrive*
  pas! **II, 2**
many, much, a lot (of) *beaucoup*
  (de), un tas (de), plein (de), **I**
map *une carte,* **I; (of a city)** *un*
  plan, **I**
March *mars* (m.), **I**
marina *un port de plaisance,* **I**
married *marié, -e,* **II, 11; to get**
  married (to) *se marier (avec),* **II, 11**
marvelous *merveilleux, -euse,* **II, 1**
math *les maths (mathématiques)* (f.), **I**
matter: as a matter of fact
  justement, **II, 2**
May *mai* (m.), **I**

maybe *peut-être,* **I**
me *moi,* **I; me too** *moi aussi,* **II, 1**
meal *un repas,* **I**
mean *méchant, -e,* **I**
to **mean** *vouloir dire,* **II, 5**
means *un moyen,* **II, 6**
measure *une mesure,* **II, 7**
to **measure** *mesurer,* **I**
meat *la viande,* **I**
medicine *un médicament,* **I**
to **meet** *faire des rencontres,* **I;**
  rencontrer, **II, 1; to meet again**
  retrouver, **II, 1**
member *un membre,* **I**
memoirs *les mémoires* (m.), **II, 11**
memory *une mémoire,* **I; memory**
  lapse *un trou de mémoire,* **I; un**
  souvenir, **II, 9**
to **meow** *miauler,* **II, 6**
merchant *un(e) commerçant(e),* **I**
meter *un mètre* (m.), **I**
midnight *minuit* (m.), **I**
milk *le lait,* **I**
millions *des millions* (m.), **II, 11**
minimum *un minimum,* **II, 6**
minus *moins,* **I**
mirror *une glace,* **II, 3**
miss *mademoiselle (Mlle),* **I**
to **miss** *manquer,* **II, 10; I miss...**
  ...me manque, **II, 9;** *regretter,* **II, 1;**
  rater, **II, 10**
modern *moderne,* **II, 9**
Mom *maman,* **I**
moment *un instant,* **II, 10**
Monday *lundi* (m.), **I; on**
  Monday(s) *le lundi,* **I**
money *l'argent* (m.), **I;** *le fric*
  (slang), **II, 3; spending money,**
  allowance *l'argent de poche*
  (m.), **II, 6**
month *un mois,* **I**
Montreal *Montréal,* **I**
monument *un monument,* **I**
moped *une mob(ylette),* **I; by**
  moped *en mobylette,* **I**
more (of) *plutôt,* **I**
more *encore,* **I; a little more**
  encore un peu, **I;** *plus,* **I;**
morning, in the morning *le*
  matin, **I**
mother *une mère,* **I**
motor *le moteur,* **II, 11**
motorcycle *une moto,* **I; by**
  motorcycle *en moto,* **I**
mountain *la montagne,* **I; in the**
  mountains *à la montagne,* **I**
mousse *une mousse,* **I; chocolate**
  mousse *une mousse au chocolat,* **I**
to **move** *déménager,* **II, 9**
to **move, budge** *bouger,* **II, 3**
movie *un film,* **I; movie theater**
  le cinéma, **I; comedy** *un film*
  comique, **I; horror movie** *un film*
  d'horreur, **I; detective film,**
  mystery *un film policier,* **I;**
  science-fiction movie *un film de*
  science-fiction, **I**
to **mow** *tondre,* **II, 5**

Mr., sir *monsieur (M.),* I
Mrs., madam, ma'am *madame (Mme),* I
murderer *un assassin,* I
muscle tone *le tonus,* II, 7
museum *un musée,* I
music *la musique,* I
musician *un(e) musicien, -ienne,* II, 2
must *devoir,* II, 2
my *mon, ma, mes,* I

N

name *un nom,* I
narrow, tight *étroit, -e,* I
natural *naturel, -elle,* II, 10
nature *la nature,* II, 9
near *près (de),* I
necessary *nécessaire,* II, 11; **It is necessary** *Il faut,* I
necklace *un collier,* I
to **need** *avoir besoin de,* I; **I/you need** *il me/te faut,* I
neighbor *un(e) voisin, -ine,* II, 6
neighborhood *un quartier,* I
neither do I *moi non plus,* II, 1
nephew *un neveu (pl. -x),* II, 6
net *un filet,* I
never *jamais,* II, 6
new *nouveau, nouvel, nouvelle, nouveaux, nouvelles,* I
new: What's new? *Quoi de neuf?* II, 9
news *les informations (f.),* I; *des nouvelles (f.),* II, 6
newspaper *le journal,* II, 1
news report, commentary *un reportage,* I
next *prochain, -e,* II, 1; **the next day** *le lendemain,* II, 5; **next to, next door to** *à côté de,* I
nice *bien, gentil, gentille, sympa(thique),* I; **It's nice weather.** *Il fait bon.* I
no *non,* I; **no problem** *pas de problèmes;* I; **no longer** *ne... plus,* I
noise *le bruit,* II, 3
nonsense *les bêtises (f.),* II, 5
noon *midi (m.),* I
normal *normal, -e,* II, 5
not *(ne...) pas,* I; **not bad** *pas mal,* I; **not so great** *pas le pied, pas terrible,* I; **not yet** *pas encore,* I
note *un petit mot,* I; **thank-you note** *un mot de remerciements,* I
notebook *un cahier,* I; **loose-leaf notebook** *un classeur,* I
nothing *(ne...) rien,* I; **It's nothing.** *Ce n'est rien,* I
nourishing *nourrissant, -e,* II, 7
November *novembre (m.),* I
now *maintenant,* I
number *un numéro,* I; **What number are you calling?** *Vous demandez quel numéro?* I; **Wrong number.** *C'est une erreur.* I; **number, piece (musique)** *un morceau (pl. -x),* I

numerous *nombreux, -euse,* II, 11
nurse *un(e) infirmier, -ière,* I
nutritive *nutritif, -ive,* II, 11

O

obligation *une obligation,* II, 5
obliged *obligé, -e,* II, 9
to **observe** *observer,* II, 2
obvious: That's obvious! *C'est évident!* II, 11
occupation *une profession,* I
October *octobre (m.),* I
odor *l' odeur (f.),* II, 6
of *de,* I
to **offer, give** *offrir,* I
often *souvent,* I
OK *d'accord,* I; **to agree** *être d'accord,* I
old *vieux, vieil, vieille, vieux, vieilles,* I; **How old are you?** *Tu as (Vous avez) quel âge?* I; **I am... years old.** *J'ai... ans.* I
omelette *une omelette,* I
on, in (a photo) *sur,* I
once, one time *une fois,* I
one, people in general *on,* I
only *seul, -e,* I; *seulement,* II, 2
open *ouvert, -e,* II, 3
to **open** *ouvrir,* I
opera *un opéra,* II, 10
opinion: in my opinion *à mon avis,* I
opponent *un(e) adversaire,* II, 2
opportunity *une occasion,* II, 6; **to have the opportunity** *avoir l'occasion de,* II, 9
opposite *le contraire,* II, 5
optimistic *optimiste,* II, 11
or *ou,* I; **or else** *ou bien,* I
orange *orange,* I; *une orange,* II, 7; **(color)** *l' orange (m.),* I
orchestra *un orchestre,* II, 3
order: to be out of order *être en panne,* II, 6
to **organize, arrange** *organiser,* I
original *original, -e (m. pl. -aux),* I
other *autre,* I
our *notre, nos,* I
outside of *en dehors de,* II, 2
overpopulation *la surpopulation,* II, 11
over there *là-bas,* I
own *propre,* II, 2

P

Pacific *le Pacifique,* II, 11
paid *payé,* II, 6
painter *un peintre,* I
painting *la peinture,* II, 2
pair *une paire,* I
pajamas *un pyjama,* I
pal, friend *un copain, une copine,* I
pants, slacks *un pantalon,* I
paper: sheet of paper *une feuille,* I
parade *un défilé,* II, 3
parents *les parents (m.),* I

park: amusement park *un parc d'attractions,* II, 3
party *une boum,* I; **The party's in full swing.** *La boum bat son plein.* I
passion *une passion,* I
Passover: Happy Passover! *Joyeuse Pâque!* I
passport *un passeport,* I; **passport check** *le contrôle des passeports,* I
past *le passé,* II, 10
pasta *les pâtes (f.),* II, 7
pastime *un passe-temps,* I
pastry shop *une pâtisserie,* I
pâté *le pâté,* I
patient *patient, -e,* II, 6
to **pay** *payer,* II, 6
peacefully *tranquillement,* II, 3
peanut butter *le beurre de cacahouètes,* I
pear *une poire,* II, 7
pen *un stylo,* I
pen pal *un(e) correspondant(e),* I
pencil *un crayon,* I
pencil case *une trousse,* I
people *les gens (m.),* I
perfect *parfait, -e,* I
perfectly *parfaitement,* II, 9
perfume *le parfum,* I
perfume shop *une parfumerie,* I
perhaps *peut-être,* II, 2
permission *la permission,* II, 2
person *une personne,* II, 6; **from Lyon** *un(e) Lyonnais(e),* II, 9
to **persuade** *persuader,* II, 2
pesticide *un pesticide,* II, 10
pharmacist *un(e) pharmacien, -ienne,* II, 7
to **phone, call** *téléphoner (à),* I
photo *une photo,* I
photographer *un(e) photographe,* I
photography *la photo,* I; *la photographie,* II, 10; **to take pictures** *faire de la photo,* I
physics *la physique,* I
piano *le piano,* II, 2
picnic *un pique-nique,* II, 10
to **picnic** *pique-niquer,* II, 10
pills *des pilules (f.),* II, 11
pilot *un pilote,* II, 11
to **pilot** *piloter,* II, 11; **automatic piloting** *le pilotage automatique,* II, 11
ping pong *le ping-pong,* II, 1
pink *rose,* I
pity *dommage,* II, 3
place *un endroit,* I; *un local,* II, 2
plan *un projet,* II, 1
planet *une planète,* II, 11
plastic *la matière plastique,* II, 10
to **play** *jouer,* I; **to play (a game)** *jouer à,* I; **to play table soccer** *jouer au baby-foot,* I; **to play (a musical instrument)** *jouer de,* I
play *une pièce de théâtre* II, 2
pleasant *agréable,* I
please *s'il vous plaît,* I

to **please** *faire plaisir* , **II, 3; Would it please you to…?** *Ça te plairait de…?* **II, 2**
pleasure: with pleasure *avec plaisir*, **I**
plus *plus*, **I**
pointed *pointu, -e*, **I**
police station *la gendarmerie*, **I**
to **pollute** *polluer*, **II, 10**
pollution *la pollution*, **II, 9**
polo shirt *un polo*, **I**
pond *un étang*, **II, 10**
poor *pauvre*, **II, 7**
poorly *mal*, **II, 1**
possibility *la possibilité*, **II, 1**
postcard *une carte postale*, **I**
post office *la poste*, **I**
poster *une affiche*, **I;** *un poster*, **I**
potato *une pomme de terre*, **II, 7**
pottery *la poterie*, **II, 2**
practical *pratique*, **I**
practice, training *un entraînement*, **II, 2**
to **prefer** *préférer*, **I**
preference *une préférence*, **II, 3**
to **prepare** *préparer*, **I**
preserved *conservé, -e*, **II, 10**
pretty *joli, -e*, **I; That looks pretty.** *Ça fait joli.* **I**
pretty, very *drôlement*, **II, 3**
probably *probablement*, **II, 10**
problem *un problème*, **I; no problems** *pas de problèmes*, **I**
to **produce** *produire*, **II, 10**
to **program** *programmer*, **II, 11**
progress *des progrès* (m.), **II, 1**
to **project** *projeter*, **II, 10**
project *un projet*, **II, 1**
projector *un projecteur*, **II, 10**
to **promise** *promettre*, **II, 7**
to **propose** *proposer*, **II, 6**
proud *fier, fière*, **II, 11**
Provence *la Provence*, **I; from Provence** *provençal, -e*, **II, 10**
province *une province*, **I; in the provinces** *en province*, **I**
pullover *un pull*, **I**
pupil *un(e) élève*, **I**
purchases *les achats* (m.), **II, 2**
pure *pur, -e*, **II, 9**
purposely *exprès*, **II, 3**
purse *un sac*, **I**
push-up *une pompe*, **II, 7**
to **put (on)** *mettre*, **I**

Q

quarter *un quart*, **I; quarter past (the hour)** *et quart*, **I; quarter of/to (the hour)** *moins le quart*, **I; a quarter-hour** *un quart d'heure*, **I**
Quebec: inhabitants of Quebec *les Québécois*, **II, 3**
queen *la reine*, **II, 3**
question *une question*, **I; What a question!** *Quelle question!* **I**

quickly *vite*, **I**
quietly *tranquillement*, **II, 3**
quiz *une interro(gation)*, **I**

R

rabbit *un lapin*, **II, 9**
race: arms race *la course aux armements*, **II, 11**
racket: (tennis) racket *une raquette*, **I**
radio *une radio*, **I**
railroad station *la gare*, **I**
to **rain** *pleuvoir*, **I; It's raining.** *Il pleut.* **I; It rained.** *Il a plu.* **II,1**
rain *la pluie*, **II, 9**
raincoat *un imperméable*, **I**
to **raise** *élever*, **II, 11**
rapidly *rapidement*, **II, 3**
rather *assez*, **I;** *plutôt*, **I**
razor: electric razor *un rasoir électrique*, **I**
to **read** *lire*, **I; I'm reading..** *Je lis.* **II, 5**
ready *prêt, -e*, **I**
really *vraiment*, **I**
reason *la raison*, **II, 6**
to **receive** *recevoir*, **I**
reception *l' accueil* (m.), **II, 2**
receptionist *un(e) réceptionniste*, **II, 6**
recess *la récré(ation)*, **I**
recipe *une recette*, **I**
record *un disque*, **I**
record shop *chez le disquaire*, **I**
red *le rouge*, **I;** *rouge*, **I**
refrigerator *un réfrigérateur*, **I**
to **refuse** *refuser*, **II, 5**
regarding *au sujet de*, **II, 2**
region *une région*, **II, 2**
registration desk *l' accueil* (m.), **II, 2**
to **regret** *regretter*, **II, 1**
regrettable *regrettable*, **II, 3**
to **rehearse** *répéter*, **II, 2**
to **release** *lâcher*, **II, 10**
relic *un vestige*, **II, 10**
remainder *le reste*, **II, 6**
remain(s): there remain(s) *il reste*, **II, 10**
remaking *la remise en forme*, **II, 7**
rendezvous *un rendez-vous*, **I**
to **rent** *louer*, **II, 1**
to **repair** *réparer*, **II, 11**
to **repeat (a grade)** *redoubler*, **II, 1**
reporter *un(e) journaliste*, **I**
research *la recherche*, **II, 10**
reserved *réservé, -e*, **II, 3**
resistance *la résistance*, **II, 3**
resolution *une résolution*, **II, 1; to make a resolution** *prendre une résolution*, **II, 1**
resort: vacation resort, camp *un centre de vacances*, **II, 1**
responsibility *la responsabilité*, **II, 5**
rest: the rest *le reste*, **II, 6**
to **rest** *se reposer*, **II, 7**

restaurant *un restaurant*, **II, 7**
restoration *le rétablissement*, **II, 7**
restroom *les toilettes* (f.), **I**
retired *à la retraite*, **I**
to **return (home)** *rentrer*, **I; (something)** *rendre*, **II, 6**
reunion *les retrouvailles* (f.), **II, 9**
Rhône: the Rhône delta *la Camargue*, **II, 10**
rice *le riz*, **II, 7**
rich *riche*, **II, 9**
ride *un tour*, **II, 3**
right *le droit*, **II, 5; right?** *huh?* **I;** *juste*, **I; right there** *juste là*, **I; to be right** *avoir raison*, **II, 1; to the right (of)** *à droite (de)*, **I; to have the right to** *avoir le droit de*, **II, 5**
ring *une bague*, **I**
river *un fleuve*, **I; Saint Lawrence River** *le Saint-Laurent*, **II, 3**
robots *les robots* (m.), **II, 11**
rock music *le rock*, **I**
roller coaster *les montagnes russes* (f.), **II, 3**
Roman *romain, -e*, **II, 10**
Romans *les Romains*, **II, 10**
roof *un toit*, **I**
room *une pièce*, **I; bathroom** *la salle de bains*, **I; dining room** *la salle à manger*, **I; guest room** *une chambre d'amis*, **I;** *l' espace* (m.), **II, 9**
route *le trajet*, **II, 10**
rule *la règle*, **II, 5**
ruler *une règle*, **I**
to **run** *courir*, **II, 7; I run.** *Je cours.* **II,3**
Russia *la Russie*, **II, 2**

S

sad *triste*, **I**
sailing *la voile*, **II, 1**
saint: Happy saint's day! *Bonne fête!* **I**
salad *une salade*, **I**
salami *le saucisson*, **I**
salesman, saleswoman *un(e) vendeur, -euse*, **I**
same *même*, **I**
sandale *une sandale*, **I**
sandwich *un sandwich* (pl. -es), **I**
satisfied *satisfait, -e*, **II, 1**
Saturday *samedi* (m.), **I; on Saturday(s)** *le samedi*, **I**
sauce *une sauce*, **I**
to **save** *économiser*, **II, AC1**
Savoy *la Savoie*, **I**
saxophone *le saxophone*, **II, 2**
to **say** *dire*, **I; Say!** *Dis!* **I; What did she say?** *Qu'est-ce qu'elle a dit?* **II, 6**
scarf *une écharpe*, **I**
scene *la scène*, **II, 9**
schedule *un emploi du temps*, **I;** *un horaire*, **I**
school *une école*, **I; (adj.)** *scolaire*, **II, 1; middle or junior high school** *un collège*, **I**

science fiction *la science-fiction,* **I**
to **scratch** *griffer,* **II, 6**
screen: projection screen *un écran,* **II, 10**
sea *la mer,* **I**
search *une recherche,* **I**
seashore: at the seashore *au bord de la mer,* **II, 1**
season *une saison,* **I**
second *deuxième,* **I; on the second floor** *au premier étage,* **I**
to **see** *voir,* **I**
seem: it seems (that) *il paraît (que),* **II, 9**
selfish *égoïste,* **I**
to **sell** *vendre,* **II, 3**
to **send** *envoyer,* **I; Everyone sends you their love.** *Tout le monde t'embrasse.* **II, 9**
September *septembre* (m.), **I**
series *une série,* **I**
serious *sérieux, -euse,* **II, 6;** *grave,* **II, 11**
services *les services* (m.), **II, 6**
to **set** *fixer,* **II, 10**
several *plusieurs,* **I**
shape: in (great) shape *en (pleine) forme,* **II, 1; to keep in shape** *garder la forme,* **I; to be in good shape** *être en forme,* **II, 3**
she *elle,* **I**
Shhh! *Chut!* **II, 10**
shirt: man's shirt *une chemise,* **I; woman's tailored shirt** *un chemisier,* **I; turtleneck shirt** *un col roulé,* **I**
shoe *une chaussure,* **I; running shoes** *des joggers* (m.), **I**
shop *une boutique,* **I; (class)** *la technologie,* **I**
shopping *les courses* (f.), **II, 5; to go shopping** *faire des achats,* **II, 2; to do one's grocery shopping** *faire son marché,* **II, 11**
shopping center *un centre commercial,* **I**
short *court, -e,* **I; short of** *à court de,* **II, 6**
shorts *un short,* **I**
should *devrais,* **II, 7**
shoulder *l' épaule* (f.), **II, 2**
shout *un cri,* **II, 3**
to **shout** *crier,* **II, 6**
to **show** *montrer,* **I**
show *un spectacle,* **II, 2;** *une manifestation,* **II, 10;** *une exposition,* **II, 9; (television)** *une émission,* **I**
shy, timid *timide,* **II, 5**
sick *malade,* **II, 1**
sign *une enseigne,* **I**
similar *pareil, pareille,* **II, 1**
since *depuis,* **II, 7;** *depuis que,* **II, 9**
to **sing** *chanter,* **I**
sister *une sœur,* **I**
site *un site,* **I**
situated *situé, -e,* **I**

size *la taille,* **I; (shoes)** *la pointure,* **I**
skating rink *une patinoire,* **I**
skeleton *un squelette,* **II, 3**
skiing *le ski,* **I**
skis *des skis,* **I; ski boots** *les chaussures de ski,* **I; ski poles** *des bâtons* (m.), **I**
skirt *une jupe,* **I**
sky *le ciel,* **I**
to **sleep** *dormir,* **I; to sleep late** *faire la grasse matinée,* **II, 7**
slice *une tranche,* **I; slice of bread and butter** *une tartine,* **II, 7**
slide *une diapo(sitive),* **II, 10**
slowly *lentement,* **II, 3**
Smile! *Souriez!* **II, 10**
to **smoke** *fumer,* **II, 5**
snack: afternoon snack *le goûter,* **I**
sneakers (high) *des baskets* (f.), **I; (low)** *des tennis* (m.), **I**
to **snow** *neiger,* **I; It's snowing.** *Il neige.* **I**
snow-covered *enneigé, -e,* **II, 3**
snowman *un bonhomme (de neige),* **II, 3**
so *alors,* **I;** *si,* **II, 11**
soaked *trempé, -e,* **II, 9**
soap opera *un feuilleton,* **I**
soccer *le foot(ball),* **I**
sock *une chaussette,* **I**
solution *une solution,* **I**
to **solve** *résoudre,* **II, 11**
solvent *un solvant,* **II, 10**
some *quelques,* **II, 9**
some, any *des, du, de la, de l',* **I**
sometimes *quelquefois,* **I;** *parfois,* **II, 10**
somewhere *quelque part,* **II, 1**
so much *tellement,* **II, 3**
son *un fils,* **I**
song *une chanson,* **II, 2;** *un chant,* **II, 3**
soon *bientôt,* **II, 11; as soon as** *dès que,* **II, 6**
sorry *désolé, -e,* **I; to be sorry** *regretter,* **I**
south *le sud,* **I**
space *l' espace* (m.), **II, 11**
Spanish (language) *l' espagnol* (m.), **I**
to **speak** *parler,* **I**
special *spécial, -e* (m. pl. *-aux*), **II, 3**
to **spend** *dépenser,* **II, 6**
spendthrift *dépensier, -ière,* **II, 6**
spin *un tour,* **II, 3**
splendid *splendide,* **II, 1**
sport *un sport,* **I; sports** *le sport,* **I; the sporty style/look** *la mode sport,* **I**
spring *le printemps,* **I; in the spring** *au printemps,* **I**
square *une place,* **I**
stadium *un stade,* **I**
stairs *un escalier,* **I**
stamp *un timbre,* **I; stamp collecting** *la philatélie,* **II, 2**

to **start** *commencer,* **I; (a car)** *démarrer,* **II, 11; to get started** *marcher,* **II, 2; to start again** *recommencer, reprendre,* **II, 1**
stationery store *une papeterie,* **I**
to **stay** *rester,* **I**
stay *un séjour,* **II, 1; stay to learn a language** *un séjour linguistique,* **II, 1**
stereo *une chaîne stéréo,* **I**
stillness *le calme,* **II, 11**
stock: to play the stock market *jouer à la Bourse,* **II, 11**
stomach ache, nausea *mal au cœur,* **II, 3**
stone *une pierre,* **I; made of stone** *en pierre,* **I**
to **stop** *(s') arrêter,* **II, 3**
stop, stopover *un arrêt,* **II, 10**
store *un magasin,* **I; department store** *un grand magasin,* **I**
storeroom *le débarras,* **I**
story *une histoire,* **I; love story** *une histoire d'amour,* **I**
straight *droit,* **II, 2; straight ahead** *tout droit,* **I**
street *une rue,* **I**
strict *sévère,* **II, 1;** *strict, -e,* **II, 5**
strike *une grève,* **II, 9; public transportation strike** *une grève des transports en commun,* **II, 9**
strong *fort, -e,* **II, 3**
strong point *un fort,* **II, 1**
student *un(e) étudiant(e),* **I**
studies *les études* (f.), **II, 2**
to **study** *étudier,* **II, 2**
stupid *idiot, -e;* *bête,* **II, 10; to act stupid** *faire l'idiot,* **I**
style *un style, la mode,* **I; stylish** *à la mode,* **I; the latest style** *la mode branchée,* **I; the style of the Fifties** *la mode rétro,* **I; the sporty style/look** *la mode sport,* **I; out of style** *démodé, -e,* **II, 6**
subject (school) *une matière,* **II, 1**
subway *le métro,* **I; by subway** *en métro,* **I**
to **succeed** *réussir,* **II, 1**
such *pareil, pareille,* **II, 10**
to **suggest** *proposer,* **II, 6**
suitcase *une valise,* **I**
summer *l' été* (m.), **I; in the summer** *en été,* **I**
sun *le soleil,* **I; It's sunny.** *Il y a du soleil.* **I**
sunburn *un coup de soleil,* **II, 1**
to **sunburn** *attraper un coup de soleil,* **II, 1**
Sunday *dimanche* (m.), **I; on Sunday(s)** *le dimanche,* **I**
super *super,* **I**
superb *superbe,* **I**
supper *le dîner,* **I**
surely *bien sûr,* **I**
surfing *le surf,* **I**
surprise *une surprise,* **I; That would surprise me!** *Ça m'étonnerait!* **II, 11**

to **swim** *nager*, I
swimming *la natation*, I; **swimming pool** *une piscine*, I
to **swing: It's going to swing!** *Ça va swinguer!* I

T

table *une table*, I; **to set the table** *mettre la table*, I; **night stand** *une table de nuit*, I
tablecloth *une nappe*, II, 10
to **take** *prendre*, I; **to take (a course)** *suivre*, II, 7; **to take (a test)** *passer*, II, 2; **to take (someone somewhere)** *emmener*, II, 3; **to take charge of** *s'occuper de*, II, 7; **to take out** *sortir*, II, 5; **to take part in** *pratiquer*, II, 2; *participer*, II, 5; *faire de*, I; **to take pictures** *faire de la photo*, I; **to take up** *monter*, I; **to take (food or drink)** *prendre*, I
to **talk** *discuter, parler*, I
tan: to get a tan *bronzer*, II, 1
tanned *bronzé, -e*, II, 1
task *la tâche* II, 5
taste *le goût*, I
taxi *un taxi*, I; **taxi stand** *les taxis*, I
tea *le thé*, I
teacher *un prof(esseur)*, I
technologies *les technologies* (f.), II, 11
telephone *un téléphone*, I
television, TV *la télé(vision)*, I; **television program** *une émission*, I; **What's on TV?** *Qu'est-ce qu'il y a la télé?* I
to **tell** *raconter*, II, 1
temperature *la température*, I; **What's the temperature?** *Il fait quelle température?* I
tennis *le tennis*, I
terrace *la terrasse*, I
terrific *extra(ordinaire)*, I
to **thank** *remercier*, I; **thank you, thanks** *merci*, I; **thank-you note** *un mot de remerciements*, I; **thanks to** *grâce à*, II, 11
that *ce, cet, cette*, I; *ça*, I; **that's** *c'est*, I; **that one** *celui(-là), celle(-là)*, I; **That's all right.** *Ça ne fait rien.* I
the *le, la, les*, I
theater: to take part in a theater group *faire du théâtre*, II, 2
their *leur, leurs*, I
them *eux, elles*, I; *les*, II, 5; **(to or for) them** *leur*, I
then *alors, puis, ensuite*, I
there *là, y*, I; **over there** *là-bas*, I; **right there** *juste là*, I; **there is/ are** *voilà*, I; *il y a*, I; **there it is** *le/la voilà*, I; **there you are** *voilà*, I
therefore *donc*, II, 6
thermos *une thermos*, II, 10
these *ces*, I; *ceux(-là), celles(-là)*, I;

these are *c'est*, I
they *ils, elles, on*, I
thick *gros, grosse*, I
thing *une chose*, I; **something** *quelque chose*, I; **the simplest thing** *le plus simple*, I
to **think** *penser*, I; *songer*, II, 10; **What do you think of that?** *Qu'est-ce que tu en penses?* I; **Do you think so?** *Tu crois?, Tu trouves?* I
third *troisième*, I; **on the third floor** *au deuxième étage*, I
thirsty: to be thirsty *avoir soif*, I
this *ce, cet, cette*, I; **this is** *c'est*, I; **this one, the one** *celui(-là), celle(-là)*, I
thrifty *économe*, II, 6
thunderstorm *un orage*, I
Thursday *jeudi* (m.), I; **on Thursday(s)** *le jeudi*, I
ticket *un billet*, I
to **tidy up** *ranger*, I
time *le temps*, I; **a long time** *longtemps*, II, 2; **all the time** *tout le temps*, II, 5; **at the time of** *au temps de*, II, 10; **Did you have a good time?** *Tu t'es amusé(e)?* II, 1; **dinnertime** *l'heure du dîner*, I; **free time** *les loisirs* (m.), II, 11; **from time to time** *de temps en temps*, II, 5; **I had a good time.** *Je me suis amusé(e).*, II, 1; **It's been a long time since I've seen you.** *Ça fait longtemps que je ne t'ai pas vu!* II, 9; **It's been such a long time!** *Il y a si longtemps!* II, 9; **one time** *une fois*, I; **on time** *à l'heure*, II, 10; **what time** *à quelle heure*, I; **What time is it?** *Quelle heure est-il?* I
timetable *un horaire*, I
tired *fatigué, -e*, I
tiring *fatigant, -e*, II, 9
to *à, en*, I
today *aujourd'hui*, I
together *ensemble*, I
toilet *les toilettes* (f.), I
tomato *une tomate*, II, 7
tomorrow *demain*, I
too *aussi, trop*, I; **too much, too many** *trop (de)*, I
tooth *une dent*, II, 7
top: at the top of *en haut de*, I
totally *tout à fait*, I
touching *émouvant, -e*, I
tour *un tour*, II, 3
tourist *un(e) touriste*, II, 3
tourist office *l' Office de tourisme* (m.), I
tournament *un tournoi*, II, 3
toward *vers*, II, 3
tower *une tour*, I
town hall *la mairie*, I
trace *un vestige*, II, 10
track and field *l' athlétisme* (m.), I
trade *un métier*, II, 6
train *un train*, I
to **train** *s' entraîner*, II, 7
training course *un stage*, II, 6

trash: It's trash! *C'est bidon!* I
tree (family) *un arbre généalogique*, I
trendy *dans le vent*, I
trip *un voyage*, II, 10; **Have a good trip! (by plane, ship)** *Bon voyage!* I
trombone *le trombone*, II, 2
true *vrai, -e* I
trumpet *la trompette*, II, 2
to **try** *essayer (de)*, II, 2
T-shirt *un tee-shirt*, I
Tuesday *mardi* (m.), I; **on Tuesday(s)** *le mardi*, I
turn *le tour*, II, 7
to **turn** *tourner*, I
twelfth *douzième*, I
twenty: about twenty *une vingtaine*, II, 9
to **type** *taper à la machine*, II, 6

U

umbrella *un parapluie*, I
uncle *un oncle*, I
to **understand** *comprendre*, II, 1
undoubtedly *certainement*, II, 7
unemployment *le chômage*, II, 11
unfair, unjust *injuste*, II, 5
unfortunately *malheureusement*, II, 3
United States: the United States *les Etats-Unis* (m.), I
unknown *l' inconnu(e)*, II, 11
unmarried *célibataire*, II, 11
until *jusqu'à*, II, 1
uprooted *dépaysé, -e*, II, 9
to **upset** *énerver*, II, 6
up there *là-haut*, II, 9
used: to get used to *s' adapter*, II, 9
used to, accustomed *habitué, -e*, II, 7
useful: to make oneself useful *se rendre utile*, II, 11
useless *inutile*, II, 1
usually *d'habitude*, I

V

vacation *les vacances* (f.), I; **Have a nice vacation!** *Bonnes vacances!* I
to **vacuum** *passer l'aspirateur*, I
vacuum cleaner *l' aspirateur* (m.), I
varied *varié, -e*, I
variety show *les variétés* (f.), I
vegetable *un légume*, I
vegetarian *végétarien, -ienne*, II, 7
vertigo, fear of heights *le vertige*, II, 3
very *très*, I
viaduct *un viaduc*, I
videocassette *un film vidéo*, I
videocassette recorder, VCR *un magnétoscope*, I
view *une vue*, I
village *un village*, I
violent *violent, -e*, I

visit *une visite*, I
to visit *visiter*, I
vitamin *une vitamine*, II, 7
voice *la voix*, II, 11
volleyball *le volley(-ball)*, I

W

to wait (for) *attendre*, I
waiter, waitress *un(e) serveur, -euse*, II, 6
to walk *marcher*, I; *se promener*, II, 7; to walk (an animal) *promener*, II, 6
walk, stroll *une balade*, I
walking *la marche*, II, 9
wallet *un portefeuille*, I
walls: city walls *les remparts (m.)*, I
to want *vouloir*, I; If you want to. *Si tu veux.* I; Do you want to . . . ? *Ça te dit de…?* II, 2; If you want. *Comme tu veux.* II, 9
war *la guerre*, II, 11
wardrobe *une armoire*, I
warm *chaud, -e*, I; It's warm. *Il fait chaud.* I
was *était*, II, 1
to wash *laver*, II, 5
watch *une montre*, I
to water *arroser*, II, 5
water *l' eau (f.)*, I; mineral water *l' eau minérale*, I
way *le chemin*, II, 7; *une façon*, II, 6; in the way of *comme*, II, 2
we *nous, on*, I
weak *faible*, II, 7
to wear *porter, mettre*, I
weather *le temps*, I; What's the weather like? *Il fait quel temps?* I; It's nice weather. *Il fait bon.* I
wedding anniversary *l'anniversaire (m.) de mariage*, I

Wednesday *mercredi (m.)*, I; on Wednesday(s) *le mercredi*, I
week *une semaine*, I; once a week *une fois par semaine*, I
weekend *un week-end*, I
to weigh *peser*, II, 7
Welcome! *Bienvenue!* I; Welcome! *Soyez le/la bienvenu(e)!* I
well *alors, bien, eh bien*, I; *enfin*, II, 3; Well done! *Bravo!* II, 6; Get well soon! *Bonne santé!* I
Western *un western*, I
what *quoi*, I; *ce que*, II, 5; *qu'est-ce que*, I; What is it/that? *Qu'est-ce que c'est?* I; *qu'est-ce qui*, II, 10; *que*, I; It's so (+ adj.)! *Qu'il/elle est (+ adj.)!* I; What a . . . ! *Quel (Quelle)… !* I; What a question/life! *Quelle question/vie!* I
when *quand*, I
where *où*, I
which *quel(s), quelle(s)*, I
white *le blanc*, I; *blanc, blanche*, I
who *qui*, I; *qui est-ce qui*, II, 10
whom *qui*, I; *qui est-ce que*, II, 10
why *pourquoi*, I
wide *large*, I
wife *une femme*, I
to win *gagner*, II, 1
wind *le vent*, I; It's windy. *Il y a du vent.* I
window *une fenêtre*, I
to window-shop *faire du lèche-vitrines*, I
windsurfing *la planche à voile*, I
winter *l' hiver (m.)*, I; in the winter *en hiver*, I
wish *un souhait*, II, 11
wish *un vœu (pl. -x)*, I; Best wishes! *Meilleurs vœux!* I; *Meilleurs souhaits!* I
with *avec*, I
without *sans*, II, 11

woman *une femme*, I
wood *le bois*, I; wooden *en bois*, I
word *la parole*, II, 11
to work *travailler*, I; *fonctionner*, II, 3; *marcher*, II, 2; to work as a mother's helper *travailler au pair*, II, 6
work *le travail*, I; Down to work! *Au travail!* I
worker: factory worker, blue-collar worker *un(e) ouvrier, -ière*, I
world *le monde*, II, 11
worried *inquiet, -ète*, II, 6
to worry *s'inquiéter*, II, 7; Don't worry! *(Ne) t'en fais pas!* II, 9; *Ne t'inquiète pas.* II, 1
wrong: to be wrong *avoir tort*, II, 1; What's wrong with you? *Qu'est-ce qui t'arrive?* II, 7; *Qu'est-ce que tu as?* II, 7
wrote: she wrote *elle a écrit*, II, 6

Y

yacht *un yacht*, II, 11
year *un an*, I; every year *tous les ans*, I; Happy New Year! *Bonne année!* I
yellow *le jaune*, I; *jaune*, I
yes *oui, si*, I
yesterday *hier*, I
yet: not yet *pas encore*, I
yogurt *le yaourt*, II, 7
you *on, tu, toi, vous*, I
young *jeune*, I; young people, the youth *les jeunes (m.)*, I
your *ton, ta, tes, votre, vos*, I

Z

zero *un zéro*, I; It's zero (degrees). *Il fait zéro.* I; It's ten below (zero). *Il fait moins dix.* I

GRAMMAR INDEX

Here is an alphabetical list of grammatical structures. The roman numeral **I** tells you that the structures were introduced in **Nouveaux copains.** Roman numeral **II** lets you know that the structures are in **Nous, les jeunes.** Following the roman numerals, you'll see *either* the number of the unit *or* the number of the unit and the letter of the section where you learned the structure.

483

en: before names of countries, I 5; as pronoun, II 2 (C15); in commands, II 2 (C15); review, II 5 (C16); in **passé composé,** II 5 (C17)

en train de: II 9 (B12)

envoyer: present, I 10; future, II 11 (B14). *See Verb Index,* 449.

être: present, I 1; requests or commands, I 6; past participle, I 10, II 1 (A14); in **passé composé,** II 1 (B7); subjunctive, II 7 (C13); imperfect, II 9 (A15); with **en train de,** II 9 (B12); future, II 11 (A8). *See Verb Index,* 449.

faire: present, I 3; talking about sports, I 3; past participle, I 10, II 1 (A14); subjunctive, II 5 (A11); future, II 11 (A8). *See Verb Index,* 449.

faut: il faut, I 2; followed by the subjunctive, II 5 (A11); imperfect, II 9 (A15); future, II 11 (B14). *See Verb Index,* 449.

feminine: gender, I 1, I 2

future: expressed by **aller** + infinitive, I 5; regular verbs, II 11 (A8); stem-changing verbs, II 11 (A8); **avoir, être, faire,** II 11 (A8); other irregular verbs, II 11 (B14); using **quand,** II 11 (B14)

gender: explained, I 1; singular noun markers, I 1; plural noun markers, I 2

imperfect: formation, II 9 (A15); **être,** II 9 (A15); using the imperfect, II 9 (A15), II 9 (B12); review, II 9 (B11)

independent pronouns: II 2 (A8); in comparisons, II 9 (A9)

indirect-object pronouns: **lui, leur,** I 11; in commands or requests, I 11, II 6 (A8); review, II 5 (C16), II 6 (A7); in **passé composé,** II 5 (C17), II 6 (C10), II 6 (C11); **me, te, nous, vous,** II 6 (A8); position, II 6 (A8)

infinitive: explained, I 3; following **aller,** I 5; with reflexive pronouns, II 7 (A7); past infinitive, II 10 (C10)

interrogative adjectives: **quel, quelle, quels, quelles,** I 11

interrogative pronouns: review, II 10 (A11); as subject of verb, II 10 (A12); as object of verb, II 10 (A12); as object of preposition, II 10 (A12)

-là: with demonstrative pronouns, I 11

le, la, l', les: as articles, I 1, I 2; as direct-object pronouns, II 5 (B10), II 5 (C16), II 5 (C17), II 6 (A7), II 6 (C10)

liaison: explained, I 2; with articles, I 2; with subject pronouns, I 3; with **aux,** I 5; with **des,** I 5; with possessive adjectives, I 6; with **y,** I 7; with adjectives preceding nouns, I 7, I 11; in **passé composé,** II 1 (B7); with **en,** II 2 (C15); with inversion, II 3 (C8); with direct-object pronouns,

II 5 (B10), II 5 (C17), II 6 (A8); with indirect-object pronouns, II 6 (A8)

lire: past participle, I 10, II 1 (A14). *See Verb Index,* 449.

lui, leur: indirect-object pronouns, I 11; review, II 5 (C16); II 6 (A7); in **passé composé,** II 6 (C10)

masculine: gender, I 1, I 2

meilleur: comparative use, II 9 (C5); superlative use, II 10 (B6)

mettre: present, I 10; past participle, I 10, II 1 (A14). *See Verb Index,* 449.

mieux: comparative use, II 9 (C5); superlative use, II 10 (B6)

negative constructions: **ne... pas,** I 3; **pas** alone, I 3; **de** after a negative instead of **du, de la, de l', des** or **un, une,** I 6; review, II 6 (B12); other words used with **ne: plus, jamais, rien, que,** II 6 (B13)

nouns: gender of, I 1; plural of, I 2; adjectives used as, I 11; comparisons of, II 9 (A9), II 10 (B5)

nouveau: I 7

numbers: cardinal numbers 0–20, I 1; cardinal numbers 20–1,000, I 5; ordinal numbers, I 2, I 6. *See Numbers,* 458.

offrir: present, I 11; past participle, 11, II 1 (A14). *See Verb Index,* 449.

on: subject pronoun, I 3; in suggestions, I 7

où: I 3, I 5

ouvrir: like **offrir,** I 11; past participle, II 1 (A14). *See Verb Index,* 449.

partir: like **sortir,** I 9. *See Verb Index,* 449.

passé composé: with **avoir,** I 10; in negative constructions, I 10, II 6 (B13); with adverbs, I 10, II 3 (B13); review, II 1 (A14), II 9 (B11); with **être,** II 1 (B7); past participle agreement of verbs using **être,** II 1 (B7); **liaison,** II 1 (B7); in questions, II 3 (C8); with **le, la, les,** II 5 (C17); with **me, te, nous, vous,** II 6 (C11); with reflexive pronouns, II 7 (A7); **passé composé** vs. imperfect, II 9 (B12); with relative pronouns, II 11 (C14)

past infinitive: II 10 (C10)

past participle: formation, I 10; irregular past participles, I 10, II 1 (A14); agreement, II 1 (B7), II 5 (C17), II 7 (A7), II 11 (C14)

pleuvoir: present, I 7; imperfect, II 9 (A15); future, II 11 (B14). *See Verb Index,* 449.

plural: of nouns, I 2; of noun markers, I 2; of adjectives, I 7; of possessive adjectives, I 6

possessive adjectives: I 6

pourquoi: I 5

pouvoir: present, I 9; past participle, I 10, II 1 (A14); subjunctive, II 7 (C13); future, II 11 (B14). *See Verb Index,* 449.

préférer: present, I 9. *See Verb Index,* 449.

0
C 1
D 2
E 3
F 4
G 5
H 6
I 7
J 8